Jewish Budapest

Dear Dad

Happy 65th Birthday.

Hope you have a wonderful day.

See you in the summer.

Love
Aaron

(Archie 4)

JEWISH BUDAPEST

Monuments, Rites, History

by Kinga Frojimovics, Géza Komoróczy, Viktória Pusztai
and Andrea Strbik

Edited by Géza Komoróczy

Central European University Press
Budapest

No. 101. "Atlantic Studies on Society in Change"
of the Atlantic Research and Publications, Inc.
Highland Lakes NJ 07422 USA
Editor in Chief Béla K. Király
Associate Editor in Chief Kenneth Murphy
Editor László Veszprémy

First published in Hungarian as *A zsidó Budapest*
in 1995 by Városháza and MTA Judaisztikai Kutatócsoport, Budapest

English edition 1999 by
Central European University Press

Október 6. utca 12
H–1051 Budapest
Hungary

400 West 59th Street
New York, NY 10019
USA

Translated by Vera Szabó
Translation edited by Mario Fenyő and the authors
Typography and cover design by István Kiss

© 1994 by Kinga Frojimovics, Géza Komoróczy, Viktória Pusztai and Andrea Strbik
English translation © 1999 by Vera Szabó and Center of Jewish Studies
at the Hungarian Academy of Sciences

Distributed by Plymbridge Distributors Ltd., Estover Road,
Plymouth PL6 7PZ, United Kingdom

Published with the support of the
Hungarian Ministry of National Cultural Heritage–
Frankfurt '99 Non-Profit Organization
for the Frankfurt Book Fair, 1999: Hungary in Focus

ISBN 963-9116-38-6 Cloth
ISBN 963-9116-37-8 Paperback

Library of Congress Cataloging in Publication Data
A CIP catalog record for this book is available upon request

Printed in Hungary by Akadémiai Nyomda Kft.

Preface to the Series

The present volume is part of a series that, when completed, will constitute a comprehensive survey of the many aspects of East-Central-European society.

The books in this series deal with peoples whose homelands lie between the Germans to the West, the Russians, Ukrainians and Belorussians to the East and North, and the Mediterranean and Adriatic seas to the South. They constitute a particular civilization, one that is an integral part of Europe, yet substantially different from the West. The area is characterized by a rich diversity of languages, religions and governments. The study of this complex area demands a multidisciplinary approach, and, accordingly, our contributors to the series represent several academic disciplines. They have been drawn from universities and other scholarly institutions in the United States and Western Europe, as well as East and Central Europe. The editor of the present volume is professor at the Eötvös Loránd University of Budapest and director of the Center of Jewish Studies at the Hungarian Academy of Sciences, his co-authors are his former students.

The editors of the series, of course, take full responsibility for ensuring the comprehensiveness, cohesion, internal balance and scholarly quality of the series they have launched. We cheerfully accept this responsibility and intend this series to be neither justification nor condemnation of the policies, attitudes, and activities of any persons involved. At the same time, because the contributors represent so many different disciplines, interpretations, and schools of thought, our policy in this, as in the past and future volumes, is to present their contributions without substantial modifications.

Béla K. Király *Editor-in-Chief*

Acknowledgments

This book was prepared and written in the Center of Jewish Studies at the Hungarian Academy of Sciences between 1992 and 1994 and reflects an important aspect of the teaching and research activity of our Center. The Hungarian version of the book appeared early in 1995, and saw a second edition within less than a year. The three young co-authors, Kinga Frojimovics, Viktória Pusztai (now Bányai) and Andrea Strbik, were still students majoring in Jewish studies back in those years, by now they are young scholars in their own right.

The editor and the four authors owe special thanks to the staff and the students of the Center, first of all, to our secretary Zsuzsa Egyed-Arányi. Without her assistance it would have been difficult to prepare and handle the complex material used for the book, including organization, library research and dealing with the photos. There were times, weeks and months, during which everyone connected with the Center was doing some research for the book. Special thanks is due to Tamás Turán and Tamás Dezső, both assistant professors, who helped in rabbinical matters and drew some of the figures, respectively.

In different phases of the preparation, substantial intellectual help came from R. Joseph Schweitzer, that time director of the Rabbinical Seminary, Budapest, now emeritus in this quality and the Chief Rabbi of Hungary; and from R. Hermann Imre Schmelzer (of St. Gallen), an alumnus of the Rabbinical Seminary in Budapest. R. Schweitzer was ready to answer our questions at all time, and furthermore, in long, detailed discussions, shared with us his recollections on Jewish life in the pre-World War II period and treasuries of his knowledge on Hungarian Jewish history. R. Schmelzer commented on the printed Hungarian version of the book in a series of long letters; his remarks proved to be most useful during the preparation of the English version.

Advice and information on earlier and contemporary Jewish life, rich in intimate, sometimes hidden details, and personal recollections were given to the editor by the late Meir Weiss of the Hebrew University (R. Pál Weisz), R. István Domán, R. György Landeszman, R. Baruch Oberlander; and in connection with his novels and stories by the late G. György Kardos. Art historian Ferenc Dávid and literary historian Miklós Szabolcsi read the entire preliminary manuscript in Hungarian, their wide knowledge was a gold mine of information. Parts of the manuscript were read by József Schweitzer and László Jólesz as well. Important information and advice relating to the architecture of the capital came from the late Gábor Preisich; to literary history from Béla Stoll; to the architecture of the synagogues and the organizing potential of the Jewish community in nineteenth-century urbanization from the late Anikó Gazda—it was our honor to edit and publish her last manuscript on this subject—; to economic history from Yehudah Don (of the Bar-Ilan University); to Jewish history of Budapest from the late Károly Vörös, from László Varga, Gyula Zeke, György Bence, György Haraszti; to the history of the Holocaust from László Karsai, who allowed us to use, and in part to excerpt, his late father's and his own collection of documents on the period following October 15, 1944, still awaiting publication; to Polish emigration during World War II from Tamás Salamon-Rácz, who as a high-ranking civil servant took part in these rescue actions; to certain moments of the Budapest stay of the Belz rebe from Joseph Silber (New York) and the writer István Gábor Benedek; to the history of the Jewish hospital from András Losonci; to theater history from Tamás Gajdó. The architect Anna Perczel's extensive research into city planning and the history of streets and houses in Józsefváros, and—already during the preparation of the English edition of our book—in certain neighborhoods of Erzsébetváros and Lipótváros, and in the old Jewish quarter proper, helped us to check and complete the available data.

Zsigmond Csoma, Zita Deáky and Gyula Zeke made available their collections of photos, that of Csoma & Deáky, a rich documentation of Jewish ethnography, and Zeke's, a representative photographic archive on Jewish urban life in the early twentieth century. Gábor Izsák put at our disposal his unpublished extensive catalogue of historical postcards of synagogues and Jewish topics in Hungary.

For the English version the editor was given very useful advice by T. Iván Berend (UCLA), Shlomo Spitzer (Bar-Ilan University) and by the respected translator of Hungarian literature Ivan Sanders (New York).

Research activity of the Center, including research for this book, has been sponsored by the Memorial Foundation for Jewish Culture (New York). The editor thankfully acknowledges institutional support from the Memorial Foundation and advice from its executive vice-president, Jerry Hochbaum; grants from the Soros Foundation (New York–Budapest); support from Brown University, Program in Judaic Studies, and its earlier director, Ernest R. Frerichs. The editor, while working on the manuscript, during his long stays there, enjoyed the hospitality, the excellent library background and the warm, cordial atmosphere at Professor Frerichs' Brown Judaic Program, that of the *Wissenschaftskolleg* (Berlin) and of the Institute for Human Sciences (Vienna).

The Hungarian version of the book was a joint publication of the *Városháza* (City Hall), Office of the Mayor of Budapest and our Center of Jewish Studies. Work on the book was first suggested by Gábor Demszky, the Mayor himself; he and his editorial staff gave us support throughout the project. Gyöngyvér Török of the City Hall helped in editorial work of the Hungarian version. The second Hungarian edition was sponsored by the literary weekly *Élet és Irodalom*.

The English translation of the book was sponsored in 1995 by the *Nemzeti Kulturális Alap* (National Culture Fund of Hungary) on the initiative of its then president, András Török. During preparation of the English edition, for additional research and updating, our Center received a special research grant from Ferenc Glatz, the President of the *Magyar Tudományos Akadémia* (Hungarian Academy of Sciences). Editorial work of the English version was supported, in preparation for the *Frankfurter Buchmesse, 1999: Schwerpunkt Ungarn* (Frankfurt Book Fair, 1999: Hungary in Focus), by the *Nemzeti Kulturális Örökség Minisztériuma - Frankfurt '99 Kht.* (Ministry of National Cultural Heritage—Frankfurt '99 Non-Profit Organization).

We would like to thank the photographers who made the original photos for this book: Zoltán Egyed, Annie Fischer-Bánó, Aliona Frankl & László Lugo Lugosi, Csaba Gedai and Endre Lábass.

Thanks are due to all those museums, libraries and institutions, which, through the generous help of their staff, have enabled us to collect and identify the illustrations used in this book and gave their permission to publish photos from their collections. These are as follows. *Magyar Nemzeti Múzeum* (Hungarian National Museum), its director general István Gedai and deputy director Tibor Kovács; its collections, the *Éremtár* (Numismatic Collection); *Középkori Régészeti Osztály* (Department of Medieval Archaeology); *Legújabbkori Történeti Múzeum* (Museum of Modern History); *Magyar Történelmi Képcsarnok* (Hungarian Historical Gallery), and in particular its earlier director, the late Gizella Cenner-Wilhelmb; *Történeti Fényképtár* (Historical Photo Archives); *Értékpapír gyűjtemény* (Numismatic Collection. Collection of Securities), and in particular Lajos Pallós.—*Budapesti Történeti Múzeum* (Budapest Historical Museum), its *Kiscelli Múzeum* (Kiscell Museum) and *Középkori Zsidó Imaház* (Medieval Jewish Prayer-house).—*Magyar Zsidó Múzeum* (Hungarian Jewish Museum), and in particular Frigyes Porscht, Anna Sándor and Róbert B. Turán.—*Szépművészeti Múzeum XX. századi Alapítványa* (Museum of Fine Arts, Twentieth-century Art Foundation), and in particular Judit Geskó.—*A Magyar Tudományos Akadémia Könyvtára* (Library of the Hungarian Academy of Sciences), Oriental Collection.—*Országos Széchényi Könyvtár* (National Széchényi Library).—*Fővárosi Szabó Ervin Könyvtár* ("Ervin Szabó" Municipal Library), Budapest Collection.—*Eötvös Loránd Tudományegyetem* ("Loránd Eötvös" University), its *Egyetemi Könyvtár* (University Library) and *Történeti Könyvtár* (Faculty of Humanities, Library of the History Department).—*Országos Rabbiképző Intézet* (Rabbinical Seminary, Budapest), and its library, in particular its director emeritus R. László Remete.—*Magyar Országos Levéltár* (Hungarian National Archives).—*Budapest Főváros Levéltára* (Budapest Municipal Archives), and in particular László Varga.—*Magyar Zsidó Levéltár* (Hungarian Jewish Archives), in particular Zsuzsanna Toronyi.—*Magyar Kereskedelmi és Vendéglátóipari Múzeum* (Hungarian Trade and Catering Museum).—*Magyar Mezőgazdasági Múzeum* (Hungarian Agricultural

Museum).—András Szántó, collector, owner of a large collection of printed postcards.—*Hild-Ybl Alapítvány Archívuma* (Hild-Ybl Foundation Archives).—*Országos Műemlékvédelmi Hivatal* (National Office for the Preservation of Historic Monuments), and its Photo Collection.—*Kunsthistorisches Museum* (Vienna). Reproductions of objects from museum and archival collections and from printed books were made by Z. László Nagy and István Móricz; by Csaba Gedai for the Hungarian National Museum, Numismatic Collection; and by the staff photographers of the collections, László Jaksity and Árpád Farkas for the Museum of Modern History; Mrs. Tibor Kolthay for the Library of the Hungarian Academy of Sciences; Mrs. András Márkus for the Kiscell Museum; by Mrs. Gábor Pechan for the Budapest Municipal Archives.

The translator of this book into English, Vera Szabó, a Yiddishist, did her best to make the material of the book accessible to the English reader. Her translation was edited by Mario Fenyő (New York), and then again and again by the editor and the authors, partly in order to update information and integrate recent research into the text of the book. Vera Benczik, an advanced student in our Department of Assyriology and Hebrew, took part in preparing the indexes of the English version.

Atlantic Press, and its director, Béla K. Király, initiated the present English edition. The publisher, Central European University (CEU) Press, its staff, the director, Klára Takácsi-Nagy, Péter Tamási publication manager, and Dolly Salgó, the proofreader, were of great help throughout the process of publishing. Typography of both the Hungarian and English versions was designed by István Kiss. We owe special and warm thanks to all of them.

The fact that there were two Hungarian editions indicates a certain interest in the book, which was well received by the public. Nevertheless, it was much disputed, first of all from the point of view whether the title *Jewish Budapest* is justified at all, and whether speaking of Jews as such in an—as critics have insisted—assimilated society was ahistoric. Yet, recent books of the type "Jewish Rome", "Jewish Venice", etc., or the Suhrkamp Verlag / Jüdischer Verlag series in German: *Jüdisches Städtebild* on Jewish cities (Amsterdam, Krakau / Cracow, Prag / Prague, Wien / Vienna), the map of Jewish Vienna, or guides to Jewish places in the United States and in Europe all speak in favor of our choice of title. Speaking of Jewish Budapest refers, on one hand, to a distinct component in the society of Hungary, and, on the other, to a Hungarian variant of the universal Jewish culture in the Diaspora.

Last but not least, the editor expresses his very special thanks to his daughter Szonja Ráhel Komoróczy, herself an advanced student in Jewish studies, for her substantial help in editing this English version and updating information on present-day Jewish life, including its reflection in English usage.

Without wanting to diminish the importance of the contribution of the three co-authors or the consultants, the editor would like to emphasize that responsibility for the data, for the views presented, and for the text with all the possible mistakes and faults rests with him.

January 16, 1999

Géza Komoróczy

Contents

A Hakdome

Buda, Óbuda, Pest: the population of the historical Budapest was rather diverse during the past centuries. Indeed, the city's socio-ethnic character can be defined in many ways. In any case, a person living in Buda, whether a subject of the Hungarian king or a citizen of Hungary, was *hungarus*, Hungarian. The inhabitants of Buda speak Hungarian—wrote Evliya Chelebi somewhat surprised in the seventeenth century, after a century or so of Turkish rule. But there were times during the occupation when Buda was a Turkish-speaking city. In those times, though, as Evliya notes, its population was mostly Bosnian. From the late Middle Ages on its burghers generally were Germans: the "Law Book of Buda" was written in German and the nineteenth-century Hungarian poet, János Arany, too, referred to Pest as a city where "there were stink and German and litter on the streets".

At the same time the medieval and modern towns eventually united as Budapest were Jewish cities, too. There was a Jewish quarter in each one of them. In Europe and over the world several great cities still have Jewish quarters or neighborhoods: Antwerp, Paris, New York (Williamsburg in Brooklyn, Boro Park or the Lower East Side and Harlem of earlier days) and have had them in the Middle East until very recently: as in Cairo or Baghdad. Despite the general modern scenery these quarters still evoke the image of the East, the Eastern Jews and the Eastern European *shtetl*.

On weekdays the streets are swarming with a busy crowd, buying and selling, hurrying to and fro. Men in black or *biber* hats, with long beards, possibly bending over the hood of a car which just broke down or in the subway—men wearing kaftans, velvet *kippah*s under their black hats, boots or breeches, black stockings. Boys with curly sidelocks among the regular metropolitan crowd, on foot, by bicycle or riding a bus. Bearded old men with beautiful, wise eyes, wearing coats from the times of Emperor Francis Joseph, long *kapote*s made of atlas or satin. Women whose head is carefully covered with kerchiefs, beautiful hats, or they are wearing wigs (*shaytl*), perhaps with their hair cut underneath.

Friday night the whole neighborhood becomes festive, traffic decreases. *Shabes*, the Sabbath, is about to arrive, everyone hurries to *shul*: the big synagogue or one of the small prayer-houses (*shtibl*) around the corner. Saturday morning shines with festivity. Men wearing their *shabesdik*, festive clothes: white stockings (*zokn*) and flat shoes (*shikh*), white wool threads, the *tsitses* hanging from under their coats. In Brooklyn or in Mea Shearim, Jerusalem, one can see men in wide, flat, fur-edged hats (*shtrayml*)—with velvet in the middle, occasionally sable tails hanging from the sides, altogether thirteen: this is what the distinguished Hasidic *rebe* wears. They too are Jews: a people.

1. Street vendors on Teleki tér, 1912. The man on the right is wearing a *kapote*

Such scenes are rare in Budapest. Occasionally one may catch a glimpse of it in the Wesselényi or Kazinczy utca, in the courtyard behind the Orthodox synagogue. An iron frame in the back of the courtyard—the frame of a *huppah*. Steps leading up to a small prayer-house and the "Hannah" restaurant. But the people in black kaftans are mostly tourists, Hasidic pilgrims visiting the graves of the *rebe* of Liszka or Kálló (*Kalev*). Similar might be the atmosphere once a year, on a late summer eve in front of the Romantic Moorish synagogue in Dohány utca, when hundreds or perhaps thousands of people gather for *Kol nidrei*. People here never wear the special garb of the Ultra-Orthodox but they, too, dress up for the festive occasion. Men in black hats, women in lace kerchiefs. Someone unfamiliar might pass by without noticing: they are gathering for a Jewish holiday, a service.

Yet a Jewish quarter does exist in Budapest; moreover, Jewish life here is not restricted to the Jewish quarter. Budapest does have a Jewish face as well: it may not be visible to everyone, but those who know about it will recognize the Jewish traits immediately.

A sefer on a hakdome iz vi a guf on a neshome, "A book without a foreword is like a body without soul"—says a Yiddish proverb. Therefore, let us continue with the following.

This book is about the Jewish face of Budapest: in other words, about the *Jewish Budapest*, about the Hungarian capital as a Jewish city. Naturally, this is only one aspect, one flavor of the metropolis. There is also a Roman- and a Greek-Catholic Budapest, a Lutheran and a Calvinist Budapest, a German, a Serbian and a Gypsy Budapest and some people may know that there was—and maybe still is—a Greek Budapest, as well.

We chose to write about Jewish monuments and relics, about the history of Jews in Buda, Óbuda and Pest: past and present Jewish life as an organic part of the life of the Hungarian capital, Budapest—be it memory or living reality. We will also write about Jewish life in general, about everyday life which is the same or very similar anywhere in the *goles*, in the Diaspora.

Our intention is not to write a guidebook, for such books already exist. Nor do we want to describe historical processes in a comparative perspective. We are to write only about those parts of the city where there is a story to tell: glimpses of Hungarian Jewish history. We will mainly talk about places where history is still visible, where it can be located, where its traces still exist or at least we know what happened there: in other words, we will describe the history of places that surround us, that are part of life in Budapest today.

We shall proceed according to the chronological sequence of the birth of Jewish quarters in Budapest.

I. Castle Hill

(1) The Old Jewish Quarter on Castle Hill (Szent György tér[1] / Szent György utca[2])

In medieval Hungary, like in the rest of Europe, the "keeping" of Jews, that is, giving Jews permission to settle down, was the right of the ruler, the king. From the fourteenth century on the king occasionally renounced this right and gave it to members of the nobility.

Jews settled in the new capital, Buda, i.e. on today's Castle Hill, after the Tartar invasion of the country (1241/42) as part of the reorganizational program under King Béla IV (1235–1270). At that time Buda was called Új-hegy (New Hill) or Új-Buda (New Buda) of "Pest"—this was how the territory that is now called Óbuda (Old Buda) gained its name. Jews may have lived here even before, during the eleventh century, but it was King Béla who first regulated the rights of Jews. By a charter issued on December 7, 1251, he allowed them to reside in the country.

King Béla granted the Jews the right to live in freedom, according to their own laws, under the special protection of the king. He allowed Jews to practice their religion, to choose their own "priests" (rabbis) and judges, to build synagogues. In certain legal disputes among Jews their own judges were allowed to decide; this basically meant that the king accepted traditional Jewish customs and law. He reserved himself the right to hand down sentences in certain serious cases. Jews were considered serfs of the Chamber (*servus camerae*), therefore they were called "Jews belonging to the Royal Chamber (*Judaei ad cameram regiam pertinentes*)". The consequence of this status was a special tax Jews were expected to pay. In commercial transactions their situation was similar to the rest of the city burghers. Several measures were taken to protect them from atrocities and abuse. King Béla's Charter of Freedom for Jews, based on the privileges issued by the Duke of Austria, Frederick II (the Belligerent) of Babenberg (1230–1246) in 1238, and its modified version from 1244 remained in effect in Hungary until the Battle of Mohács (1526); the Jewish community managed to renew it with every monarch.

A certain Count Teka / Theka (*comes* or *comes camerae* / *Kammergraf*), a rich gentleman who was supposedly Jewish at least by birth, played a considerable role in the financial affairs of the Hungarian Kingdom at the beginning of the thirteenth century, in the 1220s. King Andrew (Endre) II (1205–1235) mentions him in one of his charters under the name Teha, calling him a "Jew" (*iudeus*)[3] and "a count, because he has been placed in charge of the treasury". A coin, from the times of King Béla (*Belae rex*), i.e. Béla IV, has the Hebrew letter *tet* on its reverse, probably the initial of Teka.

2. Mint, 1515

---

[1] Hungarian *tér* means *square*.
[2] Hungarian *utca* means *street*.
[3] When quoting from Medieval sources we retained the original spelling. Consequently, several names and words are given in a form different from the classical spelling, e.g. *iudeus* for *Judaeus*.

3. Denarius of King Stephen (István) V. Obverse. Enlargement. In the mint-mark the Hebrew letter *alef*

4. Denarius of King Stephen (István) V. Obverse and reverse. Original size

5. Denarius of King Béla IV. Obverse. Enlargement. In the mint-mark the Hebrew letter *pe*

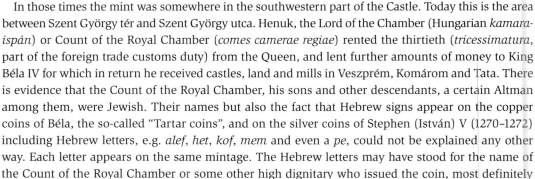

6. Denarius of King Béla IV. Obverse. Enlargement. In the mint-mark the Hebrew letter *mem*

Around 1235 this Teka can be traced in Austria, at the court of Frederick of Babenberg. He may have played a role in transmitting the charter of Frederick to Béla IV. But the main reason for issuing privileges to Jews must have been that Béla—aware of foreign models—realized that "keeping Jews", allowing Jews to live in the country entailed advantages for the Kingdom.

After the Tartar hordes left the country, the king, returning from exile, moved from Esztergom to Buda. He established several new institutions in his new residence, in the Castle of Buda, including a mint (*fabrica*). Earlier the only mint was in Esztergom. Around 1250 Béla invited *Henuk* (Hanokh / Henokh) or *Henel* (Hanele) from Vienna to Buda.[4] It seems likely that Henuk, earlier in the service of Frederick II, won his new position by lending money to the king. It must have been he who introduced minting in Buda.

In those times the mint was somewhere in the southwestern part of the Castle. Today this is the area between Szent György tér and Szent György utca. Henuk, the Lord of the Chamber (Hungarian *kamara-ispán*) or Count of the Royal Chamber (*comes camerae regiae*) rented the thirtieth (*tricessimatura*, part of the foreign trade customs duty) from the Queen, and lent further amounts of money to King Béla IV for which in return he received castles, land and mills in Veszprém, Komárom and Tata. There is evidence that the Count of the Royal Chamber, his sons and other descendants, a certain Altman among them, were Jewish. Their names but also the fact that Hebrew signs appear on the copper coins of Béla, the so-called "Tartar coins", and on the silver coins of Stephen (István) V (1270–1272) including Hebrew letters, e.g. *alef*, *het*, *kof*, *mem* and even a *pe*, could not be explained any other way. Each letter appears on the same mintage. The Hebrew letters may have stood for the name of the Count of the Royal Chamber or some other high dignitary who issued the coin, most definitely a Jew. The letter *het* could stand for Henuk, *alef* for Altman (Oltman). The letter *pe* may have stood for "Fredmanus (*iudeus comes camerae*)". Throughout the thirteenth century the king regularly appointed Jews to head the Chamber and they were put in charge of minting as well. The Bishop of Olmütz complained to Pope Gregory X (1271–1276) that in Austria, like in Bohemia and Moravia, there are too many Jews in the mints. It is possible that King Ladislaus (László) IV (1272–1290) prohibited the use of Hebrew mintages. His successor, Andrew (Endre) III (1290–1301) defended the *monetarius* people: "A Jew is in charge of our currency and it is his merit that our city is praised everywhere."

The earliest Jewish quarter of Buda was near the mint, between what is today Szent György tér and Szent György utca, on the western side. In those times—in the thirteenth and fourteenth centuries—it was called Jewish street (*platea Judeorum / Juden Gasse*). Judging from the Jewish charter issued by Béla we may assume that there was a synagogue, too. The *Illuminated Chronicle of the Hungarians* by Marc Kálti (1358) does indeed refer to a synagogue (*Synagoga Judeorum*): it mentions a certain gate which stands next to the synagogue. The building itself could have been under what is Dísz tér today or under the former building of the Ministry of Foreign Affairs, as László Zolnay, the archaeologist who excavated in the area meant. Others, e.g. András Kubinyi, a historian, locate the synagogue further to the North. The gate mentioned in *Illuminated Chronicle* as the predecessor of Fehérvári gate was called Jewish gate or Sabbath gate. (Occasionally it was called Logodi gate, after the neighboring village.)

[4] The transliteration of Hebrew names and words throughout the book follows the system applied by the *Encyclopaedia Judaica*, modified if necessary and omitting the diacritical signs. Yiddish, on the other hand, is transliterated according to the YIVO (New York) standard. The Germanized spelling of Hebrew and Yiddish, traditional in Hungary, is indicated only in some rare cases.

Another name that survives is Sabbath place, probably an open space near the Sabbath gate.

The name Sabbath gate (*Porta Sabbatina*, *Porta Sabbati* / in Hungarian: *Zombath kapw*) refers most probably to the fact that the Jewish quarter was closed for the Sabbath (from Friday evening until Saturday evening): it was surrounded by a chain or segregated by some other means, as was customary up until modern times. (In Kis-Márton/ Kismarton / Eisenstadt, today in Burgenland, Austria, one can still see pillars which held such chains.)

The enclosure for the Sabbath (*eruv*, "inclusion" or "unification") unites public and private domain and thus allows some freedom from the traditionally strict Sabbath rules. On the Sabbath it is forbidden to carry certain things from private domain (*reshut ha-yahid*), such as an apartment, to public domain (*reshut ha-rabbim*) or the other way around, because this would be considered work and thus break the commandment of resting on the Sabbath (Genesis 2,2–3; Exodus 20,10). The Sabbath chain or Sabbath rope achieves the "unification of the domains (*eruv hatzerot*)" and thus allows smaller things to be carried from one place to another within the private domain. It is forbidden to go further than two thousand cubits or steps from one's dwelling place (Exodus 16,29). Another way of ritually uniting a territory larger than the city within the Sabbath boundaries (*tehum shabbat*) is to place food on the border point, thus uniting the two separate two thousand step domains (*eruv tehumim*).

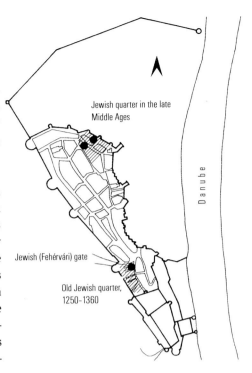

7. The two Jewish streets and synagogues on the Castle Hill of Buda

The first Jewish quarter in Buda must have evolved by the end of the thirteenth century. In 1279 the Synod of Buda, called together by the Holy See, forbade Christians to dwell under one roof with Jews and to communicate with them in a friendly manner—a sign that Jews and Christians must have lived together peacefully in Buda earlier. The growth of population and the desire to avoid conflicts must have justified segregation from the Jewish point of view as well. Moreover, the Synod of Buda ordered Jews to wear a discriminating badge: a patch of round red cloth (*circulus de panno rubeo*) on their upper garment, above their heart.

The first Jewish source concerning the Jews of Buda also dates from the thirteenth century. Yitzhak ben Moshe, author of *Or zaru'a* ("Spreading light", ca. 1260), a collection of responsa (for the source of the title see Psalms 97,11), was a rabbi in Vienna, who visited Hungary (*eretz Hagar*), Buda (*Buda* in the Hebrew text too) and Esztergom sometime before 1217. He was asked a Halakhic question (*she'elah*), whether the hot springs (in Latin texts: *calidae aquae*) may be used by women for their monthly ritual bath instead of cold water. His answer was affirmative: the Talmud, too, permits the use of the good thermal waters of Tiberias. The story bears additional information for us, namely that the Jews of Buda did not have a rabbi to decide over the important question of the daily and monthly use of the *mikveh*. In any case, the thermal waters of Buda were now considered ritually pure.

(2) Jewish Cemetery in Krisztinaváros (Alagút utca–Pauler utca–Roham utca–Attila utca)

The cemetery of the old Jewish quarter (*sepoltura Judeorum*) lay beyond the city walls, West of the Castle Hill, in Krisztinaváros, along the Szent Pál creek, which was covered and renamed Ördögárok in the nineteenth century. This is the area between Alagút utca, Pauler utca, Roham utca and Attila utca today. Its oldest known gravestone is dated 1278. It shows the name of R(av) Pesah b(en) r(av) Peter, i.e. "Master Pesah, son of Master Peter"; this is the oldest gravestone in all of Buda with a date on it. It was found in its original place (*in situ*) on the corner of Alagút utca and Pauler utca in 1894. Today it is on display in the Budapest Historical Museum.

8. The earliest Jewish gravestone of Buda, that of "Rav Pesah, son of Rav Peter", 5038 (1278 C.E.)

9. Jewish gravestones from the excavations in Buda on display in the former Lapidarium in the Round Bastion of the Fishermen's Bastion. Second from the right: gravestone of Lady Freudel (see fig. I:8 and Ch. I, 14, below)

In an appeal to the king in the eighteenth century the Jews of Buda referred to these gravestones to justify their claims for property: "The ancestors of the poor Jews received an entire Jewish street and a synagogue from the majestic and most glorious kings of Hungary; this is certain because there are five–six-hundred-year-old inscriptions on the gravestones (*die Grabinschriften in Stein gehauen*) next to the houses of that street (*nebst denen Heüsern*)"—they wrote in 1713 to King Charles (Károly) III (1712–1740) / Emperor Charles VI. The dates on the gravestones served to support the historical claims of the Jews of Buda. Being well versed in Hebrew they had no difficulty reading the text on the stones and converting the date; they used the same chronological system, the "minor era".

The Jews of Buda most probably knew not only the gravestones from the buildings of the Castle after the Recapture of Buda (1686). They must have also seen the gravestones in the cemetery in Krisztinaváros. The "five–six hundred years" may be a bit of an exaggeration compared to the reality, namely the thirteenth century, but a loose estimation to support property claims in an appeal may be acceptable. The Jewish street mentioned in the text was probably not the old Jewish street, what is today Szent György utca, but the new one, Werbőczy utca, today's Táncsics Mihály utca. The latter was referred to as *Juden Gasse* up until the mid-eighteenth century. By the eighteenth century the location of the first Jewish quarter was no longer known. Jewish gravestones were used for erecting new buildings, among others the István / St. Stephen's Chapel of Matthias Church, the houses underneath 9–11 and 13 Szentháromság utca, 6, 32 and 38 Úri utca, 1, 2 and 4 Hess András tér, 1 Táncsics Mihály utca, 4, 5 and 7 Dísz tér, 5–7–9 Színház utca (the former Carmelite monastery), 1–2 Szent György tér, throughout the Castle and even further away from the Castle, in the former summer residence of the famous novelist Mór Jókai on Sváb-hegy (19 Költő utca). The gravestones built into the houses of the Castle are partly from the Middle Ages and partly from the period of the Turkish rule. Does this mean that the construction workers picked them up from a single site? If so, the Jews of Buda must have been using the cemetery in Krisztinaváros to the very end of the seventeenth century. Another possibility is that the gravestones from the Turkish times were taken from the new cemetery, when materials were needed to rebuild the Castle district.

The Jewish cemetery of Krisztinaváros and its gravestones are mentioned by eye-witnesses as late as the beginning of the nineteenth century. In the course of some construction work at the end of the nineteenth century stones with inscriptions were found: David Kaufmann, Professor of the Rabbinical Seminary of Budapest, published them at first in a daily, the *Pester Lloyd* (1894) and later in *Archaeologiai Értesítő*, a journal of archaeology (1895). These publications were the first steps in Hebrew epigraphy in Hungary.

No Jewish cemetery from before the eighteenth century survived untouched, in its original place in Budapest or anywhere else in the country. The cemetery in Víziváros (ca. 1880) is a more recent one—found in its original place or close to it. The Jewish gravestones from medieval Buda and from the period of Ottoman rule are kept in the Hungarian Jewish Museum and in the Budapest Historical Museum. Some of the gravestones found at the end of the nineteenth century were placed in the Hungarian National Museum, while more recent findings are kept in the Budapest Historical Museum which also displayed some of the gravestones from the Round Bastion of the Fishermen's Bastion between the world wars. Some of the latter are on display at the Medieval Jewish Prayer-house (Táncsics Mihály utca) today.

Other gravestones were built into walls during the reconstruction of the Castle in the 1700s. These places are the restaurant "Fehér galamb" (11 Szentháromság utca), where four of the steps leading to the cellar were marble gravestones; some stones were located in the old part of the Hilton Hotel (2 Hess András tér), others in the former Carmelite monastery (5-7-9 Színház utca), on the ground floor corridor of the eastern wing and in the wall facing the garden, on the second floor. These stones were removed from the walls during the reconstruction of the historic monuments of the Castle Hill and placed in museums.

(3) New Jewish Quarter (Táncsics Mihály utca)

We know from the Chronicle of Josef ha-Kohen that the king of Hungary expelled the Jews from his country sometime around 1350 (Josef ha-Kohen says 5108 according to the era of creation, which is 1348 C.E.). They had to leave Buda as well. The expulsion occurred in consequence of the plague that swept over Europe in those years—reports Bonfini (*Rerum Ungaricarum decades*, II, x,199), but an additional motive of his decision was, as emphasized by a Latin chronicler, Johannes Küküllei, that King Louis Anjou (Lajos I / Lajos the Great) (1342–1382) failed in his plans to convert Jews. "(...) Striving for salvation, he wished to convert Jews to Catholicism and Christ but his plan failed because of the stubbornness of the Jews"—as quoted later in Hungarian chronicles, e.g. in the *Chronica Hungarorum* (printed by Andreas Hess, 1473), in the chapter "*De iudeorum expulsione*" and in *Chronicon Budense* (Buda, 1838) as well. We do not know whether these late explanations correspond to reality but, if they do, the "holy community (*kehal kodesh / kehillah kedoshah*)" deserves to be praised for its faithfulness.

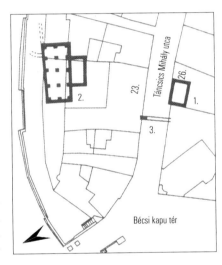

In 1364 Jews were allowed to return to Hungary. But since after their expulsion the king gave their houses to Hungarian nobles, they had to look for a new place to live. As László Zolnay put it: the Jewish quarter and the royal residence switched places. The king and his offices occupied the new palace on the southern side of the Castle. The new Jewish quarter was established on the northern side of the Castle district, around the lower part of Táncsics Mihály utca, running towards the West, near the old *Magna Curia Regis* or *Kammerhof*. This was the new *Judengasse*. Writing about the Turkish occupation of Buda Johannes Kessler, a Swiss Humanist, noted that "the Jewish street was marked off by walls and fortifications". Other sources mention a "round bastion" next to the Jewish street as well. This is possible but not very likely. More probably the observer mistook the wall of the Castle for a wall protecting the Jewish quarter, since its houses were built right on the wall, especially on the northern side.

Jews in Buda, as in several other medieval Hungarian cities (e.g. in Esztergom, Székesfehérvár, Pozsony, Sopron, Kőszeg) were serfs of the Royal Chamber; someone called them "treasury of the king". During the fifteenth–sixteenth centuries there may have been about five hundred Jews in Buda. In 1371 Louis the Great had ordered a Jewish Judge (*iudex Judeorum totius regni*) to rule over all internal matters. This high position was initially filled by the Master of royal incomes (*magister taverni-corum*), later the Palatine of Hungary. Jews retained judicial and administrative autonomy concerning internal matters. The office in charge was the *bet din*, a Rabbinical court consisting of at least three rabbis or learned persons from the community. Members of the *bet din* were called Jewish masters.

Jewish tradition, rooted in ancient customs, allows the communities themselves to retain jurisdiction. In the Diaspora this autonomy has always been rather limited by the principle of *Dina de-malkhuta dina*, "The law of the state is the Law", strictly followed by Jews in the Middle Ages as well

10. The new Jewish street (today: Táncsics Mihály utca) and the two synagogues on Castle Hill.
1: The "small" synagogue (26 Táncsics Mihály utca)
2: The "great" synagogue (23 Táncsics Mihály utca)
3: The archway between the two buildings (see fig. 30, below)

as today. Or, as Baron József Eötvös put it in 1840, "The laws of the state are *the* laws". This Talmudic legal principle (Gittin, 10) conforms to the words of prophet Jeremiah in the Bible: "And seek the welfare of the city to which I have exiled you and pray to the Lord in its behalf; for in its prosperity you shall prosper" (Jeremiah 29,7).[5] Jewish communities have always been law-abiding, loyal subjects or citizens. They turned to their own courts with questions of religious practice or with disputes within the community, involving only Jews. Rituals, religious customs and decisions of the community had to be observed by all its members, even if other communities lived according to different traditions. *Ha-kol ke-minhag ha-medinah*, "everything should follow the customs of the country" or, as a Yiddish proverb puts it, *A mineg brekht a din*, "Customs break the law". Thus the *bet din* usually ruled in cases like ritual divorce, issuing a letter of divorce (*get*), responsibility of men for the widows

of their deceased brothers (*halitzah*), converting non-Jews or children born to a non-Jewish mother to Judaism, monetary issues, inheritance, slander. The decision of the *bet din* (*pesak*) was final.

The institution of the Jewish Judge meant that Louis the Great tried to define the status of Jews "residing" (*commorans*) within the Hungarian state, giving them permanent legal status. By the late fifteenth century Buda became the center of Hungarian Jewry and also represented them at the royal court; it was always the Jews of Buda who confirmed Béla's Charter of Freedom.

In the late Middle Ages Buda was a German city and its inhabitants must have seen the ever growing Jewish

11. A former memorial slab commemorating the old Jewish street on the Castle Hill, 1866

community, supported by the king, as their competitors. Several anti-Jewish acts were recorded around the turn of the fourteenth–fifteenth centuries. A Jewish source (Shelomo ibn Verga / ben Virga, *Shevet Yehudah*, "Judah's Scepter", early sixteenth century) mentions that "in a city called Budun" a wax torch was lit in the market and it was announced that those Jews who converted before the torch burns down would be accepted as Christians but all others will be burnt. The Jews agonized: "How does the glory you are offering—replied a wise and brave Jew to the captain of the city—compare to the glory that shines on me from the LORD of the Souls if I do not become a Christian?" We may imagine the torch and the stake on the little square in front of the Vienna gate; but the story—though it may be typical of the Jews' dangerous predicament in general—is only a figment of time and imagination. In any case, a gravestone in the Jewish cemetery of Krisztinaváros calls the year 1405, the year of King and Emperor Sigismund's (Zsigmond) (1387-1437) decree, the "cursed year (*shenat kelalah*)". This decree stressed the rights of the royal cities vis-à-vis foreign merchants, placing the Jews at the mercy of the municipal administration. Soon the Law Book of Buda (*Ofner Stadtrecht*, ca. 1420) called Jews "hateful, stubborn, smelly betrayers of God" and restricted their activities. The law ordered Jews once again to wear a discriminating badge, forbade them to sell their merchandise beyond the Jewish street, to collect interest and pawn ecclesiastical objects, though punishment was to be delayed until the day of the Last Judgment. On the other hand, the law allowed Jews to buy property and decreed the death penalty for the killing of a Jew. In other words, King Sigismund wanted to restrict the commercial and financial activities of Jews—the very activities which made the presence of Jewish serfs of the Chamber desirable in the royal courts. Several Western European, Ashkenazi Jews found a home and made a living in Buda. A knight from Burgundy wrote about Buda: "There are several Jews here, they speak French well, many of them were expelled from the kingdom of France" (Bertrandon de la Brocquière, 1433). He was probably referring to the expulsion of 1394 when French Jews escaped through Northern Italy and scattered all over Europe. The first rabbi of Buda, a certain "*magister Josephus Judeus*", or "*der Jude Joseph Rabbi zu Ofen*" (1436) was

---

[5] Quotations from the Bible follow The Jewish Publication Society of America's recent edition (1962-1982), modified, if necessary, according to the documentary evidence quoted.

of French background, too. Fülöp Grünvald could confirm the Western European origin of the family and he noted that R.[6] Josef made the acquaintance of Sigismund and Queen Borbála in Constance. The other side of the story is that Emperor Sigismund—on request of the Jews—reissued the Jewish charter of Béla IV for all the Jews living in the Hungarian Kingdom several times (e.g. in 1396 and 1422).

Some time in the 1470s King Matthias (Mátyás) (1458–1490) abolished the institution of the Jewish Judge and established a new position instead, that of the Jewish Principal or Prefect (*praefectus Judaeorum* / "*obrister der judischhait*", in Old Hungarian: *az sydoknak elewthek yaroyok*) who was responsible for the Jewry of the whole country. This position was filled by the leader of the Jews of Buda (*supremus*). Mendel, "the Jew" (*Mendel Jvd*), who was appointed Prefect by the king, must have lived in Buda for a long time already and his position suggests that he must have had a leading role among the Jews of Buda. He could have been the community leader (*rosh ha-kahal*) or at least one of the *parnasim* or *shtadlanim*. He is mentioned as *supremus* in a document from 1474 and as a *praefectus* in 1482. Due to the coincidence of these two positions Hungarian Jewry was in a special situation: the Jewish Prefect, who was simultaneously the head of the "holy community", was one of the leaders of the country due to his rank. The difference between the Jewish Judge and the Jewish Prefect resulted in considerable improvement in the status of the Jewish community. Earlier, the Jewish Judge was a non-Jewish person appointed by the king to rule over the Jewish community, while the Prefect was a member of the community put into a leading position. King Matthias may have thought that he would collect more taxes from the Jews if the leader of that community were a member of the royal court. The Jewish Prefect of Buda had almost the same rank as the exilarch (*resh galuta*) in Talmudic times in Babylon: he was the real leader of the autonomous Jewish community (*universitas Judeorum*). This meant the realization of an ancient form of traditional Jewish community leadership. The Jewish Prefects of Buda, Mendel Jacob and his successors were virtually called "Prefect of all Jews" (*Judeorum prefectus universalium*), "Jewish prince" (*princeps Judeorum* / *prince des juifs*—Pierre Choque), even "Jewish king". Well, this last title was indeed an exaggeration.

12. Pointed hat (*Judenhut*) as a Jewish badge in a medieval prayerbook

(4) The Jewish Prince of Buda

Until the very end of the Jewish prefecture, that is, the Turkish occupation of Hungary, this office was held by members of the Mendel (Mendl / Mandl) family of Buda who most probably came from Nürnberg. They included Judah Mendel or "Mendel the Jew" (*Mendel Jvd* or *Judaeus*) (Prefect ca. 1480); Jacob (ca. 1495); Jacob Judah (ca. 1500); Jacob *filius Jacobi* (ca. 1515); Israel (ca. 1525); Isaac (ca. 1530). (Neither the names nor the dates are exact and we do not know the family relations either.) It must have been the king's privilege to appoint the Prefect, thus Jews still belonged under the king's authority. King Matthias called the leaders "Prefects of our Jews" (*iudeorum nostrorum prefectus*).

Leaders of the Jewish community thought that the coronation and other festivities were the most convenient time to win the good-will of the king. The Prefect was not only entitled to or interested in participating in such festivities, it was probably his duty, too. All of the Mendels lived up to their tasks and made use of their opportunities. They always acted on behalf of the Jewish community.

1458: After Matthias was elected king the delegates of the Jews, among them a certain "Men(d)el" (MWL, correctly: MN[D]L), i.e. Mendel, carrying the "tablets" of the Old Testament (*praeferens veteris testamenti tabulas*) were first to greet him in Buda and ask for the confirmation and expansion of

---

[6] R. stands for Rabbi / rabbi.

their privileges (i.e. the privileges issued by Béla IV). The strangely spelled, maybe misspelled name most probably hides the Ashkenazi name of *Mendel Jvd*, now community principal (*supremus*), later Prefect. The word *tabulae* (tablets) may refer to the double tablets from the synagogue (*shenei luhot avanim*), as mentioned in one of the sources published by Johann G. Schwandtner (1716–1791), a Viennese professor and librarian (who uses the Latin term, *decalogus*, "Ten Commandments"). Or it may mean the Torah scrolls, which sounds more likely, since the "Old Testament" is mentioned. We have only indirect evidence. It is not customary, often even impossible to carry the Tablets of the Law

(*shenei luhot ha-Torah*). In those times, even in a passage about the Jewish oath (III, 36) in *Tripartitum opus juris consuetudinarii* (1517), a normative handbook of legal customs in the noble Hungarian kingdom by István Werbőczy, a high state official, *tabulae Moysis* meant nothing but the Books of Moses, i.e. the Torah scrolls. The word *tabula* in plural could also mean document. It is likely that the Jewish delegates held the Torah in their hands.

1464: The Jews of Buda were among those who escorted King Matthias to Székesfehérvár for the coronation ceremony. Mendel was leading the king and his company, riding a horse, with sword at his side and ostrich-feather in his cap, accompanied by a *banderium* of sixteen with banners and trumpets.

Winter 1476/77: The wedding of King Matthias and Beatrix of Aragon. On Sunday, December 8, the Jewish *banderium* bade farewell to the king who was about to leave for Székesfehérvár to welcome his bride. They wanted to join the king but he ordered them to stay in Buda. Mendel, the Jew (*der Mendl Jvd*) rode into the inner courtyard of the Castle, circled around the fountain and delivered a little speech (*ain redlein*). He had thirty-one fine horses with him. On the first horse rode a boy (or Mendel's son), holding a silver sword and playing the trumpet beautifully. His trumpet was decorated with a banner. He was followed by ten other young men, all riding horses. They all wore silver belts with square buckles—of the size of a cup—holding a pitcher of wine. They carried long, silver swords with decorated hilts and scabbards on their sides. Mendel the Jew himself rode his horse in "gray (ceremonial) clothing (*in grab*)": on his head a pointed high hat lined with velvet and decorated with a buckle, on his side a long silver sword (*ain lanngs silbrenis schwertt messer*). The others rode in pairs, wearing brown uniforms and hats decorated with two white ostrich-feathers (*strawssenveder*), and a brown one between them. They spent one hour in the inner courtyard of the Castle. Then they rode to Székesfehérvár, choosing a different route (Hanns Seybold, Bavarian scribe and chronicler, 1482).

13. Jacob Mendel, "Prefect of the Jews"

14. Portrait of "Mandl Jvd" (Mendel) on his seal

King Matthias and Beatrix were crowned in Székesfehérvár on Thursday and returned to Buda on the following Sunday (December 15) with their attendants. The nobles, burghers and even the Jews departed from the city to greet the Queen, dressed in ceremonial garments. The Jews, a *banderium* of twenty-four, all of them on brown horses, holding banners, and members of the synagogue (*Judenschule*), men and women, the elderly under one "roof (*hymel*)", came carrying "the Commandments of Moses swaddled like a baby" and singing for the Queen according to their law (*nach irem Gesetze*) (Peter Eschenloer, notary of Boroszló / Breslau). The elderly stood under a canopy (*sub uno umbraculo*) surrounded by younger people, one of whom was holding a "tablet" (*tabula*) decorated with gold. Their red banner (*rubeum vexillum*) was adorned with a Hebrew inscription in guilded letters spelling "*Schina Israhel*" and "two golden stars (*duae aureae stellae*)" or "three golden stars (*drey guldin stern*)" according to other sources. (In the texts: *pes bubonis, quinque aculeis* and *truttenfuess, Dauid wappen*, that is, five-clawed owl- or fowl-foot, etc.) Pointed Jewish hats (*Judenhuett / Iudaica aurea tyara*) surrounded by golden flames ("halos") were depicted on the banners and shields. Israel rejoiced when the king approached them and they sang a song loudly (*mit lauter stym*). Seybold noted that he did not understand the song but he was told it was in Hebrew. They gave a speech in front of the Queen, too. The old man standing in the middle under the canopy held a wrapped scroll (*ain eingewickeltte tocken*) (Tuch, "kerchief"), topped by a golden plate (*ain guldins*

plech) in front of the Queen and wanted her to kiss it but the Queen did not want to do so: "(...) *de tätten die Juden die tocken auff vnnd woltten der künigin zeküssen haben geben. Sy woltt aber nicht.*" At the end of the procession rode two hundred Jews, their heads covered with prayer shawls (*ephod*) (*in capite Ephod impositum habebant*) (Schwandtner). According to another source their heads were all covered with silk and damask hoods (*seyden vnd damaschk kaputzen*), i.e. prayer shawls. They handed their present, among them two huge, live deer, to the royal couple and asked for their patronage.

15. "Wedding procession of King Matthias (Mátyás) and Beatrix to Buda in 1476." Lithograph by Béla Vízkelety, 1864

The wedding itself started on the following Sunday (December 22) and lasted until January 6. The cost of one of these feast days was covered by the Jews of Buda (Bonfini, *Decades*, IV, ɪv 35–62; Seybold; Bongars, delegate of the Elector of Pfalz).

The description of the Queen's coronation ceremony and the wedding is interesting from the Jewish historical point of view not only because it talks about the renaissance pomp and wealth of the Jews of Buda: this was natural in those times, as was the procession with a *banderium*. These descriptions, reflecting the non-Jewish observers' lack of familiarity or understanding, also preserve unique information about the religious symbols and customs of the Jews of Buda, which would otherwise remain hidden from us. Their interest, too, must have been tackled by the Jewish *banderium* since they had never seen anything like it at home. The fact that the Jewish community of Buda had a banner with an emblem is in itself a sign of the institutional strength of their position: only acknowledged communities had the right or privilege to march with a banner. The banner indicates that the status of the Jews was the same or very similar to other privileged groups. The king's court belittled or rejected them only if they insisted on executing their peculiar customs.

The way the red banner of Mendel's *banderium* is described in the sources recalls the medieval banner of the Jews of Prague which can be seen next to the *bimah* in the *Altneushul* in that city today. This banner is made of scarlet velvet, decorated by a golden embroidered six-pointed star with a golden *Judenhut* in the middle and an old Hebrew inscription: *Shema Yisra'el*. Judging from the descriptions, the banner of Buda was very similar to this one. The only difference is the inscription, though the sources do not agree on this issue. Some reports say that the text in the banner was *Schina Israhel* or, the way we would write it, *Shekhinah Yisra'el*, "God (and) Israel". Another author, Seybold, translates the inscription in Hebrew characters (*hebreysch*) in his German commentaries:

CASTLE HILL 11

"*hortts kinder Israhel*", "Hear, sons of Israel"—in Hebrew, *Shema Yisra'el*. The banner in Prague confirms Seybold's translation. The Jews of Buda could have chosen the name *Shekhinah* instead of God's name; *shekhinah* "(God's) dwelling place", symbolically means God himself. But it is more likely that the person who explained the meaning of the words to Bonfini did not understand them fully either and thus mistook the letter *mem* in *shema* for the letters *kaf* and *yod* in *shekhinah*. The strange embroidery must be a five- or rather six-pointed "shield of David (*magen David*)". The five- or six-pointed star or, for that matter, the pentagon or hexagon was an emblem in the banner and so was the pointed Jewish hat; the six-pointed star was not yet among the important Jewish symbols in those times. It is possible that Mendel's pointed hat was an ordinary, if rather fancy, *Judenhut*.

The Jews of Buda must have carried a Torah scroll with them, a real scroll in a mantle, i.e. "dressed up"; it even had a golden Torah shield. They held the Torah in front of the royal couple waiting for them to kiss it—this is how Jews themselves honor the holy book. They chanted ritual songs and prayers. They wore clothes which are normally worn to pray: the "*ephod*" or "hood" must have been the *tallit*, a huge prayer shawl which covered their head and shoulders. Though they participated in a celebration of the court, a Christian ceremony, their behavior was strictly traditional. It is obvious that leaders of the Jewish community of Buda were accepted in the court of King Matthias as Jews. True, the Queen did not want to kiss the Torah—she probably did not even understand why it is being held in front of her and rejected the obtrusive gesture. The authors who reported on the festivities, all members of the court, some of them foreigners, admired the wealth of the Jews of Buda. Their garments and accessories were completely unfamiliar to them.

1490: Ulászló II is elected king. The Jews greeted the king outside Új-Buda, carrying the "tablets of Moses" (*Mosis tabulae*) and asking him to observe their privileges (Bonfini, *Decades*, IV, x,32). September 21 (day of the coronation): The Prefect escorted the king to Fehérvár leading a *banderium* with weapons of such pomp as man had never seen.

1502: The wedding of Ulászló and Anne of Candale. The king received his bride in Székesfehérvár on September 27. The Jewish Prince was present, too, accompanied by other Jews in ceremonial garb (Pierre Choque).

The imprint of Jacob Mendel's seal is preserved on a contract (December 12, 1496); his initials in Hebrew characters are J M.

Mendel's often-mentioned sword was in possession of the Andrássy family (Manó Andrássy) until after World War I. Today the Jewish Museum exhibits a sword of honor, an antique one, with two inscriptions on its steel blade, Hebrew intarsia in silver: "Jhwh, my Lord, the strength of my deliverance" (Psalms 140,8) and, among the words of the first inscription in an oval frame, the second: "Let the name of Jhwh be blessed now and forever" (Psalms 113,2).

Was this Mendel's sword? Several older scholars expressed their opinion or hope that it was. Actually, it dates from the seventeenth century. The inscription is a fine intarsia, which could only have been manufactured together with the sword, maybe for a Jewish customer. In those times Jews never wrote down the four holy letters (the *Tetragammaton*). This way of spelling could only have been known to someone who looked it up in the Hebrew Bible. In fact, the learned customer certainly knew the continuation of the short quotations as well, which suits a sword perfectly:

"You protected my head on the day of battle."
(Psalms 140,8)

The Andrássy sword could not have been Mendel's, but it reveals much about the level of familiarity with the Hebrew Bible in the seventeenth century.

The literature mentions another sword in the Andrássy collection: a short, curved scimitar. (If it is not identical with the previous one, its location is unknown.) According to the descriptions this sword has the same inscription:

ה׳ אדני עז ישועתי סכתה לראשי ביום נשק

"H' [HA-SHEM], my LORD, the strength of my deliverance,
You protected my head on the day of battle."
(Psalms 140,8)

God's name is written according to Jewish tradition. It is impossible to tell the origin of the sword from the short descriptions.

The Mendel family had a great career: members of the family were leaders of the Jewry of Buda and Hungary for about three quarters of a century. András Kubinyi argues that it was the treasurer (*thesaurarius*) of King Matthias, János Ernuszt (Hampó), who helped them settle in Buda, possibly because of their previous business contacts. Ernuszt was a Jew from Vienna who converted to Christianity; he became a burgher of Buda, purveyor by special appointment, merchant, royal treasurer. He must have advised King Matthias to establish the Jewish prefecture. The goal of this change was to ensure the collection of taxes: this way one person was responsible for collecting taxes from the Jewish communities of several cities. In King Matthias's times there were 10–15 of them. Half of all taxes collected in Buda were paid by Jews. The situation was probably similar in other towns. This meant a lot of money. Like Ernuszt, Mendel was a financier, which is why he was in the service of the king. After the death of King Matthias someone wrote about him: "He must have been as wealthy as the two counts (*graf*) of the country together."

It was the 1251 privilege issued by Béla IV that encouraged Jews to engage in financial transactions, money-lending and pawnbroking. According to Biblical law Jews may not collect interest on loans to each other (Deuteronomy 23,20–21). Interest could be collected on certain conditions on loans of cash, but never on loans of grain; based on the principle of solidarity, there were different regulations for transactions among Jews and non-Jews, rich and poor (Mekhilta, ad Exodus 22,24). Christianity accepted the same principle. In Hungary, as well as in the rest of medieval Europe, the Christian Church forbade Christians to collect interest from each other. The privilege of Béla IV as well as the Law Digest of Buda permitted Jews to carry out financial transactions. They could take pledges for money-loans. They had to renew their claims every year, or else forfeit their right. In case their loan was not paid back, they were allowed to sell the pawn or collect their claims some other way. In the fifteenth century maximum interest rate was—according to the regulations of King Sigismund (Zsigmond)—2% weekly, which could amount to over 100% a year, although this rarely happened due to the usually shorter periods of loans. With other loans the amount of debt doubled whenever the due date was extended. The high interest rate was matched by high risk: the king, exercising his pardoning privilege, often canceled interest payments to Jews. This was called "letter-killing" (*Brieftöten*), maybe because canceling the debt meant literally punching a hole in the contract. Apart from trade which was made difficult in many ways, financial transactions were the only other way Jews could make a living; lending money to royal courts, towns and aristocrats also meant a chance to win permission to reside.

King Matthias's decree ordered the Prefect to apportion taxes among Jews. The Prefect was granted official help to collect taxes. But he also had the right to see to it that the privilege of Jews was observed everywhere. Harassment of Jews would have reduced the taxes they pay. The Prefect was a mediator between towns and Jews in legal disputes and he relayed Jewish complaints to the king. He also took measures against Jews who converted to Christianity if they meant to harm the Jewish community. In matters concerning the whole of Jewry he asked for the opinion of each community. He lent money to Christian burghers and nobles, towns and the royal court. King Ulászló owed large sums to his Prefect. Louis (Lajos) II (1516–1526) had to pledge even his silver ware. The Prefect, a man of high rank, had a say-so in state matters as well. As a privilege of his rank he and his family were exempt from the obligation of wearing identification badge, even when traveling abroad.

In Hungary, like in the rest of Europe, Jews were required to wear identification badges time and again during the Middle Ages. The first such regulation after the Golden Bull (1222) was issued by

Andrew (Endre) II on the request of Pope Gregory IX (1227-1241) in 1233 (Oath of Bereg). The Council of Buda (1279) prescribed that Jews wear a round patch of red cloth; the yellow patch marked other "Eastern" foreigners—Saracens and Ismaelites. According to the Law Digest of Buda the Jewish badge is a red coat (*rother mantel*, Jewish coat) with a yellow patch (*gilber fleck*, Jewish patch) which may not be hidden—a sign of German influence. Later it was a hood, *csuklya* in Hungarian (*capucinum quod vulgariter* cuclya *vocatur*) or a pointed hat, the Jewish hat (*Judenhut*). All these marks implied strong negative discrimination, those who wore them were placed at a serious disadvantage compared to others. The charter issued by Béla IV, naturally, did not contain anything like that; Matthias and later the Jagellos extended the privileges of the Jewish Prefect to all Jews, at first only to those living in Buda, but later, after the time of Louis (Lajos) II—despite the strong resistance of the German inhabitants of the city—to the Jews of all Hungary (1520). The burghers of Pozsony protested: Jews should not be allowed to dress the way they do in Buda, i.e. walk around without wearing the Jewish insignia. Louis II calmed them down: "Wearing the Jewish hood in this country is unheard of"—wrote Pál Várdai, at that time Royal Treasurer in Buda, later, after the Battle of Mohács, Archbishop of Esztergom. And when King Ferdinand prescribed wearing the Jewish insignia, a round yellow patch over the heart, in the Austrian provinces, his order did not apply to the Hungarian territories of the country.

(5) The Mendel Houses (23, 26, 28 Táncsics Mihály utca)

The Mendel family had several residences in the (new) Jewish street, in Hebrew *rehov ha-Yehudim*, "street of the Jews", near the city wall, on both sides of the street. We must assume the huge building-complex served multiple functions: it was the home of the Jewish Prefect, the dwelling place of people in service of the community, as well as a synagogue.

Excavations so far could uncover only parts of the buildings. Next to some buildings from times long before the Mendel family some archaeological remains were found which could not have belonged to ordinary houses of those times, for instance, arches over octagonal stone pillars. These arches served to create one large room out of several small ones on the ground floor. The "great" synagogue was built in one of the courtyards.

This was the center of the "holy community". The Prefect was entitled to appoint the chief rabbi of Buda. Ulászló even gave him the right to appoint the chief rabbi of Hungary, as an extension of the rights of the chief rabbi of Buda. He also appointed the employees of the community, in those times the cantor (*hazzan*) and other community servants (*shammash / judex ordinarius / subjudex / Meister*, in Hungarian: *kisbíró*). These servants (beadle / *shames*)—there was more than one—acted from time to time on behalf of the Prefect as delegates (*shaliah*, delegate). The building even had a jail, should the Prefect need to imprison someone (a Jew) for unpaid taxes or some other minor transgression.

*

Under the Jagellos there were several pogroms in the Jewish street. The mob never missed the Mendel Houses. One of the pogroms, that of August 1496, is described by Bonfini (*Decades*, V, v, 102-109) in the final passage of his historical work. He names general dissatisfaction as the cause of the tragic events. The Bishop of Eger as well as the king himself took energetic measures against the raging mob.

"In the street of the Jews some irresponsible Christian youngsters caused a riot, shouting disrespectfully in front of the doors of the Jews, throwing stones at their windows. When the Jews tried to chase them away, a crowd of shady characters, mostly poor people who were ready to destroy and plunder, attacked them. (...) The fight lasted till midnight. At dawn some people, not satisfied with the unsuccessful attack of the night before and hoping for more plunder, launched a new attack on the houses of the Jews; the crowd grew from hour to hour, they smashed the doors and windows, stole their belongings, jumped on the pawned articles, gold and silver dishes, silk dresses; others, waiting for the bandits at some distance from the houses, attacked them and took the stolen goods—thinking this was a safer way to rob (...). Moreover, the servants of the elegant Jews, who were ordered by their masters and the king to help fight against the riot, started plundering themselves, pretending to protect the house. Due to the horror and fear which ruled over the whole city the king decided to take measures himself and sent down the captain of the Castle with his guardsmen. The mob, seeing these men hang some of the plunderers, dispersed very quickly."

(6) "Great" Synagogue (23 Táncsics Mihály utca)

The building was found by Melinda H. Papp and excavated by László Zolnay, István Gedai and Rózsa Feuer Tóth (1964/65). Built in the fifteenth century, the synagogue stood in the courtyard of the Mendel Houses. Today it is in the garden of the former Zichy palace. Its floor lies four meters (13 feet) below ground level.

The "great" synagogue was built when the building was already owned by the Mendel family. It stood in the back of the courtyard, against the city wall. Its ground floor was one or two steps above the courtyard. Its central hall consisted of two huge naves, separated by three pillars. These pillars supported at least eight arches aligned along the axis of the building. The tall, square base held a pyramidal element and an octagonal shaft. The crossbeams and ribs holding the vault extended directly from the fluted shaft, without a crown. The vault was supported by similar half-pillars along the walls. Both the wide crossbeams and narrow-fillet ribs were jointed by deep grooves. The hall, constructed according to the strict architectonic canons of the late Gothic period, must have been at least 7.5 to 8 meters (25–26 feet) high. The size of the prayer-house (10 m × 26 m, 33 × 85 feet) suggests that it was used by a large congregation. Next to the main building there was a separate prayer room for women. Small apertures were cut on the wall between the men's and women's prayer-rooms to enable the women to hear and keep up with the men's prayer. This type of segregation was customary and can still be seen in the *Altneuschul* in Prague.

Similar two-nave synagogues were often built by Ashkenazi Jews, from the twelfth century on, wherever the size of the community, their rights and economic means allowed it—initially in Worms, Cologne, Regensburg; the Altneushul in Prague from the thirteenth century; the Kazimierz Synagogue in Cracow under Kazimierz Wielki (Casimir the Great, 1337–1370). These buildings towered over the small, 60–70 square meter (650–750 square feet) prayer-houses of the *shtetlekh* with metropolitan grandeur. The two-nave construction was intentional: a Jewish house of prayer should not look like a Christian cathedral, three naves would remind people of the holy trinity, also there should not be a transept resembling the cross. In all other respects, however, the architectural style of the age was dominant. Following foreign models meant that the Jews of Buda claimed a leading position among Hungarian Jewry.

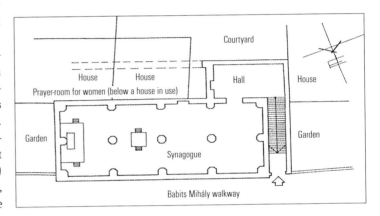

16. Ground-plan of the "great" synagogue on the Castle Hill, Buda

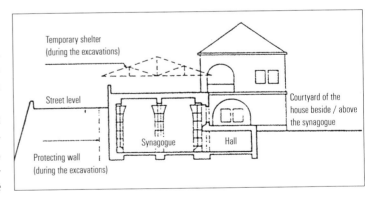

17. Cross-section of the "great" synagogue

18. Interior of the
"great" synagogue.
Reconstruction,
timber ceiling version

19. Interior of the
"great" synagogue.
Reconstruction,
vaulted ceiling version

One of the middle pillars bears two inscriptions: Hebrew letters which have been interpreted by Sándor Scheiber as numbers. One of them is a *shin* (= 300) and an *alef* (=1) giving the year 301 according to the "minor era", i.e. 1541. The other inscription is equally short, two, or rather one letter: *bat pe*. The numerical value of the letter *pe* is 80. In Scheiber's interpretation "Eighty years old". (The Hebrew expression literally means "daughter of eighty".) Based on these two inscriptions Scheiber and Zolnay concluded that in 1541 the synagogue was eighty years old, consequently it was built in 1461.

The synagogue in the Mendel House must have been built by wealthy people of refined taste for it is the most beautiful relic of the late Gothic period in Buda and there are but few as impressive in the whole of Europe. In view of its age we have to call this the "new" synagogue.

Jews returning to Buda in 1541, when the city was already under Turkish occupation, could not maintain the synagogue in its original, impressive form. The evidence for this are some minor repairs and brickwork from the Turkish period. But it is likely that they continued to use the building as a synagogue, at least for a while. This must have been the Ashkenazi synagogue in those times, the place where the chief rabbi of Buda used to preach, the building that Yitzhak Schulhof, the chronicler of the 1686 siege, refers to when he mentions "the synagogue".

The building was heavily damaged already during the 1684 siege. A male skeleton was found in the ruins covering the floor; the man was buried according to tradition, with a *tefillin* on his left arm.

20. Remains of the
southern, longitudinal
wall of the "great"
synagogue.
The date on the pillar:
301 (=1541 C.E.)

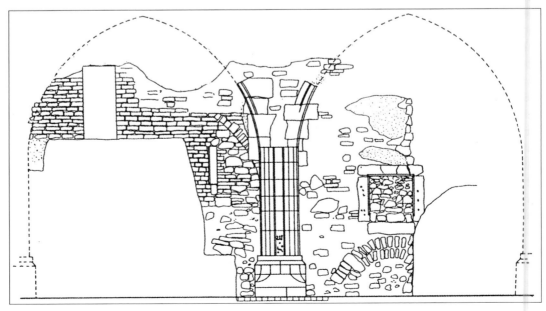

The "new" synagogue collapsed completely in 1686, as Christian armies attacked Buda.

In the synagogue there were moveable pews and prayer-stools designed for one person with a stand for the prayer-book. These were usually kept next to the wall. The pews were called *istender* (*Ständer* / *shtender*) in the language of Ashkenaz.

> "In the community of Buda (*Budun*) or in German *Ofen* (...), like in other German communities, everyone buys a place in the synagogue, he sits there, he owns that place, he can rent, sell or give away this seat as a present."
>
> (Hayyim ben Shabbetai, *Torat hayyim*, ca. 1630)

The ruins of the synagogue remained untouched during the centuries following the recapture of Buda and thus they were found in their original position during the excavations of 1964/65. Unfortunately, the almost completely excavated building had to be reburied in 1966 partly for financial reasons and partly because there is a building above one of the walls of the women's gallery today. It is known only from the descriptions and photos of Melinda H. Papp, László Zolnay and the sketches made by Aurél Török. Some of its stones, a pillar and some arch fragments are displayed in the Medieval Jewish Prayerhouse across the street.

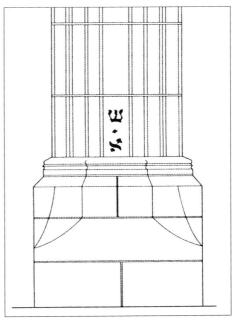

21. The Hebrew date inscription on a pillar in the "great" synagogue: *shin* and *alef*

Until the building is uncovered again it is worthwhile to have a look at the mound over the ruins. We can approach it from the Mihály Babits promenade. It can be seen in the courtyard surrounded by the house, behind an iron fence.

(7) Rabbinical Learning in Budavár

Jewish learning thrived in Buda in the times of King Matthias, the Jagellos and the Mendel family. There were Hebrew codices in the collection of the royal library (Bibliotheca Corviniana). Though Matthias must have bought or received these codices from abroad and they were probably never used by Hungarian Jews, the fact of keeping such books has symbolic relevance. It tells us that the Humanists acknowledged the importance of studying all three holy tongues. Among other Humanists an eminent Christian Hebraist, Petrus Niger (Schwartz), was active at Matthias's royal university. He had learned Hebrew in Spain, studied at German and French universities and was ordained as a Dominican friar. He was among the first European scholars who, in spite of their considerable Jewish lore, wanted to convert Jews to Christianity using the argument that the true Messiah whom Jews were still awaiting had already come. Matthias invited him from Würzburg to become the director of the university at the Szent Miklós monastery of the order in Buda. The arguments of

22. Theological dispute between Christian and Jewish scholars. Both parties draw their arguments from the Bible. The Jews are wearing the *Judenhut*

23. Fragment of a page from a Hebrew codex, possibly from Buda

Petrus's work, *Stern des Meschiach* (1477), are partly based on Jewish (Hebrew) sources.

The propaganda to convert Jews was meant as an honest attempt to integrate Jews into European society. Historically it bears witness to the influence of the Jewish community; it indicates that at least the intellectual elite realized that the presence of Jews could not be regulated by discriminative measures. The fact that arguments favoring conversion were derived from within, from Jewish texts, inspired the Humanists to study Hebrew and traditional Jewish texts. Attempts to convert Jews to Christianity were successful only among individuals, not whole Jewish communities. Whether conversion was motivated by the theological arguments about the Messiah, or by the attraction of careers open only to Christians remains unclear. On the other hand, the study of the original text of the Bible, the interest in Jewish Messianism and the Kabbalah led to the emergence of Hebraic studies in Europe, contributed to the cultural integration of early modern Europe and even gave a little push towards the social acceptance of Jews.

Sources do not mention whether Petrus had any contact with the rabbis of Buda, but it seems unlikely that King Matthias or the Humanists would have lacked all curiosity about the opinion of a group of people who honored them at royal ceremonies holding holy Jewish scripts.

Akiva ha-Kohen, son of Menahem ha-Kohen, was a noted rabbi at the end of the century. We do not know his status in Buda. According to his contemporaries and the inscription on his daughter's gravestone in Prague he was a *nasi*, prince or leader; R. Simhah later wrote that he was the head of the exiled Jews (*rosh le-kol ha-golah*). He may have been the rabbi of the Buda community for a while and thus considered a *princeps* by outsiders, just like the Prefect. R. Simhah also mentions that he used to write his name in golden letters (*be-otiyot zahav*). One of his hand-written documents (1496) survived—a certificate about someone's debt, in Hebrew. This is naturally not signed in gold. He left Buda because of certain slanders and was again accused in Prague, where he settled after leaving Buda. Was he disdainful or too ambitious? In any case, his generous, charitable acts were not forgotten.

A Hebrew-language chronicle from Prague from the early seventeenth century by an unknown author mentions that in the winter of 1497/98 R. Meir Pfefferkorn, the rabbi of Prague held lectures on the Talmud for the congregation of Buda every day; it seems that he had been invited to instruct the Jews of Buda.

At the beginning of the sixteenth century the rabbi of Buda was Naftali ben Yitzhak ha-Kohen Hircz (Herz). He corresponded with several Italian rabbis about Halakhic problems and his decisions were quoted by others too. Here are some problems R. Naftali had to solve. May a *parokhet*, a Torah shrine curtain, which is decorated by a six-line inscription embroidered with Samaritan writing (*ketivat shomronim*), be used as a curtain to cover the Ark? Is it lawful for (Jewish) merchants from the countryside not to pay the emissary (*shaliah*) of the creditor for the delivered goods, only the creditor himself? Does a prisoner, for whom a co-religionist deposited a bond, have to pay his part of the costs if he is freed some other way? The rabbi's task is to apply principles of the legal tradition and precedents to the new situation. Halakhic decisions (*pesak*) apply to a specific occasion but they serve as guidelines for other situations, too. R. Naftali's Jewish world was an international one, including Northern Italy as well as the Ottoman Empire. The rabbi of Buda had to decide about the fate of merchants and creditors, debtors and prisoners so that they could live according to Halakhah, Jewish legal tradition.

Since the Early Middle Ages it is customary in the Jewish world to ask questions about everyday life, whether they are of religious (Halakhic) or philosophical nature, from an authority, occasionally from several authorities. A query (*she'elah / rogatio*) is addressed to someone entitled to decide (*posek / paskan*). The responsum (*teshuvah / responsum*) always places the query in the context of religious law. It becomes a Halakhic treatise, generally accepted as a decision (*pesak*). The literature of "queries and replies" (*she'elot u-teshuvot*, or *shut / ShuT* according to the popular abbreviation / in Latin: *rogationes et responsa*) reflects Halakhic casuistic law. Responsa were distributed in handwritten and copied collections and later, after the sixteenth century, in print. The correspondence, which developed into a world-wide network, and later the use of the collections, ensured that the Jewish legal tradition remained uniform across the Diaspora while allowing room for dissenting and personal opinions. A responsum had to quote not only the correct Biblical passage and some Talmudic literature, but a Talmudic passage about a detail of the case as well as earlier responsa on the same question (*Shas u-poskim*). Some earlier rabbis of Buda are known only from responsa which quote them. Responsa literature is almost the only source for the internal history of medieval Jewry in Buda.

(8) In Szent György utca

In addition to the career of the Mendel family there was another great Jewish success story from before the Battle of Mohács—an early Hungarian *Jud Süss* story. Shlomo Seneor (Hebrew Shneur, like *senior*, "elder" in Latin) escaped from Spain after the expulsion of Jews (1492). He came to Buda with the help of a relative who had moved there earlier. One of his books, a commentary on the Genesis by Nissim ben Reuben Gerondi (fourteenth century)—which, being a manuscript, informs us not only about his financial situation but of his erudition as well—bears the following short note from the hand of its owner: "(...) My name is Shlomo Seneor (SH-N-Y-'-W-R), I learned Torah and Torah became my wealth." Well, Shlomo ben Efraim acquired some wealth besides

24. Imre Szerencsés's note in a Hebrew manuscript (top, right)

the Torah, too. He settled down in the Jewish street of Buda, chose a Hungarian name, Etil (Attila) and learned Hungarian as well as German. He got married, had two sons and became "a great man among Christians, someone close to the king", being a Chancellor of the Treasury in the court of Lajos (Louis) II. He then had an affair with a Christian woman and when this became public, to avoid punishment and maybe even to further his career, he got baptized (ca. 1510). His godfather was none other than Imre Perényi, Palatine of Hungary. That is how he got his new first name: Imre, in full: Imre Szerencsés (Fortunatus), Emericus Zerenczes (Zerenshes / Zerenchees), Imre the Fortunate. "This Jewish Imre (Imrich Jud) left his wife and child in the Jewish street (Juden Gasse) in Buda (Ofen)"—writes an almost contemporary chronicler, Hans Dernschwam. He took a second wife, most probably his former mistress, a German noblewoman from Kolozsvár by the name of Holdin (Held) Anna, had another son and moved to a more elegant neighborhood, to Szent György utca, befitting his new position as treasurer (*thesaurarius*), the leading figure in financial affairs of the court.

25. The Fortunate One (*fortunatus*). Man sitting under a canopy, holding a money-pouch

He was often attacked under Lajos (Louis) II. He may have made mistakes and may have given bad advice in the complicated and insecure financial situation of the king, but his enemies accused him of many things unjustly. They blamed him because there were not enough funds in the Treasury to fight the Turks, or because relief forces reached Nándorfehérvár (today Belgrade) too late and the fortress fell.

Szerencsés did not initiate the debasement of coinage—minting money worth only about half of its face-value—in 1521, although he did participate in it, but a scandal broke out and the king had him imprisoned. As Eliah ha-Levi of Stambul (Istanbul) puts it, "he was imprisoned because of a Christian woman". The Diet of Rákosmező wanted to sentence him to death by burning. This was when István Werbőczy first used (1517) the term "half-Jew" derogatorily, complaining that they are now "allowed to hold public position", that "we have to turn to them for money, for usury". But after two weeks of prison the king released Szerencsés in exchange for a large sum of money. He was celebrating his liberation with his friends in his home when the servants of nobles participating in the Diet, bailiffs, hussars and the mob fell upon his house; Szerencsés himself managed to escape but the rampage continued, gold was taken by the sackful and, on the third day, the mob broke into the Jewish street. A pogrom ensued. It was the army who stopped them after a whole day's fight. Shortly after the pogrom Szerencsés was still able to convince the magnates that he could restore the financial situation of the royal court. He based his plans on the copper mines of the Fuggers in Hungary. These were entrusted to Szerencsés on the advice of none other than Werbőczy. The success of these adventurous transactions strengthened his position. In exchange for his debts the king awarded him the thirtieth of the taxes collected in Buda and some other compensation. A few weeks before the Battle of Mohács, in June–July 1526, Szerencsés donated a large amount of money to the king to support the campaign against the Turks. This was one of his last acts.

Szerencsés died around the time of the Battle of Mohács. A rabbinical responsum later claimed that in the hour of his death, crying and praying in the presence of several Jews, he returned to the Jewish faith according to the traditional ceremony of *teshuvah*.

Still in his lifetime, a Halakhic dispute emerged in Buda about the situation of Imre Szerencsés. According to Ashkenazi custom his two sons (Avraham and Efraim), who remained members of the Jewish community, were called to the Torah by their grandfather's name rather than by their baptized father's. The sons, embarrassed since their grandfather's name was well known, did not accept this and declined to make *aliyah*. Finally, after the death of Szerencsés, the rabbi of Buda, Naftali ha-Kohen, permitted the use of the name *ben Shelomo* when calling the sons to the Torah. Other rabbis were consulted about the issue, as customary. The rabbi of Padua, Meir Katzenellenbogen (1473–1565), a cousin of R. Naftali, noted that even the king and other nobles are mentioned in blessings in the synagogue, though they are not Jews. If their names can be pronounced, R. Shlomo deserves it all the more since he did so much for the well-being of his people and he was friendly towards all honest and kind persons. His benevolence was described in a responsum by Eliah ben Benjamin ha-Levi, rabbi of Istanbul, after the death of Szerencsés: every Friday afternoon before the Sabbath he would give charity to poor Jews. After the death of their baptized father Szerencsés brought two children from Austria to Buda and raised them as Jews. He saved Jewish men and women from the death penalty. He saved the Jewish community from the charge of sacrificing Christian children; he spared no trouble or money to clear the Jews from the accusation and he was able to prove that it was the denouncer himself who tried to frame the Jews by hiding blood among them. One of his sons wrote that his father warned the Jews in a secret Hebrew letter when they were in danger. He prevented the expulsion of Jews from Prague, when the city was under Hungarian rule. Szerencsés always acted in favor of Israel, both personally and through his wealth. It was announced in every synagogue in Buda that whoever considers Szerencsés lost for Israel will be punished in person and in his belongings by the Prefect. Szerencsés was attacked by Christians, thrown into prison and almost burnt because they claimed that he was still a Jew. He could escape only at the cost of major financial sacrifice.

The decision in favor of the sons of Szerencsés embraced merit over the strict law: "We may mourn him for mixing with Christians, but we should not forget that he had always cared about the well-being of his folk and helped people close or far away from him. His deeds show that he regretted his conversion and he feared God. He deserves to be accepted in the community, not rejected." It is interesting to note that since Szerencsés was a Sephardi Jew, his second marriage would not have violated Jewish law: in those times Sephardi Halakhah allowed polygamy, Sephardim were not subject to the prohibition of Rabbenu Gershom. His only sins were that he got baptized and married a Christian woman on the second occasion. Looking at the manuscript left behind by Szerencsés we can see that all his personal notes are written in Hebrew script. The Halakhic decision in favor of his sons was later confirmed by Moshe Isserles, rabbi of Cracow. The distinguished scholar knew about the case only from R. Meir's responsum but he accepted the decision due to the authority of the rabbi of Padua: "Once he gave his permission, who can have a word after the king?" In any case, for the Ashkenazi world this *teshuvah* meant, at least theoretically, opening new doors for apostates to *return* to Judaism.

The two Jewish sons of Imre Szerencsés left Buda after the Battle of Mohács and changed their name to Zaksz (Sachs). They claimed that the name was an abbreviation of "Holy seed of Seneor (*Zera Kadosh Seneor*)". One of them, Abraham, got permission from the widowed Queen Mary to settle down in Kismarton (Eisenstadt) with his family, children, household and wealth. Some of his offspring moved as far as Vilna.

In spite of their dependence, the life and behavior of Jews, their relations with the surrounding society in the renaissance Buda of King Matthias or the Jagellos manifest the forms we see in modern bourgeois societies. Their livelihood was determined by the surrounding society and was basically restricted to professions connected to trade and finances. Otherwise there was wide room to maneuver. Beyond the ordinary members of the community, rich and poor, there were the learned rabbis, the Jewish leaders who adjusted their appearance to the expectations of the royal court where they were accepted, the Jews who converted to Christianity for the sake of a career but maintained Jewish contacts and the assimilationists who were Jewish only by birth. Though individuals left, the Jewish community of Buda remained a traditional one, surrounded by a society which can be considered bourgeois already around 1500.

A foreign responsum mentioned that in the 1500s in Hungary and the surrounding countries the *hazzan*, holding the Torah scroll, used to ask for a blessing over the king or the prince of the country and his retinue. The Jews of Buda were grateful and faithful to the ruler who admitted and accepted them.

This world did not exist in isolation. To characterize the surrounding atmosphere we should also mention an ardent enemy, the anti-Jewish demagogue István Werbőczy (1458–1541). He was a member of the gentry, a jurist and high state official. His xenophobia and his envy of successful Jews drove him to constant accusations, fighting against persons rather than for causes, even though occasionally he himself could be charged with the same violations as the accused Jews. His prejudiced views were expressed in the form of restrictive laws in the *Tripartitum opus iuris consuetudinarii* (1517). The code ruled that when a Jew appears in court with a Christian he has to take an oath prior to the process wearing a short coat, Jewish hat, barefoot, facing East, swearing on the five books of Moses, saying that the Biblical curse should strike him if he is guilty. The Jewish oath of Werbőczy was mandatory in the Middle Ages. Its text was based on the Jewish oath of Erfurt elaborated by Conrad, Archbishop of Mainz (twelfth century), and the Buda Law Book.

History played a trick on Werbőczy, for he is said to have been buried in the cemetery of the old Jewish quarter (*auf dem Judenfriedhof*), in Krisztinaváros (Hans Dernschwam, 1555). His elegant summer house and garden, which he received after the Battle of Mohács, stood nearby. (He owned another house on Castle Hill.) Werbőczy died during an epidemic (1541), but his death may have been hastened by a glass of refreshment handed to him by the pasha of Buda at a feast. The pasha did not appreciate the constant legal skullduggery of the "old jurist", he was not used to this in other countries. Whatever the case, Turkish authorities did not allow his remains within the city walls. His tomb has not been found since.

(9) Jahudiler Mahallesi

Jews did not leave Buda in the late summer days following the Battle of Mohács (Wednesday, August 29, 1526), as did so many others. Josef ha-Kohen's chronicle (1554) is explicit about this: "Jews stayed in the city." They did not escape because pogrom followed upon pogrom in Western Hungary (Pozsony, Sopron, etc.); people fled from Western Hungary to Buda instead.

After the rout of the Hungarian army and the death of the king the city must have been left without public authorities and administrative institutions for weeks. The official report of Sultan Suleiman the Magnificent (1520–1566) said, "the coward inhabitants of Budun realized that the Padishah of the world is approaching them and they scattered like the stars of the Great Bear; some of them went to the mountains or other hidden places while others entered the inner Castle begging for mercy. (...) The king, tired of his life, sent the keys of the Castle to the footstool of the Padishah's throne begging for mercy." "King" is probably meant symbolically here since the King of Hungary, Lajos (Louis) II was dead by then.

A Turkish official chronicler, *efendi* (that is, Mr.) Ferdi writes (1542):

"Nobody stayed in the Castle of Budun (...) apart from some faithless persons of easy virtue, the poor and the Jews. When the banners, shining like the Sun, came into sight around the city, the above mentioned Jews, wearing white death robes (*kittel / pallium Judaicum*) came to meet the victorious army, threw themselves to the earth and begged for mercy."

There are other chronicles of the events.

"Jews, who were numerous in Buda, fought heroically for their lives and freedom. Before Solomet the Turk marched into the city, two hundred of those who were too poor to escape occupied the Royal Castle. When the Sultan wanted to enter the Castle, he was prevented by cannonade and gunfire, even though they did not have enough food for more than a few days. The Sultan promised them their lives if they let him march into the Castle without further obstacles and he kept his promise after entering the Castle, sitting on the throne. Finally he convinced them to accompany him to Turkey."

(Johannes Cuspinianus / Spiessheimer, *Oratio protreptica*, 1527)

This diplomat, trying to convince the Christian princes with this "Stimulating Speech" to fight against the Turks, probably exaggerated the heroism of the Jews of Buda: even if they did try to defend the city they could not have done so for long. Based on various independent European, Turkish and Jewish reports which seem to be well informed about several details we may suppose that after Lajos died and the widowed queen fled, the Jews of Buda, formerly serfs of the Chamber, remained the only representatives of public authority for a while. Buda was empty, surviving members of the Royal Court having fled the country.

The Jews, realizing what had happened, went to greet the victorious army approaching Buda. An "*alaman*" of Buda, i.e. a German (Ashkenazi) Jew, Jasif ibn Solomon (Josef ben Shlomo), probably accompanied by a few members of the community, appeared before the Turks and handed them the keys of the city. He was granted exemption from taxes as a reward. Where were the keys given to the Turks? Already in Földvár, or only in Buda? The Jews visited the Turkish camp in death robes (*kittel*), in ceremonial garb. At first they only met Ibrahim pasha, but after a few days, on September 11, after a fast—the Fast of Gedaliah (Tishri 3)—, they met the Sultan who marched into Buda in the meantime. Did they really hand over the keys? Maybe. But the Padishah needed neither submission nor the keys: he was the victor.

Suleiman "was merciful" towards the Jewish population of Buda, as we know from ha-Kohen's chronicle, so he sent them to his country, Turkey. They left at the end of September (September 21/22, 1526), on the first day of *Sukkot*, by boat. The official diary of the Padishah notes as follows: "On the 14th of the month *zil hidzhe* in the year 932 (September 21, 1526), Saturday: (...) the Jews of Buda were taken to ships, to be shipped to Turkey." Cuspinianus says that the Sultan "persuaded" them to accompany him.

There were several legends about these events in Europe. According to a German newspaper of the time Suleiman "offered a choice" to the Jews: they could go with him or stay in Buda. They were to decide within three days. Of course, they all wanted to stay in Buda. Therefore the Turks came to Buda and divided the Jews into three groups. One group consisted of people older than thirty or forty years, the second group was people younger than twenty, the third group was made up of women and children. They had to decide again, this time in groups, whether they wanted to stay. Again their answer was unanimously yes. Upon this the Sultan massacred the older men and took the women, children and men under twenty with him.

Johannes Kessler in Switzerland heard that the Turks occupied Buda after a siege. Jews participated in the heroic defense of the city, though they did not have an army of their own (*kriegslüt*). "Of the three and a half thousand Jews barely twenty survived", he says. The number of the victims must be an exaggeration but it gives us an idea about the size of the Jewish community before the Turks invaded Buda. Various leaflets, the newspapers (*zeyttung*) of sixteenth-century Europe, reported similar figures. A Turkish source, Ferdi, also mentions two thousand Jewish "families" in Buda. It is possible that in Kessler's as in Ferdi's chronicle events of the weeks directly after the Battle of Mohács got mixed up with some later events. But the figures are comparable in the various European sources and Turkish reports confirm these numbers. We are probably not far off the mark if we presume that half a thousand or more Jews lived in Buda.

26. Jews and Turks defending Buda against King Ferdinand's army, 1541

Sixteenth-century European newspapers as well as later chronicles tell the story of the fall of Buda as was appropriate in the case of defeat: resorting to customary elements of journalism, with trite phraseology, exaggerating the havoc and losses suffered. The only incontrovertible fact seems to be that, after the Battle of Mohács, the Sultan took the Jews remaining in the abandoned city of Buda as hostages. Or rather he resettled them, just like the Babylonian ruler Nebukhadnezzar had resettled the craftsmen of Jerusalem (587/586 B.C.E.). Suleiman, too, needed merchants and craftsmen, which was why he took the Jews with him.

Interesting evidence of the scattering of the Jews of Buda in the Balkans and the Ottoman Empire can be found in the sixteenth-century responsa; an increased number of women whose husband disappeared (*agunot*) turned to the rabbinical courts (*bet din*) asking to be considered widows. Their husbands had disappeared several years earlier, they were not likely ever to return and the women wanted to remarry. War and deportation had ruined several Jewish families in Buda.

According to the Turkish chronicler Kemalpashazade (1483?–1534) "by leaving their home country the merchant–craftsmen escaped great poverty" (*Mohács-Name*, ca. 1530). The situation of the Jews changed after the Turkish occupation of Buda. The Turks were sure to win the Jews over to their side by granting them certain advantages:

> "It is considered a great wonder that after occupying Buda and bringing the Jews to Constantinople the Turks did not sell them as serfs but let them free; they were only obliged to pay taxes. Had they been sold into slavery, this would have caused the decline of all of Turkey's Jewry because—according to their customs—they would have been obliged to redeem them.
>
> (Hans Dernschwam, *Tagebuch einer Reise nach Konstantinopel*, 1555)

After the establishment of Turkish administration in Hungary the Jews of Buda, or rather the former Jews of Buda, were free to trade throughout the Ottoman Empire. Jewish sources mention several "holy communities of Hungarians (*ungarus*)". Jewish communities from Buda could be found in Istanbul (Constantinople), Salonika (Thessaloniki), Vidin, Sofia and Kavala (Greece) as well as in the Holy Land. Turkish documents from the mid-sixteenth century from Safed (Tzfat) mention ten to fifteen Hungarian families. They maintained contacts with the rest of their families in Buda, receiving help from them. With financial help from R. Noah from Buda Hungarian Jews opened a separate *yeshivah* in Safed (1619) and their foundation (*keren kayyemet*) helped the poor in Jerusalem, too. Some sixty Hungarian Jewish families together with R. Naftali ha-Kohen ended up in Sofia. They became members of the German (Ashkenazi) community. The fame of the Buda rabbi reached even Josef Karo or Caro (1488-1575), the author of the *Shulhan Arukh*, who lived in this area, in the Balkans, in Adrianople (Edirne) for an extended period before moving to Safed (1536).

*

The religious customs (*minhagim*) of the Jews of Buda (*benei Budun*) differed from those of other communities. Josef Caro mentions that three weeks before *Tish'ah be-Av*, between Tammuz 17 and Av 9, the Jews of Buda refrained from business and trade, though Halakhah prescribes only one day of rest. Work is not prohibited on this fast day, not to mention business, which is a "much smaller issue". But if the "Hungarians" want to make this day of mourning even harder, says Caro, they may do so. If a man gave a ring to a woman it was not considered an act of engagement among Hungarians living in Turkey, i.e. the Jews of Buda, though this custom prevailed in other communities. This resulted in disputes between them and other Jews. Hungarians interpreted the instructions regarding kosher meat somewhat loosely. Glancing onto the top of the neighbor's house from their window was acceptable to Hungarians here, just like in Buda. (The difference between Buda and the Turkish lands being that while in Buda people sleep inside the house, in the Balkans and the South it was customary to sleep on the roof most of the year.)

The "hard" pronunciation of the Hungarian Jews (compared to the pronunciation of German Jews) was striking. They said *bedzh* (as in Hungarian: Bécs) instead of Wien. Whether the Duna / Donau / Dunaj was identical with the river Tuna was debated for a long time by the scholars. This lack of clarity, too, was caused by the difference between voiced and unvoiced pronunciation. Instead of *Ofen* (Buda) they wrote *Oben*, which suggests that they pronounced the letter *b* in the middle of the word not like it was customary, as *v* (*Oven*), but in the German manner, as *f* (*Ofen*). Or the other way around, they used a voiced *v* instead of the *f* sound. The usual Ashkenazi / Yiddish pronunciation of the name is *Oyvn* / *Oyfn*.

In 1554 the Hungarian synagogue of Constantinople burned down. From this date Jews of Buda started to attend the German synagogue and founded a joint Burial Society (in Aramaic: *Hevra Kaddisha*), but when it came to electing the head of the community some tension arose and the Jews of Buda no longer wanted to belong into one group with the German and Spanish Jews. As a consequence, certain communities decided to break off all contact with the unsociable Hungarian Jews. The excommunication was lifted only later by the joint decision of the most influential rabbis of the

Balkans who quoted the Biblical story of Benjamin's tribe (Judges 20–21): never again can a whole tribe be excommunicated from Israel. Slowly, by the end of the sixteenth century, the alienation of and discrimination against the Jews of Buda had vanished.

*

As for Buda, the earlier community having left the city, practically no Jews remained. King János (John) (1526–1540) and Ferdinánd (King of Hungary between 1526 and 1564) took turns in distributing the homes of the Jews among their subjects. The new owners occasionally even went to court to argue their rights to the donation-house on Jewish street. The fortress was extended up to the Jewish cemetery. The Jewish street got a new name for a while: Szent Márton (St. Martin) utca.

After August 29, 1541, when the fate of Buda under Turkish rule was sealed, Jews started moving in from neighboring towns like Ráckeve or Esztergom or returning from other parts of the Ottoman Empire. The documents of Jews resettling in Buda show Sarajevo, Szendrő (Semendria), Belgrade, Vidin, Kavala, Sofia, Salonika, Adrianople (Edirne), Istanbul, even Safed as their former place of residence. They moved back to the place where they had lived before, the Jewish quarter, the Jewish street (the lower, north-western segment of today's Táncsics Mihály utca). This is when they carved the date, 1541, into a pillar of their old synagogue.

A German traveler, writing about Turkish Buda a quarter of a century later, states that "there are plenty of Jews and Turks in the city but only a few good Christians…" (Stephan Gerlach, 1573). Around 1569 the rabbi of Buda was R. Hayyim Hatsman ben Yitzhak. The first Jewish Prefect appointed by the Turks (*kethüda*) was Abraham ibn Jusuf. The district (*mahalle*) around the Vienna gate was named after the Jews. In Turkish it was called *Jahudiler mahallesi / Mahallei jehudian*, "Jewish city", i.e. "the Jews' street", "Jewish quarter", "Jewish street", or in Hungarian spelling *Mahalle Zsidó ucsa*. It occupied two large blocks East of the Jewish gate (*Porta Judaica*), Bécsi kapu tér, next to the city wall. It was not a ghetto, but a separate quarter. In Sándor Scheiber's opinion the new cemetery of the Jewish quarter was in Víziváros, East–northeast to it, in the space between today's Hunfalvy and Batthyány utca. But they may have used the old cemetery for a while. Why did they have to open a new cemetery? We can only guess. A possible explanation is that the bodies of those who fell during the siege of Buda (1529), Christians and Turks, were all buried in the Jewish cemetery (*judenfreithof*) which made the cemetery ritually unfit for further use by Jews. Jews lived in other parts of the city, too, in the Tabán and Víziváros which had an area called *civitas Judeorum*, and possibly around the Császár bath.

Jews of Buda who ended up in other parts of the Ottoman Empire remained attached to the city. They retained their seats in their synagogue for a long time and even paid taxes. This tradition was continued by some of their children. If circumstances allowed they moved back to Buda. It was often disputed whether they could keep their rights, whether they could remain full members of the Jewish community. The Jews of Buda would have been happy to get rid of them. Legal conflicts arising from this situation were discussed by Halakhic authorities all over the world.

From a responsum (ca. 1630) of Hayyim ben Shabbetai (ca. 1555–1647), rabbi of Salonika:

"(…) Among those who fled were people whose grandfather lived in Buda and they still have houses, shops and other property in Buda, and are still paying taxes after these to the (Hungarian) king. (…) And when the Almighty took stock of His people and Edom [the Christians] and Yismael [the Muslims] made peace [Peace of Zsitvatorok, 1606], these people took their families and set forth to return to their country and properties. Seeing this, those who stayed at home and liked to quarrel said to each other deceitfully: Let us take measures among ourselves that those who return should not be entitled to occupy their property until we discuss their cases. Those who are returning said that they would never have left if they were not forced to, they never wanted to leave the city of Budun but they were forced to, they had to save their lives.

Response (*teshuvah*): Law supports those who are returning, people who stayed in the city can not keep them from returning."

27. Hebrew manuscript
from Buda.
The date: Oven,
403 (= 1643 c.e.)

The majority of the Jews of Buda was Ashkenazi, i.e. of German origin, speaking German, just like before the Turkish occupation. Most of the Hebrew tombstones from Turkish times bear German names. Jews arriving from the Balkans, from the Ottoman Empire, however, were Sephardi (Spanish) Jews; they were identified as "guests" in the census for a while. Eastern Jews had a separate synagogue (26 Táncsics Mihály utca, where the Medieval Jewish Prayer-house is today); this was the "small" or "old" synagogue across the street from the Ashkenazi "great" or "new" synagogue (23 Táncsics Mihály utca).

By the end of the Turkish occupation the Spanish Jewish community of Buda consisted of some thirty families. They prayed according to their own rites, in their synagogue, as mentioned later by Yitzhak Schulhof (*Megillat Ofen*, "Buda Chronicle", 1686). They translated documents into their language (Ladino), if it was necessary. Memorabilia of the Jews of Buda show little Turkish influence. Maybe the name *Haszlán* (in Hungarian: Arszlán / Araszlán), which is the Turkish version of Löw / Leyb / Aryeh, "lion", or occasionally the Arabic or Turkish spelling of a Hebrew name (Ibrahim, Jakub, Jasif / Jusuf, Musi, Suleiman, etc.), or some minor spelling mistakes on the Hebrew gravestones are indicative of Turkish influence.

The Ashkenazi and Sephardi Jewish communities lived close to each other in Buda, like in other cities of the Ottoman Empire, which must have stimulated certain conflicts. R. Efraim ha-Kohen found it necessary to call for the mutual tolerance of the two different synagogue rites in a responsum (ca. 1670). If a Sephardi Jew says his prayers in an Ashkenazi synagogue, or the other way round, he is considered to have fulfilled his obligations, since there is no Halakhic difference between them which would disqualify the prayers. The *Shema* and the *Tefillah* (or *Amidah* / *Shemoneh Esreh*) are part of both rites, they are recited together with all the blessings, though there are minor variations in their texts. R. Efraim's words suggest that the Ashkenazi and Sephardi communities of Buda had close relations with each other, probably marriage and other social ties, which warranted the occasional or regular participation in the other community's rites. This was a segmented Jewish society, not segregated communities, living in the same street, their synagogues next to each other.

Isaac (Yitzhak) Schulhof's description tells us that most houses in the Jewish quarter were built from rubble-stone and had cellars for storage.

During the Turkish occupation the largest Jewish community of the three Hungarian lands—that under the Habsburgs, under Turkish rule and the Hungarian principality of Transylvania, respectively—lived in Buda under Ottoman rule. Population figures may be traced through the Turkish tax-rolls. (Jews paid a yearly poll-tax to the Turkish authorities.) Based on the documents we know of 80 permanent resident families by the end of the sixteenth century, amounting to six or seven hundred people. These numbers changed constantly but, by the time of the reconquest of Buda, the number of Jews, including Ashkenazim and Sephardim, reached and even exceeded a thousand people. In other words, Jews constituted 4–5% of the entire population of twenty thousand in Turkish Buda.

According to the Moslem tradition and general practice in the Ottoman Empire, authorities considered Jews a separate social group, an independent community. Jews were granted autonomy in their communal affairs but this status (*zimma*) meant certain restrictions on their personal freedom: *zimmi* enjoyed rights only as members of the religious community. The secular head of the Jewish community was the *kethüda*. Islam and the Turks continued the Babylonian tradition; the *kethüda* was the equivalent of the "exilarch" or the Jewish judge. But the *kethüda* was far more dependent on the Turkish authorities than the medieval Jewish judge. His decisions were oral, therefore only few of their names survived in documents: Ibrahim (Abraham) ibn Jusuf (1547), Jakub (Jacob) and Saul (1580). In Jewish communal matters rabbis were to decide. The Turkish name of the rabbi was *papas* or *hakham*, using a Greek or Hebrew term. Some of their names were preserved only in the Turkish censi: Musi (Moshe), David and Ibrahim (1580).

In the second half of the sixteenth century, when the emergence of Jewish mystical philosophy in Safed and other circumstances drew Jews from all over Europe to Palestine, the German and French *aliyah* usually assembled in Buda and formed groups here to continue their journey to Turkey. Those who spent a longer period of time in Buda waiting for their groups and occasionally participated in Jewish communal life in Buda, and their rabbis even had an opportunity to teach. Buda needed foreign rabbis anyway. Hakham Tzvi said: "No Hungarian Jew was learned enough to become rabbi of Buda."

28. Hebrew manuscript from Buda. The date: *Oven ha-birah* (Fortress Buda), 5403 (= 1643 C.E.)

During one of the sieges of Buda, in October 1598, when the Hungarian and Austrian troops—Prince Matthias (Mátyás) (1557–1619), later King of Hungary (1608–1619) and Emperor of the Holy Roman Empire (1612–1619) and others, among them Lord Chief Justice Miklós Pálffy (1552–1600) and count Ferenc Nádasdy (1555–1604), captain of Transdanubia—the famous Black Bey—tried to recapture Buda, the Jews fought against them heroically from within the city walls. Buda was not occupied.

In Vienna the Jews were blamed for the defeat. The following story is from Josef ha-Kohen's book, *Emek ha-bakhah*, "Valley of Tears" (1563/1575), from a supplement by an unknown author.

"(...) The Turks ran into the Castle. When the Jews who lived there saw this, they rose to defend their lives, saying: Let us fight for our children, wives and property and let God do whatever he sees fit. They fought against the army of the Emperor with great bravery and strength and won, so that that army was forced to run disgracefully. Then there were people in the Palace who accused the Jews as follows: Your High Majesty! The Jews supported our enemies and that is why we could not capture Buda. Therefore, all the Jews should be exiled from our country! Upon this the wise Emperor replied, like an Angel of God, as follows: On the contrary, we have to appreciate their loyalty to their Emperor. I have no doubt that if the time comes, the Jews who are our subjects will fight for us loyally, too. Therefore they should not be accused. Blessed be he who planted this idea into the Emperor's heart."

(10) The Settlement Flourished, like a Green Olive-tree

In the Turkish period the Jewish community of Buda enjoyed the right of free commerce and trade. The Jews maintained lively trade relations with other parts of the Ottoman Empire. "The Jews of Buda are exempted from the province tax", records Evliya Chelebi, and Yitzhak Schulhof wistfully remembers how the "settlement flourished, like a green olive-tree, safe and untroubled—we could truly say: Every man sat under his vine and under his fig-tree". Schulhof was alluding to a Biblical phrase (see II Kings 18,31; Jes. 36,16; Mikha 4,4) referring to the call of the Assyrian troops besieging Jerusalem to surrender, and to their tempting promises; yet Schulhof knows very well that the Jews were in exile (*galut*), even in the midst of prosperity. This was a fact known to each and every Jew; a sixteenth-century Turkish textbook (Birgevi, *Risale*) clearly states: "To be a Jew is even worse than to be a Christian."

Of course, Jews, too, had to pay the poll-tax and various other taxes—this was what the Turkish authorities gained from them. But otherwise they enjoyed religious and economic freedom within the Ottoman Empire, and they could, for example, enlist Turkish support for recovering debts from Christians. (Christians, of course, were entitled to receive similar help, if necessary.)

We know about Jewish physicians active in Buda: one of them, accused of poisoning some forty persons, was executed by the Turks in 1547—this seems to have been an obvious slander, a trumped-up charge, for according to the testimony of the single written source, all forty of the victims were named Mehmed. Gábor Bethlen (1580–1629), Prince of Transylvania, also knew of a Jewish physician in Buda (1625). The Jews of Buda apparently specialized in manufacturing decorative braids for uniforms, an article for which there seems to have been widespread demand. Evliya Chelebi records that Jewish women made a particular type of broadcloth (*shaiak or shaia*) that was unknown elsewhere. Most Jews of Buda, however, were probably money-lenders or merchants. Almost everyone borrowed from them since they always had money, all their wealth being vested in money-capital; the interest they charged was 3% a month. It was the Jews who brought felt and cotton from Vienna to Buda and to Turkey; on the way back they carried cordage, cotton, colored threads, morocco leather, Turkish scarves to Vienna. They played an active role in driving cattle to Vienna and to other parts of Western Europe. (A certain Yitzhak, a Jew of Buda, paid duty on a thousand heads of cattle in 1571.) It was the Sephardi Jews who established and maintained trade relations with the Ottoman Empire. The Jews of Buda regularly traveled to the Eszék (Essek) market by boat, bringing back articles of clothing and various garments, animal hides, metals (copper, lead, iron), they did not disdain the contraband goods that could be acquired along the southern course of the Danube either. In the Jewish quarter of Buda one could buy almost everything: Persian carpets, *kilim*, velvet, *muslin*, fine linen, *atlas*, felt, aba cloth, frieze cloth, Moroccan leather. Fruits, even the most exotic ones that grew in the remotest corner of the Sultan's empire, were sold there, as well as cattle, hide, flour, salt, timber. Credit was also available, against promissory notes. Jewish merchants played an important role in the ransoming of Christians who had been taken captive. Servants, too, were sold on the market.

Trade in wine, however, was prohibited even to the Jews. In order not to tempt the virtues of the Moslem population, the Turkish authorities forbade the use of wine even in Jewish ceremonies. "A decree came from the Emperor that anyone who has wine shall be decapitated." We can only guess how R. Efraim made *kiddush* on Friday evenings. Perhaps he used *boza*, fermented Turkish elderberry beer. Or did he risk a glass of wine, in spite of the prohibition?

Schulhof mentions that the wealthier Jews of Buda acquired Christian servants if the opportunity arose. He himself had bought a Christian servant-girl from among the Christian prisoners captured during the siege of Vienna who, after some time, had become familiar with "the laws regarding dishes and cooking prescribed by the Jewish religion". R. Efraim says that these servants were often converted to the Jewish faith by their masters.

The life of the community was regulated by the Jewish calendar. The Sabbath and other festive days were all celebrated, and the dates were given according to the Jewish calendar and the weekly segment of the Torah. The years, in accordance with the prevailing practice, were calculated according to the "minor era", starting with the Jewish creation of the world. Schulhof recounts with sorrow how on one occasion in 1683, during the Austrian–Turkish wars, everyone, including the Jews, had to bake as much bread as they could in their ovens so that the soldiers returning from battle would have enough to eat, even though that particular day happened to coincide with the day of Rosh ha-Shanah.

"It was the custom there," says Schulhof about the (Great) synagogue, "that scholars, when explaining the Bible to the congregation, did not stand before the Ark, as is our custom (in Prague), for it is disrespectful to turn one's back to the Holy Ark containing the Torah. Hence they made a lectern, two or three steps high, on the western side (i.e. on the left), where the preachers stood."

This was a minor adjustment to the Sephardi rite and, through it, to Moslem customs, to the layout of the mosque.

In his "Great lament (*Kinah gedolah*)" Schulhof mentions that hundreds of sacred books were destroyed during the 1686 siege; taking the estimated number of the Jewish community of Buda into consideration, and allowing for some exaggeration on Schulhof's part, each family had a Hebrew book, a Bible or a prayer-book (*siddur / mahzor*), most of them probably printed, although there may have been some manuscripts among them, for the victors "plastered the windows of the houses" with the pages torn from the books, perhaps with the parchment of Torah scrolls taken from the synagogue. It seem probable that the Hebrew books were kept not in the homes, but in the synagogue. The "new" synagogue even had a separate room for keeping Hebrew manuscripts no longer in use (*genizah*). The leader of the troops besieging Buda, Prince Charles of Lorraine (1643–1690), also confiscated thirty-five Torah scrolls to ensure the ransom of the captive Jews. Some codices were allegedly saved by Count Luigi Ferdinando Marsigli (1658–1730), at least according to his own account of the siege in which he mentions the library (*Discorso intorno all libreria famosa di Buda*, 1686). The numbers quoted above suggest that the holdings of the Buda synagogues reflected the situation of the Jewish community; and each congregation probably had over ten Torah scrolls.

Some Hebrew manuscripts from Buda are perhaps still hidden somewhere in the world. Sámuel Krausz, and later Sándor Scheiber, painstakingly sifted through numerous codices and their fragments in various libraries, checking old references. Based on their findings we can confidently assert that some manuscripts as well as a few printed books definitely originate from Buda—either from the palace of the Kings Matthias and Louis II, or from the Jewish quarter. The text of the colophon of two manuscripts furnishes ample evidence for this. According to the colophon of one of the manuscripts, an astronomical treatise (*Shesh kenafayim*, "The Six Wings"), currently housed in the Vatican, was copied by Yisrael ben Yosef "in the castle of Ofen" in the year 5324 (= 1564). The other, a prayer-book (*Selihot*), which is now kept in the municipal library of Mainz was copied by Yehudah bar / ben Meir ha-Kohen "in the castle of the city of Ofen" in 5403, at the very beginning, on the third day of the month of Sivan (May 19, 1643). The latter had undoubtedly been pocketed by one of the leaders of the liberating forces, General Johann von Thüngen, the military commander of Mainz, as a memento of the successful siege of Buda.

The religious laws governing Jewish life were strictly observed in the Buda community. This can be seen, for example, from the meticulous care with which the writing of place-names was regulated, for the precise spelling of each and every name was vital to the validity of a divorce certificate (*get*). The various writing systems (Latin, Arabic, Hebrew), differences in pronunciation, the occasional variations in the name, did lead to some confusion every now and then. Moreover, the rabbis would not accept the "monks' writing": every name had to be transcribed from Latin into Hebrew. A conscientious rabbi fasted before writing the divorce certificate in order to ensure that he would not corrupt the writing of the names through his own negligence. Whenever there was doubt concerning place-names, the rabbis preferred to issue two versions of the divorce certificate with the different spellings of the place-name or names in question. The eventual "refusal" (*me'un*) by a girl to stay married to the husband picked by her parents when she was a child was no longer allowed in Ashkenazi legal practice, after the fifteenth century. In Buda this was still possible as late as the seventeenth century (1676)—even if amidst considerable scandal, quarreling and passionate debates—as shown by a case in R. Efraim's responsa; in fact, the Buda *me'un* is the last known case of this practice in the Jewish world. Turkish tax rolls serve as sources indicating adherence to the dietary laws for, among other professions, they list the Jewish "butcher" (*kasab* in Turkish), implying that Buda had its own *shohet* who supplied the community with kosher meat. The inscriptions on some gravestones suggest that the dead could not always be buried within the prescribed short period of time, and had to be buried into a communal grave—undoubtedly a necessity brought on by extraordinary times. According to a decision of R. Efraim, servants who had converted were not obliged to observe the seven and thirty days of mourning (*shivah* and *sheloshim*) prescribed for close relatives when their master died.

In the seventeenth century the former Mendel Houses were connected by an archway resting on massive stone pillars. The archway spanning over the street was considered by many to mark the boundary or entrance of the Jewish quarter. One of Efraim ha-Kohen's responsa offers a vivid description of this passage:

"A question has been posed to me. Here, in the Jews' street, an arch (*kipah*) springs from the wall of the house incorporating the synagogue (*bet ha-keneset*) to the other side of the street. In other words, it is built in the following manner. A separating wall (*mehitzah*) (a buttress), one or two cubits (*ammah*)[7] thick, stands beside the house incorporating the synagogue; on the other side of the street (*le-rohav ha-rehov*) there stands another high wall (*homah*) (also a buttress), one cubit thick. An archway, perpendicular to the street, spans the street between the house incorporating the synagogue and the other side. People walk under this archway. The width of this archway and the arched wall (*homah shavvah*) is two or three cubits. A wall was erected on either side above this archway that one might cross over from the far side of the street to the side where the house incorporating the synagogue stands, and a roof (*gag*) was built over the two walls, from the two ends of the archway.

שאלה צד נשאלתי פה נרחוב היהודים משוכה כיפה ח' אצל בית שבית הכנסת בתוכה והולכת עד לד הצני של הרחוב דהיינו שעשויה באופן זה אצל בית של הצני של הרחוב למורך הרחוב ערך אמה או שתים וגם מגד הצני של הרחוב יש ג"כ חומה נטוה לרוחב הרחוב ערך אמה ועל תומה שוה אחד מגד רוחב הרחוב שאצל בית ב"ה משוכה כיפה עד לד החומה השוה של הרחוב שמגד הצני אשר עוברים שנים תחתיה וכיפה הני' וגם החומה השוה עוביה עוביה ערך שנים ושלשה אמות וע"ג הכיפה בנ למעלה מחיצה משני לדדים הכיפך והחומה שיטלין לעבור מגד הצני של הרחוב עד בתוך הבית אשר בתוכה כ"ה וגג על שני המחיצות אשר משני לדדי המחילות חומת השוה ונם הכיפה .

29. Efraim ha-Kohen, *Sha'ar Efraim*. Question: May a *kohen* enter the "great" synagogue if it is connected to the house on the opposite side of the street by an archway?

I have seen that there is some question as to what happens if someone dies on the other side when the Kohanim enter the synagogue, whether we are then faced with the same situation for which the rabbis, who were here before I came, brought a decision: that the thatch (roof) (*shindel*) be removed from the top of the wall. (...) For there is no opening on either side of the separating wall (*mehitzah*), and both are high walls, the (ritual) impurity (*tumah*) cannot penetrate the other side, where the synagogue stands, upwards from below: (the building) cannot be called a house (*bayit*) and there is no reason for us to have reservations; the Kohanim may enter the synagogue (without apprehension)."

(*Sha'ar Efraim*, 1689, Lemberg edition, 1887, question 94)

The background to the Halakhic question (*she'elah*) posed to R. Efraim is the traditional prohibition of Kohanim to come into contact with the deceased or even to be under the same *roof*. The passage supported by the archway and the *arched wall* connected the building of the synagogue with a residential building in which a death may occur. If there was a deceased in the house, the Kohanim could obviously not go to pray since the roof above the passage connected the two buildings; in this case it would have become impossible for the Kohanim to recite the daily prayers which require the presence of a congregation (*minyan*). This misgiving had already arisen earlier and, in order to solve it, the previous rabbis had ruled that the upper part of the narrow passage, the thatch roof over the archway in the street, must be dismantled. Later, the more punctilious asked R. Efraim whether the same situation does not recur with the archway and the passage (the "arched wall") itself. R. Efraim's answer (*teshuvah*) and decision (*pesak*) was reassuring: the dismantling of the roof brought an end to the "unification of the domains (*eruv hatzerot*)" and the buttress erected along the two opposite houses were, from a ritual point of view, to be considered "separating walls (*mehitzah*)", meaning that there was no need for further demolition.

In the 1670s and 1680s, in Schulhof's time, there were several Talmudic societies, similar to the *Shas hevrah*; in one of them some thirty men "studied every Wednesday night, from evening to morning, the five books of Moses (*Torah*), the prophets (*Neviim*) and the writings (*Ketuvim*) (the three great units of the Hebrew Bible, abbreviated as *Tanakh*), the Mishnah, the Aggadah, and the Midrash", and at dawn they immersed themselves in the *Zohar*, the fountainhead of Jewish mysti-

[7] 1 cubit (ammah) = ca. 50 cm (ca. 1.6 feet).

cism; when they finished their studies they stood up and sang with a resounding voice the pleasant melody of the song beginning with the line "Lover of my soul (*Yedid nefesh*)" from the prayer-book "The Gates of Zion" (*Sha'are Zion*). Others gathered for study on other days of the week: "betrothed young men and young husbands, who had recently married, some twenty of them" would study on Mondays, while the Talmudic scholars would get together on Thursdays; and thus in the community of Buda the men studied the holy writings "three nights each week in a public congregation", and they even swore an oath that this custom would never be broken. We know of at least eight or ten well-trained rabbis who were active at the same time in Buda. Renowned scholars, forced to flee from other towns, also found refuge in Buda. Rabbis (Shlomo Amarilio, David Segal) in other towns and cities spoke of seventeenth century Buda as "the great city of the wise and learned (*sofer*)". The decisions of the Buda rabbis in a given case were heeded and respected everywhere in the Jewish world; in fact, R. Efraim wrote most of his responsa in answer to questions from Jews living abroad.

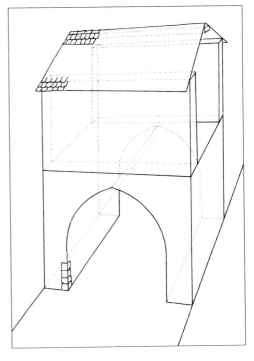

We know from these responsa that a number of "holy societies (*hevrah kaddishah*)" were active in the city, together with voluntary associations for charity (*gemilut hesed / hasadim*), for burials (*halvayat ha-met*), for caring for the sick (*bikkur holim*), as well as for caring for the poor and needy (*malbish arummim*, literally "the dressing of the naked"). These associations chose their officials each year; the finances were managed by two officials, one of them entrusted with the moneybox, most probably a wooden chest, the other with its keys. The magistrates of these associations were called *kabribashi* in Turkish ("the head of the *Hevrah*"). Each year the rabbi would give two speeches, encouraging his congregation to support the societies, and the next week a communal feast (*se'udah*) would be held where their contributions would be collected. (In contrast to the prevailing custom R. Efraim brought a decision that also rabbis other than the rabbi of the Society could be asked to give the speech.) Clothes were distributed among the poor during *Hanukkah* and the Jews of more distant lands also received help from Buda, a city that was considered "one of the most distinguished communities of the *galut*, whose members were respected and held in high esteem abroad", wrote Alexander Büchler, the well-known Jewish historian (1901).

30. Covered passageway in the Jewish street. Reconstruction

One of the greatest Talmudic scholars in Buda during the Turkish occupation was R. Efraim ha-Kohen. Born in Vilna, he soon became renowned for his Talmudic erudition. He was forced to flee the town in 1648, at the time of Chmielnicki's pogroms in Ukraine. He traveled extensively and the Buda community, aware of his reputation, invited him to be their rabbi. He accepted the invitation and moved to Buda in 1667, together with his family. His son-in-law, Yitzhak Schulhof, came to Buda with him. One of his sons, Judah, soon married into one of the town's distinguished families. Sometime earlier (1655) a Viennese rabbi forbade by *herem* (curse) the election of a rabbi who had relatives in the Buda community. This decision was necessary because any dispute that might arise among the Jews came under the rabbi's jurisdiction, and if he had relatives in the community his impartiality might be impaired, or his relatives might take advantage of this connection.

"*Az a rov tut a shidekh mitn beder, halt zikh der beder far a rov*", if the rabbi becomes related to the bath attendant, the bath attendant (the employee of the *mikveh*) soon holds himself for a rabbi—states a Yiddish proverb.

R. Efraim's predecessor, R. Simhah, voluntarily resigned from his job following the decision (*pesak*) of the Viennese rabbi. This decision, when applied to R. Efraim, generated a debate that swept through several countries, but international scholarly opinion eventually approved and endorsed the choice of the Buda community. As far as Halakhic questions were concerned, R. Efraim corresponded with almost the entire Jewish world, from Jerusalem to Venice and from Salonika to Frankfurt. He maintained that a (ritual) curse (*herem*) cannot be imposed on scholars and that a well-grounded opinion, formed in good faith, concerning matters of religious life cannot be persecuted and that he who errs should be admonished in private. His insightful Biblical and Talmudic interpretations generally show tolerance: for instance, he allowed a girl to reject a marriage that was not to her liking if she was betrothed while still a child (*me'un*). In his responsa he occasionally cites the *Zohar*; although he respected the mystic Biblical interpretations of the Kabbalah, he did not consider himself a mystic. He was invited to Jerusalem, to become the Chief Rabbi of the Holy Land, but he rejected the offer because he would first have liked to see his books printed. He died in Buda, during an epidemic. His tomb, lying somewhere near the wall of Castle Hill, was still visited in the nineteenth century—he may have been laid to rest on the highest point within the Jewish cemetery of the Víziváros. His son, R. Judah, who survived one of the sieges of Buda (1684), settled in the land of Zion but returned to Prague after the reconquest of Buda to fulfill his father's last wish that his writings be printed. His answers and decision (*teshuvot / responsa*) in matters of the Halakhah, the most important scholarly document of the Buda community that is still quoted, were printed under the title *Sha'ar Efraim* ("The Gate of Efraim") (1689). The collection of his speeches, *Mahane Efraim* ("The Camp of Efraim") has been lost.

It appears that R. Efraim did not learn Hungarian during his years in Buda, certainly not enough to write his works in that language. This suggests that members of the city's Jewish community spoke German / Yiddish among themselves. Beyond that Spanish, Portuguese, Hebrew as well as some Turkish influence can be perceived in the inscriptions on Hebrew gravestones. R. Efraim mentions that German was customarily the tongue of the *bet din*, whereas Hebrew was the language of (ritual) law, and the decisions were always translated. The minutes and regulations were always set down in Hebrew; extensive excerpts from the statutes of the community have survived as lengthy quotes in the works of R. Efraim and others.

Geographical and military borders meant little, if anything, in Jewish religious and intellectual life. The prohibition of the Viennese rabbi also aimed to keep the Jewish world universal, at least as far as the training and the contacts of rabbis were concerned, and ensured that local traditions contradicting the universal did not emerge even under the protection of the *minhag*. Visits by foreign rabbis helped maintain this universality. R. Efraim's horizon extended well beyond the borders of empires. The Jewish world was universal and uniform even in its variety.

The road from Western Europe to the Holy Land led through Hungary and, with a small detour, through Buda. The rabbis making their way from the German towns to *Eretz Yisrael*, a journey that normally entailed a lifelong commitment, would stop for a year or two at Buda and work in the Ashkenazi community.

It was not difficult to maintain contact with the Holy Land within the Ottoman Empire, and Buda was no exception. Since Suleiman had rebuilt Jerusalem and placed it under his own protection, the Jews, too, had a natural imperial framework. The Buda community made donations (*halukkah*) each year to the Jews in Safed, Tiberias, Jerusalem and Hebron, to help the poor and those who devoted their life to the study of the sacred books. Emissaries from the Holy Land would also come to Buda to collect charity. At that time the fame of Safed eclipsed even that of Jerusalem. There was a pious and wealthy man in Buda who took pains to ensure that his body (his bones?) would be taken to Safed and buried there: R. Noah, known as "the pious" by his contemporaries, who had regularly sent charity to former members of the Buda community living in the Holy Land. He died in 1630. A certain Levi traveled to the Holy Land himself to have his father-in-law buried there, at great financial sacrifice. The ship was near Sidon when the customs officials searched a woman and found her husband's bones, and he too had to pay customs' duties to avoid being harassed by the officials. The local *Hevrah* (that is, *Hevrah Kaddishah*) also demanded money for the burial place, and he had to ask for a donation from the heirs—his brothers-in-law—to cover these unexpected costs.

The Buda community also took up collections to ransom their brethren who had been taken captive (*pidyon shevuyyim*).

The redemption of all captives is a command (*mitzvah*), a sacred obligation. Maimonides says:

"One who is willfully slack in assisting in the ransom (of a captive) becomes liable forthwith for the transgression (of the Scriptural commandment): Do not harden your heart and close your hand against your needy kinsman; as well as for his failure to fulfill (the Scriptural command): Do not allow your brother to be forced to labor in front of your eyes; and: Rescue those who are taken off to die; and for his failure to heed the exhortation of the prophet: Deliver those who are bound in chains.

(*Mishneh Torah*: Zeraim, Hilkhot Matnat aniyyim, 8,10)

A number of details about life in Turkish–Jewish Budapest is known from a Halakhic work by R. Efraim's immediate predecessor, R. Simhah ha-Kohen of Belgrade (his other names, also in a Turkish series were Freudemann (Simhah) Efraim ben Gershon ben Shimeon ben Yitzhak) (ca. 1622–before 1669). R. Simhah's mother was Hungarian, the daughter of a learned rabbi who himself married into the Buda community, and who lived for some years in Buda on account of his father-in-law. In his book, *Sefer shemot* ("The Book of Names") (Venice, 1657), he surveyed the orthography of Jewish male and female names, as well as of European and Asian place-names. The practical purpose of the exercise was the regular publication of information necessary for the precise issuing of divorce certificates (*get*). The divorce certificate must contain the name of the river or some other natural feature next to the town in which the document had been issued. In order to clarify the minute details of orthography R. Simhah had to sift through his erudition, observations and recollections, including his memories of Buda. It was the fame of this book that earned R. Simhah an invitation to Buda, which he accepted. After two months, however, given the warning implied in the Vienna decision, he returned to Belgrade. The scattered references in his work constitute an encyclopedia of Jewish Buda in the seventeenth century.

In Hebrew documents Buda is generally written as Budn, pronounced as *Budun* and, in one case, as *Budan* (probably following the declined form of the Hungarian name). Sometimes the German name is used: *Ovn*, pronounced *Oven* or *Ofen*, perhaps *Ofenstadt*, the Hebrew variant being *Oven ha-birah*, Buda Castle. The two names were occasionally used side by side: "Budun or / otherwise Ofen"; and the reason why Hungarian comes first, writes a contemporary, is that in Buda Hungarian is spoken more common than German. The city was also called Old Buda (*Alt Oven*), and the adjective "old" is declined according to German grammar (Simhah ha-Kohen). In fact, the name Ofen was used more extensively in the Ashkenazi tradition, while Budun was more common in the Sephardi and Turkish tradition. The description in the divorce certificates, always referred to the river flowing near the city, as follows: Buda, that is called Ofen, lying beside the river Danube and springs and thermal springs. Buda was sometimes described as "Mount (*har*) Bud(a)". And even though the custom of using both names (Budun / Ofen) survived for quite a while in Hebrew sources even after the Turkish occupation, the name Buda gradually took precedence. R. Meir of Kismarton (Eisenstadt) argued in several responsa (*Panim me'irot*, "Sparkling faces / Faces of Meir", 1733) that although the name of the city once again became Ofen, as it had been earlier among the Ashkenazim, after Buda had been occupied by the Germans, he would nonetheless recommend the name Buda because, R. Meir argued, it was the Sephardim who had "originally" formed a majority in the town.

In spite of the unexpectedly rich excavation results there is some uncertainty in the identification of the Buda synagogues. According to one source there was an "old" and a "new" synagogue in Buda in 1647. Evliya Chelebi, too, speaks of two synagogues. R. Efraim mentions three synagogues (1674), as does Schulhof a decade later. This number would correspond to what we know of religious movements within the Jewish community of Buda. The Ashkenazi community was reorganized after 1541; the Sephardi Jews who arrived with the Turks probably had their own synagogue; and we know that the town also had a "Syrian community" (*kahal*, or perhaps more correctly: *kehillah siriatike*). However, only two buildings have so far been identified—the third may have stood outside of the Castle district, somewhere in the outlying Jewish town (Tabán or Víziváros), although its exact site has not been located yet. R. Efraim mentions that it was not customary to recite the prayers in private houses, lest the Turkish authorities become suspicious about a clandestine meeting.

(11) Next Year in Jerusalem

Around 1665 Shabbetai Tzvi (1626-1676) of Smyrna (Izmir) started proclaiming in the Jewish communities of Asia Minor that he was a direct descendant of David and, as such, none other than the Messiah. Jews from all over the Ottoman Empire, as well as Europe flocked to join his movement. He preached that the Messianic age had arrived and that for the little time left on this earth one should act exactly to the contrary of all religious commandments. His activity is mentioned by Dávid Rozsnyai (1641-1718) who happened to be studying Turkish at that time in Istanbul and who was extremely well informed: "And they brought the Jew, considered to be the king of Jews, before the emperor." Shabbetai Tzvi's fame spread quickly. His popularity did not diminish even after he converted to Islam, the faith of the sultan.

The rector of a Calvinist school in Transylvania, István Eszéki (Nagybánya), mentions the new Messiah in one of his school plays performed at Christmas, 1667 and printed in Kolozsvár (today Cluj) (1669).

> "(...) But why am I bringing up such an old issue? — Not so far, three years ago — A false preacher arose — His name was Sabetha Sebi, a swindler. — What happened, even the children know, — Because you were then completely fooled; — The Turk is still laughing at you, — He just wanted his treasury full. — He changed religion and became a Turkish Moslem — He left his mission as Messiah soon, — Because he was in great dangers, — And he saw he could not complete what he had planned."
>
> (*Rhytmusokkal való szent beszélgetés* [Holy Talk in Rhymes])

Eszéki was of course attacking not only Shabbetai Tzvi, but the Jews as well, whom he would have liked to convert. But as far as the conversion of the Jewish Messiah was concerned, his information was precise and admirably up-to-date: he must have received the news straight from Turkey. Throughout most of Europe, his non-Jewish contemporaries tended to consider Shabbetai Tzvi an impostor, swindler and deceiver.

The appearance of a Messiah in Turkey elicited an immediate positive responsum in Buda, too. A son-in-law of R. Efraim, R. Jacob ben Benjamin Zeev Ashkenazi, became a follower of Shabbetai Tzvi. Paul Rycaut, the English consul in Smyrna who in 1666 sojourned briefly in Buda on his way home, recorded in his diary that he felt a strange unrest among the Jews of Buda: as he saw it, there was hardly a single soul who was not abandoning his customary trade and preparing to travel to Jerusalem with his whole family. In their conversations, dreams and daily transactions they were preoccupied with nothing but moving to and settling in the Promised Land. One particularly notorious Shabbatean, Nehemyah Hayyon, later claimed that in the summer of 1666, on the Fast of the 9th of Av (*Tish'ah be-Av*)—the day when Nebukhadnezzar had occupied Jerusalem—the Jews were rejoicing and partaking in festive meals, flouting all religious precepts. The fanatic followers of the new Messiah killed an observant Jew—allegedly with the tacit consent, if not at the instigation of R. Jacob—who was sitting in the synagogue and refused to recite a benediction over the Messiah of Smyrna. Taking the exhortation recited on the eve of Yom Kippur and Pesah, "Next year in Jerusalem!", literally, they wanted to be in Jerusalem by the beginning of Hanukkah of the next year (December, 1666). They planned to travel through "the land of Edom", through Christian lands, probably taking a sea route, rather than through the Ottoman Empire. Poor R. Efraim must have lived through some difficult days...

Some decades later, as an established rabbi in Belgrade and, later still, as rabbi of Altona-Hamburg-Wandsbeck, towards the end of his life, R. Jacob's son, Tzvi Hirsh Ashkenazi (Hakham Tzvi, "the Wise"), became known as an implacable opponent of the Shabbateans.

(12) "Small" Synagogue: Medieval Jewish Prayer-house (26 Táncsics Mihály utca)

In the sixteenth–seventeenth centuries one of the Jewish communities of Buda established a small prayer-house in one of the former Mendel Houses, across the "great" synagogue. Hebrew inscriptions were painted in flaming red onto the medieval vaulting of the building that had formerly been a simple residential house.

One of the graffiti represents a bow, on top of it an arrow with flower-petals, in and beneath the bow a Biblical quotation, Hannah's prayer:

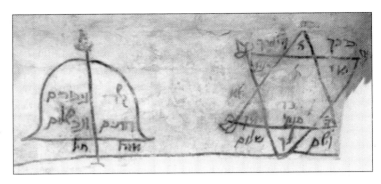

31. Hebrew inscriptions on the wall of the "small" synagogue

קשת גברים חתים ונכשלים אזרו חיל

"The bows of the mighty are broken,
And the faltering are girded with strength."
(I Samuel 2,4)

The other drawing is a star of David with the Priestly Blessing inside:

יברכך ה׳ וישמרך
יאר ה׳ פניו אליך ויחנך
ישא ה׳ פניו אליך וישם לך שלום

"The Lord Bless you and keep you!
The Lord deal kindly and graciously with you!
The Lord bestow his favor upon you and grant you peace!"
(Numbers 6,24–26)

The remnants of the building were discovered during excavations in 1964/65. Sándor Scheiber identified the script as Eastern cursive script and dated it to the sixteenth–seventeenth centuries. The content of the texts confirms this interpretation: in those times Buda was often under siege, which explains why the Jewish community was constantly prepared for war and praying for peace.

The inscriptions suggest that this synagogue was used according to the Sephardi rites (*minhag*) but it is hard to know whether it housed the Spanish or the Syrian Sephardi community. Stylistic features of the building suggest that it was built around 1400 as a residential house. Later, after the synagogue in the courtyard of the Mendel Houses was built, or even later then that, during the Ottoman rule, it was occupied by the Sephardi community of Buda. They made some minor alterations to suit the new functions. The apertures or windows of the women's gallery are still visible.

Since the renovation of the "small" synagogue in 1966, the building houses a small collection of liturgical and personal objects, mostly the heritage of the Jews of Buda.

Jewish gravestones are displayed in a small niche to the left of the entrance. The closely packed steles with their Hebrew inscriptions evoke a stylized Jewish cemetery, with the gravestones piled next to each other. Most of these gravestones were unearthed in the late nineteenth century during renovation and reconstruction work in Buda. Some were found after World War II, while clearing away the rubble of houses hit by bombs in the Castle area. They come from the medieval and Turkish period cemeteries of the Jewish quarter of Buda (Krisztinaváros, Víziváros), and they constitute a major source for the medieval history of Hungarian Jewry. Some of the stones of the "great" synagogue are displayed in the courtyard; these were removed before the building was reburied.

(13) The Gravestone of Lady Sarah (1656)

The expulsion of the Turks from Buda in 1686 also entailed the end of the earlier Jewish settlement. Their cemetery was destroyed and some of their gravestones were carried away to be used in construction work. Most were used in the buildings around Matthias Church, with some incorporated into the wall of the St. Stephen's chapel.

The gravestone of Lady Sarah was found in the wall of the ground floor corridor of the wing facing the Danube in the building at 5–7–9 Színház utca, a former Carmelite monastery. A Franciscan monastery had stood here since the thirteenth century, with Werbőczy's house next to it. During the Turkish occupation this house had been the residence of the Pasha of Buda. Both buildings were destroyed in 1686, when Buda was recaptured, and the plot, together with the ruins, was given to the Carmelite Order. The gravestones of the nearby Jewish cemetery were used in the construction of the new monastery. These gravestones were discovered in the course of clearing away the rubble and renovation after World War II. They are currently exhibited in the Medieval Jewish Prayer-house.

32. Inscription on Lady Sarah's gravestone

פה
נקברת מרת
שרה בת ר׳ שמשו
זל ונפטרת
ביום ה כב ימים
לחדש אב
שנת תטז לפ

"Here
is buried the Lady
Sarah, daughter of R. Simson,
his memory is blessed. She died
on the fifth day (Thursday), the 22nd day
of the month of Ab,
in the year 416 according
to the minor era (1656)."

(14) The Gravestone of Lady Freudel (1672)

The gravestone of Lady Freudel (1672) was formerly placed in the *lapidarium* of the Budapest Historical Museum (Fishermen's Bastion), and is currently exhibited in the Medieval Jewish Prayer-house. Broken in two, it came to light at 1 Hess András tér in 1887. The building, originally a Jesuit college, was built between 1686 and 1702, and the gravestone was incorporated into its walls. The gravestone is ornamented with three flower petals (*rosetta*), the inscription itself is framed by an arc. The most personal inscription from Buda is to be found on this gravestone.

(*Among the three flowers:*)

אור ליום ג׳ כח אלול תלב לפק

"On the eve of Tuesday, on the 28th of Elul, in 432, according to the minor era
(September 20, 1672).

(*On the upper part of the frame:*)

פה טמונה אשה חשובה הגונה

Here is hidden the valuable and distinguished woman,

(*On the left side of the frame*:)

מרת פריידל בת מה דוד זצל מק אויסי

the Lady Freudel, daughter of R. David, the memory of the just is blessed,

from the commune of Aussee,

(*On the right side of the frame*:)

אשת האלוף הגביר כהרר ליב .. ש יצו

the wife of the illustrious master R. Leb of Lichtenstadt (or Nikolsburg),

may his Rock and Redeemer guard him.

(*Within the frame*:)

על

אלה אני בוכיה מאין

הפוגה על פטירת האש

הרכה והענוגה היקרה

והישרה מנורה טהורה

המפוארה המהוללה עטר

בעלה פיה פתחה

לות ………

For these things

I weep without

intermission, because the wife has died,

the tender and delicate, dear

and straight, the pure lamp,

virtuous and laudable, a crown to

her husband, she opened her mouth (with wisdom).

(*Break*)

מעלותיה מי מנה כפה

פרשה לעני בכל עת

עונה הנמצא דוגמתה

תנצבה

Who could recount her good qualities? She stretched

out her hand to the poor always

(and at every) time. Can one find her equal?

May her soul be bound up with the bond of life."

This distinguished lady had a typically German name, and had probably moved to Buda together with her husband who, as indicated by his name, was a rabbi. The inscription reflects not only his deep grief, but also his erudition. The text, which rhymes in Hebrew, reveals a number of Biblical quotes. One rabbinical genre, displaying familiarity with the sacred texts, was to spin an entirely new text laced with Biblical words, expressions and quotes, similar to the classical Latin genre of the *cento*, a "patchwork of poems". R. Leib's quotes are the following: "for these things do I weep" (Lamentations 1,16); "without respite" (Lamentations 3,49); "dainty and delicate" (Isaiah 47,1); "a crown for her husband" (Proverbs 12,4); "her mouth is full of wisdom" (Proverbs 31,26); "her hands are stretched out to the needy" (Proverbs 31,20).

The Bible was known by all, the quotes could be easily identified and the art of Biblical citations was undoubtedly admired.

(15) Mazl Tov!

Aside from the gravestones, very few inscribed objects have survived from the period of the Ottoman rule. One of these, a golden wedding ring (*tabba'at kiddushin*), is on display in the Hungarian National Museum. It was found in 1861 in Buda during groundwork for a house (Iskola utca). The ring is from the sixteenth or seventeenth century. Nine bumps, alternating with granulation, ornament the wide solid gold hoop.

The head of the ring is a miniature house, indicating marriage. The Jewish custom of giving a ring to the bride during the wedding ceremony (under the *huppah*) is an old one, it dates back at least to the early Middle Ages. The ring is not only a symbol, it carries value too. It can only be made of pure gold or silver, it may not have a precious stone in it because the value of the latter is uncertain.

The inscription in the ring from Buda is the well known Jewish wedding greeting and wish: *Mazzal tov*—Good luck! You should be lucky! As one says today: *Mazl tov*. The word *mazzal* used to mean the lucky conjunction of the stars, *mazzalot* is the Zodiac. The word as well as the image it suggests is part of the Babylonian heritage of the Jewish tradition.

(16) The Recapture of Buda (1686)

During the earlier sieges (1598, 1602, 1684) the Austrians treated the Jews similarly to the Turks, their enemies. But even in more peaceful times, "the Hungarians, Germans and Czechs are apt to impale and roast the Jew from these lands, should he fall into their hands," writes Evliya Chelebi.

In the summer of 1686 the Jews took part, as far as the Turks allowed them, in the defense of Buda, carrying water, wood, stones and ammunition, except on the Sabbath, when they were exempt from this work. The Castle Hill could best be approached from the Víziváros. The city walls had lain in ruins since the 1684 siege, and the Christian troops began their assault from this direction. They did not bother to distinguish between the "Ismaelites" (Turks) and the Jews of Buda—neither could expect mercy. During the last phase of the siege, when the Brandenburg soldiers were fighting in the vicinity

33. Map of Buda Castle from the time of the siege, 1684 4 (the towered building on the right): *Iuden Kirch*, "the Jewish temple" (in fact, the Maria Magdolna Church)

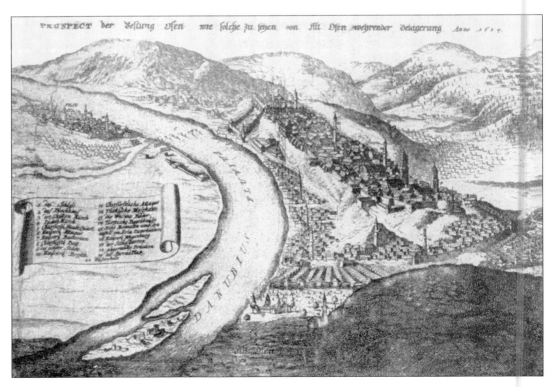

34. The victorious troops plunder, pillage and shed blood in Buda recaptured from the Turks, 1686. The Jewish quarter of Buda can be seen in the background

of the Jewish street, the Jews sought refuge in the "great" synagogue. Non-Jews, too, tried to find shelter in the building; anyone making his way there was asked whether she or he could recite the *Shema*. The artillery fire severely damaged the building: its roof and walls collapsed and countless people were buried under the ruins. On September 2 the soldiers massacred everyone they found there.

> "All the people (with Schulhof: 'the community') gathered there, from all corners of the Jewish quarter men, women and children, crowding, jostling, thronging, all breathless, fleeing the arms. Everyone was lamenting and weeping in despair, crying out for help, and the weeping rose unto the skies—such great distress as our souls suffered had not been heard before. (...) And a great many soldiers, infantrymen (called *Musketiere* in German), broke in, brandishing their destructive weapons, their guns, their naked swords in their hands, and also Hungarian hussars, holding their curved swords. And they made a bloody sacrifice in the House of the Lord: they spilled the innocent blood of the sons of Israel."

The bones that were unearthed in the course of excavations were reburied in the martyrs' plot of the Kozma utca cemetery (1968).

35. Turk and Jew (wearing a *Judenhut*) in the Buda mint. A sarcastic medal minted on the occasion of the recapture of Buda, 1686

36. A Jewish flyer urging the redemption of the Jews captured in Buda, 1686

The Jewish community of Buda was completely destroyed in 1668. The siege was called *hurban*, "destruction", as the siege of Jerusalem. The victors imposed a ransom on the Jews, an enormous amount to be paid to the commander of the Christian forces; this amount could only be raised by loans from Jewish communities abroad, and while the sum was being raised the Jews of Buda had to rely on the guarantees put up by Prague, Nikolsburg and other towns. Those who were unable to escape in time and who were not killed during the siege, were taken captive as part of the booty. Some four hundred Jews were taken captive. For many years after the fall of Buda, fund-raising continued in the Jewish communities of Europe in order to ransom the captives taken by the Austrian and Hungarian troops.

R. Efraim ha-Kohen's son-in-law, R. Jacob Ashkenazi, was captured by the Brandenburgians, but he eventually managed to make his way to the Holy Land, even if not the "next year", as he had once hoped when still under the influence of Shabbetai Tzvi's ideas; after he was ransomed, he made *aliyah*. Shemuel (Samuel) Oppenheimer (1630–1703), a Viennese banker and army contractor living in Heidelberg, was especially active in ransoming the prisoners of Buda: he undertook to muster a fully equipped musketeer for each Jewish prisoner, and offered to cancel a significant portion of the war debts of the court at the pertinent imperial committee. The prisoners who were ransomed by him and by his agents—one by the name of Sender (Alexander / Sándor) Taussig / Tauszk, an able young Jew who repeatedly courted danger in his dealings—were scattered all over the world. Some of them had the surname *Oven*, "of Buda", which they kept even after their arrival to the Holy Land.

II. Óbuda

The Golden age of the Jewish community of Óbuda came in the late eighteenth and early nineteenth centuries. In those times Óbuda was the largest Jewish community in the country, perhaps after Pozsony / Pressburg. This is when their famous rabbi, Moshe Münz, was active.

When the Turks left the country, Buda and Pest came under the jurisdiction of the Hungarian Kingdom where Jews were not permitted to settle in royal free boroughs. In fact, Jews did not settle in Buda in the eighteenth century until the times of Joseph II. Landowners, however, were not subject to the restrictions of the royal free boroughs; it was them who settled Jews on their own estates during the seventeenth and eighteenth centuries. This is how the Jewish communities of Western Hungary emerged: on the Esterházy estates in Kismarton (Eisenstadt) and in the "seven communities (*sheva kehillot*)" in Burgenland, Austria, on the estates of the Batthyány family in Rohonc (Rechnitz, Austria) and Németújvár (Güssing, Austria), under the protection of the Pálffy family in Pozsony (Bratislava, Slovakia), and elsewhere. The contractual relationship between the landowner and the Jewish community (*communitas*), defined when these communities were established, served as models for similar contracts throughout the eighteenth century. Landowners were happy to take advantage of the Jewish communities for they tied their production into the international commercial network. The Jews of Óbuda, too, settled on a manorial estate, under the protection of the Zichy family.

Some fourteenth- and fifteenth-century documents testify that Jews did live in Óbuda (*Ofen Yashan / Oven Yoshen* by its Hebrew name, *Alt Ovn* in Yiddish) before the Ottoman rule. In addition to written sources (tax registers), the goblet of their Holy Society (*Hevrah Kaddishah*) survived, to become part of the collection of the Jewish Museum in New York City. The goblet, inscribed with a date (1626), is not an ultimate proof because it may have belonged to the Jewish community of the Castle. After the recapture of Buda it was the Austrian authorities who promoted the settlement of Jews in Buda. They needed the Jews as suppliers for the army. The Jews of Óbuda came mostly from Bohemia and Moravia. Among them there was also a Sephardi Jew, an Italian merchant called David of Rome, who traded in coffee. After 1746, when Maria Theresa's decree expelled the Jews from Buda, a number of Jewish families moved to the neighboring Óbuda. Prominent eighteenth-century rabbis included Issachar Dov (Ber) Oppenheim (ca. 1740), Mattityahu Günsburg, Izsák Kicse (Köce / Kittsee / Yitzhak Katz) (ca. 1786) and finally Moshe Münz.

During the eighteenth century the Jews of Buda lived in an autonomous community. They called their city by its Turkish Sephardi name. R. Meir of Kismarton (Eisenstadt) allowed the use of both names, *Budun* and *Ofen* (i.e. *Ofen Yashan*) in divorce certificates.

The first Jew of Óbuda identified by name was a certain Jacob Flesh who delivered oil, sugar, almonds, lemon, hair powder, and other goods to the Zichy Palace in Zsámbék. The market town Óbuda, together with about ten other villages, belonged to the Zsámbék estates of the Zichy family of Zics and Vásonkő. In 1726 Count Zichy leased an abandoned ale-house (brewery and inn) to the Jews. He needed the income from the rent of the apartments and shops. Jews who chose occupations that ultimately served the landowner were not only granted rights to settle but also enjoyed certain privileges and the landowner's protection. According to the orders (1745) of Zsuzsanna Bercsényi, the widow of Count Péter Zichy, which were confirmed after her death (1746 and 1765), the Jewish community was entitled to elect public officials (*hithadshut / hishadshus*), turn to their own courts in domestic disputes and build synagogues. They were granted free practice of religion, they could run slaughterhouses and inns, they could buy a license to sell alcohol, although it was restricted to selling wine or beer to fellow-Jews. They were allowed to surround their dwelling place with a Sabbath-rope (*eruv*). In return they were obliged to pay considerable sums in the form of all sorts of annual taxes, they had to maintain a fire brigade, keep their shops closed on Christian holidays and always report giving shelter to foreign Jews. They were even allowed to own property. They retained their rights after the estate came under the control of the Treasury (1766).

In Óbuda, Jews and Christians lived side by side, they had equal rights. The partial dependence of Jews on Christian society emerged relatively late, after the 1840s and only in connection with the military tax. The head of the community was the Jewish Judge (*Juden Richter / judex judaeorum*), assisted by a council, composed of jurors and five assessors. Further organs of self-government were the larger exterior council (24 people), led by the speaker (*Vormund*) and the board of deputies (60 people). By the end of the eighteenth century the population attained almost two thousand. Ferenc Schams (1780–1839), an apothecary, estimated the population of Óbuda in 1822 at 7,356 people, including 4,000 Catholics and 3,210 Jews. Most people in the town were merchants and craftsmen by profession. The merchants were mostly peddlers, carrying "small articles on their back from village to village". They traded in hare-skin, leather, shells for making buttons, and scrap iron. Some maintained shops or inns or delivered grain and wine to faraway places. Among the craftsmen were tailors, cobblers, brandy distillers, furriers, goldsmiths, silversmiths and bookbinders. According to the 1767 census the Jewish community of Óbuda could even support two jesters (musicians).

The situation of Jews living on the estate of a landowner and under his protection was far more favorable than that of the Jews of Buda or Pest: they were less exposed to the extremes of daily events. In market towns Jews even had an opportunity for upward mobility into the middle class. True, the main attraction of Óbuda, the "harbor", was the proximity of the two bigger cities, mostly of Pest. "They lingered here like in a hallway, waiting to enter Pest and Buda, but the Germans would not let them" (Antal Szerb, *Budapesti kalauz Mars-lakók számára* [A Guide to Budapest for Martians], Budapest: Löbl Dávid és Fia, 1935).

A Hungarian saying bears testimony: "They are as numerous as Jewish kids in Óbuda."

"A large community with many persons learned and wise, rich and well-off—God Almighty should keep them", wrote a Jewish chronicler about Óbuda in 1746.

"The Jewish community of Óbuda is one of the oldest in the country and it had become independent not only as a religious congregation but as a political unit, too. They elected their own judges, they were granted self-government, later they even practiced criminal law, inflicting punishment, including caning and prison terms. They communicated with county and city officials in writing, lived peacefully, practiced their professions and multiplied. (...) They accumulated great wealth and people came from all over the world to borrow their money. The sales registers of the goldsmith Totisz, kept in our museum today, contains the names of the most prominent nobles of Transylvania from the 30s."

(Gábor Halász, *Vázlat Óbudáról* [Sketch of Óbuda], 1935)

(1) Institutions of a Jewish Community

Whenever Jews settle in a new place, they first try to establish the basis of Jewish communal life, the institutional framework of the "Holy Community"(*Kehillah Kedoshah*), to ensure life according to Halakhic rules and customs (*minhag*). The most important Jewish institutions are a prayer-room, ritual bath, slaughterhouse, and cemetery.

Building a synagogue is never the concern of newcomers but of established, wealthier communities and only if external circumstances permit. The only requirement for communal prayer is the presence of ten adult men, a *minyan*, meaning "number", "number of people". Thus, any ordinary room where there is a Torah scroll is suitable. Prayer-rooms or small prayer-houses were often set up in private homes; they served as a meeting place for the men of the community. The word "synagogue" itself, derived from the Greek *synagogue*, means "assembly", "congregation", "place / house of gathering". In large villages this room or building also served as the center of the community (*kahal / kehillah / edah*) and as the headquarters of various institutions. Ritual, educational, judicial institutions as well as tax-related issues and social welfare were directed and supervised from here.

37. Portrait of
Pinhas Leib Freudiger,
dayyan of Óbuda

38. Portrait of Mózes
óbudai Freudiger

The two most important institutions of ritual life are the ritual bath (*mikveh*) and the slaughter-house together with the slaughterer, the person in charge of ritual slaughter (*shohet*, Yiddish *shoykhet*, Hungarian *sakter*, a Germanized version of the Yiddish term). In Hungarian he is also called "metsző" [cutter] because according to Judaic law he cuts the trachea and the neck artery of the animal with one quick slice, to avoid unnecessary pain. An equally important person is the *mohel / moyhel*, the person trained to circumcise newborn baby boys when they are eight days old. Since circumcisions happen relatively rarely, not every community has its own *mohel*, he can be invited from another community.

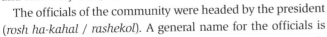

The traditional Jewish school is called *heder* "room"; here children are taught to read and write in Hebrew with the help of some simple prayers and Biblical texts, guided by the *melammed*, the teacher. The *yeshivah*, the Talmud school, is the higher institution of learning. A *boher* "young man" or *yeshivah boher*—teenager or elder boys, young men or even some of older ones—study the Talmud for several years with a rabbi. It was not customary to "maintain" a yeshiva—this was the term they used—in a large town like Óbuda or Pest because the temptations of city-life would have distracted the students' attention from the Talmud. Therefore there is no mention of a single yeshiva in the whole of Budapest, with the exception of the Orthodox school on the corner of Dob and Kazinczy utca, which used to be called a yeshiva.

39. Portrait of
Ábrahám óbudai
Freudiger

The officials of the community were headed by the president (*rosh ha-kahal / rashekol*). A general name for the officials is *parnas*. Members of the council are called "elders" (*zaken*, plural *zekenim*), the officials are *gabba'im*. It was the *dayyan* who decided in civil matters. To qualify for this position one had to have a good moral and critical sense as well as familiarity with the Talmud, Mishnah and earlier responsa. Questions of ritual were to be examined by the *moreh hora'ah*. *Gabba'im* ("tax collector", Yiddish *gabe*) were entrusted with collecting communal taxes, alms and some other organizational tasks. The full name for this position was "charity collector (*gabbai tzedakah / tsedoke gabe*)". This was a confidential post, every community had at least two *gabba'im*. It was the *gabbai* who indicated the text when the Torah is read. The sexton in the synagogue is called *shammash / shames*; he is in charge of opening and closing the synagogue, he takes care of the building. Another paid communal official or emissary (*sheliah tzibbur*) is the cantor (*hazzan / khazn*, in Óbuda: *Schulsinger*, "synagogue singer"). He is the person who leads the prayer, the services. In his modern role the rabbi is the religious and spiritual leader of the community, he preaches, conducts wedding ceremonies and burials. His original role, however, was different: he helped his congregation understand and interpret traditional texts and laws. He participated in the daily Talmud study (*shi'ur*) of the community, held lectures before Pesah and the High Holidays and gave replies (*teshuvah*, plural *teshuvot*, Latin *responsum*) to Halakhic questions (*she'elah*, plural *she'elot*, Latin *rogatio*) addressed to him. The rabbi was the president of the rabbinical court (*bet din / beys din*) which consisted of three people. Since the other two members of the *bet din* were rabbis, too, the president was usually called chief rabbi. The Turkish–Jewish name for chief rabbi (*hakham bashi*) was not unknown in Buda during the Turkish occupation. Rabbis were addressed by the title *morenu* or *morenu ha-rav*, "our teacher". In the nineteenth and twentieth centuries the Neolog communities of Pest, like the Dohány utca community, would employ a preacher in addition to the rabbi. Registers—birth- and marriage-registers, death certificates—were kept by the rabbi or his deputy. Orthodox communities would keep a register of circumcisions (*mohel* book), in addition. (Actually, keeping Jewish registers grew out of this practice.)

Óbuda was the first modern Jewish community in the region of the capital of Hungary. Here, in this market town, there was no separate Jewish quarter as there had been everywhere else, including Buda. Jews lived among the non-Jewish population but their communal life was organized around a center, the Jewish institutions. This center was in the Zsidó utca / Lajos utca, near the synagogue. The rabbi's apartment, the Jewish hospital and apothecary were on a huge ground-plot, overlooking the street, next to some dwelling houses, and the synagogue behind them; this arrangement was typical in the eighteenth century.

Next to this complex stood the slaughterhouse (*Fleischbank*) and the Jewish community house (*Gemein-Haus*). In the first half of the eighteenth century there was an additional small prayer-room and a little further, of course, the cemetery. From the second half of the eighteenth century on there was a Hevrah Kaddishah, a hospital and, due to the decrees of Joseph II, a Jewish public school in the neighborhood. This complex grew with time. Not to the North, where the St. Peter and Paul Roman Catholic Church and the Zichy Palace stood, but to the South, towards Újlak. Many Jews lived in Lajos utca, Mókus utca and Korona utca; this was the "Jewish courtyard (*Judenhof*)" where Jewish institutions, shops, beer- and wine-cellars dominated the streets.

(2) The Óbuda Synagogue (163 Lajos utca)

The first prayer-house was opened on the cartwright- ("*Wagenmeister*"-) plot in the first decades of the eighteenth century. Documents call it *Judenshul* or *oskola*, "school", though it could hardly have been anything but a traditional Jewish study house (German *Schule*, Yiddish *shul / shil / shül*), i.e. a prayer-house. It is mentioned that the "tools of the Jews", books and "robes", were kept in the "school", which confirms that it was a prayer-house. The building, with adobe walls, was probably erected for some other purpose. The first synagogue proper was built in 1732–1733 on the Zsidó tér (Jewish square) which was more or less the area South to the present synagogue, on the Danube side. The second one was built in 1769 on a privately owned lot, according to the plans of Mátyás Máté Nepauer (ca. 1719–1792). Nepauer was a popular architect, almost all the eighteenth-century churches in Buda are hallmarked by his name (St. Anne Church in Víziváros, the parish church in Újlak, St. Florian Chapel in Fő utca, the Augustine, later Franciscan Church on Margit körút). The fact that he was commissioned to build the synagogue is an indication of the developing bourgeois status of Jews. Unfortunately, parts of Nepauer's modest synagogue had to be demolished in 1817 because its walls cracked, due to poor soil conditions. The winner of the competition to design a new synagogue was

40. The Óbuda synagogue, ca. 1899

Andreas von Landherr's Neo-Classicist building, against Mihály Pollack's plan. The interior decoration was commissioned from János Maurer stucco master. A statement of the construction costs in German with Hebrew letters survived, amounting to 130,000 forints.

41. The Óbuda synagogue, ca. 1920

42. The Óbuda synagogue, ca. 1960

"Corinthian columns on the facade, acanthus decoration inside, in the middle four Napoleonic eagles on four classical columns, built in 1820. Mihály Pollack, the architect of the National Museum participated in the competition to design the synagogue, but the Jewish community opted to have a native of Óbuda build it, hence chose the plans of Andreas von Landherr, who completed the work in accordance with all modern standards. The spirit of the times accommodated the soul: this grandiose building is a bridge between ancient isolation and the universal. Not that such a move was a requirement of emancipation. It was better than equality, it was an autonomous decision." (Gábor Halász, 1935)

Consecrated in 1821 (July 20), the Neo-Classicist building—with Empire style decoration—is a typical example of late eighteenth-century synagogue with a gallery. Its ground plan is asymmetrical, it is obviously designed around the former building. The main room of the old synagogue was preserved, extended by a small room on the northern side. The L-shaped women's

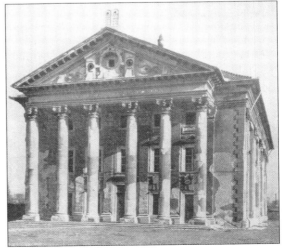

43. The Óbuda synagogue, 1981

gallery was on the northern and western sides. An open portico, supported by six Corinthian columns, was built at the entrance of the building. Fourteen chandeliers hung in front of it. When Mózes Oesterreicher, the Jewish Judge was blamed for its lavishness, he replied that religious customs required festive lighting on Friday nights. The *bimah* stood in the middle. It was made of wood, painted white with a gold trim, steps leading up to it on two sides. Empire style obelisks stood on all four corners with eagles spreading their wings on the top, the banister decorated with a lute, the wrought-iron steps with a lute and trumpet (*shofar*).

The synagogue must have been a remarkable sight near the free royal boroughs of Buda and Pest around the time of its construction. The Archduke Joseph (1796–1847), the Palatine, would proudly show it to his guests visiting from abroad. Ferenc Schams wrote in his guide-book:

"(In Óbuda) several Jewish houses stand out by their pomp from the street view, but the most magnificent novelty is the new synagogue. Contemporary Jews differ from their ancestors—very rightly, I suppose—in their principles; for while the ancient Hebrews, being monotheist, would not tolerate more than one place of worship, and their religious practice and love of their home was united in the Temple of Jerusalem, these days we find synagogues in every community of more than a few hundred members. This new synagogue is undoubtedly the most beautiful one of all the similar Jewish religious establishments in the Austrian Monarchy; not even the Jewish temple of Temesvár [today Timişoara, Romania] can compete with it in pomp, not to mention the old synagogues of Prague. The only building that may outdo it in grandiosity is the building of the Jewish community of Amsterdam."

(*Vollständige Beschreibung der königl. freyen Haupt Stadt Ofen*, Buda, 1822)

A Russian traveler, Piotr I. Keppen visited the synagogue in May, 1822, guided by the same Schams.

44. Interior of the Óbuda synagogue

In his account Keppen says that only "a synagogue in the Netherlands surpasses the Óbuda building", "its architecture is simple and grandiose, every traveler must see it"; referring to the Netherlands, the Russian perhaps meant the famous Esnoga of the Spanish and Portuguese congregations in Amsterdam.

A painting of the synagogue by F. Weiss appears on a page of the beautiful map-series by Károly Vasquez published in 1838 (in the collection of the National Széchényi Library). Among other buildings characteristic of the city, the synagogue is painted in the lower left-side corner of the frame. The painting, just like turn-of-the-century photographs, clearly shows the small, one-story houses next to the synagogue: the Jewish center of Óbuda. Samuel Kohn mentions that a lithographic print of the synagogue was a valued treasure decorating his parents' house.

The Hebrew–Yiddish register of the synagogue seats has been preserved in the Budapest Municipal Archives. The large book lists the owners of the seats and the price paid for them. The number of permanent seats is indicative of the size of the community: there were numbered places for 364 men (*shtodt*) and for 298 women upstairs on the gallery.

Renting the seats of the synagogue was part of the tax-revenues of the community. Members of the synagogue would renew their seats for the next (ritual) year at the end of the summer, before the High Holidays. The owner's name was usually inscribed into the benches, too. Each bench had a small drawer where its owner could keep his prayer-book and, if he *daven*ed every day, as was customary in the eighteenth century, his *talis* and *tefillin*. Seats were sold at different rates, the wealthier could pay more money for a better seat.

The Óbuda synagogue is one of the most beautiful Neo-Classicist buildings in Hungary.

Not far from the synagogue, in the former Zichy utca (no. 9), the Jewish community established a museum for the history of the Jews of Óbuda. Some of the ritual objects of the former synagogue and Jewish community are now in the collection of the Jewish Museum of Budapest, including Torah crowns, breastplates, a curtain of the Ark (*parokhet / paroykhes*) as well as boxes and bowls for alms. Some of the inscriptions on the goldsmith's works are "Made by Hayyim ben Yehuda and Levi, aldermen of the Óbuda Hevrah, in the year 5536 [= 1776]" (silver alms bowl); "This was given to the Hevrah Kaddishah by Moshe Abeles upon his becoming a member of the society to redeem the costs of his burial" (silver cup with cover, late eighteenth century); "Made by Moshe Kan and Moshe Tsoref [whose name means "goldsmith"], Ferenc Holics, aldermen of the Óbuda Hevrah Kaddishah, in the year 5560 [=1800]" (silver alms bowl); "Jicek Köce [Yitzhak Katz / Kittsee] donated this to the Torah study society. Cup of the blessing and the food. (The Almighty) ordered us to say a blessing upon this (cup)" (silver kiddush cup, decorated with gold, Lipót Fischer's work, Pest, ca. 1800); "A present of Mordecai Holics and his wife, Sarah, to the Hevrah of Óbuda, in the year 565 [1805]" (silver alms bowl); "The possession of Shmuel Gran's widow, Lady Rezl, her mother's name is Bele, made in honor of the Torah in the year 5574 [= 1814]" (*parokhet*). "This beautiful box was given as an offering by Yosef Gran, Mikhael Leser, Hayyim Zilc, Yeshaya Rosenthal, Avraham Spitz, David Bergl. On the first day take the fruit of the *hadar* tree" (silver *etrog*-box) (1822); "Belongs to the Society for care of the sick [*Bikkur holim*], 5582 [1822]" (*besamim*, silver spice box).

In 1848 the violence against Jews of Pozsony and Pest spread to Óbuda as well. Someone, a non-Jew, who visited the famous synagogue on a Saturday morning, wrote as follows (*Életképek*, May 7, 1848):

> "Seeing that I was not one of Israel, a man interrupted his prayer, came up to me and talked to me kindly in Hungarian. We discussed the ceremony and I was sad to hear that they may not be able to worship their God peacefully anymore for they feared the Christians' attack."

45. The *bimah / almemor* in the Óbuda synagogue

46. The former building of the Óbuda synagogue now occupied by the studio of the Hungarian Television, 1993

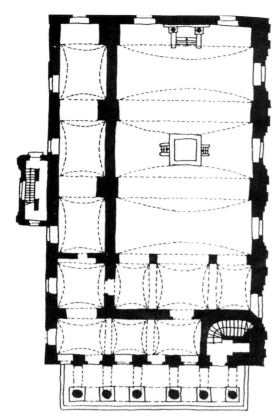

47. Ground-plan of the Óbuda synagogue

In the fall one could hear *verbunkos* or recruiting music on the square in front of the synagogue: twenty young Jewish musicians played recruiting songs led by the silver-knobbed walking stick of the Jewish Judge, inviting all to join the army, to become a hussar. At the beginning of May of the following year the Jews of Óbuda gave shelter to many of the two thousand refugees escaping the siege of Buda.

The synagogue underwent major renovation in 1900. This is when the secessionist or Art Nouveau decoration of the tympanum by Gyula Ullman was added. Before that the facade was decorated with a clock within a rosette. At the same time the old copper roof was replaced by sheet iron. The square windows on the second floor were replaced by round ones. The walls were decorated with secessionist paintings (inside) and stained-glass windows were installed. Electricity was installed to replace the old candelabra. The interior furniture was partly restored and partly replaced. The report of József Parczel, the notary of the community, serves as an important document of the renovation, in spite of the awkwardness of its intended lofty style (1901).

"The temple's interior makes a great impression on the visitor. Officials and experts made every effort and acted with great care to preserve the original character of the synagogue while up-dating it to meet all contemporary needs. The old seats had been replaced by new, modern ones (402 of them); one of them is a heavily decorated, closed seat for the chief rabbi of the community. Among the new pieces of the synagogue's furniture are a new pulpit in front of the Ark and a stand for the cantor on the right side of the widened steps leading up to the pulpit. The artistic paintings compiled tastefully from beautiful colors as well as the golden decoration on the paintings and other objects, illuminated by fifteen chandeliers hanging from the ceiling and 286 electric lamps around the walls offer a fairy-tale view. The Israelite community of Óbuda can justly be proud of its synagogue and say that *The glory of the LORD filled the house* (II Chronicles 7,1) because a special, grand pathos seizes the soul upon entering the holy temple."

48. Ark-shaped wall candelabrum from the former Jewish Museum of Óbuda (formerly 9 Zichy utca)

After World War II minor damages to the building were repaired, the roof was covered with tiles. In the 1980s a full reconstruction, or rather remodeling took place. Today visitors can only see it from the outside because it serves as a studio for Hungarian Television. The iron fence and the small houses around it were demolished.

Though the building itself stands, the Óbuda synagogue is no more.

(3) Inscription on the Facade

The facade is decorated by a Hebrew inscription. As we know, the construction of the synagogue was initiated by the rabbi of Óbuda, R. Moshe Münz. It was him who held a sermon at the consecration of the synagogue. The sermon was printed in Vienna within a year—a good sign of the importance of the event as well as of R. Münz.

The title of his sermon (*Devir ha-bayit*) as well as the Hebrew inscription on the facade of the synagogue refer to the temple of King Solomon in Jerusalem. *Devir ha-bayit* is an expression for the Holy of Holies; clearly, the consecration sermon talks about a central issue. The inscription on the synagogue is a Biblical quotation (I Kings 8,38), an excerpt from Solomon's prayer (or speech) at the consecration of the Temple of Jerusalem.

"(...) Oh, hear in heaven and pardon the sin of Your servants, Your people Israel, after you have shown them the proper way in which they are to walk; and send down rain upon the land which you gave to Your people as their heritage. So, too, if there is a famine in the land, if there is pestilence, blight, mildew, locusts or caterpillars, or if an enemy oppresses them in any of the settlements of the land. In any plague and in any disease, *in any prayer or supplication offered* by any person among all Your people Israel—each of whom knows his own affliction—*when he spreads his palms toward this House*, oh, hear in Your heavenly abode..."

(I Kings 8,36–40)

The inscription on the facade is not the full quotation, only the italicized parts. The meaning of the words taken out of context is different from their Biblical meaning.

כל תפלה כל תחינה אשר תהיה לכל האדם ופרש כפיו אל הבית הזה

"Anyone who prays or offers supplication spreads his palms toward this House."

R. Münz's sermon confirms this interpretation. He quotes a passage from the Talmud (Berakhot 6a) to support his thesis that only prayers said in the synagogue are answered. There is no doubt that it was Münz who selected the inscription on the facade. In his sermon he also refers to the rabbinical concept, ultimately rooted in the Bible (Ezekiel 11,16), that the synagogue is nothing but a "small sanctuary (*mikdash me'at*)". Münz wanted to tie the community to the *sanctuary* of Óbuda in order to preserve strict religiosity. This modern and impressive building reflects his traditionalism, tempered by the central role of the temple, unusual in Jewish tradition. It foreshadows the modernization of religious conservatism. The spreading of the palm, referred to in the quotation, is the priestly blessing. Münz's slogan is "sanctuary and a priestly gesture".

49. The sermon of R. Moshe Minc (Moses Münz) at the consecration of the Óbuda synagogue

(4) The "Dressing" of the Torah

The primary object of Jewish ritual is the Torah scroll (*sefer Torah*). It is used for the reading of the weekly Torah portion (*sidrah / parashah*) during services.

In the synagogue traditional texts appear in three forms: scrolls, the Torah rolled around two staves; the Book of Esther, a simple scroll (*megillah*); and the prayer-books (*Siddur* and *Mahzor*), a

50. Torah shield from the former Jewish Museum of Óbuda

book or books bound and sewn together from pages, either handwritten or printed. The use of Siddur, the prayer-book for regular services, and of Mahzor, prayer-book for the holidays is individual (in Hungary they are called popularly *siderli* and *mahzerli*); the Torah scroll and the Megillah, on the contrary, do have a ritual status of a sort.

The preparation of the Torah scroll for reading (*keri'a be-tzibbur*) happens according to a very old tradition. It is inscribed on parchment from a ritually clean animal (*kelaf*), always on the inside of the hide (the side towards the meat) with the tendon (*gidin*) of an equally clean animal, written in special ink with the consonants only. It has to be an impeccable text, corrected, if necessary, without interpunctuation. The manuscript may not be decorated except for the little three-pointed crowns (*tag*, plural *tagim / tagin*) which are used to ornament certain letters (*gimel, zayin, tet, nun, ayin, tzade, shin*). Some letters are only topped with one *tag*, these are called *ziyyun*, "decoration with the letter *zayin*". (Both signs are actually very tiny and thin *zayins*, one or three of them.) Tradition requires that more than one Torah scroll be kept

51. Torah crown from the Óbuda synagogue, 1806

in the synagogue. The number of Torah scrolls kept in the Ark indicates the rank of the synagogue, the wealth and devotion of the community members. It is prohibited to read from a fragmentary manuscript or printed text. At the slightest suspicion of a mistake in the text a new Torah scroll has to be unrolled. An unfit (*pasul*) Torah scroll may not be used in the synagogue.

The work of the "certified" scribe, in Hebrew: *sofer stam / soyfer stam / sayfer stam*, the word *stam* being an abbreviation from the initial letters of words for scrolls written only by a qualified scribe: *sefer Torah* (and) *megillah*, the man who copies, checks and corrects Torah scrolls, is considered a religious activity. There are stories how simple, bearded men would occasionally appear at the rabbi's house or in the synagogue, take the Torah scroll and check it to the last letter. They would correct mistakes with great care. As a reward for their activity, they accept only food, never money.

In Ashkenazi communities the Torah is always rolled around two wooden staves called *etz hayyim* "tree of life" (Proverbs 3,18), plural *atzei hayyim*. The handles below the scroll make holding it easier and serve as supports when dressing the Torah. The two scrolls are rolled onto the staves, a wide linen, silk and velvet ribbon (*vimpel / vindel* or *sash*) is rolled around them, tied with a string (*avnet*), and finally the *sefer Torah* is covered for protection by a decorated cloth, a "dress" (*mitpahat*). The staves are topped with metal finials: two "pomegranates" (*rimmon*, plural *rimmonim*), apples (*tappuah*, plural *tappuhim*); in modern times a crown or wreath (*keter* or *atarah*) was used in addition, or a helmet in Sephardi communities. These ornaments carry further ornaments: *rimmonim* have bells (*pa'amonim, sagim*), the six-pointed crown has floral designs or a wreath, animals (lion, deer, eagle) or birds, precious stones, etc. The (double) scroll itself is protected by a case (*mantel / mentele* or *meil*) made of some fine material. "We dress the Sefer Torah," wrote Bertalan Kohlbach (1866–1944), a distinguished Jewish folklorist. "We sew and embroider three sets of clothes for her: for everyday, holidays and mourning. On the 9th of Av we use the black dress, on days of repentance and reverence the white one and on the Sabbath and pilgrim holidays the ceremonial one, made of silk, velvet and brocade."

In modern Ashkenazi communities there are further accessories of the Torah scroll, such as the breastplate hung above the mantle (*hoshen / tas*) with a small plate (*shilt*) showing the weekly portion, or the pointer (*taitel / taitelboym*) forming a hand (*yad*) placed in the square hole in the middle of the breastplate. The decoration of the breastplate can be the lions of Judah with the Torah crown, two columns of the Temple of Jerusalem (Jakin and Boaz, I Kings 7,21; II Chron. 3,17), the two stone tablets of Moses and Aron (*shenei luhot*). It is forbidden to touch the letters of the Torah or even the scroll itself by hand, that is why the pointer is needed. It is the gabbai's duty to lead the *yad*. The pointer is hung above the mantle with a chain. Torah ornaments (*kelei kodesh*) are the most peculiar field of Jewish art.

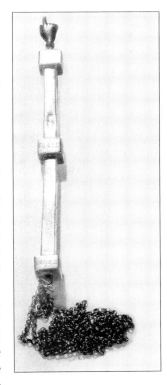

52. Torah pointer (*yad*) from the Óbuda synagogue, 1837

53. *Rimmonim*, "pomegranates", from the Óbuda synagogue, ca. 1800

54. Torah shield from the Óbuda synagogue

(5) Jewish Burghers of Óbuda

The Jews of Óbuda were not only involved in the retail trade of special commodities like sugarcane, hare-skin and sheep hide, scrap iron, etc. They played a significant role in the development of Hungarian industry.

The Goldbergers

Óbuda had several dye manufactures, which later became the foundation of the town's textile industry. The greatest fame was achieved by the company of Samuel Goldberger & Sons. Their factory was to the South of the synagogue, in Landstrasse (today 136–138 Lajos utca). It was a one-story building, referred to as the "old roller" by the residents of the neighborhood. The name of the founders is marked by a plaque on the building.

Family tradition maintains that one of the ancestors of the *Goldberger family*, a certain Perec, a goldsmith, was of Italian origin. Maybe, but it is more likely that along with most of Óbuda's Jewry he, too, came from Moravia. All we know for sure

55. Leó budai Buday-Goldberger, 1941

is that his son, Ferenc Goldberger (1755–1834) was born in Óbuda. He traded in textiles, sold blue dye on the market of Pest in the early 1780s, soon had his own wooden booth and finally found a partner, the Czech master Stibrall with whom he established the dye factory of Óbuda in Lajos utca (1785). For a long time he signed his official correspondence as Goldberg. It is possible that he acquired this name only after Joseph II's decree. When the Governorship of Pest ordered the demolition of the booths on the new market place (1798), he, too, along with the other merchants trading on the left side of the Danube applied for a permit to open a warehouse and a store in Pest. With the permission in his pocket he started his business in 1800. The Orczy House and the Király utca store were only the first steps, followed by stores on the new market place and on the corner of Nagyhíd and Deák Ferenc utca. The Goldbergers were among the first ones to install gas lamps in their stores, right after the National Theater and the Pilvax.

The blue, printed materials of the Goldbergers were very popular, especially among the Swabian, German burghers. They were prepared with genuine indigo dye, so the linen and calico did not lose its color. The founder was followed by his son, Samuel Goldberger (1784–1848), in 1825 and the latter immediately took his eldest son, Fülöp, into the business. Samuel streamlined the management while Fülöp's strength was in technical innovation. They introduced a new dyeing technique (1829), bought or built new machines, invented or introduced new dyeing recipes. The procedures were kept secret, written in German but with Hebrew characters. They increased production, employed over a hundred workers, introduced new textile products. Some of them, like the white spotted blue calico or the black kerchief with red roses, are still basic products on the Hungarian market. "The dyeing factory of Mr. Samuel F. Goldberger in Óbuda is among the most important businesses in Hungary and it is the best one of its kind, without a doubt," reported Lajos Kossuth, in his *Jelentés az első magyar iparműkiállításról* [Report from the First Hungarian Industrial Fair], 1842.

It was always the head of the family who ran the factory and the factory held the family together, more or less. In her will of 1861 written after resigning from the business Erzsébet Adler, Samuel Goldberger's wife (1788–1868), who bore him ten sons and seven daughters, included some words of admonition. She wrote that social success can only come through a loving family, through holding together and cooperation.

By the middle of the nineteenth century the Goldberger factory became one of the most important enterprises of the Hungarian economy, even the pride of the nation. When Francis Joseph I first visited the Hungarian lands after his victory in the War of Independence of 1848/49 he stopped at the Goldberger factory in Óbuda (May 7, 1857, at noon). A newspaper of the time reported about the remarkable event:

"Honored by the visit of His Royal Majesty the owner decorated his factory for the festive event. The factory has one entrance and two courtyards; its walls were covered with red–white–blue and yellow–black cloths up to the roof, like a tent, and decorated with flags, coat of arms and other objects with the picture of His Majesty. The second courtyard was covered in red velvet and smiling flowers as well as the pictures of His Majesty. The pavement was richly covered with carpets, the workers were all dressed in blue uniforms. The owner and his family welcomed His Royal Highness who dismounted to meet them."　　(in: *Hölgyfutár*, 1857)

And another, somewhat ironic account of the event from a novel written a little later, based on the memory of the local population:

"His Majesty came from the Castle of Buda. He arrived on the Danube by ship—to come by carriage on the cobblestone pavement full of pot-holes would have been too hard a lesson for the royal and apostolic bottoms. From the harbor to the decorated factory and even inside he walked on red carpet. This red strip of carpet is what people seized and what remained in their memory, this endless magic carpet which must have cost a fortune. But, after all, it was due to an emperor who assigns Hungarian noble names ending in a 'y', and that was what the Goldbergers received."

(Lajos Hollós Korvin, *Óbudai búcsú* [Carnival of Óbuda] 1958/1961)

56. The visit of His Majesty Francis Joseph I at the Goldberger factory in Óbuda, 1857

We can imagine what a sight it must have been: the streets of Óbuda South of the synagogue, between the Danube and the factory, all covered by a red carpet, the factory itself completely wrapped up. But for a textile factory no luxury in carpets was too much. The family received the title of nobility only several years later (1867).

In the last decades of the nineteenth century the company was owned by the sons of Samuel Goldberger and, after 1876, by one of the grandsons, Bertold Goldberger (1849–1913). His son and heir, the new head of the family, Dr. Leó budai Buday-Goldberger (1878–1945)—who already managed a greatly expanded operation transformed into a corporation—enjoyed a special status in Óbuda at the beginning of the twentieth century. This is how Lajos Hollós Korvin (1905–1971), also a native of Óbuda, described Goldberger's status, based partly on his own family memories. "Already born a Hungarian noble and yet a faithful Israelite", since 1932 an appointed member of the Upper House, he used to play bridge with His Excellency the Governor Miklós Horthy's son, Miklós Horthy jr., who was a member of the board of directors as well as with Baron Ferenc Chorin, the president of GyOSz (National

57. The kosher restaurant of M. Guttman in Óbuda (28 Zsigmond utca), early twentieth century

Union of Industrialists). (He himself was an executive of GyOSz.) By then, of course, he did not live in Óbuda anymore but had moved to Pest. "The people of Óbuda, however, still considered him one of theirs, him being one of the richest and most influential burghers there. Not only because his family had lived and died there for several generations but because that is where the huge factory stood, employing over a thousand people from Óbuda, and because Leó, like his father and grandfather,

58. Jewish courtyard (*Judenhof*) in Óbuda. Street view, early twentieth century

acted as a feudal patron of the people, especially the Jews. (...) Scorning him was almost equal to high treason..." The boss was a wholehearted supporter of the Jewish community of Óbuda and especially its poorer members, if they strictly observed ritual law. He was the *kvater* (benefactor) of several young men of Óbuda and he always gave graciously.

In 1944, immediately after the German occupation of Hungary several members of the Goldberger family were taken to the internment camp established in the Rabbinical Seminary. The head of the family and the company, Leó Goldberger, a Hungarian patriot, consequently a militant opponent of Zionism and Jewish emigration, died in Mauthausen. He died of starvation immediately after the liberation of the camp.

With times Óbuda became a virtual textile center. Another textile factory was founded in 1826, the Spitzer calico factory (102/B Lajos utca). In 1950, after several changes in its ownership, it was brought under state control and was turned into a textile processing plant (1 Nagyszombat utca). It was united with the former Goldberger factory (1981) and finally closed down. The building, a historic monument of industrial architecture, was used as a department store (1986) and eventually other businesses took over the place.

Around the middle of the nineteenth century the greatest competitors of the Goldbergers were the Spitzers, and later, towards the end of the century, the Freudiger family of Óbuda. Pinhas-Leib Freudiger, rabbi of Óbuda, an excellent Talmudist, bought the former Levi Lindenbaum bed-linen, underwear and clothing factory in 1883. His son, Moses Freudiger (1833–1913), chose a practical career and took over the management of the factory from his father. After the Jewish Congress of 1868/69 the Goldbergers became Neolog Jews. The Freudiger family, possibly because of their strong rabbinical heritage, chose Orthodoxy. Their capital, acquired through industrial enterprise, allowed them to play a considerable role in Jewish communal affairs. Moses Freudiger was among the founders and, for a long time, the president of the Orthodox community. He received a Hungarian title of nobility and was called *óbudai* (1908). His sons inherited the mill as well as the presidency in the Orthodox community: Lipót (1866–?) became the honorary, Ábrahám (1868–?) the acting president. The latter initiated the construction of the Orthodox synagogue in Kazinczy utca. The presidency remained in the family even through the next generation. Fülöp (Pinhas) Freudiger (1900–1976) took over his father's position.

Óbuda had more than one nationally and even internationally known sons. It was the firmly based bourgeois society that offered so many opportunities for great achievement.

All one needed was a spirit of enterprise and real talent.

Benjámin Salamon Spitzer

(1774–1820) was born in Óbuda. His father, Götzel Spitzer moved to Pest in the times of Joseph II and became the head of the Jewish community. One of his sons became a Talmudist, another made use of his German education as a clerk in the Jewish community of Óbuda; the third son, Benjámin, did not want to study so he became a peddler. As a child he would gaze at the Danube for hours. At age fifteen he went to Prague and later to Hamburg where he became a sailor. He loved the sea. "Watching the sea I keep thinking that it talks to me. This is a holy language, too"—he wrote to his Talmudist brother. He sailed around the world twice, founded a shipping company in New Orleans and got rich. He invited his brothers to America but finally it was he who returned to Pest in his captain's uniform, as a millionaire (1808). In Pest some fine business partners cheated him out of his money. Poor again, he returned to the sea, wanted to be among the "wild". He sailed to Malta, to Alexandria, from Fiume to Sicily. Once he ended up on a warship. Sailing along the coast of Morocco, a bullet took his left leg. He wrote to Óbuda (1810) asking for at least his rings which he had bought in America, for he felt disappointed in people and was longing for his memories. Around 1820 he was in Vienna for a while where he met his brothers. He was about to embark on a last trip to America to fetch his belongings before settling in Europe when he died of a stroke. His gravestone reads: "Burgher of New Orleans, American sailor."

József Manes Oesterreicher

(1756–1832), too, was from Óbuda. He was the first Jewish doctor to receive a diploma from a Hungarian university. He started his studies in Vienna but the university of Nagyszombat moved to Buda in the meantime (1777) so he defended his thesis *Analysis aquarium Budensium* [Analysis of the waters of Buda] (1781) already there, in the Castle, in the Royal Palace at that, where the university was located temporarily (February 21, 1782). In order to take the Hippocratic oath without contravening Jewish traditions, he needed special permission and a slight modification of the standard text. The newspaper of the time, *A Magyar Hírmondó* reported about this extraordinary event, on March 2, 1782: "The Royal University received a special order from His Excellency concerning the freedom of persons of other than Catholic faith to become doctors of medicine." Oesterreicher, "of Jewish faith and nationality", had been working as a physician in the Jewish hospital of Óbuda already before he graduated as a doctor. He wrote "a detailed and magnificent study about the healing waters of Buda and other places", but his scientific interest drew him to the acid waters of Füred (today Balatonfüred). The lessees of the bath, especially Count Alajos

59. Portrait and signature of József Oesterreicher Manes

Batthyány, who was otherwise a noted liberal, and later the Benedictine order of Pannonhalma, tried to hinder his activities. Only after the dissolution of the order in 1787, when a royal *physicus* was allowed to work in Füred, did Oesterreicher manage to establish a health resort which soon became very popular. Beyond being a physician he also acquired fame for his medical innovations. He described the healing power of the natural bitter salt of Buda (*sal mirabilis nativus hungaricus*, "natural Hungarian wonder-salt") (1801). He found the salt (sodium sulfate or Glauber's salt) which cures the catarrh of digestive organs on the territory Southwest to Kelenföld, on the Dobogó plain (today Gyógyvíz / Keserűvíz utca) and developed methods which would have allowed the distribution of the wonder-salt all over Europe. In 1803 he moved to Vienna. His work was acknowledged and admired even at the Emperor's court. The marshland was completely drained during the canalization of Lágymányos–Kelenföld (1821). The forgotten spring (Ilona spring) was rediscovered only several decades later in 1863. The thermal water of the spring is sold even today, it is called "Hunyadi János keserűvíz" (bitter water). Back in the nineteenth century a spa was built upon it ("Erzsébet" bitter-salt bath).

In his will Oesterreicher sounds like an enlightened Jewish burgher, faithful to tradition: "I was born to God-fearing parents in Óbuda. As an adult, I seriously examined the moral principles of the Mosaic religion and I am now convinced that they allow man to fulfill his obligations towards God, his Emperor and other People. Therefore, disregarding my personal advantages, I remain faithful to the tradition of my forefathers and I order that my corpse be buried according to the Israelite customs."

His grave is in the (old) Jewish cemetery of Vienna. The plaque marking his name in Balatonfüred was wrecked in 1944. Whatever is left from it can be seen in the Jewish Museum today. In Füred there is a new plaque on the wall of the Heart Hospital.

*

The Jewish community of Óbuda grew and flourished from the mid-eighteenth century up until World War II almost uninterruptedly. The only hard times were the three decades following the death of Moshe Münz when there was not even a rabbi. The community established all the necessary societies and welfare institutions very quickly. At the turn of the eighteenth to the nineteenth century it was still a traditional community with associations based on solidarity. The Hevrah Kaddishah was founded (or revived) in 1770. Their registers are in Hebrew. In Hungarian it was also called *Szent Testvérség* [Holy Fraternity] or *Halottas Céh* [Burial Guild]. At the end of the eighteenth century they opened a hospital (*Siechenhaus*) with 24 beds. R. Münz founded the *Óbudai Menücho Nechajno Lelki Egylet* [Menukha Nekhona Spiritual Society of Óbuda] (*menuhah nekhonah* meaning "firm tranquillity") or, as it was called, the Society to help strengthen the faith in the world to come. The task of this society was to say *Kaddish* over the deceased who died without an offspring, on their anniversary (*Jahrzeit / yortsayt*). Later they organized pilgrimages to the grave of R. Münz. The Bikur Holim Society (for visiting the sick) is equally old (1794). Several other civil and social organizations emerged in the first half of the nineteenth century. This is when the Women's Society was founded. Beyond its regular functions the Hevrah Kaddishah in Mókus utca also gave shelter to merchants and salespersons to enable them to manage their affairs in peace. At the turn of the nineteenth and twentieth centuries separate Jewish societies, institutions and associations existed in almost every sphere of life. There was the *Óbudai Zsidó Ifjak Irodalmi Társulata* [Literary Society of Young Jewish Men of Óbuda] (1905); the *Solós Szeudosz Egylet* [Shalesh Sudeh / *Shalosh se'udot* Society] (1922) in charge of giving the "third meal" on the Sabbath and organizing cultural programs; a communal soup kitchen (1923); scouts (1924); old age home (1925); the first Jewish kindergarten in Hungary (1927) and several other institutions.

The collection of the Jewish Museum of Budapest contains some beautiful eighteenth- or nineteenth-century goldsmithery from Óbuda, ritual objects of the home: a spice-box (*besamim*) for *Havdalah*, a nine-branched Hanukkah lamp (eight spouts for the candles and the ninth for the *shames*, the pilot light), a *Seder* plate and some fancy ritual objects for wealthier families.

The Jewish community of Óbuda existed independently until 1948. Today it is part of the Buda community, their synagogue is not used.

(6) The Jewish School Opened, Closed, then Reopened Again

A decree of Joseph II (1783) ordered that every Jewish community should maintain an elementary school where secular subjects would also be taught. The costs of the Jewish school of Óbuda (*Normal Schule*) were shared by other Jewish communities (Abony, Apostag, Aszód, Dabas, Gyón, Irsa, Szele, Tétény, Tinnye, Vörösvár, Zsámbék, etc.). According to the original plans the Jewish school was to be established in a newly acquired dwelling house (the house of Sekl Hollitscher, on the plot of today's 127 or 129 Lajos utca). Because of official requirements that the school building should face the main street, a different building had to be used for the school (9 Zichy utca, a lot which no longer exists). The building later served as the center of the Jewish community and the Jewish Museum of Óbuda. The school was opened in 1784. The opening ceremony took place on June 17, just a few days after Shavuot in that year, apparently the time when the traditional Jewish

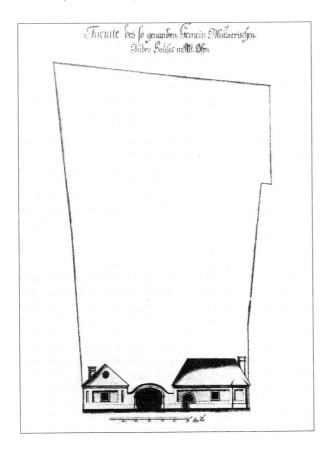

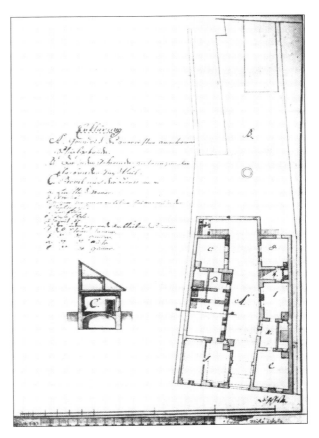

60. Facade of the building used as the Jewish school, Óbuda, 1774

school year started. The opening address was given by Mr. József Oesterreicher Manes, referred to as "Doctor R. Mones". The Jewish notary (*notarius*) listed 132 students, 113 boys and 19 girls. Secular subjects were taught beginning September 1st. Some of the subjects were school regulations, alphabet, syllabification, reading, fluency in reading German, basic rules of German orthography, German calligraphy, basic mathematics. There were two classes, each had 22 lessons a week. (The Jewish community of Prague opened a similar school just a year earlier, on May 2nd, as we know from a report in a contemporary newspaper, *A Magyar Hírmondó*.)

Members of the community thought that the school was a miracle. For days, people lined up under the windows or in front of the classroom door to listen to their children and the Christian teacher (there was no other qualified teacher in the town). The boisterous crowd created such an uproar that the principal had to announce, sticks and whips would be used to chase away whoever disturbed the classes. But the interest in the school soon decreased, fewer and fewer children attended, they were

61. Design of the future Jewish school, 1789.
Explanation:
A: "Ground-plan for the school building to be built"
B: "Premises remaining in the use of the Jewish community"
C: "Section along the m(eridian) line"

62. Beaker of the Hevrah Kaddisha of Óbuda

63. Goblet from the Óbuda synagogue, early eighteenth century

64. Tankard with lid from the Óbuda synagogue, eighteenth century

taken to private tutors. Members of the community thought the teacher earned too much and they were afraid the secular subjects would undermine the religious observance of their children. An announcement on the door of the synagogue had to warn parents that their children must not miss school. When they heard that the Emperor annulled all of his decrees on his deathbed, the brave citizens of Óbuda immediately closed down the school, and even removed the benches. They were deeply disappointed to learn that the school may not be closed after all. Their only consolation was that by then they could hire a Jewish teacher, Abraham Kohn. Josef Bach, another teacher of the school, later became the preacher of the Pest community.

The school of Óbuda used the same textbooks as other public schools. There was, however, a special textbook for Jewish children (1781) written by a "well known scholar from Berlin" who was none other than David Friedländer (1750–1834). This book taught Hebrew cursive script, the "thirteen articles of the Jewish faith" according to Maimonides, the Ten Commandments, stories, parables from the Talmud, "supplications of a sage" and other texts. It was a real *heder* textbook, but in the spirit of Moses Mendelssohn (1729–1786), based on his ideas about Jewish Enlightenment (*Haskalah*).

(7) The 1838 Flood of Pest–Buda

The ice-cold flood of the Danube in the spring of 1838 reached its peak on March 13, 14 and 15 in the inner city. The flood reached as far as Király utca. It reached some parts of the right bank, too, especially the Jewish quarter of Óbuda. The New market on the left bank of the Danube lay a little higher than the surrounding streets so it was spared by the waters, giving refuge to the Jews fleeing from Király utca. They also found shelter in the Lutheran church on Deák tér and they themselves offered help to others. The thick walls of the Orczy House resisted the waters like a fortress. The Jews of Óbuda were in much bigger danger. Many people found shelter in the new synagogue. They too participated in the rescue operations bravely:

"In Óbuda many of the Israelites distinguished themselves with their generosity. In these disastrous days the community leadership practiced brotherly compassion and engaged in helping the hungry and needy irrespective of their religion with all their means. Especially noteworthy was the wise advice and quick help of the judge Márk Boskovitz. There was no rest for anyone till all the helpless people were safe. Divine providence and the generous behavior of these gentlemen is to be praised, for no life was lost in the disaster. Two people who distinguished themselves by their extraordinary bravery should be singled out by name. Mózes Österreicher waded into the water by himself where no boat could go, to save the people and their animals in danger. Lázár Hirsch, who knew that urgent help was needed here, spent several nights on a boat to round up additional boats for the rescue operation."

(János Trattner, *Jégszakadás és Duna kiáradása Magyarországban*
[Ice-floes and the Flood of the Danube in Hungary] Buda, 1838)

Once the flood was over, Herman Lőwy, silversmith and a leader of the Jewish community, gave a silver chalice to Mihály Láng, a Lutheran pastor, to express his gratitude for the help offered by the parish to the Jews who found refuge there during the flood.

Josef Bach, the preacher of Pest, published an announcement in a newspaper in Leipzig asking for foreign aid for the poor of the city who suffered losses during the flood. The Hebrew teacher of the Óbuda school, I. H. Kohn, published an epic poem about the events of the flood in Óbuda in Hebrew (*Yemei tzarah u-mehumah*, "Days of disaster and panic"). The poem relates that a crowd sought refuge in the synagogue but the water followed them. Some tombstones and corpses were washed away from the cemetery. The poem, of fifteen verses, appeared in German translation, too. The author donated his royalties to the low-income students of good behavior of the school. Mordechai Löwy, the owner of a bookstore, described the events in a German leaflet while Fülöp / Philipp Weil, who was at home in the world of the German theater of Pest, wrote a two volume work in German about it. The first volume included all sorts of occasional poems while the second one, published for the book-fair of the following year, gave an account of the events in prose, based on newspaper clippings and other reports. The book informs us that on March 15, at the culmination of the flood, some elderly people gathered in a tent in the Jewish market and recited Psalms, as customary in times of great danger. The publication of the book was made possible by the aristocracy of the town. It was written in German not only because that was the language of the burghers of Pest, but also because it was meant to inform an international public. A German text written in Hebrew characters is an unmistakable sign of Moses Mendelssohn's influence. The fact that a "report" was written about the events in the form of a Hebrew poem, that is, the natural use of Hebrew for the literary description of an ordinary event constitutes a major step in the modernization of Hebrew literature.

Something extraordinary happened after the flood. The burghers of Buda submitted a petition to the Governorship asking freedom for the Jews to settle and buy property. The request was turned down this time, but a year later, at the Diet of 1839/40, Simon Dubraviczky, the deputy of Pest who survived the flood in the County Hall, suggested that "(...) the Jewish religion should be among the accepted ones, and (...) those of Jewish faith should be granted civil rights, (...) like other non-nobles, they should not only be allowed to buy property but, if they prove to stand in the service of country and king, they should also be eligible to receive a title of nobility". The Diet passed Act xxix of 1840.

The highest level reached by the flood was marked on several buildings throughout the city. Some of the Hungarian and German, iron or marble water marks are still visible today, but there must have been Hebrew ones, too. Only one of these survived in Óbuda, of red marble, in the Lajos utca synagogue, on the left side-wall of the stairs leading to the Ark. The location is no coincidence. The gallery of the synagogue gave shelter to many who became homeless during the flood. The slab was removed during the restoration of 1980 and it is now in the Museum of Water Use. Rumors have it that it was offered for sale by a distinguished person who had always been attracted to all kinds of Jewish memorabilia and antiques. In any case, the level reached by the flood was marked on some buildings of the Jewish quarter of Pest, too. There was one on the wall of 6 Holló utca, 3 feet above street level, but this one is in German.

(8) The New Cemetery of Óbuda (369 Bécsi út)

The cemetery is partly a historical ossuary (*ossuarium*) today.

There were three Jewish cemeteries in Óbuda. The first one was bought from the landowner in 1737 and was in use for about a hundred and fifty years, till the 1870s. It lay North to the Zichy Palace, outside the city (today the corner of Laktanya utca and Kő utca). This is where the Jewish victims of the 1831 cholera epidemic are buried. It lay South of the fire station, the former station of the river forces. This is also where the ancient Roman city was located. Gravediggers often found Roman bricks and the ruins of Aquincum were sought beneath the cemetery. It is possible that the growing archaeological interest played a role in closing the cemetery in Laktanya utca.

65. Gravestones in the old Jewish cemetery in Óbuda, Laktanya utca, ca. 1920

66. Mortuary in the Laktanya utca cemetery

67. Gravestones in the Laktanya utca cemetery, ca. 1920

68. Triple gravestone (husband, wife, child) in the Laktanya utca cemetery, 1796

69. "The former Jewish cemetery in Óbuda". Drawing of Imre Ámos, 1936

"The Jewish cemetery of Óbuda (...) lies above the former Roman city and gravediggers often found lead pipes and bricks with markings. These are remains of a magnificent bath which was possibly under the island where the shipyards stand today. (...) It is possible that later, after the closing of the cemetery, if they dig below the level of the graves, some foundations and other parts would be revealed."

(in: *Archaeologiai Értesítő*, 6, 1872, p. 88)

Today the area of the former cemetery is occupied by the southernmost monster-buildings of the Óbuda housing project.

The second Jewish cemetery of Óbuda was opened in 1888 at the foot of the Táborhegy (corner of Bécsi út and Laborc utca) and the third one in 1922.

The cemetery in Laborc utca was also demolished. Today we can only see the crumbling ruins of the mortuary, at the beginning of Laborc utca, on the left. The six-pointed star and the tablets of law can still be recognized. The ruins of the building reveal a traditional, Orthodox arrangement: the mortuary in the middle, two separate rooms (for men and women) for the ritual cleansing of the deceased (*heder taharah*) on each side.

*

There was a fourth Jewish cemetery in Óbuda, the almost forgotten tiny Pálvölgyi cemetery, the second one in chronological order. "The sloping, wild, beautiful Pálvölgyi cemetery is there only to preserve the memory of the Jews", wrote Antal Szerb. It can be seen on a map of the capital from 1909 (published by the Eggenberger bookstore), to the left of Szépvölgyi út, right next to the cave which was discovered only at the beginning of the twentieth century. It should be on the plateau West of the crevice, on the lower stretch of Pálvölgyi út. Photographs of it have survived and Imre Ámos drew a picture of it, too, in 1936. It

70. "The cemetery at the feet of Mount Matthias" (Pálvölgyi Jewish cemetery)

was opened probably around 1820 and closed down in 1938. Its official name was "Szépvölgyároki izraelita temető" [Israelite cemetery of the Szépvölgy ditch]. In the rubble over the area some pieces of rounded stones may be found even today: these could be parts of tombstones.

It is possible that there was a Jewish cemetery in Óbuda before the above-mentioned ones. When the widow of Péter Zichy leased (1732) and later sold (1737) a plot of land to the Jewish community (where the synagogue was built later), there must have been some space next to it for a cemetery for it is hard to imagine how Jews could have lived here from the beginning of the century without a burial place. But there is no trace of this ancient cemetery, it might have been completely demolished during construction work.

Jewish tradition prohibits the stirring of graves but in ancient times, in Jerusalem, it was customary to collect the bones of the decayed corpses after some time and place them into a crypt to allow the deceased to "return to their fathers" (Genesis 15,15). If the need arises graves may be relocated.

71. "The cemetery at the feet of Mount Matthias" (Pálvölgyi Jewish cemetery)

In Óbuda it was the fathers who returned to their sons, so to speak. In 1950 some eighteenth- or nineteenth-century graves and tombstones were moved from the old cemetery into the present one, right of the entrance, all in the same area. That was when the grave of Moshe Münz was transferred here, too. Today his gravestone is the only one whose inscription has been refurbished.

The new, present cemetery has a general marker to indicate the relocation of the graves: "Here are buried those members of our community who left us before 648 [= 1888] and were originally laid to rest in the first cemetery. Obeying an official order we removed their remains and reburied them here, in this common grave, in great honor."

But there were relocated graves already in the first cemetery. On July 17, 1806, decades after the expulsion of Jews from Óbuda (1745), when the cemetery of Új-Buda (*Ofen hadash*) and Krisztina-város were both full, the community of Óbuda took some of the graves to their own cemetery. They could not save all the tombstones, as we can surmise from the fact that some nineteenth-century tombstones were eventually found in their original emplacement. We know from Sándor Büchler that the following inscription was placed over the common grave in the old Óbuda cemetery in 1806,

למען
דעת כל עמי הארץ וידעו
בנים אשר יולדו : כאשר
גלתה יהודה מאובן חדש
ושועלים הלכו בבית קבורתם
ועתה
הוכרחנו לפנות עצמות
וקדשים האלה וקברנוט
פה ואבן הזאת שמנו מצבה
לעד בבני ישראל
ב אב תקס"ו לפ"ק

"So that
the people of the world and all the children
to be born should know. When
Yehuda was expelled from Új-Buda
and Jackals prowled [Lamentation 5,18] over the graves:
that was when we had to dig up the holy
bones and bury them
here. This stone was erected to commemorate
and bear witness for the sons of Israel.
On the 2nd of the month of Av, 566 (July 17, 1806), according to the minor era."

When Ignác Schreiber (1891–1922), rabbi of Óbuda, graduate of the Rabbinical Seminary only a few years earlier, consecrated the cemetery on Bécsi út, he asked the question, who would be the first one to be buried here? A famous personality? A simple man? A few days later he was hit by a streetcar and killed. He himself became the first one.

Several victims of the year 1944 are buried here, in Óbuda, or at least have memorial plaques: the martyrs of Óbuda, people murdered in the hospital of the Hevrah Kaddishah of Buda (16 Maros utca), people who perished in death camps.

We also find here the "grave" of a Torah scroll from the same year. A scroll which was damaged and desecrated, became unfit for synagogue use (*pasul*) and thus, according to tradition, had to be buried. *Po nignaz sefer Torah*, "A Torah scroll is hidden here."

(9) A Noted Rabbi of Óbuda: Gyula Wellesz (1872-1915)

In addition to R. Münz, famous for having built the synagogue, there were other notable rabbis of Óbuda. There was Illés Ádler, a striking personality who was active in Óbuda only for a decade (1896–1907) before he moved to the Rumbach utca community, and his successor, the modest but very learned Gyula Wellesz.

Wellesz was born in 1872 in Budapest. His ancestors on his mother's side were rabbis for generations. His grandfather, Avigdor Abeles, was the rabbi of Vörösvár and later the *lamdan*, teacher of the Hevrah Kaddishah of Pest. He was one of the first students of Vilmos Bacher in the Talmud-Torah and later in the Rabbinical Seminary, too. Like his master, Wellesz exhibited great interest in the history of Hebrew linguistics (David Kimhi, Avraham de Balmes) and wrote his doctoral dissertation in that field (1895). Being ordained a rabbi in 1898 he spent a decade in small towns (Csurgó, Nagybiccse). He was invited to become the rabbi of Óbuda in 1910. Some of his sermons are known to us for they were printed in theological periodicals.

Initially Wellesz's scholarly interest was directed towards Hebrew grammar but, through the study of older literature, he came to rediscover some major medieval French- and German-Jewish literary figures. He virtually rediscovered the work of a medieval rabbi of Vienna, R. Yitzhak ben Moshe (thirteenth century) called *Or zaru'a*, "Spreading light" which has, as we have seen in connection with the thermal springs of Buda, some Hungarian references. His research in linguistics shed a different light on the primary sources of the religious tradition. On the 800th anniversary of Rashi's death he was asked by the *Izraelita Magyar Irodalmi Társulat* [Israelite Hungarian Literary Society] to write his literary biography (*Rasi élete és működése* [Rashi's Life and Work], Budapest, 1906). His volume is still the best Hungarian-language study on Rashi, on all the details of this eleventh-century great master of exegesis. In his later works he pointed out the similarities of Talmudic law, Halakhah and the basic principles of Roman law. After the death of Vilmos Bacher, Wellesz was offered the chair of medieval studies at the Rabbinical Seminary, but he rejected the position because he did not consider himself suitable for the task. His early death was a great loss to the entire Jewish community of the capital.

72. Portrait of Gyula Wellesz

His grave is in the cemetery of Óbuda, in the northwestern corner, not far from the mortuary.

(10) Rabbi Münz as Supervisor of the Jews of Pest

Let us go back to the eighteenth century for a while.

In Óbuda all eyes were focused on Pest. Not only merchants and the rising bourgeoisie but R. Münz, the respected rabbi, also had an interest for Pest. It is hard not to notice that he was looking even beyond Pest.

Moshe (Moses / Mózes) Münz / Minc (ca. 1750–1831) was a famous rabbi in Brody (Galicia); he ran a yeshiva there before coming to Óbuda. He was chosen for the position at the recommendation of the rabbi of Prague (1790).

73. Portrait of Moshe Abeles, *dayyan* of Óbuda

Let us tell three stories from his long life.

The Jews of Pest came mostly from Óbuda. The first group of migrants, however, crossed the Danube only with one foot: their rabbi was still Moshe Münz. Even their Torah scroll was only borrowed from Óbuda, for money. They were mostly merchants and innkeepers and there was none among them learned enough to tend to the ritual needs of the developing Pest community, to do the ritual supervision. The needs of the Pest community met the ambitions of R. Münz. In 1790 Münz became the ritual supervisor of the Pest community. The leaders of the Pest community declared that as long as Münz remained in Óbuda he would be considered the rabbi of Pest, too. But in 1793 Farkas (Wolf / Zeev) Boskovitz (1740–1818), the son of Óbuda's Shmuel Boskovitz, moved to Pest. Several years earlier, when Münz was elected rabbi of Óbuda, the older Boskovitz was the other applicant for the position. R. Münz transferred his jealousy from the father to the son and tried to take revenge on him. True, Farkas Boskovitz was no saint either. They remained relentless in their hatred. As soon as he set foot in Pest,

Boskovitz took over the *kashrut* supervision at Moses Liebner's restaurant (checking the ritual purity

of the food and the kitchen). This was convenient for the restaurant owner because a kosher kitchen requires daily supervision and Boskovitz, living in Pest, was easier to reach than R. Münz in Óbuda. In turn, Münz announced that restaurants may only operate with his kosher certificate (*hekhsher*). None would enter a suspicious restaurant, one without a certificate. Boskovitz was then elected rabbi by the Pest community. Though his title was only preacher and supervisor (*Sermunial*

74. Portrait of Moshe Minc (Moses Münz), chief rabbi of Óbuda

Vorsteher und Versorger), his function and salary were those of a rabbi. Münz again placed the restaurant in *herem*, under interdiction. Finally, they went to court, a secular one. The authorities of Pest county ruled that Boskovitz had family in Pest, therefore he could not become rabbi here. People on the Pest side appealed the decision accusing R. Münz of lusting for power. The Óbuda community's counter-argument was that the Jews of Pest, domiciled at Óbuda, belong under R. Münz's supervision anyway. They noted with regret and indignation that religious observance in Pest decreases from day to day. The investigators in the case recommended that neither of the parties should become rabbi of Pest. Münz should not interfere in the affairs of Pest and Boskovitz should leave the city. It was in the interest of the state that everyone retain their religion and not become an atheist because then they would constitute a danger (*periculosus*) to the public good. Finally, the Governorship deprived Boskovitz of his office and called upon the Jews of Pest to chose anyone but R. Münz (1796). Boskovitz spent the rest of his life in Bonyhád writing his excellent commentaries on the Talmud and on Maimonides.

R. Münz thought that his time had arrived. He asked the seven richest Jews in the country to appeal to the king for the establishment of a rabbinate in Pest. He would fulfill this obligation during fairs while one of his deputies would function as rabbi the rest of the year. But the Jews of Pest had learnt their lesson and quickly elected Israel Wahrmann, coincidentally of Óbuda, as their rabbi (1799).

Münz actually hoped to exercise a public role and influence. Though a rabbi, he wanted to act as the secular authority. In 1791 Archduke Lipót Sándor (1790–1795), Palatine of Hungary, was planning to visit Óbuda. His ceremonial reception had to be organized. August 6, the day of his visit, happened to be the Sabbath before *Tish'a be-Av*, a day of mourning and fasting, with all kinds of prohibitions. Münz announced that he who shaves himself throughout the year should do so now, too. Failure to participate in the reception of the palatine would be considered a violation of religious law. To ease the hunger of the crowd waiting for the distinguished guest, they would make an *eruv*. As soon as the Sabbath was over, right after the *Havdalah*, everyone was to light up their windows. The preparations for the event, halakhically somewhat questionable and very complicated, were washed away by a summer shower and everything had to be prepared anew. On Saturday, the words of welcome were delivered by R. Münz in Hebrew and a German translation of it was handed over to the palatine and his attendants. They even prepared a new seal for the occasion. Münz did not have to wait long for the acknowledgment. Soon the king appointed him chief rabbi of Pest county. Now he started to demand secular (administrative) powers. The Jewish communities of the county protested. It came to light that in Óbuda serious corporal punishment like flogging and stretching on the rack were inflicted on those who violated religious rules. After this neither the county nor the Governorship agreed to the appointment of the rabbi.

But for R. Münz neither Buda nor the county of Pest was enough. He played a dubious role in a case which was debated throughout the country. Aaron Chorin (1766–1844), rabbi of Arad, published a treatise in Prague (1803) in which, with a thorough knowledge of his topic and addressing

דבר בעתו

מה טוב

ובו נכללו שני שערים

שער תורה, ושער עבודה

אל אחי

בני ישראל היודעים לשון עברי בלשונם, ואל הבלתי
יודעים לשון עברי, בשפת אשכנזי.

מאת החכן שלומס

אהרן חארינר.

DABAR BEITTO. (Ein Wort zu seiner Zeit.)

ווין

געדרוקט ביא אנטאן שטרויס, ק"ק פריס בוכדרוקער

WIEN, gedruckt bey ANTON STRAUSS, k. k. priv.
Buchdrucker. 1820.

ספר

עמק השוה

חלק ראשון

נרפס פה פראג ה'ק'ס'ג לפ'ק

Synagogus in Arad R. *Aaron Charin* in hoc opusculo,
cui titulum ex Genesi C. XIV. v. 5. *Emek Hasch-Schave*, id
est : *Vallis Schave* præfixit, tribus orationibus de rebus
potissimum metaphysicis differit. Accedit ejusdem disser-
tatio alia super tractatum Talmudicum *Seraim* dictum.
His a me lectis nihil obstare judico, quin typis committi
possint. Pragæ, 3. Maji, 1803.

Carolus Fischer,
Cæs. Regius Censor, Revisor & Translator
in Hebraicis.

Prag, gedruckt in der Eisenwangerschen Buchdruckerey, 1803.

the needs of his generation, he was critical of the common interpretation of Halakhic prescriptions. Münz agreed to the publication of his work and even wrote a preface to it. Chorin was soon
attacked for his modern views and his former supporter, who knew why, joined his opponents.
The most vehemently discussed issue was whether white sterlet or *kecsege* in Hungarian (*shtirl*)

was kosher. (The laws of *kashrut* only allow the consumption of scaly fish.) On September 1, 1805, at the
time of the national fair in Pest Münz sent for Chorin
and brought him in front of the *bet din.* He himself did
not go to the trial, just sent his emissaries. These greeted Chorin with curses already in the synagogue courtyard and, without a trial, they ruled that he was obliged
to withdraw his ideas, or his beard would be cut off.
(The cutting of the beard as a shameful punishment is
rooted in the Bible—see as a prohibition Lev. 19,27; as a
story, II Samuel 10,4–5). Münz made up a cruel, Biblical
humiliation. Chorin's excuses were not accepted, so he
had to withdraw his ideas in writing. Though the
Governorship later condemned the process, Münz considered himself the winner and from then on took every
opportunity to attack Chorin. There is no sign that he
had a bad conscience for having attacked a book that
was previously approved by him. All he achieved, however, was that Chorin became more outspoken in his
reform ideas.

75. Aaron Chorin's
advice to his genera-
tion: Title pages of
two of his books

76. Portrait of Aaron
Chorin, chief rabbi of
Arad

The conflict between R. Münz and R. Chorin was remembered for decades. Anders Lindeberg, a Swedish traveler, friend of Count István Széchenyi, wrote in his diary upon his visit to Pest–Buda in 1840:

"(...) I made the acquaintance of a Jewish chief rabbi called Aaron Chorin. He is a well-known man of letters, author of philosophical works, over seventy years old. He is one of those who had been working hard for the reform of Israelite religious law. Therefore he had to bear the fate of all reformers: persecutions, accusations of heresy. They even considered depriving him of his office and shaving off his beard, which is a great humiliation for a man in his position."

R. Chorin's grandson, Ferenc Chorin sr. (1842–1925) and his great-grandson, Ferenc Chorin jr. (1879–1964), since 1901 of the Catholic faith, were to play a major role in the Hungarian economy, specifically in heavy industry.

Moshe Münz died of cholera during the epidemic of 1831.

His commitment to Halakha was unquestionably serious and honest, but this is not enough for the evaluation of his historical role. R. Moshe Münz was deeply conservative and yet tried to introduce major innovations in Jewish customs. He wanted to reform Jewish life with the vehemence of the Roman Church at the height of its power. This principle found expression in the Biblical quotation on the facade of the synagogue. Being convinced of his truth, he used his power against his opponents. Fairness was not one of his guiding principles. He may have been led by personal ambitions, too. Had his ideas been realized, Jewish modernization would have lacked any genuine force, while the Orthodoxy would have lost its tradition of communal autonomy.

Otherwise, the developing Jewish bourgeoisie as well as the capital city stood only to gain by the fact that, in spite of Münz's efforts, the Pest community got rid of the supervision of Óbuda.

III. Király utca: The Old-Old Jewish Quarter of Pest

The term *old-old* is not used just for stylistic purposes here. It is rather a descriptive term. There have been several Jewish quarters in Pest, an *old* one, Teréz- / Erzsébetváros, a *new* one, Lipótváros, and even *newer* ones, like Új-Lipótváros. Accordingly, there is also an *old-new* one, *alt-neu* in the vernacular, which is then Lipótváros. Let us thus call the very first one, the core of Erzsébetváros, the *old-old* Jewish quarter.

(1) Marketers, Innkeepers

The first generation of Jews living in Pest was mostly migrants from Óbuda. Later, after the turn of the eighteenth and nineteenth centuries the community of Pest gradually grew to be the largest and most influential Jewish community in Hungary.

During the past centuries three types of Jewish quarters developed in what we call Budapest today. In Buda, in the Castle Hill area, *royal privileges* granted Jews the right to settle. In Óbuda Jews dwelled on a *landowner's estate*, under his protection. In Pest it was the *town* or *city* which accepted them. Before Jewish emancipation was regulated by law, Jewish communities lived in one of these three types of settlements. As Buda, Óbuda and Pest became united in Budapest (1873), all three types of Jewish quarters were present in the metropolis.

In early-sixteenth-century Venice the Jewish quarter was called ghetto (*getto*). Not long after the attribution of this name Hebrew sources connected the word *getto* to *get*, the Hebrew word for the divorce certificate. Though the two words may not have the same root, connecting them refers to the emergence of Jewish quarters through *separation*.

The location of the Jewish quarters was invariably the consequence of the legal status of Jews. Whether Jews were settled by the monarch or a landowner, it was the lawgiver who determined the location of the Jewish quarter. To ensure protection and control, this place was usually right next to the royal residence or the center of the estate, in a separate quarter of the city or the property, possibly on a previously uninhabited plot of land. Thus the Jewish quarter was located near the geographical and legal center, yet it was clearly separated both from the center and other parts of the settlement. Certain forms of segregation—for instance, the enclosure for the Sabbath, the symbolic unification of public domain among Jewish houses (*eruv*)—was fostered by the Jewish communities themselves; they had to consider security issues as well, should they need to defend themselves. Jewish quarters which survived from the Middle Ages are generally relatively independent parts of the city which surrounds them. They are a separate entity in terms of the aspect of the city, the city wall or the network of streets. The segregation is much less visible, however, in those Jewish quarters, which emerged as late as the eighteenth century. It was always individuals or families who were granted permission to settle and for them social status was the main consideration for their choice of a dwelling place, though other factors still played a role in patterns of settlement.

It is well known that the "haven" or "base" effect plays an important role in the process of immigration. Newcomers are drawn to those persons, institutions or circumstances which can offer them initial help and facilitate the process of adjustment to the new social setting without total self-rejection, without completely breaking with their original social background (change of social identity). The "base" enables them to transplant some of their cultural traditions, not just themselves as individuals. This "anchor" often means a similar way of life, which for Jews has always been determined by the laws of religious tradition (*Halakhah*). In different ages, places and communities Jews chose to adhere to the Halakhah to a greater or lesser extent, but even in the civic towns Jewish immigrants

settled in concentrated communities. This meant only informal segregation, real Jewish quarters did not emerge any more. The existing Jewish quarters developed in the Middle Ages or in the Early Modern Age. In the United States, especially in New York City, Jewish quarters evolved on the European pattern. From the Jewish point of view, Jewish parts of Brooklyn are Eastern Europe even today.

In the eighteenth century the royal free city of Pest did not have a large Jewish population. In spite of the warnings of the *Königliche Statthalterei* (Governorship) and the king, the city council tried to prevent Jews from settling and made even their temporary stay difficult. Jews who stayed in Pest overnight or in transit on their way to another destination or seeking justice at the royal court were subject to heavy taxes. The first Jewish census (1791) listed Jews both "in and outside of the city (*in und vor der Stadt*)". Jewish merchants who were not allowed to enter Pest or Buda simply settled in the nearest town, that is, in Óbuda.

They could come to Pest only occasionally. The beautiful Baroque palace of Anton Erhard Martinelli (built between 1716 and 1741) was built as a veterans' hospital (House of Invalids), since 1784 it was the barracks of the grenadiers and was named Károly Barracks after King Charles (Károly) III. (From 1894 on the building, Gránátos utca / 9–11 Városház utca, is the City Hall / Office of the Mayor of Budapest, the architect of its reconstruction was Ármin Hegedűs.) Back in 1759, the commanding officer of the House of Invalids rented the canteen to the Jews of Óbuda, that is, he put them in charge of feeding the veterans. The city council of Pest protested strongly and the Archbishop expressed his pleasure over the city's measures against the Jews. The contract had to be broken after a few years but eventually the Jews of Óbuda continued to lease the canteen of the hospital and later of the Barracks.

There were four annual national fairs in Pest toward the end of the eighteenth century. One on St. Joseph's Day (March 19), one at Medardus (June 8), a third one on St. John's Day (August 29) and the fourth one on St. Leopold's Day (November 15). In those days drive-in fairs were held in front of the Hatvani Gate (Hatvani út / Kerepesi út / beginning of Rákóczi út), while fairs with display stands were held on the Új Vásár tér [New Market Square] (today Erzsébet tér). (Later, the drive-in fairs moved a little further out, to the vacant lots along the outer segment of the road.) As for the right to visit fairs the debate between the city council and the *Königliche Statthalterei* went on for decades, the latter supporting the Jews. Finally the city had to allow Jews to participate in fairs, but they were subjected to extra taxes and forbidden to display their merchandise on stands or to buy hare-skin. Moreover, they were not allowed to sell their wares within the city walls. During the fairs (for maximum 16 days each time) the council gave them permission to open a kosher restaurant. This was rented to the Jews of Óbuda.

The Jewish community was organized around the restaurant license. City officials considered the renters (*arendatores*) of the kosher restaurant the deputies of the Jews (*Deputierte*) since it was them who were bound to the city by a legal contract. The restaurant was rented, usually for six years, to the innkeeper who placed the highest bid. Thus it was the city that indirectly appointed the leaders of the emerging Jewish community. The first official leaders were the innkeepers, Baruch Abelsberg, a grain merchant, later Marcus Sachsel (Sachs, Sachsl, Sax)—the 1787 census calls him the renter of the temporary eatery (*Garküche*)—and another innkeeper, Moises Liebner. Their position in the Jewish community was enhanced by the fact that they had exclusive sales rights for kosher meat and wine. Without them there could not have been Jewish life in Pest.

Joseph II (1780–1790), the enlightened Austro-Hungarian emperor and king—who, according to contemporary gossip knew even a bit of Hebrew, though his politics was directed at suppressing its use—issued an important decree on March 31, 1783 (26th of Adar, according to the Jewish calendar). The *Systematica gentis Judaicae regulatio* gave way to the integration of Jews into civil society, at least in the Hungarian territories of the Monarchy. Cities could no longer keep Jews from settling. Neither could Pest, and so the extraordinary growth of the Jewish community of Óbuda in the second half of the nineteenth century finally resulted in a migration to Pest. Others came from Bohemia, Moravia or the Austrian hereditary lands. They were merchants attracted by the ever expanding trade of the city. A few decades earlier they pioneered trade contacts with Turkey and contributed to the boom of the previously insignificant economy of the city. Already in the 1780s Jews of Hungary held their councils in Pest, on the occasion of the annual fairs. Thus the Jews of Pest automatically became the leaders of the whole Hungarian Jewish community.

Where the Jews of Pest should live, i.e. whether a separate Jewish quarter (ghetto) should be established for them, was debated by the city council and the representative of the emperor, the Lord Lieutenant (*főispán*) even as late as 1786. The city council asked the Lord Lieutenant to allow Jews to settle only in the suburbs, rather than in the center of the city. The Lord Lieutenant, Count József Majláth, left the decision to the city officials but called their attention to the fact that the times when Jews were concentrated in ghettos and prohibited from entering the center were over. The social integration of Jews (*bürgerliche Verbesserung*) started with the reforms of Joseph II. The first sign of change was precisely the spatial integration—that their place of settlement was no longer determined by the authorities.

It was in 1786 that the city of Pest first gave permission for Jews to settle. As opposed to the *commorans* ("who stays temporarily") who were only permitted to sojourn temporarily, Jews were *tolerated* ("allowed", "accepted"), they could rent permanent apartments, they could maintain a workshop or store, though only with closed doors, without a signboard or a shop-window. They could only engage in wholesale trade. The number of tolerated Jews grew to over fifty within a decade, while the *commorantes* numbered nearly seventy-five.

The "haven" through which the first Jews arrived to Pest was obviously the area around the Károly Barracks, East to the city wall (today Madách Imre tér–Deák tér–Király utca). The Jewish market, too, was set up here, near the New Market. Soon there were four or five Jewish restaurants. Their high ("triple") prices were subject to general complaint. Since there was no kosher slaughterhouse and the city butchery sold kosher meat only twice a week, Jews were at the mercy of the restaurant keepers. After a while they bought up all the kosher meat, rented a place for its storage and sold it in small quantities. (The ritual slaughter and handling of cows, sheep and poultry have always been very costly, as even today.) The first ritual slaughterer (*shohet, shaykhet*) of Pest was a certain Ánsil (Anshl). He was employed by the restaurant keepers to perform the ritual slaughter at the city butchery.

Towards the end of the eighteenth century the Jews of Pest, already exceeding one thousand in number, lived outside the former city wall, along the line of the previous, already destroyed wall, in a new, developing quarter of the city called Terézváros since 1777. They were rarely allowed to live in the inner city, today's *Belváros* or Downtown, except for show. For show, because the city council had to prove to the *Königliche Statthalterei* that they obeyed the law and thus placed a few individuals in the "shop-window". The center of their economic activity was the area South–Southeast to the New

Market, the northeastern corner of today's Deák Ferenc tér, the northern side of today's Madách Imre tér. The square itself was called *Zsidók piarca / Zsidópiac* [Jews' Market] in 1833 and *Zsidó tér* [Jewish square] around 1840. Other names were in use, too, such as *Kohlmarkt* [Cabbage Market]; the square in front of the Lutheran church; *Török tér* [Turkish square], named after the oldest house of Lipót-város, the Kemnitzer, later Wodianer, House, the so-called "Két Török" [Two Turks] House, etc. (A Jewish folk etymology, which explains the name *Kohlmarkt* from *kahal / kohol*, "Jewish community", that is, the "*Kahal's Platz*", may not be completely unbiased.) This was the center of the first Jewish quarter of Pest, the beginning of Angol Király utca / Három Király utca / Király utca.

78. Market on the Pest quay. Lithograph after the drawing by Henrik Weber, 1855

Jews in Pest typically traded in grain and cattle, tanned and sold leather, fur, wool, linen and other textiles. Most frequently they dealt in leather, for tanneries were not organized in guilds and did not require the permission of any guild, a trade license was enough.

"Most merchants who sold their wares to the peasants were Jews. It was interesting to see and hear how they traded. As the usual liveliness of these Hebrews mixed with the rough boorishness of the peasants, their bargaining sounded more like arguing, squabbling." (Jan Ackersdijk, 1823)

A Hungarian proverb says: "He is bargaining like a Gypsy for a horse, a Jew for wool."

The neighborhood no longer smells of tannic acid but this area (Anker köz; Két Szerecsen / Szerecsen / Paulay Ede utca; Laudon / Káldy Gyula utca; Kék Kakas utca / Petőfi Sándor utca / Kazár utca / Székely Mihály utca) remained the center of leather manufacture and trade for nearly two centuries.

In the first decades of the nineteenth century there must have been a Sabbath rope (*eruv*) in Király utca, along the invisible and unmarked boundaries of the "Jewish quarter" of the city, the district of Pest inhabited by Jews. Or maybe the whole Orczy House was considered "private territory (*reshut ha-yahid*)".

"Being an observant Jew I took every precaution not to cross the *ereb* [eruv] on the Sabbath if I was carrying something in my pocket. I mean the rope which marked the inside of the city, for had I crossed this line, it would have been considered an act of business, it would have desecrated the holy day of rest. Therefore, on the Sabbath I only dared to walk with a kerchief in my belt, my eyes fixed on the rope hanging from the pole." (Ármin Vámbéry, *Küzdelmeim* [My Struggles], 1905)

The Jews of Pest received a separate cemetery from the city already in 1788, free of charge. It was in the Váci Cemetery, somewhere around the outer tracks of today's Nyugati pályaudvar (Western Railway Station), around Ferdinánd Bridge (built in 1875). This cemetery was used only for a few decades. In 1808 a new cemetery was opened not far from the old one, within the triangle between Váci út and Lehel utca, between Taksony utca and Aréna út. Graves and gravestones of the old cemetery were carried over here (1838).

Around 1780 Jews who somehow managed to enter Pest with a temporary permit, assembled to pray, "daven" (in Hungarian *davenolni / davenen*) in a private home, in Marcus Sachsel's house. The first permanent prayer-house was established in 1784. Until 1787 it was used illegally, without a permit. Then they moved to the Heuserl (Heuszlir, Heusler) House in Király utca, into the larger room of a small apartment. They only had a single Torah scroll which they borrowed from the Jews of Óbuda, that is, from R. Münz, for a fee. They were not permitted to employ a rabbi. After a long fight with officials as well as with the rabbi of Óbuda, in 1796 the *Königliche Statthalterei* finally gave them permission to employ a qualified person to take care of religious matters. The tiny room of the synagogue soon became too small for the ever-growing congregation. It was enlarged by combining it with the other room of the apartment and later even the kitchen, so that the women could have a separate room to pray (*ezrat nashim*), as prescribed by tradition.

(2) The Orczy House

The huge building, constructed back in the 1700s, stood in Terézia- or Terézváros, on the corner of *Landstrasse* / Ország út (today Károly körút) and *König von Engellandgasse* / Angliai Király utca, right next to the *Zsidók piarca* [Jews' Market]. Originally it was two separate houses on neighboring plots of land. The plot near Ország út was purchased by István Orczy (1728), the first one in the family to acquire a title and wealth. He built a house on it. The plot next to Király utca and the corner house on it was owned by Count József Orczy (1746–1804), son of the poet Count Lőrinc Orczy, himself Lord Lieutenant of Zemplén county, founder of the Orczy Garden, the first public park of Pest. He bought it on October 8, 1795, from Anna Mayerhoffer, the daughter of the architect and builder of the house, András Mayerhoffer (1690–1771). In those days this was the building no. 333 of the city.

In the Mayerhoffer House there was an inn called "*König von Engelland*", and merchants attending the Pest fair would stay there. The inn provided some storage space for their merchandise. By the time of András Mayerhoffer's inheritor, János Mayerhoffer, the inn and tavern, the "*König von Engelland* / Angliai király" [King of England] (1 Király utca), from which the street obtained its name, had been in business for decades. It should rather be called a restaurant or café, for it had received the right to serve coffee (*jus cavenae radicitum / jus caveatum*). This right was usually connected to a store. On the first floor of the house there were stores overlooking the market and Király utca. At times there were in the Orczy House three restaurants and a café.

József Orczy joined the two buildings together—that was when the name Orczy House came into usage. He left the house to his widow and to his family that split up in various branches. The new building originally had two courtyards but the wing across the middle and the small structures in the courtyards divided them into three or—if one will—four. The second floor was added only in 1829. The second largest building of old Pest—the only one larger was the Károly Barracks—had 48 apartments with about 140 rooms, among them several luxury apartments as well as a number of storerooms. After all, being next to the market place, it was meant to be a storage space, a huge net-

79. View of the Orczy House from Károly körút

work of cellars suitable for storing wine, a slaughterhouse and a bath. There were times when there were even two baths.

The Orczys were among the influential, enlightened families of their time, like the Festetics, Podmaniczky and Ráday families. By allowing and even welcoming the settlement of Jews in their city-houses they practiced their rights as landowners, but in an urban center, and for that, under radically different circumstances. Jews renting an apartment or store in the Orczy House were in an official contractual relationship with the city, Pest. The number of Jewish renters grew with time and the Orczy House must have become a sort of a metropolitan *shtetl*, a Jewish town, a

80. The southern courtyard of the Orczy House with the gate from Károly körút

"haven", the first safe point for Jews arriving from the real *shtetlekh* in the province to the big city. Many people came here just for overnight. With time, the building was completely taken over by Jews and therefore came to be called *Judenhof*. In its heyday it was said to be "the most profitable building in the city". According to contemporary rumors, it brought one gold coin (of Körmöc, the famous gold mine in Northeastern Hungary, today in Slovakia) per hour to its owner, day and night. Due to the rents collected, the owners of the Orczy House were among the biggest taxpayers of Pest.

"Look at the citadel of the ghetto, the Orczy House. About a century ago it was built as a castle. Later, in due time, it came to be called a palace. But since the times of Emperor Francis I, one of the Orczy counts started renting apartments to newly arriving Jews, and the ancient Knights' Hall was transformed into a prayer-house. The synagogue moved in here irrevocably with all its stocks and stones, so it has been demoted to a house. Burghers of Pest look down on the place and the Jews are aware of their disdained status. How could it be called a palace, when it is, indeed, the Jewish house! They keep their rabbi here and the whole rabbinate. Their baths and schools are here, too, as well as their courtyards, the scene of debates. Along with ritual objects they sell people here, they park their carts and trade here, their study houses and welfare societies, Torah scribes and matchmakers, restaurants, cafés and bookstores, where books are read from right to left—everything is here. There are other stores, too, and a warehouse. From the cellar filled with rats up to the tower room where bats reside, everything is full of feathers, rags, wool, horn, oak-apple,

81. The southern courtyard of the Orczy House, a gravestone store at the outer wall of the synagogue

82. The northern courtyard of the Orczy House, the corner left to the Choir Temple

sugar, black pepper, cloth, linen, Halina cloth, leather, glue, starch gum. There is a doctor in the house, an apothecary, a barber, and a midwife. They have surgeons with a rabbinical diploma who perform surgery on their eight-day-old boys, they have dowry collectors and matchmakers, they have corpse washers and dressers for both sexes who, in the name of the Hevrah, perform those ancient ceremonies which are the dues of the deceased. The Orczy House has by now lost all its pomp as well as its tiled roof, and what remains from its aristocratic glitter is maybe the shining of the golden coins it brings to its owner. In the three huge courtyards of the Orczy House, Talmudists practice *pilpul*, this high form of debate, Torah scholars relate passages of the ever wise Scriptures to everyday life, Psalm sayers and Mishle[1] knowers exchange their thoughts while their carts, which brought them here from the countryside, wait for them in one of the courtyards. Cantors, slaughterers, teachers, Torah readers and Shofar blowers try out their talents here before being sent off to faraway Jewish islands for seasonal assignments or long-term jobs…"

83. The northern courtyard of the Orczy House, the Károly körút-Király utca corner

(Illés Kaczér, *Három a csillag* [Three Are the Stars. A Novel], 1955/1956)

The bath in the building must have been used for ritual purposes (*mikveh*). Its water came from a well, first dug, later bored.

The Orczy House was probably the most important commercial center of old Pest. In the nineteenth century it was called the "Jewish caravansary of Pest", the Jewish *suk, hane, locanda*; all these names refer to the Southern or Eastern character of the neighborhood.

"Approaching the house you notice already on the sidewalk which way you are heading. You stumble upon women with baskets selling not only *kosher* apples and pears but also wood cuts of popular Israelite preachers, religious flyers, offprints of some speeches and other such fruits which do not grow on trees."

(Lajos Hevesi, *Karczképek az ország fővárosából* [Sketches from the Capital of the Country], 1876)

Until 1856 leather sales were held in the Orczy House. Jewish merchants of Óbuda came here in search of a larger market. At the turn of the eighteenth and nineteenth centuries the entire Jewish community of Pest lived in Terézváros, except for maybe a few families. Quite naturally the Orczy House became the center of Jewish community life.

"(…) The Orczy House has everything that a traditional Jew may ever need throughout his life. There is flour for Passover, a bank, pocket-watches cooked according to Jewish ritual, a Jewish bookstore and even a ritual slaughterer"

—wrote a contemporary, the author of the previous quotation, a certain Lőwy who later on Magyarized his name to Lajos Hevesi (1843–1910), to become famous in Vienna as Ludwig Hevesi for his essays on modern arts, especially Art Nouveau (*Sezession*). He continues as follows:

"Many people live in the Orczy House and it is rare that someone should move out from there. The way this house is inhabited endows it with patriarchal flavor. I bet they give at least a quarter of a century notice before someone is evicted rather than six months. Let's say the grandfather gave notice and the grandson

[1] Mishle: from *mashal* (plural *meshalim*, genitive *mishle*), "proverb", "wise saying".

will move out. Therefore, this very special house offers a certain insurance to its residents, it is a community within the community, and looking at the more prominent stratum of the Israelite population of Pest we will note that they were all nurtured either in Óbuda or the Orczy House."

(Lajos Hevesi, *Karczképek az ország fővárosából* [Sketches from the Capital of the Country], 1876)

Today the image and spirit of the Orczy House can only be evoked by reading old descriptions or using our fantasy. To help us imagine what the Orczy House was like we may look at the buildings on the corner of Üllői út and József körút (49–51 Üllői út). These houses were formerly one huge building, the Maria Theresa / Kilián Barracks. After 1956, however, possibly to blur the bad memory that this was the center of military actions in 1956, the headquarters of the revolution, it was, as a symbolic revenge for the sins of the building, divided into small units to be used as offices, apartments, stores and storage space. Thus the huge block of houses, built (1845–1846) according to the plans of József Hild (1789–1867), fell apart. It is disorganized, noisy, boisterous and tumultuous, just like the Orczy House in the descriptions.

"That large, noisy house in Király utca, where we lived, was like a Shakespearean stage, divided into three levels with its three courtyards. And add to these, my dear, the iron doors of the cellars, opening onto all kinds of dark caves and caverns, the dark nether worlds of the locksmiths and a variety of workshops, the confectioneries, whence drifted the most varied odors, whence blew the illest of winds, whence resounded the rumbles and grumbles of a multitude of sounds, the clatter and chatter of knives, the wheeze and sneeze of saws, the whistle of metals and whence came only glimmers of light. Add to this the granite stairs closed within the walls of the staircases, like a stage set, illuminated by the feeble flickering of a gaslight on winter nights, not unlike a Venetian night, and where, pressed against the walls, the servant girls withstood, as martyrs, the Sunday onslaught of their ardent recruits from the Austro-Hungarian army of old. And forget not the corridors, the iron railings, the gratings and the gray walls with their falcon nests. (...) The first courtyard, especially its first two floors, was inhabited by the bourgeois elite. (...) The second was inhabited by lowlier folks, multiplying fruitfully and celebrating ceremonies of circumcision, in a blissful Hungary! In the third, the collective world of monthly beds, like an alms-house, where a certain young man could live cloistered in rabbinics, cheering his academic melancholy by reading the Sanhedrin and Pesahim, by immersing himself into the Babylonian and Jerusalem Talmud. (...) The old house! What more can I add? (...) These contours, forms and features would need a wealth of detail à la Balzac: the minute topography of the three courtyards and of the three floors, the colors of the nooks and crannies, the description of the thresholds and window sills, the evocation of wood, stone, plaster, brick, paints, waterpipes, loft ladders, roof tiles and chimneys, as the singular bits and pieces, together with the portrayal of the porter's lodge and the lavatories, as all-important elements. Each and every flat, saloon, closet, room, alcove and hiding place would need to be turned inside out, like pockets, to show the lives, the fates, the fortunes and misfortunes, the assortment of trades, of livelihoods and of peoples (...) the old with their prayers, the young with their enthusiasm, the many lodgers in their polygamy, the women with their sophisticated hairdos, the children picking their nose, the families at peace and war, the fishwives, glaziers, organ grinders, peddlers, the soothsayers with their birds, the blind singer with his high-pitched voice, and the great vitality that drove them towards and against each other. (...) The dramatic monumentality of that old building has remained with me, painted in rich colors and elaborately orchestrated, and I have since often seasoned my writings with its particular hue or sound, as a precious gift bequeathed in a testament. (...) The vision of a long-gone East arose in this house, the long-gone East with her cedar trees! A sound, a sigh, a cry burst forth, as if from the streets of Jericho, from the immense chaotic hubbub, in a sudden glint, with a mysterious echo and resonance that is none other than the reverberation of the human soul through time immemorial. (...) I no longer stand here, with a child's restless heart, on this bygone threshold, that has long disappeared, for the entire house has rolled into oblivion, dismantled to its very foundations!

(Dezső Szomory, *Levelek egy barátnőmhöz* [Letters to a Girlfriend of Mine. A Novel], 1927)

When the director of the Pozsony school district, Count József Szapáry, asked the *Königliche Statthalterei* of Pest to see to it that a Jewish school be established in Pest, Israel Wahrmann, supported by János Boráros, a liberal judge, set up the first public school of the Jewish community in the Orczy House. It was called *Nationalschule*. The opening ceremony was on November 5, 1814, after the High Holidays. The single classroom of the elementary school stood in one of the courtyards. Along with Jewish traditions and the Hebrew language, the national language and general knowledge were taught. After 1834 separate Sabbath services were held for the students of the Orczy House.

The first teacher of the school was Károly János Kohlmann. He held his position only for a short period; he was forced to resign because of his reform ideas. Prompted probably by a sudden urge, he got baptized. Later he was employed by the Central Book Examining Office as "censor of Hebrew books". He was in charge of the Hebrew publications of the University Press. He maintained a strong Jewish commitment until an advanced age. He composed an ode in Hebrew on the occasion of the consecration of the Dohány Temple (1859).

(3) Synagogue and Temple in the Orczy House

In April 1796 a new public prayer-house was opened in the Orczy House, the second one in the city. There were two rooms, one for men, the other for women. The rabbi was Israel ben Salomon Wahrmann (1755–1826), born in Óbuda, rabbi of Bodrogkeresztúr at the time of his election (1799). He headed the Jewish community of Pest (*communitas*) until his death. He was the first official rabbi of Pest, though his personal legal status was only *commorans*. It is from this time on (1802) that we may speak of an independent Jewish community in Pest. In the 1810s several legislative acts were introduced concerning the community, but its official designation continued to be "*Pester Juden / Judaei Pesthienses*" and they were not entitled to use a seal.

To control the earlier "presidents", the innkeepers, Wahrmann employed cashiers, controllers (*Gegenhändler*) and a committee of twelve representatives of the Jewish tenants (*die Deputierte*) and of five to seven elected members (*die Genannte / anashim*). These members slowly turned into the secular leaders of the community (*Vorsteher, alluf*, plural *allufim*). The board of leaders (*würklicher Ausschusskörper*) held meetings (*asifah*) at least every other week. After introducing basic rules, the members divided the work among themselves. For a while it was still the renters who represented the community vis-à-vis the city officials, and so a dual system of external representatives (*shtadlan*) and internal leaders (*rosh ha-kahal / rashekol*) developed. Soon, however, the leaders took over both functions. The name of the first *hazzan* of Pest, a certain Jacob, appears in the records of that time.

84. The southern courtyard of the Orczy House, 1928

85. The synagogue in
the Orczy House

86. The northern
courtyard of the
Orczy House during
its demolition

The organizational changes of Wahrmann correspond to the requirements of the Pesti Polgári Keres-kedők Testülete (Civil Merchants' Corporation of Pest) (around 1815) towards Jewish merchants: to wit, that they should elect three representatives whom they trust and should delegate them to the Corporation which will appoint one of the three as the "Jewish alderman (*Juden-Ältester*)", to mediate between the Jews and the Corporation. Administrative expenses of the community were partly covered by the tax collected on meat (*Fleischaccis*). Later, the system of communal leadership became more complicated, leaders were elected biannually by the general assembly (*asifah ve-edah kedoshah*). For a long time the position of the president was filled by the leaders together or in three months' rotation.

The Jewish community (*Juden Gemeinde*) achieved this designation and status on January 2, 1833, when the *Königliche Statthalterei* approved the ground rules and the new system for electing the community leaders. In those days the oval community seal showed two hands in a friendly shake above the branches of a palm-tree, the inscription *Concordia*, "Egyetértés" [Concord] and the name "Pester I. G. [*Israelitische Gemeinde*]".

Due to the constant growth of the congregation, the synagogue in the Orczy House soon proved to be too small. In 1820 a larger, Classicist style synagogue was designed by Lőrinc Zofahl. It was in the wing of the building towards the courtyard, parallel to Király utca, on the second floor, in a long room origi-nally meant to be a reception hall (*vigarda*)—this was what Illés Kaczér referred to as "ancient knights' hall". It became known as the "big" synagogue, *big* compared to the previous small prayer-room.

The "Polish" *minyan*, originally housed at 6 Király utca, moved to the Orczy House, to the prayer-room which was now free (ca. 1820). Initially they would call it the "Polish" or "new" synagogue after the *minyan* that moved in here. Later they merged with the congregation of the "big" syna-gogue (1829), their members receiving a certain number of seats. They contributed their wealth as well as their ritual objects.

During the construction work in the Orczy House (1829) the "big" synagogue became even larg-er; it had 585 seats altogether. A women's gallery was added on the newly built third floor of the house adjoining the prayer-room, and so was also a communal conference room. The synagogue entrance was on the second floor, from the balcony facing the courtyard. This traditional synagogue, operating strictly according to the *Shulhan Arukh*, was used until the Orthodox synagogue in Kazinczy utca was built. Around the middle of the century its congregation was called the "syna-gogue party", because of the debates about the synagogue construction and the order of ritual. After the "Dohány Temple" was completed, traditionalist members of the congregation stayed in the Orczy House, later on joining the Rombach utca synagogue or simply remaining in the old place. What we later call "Orthodoxy" started to form itself here, in the Orczy House.

On the other side of Király utca, in no. 6, a new congregation or *minyan* was set up in the former "Polish" prayer-room (1825). The Chesed Neurim society (*hesed ne'urim* "piety of the youth") assembled to pray in one of the warehouses in the Bácskai courtyard. Their main objection against the synagogue and the reason for their schism was the fact that in the Orczy House bachelor men were not called to the Torah on Saturday mornings and on holidays. These young men, however, wanted to express their piety and their religious pride. In their own prayer-room they introduced a shortened version of the order of prayers. In those days, after the death of Wahrmann, there was no rabbi in Pest. At Wahrmann's funeral R. Münz was among the speakers (his *hesped* appeared in print, too), but no one in Pest wanted him for rabbi. Only the whole community could have elected a rabbi. The new congregation could not employ a rabbi, but around 1827, possibly as a compromise solution, the Jewish community hired a preacher and a cantor for them.

The first preacher of Pest was Josef (Joseph) Bach (1784–1866), a Talmudist from Óbuda. He studied in Prague, returned to his home-town and became a teacher. He taught Hebrew language and the Talmud. The invitation to Pest came as a surprise.

> "I felt that the task was beyond my abilities, but my self-reliance, strong will and ambition encouraged and finally convinced me to accept this honorable task." (...) "It was my mission to show the people the beautiful precious stone of the divine Teaching that had been clumsily distorted when inserted into its setting, to make the spiritual seed of Judaism clear and easily understood in its brightness, to awaken the consciousness of people so that they be proud of their Jewishness."

A major innovation of Bach in Pest was that he held his sermons in literate German rather than in Yiddish. He published some of his early sermons in book form (*Homiletische Erstlinge*, Pest, 1827). His German sermons helped the Jews accept the idea that Yiddish could be replaced by other languages, German or Hungarian. Occasionally even Christian priests and teachers would listen to his sermons. He preached in the Szent Rókus (St. Roch) Hospital as well as in the jail, for prisoners, in order to mend their morals. Later he even gave one sermon in Hungarian, at a funeral (1844) in the courtyard of St. Roch Hospital, in front of the prison inmates. According to some he gave his Hungarian sermon over a Jewish medical student, in the courtyard of the university. But since his Hungarian was rather poor, he did not experiment with speaking Hungarian too often. As a reward for his occupation as a preacher he received a permit to settle in Pest (1833). Otherwise Bach did not leave much after him. His self-confident, solemn words about his calling contrast strangely with what some memoirs say about him: that he wore his preacher's robe for over thirty years, as a matter of pride or pettiness.

> "In his autobiography he says that he was well versed in the Talmud already as a child and it was predicted that he would become an authority on the Talmud (*talmid hakham*). This was the highest honor among Jews, both rich and poor strove to attain it. The community must have been rather lenient towards the boy or else his willpower must have left him, for he did not fulfill the expectations. His knowledge of the Talmud was no greater than his modesty, which his friends could trace in him only on rare occasions and on a small scale."
> (Sándor Büchler, 1901)

It was probably young Jewish merchants visiting Vienna who invited a cantor. In those days the rabbi of Vienna, who was born in Copenhagen, but was the son of a *hazzan* from Hungary, Isak Noa (Noah) Mannheimer (1793–1865), initiated certain innovations in the ritual. The reformed *minhag* was first introduced (1826) in the new synagogue of the city (*Stadttempel* or *Chorschul*, Seitenstettengasse). This was the "*Wiener Minhag*".

Parallel to Mannheimer's liturgical changes, the cantor of the *Stadttempel* in Vienna, Salomon Sulzer (1804–1890), introduced some innovations in the *nusah*, in the music of the synagogue. He admired the music of his contemporaries (Haydn, Schubert), he was a personal friend of Schubert. He carefully adjusted the Ashkenazi cantorial (*hazzan*) tradition to their style. His musical ideas were also formed by Christian church music. Sulzer's synagogue practice, first introduced in 1825, and his song book, the *Schir Zion / Shir Tzion*, "Song of Zion" (volume I: 1839, second edition: 1842; volume II: 1866) uses a choir and solists for the performance of traditional melodies in the synagogue. In his synagogue the usual muttering sound was replaced by silence or liturgical vocal music performed by professionally trained musicians, as at a mass. He composed new melodies, too. He used the Sephardi pronunciation in prayer and songs. (E.g. the prayer recited after the *Amidah*, the *Kedushah* [Jes. 6,3] sounded like "*Kadosh, kadosh, kadosh Adonay tzevaot*", and not "*Kudaysh, kudaysh, kudaysh Adoynoy tsövuoys*", as it sounds in the Ashkenazi pronunciation.)

"I heard Sulzer, the cantor in Vienna [in ca. 1845]. The mask concealing the innermost being is less impenetrable in the case of this artist than usual, the true features of the soul, impressed by the arcane words of ancient doctrines, shimmer through it. (...) To hear Sulzer sing I went to the temple of which he was the musical manager and first singer. I have but rarely experienced the enthrallment evoked by all chords of a religious service and of human compassion as I did on that eve. A most extraordinary choir rang out by the light of the candles, flickering as stars on the ceiling—the choky gutturals soaring as if freed from the prison cells of the soul. (...) Opaque flowers rose from the lilt of the Hebrew words and their ringing petals fluttered in the air; these jagged melodies, sparkling diphthongs and strident sounds floated through the air and brushed the ears like flickering flames. No woman could step inside this holy circle, as if male daring and temper were needed for reciting the prayer, as if more feeble forces should keep distance. (...) It seemed as if they tried to give rhythm to these impetuous entreaties with short, rapid, regular motions. It seemed as if the psalms hovered like fire-spirits above us, as if they rippled like a terrace under the steps of the Highest Being. (...) The listener prayed together with this immense chorus with his entire soul...

(Franz (Ferenc) Liszt, "A zsidó istentisztelet" [The Jewish Synagogue Service], 1859, in: *Gesammelte Schriften*, 6, 1883)

Around 1826 Pest also got a new *hazzan*, Karl / Károly Eduárd (Azriel) Denhof (1798–1840). He was a tall, corpulent young man, a "young Shaul" (see I Samuel 9,2), and he had a powerful, warm tenor–baritone voice. He knew the art of blowing the *shofar* and pronounced the words clearly—he was an ideal cantor. As a child he went to *heder* and the *Nationalschule*, he was well read in secular subjects, wore fashionable clothes and shaved his beard. He was already working as a cantor when Gábor Ullmann, the president of the community, sent him to Vienna to study. The greatly admired master, the cantor of the Chorschul taught him for several months. Sulzer taught him his own performance style which he had introduced in Vienna, corrected his Hebrew pronunciation and intonation. (As we may suspect, Sulzer also tuned him for the Sephardi pronunciation.) From Vienna Denhof went to Italy on another study tour (it was called *Kunstreise* in those days).

Denhof introduced only some minor changes in the *minhag* of Pest. To improve the musical effect, he employed two or three choirboys (*meshorer*), a bass, a tenor and later other sound ranges as well. The group of boys, who initially could not really be called a choir, recited or rather sang the *piyyutim* and the prayers together with him. Naturally, the desire for artistic perfection, which is only an addition to the perfection of the *mitzvah* (*hiddur mitz-*

87. Tribute to Salomon Sulzer. A Hebrew poem by Josef Lőwy (Nagykanizsa)

An Se. Wohlgeboren,
den Herrn Professor

SALOMON SULZER
in Wien.

Anlässlich seines 40jährigen Ober-Cantorats.

משוררים רבים קמו גם נצבי לפני הארון.
אך מי ומי ארמה לך יפה, קול ומטיב טעם?
אל נטע און כי תגיש תפלה — וישב חרון
לקרוע מחזור תורהך לששון עברה וזעם.

משוררים רבים, עמקי שפתים מאנשי הארון —
את חטאא אני מזכיר. על הקרשים° ירעמו רעם:
אכן אתה, ציר נאמן, הלא אל רממת כנרון!
לכן פי לא חנף יורך, ואדברה אך המעם. —

שלמה! אף כי זקנת, עוד קולך כשאנת כפירים.
ושיריך על הארץ מקצה לקצה נפוצו.
אתה, יצרחמו אף עשיתם, ובם יחפוצו;
עוד ארבעים שנה תקום בדור כאחד הצעירים,
ואחרי בלוחך הלא תמצא עדן, אביר השירים!
ושיריך עד בלי ירח ימין ושמאל יפרוצו. —

Gross-Kanizsa, 24. *März 1866.*

Josef Lőwy.

*) Bühne.

vah), soon led to setting up a real choir. As in Vienna, the choir in Pest was also just an extension of the *hazzan*'s function. There was no Halakhic prohibition against the choir, yet it completely changed the ceremony. Denhof's temple was nicknamed the "silent synagogue" in Pest, Denhof himself "the first choir-*hazzan* of our beloved Hungary (*der erste Chor-Chasan unsers geliebten Magyarország*)" by Ignác Reich. The congregation sat silently during the services, individual prayer was replaced by the choir. In a structural sense the Jewish prayer started to resemble the Christian ceremony. The concert-like elements of the prayer alienated some members of the congregation.

Denhof was influenced by Sulzer in other respects, too. On rare occasions he would accept an invitation to entertain at social events, in aristocratic salons, charity concerts. He once recited Eleazar's aria from Halévy's opera, the "La Juive", and rejected the fee he was offered. After the performance someone from the audience casually remarked, "Mr. Cantor, you played the Jew really well." In any case, Denhof was the first *hazzan* in Pest who discovered the opera, this "new" musical genre of the rising bourgeoisie. At Denhof's death Sulzer praised his former student in music, who was older than him, saying that he also knew the "Polish" style of synagogue singing.

88. Portrait of Karl Ed. Denhof

The Jewish community officially acknowledged the *Cultus-Tempel* on April 30, 1830. From then on the "young" or "modern" congregation was equal to the congregation of the "big" synagogue. For the first time in Pest separate services were held for women. (Since there can be no *minyan* without men, they did not read from the Torah at these services.) The acknowledgment of the community meant that they were allowed to move into the Orczy House (1830). Theirs was the new synagogue in the courtyard.

In 1829 the landlord's family called upon the Jewish community through a lawyer to rent more space in the Orczy House. In response, the Jewish community added a third floor in the central wing, extended the "big" synagogue and started to build a new synagogue in the courtyard opposite the entrance from Király utca, with 491 seats, according to the plans of Lőrinc Zofahl. The synagogue in Classicist style, with three naves divided by two rows of columns, was ready in 1830. Women were seated upstairs, in the gallery.

> "In the third courtyard of the house masons erect scaffoldings, carpenters measure the beams and mark with an enormous red pencil where the saw or the ax will play a role, painters position their pails, their color gouaches and finer paints, varnishes and brushes, with which they will paint the much-admired ornaments of the Viennese Seitenstettengasse onto the walls, glaziers carefully set into sheltered corners their panes and glasses patterned with tendrils of foliage, roses and lilies, through which the sunlight will stream mystically or, better said, faint glimmer of light, for this courtyard is but rarely visited by the rays of the sun, so that the religious service of the serene should be no less pious and devout than that of the neighboring folk. The quiet synagogue, even if on a less grand scale, is also under construction, as the noisy building in its vicinity, the first floor reserved for the men, the second, with its latticework, for the women."
>
> (Illés Kaczér, *Három a csillag* [Three Are the Stars. A Novel], 1955/1956))

"Modern" Jews, followers of the religious reform movement, occupied this new temple, named after Vienna the *Cultus-Tempel* or Choir Temple, *Kórtemplom* in Hungarian. Whoever chose to join this congregation was referred to as a member of the "temple-party" in mid-nineteenth-century debates. This group was the seed from which the Neolog community was to grow out.

"And, should thou, provincial Magyar, chance to come to Pest, the center of Hungarian prosperity and, disappointed in your hopes, find an alien soul, an alien tongue and alien theaters, do not flee at once, but make thy way to the Orczy House, where in the middle of the courtyard thou will see a pretty building, and should thou go there at sundown on a Friday eve or on a Saturday morn at ten o'clock, thou will be greeted by sweet voices; go thou and greet them at the temple, and thy fanciful soul will be refreshed by the sweetness of Asian voices. Kindred voices are they, flowers of the Orient in Pest!"

([Péter Vajda], "Keleti virág Pesten" [Flowers of the Orient in Pest], in: *Hasznos Mulatságok*, 1883)

Soon after the Neolog congregation, also the "old", traditional community found for itself a *hazzan* (1830), a "Polish" one, Dovidl Brod (David Strelisker) (1783–1848). Brod or Brodi (Bródy) was a grand

89. A synagogal cantor (*hazzan*)

cantor, an original talent. He could not read music scores but adjusted his own tunes to the traditional Ashkenazi synagogue melodies. He performed every liturgical move with personal feeling and great artistry—this too was a sign of modernity. His contemporaries called him "the best prayer leader (*ba'al tefillah*) of the century". His gravestone reads: "He was able to express all the sufferings of the Jewish people in one sound. (*Er hat es verstanten die gantze Leidensgeschichte des Judenthums in einem Ton zu erzählen.*)"

After R. Wahrmann's death the Pest community did not have a rabbi for a whole decade. Everyone agreed that it was necessary, or at least logical that every *minyan* of the Orczy House, forming virtually separate communities, have separate *hazzan*. Liturgical changes were inspired by the simultaneous wish to adhere to tradition and to modernize. The size of the Pest community grew abruptly, people were not used to seeing hundreds of men in the synagogue three times a day for prayer. The Jews of Óbuda and especially Jews from the Hungarian countryside and the "Poles" were used to a small *minyan*, to a *shtibl*. They felt strange in the huge synagogue filled with hundreds of people. They did not "visit the temple", they went to the synagogue to pray and to talk to each other. They maintained their *separate minyan* exactly because they wanted to pray *together* with each other, together with those few who prayed like they did, who were used to the same melodies. Initially these separate communities were only separate *minyans* within the Jewish community of Pest.

The position of the two established congregations in the Orczy House did not change in the mid-1830s, when a new rabbi was appointed, R. Löw Schwab (1792–1857). (The rabbi of the Pest community lived in the Orczy House, on the second floor, above the Király utca entrance.) So far neither

90. Portrait of David Strelisker

91. The northern courtyard of the Orczy House. In the middle the western side of the former Choir Temple

92. Interior of the Choir Temple. Photo taken from the gallery

93. Interior of the Choir Temple, already used as a textile depot

speculations about reform nor the actual minor changes in the ritual went so far as to cast the role of a priest on the rabbi. Therefore the rabbi of Pest could serve the Halakhic needs of both groups. Daily ceremonies were performed by the separate *hazzans* in the two communities, according to their own ways, but acting only as a *sheliah tzibbur*. Two different *nusahs*, two different orders of worship in one community, in one building was a sign that the unity of the Jews of Pest was about to end. Changes first manifested themselves in the musical traditions of the two synagogues in the Orczy House. There was no tension or personal conflict between Brod and Denhof; Denhof learned from the traditional knowledge and personal art of the older master. In any case, his performance gave evidence that bearded "Poles" were not the only ones who could stand in front of the Ark, that one did not have to be completely ignorant of the secular world to recite prayers properly. The difference between the musical styles of the two congregations was not in quality but in concept.

The congregation of the Choir Temple later became members of the Dohány synagogue. When they moved out from the Orczy House (1859), the synagogue in the courtyard was used as a storeroom, without any changes in the Ark or the gallery. Later a textile merchant used it. At least the original ceiling was covered by a vault.

The Orczy House, this two-century-old massive building was condemned in 1931. Its demolition started in 1936 (October 10) and it was soon finished. The immediate reason for its destruction was a city development plan, the construction of a new avenue (Erzsébet sugárút) leading to the Város-liget (City Park). The grandiose plans were luckily not fully realized. Some changes were carried out after World War II, but not according to the original plans.

94. Demolition of the Orczy House, 1936

95. The Orczy House. Passage between the two courtyards

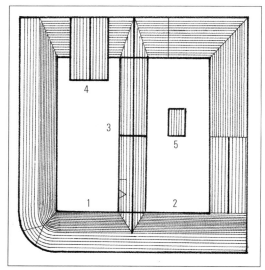
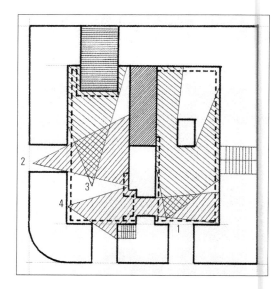

96. The Orczy House. Ground-plan based on the map fig.. III:2. Roofs and buildings.
 1: Northern courtyard
 2: Southern courtyard
 3: Synagogue
 4: "Choir temple"
 5: "Israelitische Nationalschule" (?)

97. The Orczy House. Visual angle of the surviving photos. Figs. 79, 98, 99 taken from Károly körút.
 1: Fig. 84.
 2: Fig. 86.
 3: Fig. 91.
 4: Fig. 95.

Today the Orczy House, the former center of Jews in Pest, has been replaced by the so-called Madách Houses (1938). These modern brick buildings, the robust blocks of houses, the grandiose, promising triumphal arch unmistakably reflect the German and Italian imperial style of the 1930s or the Marx buildings in Vienna. They certainly stand in strong contrast with the narrow streets of the old Jewish quarter of Pest behind them. In Erzsébetváros the aura of the nineteenth century is still preserved, despite some modernization. It is similar to the "old-new" *Scheunenviertel* in Berlin.

(4) Prayer-houses in Király utca and Its Neighborhood

In the beginning, when this whole neighborhood was still farmland with gardens, yards, stalls and silos, the predecessor of Király utca was called *Mittermayerische Gasse* or *Obermeyerhofweg* (named after the Mayerhoffer family, the former owner of the Orczy House.) In 1804 it was named *König-gasse* or *König von Engellandgasse / Engelische König Gasse* in the longer version after the "Angliai / Ángoly / Angyali király" [King of England / of Angels], the inn and tavern in the Orczy House. From the 1820s on, it used to be called *Drei Könige Gasse / Három Király utca* [Street of the Three Kings], too, after the new name of the inn. (This latter name refers to the kings at the Congress of Vienna. Emperor Francis I of Austria, Frederick William III of Prussia and Tzar Alexander I visited Pest and Buda in late October, 1814. It is the imperial visit that gave the idea for the new name. The lower part of the street was indeed worthy of that.) The section beyond the Roman Catholic church of Terézváros and Gyár [Factory] utca (today a part of Liszt Ferenc tér) was called *Lerchenfeld Gasse / Pacsirtamező* [Lark Field]. In 1874 the two parts of the street received a single name: *Király utca.* Its continuation beyond Lövölde tér is called today the Városligeti fasor.

Originally Király utca led from the inner city, the Danube bank (Híd / Nagy Híd and Új utca, today Deák Ferenc utca) to the Városliget (City Park). It was the nucleus of a grand metropolitan avenue. When the city leased the Városliget (Stadtwald / Stattvájli) [City Park] to Primate Count József Batthyány (1727–1799), the contract was based on conditions: the street leading from "Ángoly király" to the City Park should be maintained so that it could be used in every season, trees were to be planted on both sides, and it was to have proper lighting. These requirements were fulfilled probably only on the outer segment of the street, along the Városligeti fasor. When the city regained the avenue from the Primate's heritage (1805), no major construction work was undertaken for a long time. Thus the avenue developed without an overall plan, it was built according to the wishes of the owners of the lots along the street.

A radical change in the appearance of Király utca occurred only in the 1830s, especially in the years following the flood of 1838. The neighborhood became a modern, elegant quarter of the city with two- or three-story Classicist or Romantic style houses, with busy traffic. The houses here were designed by the most prominent architects of the era, Mihály Pollack (1773–1855), József Hild and Lőrinc Zofahl. Before the construction of Sugár / Andrássy út and even afterwards, Király utca was meant to be a sort of an alternate avenue. Starting in front of the Orczy House the street, as well as the side- walk, were paved with cobblestones. Later even an omnibus ran there. Only after the magnificent Sugár út was opened did Király utca lose its primary position. Artisans and middle-class people lived here. In 1882 the inner Erzsébetváros became independent from Terézváros. The natural dividing line between them is Király utca. The streets of the neighborhood are narrow and haphazard.

From the early nineteenth century on, the lower part of the area can be considered the Jewish quarter. The first prayer-rooms of the Jews of Pest were here, in Király utca, that is,

1787: in the Heusler House, owned by Count Donát Heusler;

1796: in the Orczy House.

1800: A prayer-house is mentioned in the Tomola House in Rombach utca, exactly where the syn- agogue stands today.

1800: In the Classicist building at 6 Király utca the "Polish" synagogue was opened by Hasidic Jews who came from Poland or Ukraine. Lajos Hevesi referred to Király utca sarcastically as "the street of the Polish king" (*Karczképek*, 1876). Around 1825 the "Polish" congregation moved to the Orczy House and merged with the *minyan* of the "big" synagogue. These Hasidim liked to call themselves Sephardi Jews, though actually they were Yiddish-speaking Jews following the Ashkenazi rite (mix- ing in some Sephardi elements from Palestine, Turkey). In their case "Sephardi" only meant differ- ent from the others, not following the road of modernization or reform.

1805: The prayer-house of the Chesed Neurim Society for Aid to the Sick was opened at 2 Király utca, in the building called "White Goose" or Wagner House. Most of the members came to Pest from Óbuda; they must have been hardworking, ambitious people. The *minyan* was formed from members of the Society (*hevrah*) in 1825. They assembled to pray in the warehouse in the Bácskai courtyard. When the new group was acknowledged (1830), they moved over to the Orczy House and used the synagogue in the courtyard.

1827: The building at 12 Király utca called Gömöry House (*Gömery'sches Haus*) was at one time owned by Károly Gömöry (1779–1845). It was built according to the plans of Mihály Pollack (1812), in Classicist style. Gömöry, an offspring of the famous alchemist, opened an apothecary in the building called "Arany Oroszlán" ("*Zum goldenen Löwen*"), on the second floor, in one of the luxury apart- ments. Azriel Brill (?–1853) rented this apartment too, but in his time there was a prayer-room on the first floor, not an apothecary. Fülöp Jakobovics, the director of the Jewish Hospital lived here as well. The building was also called Török House after József Török.

In 1830, when the new synagogue was opened in the Orczy House, the Jewish community of Pest decided to dissolve the private synagogues. Their purpose was to bring about the administrative and ritual unity of the community. For a while all the groups used the same prayer-room in the Orczy House, and each functioned according to its own *minhag*. The differences between the groups increased day by day, new trends and customs emerged, new groups appeared, which—while not separating themselves from the community—followed their own ritual in their own, separate prayer-room.

1842: The Shas Hevrah Talmud-Torah Society was founded in Zwei Mohren Gasse / Két Sze- recsen utca (2 Paulay Ede utca). This was a strictly Orthodox, pious Jewish community which even named itself after the Talmud (the word *Shas* is an acronym of *shishshah sedarim*, "six orders", i.e. the six divisions of the Mishnah and the Talmud). Members of the society emphasized learning, studying the Talmud throughout their lives. They studied the books, according to the widespread custom, in pairs (*zugot*). Days were divided into three parts. One part was for Torah study, anoth- er part for prayer and a third part to earn a living. Members (*haverim*, "fellows") of the Shas Society spent practically all their free time in the study house (Yiddish *shul* / *shil* / *shül*) bending over pages of the Talmud and discussing every word, like the great masters of the Talmud of yore.

At dawn the beadle (*shammash / shames*) would go from house to house banging at the door of each apartment with a wooden hammer (*Schulklopfer / shulkloper*) shouting: "*In Schul herein!* To the study house!" The inscription on the *shulkloper* actually says so: "But I, through Your abundant love, enter Your house" (Psalms 5,8). In 1887 the Society moved to the new synagogue built in the Vasvári Pál utca.

A Yiddish proverb about why it is necessary to study says: *Oykh ven der tsadik vendt zikh tsum riboynoy shel oylom mit a shayle, di tshuve git er aleyn*, "Even if a *tzaddik* turns to the Almighty with a question, he gives the answer himself."

Older people remember that at 11 Paulay Ede utca there used to be an "Israelite prayer-house". Maybe a prayer-room.

Finally, in the nineteenth century, the synagogue of the Frank (*frenk, fränk*) community was in Király utca, too, at nos. 35–37. These "Frank" Jews were actually Sephardim and followed the Sephardi, Spanish *minhag* and tradition. (They were not the baptized followers of Jacob Frank, the eighteenth-century false Messiah from Podolia.) The name *Frank* comes from the Turkish, meaning "Western (*faringi / frengi*)", a loanword from *frank*, etc. In the Mediterranean area the word has come down as a family name (*Franco*). Spanish Jews who found refuge in the Ottoman Empire after their expulsion from Spain in 1492 came to Hungary via the Balkans. Izsák (Isaac) Almuslin, who lived in Pest in the last decades of the eighteenth century, was a *frenk*, too. Here is how Adolf Ágai (1836–1916), a writer, journalist and editor, who would from time to time jot down interesting Jewish customs and items of folklore, remembered them at the beginning of the twentieth century.

> "My late grandfather on my mother's side [Ágai refers to him as don Yitzhak in other places] founded the *fränk* synagogue in Budapest back in the 30s [1830]. These Sephardi Jews, dispersed from Spain all over the world, retained their mother tongue, Spanish, with great love and care. The older generation still speaks it at home.—Old Castilian and ancient Andalusian chants and *zemirot* sounded at my grandfather's table on holidays, where we used to eat an ethnic pastry filled with spinach."
>
> (Adolf Ágai, "Az én dédatyámról" [About My Great-grandfather], 1907)

As the Jews occupied larger and larger portions of Terézváros, so grew the number of small and even smaller synagogues in Király utca and in the side streets. In the beautiful album of Karl Vasquez / Count Károly Vasquez, "Buda Pest szabad királyi várossainak tájleírása, 1838" [Depiction of the Royal Free Cities Buda and Pest], on one of the colored maps of Terézváros, a spot near the House of Invalids, South of Király utca, is called "*Synagogen*".

(5) The Orczy Café

or "Orczy'sche Cafe", or the "*Aczy'sche*" was in the Orczy House, facing the market. Its address was 17 Károly körút. It was opened as a café on the first floor of the building in 1825, but coffee was served there already earlier, since 1795. The *Orczy'sche* was the most long-lived among the cafés of Pest. It closed only when the building was pulled down. From outside it looked very simple, like the rest of the building, but inside it had a cozy atmosphere. In the nineteenth century the large mirror room was a central meeting place of grain merchants from just about the whole of Europe. "The Orczy Café was the middle of the world" (Andor Peterdi, 1934).

> "Low, rather pleasant, silent arches. The wallpaper has ripened dark like sepiolite. Customers have grown old, too. You do not see people with young faces, just old or older. Who would come here? This place has been visited by wool and leather traders from the beginning of time. This Café witnessed how billions passed from one pocket to another. This was the leather stock exchange. In good old times these courtyards housed thirty to forty wagons a day, arriving from the countryside, filled with raw hide. These three court-yards were a transit point back then..."
>
> (Zsigmond Móricz, 1935)

But not just leather was sold there. As Béla Bevilaqua Borsody, a unique historian of the cafés of Pest notes (1935), all the grain merchants of Western, Southern and Eastern Europe met here, this was the exchange for tobacco, oak-apple, feather, hide, fur, alum, natron, potash and bone black. In short, all the accessories for tanning leather were bought and sold here, wholesale, of course.

98. The Orczy House from the Károly körút. In the front, the Orczy Café

99. The Orczy House (Orczy Café), 1935

"But let's see what the waiter says.

"The Orczy Café—so says the headwaiter of the Orczy Café—*is not an ordinary café*. Take a look around—he says, pointing around the low, deep, strong, smoky groined vaults—the grandfathers of those gentlemen sitting here used to sit here as well, next to these same tables.

"The gentlemen sitting here are strange gentlemen, but gentlemen. One really cannot see the kind in other cafés. The heavy gold chains on their vests show or sustain the continual right of seniority; the gentlemen sitting here are merchants, dealers, that's true, but of the kind whose *grandfathers used to be merchants and dealers here as well*. That is, *real gentlemen*. It should not be understood as sarcasm: these seven-percent

gentries of the mercantile age stir their coffee and peek into their papers through their pince-nez sitting at the marble table of the Orczy Café with the same nobility as the impoverished country gentlemen used to do in the age of chivalry sitting at the table on the balcony of their countryside mansion. They are gentlemen, in fact, *exclusive gentlemen*, who pry into the background of the stranger that appears among themselves.

"*Sind sie ein hiesiger?*[2]—raises one of them his eyes upon me.

"Well, yes, though not exactly from Király utca, but I am myself one from Pest as well—I try to say an excuse.

"*Na und*—honors me my gentleman with one more question—*was für ein Geschäft haben Sie?*[3] (...)

"You see this café?—asks the headwaiter when he gets the opportunity to speak.—Look around thoroughly, *it has been here for more than a hundred years. This café is the ancestor of the palace of the stock market at Szabadság tér*, the place where national deals are made, where these people take a rest."

100. The Orczy Café, 1935

(...) "The Orczy House, the Dobbler bazaar, the Gozsdu courtyard—with their complicated structure of courts, shops, banisters, corridors, with the thousands of people staying around them—all *represent the ancient, magnificent forms of human settlement*, sometimes in a distorted form. Each one is a Noah's Arc in itself, filled up with all kinds and forms of human existence."

(Mihály András Rónai–Marianne Gábor, *Szülőfalunk, Budapest* [Budapest, Our Home Village], 1998)

[2] "Are you from here?" (German).
[3] "And what kind of business are you in?" (German).

Those who rented the Café included Sebestyén Bauer, József Müller, János Bartl, János Szevera and János Dörsching until finally, in 1870, the Strasser family took over and kept it for over sixty years. The first people to run coffee-rooms were Christians. Jews were banned from the coffee guild, they could not 'obtain a permit to sell coffee until 1864. Bartl came to Pest (1823) as an Austrian *cavearius* of Roman Catholic faith. He rented the hotel "Magyar Király" (Hungarian King) on the corner of Dorottya utca and Régi színház / Gizella tér (today Vörösmarty tér) in the inner city, later the "Angol királynő" [Queen of England]. He got rich, purchased several plots and built houses on Herminamező. Another renter, the Italian Szevera, was originally a butcher who traded in salami but later decided to go into the coffee business. He had another café nearby, on the corner of Váci körút (today Bajcsy-Zsilinszky út) and Hajós utca. He invested his enormous income in real estate. He bought homes in the countryside and Pest, on Herminamező, like Bartl. He lived at 20 Károly körút, on the opposite side of the square. His sister lived in the Orczy House in an apartment right above the Café. Actually, the only Jewish

101. The Strasser family, last renters of the Orczy Café

renters of the Orczy Café were the Strassers. Yet the Jewish community of Pest put up a commemorative inscription to honor János Dörsching after his death to express their gratitude for his charitable donations.

In the Strassers' time espresso and capuccino were served in the "Orczy", maybe also beer. It closed at 8 p.m. every night and remained the single "glatt kosher" café of the capital until its last day, following the Orthodox standard of *kashrut*. The guests did not remove their hats or caps. The Café subscribed to Jewish magazines. On the tables lay newspapers with Hebrew characters and Jewish playing cards (*shas*, borrowing this name from the complete Talmud, or *tiliml / tilem*, from the title of the Psalms in Hebrew); instead of figures they had fancy Hebrew letters on them. Whether they used *fledli*, false cards, none remembers today.

"This is the place where all human creatures from the East feel themselves at home, where they enjoy the atmosphere they like best, where their ears are charmed by familiar tones, though we must admit that the customers of this Café do not exchange ideas as much as they do other goods."

(Hevesi, *Karczképek* [Sketches], 1876)

Throughout the nineteenth century, even before the Strassers' time, the Orczy Café served as the Jewish cantors' and teachers' exchange, too. *Hazzanim* seeking jobs would even showcase their voice and knowledge to the emissaries of various communities. We know from diaries that the rooms of the Café and even the restrooms were sometimes filled with the familiar sound of liturgical music. Teachers were "for sale", too. To tell the truth, only those came to the Orczy House who could not find a job by invitation or recommendation. Teachers of lesser quality flocking here were called *oyfeslerer un kindershokhtim*. By ironically mixing up the compounds of two ordinary words, *kinderlerer* "(children's) teacher" and *oyfesshokhtim* "poultry slaughterers", they created "poultry teacher" and "children slaughterer".

"The Orczy coffee-house, on the Ország út [Váci körút] of Pest, was an especially noted exchange for teachers. In this dirty hall, redolent with smoke from the most diverse tobaccos which, even after forty years, to this very day, has retained much of its former appearance, jostled a colorful throng of urban and provincial Jews, sipping their coffee and making a deafening noise, chatting, speaking and shouting with unruly gestures. The rush and the crush reached its height between one and four in the afternoon at this exchange of teachers, this being the time for most appointments. The unemployed teachers sat on a bench and awaited anxiously the glance of an agent as he stepped out from the crowd and with the buyer, or better said, the future principal, stood in front of the bench and inspected the candidates, introducing one or the other to the stranger. It was a most embarrassing situation. I still recall these scenes with feelings of distaste, whenever my path takes me by the Orczy coffee-house. I sat for long hours on this bench, for many a long afternoon with an anxious heart and deep embarrassment..."

(Ármin Vámbéry, *Küzdelmeim* [My Struggles], 1905)

A former schoolmate of Vámbéry, Adolf Ágai (as Porzó, using a pen-name), seems to add some extra flavor to the description of the Café:

"Some say it is the teachers' exchange, others that it is the witness' bourse. Rumor has it that you can find a witness for any delicate case on either side. But rumors are never more than half true."

(Porzó / Adolf Ágai, *Utazás Pestről – Budapestre* [Journey from Pest to Budapest], 1912)

Ármin Vámbéry (ca. 1832–1913) himself was in search of a job on the teachers' exchange of the Orczy Café several times in the 1850s, thus also in 1852. A thorough knowledge of the Talmud was held in high esteem. Wealthier Jewish families living in rural Hungary would hire a teacher (*melammed*) for their sons, like the aristocrats who employed private tutors and governesses to educate their children. Vámbéry, who came to Pest from the provinces, took on such jobs for a year or two and earned some money for his education. When in Pest (1853/54), he lived at 7 Drei Trommel Gasse / Három Dob utca (today 10 Dob utca). Here is what he wrote about his accommodation. "It was a one-story house with a long and deep courtyard. The people who lived there could only pay their rent by subletting a bed or two, they shared their only room with one or more tenants." He would go to a café to read, to the "Szegedi" Café on the corner of Dob utca and Dohány utca (i.e. on Károly körút) for there was not enough light in his room. At the turn of the century, already as a well-known traveler and a prominent scholar, professor of Turkish studies, he lived in a more upscale neighborhood, in one of the houses on Ferenc József körút (today 24 Belgrád rakpart).

(6) Out of the Ghetto

Out of the Ghetto—this was the title Jacob Katz gave to his seminal historical study on the social integration of Jews (1973). Earlier, in 1911, back when Katz was a child in Hungary, it was the title of a novel by Tamás Kóbor (1867–1942). Though the Jewish quarter of Pest can by no means be considered a real ghetto, here, like everywhere in Europe, several obstacles stood in the way of Jewish emancipation. Clearing these obstacles opened the way for the modernization of society in general. The process of modernization confronted the Jewish community with an additional problem. Will this formerly distinct group remain at least partially unified, will its members preserve their full Jewish identity, or will they melt into the surrounding society and lose their special character?

Around the middle of the nineteenth century, in addition to tradesmen, a new class of Jewish entrepreneurs and intellectuals appeared. These people became completely secularized and adjusted themselves to the upwardly mobile, yet rooted in the national tradition, Hungarian middle-class; in other words, they became culturally assimilated. Some converted to the Protestant or, less often, to the Roman Catholic religion, yet integration did not always mean leaving the Jewish community, or at least not completely leaving it. Katz called the milieu which accepted the Jewish bourgeoisie a neutral or indifferent one, referring to the fact that only a society more or less free of prejudice would allow the integration of Jews. It was not only legal equality (*bürgerliche Verbesserung*) or, in the words of Baron

József Eötvös (1813–1871), the "bourgeois rise" of Jews necessary, but also equality of social opportunities. These opportunities, or types of careers, will be indicated here by means of short biographies.

As for the schools, where social integration begins, Jewish children in Pest could attend Jewish, Roman Catholic or Protestant schools. They could, for example, attend the Piarist school (*Collegium Pestiense*), the building of which was in the Inner City, on today's Március 15. tér (March 15 square), which was then called Galamb utca. The successor of the school, the Piarist high school—for the time being, the central building of the Faculty of Humanities of Eötvös Loránd University (1 Pesti Barnabás utca / Piarista

102. "The building of the Piarists on Városház tér", a colored lithograph by Adolf Tikáts

köz)—was built not exactly on the same lot as the former building, only next to it. During the nineteenth century several Jewish personalities attended this famous school, among others R. Israel Wahrmann's two sons, David Josef Wahrmann (1793–1852), rabbi of Nagyvárad (today Oradea, Romania), and Judah Wahrmann (1793–1868), *dayyan* of Pest.

A distinguished Jewish student of the Piarist school, Ignác Hirschler (1823–1891), the famous ophthalmologist, influential member, and for a short period even president of the Jewish community of Pest, corresponding member of the Hungarian Academy of Sciences (1869), member of the Upper House (1885), late in his life, remembering his former school writes with affliction that in the 1830s, when he attended the school, Jews were admitted as students, but the social atmosphere was definitely not *neutral* towards them, to use Katz's terminology.

> "The dark corridors of the monastery, the crosses, which I barely even dared to look at, Latin (the language of instruction), the priest-teachers of my first years, the separate Jew-bench, the cruel and cynical corporal punishment, which I feared constantly, the malicious comments on my religion, the insults, the beating and shoving of my wild schoolmates which I, being a skinny child, had to endure: all this haunted me as a nightmare. (...)
>
> I felt that the humiliation was rooted in the Jew-bench, and this had a much worse effect on the human soul and spirit, than people generally think." (*Autobiographisches Fragment*, 1891, pp. 7–8)

The social resistance with which the Jews of Pest had to contend in order to establish themselves as part of civil society could be felt already at school, and the pressure became stronger and stronger as one grew older. But Ignác Hirschler's way led only out of the "ghetto", not out of the Jewish community.

Móric Bloch / Mór Ballagi (1815–1891)

Móric (Moritz) Bloch chose a different path.

Born a Jew, died a Calvinist Protestant, he was a member of the academic elite, a professor at the Calvinist Theological Academy. An excellent rabbinical scholar, who left his Jewish faith in order to achieve high standing in the society at large and to establish himself as a secular intellectual. He was born into a poor Jewish family in Northeastern Hungary. As a young boy, after his *bar mitzvah* he made a living for himself and for the family by reading Torah (*leinen / leyening*) and studying Talmud (*lernen gemore*) in Jewish communities all over the country. In order to study he attended *yeshivot* (Nagyvárad and Pápa) for some three years—hence his Hebrew and Jewish erudition. In a biographical essay his son called him later, but still in his life-time, "a wandering *boher*". After his *yeshivah* years he became a private instructor in the house of a noble Hungarian family in the countryside.

The learned and ambitious *yeshivah boher* came to Budapest at the age of twenty-two (1837) to study mathematics at the Pest University. That is when, to pursue his secular studies, he learned Hungarian. At that time he already wrote on Hungarian national issues for newspapers (*Hasznos mulatságok*, *Pester Tageblatt*). Being a Jew he could not even get a degree in mathematics—as a matter of fact, he failed at the final examination (*rigorosum*), so he went to Paris to finish his studies (1839).

In the meantime the Diet—as the Parliament was called—in Pozsony (Pressburg) started to debate the issue of Jewish emancipation, in preparation of the Act XXIX of 1840. Also R. Löw (Arszlán) Schwab participated in the wide, general discussion. His treatise, *A zsidók. Felvilágosító értekezés* [The Jews. An Enlightening Treatise], printed in Buda, with type from the Hungarian Royal University (1840), was translated into Hungarian by Móric Bloch. He added to the translation an introduction and footnotes as well. At the request of the Hungarian reform-minded noble-intelligentsia, perhaps urged by Baron József Eötvös himself, Bloch published a pamphlet on the issue as well, under the title *A zsidókról* [On the Jews] (Buda, 1840), and that writing brought him recognition. Part of this pamphlet was given the title: "Jewish appeal to the Szittya folk"; the word *szittya*, "Scythian" was a popular name among the Hungarian nobility who boasted with their supposed Scythian origin. Péter Vajda, a reform-oriented young writer, wrote a foreword to it, as if his words were a Hungarian appeal to the Jewish people: "You are no longer step-children, you should feel this and place yourself in the center of national feelings." Bloch influenced the views of Eötvös about the Jewish emancipation. But a pamphlet was published against him too, in German: *Das religiöse Gewissen vor dem Forum des Judentums oder Dr. Bloch und die Juden* (1844). Immediately after the publication of *On the Jews* and the first volume of the Torah translation, the *Magyar Tudós Társaság* [Hungarian Learned Society], the Hungarian Academy of Sciences elected Bloch a corresponding member (1840). He was the first Jewish member of the Academy founded by Count István Széchenyi. (He became a regular member in 1858.) Even the Archbishop attended his inaugural lecture.

After becoming a corresponding member of the Academy, he became a student again: he went to Tübingen, where he studied with Georg H. A. Ewald (1803–1875), among others. Professor Ewald was Christian, a leading Hebraist of his age, his book on Hebrew grammar was well known in Hungary too.

In Notzingen, Germany, Bloch converted to the "united Protestant" faith (1843). Some (e.g. the Hungarian *Zsidó lexikon*, 1929) will know that first he converted to the Lutheran and later on to the Calvinist denomination. His decision was condemned in Hungary; it elicited several pamphlets and an open letter by Leopold Löw to József Székács, a Protestant minister in Pest. *Bloch* soon became *Ballagi* (1848) and, at the same time, an advocate of Protestantism in most of his works: as a teacher, professor and founder of institutions. For years he taught in the Lutheran Gymnasium at Szarvas, together with the above-mentioned Péter Vajda. In the War of Independence of 1848/49 he participated as a captain, served as a clerk—later on as a secretary—of the Commander-in-chief General Artúr Görgey for a while and in 1849 he was appointed secretary of the Division of the Supreme Commander at the Ministry of War. After the War of Independence and a short period of internment he engaged in running an agricultural enterprise, but soon became a lecturer at the Calvinist Theological Seminary in Kecskemét (1851) and later a professor at the Calvinist Theological Academy in Budapest, in Ráday utca (1855).

Bloch played a significant role in the Magyarization of Jewish intellectual life. His bilingual Torah edition, published in small brochures (1840–1841), contains a good Hebrew text and an excellent Hungarian translation. The former was natural since he had a thorough Jewish education, while the latter was a remarkable innovation: he took the path chosen by Moses Mendelssohn, braving conservative opinion, specifically that of the head of the Pozsony Yeshiva, Moses Schreiber (1763–1839), the Hatam Sofer,[4] who ruled against the translation of the Torah. Together with Mór (Móric) Rosenthal,

---

[4] In Moses Schreiber's popular post-mortem name, *Hatam Sofer* (*Hasam Sayfer*), the word *sofer* is the Hebrew translation of his German family name, *hatam* being an abbreviation of the title of his book *Hiddushei Torat Moshe*, "Novellas to the Laws of Moses / by Moses [that is, Moses Schreiber]".

חמשה חמשי תורה

מתורגמים ומבוארים

הונגרית

על ידי

מרדכי בלאך

חבר לעקר חכמי התנגרי'

דברים'

אפען

נעדרוקט אין דער קעניגל' אוניווערשיטעטס בוכדרוקעריא תר"ב לפ"ק.

103. Torah translation of Móric Bloch (Mór Ballagi). Two pages and the Hebrew title page of the book

104. Mór Ballagi

a teacher (*melammed*) in Buda, Bloch edited a *Siddur* in Hungarian (*Israel könyörgési egész évre* [Israel's Prayers throughout the Year] 1841; second edition, 1843) and published a grammar of Hebrew (*A héber nyelv elemi tankönyve* [Basic Grammar of the Hebrew Language], 1856). He wrote several works in the field of Hungarian grammar and linguistics and supported the idea of establishing a Hungarian Jewish rabbinical seminary. His most important work, *A magyar nyelv teljes szótára* [A Complete Dictionary of the Hungarian Language], I–II (Pest, 1866–1873), laid the linguistic foundation of nineteenth century national scholarship. His German dictionaries were widely used up until recently.

Maybe Bloch wanted to become the Hungarian Mendelssohn, maybe he wanted to create a Hungarian version of the secular, academic Jewish scholarship flourishing at that time in Germany; he was a reformer who, along with the social emancipation of the Jews, wanted to renew Jewish religion and ritual as well. In the 1840s his work followed the Jewish tradition in religious matters. His Torah edition was a traditional Jewish book in appearance, the pages to be turned over from the "back", that is, from left to right, the commentaries and notes of the translator following traditional Jewish exegesis. He could have become one of the leaders of the Haskalah, a *maskil*, like the great Master of a previous generation in Berlin or his own contemporaries. We do not fully know why he left the Jewish community. Certainly not because of yielding to the bourgeois social trend, but rather because of his ideas about religious reform; he must have thought after a while that important religious reforms would never occur in Pest. The Jewish community rejected Bloch only as a religious reformer.

His person was accepted; witness the fact that Ignác Goldziher participated in the publication of the second and third editions of his grammar. Bloch left the community but he never turned against the Jewish people or faith.

Goldziher wrote in his *Diary*:

"Ballagi distinguished himself greatly by supporting all kinds of Jewish talents. With this remarkable ambition he compensated for the fact that he left the Jewish community."

His grave is in the Kerepesi cemetery; not in Salgótarjáni utca, of course not, but in Fiumei út, in the public cemetery (plot 21).

His brother, Károly Ballagi (1824–1888) was a teacher in Calvinist Gymnasiums and a school-inspector, author of textbooks and grammars, journalist, wrote textbooks for the Jewish schools about the history of Hungary and Transylvania long after his conversion.

One of his sons, Aladár Ballagi (1853–1928), became a promoter of the conservative nationalist view of history. His father told his friends in despair that his son had become an anti-Semite. He was a professor of history at the Pest University and a member of the Academy, and for a term served as a MP. In his writings and political activities he appeared as an opponent of the Jewish community and of liberalism, often viewed as a Jewish issue.

The Wodianers

Two branches of the Wodianer family participated in the business life of Pest. The Wodianers moved to Pest from Southern Hungary. Family tradition maintains that originally they are from Spain. They moved to Hungary around the mid-eighteenth century from Moravia; this was when their ancestor, Samuel Weidmann / Woidzislav first appeared in Bács county. Their Slavic–German name means "watery", "aquatic". Later the family developed two branches. One of them traded in cereal, wool and tobacco; they delivered these goods to Pest from the South on their own barge, the other branch dealt in books and magazines. They shared only the ancestors in Bács county.

One ancestor of the grain merchant Wodianers, Fülöp, lived in Szeged at the end of the eighteenth century and was a leader of the Jewish community there, a *dayyan*. His son, Joshua Wodianer Kozma (1789–1831), inherited his deep knowledge of the Talmud. The son lived and worked in Győr and corresponded with the greatest rabbinical authorities of his time, R. Münz of Óbuda and R. Moses Schreiber of Pozsony, the renowned Orthodox leader. His commentaries on the Babylonian Talmud and the Torah were published by his son with an introduction by Vilmos Bacher (1890).

Fülöp Wodianer lived in Szeged but maintained a warehouse in Pest. His two sons married into wealthy merchant families in Pest. He was getting ready to enter the heart of the country.

After the death of their father (1820) the eldest son, Samuel Wodianer (ca. 1780–1850), tried again to apply to the Council of Pest for a permit to settle (1828). He received it a few years later and he even got a license for wholesale trade (1834) but he relocated his business to Vienna. "It is the natural wish of every person to extend his sphere of operation for his own well-being and for the benefit of the community", he wrote in his application. In the 1830s his company grew to become the most influential one in the wool trade. He delivered large amounts of goods to the Netherlands and England. In Pest he counted as a uniquely profit-oriented businessman. Soon he took over all the tobacco sales beyond the river Tisza. He was the wealthiest wholesale merchant in Hungary; he applied for membership to the National Casino, the casino of aristocrats founded by Count István Széchenyi. That his request, which was turned down at the time, counted as a bold and provocative act in the eyes of the aristocracy, is well demonstrated by a brief remark of Széchenyi in his diary (October 22, 1837), "Wodianer wants to be a member of the Casino." Wodianers's pride as member of the financial aristocracy was bolstered by his bourgeois mentality and his belonging to a high tax-bracket. In his application he brought up his love of the homeland as an argument. His summer house, 32 Budakeszi út, was built in the Classicist style (ca. 1840).

105. Mór Wodianer. A drawing by Josef Kriehuber (1800–1876), a Viennese artist, 1847

Samuel Wodianer's older son, Móric / Mór Wodianer (1810–1885) got baptized already as an adult (1839 or 1840) and "became a Calvinist" (Széchenyi, *Diary*, February 25, 1841), opened a wholesale business in Vienna, first together with his father, later by himself. Széchenyi, like members of the Batthyány family, sold wool to him (Széchenyi, *Diary*, February 10, 1836, etc.). A few years later his father also converted to the Protestant faith. Samuel Wodianer and his two sons, Mór and Albert received a title of nobility in 1844 and the name "kapriorai". A cargo boat in their family arms represented the merchandise they delivered on the Danube, tobacco and grain. From now on Samuel and Mór even more so played a leading role in the commerce of Pest, in the Union of Wholesale Merchants, in several enterprises. Mór was among the founders of the Hungarian Commercial Bank, cosponsored the construction of the Chain Bridge and the Cylinder Mill. He gave not only of his own money but took a loan from the Rothschild Bank in Vienna. He sponsored several foundations. "He makes me nervous—he is so clever and smart", wrote Széchenyi (*Diary*, August 18, 1845), who was in daily contact with Wodianer on account of the bridge and railway construction. By now the doors of the Casino opened in front of him and his family. He had lunch with Széchenyi, they visited Óbuda together. Wodianer became a Hungarian magnate, or almost.

106. Albert Wodianer

Samuel Wodianer left the former Kemnitzer House to his older son, Mór. The building stood on the lower Danube bank (Aldunasor, Nagy Híd / Deák Ferenc utca-Kis Híd / Türr István utca). Initially it housed a famous café and later, after the 1838 flood, a restaurant dedicated to the "Angol királynő" (Queen of England, that is, Queen Victoria). The building suffered damages during the siege of Buda in 1849, but it was reconstructed by József Hild (1852) and finally, after the mid-1850s, it served as the home of Ferenc Deák (1803–1876) until his death. (The building was demolished in 1940. Today an office building stands in its place.)

The acquisition of the Kemnitzer House is a story with an interesting morale. In 1835 Mór Wodianer bought the house called "Two Turks" from the heirs of the original owner, the tanner János Kemnitzer. In 1844 he bought the "Queen of England" but he had to return the "Two Turks" to the Kemnitzer heirs because the initials (J.K.) of their father were still visible in the coat of arms decorating the facade of the house. (The emblem was held by two Turkish figures—hence the name of the building.) But in 1848 Samuel Wodianer paid a high price to buy back the "Two Turks". He moved the offices of the Commercial Bank into the building and changed the initials in the arms to S.W. Clearly, both father and son strove not only for wealth and property but prestige, after a while mostly prestige.

After the revolutions of 1848 Mór Wodianer, already a Viennese banker, gained some influence in the financial and business life of the Austro-Hungarian Monarchy, particularly in railway construction and steam navigation. He was made an Austrian (1863) and later a Hungarian baron (1863). His brother, Albert Wodianer (1818–1898) inherited the company in Pest from their father. He was mostly involved in banking, hence his nickname, "the Hungarian Rothschild". He was a member of the Upper House and was made a baron (1886).

The middle son of Fülöp Wodianer, Rudolf (1788–1856), became active in business in Pest already in his father's life-time. He traded mostly in wool and grains. He set up the first wool sorting manufacture of Pest (1839) which increased the profit on foreign sales of wool. Not counting the rabbi of Győr he was the only member of the grain merchant branch of the Wodianers who kept the Jewish faith. Because of this he suffered certain disadvantages, for instance he was not allowed to transfer his property to his own name, not even in 1843. He owned a beautiful Classicist style two-story house on the lower Danube bank (Aldunasor) and another one to the North of it, on the upper Danube bank (Feldunasor), at the northern corner of the Kirakodó tér (today Roosevelt tér). The latter one can be seen on one of the colored frame-pictures (F. Weiss) on the map series of Vasquez and is noted as his property (1838). He bought it a year earlier, right after it was built. It was designed by József Hild (Tänzer House, 3 Akadémia utca–5 Arany János utca). Rudolf was not as successful as his brother and cousins, either in business or in social affairs. His rough character must have contributed to his relative failure. He did not treat his wife, who came from an equally rich grain merchant family and bore him ten children, as an equal human being, ignoring Jewish tradition and violating the unwritten laws of civil behavior. After 1853 he traded in grain and worked as a banker. There were rumors that he was unfair in business affairs. His son, Béla Wodianer (1831–1896) served as a captain in the Corps of Engineers in the War of Independence of 1848/49. After the war he bought himself some property in Maglód from his earnings, hence his noblemans' name *maglódi* when he received a title of nobility in 1869.

107. Béla Wodianer

The founder of the other branch of the Wodianers, the book-dealers, Fülöp (1822–1899), was born in Hódmezővásárhely in Southeastern Hungary. He was named after the grain merchant Wodianer who probably died only a few years before his birth. If this was the case, the other Fülöp Wodianer, the one from Szeged, must have been his uncle. He learned the printing trade in Pest, he worked in print shops in Pozsony and Vienna. In 1842 he became the printing director of *Pesti Hírlap*, a newspaper published by Lajos Kossuth (1802–1894) at Egyetemi Nyomda (University Press). In 1848 he was the printer in charge of Government publications as well as of the mint. Wearing a uniform, he accompanied the Hungarian Government to Debrecen, then Arad in its last days (his leg was wounded by a bullet in battle). After the collapse of the War of Independence of 1848/49 he threw the mint into the river Maros. He spent a few years in Arad before returning to Pest (1855). Here he opened a new print shop (1856), bought the publishing house of Robert Lampel (1874) and, by the second half of the nineteenth century, his company grew to become a most influential newspaper and book publishing house. In those days publisher, printing house and bookstore were usually united under one roof. Wodianer printed Hebrew characters from the very beginning, following in the steps of the University Press. Toward the end he spelled his name Vodiáner, though the company remained Wodianer. Its locations were Sarkantyús utca 9 / Megyeház tér 9 and later Erzsébet tér 4, both in the elegant Lipótváros. Towards the end of his life Wodianer / Vodiáner and his sons received a title of nobility (1897). The Jewish press could always count on him and his company as good business partners. They were the publishers of *Magyar Izraelita* [Hungarian Israelite] (1861), *Izraelita Néplap* [Israelite Newspaper] (1869), and initially published the yearbooks of IMIT [Israelite Hungarian Literary Society]. But they published other popular dailies, too, including *Magyarország*, *Magyar Újság*, *Kis Újság*, *Budapest*, etc.

Arthur Wodianer (1860–1921), the founder's son, followed in his father's footsteps and went to learn the trade abroad. At home he joined his father in directing the Wodianer (Lampel) book-dealer company. He established a name by publishing school textbooks. In the 1890s the company merged with the Franklin Társulat, which was heir to Landerer and Heckenast's famous publishing house.

(Back in 1848, on March 15, it was they who printed the "12 points", the proclamation of the Pest revolution.) They continued to publish Jewish periodicals, the *Magyar Zsidó Szemle* [Hungarian Jewish Review] (1884–1948) among others, and, after the turn of the century (from 1901 on), the *Évkönyv* [Yearbook] of IMIT. In the latter the name Franklin only appeared in the colophon. During the first half of the twentieth century Franklin was the main publisher of the Hungarian classics. Its headquarters was in the inner city (Egyetem utca 4, today corner of Reáltanoda and Károlyi Mihály utca) After 1909 the literary editor of Franklin was Aladár Schöpflin, the renowned critic of the great generation of writers around the literary journal *Nyugat* which promoted modernism. During World War II they did not cease to support great literature and they helped writers who suffered discrimination because of their Jewish roots.

The Wodianer House (Városligeti fasor 45, designed by Emil Vidor, 1907) was lately in the possession of the family.

Márk Rózsavölgyi (1787-1848)

Márk (Márkus) Mordechai Rosenthal was born to a Jewish merchant family in 1787 in Balassagyarmat. He was the last great musician to compose *verbunkos*, the Hungarian recruiting music. His artistic career started in Prague where he learned to play the piano on an advanced level. He earned the money for his piano education with calligraphic writing. He achieved success as an instrumental soloist, but he arrived to Pest (1806) as a salesman, not a musician. Soon he became known as a fiddler and composer (1808). A sign of his popularity is that his piece called "Hatvágás" was attributed to János Bihari (1764–1827), the famous Gypsy musician, whom he met only afterwards. Bihari was playing in the restaurant called "Vörös Ökör" in the courtyard of the Károlyi–Trattner House (Úri utca, today Petőfi Sándor utca) when he suddenly heard the sound of a violin coming from the street. He ran out and found Rosenthal there, giving a serenade. Instead of rivalry they developed a close friendship, learned Hungarian popular folk songs from each other.

For a long time "Mordchele" Rosenthal was known as the soloist of Gypsy bands. Hiring Jewish musicians for all kinds of occasions was common in Hungary, as we know from the poet Mihály Csokonai Vitéz. In his epic poem (*Dorottya*, 1803) it is Izsák (Isaac) and the Jews of Toponár, an invented place-name, who play at the carnival of Somogy county. Later Mordechai Rosenthal was the first violinist of the orchestra of the Hungarian group that played in the German Theater in Aranykéz

108. Portrait of Márk Rózsavölgyi. Lithograph by Miklós Barabás, 1844

utca. After 1814 he performed in other theaters as well, in Baja, Pécs, Fehérvár, Veszprém. He got invitations from all over Hungary. In 1817 a Gypsy musician called Csóri achieved wide popularity with his tunes at the balls of Füred (today Balatonfüred). By 1824 Rosenthal was a famous musician, he participated in a musical festival at Balaton-Almádi (today spelled as Balatonalmádi). This is when Gábor Sebestyén, the judge of Veszprém county and a "Renaissance man" named him Rózsavölgyi (Hungarian translation of Rosenthal), though officially he could not change his name until 1846. In 1825 at the Diet of Pozsony and in 1827 in Miskolc at the ball on the occasion of the Lord Lieutenant's inauguration he achieved great success playing verbunkos music "in the Hungarian style", "in the style of highway men" and on Hungarian themes. His best genres were the *csárdás* and *palotás* (dynamic and slow Hungarian dances, respectively) but he played ring dances and mixels, too. He was the one who established the classical structure of the *palotás*. In 1831 he moved to Pest for good. True, when he applied for a permit to settle (1833) and enclosed a letter of support from the Jewish community, the authorities of Pest rejected his request after some hesitation. The "Jewish Gypsy" played in Pest too, though only at the balls of the Casino, still in its original location on the Rak-piac / Kirakodó tér, the quay, on the second floor of the palace built by József Hild (Merchants' House, later: Lloyd Palace) which was destroyed during World War II. At one of his

109. "The National Theater in Pest". Drawing by Rudolf Alt, 1845

last performances (1846) Márk Rózsavölgyi was already referred to as "the old Gypsy musician with his band". His *csárdás* melodies were published by the Casino. He was the best and most prolific Hungarian *csárdás* composer, with over two hundred pieces in his oeuvre.

He was hired by the Hungarian Theater of Pest (National Theater) right from the first season in its new building (1837). The Classicist building was constructed by Mátyás Zitterbarth, near the Hatvani Gate, Kerepesi (today Rákóczi) út, on a plot of land donated by Antal Grassalkovich for the National Playhouse. Two of Rózsavölgyi's pieces were played at the opening performance (August 22, 1837). The playbill states, "... and the 'National Sounds of Joy Upon the Opening of the Hungarian Theater of Pest' by Rózsavölgyi will be performed. Between the Overture[5] and Belisar[6] a Hungarian dance will follow, taught by Mr. Szöllősy, music by Rózsavölgyi."

> "That not only Gypsies, but also Jews can become eminent Hungarian musicians is best exemplified by good old Rózsavölgyi, our beloved *Márkus bácsi* [Oncle Marc], who is also of the Eastern race. As a famous Hungarian composer and musician he Magyarized his German name Rosenthal, but he never denied his faith."
>
> (Imre Vahot, *Emlékiratai* [Memoirs], 1881)

The Hungarian cultural scene, imbued with national awakening, celebrated Rózsavölgyi's popular music. When Béni Egressy plagiarized his piece called "Honfihűség" [Loyalty to the Fatherland], critics stood on Rózsavölgyi's side. He also composed national music with Jewish themes, for instance to a poem by Mihály Heilprin (1823–1888), rabbi of Miskolc, who moved there from Poland. The poem, "Jewish song", followed the format of Mihály Vörösmarty's "Fóti dal". He dedicated "the beautiful music" to the Society to Disseminate the Hungarian Language among the Israelites of the Country (1846).

Sándor Petőfi, the Hungarian national poet, was an admirer of Rózsavölgyi's art, and a close friend of his. He praised Rózsavölgyi's performance (he used to play in the Pillvax Café, too) in *Magyar Divatlap* [Hungarian Fashion News] (1844) and a farewell poem upon the death (to cancer) of the musician.

Prose translation of the poem:

> "Old musician, what have I done to you, – That you just want to make me sad? – I was lamenting at the sound of your fiddle, – Oh, it does not sound anymore, and this is more bitter to me, – This is more bitter to me! – Wake up, old musician, my old friend, – Let us lament and cheer over your song, – You knew exactly – Where the heart of the Hungarian lies, – The heart of the Hungarian."
>
> (Sándor Petőfi, "Rózsavölgyi halálára" [Upon the Death of Rózsavölgyi], 1848)

---

[5] Mihály Vörösmarty, *Árpád ébredése* [Árpád's Awakening]. (Árpád was chieftain of Hungarian tribes during the occupation of the Carpathian basin in the ninth century C.E.)

[6] A play by Eduard von Schenk (1788–1841) (1826), staged in the translation of János Kis (1770–1846).

110. The grave of Márk Rózsavölgyi in the former Jewish cemetery on Váci út. Drawing by Gergely Pörge, 1908

His grave is now in the Jewish cemetery in Kozma utca.

The Rózsavölgyi & Co. music publishing company was founded around 1850 by the musician's son, Gyula Rózsavölgyi, and Norbert Grinzweil. The succeeding owners retained the name of the company. In 1858 they bought the music publishing company of József Wagner which published the works of Hungarian composers, including Rózsavölgyi himself. During the second half of the nineteenth century Rózsavölgyi & Co. grew to be the largest music publishing company of Hungary, official publisher of Ferenc Liszt, Ferenc Erkel, Mihály Mosonyi and others, organizer of premieres (Liszt's "Esztergom Mass", "Coronation Mass", "Legend of Saint Elizabeth"). After 1910 the new owners published the works of Béla Bartók, Zoltán Kodály, Ernő Dohnányi, Leó Weiner and László Lajtha. In the 1920s it was Rózsavölgyi & Co. who founded the Budapest Orchestra, they organized memorable concerts.

The Rózsavölgyi Music Shop (5 Szervita tér) is world famous even today for the great variety of its merchandise of scores and recordings. The building, most of which serves as a dwelling house today, was designed by Béla Lajtha (1911). Its facade is decorated with glazed brick friezes constructed by geometrical motifs borrowed from Hungarian folk art. Its original interior was designed by Lajos Kozma (1912).

Mór Freund

At no. 15 of Király utca, on the second floor of the vast, elegant building on the corner with Fekete Sas utca / Holló utca lived Mór Freund, a grain- and flour-merchant, founder of the *Gabonacsarnok* [Grain Exchange] of Pest (located on the ground floor of the Lloyd Palace). He moved to Király utca after the War of Independence of 1948/49. During the war he delivered flour to the Hungarian army's depot at Paks and, naturally, went bankrupt. Then he moved to Pest, where he opened a flour store and sold wholesale and retail, and became rich. He was among the first ones to buy a seat in the brand new Dohány synagogue. Later he moved to Lipótváros to be near the Gabonacsarnok. One of his sons was Vilmos Freund, an architect.

As the life of Freund exemplifies, adjustment to civil society, social mobility often went along with geographical mobility, moving away from the original homes. The wealthiest Jews broke out of their territorial segregation, moving to areas where the bourgeoisie lived, to Lipótváros and the distinguished Sugár / Andrássy út. But the majority of Jews stayed in the area surrounding Király utca, which remained the center of Jewish society.

(7) The Pest Reform Society

Back in the late eighteenth century the Valero brothers, István and Tamás, Italians who settled in Hungary, founded their famous silk factory on a piece of sandy ground Southeast of Király utca (Király utca–Akácfa utca–Dob utca–Gyár utca / Liszt Ferenc tér). They planted mulberry trees next to the factory and bred their own silkworms. The factory building was designed by Mátyás Zitterbarth, sr. Later (1824) some additions were made to the building, including annexes and a courtyard, under the direction of József Hild. The company grew quickly and soon the building proved exiguous. The price of land in the near-by lower part of Király utca was favorably high, so Antal Valero, the owner at the time, moved the company to Lipótváros and sold the factory building together with the plot of land. The Valero family kept living in the neighborhood, their former house, a nice Classicist building, still stands (8 Kürt utca).

This neighborhood was considered suburban in comparison to Király utca. It was here, in the Neo-Classicist building of the Valero Courtyard, "built in the fashionable Italian style" (*Feldmanns Wegweiser*, Pesth, 1859), behind the spacious, sunny courtyard with trees and flowers, where the radically modern Jewish Reform Community of Ignác Einhorn (later Ede Horn) (1825–1875), founded under the impact of the March 15 revolution of 1848, survived until 1852.

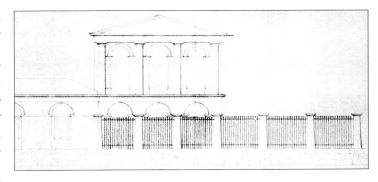

The Valero Courtyard, as the complex was called, had some Jewish ties even earlier. In the previous year (1847), during the "general famine", the Jewish community opened a "volunteer workers' house" in the factory building so that "healthy but starving people may earn their nourishment by work". About a hundred people were kept busy with fur and wool peeling. In addition, the income helped maintain a needlework school for poor girls.

The Reform congregation also had some history by then, namely in Buda, where two years earlier, on May 17, 1846, a group of young Jews, authorized by chief rabbi Löw Schwab founded the *Chevrat Tiferet Ha-Dat* (*hevrat tif'eret ha-dat*, "society to promote the glory of faith") whose goal was to introduce "up-to-date religious services (*zeitgemässer Gottesdienst*) in Buda". The community leadership acknowledged the new *hevrah* immediately and assigned the school as a prayer-room to them. Later, however, the leadership declined the request of the Society to rent the room for the whole year. They were only permitted to use the school during the High Holidays. Yet Ignác Einhorn, the young rabbinical student, preached at the services of the Buda youth society regularly, every second week, from the fall of 1846 on, and occasionally at the Öntőház utca *minyan* as well.

But the reform of ritual had even deeper roots. The Diet of 1839/40 which passed the Act XXIX of 1840 expressed that certain changes in the Jewish ritual were desirable. Of these requirements the use of the Hungarian language seemed the least problematic for Jews. On the initiative of some Jewish medical students from Pest (1843), the *Magyarító Egylet* [Magyarizing Society] or *A honi izraeliták között magyar nyelvet terjesztő pesti egylet* [Society to Disseminate the Hungarian Language among the Israelites of the Country] was founded (May 8, 1844). Its president was Fülöp Jakobovics, the director of the Jewish hospital, and it was supported by R. Schwab, too. The Society had over 400 members. They held lectures, opened a library and a reading room. The librarian was Ignác Einhorn. Initially the headquarters of the Society were in the house called "Jó Pásztor" [Good Shepherd] (today 21 Király utca), designed by Mihály Pollack (1833), later they moved to 12 Két Sas utca (today Sas utca), to the second floor of the Prix House (then only three story high), designed by József Düttrich (1819). They rented both places. In 1845 they issued an appeal:

"The knowledge of the Hungarian language is unavoidable for anyone dwelling in this country. (...) And since the language of the homeland

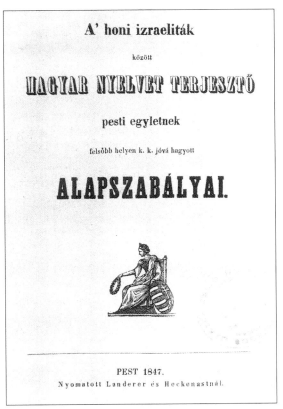

already relegated all other languages into the background in social interaction, those who are not familiar with it will pay a high price for their negligence or indifference. Namely, they will be deprived of the possibility of participating in more cultured conversation."

The new society expected "Hungarian sermons at services on the Sabbath". In a letter written in German, dated October 31, 1847, the leadership of the community agreed to their request but they strongly opposed any other reform. And yet there was no *droshe* in Hungarian at the Orczy House, not even in the school in its courtyard building.

After the revolution of March 15, on September 27, 1848, on the eve of *Rosh ha-Shanah*, Einhorn and his friends, some upper-middle-class merchants from Lipótváros, started with the services in a religious organization bearing the name *Magyar Izráelita Középponti Reformegylet* [Hungarian Israelite Central Reform Society] or *Genossenschaft für Reform im Judenthum* in German. The organization was founded already on July 8. Einhorn published a pamphlet delineating his reform ideas (*Grundprinzipien einer geläuterten Reform im*

113. Portrait of Ignác Einhorn (Ede Horn). Painting by József Borsos

Judenthum [Principles of a Refined Reform among the Jews], Pest, 1848). They rented and consecrated the abandoned building of the silk factory in the Valero Courtyard's central building, starting October 1, for their religious services which they held on Sundays (!). They did not consider their Society a closed, autonomous organization, but a "cult-leadership". They omitted almost all typically Jewish elements from the services, the Shofar and the prayer shawl, the *Sukkah* and the four species used at *Sukkot*, the circumcision (within four years 70–80 children were born to the families belonging to the Reform Society), they omitted the redemption of the firstborn, the Sabbath, they decided that holidays be started in the morning, and not at sundown, on the eve

before the actual day of the holiday, they omitted all second days of holidays, they stopped renting benches in the synagogue and, after having read the Torah in Hebrew, they translated it into German or Hungarian during services. All this happened in the spirit of the radical reforms of Abraham Geiger (1810–1874) in Germany, but occasionally went even further than the program of German reformers. Einhorn's efforts to create a secular frame for Judaism is clear. In April 1848 he even founded a short-lived weekly, *Der ungarische Israelit*, and being among the leaders of the *Magyarító Egylet*, he supported the publication of the *Első magyar zsidó naptár és évkönyv 1848-ik szökőévre* (1848) [First Hungarian Jewish Calendar and Yearbook for the Leap Year 1848] which was published by the *A honi izraeliták között magyar nyelvet terjesztő pesti egylet* [Society for Propagating Hungarian among the Israelites of the Homeland] and printed at

114. Memorial tablet of Ede Horn on the house where he was born (Vágújhely), by Kornél Sámuel, 1912

Landerer and Heckenast Press. The *First Jewish Calendar* included a portrait and a biography of Áron Chorin whom they considered the initiator of religious reforms in Hungary. Einhorn expressed his views about religious reform in a booklet (*Grundprinzipien einer geläuterten Reform im Judenthum*, Pest, 1848). Half a century later Sándor Büchler wrote about it: "The description of the function of the Jewish religion is a beautiful and attractive task that any Jewish religion textbook could take up with pride." Einhorn celebrated the Declaration of Independence (April 14, 1849) in a great sermon held on May 27, 1849.

Einhorn himself participated in the very last phase of the 1848/49 War of Independence as a field rabbi, with the rank of captain. His appointment is dated on September 11, 1849. On Einhorn's initiative, the Commander-in-chief of the last stronghold of the Army, of the Komárom Fortress, General György Klapka issued an order that all Jewish soldiers be allowed to celebrate the next Feast of Tabernacles (*Sukkot*) two days later, on September 17, 1849, in the Lutheran church. Einhorn did not leave his post until the very last day (October 3), so he had to escape after the surrender of the Fortress. He found his way to Brussels and married a woman of the Roman Catholic faith. He raised his son as a Jew, his daughter as a Roman Catholic. He achieved some fame with his knowledge in economics, finances and commercial law. After the Austro-Hungarian *Ausgleich* or compromise (1867) he returned to Hungary, already with a newly Magyarized name, as Ede Horn (1869), assuming a political role. He was elected to Parliament and, in 1875, he was appointed secretary of state in the Ministry of Commerce. He was the first Jewish official in the Government. He died the same year.

His grave is in the cemetery in Salgótarjáni utca. After his name on the tombstone it is written: "Royal Hungarian Secretary of State." Before World War II a street was named after Ede Horn in Terézváros. Earlier it was called Dávid utca, today its name is Weiner Leó utca—after the famous Jewish composer (1885–1960).

The reform, of course, could not strike roots. Or better said, it was not allowed to. The extent of religious modernism that Einhorn wished to introduce was too much even for the reformists. Löw Schwab attacked Einhorn's program in a pamphlet. R. Béla Bernstein (1868 – Auschwitz, 1944), an outstanding historian, called it a "religious upheaval".

The successor of Einhorn as rabbi of the Reform Society, David Einhorn (1809–1879), who in spite of his name was not related to Ignác Einhorn, occupied his position for but a short time. His inaugural speech was held in January, 1852, in the synagogue in the Valero Courtyard. Masses of people came to listen to him. (Three sermons of Einhorn, including this one, were found among his papers and published in the United States decades after his death.) Earlier activities of Einhorn made it clear that his ideas were close to Geiger's. For instance, he maintained that circumcision was an unnecessary anachronism. If you are born a Jew you will be a Jew even without a *berit / bris*. Soon it was R. Schwab himself who appealed to the *Königliche Statthalterei* against Einhorn. The latter's organization was declared an illegal sect and dissolved on October 25, 1852.

115. Portrait of David Einhorn, Pest, 1852

After the sudden prohibition Einhorn emigrated to America. His stops included, the *Har Sinai* synagogue in Baltimore, he sojourned in Philadelphia for a while and later went to New York, to the *Adas Yeshurun* synagogue (14 Elridge Street) at the foot of Manhattan Bridge, the predecessor of *Beth El* synagogue. Initially he experienced some difficulties amidst the American congregations, too, for he opposed slavery. Einhorn was among the initiators of the American religious reform. His Hebrew–German prayer-book (*Olat ha-tamid*, Baltimore, 1856–1858) was the model for future American Reform prayer-books. Einhorn participated in founding the first American rabbinical seminary, Maimonides College (1865). It did not survive, but a similar reform rabbinical seminary, the Hebrew Union College of Cincinnati, Ohio, was set up. Einhorn was a renowned preacher already before he came to Pest, but in the United States he was considered a religious genius. His modifications in the ritual were governed by the thesis that no lie may be pronounced in the religious service and prayer. Since prayers are archaic, some of their statements are no longer true, therefore they have to be replaced by new texts.

There is no doubt that Einhorn, like his predecessor, had to leave for political reasons. After the War of Independence of 1848/49 radical religious reformers were easily mistaken for political radicals and these were renounced by Jews as well as the Austrian authorities. Even R. Löw (Arszlán) Schwab who, upon the Declaration of Independence, had been asked by the Pest municipal authorities to hold services, and he did, in the early 1850s occasionally cooperated with the Austrian authorities, with the officials of the interior minister Baron Alexander von Bach (1813–1893) in Pest. In plain words, he denounced Einhorn in order to protect the Jews of Pest from the danger of "splintering into disorganized sects", even if by a *malshinut*, denunciation.

(8) In 1848, in front of the Orczy House

As a matter of fact, it was in Király utca that most of the anti-Jewish atrocities took place in 1848. On April 19, the second day of Passover, which has always been a holiday of the Ashkenazim, a throng of people calling themselves "Hungarian patriots" demonstrated against the Jews in front of the City Hall in the inner city. The agitation went on for days; a speaker incited the mob saying that rents were high because too many Jews had settled in Pest. At the council of the guilds and other meetings dismissal of the Jews from the National Guard was demanded. Furthermore, they even talked about the expulsion of the Jews who settled "illegally" after 1840 or arrived recently.

That day the agitated demonstrators penetrated the Jewish quarter. The mob, which assembled at the foot of Király utca, attacked ex-lieutenant Adolf Lőwinger, a member of the university's "equality battalion" at this time, who kept guard in front of the Orczy House to prevent the mob from looting the shops. False news was spread that the Jews in Király utca threw stones at passers-by and poured hot oil on them. The uniformed lieutenant tried to calm down the crowd. In response, he was beaten and thrown to the ground; only the fast intervention of the military saved his life.

The next day the mob started beating up Jews at the foot of Király utca. They ruthlessly struck everybody they caught, even women. Many ran in the direction of the hay-market (*Heu Platz* or Széna tér, today Kálvin tér), others found refuge in the brand new Calvinist church, at whose gate the pastor Pál Török (1808–1883), the future bishop, stopped the mob with unsheathed sword. (Török had already protected Jews earlier, both verbally and in writing: "Their virtues", he said in 1839, "are needed for the desirable cohesion of bourgeois society, the best means to create prosperity.")

Eventually only the energetic measures of the prime minister, Count Lajos Batthyány (1806–1849), prevented the disturbances from turning into a general political crisis. Batthyány himself spoke to the crowd, dispatched troops to maintain order, and proposed solutions to the cabinet, but he also heeded the report of the committee of the Pest municipal council which investigated the case and declared: "obliging Jews to serve in the National Guard, a noble but burdensome task, is not considered." Their inclusion in civil and political rights was not recommended because of "the separatist principles and way of life followed by them". In any case, the chairman of the Committee in Charge of Silence and Order forbade landlords in Pest to lodge Jews who were without a permit of settlement.

On the orders of the prime minister the Jews "voluntarily" withdrew from service in the National Guard; their battalion, led by Mihály Táncsics (1799–1884), who had been freed from jail shortly before and hoisted on the shoulders of the Pest youth, simply dissolved.

In September, after the Croatian invasion, Jews would not only be admitted but recruited into the National Guard.

In his diary Sándor Petőfi (1823–1849) noted about the anti-Jewish tension after similar disturbances in Pozsony a month earlier (March 20, 1848):

"The unity that has dominated the capital so far is on the verge of dissolution. I accuse you, German citizens, before the nation and generations yet to be born of having broken it! (...) They declared first that they would not admit Jews in their ranks of the National Guard, they were the first to spoil the purity of the banner of March 15! (...) But it is most depressing that everything, even the most shameful issues, sooner or later find their apostles. Some pettifoggers became zealous advocates of these revolting persecutions of Jews and are now preaching against them far and wide. These despicable false prophets accuse those that side with the truth of being bribed by the Jews. The wretched! They do not know, or they are just not willing to believe there are people more honest than themselves..."

116. Recruitment of a Jew into the National Guard, 1848

These noisy events did not come out of the blue. Citizens of Pest turned against the Jews right after March 15, the sacred day of liberty. Many Jews entered the National Guard formed on the second day of the revolution—after all, they supported the fight for liberty. But some citizens of Pest started to fear that Jews would want equality immediately. A merchant of Miskolc, whose name has not come down to us, must have come to Pest for the St. Joseph day's fair. Here is what he wrote to the principal of the Jewish school of his city in a German letter (March 17, 1848):

"When citizens here were certain that nothing could threaten the order, some people started to demand that Jews should withdraw from the National Guard (Nationalgarde), and objected to the equality of Jews. The students found out about this and they assembled. They called upon the Jews to be brave and do their best to win. (...) Some citizens tried to find arguments in the Talmud and the rituals, only Klauzál renounced them saying that they should not try to catch fish in a dry pond, if they do not like the Talmud and the Bible they should not purchase or read them. (...) Kunewalder [the president of the Jewish community] submitted his resignation from this office at the City Magistrate remarking that henceforth we were one community. This was accepted with hurrahs (mit Ellyenruf).[7] Kunewalder will join the delegation to Pozsony tomorrow."

The address of Lajos Kossuth in Parliament, which played a part in sparking the revolution in Vienna, was translated into German by a Hungarian Jew, Mór Kálozdi (Kaufmann), and was taken to Vienna by Miksa Goldner (he was to become the first physician-lieutenant in the National Guard). On March 15, while the flyer with the "12 points"—the program of the revolution—was being printed on the freshly confiscated press of Landerer and Heckenast printing house (at 3 Hatvani utca, today Kossuth Lajos utca) "a young physician of the Israelite faith" gave a speech before the crowd waiting outside. According to a famous chronicler of the event, the novelist Mór Jókai, his name was Kauders, or perhaps Kornfeld / Kronfeld, as others know, later Baron Frigyes tolcsvai Korányi (1828–1913), the famous university professor at the School of Medicine.

A few days later (on March 17) the "managing committee" of the Jews of Hungary and of Transylvania let everybody know in an announcement:

"Brave Israelite students as well as some other Israelite inhabitants from various towns have merged with all others from the very beginning. (...) They are Hungarians and not Jews, for they and we are only to be considered as a distinct denomination when in our prayer-houses we address the Almighty with our grati-

[7] A Hungarian word in the German text, Ellyen / éljen, "vivat".

tude for the grace upon the fatherland and upon us, but in every other path of life all distinction, political as well as civil and social, must be eliminated, and we are merely patriots, Hungarians, since the country has admitted us as equals with all other inhabitants."

Several Jews, Jónás Kunewalder among them, were elected to the "Board of Public Bravery" (a civil authority of the revolution). In a short while, however, Kossuth retreated in the Parliament—obviously as a result of the events in Pozsony. "Prejudice exists and even the gods fight against its blindness (...) in vain." The Diet of 1847/48 dissolved without admitting Jews into the "heart of the fatherland". The poet Mihály Vörösmarty wrote on May 13, 1848 as follows:

"There can be no more bitter mockery of the equality and brotherhood advocated than the world-wide hatred and fury against Jews, which probably rages in its wildest form in our country. After the first pure days of liberty, in which the noblest pearls of human emotions sparkled, the scum broke to the foreground, obscuring the sunshine of the idea of rights with its false demands. (...) In the name of equality they first of all began to beat and loot Jews. (...) The authorities themselves were occupied with superior tasks and thus had to give in to hatred for a while. Fearing disturbances, the otherwise liberal Diet acted in the matter with uncertain hands."

Ignác Einhorn wrote on April 10, 1848:

"Our Christian compatriots get heated about liberty, and in the flaming blaze they forge new chains for the Jew! They let the flag of equality fly high, while under its cover they gather to confine Jews in a new ghetto. They wield the sacred sword for unity and fraternity, and make the very same sacred sword block the way of Jews to the Paradise of freedom."

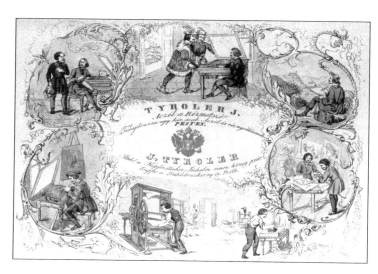

117. An advertisement for József Tyroler, engraver

Even the nationalities rebelling against the revolutionary Government attacked Jews. In Zenta, early in the summer of 1848, the Serbs slaughtered the majority of the Jewish community, among them Jakab (Jacob) Münz, the son of R. Moshe Münz / Minc. The municipal council of Pest deprived the Jewish community of its right of local authority (collecting the "mandatory tax", etc.) in a resolution and granted them only the status of "religious community" (December 21, 1848).

Jews from Pest as well as other cities and towns of the country took part and distinguished themselves in the war of independence in large numbers. The bank notes (called "Kossuth-notes") issued on October 15, 1848 by the Defense Committee were designed by József Tyroler (Tyróler) (1822-1854) and printed at the Hungarian Commercial Bank of Pest and later, in the spring of 1849, in Debrecen by Fülöp Wodianer. (Tyroler not only designed bank notes in the service of liberty but, in April 1848, he engraved in steel the portraits of Lajos Kossuth, Lajos Batthyány and Ferenc Deák, as well as a drawing of Sándor Petőfi by Miklós Barabás.) In May, in response to Kossuth's call, Jews of Pest even removed the decorations of the Torah scrolls in the synagogues, and offered 856 *lat* (ca. 33 pounds) of silver; the Hevrah Kaddishah offered an additional 1193 *lat* (over 40 pounds) of silver for the fatherland. This, of course, did not include the contributions of the Buda and Óbuda communities. A newspaper (*Életképek*, May 28, 1848) wrote that (Mór) Wodianer alone gave over 200 pounds of silver to the country. Early in the fall—according to Károly Eötvös, a great story-teller—a horse-dealer from Pest,

Arnold Brachfeld, acquired horses sufficient for a whole hussar regiment, altogether 900, in four days and delivered them to the courtyard of the Károly Barracks (Károly Eötvös, *Amit nem tud a történetírás* [What Historians Do Not Know], 1901).

A petition to the Hungarian Diet, from July 24, 1848, says:

"Being convinced of the justice of our matter we hope that you are also guided by justice when dealing with our case. Justice, which brings the equality of rights to all citizens irrespective of their differences, not just mercy, strange regulations, special rights and advantages."

In the winter and spring of 1849, during the siege of Buda and the War of Independence between the Hungarian army and Austria, Jews of Óbuda supported the National Guard by all means, including military service and financial contribution. Duke Alfred Windisch-Grätz sr., the commander-in-chief of the Austrian army, proclaimed (February 11, 1849), that Jews of Buda, Pest, and first of all, of Óbuda, in case they supported the revolutionary Government, that time in Debrecen, would be severely punished. Out of fear, 404 Jews of Óbuda signed a declaration of fidelity. Nevertheless, some Jews were sentenced to death (out of mercy, their death sentence was changed to 8–12 years "in heavy iron").

118. Portrait of Ferenc Deák. Etching by József Tyroler, 1848

A fine of 40,000 forints was imposed on the Jews. A joke circulating in Pest that time said: "As the King of Jerusalem, His Holyness the Emperor [Francis Joseph] is entitled to make the Jews pay his daily expenses."

The Habsburg dynasty decided to settle the legal status of Jews before the Hungarian legislation, even if they were motivated by political goals. Francis Joseph's constitution of Olmütz (March 4, 1849) granted the Jews full legal equality. The Diet of Hungary passed the Act of emancipation only at its very last session on July 29, 1849. The Act, submitted by the minister of interior Bertalan Szemere in Szeged, declared that "All persons of the Mosaic faith born or legally settled within the boundaries of the Hungarian state possess all of the same political and civil rights as inhabitants of any other religion." This happened exactly on *Tish'ah be-Av*, the day when the destruction of the Jerusalem Temple is mourned. The Act was moot, there was no time to put it into effect.

Bertalan Szemere writes in his *Memoirs*, 1853/54:

"The Jews, this people exiled by Christianity and the whole world, joined the defenders of human rights in masses. In spite of their being the only people that did not share in the new public freedom, they struggled for a constitution whose benefits they did not enjoy. Emancipation was declared only in July, 1849, when everything was lost. It was not a motive for the participation of Jews in the struggle, but a reward for their merits."

It might not be a coincidence that Jewish emigration to America began exactly in 1848/49 and from those two cities where atrocities took place, that is, from Pest and Pozsony.

A Central Emigration Society was founded in Pest in May, 1848 with an "appeal to the Jews of Hungary for emigration to America". In a poem Ignác Reich associated the emigration of Jews directly with their expulsion from the National Guard. "There I am free to wear the sword of protection, / There I may put on my breast the cockade of freedom." As we may expect, an anti-emigration manifesto appeared, too, written by a certain Sándor Herczfeld. "We are not going to America, we are staying right here!" (Pest, 1848):

119. Memorial of the Jewish soldiers who fell in the War of Independence of 1848/49

"We are not going to America, we are staying here, and if we are driven out of the towns and villages by the murderers, robbed of our properties earned with sweat and blood by some cowardly thieves, then we will go to the caves, the forests, live on roots, but we will not emigrate with a faint heart, we will not leave our beloved sweet homeland because it is being threatened by grave danger..."

Those who left were to try their luck. They hoped to find better opportunities than those they left behind, after the riots of the recent past. Besides the freedom of worship in the United States, many were driven there because their traditions were not threatened by reforms. In Pest a special board of the Emigration Society disseminated information regarding the circumstances (travel, settlement, possibility of acquiring land), kept record of those wishing to emigrate, raised funds to help defray the expenses. Within two or three years thousands of Jews left Austria-Hungary for the United States. The political exiles who had been fighting in Kossuth's army tried to reach the western hemisphere via Italy or Turkey. Like other Hungarian immigrants, from Ellis Island the Jews also made their way to New York, Philadelphia and Cleveland. Most of those remaining in New York settled on the Lower East Side. Though their mother tongue was Yiddish rather than Hungarian, they always joined the Hungarian societies or founded their own Hungarian–Jewish ones. Along with their new American identity, they remained true to their two former identities as well, to their Jewish roots and to the Hungarian culture, one for a short while, another for long.

IV. The Jewish Triangle in Pest

By the mid-nineteenth century a dense Jewish quarter evolved in Teréz- and Erzsébetváros (at that time the latter was still part of the former), extending from the mouth of Király utca to István tér / Klauzál tér. This was the new Jewish quarter of the old Pest, "*Alt-Neustadt*", *old-new* Jewish quarter, meaning *old* in comparison to Lipót- / Új-Lipótváros and *new* compared to the original core of the Jewish quarter, the *Zsidópiac* (Jewish market) and the lower part of Király utca. We chose to call it a "Triangle" because the three grand synagogues or temples, the "Dohány", the "Rombach" and the "Kazinczy" are its geographical as well as spiritual cornerstones, symbolizing the three major religious wings in the history of Hungarian Jewry in modern times. This Triangle embraces 150 years of Hungarian Jewish history.

(1) Synagogue or Temple?

There is some ambiguity about the use of these terms. Ever since the second Temple of Jerusalem was destroyed by the Romans (70 C.E.), there is no Jewish temple (*heikhal*) in the literal sense of the word. Synagogue is a Greek word (*synagoge*), seldom used in Hebrew or Yiddish. Its Hebrew equivalent is *bet ha-keneset*, "house of assembly", or *bet tefillah*, "house of prayer". The Ashkenazi (Yiddish) term for prayer-house is *shul / shil / shül* (German *Schule*) meaning school, study house (*bet ha-midrash / beis-medresh*). The word *temple* (*Tempel*) was first used in German (Seesen, Westfalen,

120. The "Jewish Triangle" in Pest.
The "Triangle":
1: Synagogue in Dohány utca, 1859
3: Synagogue in Rumbach Sebestyén utca, 1872
4: Orthodox synagogue in Kazinczy utca, 1913
Other places of interest of the Jewish community:
2: Heroes' Temple, 1931
5: Hungarian Jewish Museum, 1931
6: Graveyard, 1944/45
7: Goldmark Hall, 1931
8: Ghetto Memorial, 1985
9: Holocaust Memorial, 1989

1810) and spread quickly among the German reform movements. As for the sociological context of the words, a (Neolog) rabbi recently argued that it may be more "elegant" to use *synagogue* in an analytical text, but no one would ever say in Hungary: "I am going to synagogue", except maybe someone who never goes. Those who do go today say *temple*. This word corresponds best to the cultural context, too. If there is a distinction to be made, then the Orthodox usage is *shul* and the Neolog one is *temple*: Rombach *shul* but Tabak *templ*.

The growth of the Jewish community of Pest both in number and in wealth made warranting the construction of a new temple, one that matched the community in size and appearance. By the mid-nineteenth century at least 40,000 Jews lived in the capital. Two opinions seemed to have crystallized within the Jewish community, the "synagogue-party" and the "temple-party". The formation of various religious tendencies within the Hungarian Jewish community and their institutional separation was most evident in Pest, the largest community. Here, some signs of the future split appeared already in the first half of the nineteenth century, although the formal split was to occur later.

Löw Schwab, or Arszlán Schwab, as he was called on the title page of the Hungarian translation of one of his works, with an archaizing Hungarian form of his first name, was elected chief rabbi

of Pest in 1836, ten years after Wahrmann's death. He studied in Moses Schreiber's famous yeshivah but became an advocate of moderate reforms as long as these did not violate the laws of the Torah. He supported assimilationist tendencies, held his sermons (*derashah / droshe*) in literary German rather than in Yiddish, and even though he himself spoke no Hungarian, he encouraged his congregation to Magyarize themselves. For him Magyarization meant loyalty to Hungary as its citizen and cultural identification, as it did for Móric Bloch, but he did not consider the Hungarian language itself an important element of modernization. When the community invited him to become their rabbi, nobody asked if he knew Hungarian, and nobody expected him to learn it. He replied to the letter of invitation in Hebrew. Reform *per se* was not an issue for him, but he did not oppose it either. Schwab was invited to be the rabbi of the whole community, thus he felt obliged to head the progressive party as well, those who yearned for a new synagogue / temple.

121. Portrait of R. Löw (Arszlán) Schwab

In 1837 the community rented the plot of land where the Dohány synagogue stands today from Baron Antal Baldacci (Baldácsy), a landowner, for 32 years. A few years later, in 1841, they rented the neighboring plot, 12 Pfeiffer Gasse / Sipos utca (today Síp utca), too. Since in 1840 a law was enacted which made it possible for Jews to own property (Lajos Kossuth called Act XXIX of 1840 "a tiny result of great words", *Pesti Hírlap*, April 24, 1841), the Jewish community bought both plots in 1844. They were planning to build a school there, but finally decided in favor of a new synagogue. The Jewish community set up a committee headed by Dávid Öszterreicher whose task was to determine which tendency the new synagogue should follow. On the suggestion of R. Schwab the synagogue construction committee decided on September 3, 1845, that the new synagogue would be built according to the *Wiener Minhag*, with a choir and an organ to enhance the festive mood, but in all other respects the traditional ritual would be observed. Followers of the other, even more traditional tendency would have a separate synagogue built. In 1850 the committee was set up again, this time headed by R. Schwab himself. Among its members were Joszéf Bach, Sámuel Löw Brill, the new rabbi of the community, and Júda Wahrmann, the *dayyan*. They again decided to have a "cult" temple built and the community leadership confirmed it. These decisions prove that followers of the modern tendency were in the majority at the Orczy House, that their opinion was decisive for the Pest community by the mid-nineteenth century. Finally, in 1853 the *Königliche Statthalterei* authorized the construction. There was no doubt that a *temple* would be built.

(2) The Dohány utca Synagogue (2 Dohány utca; office: 12 Síp utca)

Three architects were invited to the competition for the commission to design the synagogue in Dohány utca. József Hild, the popular and highly respected architect of great Hungarian cathedrals and of several buildings in Pest, designed his synagogue in the Classicist style. The young Frigyes Feszl (1821–1884), who built the Vigadó, a theater in Lipótváros, in the very center of the city a few years later (1865), designed a Romantic temple decorated with Venetian and Byzantine elements. Ludwig Förster (1797–1863), the renowned Austrian architect whose plans were probably requested by József Löb Boskovitz, the president of the community, imagined a temple in the "hemispheric" style associated with Romanticism and enriched with Oriental elements.

The first task to be solved by the three architects was to find room for both the office building of the Jewish community and the synagogue on the asymmetric lot. Dohány utca used to serve as a shortcut between Hatvani út and Ország út / Károly körút, people would simply cross the intersection diagonally. Because of this diagonal cross-street it was especially hard to find a suitable plot for an impressive building on the corner of Dohány utca and Ország út. Hild maintained the asymmetry

122. Dohány utca synagogue. Design by Frigyes Feszl, 1851

by placing the synagogue at the edge of the lot in his plans. Feszl and Förster, on the other hand, both found a harmonious position for the temple by placing it between the two office buildings in an upside down U-shape courtyard. In Förster's design the facade of the synagogue did not face the street, it was turned towards Károly körút. This arrangement overcame the difficulties caused by the shape of the plot.

Ultimately it was Förster who was asked to prepare the blueprints. According to his specifications enclosed with the plans the interior and proportions of the Dohány Temple follow the Biblical description of Salomon's Temple (I Kings 6–7; II Chronicles 3). He wanted to rebuild the *heikhal*. Nevertheless, he used the most modern technical devices (cast-iron structures, lighting from upstairs, natural color bricks) and invented a new, Orientalizing style influenced by excavations in Mesopotamia (Ninive, Khorsabad) which came to be known in Europe around that time, and by ancient Moslem architecture. His work was

123. Dohány utca synagogue. Colored engraving by Ludwig Rohbock, 1859

based on thorough historical and archaeological knowledge. Thus, as Ferenc Dávid noted, he managed to accomplish the goals set by the historicizing architectural styles half a century earlier. He tackled a major architectural task by integrating the third great architectural tradition, the Oriental–Byzantine style, in a modern metropolis (the other two being the style of Greco–Roman antiquity applied to museums or public buildings, and the medieval Romanesque or Gothic style for Christian churches). The popular name "Moorish style" is only applicable to certain elements of the ornamentation on Dohány Temple.

The community favored Förster's plans. The Jewish bourgeoisie of Pest consciously accepted cultural assimilation as a way of integration into Hungarian society. They felt that the style of Förster's synagogue in Vienna (Tempelgasse,

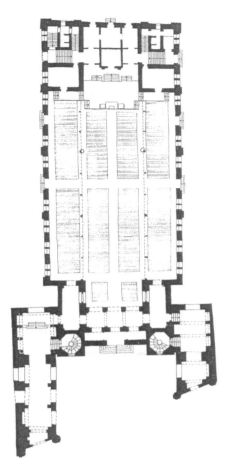

124. The original ground-plan of the Dohány utca synagogue

1854–1857) suited them. The synagogue in Tempelgasse and in Dohány utca were the first monumental examples of the European synagogue style in the ensuing decades and they strongly influenced several synagogue designs later as well. The *Central Synagogue* in New York (East 50th Street), for instance, is an exact copy of the Dohány Temple. A guide book of the time says that if the square in front of it would be a bit bigger, it were the most impressive building in Hungary (*Kalauz Felső-Magyarország vasútain Budapesten és a Dunán utazva* [A Guide Book to Traveling on Upper Hungary's Railway in Budapest and along the Danube] Budapest, Pesti Könyvnyomda, 1873). The facade of the three-nave building on a pseudo-basilican system is flanked by two narrow towers containing staircases. According to Förster's explanation these are the equivalents of the two front columns (Jakhin and Boaz, I Kings 7,21; II Chronicles 3,17) in Salomon's Temple in Jerusalem. The two towers in the Dohány Temple are important ingredients of the system of symbols of the emancipation and are first applied in a Hungarian synagogue here. These towers made the synagogue resemble a Christian church. The exterior is covered with different color burnt bricks, a popular material of the time, whereas the patterns were copied from recently excavated ancient Near Eastern monuments. The wide, solemn hall leads to a large interior fenced by galleries on three sides, the sanctuary in the eastern end covered by a dome. The women's galleries on the second and third levels above the entrance are held by thin iron pillars, the flat ceiling is made of bricks upheld by an iron beam skeleton. The daring designed structure of the synagogue offers a well-lit, open space so that one can see everything from the galleries.

Frigyes Feszl (1857–1859) was entrusted with the interior design. Problems arose between the leaders of the Jewish community and Förster and so they preferred to offer the rest of the work to Feszl. There is special emphasis on the Ark which is almost a small temple in itself. Reporting on the history of the construction of the Dohány Temple Dénes Komárik wrote that "the Ark was a richly decorated central edifice with a fine structure topped by a dome (...) which has a monumental effect due to its proportions and size in relation to the Temple itself. Next to the Vigadó it is Feszl's most important architectural achievement."

The construction costs were partly covered by the revenues from the sale of the seats. Yet there were not always enough funds for the best materials, thus Ignác Wechselmann, in charge of construction, was occasionally forced to use materials of an inferior quality; for instance, the walls were covered with thick colored cardboard instead of marble or cast stone. The carved *shulhan*, "table" or pulpit, an extraordinary piece of furniture, is also Feszl's work (1859).

The organ bears a specific importance in the Dohány Temple. It was a scandal for the Orthodoxy to follow customs of the gentiles (*hukkot ha-goyim*) (Leviticus 18,3), in this case of the Christians, and to disturb the sanctity of the Sabbath by any kind of work, even by playing an instrument. On the other

125. Dohány utca synagogue. Engraving by G. M. Kurz, 1860

126. Dohány utca synagogue and the neighboring houses, ca. 1890

hand, the organ became a symbol of the reforms for Neolog Jews who wanted to modernize the service. Hungarian rabbis were involved in the discussions about the permissibility of the organ in the synagogue service already decades earlier. In 1818, when in the Beer House in Berlin the organ was to be installed, R. Eliezer ben Farkas Liebermann of Homonna was one of the authorities asked for his opinion. He forwarded the question to R. Kunitzer of Óbuda and R. Chorin of Arad, and both of them approved. In the "Dohány" the organ pipes were originally placed behind the Ark, but the new pipes, installed during remodeling in 1902, were put above the wings of the Ark. The choir used to stay on the first floor, but on some ceremonial occasions they came forward to the stand in front of the Ark.

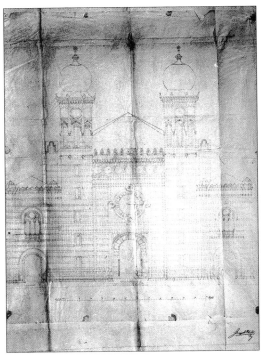

127. Ludwig Phillippson's choral work for the consecration of the Dohány utca synagogue, 1859

128. The original design for the facade of the Dohány utca synagogue, by József Hild, 1857

A huge (12 m diameter) triumphal arch divides the sanctuary from the nave, like the apse of Christian churches. The synagogue used to be called, not without a tinge of irony, the "Israelite cathedral".

The curtain (*parokhet*) is lifted from the Ark automatically upon opening. The "Dohány", like most of the synagogues, has several *parokhets*. Donating a curtain is a pious act. The synagogue's original embroidered *parokhet*, hard like the "iron curtain" in a theater, now can be seen in the Jewish Museum. (It had been put on display in the entrance hall—propped against the wall—decades ago.) The embroidery on a recent *parokhet* depicts the Ark itself.

The inscription on the facade above the entrance reads:

ועשו לי מקדש ושכנתי בתוכם

"And let them make Me a sanctuary that I may dwell among them."

(Exodus 25,8)

On the arch in the nave:

ממזרח שמש עד מבואו מהלל שם ה'

"From East to West the name of the LORD is praised."

(Psalms 113,3)

On the rostrum:

קחו עמכם דברים ושובו אל ה'

"Take words with you and return to the LORD."

(Hosea 14,3)

Above the main entrance there is a date (a *chronogram* constructed by the letters of the very inscription): 618 (= 1858).

The consecration of the *Istenháza / Gotteshaus*, "House of God" in Dohány utca was a major social event in the city. It took place on September 6, 1859 (7th of Elul, 5619), Tuesday morning at 9 o'clock.

Here is what József Katona, chief rabbi of the Dohány Temple after World War II, wrote about the lights of the synagogue in an essay on the history of the synagogue (1949):

129. Mór Friedmann, chief cantor (*hazzan*) of the Dohány utca synagogue. Lithograph by Miklós Barabás, 1860

"The flickering lights of gas lamps, the fifty-four chandeliers and bracket lamps together with the two candles in the huge golden candlesticks in front of the Ark caressed the sunrays shining through the three enormous skylights in a flood of light. The varicolored light pouring in through the stained glass windows all around enveloped the thin pillars and the soaring arches, the arabesques around the wall and the lattice-work along the arches."

The person who did most for the event, R. Schwab, did not live to see it happen. The keynote speech was delivered by his successor, chief rabbi Meisel, who arrived in Pest only three weeks earlier. He remained the chief rabbi of the Dohány Temple until his death. Joseph Bach also delivered a short speech. The *hazzan* was Mór Friedmann (1826-1891), a former pupil of Sulzer. There was a men's and a boys' choir. The organ, considered a symbol of ritual reform, was played by Gotthard Wöhler (?-1888), the music critic of *Pester Lloyd* and instructor at the Nemzeti

Zenede [National Music Institute]. Twelve Torah scrolls were placed in the Ark, all of them donations from members of the congregation.

> "It was the cantor and some community leaders who carried the scrolls, accompanied by solemn singing. The procession was led by young men carrying lit candles. They stopped in front of the sanctuary where the honorable chief rabbi lit the star-like sanctuary lamp hanging from a silver chain. Psalms sounded during this ritual, too." (*Magyar Sajtó*, September 7, 1859)

The Jewish merchants of Pest kept their stores closed on that day. An enormous crowd participated in the ceremony and, during the following days, proud and curious people poured by hundreds to Dohány utca to see the new temple.

The Dohány Temple has remained the largest synagogue in operation in Europe until today. Its dimensions are 27 × 75 m (88 × 246 feet) on the perimeter and it holds about three thousand people. The only larger synagogue in the world is Temple *Emanu-El* in New York (Fifth Ave. / East 65th Street), but only by size and not by the number of people it can hold.

130. Consecration ceremony of the Dohány utca synagogue. Engraving by Alajos Fuchsthaller, 1859

For decades the "Dohány" symbolized the endeavor of the majority of Pest Jews to become part of the Hungarian nation. On December 20, 1860, the festival of Jewish–Hungarian brotherhood took place in the Dohány Temple. On this day even the "Szózat" was recited, the second most important national poem after the national anthem, sung by the choir to the music composed by Ferenc Erkel. Memorial services were held here for some great Hungarian leaders; on April 8, 1861, for Count István Széchenyi, on June 6 for László Teleki. On June 2, 1866, Sámuel Kohn, who was elected the Hungarian preacher of the synagogue a few days later, delivered the first Hungarian sermon (*droshe*) in Dohány utca. Later, on February 6, 1876, and April 5, 1894, memorial services were conducted for

131. "Memorial services for László Teleki in the Israelite temple of Pest." Lithograph by Ede Langer, 1861

132. Interior of the Dohány utca synagogue. Photo, ca. 1900

133. A *parokhet* for weddings in the Dohány utca synagogue

Ferenc Deák and Lajos Kossuth as well. The restoration of Hungarian constitutionalism and the emancipation of Jews (1867) were also celebrated here, as was the millennium of the Conquest of Hungary in May 1896.

For a few more decades there was not only a Hungarian but a German preacher, too, for the benefit of those members who were not yet Magyarized—and initially they must have been the majority. From 1870 to his death the German preacher of the Dohány Temple was Mayer (Meir) Kayserling (1829-1905), an outstanding student of Sephardi Jewish history and literature. He was considered a major authority in his field among German-Jewish scholars. His works were published in German and are widely read even today, in Spanish and Portuguese translation too. His invaluable collection of books was donated to the library of Hebrew Union College in Cincinnati, Ohio. He is buried in the cemetery in Salgótarjáni utca. His portrait is hanging on the wall on the third floor of the Síp utca community building.

In the period between the two world wars there were always four rabbis in the Dohány Temple simultaneously, two chief rabbis and two rabbis. The two chief rabbis, Simon Hevesi and Gyula Fischer (1861-1944), seemed almost as if they were in an oratorical contest. Their pulpits stood at the opposite corners of the nave. They gave sermons every other Sabbath in turn. Both were excellent preachers, the synagogue was often filled just for those 30-40 minutes when they gave the *droshe*. They both had their own fans, it is said that people only listened to the *other* one to strengthen their preference for *their* rabbi. As we may surmise, they did not care for each other too much.

In the final year of World War II, during the summer of 1944, the Dohány Temple was transformed into a military command post. A forced labor battalion was housed here and the Germans used the building as a detention camp. After the termination of the ghetto it again functioned as a prayer-house, services were held on every Sabbath. Since then the damage caused by the war has been repaired and the synagogue serves its original, liturgical purpose.

Ever since it was built, but especially since the other two corners of the Jewish Triangle came into being, it is understood that the Dohány Temple is the main synagogue of Hungarian Jewry. Its rabbi, though not always officially, was the "leading" or "national" chief rabbi of Hungary. To some extent this is an adaptation to the national organization of the Christian churches and the state requirements after the 1868/69 Congress. Not that the original Orthodox concerns are no longer applicable; a true Orthodox would not set foot in the Dohány Temple, certainly not an Orthodox who emigrated from Pest. The famous or notorious prohibitions (*takkanot*) of the Orthodox conference in Nagymihály (Michalovce, today in Slovakia) on November 28, 1865, seem to be in effect to this day. But visitors from abroad or younger people are not bound by the *pesak* or convention anymore, Israeli tourists just laugh at the organ. For them the largest synagogue is unquestionably the center of Pest Jewry.

Today the Dohány Temple is filled only on High Holidays. On weekdays people pray at home, in the "*Hősök*", the Heroes' Temple, in the small prayer-room in Wesselényi utca or in a synagogue near their home—if they pray at all. But on High Holidays it is important for the whole congregation to come together. Jews who come home for the holidays from abroad pray here too, unless they or their parents have their own synagogue. At such times it is difficult if not impossible to keep the women's gallery (*ezrat nashim*) separated. Women, girls who are not used to strict regulations often come down from the gallery and mingle with the men. On High Holidays the congregation appears to be large and thriving. Today for some Jews-by-birth, showing up here on the eve of High Holidays might be the only religious—or pseudo-religious—component of their Jewish identity.

In the mid-1990s the synagogue has undergone major renovation, both inside and outside. The exterior work was finished by 1994: the building was covered with a new layer of dark red bricks similar to the original. Most of the rubble was cleared from the interior by 1993, and in that year one could see, even through the forest of scaffolding, the painted ceiling in its original glory with its subtle hues and varicolored Romantic or Moorish patterns. During the excavations necessary for the renovation a considerable part of the post-1869 archives of the Pest community were found in the northern wing of the Dohány utca front building; the archive was hidden sometime between 1949 and 1952 for fear of the expected anti-Zionist purges. Construction workers found the first lists of seat rentals as well. According to some sources there was a ritual bath (*mikveh*) in or near the building but so far no trace of it has been found. In 1996 the renovation works were completed. The (re-)opening ceremony was held a few days before Rosh ha-Shanah, on the 22nd of Elul 5756 (September 5, 1996), in the presence of the President of the Hungarian Republic, Árpád Göncz, and the former Prime Minister of the State of Israel, Yitzhak Shamir; their entry was greeted with a warm applause. The synagogue was crowded, the balconies—in part inaccessible for decades—as well, there were people waiting even on the square in front of the building, among them prominent members of the Orthodox community. In his inaugural sermon R. Joseph Schweitzer, the Chief Rabbi of Hungary, referred to the Dohány Temple as a symbol of emancipation.

134. "A seat for prayer", reservation for a year in the "Temple" of Pest, i.e. in the Choir Temple in Orczy House, 1845/46

Today the "Dohány" is the representative prayer-house of the (Neolog) Jews of Budapest, and at the same time the scene of concerts, Jewish or not, liturgical or not, several times a year.

(3) A Small Portrait Gallery of the Rabbis of Dohány utca

On the second floor of the Jewish community's office building at 12 Síp utca, to the right of the stairs, there are some portraits hanging on the wall across from the office door of the Dohány Temple's chief rabbi; photos or unsophisticated paintings, a portrait gallery of rabbis. Let us say a few words about some of the distinguished men depicted here.

Sámuel Löw Brill (1814–1897)

To say the truth, R. Brill never was a rabbi of the Dohány utca synagogue, still, as a *dayyan* there, he belongs to the circle of the rabbis around this main temple of Pest Neolog Judaism. He was born at 12 Király utca, the former apothecary building (it was called the "Arany Oroszlán" [Golden Lion] back then) and lived in the very same apartment throughout his entire life. His father, Azriel Brill, was a famous rabbi and a learned scholar himself. He composed a sheet of historical and geographical survey of Hungary in Hebrew, published under the title *Ein ha-aretz* ("A View of the Country"), in 1821 in Buda. He took good care of his son's education; in addition to Biblical and Talmudic scholarship he was taught secular subjects, too. Before going to study at the *yeshivot* in Kismarton (Eisenstadt) and Pozsony (Pressburg), Sámuel Brill completed the first six secondary grades at the Lutheran Gymnasium (secondary / high school) in his neighborhood, on Deák tér. In Pozsony he studied "at the feet" of Moses Schreiber, the *Hatam Sofer*. He also studied at the distinguished university of

Prague, focusing on traditional Biblical studies and philology. After his return to Pest he became a *dayyan*. Together with his two colleagues he was in charge of handing down Halakhic decisions (*pesak*). Unfortunately he failed to publish his responsa (*teshuvot*), as customary, so we know very little about his religious views. Before the 1868/69 Congress he was expected to take the Orthodox point of view but surprisingly, already on the very first day, he sat on the "right side", among the reformists, and supported the progressive party throughout the Congress. Finally he was elected president of the Pest community's *bet din* in 1874. He participated in the work of the committee in charge of setting up the Rabbinical Seminary (1877) and later taught Talmud there. Goldziher mentions in his *Diary* that, from 1865 on, he visited Sámuel Brill's *shi'urim*.

> "Brill quite correctly concentrated on a single page for weeks, digressing in various directions and returning again and again, thus covering a wide range of fields. The classes were usually followed by witty conversations. The rabbi opened the wonderful treasure-house of his knowledge of Jewish literature for us; it could only have been hidden from such an ignorant crowd as the Jews of Pest. He was not only well versed in Talmudic literature but also read modern Jewish literature, as well as many classical German writers. Despite of his relatively modest financial means Mr. Brill accumulated a surprisingly rich library which included several first editions and rare prints from the entire range of Jewish scholarship. These served as lighthouses during our journey among his shelves, while Brill casually conversed with us."

Brill used to give these Talmud classes in his home in Király utca. His students, including Ignác Goldziher and Vilmos Bacher, could glean a great deal of knowledge even about the yeshivah's methods. Brill's invaluable book collection enriches the library of the Rabbinical Seminary today.

His grave is in the cemetery in Salgótarjáni utca, among the graves of other members of the Rabbinical Seminary.

Wolf Alois Meisel (1816–1867)

Meisel Farkas Alajos / Wolf Alois Meisel / Benjamin Zeev Meisel was invited to the Pest community from Stettin, a German city that time (today Szczecin, Poland) in 1859, first only for a probationary sermon and later, in view of his great success, for a permanent position. In spite of his authority and influence, the Jews of Pest did not appreciate the outspoken Lipót Löw (1811–1875). Some said that he was cantankerous, so they found themselves a foreign rabbi. Meisel was the first rabbi of the Dohány Temple, or actually chief rabbi, because Júda Wahrmann and Sámuel Löw Brill were still alive when he came to Pest. Meisel learned Hungarian after a while but, despite of his efforts, he only spoke a broken Hungarian which did not make it any easier for him to strike roots among the rapidly Magyarizing Pest Jews. He held his literary sermons in German, in a rather low tone. He wrote poems, too, and published a religious newspaper (*Ha-Karmel*) in his mother tongue. His religious views as well as his linguistic isolation brought him closer to the traditional party, but his major ambition was to keep a balance between traditional and modern Jews. He preached in the Orczy House and Dohány utca simultaneously. He objected to giving sermons in Hungarian—it is not hard to see why. He encouraged the "synagogue party" to keep their

135. Farkas Alajos Meisel, the first rabbi of the Dohány utca synagogue. Lithograph by Miklós Barabás, 1859

promise and build a new, worthy prayer-house for the conservatives who stayed in the Orczy House. The construction of the synagogue in Rumbach Sebestyén utca was partly the outcome of his efforts. In addition, Meisel revived the Talmud-Torah of Pest, he founded the women's society (1866), the girl's orphanage (26 Damjanich utca) (1867) and the teachers' society, he spoke in favor of Hungarian language instruction in the Jewish schools. Once on April 14, 1860, he held a *bat mitzvah* ceremony for girls, modeled after the boys' *bar mitzvah*, probably the very first one in Pest. Charity was close to his heart, too: he founded a soup kitchen (*tamhuy, Suppen-Anstalt*) at the Teachers' College.

R. Meisel wanted to restore the authority of the rabbi at the expense of communal authority. He even submitted a petition to the *Königliche Statthalterei* in 1863, stirring indignation among his congregation and especially with members of the community leadership. It resulted in a nation-wide scandal. Meisel was ahead of his time in requesting state support for the authority and influence of the rabbi. His contemporaries suspected that it was due to Meisel's petition that Ignác Hirschler, the impeccable and fearless president of the community, was relieved of his duties. Meisel did not oppose the election of Sámuel Kohn as a preacher but his jealousy grew slowly, since Kohn spoke Hungarian fluently and thus became increasingly popular among their shared congregation. R. Meisel died in the Orczy House, right after he delivered a sermon.

Sámuel Kohn (1841–1920)

The historian Sámuel Kohn is one of the most prominent personalities even among the great rabbis of the Dohány Temple. He was born in Hungary, studied at various *yeshivot* (Kismarton / Eisenstadt, Pápa) and later at the Rabbinical Seminary in Breslau, where he earned a doctorate in 1865. The community of Pest invited him upon the recommendation of the Seminary's director, Zacharias Frankel (1801–1875) to become a preacher with R. Meisel. Kohn was exactly the opposite of Meisel in matters of Magyarization. Though he preached in German (his contract required him to do so), he may be credited with introducing Hungarian to the Dohány Temple. He participated in the 1868/69 Congress, he was among the founders of the Rabbinical Seminary in Budapest and taught rhetoric there (1899–1905), but he

136. Sámuel Kohn as the central figure on a tableau of the "Young Hungarian Israel", 1868

was most important as a historian. His major works are *Héber kútforrások és adatok Magyarország történetéhez* (1881) [Hebrew Sources and Data Relating to the History of Hungary], *A zsidók története Magyarországon a legrégibb időktől a mohácsi vészig* (1884) [The History of Jews in Hungary from the Beginning until the Battle of Mohács], that is, until 1526, and *A szombatosok története* (1890) [History of the Sabbatarians]. All of these are collections of sources with historical interpretations. One of his contemporaries, Pál Tencer, had words of praise for Kohn the writer rather than the preacher (1869).

> "When he spoke at the Congress (of 1868/69), all the deputies and the audience on the overcrowded balconies fixed their gaze on his interesting, pale face. Were the synagogue sermons of our honorable preacher as popular as his lectures at the Congress, he would be the most prominent preacher of Hungary. It seems that Dr. Kohn affects the mind rather than the heart."

Kohn was the first scholar to write an overall history of Jews in Hungary. But as a historian he fell victim to the ideas of emancipation. He projected the principles that prevailed following the Congress back onto early Hungarian history. He saw a common Jewish–Hungarian past

137. Sámuel Kohn, ca. 1875

138. Sámuel Kohn in the 1900s

139. "Chief Rabbi Sámuel Kohn, of the Dohány Temple, on the occasion of the Millennial procession (1896)"

since the Khazar Empire and the Conquest of Hungary in 896 C.E. His great historical dream blunted his critical analysis. Though he did not overlook the sufferings of the Jews, he always emphasized Hungarian national traits rather than Jewish motifs in the history of Jews in Hungary.

"As Hungarians of the Jewish faith (...) we celebrate the millennium of our beloved homeland conquered by the troops of our father Árpád. Allies of the Jewish faith were among the fighters, as some historical sources testify. (...) This land is our holy land. (...) Its stones tell the story of heroic battles, its earth contains the ashes of our ancestors, too, who had been laid to rest here over the past thousand years."

(Sámuel Kohn, in: *Egyenlőség*, May 15, 1896)

Kohn finished the second part of his *History* dealing with the period after Mohács but it was not published. Only parts of it were found in the manuscript collection of the Hungarian Jewish Archives. For an extended period Kohn and Goldziher were neighbors in Holló utca. There is an inscription in his memory on the wall of the house exactly where his apartment used to be. The inscription, probably prepared by Károly Sebestyén, translates, in prose, as follows:

"In this house lived – Dr. Sámuel Kohn, – chief rabbi of the Israelite community of Pest, – historian of Hungarian Jewry, – for over half a century. – He devoted himself to our faith and spread the Word of the Lord, – He was a father and a pastor of his community. – God lit the warmth of his heart– and gave him an eloquent tongue."

Simon Hevesi (1868-1943)

Originally his name was Handler and his first articles appeared under this name. His pen-name was *Homo Sum*, "I am a *mentsh*", his Jewish name was *Tzadok*. This name is taken after no lesser a figure than the high priest of David and Salomon (II Samuel 8,17). He was a student of Vilmos Bacher at the Rabbinical Seminary. After his doctorate (1892) and rabbinical ordination (1894) he was active as a rabbi for a decade, first in Kassa (today Košice, Slovakia), then in Lugos (today Lugoj, Romania), where he succeeded Lajos Venetianer. He was invited to Pest in 1905, after the Palestine excursion organized by József Patai, first for an introductory sermon, and after that, to be rabbi in the "Dohány". He was appointed chief rabbi in 1921. He taught rhetoric and philosophy at the Rabbinical Seminary of Budapest and co-edited some of the most important Jewish periodicals of the time (*Magyar Zsidó Szemle, Jabne*). In 1925 he competed with Immánuel Löw (1854–1944), chief rabbi of Szeged, for the seat reserved for Neolog Jews in the Upper House. He was not elected, which was a great disappointment to him, even though a new title, "leading chief rabbi" was invented for him (1927) as a compensation.

He was the greatest preacher of his time, his sermons, whether in the synagogue, at funerals or at secular events, brought him fame. His beautiful, sonorous voice filled the Dohány Temple. His speeches were always polished. Oratory probably fascinated him more than the literary genre, the content of his speech was more important to him than its form. He prepared an abridged version in Hungarian of Maimonides's famous *Guide of the Perplexed*, originally written in Arabic and known as *Moreh nevukhim* by its Hebrew title (*Dalalat alhairin*, 1928). He was an advocate of religion guided by emotions, he countered doubt with feeling. He opposed Zionism because he thought it lacked a religious base, but he was not against life in Palestine. Though he felt at home on the pages of *Egyenlőség*, occasionally he wrote also for *Múlt és Jövő*. He lived in a luxury apartment in Pest at 5 Vilmos császár út (today Bajcsy-Zsilinszky út), within walking distance from the synagogue, to be able to observe the traditional prohibition against travel on the Sabbath.

His grave is in the cemetery in Kozma utca.

Simon Hevesi was an important figure in Jewish public life of Pest in the first decades of the twentieth century. He founded the *Országos Magyar Izraelita Közművelődési Egylet* (Hungarian Israelite Cultural Society or OMIKE) (1910), its club house was at 11–13 Üllői út, after World War II at 84 Dózsa György út, for a while, and was its director of religion until his death. The OMIKE maintained several Jewish cultural and social institutions in the interwar period such as a dormitory for students, the Mensa Academica (canteen for Jewish university students), the Ambulatorium (outpatient care for Jewish students), a library and a reading room, a cultural center, a school for graphic design, schools for apprentices. During the period of the anti-Jewish laws OMIKE organized artistic productions. The institutions of OMIKE made it possible for Jewish youth studying in Pest to visit educational and cultural institutions without giving up their Halakhic lifestyles, that is, without violating the dietary laws.

The daily work of the OMIKE's institutions was coordinated mostly by Ármin Frisch (Friss) (1866–1948), a teacher and historian of religion. His main work, *Izráel szellemtörténeti fejlődése* ("History of Ideas of Israel", 1940), has not been published yet.

R. Hevesi's son, Ferenc Hevesi (1898–1952), received his rabbinical ordination in 1922 and became a rabbi in the Dohány utca synagogue, beside his father, in 1930. His main literary work is a history of Jewish philosophy in antiquity (1943). After his father died, he was appointed the chief rabbi of the "Dohány" and remained in office until 1947.

(4) The Reading of the Torah

The central feature of Jewish religious practice is the reading of the Torah (*keri'at ha-Torah*). This is also the most important communal ceremony. It takes place in the synagogue or prayer-room, its order is determined by several ancient rules. Reading the Torah regularly on the Sabbath is documented since the first century C.E. in Josephus (*Contra Apionem*, 2,175) and the New Testament (Acts 15,21).

In the ancient Palestinian tradition the entire text of the Torah was completed in three years. However, it was the Babylonian tradition which spread throughout the world, according to which the Torah is read in yearly cycles. As in Babylonia, the text is divided into 54 large units. These units are called "weekly portion (*sidrah*)". Each week one portion is read on four different days. The whole *sidrah* is read on the morning of the Sabbath, parts of it on Sabbath afternoon, and on the preceding Monday and Thursday mornings. These latter two were the market days in Babylonia, the Torah was read then so that everyone could hear it in the synagogue. A *minyan*, the presence of ten adult males (Numbers 10,27), is essential at the reading of the Torah.

The cycle of reading the Torah always starts in the fall, on the first Sabbath after *Sukkot*, and ends on *Simhat Torah*. The whole text needs to be read in the original Hebrew, selections (*inyan*) are not enough, nothing may be omitted. On weekdays and on Sabbath afternoon, however, only the first three parts of the weekly portion, the *parashah*, are read. In the years when the number of weeks is less than that of the portions because some holidays fall on Shabbat and other sections are to be read, two concluding weekly portions are read on some of the Shabbaths. In leap-years, when there are more weeks than *parashot*, the new cycle is started earlier.

In ancient times it was customary to provide a simultaneous interpretation of the reading of the Torah in the vernacular; this is the origin of the Aramaic translations (Targum) and this "explanation" was the basis of the sermon (*derashah*) in the temple. In the nineteenth century in Germany some radical reformers tried to introduce reading the Torah in German translation, but by today the Hebrew text is commonly accepted by all Jewish congregations, at least in Hungary. The fact that not everyone understands the text only strengthens the ritual character of the reading of the Torah. Following the tradition of the Targums, a new custom has been introduced in the Rabbinical Seminary recently: the Hebrew text is accompanied by Hungarian explanations.

The first step of the ritual is opening (*petihah*) the Ark (*aron ha-kodesh*) and the removal of the Torah scroll from it. At this time the whole congregation rises, even those who cannot see the scroll from their places. Bells remind them to do so, the tiny ones (*pa'amonim, sagim*) that decorate the crown or *rimmon*. As the dressed Torah scroll is being carried towards the rostrum (*bimah*), everyone tries to get near it and to touch it, if not directly by hand then with his prayer-book or with his prayer shawl, rolling its fringes around his finger. Then the devout kiss the *Siddur*, the *tallit* or the fingernail of his index finger. In some communities only children kiss the Torah scroll. On the *bimah* the Torah scroll is placed on a Torah reading stand and its decoration is removed. In Ashkenazi communities the Torah scroll is laid on the stand while reading, in Sephardi ones it is held upright.

A set number of persons from among the members of the congregation and the honorable guests are asked to read the Torah. Generally three or four, five on holidays, six on the Day of Atonement (*Yom Kippur*) and seven on Sabbath morning. Being asked to read is a great honor. The formula is "so-and-so please rise (*ya'amod* XY)" and the person is called by his Jewish name together with his father's name, rabbis by their title (*morenu ha-rav*), doctors (Dr.) as well. Those who are chosen, walk *up* to the *bimah*, that is why this ceremony is called "calling up (to the Torah)" (*aufruf / ufruf*) and ascension (*aliyyah*), respectively. The person who ascends is an *oleh*.

Each weekly portion is divided into seven shorter units (*parashah*). The part read by each *oleh* is called *aliyyah*, just like the ascension itself. In Hungarian it used to be called "a lesson". No one may read less than three verses.

People are asked to read according to a fixed order following the Bible (Deuteronomy 31,9). The first reader must always be a *kohen*, after him a *levite*, and finally any *Isra'el*. If no Levite is present, he can be replaced by a Kohen. If, however, no Kohen is present, the order of the reading is canceled (*nitpardah ha-havilah*) and any ordinary Israelite may be called to read. Close relatives are generally not asked to read together. The *oleh* tries to get to the *bimah* along the shortest possible path. On his way back, however, he takes the longest possible way and even makes detours (Ezekiel 46,9).

The attention of the congregation centers on the person who is honored by being called to read from the Torah. Therefore, it is customary to call on people to whom something extraordinary has happened on that specific week, e.g. they had their *bar mitzvah*, their wife gave birth to a baby, they pray for a sick person, their period of mourning is completed, they say *Kaddish* for their father or they have a *Jahrzeit*. He who is getting married soon is called to the Torah a few weeks in advance. This ceremony renders the Sabbath in the synagogue family-oriented. The most valuable *aliyyah* is always the third one on a weekday and the sixth on the Sabbath. In larger communities, where the five remaining *aliyyot* are not enough, the Kohen leaves the prayer-room for a short while, thereby allowing ordinary Israelites to be called to read instead of them and the Levite. Another solution is to introduce additional *aliyyot* (*hosafah*, in plural *hosafot*), or to call one more person than necessary on that day. The last *oleh* is then called "the last one (*aharon*)". In Hungary, after reading from the Torah it is appropriate for the *oleh* to return the honor by offering a donation (*nedavah / nedove*). The act is called *snóderolni, shnodern* (from the Hebrew *she-nadar*, "he who promises / offers"). The *gabbay* immediately announces the amount and later—at the next possible opportunity—registers and collects it. Once a year, always on one of the Sabbaths of the High Holidays, an *aliyyah* can be obtained solely by donation. This money is for the maintenance of the synagogue. It is a special honor (*kavod*, pronounced as *koved*) to be called to read the Song of Moses (Exodus 15,1–21) or the Ten Commandments (Exodus 20,1–14; Deuteronomy 5,6–18). During these readings the community stands.

While the Torah is read there are always at least three people standing on the *bimah* behind the pulpit with the scroll, naturally wearing a *tallit*. These are the *gabbay*, the reader (*ba'al kore*) and the *oleh*. All of them have to stand (Deuteronomy 5,28). The *oleh*, the person who is called to read from the Torah, holds the rod (*etz hayyim*) of the scroll nearest to him with his right hand. The *gabbay* does so too and he leads the *oleh*'s eyes by the *yad*, the Torah pointer, always holding its "fingertip" above the text. The previous *oleh* remains standing nearby until the next *aliyya* ends.

Before it comes to reading from the Torah the text of the weekly portion has to be examined. Whoever is called upon to read starts by reciting the blessing. The congregation usually pays no attention to this; there is constant murmuring, prayer, conversation, pacing up and down. But when the reader finishes the blessing by saying *amen*, suddenly everyone stands still.

Now comes the reading of the portion. Being called to read from the Torah rarely means that the person actually reads his part. Most of the time he just recites the blessing. The text itself is read by the professional reader, in older days the *oleh* occasionally used to repeat it sentence by sentence.

Reading the Torah has a specific mode (*cantillatio*). This mode differs from country to country, from community to community. It is impossible to learn it from books, only from living tradition, from other readers. The indication of the melody (*ta'amei ha-mikra / trop*) in manuscripts and some printed editions is not enough. Incidentally, the intonation of reading the Torah and the *Haftarah* differ. (The *trop* for reading the Megillot is different as well.)

The *oleh* touches the spot of the scroll where his part of the text begins and ends with the fringes of his *tallit* and kisses the fringes afterwards. After finishing his *aliyyah* he stays on the *bimah* until the next part is read and returns to his seat only afterwards. He backs off to his seat to avoid turning his back to the Torah. As he passes, people greet him saying: "Be strong (*yeyashsher kohakha*)"—in Pest this sounds "*shkayakh*" or "*shkayekh*"—or "Be strong (and) blessed (*hazak u-varukh*)", because studying the Torah gives strength and is a blessing. The answer is: "Be blessed." The last *aliyyah*, the final part of the weekly portion, has a special name, "closing (*maftir*)".

140. Lifting of the Torah scroll (*hagbahah*). Lino-cut by Imre Ámos, 1940

If more people need *aliyyot*, this one is simply repeated. Between two *aliyyot* the scroll is always covered. (The word *shkayekh* is often used in secular contexts as well, sometimes just as congratulation after lectures, etc.)

The final act of the ceremony is lifting (*hagbahah / hagbe*) and rolling (*gelilah*) the Torah. The *magbiah* lifts the scroll, he shows it to the community who say: "This is the law which Moses set before the children of Israel" (Deuteronomy 4,44). It is then rolled—the beginning of the next weekly portion is to be between the two scrolls—and dressed up. Lifting the Torah is a ceremony on its own. It is a gesture of reassurance, based on a word pun, that is, the double meaning of a Biblical verb (*yakim*, "to lift" and "to maintain"): "Cursed be he who does not *maintain* the words of this law" (Deuteronomy 27,26). By looking at the text of the lifted Torah scroll the congregation can make sure that the Torah from which they read was the real Torah.

There are two parts of the Torah which no one likes to read because it predicts punishment for Israel if they violate the divine law (Leviticus 26,14–43, Deuteronomy 28,15–69). Nevertheless, these parts have to be read, too. A practical solution is that when it comes to these terrifying passages, the leader of the ceremony asks the congregation, "Who would like (to read) (*Mi she-yirtze*)?" It is always the beadle (*shames*) who responds to the question and he reads the text in a faint voice. There are two other parts of the Torah (Exodus 32,1–33,6; Numbers 11) dealing with the disobedience of Israel which are also read in a low voice.

The reading of the weekly portion is followed by the real closing (*maftir*), the reading of a concluding, explanatory, supplementary passage from the Bible (*Haftarah*, plural *Haftarot*). This is read by the *ba'al maftir* or *maftir*. In a sense, to be called to *maftir* is an even bigger honor than to receive an *aliyyah* because the *maftir* often gets to read the *Haftarah* by himself. These texts are taken from the Prophets (*Nevi'im*) and their topic or tone is similar to the weekly portion. The *Haftarot* may be read from a printed book as well. The first reference to reading *Haftarot* dates from the first century C.E., in Christian scriptures (Luke 4,17; Acts 13,15). Jewish Torah editions contain the texts of the *Haftarot* in an appendix. The Torah scroll is placed back into the Ark only after the reading of the *Haftarah* is completed and the concluding blessings are said.

It is customary that men, during the pregnancy of their wives (while they *carry* a child), help *carry* the Torah scroll to and from the Ark as often as they can. The reward for the pious service should be an easy delivery.

(5) Rejoicing of the Torah

The last day of the Days of Awe (23rd of Tishri) is a joyous festival day, *Simhat Torah*, "the rejoicing of the Torah". This day brings even more people to the synagogue than the preceding holy days except, perhaps, Yom Kippur. People come to rejoice, be happy. Already on the eve of the holy day of the Torah all the Torah scrolls are removed from the Ark and the rabbi, together with his congregation, circles the *bimah* seven times (*hakkafot*) holding them. People celebrate, sing, dance, try to touch the Torah scroll. Children participate in the procession, too, flourishing small Simhat Torah flags, recently even flags of Israel, shouting with joy. In some cases it is allowed to sing songs that do not belong to the ritual. Everyone may rejoice over the Torah as he or she wishes. The *mehitzah* (partition) may be ignored even in Orthodox communities. The scrolls are brought up to the women's gallery as well.

For the reading of the Torah the congregation dissolves into small *minyan*s so that everyone may receive an *aliyyah*. They follow the words of the Torah literally (*kol yisra'el*, "whole Israel"), therefore even children (*kol ha-ne'arim*) receive *aliyyot* together with their father, under their father's *tallit*. The last weekly portion of the Torah (*Ve-zot ha-berakhah*) is read again together with the first portion of the next cycle, the story of Creation (*Bereshit*). It is the two "bridegrooms (*hatan*)" who finish the ceremony of reading the Torah. One of them is called the "bridegroom of the Law (*hatan Torah*)", he reads the concluding part of the last portion. He is usually surrounded by all the children (*im kol ha-ne'arim*). The other "bridegroom" is called the "initial" or "he who starts (*mathil*)" or "bridegroom of Bereshit (*hatan Bereshit*)"; he reads the first portion, the story of Creation. "*Va-yehi erev, va-yehi voker*", which the whole congregation repeats with him aloud. The two bridegrooms are usually prestigious members of the congregation, they were called to the Torah already on the Day of Atonement, and sit in front of the *bimah*, on separate chairs. When their turn comes, their friends surround them. A canopy (*kilah*) is held above their heads, after all, they are bridegrooms. (In small communities it is customary to honor recently married men by asking them to be the *hatan*.) In the foreground of the synagogue a festive table, a feast (*neilat ha-hag*) or *kiddush* awaits the congregation, as is customary after services on holidays. The two "bridegrooms" are in charge of setting it up. The *hatan*, "bridegroom" in the expression *hatan Torah* might originally have been *hatam*, "seal / sealing (of the Torah)", namely the one who sealed or "closed" the Torah scroll after completing the reading cycle. This word then became confused with *hatan* and moments of a wedding ceremony were added. *Mathil*, by the way, does not mean "bridegroom" either, it means "he who starts" the new cycle.

The joyous song of the celebrating congregation can be heard in the street, too. *Am Yisra'el hay*, "the Jewish people lives."

(6) General Jewish Congress, 1868/69

The sessions of the first congress of Hungarian Jewry called *Izraelita Egyetemes Gyűlés* or *Magyarországi és Erdélyi Izraeliták Országos Kongresszusa* (*Landes-Congress der Israeliten in Ungarn und Siebenbürgen*) [General Jewish Congress] by its official name, were held in the inner city, in the main auditorium of the County Hall (today 7 Városház utca, the building of the Local Government of Pest County) between December 10, 1868 and February 23, 1869. This first congress also proved to be the last, so far. The Neolog organizations did have another general congress in 1930, and after World War II, in 1950, the organizations of the Neolog and Orthodox communities were united at a general assembly, but none of these meetings were fully attended. True, the General Congress, called together precisely to create a unified organization of Hungarian Jewry, ended with the final and official split of the various Jewish communities. Nevertheless, the Congress was the most important official event in the history of Hungarian Jewry.

141. Portrait of Ignác Hirschler, 1868/69

220 delegates from all over the country attended the General Jewish Congress. Its costs were covered by loans taken from the school fund. 132 deputies, members of the progressive party, sat on the right side of the hall, the others, the traditionalists on the left side. Ignác Hirschler, the famous ophthalmologist, played a central role in the Congress; he was elected its president. Later he became a corresponding member of the Hungarian Academy of Sciences (1869), and a member of the Upper House in 1885. The vice-president of the Congress was Mór Wahrmann, businessman, member of the Jewish community leadership. During the Congress he led the delegation of Hungarian Jewry which met His Majesty Francis Joseph I. (1848–1916), Emperor of Austria and King of Hungary.

The site of the Congress itself signaled that the event was considered important by the state. The General Jewish Congress was preceded by the law of emancipation (Act XVII of 1867). This law made all Israelites equal to the Christians "in practicing all civil and political rights". (Formally, the Jewish oath prescribed by the *Tripartitum opus juris consuetudinarii* was terminated then, by § 242, Act LIV of 1868, and later decrees.) After the establishment of legal equality it was necessary to find a place for the Jewish communities within the structure of the state. Baron József Eötvös, Minister of Religion and Education, felt that the Jews should also have an organization similar to other religions, representing them vis-à-vis the state. The Jewish community would be free to decide in internal matters, they would be autonomous and self-ruling.

> **XVII.**
>
> **Törvényczikk**
>
> **az izraeliták egyenjogúságáról polgári s politikai jogok tekintetében.**
>
> **1. §.**
>
> Az ország izraelita lakosai a keresztény lakosokkal minden polgári és politikai jog gyakorlására egyaránt jogosítottaknak nyilváníttatnak.
>
> **2. §.**
>
> Minden ezzel ellenkező törvény, szokás, vagy rendelet ezennel megszüntettetik.

142. The law of emancipation (Act XVII of 1867)

Here is an excerpt from the opening address of Baron József Eötvös (December 14, 1868):

"The state offers you the opportunity to rule independently in all of your religious matters and determine how you wish to organize and govern your communities by your own ideas and principles, which no other country ever offered to your co-religionists. I have great confidence and trust that freedom will soon bring its fruits to your community as it affects favorably all noble human ambitions, and your organizations as well as your spiritual and intellectual life will quickly develop. Since the blessings of freedom is even dearer to a people who had been repressed for the last two thousand years, it is my conviction that precisely this freedom, granted by the constitution of Hungary, will bind the Israelite citizens of our country to the homeland in all circumstances."

(Pál Tencer, Ed., *Album*, I, 1869)

According to the minutes of the Congress the address of Eötvös was followed by "long, enthusiastic applause and hurrahs, people exclaiming: Long live the homeland!"

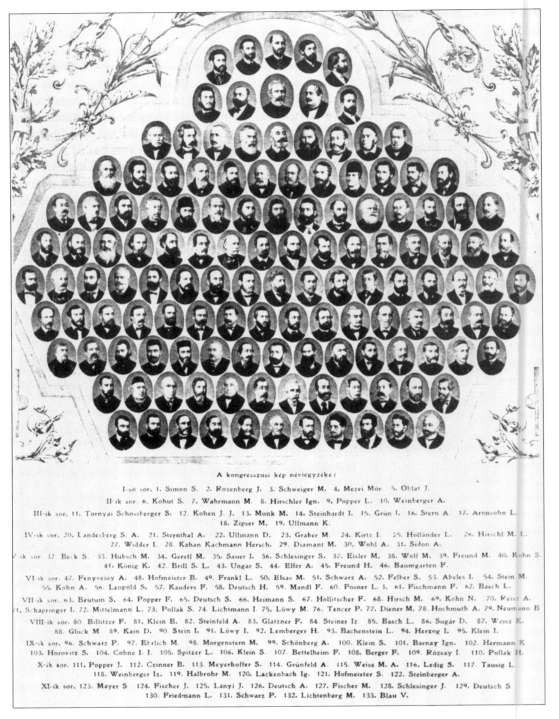

A kongresszusi kép névjegyzéke:

I-ső sor. 1. Simon S. 2. Rozenberg J. 3. Schweiger M. 4. Mezei Mór. 5. Oblat J.

II-ik sor. 6. Kohut S. 7. Wahrmann M. 8. Hirschler Ign. 9. Popper L. 10. Weinberger A.

III-ik sor. 11. Tornyai Schossberger S. 12. Kohen J. J. 13. Munk M. 14. Steinhardt I. 15. Grün I. 16. Stern A. 17. Aronsohn L. 18. Zipser M. 19. Ullmann K.

IV-ik sor. 20. Landesberg S. A. 21. Sternthal A. 22. Ullmann D. 23. Graber M. 24. Kirtz I. 25. Holländer L. 26. Hirschl M. L. 27. Widder I. 28. Kahan Kachmann Hersch. 29. Diamant M. 30. Wohl A. 31. Sidon A.

V-ik sor. 32. Beck S. 33. Hübsch M. 34. Gerstl M. 35. Sauer I. 36. Schlesinger S. 37. Eisler M. 38. Wolf M. 39. Freund M. 40. Kohn S. 41. König K. 42. Brill S. L. 43. Ungar S. 44. Elfer A. 45. Freund H. 46. Baumgarten F.

VI-ik sor. 47. Fenyvessy A. 48. Hofmeister B. 49. Frankl L. 50. Elsas M. 51. Schwarz A. 52. Felber S. 53. Abeles I. 54. Stein M. 55. Kohn A. 56. Leopold S. 57. Kauders F. 58. Deutsch H. 59. Mandl F. 60. Posner L. I. 61. Fischmann F. 62. Basch L.

VII-ik sor. 63. Beutum S. 64. Popper F. 65. Deutsch S. 66. Heimann S. 67. Hollitscher F. 68. Hirsch M. 69. Kohn N. 70. Reisz A. 71. Schapringer I. 72. Mittelmann L. 73. Pollak S. 74. Lichtmann I. 75. Löwy M. 76. Tencer P. 77. Diener M. 78. Hochmuth A. 79. Neumann B.

VIII-ik sor. 80. Billitzer F. 81. Klein B. 82. Steinfeld A. 83. Glatzner F. 84. Steiner Iz. 85. Basch L. 86. Sugár D. 87. Weisz K. 88. Gluck M. 89. Kain D. 90. Stein I. 91. Löwy I. 92. Lemberger H. 93. Bachenstein L. 94. Herzog I. 95. Klein I.

IX-ik sor. 96. Schwarz P. 97. Ehrlich M. 98. Morgenstern M. 99. Schönberg A. 100. Klein S. 101. Barnay Ign. 102. Hermann K. 103. Horovitz S. 104. Cohne I. I. 105. Spitzer L. 106. Klein S. 107. Bettelheim F. 108. Berger F. 109. Rózsay I. 110. Pollak H.

X-ik sor. 111. Popper J. 112. Czinner B. 113. Meyerhoffer S. 114. Grünfeld A. 115. Weiss M. A. 116. Ledig S. 117. Tausig L. 118. Weinberger Iz. 119. Halbrohr M. 120. Lackenbach Ig. 121. Hofmeister S. 122. Steinberger A.

XI-ik sor. 123. Mayer S. 124. Fischer J. 125. Lányi J. 126. Deutsch A. 127. Fischer M. 128. Schlesinger J. 129. Deutsch S. 130. Friedmann L. 131. Schwarz P. 132. Lichtenberg M. 133. Blau V.

143. Tableau of the participants of the General Jewish Congress, 1868/69

The task of the Congress was to make decisions on pressing issues arising from the *Ausgleich* of 1867, from the compromise between Austria and Hungary and Jewish emancipation, the granting of civil rights to Jews. Hungarian Jewry had to be fitted into some organizational framework, their representation in the modern constitutional state had to be solved. Minister of Religion and Education Eötvös, ultimately responsible for initiating the Congress, held that a decision about the organization of the Jewish community did not have to, indeed, should not, depend on religious principles. Therefore, no rabbis participated in the discussions. Yet, since the beginning of the nineteenth century, modernization had always presented itself as a religious problem for the Jewish community.

Traditionalists considered every innovation in ritual or administration as breaking religious tradition, while the progressive party only wanted modest reforms, adjustment to the modern world without disregarding tradition.

It was precisely because of the religious elements of modernization that the Congress did not lead to unification. Hungarian Jewry split into two, or rather three factions.

The traditionalist group formulated segregation as a program long before the Congress convened. The Congress only had to finalize the split (*perud*). Those who wished to adhere to tradition to the extremes ruled that an undisturbed, fully religious life could only be led in a

144. The scene of the General Jewish Congress: County Hall in Pest. Lithograph after Rudolf Alt's drawing, ca. 1853

traditional Jewish community and such a community did not acknowledge any authority other than the Bible, the Talmud and the Shulhan Arukh. They rejected the innovations of modern Jews concerning synagogue construction, order of ritual and other details which were already the established practice in Dohány utca, and they would not accept the new type of rabbinical training either.

Actually, modernization of Jewish life in Hungary started decades earlier, along German patterns. Its results were obvious in Pest. Little less than ten years before the Congress the Dohány Temple was built with two towers—contrary to all previous custom. The rostrum for the reading of the Torah (*bimah*) was placed in front of the Ark, not at the center, like before. The women's gallery was not segregated by a grill (*mehitzah*), though in Orthodox circles even the density of its bars was prescribed. (True, the gallery in the Dohány Temple is fairly high up.) They used a choir and an organ during services and later on they even changed the language of the sermon from Yiddish, the only appropriate language for the Orthodoxy, into Hungarian or German. Rabbis dressed in a robe for services, like Protestant (Evangelical or Lutheran) pastors.

The traditional framework of Jewish life was constantly stretched in Pest by modern, progressive members of the community, mostly influenced by German reforms, but not merely by copying the foreign model. Ideas were taken from several regions and adjusted to different circumstances. Altering the ceremonial hymn and introducing a choir were only the first steps (around 1830). Further changes were the gradual reduction of sermons in Yiddish ("jargon") around 1840; placing the *bimah* in front of the Ark (in the newly built synagogues); the reorganization of the prayer-book (omission of certain *piyyutim*), etc. Slowly they stopped selling the *aliyyot* for money (the goal of which was

145. The scene of the Orthodox convention after they left the General Jewish Congress: Hotel Tigris. Lithograph after Rudolf Alt's drawing, ca. 1853

collecting alms), no one knocked on people's door in the morning to call them to prayer (*Schulklopfen*), weddings were held inside the synagogue rather than in the courtyard, burials were not held immediately after death, etc.

Beyond these formal changes in the details of ritual, which are by no means insignificant, there were other, more fundamental changes. In Germany reforms altered the role and position of the rabbi in the life of the community. Traditionally, the rabbi and the *dayyan*, his deputy, were legal personalities. Trained in Halakhah, their job was only to respond to Halakhic questions and decide in ambiguous cases. Prayer and ritual were taken care of by the "emissaries of the community", actually the *hazzan.* The rabbi himself had hardly any duties in the synagogue. He was by no means a preacher (*darshan*). He held only two or maybe three sermons a year, one before *Pesah*, on *shabbat gadol*, one before *Yom Kippur*, on the Sabbath of return (*shabbat shuvah*, see Hosea 14,2) and one on the eve of *Kol nidrei*. The community's needs for interpretive sermons were satisfied by wandering preachers (*maggid* or *mokhiah*). Their sermons were not part of services, they were given on Sabbath afternoons. German reforms slowly transformed the rabbi into a preacher, much like among Protestants. His audience required the rabbi to speak German or Hungarian instead of Yiddish. The Magyarization and middle-class assimilation of the rabbi and the congregation took place concurrently, influencing each other. The rabbi was no longer evaluated according to his in-depth knowledge of the Talmud (Halakhah) but by his talent as a speaker. (R. Meisel was painfully aware of this change in the Dohány Temple.) As the sermon became the central element of services, prayers and the rest of the ceremony had to be shortened. The rabbi of the Jewish *temple* became more and more of a *priest*.

Traditionalists firmly rejected every form of change or innovation, be it wedding inside the synagogue, studying secular disciplines or establishing a rabbinical seminary. They even forbade wearing modern, worldly clothes, Magyarizing one's name and using Christian dates on letters.

Most of the traditionalists left the Congress even before discussing the agenda, expressing thereby that they did not wish to belong into one organization with the progressive Jews who outnumbered them at the Congress. They did not go far, only as far as the Hotel Tigris (5 Nádor utca, today an office and apartment building). They held their separate conference in the ballroom of the hotel. They chose a different path.

The Congress, following the recommendation of Eötvös, adopted a resolution about setting up a national organization of Hungarian Jewry (Israelites). It decided about the structure of the individual communities within this organization and about the utilization of the school fund established by Francis Joseph. Among the plans were founding a Rabbinical Seminary and organizing a Jewish school system. They passed the so-called Congress Statute which determined the structure of the individual Jewish communities under the administration of the National Israelite Office. The country was divided into 26 community districts, Pest being the VIth. Pest, Buda and Óbuda formed separate Israelite communities, and other small towns around Pest joined the capital only later.

Though the organization of the Jewish communities on a regional-administrative basis as approved by the General Jewish Congress was created on the initiative of the Government, it was not at all alien to Jewish tradition. In other Eastern European countries with a large Ashkenazi Jewish community central administrative organs were instituted over the individual communities (*kehillah*) according to regions (*galil*) and country (*medinah*), on the pattern of the centralized authority of the state. Halakhic authorities found it admissible that decisions concerning the whole community be made by a central authority while leaders of the individual communities were only in charge of executing those decisions. The national organization never intended to take over the role of the rabbis, yet its existence and position contributed to the decrease of rabbinical authority and the gradual decline of communal autonomy. In spite of the changing circumstances this tendency seemed to prevail.

After the 1868/69 Congress Hungarian Jewry split into three different organizations—a unique development in Europe. Those who followed the decisions of the Congress were called *Neolog*s (or with official term *Congress community*); those who left the Congress were called traditional, Orthodox, or autonomous Orthodox Jews, and the third group, those communities who wished to maintain the situation before the Congress were called *status quo ante* (i.e. *ante congressum*) communities, "(adhering to) the (legal) status before (the congress)", or in short *Status quo*, sometimes written in one word: *Statusquo* and pronounced as *státeszkvó*. The word *Neolog* (with Hungarian spelling: *neológ*) is a Hungarian historical reference; it refers to advocates of the language renewal movement half a century earlier who were called *neologus*, i.e. "person using or creating new words". In the Hungarian Jewish context it was—and still is—used instead of the term *reform* which had already been discredited by the Reform Society.[1] The Orthodox, as the name indicates, consid-

---

[1] In our time, the Neolog community in Hungary is affiliated with the U.S. Conservative Judaism.

ered themselves custodians of the *real* faith. (The Hebrew names, *shomrei shabbat*, "those who observe the Shabbat", or *yere'im*, "the faithful ones", refer to the same conviction.) The organization of the Congress (Neolog) community started to operate according to the Congress Statute (1869). They considered themselves representatives of entire Hungarian Jewry, calling themselves just *Israelite community* rather than *Congress-Israelite community*. Later, in 1871, the Orthodoxy also created a central organization. The *Status quo* communities formed their organization only much later, in 1928, but they showed a more or less uniform character from the very beginning. None of the organizations distinguish between Ashkenazi or Sephardi communities but the regulations of the Orthodox organization named both as belonging under their jurisdiction.

Based on regulations of the General Jewish Congress the organization of the Congress communities ruled that each and every Israelite was obliged to be registered in the community of his residence, or if there was not any, in the community where other members of his city were registered. Israelites residing in a given city were not allowed to belong to more than one community. The community may not reject anyone who wishes to become its member. In this sense the new type of Jewish community retained the role of the old one. There was no Jewish life outside of the official Jewish community. Apart from the capital there were only a few large cities where several Jewish communities operated side by side.

In Hungary, where the majority of Jews were Ashkenazim, origin and historical background resulted in further differences. Jews living in the northeastern part of Hungary were generally called *interlendish* in Yiddish (German *unterländisch*), while communities in the western and central regions of the country were the *oyberlendish* (German *oberländisch*). Referring to geographical setting as related to Austria, these familiar terms later came to be used to distinguish the dialects of Yiddish spoken in Hungary. Jews living in the "low-land", the northeastern part of Hungary, came mostly from Poland or Lithuania; they spoke (Eastern) Yiddish, lived a rural life preserving the customs of the *shtetl*, often strongly bound to Hasidism. The Jewry of the "upper-land", of the territories in the West, including Budapest, came mostly from the more developed cities of Moravia, Austria or Germany, from territories with a more advanced industrial and bourgeois society. Jews in Bohemia and Moravia spoke mostly German or Western Yiddish and they were culturally German-oriented. They were used to urban life and lived in a somewhat more individualized, middle-class society. From the mid-nineteenth century on the tension between these two groups of Jews was as great as that between Jews and the non-Jewish social environment. The urban, bourgeois Jews of the capital despised the rural Jews, resorting to pejorative terms such as *pólisi* (Polish). The use of the Viennese choir, German sermon, the construction of temples in a modern architectural style, reforms of the ritual and other changes, i.e. the Hungarian version of the nineteenth-century Jewish religious reform movements, referred to as Neology, developed among the *oyberlendish* Jews of Pest, while the Hungarian Orthodoxy, or rather Neo-Orthodoxy, which later became the source of new radical Orthodox movements, was more widespread among the *interlendish* Jews who did not participate in the process of modernization, that is, mostly the Jewry of the eastern territories.

Apart from the three institutionalized movements Hasidism was also present in Hungary. Hasidic ("pious") Jews always gather around a rabbi (*rebe*), their religious and spiritual leader, the head of their community. If they need to decide important questions or even minor, everyday matters, they consult their *rebe*. They even ask him how they should live. Many of them study, of course, but for a pious Jew (Yiddish *hosed*) his *rebe* is the source of all knowledge, he is the ultimate arbiter, he, rather than the individual *Hasid*, maintains contact with God. Therefore, his word is sacred. This kind of religious community is centered around a person, it excludes territorial organization. Without a *rebe* there can be no *Hasid*. Hasidim did not have a voice in Jewish public life in Hungary, though their number was significant, especially in the countries of Northeastern Europe. The so-called "Sephardim" of Pest were actually Hasidim, Yiddish-speaking Ashkenazi Jews living far away from their *rebes*, and their local leaders could not be compared to some of the great Eastern European *rebes*. During World War II there were several real Hasidim among the Jewish refugees from Poland, Slovakia and Ukraine who found temporary refuge in Budapest.

The central organization of the Neolog communities established after the Congress and called by various names exists even today, holding together Neolog Jewry quite like the Christian churches. This centralized structure suited the Government of the Dual Monarchy. Through modernization and equal rights the Jewish community became a well-organized religious group, just like Eötvös suggested in his opening address.

A quip from the years following the Congress: "Why is the Jewish community of Pest the luckiest one in the country? Because its rabbinate consists of *Kaiser-* and *Kohn-igliche* rabbis." This quip, obviously from the 1870s, is actually a pun on the names of Mayer *Kayser*ling and Sámuel *Kohn*, then preachers at the Dohány Temple. It seems to confirm the general opinion that the Jewish community was permeated with the K. u. K.[2] mentality. The reforms initiated by József Eötvös integrated the Jewish community into the state organization.

The concerns of the Orthodoxy about the organizational changes initiated at the Congress were basically justified. It was the Christian, and not the bourgeois state which offered Jews entering bourgeois society the opportunity to modernize. The choice was either accepting emancipation and restricting Judaism solely to religion, or pursuing Judaism as an all-comprehending form of life at the price of relative isolation and restricted cultural modernization.

The various Jewish groups had been fighting over the interpretation of Halakhah already before the Congress and even more so afterwards, trying to present it as if the other party was turning its back on Jewish tradition. Moshe Schick (Sik) (1807–1879), the rabbi of Huszt in Northeastern Hungary, talked about the Neologs as if they were a separate sect or religious group (*kat*) no less different from Jews than Protestants are from Catholics. This came as a shock since, despite of the debates within the community, nobody had ever before questioned the unity of Jewry. The Orthodoxy or rather Neo-Orthodoxy, as Jacob Katz and Michael K. Silber called them, forming alongside the reform movements, had its share in casting Jewry into being a religious confession at least as much as the Neolog, whom they accused of doing so. After a decade or two the heated debate between the Orthodoxy and Neology died down and the groups isolated themselves completely from each other.

Following the Congress the Government regulated several questions which had earlier belonged to the sphere of Halakhah or tradition. The issues included marriage and divorce (1878), birth registration (1885), Saturday as a school day (1885), the Talmud-Torahs (1887), the organization of the individual Jewish communities (1888), religious education, etc. All of the Jewish communities, whether they were Neolog, Orthodox or *Status quo*, became an organizational part of the state, maintaining their freedom only in matters of religious faith, which in case of Judaism is hard to divide from the organization and from the way of life.

A few years after the General Jewish Congress the Minister of Religion and Education issued a decree which stated that the officially accepted name, *Israelite religion*, should be used in every official document and previously fashionable terms like "Hebrew" or "of the Mosaic faith / religion" should be dismissed in the future. "Jewish" was no longer acceptable; during the trials of Tiszaeszlár (1882/1883) the word *Jew* "acquired such hateful and contemptuous connotations that it became a term of disparagement" (Aladár Komlós).

"In the age of liberalism Jews cherished the illusion that emancipation finally allowed them to enter the family of European nations. It seemed that ancient anti-Jewish sentiments had finally disappeared and the Jewish community could become part of the state and of society as just another religious group. Since religion seemed to be the only criterion of Jewish life, many believed that only the uniformity of religious ideas could hold the Jewish community together. Since this was missing, Orthodoxy denied Jewish unity. As a reaction, anti-Semitic movements arose in Berlin wishing to deprive all Jews of their political rights. They found an echo in Hungary, too, under the leadership of Győző Istóczy. Hungarian Jewry had several occasions and good reasons for feeling disillusioned. The religious split may have been prevented by awakening Jewish solidarity, but it was too late. It was only our generation that realized and only through the ultimate persecution of Jews: in spite of all differences world Jewry has a common fate." (Jacob Katz, 1991)

[2] *Kaiser- und königliche*, "imperial and royal", as it was institutionalized in the Austro-Hungarian Monarchy after 1867.

(7) What is Jewish?

The processes by which Hungarian society accepted or, using historical vocabulary, "tolerated" and "admitted" the Jews, are consequences of the 1868/69 Congress resolutions.

Act XVII of 1867 identifies the Jews as a separate ethnic–religious group (*corpus separatum*). They were treated as foreigners or were accepted, tolerated (this applies to other minorities as well). After the law of emancipation and the Act XLII of 1895, the so-called law of reception, the word *Jew* only meant "someone of the Israelite faith". With the progress of secularization the meaning of *Jew*, *Jewish* changed. After Act XXV of 1920, the so-called *numerus clausus* law, it came to designate a vaguely defined social category even in legal terminology. The restrictive provisions of the *numerus clausus* law were repealed by Act XIV of 1928 only to be followed by the anti-Jewish legislation a few years later, bringing on even more severe restrictions for Jews for several years. After World War II and the Holocaust, Hungarian legislation restored the legal status of Jews as it was between 1867 and 1920, but the general attitude of the society at large remained similar to that of the 1920s.

The self-definition, or rather self-definitions of Jewry is an open question even today. Actually, not even religion is defined unambiguously. The "surrounding" neutral society has yet to find a strategy for accepting all the Jewish groups or communities that exist independently and are so different from one another.

Today several kinds of Jewish identities may exist: religious, ethnic, linguistic, cultural, sociological, emotional, based on background, etc. Theoretically all of these exist simultaneously, although not all of them are recognized equally and their criteria of definition differ as well. Forms of identity change along with the changing situation and it is in our common interest to maintain options of change, pluralism and personal decision.

(8) Theodor Herzl in Pest

In the second half of the nineteenth century the Wesselényi utca started somewhat farther back than today, at Síp utca, the next intersection on Károly körút being Dob utca. (The segment of Wesselényi utca extending to Károly körút was opened only in 1897.) Photographs from the turn of the century show that an insignificant two-story house joined the block of buildings right next to the entrance of

146. The house where Theodor Herzl was born

147. Theodor Herzl. A childhood photo, 1865

the synagogue towards Károly körút, where the building of the Jewish Museum now stands. Another house stood beside it. The name of Samu Schiller, written on the signboard above of one of the shops in no. 4, can be made out on an historic photo of that house, the house where Theodor (Binyamin Zeev) Herzl (1860–1904) was born and where he spent his childhood. According to his elementary school grading records, street address of his parents' home was 47 Ország út.

His father, Jacob Herzl, was born into a German-speaking family in Moravia. They lived in Zimony. Herzl first moved to Debrecen and only later, in 1856, did he settle in Pest. A wholesale timber merchant, he amassed an impressive fortune. He also dabbled in financial transactions, almost going broke once, but then rising again to become one of the wealthiest citizens of Pest. His mother, Jeannette (Johanna / Anna) Diamant was the daughter of a well-to-do clothier in Pest. In his *Altneuland* Herzl evoked various events of his childhood in Pest, such as the Sabbaths spent at the neighboring Dohány Temple, the holidays and the Seders with his family. Theodor was first sent to the Jewish Elementary School of Pest, and he began his secondary schooling in the *Pest városi nyilvános Főreáltanoda*, a Municipal School (today the Eötvös József High School, 7 Reáltanoda utca), which, however, as he later recounted in his *Autobiography*, he disliked owing to the

148. Theodor Herzl's parents with their two children

strong anti-Jewish atmosphere. (One of his teachers referred to the Jews as "heathens", no better than idolaters or Moslems.) He was a private pupil for shorter or longer periods of time. From the second semester of the 1875/76 school year on he attended the Lutheran Secondary and High School (the Pest Evangelical Gymnasium of the Augustan Confession), which was regarded as the best secondary school, and in 1878—after the family had already moved to Vienna—he graduated from this school as a private pupil. The school was located on Deák tér, in the neighborhood of the Teréz- and Lipótváros, and later in the Fasor (today Városligeti fasor); between a third and a half of the students were Jewish.

149. Theodor Herzl's sketches on one of his school essays, 1874

Herzl grew up speaking three languages: both German and Hungarian were his mother tongues, and he also had a spattering of Hebrew which he learnt at home, at least enough to read the prayer-book. As a child he wrote his letters to his father in Hungarian, and in his later letters to his parents, although written in German, he used Hungarian terms of endearment. He was eight years old when, together with his father, he became a member of the Hevrah Kaddishah of Pest. One surviving relic of this time is the invitation to his *bar mitzvah*, held on May 3, 1873, in which the event is described as a "confirmation", according to the then current Neolog usage. It is uncertain, however, whether the *se'udah* or reception, planned as a major social event, had indeed taken place. It is quite possible that due to the cholera epidemic that had reached its peak at that time (October, 1872 to November, 1873) only members of the immediate family attended the ceremony. In any case, a minor detail on the invitation reveals that by this time the Herzl family had moved away from Dohány utca. The address given is a much better one: *Thonethof*, Mária Valéria utca, 4th floor. The Thonethof is the house on the corner of 3 Vigadó tér and Mária Valéria utca (today 10 Apáczai Csere János utca), still one of the most beautiful buildings in the area. From Dohány utca the family had moved to a more fashionable neighborhood, to Lipótváros, to the immediate vicinity of the Vigadó,

150. The Herzl family's new home on the Danube embankment: The *Thonethof*, 4th floor

even if the third floor was not the best. (The family, and Theodor Herzl himself, owned some estate in Budapest in ca. 1880, such as the house at 96 Andrássy út. Later it was sold to Duke Philipp of Saxe-Coburg.)

At the Realschule Theodor, his sister, his cousin and some of his friends founded a students' literary club, resembling a literary society, which they called *Wir / Mink* [Us] (1874), of which Herzl became the president. They staged Hungarian and German plays, recited poems and read essays.

Herzl's Hungarian school papers (some of which are now housed in the Central Zionist Archives in Jerusalem) were written in the flowery literary style of the period of the compromise of 1867. His Hungarian was impeccable and exceptionally good. When the family moved to Vienna after his sis-

ter's death, he tried to leave Budapest behind spiritually too. He had equal opportunities for intellectual activity in German and Hungarian, but he consciously chose a career as a German journalist. At first he only returned to Budapest for short visits on his sister's *Jahrzeit*. Soon the time came when he felt—or so he said—that he became a railwayman at Keleti pályaudvar (Eastern Railway Station).

As a Viennese journalist and writer, Herzl was the first one to develop and mold the Zionist concepts and ideals that had long since ripened among the Jewish intellectuals of Western Europe, Russia and Galicia into a coherent plan of action. He was also able to publicize these concepts (*Der Judenstaat*, February 1896). The chronicler of his youth in Pest, Andrew Handler, however, argued that his experiences in the secondary school classes—the political anti-Semitism that manifested itself in the Hungarian Parliament in the late 1870s and the reactions to it—were instrumental in shaping Herzl's personality. One might even go as far as to say that the experiences from the *Alt-Neustadt* of Pest greatly influenced his thought and prompted him to start thinking about a Jewish *Altneuland* (the title of Herzl's utopian novel, published in 1902). Herzl organized the Zionist movement around 1895. The

151. Herzl as student of the Lutheran High School, 1876

First Zionist Congress opened in Basel on August 29, 1897.

The Zionist point of view meant a repudiation of the assimilated Hungarian Jewish position. It is thus understandable that Herzl found hardly any followers in Budapest. At the height of his fame he wrote with bitter irony that in twenty years a sign proclaiming "To let (*Zu vermieten*)" would be hung on the house where he was born. He was particularly shaken by R. Sámuel Kohn's scornful remarks against the Zionist movement even from the pulpit. Still, when in 1900 he felt that Ármin Vámbéry's Turkish contacts might come in handy for the realization of the Zionist program—Palestine being under the authority of the Turkish Sultan at the time—he approached the professor in patriotic Hungarian–Jewish terms, a combination of German and Hungarian: "Mein guter Vámbéry bácsi". In an imaginary letter, written on the Vienna express after their first meeting on June 17, 1900, he wrote:

"Kedves Vámbéry bácsi, das ungarische Wort ist gut: zsidó*ember*.[3] Sie sind einer, ich bin auch einer. Darum haben wir uns so schnell u[nd] voll verstanden—vielleicht noch mehr im Menschlichen als im Jüdischen, obwohl dieses bei uns beiden stark genug ist." [My dear Uncle Vámbéry, the Hungarian word zsidó*ember* [a Jewish *person*] is most expressive. You are one, and so am I. That is why we understood each other so quickly and so perfectly—perhaps even better as human beings than as Jews, even though the latter be strong enough in both of us.]

They had probably reached an understanding and, after this meeting Herzl always referred to Vámbéry as "Schlesinger", an almost secret code name, and Vámbéry, too, cabled him under this name. (Vámbéry had originally been called Wamberger.) As it happened, Vámbéry was ready to help him with his plans, for even at the height of his fame he never forgot his humble Jewish origins, regardless of his religious beliefs.

The city of his youth, as Herzl used to call Budapest in his diary, assumed a special significance in the pursuit of his Zionist aims and organizational work, and his journeys to Istanbul always led through Pest. Although he spoke of his home-town but reluctantly, several of his remarks reveal that throughout his life, and in whatever he did, his childhood environment was the measure of his achievements. The Hungarians (i.e. the Hungarian Jews) would be the Hussars of Judaea. In Hungary

---

[3] Italics by Herzl.

Zionism could hardly be anything but red–white–green. After all, Herzl too—as he himself admits—was a "Pest Jew".

In an interview given to Miksa Szabolcsi, Theodor Herzl predicted:

"Hungary will soon experience such a bout of anti-Semitism that ours (the Austrian) will seem insignificant in comparison. If I were to urge political Zionism, people would say that this anti-Semitism had been stirred up by Zionism. I don't want this. You, Sir, and the Hungarian Jews will eventually come to us, for anti-Semitism will drive you into our arms." (*Egyenlőség*, 1904 / *Múlt és Jövő*, 1941)

A commemorative inscription in the stairway of the Jewish Museum marks Theodor Herzl's birthplace. Prior to World War II the slab was on the street in front of the museum, on one of the pillars of the arcades, but it was later moved inside the building, to a landing along the staircase. During the reconstruction of the museum the slab was once again moved, this time to a lower landing, close to the entrance, and was provided with a small edge, on which there are always a few pebbles.

*

One of Herzl's cousins was Jenő Heltai (Herzl) (1871–1957), the writer, an acknowledged master of chansons and of an urbane literature sparkling with wit. They had a cordial relationship. Jenő Heltai asked to be allowed to translate Herzl's plays into Hungarian. He received this permission and authorization in 1891, but on one condition: "... as a translator, choose a pen-name for yourself, because you cannot use the name Jenő Herzl. I wish to avoid any crude jokes about the Jewish–German–Hungarian family. You are hardly striving for literary laurels in this case. You will undoubtedly be satisfied with receiving your fee and establishing contact with the National Theater." Some years later, when Heltai was preparing to travel to Paris as a correspondent, Herzl provided him with good practical advice.

Much later, in an interview, Heltai revealed what Herzl had told him about his Zionist projects in Vienna (1895).

152. Herzl's advocate at the Sublime Porte: Ármin Vámbéry, Oriental scholar and traveler

"After the excellent lunch we took a stroll. I realized only later that it was no accident that we roamed the streets of the Jewish quarter in Vienna. (...)

"Listen to me now. You're my cousin, we're branches of the same tree. I'll tell you about the great enterprise that I've embarked on.

"I listened to Theodor in surprise. I thought he wanted to tell me about some great literary or theatrical enterprise. (...)

"I'm going to create the Jewish state.

"I have to admit that even today, after almost seventy years, I can still hardly grasp the significance of this sentence. (...)

"You will have to spread this idea in Hungary. You will have to win over the entire Hungarian Jewry for this movement. (...)

"I can't accept, I replied, for I have no such feelings either in my heart, in my mind or anywhere else that would encourage me to take on this task. I have to tell you in all honesty that I'm not Jewish. I'm Hungarian.

153. Theodor Herzl's letter to Adolf Ágai, 1889

"Beware! Don't forget my words. (...) You say that you're not Jewish, but Hungarian. I've heard the same sentiment expressed in several European tongues, but beware! The time will come when your nose will be rubbed into the fact that you're not Hungarian! (...) But it'll be too late by then!

"I have often recalled this conversation. (...) And not much time had to pass for me to realize that he was right.

"But by then it was truly too late."

(Andor Zsoldos, *Theodor Herzl. Emlékezések* [Recollections on Theodor Herzl], New York, 1981)

(9) The Rombach (11–13 Rumbach Sebestyén utca)

Sebestyén Rumbach (1764–1844) was a medical officer in Pest. His name became widely known after the first chalybeate spas in Pest. A street was named after him already in his lifetime, the one where he owned several houses. His street was originally a narrow alley opening from Király utca, which in 1850 was extended to Dob utca; in 1899 the segment to Wesselényi utca was also built. Between 1817

154. Facade of the Rumbach Sebestyén utca synagogue, 1981

155. Facade and towers (Yakhin and Boaz) on the street front of the Rombach utca synagogue

and 1939 it was called Rombach utca / *Rombachgasse*, hence the synagogue's names: "Rombach synagogue", "Rombach Temple" or just "the Rombach".

With this synagogue the leadership of the Pest community fulfilled a promise it had made when building the Dohány Temple. The traditionalist members of the community remained in the Orczy House even after the Dohány Temple had been built. The leadership threatened to cease payment on the lease of the old premises, and that it would move the prayer-house to the former premises of the Cult temple. Perhaps they wanted to persuade the traditionalists to join them not only in the new building, but also to accept their ritual and attitudes. R. Meisel, too, considered the Orthodox demand for a separate building justified. In the summer of 1867, twenty-four members of the congregation in the Orczy House finally purchased the Kehrn–Tomola lot in Rumbach Sebestyén utca (which at that time was no. 8). (The building was used as a prayer-house for some time, but from 1840 on it housed the kindergarten of the community.) The Committee for the Construction of the Synagogue was formed the same year and a competition was announced. The Committee accepted the design submitted by Otto Wagner, the Viennese architect (1841–1918). In March 1868 the prize-winning design was placed on display. Construction work was begun on May 1, 1870. Felix (Bódog) Buzzi (1829–1875) was contracted to build the synagogue based on the design drawn up by Wagner and Mór Kallina (1844–1913). It took the authorities two months to issue the necessary building permit. The building was completed in 1872 and it was consecrated on Tuesday, October 1 (the 28th of Elul), although some minor details were finished only after the High Holidays. By Rosh ha-Shanah of the next year (633 of the "minor era", i.e. 5633 of the creation = 1873 C.E.) the synagogue was completely finished.

In contrast to the Dohány Temple with its basilica-like ground-plan (incorporating a longitudinal nave), Otto Wagner consciously chose a different, centralized structure, even if he, too, adopted elements of the Romantic–Orientalizing style. His partly Classicist, partly Byzantine ground-plan reflects a

156. Frieze on the facade of the Rombach utca synagogue before the recent restoration

new tendency in Jewish architectural tradition. It is fairly obvious that both the contractor and the architect had in mind a building that would in no way be inferior to the Dohány Temple. It may be smaller, but certainly not poorer. At the same time, they also wanted to comply with the wishes of the traditional congregation. It is only fair that a prayer-house of similar size and beauty be maintained for the followers of both tendencies, stated the petition of the traditional congregation (1859).

157. The Tablets of the Law on the facade of the Rombach utca synagogue after restoration

As a piece of architecture the "Rombach" was indeed a work of art. Its internal layout corresponded to the Orthodox ritual requirements, with a separate women's gallery and the *bimah* standing in the center; but even so, spatial unity was created for the entire congregation. The Orientalizing, Moorish ornamentation echoes the medieval decoration and arabesques of the Alhambra, while the conspicuous wall covering conceals a very modern and emphatically light structure, just like the Dohány Temple. The position and size of the windows is especially praiseworthy. Artificial light was not needed during services. Saturday mornings the sunlight streamed through the windows directly onto the stand where the Torah was read.

An apartment house was built on the street-side of the building, containing the rabbis' flats, as well as the Teachers' Training Center for some time, the Talmud-Torah of the synagogue in the tower, a house of study for the religious education of the employees of the synagogue, as well as the girls' primary school of the community.

158. The "Moorish" ornamentation of the Rombach utca synagogue tower

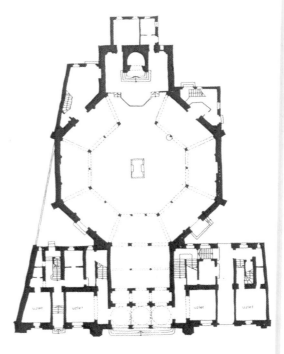

159. Interior of the Rombach utca synagogue, ca. 1895

160. Ground-plan of the Rumbach Sebestyén utca synagogue

Like the Orczy House, the "Rombach" synagogue and its neighborhood were threatened by various projects of urban planning, such as the plans for the Erzsébet sugárút / Madách út promenade. The "Rombach" nonetheless went ahead with various improvements. The building, particularly the heating system, was technically modernized, a house of study (*bet ha-midrash*) was built in the courtyard, to the right of the building, as well as a *Sukkot* room with removable roof that could also be used in winter (it was used for choir rehearsals).

The General Congress of 1868/69 was held during the construction work. The "Rombach" synagogue did not secede from the Pest community, but neither was it Neolog. Perhaps it stood closest to the *Status quo ante* communities, but was never actually linked to them organizationally. In the late nineteenth century the popular German guidebook (Karl Baedecker) described the "Rombach" as an Orthodox synagogue. The strict Orthodox, however, never accepted the synagogue as one of their own. Only a part of the traditionalist congregation joined the "Rombach", while the holdovers, those who remained in the Orczy House—the true Orthodox in the strict sense—continued to use

161. Interior of the Rombach utca synagogue, ca. 1949

162. The former Ark in the Rumbach Sebestyén utca synagogue, 1974

163. The former *bimah* in the Rombach utca synagogue, 1988

164. The northeastern corner of the women's gallery in the Rumbach Sebestyén utca synagogue, 1971

their old synagogue until the new synagogue of the "pious (*yere'im*)" in Kazinczy utca was completed. In one of his responsa (*teshuvah*) the rabbi of Szatmár, Yehuda Grünwald (1845–1920), mentions that there is one synagogue in Pest that has been built in the traditional way and is named after Rambam (Maimonides), but since the congregation adopted some minor changes introduced by the reformers, a truly pious Jew would not pray there. In fact, there is no "Rambam" synagogue in Pest. Was Grünwald perhaps thinking of the "Rombach"? If he saw the name written in Hebrew letters and had no inkling of what the name was, instead of Rombach, written in Hebrew רמבה, he could easily have read רמבם , or perhaps רמב״ם (RAMBAM / R. Moshe ben Maimon / Maimonides). The community's new synagogue was another step away from Orthodoxy. Orthodoxy retained the shabby "great" synagogue in the Orczy House and probably soon formed the idea of building a new synagogue. The congregation of the "Rombach" was originally made up from among the traditionalist members of the Pest community who stood close to Orthodoxy and who were joined by members of the Óbuda community, the Orthodox from Northern and Northeastern Hungary who had recently moved to Pest, as well as the traditionalists from Western Hungary. Their ranks included merchants, artisans and intellectuals, they spoke Yiddish, German and Hungarian. Although Magyarized to some extent in their language and customs, they clung to their traditions and familiar ceremonies in their religion. They kept their special ceremonial hymns and melodies, and also had their own prayer-book (*Derekh Hayyim*, "The Path of Life"). The "third meal" on the Sabbath was held in the building.

The "Rombach" rabbis were all renowned personalities. No rabbi who had graduated from the Rabbinical Seminary could ever hope to be called to serve in this synagogue for the traditional attitude would never allow it: in their eyes the Seminary was far too liberal. The malicious gossip (*leshon ha-ra*) at the time was that only *negative qualifications* entitled one to become a rabbi in the "Rombach": no rabbinical diploma. However, none of the synagogue's rabbis can be said to have been ignorant.

In accordance with the traditions of the Pest community and the Dohány Temple, there were two rabbis at the "Rombach", with a slight difference in their views and attitudes. The first pair, from 1872 on, were Sámuel Löw Brill and Lajos Eleázár Pollák (1822–1905).

Mózes Feldmann (1860–1927) was the rabbi of "Rombach" since 1900. At his earlier post, in Galánta (today in Slovakia), he held a yeshivah and after he moved to Pest he took over Brill's place and responsibilities in practical matters; he was the head of the Pest rabbinate and taught liturgy in the Rabbinical Seminary for a while (1921–1926). He left a number of Hebrew treatises on Halakhic topics

in manuscript. His attitude in religious matters was strictly traditional; he undoubtedly helped keep the balance between the modern orientation of the community and the more traditionalist members of the congregation.

Illés Adler (1868–1924) was invited to the "Rombach" from Óbuda. He was actually the fellow-rabbi of Feldmann. His contemporaries regarded him as one of the best preachers. Adler lived at 35–37 Király utca; his walk home from the synagogue on Saturday morning, followed by his congregation, was almost like a royal procession. For his funeral the entire Jewish quarter turned up. His followers kept vigil, "sat" beside his body at the Jewish hospital until the next day and followed the hearse down Andrássy út and Király utca to the "Rombach". His catafalque was set up on the porch of the synagogue and his followers bade farewell one by one. The procession of the crowd lasted long into the night. The next day, following the memorial service at the "Rombach", the crowd attended the official ceremony of the Jewish community held in the Dohány Temple. Thousands and thousands of people followed the hearse along Rákóczi út to Népszínház utca, and only here did they board the streetcar for the Kozma utca cemetery.

Towards the end of World War I, R. Alexander Fischer of Gyulafehérvár (today Alba Julia, Romania), the renowned rabbi of a *Status quo* community, was elected rabbi of "Rombach", but he could not accept the invitation because of the newly established borders. (His sons, Joseph Fischer and Tivadar Fischer, became this way leaders of Hungarian Jews in Transylvania for the decades to follow.)

Benjámin (Betzalel ben Tzvi) Fischer (1878–1965) was the very last rabbi in the "Rombach": the customary two rabbis in one person. He was active here for half a century. It is said that at his inauguration in 1926 the police had to control the crowd. Great expectations preceded his coming and he remained widely popular. He lived at 4 Holló utca, in the same house where Kohn and Goldziher used to live earlier. Fischer's ideal was the Neo-Orthodoxy of Frankfurt and of R. Samson Raphael Hirsch (1808–1888) in particular, who was able to present traditional ceremonies and ways of life as an attractive alternative to the Neolog movements. Two decades after Hirsch's death it was written about him that "he was the Péter Pázmán of the German Jews" (*Magyar Zsidó Szemle*, 1907, p. 353)— Pázmány was an eloquent Roman catholic archbishop in the seventeenth century. He argued that until the coming of the Messiah, Jewry is not a nation, but a religion, and thus the laws of tradition cannot be changed, although it is permissible for Jews to align themselves with national or political movements and to participate in secular life. Fischer followed these ideals. He always preached in Hungarian, with the exception of the traditional days of the rabbinical *droshe* (*shabbat gadol* and *shabbat shuvah*) when he used Yiddish. He must have been the very last one to speak Yiddish from a non-Orthodox pulpit.

The choir of eight and later of six men and almost thirty boys in the "Rombach" was a small concession to Neology. Women could not sing in the choir and there was no organ either. Members of the choir wore uniform gowns and stood in front of the Ark. They took great care to remain solemn at all times. Three of the six *gabbayim* were always present when the Torah was read, dressed in dark robes and a top hat. The *hazzan* was always excellent. Although rooted in Polish tradition, the melodies reflected the somewhat newer style introduced by the extremely popular Louis Lewandowski of Berlin (1821–1894), whose works were in the manner of Felix Mendelssohn's great choirs. Lewandowski's adaptations (*Kol rinnah u-tefillah*, "The Sound of Supplication and Prayer", 1871; *Todah ve-zimrah*, "Thanksgiving and Song", 1876–1882) are still standard elements in the repertoire of the Jewish choirs of Pest.

168. The Rumbach Sebestyén utca synagogue prior to its renovation, 1988

"Rombach utca represented an entirely different world in my childhood. On weekdays I entered this narrow street of the Jewish quarter only when, three times a week, I attended the Talmud-Torah in the rooms of the temple's tower. The street was permeated by the fragrance of textiles and fresh cotton prints. All kinds of felts, rolls of linen cloth and Norinberg [Nuremberg] packages [haberdashery, trinkets, toys] would arrive on the most amazing vehicles, pushcarts and enormous carts drawn by huge Brandenburg horses. On weekdays the street would resound with the cursing of the drivers and the noise of the packing men.

"But what a change came over the street on holy days! You could hardly recognize it. Gone was the dirt, all the shops were closed, and the street became a promenade. Holding a voluntary recess during services, the young ones would stroll up and down, while others waited for temple tickets to be smuggled out, enabling them to pray in a 'forbidden' way during the High Holidays. At these times the Rombach utca became one large synagogue, for the prayers were said not only inside the synagogue, but in every house where there was either a permanent prayer association or some kind of supplementary prayer-house for the occasion. When I walked down Rombach utca early in the morning on the days of *Selihot* or the High Holidays, loud, penitent sighs, strains of solemn melodies would sound from the open windows in the cool autumn morning. (...)

169. The Rumbach Sebestyén utca synagogue after its renovation, 1991

"The Rombach utca temple faithfully fulfilled the purpose intended by its founders. It preserved tradition: the old synagogal songs, the style of the old sermons and the ideals of the old, traditional men. (...)

"Happy is the eye that witnessed this, exclaimed the medieval *piyyut* poet remembering the sublime ceremony of the High Priest on Yom Kippur when the Temple in Jerusalem was still (...) standing. Happy is the eye that witnessed this, I sigh. Happy indeed, who saw the manifestations of the creative powers of the traditional kernel of Pest Jewry."

(Ernő Munkácsi, 1943)

The "Rombach" congregation still sticks together, even years and decades after the closing of the synagogue. On weekdays the morning prayer (*shaharit*) is held in the small *bet ha-midrash* in Wesselényi utca, together with the congregation of the Dohány Temple. The Sabbath morning services are also held there, but separately. On the High Holidays services are held in the Heroes' Temple, again separately.

*

In the summer of 1941 Jews of "unclear citizenship", namely the Jewish refugees from Poland, Germany, Slovakia, Carpatho-Ukraine and, from Hungary itself, who tried to escape to Palestine or elsewhere, were interned on the orders of the Minister of Interior: they were transported to gathering points to facilitate their resettlement to "Galicia" which, at the beginning of the war, was under German–Hungarian occupation and military administration. One of the detention centers was established at the Rumbach utca synagogue. Similar refugee camps were set up at 46 Columbus utca, 39 Magdolna utca, 39 Páva utca, Szabolcs utca (by the Jewish hospital) and later in Damjanich utca, and Ó utca. The operations were directed by the *Külföldieket Ellenőrző Országos Központi Hatóság* (Office for Aliens' Control or KEOKH). At these gathering points the basic provisions were supplied by the Pest community and the *Pártfogó Iroda* (Office for Patronage or MIPI). Endre Bajcsy-Zsilinszky, an MP, visited the Jews who were detained in Rumbach utca and tried to intercede on their behalf with the Prime Minister, László Bárdossy, but without success.

In July and August, 1941, the interned were taken to Kőrösmező (called *Yasene* in Yiddish), or more exactly, to Havasalja, a district of Kőrösmező, in order to be deported within a few days via the Tatár-hágó (Tartar Pass)—to expel them to the other side of the pre-war border, over the river Dniester. They were told that they would be settled in the villages of Podolia and there were in fact a number of families who were allowed to move into abandoned houses. A number of prominent people, including the former MP and Christian-socialist politician Margit Slachta, made desperate efforts to save—or at least to help—the inmates in the camp at Kőrösmező.

> "We saw people holding their citizenship papers, one-armed veterans, old men who could hardly move, children stricken with measles, all waiting for hours to be sent further after a two-day journey in an open truck under the pouring rain. We saw a gallows with a crow dangling from it set up at the railway station to make fun of these unfortunates, we saw the abandoned houses with boarded up windows at Karácsony-falva, whose owners had been deported at night or at dawn, we saw the women's concentration camp at Ricse, (...) I saw the long line of wagons in which these unfortunates were taken there, (...) I saw how they were packed on to the trucks, guarded by gendarmes and soldiers with bayonets, while the villagers looked on, when orders had already been given to call off the action. I saw a group of people whose documents were confiscated by the district administrators, and saw these people subsequently deported (...)."
>
> (Margit Slachta's letter to Mrs. Horthy, August 13, 1941)

In the meantime, the German military command had decided to call off the operation because they feared that their supply lines would be in jeopardy. They offered to transport the deported Jews back to Hungary. The Hungarian military commander rejected the offer. On August 27–28, units of the German army then proceeded to murder an estimated 14,000 to 16,000 Jews in Kamenets-Podolsk and in neighboring villages—"alien" Jews and Hungarian Jews from the Budapest detention centers, from the Kárpátalja region (Carpatho-Ukraine) and Máramaros (Maramureş, today in Ukraine and Romania). The protests forced the Hungarian authorities to eventually call off the deportations and some of the survivors returned, but the internment camps, including the one in Rumbach utca remained and the deportation plans were not completely discarded either. With the deportations to Kőrösmező the Hungarian Government merely helped the Germans implement their plans for resettling all the Jews in the East from where—or so they said—they came. The action was a prelude to the Holocaust.

(10) In the Synagogue

The conventions that governed the layout of the synagogue, regardless of whether it was a humble prayer-room or a magnificent temple, evolved over the centuries. The basic model was the Temple in Jerusalem, destroyed in 70 C.E. and, as time passed, its idealized image as conceived from descriptions in the Bible.

Old synagogues were built to open onto a court-yard. The courtyard not only separated it from the non-Jewish world but also simplified certain ceremonies such as weddings and *Sukkot*, which are traditionally held in the open. The courtyard, no matter how small, lent an air of intimacy to the synagogue and evoked the courtyard of the Temple in Jerusalem. The synagogues in the Orczy House, especially the "big" one, fitted perfectly into this tradition. There were several synagogues opening onto a smaller or larger courtyard (Dessewffy utca, Vasvári Pál utca, Újlak: Lajos utca, Teleki tér, Újpest, etc., as well as Rumbach Sebestyén utca, Kazinczy utca, etc.). In many cases the various buildings serving the Jewish community, such as the "*matzo bakery*", the kosher butcher, the school (*heder*), etc., stood in the immediate vicinity of the syna-gogue, as in Óbuda and also in the Orczy House. Under urban conditions, however, the spatial unity of these institutions gradually ceased and now only the Orthodox quarter around Kazinczy utca pre-serves elements of this traditional layout.

170. Interior of the Rumbach Sebestyén utca synagogue: The Ark and the *bimah*, ca. 1985

Since it is a holy place, there is no *mezuzah* on the synagogue; although there must be one on the study house (*bet ha-midrash*).

The traditional requirement for a window in the room where one prays stems from the Book of Daniel (6,11). Since the Middle Ages the windows in the synagogue are built high and it is impossible to either gaze out through them or for anyone to peek in. In a prayer-room a simple curtain, opaque glass or a paper cover will do. According to Jewish mystic thought (*kabbalah*) the synagogue should have twelve windows in order to enable all twelve tribes of Israel to conduct the ceremony in their own fashion. This tradition was given a new twist in Budapest in the relief depicting the Twelve Tribes of Israel that adorns the external walls of the Goldmark Hall. The same tradition is reflected in Chagall's stained glass windows made for the Hadassah hospital of Jerusalem.

When building a synagogue, if it was not a simple temporary prayer-room, the architect was expected to bear in mind the image of the Temple, a "little sanctuary (*mikdash me'at*)" (Ezekiel 11,26). This ide-alized image, however, could not be realized in prac-tice, for the building itself had vanished without a trace, and the Biblical descriptions were not suffi-ciently detailed for an architectural reconstruc-tion; this is the main reason for the divergences in the appearance and style of individual synagogues. They do, however, share one structural feature in their ground-plan. Compared to the courtyard and hall (*ulam*) of the Temple, the courtyard of the synagogue, if it happens to have one, and its hall are proportionately much smaller, while the inte-rior is relatively large. There is no Holy of the Holies (*kodesh ha-kodashim / devir*), there is no holy space (*heikhal*); instead, they are equipped with an *aron*, a *dukhan* and a *bimah*. Regardless of whether the ground-plan follows a basilica-like or a centralized layout, these liturgical spaces are as a rule aligned along the length of the building.

171. Plaque on the eastern wall in the prayer-room of the Nagy Fuvaros utca synagogue

The two most important elements of the synagogue's interior space are the rostrum (*bimah*), where the Torah is read and the holy Ark, where the Torah scrolls are kept. The Ark (*aron*) was always set against the main wall, the eastern side of the building, while the position of the *bimah* was and still is subject to heated debates.

The terms for the elevated platform or rostrum (*bimah* / *almemor* / *melemmer*) go back to Greek (*bema*) and Arabic (*al-minbar*). In traditional synagogue architecture and in Orthodox synagogues the *bimah* is located at the center of the building, while in a longitudinal hall it stands closer to the Ark, roughly one-third of the way down the nave. Influenced, no doubt, by the interior layout of Christian churches, the Neolog movement has placed the *bimah* in front of the Ark, albeit it took care to draw arguments from rabbinical tradition to justify this change. It is important that the *bimah* be a rostrum, an elevated platform that lies above the floor of the synagogue; this separate space symbolically raises it above ordinary space, placing the ceremony of reading the Torah on a different plane. This separation enables the congregation to remain seated while the Torah is read. There are columns at each corner, or at least an indication of columns. The one-time central location of the *bimah* is reflected in that it was often erected between the columns supporting the roof. On this rostrum stands the *shulhan*, the reading table or pulpit, with a small ledge (*zer*) at its upper end, covered with an embroidered cloth (*mikhseh* or *mappah*), onto which the Torah scroll is placed. On the New Year the *shofar* is blown from the *bimah*.

A special double chair, Elijah's chair, usually stands in front of the *bimah*: this is the "place of honor (*moshav kavod*)", where the prophet and the godfather (*sandak*) usually sit. The two "bridegrooms" (*hatan Torah* and *hatan Bereshit*) who are called to read from the Torah at the end of one yearly cycle and the beginning of the next one, are seated on a similar chair. "To sit in front", "to be seated in front" has been a great honor since Talmudic times.

The "chest (*tevah*)", or the "Ark of the Holy (*aron ha-kodesh*)", or, more rarely, the "sanctuary (*heikhal*)" is always set against the eastern wall. During prayer (first of all, the *Shemoneh Esreh*) the entire congregation faces East, towards Jerusalem. The *aron* is usually an ornate construction: the Torah scrolls, the most precious possessions of the synagogue, are locked away behind a door and an elaborately embroidered curtain (*parokhet* / *paroykhes* / *velum*). The Ark is traditionally made of *shittim*-wood, that is generally translated as acacia (?). Should it for any reason become damaged, it cannot be reused for making any secular article, not even a reading table for the Torah. Some sort of platform (*dukhan* / *dukhen*) usually stands in front of the Ark. The inaccessible, holy sections of the Temple in Jerusalem, too, were separated by a curtain (Exodus 26,31–37). As in the case of the *bimah*, its role was to divide the secular from the sacred space. (In Christian Orthodoxy the iconostasis plays a similar function and it, too, goes back to the curtain of the Jerusalem Temple.)

In European synagogues the *shivviti* and *mizrah* plaques are on the eastern wall. The *shivviti* plaque in front of the *hazzan*'s table marks the direction of the prayer. Its text is a verse from the Psalms: "I have set (*shivviti*) the LORD always before me" (Psalms 16,8), a part, as well as a reminder, of the daily prayers. The *mizrah* ("East") plaques designate the direction of Jerusalem. In some synagogues there are separate *shivviti* and *mizrah* plaques on the eastern wall. Both are made with exceptional care. The *shivviti* plaques were often gems of calligraphy, describing the entire order of the service, written in beautifully shaped letters, and decorated with pictures of a *menorah* or of Biblical creatures, and with the *Tetragrammaton*, JHWH, in a frame in the center. In most synagogues the schedule (*zeman*) or order of the service is likewise set down on a separate plaque. (In some Jewish homes a panorama of Jerusalem or a *mizrah* plaque is found on the eastern wall, not only as a piece of decoration, but also to mark the direction to be faced during prayers.)

In the Dohány Temple, the Rabbinical Seminary and some other synagogues there are benches or chairs, set on a platform (*safsal* and *katedra*) and flanking the Ark; a separate place, on the right, directly beside the Ark, for the rabbis, the *dayyans* and other learned men; and for the *parnas*, the president and the leadership of the community, on the left. The pulpit (*omed* / *stender* / *Ständer*) where the rabbi or the preacher stood when speaking, is generally in front of the Ark, on the platform itself, but always above the level of the floor and always facing the congregation: traditionally, there are seven steps leading up to it.

The lamps (*menorah*, plural *menorot*) near the Ark recall the oil-lamps of the Temple: the eternal light (*ner tamid*) (Exodus 27,20; Leviticus 24,2) and the seven-branched candelabrum. In some synagogues a *Hanukkah* candlestick is also placed here.

It is an old tradition, almost a commandment, that every man should have his own seat (Yiddish *shtot*). Nowadays, when instead of chairs, most synagogues have benches, these are provided with a reading surface and a drawer. According to the Babylonian Talmud (Berakhot 6b), one should make provisions for a permanent place of prayer, and the Jerusalem Talmud is even more explicit: one should designate a place for oneself. Anyone who can afford it buys the place for himself for the entire year. The bench fee is part of the community tax; and should one go to *shul* every day, he can keep his prayer-book, his *tefillin* and *tallit* in his own bench.

The women have a separate section (*ezrat nashim*); this is usually the gallery, although in earlier times this may have been a neighboring room, perhaps not even opening into the men's prayer-room or separated from it by a grating or partition screen (*mehitzah*). (In Hunyadi tér, Visegrádi utca, or in the Orthodox old-age home in Alma utca similar constructions are applied.) The women's gallery had its own entrance and staircase. Women enjoy greater freedom in the synagogue than men, they come and go as they please and are even allowed to talk. Today in Budapest in many synagogues the women's section (*azarah / ezrat nashim*) is simply the left side or the back part, sometimes without any partition. Young girls do not have a separate place; together with the boys who are not *bar mitzvah* they can sit wherever they like, they can even walk around quietly during services. In Ashkenazi synagogues there is usually a learned woman (*forsagerin / forzogerke*) who, on the women's gallery, recites the prayers, sentence by sentence, for the others to repeat them after her.

The synagogue, or the prayer-room, was traditionally the center of the Jewish community, and the stage for each and every event of community life. This is where people recited prayers three times daily, where they studied in their free time, where the *bet din* met for counsel and announced its decision, where the punishments, including the floggings, were administered, and where the ritual penitence was performed on *Yom Kippur*; where travelers, scholars, merchants, emissaries, who on a Friday evening could not continue their journey, were offered shelter and lodging in a separate room (*hekdesh*).

The most important prayer in the synagogue is the *Amidah*, "Standing (prayer)", which has to be recited standing; since the destruction of the Second Temple this is *the* Prayer (*Tefillah*) that takes the place of the Temple service. It is also called *Shemoneh Esreh*, "Eighteen (scil. benedictions)", for it originally contained eighteen short benedictions to which a nineteenth was added later. The prayer itself dates from the time of the Second Temple and attained its final form after the fall of Jerusalem around 100 c.e. The nineteen formulae, all different but sharing a similar structure, cover the entirety of the personal and the communal sphere. It is a classical Jewish prayer (*tefillah*): benediction (*berakhah*), supplication (*bakkashah*) and thanksgiving in one (*hodayah*, literally "glorification" or "praise").

The *Amidah* is recited three times daily, in the morning service (*Shaharit*), in the afternoon service (*Minhah*) and in the evening (*Ma'ariv*). (On Shabbats and on holidays there is a fourth occasion as well, namely in the "additional prayer", the *Musaf.*) The first time, in the morning, everyone recites it for himself, quietly (*tefillah be-lahash*) as a personal prayer, with only the lips moving (I Samuel 1,13), and the *hazzan* recites it aloud (*hazarat ha-shatz*); during the evening service the *hazzan* does not repeat it. The daily service is built around this prayer, instead of the sacrifices made in the Temple. It is desirable, but strictly necessary only for the repetition, that there be a full *minyan*.

There is a strictly regulated choreography for this particular prayer. Everyone turns towards the East, towards Jerusalem, takes three steps backwards, and three forwards as if approaching a throne. Then bows four times (at the beginning and the end of the first and of the penultimate benediction) and at the end of the prayer again steps three steps backwards, bows to the left, to the right and to the front. The benedictions begin with the words: "*Barukh attah Adonay*, Blessed art Thou, Lord our God." When the first word is said (*barukh*), the knees are bent, the head is bowed during the second (*attah*), and one stands up straight for the third, the mention of God (*Adonay*). When standing, the feet remain together. One must not stand close to someone else and, while preparing for the prayer, one must make sure that the prescribed "four handbreadths (*ammah*)" are there. There must be no noise or chatter during the recital of this prayer or during the reading of the Torah. If there is a *minyan*, everyone says the prayer together when it is repeated (*tefillah be-kol*). In the diaspora, the Priestly Benediction is usually recited on the High Holidays by the Kohens before the last, the nineteenth, benediction. A pious custom is to recite one's own Biblical verse or *pasuk*, whose first and last letters are identical with the first and last letters of one's name, after the *Amidah*. As an explanation for this custom, Rashi cited a passage from Micah (6,9), "Then will your name achieve wisdom."

It is customary to sway (German *schaukeln*, Yiddish *shokeln*, in Hungary some people say *soklolni*) rhythmically during prayer (*daven*) in the temple and cemetery, but also at home and during "studying", while reading the Bible or the Talmud. One must bow, whether symbolically or actually, during the recital of some prayers, but bowing *per se* is more of a custom than a prescription, based on a passage from Psalms (35,10): "All my bones shall say, LORD...", i.e. words of praise. The ritual act of prostration calls to mind parallels in the history of religions.

In traditional liturgy everyone recites the prayers to himself, according to his own rhythm, during the service. This custom still prevails in Orthodox congregations. The softly whispered prayers blend into a barely audible murmur. It is the task of the prayer-leader, the person who officiates as a reader (*sheliah tzibbur*), to keep a certain order among individual prayers. This person can be anyone. He, too, recites the prayers in a low voice, together with the others, but repeats aloud the last words, so that one may know where the others are. A certain unity is given to the individual rhythm of the prayer by the *Amen* pronounced at the end of certain passages.

The synagogue is a house of study or a house of prayer, and not a residential building. Yet anyone who studies or prays there practically lives there. In an old-fashioned *shul* one could eat his meals and stay overnight, if necessary. One could hold a conversation in the courtyard or in the lobby even during service. In this respect, the synagogue is truly a place of assembly, enabling people who would not otherwise meet, to be together. But nobody can simply enter the building seeking shelter from the rain, or take a short-cut through the synagogue. Anyone crossing a synagogue has to recite at least one benediction.

Near the entrance stands a ritual basin for ritual hand-washing (*kiyyor*). (The Hebrew word, a Sumerian loanword, originally denoted one of the ritual vessels of the Temple.) The collection plate or box (*kuppah*) is generally next to the door, too.

Upon entering, a Biblical verse is recited: "How fair are your tents, O Jacob, your dwellings, O Israel!" (Numbers 24,5), and upon leaving, another one: "Happy are those who dwell in Your house; they forever praise You" (Psalms 84,5) and "Righteous men shall surely praise Your name, the upright shall dwell in Your presence" (Psalms 140,14), are said. It is customary to hurry on the way to the synagogue, to proceed as slowly as possible when leaving and also to sit down for a moment in quiet contemplation, or to loiter and chat with the others in the lobby, in the courtyard or in front of the entrance.

(11) The Priestly Blessing

Only a *kohen* may recite it, hence its name: "Kohanite blessing (*birkat kohanim*)", sometimes known also as "Aaron's blessing", since according to the Bible, the *kohanim* are the descendants of Aaron, the first High Priest. It is sometimes called *dukhenen*—or *dühenolni* in Hungarian—for the Kohen stands on the platform (*dukhan*) in front of the Ark in the synagogue.

The blessing itself consists of fifteen words and three short sentences (Numbers 6,24–26), the first of which is one of the earliest surviving Biblical verses. In 1986, the Israeli archaeologist of Hungarian ancestry Gabriel Barkay found two fine and tiny silver sheets, each rolled together into an amulet, bearing the words of the Priestly Blessing, in one of the burial sites carved into the rock at the edge of the Hinnom valley (*Gei Hinnom*), southwest to the Old City of Jerusalem. Although inscribed with only some portions of the Priestly Blessing, these silver sheets, dating from the last quarter of the seventh century B.C.E., have conclusively proved that the text of the blessing was exactly the same in the time of the First Temple as recorded in the earliest surviving Biblical manuscripts that were younger by ca. one and a half thousand years. And even though it is not the earliest passage of the Torah, it remains, for the time being, the earliest linguistic remnant.

The recital of the Priestly Blessing is the task of the *kohanim*; it is recited before the very last benediction in the *Amidah*. (In Jerusalem every day, in Israel every Shabbat, and in the Diaspora on the High Holidays only.) They remove their shoes—a heritage of the Orient—, and wash their hands. A Levite (or if there is no Levite, someone else) pours the water from the jug. Since the destruction of the Temple this has remained basically the only service performed by the Levites. They ascend the *dukhan* before the *Amen* of the previous benediction, and the *hazzan* then calls them at the appropriate time. All the *kohanim* who are present in the synagogue are there. They turn towards the community, stretch out their hands at shoulder height with palms facing forward (*nesi'at kappayim*). The hands are held touching at the thumbs, with the first two fingers of each hand separated from the other two. According to a *midrash*, the LORD looks down on the congregation through their fingers. The fingertips point downwards, the right hand is held slightly lower than the left. The synagogue has to be absolutely quiet, nothing is allowed to distract the congregation's attention. If the *kohanim* recite the blessing themselves, the *hazzan* does not participate, although the prevailing custom is for the *hazzan* to say each word of the Priestly Blessing which is then repeated aloud by the *kohanim*, with a small pause between each word for the sake of emphasis and clarity. The

172. Pitcher (ewer) and bowl of the Levites

tallit is drawn over their head and their arms, so neither their face nor their blessing hands can be seen. It has become a custom not to look at the *kohanim* and, also, for members of the congregation to cover themselves with the *tallit*. The congregation responds with an "Amen" after each of the three sections. This blessing may only be recited in Hebrew.

Passed down from father to son and preserved also in certain surnames (Cohen, Kahana, Kohn, Kogan, etc., in Magyarized names, like Kelemen or Kende, retaining only the initial), the tradition of a Kohanite lineage is still strong, and indicated also on tomb-stones; in deeply religious circles this tradition is mostly maintained by the Priestly Blessing and certain prohibitions. The prestige it conveys may be no more and no less than that of genealogies in general. Kohanite names amount to about two to three per cent in each Jewish group of some size and it is most unlikely that anyone would take a Kohanite name unlawfully, for it entails real disadvantages besides the barely tangible prestige.

(12) Tallit, Tefillin—Shema, Kaddish

The prayer shawl (*tallit / tales*, plural *tallitot*) was a rectangular mantle, a simple outer garment similar to the Romans' *pallium*, worn by men. Later, following the instructions set down in the Torah (Numbers 15,37–40), its use became exclusively ceremonial. Traditionally only men wore it, although Reform Judaism in the Western world has extended the right to wear a *tallit* to women as well (but still an exceptionally rare sight in Budapest). The size of the rectangular wool or linen shawl varies: it should be large enough to cover the entire body, but definitely to cover at least the head and the shoulders, and it should be at least a "handbreadth" shorter than the lower edge of one's garment. Among Ashkenazi Jews black or blue stripes are woven into the *tallit*. There are fringes or tassels at the corners (*tzitzit*, plural *tzitziyot*, *tsitses* in vernacular), eight in each corner (Numbers 15,38–39), with five knots on each. There is a separately sewn ornate band along one side, the "wreath (*atarah*)" that covers the forehead. During prayer the *tallit* covers the shoulders or sometimes also the head—

"in the manner of the Arabs (*ke-atifat Yishma'elim*)". Only married men must wear the *tallit*, but in many communities, such as the Hasidim, children after their *bar mitzvah* are required to wear one, too. This is the *tallit gadol*, "the great prayer shawl", worn only during the morning prayers. The *Shema* can be recited without a *tallit*, but if it has already been put on, the fringes must be pressed to the eyes during the recital of the prayer. During the day, the *tallit* is kept in a special case, an embroidered pouch; in the morning it is not too difficult to notice men hurrying to the temple, carrying a *tallit* pouch. They can obviously be identified as Neologs, for an Orthodox person would not carry anything on the Sabbath, he would keep his *tallit* and his prayer-book in the *shul*. This is why he needs his own, permanent bench and a drawer in his bench. According to tradition, the deceased has to be buried wrapped in the *tallit* that he wore in his lifetime. On

173. All one needs for the morning prayers: *tallit*, prayer-book (*Siddur*) and *tefillin* (in a velvet bag) in the winter prayer-room of the Kazinczy utca synagogue

Yom Kippur one wears a *tallit* with white stripes against a white background.

The "small *tallit*" (*tallit katan / tales koten*) is a simple rectangular piece of linen (*arba'a kanfot / arba kanfes*) with the prescribed fringes at the corners and a slit along middle, allowing it to be worn. This is worn also during the day, in some families even three- or four-year-old boys are given one; the most religious have the fringes outside, so that one may "look at it" (Numbers 15,39). They are a reminder of the religious rules (*mitzvah*). The common Ashkenazi name for these fringes is *tzitzes* (*tzitzit*) or Yiddish *tsidekl* (German *Leibzudeckel*). The Hungarian word is *tzidakli*. The Halakhic obligation is that during the day men are obliged to wear the fringes on any rectangular garment they might have on, but whether this garment is a *tallit* or a *tzidekl* is not specified. And if one does not wear a rectangular garment, there is no obligation whatsoever.

The phylacteries are used during the morning prayers, except on the Sabbath and during festival days. Their Hebrew name is *tefillin / tfilin*, from *tefillah*, the Hebrew word for "prayer". The ancient Greek word (*phylakterion*) first occurs in Matthew (23,5), suggesting that it had at one time been worn as an amulet. *Tefillin* from the first century B.C.E. have been found in the caves along the Dead Sea. A *tefillin*

174. Laying of the *tefillin* (*shel yad*). Lino-cut by Imre Ámos, 1940

consists of two small, cubic leather cases or boxes (*bayit*, "house"), made from the hide of ritually cleansed animals, both of which contain four short Biblical verses written on parchment according to the same strict rules as the writing of the Torah (Exodus 13,1–10; Exodus 13,11–16; Deuteronomy 6,4–9; Deuteronomy 11,13–21); the most important being the *Shema Yisra'el*. Each case has a strap (*retzuah*) attached to it. The *tefillin* is the sign (*ot*) on the hands and the head, as prescribed in the *Shema Yisra'el* (Deuteronomy 6,8). There are two kinds of *tefillin*: the *tefillin* of the head (*tefillin shel rosh*) which, as shown by its name, has to be placed in the center of the forehead. The leather case itself is divided into four small compartments (*titorah*, "bridge"), and each of the four Biblical verses is written on a separate piece of parchment that is carefully placed inside these compartments according to a strict order. The leather case of the *tefillin* of the hand (*tefillin shel yad*) has but a single compartment and thus the Biblical verses are written on one piece of parchment and the verses follow one another. This *tefillin* goes on the left upper arm, as near to the heart as possible. Its strap must be wound around the arm seven times. Ashkenazi Jews wind the strap outwards, the Sephardim inwards. The end of the strap is wound around the wrist and the three middle fingers of the left hand to form the Hebrew letter *Shin* (standing for *Shadday*, "Almighty"). The strap of the *tefillin* of the head is a leather band—circular in diameter—that has to be knotted (*kesher*) above the neck; the strap of the *tefillin* of the hand is flat. The leather cases and the straps are black, and the top of the leather case has to be stitched with twelve stitches. First the *tallit* has to be put on, then comes the *tefillin* of the hand. There is still no agreement on the order in which the two verses from Deuteronomy should be written on the parchment and this is the reason for the two types of *tefillin* of the head. (The *tefillin*

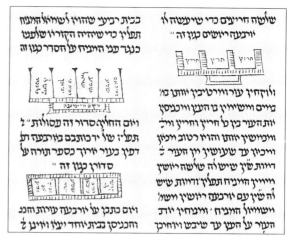

found together with the Dead Sea scrolls have not resolved the debate, for they include both types.) The very pious solve the problem by wearing both types of *tefillin*, either at the same time, or changing them during the recital of the prayer. Both cases are inscribed on the outside, with the letter *Shin*, an abbreviation for *Shadday*, or the whole word; on the *tefillin* of the head the letter appears on both sides, with four tiny stems on the left. Every man is obliged to lay or don (Yiddish *legn*, in Hungarian *légol*) the *tefillin* after his *bar mitzvah*, and most boys begin to practice how to do this well before the actual ceremony. No harm can come to one who has the *tefillin* on his head, says the Talmud (Menahot, 43b), the *tefillin* on the arm, *tzitzit* on his garment and the *mezuzah* on his doorpost; he is surely protected against all evil.

A sad story contradicts this pious tradition. In his *Utazás Pestről – Budapestre* [Journey from Pest to Budapest, 1912] Adolf Ágai recounts that in the spring of 1848, at the time of the siege of Buda, the captain of the Hungarian patrol caught a suspicious looking man at Normafa, in the Buda hills. He was a Jew, who had a peculiar little pouch in his bag that he tried to hide from the armed soldiers. "It contained the tefillin: the phylacteries used by Jewish men, wound around his arm and his head." The peddler always had his phylacteries with him. The soldiers, however, took him for a spy, carrying classified military information in the "box" and immediately hung him on a tree.

The *Shema Yisra'el* or *Shema* is the most important Jewish prayer. "Hear, O Israel...". Three quotations from the Bible, called *Shema* (Deuteronomy 6,4-9), *Ve-hayyah* (Deuteronomy 11,13-21) and *Va-yomer* (Numbers 15,37-41) after their first words, encapsulate the most important teachings, commandments and traditions of Judaism. This is the very first prayer one learns as a child and the last prayer one recites on the deathbed, encompassing human life itself. It structures daily life, being the focal point of the morning and evening prayers. Two short benedictions have to be recited before and one after the recital of the *Shema*. If one is praying alone, three words, *El melekh ne'eman* (the LORD is a righteous king) are said right before reciting the *Shema*, and if there is a *minyan*, the three last words, *ha-Shem Elohekhem emet*, "the LORD, your God, is righteous" are repeated. Together with these three words, the *Shema* contains a total of 248 words, corresponding—according to tradition—to the limbs of the human body and to the number of positive commandments. It is customary to cover one's eyes during the recital of the first verse so that nothing can distract from the most important statement: "YHWH, our God, (is) the only YHWH." The last letter (*ayin*) of the first word (*shema*) and the last letter (*dalet*) of the last word are generally written slightly larger than the others for emphasis. When the two *tefillin* are mentioned, everyone touches his own *tefillin* and when the *tzitzit* are mentioned in the third section, the *tsitses* on the prayer shawl are kissed. It is forbidden to interrupt the *Shema*, and the *Amidah* must begin immediately after its last words.

The *Kaddish* is not simply a mourner's prayer, as is often thought, and it is not even a funeral prayer. It is an affirmation of faith (*doxologia*), a glorification, a sanctification. "Magnified and sanctified be...". The text is neither Biblical, nor Hebrew, but Aramaic, from the Talmudic Age. The text

175. Arrangement of the *tefillin* boxes. Explanatory diagrams from the manuscript of *Mishneh Torah* by Maimonides

and its role in the ritual is the sanctification of God's name. According to the traditional explanation, it is written in Aramaic because this is the one language the angels do not understand and thus this prayer rises directly to God. At the time that this prayer was formulated, Aramaic was the vernacular and anyone could easily learn and memorize it, for everyone spoke Aramaic. The prayer can only be recited if there is a *minyan* and the congregation has to turn and face Jerusalem. The *Kaddish* has five basic variants:

(i) *Kaddish de-rabbanan*, "the scholars' *Kaddish*", originally a prayer of glorification recited at the end of one's studies; it is still customary to recite it after any Talmudic passage that appears in the synagogue service.

(ii) *Kaddish shalem*, "complete *Kaddish*", recited by the *hazzan* at the end of the synagogue service.

(iii) *Hatzi Kaddish*, "half (short) *Kaddish*", a shorter version of the *Kaddish* recited at the end of certain parts of the synagogue service.

(iv) *Kaddish yatom*, "mourners' *Kaddish*", the mourner's (*yatom* / *yosem*) prayer of glorification during the synagogue service.

(v) *Kaddish le-ithaddata*, a more extended version of the mourners' *Kaddish*, is part of the burial ceremony; the same prayer is customarily recited at the end of the study of a Talmudic treatise.

There is no reference either to death or to the deceased in the text of the *Kaddish*; this prayer is only concerned with the glorification of God. The mourner is comforted by the divine world order. Both the complete and the short *Kaddish* are recited during the synagogue service, the latter several times. The mourning son has to recite the *Kaddish* daily during the year after the funeral, following the thirty days of full mourning, i.e. for eleven months, and then once a year, first time at the anniversary of the funeral, and then on the day of the death.

A few words from the beginning of the mourners' *Kaddish*:

יתגדל ויתקדש
שמה רבא בעלמא
די ברא כרעותה
וימליך מלכותה
בחייכון וביומיכון
ובחיי דכל בית ישראל
בעגלא ובזמן קריב
ואמרו אמן

Yitgaddal ve-yitkaddash
shemeh rabba be-alma
di-bera ki-re' uteh
ve-yamlikh malkhuteh
be-hayyeikhon u-ve-yomeikhon
u-ve-hayyei de-khol bet Yisra'el
ba-agala u-vi-zeman kariv.
Ve-imru amen...

"Magnified and sanctified be
His great name in the world
which He created according to His will,
and may He establish His kingdom
in your lifetime and in your days
and in the lifetime of all the house of Israel
speedily and at near time.
And say ye, Amen..."

(13) Orthodox Synagogue in Kazinczy utca (29-31 Kazinczy utca)

The small area enclosed by Kazinczy utca (formerly called *Kreutzgasse / Nagy Kereszt utca*) and Dob utca (formerly called *Drei Trommel Gasse / Három Dob utca*) is the center of Budapest Orthodoxy; it has retained many essential features of a traditional Jewish community even in the midst of a modern city. The *shul*, where the daily prayers are recited, cannot be too far from the home. This pattern was established jointly by the necessities of Jewish religious life and the non-Jewish environment. Surrounded by a wall, the Jewish quarter was impenetrable from the outside and fulfilled a double

function: to enable the practical fulfillment of religious commandments and, at the same time, to protect members of the community from the mocking eyes or possible attacks of the outside world, owing to the legal position of the Jewish community prior to their emancipation in 1867. More often than not the wall was formed by the residential buildings; the community's most important institutions, such as the synagogue, the school, the *mikveh*, etc. lay in the area enclosed by these houses.

In Budapest the center of the Orthodox community reflects a similar spatial organization amidst modern urban condi-

176. The Orthodox school in the court-yard of the Kazinczy utca synagogue

177. Facade of the Orthodox school, with clock

178. Maharam (Morenu ha-Rav Moshe) Trebitsch, a graduate from the *Hatam Sofer*'s Yeshivah

179. The office building of the Orthodox community of Pest in Dob utca

180. Interior of the Kazinczy utca synagogue

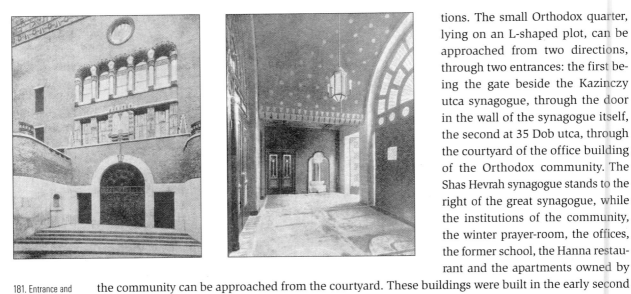

181. Entrance and detail of the facade of the Kazinczy utca synagogue, 1913. The (pseudo-) rosette window is decorated with a *menorah*

182. Entrance hall with an ornamental fountain in the Kazinczy utca synagogue, 1913

tions. The small Orthodox quarter, lying on an L-shaped plot, can be approached from two directions, through two entrances: the first being the gate beside the Kazinczy utca synagogue, through the door in the wall of the synagogue itself, the second at 35 Dob utca, through the courtyard of the office building of the Orthodox community. The Shas Hevrah synagogue stands to the right of the great synagogue, while the institutions of the community, the winter prayer-room, the offices, the former school, the Hanna restaurant and the apartments owned by the community can be approached from the courtyard. These buildings were built in the early second decade of the twentieth century. The school was completed first, in 1911, followed by the office building in 1912. The architects and the year of construction (673 of the "minor era" / 1913 c.e.) are commemorated on a slab set on the facade of the building. Having won the competition for planning the synagogue, Béla Löffler (1877–?) and Sándor (Samu) Löffler (1877–?) were commissioned. Their victory could in part be attributed to the fact that the other architects who had entered the competition were not members of the Orthodox community. The construction of the synagogue, based on the Löfflers' designs, was finished in 1913 and the building was consecrated on the Friday preceding the High Holidays (September 26, 1913). From that time on, until recently, little was done against the decay of the building, including harms caused by World War II.

After the renovation of the courtyard and the adjoining buildings, the reconstruction of the synagogue itself was started in 1997. The works aim at restoring the original architecture and decorative design. The entrance hall, in ruins and inaccessible since World War II, is the first to be finished.

The fact that the distinctive synagogue of the Orthodox community was finished some fifty years after the Neolog temple in Dohány utca would indicate that Orthodoxy gained ground but slowly in the capital's urban atmosphere. The roots of Hungarian Orthodoxy were mainly to be found in the towns and villages of Hungary, and not just in Northeastern Hungary. Budapest

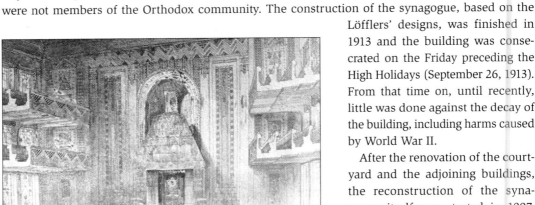

183. Interior, with the Ark, in the Kazinczy utca synagogue. Drawing by Sándor Skutetzky and József Porgesz for the architectural competition, 1910

184. Interior of the Kazinczy utca synagogue with the *bimah / almemor*

had the largest Jewish population, most of whom were members of one of the Neolog communities; in contrast, the rural Jewish population tended to be Orthodox and vastly outnumbered the Neolog. Modeled as it was on the state organization, the administrative center of the Orthodoxy could hardly have been outside the capital, even if the most renowned Orthodox rabbis were, with a few exceptions, active in the provinces, mostly Eastern Hungary. An authoritative handbook, Pinhas Zelig Schwartz's *Shem ha-gedolim* (Paks, 1913), lists twenty-five Orthodox rabbis in the capital in the early twentieth century. Budapest may have been the center of Hungarian Orthodoxy, but the Orthodox community of the city was in no way regarded as being particularly significant.

Orthodox Jews have always taken great care in their choice of home. The Kazinczy utca area used to be a true Orthodox neighborhood. The central institutions—such as the Central Office of Orthodoxy, formerly in Terézváros (19 Eötvös utca)—were moved here, as was the Hevrah Kaddishah (12 Dob utca). A "*matzo* bakery", as it was called in Hungarian, and a kosher poultry

185. The Ark and the eastern wall in the Kazinczy utca synagogue

186. Door of the Ark in the Kazinczy utca synagogue

187. Winter prayer-room in the Kazinczy utca synagogue

188. Interior of the Kazinczy utca synagogue: view from the second-floor gallery

189. Interior of the Kazinczy utca synagogue: view from the steps of the Ark

butchery were built in the courtyard of the Kazinczy utca–Dob utca complex. The ceremonial hall of the community was on the top floor of the office building. Together with the neighboring blocks, Kazinczy utca was the street of the silversmiths and jewelers. The time-worn, occasionally neglected facade of the houses reflected a certain stand, even good taste. The Orthodox building complex designed by the Löffler brothers was an outstanding example of Art Nouveau (*Sezession*), and it did not contradict the taste of the commissioners or the community.

The facade of the Kazinczy utca synagogue is an outstanding example of late Art Nouveau in Hungary. The Art Nouveau-design letters of the Hebrew inscription on the frieze harmonize well with the architectural style of the facade.

אין זה כי אם בית אלהים וזה שער השמים

"This is none other than the abode of God,
and that is the gateway to heaven."
(Genesis 28,17)

The ground-plan of the synagogue is traditional. The rostrum (*bimah*) stands at the center; five steps lead up to it. The Ark is along the eastern wall. The lobby is flanked by the stairways leading to the women's gallery. The two-story gallery is supported by reinforced concrete pillars, a practice conforming to nineteenth-century interior design. The synagogue could seat 479 men and 522 women.

The Kazinczy utca synagogue continues to be the most important religious center of Budapest Orthodoxy. The various other institutions of Orthodoxy lie around it. A religious school, a "small yeshivah (*yeshivah ketanah*)" is maintained for children. Visiting rabbis from Israel recently set up a "circle" or *Kolel* for educating grown-ups. The synagogue itself is only used on the High Holidays and other festivals; services are normally held in the Shas Hevrah Synagogue in the summer and in the small prayer-room in the winter.

(14) Mikveh (16 Kazinczy utca)

The only "public" ritual bath (*mikveh*) of the capital is in Kazinczy utca, not far from the synagogue, used by the Orthodox community. Before World War II there was another *mikveh*, at no. 40. This

one had to be used as a mortuary in the days of the ghetto and was pulled down after the war. Today some kind of a shed made of aluminum stands in its place. The Orthodox community opened its ritual bath with state-of-the-art facilities in 1928. The present bath has been rebuilt several times after World War II, observing traditional rules.

The *mikveh* does not serve hygienic needs, it is for ritual purification. Only natural, "living" waters are suitable for this purpose, water from rivers, wells or rain water. Still water, or water that comes through a metal pipe, may not be used. The *mikveh* has to be deep enough so that one is submerged in the water even when standing. Steps should lead into the water. The use of the *mikveh* is mandatory in Orthodox circles. Women visit the *mikveh* after their period of purification and the following seven days, fourteen days altogether, of separation from their husband (*niddah*) (Leviticus 15,19–24); young women first visit the *mikveh* before their wedding and then after the

190. Ritual bathing (*mitzvat niddah*)

bridal night. Pious men immerse themselves in the *mikveh* on Friday and before holidays, most of them definitely before *Yom Kippur*. Hasidim may go every day or at least in the morning of the days when the Torah is read (Monday, Thursday).

One must go to the *mikveh* clean, after thorough washing. Jewelry or any other object must be removed from the body, the hair must be opened and combed, nails cleaned. Immersion (*tevilah / toyvl*) in the *mikveh* should be full, the head and the hair should be three inches below the surface. (In the late 1990s, there are about a dozen women using it regularly.) Immersion in the *mikveh* is a part also of the ritual when someone converts to the Jewish faith (*giyyur / gier*), both for men and women.

There used to be several ritual baths in Budapest, many people needed it. It is almost certain that every traditional (Orthodox) Jewish community maintained a *mikveh*, even in Pest, usually not far from the synagogue. There was one in the former Orczy House, another one in the nearby Mestetics Bath and a further one in Két Szerecsen utca / Paulay Ede utca (this latter one came to be replaced by the headquarters of the "Hunyadi János" Bitter Water company). It was easy to bore a well in the soil of Pest. From the river-bed nearby the neighborhood was supplied with water abundantly. In a few houses, like in 31 Paulay Ede utca, there is still a well in the basement, rich in fresh—living—water.

(15) Wedding

In Ashkenazi communities Orthodox Jewish weddings are held under the open sky, the only roofing may be the canopy, the *huppah*. In the towns of Judah and in Jerusalem you hear

קול ששון וקול שמחה
קול חתן וקול כלה

"The sound of mirth and gladness,
the voice of bridegroom and bride"

—as the traditional inscription on the beautiful *Jugendstil* iron *huppah* (*hüpe* in Hungarian) frame in the courtyard of Kazinczy *shul* quotes the Bible (Jeremiah 33,11 or—in another context—Jeremiah 7,34). The same inscription is generally inscribed on the betrothal plate which is broken at the engagement ceremony. (Luckily, not all of these plates were broken, some are exhibited at the Jewish Museum and other places.)

In the past all marriages were arranged, even in large cities. A good match (*shiddukh / shidakh*) was the result of careful consideration of the financial and social status of the parties. The dowry and the wedding gifts were also settled in advance. The parties were introduced to each other by the matchmaker (*shadkhan / shadkhen*), parents first, the couple afterwards. After Bernard Malamud's short story, *The Magic Barrel* (1958) became popular in Hungary and the musical *Fiddler on the Roof* was staged in Pest, Hungarians learned the "matchmaker" by the English name. But the profession is not practiced anymore. (Sándor Scheiber used to say ironically: "In my youth I wished to be a world-famous scholar and rabbi, but I became a famous *shadkhen*, the best one in Pest." As a matter of fact, several couples found each other at his frequented Friday evening gatherings in the Rabbinical Seminary, where he would give a *kiddush* with cocoa and *hallah*. The wedding greetings constitute a big part of the sermons in his literary remains.) According to tradition, a real *shidukh* is made by the Heavenly Sound (*bat kol*) forty days before the parties are born. The *shadkhen* only discovers the match and helps them

191. The back wall of the Kazinczy utca synagogue

come to an agreement. His (or her) role was often just to provide a proper appearance to the agreement. A *shadkhen* was often employed even if the bride and groom knew each other already, even if they had found each other on their own. Employing a *shadkhen* meant that the young couple behaved appropriately in other respects as well. *Shadkhones* used to be a real (part-time) job. The *shadkhen* lived from traveling a lot, knowing many people, taking and bringing news, talking to everyone about everyone else, indeed, gossiping, mixing and intriguing. A fee was due for the successful match. It was most natural that relatives should mediate matches. Decades later, even after their relationship grew cold, Ignác Goldziher would still recall in conversations that Vilmos Bacher met his wife at his house. Not that they wanted to marry off anyone who did not wish to get married. This is forbidden by Jewish law. But traditional way of life did not offer many opportunities for young people of the opposite sex to meet. Mediation made up for this. In large cities it was even desirable that the parties get to know each other well in advance. A popular meeting place was the café, for instance the "Café Herzl" in the Gyertyánffy House in Pest.

The first step toward a marriage is the agreement between the parents. The parents put down the terms of the marriage in writing (*tenayim / tnoim*): they agree on the dowry (*nadan / nadn*) and the fine in case the groom breaks the betrothal (*knas*). This is not a marriage contract and it is not accompanied by a ceremony, though occasionally they break the betrothal plate. Now the date of the wedding can be set. On the Sabbath before the wedding the groom is called to the Torah in the synagogue and he uses the opportunity to announce the upcoming event. After the *aliyyah* the women, sitting upstairs in the gallery, throw nuts, peanuts and almonds at the groom (*bavarfn*). In the evening, after the Sabbath, there is a bachelor party (*forshpil*) at the groom's house.

192. Frame of the wedding canopy (*huppah*) in the courtyard of the Kazinczy utca synagogue

Weddings are not held on days when legal acts cannot be carried out (Sabbath, holidays, days of mourning). There are no rules as to the specific time when the ceremony should take place. It can be during the day or at night, but not at sundown because this is when the calendar day changes and so the above-mentioned condition may not be met. Tuesday is often chosen as the wedding day because it is considered a day doubly-blessed: in the Biblical story of creation God said "it is good" twice (Genesis 1,10 and 12) on the third day. According to Jewish tradition (Numbers 5,18), the bride's hair has to be cut on the day of the wedding, completely or very short, a practice still observed in strict Orthodox circles. From then on she wears a wig, or covers her head with a hat or a kerchief, for the rest of her life.

"The day of the wedding has arrived (...) The musicians played a haunting Eastern tune as the braids of beautiful Hannika[4] were untied, to be cut according to the ancient tradition. (...) Covering her head with a golden-striped headband, the rabbi blessed her; bride and groom, dressed in the burial clothes, were led under the wedding canopy, which stood under the open sky. Music sounded everywhere, the cantor sang Hebrew songs specially made for such occasions...

(Mór Szegfy, "Az elátkozott bachúr. Eredeti beszély" [The Cursed Bahur. An Original Short-story], in: *Első magyar zsidó naptár és évkönyv*, Pest, 1848)

As part of the religious ceremony, the groom (*hatan / khosn*) and the bride (*kallah / kale*) fast the day of the wedding; the bride, for the first time in her life, goes to the *mikveh*; like people before dying, bride and groom both confess their sins (*vidduy gadol / vide godl*) so they can start their new life pure. During the ceremony—under the *huppah*—the groom wears his *kittel* and puts on his *tallit / talis* too. (For one year after the marriage he is not going to wear his *kitl* any more, not even on Rosh ha-Shanah and Yom Kippur.) At some places the bride, too, is dressed in white linen (*sarganit / sargones*)—these are also burial clothes.

[4] Hungarian nickname for Hannah.

There is no rule that the ceremony has to take place in a synagogue. Yet in Hungary since the mid-nineteenth century, the Neolog custom has been to hold weddings in the synagogue. Attached to most synagogues there is a special room where the bride's girl-friends dress her and prepare her for the ceremony. When she is ready, she sits in the bride's chair (*kisse shel kallah*) and waits for the groom who comes here to meet her. He may only enter upon her permission. According to the ceremonial order they see each other now for the first time. Since the deception of Jacob (Genesis 29,16–26) it is customary for the groom to look at his bride right before the wedding, to see whom he marries. It is his duty to put the cap (*kepele*) or veil (*vual, shleyer, dektikhl*) or kerchief (*bindalik*) on the bride (*kale badekn* / German *bedecken*). Then comes the "acceptance of the deal (*kabbalat kinyan*)". This symbolic act takes place in the hall of the synagogue. In the name of the bride's father one of the witnesses hands over a glove or a kerchief to the groom (*kinyan sudar*), but it is enough if the groom, the "buyer", lifts up the edge of the coat of the witness (*kinyan hagbahah*) or pulls it towards himself (*kinyan meshikhah*), because the edge of the clothes symbolizes the acquisition (*kinyan mesirah*). Actually, the bride's gift to the groom is usually a "kerchief", a beautiful *tallit*. The gifts of the *hatan* and *kallah* to each other (a *Siddur*, a ring and a *tallit*) are called *sivlonot / siblonot*, "symbols" (Greek *symbolon*).

193. The courtyard of the Kazinczy utca synagogue: view from beside the *huppah* frame

Since the mid-nineteenth century the wedding canopy has always been set up in front of the *bimah* in the Neolog synagogues of Pest. It is only in Kazinczy utca that we find a permanent *huppah* in the synagogue courtyard—Orthodox Jews usually perform the wedding ceremony in the courtyard. In the Pest community Löw Schwab was the first one to bring the *huppah* and the entire ceremony inside the synagogue. The interior has to be illuminated as brightly as possible. Bride and groom do not go under the *huppah* together, they are led there by the *unterfirer*, the groom usually by his father or sometimes by his father-in-law as well. The bride arrives last. She is led to the *huppah* by the best man (*sosebin*), usually her father or an older male relative. (The word *sosebin* is of Babylonian origin, *susapinnu*, and comes from Talmudic language.) The bride, occasionally together with her mother and mother-in-law, circles around the groom, who is waiting for her under the *huppah*, seven times (Jeremiah 31,21). If one of the parents is not alive, a burning candle is brought to the ceremony symbolically, even if there is daylight. During the ceremony everyone remains standing, the parents next to the *huppah*. To perform the wedding ceremony it is not necessary to have a *minyan*, but there are usually more than ten people—who would not attend a wedding? The *mitzvah* of going to a wedding comes before Torah study.

The ceremony itself begins with a blessing. The rabbi, or someone else makes *kiddush* over the wine (*birkat erusin*, "blessing over the wedding", or rather "the engagement"), then the groom's father raises the wine to his son's lips, then his wife to the bride's lips and they both drink.

In the description of a wedding in Pest by Lázár Petrichevich Horváth we can identify the Choir Temple in the Orczy House. His vivid description evokes the synagogue and the ceremony fairly realistically:

"Upon the invitation of some refined Israelite families of Pest I attended a few weddings recently. The prayer-house was filled with people. (...) On a stand guarded by a wooden fence there stood the choir, forming a semicircle. They were grinning boys, dressed in black robes, and adult men for the solo parts, all wearing a black beret. Among them stood the chief singer in the same garb but decorated with silver lining. (...) To the right (of the stand) sat the men, on the other side the women, relatives and acquaintances. (...) When time came, the huge doors of the main entrance opened and in poured a crowd of wedding guests, men and women separately. The bride stood out from the crowd by her graceful figure and ethereal stature like a Lebanese cedar tree [sic!]. Her well-proportioned body was concealed by a fluffy snow-white silk dress, her beautiful, marble-like shoulders and arms under a veil which fell from her abundant hair. The angelic head

194. A printed wedding invitation, eighteenth century

חתן
ופה רל,הישץ כרה מטהן,וטיראב שום
נבא על ראש שמחתיואל הנשתה אשר אבי עשה
שא למז ט אתהכלה

was crowned with a white wreath, her chest covered with rosebuds. (...) The sublime song of the young choir filled our heart with harmony, alternating with the soloist who sang artistic cascades of sound (*Tonrouladen*) in deeply emotional tones. In front of them was the Ark containing the Tablets of Moses, covered with gold-embroidered scarlet drapery, and the Hebrew inscription of the holy doorstep, which signals God. The couple to be wedded and their parents stepped ahead. An honorable high priest preached about pure morals and the obligations, joys and burdens of married life. He asked the couple whether they loved each other truly and faithfully. After a loud but simple 'yes' and the exchange of rings his patriarchal role ended." (in: *Honderű*, 1847)

The ceremony thus described by Petrichevich Horváth contains all the innovations of a Neolog ceremony. Members of the Cult temple held weddings inside the temple since 1832.

According to the Mishnah (Kiddushin 1,1), a marriage is considered valid if one of three legal acts take place: "purchase" (Deuteronomy 22,16), "document" or "being together". All of these need to be incorporated into the wedding ceremony in a symbolic form. Three moments of the ceremony have legal validity, the "betrothal (*erusin*)" or "separation (*kiddushin*)", that is, the giving of the ring; the "uplifting (*nissuyin*)", taking the bride into the house symbolized by the *huppa* and reading the marriage contract; and finally "being together (*yihud*)".

It is the groom who buys the wedding ring, but he buys only one, for traditionally only the wife wears it. It is a symbolic certificate of the purchase. The wedding ring (*tabba'at kiddushin*) is a valuable gift which becomes the property of the wife; it cannot be taken back in case of a divorce. Some of them are not even suitable for wearing one, for instance, because it is topped by a tiny castle, made of gold. Its inscription, like on the ring in the Hungarian National Museum, says: *Mazel tov*. At the ceremony the rabbi holds it up so that the guests can ascertain that it is really a valuable piece. Then the groom pulls it on the bride's finger, on the index finger rather than the ring finger.

אני לדודי ודודי לי

Ani le-dodi ve-dodi li.
"I am my beloved's
and my beloved is mine."
(Song of Songs 6,3)

According to more recent European customs the husband receives a wedding ring from his wife, too, namely on the Sabbath following the wedding. As we can see in Petrichevich Horváth's description, in the Cult temple of Pest husbands received wedding rings from their wives during the ceremony already at the mid-nineteenth century.

The marriage certificate (*ketubbah*, Greek *gamiskos*) is written in Aramaic—this is a two-thousand-year-old tradition. Nowadays there is a printed form which needs to be filled in, but originally the groom wrote it by hand or dictated it to a professional scribe. The document determines the obligations that the husband takes upon himself by wedding his wife, as well as her rights. Formally it is a declaration, not a mutual contract. It is read aloud as a part of the ceremony and signed by two witnesses who may not be close relatives. The Jewish names are used here, in Hebrew letters. Finally the document is handed over to the wife who will keep it. The seven blessings (*birkat nissuyim / birkat hatanim / sheva berakhot*) are recited over a new cup of wine. They can be said by guests, too.

The parents of the couple lift the cup to the lips of the groom and bride. After that, still under the *huppa*, the groom breaks a glass cup by stepping on it, symbolically recalling the destruction of the Temple. In some synagogue courtyards there was a special place (*Traustein*) for breaking the glass. Now people can wish good luck to the newly weds saying: *Mazel tov*, "Good luck" or "Congratulations". After that the symbolic consummation of the marriage (*yihud*) takes place. The couple retreat to a closed room for a few minutes. The husband "visits" his wife and "they are together", they break the fast with a bite to eat. Two guards stand in front of the door so they will not be disturbed.

Before the wedding feast everyone eats a piece of the wedding *barches* (*hallah*). The young couple gets one plate of chicken soup, the "golden soup" (*goldene yoykh / goldzip*): this is the first meal eaten from the same plate. The groom, if he is talented, gives a short speech (*derashah / droshe*) on a Biblical topic or sings something. The longer his performance the better he fulfills his obligation. The gifts given to the couple at the wedding are actually a reward for the speech, hence the name *droshe geshank*, "speech gift".

Musicians (*klezmer*, plural *klezmorim*) are indispensable participants at a wedding. They are not necessarily Jewish; in Transylvania they were often Gypsies or other non-Jews playing specifically Jewish melodies, pieces that resemble Slavic tunes but with a syncopated rhythm. The musicians escort the groom and bride to the ceremony, they play during the feast (*se'udat hatan*) and throughout the night, which is not at all customary on other holy days. At a traditional Orthodox wedding, of course, men and women sit at different tables. The Hebrew name for the dance house, *bet hatunot*, indicates that apart from the dances of Hasidim on *motza'e shabbat* or *motse-shabes*, dancing was mostly customary at weddings. Traditionally men and women would dance the ring dance in separate groups, especially in Orthodox communities (*kosher tants*), bride and groom sitting in the middle. The only couples' dance, the bride's *mitsve tants*, is the highlight of the evening. The *badkhen* or *marshalik* calls the guests one by one to dance with the bride. Even beggars take their turn. During the *mitsve tants* only two people dance, the others stand around, watching them and clapping the beat. A very special moment is the dance of the rabbi and the husband with the young wife as well as the dance of the in-laws (*mekhutonim tants*). Men and women do not touch each other during the *mitsve tants* either. The wife holds a kerchief (*sudar*) in her hand, she holds it high so her partners may grab it. All men, including the groom, wear white gloves. At Hasidic weddings there are other dances as well. They dance with the braided *hallah* (*koylitsh tants*), there is an "angry" dance (*broygez tants*), a "clapping" dance (*klapper tants*), a "bottle" dance (*flash tants*), etc. A proper wedding, at least in the countryside, used to last for seven days, based on Biblical tradition (Genesis 29,27; Judges 14,12). Nowadays, this custom prevails in Orthodox families, where a *se'udah* is organized for the young couple every evening for a week after the wedding, and the seven blessings (*sheva berakhot*) are said at the conclusion of their meal each time.

The Biblical Patriarchs, Abraham, Isaac and Jacob, lived in polygamy. Rabbinical tradition also allowed men to have four wives simultaneously and this rule still prevails in Islam. In Ashkenazi Judaism, however, it did not become general practice. It would have been a terrible burden, because Jewish law protects the rights of wives. In Europe polygamy was also in conflict with Christian law and customs. Ashkenazi Jewry eliminated polygamy. In one of his decisions (*takkanah*) (around 1000 c.e.) Rabbenu Gershom ben Judah placed a curse (*herem*) on those who married more than one wife until 1240 (the end of the fifth millennium according to the Jewish calendar). His prohibition was then renewed and it is in effect today, until the Messiah comes. Furthermore, Rabbenu Gershom prohibited divorcing a wife unless she agreed to it. He also forbade reading others' letters. He was called the light of the Diaspora (*me'or ha-golah*) because everyone lived according to his teachings and every Jew was considered a disciple of his disciples (Rashi). Gershom's decision certainly played a part in the fact that Jewish law evolved differently in Europe than in Moslem countries, that the customs of Ashkenazi and Sephardi Jews differ considerably.

Divorce (*gerushin*) is a legal possibility in Judaism. A marriage is legally annulled by the divorce certificate (*get*) (Deuteronomy 24,1). (Hebrew *get* is an old loanword from Mesopotamia, from the Akkadian *gittu*, "one-column tablet", "document written on parchment".) It has to be declared in the presence of three rabbis and a scribe (*sofer*). A *get* is valid if it consists of 12 lines (the name of the witnesses is on the thirteenth line), written in a column form in black ink, with goose quill. Certain letters have fixed positions, there cannot be any corrections in it. It cannot be written in the evening or a day before a holy day. The document is handed to the wife and then immediately taken from her and it is stabbed several times so it may not be misused. Then both parties receive a certificate (*petor*, "exemption" / *setar pitturin*, "proof of exemption"). In his well-known poem "Elbocsátó szép üzenet" [A Nice Farewell of Divorce] (1912) written to Léda (Adél Brüll), Endre Ady (1877–1919)—a famous poet of gentry origin—created a special literary *get*, a poetical equivalent of the religious divorce letter to break up with his (Jewish) mistress.

Jewish marital law differs radically from civil law in two respects. One of them is called in-law or levirate marriage (*yibbum*); it is in effect even today, at least in principle. If a first-born man dies without an heir, his younger brother is obliged to wed the widow (*yebamah*) so his brother's name should be carried on (Deuteronomy 25,7–10). The younger brother may be exempted from this duty but only in a legal form. The *halitzah* ceremony needs to be carried out as specified in the Book of Ruth. (According to an ancient custom, whose origins are not known, the widow pulls off the shoe from the right foot of her brother-in-law and throws it away.) After that the widow may marry whomever she wishes to. The other major difference is the law concerning the *agunah*. A woman whose husband disappeared or died without a witness may remarry only after a formal divorce. This act replaces the *get*. It must be a complicated process because basically the husband has to be declared dead. After World War II it was especially difficult to clarify the situation of women whose husband had died in captivity, forced labor or death camps. In such cases the rabbinical court (*bet din*) is required to intervene.

V. Erzsébetváros

This district was the scene of Jewish life in Pest. Back in the eighteenth century Jews had no other choice—the market and the restaurant chained them to this location. Even later, it was the merchants and the high concentration of inns, restaurants and cafés, that preserved the Jewish character of the neighborhood.

(1) Shops and Nightclubs, also Cafés, Restaurants, etc.

Initially the new Jewish quarter barely extended beyond its original center, the immediate surroundings of the Orczy House. Jews were not the only ones to live in Terézváros / Erzsébetváros, there were also Greeks, Armenians, Romanians—everyone who came to Pest for the fairs. It was these people who were to form the core of the bourgeoisie. Slowly, as the area towards the Körút (Ring) and even beyond it developed, the "Jewish triangle" as a whole took over the role of the Orczy House. The Roman Catholic church in Terézváros and Nagymező utca, a major artery by then, formed a clear division between two zones connecting the new parts of Király utca to Andrássy út at the same time. The parts of city beyond the church, further to the Northeast, were clearly the outcome of the emerging needs of an urban bourgeoisie during the second part of the nineteenth century, and Jews were part of this bourgeoisie.

Among the inhabitants of Király utca, in apartment houses owned mainly by the German-speaking bourgeoisie, there were merchants of cloth and leather, factory owners, rabbis and engineers, Hasidim and eventually even middle-class Jews who became the concert-going crowd of Pest.

> "They were the simplest Jewish merchants, artisans who spent the entire day in their workshops together with their apprentices, servants and store-clerks, only concerned about their daily income which they then spent immediately; bushelmen, cleansers, poor women, peddlers"

195. The outer edge of the Jewish quarter around Király utca: "Nagymező utca with the Terézváros Church". Painting by Albert Schickedanz, ca. 1880

—this is how Ármin Vámbéry described the population of the area in the 1850s.

The official census usually indicated profession. The 1820 census, for instance, listed the following professions next to the names of persons living in and around the Orczy House: rabbi, prayer leader (*hazzan*), beadle (*shammash / shames*), community officer, parchment maker, calligrapher, i.e. Torah-writer (*sofer / sayfer*), slaughterer, poultry-*Schachter*, *hallah*-baker, school servant, tax collector, doctor, hospital caretaker, nurse, burial clothes tailor (*Leichenhemds*- [i.e. *kittel*-] *Schneider*), sexton, musician, veteran soldier, merchant, clothing merchant, kosher milk deliverer, innkeeper, secondhand dealer, general storekeeper, peddler, salesman, midwife, pedicurist and corn remover, medical student, surgeon, student, beggar, servant, coachman, maid, etc. Family members are also indicated. Among the servants one can find Christian persons, too. There were some additional professions listed for persons living in other locations: medical practitioner, surgeon, midwife, dance instructor, leaf-gilder, silver cleaner, pipe-maker, umbrella-maker, button-maker, watch-maker, watch case-maker, hat-maker, carpet-mender, feather store keeper, wool-cutter, wool-selector, brandy distiller, chocolate factory owner, cigar factory owner, starch factory owner, penholder factory owner, vinegar distiller, glue boiler. All of them were Jews.

But the real Jewish trade was the art of the tailor. A somewhat anti-Jewish missionary broadleaf from the late eighteenth century, which will be discussed later, states:

> "The most common occupation among Jews is tailoring. They trade in secondhand clothes at many places (...) ; they buy the used items from those who got bored with them and pass them on to others at the flea-market, making a modest profit"
>
> (Paul Medicei, Miklós Rosthy & "a priest from the bishopric of Pécs",[1] *A zsidóknak szokási és szer-tartási* [Customs and Rituals of the Jews], 1783)

An 1846/47 census taken in Pest, more or less in the Jewish quarter around Király utca, lists altogether 422 Jewish "masters" and 607 "apprentices", of whom 204 were tailor masters and 410 tailor apprentices. It is hard to imagine what this many people sewed and for whom. Did they supply the whole city with clothing?

Such a huge crowd of people cannot live without certain services. Thus, several barbershops were opened in Király utca and the neighborhood. There might have been customers sitting in the street in front of the Orczy House as well, but the more successful masters opened a shop.

> "A local specialty is the barber shaving without a knife. There are numerous barbershops where Orthodox customers, who would not allow a razor to touch their face, are shaved with orpiment."
>
> (In: *Egyenlőség*, January 20, 1934)

196. Gömöry House, 12 Király utca

Actually, it was only scissors which were halakhically problematic, because the Torah (Leviticus 19,27) only prohibits cutting or spoiling the sidelocks (*pe'ah*) and the beard. According to the extrapolated interpretation this implies the prohibition of cutting one's beard, too, shaving with a knife. The electric razor resolved all religious concerns, even those of the strictly traditional modern man. Everyone may shave now, yet it is still good to have a nice long beard!

August Ellrich (*Die Ungarn, wie sie sind*, Berlin, 1831) and other reports from the 1830s (quoted by Béla Bevilaqua Borsody, 1935) said that in Király utca one could see men dressed in clothes reminiscent of Lessing's *Nathan der Weise* (1779), selling vials of perfume, Turkish handicrafts and other Eastern merchandise. Their Polish co-religionists, who had a typical glib tongue, sold rings and glass beads. People were hurrying to and from the stock exchange, speculating, peddlers offering their ware, Jacob's sons making magic without calling themselves magicians. Two decades later *Hartleben's Polyglotte-Führer* (1852) described an equally vivid scene in Király utca: swarms of people and strikingly large numbers of cafés, alehouses and wineshops.

And something else:

> "In Erzsébetváros soup kitchens and cafés vie in numbers. The district is a worthy daughter of Terézváros in this respect. (...) Sugared water is the main drink in its cafés. The Orthodox usually gather in the Orczy Café drinking sugar water, while more modern winds blow in Szegedi Café where some might even order an espresso. (...)

[1]The priest can be identified as János Lethenyei (1723–1804), a Roman Catholic parish priest.

Everyone is out in the street all day long. People stand, sit, chat, drink coffee, knit, sew, receive guests, lend and borrow things in the doorway of shops and houses. While the normal medium of exchange is money, the merchandise here is different: wooden spoons, onions, half a lemon, a washbasin, two eggs. There is no interest on these deals and no bills or receipts. If the loan is not repaid when due, it would occur to no one to file a suit in court. The problem is resolved in the courtyard, with the assistance of the women of the neighborhood."   (Ödön Gerő / Viharos, *Az én fővárosom* [My Capital City], 1891)

The Gyertyánffy House, located at 6 Deák Ferenc tér (corner of Király utca and Bajcsy-Zsilinszky út), used to be owned by an Armenian family. It was built in 1815 at the site of today's Anker house, right next to the Jewish market, close to where the flea-market found its place later. It was called "*Am Judenhof*" or "a Zsidópiac mellett(i ház)", that is, "(the house) next to the Jewish market", although the Hungarian name is not an exact translation of the German. *Judenhof* actually means "Jewish courtyard", not "market". This was the first five-story dwelling house in Pest. The owner must have expected a considerable income from the rent when he built the huge house, similar to the Orczy House. His calculations proved correct. It was in fact Jews who rented apartments in his building, and somewhat wealthier families than the ones who lived in the Orczy House at that. Among them was Albert Hoffmann, the surgeon of the Jewish hospital in the 1820s. The owners of Gyertyánffy house were among the highest tax-payers of Pest, like the Orczys.

Next to its entrance in Király utca, there were two cafés, the Orczy Café to the right and the "Herzl", nicknamed the "Jewish Café", to the left. The "Herzl", just like the "Orczy", was for a long time rented only to Christians, but the first recorded lessee was a *Marrano*, a certain Filippi Giuseppe, who moved to Pest from Szeged. The Café was nicknamed after him, the first Jewish *cavearius*, rather than after its Jewish customers. After all, customers of the "Orczy" were all Jewish, too. These two cafés were the business centers of the Jews of Pest during the first half of the nineteenth century. "In Pest, decisions about the great national fairs are made in cafés", wrote Ellrich in 1832.

Since all civic forums were closed to the Jewish participants of the by now flourishing business life, they were forced to negotiate their deals outside of the guild, as if they had not been professionals. The café was a public place, a free market and a stock exchange where business partners found each other easily. Later, around the middle of the century, when some of the modern commercial centers like the *Gabonacsarnok* (Grain Exchange), the Lloyd Society and the stock exchange were opened and Jews were no longer banned from these institutions, the atmosphere of cafés became more subdued. True, confidential conversations were still carried out within the walls of the café for several more decades, and the tradition continued well into the twentieth century when the cafés on Andrássy út came into fashion. But by then the café was less of a business center and more of a place for social life.

197. Small shops, 25–27 Király utca

198. Shops, 3 Király utca

Gyula Krúdy would often mention the Jewish café in Gyertyánffy House at the turn of the century. The "Herzl" was never anything but a café. No billiards was played there. Coffee was served with whipped cream and cinnamon-raisin *hallah*, or *barhes* in Hungarian. It was known as a respectable place and a major meeting point, almost an *exchange*, of the *shadkhanim* of Pest. The matchmakers must have exchanged their "merchandise" here. It was the *shadkhen* who introduced young people to be married to each other. They usually met in a café for the first time.

A local joke about the efficient *shadkhen* in conversation with a young man (it is a well-known wandering anecdote, indeed, it was used by Malamud as well, in his *The Magic Barrel*):

"I have a good *shidakh* for you: she is a real beauty."
"No, thank you."
"I have a rich one as well, with a huge dowry."
"No, thank you."
"But she is a real treasure!"
"No, thank you."
"I see, you want someone from a fancy family. I have one like that, too."
"No, thank you. I would only marry out of love."
"I have that *in stock*, too!"

In the nineteenth century, but even in the decades preceding World War II, at least a quarter or even a third of the population of Király utca was Jewish, in some buildings even more. The area was mostly filled with small stores selling simple, cheap merchandise, secondhand clothing and the like. Earlier Jewish merchants would be traveling salesmen selling expensive, luxurious articles in mansions rather than ordinary homes—even if they had to enter through the back door—, or they would go to fairs, spending a week or two in each city. The Jews of Pest had their own little stores in Király utca first, close to their apartments or actually in front of their apartments, facing the street. A small storage space was attached to all of these stores, a room without a window in the back, or a separate place which opened from the courtyard. Here it was no longer the merchant who went after the customer, but the other way around, customers came to the store for what they needed, the need went after the ware. The market became more open, thanks to the storage rooms there was a wider selection of goods, and since there were more stores selling the same type of wares, competition started to grow. Better quality and better service became decisive factors. There was a demand for luxury items as well, including fine underwear, or colonial articles, such as black pepper, ginger, nutmeg, sugar-cane, coffee beans and the like. These small Jewish stores along the Király utca and the neighboring streets were a new phenomenon in the commercial life of Pest, giving it an urban, petty-bourgeois character. These stores defined the image of the area for the following century.

Here follows an excerpt from an inventory compiled by the union of licensed merchants, of the merchandise held in stock by their members in 1803:

"Király utca, Ádám Glasser, Jewish grocer, 20 pounds[2] refined sugar, 2 pounds coffee, 1 pound black pepper, 1 pound allspice, 3 pounds ginger, 1 pound rock-candy, 2 *lats*[3] nutmeg, 1/4 pound cinnamon, one eighths of a pound cloves. The Jewish woman says that she has only a little sugar and coffee in stock today, but a supplier, Tauscher, promised to deliver more today or tomorrow."

The stores and dim warehouses of Király utca supplied the nearby flea-market. Although there was a Penny Market Street in the Inner City (today Párisi utca), the real penny market was where the Opera House stands today (22 Andrássy út). This was the market of the poor. Auctions were held here as well, but it was mostly secondhand clothing and household objects that were on sale. It was not like the flea-

[2] 1 (Viennese) pound = 0.56 kg or ca. 20 oz.

[3] 1 *lat* (an old Hungarian weight) = 1/32 pound (17.5 gr or 0.6 oz).

market in a modern metropolis, where collectors or the more affluent search for some unique piece, it was just the market of the poor. When the plot was designated for the Opera House and construction work began, the penny market had to move to the edge of the New market (1870). For a few decades this became the scene of the flourishing Jewish market. Even a few gentlemen from the *Belváros* (Downtown) came here to buy, maybe even to sell. Whatever you could buy here was a treasure trove, a *metsie*, if only because of its price. On the other hand, many people gained a modicum of wealth from the cheap merchandise observing the golden rule: low price—high turnover—high profit. The peddler (Hungarian *handlé*, German *Händler*) was an essential member of the penny market. He went from street to street and knocked on the doors every day, buying everything that was for sale or taking what people meant to throw out anyway. He then took whatever he collected to the penny market and gave it to those who had a warehouse, a booth or a stand. They sorted out the merchandise and put it on display so people could choose. It was only towards the end of the nineteenth century that the penny market in the middle of the city became a nuisance. It was then moved to a less central location, to Teleki tér (1898).

199. Porter. Drawing by Hermann Struck

An elderly lady who had always lived in the building at the corner of 34 Király utca / 1 Székely Mihály utca, remembered in 1985 as follows:

"Everyone was a merchant here. They sold all kinds of clothes, fur and winter coats. There was an 'installment man', his name was Deutsch, who specialized in selling his merchandise on installment. He sold feather bedding, quilts, shirts, nightgowns, underwear—whatever you wanted. You bought something, paid a certain amount and came back at the end of the month or at the beginning of the next. Everyone was a merchant here. One made ties, the other sold lemons. When the Jewish holiday came, they put up a tent here in the rear of the courtyard. Then came the *shakhter* and he slaughtered the poultry. (...) All along Petőfi [/ Kazár] utca they sold used clothing. The people who used to live in our house always kept their store open on Saturday, they were not so religious.

We could say they were Neolog. Of course, there used to be Orthodox people in the neighborhood, too, back in those days, they kept their stores closed on Saturday."

A joke about the storekeeper who is open on Saturday.

"Reb Yitzhak, it is *shabes* and you are making business?"
"Look, I am selling these clothes half price—you call this business?!"

A Yiddish proverb says: *Az men hot gute skhoyre, hot men nit keyn moyre*, "If you have good merchandise, you have nothing to fear."

"This narrow street was filled with coaches—various conveyances seen all over the city. Huge wagons loaded with enormous quantities of wares, transporting them from one place to another, as if they were hoping to find a warehouse where they could dump their merchandise. Small carts stood in front of every store loading and unloading all day long, as if the whole street had intended to move out within a single day. Mail coaches standing around the corners were pouring out all kinds of packages with all the wares of the world. Boxes of lemons, oranges and figs piling up in every courtyard, one store next to the other, where a variety of goods were sold by salesclerks who looked exactly alike, who were all born and raised here, wearing identical caps. And the trolley bus rode along Király utca in the midst of the crowd and the seemingly chaotic mess as if it did not care the least that people were crossing the street, strolling up and down, shouting from one side of the street to the other, pushing strollers, leading children, staring at store-windows and shopping as if this had been their last day in Király utca... Getting acquainted with clothing stores, herring and grocery stores and courtyards and the endless, iron-fenced balconies bending over the courtyards, storage space and workshops..."

(Gyula Krúdy, Boldogult úrfikoromban [Back in My Happy Youth Days], 1930)

At the end of the nineteenth century the growing traffic of the Inner City, Terézváros and Erzsébetváros was serviced by various coachmen, carriers, porters and deliverymen. One of their meeting places was the small area surrounded by Király utca, Bajcsy-Zsilinszky út, Paulay Ede utca and Andrássy út.

One of the coach houses or stalls stood in the courtyard of 3 Bajcsy-Zsilinszky út, a building designed by Miklós Ybl. The stall was in the huge cellar. There was a carved stone water basin and a well next to a smithery in the courtyard. For at least half a century the coach house belonged to Jewish owners (Holzer / Braun), and the majority of the coachmen were Jewish, too. There were similar stalls at 4 Ó utca and 23 Dessewffy utca.

The building at 26 Király utca was called the Jálics House. Ferenc András Jálics (1795–1874), a wine merchant, commissioned its plans (1840–1846) from the architect József Hild. Jálics owned the largest wine-cellar in Pest in the nineteenth century. It was a long chain of vaulted cellars spanning as far as the Két Szerecsen utca / Paulay Ede utca, with wooden staircases, a winch to lift barrels, a coach house and a stall. A popular restaurant called "Jálics Cellar" operated in the house, noted for the fact that the Prince of Wales had a luncheon there in 1873 on his first visit to Pest. Ferenc Jálics was born to a bourgeois family that received a title of nobility; he acquired considerable wealth as a wine merchant and was among the highest tax payers of the city for the rest of his life. Though Jálics himself was not Jewish, he had family connections with several Jewish merchant families through the marriages of some of his offsprings. For a few years after World War II (sometime between 1946 and 1950) there was even a prayer-room in one of the apartments on the first floor of the Jálics House. (After World War II, up to recently, the part of the former wine cellar opening to Paulay Ede utca was used as a prison.)

At 43–45 Király utca lived the architect Lipót Baumhorn (1860–1932) for a short while, a major figure of *fin-de-siècle* Hungarian synagogue architecture.

The corner building at 47 Király utca and 12–14 Csányi utca is called the Pekáry House. It was built in 1847/48 according to the plans of Ferenc Brein for Imre Pekáry, a former deputy police chief for the municipality. According to an inscription next to its entrance, the building is the work of Ágoston Pollack (1807–1872). This three-story Romanticist *cum* Neo-Gothic house must have been one of the most beautiful buildings in its time, in a way concluding the first segment of Király utca. The six-

200. The Anker House. Drawing by Gergely Pörge, 1908

201. A Jew in Pest, Váci utca. Cartoon by Mihály Szemlér, ca. 1860

202. Pekáry House, 47 Király utca. Colored engraving by Ludwig Rohbock, 1859

203. Pekáry House, 47 Király utca, 1896

pointed star decoration on the balcony above the entrance and on the bracket-supports of the windows are remarkable. It is hard to know whether these had originally belonged to the building or were added later, just like it is unclear when the two brave Hungarian soldiers were placed in the little cabin above the entrance. A Jewish and a Hungarian symbol come together here, on the edge of the Jewish quarter. Were they possibly added during the reconstruction in 1870? Old drawings are not clear enough to decide this question, but a description of the building by Lajos Hevesi suggests that they were probably original.

"There is a castle here, built in Gothic style, with pinnacles, balconies, lancets and small statues. It is a peculiar kind of Gothic, it is hard to tell whether it comes from the East, West, South or North. Some Israelite elements, however, may clearly be detected in its architecture, especially the ones which are hanging from its windows."

(Hevesi, *Karczképek* [Sketches], 1876)

In any case, towards the end of the nineteenth century the Pekáry House was inhabited mostly by Jews. This is where the Jewish young men's association held its meetings and there was a prayer-room, too, in one of the apartments. For a few years after the very end of 1899, when he married Arabella (Satanella) Spiegler (Bogdán), this was the permanent address, though not the permanent residence, of Gyula Krúdy, and also one of the settings of his charming short-stories about Pest of the *fin-de-siècle*. Arabella / Bella was the "daughter of a dye factory", as the writer puts it. He meant the dye factory of Óbuda, of course. This is how Krúdy got acquainted with the life of Király utca, its busy inns and restaurants. This is how he heard of the visit of the Prince of Wales told again and again.

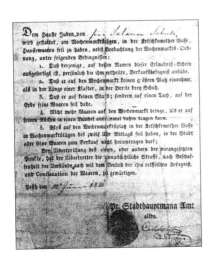

204. License issued to a Jewish peddler (*Hausir Jude*) by the Pest Municipal Magistrate

205. The Király utca near the Terézváros Church. Photo, ca. 1900

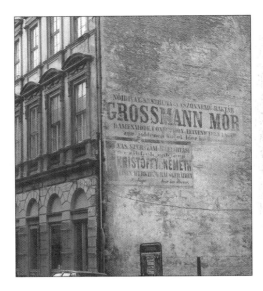

206. Jewish peddler carrying a pack that complies with the license of the Pest Municipal Magistrate, 1868 (see fig. 204, above)

207. Mór Grossmann's shop "Gilt Ball" for linen and lingery, 28 Király utca, ca. 1910. Advertising on a partition-wall recovered in 1997

208. *Handlé* [Peddler]. Drawing by János Jankó, 1867

On the corner of Király utca and Liszt Ferenc tér (8 Liszt Ferenc tér) stands the building of the Zeneakadémia (Hungarian Music Academy). The lot used to belong to the Valero silk factory. The Music Academy was built in 1907 at the site of a two-story house which accommodated a prayer-house (*bet ha-midrash*) and the (Jewish) Institute for the Blind. There was a small store which opened on Király utca, where products hand-crafted by the Jewish blind were sold.

Like the literary matinees organized by the *Nyugat* over several decades, Saul Tchernichowsky's (1875–1943) poetry reading was also held at the Music Academy, upon his visit to Budapest in 1924 (January 13). The evening was organized by *Múlt és Jövő*, he was introduced by József Patai. Hungarian translations of his poems were recited by Mari Jászai and other personalities, artists of the Opera House performed musical pieces, and Tchernichowsky himself recited some of his poems in Hebrew. The Russian-born modern Hebrew poet lived in Berlin at the time, but Patai's choice was not just a matter of geographical proximity and their personal acquaintance. Unlike Bialik, whose poetry was strongly rooted in religious tradition, Tchernichowsky was a secular Hebrew poet. A few years later, after the death of Mari Jászai (1850–1926), one of the organizers of the reading recalled the performance of the leading Hungarian actress:

"She appeared on the side of the great Hebrew poet and returned the laurels of success, in the midst of a storm of applause, to the guest with a royal gesture."

209. Traffic and the throng in Király utca. Drawing by Karl Klic, ca. 1868

210. Building of the (Israelite) Institute for the Blind, 64 Király utca, ca. 1900

164 ERZSÉBETVÁROS

The outer part of Király utca, the segment between Nagykörút and Városliget was the entertainment district. It was a transition between the Jewish quarter and the more lighthearted Városliget.

At 71 Király utca was the Király Theater, where operettas were performed. There were several small nightclubs and bars (Éden Theater, Rémi Bar, Somossy Music Theater) but this was the first cosmopolitan comedy theater in the capital; it opened on November 6, 1903. Several famous Hungarian operettas had their premieres or even world premieres here, like "János vitéz" by Károly Bakonyi–Jenő Heltai–Pongrác Kacsóh on November 18, 1904—this operetta was performed 689 times–, or "Gül Baba" by Jenő Huszka in 1905, "Víg özvegy" [The Merry Widow] by Ferenc Lehár in 1907, "Luxemburg grófja" [The Count of Luxembourg] by Ferenc Lehár in 1910, "Leányvásár" [The Marriage Market] by Victor Jacobi in 1911, "Szibill" [Sibyl] by Victor Jacobi in 1914, "Csárdáskirálynő" [Czardas Princess] by Imre Kálmán in 1916, "Mágnás Miska" by Albert Szirmai in 1916 and "Sztambul rózsája" [The Rose of Stambul] by Leó Fall in 1917. They put on close to 250 plays altogether, even a jazz-operetta. The famous Sári Fedák, Márton Rátkai, Vilma Medgyaszay and Árpád Latabár performed on this stage. The Theater was closed in 1936. Part of the building was pulled down in 1941 and the rest was reconstructed. Today there is a service station in the building. An inscription on the wall commemorates the Király Theater.

211. Imre Kálmán. Photo, 1912

77 Király utca was the address of the "Tátra" Café and nightclub since 1901 but in 1921 Jakab Grüner founded the cabaret "Trocadero" in its stead. It was Imre Harmath's rather weak show that bombed and chased away the guests of "Trocadero", so that it soon had to be closed. A year after the great fiasco, in 1922, Béla Salamon launched a cabaret show in the newly opened "New Trocadero". A few years later it had to be renamed ("Pengő Cabaret", 1926).

(2) Purim in Király utca

Purim (*pirem / pürem*) is a merry Jewish holiday. It could not be compared to any particular non-Jewish holiday but bears similarities to certain elements of several of them: Saturnalia and New Years' Eve, Carnival and the Nativity play at Christmas. (Christmas eve is called *nitlnakht* in Yiddish, from Latin *natalis dies*, Jesus's birthday.) Hanukkah is not exactly the day of devout prayer, but even so part of it takes place in the synagogue. From there and from private apartments people pour in to the streets by the evening.

Purim is in the Spring, in Adar or in a leap year in the second Adar. In Babylonia this was the last day of the year, this is when people welcomed the new year and their fortune was determined. The name *purim* comes from the Akkadian (Babylonian) *pūru* "lot", "drawing of lot". By casting lots Haman wanted to determine the day when he should massacre all the Jews in the Persian empire (Esther 3,7). Esther, the Jewish queen and Mordecai, a high official in the royal court, prevented him from carrying out his plan. Haman and his ten sons were hanged and all the enemies of Israel died with them. The word *homen* means "anti-Jewish" in vernacular.

The day before Purim is a fast day, Esther's fast (*ta'anit Ester*). On 14th of Adar the synagogue is

212. Boy wearing a Purim mask, carrying *shlakhmones* in one hand and a rattle in the other. Lino-cut by Imre Ámos, 1940

PURIM DARF MAN ALLES TUN MAGYATEKÁBOL NACH JONTEF STELLT SACH ERAUS WER E ASES PONEM WAR!

213. "On Purim you may do as you like, but after the holiday we will know who behaved improperly." Color drawing by Lipót Herman

decorated with colorful banners. Part of the ceremony is reading the Book of Esther twice, once in the evening and once in the morning. Like the Torah, the Book of Esther is written on a scroll (*megillah*), but it is only rolled onto one rod, not on two, like the Torah, and it is completely unfolded before the reading starts, like an ordinary letter (Esther 9,29). Old Megillah manuscripts, including one in the Kaufmann Collection in the library of the Hungarian Academy of Sciences, are illustrated with scenes of the story. In the Kaufmann Megillah the word *hamelekh*, "the king", is written above each picture, meaning the Almighty, of course, and not Ahasuerus, the Persian king. The Book of Esther can be read in Hebrew, like all books of the Bible, though also in Greek or any other language, even in Hungarian, if the community does not understand Hebrew. The four sentences (Esther 2,5; 8,15–16; 10,3) which tell that Mordecai delivered the Jews from destruction are always read in a loud voice, the congregation practically shouts it together with the *hazzan*. The names of Haman's ten sons (Esther 9,7–9) have to be uttered in one sequence. This results in much noise and uproar, but the tumult is even greater when the name of Haman is uttered, the vicious minister who plotted against the Jews and almost succeeded in convincing the king to massacre all the Jews in his kingdom. Whenever the hateful name is pronounced, children start to "beat Haman (*shlogen Haman*)", whistle, beat the pews and make loud noises with rattles (*homenklaper*). Even the Hebrew inscription on the rattle curses Haman: *Arur Haman!*

Here is a brief quote from an eighteenth-century Italian pamphlet which tried to argue against Jewish "errors" by disseminating Christian doctrines selected to convert the "pagans". It was written by an anti-Jewish convert, a certain Paul Medici or Medicei (Paolo Sebastiano Medici), and was later translated into Latin (Nagyszombat, 1758) by Miklós Rosthy, a monk belonging to the order of the Hermits of St. Paul in Hungary. From the Latin version two priests, a Roman and a Greek Catholic one, prepared two Hungarian translations, one published in Pécs by János Angyal in 1783, the other in Ungvár by the "Kelet" publishing house in 1889. The book describes Jewish customs in detail. That it was published twice within a century in Hungary suggests that the Hungarian public, even in Ungvár at the end of the nineteenth century, knew more about Jewish ritual from polemics than from first-hand experience, that they viewed Jewish religious practice as something exotic and strange.

"Every time they mention Aman's [Haman's] name while reading, they start stamping their feet, the children start clapping the benches with some kind of a hammer specially prepared for the occasion, as if beating the heads of their enemies. The last sentence of the reading is: Cursed be Aman, blessed Mardocheus, (...) cursed be the evil and blessed be the Jews."

(Paul Medici, Miklós Rosthy & József Fesztóry, *A zsidók szertartásai és szokási* [Customs and Rituals of the Jews], 1889)

If this is what the synagogue ceremony sounded like, one can only imagine the turmoil in the Orczy House or in one of the prayer-rooms in Király utca. The sight of the celebration in the streets and courtyards in the evening and into the night is best left to the imagination!

In the following passage József Kiss describes a Purim celebration in Király utca in the 1860s:

"(...) There is one night in the year when Király utca and Két Szerecsen utca appear in a somewhat more provocative light than usual, when the modern city is decorated with a dash of medieval colors. This is the night of the Jewish carnival, of Purim.

"We see children running around with loads of cakes and cookies, their faces shining from the joy of the day. When two kaftans meet, they greet each other with a *güt pürim* (*pürem*) and proceed.

"Here and there a larger crowd of people assemble—depending on where a more exciting costume has drawn their attention. Indeed, the street is filled with costumes and masks: harlequins, chimneysweepers, peasant boys and girls, Slovaks and some strange creatures patched together from various remnants, walking around in the crowd like a living riddle. Those familiar with the Purim-crowd would not be surprised to hear that the masqueraders are often threatened by violence. Therefore, each group is accompanied by a guard as they stroll from café to café, though minor incidents may occur occasionally, and the city police department orders some mounted patrols to guard Király utca throughout the night. But more serious confrontations never occur.

"The crowd is densest in front of cafés where music and singing filter out to the street. People form a circle around the masqueraders to watch them perform St. David's dance and at times the audience joins them. In front of the Teleki Café three or four Polish Jews stand in kaftans. They hum a *nigun* and begin to dance—their long, curly sidelocks swaying. They do not seem to feel the cold: they are heated by the day's joy and the significant amount of wine they have already consumed. They take sips of wine and dance around and around until one of them loses his balance and they all fall on top of each other, piled up in the street.

"Hurrah!—sounds suddenly from Kék Kakas utca. A group of masqueraders from Két Szerecsen utca approach Király utca. There are twelve girls and three or four men; the men are wearing masks which are already in shreds, the women's faces are painted with thick red and white paint. Some are dressed as *débardeurs*, others are wearing dresses with long tails. They head toward the Teleki Café in high spirits, dancing, jumping up and down, whooping it up. The excited and curious crowd from Király utca marches to greet them in Kék Kakas utca, but the lively procession rolls against them forcing them back into Király utca...

"These images and scenes recur every year in Király utca, keeping up the joyful tradition of Purim night. This will remain so forever, even if the Messiah should make up his mind one day and drop in on Király utca."

(Rudolf Szentesi [József Kiss], *Budapesti rejtelmek* [Mysteries of Budapest], Second part, III, Chapter 8, 1874)

Notes:
Kék Kakas (Blue Rooster) utca: Székely Mihály utca
Két Szerecsen (Two Blacks) utca: Paulay Ede utca
The "Teleki" used to be a café of questionable reputation on the corner of Kék Kakas utca and Király utca. (There is a restaurant in the building today.)

Late in the afternoon some special Purim foods are served at home (*se'udat purim*): boiled beans, as a reminder that this was the only kind of kosher food Daniel and Esther could eat at the royal court, fish, since this is the sign of *adar* in the zodiac, sweet stuffed cabbage (*megillokraut*) and special cookies: "Haman-ears" (*oznei Haman* / *hamanoren*) or "Haman bag" (*homentash* or *Mahntasche*, *Mohntasche* in German) a three-cornered pastry filled with poppy-seed, prune jam or stewed prunes, *beigli* and *kindli*, or *leikekh* / *lekekhl*, honey cakes forming Haman or Esther. The *malkhesbreitel* is the crown of Queen (*malkhah* / *malkhe*) Esther. Made of pastry (*breitel*), of course.

The only thing one should abstain from on Purim is water. Drinking (*mishteh*) is not only allowed on this day, it is almost a religious duty. Even the Shulhan Arukh acknowledges that the celebration of Purim demands that one should imbibe to the extent one no longer knows (*ad de-lo yada*) whether he is praising Mordecai or cursing Haman. This is gallantly interpreted as mixing up the blessing (*Barukh Mordekhai*) with the curse (*Arur Haman*), since the numerical value of the letters is in both equal to 502. Nowadays the street festivities on Purim in Tel-Aviv are just called *Adloyada*.

Even the Talmud has something humorous to say about excessive drinking on Purim. Rabbah and R. Zeira were sharing their festive Purim meal. Rabbah became heated from the wine and suddenly killed R. Zeira. When he woke up the next morning and saw what he had done, he begged God to have mercy on him, so God redeemed R. Zeira from the dead. The two met again the following year, right before Purim. Rabbah said to Zeira: "Let us celebrate Purim together again." Zeira replied: "Are you out of your mind? Miracles do not happen every year." (Megillah 7b.)

On Purim people send gifts to each other (*mishloah manot / shlakhmones*): two "portions (*manah*)" or kinds of sweets, cookies or fruits to at least one person. (The two things or "portions" sent require a different blessing to be said over them. So if one is a cake, the other should be a fruit. Or if one is an apple, a fruit of a tree, the other can be a banana, which is a fruit of the ground, or a candy, etc.) This is not just a folk custom but a commandment (*mattenot la-evyonim*): everyone is expected to give charity to the poor (Esther, 9,22), at least three "portions", because it is mentioned three times in the Bible (Exodus 30,11–16), or as many portions as there are family members. A "portion" is traditionally measured by money, it is worth "half a shekel (*mahatzit ha-shekel*)". Non-Jewish beggars get presents too. The festive Purim dinner has to be very rich. No one is allowed to say "thank you", because whoever gave the meal was fulfilling a commandment (*mitzvah*), and should be himself— or herself—thankful for the opportunity.

The *purimshpil* is another opportunity to wear masks and act out funny scenes. Originally it was the story of redemption that was remembered on Purim. From the fifteenth–sixteenth centuries on the story known from Book of Esther was performed in Ashkenazi communities, naturally in Yiddish, in rhymes. It was a real theater, with a prologue, scenes and an epilogue. The actors were always men, *yeshivah boherim* in masks and costumes. The play was led by a narrator (*loyfer, shrayber*) or a jester (*payats*) and coarse jokes were an integral part of it. Traditional genres were made fun of. Even stories from the Torah could be performed satirically (*purim Torah*), and even the rabbi could be presented as a fallible or ridiculous figure (*purim rabbi*). In Eastern Europe, R. Elimelekh is a similar, although Hasidic, figure in Jewish popular songs. Occasionally the rabbi gave his kaftan as a symbol of his power to the *gabbay* who acted in his stead, making fun of the situation. Or it was a *yeshivah boher* who entertained his colleagues by parodying the rabbi. A pseudo-Talmudic tractate called *Massekhet Purim* discusses drinking wine at length, in a serious tone, like a real tractate (*massekhet*). Other Biblical stories were acted out, too: Joseph sold by his brothers, David and Goliath, Hanna's getting pregnant, Salomon's verdict or any other story known widely enough so that people would understand the parody. On this day the Bible and texts of prayer and ritual were brought out to the street as a source of fun. They became sort of a Haggadah "for the night of drunkards (*haggadah le-leil shikkorim*)". The improvisations were coordinated by the *badkhen* or *marshalik*. Somewhat risqué songs were performed in a *hazzan*-like style, mockingly.

It is probably the practice of excessive drinking that Miksa Szabolcsi had in mind when he compared Zionism to a *purimshpil* in an article in *Egyenlőség* on September 5, 1897.

A Jewish–German proverb says: *Purim darf man alles tun, nach jontef stellt sach eraus, wer e asesponem war*, "On Purim you may do whatever you like, but after Purim we will know who behaved inappropriately."

Every year in the spring there are cantorial concerts in Budapest—is this tradition somehow connected to Purim? Maybe.

Purim can only be enjoyed in a crowd. "A numerous people is the glory of a king" (Proverbs 14,28). On Purim this was meant literally. By the evening everyone was in the street, youngsters running around with rattles (*homen-klaper / grager*), Haman's name inscribed on the soles of shoes so that they can step on him, children going from house to house asking for gifts. Everyone was dressed in a costume or mask, people would repeat riddles while carrying around an effigy of Haman on a rod which they threw into the fire at the climax of the celebration.

In the eighteenth century the cities populated by a bourgeois society, outraged by these customs, often called for banning of the noisy Purim plays.

Every word József Kiss wrote was true. And for that matter, a document from 1883 is preserved in the archives of the Hungarian Royal Police: a petition handed in by the police chief of the districts VI and VII, that is, Terézváros and Erzsébetváros, asks his commander to prohibit any masked procession on Purim.

(3) 4 Holló utca

In the nineteenth century Holló utca was the goldsmiths' (*tzoref*) street. Some excellent wire-drawers (*Goldzieher*), gold leaf gilders (*Goldschläger*), chain makers, planishers and galvanizers had their workshops here, even small factories. Why Ignác Goldziher chose to move here as an adult is hard to imagine. Indeed, there had been goldsmiths in his family, but the last one was in Hamburg in the sixteenth century. His father, a leather merchant in Lipótváros, moved to Pest from Székesfehérvár. In any case, his family name fitted into the area.

Ignác / Ignaz (Isaac Judah) Goldziher lived on the second floor. His neighbor was none other than a good friend and colleague of his, R. Sámuel Kohn. They both rented their apartments from the owner of the building, the Jewish Boys' Orphanage.

They lived just a few minutes from their offices, Goldziher being the secretary of the Budapest Neolog Jewish community for thirty years (November 1875–1905) and Sámuel Kohn the rabbi of the Dohány Temple. They did not want to own an apartment anywhere else, for it was convenient for them to live in the neighborhood. In those decades the two neighbors maintained a rather formal relationship, calling each other "*Herr Doktor*" and "*Sie, Goldziher*", but a friendly one. Goldziher, who in his *Diary* seldom had a good word for any of his Hungarian colleagues, once referred to Kohn, to whom, incidentally, he owed his high position as secretary of the community, as "my guardian angel sent by God" (1908).

After 1905 Goldziher would leave Pest at the beginning of May and return only mid-September. When not abroad, he used to spend his summers in Zugliget, where he rented a residence at 21 Zugligeti út from Alfréd Wellisch, its owner–architect. The place was ideal for "idle rest", he wrote in a letter. Actually, he wrote his most important works here.

214. 4 Holló utca. Floor mosaic in the shape of a six-pointed star on the ground floor in the stairway

Throughout his life Goldziher was tortured by the nostalgia of two commitments: his love of Islam and his ties to Western scholarship.

Ever since he traveled in the Middle East as a young man in 1873/74, he could not tear himself away from the world of Islam, from Syria, Palestine and Egypt. It was not just the topic of his scholarly research; he also felt a certain longing for Islam. There is not a single Jewish symbol in his *ex libris*. It shows a human figure in the position of Moslem prayer and the text is a quotation from the Koran, from Joseph's story (Sura 12,18), the words given into Jacob's mouth: "(...) Come, sweet patience! / And God's succor is ever there to seek against / that you describe." When the sheik of the Azhar mosque and university in Cairo asked Goldziher what his religion was, he gave him a wordy and circumspect answer: "My name is Ignatz *al-Madzhari*, I was born a son of the People of the Book (*ahl al-kitab*), and I believe that I will be redeemed together with those who believe in One God." He did not tell the full truth, but he did not deny it either. He just formulated his answer as if there was no difference between Judaism and Islam. His scholarly work reveals a deep and original insight into Jewish tradition, often interpreting Islamic teachings with the help of Jewish material. In his *Diary* he made several negative and critical comments concerning Rabbinical Judaism, but he was never inclined to leave the Jewish community, to become Christian like Ármin Vámbéry, his former professor, or Moslem, like the Arabic scholar Gyula Germanus did later (via Protestantism).

215. Vitus Srágó Feis Phoebus Goldzieher (?–1844), Ignác Goldziher's grandfather

The same applies to his nostalgic feelings towards Western scholarship. He got acquainted with this world in his youth; upon the recommendations of Mór Ballagi and Ármin Vámbéry he won the

216. R. Nathan Mayer
(Meir) Goldziher,
Ignác Goldziher's
uncle

217. R. Meir Hirsch
Henrik Goldziher
(1816-1884), Ignác
Goldziher's oldest
uncle

218. Izsák Goldzieher
(1820-1892), Ignác
Goldziher's uncle

219. Mrs. Adolf
Goldziher née
Katharina Gütl Berger
(1814-1884), Ignác
Goldziher's mother

220. Adolf Goldziher
(1811-1874), the old-
est son of Vitus
Goldzieher, Ignác
Goldziher's father

221. Mrs. Nátán
Glück née Mária
Goldziher
(1852-1884), Ignác
Goldziher's younger
sister

scholarship sponsored by Baron József Eötvös in 1868, which enabled him to study at the universities of Leipzig and Leyden. He was an internationally acknowledged genius of Islamic scholarship who had several opportunities to go abroad, as did Aurél Stein later. He proudly records several such invitations in his *Diary*. But apart from attending scholarly conferences, he never left Hungary. József Somogyi, Goldziher's student and the publisher of his collected works, quotes one of his sayings, "Scholarship does not have a home, but the scholar does." He was elected a member of the Hungarian Academy of Sciences not long after he returned from Leyden (corresponding member in 1876, ordinary member in 1892) and became a lecturer at the university (*Privatdozent*) as well, although he was appointed a full professor only later, in 1905. He remained an employee of the Pest Jewish community and stayed in the Jewish quarter.

In any case, even though he could not conceal his pride—at least not from the pages of his *Diary*—over the fact that, as dean of the Faculty of Humanities in 1917–1918, he wore a Hungarian national gala outfit and a sword, he always watched out for the opinion of his co-religionists at home. His narcissism was similar to Joseph's feelings towards his brothers in the Biblical story (Genesis 42–45). The Jewish quarter of Erzsébetváros was his natural environment.

Here is an excerpt from his *Diary*:

"An officer dressed in a hussar uniform came to pick me up from my apartment. I rode with him in an open carriage all along Dob utca, guarded by two long lines of Polish co-religionists along the street. I wonder what they thought when they saw my hat trimmed with egret feathers. Surely not that it's *me* who is in *goles*. In any case, I heard that I had a very honorable and very Hungarian appearance."

(September 10, 1917)

In these words, "Polish" means, of course, Orthodox or Oriental Jews.—Another excerpt on the same topic:

"I rode along Holló utca and Király utca in a fancy carriage sitting on the driver's seat next to a hussar, wearing a gold necklace, and felt the eyes of the poor Jews on my back who were faithfully carrying home their *lulavim* for the upcoming Sukkot. What can this mean? The old *secretary* wearing a gold necklace, riding with a striped hussar? I swear that I would much rather walk down there with a *lulav* in my hand than ride up here, seemingly proud, parading in a gold necklace with a hussar."

(September 30, 1917)

Compared to the previous generation of young, talented Jews in Pest who tried to fulfill their ambitions and enter bourgeois society by breaking *Out of the Ghetto*, we must note that despite his inner struggle, Goldziher never questioned his being Jewish. The writer Géza Hegedüs, a late and distant relative of Goldziher, wrote later that "he believed that a decent person remains faithful to the Jewish community, the Hungarian homeland and the name he inherited from his forefathers". His contemporaries remembered that on the High Holidays Goldziher never went to the Dohány Temple, he always prayed at one of the small, more traditional prayer-houses, of which there were many in the area. True, as a university dean he participated in the "Gnostic, Neo-Platonic, anti-monotheistic religious festivities of the government" even on the day of Rosh ha-Shanah, with pangs of conscience, to contradict the common accusation that "Jews cannot fully behave as citizens of Hungary". He wanted to adjust to his environment, yet he did not want to change. In spite of his being the dean he did not participate in the procession on Corpus Christi. "(...) I would surely die of it. Believing in one God, being a purist and a Jew, to participate in a procession celebrating a God turned into human? I stayed away from this misfortune. I refused to defy my own faith." Or, "I might be overstating my spiritual apprehension towards participating in processions organized by the Cardinal Prince Primate which are of national, and not of religious character, (...) but I never marched under the cross and its eucharistic version."

222. A certificate by Moses Schreiber, chief rabbi of Pozsony (the *Hatam Sofer*), 1828

223. Ignác Goldziher's childhood pledge to his father

224. Adolf Goldziher's letter to his son, October 5, 1868

225. "My son, Jichak Leib (...) was born to me in good hour, on the holy Sabbath (...) on the 12th of Tammuz, 610 according to the minor era (= 1850 C.E.). May God protect him (...)."

226. Ignác Goldziher delivers his *bar mitzvah* sermon in the Székesfehérvár synagogue, 1863 (The photo was apparently made at a photographer's studio with stage props)

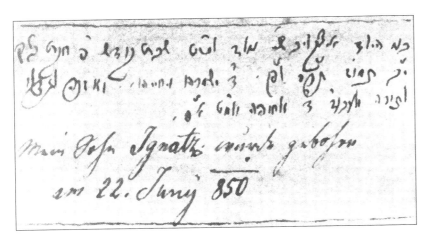

227. Ignác Goldziher
at age 16, 1866

The spirit of German reform Judaism was actually closer to Goldziher than the strict conservatism of some in his community, and scholarly research was, of course, more important for him than the academic intrigues of Hungarian high society. But he did not want to break with tradition, and neither did he want to leave Hungary. He tried to think of both in better terms, he tried to improve them. Goldziher's career can best be examined from the window of his apartment in Holló utca.

The original slab on the wall of his house in Holló utca proudly tells us in verse that Ignác Goldziher, university professor, "spent a lifetime in this house", that

"Night and day here worked, researched, the great scholar of the East – Here matured quietly the great works of his genius – And while his name spread brilliantly conquering the whole world – He himself stayed put faithfully on this native soil."
(Translated by Raphael Patai)

Raphael Patai quotes this verse in his memoirs, using the last line to criticize the officials of the Pest Jewish community for their anti-Zionist attitude. It is true that the inscription was put up by the community and its text written by Károly Sebestyén, but Goldziher's *Diary* is a proof that he shared those ideas.

According to the testimony of the *Diary*, Goldziher always had a negative opinion of the Pest Neolog Jewish community, of which he was the secretary for thirty years. Some of his complaints, however, were not completely justified. It would have caused an international scandal if the Rabbinical Seminary

228. Ignác Goldziher
upon receiving his
doctor's degree in
Leipzig, 1870

229. *Ex libris* of Ignác
Goldziher

had appointed professors without *semikhah*, rabbinical ordination. He called Vilmos Bacher, with whom he had studied Talmud together for years, *boher* in his diary. This, and his often even more sarcastic comments about Bacher are somewhat unjust. He scornfully refers to Wahrmann as a "Pole (*Pollack*)", meaning "Polish", though even the latter's grandfather, the rabbi of Pest, was born in Óbuda. (He must have had Wahrmann's two uncles in mind, who were living in Galicia in the 1830s, although that still does not justify his mockery.) An anecdote survived about how Goldziher, in an informal gathering of his friends, said farewell to his position in the Jewish community with a Biblical pun. He quoted Exodus 31,17, "it shall be *aus* for all time between Me and the people of Israel", but distorted the pronunciation of the Hebrew word *ot / oys*, "sign" into the German–Yiddish *aus*, thereby changing the meaning. Instead of "it shall be a *sign* for all time between Me and the people of Israel" he said "it shall be *over* for all time between Me and the people of Israel". Of course, nothing was *over*, and that was Goldziher's own wish. His complaints, whether justified or not, made him angry and passionate, but they never influenced his sober decisions.

Until the day of his death Goldziher remained who he was at his birth. In a letter written in 1889 he says, "As for my nationality, I am a Hungarian from Transdanubia, and my faith is Jewish. Leaving Jerusalem I said I was going home."

In his will written in 1901 Goldziher directed as follows:

"Over my coffin I ask that my good friends recite Psalm 23, and the same when they bid farewell to it. On my gravestone they should inscribe verse 4 of the same Psalm in the original Hebrew. My child understands the importance of this Psalm in my life. It accompanied me throughout my life, supported me in hardships and encouraged me to win in spite of all ill will."

Not long before he wrote his will, Goldziher translated this verse of the Psalms into Hungarian and read it at the funeral of David Kaufmann.

"Though I walk through a valley of deepest darkness,
I fear no harm, for You are with me."

(4) Secondhand Bookstores, Book Sellers

Király utca was also the home of Jewish bookstores. The best ones, Benő Neumann's and Ignác Schwarz's, were right at the beginning of the street, opposite the Orczy House, at nos. 6 and 8, but there were several others, too, because wherever there are Jews, lots of bookstores are needed. Today, there is a secondhand bookstore with a selection of Hebrew books in the neighborhood, but this is not like it used to be, the choice is much poorer. In a real Jewish bookstore there are not only prayer-books and various Bible editions, but also the Talmud, Maimonides and the Shulhan Arukh along with all the publications of Hebrew printing houses, collections of responsa, rabbinical Bible commentaries, religious tractates and disputes, as well as modern Hebrew and Yiddish literature. Such stores can be found in Brooklyn or in the vicinity of the synagogues of Paris, London and Jerusalem. The crowded shelves of small Hasidic bookstores in Me'ah She'arim still retain a piece of Eastern Europe. A Jewish bookseller is not really a merchant but rather a scholar who knows what books are worth.

Zoltán Trócsányi (1886–1971) drew the portrait of a bookseller, a *bouquiniste* or *moykher sforim* in Király utca.

"A professor of linguistics at the Budapest university mentioned the following case. While reading a Hebrew book I came across particular and surprising quotations from another Hebrew work I had never heard about, whose title I had never seen in bibliographies, and which I would hardly find in the scholarly libraries of Pest, or the world-famous Kaufmann Hebrew collection of the Academy and the foreign library catalogues. I was rather annoyed since the quotations from the Hebrew book seemed to provide rather significant data for my essay in progress. I nearly gave up hope of finding this book so valuable to me, and for which I would have been ready to offer millions, when it came to my mind that I should have a look at the holdings of the secondhand booksellers of Pest.

"Since it was a Hebrew book, I made my way to Király utca as a matter of course. In a miniature bookstore where there was scarcely room for four side by side, a peculiar turn of fortune threw the desired book into my hands. It lay in the rear of one of the shelves, was a bit ragged, and it was obvious that its owner was not aware of its value, just like I had not been aware of it a few weeks earlier, and probably no one but me is aware of it even today.

"There were just the two of us in the store, the old long-bearded bookseller and I. First we talked about indifferent matters, in Hebrew, of course, then I turned to the bookshelves and began to browse, while the old man was deeply involved in reading a Hebrew book. Suddenly my hand jerked hard, my breath stopped, a flutter came over me, but at the next moment I stole a glance at the old man to see whether he had noticed my excitement because if he didn't, this treasure of a book so longed for would belong to me for a few thousand crowns. He did glance at me, but the next moment his eyes were on his book again. I, too, went on searching among the dirty, dusty covers and meanwhile I kept examining the old man's face, but it remained cold and indifferent. Or was there a cunning smile in the corner of his eyes?

"I made up a scheme: I would choose some more books, shudder or tremble each time I touch one of them, and at the sight of one book, the least interesting one, I would even cry out. I did so, glancing at him secretly, but he was reading on motionless, he did not even look up, with a cunning smile under his mustache.

"I could not bear to continue the game too long, so I put the pile of books in front of him: interesting and uninteresting ones, among them my treasure, which ten minutes earlier had not even been worth 2 thousand crowns.

"The old man sorted out the pile. The one I was really interested in, he set aside, dusted the thick, black, decades-old dust, looked me in the eye and said it was not for sale. Next he opened the drawer of the desk and put the book in there carefully.

"We stared at each other above our spectacles.

"It isn't for sale, he repeated, but for the other ones I charge a cheap price. I gathered all my self-control so that my face remained indifferent, but I felt he was the better gambler and had noticed earlier that I had found something extraordinary, dear to me. Now, he read the confirmation of that experience in my eyes. What could I do? I purchased two insignificant books, which I needed not at all, and said farewell to him. A few paces from the door I stopped, half expecting to hear him call me back. He did not. I kept on standing there, and finally I turned around.

"He, too, must have changed his mind meanwhile, thinking I might find the same book in the neighboring bookstore, so after an hour's bargaining the book became mine for a fortune."

(*Magyar régiségek és furcsaságok* [Hungarian Antiquities and Peculiarities], Fourth series, Budapest: Dante, n. d., pp. 140–145)

Who might have been the scholarly professor mentioned in this sketch? We can only guess. From the prices we may assume that the event must have happened during the years of inflation following World War I. Who needed rare Hebrew publications in Pest then? Goldziher, Sámuel Kohn and Sándor Büchler (1870–1944) were still alive, but in those years the first person to come to mind would be Miksa (Meir Tzvi / Max) Weisz (1872–1931), the well-known Hebrew bibliographer, who catalogued David Kaufmann's library. We might also consider Sámuel Krausz (Samuel Krauss) (1866–1948), or maybe Kayserling as possible characters in the story. But either way, a sketch does not need to refer to an exact date or person, it is literature, after all. In fact, of the above personalities only Goldziher was a professor at the Pest university, yet it is just him who can hardly be imagined in the above scene. Büchler, an excellent historian who wrote the history of the Jews of Pest and Buda in a brilliant book (1901), was the rabbi of Keszthely and obtained the title of honorary lecturer (habilitation) in 1914 only with the backing of his wife's uncle, Goldziher. (He perished in Auschwitz in 1944, the year when all of Hungary's Jews were deported from the countryside along with all the members of his community.) Krausz, a scholar of Talmudic antiquities, had been active in the Viennese Rabbinical Seminary since 1905. Miksa Weisz was a professor at the Rabbinical Seminary of Pest. There was no place for Jewish studies at the university of Pest then. The Jewish bookworm

231. Portrait of Sándor Büchler at the time he wrote his major work, *A zsidók története Budapesten* [The History of Jews in Budapest] (1901)

of Király utca must have received his title of university professor of linguistics as a matter of poetic license, gently making the reality of Pest blush. Jewish or Hebrew books were still available in Király utca in the 1940s, both *ante* and *post* (scil. the Holocaust), as they are today, but we should not expect anymore to find a rarity there. True, today even a formerly ordinary publication printed by the Schlesingers or Katzburg can be considered a rarity.

The most famous secondhand bookseller of Pest, however, did not sell his books in Király utca. Bence Szabolcsi (1899–1973), an eminent scholar of music history, earned his living in the late 1930s as a bookseller, though not exactly voluntarily, since he could not get a job that would correspond to his standing in scholarship. He collected and sold books, assisted customers and offered his advice to those who turned to him with questions. The small shop on Vilmos császár út / Bajcsy-Zsilinszky út used to belong to his father-in-law, A. Andor Győző, one-time publisher, and it remains a home for books even today.

Andor Győző's firm was founded in the building at no. 40 in 1898, and had functioned there for three decades until they moved to no. 34, in 1928. Here they became the neighbors of Hungaria Newspaper Printing House and the editorial offices and publisher of the journal *Múlt és Jövő* for a few more years, and here were the offices of the famous *Nyugat* and the Nyugat Publishing House and Literary Co. during the entire time of its existence, between 1908 and 1948. It was A. Andor Győző's company which published the ever so important reference works of the interwar period: *Művészeti lexikon* [Encyclopedia of Arts] (1926, second edition: 1935), *Irodalmi lexikon* [Encyclopedia of Literature] (1928), *Színházi lexikon* [Encyclopedia of Theater] (1930), *Zenei lexikon* [Encyclopedia of Music] (1930–1931, second edition: 1935). Bence Szabolcsi was an editor of the latter.

Though Mihály Reményi's store at 58 Király utca was not a secondhand bookstore, it deserves to be mentioned here. Reményi collected and sold musical instruments there, new and antique pieces, about a hundred old violins—it was almost a museum. In the summer of 1944, in a decree issued to the Commissioner of Confiscated Jewish Works of Art, the secretary of state of the Ministry of Education and Religious Affairs ordered that this "collection unique under the circumstances of the country" be handed over to the College of Music. The order was carried out.

(5) Hebrew Printing Houses

Hebrew type-setting and printing in Pest begins with János Tamás Trattner's (1717–1798) printing house. The printing house privileged for printing missals, located at the corner of Úri utca (today Petőfi Sándor utca) and Gránátos utca (today Városház utca), had only a modest set of Hebrew characters and could only print words or short quotations, examples. (This printing house later moved to the Károlyi–Trattner house at 3 Petőfi Sándor utca.) The Hebrew printing business was carried on

232. Wholesale and retail stationery, lithographs and printed books, 1901

by the founder's relatives, Mátyás Trattner (1745–1828) and his son, János Tamás Trattner (1789–1825), then his son-in-law, István Trattner-Károlyi (1794–1863). Mátyás Trattner had been the head of the University Press earlier, so we can say that Hebrew printing was in the hands of the Trattners during the first half of the century.

The University Press, which was moved from Nagyszombat to Buda together with the university, was equipped just like the Trattners' printing house. At the end of the eighteenth century it was their privilege to publish Hebrew textbooks. The demand of Pest Jews for prayer-books was satisfied by firms in Vienna and Pozsony. Yet in the end it was still in the framework of the University Printing House that Jewish book publishing developed.

Éliás (Eliyah) Rosenthal (1758–1833), the son of Naftali Rosenthal (1727–1798), the famous rabbi from the town Mór, was a merchant and brewery lease-holder in Komárom. He acquired a thorough Talmudic education in the yeshivah of Pozsony, but was also acquainted with the enlightened ideas which urged the civil emancipation of Jews. He called together the great Jewish "synod (*asifah*)", a national assembly, for the spring of 1790 to formulate the wishes of the Jews. They consulted French Jews on ambiguous issues and, within three weeks, handed in a petition to the Diet of Pozsony. They requested religious, commercial and personal freedom, rights to settle and permission to turn to the rabbinical court in legal disputes. They cited the privileges enjoyed by Jews in medieval

233. The publishing house of the Singer and Wolfner company, ca. 1912

234. Interior of the Singer and Wolfner publishing house, 1912

Hungary in support of their request. Although the petition had no practical results, the discussions and the appeal made Rosenthal's name well known all over the country. In 1804 he moved to Pest and opened a stationery and bookstore. His father had been on friendly terms with Moses Mendelssohn in his youth, they had studied together and also remained in correspondence later, which determined his son's orientation. But Naftali Rosenthal's family education and the Jewish enlightenment (*Haskalah*) of the town Mór could only bear fruit in Pest. In 1807 Éliás applied to the *Königliche Statthalterei* for permission to publish Hebrew books. He joined with Trattner and they invited a typographer, Sámuel Falka of Bikfalva (1766–1826), the well-known classicist letter-cutter from the University Press, to join. The first Hebrew book they published together was R. Münz's address on the victory over Napoleon in 1814. Their rabbinical adviser was R. Münz. Rosenthal was a real scholar–publisher. The fame of his library reached abroad, even Leopold Zunz (1794–1886), the first scholarly authority of the *Haskalah*, praised it. He could not enter the field of Jewish politics, so he withdrew into his books. His brother, Salamon Rosenthal (1764–1845), followed him to Pest in 1819. He was engaged in scholarship, wrote and collected books as well. He was interested in Hebrew as a living language, so he translated Mendelssohn's *Phaedon* and the works of Kant into Hebrew. He was well versed in Christian Biblical scholarship, read Mendelssohn's works, but opposed liturgical reforms and textual criticism. He even published a book against reforms (*Bet Oven*, Buda, 1839). In Pest of the 1820s Hebraic studies were not associated with either the university or the *yeshivah*. They were born within the realm of book publishing and collection—and this was a first sign of the modernization of traditional Jewish scholarship.

Thanks to Rosenthal's assistance, a few years later the University Press had already been publishing prayer-books, a Haggadah and other Hebrew books, such as Azriel Brill's short history and survey of Hungary in 1821. They tried to keep pace with the fashionable movements of Hebrew printing, in 1842 they bought a new set of letters and even printed pulp fiction in Rashi letters, but in the 1870s, when there were already several other Hebrew printing houses, they withdrew from the market of Jewish book publishing. They moved to 10–14 Dohány utca only much later, in 1950, when they merged with the former Forrás Printing House.

Also the printing office in Dohány utca has an exciting story. Before World War I it was the address of the Fried and Krakauer Printing House, then of the Gutenberg and the Forrás typographies. (Forrás was run by a certain Forrai—obviously a Magyarized name.) Several Jewish community and Zionist papers were published here in the course of time. Originally it had belonged to the Tolnai Printing House, where the magazine *Tolnai Világ-Lap*, the most popular Hungarian weekly for decades, was printed. The owner and editor, Simon Tolnai (1895–1944), initially lived almost next door, at 10 Síp utca, but later he moved to a more distinguished neighborhood, to 12 Erzsébet királyné útja. When the Tolnai Printing House was nationalized (1941), confiscated, to be exact, it was named Forrás Könyvkiadó és Nyomda [Forrás Publishing and Printing House]. In 1944 the *Tolnai Világ-Lap* (*Világ-Lapja*) could only be published under the title *Világlap*, dropping the already deported Tolnai's name from the title, but it continued to appear until as late as December 20. In the Fall of the same year Tolnai was deported to Mauthausen and killed there. Today the building houses the University Press. For a short while, around 1955, the Jewish community newspaper with the meaningful title *Új Élet* ("New Life") was published here. Maybe it is not a coincidence that a restaurant at 5/B Dohány utca, very near both to the former Forrás Printing House and to the synagogue, was also called *Forrás* ("source", "origin"). There is still a restaurant at this address today, though a Korean one.

The University Press maintained contacts with the descendants of the Wodianers, who did the most in Pest to promote the Hebrew language and Jewish book publishing and press in general.

There were numerous small Jewish printing shops in Pest, naturally in the Jewish quarter and its vicinity. They often consisted of only one small room opening onto the street or the courtyard, and though their names and places changed frequently, the character of printing manufactures or printing industry remained the same until the end of World War II, sometimes even later, until the nationalization of minor plants.

Printing establishments around Király utca which published or printed Jewish newspapers in the decades between the Congress of 1868/69 and World War II are listed below. Names are given according to the imprints. This list is far from complete, it serves merely to indicate the range of Jewish printing, to show the density of printing houses of all sorts in such a small neighborhood. In the names below *Nyomda* is the Hungarian word for Press or Publishing House.

18 Dohány utca: Tábori Nyomda
44 Dohány utca: Neuwald Illés Utódai (Successors of Illés Neuwald).—They developed a version of Art Nouveau in Hebrew book publishing
27 Hajós utca: Kellner Albert Könyvnyomda (Albert Kellner Printing House).—The third floor of the building was built for Mr. and Mrs. Albert Kellner, née Etel Klein, in 1927. Later (1946) Folio Nyomdai Műintézet (Jakab Schwarz)
9-11 Horn Ede (today Weiner Leó) utca: Igazság Nyomda
5 Kazinczy utca: Hoffmann és Tsa. [Associated] Nyomda
35 Kazinczy utca-28 Dob utca: Katzburg Nyomda
21 Kertész utca: Spatz Henrik Könyvnyomda. (Housed perhaps in the rear of the block)
1 Király utca: Jos. Schlesinger bookseller's firm
9 Király utca: Viktória Nyomda
18 Király utca: Ferdinánd Gevürcz Könyvnyomda.—Besides the Katzburg Nyomda this is the most important Hebrew printing house of the interwar period. Hebrew parts of scholarly books were usually typeset and printed at Gevürcz (Gewürcz) Printing House
19 Király utca: Admirál Nyomda
26 Király utca: Schwarcz és Krausz Nyomda
47 Király utca (Pekáry House): Eckstein Bernát és Fia Könyvnyomda
Lipótvárosi tér (today 2 Szent István tér): Benndiner Testvérek és Grünwald A. Nyomda
3 Nagymező utca-55 Paulay Ede utca: Általános Nyomda / Hírlapnyomda. (In the building opening to both streets there was a newspaper editorial office, too)
2 Ó utca: Neumayer Ede Könyvnyomda
5 Ó utca: Neuwirth Nyomda.—It was they who printed most of the publications of the Rabbinical Seminary and other Jewish scholarly works
12 Ó utca: Európa Irodalmi és Nyomdai Rt. [Co.]
50 Ó utca (on the corner of Gyár utca and Ó utca): Gross és Grünhut Nyomda
14 Révay utca: Corvina / Korvin Kő- és Könyvnyomda (Ignác Schlesinger).—The Press moved into this house from Rostély utca (today Gerlóczy utca) around 1892. In the nineteenth century they published, among others, the *Izraelita Tanügyi Értesítő* [Israelite Educational Newsletter], the journal of the Izraelita Tanító Egyesület [Society of Israelite Teachers]. After World War II the Akadémiai Kiadó, the bookstore and printing house of the Hungarian Academy of Sciences took over the space in Gerlóczy utca and held it until 1996. The building in Révay utca was occupied by the Korvin Testvérek

Könyvnyomda / Grafikai Intézet [Korvin Brothers Printing House and Graphic Institute] around 1920. The two companies, Corvina and Korvin, may have been related to each other. (Both names refer to King Matthias, called Corvinus, of the fifteenth century and his famous library.) The editorial office and publishing house of the journal *Múlt és Jövő* was also here for a short while around 1930
8 Rumbach utca: Pannónia Nyomda

These small printing offices marked the location of the future press quarter in Teréz- and Erzsébetváros already back in the mid-nineteenth century. The printing houses of the previous century had been mostly in Belváros (Downtown), but modern printing industry needed larger space, available only in the vicinity of the small Jewish printing houses. Sizes and proportions became worthy of a metropolis in the headquarters of Athenaeum (Miksa utca, built in 1898) and the other press palaces on Nagykörút.

The Löbl Printing House and Stationery, the company of Dávid Löbl and Son (Marcell) was first located at 19 Andrássy út, then on the corner of Andrássy út and Nagymező utca. It was founded by Dávid Löbl in 1875. The headquarters were designed by architect Frigyes Kovács in 1899. The printing press was on the ground floor, its rooms opening from the courtyard; on the first floor there were nice apartments for the family, and on the upper two floors, rented apartments along the outside balcony. A building in the courtyard, more exactly on the ground floor, was built by Löbl's widow following Sándor Löffler's plans in 1924. In its golden age during the interwar years, the printing house was managed by the founder's grandsons, Ödön Löbl / Landy (1904-1966) and Dezső Löbl / Landy (1908-1990). At that time it was one of the master printing houses of Pest. They founded their own publishing house, Officina in 1936. Their typesetters could hand typeset even Greek and Hebrew texts, without any mistake. They published works edited by Károly Kerényi, the *Kétnyelvű Klasszikusok* [Bilingual Classics] series, and several other bibliophile serials like the *Officina Képeskönyvek* [Officina Picture Books], *Officina Hungarica*, etc. They also printed contemporary literature, among others Attila József's last volume of poetry, *Nagyon fáj* [It Hurts Too Much] (1936) and—between 1936 and 1938—the issues of a journal edited by Ferenc Fejtő and Attila József, the *Szép Szó* [Artistic Word]. They offered the best quality in everything. They were at work until as late as early spring, 1944, publishing Antal Szerb's *Száz vers* [One Hundred Poems], a bilingual anthology of classical poetry and a soft voice of protest against the barbarous age. The printing house consisted of just three rooms opening to the courtyard, and employed only a few people. After World War II it was Imre Román who headed Officina for a while. They published Jenő Lévai's volumes, *Fekete könyv* [Black Book], *Szürke könyv* [Gray Book], *Fehér könyv* [White Book] and *A pesti gettó csodálatos megmenekülésének hiteles története* [An Authentic History of the Wonderful Escape of the Pest Ghetto], which documented the persecutions of Jews and the rescue operations in 1944. Today we can still see the owner's initials, L. D., on the original iron gate of the building. Around 1980 the portrait of János Gutenberg and a few letters of his name could still be seen in a relief on the facade above the second floor.

The most important Orthodox printing press was the Katzburg Nyomda: an Orthodox press in an Orthodox environment, in the corner building at 35 Kazinczy utca–28 Dob utca, right next to the Orthodox synagogue and the community offices. The printing press was established by R. Dávid Cvi Katzburg in Vác in 1892. R. Katzburg wrote several theological works in Hebrew; for him the printing house was a means of spreading his ideas rather than a source of income or a business undertaking. He also published an international bi-weekly in Hebrew under the traditional title *Tel Talpiyyot* ("arsenal", "armory") (see Song of Songs 4,4 / Talmud, Berakhot 30a). After a time, the Vác typography was closed and following World War I the family founded a new Hebrew typography in Pest, in Kazinczy utca, then headed by Meshullam Zalman Katzburg. In 1934, the Katzburg family made *aliyya* and the typography was entrusted to a relative, Salomon Katzburg. Later on, a son of the former printer, Nathaniel Katzburg, became a professor for Hungarian Jewish history in Israel.

The Schlesingers were a typical prayer-book publishing company. It was founded by Joseph Schlesinger in 1858 in Vienna. The family, originating from the Austrian-Hungarian-Slovakian-Moravian quadrangle, was present in contemporary Jewish and secular life in various ways. Akiba Joszéf

Schlesinger (1837–1922), a follower of the Hatam Sofer, opposed the Jewish enlightenment and adhered to the traditional Jewish religious and social community (*kolel ha-ivriim*). He was an early propagator of Zionist ideas, moved to Palestine in his early youth, in 1870, contributed to the renewal of the Hebrew language and the foundation of the Jewish settlement in Palestine, the *yishuv*. Others in the extended family made their careers in the world of journalism, banking, economy, and sciences. The publishing house opened its Pest branch (Schlesinger Jos.) already before the Austro-Hungarian *Ausgleich* of 1867. Their books were published unchanged for decades: *Pesah Haggadot* and prayer-books in various editions.

Among the editions of the Schlesingers the prayer-books were especially popular. Arnold Kiss, rabbi of Buda, wrote prayer-books in Hungarian for women and girls: *Mirjam. Imádságok zsidó nők számára* [Miriam. Prayers for Jewish Women] (1899) and *Noémi. Imádságok zsidó leányok számára* [Naomi. Prayers for Jewish Girls] (1906). Simon Hevesi's prayer-books carried a literary value: *Ateret shalom ve-emet* (1911); *Siddur tefillat Yisra'el. Üdvnek, igazságnak könyörgése* [Prayer for Salvation and Truth] (1913); *Örök áhítat. Könyörgések és rövid fohászok könyve zsidó nők és leányok számára* [Eternal Devotion. Book of Prayers and Short Supplications for Jewish Women and Girls] (1918), etc.

Under the early Zionist influence around 1890 the catalog was extended by language textbooks and prayer-books called *Kol Yehudah*, "The Voice of Juda", which were circulated in a German and a Hungarian version. The Hungarian version, a thin brochure, is used in teaching Hebrew on an elementary level even today.

The company did not pay much attention to textual correctness, their Hungarian translations sometimes did not even reach the journalistic level, but these books were not meant to be literature, only aids to religious life. The Pest headquarters of the Schlesinger company were in the Orczy House (1 Király utca) for a long time, then they moved to 14 Révay utca, to the same building where the Niszel's offered kosher food, on the first floor. Because of the growing anti-Semitism, and probably also encouraged by their North-African business contacts, the company moved to Tel-Aviv in the late 1930s. Today they supply both the Israeli and the Hungarian market with Hungarian-language religious books. They mainly reprint their old editions, maintaining the continuity of Hungarian Jewish book publishing. Their store at 72 Allenby Road is one of several tiny Hungarian isles in Tel-Aviv.

(6) The Jewish Home: the Mezuzah

A Jewish home, at least a traditional one, can be recognized already at the door. There is a *mezuzah* on the right side of the doorpost. Actually, the word literally means "doorpost". This mark is commanded by the Torah, in *Shema Yisra'el*, "inscribe them on the doorposts of your house and on your gates" (Deuteronomy 6,9; 11,20). In ancient times a *mezuzah* was posted only at the entrance, but this custom had changed a long time ago and now people affix a *mezuzah* on the doorpost of every dwelling room (but not on the doorpost of a bathroom, or a small pantry, storage room, etc.). The small *mezuzah* case may be of gold or other precious metal, or just simple wood. The text of the *Shema Yisra'el* (Deuteronomy 6,4–9; 11,13–21) inside the case is traditionally written on a small piece of parchment in 22 lines, continuously. On the back side of the scroll, yet visible from outside, there is the letter *shin* for *Shadday*, "Almighty" or as an abbreviation of *shomer delatot Yisra'el*, "Guardian of the doors of Israel". Some of the modern mass-produced *mezuzot* only have a *shin*. The *mezuzah* has to be mounted on the doorpost within thirty days after moving into a new home. It has to be affixed to the upper third of the doorpost so that it would lean inwards, symbolically spanning the doorpost. Pious Jews touch the *mezuzah* every time they enter or leave and then kiss the fingernail on their index finger. The *mezuzah* has to be checked once every seven years to ensure that the writing on the parchment is still legible. The text of the *mezuzah* has to be written and corrected with the same care as the Torah scroll.

235. *Mezuzah.*
Margit Tevan's work

(7) Oneg Shabbat

The Sabbath (*shabbat / shabes / shabos*), the day of rest, is a holiday to celebrate at home; both the original meaning of the word and its Biblical description is "rest" (Genesis 2,1–3). Rabbinical tradition holds that "if you observe the Sabbath it is as if you would comply with all the laws of the Torah" (Pesikta). In fact, Jewish life has always been organized around the Sabbath.

It starts Friday evening (*leil shabbat*). Like every day, Saturday also starts at sundown (*erev shabbat*). The lady of the house lights the Sabbath candles (*nerot*) a few minutes before sundown, since it is not permissible to work or light a fire on the Sabbath. Minimum two candles in two separate candlesticks are necessary for this, a two-branched one is not suitable. They do not have to be fancy but in most households there are nice Sabbath candlesticks. The reason for having two of them is that in the Bible the two versions of the Ten Commandments use two different words for commanding the Sabbath observance: *zakhor*, "remember, do not forget" (Exodus 20,8) and *shamor*, "guard, observe" (Deuteronomy 5,12). The woman's head is covered with a kerchief, she does not blow out the match, after kindling the lights she draws three circles around the flame with her hands, then covers her eyes, palms inside, and recites the blessing.

This last hand movement resulted from a two-thousand-year-old Halakhic debate. In the late Second Temple period, in the first half of the first century B.C.E. there lived two great Halakhic authorities, Hillel and Shammai, who usually reached opposite decisions. Shammai generally liked to interpret the law strictly on the basis of the written word, whereas Hillel was somewhat looser in the details of his interpretations. The debate about kindling the Sabbath lights was about what comes first: lighting the candles or the blessing. Tradition accepted Hillel's answer and thus the candle is lit first, but Shammai's reasoning was also appreciated, hence covering one's eyes during the blessing. The candles then stay on the dinner table until they burn down completely, it is forbidden to extinguish them. In some places floating wicks or oil-lamps are used instead of candles. In the Ashkenazi areas these lamps usually had six burners, hence the name of the six-pointed yellow brass chandelier: *Judenstern*.

The Sabbath is greeted in the synagogue (*kabbalat ha-shabbat*) as part of the Friday night service. People sing "Come, my bride... (*Lekhah dodi*)" and turn to the West, or towards the door standing on their toes to catch a better glimpse of the Sabbath Queen who is to arrive. This song originates from the sixteenth-century mystic tradition, and spread among Ashkenazi Jews from Safed. After the evening prayer people are accompanied home by angels. At home they again sing the song that welcomes the angels of Sabbath peace, *Shalom aleikhem mala'akhei ha-sharet*. There is even a special greeting for Friday night: *shabbat shalom* or *gut shabes / git shabes / shabes* in Yiddish, in Eastern Europe, in Pest, even nowadays.

You shall call the Sabbath a delight (*oneg*), we read in Isaiah 58,13. This term, *oneg shabbat*, the joy of the Sabbath, has become the center of all the rituals on the Sabbath eve. The festive meal is a great joy, only enhanced by wine (Song of Songs 1,2). A blessing (*kiddush*) is recited over a cup of wine at the dinner table. This wine, always in small quantities, is regarded as a religious obligation in Jewish homes. There are stories about pious but poor men who sold even their clothes in order to be able to greet the Sabbath with wine. In most homes there is a special silver cup for making *kiddush*. The *kiddush* cup is filled to the brim.

Yet another blessing at the Sabbath dinner table is recited, like each time, over bread, only that now there are two loaves (*lehem mishneh*). The number two is related to the Biblical story of the *mannah* (Exodus 16,11–27) which says that a double portion fell for the Sabbath. The traditional Sabbath bread is braided and dipped in egg-white. It is called *hallah* or *hallot* in the plural (Numeri 15,20), since two of them are needed. This is the name of the dough or leaven saved for the food offering at the Temple, too. In Pest it is a bit different from the rest of Eastern Europe: its dough is not sweet, it is sprinkled with poppy seed and is called *barches*. (The word *barches*, with German–Hungarian spelling, is the Western Yiddish equivalent of *hallah*.) It is not clear whether the word *barches* comes from the Hebrew "blessing", *berakhot* in the plural. A similar bread is baked for the third Sabbath meal, but somewhat smaller—it is called the *shalesh-südes barchesl*—and for other holidays too, only then one loaf is enough for the blessing and it may be decorated.

On Friday night the two loaves are covered with a special cloth, a *hallah* cover (*mappah*) with an embroidered inscription. This cover is only used during the *kiddush*. Slicing the bread is a ceremony, too. The host, the master of the house, takes the loaves from under the cover, cuts one of them where its form is most perfect, recites the blessing, slices or breaks further pieces, dips a piece in salt and eats it; then he gives everyone else a piece. The first of the three Sabbath feasts, the *shalosh se'udot*, may begin now.

Traditionally Friday evening is the time of Torah study at home. At this time the "great edition of the Scripture", the *Mikra'ot gedolot* is used for study, which contains all the major medieval commentaries and other exegeses. The first "Great Bible" was published by Daniel Bomberg in 1524/25 in Venice. This edition was highly respected and it was reprinted several times.

In addition to all the other joys of the Sabbath, the *Shekhinah*, the Divine Presence, dwells in the bedroom of married couples.

Having three meals on the Sabbath is a religious obligation. The first two, the Friday dinner and Saturday lunch, have to be prepared in advance, since it is forbidden to cook on the Sabbath. Only food already prepared may be served (Exodus 16,29), something that does not require reheating, something that keeps warm. That is how *tshulent* (*sholet* in Hungarian), cooked and kept in the fireplace, has become a traditional Sabbath lunch. The order of the meal is the same as on Friday night, only the ceremony is simpler. Wine is not required to make *kiddush*, any kind of drink is suitable.

Both *se'udot* are eaten at a leisurely pace; people nibble on the food for a long time and stay at the table even after they finished eating. They chat, sing Sabbath songs, *zemirot*. At the very end of the meal people recite the Grace after Meals, the *Birkat ha-mazon*, usually with more singing than on weekdays. The ritual of *mezumen bentshn*, "invitation to blessing", becomes an obligatory part of the meal wherever there are more than three people. If there are guests, it is not the host who leads this ceremony but the most respected guest, a *kohen* or a *talmid hakham*, if any be present. The leader of the ceremony invites people to say the Grace—hence the name of this ceremony (*birkat zimmun*). The Grace after Meals is usually introduced by one of the Psalms, Psalm 137 on weekdays, recalling the destruction of the Temple and the Babylonian captivity, and Psalm 126 on the Sabbath and on holidays. The decoration and value of *Birkat ha-mazon* manuscripts is similar to that of the Pesah Haggadot.

The Jewish Museum of Budapest published a facsimile of the *Birkat ha-mazon* kept in its collection in 1991—a beautiful volume. It was a "small (wedding) gift" (*minhah ketanah*) given by a groom to his bride in Polna, Moravia (today in the Czech Republic), in 1751. It is the work of a famous master from Vienna. It contains not only the Grace after Meals but gives instructions for the three ritual duties of a woman: *mitzvat hallah*, the separation of the dough, *mitzvat niddah*, the ritual bath, and *mitzvat hadlakah*, the kindling of the Sabbath lights. The text of the Grace is written in square Ashkenazi script, the instructions in *Tzenah u-Renah* letters, and the booklet is richly illuminated with miniatures.

The third meal is traditionally called *shalosh se'udot* (*shalesh südes*), which actually means "three meals"—the grammatically correct form would be *shelishit*, or in full: *se'udah shelishit*. (Today in Budapest this form, under Israeli influence, became widely used.) This meal is just a symbolic one, it is eaten Saturday late afternoon. The typical food is *gefilte fish*, or fish spread. József Kis, and others from the older generations mention pike filled with walnuts. This is the time when Jews visit each other. Men study the Talmud together, women read the *Tzenah u-Renah* or chat, children play. If the community has a visitor, a rabbi or a *talmid hakham*, this is when he gives a talk.

The *maggid*, the wandering preacher of old Eastern Europe, used to give his sermon and tell his tales in the prayer-house. To attract the audience, his moral lessons (*musar*) were sometimes phrased in a humorous manner.

(8) Havdalah

The Sabbath also ends with a ceremony. A blessing, *havdalah / havdole*, "distinction" is recited, the candle is put out. This happens already after sundown, since it is not permissible to light a fire during the Sabbath. A blessing is recited over a full cup of wine, over the spices (*besamim*) and over the light, i.e. the candles, and a final one over the distinction between the Sabbath and the other six days of the week, between sacred and profane.

The core of the ceremony is extinguishing the *havdalah* candle: a few drops of wine are used to do this. During the blessing over the light everyone is watching the flame of the candle reflected on his or her nails. A sign of darkness is when the candle flame becomes visible; that is, when the day of rest is over. Havdalah candles are of a special kind, multicolor, braided candles with a special case called *havdole holts* in Yiddish.

After the candle is extinguished people pass around the spices (*besamim*) in a little container (*hadas, besamim, besamim-biks*) and everyone gets to smell it. Cloves, cinnamon, laurel or even

236. *Havdalah.* The man holds a *besamim*, the boy a braided *havdalah* candle. Imre Ámos, lino-cut, 1940

fresh lemon peel may be used for this purpose. An *etrog* pinned with cloves is a special *havdalah* spice. This way the *etrog* used at Sukkot stays fresh for a whole year. Smelling the spice box perpetuates an ancient custom. In the Ancient Near East it was customary to burn incense in the house after heavy meals, to eliminate the smell of food. The *besamim* is its Jewish version. These spice boxes shaped after houses, towers or fortresses, usually made of silver, are the most beautiful decorative objects of the Jewish home. (The *tower* referred to is that in the Song of Songs 5,13.)

But the joy of the Sabbath is not over yet, people should still stay together. These ceremonies are followed by the song of the Prophet Elijah, *Eliyahu ha-navi.* Why him? Because tradition holds that the Messiah will not come on the Sabbath when the creation is finished, perfect. And the Messiah would not violate the Sabbath by riding either, he would rather come on a weekday.

After the *havdalah* blessing everyone present wishes a good week to everyone else, *shavu'a tov* in Hebrew, or *a gite vokh* in Yiddish. The wife might turn to her husband and asks for a new dress; he cannot deny any request made at this time. And those who miss making *havdalah* Saturday evening need not worry, for they can make up for it until Tuesday.

The great meals on Saturday at night have a tradition mainly in Hassidic circles. They gather at the *rebe*'s and eat from *his* table, from his plate, striving to partake in the remnants of his food (*shirayim*). If the *rebe* so much as touches a fish, the leftovers are considered remnants because the Torah says "... all the fish of the sea—they are given into your hand" (Genesis 9,2). Now, that the Sabbath is over, they want to extend the evening (*tosefet shabbat*). This feast, bidding farewell to the Sabbath Queen (*melavveh Malkah*), may last for hours. This is when Hasidim would dance their ring dances, probably a rare sight in Budapest; circle, because everyone is equal, there is no first or last, beginning or end, at first slowly, step by step, then faster and faster, to the point of exuberance.

(9) Hanukkah

The celebration of Hanukkah, between the 25th of Kislev and the 2nd of Tevet, is usually in December. This is a home holiday, Hanukkah must be celebrated at home, where one sleeps and eats. It is a semi-holiday, that is, work is not prohibited during its eight days. The story of the holiday is a mythical episode of a well-known historical event described in I Maccabees. It happened in the times of the Syrian king Antiochos Epiphanes (175–164 B.C.E.), whose name *epiphanes*, "the emanating God" was distorted to "furious", *epimanes* by his contemporaries. He wanted to put an end to traditional cults and religions, but a Jewish priest, a certain Mattityahu in Modiin, along the road between Jerusalem and Tel-Aviv, defied the officially required swine sacrifice. There was someone in the community who would have carried out the sacrifice but Mattityahu killed him as he stepped to the altar. His son, Judah, later named Judah Maccabee ("hammer"), along with four of his brothers and some others, started a heroic fight against the foreign ruler. In 165 B.C.E., after three years of fighting they even managed to capture Jerusalem. They entered the Temple where a statue of Zeus occupied the place above the sacrificial altar, on orders of Antiochus Epiphanes. They cleaned the Temple of the remains of the foreign cult, carried out the process of ritual cleansing and re-consecrated it. They had no opportunity to celebrate Sukkot during the war, so they made up for it now. When they wanted to kindle the flame of the *menorah*, they found only one jug of pure oil in the cellar of the Temple. It still bore the seal of the High Priest. Legend maintains that the oil, which normally would have lasted for but one day, burned for eight days in the lamp. (Shabbat, 21b)

Hanukkah, "dedication" (Numbers 7,10), is none other than the celebration of the altar's consecration (I Maccabees 4,59) and of the cleansing of the Temple (II Maccabees 1,18), in the oldest sources. In the New Testament, John's Gospel (10,22) calls it a consecration, too. Josephus calls it *Phota*, the Festival of Lights (*Jewish Antiquities*, XII, 7). In fact, it is the festival of lights (*hag ha-urim*) in Jewish tradition. It is centered around the light of the Hanukkah lamp. The religious duty is to kindle fires, as the Talmud says (Shabbat, 21b): there should be a lamp for each person and household. But the pious have a lamp for each member of the household. And the most zealous light a lamp for each member of the household every day. At Hanukkah it is customary to celebrate other major events or personalities of Jewish liberation as well, Judith, among others, the brave woman who saved her city, Bethulia (Beth El) for offering herself to Holofernes, the leader of the "Babylonian" army and beheading him in her own bed. (The story, which may well have happened, though it is not confirmed in historical sources, is told in Judith's Book, in the Septuaginta). Judith is often depicted on candlesticks, especially Baroque ones, along with Aaron, who is portrayed for his role in abolishing idolatry.

The Hanukkah candlestick (*menorat hanukkah / hanukkiah*) is to be placed outside the door to display the wonder of the holiday (*pirsum ha-nes*), on the left side, opposite the *mezuzah*, to enable other people to see it, too. If it is not by the door, it should be in a window overlooking the street, on the sill, and if not there, at least next to the door inside the room. Whoever passes between the *mezuzah* and the Hanukkah lamp will be safe. The Hanukkah candlestick has eight branches; a ninth one, the servant flame (*shames*), is smaller than the others and is usually apart from them. On the eight days of the holiday more and more candles are lit, all from the *shames*. By the eighth evening eight candles are lit. The flames have to be at the same height. If the candles are in a row, they have to be lit one by one from the right to the left, like writing. On the Sabbath of Hanukkah, on Friday night, the Hanukkah candle is lit before the Sabbath candle, although there is debate on this issue. Another debate concerns whether to light eight candles on the first day, and from then on decrease the number from day to day (this was Shammai's view) or, according to Hillel, light one candle on the first day, and add a candle every day. Tradition follows Hillel's ruling. The holy flames may not be used for secular, practical purposes, for instance, it is not permissible to light another candle from them or to work by the light of Hanukkah candles. And the other way round, candlesticks used for other occasions may not be used to fulfill the Hanukkah obligation.

Several versions of the Hanukkah lamp or candlestick have developed over time. There should be one in every Jewish home. It may be inherited from a grandmother. Among Eastern European families, as in Pest, it is often made of brass, like the Menorah of the Temple in Jerusalem depicted on the Arch of the Roman Emperor Titus (79–81 C.E.), on the Roman Forum. Silver is often used instead of the thick brass. Galician families would have their Hanukkah candlesticks made of thin silver. Modern Israeli Hanukkah candlesticks are popular these days, with new shapes and designs. In many a household the only object that still recalls the Jewish background of the family is the Hanukkah candlestick.

On the days of Hanukkah one should eat foods that are baked in oil: *latkes*, ground potatoes mixed with onions and baked in a small, round, flat form, or *sufganiyyot*, donuts. Equally popular are dairy foods. Playing cards or other games is permitted on Hanukkah even in the strictly traditional Ashkenazi world. (According to the strict tradition, one may only play cards in the evenings of Sukkot, Hanukkah and Purim, on the intermediate days of longer holidays and on Christmas eve. And in one's own bedroom. Except, of course, a gambler or *zocker*.) Biblical riddles, assignments and other intellectual challenges (*katoves*) were considered games, too. It was customary to send gifts, usually in the form of cash, to the officials of the community on the first night of the holiday (*ma'ot hanukkah / khanukegelt*), and parents or guests would also give some change to the children of the house, usually shiny coins, to match the holiday. In the evening children play with the teetotum or *dreidel / dreidl / trenderli / sevivon*. The four Hebrew letters on its four sides, *nun-gimel-he-shin* or *pe* could be read as an acronym for the sentence recalling the consecration of the Temple in Jerusalem: "Great (**G***adol*) wonder (**N***es*) happened (**H***ayah*) there (**Sh***am*) / here (**P***o*)", but they are also the initials of the words indicating chances in the game: "nothing (***nisht***)", "all (***gants***)", "half (***halb***)" or "lay (***shtel ayn***)".

In the evening it is customary to sing *Ma'oz tzur yeshu'ati*, "Mighty Rock of my Salvation", a song of medieval origin.

Whether Hanukkah has anything to do with Christmas is a question frequently asked by Jews as well as Christians, because the two holidays occur almost at the same time, sometimes on the very same days. In fact, Hanukkah is often called the "Jewish Christmas". A common element is that both holidays are connected to the winter solstice (*solstitium*, December 21); this turning point was celebrated in antiquity, and in all cultures. But Hanukkah, even if lighting a flame is a Hellenistic custom, originated to celebrate the rejection of foreign cultures, while Christmas is the birthday of Jesus—the two have nothing to do with each other. In Budapest the two religious groups kept these holidays apart, even in the years after World War II. As a symbol of middle-class adjustment, the Christmas tree was taken into the homes of Jewish families in the city, but it did not replace Hanukkah. It was never taken very seriously, it was only for the sake of the children so they would not have to keep quiet among their Christian schoolmates. Today Hanukkah is experiencing a revival. Mostly celebrated by the youth, it is making a comeback into the home. Walking along the streets of Pest in the days following December 25, if that is when Hanukkah is that year, one may see not only Christmas trees in the windows, but also Hanukkah candlesticks.

(10) Seder

Though the Seder is traditionally a family celebration, it is becoming more and more of a communal event in Budapest these days. There are two Seders, on the first two nights of Pesah, the 14th and 15th of Nisan. Pesah or Passover celebrates the exodus from Egypt, *yetzi'at Mitzrayim*, redemption from captivity, freedom. The exodus was the most important moment in the ancient history and mythology of Israel. Even the Ten Commandments refer to this event. In its first sentence, Exodus 20,2, the Almighty defines himself as the one who had brought Israel out of Egypt. Pesah is the festival of unleavened bread, *hag ha-matzzot*. It preserves the memory of New Year in the Ancient Near East: *Nisan* was the first month of the year in Babylonia, and it is mentioned in the Bible, in Exodus 12,1. Its rituals, the sacrifice of the lamb and eating unleavened bread, are rooted in the ancient life style of the Jews in agriculture, husbandry and shepherding. Passover is one of the oldest Jewish holidays. There is mention of it in historical sources as far back as the period of the First Temple. Apparently King Josiah was probably the first one to celebrate Passover (II Kings 23,21–23) when he found the scroll containing the Law of Moses in 622–621 B.C.E. In the Second Temple period thousands and thousands of Jews would flock to Jerusalem for the holiday, bringing their first-born lamb with them. The sacrificial parts (*korban*) remained in the Temple, while the rest was taken home and the family prepared a festive, sacrificial meal of it, which they ate together. Josephus described this ceremony vividly in his *Jewish Antiquities*, XVII, 9. Except for the sacrifice, the order of the ceremony is practically the same even today as recorded in the Mishnah (Pesahim) around 200 c.e. The prayer for dew (*tal*), replacing the prayer for rain, has been incorporated into the synagogue services since then.

The sequence of Pesah is determined by two Biblical precepts. Every single element of the celebration had been deduced from these laws and maintained by tradition. One of the regulations stipulates unleavened bread, *matzzot*, for seven days (Exodus 12,15); another one is to make sure that there is no food containing yeast (*hametz*) in one's home during that time (Exodus 12,19). Unleavened bread was, and still is, a common food in the Near East; it is eaten by Arabic (*hobes*), Iranian (*sangaki*) and Turkish nomads or Armenian (*lavash*) villagers and even city-dwellers. In Jewish tradition unleavened bread was related to leaving Egypt.

The Sabbath before Passover is called *shabbat gadol*. This is a special day. In traditional Ashkenazi communities the rabbi holds his Halakhic speech in *shul* on that day. After *shabbat gadol*, preparations for Passover start slowly. During Passover all kinds of foods which contain the slightest amount of leaven or raised dough (*hametz / homets*) are considered taboo, *hefker*. There should be none (*bal yimmatze*) in the household and none should be seen (*bal yera'eh*). All kinds of cereal (wheat, rye, barley, oat and millet) and foods made of them count as leavened. Opinions differ about rice, millet, corn and legumes, which are considered leaven in the Ashkenazi tradition, but not among Sephardis. The apartment has to be completely cleaned of *homets* to become suitable for celebrating Passover, to become *pesakhdik*. Whatever *hometsdik* food remains in the apartment needs to be segregated, locked away or sold—even if symbolically—to a non-Jewish person for the duration of the holiday (*mehirat hametz*). The selling is done either directly or—as usual—through the mediation of the rabbi. The partners write a sales contract (*shetar mehirah*) specifying the leftovers to be sold and some guarantees. (As a matter of fact, this sale is a practical way of by-passing the difficulty in getting rid of all *hametz* in the household.) There is also a formula (*kol hamirah*) by which all *hametz* that accidentally stayed in one's possession is annihilated, becomes "like dust of the earth". This is not just a regular clean-up, but a ritual. On the eve of the holiday the house is thoroughly searched for *hametz*, which is then annihilated (*bittul hametz*) and burned (*bi'ur hametz*), mostly with the participation of men, on their responsibility. The search (*bedikat hametz*) takes place at candle light. All the hidden corners and shelves are thoroughly inspected and cleaned. A piece of bread is always left somewhere, intentionally, to make sure that the commandment can be fulfilled ritually as well. This piece is then burned ceremonially. Symbolic and actual preparations for Passover vary not only from community to community, but also from family to family. Foods bought at supermarkets need to be inspected, too, to make sure they contain no ingredients or preservatives with leaven (*ta'arovet hametz*). Whiskey, vodka or any liquor made of corn is out of question on Passover, only kosher wines, plum and apricot brandy may be consumed. The rabbinate issues a special certificate (*hekhsher*) for foods which comply with the Passover dietary laws, these are called *kosher le-pesah* (or, as on the label of the Hungarian kosher Slivovitz, *shel pesah*).

Naturally, along with the apartment all the dishes have to be cleaned for Passover, too. Households that have an extra set of all kitchen utensils for Pessah are generally rare in Budapest. Cleaning, kashering the dishes for Passover is the same procedure as when *milkhigs* and *fleyshigs* accidentally mix, only now it has to be applied to all dishes. Different ways of kashering have evolved over time, but all of them are deduced from a Biblical precept in Numbers 31,23. The basic principle is quite simple: each dish needs to be cleaned the same way it came into contact with *hametz* (*ke-volo kakh polto*), immersing it in boiling water (*hagalah*), heating it in fire (*libbun*), washing in boiling water (*iruy*), soaking and washing in cold water (*milluy ve-iruy*). There are thorough instructions for each procedure. Dishes made of porous materials, e.g. pottery, porcelain or ceramic, may not be kashered at all. That is why in "decent" Jewish households there are special dishes, at least tableware, for Passover, usually of better quality.

The unleavened Passover bread, *matzzah*, plural *matzzot*, in Yiddish *matzo / matses*, is also called the "bread of poverty", *lehem oni*, because it is made of nothing but flour and water. A strictly traditional man would always make *matzzot* himself, he would never trust anyone else with this task. If he does not live off the land, which is usually the case with urban dwellers, he inspects the flour very carefully before buying it, even in the store of the Rabbinate, checking the sack to make sure the flour is not lumpy. The wheat has to be separated from the time it is harvested (Exodus 12,7), ground in a specially cleaned mill, the flour placed in a carefully dried sack so it would not come in contact with even a drop of water. Only carefully "safeguarded *matzzot*", *matzzot shemurot / shmure matse / shmire matse* is a hundred percent kosher.

237. Children with *matzzot*. Greeting card for Passover, 1908

On the morning before the holiday, whoever does not have an oven rushes to the bakery. At the turn of the century a special government decree was issued to allow, despite the prohibition to work on Sunday, the manufacture and sale of the "Israelite Passover bread" on Sundays and even on the day of St. Stephen, King of Hungary, because "the needs of the population required continuous production". Today one of the most important services of the Orthodox community of Pest is the matzah bakery—there is only one in Budapest. At the time of the construction of the Kazinczy *shul* a matzah bakery was set up on the first floor of the office building. The central matzah bakery of the Pest Jewish community operates by machine. Moses Glasner, rabbi of Kolozsvár, allowed the use of machinery for making *matzzah* in one of his responsa early in the twentieth century.

In a room where sunlight does not penetrate, the men, standing next to each other, knead the dough out of matzah meal and cold, filtered water, possibly from a well (*mayim she-lanu*), just enough to keep the dough together. The women assist them. They roll out the dough sheet by sheet and pinch it to prevent blisters, because this would be fermentation. They bake it in the oven, fold them into dry kerchiefs and take them home. Hand-made *matzzot* used to be round; square *matzzot* only came into fashion with the baking machines. Old *matzzah* kerchiefs used to be round, too. In some places *matzzot* are decorated with Jewish religious symbols, symbols of Pesah or inscriptions; these are only pinched into the dough, of course. According to the careful calculations of rabbinical authorities, no more than 18 minutes should elapse between pouring out the matzah meal and the finished product. That is why *matzzot* are prepared in a hurry. The haste is a solemn one, because preparing *matzzah* is a great *mitzvah*. The most precious matzah, the *mitzvah-matzah* is prepared in the last minutes before the holiday starts. All the men, even young boys are at the bakery, all dressed in black. They sing verses from Psalms while baking, and they keep repeating the sentence: "This matzah is made for Passover." *Matzzah ashirah*, "rich matzah", is prepared for the sick and the elderly, with eggs or fruit juice instead of water.

The freshly made matzah is first eaten at the Seder. Some people use "broken" *matzzot* (*gebruk*) to prepare other dishes during Passover, such as matzah balls, while others insist that matzah may only be eaten at ceremonial dinners. But whatever tradition the community or family follows, matzah becomes an ordinary food after Passover. It is eaten with jam or butter, soaked in coffee with milk or just plain—not because of any religious obligation but for pleasure.

In the Diaspora there are two Seders, both with the same ceremonies. The most recent custom in Budapest is that two public Seders are held in most communities, to meet the needs of every member of the congregation. These community Seders are held for dozens or a few hundred people. Nowadays for most people in Hungary Pesah means, instead of making it at home, going to an official Seder for one of the nights, for whichever they manage to get a ticket.

The word *seder* means "order", the fixed order of the ritual on both evenings. The story of the exodus from Egypt (Exodus 12) is at its center, it must be told during the dinner. As the Talmud says, in all times, in every generation every Jew has to feel as if he himself had personally lived through the redemption from Mitzrayim. The Almighty, blessed be His name, redeemed not only our forefathers, but us, too (Pesahim 10,5). The Pesah Haggadah ("story") tells the story of the exodus and supplies the framework for the Seder. The Bible commands the head of the family, the father or some other authority to lead the ceremony: "And you shall explain to your son on that day" (Exodus 13,8). Communal Seders are led by the rabbi; he sits at the head of the table, wearing his white *kittel* with gold and silver lining.

The Seder should not be memorized nor held by heart. Everyone should hold a Haggadah. There are various Pesah Haggadah editions—some are masterpieces of Jewish book-lore, others are just ordinary editions—but there is one in every Jewish household. Illustrations are not forbidden in the Pesah Haggadah manuscripts. Actually, the prohibition to make a graven image in Exodus 20,4–5 refers only to idolatry, not to decoration or illustration. Most of the Haggadah editions are richly illustrated, the firmly traditional ones only with flowers, but after the Middle Ages even printed editions are illuminated with miniatures or drawings illustrating the story itself. In the Ashkenazi world the Hebrew text of the Pesah Haggadah was often printed together with its Yiddish translation and more recently with translations into other languages, e.g. Hungarian. Should someone not be able to follow the Hebrew text, she or he should still be able to understand the story. The ceremonial text is traditionally chanted. At public Seders the *hazzan* is asked to read. In big cities parodies of the Seder ceremony emerged, there are even printed Haggadah parodies.

The Seder may only be held in the evening. The Hebrew term even says "at night (*laylah*)". The sacrifice in the temple required that the meat of the lamb be eaten in the evening or at night (Exodus 12,8). To explain the unusual timing, the Haggadah tells a story about a debate among four Talmudic sages (*tannaim*) which caused the ceremony to extend deep into the night. This is happening at every Seder ever since. There are two extra tall Seder candles on the table; they have to last throughout the long ceremony.

238. Passover on a page of the Kaufmann Haggadah. Preparations for the holiday. Figure on the left: a family at the Seder table. The ceremony is lead by the head of the family. Miniature, fourteenth century

The ceremony itself is combined with dinner. The table is laid with beautiful, fancy tablecloth, plates and silverware. The matzah stand is placed in the middle, with three layers for the three leaves of matzah, and so is the Seder plate (*ke'arah*), which is decorated with inscriptions and symbols (*simanim*) indicating the special Seder menu. The round matzah stand came into fashion in Vienna. The Seder plate could be placed on top of it or its top layer could be the Seder plate itself, with a tiny bowl for the *haroset*. There is an extra cup on the table for the Prophet Elijah (*koso shel Eliyahu*), which is filled with wine along with the participants' cup. The Prophet Elijah represents the Savior (*go'el*) at the table. His cup is bigger and fancier than the participants' cup. Either there are four cups for everyone on the table (*arba kosot*), or the one cup has to be filled four times—because the ritual requires drinking four cups of wine during the Seder. These four cups refer to the "Pharaoh's four cups" which Joseph mentions in the scene of his dream interpretation (Genesis 40,11–13). Another reason for the four cups is that there are four different terms in Exodus for the redemption from Egypt (Exodus 6,6–7). There is a fifth term with similar meaning in Exo-

239. Seder plate (*ke'arah*) and rack to hold matzzah

dus 6,8, which is signaled by Elijah's cup. There was a Halakhic debate whether this fifth cup is needed, but the question was left open: Elijah will decide when he comes. That is why his cup is the fifth one. In any case, the glasses should be filled preferably with red wine, to recall the blood of the lamb slaughtered before departing from Egypt (Exodus 12,7) or the Red Sea. Very often, however, white wine was used instead of red, to avoid any suspicion of human blood sacrifice. Though the cups are filled completely each time, one does not have to drink every drop of it. Children drink grape juice instead of wine or they eat nuts, candies.

One has to recline at the table, at least once, symbolically. This position recalls the ancient practice when it was the privilege of the free to sit on a dining couch (*kline*) and eat in a reclining position. At the Seder everyone, but at least the leader of the ceremony, sits on a chair (*hesebet*) propped up on cushions, leaning to his left, "reclining (*mesubbin*)". This is a symbolical indication that at the redemption from Egypt the slave became a free man. At the Seder people usually do not pour wine for themselves, only for the person sitting next to them: a free human being is being served, after all.

The Seder night has to be different from all the other nights—that is why it is a holiday, after all. To emphasize this difference, it is customary to move things to a different place than normally; for instance the table is placed into a different position, it is set differently, the meal is different from other days and is served in a different order. The Haggadah and occasionally the Seder plate itself are inscribed with words indicating the special order. There are four questions (*di fir kashes*) asked during the Seder: *Mah nishtanah...,* "Why is this night different from all other nights?" Originally the questions could refer to anything, even the position of the table, but later tradition fixed the answers, which explain the symbolism of the Seder ceremony and foods.

Symbolic Seder foods are the roast lamb meat or bone (*zero'a*), the unleavened bread (*matzzah*) and the bitter herbs (*maror*), in Hungary usually horseradish. Three leaves of *matzzot* need to be eaten, that's why the word is used in plural. Usually two pieces of bread (*lehem mishneh*) are specified for the ritual (Exodus 16,22), the third one is for Pesah night (Deuteronomy 16,3). But there are other explanations. The three leaves may symbolize the ritual triple division of Jewish society. The place of the ritual dishes is indicated by inscriptions and pictures on the Seder plate. The order of dishes on the Ashkenazi and Sephardi Seder plates varies. The roasted shank-bone is not a food to be eaten, only a symbol re-calling the sacrifice in the Temple, like the roast egg (*beitzah* / Aramaic *beya*) which was also an accessory of the sacrifice in the Temple (*hagigah*). The Hatam Sofer held the egg an extremely important component of the Seder, because the egg differs from every other food in that the more it is cooked the harder it becomes, much like Jews who harden to every persecution. In addition, there is a special mash of apples, ground almonds, raisins, figs, cinnamon and wine called *haroset* or *haroyses* on the Seder plate, to symbolize the clay used for laying bricks in Egypt, and vegetables, celery, onions, radish, parsley or lettuce (in one word: *karpas*) dipped in salt water before it is eaten; tiny bowls or cups of salt water are placed on the table for this purpose. The *maror* is put in the middle of the Seder plate.

The "four questions" are asked by four children, usually by the youngest one, each question representing a particular attitude towards tradition: the wise, *hakham* asks: "What is the meaning of the exhortations, laws, and rules which the LORD and our God has enjoined upon you?" (Deuteronomy 6,20.) The evil (*rasha* / *roshe*) asks: "What do these ceremonies mean to you?" The simpleton (*tam*) asks: "What is this?" And the fourth "cannot even ask (*she-eino yode'a li-she'ol*)". These types, especially the *roshe* and the *she-eino yode'a li-she'ol*, often appear outside of the Seder ceremony as well, in parables. These questions and the answers are sounded to enhance awareness of the common roots and common fate. The *roshe* asks what the ceremonies mean to *you*, not *us*, thereby isolating himself from the Jewish community. "Had he been there in Egypt, he would not have been redeemed."

Rabbit chase, *Jakenhaz* (from the German *jage den Hasen*, "chase the rabbit"), is a type of picture decoration on medieval Passover Haggadot. The name itself is a German-Yiddish acronym which refers to the case when the Seder falls on the evening after Sabbath. The acronym is put together from the initials of the Hebrew words describing the first part of the Seder ceremony: *yayin*, "wine", *kiddush*, "blessing", *ner*, "light", *havdalah*, "separation", *zeman*, "time", i.e. before the Seder starts one has to say farewell to the Sabbath, to "part" (*le-havdil*) the day from the night (see Genesis 1,14), to separate the day from the following holiday night. "Time" here means "the time of our freedom (*zeman heruteinu*)", the holiday ritual itself.

The Seder evening is full of action. At first the leader of the ceremony, the *orekh ha-seder*, washes his hands at the table, in a bowl. He breaks the middle matzah into two and hides one of the pieces; this will be used only at the end of the dinner. He lifts the other half, a symbol of the bread of poverty, *lehem oni*. He lifts the shank-bone, explains what the Passover sacrifice means, what the matzah and the *maror* symbolize. He puts the *matzo* on his shoulder for a moment to show that at the time of the exodus people could not wait for the dough to rise, they had to leave in a hurry (Exodus 12,34). And the bitter herbs represent the bitter life in captivity. He proceeds to read the story and when he gets to the ten plagues, he dips his finger into his cup at the mention of each plague and sprinkles the wine on his plate. The matzah needs to be eaten in a special way, too: a "sandwich" is made from part of the whole matzah and the broken one, with a little *maror* in between: this is called "Hillel's sandwich" or *korekh*—this is how the great master mourned the destruction of the Temple, the ceasing of the sacrifice. As the dinner itself gets under way, the door is opened to let anyone in need, and especially the Prophet Elijah, enter and take a seat at the table. At the very end of the meal the children search for the hidden part of the middle matzah, the *afikomen / afikaymen*, which is then shared by the participants after the dessert. The word comes from the Greek *epikomion*, which means dessert, last dish. It is customary in some places for the children to steal and hide the *afikaymen* at the beginning of the meal so that they can return it only upon a ransom or, so that they would have to search for it and get a present if they find it.

The Haggadah binds the ceremony, including the blessings, the meal and the story together. Its traditional text has evolved over several centuries, the latest layer was added already in the Early Modern Age: these songs, traditionally sung after dinner, were accepted into the order subsequently (*nirtza*) and have become very popular: *Ki lo na'eh, Addir hu, Ehad mi yode'a* and *Had gadya.*

The Seder ends with a farewell greeting: Next year in Jerusalem—*Le-shanah ha-ba'ah bi-(Ye)rushalayim!* The various nineteenth-century reform movements wanted to change this part because Jerusalem seemed so far away for people living in the Diaspora. A late artifact of reform ritual is the Haggadah published by the Kner Publishing House of Gyoma in 1936 (*Haggáda peszach estéjére* [Haggadah for the Evening of Pesah]), meant more for reading than for actual use during the ceremony. The ritual material was compiled by Ernő Naményi (1888–1957), distinguished economist, historian of Jewish art, who worked at the Jewish Museum at the time, but Bernát Heller also gave his authorization. The text was translated, sometimes edited by the writer Károly Pap. Instead of "Next year in Jerusalem" he quoted the words of Jeremiah, the prophet's warning to the Jews of Babylonia: "And seek the welfare of the city to which I have exiled you and pray to the LORD in its behalf; for in its prosperity you shall prosper" (Jeremiah 29,7). The editors of the Kner Haggadah accepted life in the Diaspora. A few years later, in 1942, the Haggadah published by the *Országos Magyar Zsidó Segítő Akció* (OMZSA, a solidarity organization) formulated it again in harmony with the tradition: "Today we are still here, but tomorrow we will be in the land of Israel." (Contributors to this edition were, among others, the art historian Ernő Munkácsi, the music historian Bence Szabolcsi.)

Ever since the State of Israel was founded, and especially in the past few years, people in Hungary joyfully utter the three words at the end of the Seder and at Yom Kippur, too, but most of them only have their next year's visit to Israel in mind.

(11) Jewish Names

According to the Pesah Haggadah part of the reason why the Jews remained Jews during the captivity in Egypt is that they did not give up their Jewish names. This reasoning is supported by the lists of names in Exodus. But actually, Jews living in the Diaspora always had names similar to the names of the surrounding people. There were differences only in some name-giving customs.

Jews in Hungary, like in the rest of the world, traditionally give their children two names, in addition to the family name: a civil and a Jewish name. Some Biblical examples for changing names are Abram and Abraham (Genesis 17,3–5), Jacob and Yisrael (Genesis 32,18–30), Saray and Sarah (Genesis 17,15), etc. The civil name (*kinnuy*) is usually a Hungarian name, preferably a not too Christian one. (Christina for instance would not be a suitable name.) This name is used in official documents and in everyday life. In the Ashkenazi world this name is also called cradle name (*shem ha-arisah*). The Jewish name (*shem ha-kodesh*) is always a Hebrew one, but its sound or meaning is usually close to the civil name, or at least they have the same initial. It is recorded in the documents of the Jewish community and used mostly in the synagogue, e.g. when someone is called to the Torah. The Hungarian equivalent of Josef is József, Yitzhak or Isaac corresponds to István, Moshe or Moses to Mór. István and Mór, like several other non-Biblical names, are considered "foreign names (*shem la'az*)" from the Jewish point of view. In Ashkenazi communities an infant, most often the firstborn, is named after a deceased member of the family, in order to preserve the names of the ancestors, but this was not a strict rule and was applied more often to the Hebrew name than to the civil one. In any case, the names of the firstborn in a given family usually did not show a great variety. Thus the fifteenth–sixteenth-century family tree of the Mendels is hard to decipher because of that. It is, however, very rare among Ashkenazi Jews to name a son after his father in his lifetime. The Jewish name is used at ceremonies together with the father's name anyway, Josef *ben* Jacob, or Sarah *bat* Jacob ("son" or "daughter" of Jacob). (The Aramaic form of *ben* is *bar*, the Arabic version used in medieval Jewish names is *ibn*.) Converts (*ba'al teshuvah*) may be called *P. ben Avraham*, or *Avraham avinu*, "X, son of our father Abraham". Ancient and medieval ritual name-giving customs survived the reforms of the eighteenth century and the introduction of secular names.

In the Austro-Hungarian Monarchy it was Joseph II's edict, issued on July 23, 1787, which ordered everyone to have a family name (*Vorname*). Whoever refused to choose one was given a name by the Austrian officials, usually a strange or odd German word. This is how Abraham, a Jew in one of Mór Jókai's novels, was named *Rothesel*, "red donkey", which he was able to change to *Rotheisen*, "red iron" only with a great deal of difficulty. Occasionally a person's Jewish name or his occupation became the family name, thus Hebrew *Asher* became Ascher, Anschel or Ancsel, a *sofer* was named Schreiber, a *hazzan* would be called Singer; the list of German names made out of occupations is almost endless.

There are certain typical Jewish names which, all appearances to the contrary, are actually abbreviations or acronyms.

Back / Bak / Bock: *ben kedoshim*, "son of martyrs"
Basch: *ben Shammay / Shlomo / Shemu'el / Shime'on*, etc.
Bloch: *ben Leib kohen*
Braun: *ben R. Nahman*, "Rabbi Nachman's follower"
Brill: *ben R. Yehuda Levi Leib*
Katz: *kohen tzedek*, "true priest"
Pach: *poteah hotam* "seal engraver"
Sachs / Zaks: *zera kedoshim*, "seed of martyrs"
Schatz: *sheliah tzibbur*, "leader of the community", "prayer leader"
Schick / Sik / Schück: *shem Yisra'el kadosh*, "the Jewish name / the name of Israel is holy"
Schön: *sheliah ne'eman*, "true leader"
Siegel / Segal / Segall / Chagall, etc.: *segan levayya*, leader of the Levites (*sagan* is a loanword from Ancient Mesopotamia, Sumerian and Akkadian, originally denoting a dignity).

Around the mid- to late nineteenth century in Hungary, like in other European countries, it became a custom and even fashionable to change a foreign-sounding family name to a Hungarian one. The Magyarization of family names was a gesture of good-will towards the surrounding society, a means of cultural integration and in certain cases a social requirement. German, Slavic, Romanian and Jewish family names were Magyarized, though only a small percentage of the Jews, and mostly those living in the capital changed their name. Other Jewish name-giving customs had been retained. Already during the first anti-Semitic atrocities after World War I the German–Jewish originals of Magyarized Jewish names were used mockingly, with the intention of ostracizing these people from Hungarian public life. At the time of the (Anti-)Jewish Laws a Hungarian name no longer represented protection for Jews. After World War II Jews in Israel often translated their original English, German, Hungarian, etc., names into Hebrew, e.g. Landler became Artzi, Schwartz or Fekete became Kaddari.

(12) Berit, Pidyon ha-ben, Bar mitzvah

A Jewish boy receives his Hebrew name at circumcision (*berit, berit millah, bris, circumcisio*). The Hebrew name of Jewish girls is first announced on the first Sabbath after her birth, when in the synagogue her father is called to the Torah. The name of the two ceremonies is *shalom zakhar* and *shalom nekevah*, the perfect condition of the man and the perfect condition of the woman.

Circumcision takes place on the eighth day after birth. This period has traditionally been determined by the story of Isaac / Yitzhak in Genesis 21,4 and has always been strictly observed (Genesis 17,12; Leviticus 12,1–2). The only reason for postponing the ceremony may be the poor health of the newborn. Not even the absence of the father can be a hindrance, and the *bris* gets priority on Sabbath and on all holidays; it must take place even if it falls on Yom Kippur. But the source of Jewish identity is not the circumcision. A Jew is someone who is born to a Jewish mother or someone who has converted to Judaism according to the law prescribed by Halakhah. Circumcision is only a sign, as its name indicates, the sign of the covenant (*berit*).

The surgical procedure itself is carried out by a qualified person, the *mohel / mayhel / mayl*, but if none is available, the *shakhter* may perform the ceremony. If the *bris* falls on the Sabbath it is usually held in the synagogue, at least in smaller communities, as is sometimes also the *se'udah*, the feast

following the ceremony, which is otherwise given at the home of the family. In big cities it is mostly held at home, in the presence of guests. The guests are traditionally not invited to the *bris* in writing, they are only informed of its time, but it is customary to attend so there should be a *minyan*. The time of the *bris* is usually as early in the morning as possible—by way of indicating that the father is in a hurry to fulfill the commandment.

Two nicely decorated chairs are placed in the room where the newborn man is welcomed, the right one is for the Prophet Elijah (*kisse shel Eliyahu*), the left one is for the *sandak*. Elijah is the witness for every act which concerns the covenant (Pirkei de Rabbi Eliezer, 29). The godparents, the *kvater* and the *kvaterin*, bring the child into the room where the circumcision is to take place and hand him to the *sandak*. The *mohel* places him on Elijah's chair. Those present greet the baby in Hebrew, *barukh ha-ba*, "blessed be he who comes". The *sandak* holds the baby "on his

240. Elijah's chair (*Kisse shel Eliyahu*). Carpenter's work from Pest, 1827

lap, *al ha-birkayim*". This is usually just a symbolic act and after holding the baby for a minute the *sandak* places him on a table where the very ceremony, that is, the operation, can be better performed.

The instruments of the *mohel* are a sharp knife (*izmel* or *sakin*), a shield with a slit, a small bowl, and antiseptic powder. The *bris* consists of three steps, the *millah*, the cutting of the foreskin, the *periah*, the tearing of the soft membrane that covers the glans and the rolling back of the corona, and the *metzitzah*, the sucking of the wound. Naturally the framework of the ceremony is the blessing: the *mohel* recites the blessing over a cup of wine and when he is finished, he dips his finger into the wine and wets the lips of the baby with it. (In 1899 a decree was issued by the Hungarian Minister of Interior prohibiting the application of wine from the mouth but, only a year later, the decree was redrawn because "officials of the Jewish community can and wish to take care of the hygienic issue at the ceremony.")

The ceremony itself does not take long. (The verb for it in Hungarian is *malenol*.) Those present are standing during the whole time. Afterwards a feast (*se'udah*) is offered (see Genesis 21,8). Traditionally there are peas among the dishes served here—peas cooked in salt water and spiced with black pepper (*zokher*-peas). Except for Yom Kippur, one may even break a fast because of a *berit se'udah / bris süde*. Traditionally people drank wine at a *bris* but, since the nineteenth century, probably under Russian–Polish influence, *vodka* or just any *braiges* have become fashionable at the *se'udah*. (Of course, the blessing, the *brokhe* is still recited over a cup of wine.)

It is customary for the *mohel* to visit the family on the evening before the *bris* and to place his knife under the pillow of the baby. This is not only to protect him from the evil eye but also because if the *bris* falls on a Sabbath, the *mohel* should not violate the prohibition of work by carrying his instrument. The baby's father and other relatives keep vigil during the night preceding the *bris*—this is called the *vakhnakht* in Yiddish. They watch over the baby at candlelight, eating beans or peas. The evening before the circumcision is called "*erev zakhar*, men's night".

It is a great honor to be asked to be the *kvater* or the *sandak*. They should bring plenty of presents, if possible. They should also pay attention to the development of the child later, they will be the first to help if he is in need. It does not bring luck if a family asks the same person to be the *sandak* more than once. The cup over which the *mohel* recites the blessing is usually a gift, probably the kiddush cup of the son. After the ceremony the piece of foreskin (*orlah, praeputium*) needs to be covered with sand, this recalls the promise of the covenant in Genesis 22,17: "I will bestow My blessing upon you and make your descendants as numerous as the stars of heaven and the sands on the seashore..." In several German communities it was customary to cut the diaper—which was used at the circumcision and which is usually made of some fine material—into four strips, saw them together as a long runner, embroider an inscription into it and give it to the synagogue on the first birthday of the baby to be used as a Torah wrapper (*vimpel*).

After World War II European Jews, including Hungarians, often omitted to have their sons circumcised. It was not easy to forget the crude words which sounded ever so often during identity checks and round-ups in the streets of Budapest in the fall of 1944: "Down with your pants!"—A circumcised kid's remark coming home from kindergarten in the 1990s: "Mom, that boy's stick has closed its eyelids."

The circumcision of those who choose to have a *bris* as an adult or those who convert to Judaism is conducted in a hospital. In case of someone is circumcised only for medical reasons, without the religious ceremony, the act of the ritual circumcision will only be symbolic, a pinprick of blood (*hatafat dam berit*).

There is a joke, albeit a rather awkward one, redeemed by the fact that it can only be understood by those familiar with the technical terms (which makes it a rather pedantic joke):

"Which is the worst *mitzvah*? To do the *metzitzah* at the *bris* of an adult *ba'al teshuvah*."

Another joke which Sándor Scheiber used to tell about Arnold Kiss is quoted by the late István Y. Kertész in his collection of Jewish jokes as follows:

"A son is born to a young Jewish couple in Buda. Their rabbi, Arnold Kiss, offered to organize the *bris*, but the father hesitated. At first the baby was too weak, then the father had to go on a business trip, finally the family went on vacation. It became clear that they had no intention to have the boy circumcised at all. Suddenly they disappeared for a few months. Upon their return they claimed the boy had already been circumcised. Upon this Arnold Kiss replied: No problem, we will do a *re-bris*, then!"

One month after the birth of the firstborn son (*bekhor*), when it is clear that he will survive (*ben kayyamah*), he has to be redeemed from his duty of Temple service (Numbers 18,15–16). *Kohanim* and Levites are exempt from this obligation, it only applies to the son born to an Israelite mother from her first pregnancy, to the son "who opened (her) womb (*peter rehem*)" (Exodus 13,2). The redemption of the firstborn (*pidyon ha-ben*) costs five shekels (Leviticus 27,6) and any *kohen* may receive it. The ceremony is incorporated in a *se'udah*, the *kohen* recites the priestly blessing upon this occasion. It was customary and, since the eighteenth century almost a rule, that the *kohen* returns the five shekels to the father afterwards, though it is forbidden to request it. R. Jacob Emden's (1697–1776) argument to support this custom was that no *kohen* can be fully sure of his lineage and therefore none can demand the payment due only to a *kohen*.

Being the firstborn son confers a special status within the Jewish community. The firstborn has to fast on the day preceding Passover; this is to commemorate the fact that, according to the Biblical story of the exodus, all of the firstborn Egyptian boys died during the tenth plague, but God saved the Jewish firstborn and therefore he requires their services (Exodus 11,5; 12,12). The fast of the firstborn (*ta'anit bekhorim*) can be redeemed by a *se'udat mitzvah* on the same day, like a *se'udat berit, pidyon ha-ben* or a *se'udat siyyum* given at the completion of the study of a Talmudic tractate.

The first—ritual—haircut (*halakkah, opsherenis* in Yiddish) follows when the boy became three years old. (His sidelocks remain untouched.) In Budapest the public haircuts of the sons of the young Hasidic rabbi, certainly the first ones after long decades, became a social event of the 1990s.

The *bar mitzvah* is the ceremony of becoming an adult in the religious–ritual sense. It takes place when the son turns thirteen. He is called to the Torah for the first time now. He recites the blessing and reads from the Torah and the Haftarah. He may give a short sermon, receives a nice present. From then on he is a member of the community, he is "big, grown, *gadol*". He enjoys all adult rights and he must fulfill all the obligations—that's what the term *bar mitzvah* refers to, "son of the *mitzvah*", "son of the commandment". He is responsible for his acts. Since the nineteenth century girls also become *bat mitzvah* at age twelve.

By the time of their *bar mitzvah*, boys of Orthodox background had usually been studying the Torah and the simpler Talmudic texts for seven or eight years. An exceptionally talented boy (*illuy*) could give his first *devar Torah* on the occasion of his *bar mitzvah* at the *se'udah* or in the synagogue. A good example of a child's erudition is Ignác Goldziher's exegetic study published in Pest.

(13) Kosher and Treyfe

Jewish eating customs are regulated by the laws of *kashrut*. The word *kasher / kosher*, "appropriate", "flawless" means that the item is ritually clean. Not only food can be kosher but a Torah scroll, *tefillin, mezuzah, mikveh* or *tzitzit* as well, if they comply with the ritual requirements.

All the dietary regulations are based on the laws of the Torah. First of all, vegetables and all kinds of vegetable products are suitable for consumption (Genesis 1,29). Furthermore, the meat of animals which the Torah names for that purpose or to which it generally refers are also edible. These animals are clean (*tahor*). The Torah also has a long list of animals which are not suitable for human consumption (*tame*, Deuteronomy 14,7–8). Some birds are forbidden (Leviticus 11,13–19; Deuteronomy 14,12–18), but most are clean. Among animals living in water only those which have fins and scales are edible (Leviticus 11,9–12; Deuteronomy 14,9–10). Finally, from among the insects only some large locusts may be eaten (Leviticus 11,21–22). Based on this list there is consensus on what may be eaten and what should be avoided.

WEN SCHEILE, Schon TREFE

241. A housewife asks the rabbi to check the ritual purity of her chicken. Drawing by Lipót Herman

Serious Halakhic debate arose only in connection with sterlet, in Yiddish called *shtirl*. Lipót Löw even quoted the debate in the title of his study: "*Der Stör* [sterlet] *als Friedenstörer.*" There were plenty of this species of fish in Hungary. Sterlet used to come up from the Black Sea through the Danube to spawn here; one could catch them at Vizafogó (at the Újpest embankment, between Dráva utca and Meder utca) and sterlet were spawning in every river. Since their skin does not completely meet the requirements of the Torah for scales, the consumption of sterlet in Ashkenazi communities was generally forbidden while the Sephardim would allow it. R. Áron Chorin also decided in favor of the sterlet eliciting the anger of R. Münz. The difference in opinion has been maintained until today: eating sterlet is generally accepted, except in strictly traditional Ashkenazi communities.

The strict prohibition to prepare or eat meat and milk (*basar ba-halav*) together is also based on the Torah (Exodus 23,19; 34,16; Deuteronomy 14,21). Meat and dairy have to be separated, there must be an interval between eating them. Not only meat and dairy foods, milk, cheese, butter, etc. have to be kept apart, but the dishes in which they are cooked or stored as well. Therefore, a Jewish household has two sets of dishes, a *fleyshik* and a *milkhik* one, in Hebrew called *basari* and *halavi* (though in Budapest no one used these terms but always the Yiddish names). Foods that contain neither milk nor meat are called *parve* and may be eaten together with dairy as well as meat dishes. Such foods are fish and eggs, any kind of fruit or vegetable, spices and grains, sugar, coffee, tea, jam, mustard, oil and natural fruit juices. Some fancy, pewter, china or ceramic plates come already with the inscription *basar*, "meat" on them. In some wealthier households there used to be separate dishes for the non-Jewish servants with the inscription ש״ג , an abbreviation for *shel goy*, meaning "of the gentile", since the laws of *kashrut* do not apply to non-Jews employed in Jewish households.

Extreme observance of *kashrut* has also been made fun of.

"Three men, each from a different community, run into each other in the street. One of them says as follows: Our rebe is so pious that he has two separate kitchens, one for meat and another for dairy. The second man replies: Two kitchens? That's nothing, our rebe has two servants, one for meat and another for dairy. The third one boasts: That's all nothing compared to our rebe who is so pious that when he teaches in the yeshivah and the text states *basar ba-halav*, he says *basar*, then waits six hours before uttering the word *halav*."

The six hours that the rebe in the joke waited between uttering the words meat and milk is actually a commandment when it comes to eating. Today, most people wait only three hours between meat and dairy meals.

Another set of traditional regulations concerns slaughtering animals (*shehitah*). The clean animals are suitable for consumption only if they are slaughtered properly. The slaughterer (*shohet*) has to kill the animal making sure he causes the least amount of pain. His knife (*halaf*) has to be very sharp. Its edge must be inspected with the finger pad and the fingernail to make sure that it is not jagged (*pegimah*).

Here is an excerpt from a description of the Pest Slaughterhouse on Soroksári út (built in 1870–1872):

"(...) A white-bearded Jew sits peacefully around the middle of the corridor in front of the gate checking on his nail to see if the knife's hairbreadth edge is sharp enough, for he needs to cut the throat of the animal all the way down to the spine with a single cut, murmuring a blessing, as commanded by the law of Moses."

(Porzó / Adolf Ágai, *Utazás Pestről – Budapestre* [Journey from Pest to Budapest], 1912)

In fact, the most important thing at slaughtering animals is the knife. In small towns the custom was that when a learned guest arrived to the house and the rabbi wanted to offer him a meal with meat, he would send for the *shohet*, ask him to bring his knife and place it on the table as a proof of the ritual observance. The purpose of ritual slaughter is to drain the blood from the flesh of the animal completely. The throat of the healthy animal has to be cut with one quick movement. Then the *shohet* holds the animal upside down pouring out all the blood and covers the blood with earth (*afar*, "dust") (Leviticus 17,13). Next, after cutting the animal open, he examines (*bedikah*) the sensitive parts (trachea, lungs, heart) to see if there is any trace of injury (a cleft, scar or bruise) or poisoning. The fat parts are removed (*nikkur*), the tendons cut (*reinigen*). Finally, the meat has to be soaked in water, then in salt (*melihah*) to cleanse it from the least drop of blood (*kashern*). Meat that is not slaughtered or prepared properly is *terefah*, "torn" (Exodus 22,30), or *treyfe* in Yiddish, *tréfli* in Hungarian. The word originally referred to the flesh of animals torn apart by other animals. The flesh of animals which died (*nevelah*) and were not slaughtered for the specific purpose of human consumption may not be eaten at all.

242. The kosher-border on István tér (today Klauzál tér). Goose is sold on the right side, pork on the left

The person who examines the body of the animal is called *bodek*. An anecdote about Ignác Goldziher explains the difference between *slaughtering* and *examining*. Professor Goldziher used to show compliance at examinations. Asked why he never failed students, he answered: I am just a *bodek*, and not a *shohet*.

Ritual slaughtering has to be provided for every community. The *shohet* needs a special permit (*kabbalah*) to practice his profession and he is constantly supervised. It is a position of responsibility, a *shohet* is held in high esteem, almost like the rabbi or the *hazzan*. He puts his own seal on the meat guaranteeing that it is kosher, taking personal responsibility for its ritual purity. (Museums collect kosher meat seals. A such seal from the early-twentieth century from Budapest was taken to New York and is now on display in the Jewish Museum there.) Some operations which had been the housewife's task are lately done by the *shohet*. He kashers the meat and sells it ready to eat. Strictly traditional Jews do not accept food or wine prepared by non-Jews. In addition, there are various levels of *kashrut* and not all of them are acceptable to every Jewish group. The term *glatt kosher* refers to the most strictly kosher kind of food.

The border of the Jewish quarter in Erzsébetváros was the *kosher-border*, too, clearly marked by eating customs.

"The greatest satisfaction of the Erzsébetváros woman comes from the sight of her goose cut into pieces. She does not rejoice over the meat itself but can't wait for the moment when she can start boasting to her neighbor about the great amount of fat, the size of the liver and the red, crispy crackling that she obtains from it."
(Ödön Gerő / Viharos, *Az én fővárosom* [My Capital City], 1891)

Here is how Adolf Ágai describes István / Klauzál tér, which was an open-air market before the covered market hall was built in 1897, and the largest food outlet of the city:

"The market is divided into two sections: the northeastern part is Christian, the southwestern, Jewish. Over there you see the carcasses of long, fat hogs hanging, especially in winter time, hecatombs of fat geese, slaughtered kosher style. We don't hear their gruntling, they don't hear our cackling anymore."
(Porzó / Adolf Ágai, *Utazás Pestről – Budapestre* [Journey from Pest to Budapest], 1912)

As regards wine, an old principle is in effect: Jews may not participate in pagan sacrificial ceremonies (*libatio*) and therefore they are not allowed to drink wine which may have been used for such a purpose (*nesekh*). In ancient times it was even forbidden to trade in wine of doubtful origin

243. Signboard of the Orthodox kosher butchery, 41 Kazinczy utca

(*stam yeinam*), made by non-Jews. The custom, that Jews would drink from an open bottle of wine only if it was not touched by a non-Jew, has not disappeared from Pest completely. It is still practiced among older or very traditional Jews. A host is definitely polite if he allows an Orthodox guest to open and pour the kosher wine himself. *Kosher le-pesah* wine, used for the Seder, is handled with extra care; only Jews may participate in its production, observing all ritual prescriptions and every move is supervised by the rabbinate.

Famous kosher wines are the Verpeléti Riesling once served at Niszel's in Terézváros, and now sold on Klauzál tér, also from Verpelét, and recently from Eger as well (Cabernet Sauvignon). These and the kosher Slivovitz (plum-brandy) are the best alcoholic drinks available in Pest.

(14) A Hat, a Skullcap

Jewish hat-wearing customs have changed radically over the centuries. In the Ancient Near East, in Babylonia, only Torah scholars wore a hat, it was a sign of their wisdom. In the Middle Ages the discriminatory *Judenhut* was forced upon the Jews to humiliate them. The disgrace, however, came only from its unusual shape, because in those days everyone wore some kind of a head-cover. But it was only in the Modern Age that covering one's head became a religious prescription and a general custom among Jews. To be sure, it was rooted in some kind of traditionalism, adherence to medieval or early modern practice. This was all the more so in Eastern Europe.

It is since the seventeenth or eighteenth century that Jews cover their heads permanently, that they never remove their hats, not even when civility allows non-Jews to do so. It was said that this is to distinguish them from the non-Jews (*hukkat ha-goy*) who pray with their heads uncovered. For Orthodox and Hasidic Jews wearing a head-cover is not an option but a must. An uncovered head (*kallut rosh / kales rosh*) means negligence, or in case of a married woman frivolous behavior. The black velvet hat of Hasidic men is a sign of extreme piety, and so is the rebe's flat fur hat (*shtrayml*). It can be made of fur of beaver (*biber*) or sable (*soibel*), if the rebe can afford it, or just of plush (*spodak*).

The various reform movements, including the Neologs of Pest, prescribe covering one's head only in the synagogue and during prayer. Some religious Jews wear a skullcap or hat while eating, although this is just a custom, not a commandment. Some wear it while singing *Hatikvah*,[4] some even during cantorial concerts. The prescription is to cover one's head in the synagogue or in a room where there is a Torah scroll, during prayer or Torah study, or even if a text is studied which contains quotations from the Torah. Thus we could say that the practice of covering the head is the civilian version of wearing a *tallit*.

Jewish head covers have changed over time and from place to place, and so have their names. In Budapest the most widespread version was the small black yarmulke of the rabbis. It was called *keppel*, *kapele* or *kapedli* in Hungarian or *pileolus* by its archaic Latin–Christian name. People wore it only at home and replaced it with a black hat when on the street. Hasidim wear a similar but larger velvet skullcap and they keep it on their head even under the hat, to prevent accidentally remaining with head uncovered.

Here is an excerpt from a description of the people in the Orczy House:

> "The ancient yarmulke peeps out from under the brim of his hat, on the back of his head. Like a bold spot made of silk, it is always there, even at night when he sleeps."   (Hevesi, *Karczképek* [Sketches], 1876)

In other parts of Eastern Europe the Yiddish term *yarmulke* was more widespread. *Shabesdekli* or beanie was mostly used by outsiders and often mockingly. In the nineteenth century, in upper-middle class synagogues of large cities, a top hat was not a rare sight, especially on holidays. Today the term *kippah* is used most often, and along with the term the colorful Israeli crocheted skullcap (*kippah serugah*) originally fashionable among religious Zionists.

244. Mug for ritual hand-washing, eighteenth century

There is even more uncertainty about the female head-cover. In Orthodox and Hasidic communities married women are forbidden to leave their heads uncovered or their hair down. But it is only in some extremely rigorous circles where women are required to cut their hair and wear a wig (*shaytl*), a kerchief or a silk hat (*kupka*) instead. This custom was opposed even by Moses Schreiber, the Hatam Sofer himself. Yet many people have followed this custom even until recently. The general practice, however, is still what has survived from the seventeenth and eighteenth centuries: married women wear elegant dark hats or lace kerchiefs in synagogue. We can still see older ladies in such hats in the Dohány Temple or at the Rabbinical Seminary synagogue.

The *kippah* has become a symbol of proud, self-conscious Jewish identity all over the world; it signifies overcoming fear, the anxiety of the ghetto. This show of moderate confidence is still a rare sight in Budapest, usually in the vicinity of synagogues, at the time of services.

(15) The Synagogue in Vasvári Pál utca (5 Vasvári Pál utca)

The building used to house the Budapest Talmud Association founded in 1842, as the inscription on the facade still tells us. In 1887 a prayer-house was built in its courtyard, for Orthodox members of the congregation. It was a Shas Hevrah synagogue, its members came not merely to pray; they spent most

---

[4] *Hatikvah / Ha-Tikvah*: "Hope" (*ha-tikvah*), Zionist hymn, its text was written by Naphtali H. Imber, music by Samuel Cohen (1886). Today the national anthem of the State of Israel.

245. The Budapest Talmud Association's house in Vasvári Pál utca

246. Interior of the Vasvári Pál utca synagogue

of their time here, studying. The women's gallery is in the back, protected by a partition (*mehitzah*). Steps behind the synagogue lead up to it. People used to come here from as far as Lipótváros.

The synagogue is still in use. Since 1992 its rabbi is the Lubavitcher *shaliah* to Budapest. The synagogue was nicely renovated in 1993 and re-opened before the High Holidays.

It is interesting to note that there is a Sukkot room in the building, opening from the stairway. It was set up in one of the rooms of the former apartment of the *shames*.

(16) Sukkot

Sukkot / Sukkes / Sükes, the Feast of Tabernacles or by its older name the Feast of Booths or the Harvest Feast, *hag ha-asif*, or simply the Feast, *hag*, celebrates the harvest of cereal, it is "a time of rejoicing". It lasts for seven days, between 15th and 21st of Tishri (September / October). The first two are full holidays, the remaining five are *hol ha-mo'ed*, semi-holidays during which work is permitted. In addition to Passover and Shavuot this used to be the third Pilgrimage Festival, one of the three *regalim*. This holiday is spent in a tent, the *Sukkah*, to commemorate the wanderings in the wilderness (Leviticus 23,33–43; and especially, 23,42; see further, Numbers 29,12–38; Deuteronomy 16,13–15).

The tent is set up in the courtyard of one's house. This is considered the home of the family during the holiday. Between the World Wars there was a Sukkah in almost every house, in every courtyard in the neighborhood of Király utca and the outskirts of Józsefváros, or maybe on the balcony, as is customary in some cities these days. It must have looked like Williamsburg in Brooklyn, New York, where the Satmar (Szatmár) Hasidim live today, or Jerusalem: full of tents at Sukkot time, even on the balconies several floors up.

There are detailed instructions in Talmudic tradition concerning the building of the Sukkah. Each person should set up the Sukkah for his family himself. It is important that everything in the tent should be temporary. It should be made of natural wood not used for any other purpose—twigs or branches of trees or reed, but not flowers which fade too quickly. It should have at least two sides. Its covering has to be of material that grows from the soil. It should be thick enough to provide shade but shear enough to enable one to see the stars. That is why it must be built under the sky, not under a roof or another balcony. The inside of the Sukkah is decorated with fruits, plenty of apples, nuts and grapes. The most popular decorations are the seven species of the land of Israel, that is, wheat, barley, grapes, figs, pomegranates, olives and dates (Deuteronomy 8,8). These may not be eaten during the holiday.

There should be portraits of the "guests (*uspitzin*)" on the walls of the tent, like the guests invited by Abraham to his table (Genesis 18,4). In the sixteenth century Isaac Luria of Safed initiated the ceremony of inviting Abraham, the five true men (Isaac, Jacob, Josef, Moses and Aaron) and David. One of them should come each day. The *uspitzin* may be seven poor men instead of them or rather representing them, a different one every day. If someone has the same name as one of the guests, he is greeted with a glass of wine.

At least two full meals must be taken in the Sukkah and one should sleep there, too. In countries of the North it is difficult to fulfill all of these requirements so there are some traditional concessions. For instance, it is permissible to celebrate in someone else's Sukkah, in bad weather it is not necessary to be "outside", etc. As a practical and comfortable solution, it became customary to build a special "Sukkot-room" into houses. In Hungary such a Sukkot-room survived in Olaszliszka, in the house of Hershele Friedmann, the Hasidic *rebe* of the town, who died in 1874. Both here and in the Sukkot-room of the synagogue in Vasvári Pál utca the roof is removed for the days of the holiday by means of a cogwheel and pulley. The "Vasvári" Sukkot-room must have been used by the whole congregation, not just the people living in the building. A Sukkah is erected in the courtyard year by year even today.

Here is how Imre Ámos (1907 – Lager Ohrdruf, Thüringen, 1944/45) recalled a childhood memory in one of his poems written in 1942 while a forced laborer in Ukraine. The grandfather whom he remembered was the elementary school teacher and the *hazzan* in Nagykálló.

In prose translation:

"(...) I suddenly remember – (...) the overpowering smell of a tent, holiday of tabernacles, – my snow-white grandfather – is tying a thatched roof over the plank walls, – placing decoration on top, quince, pears, bottles of wine and water, – and linden-flower honey awaiting the holiday."

Already on the first morning of the holiday participants are holding a palm branch (*lulav / lülov / kappot temarim*) in their right hands and an *etrog / esrog* in the left while reciting the blessings. The *lulav* is held—bound—together with a myrtle branch (*hadas*) from the left, a willow branch (*aravah*) from the right. The *etrog* is a kind of a citrus fruit with a strong lemony-spicy smell. It is also called "Adam's apple", straight from the Garden of Eden. Its Latin name is *citrus medica*. A small bump on its lower part is called "Adam's bite". These four species, the *arba'a minim*, are a part of the ritual. The smell, the ripe fruits recall the atmosphere of the old Eastern harvest festival, despite the great distance from the Middle East. During the holiday services these four species and a Torah scroll are carried around in the synagogue (*hakkafah / hakofe*), asking for God's help (*hoshannah*, "Save, I pray").

247. *Etrog* container, Óbuda, 1865 (according to the inscription on the box)

The feast in the Sukkot-room, under the open sky, in the company of friends and family, is a real Diaspora celebration; there is a nostalgic mood recalling the pilgrimages to Jerusalem, the *aliyyah*. One of the commandments for the pilgrimage festivals is to rejoice (*simhah*), eat and drink lots of meat, wine and sweets, give presents to the women and the children, let there be music, dance. A Sukkot is a major harvest festival even in the big cities.

The last day of the week of Sukkot is *Hoshanah Rabbah*, "great liberation". People are dressed in white, in *kittel*, on this day. All the Torah scrolls are taken out of the Ark and a burning candle or wick is placed into the *aron*. Instead

248. Tabernacles.
Lino-cut by
Imre Ámos, 1940

of one, there are now seven *hakkafot*. On this day, the Almighty seals the book where everyone's fate is written. The *lulav* is put aside, and is replaced by a bundle of willow twigs called the *aravot / aroves* or *hoshannot / hoshanes*. The congregants are waving or "beating" them against the ground or the benches in the synagogue (*shanesklopfen*) while reciting Psalms 118, verses 1–2 and 25.

Traditionally this night is spent in the Sukkah or in the synagogue. One should observe the sky, to see when it opens. This is how we can find out about our fate for the coming year. Or the message comes on a *kvitl*, a note, which is why people wish each other "*a git kvitl*".

After the holiday, the willow leaves are used to prepare analgesic ointments while the twigs are preserved until next Passover. The fire in the *matzo* oven is lit from these twigs. It is also customary to give the *etrog* to a pregnant woman who bites off the edge (*pitum* or *pitom*, a small bump on the lower part of the fruit), so she should give birth to a boy and should have an easy delivery.

There is a Yiddish saying: *Esroygim nokh sukes*, "Etrog after Sukkot", an English version of which could be "mustard after meat". And another one which must have been used fairly often in Pest during the past fifty years: *Vos tut kol on an esrog? Men begeyt zikh*, "What does the community do without an etrog? One lives without one."

In the Diaspora, Sukkot is immediately followed by two more festival days. The eighth day is *Shemini Atzeret*, which is the beginning of the season when people pray for rain (*geshem bentshn*), 22nd of Tishri. 23rd of Tishri, *Simhat Torah*, the "Rejoicing of the Torah" is the last one in the long series of the autumn high holidays. The prayer for rain is recited until the first day of Passover as part of the *Amidah*, and then it is replaced by the prayer for dew. On the day of rejoicing it is customary to eat cabbage in any form, stuffed cabbage, cabbage strudel and the like.

VI. Józsefváros

In the inner parts of Józsefváros there was no Jewish quarter. On the contrary, this district—being an extension of the Inner City—was an upper-middle class area.

Józsefváros is the location of the *Magyar Nemzeti Múzeum* (Hungarian National Museum) and was that of the first *Nemzeti Színház* (National Theater) on Kerepesi út (today Rákóczi út). The Parliament used to be here, at 8 Főherceg Sándor utca (today 3 Bródy Sándor utca), in a building occupied today by the Italian Cultural Institute. The *Nemzeti Lovarda* (National Riding Hall), built in 1858 and destroyed during World War II, stood here in Öt Pacsirta utca (today Pollack Mihály tér) as did the *Nemzeti Sportcsarnok* (National Sport Hall) at 26 Szentkirályi utca. The great nineteenth-century architect, Miklós Ybl (1814–1891), designed several palaces here, including the Károlyi Palace in Öt Pacsirta utca (40 Esterházy utca / 3 Pollack Mihály tér) in 1859; the Festetics Palace, built between 1852 and 1865 (26 Esterházy utca / 10 Pollack Mihály tér); the Pálffy Palace in Öt Pacsirta utca (44 Esterházy utca / Dienes László utca / on the corner of Esterházy and Reviczky utca) in 1867. This was the district where in the last third of the nineteenth century the new university campus—buildings of the Medical School and the clinics—were built, along with the Biochemical and Biophysical Institutes of the Pest University and the Technical University. (The main building of the Pest University was in the Inner City, in Papnövelde utca.)

There is only one Jewish institution among all these imposing and elaborate buildings: the Rabbinical Seminary. Its facade and entrance face the former Főherceg Sándor tér (today Gutenberg tér). Its setting in the "national quarter" and its orientation toward West, toward the representational section of the neighborhood, indicate the status of the Seminary among the other national institutions. There is no doubt that the Rabbinical Seminary was intended to be a particularly significant and representative institution of the nation.

(1) The Rabbinical Seminary of Hungary (27 József körút)

The Seminary, *Országos Rabbiképző Intézet* in Hungarian, is located in the block between József körút / Bérkocsis utca / Gutenberg tér / Rökk Szilárd utca. Originally it was built on a smaller plot and its address was 19 Bodzafa utca, the former name of Rökk Szilárd utca. Apart from the Seminary numerous other Jewish educational institutions found a home here after World War II, including the Jewish community high school named—until recently (1998)—after Anne Frank. (In that year the school moved to its new location and received a new name, that of Sándor Scheiber, an one-time director of the Seminary.)

249. Building of the Rabbinical Seminary, 1877

The block actually consists of two buildings: 27 József körút is a four-story corner building, built in the late nineteenth century as a tenement house. In 1918 József Freund, the president of the Jewish community of Óbecse, who happened to be Sámuel Kohn's cousin, and his wife purchased the building and donated it to the Rabbinical Seminary and the Teachers' College to be used as a dormitory. A slab commemorating the donors can be seen above the entrance, and their

250. József Freund of Óbecse, the founder of the boarding school of the Teachers' College and the Rabbinical Seminary, wearing Hungarian national gala dress

portraits, painted by Fülöp Szenes around 1920, are hanging on the wall of the Seminary's main office. The original building of the Seminary was the other one, the one on the Bérkocsis and Rökk Szilárd utca side. This one was built in 1877 according to the plans of Ferenc Kolbenmeyer and Vilmos Freund, in the strict geometric style of other public and educational buildings of the time, but adorned with Oriental and folk elements. It was joined to the house on József körút only later. There is a synagogue in the courtyard.

For the past century the Rabbinical Seminary has been a major institution of Jewish learning in Hungary and Central Europe.

The Institute or Seminary, by its commonly used names, was earlier named after Emperor and King Francis Joseph I. There is a story to this choice of name. After the War of Independence (1848/49) Baron Julius J. Haynau (1786–1853), the commander-in-chief of the Austrian occupation forces, ordered by a decree of the Ministry of War on September 17, 1849 that because of their participation in the War of Independence, the Jews—actually, the Jewish communities of Arad, Cegléd, Kecskemét, Irsa (Albert-Irsa / Albertirsa), Nagykőrös and first of all, Pest—should pay 2,300,000 forints as war indemnity. This amount was actually nothing else but the debt that the Jewish communities owed in 1846 when the toleration or chamber tax (*taxa tolerantialis*) was suspended. The debts had been accumulating since 1828 and, though King Ferdinand V would have been willing to reduce them to 1,200,000 forints in his time, the debts were not paid before the 1848/49 Revolution and War of Independence started. Immediately after the restoration of "silence and order" on July 19, 1849, Haynau demanded that, "as a well deserved punishment and a warning to other Jewish communities", the Jewish communities of Pest and Óbuda pay by providing expensive uniforms and other items of clothing, shoes, trousers, shirts, jackets, etc. "for having supported the rebels in many ways". In addition, he insisted that they pay the full amount of the toleration tax debt. Francis Joseph, however, on September 20, 1850, agreed to the more favorable offer made by his predecessor and consented to the deal according to which the Jewish community would pay back the 1,200,000 forints within five years; once the debt was fully paid, he would return all of it to the Jewish community in the form of a contribution to the Jewish School Fund, established in 1856. The Institute took on Francis Joseph's name only in 1917, after his death, with the permission of King Charles (Károly) IV (1916–1918). The Seminary has always been supported financially by the Government.

251. József Freund of Óbecse and his wife in the Holy Land, dressed as Beduins

It took a decade and a half of debate for the Jewish community to decide what the appropriate way of using the donation of Francis Joseph for an educational institution would be and whether a Rabbinical Seminary would be acceptable for traditional Jewry. As a result of the Jewish Enlightenment, the *Haskalah*, and despite the strong opposition of the Orthodox, university level institutions were founded to train rabbis all over Europe. The immediate models of the Pest Seminary were the rabbinical seminaries of Breslau (Wrocław), founded in 1854, and Berlin, founded in 1872. There had been plans to establish a modern rabbinical school even earlier, in 1806, when David ben Meir Friesenhauser (1750–1828), a mathematician and Talmud scholar, handed in his proposal to Archduke Joseph, the Palatine, head of the royal administration in the

Hungarian crown lands. He was modeling his plans on the *Freischule* of Berlin (1778) and other German institutions. After several years of hesitation, the *Königliche Statthalterei* rejected the plan arguing that such rabbinical training institutes would merely enhance the separation of Jews. In 1844 the Upper House gave its consent and, in 1864, after the School Fund was established, the plans for the Seminary were actually laid out.

The debate within the Jewish community was not settled until the 1868/69 General Congress. The Rabbinical Seminary became associated with the Neolog movement. Francis Joseph gave his permission for it in 1873. The Orthodox rabbis condemned the Seminary (*issur*). József Schweitzer writes that, upon hearing that the foundations of the Rabbinical Seminary had been laid, R. Moshe Schick (Sik) cried and tore his clothes, R. Hillel Lichtenstein of Szikszó ordered a fast and R. Menahem Eisenstatt of Ungvár (today Uzhhorod, Ukraine) called upon his congregation to repent (*teshuvah*). Orthodox Jews felt that the whole of Jewry had suffered a loss, that it is time for all to mourn. A Hungarian Orthodox rabbi is not permitted to enter the Seminary or any Neolog synagogue until today. This prohibition does not apply to foreign rabbis, even if they are of Hungarian origin, which is why the Seminary can host several Hungarian Orthodox professors, rabbis who come home to visit.

252. Lajos Blau as a student of the Rabbinical Seminary, ca. 1885

253. Lajos Blau as a field rabbi in his military uniform

The Rabbinical Seminary was finally consecrated on October 4, 1877. It was a major social event. Greetings of the *Jüdisch-Theologisches Seminar* of Breslau were delivered by Heinrich Grätz (1817–1891), the great Jewish historian of his time, professor of the Seminary. On the following day the synagogue was also consecrated and the *ner tamid* was lit. The King (and Emperor) himself honored the Institute by his visit a few weeks later, on November 15. Legend has it that professor Vilmos Bacher, whose mother tongue was German and who wrote almost all of his works in German, greeted His Majesty in Hungarian, for patriotic reasons.

Traditionally the consent of three rabbis is necessary to issue rabbinical ordination, to give *semikhah* (*smikhe*). Following this tradition, there were exactly three professors when the Seminary was founded: Moses Bloch taught Talmud and Halakhah; Vilmos Bacher, professor of Bible studies, Biblical exegesis and homiletics; and David Kaufmann, professor of medieval Jewish history and philosophy of religion, the "Codices". The latter became the preacher of the Seminary's synagogue, at his own request. The traditional fields of rabbinical training are Bible, Talmud and the "Codices", *Shulhan Arukh* among them. Everything else serves either to lay the foundations or to support and supplement these. After a time several other rabbis joined the faculty as teachers. Complete academic freedom allowed every professor to develop his curriculum according to his own interests. Bloch used to teach in German, and so, even during the years between World War I and II, the unwritten law of the Seminary was that Talmud must be taught in German.

254. The "Eastern Wall" in the Rabbinical Seminary's synagogue

The best description of the Seminary at the turn of the century may be found in a novel by Arnold Kiss, *Fehér szegfű* ["White Carnation"], published in 1917. In 1986, on the occasion of the Seminary's centennial, Moshe Carmilly-Weinberger edited a scholarly account of the history of the Seminary with appendices and a bibliography. The Seminary's everyday life during the interwar years is described in detail by Ervin György (Raphael) Patai in his memoirs *Apprentice in Budapest. Memoirs of a World That Is No More*, published in 1988.

Originally the Seminary had two divisions, a lower and an upper one. The lower division, which offered a five-year program of study, was the equivalent of the upper division of the classical Gymnasium, *gimnázium* in Hungarian, a German-type secondary / high school, but the curriculum was supplemented with the study of Jewish languages, religion and traditional texts. Students graduated with a high school degree at the end, which enabled them to proceed to their rabbinical training in the upper division. There, after five years of study of Mishnah, Talmud, Midrash, Maimonides and *Shulhan Arukh*, as well as some other subjects like history, Arabic, Greek and Latin and having met all the rigorous requirements, the candidates were ordained as rabbis by three authoritative rabbis. Another condition of their ordination was that they had to earn a doctoral degree (Dr. phil. / Ph. D.) from the Faculty of Humanities of the Pest University.

Bloch was followed by Bacher in the rector's chair. He did not move into the Seminary building but lived in the neighborhood, at 9 Erzsébet körút. It was under his rectorship that the philological approach, the publication of documents with commentaries in the spirit of the Breslau *Seminar* became an established practice in Hungarian Jewish scholarship.

The third rector was Lajos Blau (1861–1936). In the wide range of the fields of Jewish scholarship he chose the history of the forms of Jewish written records, originally the history of the Hebrew book, from which his interest turned towards papyrus records, amulets and magic spells, marriage contracts, divorce certificates, etc. His thorough knowledge of Talmud enabled him to reconnect this offshoot of Jewish studies to the mainstream.

For decades the only institution in Hungary where serious, internationally acknowledged research and education took place in the field of medieval Jewish literature, Semitic linguistics and Arabic studies was the Rabbinical Seminary. Initially they even taught cuneiform writing and Accadian. It was customary to send the best students to Breslau for a year so they could broaden their fields of study and get acquainted with German scholarship. Many of the professors of the Seminary were eminent, internationally recognized scholars. The best known Hungarian scholars in the field of humanities were Vilmos Bacher and Ignác Goldziher.

The rectors of the Seminary were:

Moses Bloch: 1876–1907
Vilmos Bacher: 1907–1913
József Bánóczi and Gyula Fischer (executive director): 1914
Lajos Blau: 1914–1932
Simon Hevesi (executive director): 1932–1933
Mihály Guttmann (1872–1942): 1933–1942
Sámuel Löwinger: 1942–1950
Ernő Róth and Sándor Scheiber (alternate years): 1950–1956
Sándor Scheiber: 1956–1985
László Salgó (1910–1985) (executive director): 1985
József Schweitzer: 1985–1998
Alfréd Schőner: 1998–

During its entire existence the Rabbinical Seminary ordained three hundred rabbis altogether, and not only Hungarians. The number of students was the largest between the two World Wars, exceeding one hundred at a time. Tableaux of former students and professors decorate the walls of the Seminary's office and corridors: a picture gallery of Hungarian Jewish history and scholarship.

Some of the Seminary's professors were strictly traditional, others allowed themselves more freedom. There is an anecdote, a true story, according to which Gyula Fischer and Ármin Hoffer (1870–1941) were once examining an applicant who came in wearing a hat and failed to remove it. "This is not a pub, dear colleague", said Fischer who did not adhere to traditional clothing, turning to Hoffer for confirmation. A professor's or rabbi's authority may not be questioned, but facts are even more important. Therefore Hoffer very politely replied: "That is correct, the Rabbinical Seminary is, indeed, not a pub. It is a *bet ha-midrash*", a house of learning.

Goldziher was not a rabbi and thus could not be appointed a professor at the Seminary, so he taught philosophy of religion as a visiting lecturer. (He never wore a hat while in the Seminary.) After his death, Bernát Heller took over this subject. His students relate that Heller never sat down on the chair behind the lecturer's desk, as customary, only *next to it*, to the side. He did not consider himself worthy of his master's seat.

Zionist ideas were barred from the Seminary for a long time. Zionism started spreading among the students already in the years preceding World War I, but met with nothing but mockery from the faculty. According to their interpretation, Zionism was nothing but a nostalgic yearning for the Holy Land. But times changed. By the late 1930s students of the Seminary who came from the strongly Zionist Jewish high schools of Ungvár and Munkács spread their views, Hebrew also became a spoken language in the Seminary and it was clearly associated with Zionism.

There was even a minor debate between two of the professors, Simon Hevesi and Ármin Hoffer. Hevesi strongly opposed Zionism and hoped to gain Hoffer's support, the latter, however, answered with a Biblical reference, that is, with Balaam's prophecy (Numbers 23,9), saying that the Jewish people would dwell "apart", dispersed and would not be reckoned among the nations. Hevesi laughed and they shook hands. Zionist thinking had to be accepted along with Hungarian patriotism.

The leading Hungarian rabbis joined the *Magyar Zsidók Pro-Palesztina Szövetsége* (Pro-Palestine Association of Hungarian Jews) organized in order to support the newly established Hebrew University in Jerusalem; Bernát Heller was on its board of directors. Mihály (Michael) Guttmann was invited to teach Talmud in Jerusalem (1925), he was one of the very first professors in the Institute of Jewish Studies there. The reservations of the Budapest rabbinate towards Zionism, which, by the way, was shared by the majority of Budapest Jews, was not in contradiction with Jewish tradition. On the contrary, it was more a cautious defense of it.

255. Portrait of Gyula Fischer. Drawing by Raphael Patai

256. Portrait of Ármin Hoffer. Drawing by Raphael Patai

In Pest the Zionist movement was formulated in secular, sometimes even anti-religious terms, based on Socialist ideas and influenced by the then fashionable, and at that time still innocuous German racial theory. The Orthodoxy, on the other hand, considered it completely impertinent that human intervention should promote something Jews have been expecting during the past two thousand years to happen with the arrival of the Messiah. Their reaction to Theodor Herzl's ideas was that "no artificial movement can change the fate which the Almighty chose for Israel" (*Zsidó Híradó* [Jewish Courier], July 1, 1897). In the mid-1930s giving up the established European way of life, leaving one's home only to confront the Arabic population of Palestine did not seem a better way to preserve Jewish traditions and religious life than did civil life in Pest, Hungarian citizenship and cultural integration and staying in Eastern Europe where Jews had lived for centuries. The debate, however, was decided not by arguments but by an unexpected turn of history. In Budapest it happened in 1944. It happened in a way which none, not even the Zionists, could have imagined a decade earlier.

The Rabbinical Seminary's interior is a valuable historic monument. Though the walls were (re-)painted in 1993, the building is still wanting renovation and modernization. The main lecture hall, called, with some exaggeration, the "great lecture hall", retained until recently the atmosphere of a nineteenth-century school or college: the professor's huge desk in the middle, separated from the room by a wooden banister, is a relics of the nineteenth century. (The hall was renovated in 1998.) There is no another class-room or lecture hall in Budapest older than this one. (Extensive renovation works were started in the building in 1998. To great sorrow, first the books were removed from the shelves to the basement for an indeterminate period.)

The main wall of the Ceremonial Hall is decorated by a portrait gallery of the Institute's notable professors. The bookcases are loaded with precious old manuscripts and prints. Some are covered with antique curtains of the Ark (*parokhet*). It is like yet another Jewish museum. Lectures and celebrations as well as Friday night *kiddush* and the annual Seders are held in the Ceremonial Hall. Here in the Seminary stood Goldziher's former desk for a long time—now removed to one of the rooms of the Hungarian Jewish Archives in the Jewish Museum.

Ever since its founding in 1894, the *Izraelita Magyar Irodalmi Társulat* (Israelite Hungarian Literary Society, abbreviated as IMIT) had always had close ties with the Seminary, especially through the person of Vilmos Bacher. The Yearbooks of the society (IMIT. *Évkönyv*) were edited here, as was the *Magyar Zsidó Szemle* [Hungarian Jewish Review], the most important Hungarian Jewish scholarly periodical of which 65 issues were published between 1884 and 1948.

The successor to the former *Zsidó Gimnázium*, the "Anna Frank" High School, which occupied most of the building until recently, was originally the heir of the rooms belonging to the Teachers' College in the aftermath of World War II. The Teachers' College was established at the order of the *Königliche Statthalterei* from the School Fund as a Royal Jewish Model Higher School, a training school, a girls' school and a Teachers' College in 1856 and opened in the following year. The educational institutions of the Jewish community were planned on the model of the state educational system. The Teachers' College was originally located at 17 Lázár utca (today 10 Dalszínház utca), then at 9 Rombach utca, and finally, when the Rabbinical Seminary was set up in 1877, it moved to the ground floor rooms in 2 Bérkocsis utca. Placing the two most important Jewish higher educational institutions into the same building was a fortunate move. The original idea of a Jewish Teachers' College

257. Ceremonial Hall of the Rabbinical Seminary

was at least partially revived in 1990/91 when a new Teachers' College was established at the Seminary: the Pedagogium. Today, the Pedagogium is to occupy the whole building in Bérkocsis utca, that is, to re-occupy—as a faculty of the Jewish University—the place and facilities of the former Teachers' College.

The intellectual potential of the Teachers' College was enhanced by its distinguished leaders. One of its directors was József Bánóczi (1849–1926), a corresponding member of the Hungarian Academy of Sciences (1879), notable literary historian, philosopher and pedagogue who deserves much credit for promoting Jewish intellectual activity in Hungarian. Another prominent director was Samu (Samuel) Szemere (1881–1978), philosopher and literary critic, during the second part of his long life an excellent translator of the works of classical philosophers, including Baruch Spinoza (1632–1677) and a lecturer at the Rabbinical Seminary. In 1953, the publication of his translation of Spinoza's treatise on the Bible, the *Tractatus theologico-politicus* (1670), was meant to encourage serious, objective and deep Bible studies even in the atmosphere of the full rejection of any sacred tradition in Hungary.

Today the only specifically Jewish reference library in Hungary is the one housed in the Rabbinical Seminary. The library evolved from the collection of Lelio della Torre (1805–1871), rabbi of Padua. With its some seventy thousand volumes—the exact number is hard to determine—it is a significant collection, though its finest holdings date from the nineteenth century. There is no other library anywhere in the area where one might find treatises by Hungarian rabbis in Hebrew or the prestigious and massive Talmud editions of famous Eastern-European publishing houses, including the Romm Press of Vilna. The former private collections of Moses Bloch and Vilmos Bacher enhance the Seminary's library, too. Before the renovation the stacks occupied three levels. The "cellar" and the "main floor", i.e. the second and the third floors of the building, could only be accessed from the third floor of the building, and there was also a gallery opening from the "main floor" and constituting the third, "upper floor" of the library.

Adolf Eichmann, who had been collecting materials for a future "Central Museum of the Extinct Jewish Race" at the Jewish Research Institute in Frankfurt am Main since 1941, confiscated some Torah scrolls of the Orthodox community from Fülöp Freudiger as soon as he set foot in Budapest and also removed a few thousand volumes from the Rabbinical Seminary and other Jewish collections to Prague. It is not clear who made the selection of these works. At the beginning of the German occupation Eichmann visited the Seminary, had a look at its library and had the inventory lists taken to his office, but maybe it was not him who decided which books to take. A part of the "Eichmann collection" was stored in the cellars of the Dreher Brewery in Kőbánya. In Prague the plundered books were kept in the depot of the *Treuhandstelle*; after the war, the Jewish Museum of Prague took care of the majority of the "collection". Finally, in 1989, it was brought back to Budapest unharmed, with some help from the Hungarian state. But those who expected to find some lost treasures were disappointed a little: the "Prague collection" contained mostly books of secondary importance and lesser value only. Whoever selected them for the strange German transport must have been aware of what he / she may give over to the Nazis. Nevertheless, in the "Eichmann collection" there were some rare books as well: a series of rabbinical responsa, old editions of the *Mishneh Torah* and the *Shulhan Arukh* and the correspondence of the Salonika (Thessaloniki) Jewish community from the 1930s brought to Budapest by someone who managed to escape the deportation.

258. Former office of the director of the Hungarian Jewish Archives in the Rabbinical Seminary

During the second half of the 1980s the library more or less recovered from decades of neglect and by now there is even a small reading room to serve the needs of readers. The post-war collection of the library is rather poor, yet this should one day become the kernel of a Hungarian Jewish Library.

In the last year of World War II, on March 21, 1944, two days after the German occupation of Hungary, the Germans set up an internment camp in the building of the Seminary for prominent members of Pest Jewry and the financial aristocracy ("*die Prominenten*"), approximately two hundred people. They were held hostage here, either because the Germans wanted a ransom for their heads or because they wanted to prevent them from organizing some kind of resistance or uprising. The Institute's kosher kitchen was in charge of cooking for the inmates who changed every few weeks. People were not released from the Seminary's camp, only taken to a different one, to Kistarcsa or to some other place. The first Hungarian transport to Auschwitz left from Kistarcsa on April 28, 1944 and some of the Rabbinical Seminary's inmates were among the deported. The last train on July 19 also carried some Jewish prisoners from Rökk Szilárd utca.

At Sárospatak in Northeastern Hungary a slab on the walls of the Calvinist College preserves the memory of those former students who were taken captive by the Turks and sent to the galleys. The Rabbinical Seminary also had students who, instead of graduating and becoming rabbis or scholars, ended their lives in concentration camps. Their memory is kept only by the class tableaux on the walls.

The Seminary's synagogue does not belong to any district, but it does have a regular congregation in which young people prevail. In his time Sándor Scheiber managed to make the Seminary the center of Jewish social life on Friday nights. For the Neologs, every Friday night spent here was a real *oneg shabbat*, a really joyful Sabbath with him. Scheiber, though a rabbi, turned to the youth more like a professor and scholar, lovingly. Whoever was lucky enough to have participated in at least one of his famous Friday evening *kiddush* ceremonies in the modest but cozy Ceremonial Hall of the Seminary, knows that Scheiber's greatness lay precisely in that he could make knowledge the power of maintenance. The noble tradition of the Rabbinical Seminary stayed alive even in those difficult years, and it was continued by R. Schweitzer up to today.

Moses (Moshe) Arjeh Bloch / Mózes Bloch (1815-1907)

He was no young man anymore when he accepted the invitation to come to Budapest. He had been active as a rabbi in Moravian Jewish communities for over two decades, and even ran a grand *yeshivah* at his last place, Leipnik (Lipnik nad Becvou, Czech Republic). His person was sort of a bridge

between the traditional *yeshivah* and the modern, university-like rabbinical seminary. Neolog leaders probably chose him with the expectation that his person might bring the Orthodoxy closer and reduce their hostility towards the Seminary. Their hopes were not fulfilled. Bloch was identified with the Seminary. "His triple home, the school, the synagogue and his family, all housed in one building, surrounded him completely"—wrote Mihály Guttmann, Bloch's student and successor as director of the Seminary on his professor's first *Jahrzeit*. Moses Bloch was a Talmudist to the core. In his scholarly work he never dealt with anything but Halakhic questions, not even in his years in Budapest. He attempted to apply Jewish law to the modern civil society. His two major works, *Sha'arei torat ha-takkanot*, "Introduction to the Law of Decisions" (1879–1906) and *Sha'arei ha-ma'alot*, "Introduction to Holiness" (1908) ensured his place among the greatest scholars of Jewish legal history. Bloch edited the responsa of R. Meir ben Barukh, the thirteenth-century rabbi of Rothenburg—those Halakhic decisions which had defined the precepts of practical (business) life of Ashkenazi Jews for centuries (1885, 1891). Bloch meant to pave the way for Jews in the modern world by structuring tradition. His studies on various topics were published in the Yearbooks of the Seminary in Hungarian as well as in German. The topics included law and order (1879), civil law (1882), law of inheritance (1890), law of treaties (1893), property law (1897), criminal law (1901), custody (1904) and ethics from the point of view of Halakhah (1886). All of his works aimed at fitting Jewish law into the framework of European legal tradition—a pioneering idea in his time which was the central program of *Wissenschaft des Judentums* in the nineteenth century. The faculty of the Seminary in its first decade was committed to this program.

259. Portrait of Moses Bloch

The tomb of Moses Bloch is in the Salgótarjáni utca cemetery.

David Kaufmann (1852-1899)

He was born in Moravia, attended the famous Breslau *Seminar* at the age of 15 and was ordained there in 1877. He received his doctorate in Leipzig in 1874. When the Budapest Rabbinical Seminary opened, Kaufmann was invited to teach Jewish religious philosophy and Jewish history upon the recommendation of his professors in Breslau. He was among the greatest scholars of his time and also among the most prolific; he wrote thirty books and over half a thousand essays. He was proud that he wrote part of his scholarly work in Hebrew. Living in Budapest as *Dávid* Kaufmann, he learned Hungarian quickly; the summers spent on the Great Hungarian Plain helped him acquire the language. His enormous talent made him popular among the Hungarian Jewish intellectual elite. His marriage to an offspring of the Gomperz family gave him access to considerable wealth, enabling him to assemble an invaluable collection of manuscripts and books, a real treasure house of Jewish scholarship. Like his great contemporaries, Bacher and Goldziher, he too kept track of developments in international scholarship. From 1892 until his death Kaufmann was the editor (from Budapest) of *Monatsschrift für die Geschichte und Wissenschaft des Judentums*, the most important scholarly periodical of the time, founded back in 1851 by Zacharias Frankel, a major figure of the first period of *Wissenschaft des Judentums*. Kaufmann, like most Moravian Jews, was educated in the spirit of the German Jewish Enlightenment and brought the ideas of Haskalah with himself to Budapest. Ways of cultivating Jewish history and literature are always determined, among other things, by the scholarly and critical norms of the period. The goal is to explore Jewish tradition, to keep it alive and thus enrich contemporary Jewish life. Kaufmann initiated new fields of investigation. He set the framework for studying the history of Jewish art and studied medieval Jewish gravestones in Buda, approaching Hebrew epigraphy in a scholarly way. His untimely death was the result of an accident.

His grave is in the Salgótarjáni utca cemetery.

Vilmos Bacher (1850-1913)

Vilmos (Wilhelm) Bacher grew up in the milieu of the Haskalah and of Hungarian national tradition. His father, Simon Bacher (Bachrach) (1823–1891), was among the first to enrich the revival of Hebrew literature with translations of Hungarian poems. The "Nemzeti Dal" [National Song] by Sándor Petőfi, the "Szózat" [Summons] by Mihály Vörösmarty and the poems of János Arany could now be read and heard in the language of the Bible. He also translated Hungarian folk-songs and Lessing's "Nathan der Weise", the *intellectual bestseller* of the Haskalah, into Hebrew. The language of these translations may sound archaic today, like the language of the originals. Vilmos Bacher collected his father's translations after his death and published them in three volumes, with his own introduction, under the title *Sha'ar Shime'on* in 1894. The family had originally lived in the Rhine valley, but moved to Liptó county, Hungary (now in Slovakia), during the childhood of Vilmos. Simon Bacher moved to Pest in 1874, where he was put in charge of the finances of the Jewish community until his death.

The son, Vilmos Bacher, studied in Breslau. He too was attracted to the *Seminar*, he received rabbinical ordination (*semikhah*) here and could also become acquainted with the contemporary Jewish scholarship on the Talmud and the medieval Jewish languages of the East, Arabic and Persian. He was a classmate of Goldziher, first in Pest, in Vámbéry's classes, later in Breslau. At that time they were still best friends. They ran a Hungarian association in the Seminar, the *Boroszlói Magyar Olvasó Társulat* (Hungarian Reading Society of Breslau). When Bacher left, he took the papers and the seal of the society with him. In 1876/77 he succeeded Lipót Lőw in Szeged before being invited to a chair at the Seminary in Pest.

As a young man Bacher followed in his father's footsteps. He wrote poetry in, and translated into, Hebrew and German. His first Hebrew translation published was Schiller's "Der Jüngling am Bache" in 1865. The very same poem was translated into Hungarian earlier by Sándor Petőfi, and so the young Bacher was attracted to Schiller's poem not only because his name was part of the title but also because of his predecessor Petőfi, some of whose poems, e.g. "Reszket a bokor" [The Bush Trembles] and "Szabadság, szerelem" [Liberty, Love], he translated into Hebrew. He toasted Goldziher on his 20th birthday in Hebrew and Persian verse. He wrote a Hebrew elegy upon the death of Baron József Eötvös, a fan of his father. Several of his Hebrew poems and translations, some thirty altogether, remained unpublished and are kept at the Rabbinical Seminary today. The young scholar acted out his love for poetry in analyzing Persian verse.

Bacher's greatest scholarly achievement was the analysis and systematization of Aggadic traditions in the Talmudic literature with the application of methods used in contemporary philology and historical criticism. The collection of precepts of Jewish life, the Mishnah, eventually became a subject of

תְּפִלַּת הָאָרִין.
שִׁיר מֵעֵשְׂרוֹת הַמְּצוּנָּקָה אֲשֶׁר עָבְרוּ.
Kölcsey.
בָּרֵךְ אֱלֹהִים אֶת בֶּן אֶרֶץ הוּנְגַּרְיָה
בְּרוּחֶךָ סָמְכֵהוּ בְּתַעֲצוּמוֹת וָעֹז
וּזְרוֹעַ עֶזְרָתְךָ נְטֵה לוֹ כְּמוֹשִׁיעַ
בְּהִלָּחֲמוֹ עִם אוֹיְבָיו יַעֲשֶׂה נִפְלָאוֹת.
מֵאָז דָּפְאוּ רֹאשׁוֹ יְמֵי עָמָל וְרָעָה
רְצֵהוּ כְאָב נֶאֱמָן תֶּן לוֹ שְׁנוֹת שָׂשׂוֹן
עוֹנוֹ כְּבָר נִרְצָה בְּכֹבֶד הַתְּלָאָה
נִלְחָצָה נַפְשׁוֹ בֵּין קִירוֹת הָאָסוֹן.

שִׁיר הַבָּצִיר.
Vörösmarty
פַּגְּנֵי שִׂמְחָה יַטִּיף יַיִן
לִנְפָשׁוֹת
טוֹב כִּי כֵן הוּא גִּיל וָעֵדֶן
בְּכוֹסוֹת.
תַּעֲלֶה מַעְלָה שִׂמְחָתֵנוּ
שָׁמַיְמָה
וְרִגְבֵי דְאָגָה נַשְׁלִיךְ אַרְצָה
הַפָּעְמָה.

לַגּוּף יִתְּנוּ חֹזֶק מִסְעָד
מַאֲכָלִים
אַךְ הַיַּיִן יְחַדֵּשׁ חַיִּים
לָאֻמְלָלִים.
בְּנִי אִם אַחַת יַיִן וָנֶפֶשׁ
כְּאָה וְאָחוֹת
עֵדָנִים יִתֵּן כְּטַל שָׁמַיִם
בְּצַחְצָחוֹת.

260. Two Hebrew translations by Simon Bacher: "Himnusz" [Anthem] by Ferenc Kölcsey and "Fóti dal" [Song of Fót] by Mihály Vörösmarty

261. Vilmos Bacher
as a field rabbi dur-
ing the occupation of
Bosnia, 1878

262. Vilmos Bacher
in his study

discussions. These debates are recorded in the Gemarah, which, together with the Mishnah, forms the Talmud. The Gemarah contains the opinions of several scholars from different generations. Bacher established the historical sequence of this material, separating the various chronological layers, identifying the individual masters by name and determining which saying belongs to whom. His posthumous book *Tradition und Tradenten in den Schulen Palästinas und Babyloniens* (1914, reprint 1966) remains a classic in the field.

Bacher was also interested in the medieval history of Hebrew linguistics, which complemented his studies of the history of Biblical commentary. This material led Bacher to the area of Arabic studies. He deserves credit for rediscovering Jewish–Arabic and Jewish–Persian cultures. He was the first to undertake a systematic analysis of medieval science and poetry in the three major languages, Arabic, Persian and Hebrew. It was Ármin Vámbéry who guided both Bacher and Goldziher as polyglots in the Near Eastern languages, although not even Goldziher could keep up with him. Bernát Heller compared the role of Ármin Vámbéry in the careers of Bacher and Goldziher to that of Elishah ben Abuyah in the studies of the second-century R. Meir: they, the heretics-to-be, paved the way for their faithful students.

On top of his scholarly work Bacher was also actively involved in organizing and maintaining institutions which made culture accessible to the wider public. He became the director of the Talmud-Torahs in 1885; in 1884 he and József Bánóczi launched the journal *Magyar Zsidó Szemle* (Hungarian Jewish Review); he was among the founders in 1894 and, for a while, the president of the Israelite Hungarian Literary Society.

Bacher left his library to the Rabbinical Seminary in his will, and his family preserved the *Hand-Exemplare* of his own works, the volumes he himself used. These volumes are full of glosses in Bacher's beautiful handwriting, in German and Hebrew, often in Hebrew cursive; the margins are filled and even some pages were inserted later. He kept reviewing his works until the day of his death.

Simon Hevesi wrote in 1910, on Bacher's 60th birthday, as follows:

"The teachings of the wise (...) came down to us in short words. These words are only reminders. Every text is like the excavation of a burial site containing human remains. (...) Digging can only rescue the mortal remains, the linguistic expression; the real spiritual work is to reconstitute the whole set of ideas from the fragments. This master of Biblical exegesis, student of other great interpreters of the Bible, discoverer of the *aggadot* of the fathers (...) penetrated the spirit of past centuries, past authors and enriched our Jewish and universal culture—and there is no contradiction here—with these treasures."

Only a few years later, in 1913, at Bacher's funeral, Hevesi wrote:

"This was Vilmos Bacher, the son of Simon Bacher, a learned man, explorer of tradition, poet of the rose gardens, ardent exegete with a deep soul. He was a universal authority. He understood the unity of the difficult, thousand-year-old literature of Jewry whether written in Hebrew, Aramaic, Arabic, Persian, Greek or any of the modern languages. He could separate the layers of Bible, Midrash, Mishnah, Talmud, commentary and philology: he saw all of Jewish literature as a living unity, as one with his own soul."

His grave is in the Salgótarjáni utca cemetery.

*

The most important evidence of Bacher's philological insight and thorough knowledge of Hungarian is his translation of the Bible published by the IMIT, in four volumes, between 1898 and 1907. Bánóczi and Sámuel Krausz assisted him in the project. This is the best "Jewish" Bible in Hungarian until our days. It was newly published, together with the Hebrew text, in 1994. (Unfortunately, the names of the editors and contributors, as well as that of IMIT, was hidden in the epilogue.)

A second edition of the IMIT Bible came out in 1925, containing only the first two volumes. Its text was partially revised, simplified or even re-translated by Lajos Blau and others. This was a "youth and family Bible", as the subtitle informs us (*Ifjúsági és családi Biblia* in Hungarian).

Another new translation of the Bible was published almost at the same time. This *Szentírás a család és az iskola részére* ("Holy Script for Family and School") was edited by Bernát Frenkel (1881–1961). It was first published ca. 1915 in Vienna, then ca. 1925 in Pest, where the address of the editorial office is given as 5 Teleki tér; finally there was a third, abridged edition under the title *Kis Szentírás* ("Little Holy Script") around 1935.

There was only one edition of the Hebrew Bible in Hungary after these volumes, a five-volume Torah edition: the Hebrew text with Hungarian translation, which basically follows the IMIT translation, and with commentaries by Joseph H. Hertz, chief rabbi of England. (First edition: 1939; second edition: 1942; reprint, on the initiative of Sándor Scheiber: Akadémiai Kiadó és Nyomda, 1984; a new reprint, published in 1996 by the Budapest Chabad Lubavitch Center, with the title *Zsidó Biblia*, in a somewhat incorrect way since it does not contain the Prophets and the Writings.)

Bacher's Hungarian Bible is a brilliant translation, a philological masterpiece, but it could not knock out Gáspár Károlyi's 1590 Calvinist Bible translation and its numerous revisions, with their faulty Hungarian texts, not even from the hands of the Jews.

Sámuel Lőwinger (1904-1980)

He was ordained rabbi in 1931. He taught Bible and Talmud at the Rabbinical Seminary and was appointed director of the Institute in 1942. After World War II he assumed the task of reconstructing the Seminary and giving education and scholarly life there a fresh start. In 1950 he moved to Israel and was appointed director of the manuscript division of the National and University Library in Jerusalem. As a scholar his main interest lay in Biblical manuscripts. He spent years studying the famous Codex of Aleppo, which is one of the oldest copies of the traditional (*Masoretic*) texts of the Hebrew Bible, from the tenth century. It survived in the oldest synagogue in Aleppo (Mustariba, from the fourth century C.E.), which was burned down by the mob, assisted by the local authorities, during a pogrom in 1947. Then the manuscript disappeared and found its way to Jerusalem where it was printed in two facsimile editions and became a main source in the study of studies into the history of the Bible text. It was Lőwinger who prepared the catalogue of the Hebrew manuscripts of the Vatican and of the *Jüdisch-Theologisches Seminar* of Breslau that were rescued to Jerusalem.

Ernő Róth / Abraham Naftali Zwi Roth (1908-1991)

Among the directors of the Rabbinical Seminary Ernő Róth was, unquestionably, the last great scholar of Halakhah. The directors after him distinguished themselves in other fields. Róth was for his generation what Bloch, the Seminary's first director, had been for his own. They differed only in one aspect, that while Bloch wrote or edited mostly books, Róth was better at writing short papers and essays which dealt with contemporary Halakhic questions, embedded in their historical context. For a while Róth was the *paskan* (*paskener*), the *decisor* (arbitrator) of the Pest community

263. Portrait of Ernő Róth, 1942

and so his essays are reminiscent of the traditional genre of Halakhic decisions or responsa. Before coming to the Seminary, he studied at various yeshivot, including his father's. He received his *semikhah* from three learned rabbis and, moreover, earned a degree at the Seminary. He was appointed a professor there upon completion of his studies, as successor to Ármin Hoffer. He taught Talmud and other Halakhic literature, never separating the text from the problem. He immersed himself in legal and religious questions regarding the Holocaust. No one in Hungary could rival the depth of his Halakhic knowledge. He and Scheiber took turns as directors of the Seminary for six years. The rotation proved to be difficult, for there was tension between them. Along with thousands of other Jews Róth decided to leave the country in the Fall of 1956. In Germany he was also acknowledged as a Halakhic arbiter. His scholarly work consisted of cataloging the Hebrew manuscript collections of German and Austrian libraries. This work meant not only listing the items, but also identifying their content, exploring the manifold relations between manuscripts and recognizing original texts, all of which require a thorough acquaintance with traditional texts.

After he left Budapest, no one in the Seminary wanted—or dared—to mention Róth in public, nor wanted to remember him. He may return one day through the spirit of his lucid Halakhic essays.

(2) Hungarian National Museum: A Roman Gravestone from Aquincum (14-16 Múzeum körút)

There are no distinctly Jewish objects displayed in the exhibition of the Hungarian National Museum called "History of Hungary, 1703-1849". None of the artifacts are identifiably Jewish, as if Jews had not lived in Hungary during that period. Yet there are several objects in the collection, in storage, which do preserve the memory of Hungarian Jewry. There is even a piece from Roman times on display.

Since the third century C.E. we may speak about a considerable population of Jews on the territory of Pannonia. Jews arrived in the Province as soldiers of the Roman Empire or as merchants and craftsmen serving the needs of the army. We are informed about their being Jewish from the symbols on their gravestones—a *menorah*, *lulav*, *etrog* or *shofar*—as well as the Greek expression *Heis Theos* ("God is one" / "There is only one God") in an inscription from Aquincum, the Roman city North of Óbuda, which echoes the first sentence of the *Shema* (Deuteronomy 6,4). It most probably dates from the fourth century C.E. and was cut in Aquincum itself. It has an adventurous story. It came into the possession of the Counts Szapáry around 1830–1840, when they bought it at an auction in Pest. It was fashionable then to collect all kinds of antiquities, including architectural remains. They took it to their estate in Albert-Irsa and built it into the wall of a small chapel in the park of their palace.

They may have thought it was a Christian relic. The first one to write about it as an antiquity was Károly Wolff (Vajda), the tutor of Szapáry's children. He mentioned it in the newly launched journal *Egyetemes Philologiai Közlöny* in 1878, but it was only years later, in 1891, that Róbert Fröhlich realized that the *menorah* indicates the Jewish origin of the piece. In 1904 Sámuel Krausz (Krauss), a great scholar of Jewish antiquities, for a while professor at the Jewish Teachers' College, later on at the Rabbinical Seminary of Vienna and, after the *Kristallnacht*, from 1939 on, at Cambridge University, established that the gravestone was from Aquincum. The gravestone achieved some fame in international scholarly circles because of the human figures represented on it. Sándor Scheiber was the one who finally uncovered its secret in full.

The Aquincum stele was used twice. First it was placed over the grave of a non-Jewish family's son who died at an early age. The family members included their own portraits in the relief. Later the stele was used by a Jewish family. It was customary at that time to recycle valuable gravestones—it must have been easier than to carve a new piece. The scene of the stele must have fitted the Jewish family's case; they must have wanted to dedicate the stone to the memory of their son and themselves. They just had a *menorah* carved next to each of the original portraits to make it clear that they were Jewish. They did not remove the old inscription which by then could have been underground, but merely added their own text next to the portraits. The Greek names of the parents clearly reveal Hebrew names: ANESTASIOS / Anastasius, that is, Elyakim; DEKUSANE / Decusane, that is, Tzidkah. The son, as was often the case among romanized Diaspora Jews, had a Biblical Hebrew name, Benjamin.

The original inscription on the lower portion of the stele has no Jewish elements, which confirms that the *menorah*s next to the human portraits were added later. The new inscription is in Greek. The expression "God is one" is also inscribed three times, each time with the same spelling mistake in the Greek text. From our perspective it is especially interesting that a Jewish gravestone should be decorated with human portraits, even if we know that these were originally carved for non-Jews. This Jewish family of the fourth century had no compunctions about using a gravestone which depicted humans, obviously themselves. It seems that the Biblical commandment, "you shall not make for yourself a sculptured image" (Exodus 20,4–5) was interpreted strictly only in late antiquity.

There can be no doubt that the stele stood over the grave of an assimilated Jewish person, one who adjusted his habits to that of the Roman province.

264. Jewish gravestone from Aquincum (?). Detail

265. Jewish gravestone from Aquincum (?)

MHMORIA ANЄCTACIO ЄT ΔHKOYCANI
ЄT BHNЄIAMI ЄT ΦЄIΛЄIω
NOCTRω

ЄIC   ΘЄωC

ЄIC ΘЄωC   ЄIC ΘЄωC

266. Three engraved *menorahs* and Judeo-Greek inscriptions on the Jewish gravestone from Aquincum (?)

VII. Terézváros

(1) Sugár út / Andrássy út

The Sugár or Andrássy út is a magnificent product of conscious city planning. This is the most beautiful avenue in Budapest. Its beginning used to be called Könyök utca in the times when it was just one of the minor unorganized roads. József Kiss lived here, in Könyök utca, on the edge of the Jewish quarter, around 1865 when he arrived to the capital.

The plan of an avenue was first proposed by Lajos Kossuth in 1841 and then in 1868 by Prime Minister Count Gyula Andrássy, after whom the avenue was named in 1885. To ease the traffic of Király utca which had by then become very dangerous, in 1869 Ferenc Reitter suggested the construction of "a Promenade leading from the church in Terézváros to the Városliget". The *Fővárosi Közmunkák Tanácsa* (Council for Public Works in Budapest), founded in 1870, whose chief engineer was Ferenc Reitter, included in its plans the construction of wider roads in the city. In 1870 the Diet approved the plans for Sugár út and preliminary financial arrangements were made (appropriations, bank loans, etc.). Two years later the construction work began. The European economic crisis in 1873 slowed the progress down considerably; nevertheless Sugár út was opened for the public in 1876. By 1885 all of the 115 houses along the avenue were ready. The Diet also contributed to the project by completely or partially exempting the houses along Sugár út from taxes for thirty years.

The plan for an avenue grew out of the need to connect the overcrowded Inner City (Downtown) with the Városliget, the wooded recreation area of Pest. Earlier, for the preceding one hundred years, this function had been fulfilled by Király utca. But Király utca was a part of the Jewish quarter and, in the years following the Austro-Hungarian *Ausgleich* or compromise (1867), when the Hungarian aristocratic and gentry political elite was in the process of securing their representative space in the capital, they did not feel like riding through the Jewish quarter on their way to the Városliget. And yet the requirements of the Jews of Budapest, or at least of the wealthier ones, seem to have played an important role in the construction of Sugár út. At a time when the Jews were gradually gaining official acceptance and becoming culturally assimilated, living in the new, exclusive street was a way of identifying with the upper class. Next to the houses of the *noblesse d'épée* and of the financial aristocracy (the Koburgs, the Pallavicinis) about three fifth of the houses on Andrássy út were owned by Jews. Also, several of the executives and owners of the banks that financed the construction were Jewish, along with some of the architects, including Vilmos Freund, Mór Kallina, Zsigmond Quittner.

Some of the buildings on Andrássy út are especially significant from the point of view of Hungarian Jewish history.

(2) Wahrmann Palace

267. Portrait of Mór Wahrmann, 1868/69

Mór Wahrmann (1832–1892), an important public figure of his time, purchased this plot of land in 1882. He was the grandson of Israel Wahrmann, the first rabbi of Pest, the son of Mayer Wolf Wahrmann, a wealthy merchant, and himself became a well-to-do textile merchant and industrialist. He grew up speaking German at home, but he went to a Hungarian school, the Lutheran Gymnasium, and learned Hebrew from a private tutor. He also studied humanities at the Pest University. Already in 1847, at the age of 15, he started working in his father's linen-, sack- and huckaback-store at 1 Váci körút (today Bajcsy-Zsilinszky út), in the building which was later replaced by the Anker Palace. The company expanded and prospered in his time greatly. He was one of the founders of the *Pesti Lloyd Társulat* (Pester Lloyd Society) in 1853, the commercial federation of

Budapest which launched the *Pester Lloyd* in 1854, the German language daily of Pest in a morning and an evening edition. After his father's death in 1859, Wahrmann became the sole owner of the business with even more wealth and influence. He moved the company, Wahrmann u. Sohn, to Lipótváros, to the house right across the Basilica (10 *Drei Kronen Gasse* / Három Korona utca / Nagy Korona utca, today Hercegprímás utca). He lost his wife soon after their wedding in 1865. Wahrmann wanted to preserve her memory in a new enterprise, the Lujza Steam Mill.

Before moving to Andrássy út, Wahrmann had another apartment in Lipótváros, right next to the building of the Hungarian Academy of Sciences. Here, at 3 Akadémia utca–5 Arany János utca, he opened his new store. The offices were on the first floor, his apartment on the second. (Many, many years later, between the two world wars, another wealthy leader of the Jewish community, Samu Glückstahl rented the same apartment. Today only the building is the same: the Tänzer House, built by József Hild in 1836. A few years ago it was occupied by István Csurka and his right-wing party, their pub and restaurant.)

Wahrmann was always in favor of economic independence from Austria. He was a leading personality at the 1868/69 General Congress, its vice-president, the head of the Jewish delegation sent to King Francis Joseph I. He spoke up for the emancipation of Jews in the Jewish press already earlier and now came to the conviction that this can only be achieved through social assimilation. He won the support of Ferenc Deák—the most influential politician of the period—by his participation in the Congress.

268. Portrait of Mór Wahrmann

In 1869 he was elected the delegate from Lipótváros to the Parliament—the first Jewish MP in the Hungarian Parliament. (He won a mandate four times afterwards.) As for Deák's support, rumor has it that as opposed to his childhood friend and now his rival, Miksa Falk (1828–1908), whom Wahrmann asked to be the editor of *Pester Lloyd*, Deák thought that Wahrmann was the "real Jew" and that was why he had a better chance to get elected in Lipótváros.

Here is how Deák responded to Pál Tencer's request in the name of the rival candidates to choose between them:

> "I do wish that at the next elections some commercial personality be elected to Parliament because commercial interests are becoming more and more important to our country. (...) I find it desirable to enact the equality of the Jews in this respect soon..."

Apart from being an MP, Wahrmann was also the president of the *Budapesti Ipar- és Kereskedelmi Kamara* (Budapest Chamber of Industry and Commerce). He played an important role in financial matters. He was an expert in banking, knew the international monetary system well. On July 14, 1869, he held his maiden speech in Parliament about minting gold coins. He was the model for Adolf Ágai's "Börzeviczy W. M." (Moritz W. of the exchange market) in the satirical journal *Borsszem Jankó*.

269. Mór Wahrmann. Cartoon

270. Miksa Falk, editor-in-chief of the *Pester Lloyd* and Hungarian language teacher of Queen Elisabeth, wife of King Francis Joseph. Photo, ca. 1880

Lajos Szabolcsi wrote about Wahrmann in his *Memoirs* (1940/1942):

> "His (Wahrmann's) personality meant the power and pride of reviving Jewry. He sat in his presidential chair with the halo of power over his head, his influence and wealth shining on him. (...) Wahrmann *was* power, influence, authority and wealth."

According to a Yiddish saying: *An oysher hot umetum a daye*, "A rich man's opinion counts everywhere." Or to another one, *Gelt halt zikh nor in a grobn zak*: "Money stays only in a thick sack." As a matter of fact, Wahrmann was one of the wealthiest men of his age. A detailed city map from the year 1872, drafted by Sándor Halácsy, marks the huge blocks in Terézváros between today's Eötvös utca, Szondi utca and Bajnok utca as "Wahrmann's lots".

When in November 1883, upon the recommendation of Prime Minister and Minister of Interior Kálmán Tisza, Wahrmann was elected president of the Pest Jewish community, his rival was Ferenc Chorin, sr. During Wahrmann's presidency (already from 1876 on) the secretary of the community was Ignác Goldziher. In his *Diary* Goldziher did not have a single word of acknowledgment for Wahrmann. He called Wahrmann "His Wealthiness", "Polish moneybag" and complained that he tortured him. Their contemporaries, however, did not make a distinction between them, in their eyes it was the "Wahrmann–Goldziher regime". After all, both of them enhanced the Pest community, it was during their time that the community became the most powerful Jewish institution in Pest. In their time the Pest community was identified with Neolog Jewry.

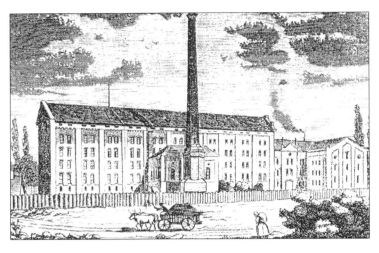

271. The Pannonia Steam Mill, 1864

As an MP Wahrmann always spoke up for the interests of Hungarian Jewry and freedom of religion. He would often start his arguments by saying, "As the Honorable House knows, I am a Jew myself." The minutes of the Parliament testify that this statement was often followed by applause from the MPs. He never attended Parliamentary sessions on Yom Kippur—he spent this day at the Dohány Temple. Of course, he was often called to read from the Torah on Sabbath, and he always knew his duty, when it came to giving *shnoder* or alms. It was him who first—in 1872—proposed in the Parliament the unification of the capital, that is, joining Buda and Óbuda to Pest. During the trials of the Tiszaeszlár blood libel he would indulge in sharp retorts to the anti-Semitic speeches of Győző Istóczy. Istóczy provoked him to a duel, and the small, corpulent Wahrmann accepted the challenge (1883). The duel took place near Ercsi, on a forest clearing. The infraction was later tried at the Court of Székesfehérvár. The penalty for the illegal duel was eight days of imprisonment for both parties.

272. Mór Wahrmann dozing off at the (private) concert given by the [Jenő] Hubay-[Dávid] Popper Quartet, ca. 1888

At the preparation of the emancipation law (Act XLII of 1895) Wahrmann was opposed by some younger members of the community who wanted civil equality for all Hungarian citizens of the Jewish faith, not just for the wealthier classes. Wahrmann was afraid that they might provoke a new anti-Semitic movement, that his position may be questioned along with what he stood for: the integration of Jewry into the Hungarian society according to financial status. His opponents thought that Wahrmann was haughty and refused to reelect him as president in 1892; but the new president was also from the generation of the Congress. Wahrmann was already ill at that time and he passed away a few days later. In his will he left a considerable sum to the Hungarian Academy of Sciences to support various projects. His foundation was abolished in 1949 during the nationalization of all foundations. At the Rabbinical Seminary Simon Hevesi, the future rabbi of the Dohány Temple, felt honored to deliver his eulogy (*hesped*) on December 22, 1892. All of Wahrmann's three children converted to the Roman Catholic faith, the two sons immediately after their father's death, the beloved daughter, Rebecca (Rifke / Regina / Rene) only a few years later.

The architects of the three-story Wahrmann Palace on Andrássy út were Vilmos Freund and János Kauser. The construction was completed in 1885. The Flora-statues of Alajos Stróbl still stand next to the entrance. A noteworthy aspect of the house is its original wrought iron banister in the staircase decorated with iron flowers and dragons, the lamp posts and the few remaining stained glass windows, the latter from the workshop of Ede Kratzmann. The walls facing the courtyard on the third floor are decorated with murals depicting mythological scenes. The owner of the house used to live on the second floor. This luxurious, elegant apartment is remarkable even in its current condition. Every detail suggests that its owner lived up to his social rank and financial status. The enormous halls were the scene of high life: fine balls with elegant people, maybe even concerts. The walls and the ceiling are covered with costly wood carvings, as are the two fire-places. There used to be some famous paintings as well. Wahrmann was a passionate art collector and after his wife's death these paintings were his only consolation. The meandering decoration around the window-frames could even be mistaken for swastikas a few decades later. The community president's taste conformed to the fashion of his times.

273. Mausoleum of Mór Wahrmann

Wahrmann's grave is in the cemetery in Salgótarjáni utca. The tomb is the work of Zsigmond Quittner.

Wahrmann's memory is preserved by a street name, too, and at an unexpected place at that, in Új-Lipótváros. Earlier a larger street was named after him in the northern part of this developing area, close to his former lots. After World War II, in 1952, this street was renamed after Victor Hugo and Wahrmann was compensated thirty years later by a small street nearby, North of Szent István park, at the corner of Pozsonyi út and Victor Hugo utca: the Wahrmann Mór köz (lane). There are only two houses in this lane.

(3) 43 Andrássy út and Two Neighboring Buildings, nos. 39 and 41

The three-story house was built in 1880, in early eclectic style. On the third floor was József Friedmann's kosher inn, the Karmel, with 24 guest rooms. The painted ceiling of the beautifully reconstructed doorway is a major tourist attraction.

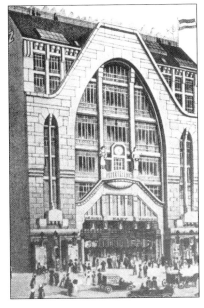

274. The Párisi Nagy Áruház (Department Store) on Andrássy út

The neighboring building, no. 41, was designed between 1880 and 1885 by Mór Kallina, one of the architects of the "Rombach" synagogue. In 1904 the Goldberger family—owners of the textile factory in Óbuda—purchased the building. Except for Leó Goldberger, who chose to live in a more peaceful area, at neighboring 45 Benczúr utca, the family lived here until the deportations, the survivors even until the nationalization in 1948. Today the building is in poor condition, so it is worthwhile to have a look at it only from the outside.

It was the Goldbergers who ordered the construction of the *Párisi Nagy Áruház* (Paris Department Store) in 1911, right next door. The predecessors of the store were a small and cramped bazaar on the corner of Kerepesi út / Rákóczi út and Klauzál utca and the Párisi Nagy Áruház on Rákóczi út which burned down in 1903. The previous building on the Andrássy út plot was the Terézvárosi Casino. This was designed by Gusztáv Petschacher (1844–1890), the frescoes on the ceiling of the ballroom were painted by Károly Lotz (1887–1904), the other frescos

by Árpád Feszty (1856–1914). During the construction of the Department Store the ballroom
facing Paulay Ede utca was retained and incorporated into the new building. The latter, an Art
Nouveau building, easily admitted a historicizing element. The blueprints of the department store were prepared by Zsigmond Sziklai
(1864–?), the contractor was the Casino's architect, Gusztáv Petschacher. The interior space is
open, divided by galleries. The five-story building encompasses a courtyard covered with
glass, and the elevators are also made of glass
and mirrors. On top of the building there is a lookout. The Párisi Nagy Áruház was the first modern
department store building in Budapest, it belonged to the Goldberger factory. For some decades, until
recently, it was called *Divatcsarnok,* today its name is *Párizsi Nagyáruház.*

(4) The Transformation of Terézváros

The elegance of Sugár / Andrássy út spread to the surrounding areas as well. By the end of the nineteenth century the neighboring streets were filled with palaces. Next to these Neo-Baroque palaces
some smaller, three–four-story houses were built in the same style, though on a smaller scale and
often of lesser quality. The image of the city changed, and so did its population. Government employees and other officials moved here, but the Jews stayed, too. The old Jewish population extended
the Jewish quarter around Király utca towards North–Northwest, but they did not leave. Some of
them, those who were already part of the new order of the "official Hungary", moved into these new
houses either as tenants or as owners. These people were no longer just members of the Jewish community: they had a civil status, even if a low one. The neighborhood around Andrássy út was like a
social staircase for the upwardly mobile Jewish middle class. They became gentlemen without leaving their original environment. Many of them still attended their old synagogue, mostly the "Dohány",
the most distinctive one. Of course, the percentage of Jews within the general population was much
lower here than in Király utca.

The elegant avenue cut through Terézváros, but it did not divide the Jewish quarter. The Jewish
quarter was barely affected whether architecturally or socially. Terézváros spreads more or less sym-
metrically on both sides of Andrássy út and the Jewish world of these two half districts did not differ greatly either. On both sides the streets belonged to the lower-middle class, craftsmen, small businesses, workshops. As if the Jewish quarter of Teréz- and Erzsébetváros had simply spread to the
other side of Andrássy út, towards North.

(5) The Baumgarten Foundation

The house at 15 Szerecsen utca / Paulay Ede utca used to belong to the Baumgarten family. They
moved to Budapest from the Rhine region and remained attracted to the German culture. In the last
third of the nineteenth century the wealthy branch of the family consisted of several brothers. Alajos
Baumgarten, "landlord and grain merchant", owned two other houses as well, the buildings at
15 Nagy Korona utca / Wekerle Sándor utca, (today 13 Hercegprímás utca), and the one at 11 Erzsébet
tér. His brother, Ignác Baumgarten, was a grain merchant too. Half of the building in Szerecsen utca,
built in 1897, was owned by Lajos Baumgarten, the third of the brethren, and the other half, by Ignác
and his five children. Lajos Baumgarten owned several other valuable buildings as well. (The
Szerecsen utca house became the property of a certain Mór Vasvári.)

The actual Baumgarten House was the palace in Lipótváros, at 15 Nagy Korona utca / 13 Herceg-prímás utca. Fülöp Baumgarten commissioned the plans from Lőrinc Zofahl. The Neo-Renaissance-style building was completed in 1861. At the level of the second and third floors the facade is decorated with three Ionic half pillars. In the courtyard there is a well made of red marble, like in several other houses in Terézváros. The owner of the house—as it was customary—lived on the second floor.

A typical way of bourgeois social mobility was the one which the Baumgartens took. They invested the money gained from trade into real estate in Budapest. The income from renting houses was competitive with that of landowners. Owning a house meant a considerable income, and two or three houses could mean a whole fortune.

One member of the family, Ferenc Ferdinánd Baumgarten (1880-1927), an aesthete and literary critic who spent much of his youth in Berlin and Munich, and wrote his literary essays and studies in German, in 1923 bequeathed all of his wealth of 1,200,000 pengő for a foundation to promote contemporary Hungarian literature.

> "It is difficult to tell his nationality. He was born a Jew, son of a homeless, wandering race. His language, culture, field of interest and literary oeuvre were German, and he felt one only with the Weimar Germany, the republic which evaporated in front of our very eyes. Yet, by an act of generosity, he turned not towards German but Hungarian literature, and also his remains are buried in Hungarian soil. Where did this homeless soul belong, where were his true roots which could never be severed throughout his wanderings? (...) Baumgarten belonged to Pest. He was a citizen of Pest in the noblest and rarest definition of the word, he was a conscious heir to the bourgeois traditions and behavior of old Pest. He was a late offspring of a patrician family of old Pest..."
>
> (Antal Szerb, 1937)

The interest on the assets of the Baumgarten Foundation has been supplying grants since 1929 continuously until after World War II, when the Foundation was terminated in 1949. The Baumgarten Award given annually on January 18, the anniversary of the founder's death (that is, on his *Jahrzeit*), and the monthly scholarships offered for outstanding Hungarian poetry, prose and criticism meant an acknowledgment of the highest order and an important means of support.

> "This is not about *rewarding talent* or giving alms providing temporary relief from financial difficulties. This means freedom, independence and work opportunity for the Spirit." (Mihály Babits, 1927)

The board of trustees of the Baumgarten Foundation consisted of Mihály Babits, Aladár Schöpflin and the lawyer Lóránt Basch, who made their decisions according to the aesthetic principles of the distinguished literary periodical, *Nyugat*. The Baumgarten Award meant literary prestige and respect for the recipient.

The Foundation maintained an excellent library of Hungarian literature in Lipótváros (1 Sas utca), which also became a central meeting point for writers and literary critics. The Baumgarten Library and its reading room occupied two rooms on the second floor of the building: the bookshelves and the librarian's desk were in the inner room, while the readers' desks equipped with green lamps were in the front room. The two were separated by a tile stove heating both of the rooms and a wooden counter. It was a friendly place, open three times a week, twice in the afternoon and once in the morning. Librarians were appointed for three years; this position was itself a sort of stipend, as well.

Between 1942 and 1944 the librarian of the Baumgarten Foundation was Gábor Devecseri (1917-1971), the outstanding, philologically accurate and poetic translator of the epics of Homer into Hungarian. Here is how he remembered the Baumgarten Library in his memoirs.

> "Apart from the books of Ferenc Baumgarten, the library on the second floor of the Sas utca building also housed the collections of Árpád Tóth, György Király and Dezső Kosztolányi and, in the final years, the books and office furniture of Mihály Babits were also kept here, in a separate room. Promoters of literature dropped by one after the other in this half library, half shrine. Writers and scholars came here to read and

to open their hearts, to report the great news happening in some faraway corner of the literary world and some nasty news about their colleagues next door. (...) The newly acquired wonderful collection of English books entered the library with the catalogue of Mihály Babits. (...) The collection was first organized by György Sárközi, the first librarian, but all the following librarians, Endre Illés, László Fenyő and the others added some imprint of their personality. Among poets of the immediate and distant past Ferenc Baumgarten, Zoltán Ambrus and Ernő Osvát were gazing at the readership from the walls. (...) The library lived. Now, after its death by fire, it is hard to describe the treasures lost."

("Egy könyvtár emléke" [Recollection of a Library], in: *Lágymányosi istenek* [Gods of Lágymányos], 1967)

The building at 1 Sas utca was hit by a bomb in the summer of 1944 and it burned down completely, along with the whole library.

Next to the entrance of the house built on its place there is a slab (1989) commemorating Ferenc Baumgarten's merits.

(6) Parisiana (35 Paulay Ede utca)

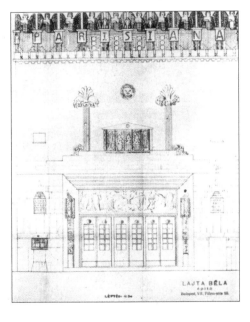

276. The Parisiana Nightclub. Design by Béla Lajta, 1908

The Parisiana Nightclub opened in 1909. It was built according to the design of Béla Lajta in the place of Adolf Friedmann's earlier variety theater of 1896. Lajta's building in itself has little to do with the Jewish community, and even less with Judaism. On the contrary, it served the worldly, mundane entertainment needs of the rising bourgeoisie in a way the synagogue did and could not, no matter how Neolog it might have been. Nevertheless, bourgeois development in Hungary, and especially in Budapest, was carried out partially, if not mostly by Jews, and the Parisiana's architect himself was Jewish. True, he did not build the Nightclub as a Jew. His task was an architectural one, to plan a tasteful and stylish building with modern, up-to-date technique.

Talking about the Parisiana is a good opportunity to formulate our opinion that Jews who participated in shaping the face of the city around 1900 did not do so to create Jewish values. Those who engaged in trade and export, prominent figures of the stock exchange may very well have been of Jewish origin or faith, but their professional life had nothing to do with this fact. They participated as citizens, and with a strong Hungarian national identity at that. The face of Budapest created mostly by the Jewish bourgeoisie shows no Jewish traits whatsoever. Much like Mihály Pollack and József Hild had earlier planned buildings for their Jewish customers, including the Jewish community, in the style of the period, so did these modern architects who happened to be Jews shape the city's face according to contemporary style. The difference between the facade of the Parisiana and the neighboring buildings is not that one is Jewish and the others are not, but that one is a modern, Art Nouveau building, while the others are Neo-Baroque.

Lajta chose the Near Eastern version of Orientalizing Art Nouveau for the Parisiana. The architectural remains of this Orientalizing style are the large, plain rectangular walls, frequent repetition of the same architectonic and decorative elements, and some motifs typical of Ancient Mesopotamia, such as the "*zikkurrat* motif", terraced rectangles. These designs, observed in the Mesopotamian collection of the Louvre, recalled the air of Paris, as did the Art Nouveau (*Sezession*) in general. The Art Nouveau in the Parisiana can be traced in a mixture of many kinds of noble materials, marble, metals—copper and aluminum—, glass, etc. used as shiny surfaces, bright colors, and of Hungarian folk motifs as decorative elements.

"Its white marble facade adorned with those angular, dim statues makes it look like a Masonic lodge or a pharaoh's tomb"

—wrote Endre Nagy about the building in Szerecsen utca in his novel *A kabaré regénye* [Novel of the Cabaret] in 1935. It seems that the building reminded him of an international style and he associated freemasonry with cosmopolitanism.

Lajta's choice of style strongly influenced the bourgeois architecture of the period. Even Jewish community buildings were built in a later version of that style, like the Orthodox synagogue in Kazinczy utca and the Heroes' Temple in Wesselényi utca.

Here is what the art historian Ferenc Dávid said about the original building of the Parisiana on the occasion of its recent renovation for which he was doing the research into the architectural history of the building:

"The theater is the type of building which is the best at expressing the victory of the bourgeoisie over the aristocracy, because this is the home, or rather the temple, of culture and education... This new genre of architecture was adopted from the palaces, from the castles. The theater became the center of social life in the city, the scene of the new kind of festivals, of splendor, thus understandably, a place of luxury and magnificence. The nightclub, the bastardized version of the theater and the *liebling* of large cities is equally luxurious, but of course it is only a cheap imitation of the theater with brash colors, gold, velvet and mirrors."

Lajta created a well-planned nightclub on the relatively small plot. In the front of the building there was a smaller room with a separate entrance from a separate staircase. The main entrance opened into a foyer with a gallery. The main hall itself was an especially gaudy room: high ceiling, trapezoid-shaped, huge marble surfaces with golden, layered rims. Against the back wall there were some boxes and a tiny stage in the front.

In 1921 the building was transformed into a theater, according to the plans of László Vágó. It was called "Blaha Lujza" Theater. Two extra floors of balconies were added in the main hall and the angular forms were replaced by the Neo-Empire style. There were only some minor changes to the facade: an inscription and a small glass canopy over the entrance. Later the name of the building was changed as well: it was called *Kristálypalota*, "Crystal Palace" or *Táncpalota*, "Dance Palace". Some additional changes between 1950 and 1962 ruined the facade completely. In 1991 the Municipality reconstructed the building with its original facade and the nicely structured foyer, but kept the theater as designed by Vágó. The new theater building—called "Arany János" Theater until 1994, today New Theater—restored the historical presence of Art Nouveau in the face of Budapest.

277. The facade of the Parisiana, ca. 1910

278. The facade of the Theater in Paulay Ede utca after the 1991 restoration

279. Foyer of the Blaha Lujza Theater. Design by László Vágó, 1921

(7) Two Jewish Journals: *Egyenlőség* and *Múlt és Jövő*

Egyenlőség—meaning "Equality"—was the most important organ of Hungarian Jewish society in the decades between 1881 and 1938. It came to existence at the time of the Tiszaeszlár blood libel in 1881 and its trial in the following two years from the daily reports written by Móric Bogdányi. The paper grew out of Móric Bogdányi's daily bulletins. Shortly after the case ended, Miksa Szabolcsi (1857–1915) took over the editorial tasks (1884). His thorough knowledge of Jewish traditions which he acquired in yeshivas was paired with an instinctive talent for journalism. His son, Lajos Szabolcsi (1889–1943) con-

tinued the work after his death. The editorial office itself was for a long time located in Szabolcsi's home at 2/A Lövölde tér. The readership of *Egyenlőség* came from among the Neolog Jews of Pest, those Jews who wished to integrate into Hungarian society. *Egyenlőség* fought for Jewish emancipation in Hungary. Its cause was supported by Hungarian parliamentary forces as well as a wide range of social groups. It was a forum for the literature produced by emancipated Hungarian Jews. Among its contributors were Adolf Ágai, Ignotus (Hugó Veigelsberg), József Kiss, Tamás Kóbor, and the prominent novelist of Jewish life, Péter Újvári (Pinhas Judah Groszmann) (1869–1931). In its time *Egyenlőség* was the only prominent Jewish confessional newspaper, with a circulation of up to 40,000 copies. Perusing it today we can see that even its advertisements are of interest, they serve as historical documents of a sort. Lajos Szabolcsi also published the Hungarian translation of Heinrich Grätz's monumental Jewish history representing the view of the *Wissenschaft des Judentums* on history, *A zsidók egyetemes története 6 kötetben, Grätz nagy műve alapján és különös tekintettel a magyar zsidók történetére* [The Universal History of Jews in 6 Volumes, Based on the Monumental Work of Grätz with Special Emphasis on Hungarian Jews] (1906–1908). The additional chapters on Hungarian

280. Portrait of Miksa Szabolcsi

Jewry were written by Károly Sebestyén "adapted from Sámuel Kohn's book", as the title page informs us.

The editors of *Egyenlőség* were distrustful of Zionism and even rejected it, they were afraid that the movement would jeopardize their main issue, the fight for emancipation and the integration into Hungarian society. But they did not reject any aspect of Jewish tradition. Miksa Szabolcsi himself organized the first Jewish pilgrimage to Palestine in 1905. 145, mostly Neolog Jews joined the three-week trip on a rented private ship between Fiume, Haifa and back. This first large group of European Jewish pilgrims to Palestine was greeted by the honorary consul of Austria-Hungary in the port, whence they proceeded to Jerusalem. These emancipated, Europeanized Jews from Pest were deeply moved by the sight of the "Holy Land".

"We heard mothers trying to take their children home from the playground in Hebrew, we heard these tiny little men chasing each other in Hebrew, playing ball in Hebrew, telling each other in Hebrew what their father had brought home from the fair and occasionally even beating each other in Hebrew. I heard a mother singing a lullaby to her child in Hebrew, a language in which some Jewish scholars can hardly even mumble."
(Miksa Szabolcsi, in: *Egyenlőség*, May 14, 1905)

Egyenlőség was closed down after the passing of the First (Anti-)Jewish Law in 1938 and with it perished the last hope for *equality* as well, for the time being.

Bence Szabolcsi, Miksa Szabolcsi's son, was another prominent member of the Szabolcsi family. He was elected a member of the Royal Asiatic Society in 1936 for his achievements in the field of Jewish musicology and folklore. Bence Szabolcsi was a great scholar of music history, a member of the Hungarian Academy of Sciences (from 1948 on a corresponding member, from 1955 on, regular), a professor at the Music Academy (1945). Before World War II—besides his research in music history—he also published essays on the history and current problems of Hungarian Jewry.

*

Múlt és Jövő ("Past and Future") was created almost in opposition to the forces of *Egyenlőség*. During its entire existence between 1911 and 1944, it was published and edited by József Patai (1882–1953), a former contributor of *Egyenlőség*, who also determined the image of the journal. The editorial office moved several times: from 6 Podmaniczky utca, they moved to 14 Révay utca and then to 34 Vilmos császár út (today Bajcsy-Zsilinszky út). Young Jews, whose taste was formed by the Art Nouveau, as the cover of *Múlt és Jövő* reveals, became increasingly dissatisfied with the harmful side effects of assimilation and, in search of wider perspectives of Jewish life, they turned towards Zionism and Palestine. *Múlt és Jövő* regularly published reports and photos about the *halutz* movement, about Jewish pioneer settlers in Palestine and the latest developments in the construction of *Eretz*. *Múlt és Jövő* was the Zionist journal of Pest, helping to define intellectual and emotional approaches to Zionism. The Jewish intellectuals of Budapest joined mainstream Zionism through this Hungarian language literary and cultural journal. Patai's home, for a while at 18 Fillér utca–22 Nyúl utca, was almost like a second editorial office of *Múlt és Jövő*. Patai himself moved to Palestine in 1940 but continued to participate in the publication of the journal from there. *Múlt és Jövő* ceased publication at the time of the German occupation; the last issue came out in March 1944.

281. Portrait of József Patai. Photo, ca. 1915

Patai's literary career started in 1902 with some poems written in Hebrew. Immediately after his first trip to Palestine in 1926 he became a strong advocate of the Zionist ideal and its practical realization. In 1927, with the support of Károly Baracs and others, he organized the Pro-Palestine Association of Hungarian Jews, which offered an organizational framework for intellectuals who wished to express their consent and support. The leadership of the Jewish community of Pest opposed Zionism and it took them almost a decade to reconcile with Patai and the Zionist movement. The Pro-Palestine Association became an advocate for the Hebrew University of Jerusalem, founded only a few years earlier, in 1925. József Patai's son, Ervin György or Raphael Patai (1910–1996) studied there after completing his years at the Rabbinical Seminary of Pest and the usual year in Breslau. He also earned a doctorate at The Hebrew University in 1936. (The title of his thesis was *Ha-Mayim. A Study in Palestinology and Palestinian Folklore*.) For a few years he traveled back and forth between Budapest and Palestine until he finally settled down to pursue scholarship abroad.

Egyenlőség served the case of the rights and adaptation of Hungarian Jews at home, in the Diaspora, while *Múlt és Jövő* helped promote the idea of a Jewish homeland and state. Both journals, both trends had readers and followers, sometimes the same people. The historical events in Hitler's Germany and in Hungary did not *decide* the debate, they only *ended* it brutally.

(8) Café "Japán" and Ernst Museum

The Café "Japán", located at 45 Andrássy út, on the corner of Gyár utca / Liszt Ferenc tér was among the most famous literary cafés of Budapest in the interwar period. Opened in 1890, it received its name after the Orientalizing pattern of the tiles covering the walls. In 1909 Richárd Weisz (1879–1945), a wrestler and weight-lifter, Olympic champion (London, 1908), member of the *Magyar Testgyakorlók Köre* (MTK) (Circle of Hungarian Exercisers), bought the place with the financial help of Alfréd Brüll. Weisz's family also owned the Hotel Continental in Lipótváros, where the *Nyugat* was edited at that time. For a while Richárd Weisz himself worked there, at the bar. In "Japán" he kept strict order, but he was also very kind to the artists. After World War I his debts increased to the point where he had to sell the Café.

There are stories about how Weisz would walk around the streets of Budapest in the fall of 1919 with a board proclaiming: "I am Jewish." Hardly anyone would dare provoke *him*, after all.

In the "restaurant and café" period of literature the "Japán" and the "Continental" were tied not only by the common ownership but also by their guests. The architect Ödön Lechner, former master of Béla Lajta; the painters Pál Szinyei Merse and Károly Kernstok; and later the writers Ferenc Molnár, Lajos Nagy, Attila József, and the opera singer Mihály Székely would visit these places regularly.

The former interior of the former café cannot be recognized anymore. The rooms house the *Írók Könyvesboltja* (Writers' Book Store) today.

One of the regular visitors at the "Japán" was Lajos Ernst (1872–1937) whose family history is almost the Pest-Jewish version of *The Buddenbrooks*. At the beginning of his career in arts, between 1907 and 1912, he was the director of the National Salon but there he was confronted by the official academic art. In these years he managed to establish the largest and richest private collection of art history and contemporary art using the income of his father, a rich grain and flour merchant. Leaving the National Salon in 1912, he had the Ernst Museum built right next to the Café Japán, at 8 Nagymező utca, to house and exhibit his collection there. The building itself was planned

282. Regular guests of Café Japán, ca. 1912. Among them Pál Szinyei Merse (second from the left) and József Rippl-Rónai (with a cane)

by Gyula Fodor (1872–1942), the benches in the foyer by Ödön Lechner, the stained-glass windows of the staircase by József Rippl-Rónai (1861–1927). There were apartments in the house, among them two huge and well-lit studio-apartments on the top floor, which were used for decades by the painter Adolf Fényes (1867–1945) and the graphic artist István Zádor (1882–1963).

On the second floor of the building, next to the Museum proper, Lajos Ernst opened the first modern art gallery of Budapest, an excellent exhibition hall destined for showing Hungarian contemporary art. The gallery functioned successfully for decades; after 1917 there were even auctions held here. This is where the collection of works of the painter Lajos Gulácsy (1882–1932) was exhibited in 1922, and this is where the art of Tivadar Csontváry Kosztka (1853–1919) was on display in 1930, first time after his death. Lajos Ernst could not cope with the effects of the great depression and committed suicide in 1937. Today, pieces from his collection enrich the Hungarian National Museum, the Museum of Applied Arts, the Museum of Fine Arts and the Opera House. The Ernst Museum itself has remained a prestigious gallery of contemporary art.

(9) Behind Andrássy út

At the turn of the nineteenth and twentieth centuries there were no traces left of the dirty and smelly trades and shops of the preceding century North of Andrássy út, and the industries that maintain every-day Jewish life decreased in number, too. One had to go a little further to find a grocery, a kosher butcher or a *mikveh*, beyond the elegant Andrássy út. However, the minor streets here, from South to North, Révay utca (formerly Rettig Gasse / Retek utca), Lázár utca, Ó utca (formerly Neu Gasse / Új utca, later on Alt Gasse), Zichy Jenő utca (formerly Neu Gasse / Új utca) and Dessewffy utca (formerly Drei Herzen Gasse / Három Szív utca), and the small cross-streets, Káldy Gyula utca (formerly Laudon utca), Dobó utca and Dalszínház utca, as well as the main arteries, Hajós utca, Nagymező utca and Gyár utca / Jókai utca were hardly better than the *old-old* Jewish quarter nearby, full of the same kinds of shops, and they were certainly not to be compared to Lipótváros or to Andrássy út itself. These were service roads of the latter. The railroad came all the way into Gyár utca, flooding the city with people from the countryside in search of work, buying and selling. The people living here were not only those who could not afford to live in the palaces of Andrássy út, not even on the top floors, or people who were not welcome to live there; they were also, and mainly, the people whose services were used by the aristocracy of the mansions. They were servants and employees, who were certainly considered better than the population of Király utca or Szerecsen utca.

As we take an imaginary walk along these streets the scene is fairly uniform. We know from historical sources that in Dessewffy utca alone there was a paper factory (at 37), a book bindery (at 6), a textile and garment shop (at 30, in Margit Courtyard), a lace manufacturer (at 3–5), a washing and dying workshop (at 14) and a precision instrument workshop (at 79), etc. As far as we can tell on the basis of names, secondary sources and the changes in ownership during World War II, all of these manufactures were owned by Jews.

The most precious manufacturer of Terézváros was at 32 Dessewffy utca: the *Első Magyar Betűöntöde Rt.* (First Hungarian Type Foundry Ltd.). The workshop was founded in 1898; they also did some printing, but were primarily focused on type casting. The owner, Salamon Löwy (1874–?) was the best of his profession in interwar Hungary. He delivered types to several printing houses. Even Imre Kner (1890–1945), the famous typographer of the Gyoma Printing House, borrowed Hebrew fonts from him.

In 1857 the *Minta Elemi Főtanoda* (Model Higher School) was opened in Lázár utca, at the corner of Lázár utca and Hermina tér (today 10 Dalszínház utca, next to the far left side of the Opera House). Two years later the school was renamed National Israelite Teachers' College. Later the school was moved to Józsefváros, right next to the building of the Rabbinical Seminary.

In Dessewffy utca there were numerous brothels, too, at nos. 9, 22, 35 and 49 among others. This neighborhood was not the closed world of Király utca anymore, but nor was it shining with the elegance of Andrássy út, either. It was beyond the elegant, luxurious quarter, with all the typical characteristics of transition. The brothel was just another, fairly common institution of urban life: in the nineteenth century there were several other similar "houses" nearby, e.g. a building with a large hall at 30 Nagymező utca (today the restaurant "Lila Ákác" [Wistaria]), or at 4 and 62 Nagymező utca, or just small, furnished rooms for an hour.

The business of paid love is old in this neighborhood, the red-light district is certainly older than the Jewish quarter. In 1808 the Pest Civic Commercial Board protested that there were some good-for-nothing who joined with a woman, sometimes even under the bonds of marriage, to open a decorating store or something of the kind, which was only a facade to a chamber inside, avoiding exposure and shame. As we saw in the Purim description from *Budapesti rejtelmek* [Mysteries of Budapest], the pubs and dens of iniquity in the Terézváros were frequented by drunkards, thieves, gamblers and the like.

> "This is where all the international café-muses dwell, here are the various music halls and nightclubs with their loose manners and juicy jokes; here, in Erzsébetváros, is the nest of some female bands of dubious character."
> (Jenő Rákosi, in: *Az osztrák-magyar Monarchia írásban és képben* [The Austro-Hungarian Monarchy in Words and Pictures], 1893)

There was a great variety of playhouses, brothels, dining places, pubs and similar institutions.

The most famous one was the "Blaue Katz" / "Kék Macska" [Blue Cat] at 10 Király utca, where all kinds of guests were entertained for over a century. In 1861 it became a music hall ("Dalcsarnok"). "People from all over delighted in this wild animal. But it should rather have been called the blue pig, since the sounds that were heard there were more similar to grunts than to meows. Even a soldier would have been embarrassed to hear them" (Porzó / Adolf Ágai, *Utazás Pestről – Budapestre* [Journey from Pest to Budapest], 1912).

Otherwise this was where the delivery boys, messengers and porters used to assemble. People today hardly know what a porter was, except for those who read the works of Gyula Krúdy. These "red-cap" porters not only carried heavy packages home from the market but they also delivered all kinds of perfumed letters, flowers, manuscripts and the like. Theirs was a confidential job. The porters, wearing a red cap with an identification number, used to stand all around the city at busy corners or in front of cafés, waiting for someone to request their services. They usually got paid twice, both by the sender and by the receiver.

From the gloomy contemplations of Móczl Füttylesi ("who waits for a whistle"):

> "If someone whispers an order, I can already feel the double payment for my services in my hand. He who shouts out loud is a shabby customer. It is the same at the papers—articles that are discreetly suggested are better rewarded than the yelling of the opposition."
> (*Üstökös* [Comet], January 11, 1891)

There were two classes of coachmen. One drove the hansom cab, pulled by a single horse, carrying one or two passengers in the back, under a leather hood; the other drove the more elegant two-horse hackney carriage where the passengers rode in a closed cabin with a glass window. In Pest the hansom cab was more in fashion. The coachmen were simple people, and modesty was an essential requirement in this profession, too.

(10) The Synagogue in Dessewffy utca

The building which stands in a courtyard was originally a coachmen's stable: the typical architectural design of the stables can still be traced on the arched, red-brick wall of the synagogue. The syna-

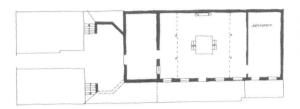

gogue was opened in 1870, and it was mostly the "red-cap" porters from the neighborhood who came here to *daven—* movers, porters, and delivery men. It was actually called the Porters' Synagogue. Their union was called *Nosei Massa*, "Carriers of Load". The building also housed the headquarters of the *Budapest Székesfővárosi Közszolga Ipartársulat Betegsegélyező és Önsegélyező Egyesülete* ("Sick Fund and Self-aid Society of the Budapest Public Servants' Industrial Association").

283. Ground-plan of the Dessewffy utca synagogue

284. The new marble *almemor* of the Bikur Cholim Synagogue in Dessewffy utca, ca. 1935

Around 1910 a new association was formed under the name *Aur Chodesch* (or *hodesh*, "the light of new moon") with different, middle class members. They joined the synagogue, but within a few years the Public Servants' Aid Society was again in charge of the house. In 1925 the Bikur Cholim Society took over the synagogue, enlarged and reconstructed it and added a hall and a new *bimah* made of Carrara marble around 1935. Older people still refer to it as the Carriers' Synagogue. In any case, it is a simple, friendly, *heimish shtibl*, an Orthodox prayer-room. From the courtyard it has the atmosphere of a manor house. The original porter's cubicle or office left of the entrance from the street is used today as a Talmud-Torah and a youth club.

(11) A Kosher Eatery: "The Niszel"

At 14 Révay utca, in the early 1950s there was "the Niszel / Niszl", the only kosher eatery of the period. Earlier their business was in Rombach utca, right next to Stern's restaurant; though it did not compete with that in elegance. (During the weeks of the Pest ghetto in 1944 both Stern and Niszel served as public kitchens.) Niszel's son-in-law also had a small kosher kitchen on the corner of Király utca and Kazinczy utca. After the war the two firms merged. The new eatery was run by the son-in-law, Mr. Goldmann, and the old Niszel remained, probably as a co-owner, merely as a decoration of the restaurant.

The area is clearly an extension of Teréz- and Erzsébetváros. It was the home of small trade. No. 16 was Schottola's rubber store, at no. 6 one found Glückstahl's clothing store and several tailors. No. 14, the location of Niszel's, was on the left side of the street, right across Dobó utca. A rather insignificant building, but there is a spectacular Neo-Gothic ornament on the facade. At the end of the nineteenth century its owner was the Biach family. The restaurant was to the right of the entrance, the kitchen had a separate door to the courtyard.

"The only light in the bleak room was supplied by some weak light bulbs hanging from the ceiling on wires. Straight-backed chairs, cheap wooden tables—the furniture was plain and lacked any adornment, comfort or coziness except for that one red velvet sofa which stood along the thin wall dividing the kitchen from the room. Old *Niszel bácsi* [Uncle Niszel] sat here, next to the fireplace, all day long, wearing his always-clean Sabbath silk kaftan and his obligatory hat. With his winter-white beard covering his chest he looked more like one of the Biblical Patriarchs than a restaurant owner. He did not care about business or other such worldly matters. He was way over eighty, maybe even over ninety. He was only concerned with eternity, the heavenly Jerusalem and the like. He was usually leafing through his Hebrew prayer-book, interrupting this devout activity only at dinner time..."   (István Lakatos, *Farsang* [Carnival. A Novel], 1982–1992)

It is rare in the literature of the generations after Gyula Krúdy, the writer who devoted long sections in his novels to describing fine food, but Niszel's eatery is mentioned by several authors in the early 1950s on the basis of personal experience. Being close to the Opera House and the Vidám Színpad (Comedy Theater), it was favored by artists, singers, actors, writers and other Bohemian intellectuals. They liked its unusual atmosphere, the Jewish nostalgia and the good food. It was visited not only by Jews but by all kinds of folksy characters.

The variety of strictly kosher dishes must have been something extraordinary in the midst of the sea of boring food offered by regular restaurants. Here one could order meat soup with *matzah* balls, fried goose liver, stuffed goose neck, stuffed turkey neck, *halzli* (*helzl*) spiced with garlic, ox tongue in almond-raisin sauce, *flódni* (*fladen*), kindli and other such delicacies.

There were, however, some drunkards and evil tongues who came to Niszel's. They spread all kinds of *rumors* about the quality of food.

According to a Yiddish saying: *In eyn tsholent un in a shidekh kukt men nisht tsufil arayn*, "Do not look into a *tsholent* and a marriage too closely."

"(...) It was a simple room with no decoration, just the smell of cooked vegetables. On the checkered wax tablecloth covering one of the tables there was a bowl decorated with Hebrew letters, in it a few stale biscuits. The lack of certain pieces of furniture in the eatery was compensated by the total exclusion of the outside world. There were no pictures on the walls, no appeals and no warnings. Above the swing-door leading to the kitchen, however, there was one single sign, as customary in state restaurants calling our attention to some important article of the Constitution [of 1949]. But *Mandel bácsi* [Uncle Niszel] on his sign only wished to say: "We clean *talesim* and add fringes, we embroider *tales* sacks." Fringing the prayer-shawls and embroidering the velvet sacks was, no doubt, the evening occupation of *Mandel néni* [Aunt Niszel]. (...) They only served one kind of wine, the transparent, tart Riesling, which they harvested in the Verpeléti Vineyard of the Jewish community, under strict rabbinical supervision. Next to the *tsholent* this wine was the second greatest attraction of Mandel bácsi's tiny restaurant. (...) The biscuits were baked at a bakery in Síp utca, from goose fat and goose crackling."   (G. György Kardos, *Jutalomjáték* [Benefit Performance. A Novel], 1993)

At Niszel's, some priority was always given to the Orthodox Jewish customers. Rabbinical students came here to eat regularly. On Jewish holidays, at Purim or Passover, and maybe for weddings, the restaurant was closed to the public, these were held privately. On these occasions "the Niszel family put out the damask tablecloth, the best silverware, the candlesticks and the like". Some people recall that on these occasions the restaurant was filled with men wearing black silk kaftans and black hats, sometimes maybe even with Hasidim in fur hats.

Here was the editorial office and publishing house of *Múlt és Jövő* from 1920 for about 15 years, as well as Ignác Schlesinger's Corvina / Korvin printing and publishing house (named after the famous library of King Matthias in Buda, fifteenth century). Their books were "Orthodox kosher", just like Niszel's food, they were meant for the same public. The explicitly kosher restaurants of Révay utca might have been the literary–press–editorial cafés of the Orthodox and Zionist intellectuals of the capital in the 1930s. A journalists' club and a fast-food restaurant. After the war the customers of the eatery underwent a slight change—this was when the non-Jewish Bohemians started coming. They knew that the wine, the Verpeléti Riesling here was crystal-clear and kosher, like before.

NISZEL אָרְטַה· כַּשֵׁר **étterme**
BPEST, VI., RÉVAY-U. 14.
(Tel.: 120-092.) Reggeli kávé, ebéd, vacsora. Kitünő hegyi, homoki borok, kisüsti pálinkák, Dréher-sör. Lakodalmak, bankettek házon kivül is mérsékelt árban.

285. An advertisement of the "orth. kosher" restaurant Niszel

A nasty remark about Niszel's, from the old days, says: "What is the difference between Niszel's and the Ritz?—At the Ritz you see, through the windows, what people eat, but you can't hear it. At Niszel's you can't see it, but you hear it."

There was another famous kosher restaurant in Terézváros, that of Jakab Neiger & Co. It opened in 1887 and served the distinguished Jewish guests for half a century. Its original location was 55 Andrássy út, at the corner of Eötvös utca, then it moved to 17 Eötvös utca and finally in 1910 to 4 Teréz körút. It was more elegant than Niszel's, with large window-panes facing the boulevard. It was customary to give the *se'udah* after a *bar mitzvah* here, if not at home. It was called the "ritual restaurant", which is just a "coded" name for kosher, that is, Jewish.

I:1. Castle Hill: Interior of the Medieval Jewish Prayer-house (the former "small" synagogue)

I:2. Jewish male attire from Transylvania, seventeenth century. The dress has a definite Turkish character

I:3. Jewish female attire from Transylvania, seventeenth century

49. A Iew. Merchant.

50. A Iew's Wife.

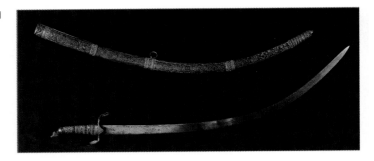

I:4. Sword, engraved with Hebrew inscription, and its scabbard, seventeenth century

I:5. Hebrew inscription on the sword blade

I:6-7. A wedding ring with Hebrew inscription

I:8. Inscription on Lady Freudel's gravestone, 432 (= 1672 C.E.)

II:1. Óbuda: Town map. (Detail), 1831

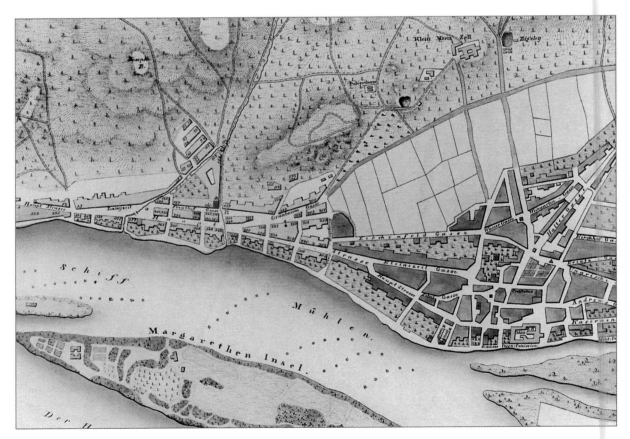

II:2. "The Temple of
the Israelites in
Óbuda."
Illustration on the
map by Karl Vasquez,
1838

II:3. Ark curtain
(*parokhet*) from the
Óbuda synagogue,
1772

II:4. Óbuda: Location
of the old "Israelite
cemetery" (Pálvölgyi
Jewish cemetery) in
the Pálvölgy–Mátyás
hegy–Zöldmál
triangle

ÓBUDA 231

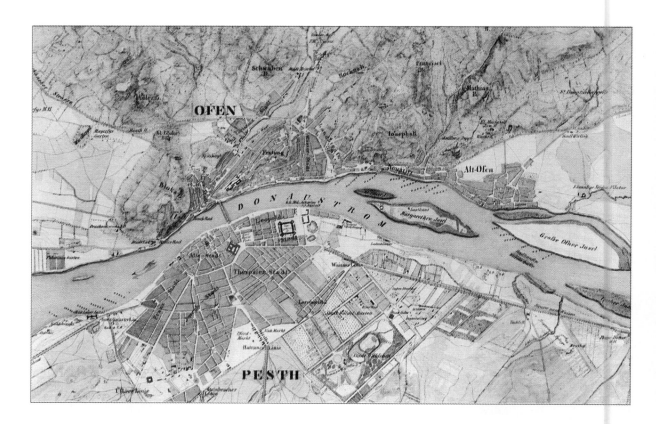

III:1. Óbuda, Újlak,
Buda and Pest.
A map by Karl
Vasquez, 1838

III:2. Neighborhood of
the Károly Barracks
and the Orczy House
on József Homolka's
city map, 1896.
(Detail.) The ground-
plan of the Orczy
House survived on
this map only

232 KIRÁLY UTCA

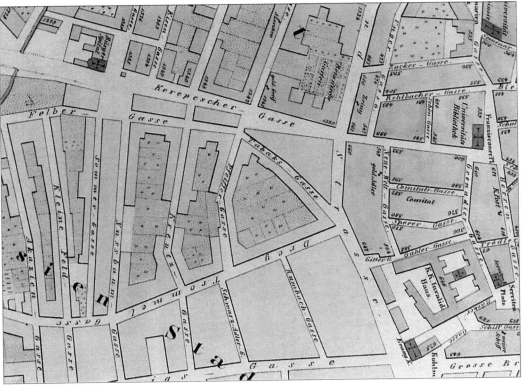

III:3. Theresienstadt / Terézváros. Apartment blocks and gardens between Kerepesi út and Király utca in what later became the Erzsébetváros. A map by Karl Vasquez, 1838. (Here rotated to the right by 90°)

III:4. Tannery, early nineteenth century

III:5. Sexton (*shammas / shames*) holding the gavel used for summoning the congregation to prayer (*Schulklopfer*). Jewish costume from Western Hungary, 1808

III:6. "The Israelite
Temple in Pest."
Lithograph by Antal
József Strohmayer,
1833

III:7. "Sámuel
Wodianer's house."
Illustration on the
map by Karl Vasquez,
1838

III:8. "Rudolf
Wodianer's house
on the Danube."
Illustration on the
map by Karl Vasquez,
1838

Wodianer Sámuel háza.
Das Sámuel Wodianer'sche Haus.

Wodianer Rudolf háza a' duna mellett.
Das Rudolph Wodianer'sche Haus an der Donau.

III:9. "J. A. Valero's
silk factory in Király
útsza." Illustration on
the map by Karl
Vasquez, 1838

III:10. Coat-of-arms of
the Wodianer family,
1844. From the *Liber
regius*

Valero J. A. Selyemgyára a királyútszában.
J. A. Valero Seidenfabrick in der königsgasse.

IV:1. Position of the hands when reciting the Priestly Blessing (*birkat kohanim*). Stained-glass window in the synagogue of the Rabbinical Seminary

IV:2. The Dohány utca synagogue, ca. 1860

THE JEWISH TRIANGLE IN PEST   235

IV:3. Colored bricks
and ornamental pat-
tern on the exterior of
the Dohány utca syn-
agogue during the
renovation, 1994

IV:5. Ark in the
Dohány utca syna-
gogue. Designed by
Frigyes Feszl

IV:4. Design of the
synagogue on the
curtain of the Ark in
the Dohány utca syn-
agogue

IV:6. Eternal light
(*ner tamid*) in the
Dohány utca syna-
gogue. Designed by
Frigyes Feszl

IV:7. Torah scrolls in
the Ark

IV:8. Stained-glass
window in the
Rumbach Sebestyén
utca synagogue

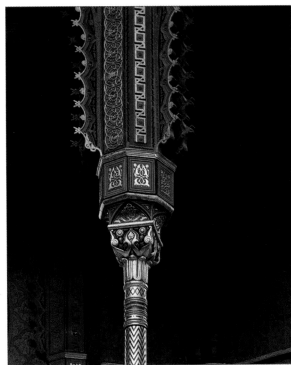

IV:9. Pillar in the
Rumbach Sebestyén
utca synagogue.
(Detail)

V:1. Betrothal plate

V:2. Spicebox
(*besamim*) for the
ritual of bidding
farewell to the
Sabbath (*Havdalah*)

V:3. Setting aside a portion of the dough (*mitzvat hallah*)

חוכין הין דעש הייליגן וחנד דיש דוח החטטני־ הייליגט
יין הייליבן נחמן פון כווייטן מין חול־כו געכן די חב טיידוכגין
בן כהן דער דח חיז
יין פון חונריינקייט
גרוטין פריידין ·
טפר זחוןונג כל
שרחל תמן וחמן
רני מובן
מזומן לכים
הצוה ·
להפריש החלה מעיסה כמו שצוה
נו הבורא ברוך הוא וברוך שמו ·

V:4. Purim in the synagogue: when Haman's name is mentioned, everyone stamps their feet and boos. On the women's gallery, musical instruments are used for making noise

אָרוּר אָרוּר הָמָן אֲרוּרָה אֲרוּרָה זֶרֶשׁ
וּבְרוּכִים כָּל יִשְׂרָאֵל אָמֵן :

V:5. Purim. Sending a gift of food (*mishloah manot*). The two persons are evidently carrying the two trays laden with food to each other, and both seem to be in a hurry

וְשָׁנָה כִּימִים אֲשֶׁר נָחוּ בָהֶם הַיְהוּדִים מֵאֹיְבֵיהֶם וְהַחֹדֶשׁ אֲשֶׁר
נֶהְפַּךְ לָהֶם מִיָּגוֹן לְשִׂמְחָה וּמֵאֵבֶל לְיוֹם טוֹב לַעֲשׂוֹת אוֹתָם יְמֵי

V:6. *Droshe,* with a moral lesson

V:7. Seder plate: ritual hand-washing. Hand-painted Herend porcelain, mid-nineteenth century

V:8. Celebration of the Seder and the meal. A *Judenstern* lamp hangs from the ceiling.

VI:1. The former desk of the professor in the main class room of the Rabbinical Seminary

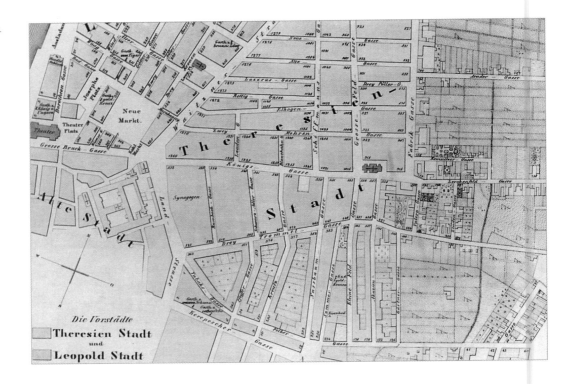

VII:1. Terézváros.
A map by Karl
Vasquez, 1838

VII:2. Interior of the
"Paris" department
store, ca. 1910

VII:3. 23 Andrássy út, staircase of the Wahrmann Palace

VII:4. Wahrmann Palace, etched-glass window in the staircase

VII:5. Wahrmann Palace, wrought-iron handrail in the staircase

VII:6. Courtyard of the Dessewffy utca synagogue

VIII:1. "Who is the mightier of the two? The rashekol or the king?" Lipót Herman's drawing to illustrate a Jewish saying

DER KÖNIG IST REICH, ABER RASEKOL KANN ER OOCH NICHT SEIN.

Ullmann uj háza a' dunaparti kirakó révnél.
Das von Ullmannische haus am Donau Ausladungsplatz.

VIII:2. "[Mózes / Móric / Mór] Ullmann's new house on the Danube bank." Illustration on the map by Karl Vasquez, 1838

VIII:3. Hunyadi tér synagogue: reading desk and the Ark

VIII:4. Zionist badges. The inscription on the round badge: "Your people, Israel, is the only one on the earth" and "One Torah, one Law"

VIII:5. Label of the "Zion" schnapps. "Be thankful unto Him and bless His name. For its taste (ta'amo) is good"

VIII:6. From the collections of the Jewish Museum: Curtain (parokhet) of the Ark, 1826

VIII:7. Ark in the
Heroes' Temple

VIII:8. From the
collections of the
Jewish Museum:
Marriage contract
(*ketubbah*). Verona,
5441 (=1680/81 c.e.).
The frame is
decorated with the
signs of the Zodiac

VIII:9. Lantern in the
Heroes' Temple

VIII:10. Memorial
inscription above the
entrance to the
Heroes' Temple

X:1. Ark in the prayer-
room of the Nagy
Fuvaros utca
synagogue

X:2. Interior of the
Nagy Fuvaros utca
synagogue: the
bimah

X:3. Plaque with the
order of prayers in
the Nagy Fuvaros
utca synagogue

X:4. Parokhet in the
Nagy Fuvaros utca
synagogue. (Detail.)
Crown of the Torah
(*keter Torah*)

X:5. 14 Fecske utca.
Six-pointed star
stained-glass window
in the staircase

X:6. 7-9 Dobozi utca.
There was an
Orthodox prayer-room
in the courtyard wing
of the building

XI:1. Share issued
by the Buda Jewish
Community for
building a synagogue
(1907)

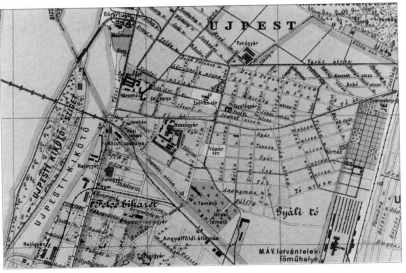

XI:2. Újpest in the
early twentieth
century

XII:1. "It's hard to be a Jew." Lipót Herman's drawing to illustrate a Jewish saying

XII:2. "Do not leave your brother behind!" An OMZSA poster, ca. 1940

XII:3. The Nagybátony-Újlaki Brickyard. Water-color by Adolf Tikáts, ca. 1910

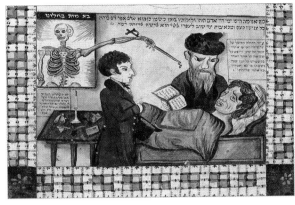

XIII:1. The Golden Book (*pinkas*) of the Nagykanizsa *Gemilut Hasadim Hevrah Kaddishah*, 1792/93. Illustration to the description of hell (*Ge-Hinnom / Tofet*)

XIII:2. Dying

XIII:3. Vigil by the deceased

XIII:4. Washing the dead body

XIII:5. On the way to the cemetery

XIII:6. Burial

XIII:7. In the
cemetery

XIII:8. Condolences

XIII:9. Sitting *shivah*

XIII:10. Black balls for
drawing lots (*goral*)
in a silver collection
plate. The balls are
inscribed with the
names of the Burial
Society's members

XIII:12. Salgótarjáni
utca cemetery.
The entrance house.
Designed by Béla
Lajta, 1908

XIII:11. *Derekh koha-
nim* in the Csörsz
utca cemetery

XIII:13. The entrance house from closer

XIII:14. The entrance of the mortuary. Designed by Béla Lajta, 1908

XIII:15. Stone table for washing the dead body (*taharah*) and fireplace for heating water

XIII:16. Candelabrum in front of the mortuary, 1994

XIII:17. Funeral prayers on the wall of the mortuary

XIII:18. Old graves in the Salgótarjáni utca cemetery

XIII:19. Tombstone of Vilmos Bacher and his wife in the Salgótarjáni utca cemetery. Front side (!) with inscriptions in Hebrew

XIII:20. Tombstone of Vilmos Bacher and his wife in the Salgótarjáni utca cemetery. Reverse side (!) with inscriptions in Hungarian. Designed by Béla Lajta, 1912

XIII:21. Tombstone of Henrik Lajta in the Kozma utca cemetery (1921). Designed by Béla Lajta

XIII:22. The Salgótarjáni utca cemetery

VIII. The Pest Jewish Community

After the General Congress of 1868/69 the whole of Budapest Neolog Jewry was organized in one community called *Pesti Izraelita Hitközség*, Israelite community of Pest. The word "Israelite" was usually abbreviated (izr.) in those days when used in writing. The new community was not organized any differently from the way it was early in the nineteenth century, except that it was much larger. While earlier all the *"Pester Juden"* would have fitted into the Orczy House, by the late nineteenth century the Pest Neolog Israelite community was spread all over the town. The Pest community was formed before the unification of Budapest—this may be the reason why Buda and Újpest—along with the Orthodox communities (*kehal / kehillot yere'im*)—remained autonomous, separate bodies. Otherwise all other synagogues or prayer-houses throughout Budapest belonged to the Pest Israelite community. An even more important difference was that, as a result of the law of emancipation, in 1867 the Pest community was free to break out of the former Jewish quarter, they could plan their future anywhere in the city. Around the turn of the nineteenth and twentieth centuries some of the new institutions of the Pest community were built in the newly developed, more elegant and fashionable areas of the city.

József Homolka's 1882 map, reprinted in 1896, the year of the millennium of the conquest of Hungary, indicates fifteen large public buildings that were in the possession of the Jewish community. These were synagogues ("Dohány", "Rombach"), prayer-houses (Kazinczy utca), the Rabbinical Seminary, *Hevrah Kaddishah* (Nagy Korona utca, Damjanich utca), hospital (Aréna utca / út, today Dózsa György út), orphanage (for boys) (Holló utca), *Árva Leányház* (Girls' Orphanage, Damjanich utca), the Institute for the Deaf and Dumb and cemetery. No other religious group had that many institutions marked on the map.

In the mid-nineteenth century the Jewish quarter of Pest grew concentrically, street by street, the center being the lower section of Király utca, the later Erzsébetváros. This pattern changed by the end of the century. The Jewish community started to plan its institutions in terms of the whole city, some important, strategic buildings were built in the new neighborhoods. They did not care, since after Act XVII of 1867 they did not have to care, whether these were close to the Jewish quarter or not.

The central role of the two great synagogues, the "Dohány" and the "Rombach", became quite evident under the changed circumstances. It should not surprise us that the Dohány utca synagogue was called the "Israelite Cathedral". It may as well have been "Jewish Basilica". Much like the Roman Catholic Basilica in Lipótváros, the "Dohány" was not a local or neighborhood temple, it belonged to the whole city. In the interwar years even the official term used by the Jewish community for these two synagogues was "the two central main temples." Consequently both temples were used as "holiday synagogues", mainly on the High Holidays. People would not go as far as the Dohány Temple every day for *shaharit* (in the interwar years the number of people who did go to synagogue daily was still quite high). Due to the inner dividedness of the Jewish community of Pest, to the presence of both modern and traditional tendencies within the Neolog community, the "Rombach" received a similar status to that of the "Dohány". The two synagogues represented two styles of holiday services. From more distant parts of the city several people had to travel to get to either the "Dohány" or the "Rombach" on holidays.

On weekdays, services were held in the small local synagogues and prayer-houses all over Budapest. But on the Sabbath and the High Holidays, these places could not accommodate all of the Jewish public. Among others, newspaper advertisements testify that in the interwar years the Jewish community often had to rent larger rooms to conduct services. Just in vicinity of the fashionable Városliget (City Park) such places included 7 and 17 Aréna út (Erzsébetvárosi Casino), 47 Hermina út (Adolf Völgyesi's restaurant "A Zöld Vadászhoz" [The Green Hunter]) and another restaurant at

67 Hermina út. The Jews of Lipótváros rented the Vigadó, the Buda Jews went to the Budai Vigadó at 8 Corvin tér. (This latter building, by the way, was designed by Mór Kallina and Aladár Árkay in 1900.) In 1937, for example, apart from the synagogues and the prayer-rooms of all the Jewish schools, orphanages and hospitals, High Holiday services were held at the Vigadó, the Goldmark Hall, at the school in Wesselényi utca (in the big gym), in the Ceremonial Hall of the boys' elementary school at 31 Eötvös utca, at 32 Akácfa utca, 65 Csáky utca, 48 Damjanich utca, 67 Reitter Ferenc utca, as well as in the prison in Markó utca and the *Tolončház* (Detention Barracks) in Mosonyi utca. Complaints were regularly filed in the reports of the Pest community that "secret" services are held at some places without the consent of the Rabbinate.

Jewish candidates were generally elected to the Parliament from Lipótváros, but not from Terézváros or Erzsébetváros, where it would have been natural because of the number of Jews among the constituents.

Jews were at home all over Budapest, nevertheless Erzsébetváros always remained the center of specifically Jewish affairs. From Király utca and the Orczy House the center shifted a bit to the South, to the area around Síp utca and Dohány utca.

(1) 12 Síp utca

The plot of land adjoining the plot of the Dohány utca synagogue on the eastern side was acquired by the Pest Jewish community in 1841. In 1854 a kindergarten and a girls' and boys' school were established there, in a one-story building in the rear of the plot, approximately where the small classroom of the Talmud-Torah is located today. They operated there until 1869.

Initially the administration of the Pest Jewish community was run in the "community room (*Kohols-Zimmer*)" of the Orczy House. Later, when the Dohány Temple was completed, the offices moved there, to the wing towards Károly körút. In 1891, during the term of President Mór Wahrmann, the construc-

286. 12 Síp utca

tion of a new central office building at 12 Síp utca was completed. Now the new building finally provided appropriate space for the offices. The big, four-story building in the Síp utca bearing signs of the late nineteenth-century Eclectic style has been the headquarters of the Pest Israelite / Jewish community, of the *Magyarországi Zsidó Hitközségek Szövetsége* (Alliance of Jewish Communities of Hungary) and the real center of the Neolog Jewish communal life—whatever the circumstances be—for more than a century.

The offices of the Rabbinate and the Hevrah Kaddishah are on the second floor, the office of the President, his Secretariat and the Conference Room are on the fourth floor. Jewish birth, circumcision, marriage and death registers are kept here, in the offices on the first floor, and here are the Jewish welfare institutions as well as the editorial office of *Új Élet* [New Life], the biweekly Jewish newspaper founded in 1945. The building has been the home of several other Jewish institutions and organizations from the beginnings. Today, among others, the *Joint* (Joint Distribution Committee of American Funds) and the Central and Eastern European Office of the World Jewish Congress have their offices in this building.

A slab on the corridor in front of the Secretariat commemorates those who were killed here in 1944 when the building was hit by a bomb during the siege of Budapest.

By the late nineteenth century the Jewish community organization of Pest became the largest in the world, and so its administration and bureaucracy were burdened with maintaining the institutions, *kashrut*, the cemeteries, etc. The institutions divided the work among themselves and left the rabbis only with functions similar to those of priests, that is, the spiritual care of the flock. The real power, or at least influence, was in the hands of the community leaders. The community could not have functioned without a strong central organization, yet, for more than half a century, "Síp utca" was blamed, reproved, sometimes cursed, among the Jewish public. "Síp utca" has always been involved in political issues concerning Jews. Lajos Szabolcsi, the editor of *Egyenlőség*, recalls the political struggles of "Síp utca" in his *Memoirs*, just as the journal used to, not only reporting about all important events, but also taking an active part in the struggles and debates. The community leadership often went beyond its everyday tasks and bore responsibility for some political moves that proved to be decisive in the fate of Hungarian Jewry. After the Tiszaeszlár blood libel trials in 1882–1883, "Síp utca" became the representative of the entire Jewry in Hungarian political life. One could say, the capital of Jewish population of Hungary.

287. Entrance to the office building of the Budapest Jewish community, view from the courtyard

"Síp utca" took part in preparing the draft of the Law of Reception (Act XLII of 1895) that declared "the Israelite religion an officially accepted religion". The legal status of the Jewish religion was thereby established. Originally the Hebrew language had no term for faith or religion. Later a Persian loanword from the sixth or fifth century B.C.E. was used to designate the notion of *religio*, religion: the word *dat*, which originally meant "ruling" or "law". Traditional Judaism was not a religion, it was both more and different: it was a religious way of life. The Reception accepted only certain elements of Jewish life. It made the Jewish religion and its institutions equal to those of Christian churches within the framework of the Constitution. (The term used in the Hungarian Constitution for religions that could be officially practiced in the country is *religio recepta*, "accepted religion".) But there were negative aspects to the laws of emancipation (Act XVII of 1867) and of Reception (Act XLII of 1895), too. Since the latter Act (§ 3) explicitly prohibited rabbis (Jewish "pastors") ordained outside of Hungary to practice in the country, Hungarian Jewry became isolated, their ever so important contacts with the rest of world Jewry were cut off. That is, Judaism was turned into a national church in Hungary. And another, though unintended consequence of this law was that it made every aspect of Judaism suspicious, which did not fit into the traditional Christian definition of religion. Ultimately the Reception, so much and for so long desired by the Jewish community, forced the Christian concept of religion onto Hungarian Jewry.

After World War I it was the Jewish community that organized, with the backing of the editors of *Egyenlőség*, the protest against the law of *numerus clausus* (Act XXV of 1920), which aimed at establishing—as they put it—"sound proportions" in intellectual professions as to ethnic background of persons concerned. Only under international pressure could they reach that the disadvantages of this discriminatory law be somewhat eased years later.

By the years immediately preceding World War II practically no Jewish activity was possible outside of "Síp utca". Even the Zionist organizations were housed here; emigration, aid and welfare, rescue operations were conducted from here.

Here, in the middle of the Pest ghetto, were the headquarters of the Jewish Council appointed by the Germans instead of the Jewish community leaders. German soldiers were not allowed to enter the building without permission. After World War II "Síp utca" and the Rabbinical Seminary were the only Jewish islands in the sea of overall official hostility towards Jewish life.

The Jewish community was the political organization of the religious (Neolog) but socially assimilated Hungarian Jewry. It always maintained the religious institutions for those who needed them and who contributed to their maintenance. Under the circumstances it was impossible to identify

Jews as a distinct social group, at least such a self-definition was not possible. Only anti-Semites could tell exactly who the Jews were. It made no sense to talk about issues concerning Jews in a wider sense than those who were official members of the "Isr." community. Whoever did not belong to the Jewish community had to cope individually, his or her social situation did not, could not concern the Jewish community. They viewed Zionism with reservations, sometimes even with hostility. The realization that being Jewish could mean something other than going to the Dohány Temple on the High Holidays wearing a hat came only too late, when the word "Jewish" had already assumed a threatening overtone. And even then their reaction to the social challenge did not go beyond escape into cultural Judaism, as it happened in many other Jewish communities across Europe as well. And in 1944 the Jewish community was simply unable to handle the situation properly. The faith in legality and the Constitution was so firm that it muted even the most basic sense of danger.

There were only a few who dared even imagine a relatively autonomous Jewish life within Hungarian society—the literary gentlemen Béla Tábor (1907–1992) and Aladár Komlós were among them:

> "Hungarian Jewish assimilation started to show some awkward traits only when Jewish education intentionally tried to blur the memory of our separate origins and duped the Jewish masses into believing that Hungarian Jews are just another confessional group among Hungarians, like the Catholics or Protestants. And so the remedy is clear. In order to come to terms with our Hungarian character we must also be aware of our Jewish identity."
>
> (Aladár Komlós, in: *Ararát*, 1943)

It is the irony of history that later, in the years following World War II, even under the communist regime, the one time liberal law of Baron József Eötvös provided the legal framework for a development contrary to the original intentions. The Jewish community of Pest as well as of the country—despite all their reservations—became dependent on the state, just like the Christian churches; its moves were indirectly controlled by the will of the state. The community managed to take care of its tasks, to maintain religious life and to support the needy, but it was in no position to pursue independent Jewish policy.

(2) Assembly Hall

The Assembly Hall on the second floor of the Jewish community building complex (the building in Wesselényi utca) is used on special occasions. The walls of the beautiful, large North–South Hall are decorated with dark, colorful Romantic patterns. The plane of the wall is divided by half-pillars and brackets for lamps; the ceiling is coffered. At the upper end of the northeastern room there is an imposing semicircular presidential table, with a separate seat at the side for the notary—it is a cabinet-work masterpiece from the early twentieth century. Meetings of the community's *parnasim* used to be held here. The room can be transformed into a prayer-room. The wall on which the Ark stands can be joined together with the Assembly Hall. There are dark oil paintings all around the walls, an official portrait gallery of the community's presidents. One of the *rashekols* is, in fact, wearing his Hungarian national gala-costume. The signatures of Antal Zilzer (1861–1921) and Frigyes Frank (1890–1976) are legible on some of the paintings.

After the General Congress of 1868/69 the Neolog Jewry of Pest formed one unified organization, the Pest Israelite community. However, it was too large both in number and in territory to be uniform. The Jews of Pest followed two different directions already back in the heyday of the Orczy House and the divergence became crystal clear after the construction of the Dohány and Rombach Temples. In the nineteenth century the newly emerged communities created new prayer-houses or synagogues. Finally in 1920 the separate Jewish communities within the Pest Jewish community organization were reorganized by districts. These districts corresponded both to the area served by the synagogue in question and to the administrative divisions of the capital.

After the General Congress of 1868/69 the Pest community was led by a board of representatives (*képviselő-testület*) or General Assembly. Initially the board consisted of 150, later—between World War I and II—of 350 members, who were elected for five year terms. Because of the large number of members the board could not meet often. Therefore, a smaller committee of 45, later of 100 members, was elected, with a 5-, later on, 15-member executive board (*elöljáróság*). The organization was headed by a president and two vice-presidents as well as a secretary who functioned as an executive director. The organization was divided into various departments whose work was directed by the president. In the interwar years there were ten departments with some five hundred employees in "Síp utca" and other community offices. The departments were as follows: presidential, ritual, teaching of religion, educational, charity, organizational, cultural, fund-raising, economic and fiscal. The budget had to be approved by the board of representatives. The president and the executive board had to give a yearly report about the income and expenditures of the community.

288. The presidential table in the Assembly Hall

The community was organized according to regions. To live as a Jew, whether in the legal or in the ritual sense of the word, was possible only as a member of the community. By the interwar years the three Neolog Jewish communities of Pest, Buda and Óbuda became less segregated. Several members of the Pest community lived in Buda, in the better parts of the city. Nevertheless, the districts themselves were relatively autonomous. They had their own presidents, magistrates, societies, etc.; and even the district-rabbi—though appointed by the central organs of the Pest community—was selected and recommended by the individual communities. The Pest community was in charge of registering birth, circumcision, etc. and of *kashrut*. The community rabbi or central rabbi ranked higher than a district rabbi, therefore he was elected by primary elections: he was elected by the whole community or its board of representatives, and served in the central synagogues, but was also entitled to preach in any of the district synagogues. District rabbis were appointed only to serve in their own synagogues. Simon Hevesi was the first to be appointed the leading chief rabbi, and soon after, to spare his feelings, they appointed Gyula Fischer as well—thus the Dohány Temple had two chief rabbis and two rabbis at the same time in the interwar years.

It was generally the head of the family (*ba'al ha-bayit / balebos / balbos*) who counted as a community member. Community tax was paid according to the families. Earlier it was levied or divided (*repartitio*), but since 1861 it is paid in proportion to the declared income (*fassio*) or by voluntary contributions. Community tax arrears were collected just like public tax arrears. Every member who paid taxes had suffrage in the community, and so did the "intellectuals" (in 1861 called "honoratior", in 1932, "intellectual"). By the last decades of the nineteenth century the size of the community made it impossible to hold primary—that is, direct—elections every year, thus leaders were elected according to the representational principle. The Assembly Hall was the scene where representative power was shown.

(3) The Sequence of the Rashekols

The organization of the Pest Jewish community emerged gradually. The community itself was not founded by one single act; it evolved with the Jews who happened to live in Pest, in the shadow of the Óbuda community, and then, because of the increasing number of community members, the number of officials and departments had to be increased continually as well. Initially Pest Jews only had representatives, then there were magistrates who led the community on a three-month rotation.

The position of the president was introduced only in the 1830s. In the nineteenth century the board of leaders (*würklicher Ausschusskörper*) as well as the president were elected for three years—like the Diet at that time. Re-election was always an option, though.

Here follows a list of the presidents (*rosh ha-kahal / rashekol*) of the Pest Jewish community / Pest Israelite community. The first few persons on the list below were not presidents proper, but members of the board of leaders and took turns in holding the executive power.

Marcus Sachsel (Sachs, Sachsl, Sax) (?–1819) was the leader of the Pest Jews due to his status as a restaurant owner for about two decades starting probably in the mid-1780s.

Joachim Kadisch (1785–1853) was a retailer and a member of every board of leaders since his youth, in the first decades of the nineteenth century.

Izsák Breisach (1758–1835) was a grain trader and a member of the board of leaders in the first decades of the nineteenth century.

Ádám Mauthner (1766–1831) was a textile manufacturer and a member of every board of leaders for two decades, starting 1811.

Mózes Ullmann (1783–1847) was a grain trader, member of the board of leaders between 1806 and 1823, its leader for a while. He delivered food for the army, had a leading role in tobacco trade, but he also dealt in salt and wood. József Deyák, his competitor whom he pushed out of the Viennese tobacco market, published a book that attacked him with "harmful remarks", but the *Königliche Statthalterei* (Royal Governorship) seized the book. Some tension arose between Ullmann and Salamon Rosenthal, an influential member of the community, a renowned scholar and Hebraist; as a result, Ullmann got baptized in 1825 under the name Mór (Móric) János (sr.). Following

his baptism he won civil rights in Pest as a home-owner in Terézváros and received a title of nobility with the name *szitányi*. In 1832 he divorced his wife (née Veronika Hirschl) who did not leave her Jewish faith, but he continued to take care of his family and did not break off contacts with them. One of his daughters from his first marriage married his younger brother, Gábor Ullmann, another married Mór Wodianer. His role in Hungarian business life was probably even more important than earlier in Jewish public affairs. He built a huge tobacco warehouse (*Silo*) in the northern suburbs of Lipótváros (today Új-Lipótváros), in the area around today's Pozsonyi út and Katona József utca. (The building, which occupied two blocks, was demolished only in 1933 when Katona József utca was to be extended all the way down to the Danube. Some twenty, six-story tenement houses were built in its place.)

289. Mór Szitányi Ullmann, a former Board member of the Pest Jewish community. (The portrait was painted after his baptism)

We can imagine the profits Móric Ullmann gained from such a huge amount of well-stored tobacco. It was Ullmann who suggested that the minutes of the *Kereskedők Testülete* (Merchants' Corporation) be kept in Hungarian. In 1837 he initiated and helped to organize the construction of the first railroad line in Hungary, between Pest and Vác. On the stocks of the *Magyar Középponti Vasúttársaság* (Hungarian Central Railway Company) one can read: "Founded by Móric Ullmann." Ullmann's house on the Rak-piac / Kirakodó tér (today between Vigyázó Ferenc utca and Zrínyi utca), designed by József Hild in 1835—later the home of Count István Széchenyi between 1836 and 1848—is marked on the city map of Vasquez. (The building was damaged during World War II and finally demolished. An ugly, dark-green office building stands in its place today.)

Móric Bauer (1786–1833) was a retailer. As a community leader he was mainly occupied with the organization of the community itself.

Gábor Ullmann (1792–ca.1837) was the first actual president, between 1833 and 1836. He was a wholesale merchant, brother and son-in-law of Mózes / Mór Ullmann, president of the union of Jewish merchants for a while around 1830, and the leader of the community at the same time. In 1833 he introduced new statutes abolishing the domination of the renters and based community leadership on the representational system. Upon this the "*Isr. Gemeinde*" elected him the first president (*Vorsitzer*) right away. He closed private prayer-rooms, founded the Choir Temple and soon found a suitable place for it in the Orczy House.

József Löb Boskovitz (1789–1862) was president from 1836 to 1839. He enhanced the role of the Pest community in the leadership of Hungarian Jewry against Pozsony (Pressburg, now Bratislava).

Dávid Österreicher (Ösztreicher) (1794–1867) and **Herman Lőwy** (1785–?) were presidents from 1839 to 1845. The *Kézműves Egylet* (Craftsmen's Union) was founded under their term, in 1842. Österreicher played an active role in founding the *Magyarító Egylet* (Magyarizing Society) in 1844.— Herman Lőwy was a silversmith and a Talmudic scholar, member of the board of leaders from 1836, a close friend of the new rabbi, Löw Schwab.

Herman Lőwy and Jónás Kunewalder were presidents between 1845 and 1848.

Jónás Kunewalder was the president of the Pest Jewish community when the Jewish communities of Hungary decided, at a national assembly held between March 4 and 14, 1846, to request the abolition of the toleration or chamber tax (*taxa tolerantialis*) from the Emperor. This tax had been introduced by Queen Maria Theresa (1740–1780), first as a one-time tax to cover military expenditures (1743, 1746), then as a regular tax in 1749. The Hebrew and Yiddish names of the tax refer to its origins: *ma'ot malkah / malkagelt*, "the Queen's money". The "Jewish tax" was levied on the whole Jewish community, and collecting it was the task of the community leadership. Its sum increased gradually until 1828, when the community stopped collecting it. At the 1832 Diet Ferenc Kölcsey and Ferenc Deák suggested that the *taxa tolerantialis* be abolished. Accepting a proposal by Simon Dubraviczky (1791–1849), the deputy of Pest, the Diet of 1839/40 passed a resolution condemning the tax. Having witnessed the helpful and charitable behavior of the Pest Jews at the time of the 1838 flood, Simon Dubraviczky did as much as he could to advance the emancipation of the Jews. Emperor and King Ferdinand V (1835–1848) would have been willing to abolish the toleration tax at the request of the Pest Jews, had they agreed to pay their debts, amounting to 2,554,293 forints and 4.5 (!) koronas. Finally a compromise was found, the Jewish community had to pay back 1,200,000 forints in installments within eleven years. The King in turn abolished the toleration tax on June 24, 1846. At the suggestion of Kunewalder the Pest community offered to pay the debts back within five years. On August 19, 1846, thanksgiving services were held in the synagogues. During the next year and a half, however, the community was unable to collect even half of the amount due. Count Lajos Batthyány suspended demanding payments from the Jews in 1848, but after the Hungarian defeat in the 1848/49 Revolution and War of Independence General Haynau again insisted on collecting the whole sum in the form of military contributions. Kunewalder himself came from Óbuda. Both he and his brother were citizens of Pest and prestigious royal free purveyors. Kunewalder was among the leaders of the *Pesti Nagykereskedők Testülete* (Corporation of Wholesale Merchants of Pest), elected member of the *Védegylet* (Protective Tariffs Society). He lived in the Kunewalder House on Ország út (that part of the street is called today Múzeum körút), near the National Museum, where some university buildings stand today. His offices were near the Inner City, in the elegant house of the Wurm Courtyard (Mária Valéria utca / 15A–B Apáczai Csere János utca and 6A–B Dorottya utca). He became widely known after his political role in the revolution of March 15, 1848. He advocated his ideas about the melting together of Jews and Hungarians in a pamphlet published in Pest on March 22, 1848: *Moses vallású magyarokhoz* [To the Hungarians of Mosaic Faith]. A few days later, on April 6, in the intoxication of equality he and his family suddenly got baptized at the St. Roch (Rókus) Church. Some of the newspapers reported this event, for instance, the *Reform*, April 9, 1848. He was occasionally called János—this may have been his Christian name. Later he became a successful businessman in Austria.

M. [Móric / Moritz?] **Á. Weisz** (1811–1876) and **József Stern** were leaders of the Jewish community from 1848 to 1851. Weisz was a merchant; he led the community during the 1848/49 War of Independence. He was deprived of his office on May 31, 1851 by Austrian officials. He was elected a member of the board of leaders several times later on.

József Löb Boskovitz was the president of the Jewish community, appointed by Austrian officials, between 1851 and 1858. His task was to set up an organizational structure for the Jewry of Pest. The Municipality stood by its earlier decree according to which the Jewish community was no more than a religious community; this excluded the possibility of autonomy. Later the Municipality even insisted that a police agent be present at every single meeting of community officials. The first indirect elections for the leaders of the Jewish community were held on November 25, 1858. The "primary electors (*Urwähler*)" elected the "electors (*Wahlmänner*)" who then voted for the actual leaders.

Fülöp Baumgarten was president in 1858.

Dávid Fleischl (1800–1868) was president from February to October, 1859. The Dohány Temple was consecrated during his short presidency.

Sáje Wolf Schossberger (1796–1874) was president from October, 1859 until 1861. He was appointed by the *Königliche Statthalterei* and in the following election was not re-elected for a further term.

Ignác Hirschler was president between 1861 and 1863. It was during the term of this excellent ophthalmologist that the Pest Jewish community regained its autonomy. In 1862 they passed a resolution that a Hungarian preacher be hired for the Dohány Temple, although it took another two years for it to be realized. The *Königliche Statthalterei* annulled Hirschler's election because he was viewed as an advocate of Hungarian political aspirations. In 1865 the community elected him the president again, but this time he rejected the honor. He lived in Lipótváros, at 2 Tüköry utca, and after 1882 at 6 Akadémia utca. His portrait hangs in the Assembly Hall of the Síp utca community building.

290. Portrait of Sáje Wolf Schossberger

Simon Vilmos (earlier Sáje Wolf) **tornyai Schossberger** was president between 1863 and 1865, appointed by Francis Joseph I. He tried to keep a balance between the trend toward Magyarization and Austrian rule. "As a community leader he was able to show that he supported the Austrian Government and the Hungarian *Königliche Statthalterei*, but not even his enemies could accuse him of being inclined to Orthodoxy. He gave ample evidence that he supported the progressive party" (Pál Tencer, 1869). He acquired his wealth from trade in tobacco and liquor, multiplied his capital by participating in railway construction and invested in real estate. He was the first Hungarian Jew who, in 1863, received a title of nobility and the name *tornyai* without converting. In the 1865 presidential elections he was not re-elected. The opposition of the Jewish community was not directed against him personally, it was just that they did not favor the intervention of state administration into their internal affairs. Schossberger was elected a member of the General Assembly of the community for several years afterwards. His portrait can be seen in the Síp utca community building. His son, Zsigmond Schossberger received the title of baron in 1890. The family owned several tenement houses in Lipótváros, e.g. Fő utca / 4 Arany János utca; 20 Nádor utca.

291. Portrait of Ignác Hirschler

Jakab Lányi (1816–1879) was president from 1865 to 1873. He was a banker. By electing him president the community gently rid itself of direct Austrian supervision. The General Congress of 1868/69 was assembled, the synagogue in Rombach utca was consecrated and the Girls' and Boys' Orphanage was opened during his term.

Ármin Neuwelt (1815–1888) was president between 1874 and 1883. He was a wholesale merchant. The Institute for the Deaf and Dumb and the Rabbinical Seminary were opened during his term. His portrait, an oil painting by H. Weiss, is exhibited in the Assembly Hall of the Síp utca community building.

Mór Wahrmann was president between 1883 and 1892.

Fülöp Weinmann (1839–1911) was interim president in 1892.

Zsigmond Kohner (1840–1908) was president between 1893 and 1906. He was an industrialist and a banker. The Old Age Home and the "Bródy" Children's Hospital were opened during his term, the IMIT and the *Ahavas Reim Society* were also founded at that time. His portrait is exhibited in the Assembly Hall of the Síp utca community building.

Fülöp Weinmann was president from 1906 to 1911. He was a lawyer, then a judge and finally a notary public. During his presidential term the Institute for the Blind, the "Alice Weiss" Maternity Home and the Hospital and Nursing Home were opened. His grave is in the Salgótarjáni utca cemetery, in the row of the members of the Rabbinical Seminary and of the community leadership. His portrait hangs in the Assembly Hall of the Síp utca community building. After his death there was no president for a year.

Lajos Adler (1837–1927) was president from 1912 to 1919. He was a banker. The founding of a "Unified Hungarian Israelite Church" was initiated by the Neolog community during his term, but this rather naïve idea was completely eradicated after World War I.

Ferenc Székely (1858–1936) was president from 1919 to 1921. He was a banker. He wrote on economics and, as a young man, for *Borsszem Jankó*, the satirical journal of Adolf Ágai. His portrait hangs in the Assembly Hall of the Síp utca community building.

Sándor Lederer (1852–1927) was president between 1921 and 1927. Based on a resolution passed on February 15, 1920, the synagogue districts of the Pest community were organized during his term. His grave is in the Salgótarjáni utca cemetery, in the row of the members of the Rabbinical Seminary and of the community leadership. His portrait hangs in the Assembly Hall of the Síp utca community building.

Aladár Kaszab (1868–1929) was president in 1928 and 1929. He was an industrialist. He became already popular in the community for having set up a foundation for outpatient care. His grave is in the Salgótarjáni utca cemetery, in the row of the members of the Rabbinical Seminary and of the community leadership. His portrait hangs in the Assembly Hall of the Síp utca community building.

Samu Glückstahl (1864–1937) and **Marcell Hajdú** (1871–1936) were vice-presidents, interim presidents in 1929. Samu Glückstahl directed the construction works in Dohány utca and Wesselényi utca. His portrait hangs in the fourth floor Conference Room of the Síp utca community building.

Samu Stern (1874–1947) was the president of the Jewish community between 1929 and 1944, and of the Jewish Council from March to October, 1944. He was also elected president of the VIth district and the Central Office in 1932. The new statutes, the "constitution" of the community, were accepted in 1932, during his term. He was one of the most important entrepreneurs in the interwar years. A considerable part of Hungarian agricultural export was in his hands; he was called "milk- and egg-king", or somewhat pejoratively "the milkman". He lived in Új-Lipótváros, at 28 Nádor utca. He had excellent contacts in high political circles. During World War II and in 1944 he was convinced that the leading politicians of the country would intervene on behalf of the Jews and thus his contacts could be of service to his co-religionists. In this hope he did everything he could to keep the Jews calm, by this conforming to the wishes of the Germans.

Lajos Stöckler (1897–1960) was appointed president of the Jewish Council in October, 1944. From July 22 on he had been a member of the Jewish Council, more exactly of the Interim Executive Committee of Hungarian Jews; in October, 1944 he was appointed chairman of that committee. As a World War I veteran who had fought at the front he was expected to be a firm leader. After the war, on the first meeting of the Assembly of the Pest community on March 26, 1945 he was elected the president of the community. At the same time he became the president of the current national organization of Hungarian Jews, first of the *Magyar Izraeliták Központi Irodája* (Central Office of Hungarian Israelites, MIKI), later of the *Magyar Izraeliták Országos Irodája* (National Office of Hungarian Israelites, MIOI), and from 1950 on, of the *Magyar Izraeliták Országos Képviselete / Központja*) (National Bureau / Center of Hungarian Israelites, MIOK). At the end of 1949 the Pest and the Buda communities joined as the *Budapesti Izraelita Hitközség* (Budapest Israelite community), and Stöckler remained its president. In January 1953 he was accused of Zionist conspiracy and arrested by the State Security Authority. Beginning with the presidency of Samu Stern, throughout the year of German occupation and Arrow-cross rule, until the 1989 transformation of the Jewish community, the president of the Budapest community and of the current national Jewish umbrella organization was always the same person.

Lajos Heves (1900–1965) was president between 1953 and 1957, during the worst years in the postwar period. Son of the Neolog chief rabbi in Szolnok, he was a lawyer, in ca. 1950 his license was canceled by the authorities, and he could return to his original profession after his presidential term had suddenly ended. (He resigned after a long hearing, perhaps on the initiative of the State Security Authority, at the State Office for Church Affairs.)

Endre Sós (1905-1969) was president from 1957 to 1965. Before World War II he was a brilliant journalist. As president of the community he failed to represent the Jews.

Géza Seifert (1906-1976) was president from 1966 to May, 1976. He, too, was a lawyer.

Imre Héber was president between March 15, 1977 and June 30, 1985.

András Losonci was president from December, 1985 to 1989. He, a respected medical doctor, was the director of the Jewish Hospital before his election and occupies the same office ever since.

Lajos Kéri is president since 1989.

(4) Population

The Jewish population figures in Pest were recorded in official documents in the nineteenth century. In the eighteenth and early nineteenth centuries censuses—or conscriptions—were often taken of

the Jews with the explicit purpose of imposing various taxes upon them, such as the toleration tax. Jews were also included in the overall population census of particular towns and cities. The annual registers of taxpayers kept by the Jewish community are, in this sense, also official records. These community tax registers generally specified the number of family members and thus their population figures are more or less reliable. Another good source are the census figures, which specified the number of persons following the—as it was called—"Mosaic faith".

József Kőrösi (1844-1906) (later József szántói Kőrösy), director of the Municipal Statistical Office from 1870 on, internationally acknowledged in his field of study, statistics and "demology" (that is, demography), devoted special attention to data pertaining to the figures, the profession and the settlement patterns of the population of "Mosaic faith" in Budapest.

292. Portrait of József Kőrösi (Kőrösy)

"József Kőrösy had a very special relationship to Judaism. He did not register his children as Jews on their birth certificate for he held that one should decide this particular issue as an adult. When his children were eighteen, though, he explained to them the options they faced—and all of them chose to be Jews. (...) At the same time, he often donated significant sums for Jewish causes. He proved that also in Hungary an important institute can have a Jewish director without having to convert and that he could uphold his own and his family's Jewish identity without observing the formal *mitzvot*." (Ferenc Kőrösy, 1984)

As a social scientist Kőrösy was particularly interested in the process of assimilation of the ethnic minorities in Hungary. He worked out a number of analytical methods for measuring Hungarian identity. In a study published in 1882 he compared the knowledge of the Hungarian language within the larger religious denominations according to data of different censuses. His correlation analyses showed that 93% of the Calvinists, 79% of the Jews, 77% of the Lutherans and 67% of the Roman Catholics spoke Hungarian in Budapest. He considered the knowledge of Hungarian, whether as mother tongue or as an acquired language, to be one of the most important elements of cultural and national identity. He used this element as an indicator of the acculturation or integration of foreigners (non-Hungarians). As far as the Jews were concerned, he only regarded the Hasidic Jews of the northeastern counties as "foreigners".

"Hungarian Jews can be divided into two widely differing groups not only in terms of religion and administration, but also in terms of social, cultural and ethnic relations. (...) While the progressive wing of the Jews adjusts to the nation as far as language and feelings are concerned, participating enthusiastically in its cultural, scholarly, artistic and literary life, the leaders of the Hasidic denomination (...) have explicitly forbidden the use of Hungarian or German in their temples."

Kőrösy's scholarly works and statistical analyses investigated and, at the same time, tried to promote Jewish religious modernization as well as the cultural and political integration of the Jewish population into the Hungarian nation. His general conclusions were in harmony with the prevalent social attitudes of the age. Budapest Jewry definitely interpreted the differences between Neolog and Orthodox as an issue of modernization and culture.

Following World War II and the Holocaust, between 1947 and 1949, the statistical department of the Hungarian branch of the World Jewish Congress (then based at 7 Wekerle Sándor utca / Nagy Korona utca, today Hercegprímás utca) prepared a report on the number of survivors and on the situation of the Jewish religious communities that had been reorganized around 1947. The report was prepared under the guidance of Zsigmond Pál Pach, on the basis of their own surveys and on a meticulous study of the historical sources and archive records.

On the basis of the available registers and census data, the Jewish population of Budapest during the past one and a half centuries can be reconstructed as follows (the figures are rounded):

Date	Population figures	In percentages	Date	Population figures	In percentages
1825:	8,000	(8%)	1910:	204,000	(23%)
1840:	10,000	(9%)	1920:	216,000	(23%)
1850:	17,000	(11%)	1930:	204,000	(20%)
1869:	45,000	(16%)	1941:	184,000	(15%)
1880:	71,000	(19%)	plus[1]	62,000	(5%)
1890:	102,000	(21%)	1945:	86,000	(7%)
1900:	166,000	(23%)	1949:	101,000	(6%)

In Pest the Jewish population rose at a relatively rapid rate during the Austro-Hungarian Monarchy. Natural population increase played an important role, as did inner migration, that is, moving to the cities from the provinces. The provinces basically meant Northeastern Hungary with its Orthodox, and mainly Hasidic population and the eastern territories of the Monarchy, the Polish border region, the Máramaros region and Galicia, which was incorporated into the Monarchy in 1772. As a matter of fact, there was little direct migration from Galicia to Pest in the nineteenth century. It was the second or third generation, who already had been living in Hungary for some time, that made the move to the capital. Altogether 400 persons whose mother tongue was Yiddish were registered in Budapest in 1941, when Hungary entered the war. During the time of the Austro-Hungarian Monarchy the assimilative Hungarianization of Jews living in the border-region was officially encouraged by the Hungarian state, since this increased the ratio of the Hungarian-speaking population in regions where otherwise ethnic minorities formed a majority.

293. At the door of a Dob utca Orthodox prayer-room. Photo, ca. 1910

Eastern Jews from Galicia, called *Galitzianers* or *Polish* (*pólisi* in Hungarian), later on—using a romantic euphemism ironically—"Khazars" or "Kozars",[2] were often snubbed, treated with suspicion, and clearly disliked by the more urbane Jewish population with more of a bourgeois mentality who had lived in Pest longer. An article in the 1911 issue of the *Magyar Zsidó Szemle* struck a rather sarcastic tone about the Polish Jews:

[1] Not necessarily Jewish by religion, but defined as such by the (Anti-)Jewish Laws of 1938–1941.
[2] Based on the nineteenth-century assumption that Jews of Lithuania were of Khazar origin. The Khazars were a Turkish people who—or only the royal family of whose—converted to Judaism in the eighth century. The Hungarian tribes lived in the framework of the Khazar empire for a time, so assimilationist Jews in Hungary, including the historian R. Sámuel Kohn, referred to that connection as a historical primer for their integration into the Hungarian society.

"(...) If a Polish Jew introduces himself to one of his kin (...) he never begins by saying who he is and whence he comes, but starts by extolling one of his grandfathers, usually a great *gaon*,[3] throwing in for good measure an uncle or two, the author of some *sefer*[4] or other, continuing with his connections with the family of a *baal shem*,[5] and only after these and that he has taxed his listener's patience to the utmost does he reveal his own name, his *Heimat* and *Sippschaft* [homeland and family]..."

In the library of the Rabbinical Seminary, where only scholars would leaf through the scholarly journals, someone wrote the following remark on the margin of the above-quoted passage: "A perfect example of the devious *kaftannik*."

At first glance, the main targets of anti-Semitic incitement in general were the Polish Jews. A few words from József Patai's reminder and warning from the year 1918:

"When Jew-baiters speak or write of Galitzianers, they have in mind not the few hundred Galician refugees, who happen to stay here, but the children and grandchildren of the Galitzianers of yesterday, in other words, the whole of Hungarian Jewry, fathers and sons."

(József Patai, "Az antiszemitizmus Magyarországon, a galiciaiak és a morál" [Anti-Semitism in Hungary, the Galicians and the Moral], in: *Harc a zsidó kultúráért*, 1937)

294. Leaving Judaism. "Mr. Meshümed and Mrs. Meshümed." Cartoon, late nineteenth century

Before World War I, but especially in its aftermath, many Jews considered conversion to Christianity as a viable course for social assimilation. In the case of certain positions or jobs it was an explicit or implicit prerequisite that the candidate be the member of a Christian denomination. The Jewish community considered conversion a "religious rebellion (*shemad / shmad*)". By the 1930s conversion was, more often than not, dictated by downright fear. According to official data and other sources, the Third (Anti-)Jewish Law, passed in 1941, affected some 62,000 persons, 18,000 of whom were born to Israelite parents, implying that their conversion had been fairly recent. This figure corresponds more or less to the decrease in the number of persons affiliated with the Jewish community in the period between 1920 and 1941. The number of conversions rose steeply in 1944, although the hopes attached to conversion proved illusory.

The population figures for the year 1944 must be treated separately. In April the Jewish communities in Hungary were ordered to provide official population data to the German authorities. According to the figures received from the Pest community the number of taxpayers was 54,000, while the overall population figure was indicated as 162,000. The actual number of Jews living or staying in Pest must have been much higher, given the number of refugees and the number of persons from the provinces and from abroad in hiding. (The majority of Jewish refugees in Hungary came from Poland and a significant number among Polish refugees staying in Hungary were Jews.) The ranks of the Pest Jews was also swollen by those who were given a Jewish identity by the (Anti-)Jewish Laws, either because they themselves, or their parents or grandparents were of Jewish origin.

[3] *Ga'on*, "religious leader", "famous scholar".
[4] "Book (of religious content)."
[5] *Ba'al shem*, "famous person".

(5) Prayer Groups, Organizations, Institutions

In the last third of the nineteenth century the great new synagogues and places of worship for the High Holidays were able to meet the religious needs of the observant members of the Jewish community of Pest, whose numbers had swollen enormously. The Jewish community also maintained the necessary infrastructure for leading a traditional Jewish life and operating smoothly, without encountering major difficulties. Kosher meats and other foods were available in the shops almost as a matter of course; ceremonies—such as weddings, circumcisions, *bar mitzvahs*, burials—calling for institutional participation gave little cause for concern. Even though its policies did not always meet with general approval, the leadership of the Jewish community also undertook the political representation of the community. The problems encountered in metropolitan life were of an entirely different nature.

The fast-growing population of the Pest community made it almost impossible to maintain the traditional life-style of a small community. Besides the need for a main synagogue that could be visited on the High Holidays, Jews who strictly observed the traditional obligation of the recital of prayers, also needed a place of worship that could be visited daily. The morning service (*shaharit / shakhres*), that marked the beginning of the day, called for a more intimate place of worship, no more than a few minutes from one's home, where a *minyan* would be sure to gather for the service. The metropolitan Jewish community could preserve the important elements of traditional life only as an intricate network of smaller communities. For Jews adhering to their traditional way of life a small place of worship in the neighborhood was far more important than large synagogues. For those living in the same neighborhood it was enough to find an occasional place, such as a room in a larger apartment, an empty warehouse or the like, as was the practice for some time in Király utca. Obviously, these separate places of worship early in the nineteenth century were the forerunners of new synagogues. Once the occasional place of prayer, as well as the congregation, proved lasting, the premises were remodeled into a real synagogue and a permanent "prayer-association" or "prayer-group" was formed. These were the small groups or cells of traditional Jewish life (*yidishkeyt*).

The statutes accepted by the General Congress of 1868/69 allowed the formation of separate congregations (called *imaházi egyesület*, "prayer-house association" in Hungarian) within the framework of the larger Jewish community, even by establishing a separate place of worship, by employing a ritual slaughterer, a preacher or a *dayyan*. Generally these

295. Outside corridor in 17 Síp utca. Photo, 1997

congregations had a charitable side, like smaller organizations within any major denomination. There was no further rift within the Neolog community. The variations of religious life were embodied in different synagogues and congregations.

A synagogue was opened in 1870 in the courtyard of 23 Dessewffy utca, for the *veres sipkás* or "red-cap" porters, messengers and delivery boys or porters working in the more elegant parts of Terézváros. It seems likely that these simple men did, indeed, go to the synagogue daily, and some of them prayed three times daily as prescribed, even on weekdays. There can be no other explanation for the fact that a synagogue was established near their stand, in a building whose social prestige obviously ranked below that of the majority of the bourgeois apartments in the vicinity. The "Dessewffy" shows that these places of worship were warranted by a genuine need.

Several Neolog places of worship and congregations were established on the territory of the Pest community. (The Hebrew–Hungarian, in cases also German, names below, *with italics*, hold up the original spelling with respect to its historical value.)

In Erzsébetváros:

37 Kertész utca: *Chinuch Neorim Egylet* (Association for Education of the Youth) (*hinnukh ne'urim*, "education of the youth");

12 Síp utca: *Áhávász Réim Országos Felebaráti Szeretet Egylet* (National Association of Fraternal Love) (*ahavat re'im*, "fraternal love");

44 Wesselényi utca.

All three were schools. In general, all Jewish schools had a synagogue or a prayer-room, and even if it was not filled on weekdays, the parents and other people from the neighborhood certainly recited their prayers here on the Sabbath.

Other places of worship could be found in Erzsébetváros at

32 Akácfa utca;

57 Dob utca;

26 Erzsébet körút: *Zion Jótékonysági Egylet* (Zion Charity Association);

27 Erzsébet körút;

1 Holló utca: *Linász Hacedek Imaegylet* (Vigil of Truth Prayer-Association), an Orthodox prayer-house (*linat ha-tzedek*, "vigil of truth");

11 Két Szerecsen utca (today Paulay Ede utca): *Titen Emesz Egylet* (To Give Truth Association), an Orthodox prayer-house and congregation (*titten emet*, "You will give truth to Jacob", see Micah 7,20); *Talmud-Tóra Egylet* (Talmud-Torah Association);

6 Király utca: *Chevre Misnajesz*, an Orthodox prayer-house (*hevrei mishnayot*, "friends of the laws");

7 Király utca: *Chevre Töhilim Egylet* (Friends of the Psalms Association), an Orthodox prayer-house (*hevrei tehillim*, "friends of the Psalms");

17 Wesselényi utca.

In Outer-Erzsébetváros:

2 Bethlen Gábor tér (or simply Bethlen tér, that is, the Bethlen tér Congregation in the building of the Institute for the Deaf and Dumb);

7 Huszár utca: *Szombat Megtartási Egylet* (Association for the Observance of the Sabbath), an Orthodox prayer-house (*shomrei shabbat*, "keepers of Shabbat", "strictly Orthodox men").

In Terézváros:

67 Andrássy út;

corner of Andrássy út and Epreskert utca (today 5–7 Munkácsy Mihály utca, the building of the Jewish Orphanage);

3 Hunyadi tér: *Hazkárah Egylet / Imaegyesület* (Association / Prayer-association for Commemoration) (*hazkarah*, "commemoration" / "prayer for the dead");

1/B Teréz körút.

After World War I

In Erzsébetváros:

4 Jósika utca: *Kattler Erzsébet Templomegyesület* ("Erzsébet Kattler" Temple Congregation), an Orthodox prayer-house founded by Bernát Kattler in memory of his daughter Erzsébet;

16 Nefelejts utca: *Réim Ahuvim Egylet* (Affectionate Friends' Association), an Orthodox prayer-house (*re'im ahuvim*, "affectionate friends").

In Lipótváros:

23 Alkotmány utca: *Budapest-Lipótvárosi Imaház-Egyesület* (Prayer-house Association of Budapest-Lipótváros);

33 or 34 Arany János utca.

In Városliget (City Park):

49 Hermina út: MIKÉFE Imaegyesület (Prayer Congregation), etc.

AFTER WORLD WAR II

22 Akácfa utca: *Or Chadas Templomegyesület* (New Light Temple Congregation), an Orthodox prayer-house (*or hadash*, "new light");

64 Rákóczi út: *Somre Sabosz* (Observance of the Sabbath), an Orthodox prayer-house (*shomrei shabbat*, "keepers of Shabbat", "strictly Orthodox men");

15 Koltói Anna utca: *Sevesz Achim* (Brethren's Union), an Orthodox prayer-house (*shevet ahim*, "being together with brethren") (for the name see Psalms 133,1); etc.

*

The growth of the Jewish population of the Outer-Erzsébetváros (*Istvánmező*, the neighborhood of István út) called for remodeling of the old prayer-room in the right wing of the Institute for the Deaf and Dumb into a special district synagogue (1931). The winter prayer-room and the Cultural Center of the district were built at the same time. There can be no doubt that the *Imaegylet / Templom-egyesület* (Prayer / Temple Association) here was the forerunner of the distinguished Bethlen Gábor tér synagogue, and it also determined its location. An Orthodox synagogue, *Bész Hakneszesz* (*bet ha-keneset*, House of the Congregation), with a large room on the ground floor that could be accessed from the courtyard, was established at 48 Garay utca near the Garay tér market (the premises formerly functioned as the warehouse and showroom of the Rieger Organ Factory [1873]).

Most of these prayer-associations had a definite character of their own. Members of the *Shas Hevrah* studied the Talmud. The *Hevrei tehillim*, the Psalm Association read the Psalms each week, according to a strict sequence (Psalm 24 on Sundays, Psalm 48 on Mondays, Psalm 82 on Tuesdays, Psalm 94 on Wednesdays, Psalm 81 on Thursdays, Psalm 93 on Fridays and Psalm 92 on the Sabbath).

A prayer-association could also be formed where the congregation was not large enough to maintain a synagogue. One such case is the prayer-association at 83 Thököly út. The *Bész Sömuel Ima-egylet* (Bet Samuel Prayer-Association) (*bet Shemu'el*, "House of Samuel") bought a villa in 1930 and transformed it into a synagogue, while the villa-character of the building remained intact. Similar smaller congregations, almost-synagogues, were to be found in several places:

32 Szatmár utca: *Erzsébet királyné úti / Szatmár utcai Imaház Egyesület* (Prayer-house Association);

8 Utász utca: *Utász utcai Imaegyesület* (Prayer-association);

12 Bosnyák tér: *Zugló és Környéke Izraelita Templomegyesület* (Zugló and Neighborhood Israelite Temple Association);

4 Luther utca: *Haladás Imaház* (Progress Prayer-house);

15 Sobieski János utca: *Ferencvárosi Izraelita Imaegyesület* (Israelite Prayer-association of the Ferencváros), founded by Mór (Moritz) Burger;

35 Soroksári út: *Soroksári úti Imaház Egyesület* (Soroksári út Prayer-house association); etc.

The Jewish community of Pest registered over 40 such congregations in the interwar period.

Observant Jews, who recited their prayers daily, generally spent the High Holidays in their accustomed, neighborhood *shul*. Other Jews, however, who only visited the synagogue on the High Holidays, generally preferred to visit a special, representative synagogue on *Rosh ha-Shanah* and *Yom Kippur*. Again, a genuine need called for the building of the Heroes' Temple right next to the Dohány utca synagogue—this became the district prayer-house of the Wesselényi utca neighborhood. The "Rombach", though the number of its tax-paying members was less than half of that in the Dohány utca synagogue, always was more of a *kile* than the "Dohány" did: it was a simple place of worship, with an appropriate room for everyday prayers. Probably this is why the community liked it more than the Dohány Temple. And it was only an ironic twist of fate that the Heroes' Temple—or the small prayer-room in the building housing Goldmark Hall—eventually united the rest of the congregations of both the "Dohány" and the "Rombach" for daily prayers: the survivors of the "Rombach" community use that room as their place of prayer.

In the early 1930s even the former Reform Association seems to have been revived in Pest. Ernő Naményi, himself a rabbi's son, organized a small group called the *Ézsajás Vallásos Társaság* (Isaiah Religious Association), with probably a considerable membership, definitely more than needed for a *minyan*. Their ranks included several wealthy Jews, high up on the social ladder. They held Reform services, or as they preferred to call it, "friendly gatherings for religious purposes", in private apartments. They consciously revived the traditions of the Pest Reform Association and of Ede Einhorn / Horn. Naményi outlined their history in a lecture held at the IMIT and in an article published in 1941. They submitted a petition to the Jewish community of Pest to be allowed to hold services on Fridays and holidays according to their own concept in one of the synagogues. Since they were extremely secretive, their main ideas are known only from an article written by Naményi (*Egyenlőség*,

296. The Hunyadi tér synagogue. Prayer-room of the Hazkarah Prayer-association

May 19, 1934). There does not seem to have been anything particularly original in their activities: brief services with prayers recited in Hungarian, lots of Bible exegesis, Psalms instead of the medieval *piyyutim*, no separation of men and women, no hat and the omission of all elements referring to Zion from the service for, as Naményi once pointed out, "religion and Zion have nothing in common". These are all elements that have been since then incorporated into various tendencies of "Reform Judaism" abroad. Naményi cited England where "also women can deliver a sermon". Why did they choose the name Isaiah? Perhaps because it was the prophet Isaiah who spoke most often and most effectively of the salvation of Israel. It is a fact that this *religious* group was never formally organized into a congregation since the Neolog community of Pest strongly clung to its traditions and did not tolerate any kind of *Neo-Neology*.

The Association, and Naményi himself, played a key role in the publication of the Kner's *Haggadah* (1936). Their story, although veiled in the mists of the past, shows that in the interwar period even the assimilated Jews of Pest tried to find new variations to the traditional forms of maintaining a Jewish identity. To quote Naményi: "We are not one *iota* worse or less religious Jews than those who diligently visit the synagogue." However, events soon took a turn for the worse, leaving no opportunity for separate organizations or for a slightly different identity.

Buda remained an independent community in the interwar period. It was smaller than the Pest community and it could not entirely cut free from the unified structure of the capital. Many of its members visited the Dohány utca synagogue from time to time. There were no significant differences between the rabbis' status in the two communities.

*

As a result of the organizational reforms following World War I, the Pest community was divided into eight administrative districts ("temple districts") around 1940. These districts were as follows: the Belváros (Inner City) district, the Csáky utca district, the Aréna út district, the Inner-Erzsébet-város, the Bethlen Gábor tér district, the Nagy Fuvaros utca district, the Páva utca district and the Bosnyák tér district. There was generally also a cultural center beside the district synagogues. Various activities were organized around the synagogues and the culture centers.

Each district maintained a handful of associations or societies with a religious and / or charitable purpose. One good example is the Nagy Fuvaros utca synagogue in the more densely populated

Outer-Józsefváros, a synagogue that seems to have functioned as a smaller center within the capital. (The rabbi here was Lajos Scheiber, father of Sándor Scheiber.) There were associations here like the *Józsefvárosi Izraelita Imaház Egyesület* (Józsefváros Israelite Prayer-house Association), the *Józsefvárosi Izraelita Szeretet Nőegylet* (Józsefváros Israelite Women's Charity Association), the *Józsefvárosi Izraelita Nőegylet* (Józsefváros Israelite Women's Association), etc. All of them were based at 4 Nagy Fuvaros utca. Other district synagogues fulfilled a similar role.

*

Traditional Jewish solidarity found expression in the activity of various volunteer associations and societies. *Kol Yisra'el arevim zeh ba-zeh*—"Jews are all responsible for one another" (Talmud, Sanhedrin, 16b). One variant on this maxim is *Kol Yisra'el haverim*, "Jews are all companions to each other", and a Yiddish proverb, *Tsvishn yidn vert men nit farfeln*, "One cannot perish among Jews." The narrowest, most natural circle of solidarity has, obviously, always been the family. For long Jewish tradition has been concerned with harmonizing the interests of family and community. The Bible explicitly states: "Do not turn your back on your own" (Isaiah 58,7). At the same time, the ancient principle that relatives could not officiate together, could not be witnesses, not even at a wedding, was also strictly observed. Anyone who had relatives in the community, could not be appointed rabbi—as set down in a *pesak*, a rabbinical decision, in Buda in the seventeenth century. Brother or brother-in-law amounted to one and the same in this respect. Solidarity within the family was strong, especially if help was needed to set up an independent livelihood, although the traditional framework for solidarity was erected from the intricate network of community relations. Conditions in the Diaspora called for the preservation of such networks. The binding link was the *mitzvah*, the command of hospitality and charity.

The size of the Jewish population of Pest and their breakdown by profession and residence eventually led to the establishment of non-religious groups and organizations. Certain institutions were called to life by the Jewish community itself, while others were formed as civil organizations. The structure of Jewish society in Pest and, in a wider sense, in Budapest during the Austro-Hungarian Monarchy was somewhat more articulated than that of other social groups. The tradition of solidarity, as well as of an urban lifestyle and the adoption of Western, especially German, models, played important roles.

The organizations and institutions of solidarity emerged much in the same way in Pest as they did in Óbuda at the turn of the eighteenth and nineteenth centuries. First to be organized was the *Hevrah Kaddishah*, followed by the *Bikkur Holim* and the school. At first, these institutions and organizations were restricted to Terézváros (in an area that later became Erzsébetváros), but they eventually fanned out from the Király utca neighborhood.

The oldest among the Jewish charitable institutions was—as everywhere—the *Hevrah Kaddishah*. The dead have to be buried in every community and, consequently, each has a Hevrah Kaddishah or a similar association. The *Bikkur Holim* associations likewise have a long tradition, as they were generally formed right after the *Hevrah*. The name, "Visiting the Sick" (*bikkur holim*, "examining / caring for / visiting the sick"), comes from the fulfillment of a religious commandment, a *mitzvah*. The *Bikkur Holim* took upon itself caring for the sick, the maintenance of hospitals and providing kosher meals for hospital patients. The Hevrah Kaddishah Jewish Holy Brotherhood of Pest was organized in 1788, before the community itself was established. It looked after the cemeteries as well.

A communal census from 1833 (published in *Egyenlőség*, January 27, 1934) registered the societies and associations in the city; their function or role are indicated by their Hebrew and German names (in the following list the names are given according to their original Hungarian or German spelling):

Chevrah Kadischa—Heilige Brüderschaft: burial society (*hevrah kaddishah*, "holy brotherhood")
Menachem Avélim—Tröster der Trauenden Verein: (*menahem avelim*, "comforter of the mourners")
Bikkur Cholim—Kranken Besuch Verein: hospital-care society (*bikkur holim*, "visiting the sick")
Cheszed Neurim—Verein der Ledigen: youth's association, a society for the religious education of
     young people (*hesed ne'urim*, "devotion of the youth")

Sandekóausz—Verein zum Gevattersein: members of this society undertook the duties of the *sandak* at the circumcision ceremony of a newborn boy of parents in need (*sandekaut / sandakut*, "godfathers' association").—It is known that in the early twentieth century Leó Goldberger was the *sandak* for several children of his factory's workers, as well as for some other kids of Óbuda Jews

Háchnószász Kálló—Braut-Ausstattungs-Verein: (*hakhnasat kallah*, "providing dowry for the bride")

Ánsé Mókaum—Armen Hausirer Verein: Association of Peddlers in Need (in Óbuda) (*anshei makom*, "men of the place")

Ánsé Córó—Invaliden Verein: Association of Disabled (*anshei tzarah*, "people in need")

Nauszóim—Nause Masso / Träger Verein: Porters' Association (*nosei massa*, "carriers of load")

Háchnószász Aurchim—Fremde Begastung Verein: a society that provided accommodation, etc. for travelers who happened to stay in the city for Sabbath or a holiday (*hakhnasat orhim*, "taking care of travelers"). Earlier, or in towns, villages, there was a modest room beside the synagogue or prayer-house (called *hekdesh*) awaiting travelers

Éc Chájim—Baum des Lebens: society that supported students in a *Yeshivah* (*etz hayyim*, "rod of the Torah scroll")

Taumché Jeszaumim—Waisen Unterstützungsverein—Orphanat Institut: (*tomkhei yetomim*, "supporters of orphans")

On January 1, 1863, the *Pesti Izraelita Betegápoló és Temetkezési Egylet* (Israelite Nursing and Burial Association of Pest) elected Mór Jókai as an honorary member. In his speech, the renowned writer remarked:

"We Hungarians have indeed much to learn from the social life of the Jews. How a kinless nation can protect itself by solidarity, how to heal its wounds by its inner strength, and how to mitigate the anguish of loneliness by communal compassion..."
(*A Hon*, January 2, 1863)

Jenő Rákosi, the conservative author of a chapter on "The Districts of Budapest" in the deluxe book *Az Osztrák-Magyar Monarchia írásban és képben* [The Austro-Hungarian Monarchy in Writing and Pictures] (1893) noted with admiration:

"Here, in Dohány and Rombach streets are the splendid synagogues. One of the remarkable features of this district is the abundance of charitable institutions, such as an almshouse for the poor, a shelter for the homeless, Protestant and Jewish orphanages, the national training institute for housewives, the Jewish Institute for the Deaf and Dumb, etc."

Around the middle of the nineteenth century some of these associations became official institutions, most often thanks to a generous private endowment. The largest and most important among them, the *Hevrah Kaddishah*, became inextricably linked with the Jewish community and its organizations. In 1869 the *Hevrah Kaddishah* established an *Aggok háza* (Old Age Home) from a private endowment by Ármin Kann. Its office building before World War II (27 Erzsébet körút), where it moved in 1931 coming from the Orczy House, is currently a movie theater. The Orthodox community had its own *Hevrah Kaddishah*, based at 12 Dob utca, while the *Hevrah Kaddishah* of Óbuda had its offices at 6 Mókus utca.

The activity of the *Bikkur Holim* associations in Pest were closely linked to the Orthodox community. They were, for a long time, based in the Orczy House. The national organization, *Országos Bikur Cholim Betegeket Gyámolító Egyesület* (National Bikkur Holim Association for Care of the Sick), was founded in 1871, moving out, when the Orczy House was demolished, to new premises at 34 Erzsébet körút. Founded in 1901, the *Áhávász Réim Felebaráti Szeretet Egylet* (Association of Fraternal Love) of Pest played a similar role in the Neolog community: to provide kosher meals for poor Jews in the hospitals and to assist the poor and their families upon leaving the hospital. This organization was based at 12 Síp utca. Founded in 1872, the *Első Pesti Izraelita Pincér-, Betegsegélyző és Halotti Egylet* (First Pest Israelite Waiters', Sick Relief and Burial Association) was a kind of cross between the

Hevrah Kaddishah, the *Bikkur Holim* and a trade union. This organization also reflects the importance of trades within the Jewish population.

From the mid-nineteenth century on an increasing number of women's associations were formed, with separate girls' associations; cultural and educational associations appeared in major towns and cities from the end of the same century. The women's associations undertook several tasks, ranging from the support of hospitals and children's homes to orphanages and homes for the elderly. Most of the welfare institutions (such as soup kitchens, old age homes, shelters, etc.) were supported by these women's associations. Based at 12 Síp utca, the *Magyar Izraelita Nőegyletek Országos Szövetsége* (National Alliance of Hungarian Jewish Women's Associations), founded in 1922, had some eighty member-associations. The *Pesti Izraelita Nőegylet* (Jewish Women's Association of Pest) was founded in 1866 and had its offices in Terézváros (41 Dessewffy utca) in the interwar period. This association maintained the *Leány árvaház* (Girls' Orphanage), which, founded in 1867, offered accommodations to one hundred girls, first in a building at 26 Damjanich utca and, later, at Jókai út / 29 Uzsoki utca, a new building whose construction was funded by Klára Hirsch, the widow of Count Mór Hirsch, and finally at 149 Hungária körút. It also maintained a public hospital, the *Weiss Alice Gyermekágyas Otthon* ("Alice Weiss" Maternity Hospital) (1910); a *Leányotthon* (Girls' Home) (1923); a soup kitchen for the needy, regardless of religious denomination (41 Dessewffy utca); an employment agency for Jewish women (41 Dessewffy utca). The *Belvárosi Izraelita Nőegylet* (Inner City Israelite Women's Association) (2 Havas utca) maintained two homes for apprentices (18/B Lónyai utca and 9 Károly körút). The *Budapesti V. kerületi Izraelita Nőegylet* (Budapest Israelite Women's Association of the Fifth District), founded in 1909 (38 Sziget utca, today XIIIth district, Radnóti Miklós utca), maintained an old age home. The *VII. kerületi Izraelita Nőegylet* (Seventh District Israelite Women's Association) (2 Bethlen Gábor tér) supported a soup kitchen, a day-care center for children and a women's old age home (27–29 István út). The *VIII. és IX. kerületi Izraelita Nőegylet* (Eighth and Ninth District Jewish Women's Association) (39 Páva utca) supported a women's old age home, a men's old age home, an apprentice home and a day-care center for children. In the interwar period there were also women's associations in Józsefváros, in Angyalföld, on Erzsébet királyné út, in Szatmár utca, in Kőbánya, in Buda (22 Keleti Károly utca) and in Óbuda, etc. Before Passover the *matzzah* was sold, distributed in, and sent out to other communities in the province from, the Bethlen Gábor tér Jewish school. Its building developed into a welfare institution and functioned as such during and after the Holocaust.

297. Manfréd Weiss, generous benefactor of several foundations, with his family. His wife, Alice Weiss, née Wohl, and their children; from right to left: Elza, Marianne, Jenő, Alfonz

Beside the *Magyar Zsidó Ifjak Egyesülete* (Hungarian Jewish Youth Association) (1902), the Orthodox *Chinuch Neorim Egylet* / Association (37 Kertész utca), which undertook religious education outside the family, can also be regarded as a religious youth organization. Jewish scout troops were—in accordance with the organizational framework of the scout movement—generally linked to a school in the interwar period. In terms of religion, these scout troops stood under Neolog influence. The manual for the Jewish scouts was written by Pál Vidor, a rabbi in Buda (1938). The Orthodox considered the scout movement far too secular. The youth organizations of the Zionist movement tried to instill a strong Jewish consciousness into their members (*ha-shomer ha-tzair*, "youth guard", or *shomer* for short), but not in a religious spirit.

The *Magyar Izraelita Egyetemi és Főiskolai Hallgatók Országos Egyesülete* (National Association of Hungarian Jewish University and High School Students, MIEFHOE) played a unique role in the 1930s. Their offices, located at the center of the university district (10 Királyi Pál utca), were more like a club, the scene of political discussions: a constant bustle filled its rooms, with animated debates over the options of Jewish life and political events in Hungary. The young intellectuals who came here were also influenced by the spirit of socialism. Although not all of them were observant, their main purpose was not to abandon Judaism. This, by the way, was less and less of an option given the deteriorating political situation. They railed against the leadership of the Jewish community, the conservatism of the influential Jewish financial elite and in general attempted to channel new ideas, ranging from those of Freud to socialism, into the mainstream of Hungarian intellectual life. With the approach of war, following the enactment of the (Anti-)Jewish Laws and the outbreak of World War II, this lively and learned group dispersed: some joined the Zionist movement, others the Social-Democrats, and some, as Endre Ságvári (1913–1944), participated in communist organizations—in July, 1944 Ságvári himself was shot and killed by the gendarmes sent to arrest him–, and others rallied around the Rabbinical Seminary. Those who survived the forced labor battalions and the deportations became members of the intellectual elite in Budapest, in Israel or in the United States.

The *Patronage Egyesület* / Association (1910) looked after children who had been abandoned or were in an endangered situation, perhaps under police supervision or under arrest.

Summer camps for children were organized each year by the *Izraelita Szünidei Gyermektelep Egyesület* (Israelite Children's Vacation Home Association), founded in 1909 (12 Síp utca; later, after World War II, 11 Barcsay utca). Their summer camps were at Diósjenő—a village and mountain resort North of Budapest—and at Lake Balaton.

*

The Jewish community of Pest was always in charge of several foundations. There were times, around 1930, when the number of these foundations was as high as 750, a special department had to be created for them in Síp utca. The largest foundations, such as the *Vakok Intézete* (Institute for the Blind), the hospitals, the Jewish High School, etc., became—in consequence of the war bond losses and the inflation in the wake of World War I—budget institutions. Decisions on the disbursement of the smaller foundations had to be made yearly. The Census of Jewish communities in April, 1944 registered the following private endowments and foundations in Pest: public welfare, charity, support for widows and orphans, rent aid, relief loans, provisions for brides without dowry, clothing aid, grants for students, education aids, scholarships, support for high school studies, scholarships for students at the Teachers' College, textbook aid, childcare aid, contributions to the cost of hospital treatments, of purchase of drugs, subvention of the tuberculosis institute, support for the cost of treatment in tuberculosis sanatoriums, support for college students affected by tuberculosis, construction of an isolation ward, recital of the *Kaddish* for the dead, etc.

The building of the Boys' and Girls' Orphanage and its real estate properties (Vilma királynő út, today 25–27 Városligeti fasor; 5–7 Munkácsy Mihály utca; 4 Holló utca) were in part utilized as apartment buildings, with the income earmarked to cover the costs of the Orphanage. In the aftermath of World War II, when a place in the orphanage was vital for many Jewish children, the Jewish community maintained orphanages and student homes in several buildings all over the city. In 1958 the community received the large building on the corner of 88 Dózsa György út and 35 Délibáb utca. After these children and boarding students from the provinces grew up, the institution was moved to the fourth floor of the Rabbinical Seminary building. At present, however, it only exists on paper for there are no longer Jewish orphans who would need it.

The *Országos Rabbi Egyesület* (National Association of Rabbis) (7 Wesselényi utca) was the lobbying organization of the rabbis, while the *Izraelita Felekezeti Alkalmazottak* (/ *Hitközségi Tisztviselők és Alkalmazottak) Országos Egyesülete* (National Association of the Employees (/ Officials and Employees) of the Israelite community) (12 Fő utca), founded in 1911, represented and defended the rights of the other employees of the Jewish community. The pension office of the employees of the Jewish community and of the Hevrah Kaddishah was created in 1852 and, even though its assets melted away with time, the Pest community continued to disburse the annuities after World War I.

The *Izraelita Magyar Irodalmi Társulat* (Israelite Hungarian Literary Society, IMIT) was closely linked to the Rabbinical Seminary; however, in the interwar period the society already pursued its activities independently, organizing public lectures, publishing its own yearbook (*Évkönyv*) and, most important, assisting with the work of the Jewish Museum. It had its own offices at 56 Erzsébet körút.

Shortly after the creation of the Rabbinical Seminary, an association for the support of its students, the *Écz Hájjim Segélyező Egyesület* (Aid Association) was also founded (1879); its mission was to maintain the students' canteen at the Rabbinical Seminary and to provide scholarships and grants for the needy students. The National Association of Hungarian Jewish University and High School Students (MIEFHOE) (22 Síp utca) was established for the benefit of Jewish students studying at other institutions, moreover, to encourage them to preserve their Jewish identity. The *Országos Magyar Izraelita Közművelődési Egyesület* (National Hungarian Israelite Public Education Association, OMIKE) provided kosher meals for students (*Mensa Academica*: 11–13 Üllői út) and financed a student home and a library.

Established in 1913, the largest charitable foundation of Pest Orthodoxy, the *Orthodox Népasztal* (Orthodox Soup Kitchen) (13 Wesselényi utca) provided meals for the needy, prepared according to the strictest rules of *kashrut*. Without this soup kitchen provisioning the Pest ghetto in the winter of 1944/45 would hardly have been possible.

*

In 1848, when the *Első magyar zsidó naptár és évkönyv* [First Hungarian Jewish Calendar and Yearbook] was published, there also was—according to an advertisement—a "Palestine *pushke*" (Palestine savings box) in the Óbuda community: "Its aim is: to assist the poor of Palestine and to train them in various crafts. Source of founds: on the occasion of weddings and circumcisions, and it shall also be set up on 12 other instances during the year."

The Zionist movement found an appropriate base in Jewish tradition on which to build in the Diaspora, for the Talmud prescribed the obligation of solidarity, the support of the Jews living in Palestine instead of the tax to be paid to the Temple. There were several foundations established for making the life of the settlers easier, for covering the costs of land purchases and the costs of immigration: the *Keren Kayemeth Leisrael / Jewish National Fund* (*keren kayyemet le-Yisra'el*, "fund for the creation of Israel") (1901) and the financial branch of the World Zionist Organization, the *Keren Hayesod / Palestine Foundation Fund* (*keren ha-yesod*, "plot / land fund") (1920). Their Pest offices were in the very center of the Jewish quarter (36 Király utca).

The Zionist movement itself was slow to take roots in Budapest. Even though there were a number of Zionist organizations, their membership came mostly from towns in the countryside. The *Egyesült Magyar Ciónista [sic!] Szövetség* (United Hungarian Zionist Movement) was based in Pest (11 József körút, I/5). Besides various sports organizations it was the *Magyar Zsidók Pro Palesztina Szövetsége* (Pro-Palestine Association of Hungarian Jews), established by József Patai after World War I, that spared no effort on behalf of Palestine. The two main departments of the "Pro-Palestine", called *Kolonizációs szakosztály* [Department for Colonization] (*Keren Kayemeth Leisrael*) and *Újjáépítési* (*Palestina felépítési*) *szakosztály* [Department for the Rebuilding / Building of Palestine] (*Keren Hayesod*) were identical with the foundations of the Zionist movement. They had their own library, cultural, university and trade departments (93 Király utca). They appealed for funds regularly. The small blue-and-white tin cans (*pushke*) in which donations were collected for the settlements in Palestine (*yishuv*, "settlement") appeared in Hungary as well. There are several such *pushkes* in the collection of the Jewish Museum, all of them rather worn, reflecting their long use. (In all fairness it must be added that there was always grumbling over the amounts of *shekalim* collected in Hungary, and especially in Budapest.) The money collected in Hungary helped support the Hungarian *olim* or their children and grandchildren, the *sabras* already born in the land, living in the "Hungarian houses (*battei Ungarn / beys ingern*)" in the quarter Mea Shearim (*me'ah she'arim*, "hundred gates", or "hundredfold", see Genesis 26,12) to the Northeast of the Old City in Jerusalem, established in the early twentieth century; the funds also helped other *halutzim*, and *aliyyah* in general, not only the *olim* coming from Hungary. During the war, and especially in 1944, several leaders of the "Pro-Palestine" also played an active role in organizing emigration as part of the overall activity of the Zionist movement. Also the *Magyar Izraeliták Szentföldi és Egyéb Településeit Támogató Egyesület* (Association for Hungarian Israelite Settlements in the Holy Land and Elsewhere) (12 Síp utca) served purposes of the *aliyyah*. (The name of the Association demonstrates that there was no final decision in favor of Palestine yet.)

The "Pro-Palestine" maintained the Javne Publications Committee. Their series, the Javne books, included several books for fostering Jewish values and promoting emigration to Palestine or, as it was called in Hebrew, to *Eretz* (the "Land"), as well as various publications on Jewish history and tradition. In hindsight, their most valuable book was a volume of poetry translation by László Kardos, *Héber költők antológiája* [An Anthology of Hebrew Poetry] (1943), compiled with the help of the then chief rabbi of Debrecen, Pál Weisz (later, in Israel, Meir Weiss). Translated from the original Hebrew, it was the first Hungarian translation of medieval and modern Hebrew poetry, conforming to the high standards set by *Nyugat*, the most prominent literary periodical of the time.

For religious reasons Hungarian Orthodoxy strongly opposed Zionism; it also opposed the political and economic organizations of the Zionists. According to a statement by one of the leaders of the Central Office of Orthodoxy:

> "We, pious Jews believe and profess that the country of the Jewish people will be restored, our magnificent Temple will be rebuilt at the time that best pleases the Almighty. But, in our opinion, human effort, human will, human action can in no way influence this. (...) It is to be hoped that also the masses bringing sacrifices under the banner of Zionism will perceive that no matter how strong their affection for the ancestral Holy Land be, Jewish traditions cannot be upheld in any other manner than by pious Jewish persons, who, after spending their lives in hard labor in various countries where their cradle was rocked, make the pilgrimage in the vale of their life to the Holy Land of ancestral traditions to spend the rest of their days in atonement, in the study of the holy books. Jewish relief cannot, should not aim to do more than assist our elderly co-religionists in studying[6] in the Holy Land."
>
> (*Egyenlőség*, 1930)

(6) The Jewish Hospital

The first hospital of the community was established in the Orczy House in 1805: it was a single room with four beds, presumably for men. By 1809 it had a separate building. The hospital then moved several times: in 1815 to Kreutzgasse / Nagy Kereszt utca (today Kazinczy utca), in 1827 to Nussbaum Gasse / Nagy Diófa utca, and finally in 1830 to Dohány utca. In this building, no. 307 according to the old numbering system, the hospital had two large sick-wards and a small private ward on the second floor. During the 1838 flood patients of the hospital have to be taken to the Jewish school in Könyök utca. By then the community had already received permission from the Municipality to build a hospital (1838) and, two years later, they also got permission to buy a plot of land (1840).

The first independent hospital building stood at 19 Gyár utca (today the corner of Jókai utca and Aradi utca), a plot owned by Dávid Österreicher, president of the community. As in the case of the Dohány Temple, the construction of the hospital was promoted by R. Löw Schwab. Archduke Joseph, the Palatine, was present at the laying of the cornerstone on September 21, 1841. The construction of the two-story building, according to the plans of József Hild, was completed within four months. It counted as a large, well equipped hospital. There were four large sick-wards on the second floor, two for men, one for women and one for people with skin disease; moreover, there were six smaller rooms, apartments for doctors and nurses, a large prayer-room, a pharmacy, a room for outpatient care, bathroom, mortuary, pantry, storage rooms, carriage stalls and a garden.

> "On September 21 the cornerstone of the new Israelite hospital was laid in the Thereza district by His Majesty the Archduke. His Majesty was greeted by an Israelite assembly outside and by the chief rabbi him-

---

[6] That is, studying the Talmud, etc.

self inside the building, amidst the cheers of the crowd. Martial music and the noise of mortars accompanied the celebration."

(*Nemzeti Újság hazai s külföldi tudósításokból*, vol. 36, 1841, no. 77, 25th of the Month of St. Michael)

"(...) We saw the pretty building and its spacious courtyard, and we must admit that there could not be a better place for the hospital than here; the building is not in lack of natural light, and this helps the sick body heal. We wish the brave Israelite community much strength and will-power so that they may establish other similar humanitarian institutions; we also express our gratitude to them for having built up this excellent institute for the suffering humankind and especially their co-religionists; and finally we have only one wish, that at future celebrations of this sort not only the cheers of the people should come from Hungarian hearts in the Hungarian language but the speeches, too. They must never forget: it is their holy duty to become Hungarians, even in their language." (*Világ*, 1841, p. 306)

The advice of surgeon professor János Balassa (1814–1868) was often requested and occasionally he was even asked to perform surgical operations himself. Women patients were consulted by Ignác Semmelweis (1818–1865), the famous professor of gynecology who first introduced clinical disinfection at childbirth. In 1863 an ophthalmology department was set up. Queen Elizabeth visited the hospital in 1866, at the time of an epidemic, and she praised it for its cleanliness. In 1884, at the time of the construction of Teréz körút, the Municipality appropriated the garden of the hospital so it had to move. The Jewish community bought part of the municipal tree nursery on Aréna út in 1886 and a new Jewish hospital was built here, one that was expected to be permanent.

298. Buildings of the Jewish hospital, 1896/97

299. A pavilion of the Jewish hospital, 1896/97

300. Sick-ward in the Jewish hospital, 1896/97

301. Entrance to the former prayer-room of the Jewish hospital

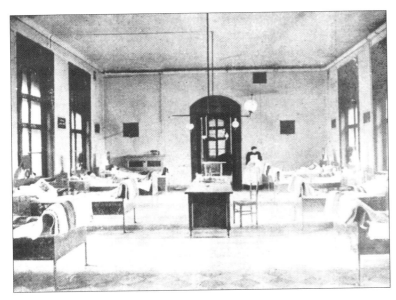

302. Interior of the prayer-room of the Jewish hospital

The former buildings of the Jewish hospital now belong to the "Imre Haynal" Medical University today. Though the interior of the buildings underwent major remodeling several times and the equipment has certainly changed, the original architecture of the buildings is mostly untouched. Even the memorial inscriptions of the donors were for a long time visible above the doors of the sick-wards.

The Orthodox community—for ritual reasons—developed its own hospital network. Their hospital and sanatorium was opened in Buda, near the Városmajor Park (64–66 Városmajor utca) in 1920. A year later the Orthodox *Ambulatórium* (outpatient clinic) was opened at 32 Kertész utca:

"The sanatorium of Orthodox Jewry is located among the elegant villas of the peaceful Városmajor. The institute itself is like the mansions around it: peaceful and elegant. The noise of one's steps is absorbed by thick, soft carpets; the corridors are decorated with tropical plants and the mirrors along the walls make them seem endless."

(*Múlt és Jövő*, 1926)

Today the Jewish hospital is on Amerikai út, in the smaller buildings of the "hospital district" planned by Béla Lajta, which after World War II remained in the possession of the Jewish community.

(7) Schools

Like every Jewish story in Pest, also the history of Jewish schools goes back to the Orczy House. The first Jewish community schools were here and in Könyök utca. By the 1830s these could by no means fulfill the educational needs of the upwardly mobile Jewish society. Jewish youth had to attend either the Piarist or the Lutheran secondary / high schools to receive secondary education. Approximately 10% of the students of the former and 30% of the latter were Jewish every year. When the *taxa tolerantialis* was waived

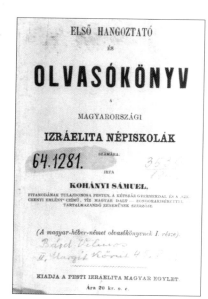

303. Title page of a Hungarian-Hebrew-German primer for the Jewish public schools, 1861

and the royal promise of the Jewish School Fund seemed close, around 1856, rabbis who felt responsible for the Jewish future and who were open to new ideas started to dream and plan a modern Jewish school system.

On September 21, 1851, after several initial proposals, a conference of mostly rabbis outlined the school program of the Jewish community. Participants of the conference included R. Löw Schwab (Pest), R. Lipót Lőw (Szeged), who wanted to establish a modern Jewish school in every community, R. Majer Zipser (Székesfehérvár), the president of the municipal assembly of Pest, the head physician of Pest, the supervisor of the schools of Pest and other official personalities. Lipót Lőw proposed the establishment of modern versions of the *heder* and the *yeshivah*. In his opinion Jewish schools had a triple task: to provide human, Jewish religious and Hungarian national education for the Jewish youth. Ábrahám Hochmuth (1816-1889), rabbi of Miskolc and later of Veszprém, maintained that the most important task was the establishment of a Jewish Teachers' College.

More traditional circles expressed strong dissent because of the focus on secular subjects in the discussions. The debate over the educational institutions was the first major episode in the historical confrontation between Hungarian Orthodox and Neolog Jews.

The Jewish schools were finally established in accordance with the proposals of 1851. Though no *yeshivah* was established, its German version, the Rabbinical Seminary, soon took over its function. A decree of the Austrian Minister of Culture issued in 1856 made the establishment of a Jewish school all the more urgent because it ordered that Christian schools were only permitted to admit Jewish students if there were enough to form a separate class, so that their presence would not hinder the education of the others in the Christian spirit.

In the 1850s, in addition to the boys' four-year elementary school a two-year division in sciences was opened in the Jewish community school. New schools were opened later at 12 Síp utca and in Nagymező utca. The girls' school was opened in 1860, initially only as a two-year elementary school. Approximately seven hundred Jewish children were educated in these two schools, about one tenth of all the Jewish schoolchildren in Pest. In addition there were several private schools for Jews enrolling dozens of children. In 1861 the *Első magyar-izraelita naptár és évkönyv* [First Hungarian-Israelite Calendar and Yearbook] mentioned such schools at the following locations: 3 and 5 Király utca, 7 Két Szerecsen utca, 7 and 8 Váci út, 44 Ország út, etc. These schools must have been in private homes. Most Jewish children, however, attended schools of other confessions. The old Jewish school in Óbuda was still functioning. All of these Jewish schools were near a synagogue and they supplied the students with kosher meals.

The most controversial topic of the last decades of the nineteenth century were the "clandestine"—that is, illegal, prohibited, secret—Jewish schools. Many people refused to accept that, according to state regulations and the spirit of the 1868/69 General Congress, attendance at schools that complied with the state requirements became compulsory also for Jewish children. Rabbis, teachers and parents alike adhered to *heder*-type schools. These were usually in private homes and they exempted themselves from the control of educational authorities. They rejected secular education. Naturally, they did not stay alive for a long time, soon the need that called them into being ceased to exist. The Jewish community then established Talmud-Torahs for the teaching of Jewish religious tradition.

10 Dalszínház utca: on June 14, 1856, the Jewish community purchased this building in Lázár utca, at the corner of Hajós utca and Hermina tér, close to the place where the Opera House was later built, and on October 8, 1857, they opened the *Minta Elemi Főtanoda*, the Model Elementary School. This was a state-supported Jewish school, the salary of its teachers came from the state. This school was later transformed into the *Országos Izraelita Tanítóképző Intézet* (Hungarian / National Israelite Teachers' College) where instruction started on October 24, 1859. The first class of students, 25 persons, graduated two years later, in 1861. Their Hebrew teacher was R. Meisel. Starting with the 1870/71 academic year the training period was extended to three years and in 1881 to four years.

At a conference held on November 13, 1860, in the beautiful auditorium of the City Hall, the *Magyar Zsidó Egylet* (Hungarian Jewish Association) formulated a plan to improve the national and Jewish character of education in the Jewish schools. The language of instruction became exclusively Hungarian, but more emphasis was placed on Hebrew, Bible and Talmud classes. The goal was to attract Jewish students from the Christian schools and ultimately to set up a separate Jewish secondary / high school. A few years later, in addition to the five schools run by the community, there were eight Jewish private schools in Budapest. In 1868 the Minister of Religion and Public Education, Baron József Eötvös, released the Jewish schools from the supervision of Roman Catholic authorities and created a special Jewish school inspectorate. Sámuel Kohn was appointed inspector of the Pest Jewish schools and he now devoted much of his attention to this task. The *Országos Izraelita Tanítóegyesület* (National Israelite Teachers' Society) was founded in 1866, with R. Meisel of the Dohány Temple as its first president. From the late nineteenth century on its headquarters were in the new Jewish school building at 44 Wesselényi utca.

Following the resolutions of the 1868/69 General Congress the curriculum of every type of Jewish school was defined in conformity with the Austro-Hungarian school system. Of course, the curriculum has changed with time, but the school system is more or less the same ever since. Knowledge of Biblical Hebrew was a basic requirement, approximately at the level Latin was required in the (German) classical *Gymnasium*. One sixth of the classes was in Hebrew. After the split of Hungarian Jewish society following the Congress, the schools, which had previously belonged to the Pest community, now came under the jurisdiction of the Neolog community. In the generally high level public schools, which were also quite popular among Jews, as well as in municipal and other confessional schools "religion" was among the subjects taught. Talmud-Torahs, where Jewish religion was taught, served to supplement the curriculum of non-Jewish schools, but were completely independent from them. *Talmud-Torah*, "learning the Torah", was essential for those who studied in non-Jewish schools; this was where the foundations of their knowledge of Bible and Hebrew were laid to enable them to cope with the Biblical, Talmudic and Medieval Hebrew texts prescribed for Jewish students attending non-Jewish schools.

The supervisor of Jewish studies at these schools was Mór Kármán (1843–1915), a university professor and an important personality in Hungarian education. Special textbooks were written for the instruction of Hebrew language, Bible and Jewish religion, there was even a prayer-book edited for students in 1873, with Hungarian titles. One of the first Hebrew school-grammars was written by Márk Handler (1837–1911), rabbi of Tata, R. Simon Hevesi's father.

Jewish students who attended public or Christian confessional schools had to go to classes on Saturday, just like the other students, but sons of rabbis and those who were themselves preparing to become a rabbi were exempted from writing and other "work" by a ministerial edict in 1885. In 1886 leaders of the Jewish community, Wahrmann and Goldziher, united in their petition to the Minister of Religion and Public Education, Ágoston Trefort (1817–1888), asking that the exemption be extended to all Jewish students. The minister did not respond to the request. It was only the next minister, Count Albin Csáky (1841–1912), who granted general exemption from school on Saturday for all Jewish students in 1893 during the debates over the Law of Reception. He also exempted Jewish students from school on the High Holidays: the two days of *Rosh ha-Shanah*, *Yom Kippur*, the first and last two days of *Sukkot*, the first two and last two days of Passover and the two days of *Shavu'ot*. (It is remarkable that he followed the Ashkenazi calendar and thus granted exemption for the second days of holidays, too.) This tolerant solution remained in effect throughout the country until the years following World War II. In small towns and in the countryside older people remember even today how they envied those few Jewish students who survived the Holocaust for not having to write in school on Saturday, for being allowed just to sit there. In Pest the situation was not so idyllic, of course. After the nationalization of all schools in 1948 this privilege, too, was withdrawn.

Jewish schools in Pest followed the model of German-Austrian enlightenment, Moses Mendelssohn and Emperor Joseph II, from the very beginning. There was no question that they should fit into the European educational system. After the reforms of Baron Eötvös, this became a legal obligation. How traditional Jewish learning, the study of Hebrew, Torah, Bible, Mishnah and Halakhic literature might fit into this system remained an open question.

> "At the age of five the Scripture, at ten, Mishnah, at thirteen, the *mitzvot*, at fifteen, the Talmud, at eighteen the wedding canopy (*huppah*)"

—this is how the Mishnah, the Wisdom of the Fathers (*Pirkei Avot*) (5,21) prescribes the first segment of a Jewish man's life. Learning here is not preparation for life but a segment of it, divided by the *bar mitzvah* and the *huppah*. Talmud study continues even after marriage. Traditional institutions of learning are the *heder*, the *yeshivah* and the various *Shas Hevrah* societies.

Ignác Goldziher's memories of his early Hebrew studies are recorded in detail in his *Diary*. Here are some excerpts from the several page description:

> "In our family religious life included the study of religious literature and so my father used to steal an hour here and there from his business activities for that purpose. (...)—At the age of four I already knew the letters.

At five I finished the first Book of Moses. (...)—I read through the Bible in the original and then, when I was eight years old, I was introduced to Talmud study. (...)—When I turned twelve, I started reading (Yehudah ha-Levi's) *Kuzari*. A year later I grabbed the *Moreh nevukhim* (Maimonides), I read through it carefully and made notes for myself."

And so on. Goldziher was twelve when his first treatise was published with the title "*Sihat Yitzhak. Abhandlung über Ursprung, Eintheilung und Zeit der Gebete*" [Reflections of Isaac.[7] Treatise about the Origin, Division and Time of Prayers] (Pest: Johann Herz, 1862). Goldziher's father wanted to make a scholar out of his son and also he himself was consciously preparing to be one, nevertheless, in the framework of traditional life learning was a continuous occupation not only for scholars but also for ordinary Jews.

304. Temporary building of the Jewish Girls' High School (5-7 Munkácsy Mihály utca)

This way of life and the traditional ways of learning could not be maintained within the European school system. A new form of Jewish education had to be developed.

In the modern era, the Talmud-Torah became a supplementary Jewish school. Its organization and curriculum were determined by the new situation. In the Talmud-Torah, basics of Jewish tradition were taught, after regular school hours, independently from any other school. Goldziher, the Secretary of the community, wanted to extend the curriculum and transform the Talmud-Torahs, which have been functioning for half a century by then, into an eight-year preparatory school for future rabbinical students and community officials. What he had in mind was probably a modern, civil version of the *yeshivah*. Theoretically the Pest community accepted Goldziher's recommendation, but then they asked Vilmos Bacher to elaborate a new curriculum for the Talmud-Torah in 1885.

305. Design for the planned reconstruction of the Jewish Girls' High School, 1923 (see fig. 304, above)

Bacher suggested a two-year program of five classes weekly, which concentrated on the prayer-book, the Bible (Torah and Prophets) and sections of the Mishnah. Others, who opposed Goldziher's modernization plans, emphasized that everybody needed a thorough Jewish religious education, that the difference was not between rabbis and lay people but between the learned and the ignorant, the *talmid hakham* and the *am ha-aretz*. The Jewish public expected the Talmud-Torah to prevent a major religious and educational division between clergy and lay people, as happened with Christianity. The debate went on for years, with participants from all over the country. Goldziher meant well, but his ideas went to the extremes of assimilationist—or maybe academic—modernization. Bacher's plan was more faithful to the spirit of tradition and seemed more realistic, too. It was around the time of the debate that the discord between Goldziher and Bacher led to a final break between Goldziher and his former best friend; it was not due to lack of loyalty on Bacher's part.

The six-year girls' *polgári iskola* or higher elementary school was formed out of the girls' school in Síp utca in 1875. Initially it was housed in Rombach utca / Rumbach Sebestyén utca, in the building of the synagogue. When the Wesselényi utca boys' school building was opened, the girls' school moved into the building of the former boys' school at 12 Síp utca. It was only in 1921 that they finally got a building of their own, again in Rumbach Sebestyén utca.

[7] Goldziher's Hebrew name was Yitzhak (Isaac).

The new six-year boys' *polgári iskola* or higher elementary school of the Jewish community opened on December 1, 1896, in the heart of Erzsébetváros, at 44 Wesselényi utca, on the corner of Wesselényi utca and Kertész utca. The first and second years of the higher elementary school were actually created by renaming the fifth and sixth grades of the elementary school. The building itself was planned by Vilmos Freund. It was a perfect school building. A synagogue was consecrated on the fourth floor. The school was nationalized in 1948. Since 1990 it again gives home to a Jewish (Orthodox) school, the *Masoret avot* American Endowment School.

By the early 1930s the Jewish community of Pest finally had a whole network of schools that satisfied all needs. There were six *elementary* schools; three *secondary / high* schools (that of the Rabbinical Seminary, and the Boys' and the Girls' *Gimnáziums*); the Teachers' College and its elementary training-school; further elementary schools of the Jewish communities of Buda, Óbuda and Kőbánya; the Orthodox boys' and girls' secondary school (both in Erzsébetváros), as well as some schools for special education like the Institute for the Blind, the Institute for the Deaf and Dumb, the Orphanage, and finally the preparatory school (*polgári előkészítő iskola*), the school of gardening, the women's school of commerce. Counting the boys' and girls' schools separately, and including the Orthodox schools, this amounts to 14 elementary schools.

The first institution for Jewish vocational training, *Magyar Izraelita Kézmű- és Földművelési Egyesület* (Hungarian Jewish Crafts and Agricultural Union, MIKÉFE) was founded on November 1, 1842, at 49 Hermina út, on the initiative of the Jewish community. Before then, Jewish craftsmen had to compete with professional guilds that protected their interests, among other methods, by not accepting Jews as members. Lajos Kossuth strongly backed MIKÉFE; Count Lajos Batthyány admitted it into the *Országos Iparegyesület* (National Industrial Association) in 1843; Palatine Joseph decreed that their students be allowed to take the master's examination. At first they took care of the education of Jewish artisans, but in 1862 also the training of Jewish agricultural workers was organized.

306. The synagogue in the MIKÉFE school and dormitory for apprentices, 48 Damjanich utca

307. Memorial leaf in honor of Moses Montefiore on the occasion of his visit to Pest in 1863

On one of his trips to Palestine, after his wife's death, Sir Moses Montefiore (1784–1885) spent a few days in Pest on his way. Here he created the Moses and Judith Montefiore Foundation in 1863 to support MIKÉFE, which had the same goals as Montefiore himself: both wanted to expand Jewish artisanry and farming, only one in Palestine and the other in Hungary. (On the same trip Montefiore said *Kaddish* over his wife in Nagykanizsa.)

MIKÉFE was the first in Hungary to establish a school and dormitory for apprentices (48 Damjanich utca) in 1892. The building served as an industrial vocational school for years even after World War II and also trained gardeners: in 1908 MIKÉFE bought some 130 acres of land at 130–134 Keresztúri út, where they had flower and vegetable gardens, a tree nursery, vineyards, hothouses, agricultural land, a dairy and poultry farm and an apiary. Today this belongs to the *Fővárosi Kertészeti Vállalat* (Metropolitan Horticultural Co.).

The *Országos Izraelita Patronázs Egyesület* (National Israelite Patronage Union) was founded in 1910 to embrace the cause of children who were under police investigation or needed care of some sort. Soon it was to provide for war orphans, too. Its headquarters were at 4 Nagy Fuvaros utca. The Patronage Union had two vocational schools in Nagy Fuvaros utca and in Lajos utca, a girls' home in Hernád utca, a nursery in Róna utca, a day-care, a special nursery and a vocational counseling center, this latter one in the vocational school of MIKÉFE.

At the time of the (Anti-)Jewish Laws the community had to set up additional schools to offer equal opportunities to those who were now expelled from non-Jewish institutions. In 1939 a four-year engineering school with two classes was opened for boys and a vocational secondary school for girls. The boys' school was in the basement of the Jewish High School until 1940/41, when the workshop was moved to Mexikói út. The girls were taught embroidery, the use of educational films and folk art in school. Some of their teachers also taught at the Jewish high school.

Immediately after the First (Anti-)Jewish Law was passed in the fall of 1938, the ORT opened a vocational school in Budapest, at 32 Erzsébet körút. The ORT started its activities in Russia in the 1880s, even its name is a Russian acronym: *Obshtshestvo Rasprostraneniya Truda sredi yevreyev*. In an atmosphere of pogroms and discrimination it helped Jewish youth by providing vocational training. In the 1930s its headquarters were in Switzerland. In Budapest the ORT established schools for beauticians, embroiderers, underwear-, layette- and corset-makers, hat-makers and ritual poultry slaughterers. In Bonyhád they opened an agricultural school. These schools operated until 1949, with an interruption in 1944, of course. Some two thousand people earned certificates from them. Using the Russian / international acronym, it was called **Or***szágos **T***ovábbképző **B***izottság (National Committee of Continuing Education, ORT) in Hungarian.

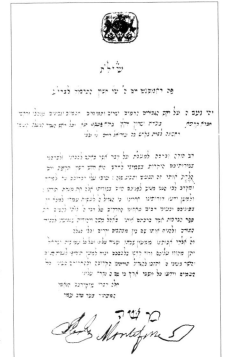

308. Moses Montefiore's letter to the Pest Hevrah Kaddishah

After World War II the *Magyar Cionista Szövetség* (Hungarian Zionist Alliance) set up its own school in Pest, an elementary school and a high school. The *Tarbut*, "civilization" schools had relatively few pupils. Emphasis was placed on Hebrew, even some of the subjects were taught in Hebrew. The Pest Tarbut School (*Gimnaziyah shel ha-Tarbut*) in Rökk Szilárd utca, in the building of the Rabbinical Seminary, was named after Ignác Goldziher. Its director between 1945 and 1948 was István Hahn (1913–1984), a professor at the Rabbinical Seminary until 1948 (and in the second, secular half of his life, professor of ancient history at the Eötvös Loránd University). Hungarian literature was taught by Sándor Scheiber, Bible and history by Hahn. Along with many other Jewish schools, the Tarbut School was nationalized in 1948 and closed down after that.

(8) Zsidó Gimnázium: The Jewish Secondary / High School

Whether a separate Jewish high school should be established was debated for several decades before and around 1900. Mór Wahrmann, the president of the community, opposed the idea, arguing that the establishment and maintenance of secondary / high schools was the task of the state, this is what taxes were for, and Jews also paid taxes. Yet in 1887 a commission was formed to advance the case of the school, starting an extended controversy. The majority of the community agreed with Wahrmann that a confessional school would hinder the adjustment to Hungarian society, and that was the opinion of the non-Jewish public, too. But in 1892 Knight Antal Freystädtler de Kövesgyűr (1825–1892), landowner, made a large donation (10-years' interest on 1,000,000 forints or, in another national currency, 2,000,000 koronas) to an endowment, thereby establishing the financial basis. Though he originally wanted to donate the money for the Hospital, Sámuel Kohn dissuaded him from his intention and so he gave it for the school. A year later Sándor Wahrmann gave an additional 600,000 forints to the Endowment, in memory of his brother Mór Wahrmann, the deceased community president, and there were other donors, too. Although the funds became available only ten years later, planning began immediately. Goldziher wanted to expand the lower division of the Rabbinical Seminary into a high school; Mór Kármán backed the idea of separate classical and science high schools;

Bernát Munkácsi (Munk) (1860–1937), the respected Finno-Ugric linguist, since 1890 the educational supervisor of the Jewish community, proposed to establish an independent Jewish high school in the Wesselényi utca building. In 1909 R. Sámuel Kohn and Fülöp Weinmann, the president of the community, won over Count Albert Apponyi, Minister of Religion and Education, the curator of the Freystädtler Endowment, for the plan of a new, independent secondary / high school—the *Pesti Izraelita Hitközség Alapítványi Gimnáziuma* (Pest Israelite Community's Endowment Secondary / High School).[8]

In 1909 the Endowment and the community signed the contract and a year later, when they received all the necessary permissions, the community bought the plot of land on the corner of Abonyi utca and Bálint utca (later Szent Domonkos utca, today Cházár András utca) in the vicinity of the Városliget (City Park). Béla Lajta drew up the

309. Bernát Munkácsi. Photo, 1885

specifications for the design competition and he made his own plan, too. Construction work began in 1912, but only the foundations and the main walls were built by 1914 when the war broke out and the construction had to be interrupted. A temporary roof was devised until after the war. Then a new architect took over, Ármin Hegedűs (1869–1945), who was to become a kind of semiofficial architect of the Jewish community until a struggle about budget ended his cooperation. Hegedűs consulted Lipót Baumhorn about changes to the original plan, but basically followed Lajta's design and remained faithful to his style. (Records of the construction, including some records of a lawsuit, are kept in the Hungarian Jewish Archives.)

To ensure the future, the school was opened in September, 1919, the Boys' *Gimnázium* at 44 Wesselényi utca and the Girls' *Gimnázium* at 12 Síp utca, years before the actual school building was completed. The boys moved into the new building in 1923, though it was not complete even then. An elderly law-

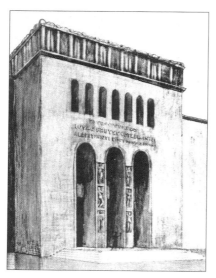

310. Main entrance of the *Zsidó Gimnázium* / Jewish High School on the original plan of Béla Lajta, 1913/14

yer who attended the Boys' *Gimnázium* in those early days recalled in 1993 that the students of the new *Zsidó Gimnázium* immediately became friendly with the students of the neighboring St. Stephen High School (15 Ajtósi Dürer sor) and they mutually visited each other's Friday night services and Sunday masses.

The construction of the Girls' High School was supposed to be financed from the money (1,000,000 forints) left by Dávid Kaufmann's mother-in-law, Róza Gomperz, in her will in 1917 for that purpose. However, the money lost its value by the end of the war; it only served as a reminder of the moral obligation. A new concept of the school was then developed. It is documented on the inscription of a slab kept today in the stonework repository in the front rooms of the mortuary in the Kozma utca cemetery. It says that "in 1927 the community decided that since the endowments that were set up to finance the construction of the *Gimnáziums* lost their value,

[8] The *Gymnasium* (in German) / *gimnázium* (in Hungarian) is a nineteenth-century category of schools. Its first 4 grades, enrolling children of ages 10 to 14 years, correspond to a secondary school, and the second 4, enrolling children of ages 14 to 18 years, correspond roughly to a high school. There were so-called classical *Gymnasiums*, teaching among others Latin and Greek, and so-called *Real-Gymnasiums*, focusing on sciences. The graduation (*Abitur* / *érettségi*) opened the way to further studies on a university level or to service in public administration and to the middle class in general.

the community would finish the building from its own resources; it would house the Girls' *Gimnázium* next to the Boys' and would maintain both from its own resources." Earlier the Girls' *Gimnázium* was thought to be sited in Munkácsy Mihály utca, but the final decision was to build it as an annex at the Boys' *Gimnázium* on the corner of Szent Domonkos utca / Abonyi utca. The school was ultimately finished from loans that the community received from England, as were other con-

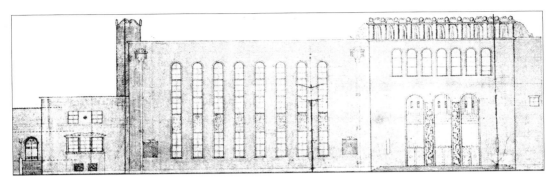

311. Facade of the Jewish High School in Szent Domonkos utca. Plan by Béla Lajta

struction works in Síp utca, Wesselényi utca and Dohány utca. The Girls' *Gimnázium*, which was accommodated first in Síp utca, after 1921 in Munkácsy Mihály utca, in the building of the boys' orphanage, and finally moved to Cházár András utca in 1931.

The large, U-shape complex was the most modern school building at the time of its completion in 1931. The entrance to the three-story Boys' *Gimnázium* was designed by Lajta. Between the three arches of the entrance two *menorahs* are formed out of the brickwork of the wall, in the wood carvings above the arches there are inscriptions with the Hebrew words: Torah, Work (*avodah*), Pious deeds (*gemilut hasadim*) and the pertinent symbols: a Torah scroll, a plummet, goblet and bread, respectively. There used to be a *menorah* above these, too. The carved-stone arches are decorated with Hungarian folk art motifs, with a six-pointed star on top of each. The separate entrance to the four-story Girls' *Gimnázium* opened from a lane branching from Abonyi utca, that is, it was located in the farthest from the Boys' *Gimnázium* end of the complex. The girls' entrance is adorned with the figures of famous Biblical women: Rachel, Miriam and Esther.

The synagogue was located in the Cházár András utca wing, above classrooms and laboratories. Majestic red-marble steps lead from the entrance hall up to the synagogue on the second floor, today an Assembly Hall. The gallery has been preserved, but the semicircular niche, once the place of the Ark, has been transformed into a stage. There is a small tower on the western side of the synagogue; one can see only from the courtyard that it is a chimney.

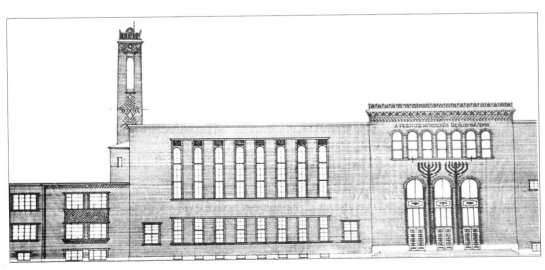

312. The entrance from Szent Domonkos utca on the design by Ármin Hegedűs & Henrik Böhm, 1928

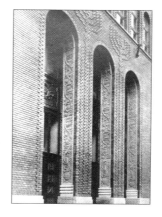

313. Hall of the Jewish High School, second floor. In the back the doors of the synagogue

314. Main entrance of the Jewish High School

315. Interior of the synagogue of the Jewish High School, shortly after its completion

The marble staircase, as well as all the corridors and entrances to the classrooms, are built in the early-modern style of Lajta. Originally there were twelve classrooms in both schools, and in addition to them a library, laboratories for physics and geography, instrument cases for art history, music, a natural history collection purchased from the László (King Ladislaus) High School and a special butterfly collection. The boys' gym was located in the eastern-wing basement (Cházár András utca), the girls', in the western wing. Above the entrance to the latter, opening from the courtyard, there is a brickwork relief depicting "Judah's Lion" (Genesis 49,9). The library was not just a simple school library. After World War II it served to the entire Jewish community, with over ten thousand volumes. Two apartments for janitors were built in the western wing, as well as offices and staff rooms. The school had a large courtyard and a garden.

The Girls' *Gimnázium* functioned as an independent institution. Separation was maintained, wherever applicable, with all religious strictness. The building, which architecturally formed a single unit, was divided inside, on the aisles where the classrooms were located, by a partition (*mehitzah*). There was a door on this partition wall, always closed, to be used only by teachers. There were separate classrooms, laboratories, etc. for the girls. Services were also held separately, first for the girls and then for the boys.

The synagogue originally was decorated with sixteen large—six meter-high—stained-glass windows, each divided into three sections. They were designed with great care, maybe after the scholarly-accurate, beautiful flower ornaments in Immanuel Lőw's synagogue in Szeged. Salamon Widder's concept was to have the holidays depicted in the lower row facing the courtyard; the more noteworthy weekdays in the lower row facing the street; the symbols of Israel's twelve tribes in the middle row; and Palestinian landscapes in the upper row. The graphic artist was Andor Szőke, an architect. Donations had to be solicited to finish the construction; the contributors' names are marked.

The school was dedicated on June 7, 1932, on an adequate date to start learning in a Jewish institution, for it was just before *Shavu'ot*, which fell on June 10 in 1932. Since the funds that were to

316. The synagogue of the Jewish High School

317. The synagogue of the Jewish High School. Photo, ca. 1935

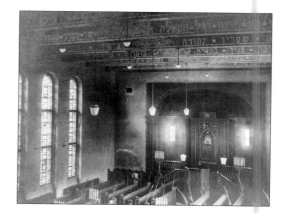

318. Charity
(*tzedakah* / *tsdoke*).
Stained-glass win-
dow in the syna-
gogue

319. The inner court-
yard of the Jewish
High School

sponsor the schools lost their value and it was now the Pest Israelite community that maintained the schools, they were officially named *Pesti Izraelita Hitközség Reálgimnáziuma / Leánygimnáziuma* (Boys' / Girls' *Gimnázium* of the Pest Israelite community).[9] The official addresses of the schools were 8–10 Szent Domonkos utca and 7–9 Abonyi utca, respectively. In 1940 the Girls' *Gimnázium* opened a special branch in 21–23 Személynök utca (today Balassi Bálint utca). During the war the two schools enrolled over one thousand students all together. Naturally, Saturday was free, but classes were held on Sundays. Only in 1939 did the High School obtain permission to introduce five-day work week.

There were morning services (*shaharit*) at the high school every day, with students assigned for the purpose, and Sabbath morning services with many participants. Many of the boys had their *bar mitzvah* here and they were often called to the Torah, too; they knew the traditional cantillation. The first class of boys who graduated in 1927 bought a Torah scroll for the synagogue and so did the girls a year later. Hanukkah and Seder evenings were celebrated together and there was always a *siyyum* before Passover. On *Lag ba-omer* there used to be a communal excursion to the mountains. Occasionally the students had their own *oneg shabbats* on Saturday afternoons.

Hebrew was, naturally, among the subjects taught at the High School. Its first teacher was Salamon Widder (1880–1951), an eminent Hebraist, who majored in German. He surprised many in the community by teaching classical Hebrew—the Hebrew of the Bible and the Mishnah—as a living language. Spoken Hebrew was only taught in *interlendish* schools in those days, at the Teachers' College in Miskolc and in the Jewish high schools of Ungvár and Munkács. In any case, students of the Jewish High School learned a decent *Hebrew* from him and his successors; they probably did not have any problems later with *Ivrit* either.

Among the teachers of the Jewish secondary school was Mihály Fekete (1886–1957), a university professor (1912–1919), who emigrated to Jerusalem in 1928 and became a professor of mathematics at the Hebrew University of Jerusalem, and later its rector (1946–1948); Ödön Beke (1883–1964) and D(avid) Raphael (Fokos-) Fuchs (1884–1977), linguists; Aladár Komlós, a literary historian; and József Turóczi-Trostler (1888–1962), a German philologist. The first principal of the school was Bernát Heller until 1922, when he was appointed a professor of the Rabbinical Seminary. He was then followed by Salamon Goldberger (1872–1945), a former student of Mór Kármán. The school experienced a great organizational and spiritual development under him. It was Goldberger who translated the greatest archaeological bestseller of the 1920s, Leonard Woolley's *Ur of the Chaldees* into Hungarian (published by Officina, 1943), a book that counted as a sensation in the popular literature on the history of Ancient Mesopotamia and on the historical background of the Bible. In 1940 D. Raphael Fuchs became the director of the Boys' High School. He was followed in 1948 by Fülöp Grünwald. The Girls' High School was headed by Kálmán Wirth (1876–1944) between 1920 and 1939, when he was succeeded

[9] In the name of the first, the Boys High School's, the word *reál* meant that no mandatory Greek and only four-years Latin were taught and an emphasis was put on sciences.

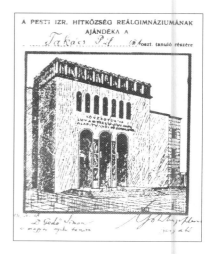

320. The staircase, view from the courtyard

321. The entrance to the gym from the courtyard in the Girls' High School

322. Sticker in the books presented as awards at the end of the school year, 1931

by the rigid Jenő Zsoldos (1896–1972). Zsoldos became the principal of both schools in 1957 and then of the united schools until 1965, when he retired. He saw to it with great care that, as conservative tradition requires, girls and boys should not mingle with each other in school or even outside of it. In this respect he had little success, indeed. His handbook for teachers, *Magyar irodalom és zsidóság* [Hungarian Literature and Jewry] (1943) is a valuable intellectual contribution as far as it demonstrated the assimilation process and acceptance of Jews in the shadow of the imminent exclusion. The faculty and principals of the Jewish secondary schools were all celebrities of Hungarian scholarship and of Jewish education.

On the occasion of the Roman Catholic Eucharistic Congress held in Budapest between May and June, 1938, the entire building of the Jewish High Schools was used to lodge the guests. The building of the Boys' *Gimnázium* was requisitioned by the army in 1941, the Girls' building a year later, in 1942. The latter was then used as a military hospital, a protected house of the International Red Cross, a transit (*gyűjtő*) station / camp for forced laborers, barracks for the forced labor unit in charge of collecting clothing, a Soviet (Red Army) military hospital. On the day of the German occupation of Hungary, on Sunday, March 19, 1944, students were sent home with the excuse that there was a shortage of coal. The next day, on Monday, the birthday of Lajos Kossuth was brought up as justification for canceling classes, and even though classes started again on Tuesday, final reports for the school year were distributed as early as April 4. April 5 was the first day when the yellow stars had to be worn. But the graduating class did take their final exams that year, too, teachers and students wearing the yellow star.

Immediately after the war all the classes were transferred to the "Wesselényi" except for students of the special branch in Személynök utca who were offered a place in the public school at 21/B Hollán Ernő utca. In 1946 the two Jewish schools could return for a short while to their old building. The graduating class lined up under three flags that year, red–white–green, blue–white and red, symbolizing three different political orientations: national Hungarian, Zionist and communist, respectively. But very soon, in 1952, everyone had to move over to Rökk Szilárd utca from where the Teachers' College had disappeared without trace by then. The two schools were united in the 1959/60 academic year and in 1965 it was named after Anne Frank (1929–1945). The building in Cházár András utca–Abonyi utca was occupied by another school already in the years following the war, the *Nemzetiségi Tanító-képző* (Teachers' College of Nationalities) and then, between 1952 and 1956, it was used by the legal successor to the former *Angolkisasszonyok kir. kath. Tanítóképző és Gyakorló Általános Iskola* (Royal Catholic Teachers' College and Training-school of the English Young Ladies) as well as the István I (today Szent István) Secondary / High School. Radnóti Miklós Secondary / High School, the training-school of Eötvös Loránd University, was organized from parts of these schools in 1961.

"*Zsidgim*", the term of endearment for the *Zsidó Gimnázium*, is still used by its former students, wherever they may dwell in the wide world. The Jewish secondary school was one of the most important institutions to maintain Jewish identity in Budapest. Its former students formed an alumni association in 1927, published a calendar for almost twenty years, until after World War II, and most of them would probably be willing to contribute to the development and maintenance of the school today.

The building itself underwent certain alterations since then. The stained-glass windows of the synagogue have been moved to the Jewish Museum, but neither Béla Lajta's art nor the Jewish symbols could be removed. The brick six-point star on the wall of the synagogue and the *menorah* decorations are still there, as is the molding of the roof, which resembles the molding of the Heroes' Temple. The *menorah* and the symbols of the twelve tribes,

323. The entrance to the Girls' High School. On the columns: Rachel, Miriam and Esther

the wrought-iron gates are still there and some documents are displayed in the hall to remind the visitor that this was once the Jewish high school. Most recently the "Radnóti" and the *Magyar Zsidó Kulturális Egyesület* (Hungarian Jewish Cultural Association, MAZSIKE) put up a slab to the right of the entrance with the inscription: "In memory of the home of Hungarian Jewish culture, the Jewish Gymnasium of Budapest (1919–1949)." The Hebrew text on the slab runs as follows:

כי היא חכמתכם ובינתכם לעני העמים

"(...) For that will be proof of your wisdom and discernment to other peoples..."
(Deuteronomy 4,6)

Although the words are not spelled out, whoever reads this Biblical quotation knows that the preceding words are, "(...) the laws and rules, as the LORD (...) has commanded", i.e. commanded *Israel*.

The message is hidden, but neither the community nor the alumni of the Jewish Secondary / High School give up their claim to the school that they had built for themselves. The former *Zsidó Gimnázium* still belongs to the Budapest Jews.

(9) The Age of Design and Construction

In 1867 the law of emancipation practically opened up the city of Pest for the Jewish community; new institutions no longer had to be confined to the Jewish quarter. The community, thanks mostly to the donations of private individuals for communal purposes, was in a position to choose good spots for its institutions. The *visible* Jewish Pest meant mostly the Jewish institutions. The city expanded towards the East as far as the "Liget" (Városliget / City Park) and beyond. Damjanich utca was still bordered by trees along its entire length; the green was reduced only later. The two Jewish orphanages and the vocational school were built here, in Damjanich utca and Vilma királynő út, while the Jewish hospital was somewhat further away, in Szabolcs utca; even further, in streets recently gained from the sandy fields of Herminamező were the Old Age Home, the Girls' Home, the Institute for the Blind, the Hospital and Nursing Home, and the Shelter. Even though the railroad lines from the Western Railway Station had already split Herminamező in 1847, the area was still a peaceful, quiet zone with elegant villas.

Around 1900 the Pest community was considering two major architectural projects. One of them, a synagogue in Lipótváros, was not carried out, but the other one, the renewal of the area in the "Jewish triangle", was completed by the early 1930s.

"Jewish architecture has only lately come into a position where it could be applied to Jewish institutions as well. Our temples, schools and other religious public buildings are no longer hidden in dark courtyards or narrow lanes. Architecture was probably the last one to get out of the ghetto. (...) In this new era of the Pest Israelite community's undertakings we intend to place great emphasis on architecture. We adopted major architectural projects in the spirit of our general program: out of the ghetto! (...) These constructions are planned in the spirit of freedom and pride. Out of the ghetto! Faithful adherence to the religious traditions of our forefathers, but open window to the spirit of modernization in our economic conduct. (...) The goal is to unite the new Cultural Center and the Dohány Temple (...) in harmony with the greater architectural beauty of our denomination, our community and our beloved capital."

(Aladár Kaszab, in: *Zsidó évkönyv az 5689. bibliai évre* [Jewish Yearbook for the Biblical Year 5689], 1928/29)

324. Middle-Eastern type bazaar at the corner of Dohány utca and Wesselényi utca, on the plot where the Jewish Museum was built later

By the time when it came to construction on the corner plot of Wesselényi utca's new, lower part and Dohány utca, commissioners and architects alike gave up their insistence on the historicizing Jewish architectural styles of the previous decades. They maintained only so much of tradition, including Lajta's Hungarian folk-art style, as was necessary to indicate continuity and coherence. This time the Jewish society of Pest created a modern style, which was to become classical. This was the last time before World War II—and until recently—that the Jewish community of the Hungarian capital actively participated in the creation of its own space and in shaping the appearance of Budapest.

By that time there were quite a few architects in Budapest who were committed to modern architecture. The mainstream Neo-Conservativism, the historical styles and even Ödön Lechner's national architecture had become barren. There were architects who were familiar with the latest trends, e.g. the Weimar *Bauhaus*, the program of the CIAM (*Congrès Internationaux d'Architecture Moderne*) and its executive branch, the CIRPAC (*Comité International pour la Réalisation des Problèmes d'Architecture Contemporaine*), or the Hungarian *Egyházművészeti Hivatal* (Office for Ecclesiastical Art in Hungary) founded in 1929 to reinvigorate the art of the Roman Catholic Church, and the Roman School. These architects maintained that even the task itself should be formulated by the architect rather than the commissioner. Functionalism operated with simple forms. Residences were built for the upper-middle class in Új-Lipótváros. Functionalism almost overcame the neo-historic styles even in the case of public buildings like temples, hospitals, or office buildings.

The real architectural breakthrough was the design of an Orthodox synagogue by Lajos Kozma (1884–1948), even though it was never realized. Until then Kozma had planned only one synagogue, and even that only abroad, that is, outside of post-Trianon Hungary, in Kassa (1925–1929). With its irregular, quadrangular ground plan, asymmetric facade and flat roof, the synagogue that he planned for Pest in 1928 was a complete stylistic departure from his previous works.

After the Great Depression major construction projects were initiated in Budapest. The great projects of the Jewish community, construction on the corner plot at Wesselényi and Dohány utca and elsewhere came just at the right time. There were architects in Budapest who had studied or at least seen modern architecture in the West and who were able to carry out the architectural tasks set by the Jewish community in a modern way. The climate in which the conservative Neo-Baroque style of the time was rejected was described clearly by Kozma during a debate about the Kassa synagogue.

"(...) Many of those modern architects who had already practiced stylish, modern architecture back in the days of peace [i.e. before World War I] returned to traditional taste in the rather depressing atmosphere of the national revival following the Commune [1919]. (...) Several years had to pass before they were in a position to rejoin the flow of great Western architectural innovations."   (In: *Tér és Forma*, 1929)

In 1927, following some internal dissension during the presidential term of Sándor Lederer, the Jewish community received a significant loan from London. Memoirs mention 300,000 pounds sterling or a million dollars, but the documents are more accurate: it was 200,000 pounds equaling 5 and a half million pengő. The construction works around Wesselényi and Dohány utca were financed out of this money: the Heroes' Temple, the Museum, the Cultural Center (Goldmark Hall) as were

some of the buildings further towards the Városliget (City Park): the Boys' and the Girls' High School, the synagogue on Bethlen Gábor tér and the buildings of the Jewish Hospital. The large projects were completed by 1931–1932. The community started repaying the loans in the late 1930s. Samu Stern, businessman and leader of the community, could not have imagined otherwise, but at the outbreak of World War II the transfer of funds stopped and even though the community saved the amounts due together with the interest, this money was lost and there are no data about payments after the war.

This wave of projects came as an awakening from the depression following World War I and the officially sponsored anti-Semitism after 1919. It is no coincidence, therefore, that the projects were centered around the memorial of Jewish soldiers who fell in World War I, the Heroes' Temple.

The community had been considering some projects on the corner plot of Wesselényi and Dohány utca ever since the 1910s; Béla Lajta's plans were discussed among others, but there was not enough money and time for it. The community acquired the plot for permanent rent already early in the century and the question of ownership was settled, too. Some old buildings, including Herzl's birthplace, had to be demolished in order to clear Wesselényi utca towards Károly körút, but this only improved the cityscape; its nineteenth-century character was finally transformed. Meanwhile the Viktória Insurance House was erected on the opposite side of Dohány utca (the work of Géza Györgyi, 1912). The one-story, bazaar type row of stores and the cramped, crumbling tenement houses behind them did not befit the new image of the Jews of Pest and were in shameful contrast to the beautiful Dohány Temple.

In 1928 the Jewish community set up an *Építő Bizottság* (Construction Committee) of experts, including several professors of the Technical University, to evaluate the plans. The work of the Committee was coordinated by Samu Glückstahl, vice-president of the Jewish community, lawyer

325. The Károly körút wing of the Dohány utca synagogue: the old office building of the Jewish community

326. Competition design by Béla Tauszig (Taussig) & Miklós Róth for the planned building on the corner of Dohány utca and Wesselényi utca

327. Design by
Marcell Komor &
János Komor

328. Design by Dezső
Jakab & Aladár Sós

and a member of the Upper House. An open competition was announced, in which anyone but converted Jews were invited to participate. Though a large number of drafts were submitted and though they came from the cream of Jewish architects, the competition had to be repeated three times until a final version was accepted. Some of the plans submitted are preserved among the so far not completely organized materials of the Hungarian Jewish Archives. Marcell Komor, for instance, would have built the Heroes' Memorial Temple on a rectangular ground plan, with a Baroque dome. He would have retained the wing building of the Dohány Temple, thus creating an enclosed space on the corner plot. Dezső Jakab would have conformed to the style of the Dohány Temple and he, too, would have built a closed complex. Ferenc Faragó planned Babylonian-style large walls with moldings and thin arched gates, with a double pool in front. He borrowed the idea of the dome as well as the pool from Moslem architecture. László Vágó visualized a *Kultúrpalota* (Cultural Palace) next to the synagogue and he would have left the space behind the "Dohány" and the Heroes' Temple open, as an extension of Rombach utca. Ernő Román, too, planned large walls, a dome and arched gates. The Construction Committee brought its final decision in December, 1929. There were no prizes, only rewards for eight works. After a second round of competition, this time only for a select circle

329. New buildings
in Wesselényi utca.
Design by Marcell
Komor & János
Komor

330. Design by Ernő
Román

of architects, the plans were commissioned from László Vágó and Ferenc Faragó (1902–?), jointly. Their original plans were so similar that they had no trouble coordinating them, one doing the Heroes' Temple, the other concentrating on the courtyard and the arcades. They also agreed on how to incorporate the style of the Dohány Temple, which had already been determined by Förster's work. Construction work started in August, 1930, and it was all completed within a year, so that on September 12, 1931, *Rosh ha-Shanah* services could be held in Dohány Temple undisturbed.

Some alterations were made to the Dohány Temple itself. The greatest change was the fourth manual of the organ on the upper women's gallery, almost sixty meters from the main organ, and that location gave the instrument an extraordinary sound. (The original organ needed to be repaired already in 1902.) The new parts were manufactured in Ottó Rieger's organ factory. This was the most beautiful and up-to-date organ in all of Hungary at the time. New lights were installed, too, including a spotlight above the Ark. The inside walls were repainted. A significant addition was the wedding gate outside the synagogue opening to Wesselényi utca leading to the bridal room. These alterations did not exactly bring the temple closer to the Orthodox ideal but their representational value was all the more significant, and they signaled that Jewish religious practice was becoming increasingly similar to the rituals of other churches. The two staircases leading up to the women's gallery were built, along with a small assembly room for the women upstairs. A driveway in front of the back gate was also incorporated in the plans but this one, thank God, was not realized.

The neighborhood of the synagogue changed completely. In order to carry out the final plans of Vágó and Faragó, the right wing of a community office building next to the synagogue entrance had to be pulled down. Approximately twenty meters (65 feet), in the width of two windows of the wing, were pulled down; it was rebuilt in the same style, only the front wall was now parallel to the front wall of the synagogue, not the street. Basically they cut off a slice that was protruding from the building. The reconstruction improved the appearance. A small square was created in front of the Dohány Temple, which was called *piazetta giudaica*, after Vágó's Italian style. József Patai wanted to name the square after Theodor Herzl, but this happened only in 1994.

331. The first design by László Vágó for the planned building on the corner of Dohány utca and Wesselényi utca

332. Design by Ferenc Faragó & György Polacsek

333. The new ground-plan of the Dohány utca synagogue after the reconstruction. Below the rule: the demolished part of the building

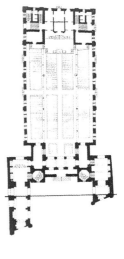

334. Arcades in the Károly körút wing of the Dohány utca synagogue, which was later demolished

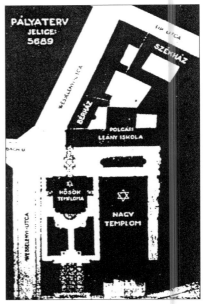

335. Backyard of the Dohány utca synagogue, where the Heroes' Temple was to be built

336. Competition design by László Vágó for the reconstruction of the corner of Dohány utca and Wesselényi utca

The Jewish Museum was built to the left of the synagogue, exactly on the corner of Wesselényi utca and Dohány utca. During its construction this building was referred to as the cultural house or cultural palace, but finally it became the Museum. An exhibition hall was planned for the upper floor, above the arcades, and a Jewish library for the third floor, but these were never realized. The building harmonizes with the synagogue completely, it appears as if they had been built at the same time, based on the same plan. The arcades facing the street "offer a good site for placing memorials", as Glückstahl said before the consecration. No one imagined back then that the Holocaust Memorial would be placed here.

The most difficult task was to build up the Wesselényi utca front. The Jewish community obtained this plot from the Budapest Municipality and a small synagogue was supposed to be built on it—the Heroes' Memorial Temple. In front of the temple, but behind the Museum, there was space for a small courtyard, framed by white cast-stone arcades. Originally it was meant to be a foyer to the Heroes' Temple, Vágó called it the "Heroes' Courtyard". A few decades later people confined to the Pest ghetto were buried here. After the war, survivors placed slabs on the wall of the synagogue in

337. Reconstruction of the corner of Dohány utca and Wesselényi utca
1: Dohány utca synagogue
2: Heroes' Memorial Temple (today Heroes' Temple)
3: Cultural Center (today the Jewish Museum)
4: Heroes' Garden (today Memorial Garden)
5: Goldmark Hall, etc.

338. The Cultural Center. Design by László Vágó & Ferenc Faragó

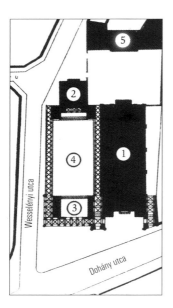

honor of the victims, and lit candles. The Heroes'
Courtyard became a memorial garden for the
tragic victims of the year 1944.

The Heroes' Temple is situated between the
Jewish Museum and the Cultural Center. Its
main entrance opens from the arcaded courtyard. There is a special gate from Wesselényi
utca into the courtyard. Its back wall is very
close to the back wall of Dohány Temple.
Behind the Heroes' Temple and the Cultural
Center there is some open space: the back gate
of Dohány Temple opens here, but one can
also enter the courtyard and Heroes' Temple
from here.

From the other side of the small square access
to the Cultural Center can be gained through
three gates with a semicircular arch. The little
square was meant to be concealed from the
street by a fence and a wall would have kept off

the inquisitive eyes from the houses opposite. It was meant to be a special place for weddings, memorial ceremonies and the like. The fence was erected only some fifty years later, when the memorial
of the Pest ghetto was already here. One can still see the balconies of the neighboring houses in the
background.

339. The Cultural
Center, 1931

The Cultural Center itself was formed by the back building, behind the community office complex
at 12 Síp utca, where the girls' school had been earlier. Its main attraction is Goldmark Hall on the
third floor. There is also a Talmud-Torah and a prayer-room on the first floor and some offices on the
second floor. The facade of the building faces the Rumbach Sebestyén utca.

(10) The Heroes' Temple

The *Hősök Temploma* / Heroes' Temple was the last synagogue built within the "Jewish triangle"—
called *Temple* from the very beginning on, and not *synagogue*.

The term "heroes" refers to the brave Jewish soldiers who fought in the ranks of the Hungarian
army in World War I, the "ten thousand heroes" as they were called in those days. This number was
calculated on the basis of the lists of martyrs of the Jewish community printed in each issue of
Egyenlőség, throughout the war. The Jewish community erected the Heroes' Memorial Temple—as it
was called in the official parlance—in their memory, fulfilling the wish of the Government that every
religious community commemorate its own martyrs. This program not only served to honor the dead

340. Heroes' Temple.
Competition design
by Ferenc Faragó &
György Polacsek

341. Heroes' Temple.
Competition design
by Ferenc Faragó

342. Heroes' Temple. Competition design by Ferenc Faragó (another version)

343. Heroes' Temple: the arcades in Wesselényi utca. Photo, 1931

but to support the official slogan that "the country was bleeding from a thousand wounds". Instead of a memorial the Jewish community decided to build a temple, thus advancing the official Hungarian cause while serving the Jewish community.

The large memorial slab of the martyrs, with Hebrew and Hungarian inscriptions, is in the courtyard by the Dohány utca entrance, on the side walls of the synagogue and the Museum. After 1944/45 the courtyard has been only referred to as *the graveyard*.

The altogether modern architectural style applied by Ferenc Faragó bears certain traits of Ancient Near Eastern, Babylonian style. In this sense it does not tie in with Vágó's previous works but more with Béla Lajta's "Parisiana" or with Löffler's style as manifested by the facade of the Kazinczy utca synagogue. The temple is a large simple block with three thin, tall semicircular gates, similar style double arcades facing Wesselényi utca and a false arcade towards the Dohány Temple, the molding on the temple and on the arcades, as if some of the sketches, photographs taken at archaeological sites would have come alive. But this kind of crenellation was not used for temples in Mesopotamia: it was used for city walls, gates and bastions. This choice of stylistic elements still points to the romantic dream of finding, or rather establishing a specific Jewish architectural style. Modern aspirations, the

344. The facade of the Heroes' Temple. Design by László Vágó & Ferenc Faragó. Photo, 1931

345. View of the entrance to the Heroes' Temple from the arcades in the garden. Photo, 1931

346. View of the entrance to the Heroes' Temple from the arcades in Wesselényi utca. Photo, 1935

347. Heroes' Temple: portico with colonnade on the Wesselényi utca side of the garden. Photo, 1935

love of simple, geometrical forms have become stronger than the urge to historicize, or perhaps we may say that certain Babylonian elements can be recycled. The simplicity of the Heroes' Temple seems to announce the return to a new classicism after Art Nouveau. Contrary to the original plans no pool was built in the courtyard in front of the synagogue, but the dome preserved a bit of the Moslem mood.

The ground plan of the synagogue is a wide rectangle. The huge Ark, covered in green marble, forms a single block with the tablets of the law (*shenei luhot*) and they are, somewhat unusually albeit in harmony with traditional orientation, along the longer wall, across the entrance. There is a giant *menorah* on both sides of the entrance. Benches are forming two rows. On the side walls there are three sets of tall windows, light blue and white glass panes with a pattern of six-pointed stars. The grate dividing the small gallery behind the *aron* from the interior space also forms six-pointed stars; the harmonium was placed up here. Behind the Ark there is a special bride's room. On the upper level there is another prayer-room, for winter. There is no separate women's gallery, the women sit on the left side. The aisle between the benches serves as a symbolic partition (*mehitzah*).

The wall above the entrance, opposite the Ark, is decorated with Hebrew inscriptions written in huge letters and in a six-pointed star form. These Biblical quotations commemorate the heroes who fell in the war.

איך נפלו גברים בתוך המלחמה

"How have the mighty fallen!"

(II Samuel 1,25)

לפני שמש ינון שמם

"May His name be eternal."

(Psalms 72,17)

זכותם וצדקתם עמדת לעד

"Their deeds and beneficence are everlasting."

(Psalms 111,3)

יחיו מתיך נבלתי יקומון
הקיצו ורננו שכני עפר כי טל
אורת טלך וארץ רפאים
תפיל

"Oh, let Your dead revive! Let corpses arise!
Awake and shout for joy, You shall dwell in the dust!
For Your dew is like the dew on fresh growth;
You make the land of the shades come to life."
(Isaiah 26,19)

The interior is covered by a dome, also decorated with Hebrew inscriptions,

כי עמך מקור חיים באורך נראה אור
"With You is the fountain of life;
by Your light do we see light.
(Psalms 36,10)

שלח אורך ואמתך המה ינחוני
"Send forth Your light and Your truth;
they will lead me."
(Psalms 43,3)

נשא לבבנו אל כפיים אל אל בשמים
"Let us lift up our hearts with our hands
to God in heaven."
(Lamentations 3,41)

צמאה נפשי לאלהים לאל חי
"My soul thirsts for God, the living God."
(Psalms 42,3)

The famous expression in the quotation from *Ekha,* the Lamentations, known in Latin as *Sursum corda,* is especially remarkable for a Hebrew philologist. The first part of the Hebrew text literally means "Let us lift up our hearts *to* the hands"—*el* in Hebrew. This appears to be a miss-spelling in the original text and even old, authoritative translations correct this mistake to "*...on* (our) hands

(Hebrew *al*)" or "...*with* (our) hands (Hebrew *im*)", or they simply omit the two letters in question before the word "(our) hands", giving the expression a meaning that could refer to the gesture of prayer. Sándor Scheiber was even more radical when he quoted the verse: following a paper by R. Gyula Wellesz in *Magyar Zsidó Szemle* (21, p. 150), he translated it as "Let us lift our hearts and *not* (Hebrew *lo*) the hands...". Those who chose this Biblical verse could have opted to correct or omit the dubious two letters, as they are corrected in almost every recent Bible edition. But no, the Neolog rabbis of Dohány utca and the Pest community were to follow the *lectio difficilior*, the Biblical text to the very last letter. This was intended as an indication that they remained faithful to the spirit of the Tanakh.

The white of the limestone walls is complemented with the gold of the decorations and some blue, for instance, the blue of the twelve-pointed star lantern hanging from the dome. This azure has already appeared in the coloration of the synagogue on Aréna út and was becoming more and more popular in Pest. Here, next to Síp utca, it would be hard to argue that it was the blue of Zionism, but it is certainly a Jewish- or Israel-blue.

(11) Hungarian Jewish Museum / National Jewish Religious and Historical Collection (2 Dohány utca)

The establishment of *Magyar Zsidó Múzeum* (Hungarian Jewish Museum) was first suggested after the ecclesiastical art exhibition organized during the Millennial Festivities in 1896, celebrating the 1000th anniversary of the conquest of Hungary. The Museum collection was to serve a twofold purpose: first, the acquisition and exhibition of Jewish religious relics and secondly, the preservation and meticulous study of the sources of Hungarian Jewish history.

On December 1, 1909, at a meeting of the Israelite Hungarian Literary Society (IMIT), a Museum Committee was formed, with Bernát Alexander, Vilmos Bacher, Lajos Blau, the painter Adolf Fényes (the grandson of rabbi Israel Wahrmann), Bertalan Kohlbach, Henrik Marczali, Miksa Szabolcsi, Ede Telcs, Lajos Venetianer and others, with the purpose of planning and preparing. "The Hungarian Jewish Museum will be an institution, which, besides its denominational character, will contribute to the enrichment of national culture with its universal scholarly values"—so proclaimed the appeal of

the committee. The most valuable artifacts deposited in the Museum from the very moment of its birth were from the collection of the religious objects of the Pest Hevrah Kaddishah.

349. Jewish Museum. Stained-glass windows

Following a long period of collection work, the first exhibition of the Museum opened on January 23, 1916, in temporary premises, in a three-room apartment (23 Hold utca). The Museum moved to its current location in 1931. Before this move, following the cancellation of the lease in Hold utca, the greater part of the collection was kept in crates in the Jewish school in Wesselényi utca, until the new exhibition halls were completed in the Museum building. The Jewish Museum was planned by László Vágó and Ferenc Faragó (who designed also the interior). The rather high ceiling of the staircase was in part an architectural necessity: the halls and rooms of the Museum were above the high arcades. As far as its outward appearance was concerned, the building harmonized perfectly with the Dohány utca synagogue, with its matching red bricks and ornamental pattern, while the arcades established harmony with the Heroes' Temple. Above the exhibition halls there is a glass-roofed upper floor that was originally meant to hold the Jewish Library, but which was eventually also utilized as an exhibition hall for the Historical Portrait Gallery. The new collection of the Museum was opened for the public on December 26, 1932. In its new building the Jewish Museum was formally owned by an *Országos Magyar Zsidó Múzeum Tudományos és Művészeti Egyesület* (Arts and Sciences Society of the National Hungarian Jewish Museum) created specifically for the purpose. In the 1930s the Museum remained open on Saturday mornings, most probably to be able to receive a larger number of visitors or to attract secular Jews in order to bind them at least to their cultural heritage.

The exhibition hall on the main floor had stained-glass windows. Some of these commemorated the names of the donors who contributed to the construction of the building, while others depicted scenes from Jewish religious and folk life. The entire bequest of Izsák Perlmutter (1866–1932), not only his paintings, but also some of his real estate came into the possession of the Museum, including the apartment house at 60 Andrássy út (later housing the offices of the Arrow-cross Party and, still later, the headquarters of the State Security of the communists).

Before World War II the Jewish Museum organized several exhibitions and hosted a number of cultural events. These included a retrospective of Perlmutter's oeuvre, an exhibit on the Emancipation (March 1938—an indirect protest against the proposed Anti-Jewish Law and an appeal to Hungarian history), a Lipót Lőw memorial exhibition (September, 1942), a József Kiss memorial exhibition (1943). An exhibition of new works by the OMIKE Arts Group was first held in December, 1939, and every year after that. In one of his reviews, the art historian Ernő Naményi succinctly remarked that "art cannot be classified according to the religious affiliation of the artist", but it remains a fact that Imre Ámos' drawings, including his series *Ünnepnapok* [Festive Days], as well as the works of Margit Anna (1913–1991), Endre Bálint (1914–1986), György Goldmann (1904–1945), Lipót Herman (1884–1972) and Lajos Vajda (1908–1941) could only be seen at these OMIKE exhibitions.

With the help of colleagues in the Hungarian National Museum, the collections of the Jewish Museum were packed into crates and hidden in the cellars of the National Museum in 1942. Only a few of the more valuable manuscripts and literary documents were lost during the war, including a few charters pertaining to the Jews from the period of the dynasty of the Árpáds (eleventh to thirteenth centuries) that had been deposited in the safe of a bank. In 1944 the building of the Museum became a district area of a forced labor battalion. A few of the people who had been herded into the Dohány utca synagogue for deportation managed to escape through a breach in the wall made by these conscripts, since the building of the Museum was facing open space. The Arrow-cross men sealed the door of the synagogue in the Dohány utca and used the back entrance beside the Torah Ark. The Jewish Museum was the single tiny chink in the wall of the Pest ghetto.

"Ernő Naményi, this outstanding man with a crystalline character, a renowned Jewish art historian in his own right, proved his courage on several occasions during the German occupation. I was present when the Museum was visited by an official of the seventh district who sympathized with the Arrow-cross movement and his colleagues. He asked: Is there anything of value here? And Naményi answered: Nothing here actually has a market value. The official randomly pointed to a Roman stone from Esztergom. What about this? Naményi: It would not fetch more than a few pengő on the Teleki square. The official: Ah, but we're going to sell it to the British Museum and not on Teleki square. Naményi: Sir, the British Museum is not engaged in the purchase of stolen goods. If I had not heard it with my own ears, I would never have believed it."

(Sándor Scheiber, in: *Magyar Könyvszemle*, 1970)

Restoration work after World War II was finished by the summer of 1947, and the new exhibition was opened on June 4, 1948. The Museum at first only staged temporary exhibitions (Synagogal Art in Hungary, 1949; The Art of the Seder, 1949; Children's Drawings from Theresienstadt, 1966; Izsák Perlmutter, 1967). Later on, visitors could also view the new permanent exhibition that has been reorganized several times since then, as well as an exhibit on the Holocaust in Hungary (called Anti-

Fascist Exhibition) in a rather small chamber of the synagogue tower that opened into the Museum. The upper floor, where the glass-roofed rooms would have provided excellent premises for a library or for an exhibition hall, were until recently used as storage space, filled to the brim with the Museum's collections not on display or bequeathed to the Museum.

The permanent exhibition of the Museum is divided into three larger thematic units: ritual artifacts and objects of the Sabbath and the High Holidays; relics of Jewish life; and documents of the Holocaust (Shoah). As part of the reconstruction of the Dohány utca synagogue, several rooms were added to the Museum in 1995. A new historical exhibition was opened, covering the history of Jews in Hungary from the Roman times to the present, in part based on photographs and documentary evidence.

350. Portrait of Bernát Mandl

Outstanding pieces among the Museum's collection are the Seder plates of Herend porcelain and Pápa ceramics, a large collection of *parokhets* from Hungarian synagogues, a collection of *hanukkiahs* and candlesticks, as well as several superbly illustrated *ketubbot*, in part from abroad, e.g. from Italy.

Before World War II the Jewish Museum published an historical and art history journal of its own, *Libanon* (1936–1943). The new acquisitions of the Museum were regularly listed in the IMIT. *Évkönyv*. After World War II the most important scholarly publication is a catalogue of the permanent collection published in 1987 in Hungarian and in English and German versions.

For the period prior to the end of World War II, it is sometimes difficult to identify the administrative and scholarly directors of the Museum's collections. In most cases, officials of the Pest community, of the Arts and Sciences Society and, occasionally, of the IMIT acted in the name of the Museum. At the same time, the museological and scholarly tasks in connection with the collections were performed by the current *őr*, keeper or keepers of the Museum, often in their spare time, since they held salaried jobs elsewhere. (The Hungarian word *őr*, an equivalent of Latin *custos*, "keeper" was generally the title of the scholarly leader of the collection.) The following list of directors, etc. can be compiled as follows:

Bertalan Fabó (director): 1915–1921
Bertalan Kohlbach and Bernát Mandl (fellows): 1915–1929
Frigyes Kürschner (director): 1921
Miksa Weisz (director): 1921–1932
Bernát Mandl (director): 1932–1934
Aladár Fürst (keeper): 1932–1939
Jenő Kolb (keeper): 1932–1942
Fülöp Grünwald / Grünvald (keeper): 1932–1948
Ernő Munkácsi (executive director): 1934–1942
Ernő Naményi (director): 1947–1948
Fülöp Grünwald / Grünvald (director): 1948–1963
Iván Róna (keeper): 1948–1963
Ilona Benoschofsky (director): 1963–1994
Róbert B. Turán (director): 1994–

351. Pass issued to Fülöp Grünwald by the Jewish Council in 1944

Ilona Benoschofsky (1913–1997) was the first woman appointed to a higher position in the Pest / Budapest Jewish community. Sister of R. Imre Benoschofsky of the Buda community, a psychologist by training, she published studies on the trauma of young girls caused by the deportation, to become herself a few years later (1953) one of the victims of the Zionist trials in Hungary. As the director of the Museum she was engaged in organizing the collection and publishing documentary evidence on the Holocaust.

On the night of December 11/12, 1993, the permanent collection of the Museum was robbed—in spite of heavy locks, alarms and a constant police watch. (The alarm system was disconnected that night.) The apparently professional robbers entered the Museum by climbing up to a window on the scaffolding built around the building. 178 invaluable *objets d'art* were stolen from the showcases. The event was shocking both for the Jewish community and for the society at large. A new—substitute—exhibition of the Museum was opened on April 15, 1994. The empty cases were filled up with material from the storerooms and from the cupboards of the Jewish community. In June, 1994 the police found the greater part of the stolen objects in a village near Bucharest and by August the objects were returned to the Museum and were put on display in the Assembly Hall of the community building for a few weeks. The case remains mysterious.

The new permanent exhibition, on the main floor, was opened in March, 1995 in the newly renovated building. These rooms house the collection of ritual objects and a documentary exhibition on the recent history of Jews in Hungary. Some old-new stained-glass windows, rescued from other buildings, were installed. The upper floor was opened in 1997 and is used again as exhibition hall for temporary exhibitions. The first major exhibition here was a collection of contemporary Jewish art in Hungary (1997–1998), accompanied by a symposium on the problematics of Jewish identity in art.

(12) Sabbatarian Codices

The collections of the Jewish Museum also include a handful of Sabbatarian codices: hymnals and prayer-books that had been used by the "Judaizing" congregation in Transylvania. Sabbatarianism was the last offshoot of the primary Reformation movement in Hungary, appearing at the close of the sixteenth century in Transylvania. The consistent application of the main principles of the Reformation—that is, reverting to the Bible, to the original, written revelation—eventually led to the incorporation of several elements from Jewish tradition and religious practice into the liturgy, the prayers and the songs of the Christian "sect" and, finally, to a complete abandonment of Christian doctrines, liturgy and religious calendar. The most influential figure in the Sabbatarian movement was Simon Péchi (ca. 1570 – ca. 1642/43), Chancellor of Transylvania under Prince Gábor Bethlen, who—drawing from his peerless knowledge of Jewish tradition—incorporated elements of Talmud into the customs of his congregation and also molded the lifestyle of the community on that of Sephardi Jews. In the 1590s Péchi traveled extensively along the Southern Mediterranean, visiting all major centers of Sephardi Jews, acquiring an excellent knowledge of Hebrew and a good Jewish education in the Jewish communities of Istanbul and North Africa. Jewish ritual literature was first heard in Hungarian in his beautiful wording. The Sabbatarian denomination survived in Transylvania until the nineteenth century in Bözödújfalu, in the Udvarhelyszék region, to become Jewish after the law of emancipation in 1867.

"They cling to their religion, to their ancestral customs, they circumcise themselves, they celebrate the Sabbath, eating only the meat of animals slaughtered by themselves or a rabbi, and marry only among themselves (or occasionally with Jews), smoking no pipe on a Saturday, cooking no meals on Friday eve after sunset; none of them are in the fields, but gather together for prayer in secret chambers of their houses where they keep their books, guarding jealously the forbidden rituals of their persecuted faith. (...) On Fridays, with the rise of the evening star, a candle burns in every window and the *shabbat* begins; and like the Jews, draping themselves in shawls, with elbow-thongs [*tefillin*], they recite their noisy prayers. (...) Many of them are outwardly Unitarian, Catholic or Protestant and they feign to celebrate their holidays. Otherwise they are extremely diligent, well-to-do, honest and virtuous people, enjoying the respect and admiration of others. (...) Neither persecution, nor the confiscation of their animals, nor emigration, nor even death has shaken their faith."

(Balázs Orbán, *A Székelyföld leírása* [Description of the Székely Land], I, 1868)

Published by Mór Ráth, Balázs Orbán's book first appeared in Pest. The Jewish community of Pest, however, in the excitement over the events of the 1868/69 General Congress and in a state of disunity rather than integration, took little notice of the Sabbatarians and, as Sámuel Kohn himself admits, only became interested after a series of articles had been published about them in various Viennese papers. Kohn, too, only wrote his all-encompassing historical study many years later, in 1890. The Sabbatarians came to be known in Hungary through Zsigmond Kemény's historical novel, *A rajongók* [The Ecstatics] (1858).

Using the chances opened by Act XVII of 1867, the remaining Sabbatarians formally converted to Judaism (May 2, 1868). Their prayer-books and hymnals, hand-written copies used in their daily liturgy until then, became dispersed in various libraries in Transylvania (Kolozsvár, Marosvásárhely), Budapest (Széchényi Library) and Kalocsa (Diocesan Library), and a manuscript even made it to the British Museum; a few hymnals were either lost or still lie somewhere undiscovered. Some late hymnals are now kept in the Jewish Museum and in the Library of the Rabbinical Seminary. A new edition of Péchi's prayer-book was prepared by Mihály Guttmann (1914) when he was teaching in the Rabbinical Seminary. Péchi's translation of the Psalms was published by Áron Szilády (1913), while the liturgical songs, the entire material of the Sabbatarian hymnals were edited by Béla Varjas and commented by Sándor Scheiber (1970). The latter and László Márton Pákozdy devoted several studies to Sephardi Jewish elements in their creed. Recently Péchi's translation of the *Pirkei Avot* was published from a seventeenth-century manuscript.

The Sabbatarian-Jewish community in Bözödújfalu survived as Jews-by-decision until 1940. By that time there were only thirty-two Jewish families and five families who had not converted to Judaism. Much like most of the Jews in Northern Transylvania, annexed by Hungary in 1938, the Bözödújfalu Sabbatarian-Jews were herded into the ghetto in the spring of 1944 (May–early June), although a few of them were taken off the freight-cars before the transport left for Auschwitz. Most of them were nonetheless deported, a few survived and went to Israel. A true history of their last decades was written by András Kovács (himself a Sabbatarian) in his book *Vallomás a székely szombatosok perében* [Testimony in the Trial of the Székely Sabbatarians] (1981). The village Bözödújfalu itself was destroyed in the 1980s due to the construction of a water reservoir, water covered up the houses of the whole village. Sabbatarian-Jewish gravestones with Hebrew inscriptions are still standing in the cemetery on the slopes of the Mountain Piritó; some of them are included in Lajos Erdélyi's album of photos: *Régi zsidó temetők művészete* [The Art of Old Jewish Cemeteries] (Bucharest: Kriterion, 1980); *Az élők háza* [House of the Living] (Budapest: Héttorony Kiadó, 1993).

(13) Goldmark Hall (7 Wesselényi utca)

The Cultural Center (*kultúrterem*) on the third floor of the new building complex of the Jewish community in Wesselényi utca was named after the composer Károly Goldmark. This building was almost completely reconstructed from the girls' school that was in the back of the Síp utca plot, adjoining the community office building. At the time of construction there already was a building standing in Wesselényi utca, no. 9, at the corner of Síp utca and Wesselényi utca, built in 1899 (and later, after the community's construction works were all done, renovated in 1935), that building, an apartment house, was to be build round by the new buildings. The plans for the Cultural Center were designed at the architectural studio of Béla Tauszig (1883–1973) and Zsigmond Róth (1885–1970). The ideas of László Vágó and Ferenc Faragó, the architects of the neighboring building, must also have been taken into consideration. The construction work itself was carried out by the company of Fejér & Dános in 1931.

The northern facade towards Wesselényi utca is adorned with a cast stone relief with the symbols of Israel's twelve tribes.

A heraldic depiction of the twelve tribes is rare in old Jewish art, because in the society of the Diaspora tribal divisions no longer existed. The only division was ritual, according to which religious roles were defined, the order of reading the Torah established. Thus the Jewish people are divided into Kohanim, Levites and Israelites, the "common Jews". The first two groups do have symbols, but these, of course, do not apply to the whole population. The five- or six-pointed star has never been a commonly accepted symbol either. Furthermore, though the tradition that Israel consisted of twelve tribes is firmly established, there has always been some uncertainty about the identity of those tribes. Classical texts themselves have various lists. The Levites have long ceased to exist as a tribe; it was exactly because they were not part of tribal division that they could take over a certain role in the cult, carry out certain practices. Though Joseph was considered Jacob's son, he was not a tribe. His two sons are listed instead of him in old registers. A special difficulty is presented by the "lost" tribes, the ones taken into Assyrian captivity. Without them there are not twelve. And in the Diaspora the twelve tribes became no more than a literary tradition. The heads of some tribes are nothing but names. Yet the

352. Goldmark Hall, designed by Béla Tauszig, ca. 1929

unity of the otherwise fairly diverse Jewish people is still derived from the twelve tribes, the sons of Jacob (Israel). The iconography of the twelve tribes was invented by European cultural Jewry. The architects of the Cultural Center in Wesselényi utca elaborated quite an original version. Wherever possible, they based the icon directly on Biblical tradition. Jacob's blessing in Genesis 49 offered applicable solutions in six cases: Judah, Zebulun, Issachar, Gad, Naftali and Benjamin. These tribes had a strong tradition of iconography in the Middle Ages, too; the contributions of Jewish and Christian artists would be hard to separate. But in the case of the other six tribes the Biblical text was of no help, so other sources had to be searched. Reuben's icon was taken from a *midrash* on Jacob's blessing, Simeon's from another Biblical story of the patriarch, in Joseph's case it is an abstraction based on the Biblical text, Asher's sign is an interpretation of a Biblical term, Levi's is a medieval and modern Jewish symbol and finally Dan's mark is based on classical European iconography.

The sequence of the symbols follows Jacob's blessing, thus the relief is to be read horizontally, from right to left, not vertically, as the two columns would suggest.

Reuben: eagle (Genesis 49,3, according to a *midrash*)
Simeon: arrow and shield. These are not mentioned in Jacob's blessing, they must come from a free interpretation of Dinah's story (Genesis 34)
Levi: pitcher. (This is the symbol of Levites in medieval and modern Jewish art, e.g. on gravestones)
Judah: lion (Genesis 49,1)

353. The Twelve Tribes of Israel. Design for the ornamentation of the Wesselényi utca facade of the Goldmark Hall

Zebulun: sailing ship (Genesis 49,13)

Issachar: donkey (Genesis 49,14)

Dan: scales. (This is not mentioned in Jacob's blessing. Scales are the symbol of Iustitia or Justice in European iconography. Here it is associated with the etymology of Dan's name, "to judge", "judgment")

Gad: (military) tents. (Associated with Genesis 49,19)

Asher: ear of wheat. (According to Jacob's blessing, "Asher's bread is rich" or "abundant". The original meaning of the latter word in Genesis 49,20 is "oily". Traditionally the symbol of Gad's tribe is an olive tree, also supported by the text of Moses' blessing (Deuteronomy 33,24). In Wesselényi utca the architects based their interpretation on the word "bread" rather than on "oily", giving thereby a Hungarian connotation to Jacob's blessing, for wheat / ear of wheat was a symbol of the fertility of the Hungarian soil)

Naftali: hind (Genesis 49,21)

Joseph: crown. (This motif is not mentioned in Jacob's blessing, but it corresponds to the image of Joseph's position among his brothers, depicted in several Biblical stories and especially in Joseph's dreams (Genesis 37,7 and 37,9)

Benjamin: wolf (Genesis 49,27)

354. Facade of the Goldmark Hall on the Wesselényi utca side

The exact notion of ideas of the commissioners, of the architect or of the relief designer at the time of planning are unknown, but the motifs of the Classicist, national, post-Art Nouveau relief clearly indicate that they were following a conscious approach. They reinterpreted Jewish art tradition based on the Biblical text. Their iconographic program revived the idea of the unity of the Jewish people. The Bible says that in the desert the Jewish people assembled around an emblem (*nes*) or a sign (*ot*) (Numbers 2,2; 21,8). The emblem, says the Prophet Isaiah (5,26), will gather the people even from faraway lands, the edge of the world. According to Jeremiah (4,6) the emblem needs to be taken to Zion. The symbols of the twelve tribes are like an emblem themselves. Israel is a cultural unity, it merging with European and Hungarian cultural traditions. Israel, as the emblems advocate in Wesselényi utca, is held together by a shared culture, shared traditions. Incidentally this iconographic program did not contradict Zionist ideals. Zionism did not choose an emblem but colors—blue and white. In those days the six-pointed star was not yet accepted as a Jewish national symbol widely. And yet the relief on the wall of Goldmark Hall promotes a Hungarian version of Jewish unity. Its Jewish symbols revealed themselves only to those who were thoroughly familiar with tradition. The relief on the street wall of Goldmark Hall reveals a hidden Jewish identity; but for an outsider it only indicates assimilated Jewry.

355. Asher, Naphtali, Joseph, Benjamin

The Cultural Center was named after a Jewish composer, Károly Goldmark (1830-1915), son of the *hazzan* of Keszthely, brother-in-law of Mór Friedmann, the chief cantor of the Dohány Temple. He was occupied with issues such as possibilities of reconstructing the music of the ancient Temple or creating a specific Jewish musical style. He, too, like many architects of the time, thought that the Eastern, Oriental style was suitable for that purpose. After "Sakuntala", composed in 1865 in a romantic Middle-Eastern style, he turned to a Jewish topic and composed the opera "Sába királynője" [Queen of Sheba] in 1875, still performed around the world today.

One of the first major events at the new Goldmark Hall was a lecture given by the Protestant Bishop Dezső Baltazár (1871-1936) on March 1, 1933. He was invited

by the Pro-Palestine Association. The title of his talk was: "The universal mission of Jewry, with or without a land." In his eulogy József Patai referred to Baltazár as a *goy tzaddik*, a "righteous gentile" and one of the "pious gentile friends of the Jews (*hasidei ummot ha-olam*)", quoting the Prophet Isaiah (9,2). By that time open support for the Jewish cause, let alone Zionism, was considered a demonstrative, not to say provocative, act.

> "Already at 6 o'clock Wesselényi and Síp utca were darkened by the crowd waiting for the doors to open. Only the police could stop the siege. The scariest moment was when the crowd opened the doors and poured into the hall. Everyone squeezed in somehow, pushing the chairs aside and standing in the middle of the room leaning on one another. One began to wonder whether the Goldmark Hall would be able to withstand the attack. Leaders of the Pro-Palestine Association could hardly get into the room. All of the neighboring rooms and corridors were open and jam-packed with people; thousands and thousands rallied in front of the building, trying to get in, and did not give up the hopeless fight until the lecture was over. And inside the hall, people were devoutly clinging to each word of Bishop Baltazár. Not a sound came from the packed room." (József Patai, *Harc a zsidó kultúráért* [Fight for Jewish Culture], 1937)

(14) Time Reckoning, Calendar, Luah

The Jewish calendar, in its ancient form, follows the sequence of the seasons. In fact, the sequence of holidays is connected with the seasons. Yet the Moon cycle has become the basic unit of time reckoning. The first day of the month (*rosh hodesh*) is itself a holiday. The difference between the Sun cycle (365 days) and the twelve-months year (354 days) is reconciled by the occasional intercalation of a leap month. This system helps keep the holidays bound to seasons, somewhere near their natural dates. The sequence of the leap months follows an ancient system taken over from Babylon of the Persian period. According to this system, in every nineteen-year calendar cycle (*mahzor hammah*, "Sun-cycle") there are seven leap years. (These are called in Hebrew *ibbur*, in Yiddish *iberyor*, combining the Ashkenazi Hebrew word and the Yiddish *yor* / German *Jahr*; the Hungarian *Jüdisch-Deutsch* used the same word as *Überjahr*, instead of the German *Schaltjahr*.) Every third, sixth, eighth, eleventh, fourteenth, seventeenth and nineteenth year of the cycle has an additional or leap month. Thus the leap years comprise thirteen (Moon-)months. The leap month is always the last month in the calendar year, Adar, and it is simply called "second Adar", Adar II (*adar sheni* or *adar bet* / *ve-adar*). The original month Adar is then called "first Adar" (*Adar rishon*). In a leap year Purim is in the thirteenth month, in Adar II. There are also other restrictions in the calendar. Because of the prescribed fast or prohibition of work certain holidays may never fall on Friday, since a holiday would make preparations for, or celebration of, the Sabbath impossible. The New Year may not fall on Sunday, Wednesday or Friday; Pesah, on Monday, Wednesday or Friday, etc. Otherwise, the date of holidays is tied to days of the (Moon-)month. It is essential, precisely with respect to the holidays, that there always be exactly 177 days between 1st of Nisan and 1st of Tishri. Therefore two months, Heshvan and Kislev, are alternately 29 or 30 days long.

The currently used Jewish chronological system was established in the second and third centuries C.E. in a historical work called *Seder olam*, "The Order of the World" or *Seder olam rabbah*, "Great Chronicle of the World". Based on this work, but only from the Middle Ages on, rabbinical chronology begins with the date of Creation—calculated on the basis of the chronological data in the Bible—on October 7, 3761 B.C.E. Thus 2000/2001 of the civil calendar (C.E.) corresponds to 5761 in the Jewish calendar. Since the Middle Ages, the thousands are often omitted in Jewish dating, the year 5759 (1999 C.E.) appears as 759. This dating is called "according to the minor reckoning" or "minor era", לפ״ק (LP״Q), an abbreviation from *li-frat katan* in Hebrew. From this it is easy to convert a Jewish date into the Gregorian calendar. In the dates after the beginning of the fifth millennium "of the creation", 1240 C.E., one just adds 1,240 to the date according to the "minor era". For example, the date on the pillar of the "great" synagogue in Táncsics Mihály utca (fig. 21, above) is: 301. This is according to the "minor era" and corresponds to year 5301 "of the creation", meaning 301 + 1240 = 1541 c.e. More exactly, September, 1540 to August, 1541, since the Jewish year starts in August or September; 1540/41 c.e., in short.

In dates according to the Gregorian calendar, Jewish authors try to avoid using the formulas "before the birth of Christus" or "in the year of (our) Lord (Jesus)", abbreviated as b.c. or a.d. (Latin *anno Domini*), respectively. Instead, a neutral term is preferred, e.g. in English b.c.e., "before the common / civil era' and c.e., "(of the) common / civil era".

The Jewish calendar system is basically of Mesopotamian origin, the names of the months are from Babylon, too. The name of the calendar chart, *luah*, is also an Akkadian loanword in Hebrew. (Akkadian *lēhu* was a wooden tablet covered with wax on which notes were taken concerning rising of the stars.) After the destruction of the Second Temple it was the Palestinian Patriarch who controlled the Jewish calendar. He proclaimed the date of the new year, and Jews all over the Diaspora followed this date. When Christianity became the official state religion in the Roman Empire, Constantius, the son of Constantine the Great (337–361 c.e.) forbade Hillel II (320–365 c.e.), the Patriarch (*nasi*) at the time, to proclaim the new year (358 c.e.). This is when the unified Jewish calendar, which can be used anywhere in the world, was established. And to avoid fatal mistakes in calculating the holidays, every major holiday in the Diaspora has been doubled, lasting for two consecutive days. The second day (*yom tov sheni shel galuyot*) ensures that the unity of the calendar is maintained. In fact, for the past two thousand years, *Rosh ha-Shanah* has always been on the same day all over the world. Each calendar cycle lasts nineteen years. Every synagogue or congregation issues their own calendar for the cycle, for the year. The printed *luah* sums up the Sabbath and holiday sequence, thus it is really a synagogal calendar. In 1944 the *luah* for the coming year could not be printed in Budapest. The rabbinate, under the leadership of Chief Rabbi Zsigmond Groszmann, decided to prepare the *luah* in manuscript form and make copies of it for every rabbi, synagogue official and community leader. After the State of Israel was established, duties of calendar preparation returned to Israel, as it used to be in the period of the Patriarch Hillel II. The Hungarian *luah* follows the Ashkenazi ritual.

In the Jewish ritual the day always begins in the evening, at sunset, as the story of Creation in the Bible states: "and it was evening, and it was morning" (Genesis 1,5). The seventh day, the Sabbath, also starts and ends in the evening, as do all the holidays: *bejön* ("comes in") and *kimegy* ("goes out") in Hungarian (with mirror-translations from Hebrew). Saturday is the seventh day of the week, and the new week starts after *havdalah*. In contrast to Hungary, in some countries Sunday is, in fact, the first day of the calendar week. The system of weeks is independent of the Moon cycle. The Bible deduces it from the story of Creation (Genesis 1,1–2,3). Though it is possible that it has developed along Babylonian rituals related to the lunar cycle, its exact origin is not known. The first definite data about the clas-

356. The first *luah* of Pest, 5608/608 (=1848)

Naptár Izraeliták számára.		Hó és hét napjai.		Katholik. Naptár.	Protestant. Naptár.
ת״ר״ח. **Elul,** אלול. **Őszelő,** September, Szent Mihály' hava.					
Tisri' תשרי Móledje: Szerdán, September 27-én, éjszaka 12 óra, 54 perczkor.					
Softim, 1.P.א״פ שופטים	ב ד	Péntek Szombat.	1 2	Egyed apát Zénó vért.	Egyed Absolon
Ki-Técze.2.P.ב״פ כיתצא	ה ו ז ח ט י יא	Vasárn. Hétfő Kedd Szerda Csötört. Péntek Szombat.	3 4 5 6 7 8 9	A. 12 Őrangy. Alb. Rosália Donát, Victor Zakariás Regina szüz Kisasszony Gorgon	Mansvét Mózes Hercul. Magnus Regina Kisasszony Bruno
Kithoba 3. 's 4. Perek. כי חבא פ״ג רד'	יב יג יד טו טז יז יח	Vasárn. Hétfő Kedd Szerda Csötört. Péntek Szombat.	10 11 12 13 14 15 16	A. 13. Mária neve Emilia Guido Morily püsp. Szent kereszt fel. Nikita Kornél és Cypr.	Jodok Protus Syrus Lóránd Salamon Nikodem Eufemia
Niczawim és Wajelech 5. 's 6.P.פ״ה רד' נצבים וילך	יט כ כא כב כג כד כה	Vasárn. Hétfő Kedd Szerda Csötört. Péntek Szombat.	17 18 19 20 21 22 23	A. 14. Lambert p. Tamas érs. Január Eustach. Máté sz. követ Móricz Thekla, Polyxena	Lambert Titus Fidonia Fausta Máté Móricz Thekla
A' bánatimádkozások megkezdődnek משכימין לסליחות	כו כז כח	Vasárn. Hétfő Kedd	24 25 26	A. 15. Gellért pus. Kleofás Justina	Gellért Kleofás Cyprián
Újév előestéje זכור ברית ע׳ר׳ה	כט	Szerda	27	Kozma és Demj.	Kozma 's D.
Újév 1-ső napja א׳ דר״ה ת״ר״ע	א	Csötört.	28	Venczel, Salamon	Salamon
Újév 2. napja ב׳ דר״ה י״ר״ת	ב	Péntek	29	Mihály főangyal	Mihály
Hásinú שובה שבת האזנו	ג	Szombat.	30	Jeromos, Zsófi	Zsófi

sical Jewish system (prohibition of legal acts on the Sabbath, etc.) are from the time of the Babylonian captivity, sixth–fifth centuries B.C.E., in cuneiform texts.

Rabbinical scholars generally did not even use months and days when indicating a date; they just gave the name of the weekly portion (e.g. *Bereshit*, etc.) and the name—in Hebrew, the number—of the day. This traditional dating, widely used in earlier periods, is now much less known. May 9, 1991, the day when the community decided to change its name and to use in all official documents from that time on the word *zsidó* instead of *izraelita* was 25th of Iyyar, 5751, according to the rabbinical dating *yom H* [fifth day] *Be-har-Be-hukkotay* [Leviticus 25–27], 751.

In some dates the day is indicated simply by the Hebrew letter of the same numerical value. E.g.
Tu bi-Shevat: 15th of Shevat, as Tu ט״ו / TV = 15, the New Year of the Trees
Zayin Adar: 7th of Adar, as ז׳ / Z = 7, anniversary of Moses' death, festival of the *Hevrah Kaddishah*
Lag ba-omer / Lagboymer: the 33rd day of the *omer*-counting period, as ל״ג / LG = 33
Gezerot tah-tat: 1648–1649, as ת״ח / TH (*tav* and *het*) = 408 (1648 C.E.), ת״ט / TT (*tav* and *tet*) = 409 (1649 C.E.), the years of the Chmielnicki Cossack pogroms according to the "minor era"
An exception is the 9th of Av: it is not *tet-Av*, it is, with the numeral, *tish'ah be-Av*.

The traditional Jewish calendar determines certain aspects of everyday life as well. The commemoration of the deceased (*mazkir*) is always held on the anniversary of the death—according to the Jewish calendar (*Jahrzeit* for Ashkenazi Jews, *anos* for the Sephardim). In Israel, to avoid conflict with the synagogue calendar, the Jewish calendar is generally used for all kind of anniversaries. In 1949 the *Kneset* determined Israel's Independence Day (*yom ha-atzma'ut*), on Iyyar 5. The Remembrance Day of the Holocaust (*yom ha-sho'ah*), a day of mourning since 1951, is on Nisan 27. These holidays are observed by Jews all over the world. Nevertheless, the anniversaries of the Six-Day War (June 5–10, 1967) and of the Yom-Kippur War (October 6–24, 1973) are always commemorated according to the civil calendar, though it would have made sense to tie these to the Jewish calendar, too.

(15) Order of Holidays

Traditional Jewish life, in the synagogue as in the home, is closely connected to the calendar. Without the calendar several elements of Jewish ritual and other customs or practices would be hard to understand. Below follows a list of the months and the dates of the main holidays (*yom tov*). Some holidays that are not mentioned elsewhere in the book are explained here in brief. For a complete liturgical calendar, however, readers are advised to turn to the *luah*. It is a characteristic of the Jewish calendar that the dates of holidays are fixed according to the Jewish liturgical year. The civil calendar, based on the Christian one, for which the Roman calendar served as a model, radically changed this tradition, allowing only Easter to remain unfixed.

I: Nisan (March / April), always a "full (*male*)" month, i.e. it has 30 days

In this month no eulogies (*hesped*) may be held over the dead. There is no fasting, not even on a *Jahrzeit*.

15: Fasting of the firstborn. And usually a feast.

"Every firstborn Israelite (*bekhor*) has to fast on the day before Pesah. This fast is not observed as strictly as the one on *Yom Kippur*; after all, tradition itself offers easy ways for the firstborn to avoid fasting. Heavenly feasts can exempt them from the obligation. A holiday meal at a wedding or a *bris* counted as such a heavenly feast. (...) Another way of securing exemption from the fast is to complete some activity dear to the Almighty, for instance to finish the study of a Talmudic treatise, an order of the Mishnah or a book of the Bible. [In this case, the meal is called *siyyum*.] Any Jewish community that takes itself seriously needs to provide an occasion for such a celebration, therefore it is quite natural that the Pest Jewish community may not be so Neolog as to make their *bekhorim* break the commandment of fasting. (...) So, on the coming of the breadless days, the Pest community organizes a *siyyum* in the grand hall of the Síp utca school, starting at 6:30 in the morning. The *bekhorim* had better remember this because at the *siyyum*, upon completing the godly act, the pious traditionally indulge in fine liquors and delicious, fluffy cakes."

(*Egyenlőség*, March 19, 1899)

15-22: *Pesah* or Passover. The first of the three pilgrimage holidays (*shalosh regalim*). The first *Seder* takes place on its first day. On the intermediate days (*hol ha-mo'ed*) work is not forbidden.

16: The counting of the *omer* (called *sefirat ha-omer*) starts on the evening of the second day of Passover (Leviticus 23,15–16). This holiday used to mark the beginning of the barley harvest (Deuteronomy 16,9–10); hence the counting of the *omer* is the harvest itself. The description of the Mishnah (Menahot 10,3) suggests that it was considered more important to start the harvest on time than to observe Sabbath or holiday. That explains why tradition fixed the beginning of the *sefirah* on the evening of Passover. During the period of "counting" one is not allowed to work between sunset and sunrise. This period is similar to the period of mourning when no celebrations, weddings or other public festivals are to be held, there should be no music, people must not wear new clothes or cut their hair.

According to Jewish tradition those events in which masses of Jews perished took place in these weeks: the revolt under the leadership of Bar Kokhba (Koseba) against the Romans (132–135 C.E.) in which twenty thousand disciples of R. Akiva died—obviously soldiers of the army; the massacres of the crusaders in Europe (1095/96) and in the Holy Land (1099); the first wave of the bloody pogrom of the Cossack leader Bogdan Chmielnicki of Zaporozhe in Ukraine (May–November, 1648). It is no coincidence that Israel set the Holocaust memorial day in this period.

It is customary to prepare various memorial calendars for the altogether 49 days of the *omer*-counting period. In synagogues one can always see such a *sefirah*-table and every day it is announced exactly where they are in the period on that day. On the second night of Passover or on the intermediate days it is customary to read the Song of Songs because of its lines evoking Spring (2,10 ff.). For this reason the text of the Song of Songs is often printed in various Haggadah editions.

II: Iyyar (April / May), always a "defective (*haser*)" month, i.e. it consists of 29 days

18: *Lag ba-Omer*. The 33rd day of the *omer*-counting period. It is a semiholiday when work is not forbidden. This is the memorial day of the death of R. Akiva's student, Shimeon bar Jochai (second century C.E.). In the schools of Ashkenazi Jewry this day is a holiday, the pupils go on excursion or athletic contests are held. In Israel this day is traditionally commemorated with a pilgrimage to Meron (Galilea), to the grave of Shimon bar Jochai. As part of the celebration the pilgrims light bonfires, they burn silk and cotton bands dipped into oil (*hadlakah*) and there is dancing. This holiday is especially important for Hasidic Jews, since tradition regards Shimeon as the author of the *Zohar*, "The Book of Splendor" (*Sefer ha-Zohar*), the kabbalistic *midrash* on Genesis (thirteenth century C.E.).

III: Sivan (May / June), always a "full" month, i.e. it consists of 30 days

6-7: *Shavu'ot* (*shvües / shvues / shvies*). The second pilgrimage holiday. The memorial day of the handing down of the Ten Commandments and of the Torah (*zeman mattan Torateinu*); actually, this day is the festival of the end of the harvest (*hag ha-katzir*) (Exodus 23,16) and of the first crop of the year (*hag ha-bikkurim*). It falls on the fiftieth day (*pentekoste*, i.e. *hemera*) of the *omer*-counting period, at the end of the seventh week, hence its name is also: "the festival of weeks (*shavu'ot*)". In the Second Temple period every male Israelite brought offerings of every kind of new crops to the Temple of Jerusalem. It must have been a colorful, joyful holiday with immense feasts of various dishes prepared from the new harvest and of plentiful milk (Leviticus 23,10–22; Numbers 28,26–31,

Deuteronomy 16,9–10). The tax payable to the priests evolved from the traditions of Jerusalem connected to the celebration of the new harvest. The income-tax played an important part in the life of Jewish communities. It made the rabbi's job desirable. The Bible prescribes the tax payable to the priests (*terumah*) of the Temple only in generalities (Deuteronomy 18,4). The amount of the tax payable to the community rabbi was determined on the basis of general customs. It was much lower than the Christian priestly tithe in medieval Europe, generally one fiftieth of the income. Fortieth part was considered generous, a sixtieth somewhat stingy.

There is an old saying about holidays.

"Which is the best holiday? *Shavu'ot*. Why? Because during *Pesah* you may not eat leavened bread. At *Sukkot* you are only allowed to eat in the Sukkah. On *Rosh ha-Shanah* you have to wait until the long ceremony is over and the *shofar* is blown before you can eat, and on *Yom Kippur* you must not eat at all. On *Shavu'ot*, however, you can eat what, where and when you want to."

Though there is a tradition, a *minhag*, of eating dairy products only. For this there are several explanations, the commonly accepted pious one being that since the Torah was given on the day of *Shavu'ot*, the sons of Israel already knew the laws of *kashrut*, yet they did not have time to prepare their utensils and the meat to be suitable.

The three days preceding *Shavu'ot* are the days of *hagbalah*, marking the boundaries. In course of the preparation for the holiday everybody gets a haircut, buys new clothes. On the night of the holiday they stay awake the whole night and study the Torah (*tikkun leil shavu'ot*). As a general custom, children started Torah study on this day; they started learning the Hebrew letters. Letter-shaped sweet cakes were made for them and boiled eggs with Hebrew words or quotes on their shells. Ashkenazi Jews decorate their synagogue with green plants or flowers. In former times they used to hang up varicolored eggs, egg-shells pinned with bird's feathers. These were sort of egg-shell birds based on the Biblical text (Exodus 19,4): God brought Israel out of Egypt on eagles' wings. On this day the Ten Commandments are read during services. In former times it was a part of the daily prayer, but later it was left out because it was feared that people might think that these were more important commandments (*mitzvot*) than the others. Dairy dishes make the holiday menu: dishes made with milk, cottage cheese or regular cheese; pancakes with cottage cheese (*palacsinta* in Hungarian) are popular in Hungary. The reason for this custom is not known but it goes back at least to the sixteenth century. We find mystics referring to the Song of Songs (4,11) to recommend light dairy dishes for those who are engaged in Torah study, to match their moderate, ascetic life. The *hallah* is baked long and narrow on that day. *Latkes*, mostly called *hremzli*, used to be triangular on this occasion. Traditionally the celebration of *bat mitzvah* takes place on *Shavu'ot*, unlike *bar mitzvah* that as a rule follows the birthday; in Hungary, there is usually one big communal *bat mitzvah* for all the girls of the community, held once a year.

IV: Tammuz (June / July), always a "defective" month, i.e. it consists of 29 days

17: Day of fast. The memorial day for the two breachings of the walls of Jerusalem. The first siege was lead by the Babylonian King Nebukhadnezzar / Nabû-kudurri-usur II (605–562 B.C.E.) in 586 B.C.E., the second one by Emperor Titus in 70 C.E. There are references to this and other fast days connected with the Babylonian siege already by the Prophet Zechariah (8,19). Though he spoke of more than four fast days, tradition formed the notion of the "four fast days" or "four Biblical fast days" based on his text. These four historical fast days are the 17th of Tammuz, 9th of Av, 3rd of Tishri and 10th of Tevet. The memorial days connected to the events of the occupation of Jerusalem by the Babylonians suggest that fast as mourning service (*ta'anit*) evolved after the loss of Judea's independence. There is no doubt that this commemoration started in the sixth century B.C.E., therefore the historical fast days may be regarded as the oldest Jewish rituals. In later times the dates of other mournful events became associated with the already traditional holidays, only with certain adjustments. The story of the Golden Calf (Exodus 32) and the breaking of the first tablets of the

Law (Exodus 33,19) are tied to this date, too. Legends survive (Taanit 4,6) about a certain *Apostomos* who burnt a Torah scroll on this day and installed an idol instead in the Sanctuary.

19: From 19th of Tammuz until 9th of Av, the three weeks (*drayvokhn*) are mourning days.

V: Av (July / August), always a "full" month, i.e. it consists of 30 days

9: *Tish'ah be-Av*, "9th of Av". Fast day. Originally the memorial day of the destruction (*hurban*) of Jerusalem according to the date (586 B.C.E.) set by Jeremiah (3,12). This day is preceded by nine dairy fast days (*nayn teg* in Yiddish) starting at the beginning of the month, during which one is not allowed to eat meat. On *Tish'ah be-Av* the abstinence from food starts at sunset and lasts for a whole day, just like on *Yom Kippur*. Mourning is the same as for the dead. One should not wear leather shoes, one must sit "on the ground", etc. We must not greet even friends long not seen with excessive joy. In the synagogue the curtain is removed from the Ark, the decoration from the Torah scroll. The Torah scroll is placed not on the Torah reading table, but on the floor. Everybody sits somewhere else than usually. It is not necessary to wear *tallit* and *tefillin* (except for the *minhah*, when it is compulsory), the *hazzan* recites the prayers with a stifled voice. Reading from the Torah is not allowed on that day, since that is joyous; only mournful Biblical texts are proper, e.g. from Lamentations.

In Jewish tradition *Tish'ah be-Av* became the mourning holiday *par excellence*. According to the Mishnah (Taanit 4,6) Israel learnt on this day that the generation that left Egypt must not enter the Promised Land (Numbers 14,35). Nebukhadnezzar and Titus destroyed Jerusalem on this day. Bethar, the last remaining fortress of the Bar Kochba revolt, fell on this day (135 C.E.). Emperor Hadrian (117–138) established the Roman Jerusalem on this day (136 C.E.), whence he expelled the Jews and even changed the name of the city for (*Urbs*) *Aelia Capitolina*. Later the ceremonial burning of the Talmud in Paris (1242) was consciously scheduled by their adversaries for this day, and the expulsion of the Jews from Spain (1492) is commemorated on it. According to the Talmud (Taanit 29a) it was on this very day that Tinneius Rufus, the Roman governor (*procurator*) announced the prohibition against circumcision, which eventually caused the revolt led by Bar Kochba, and it was also on *Tish'ah be-Av* that he plowed the Temple-hill following the suppression of the revolt.

Following the heyday of Shabbetai Tzvi's messianism some particularly rigorous mourning customs were instituted among Central and Eastern European Orthodox Jews. Since the joyful holiday introduced by Shabbetai Tzvi found a considerable number of followers in the Ashkenazi world, including Buda, it was feared that this custom would continue and they wanted to prevent the survival of the popular notion with rigorous mourning. Mourners slept on the floor at night and with a stone for pillow. Preparations for the mourning and the fast started on the first day of the month. The dinner preceding the fast (*se'udah mafseket*) was very simple, meat and wine was never on the table, only one simple dish was served, never two different kinds, maybe a hard-boiled egg with slices of bread sprinkled with ashes. On this day Ashkenazim greet one another saying: "*Tzom kal*, Have an easy fast!" Work is not prohibited on this day but it is not a day conducive to starting on a new venture.

Traditionally, the breaking of a glass at weddings is a reminder of the destruction of the Temple. And for the same reason a piece of the wall in every house is left unplastered (*zekher hurban*).

VI: Elul (August / September), always a "defective" month, i.e. it has 29 days

This whole month passes with preparations for the Days of Awe. In this month, from the Sunday before Rosh ha-Shanah, *selihot* (*slikhes*) are recited and the *shofar* is blown in the early morning service.

VII: Tishri (September / October), always a "full" month, i.e. it consists of 30 days

1–2: *Rosh ha-Shanah*, "new year", the beginning of the Jewish ritual year (Leviticus 23,24). This is the first day of the High Holidays or the Days of Awe, *yamim nora'im*, which end on *Shemini Atzeret*. Awe permeates these days, for it is now that one's fate for the coming year is decided.

People wish each other a happy new year: *le-shanah tovah tikkatev* (in plural *tikkatevu*, for women *tikkatevi*, in plural *tikkatavna*) *ve-tehatem* (*tehatemu*, *tehatemi*, *tehatemna*, respectively), "You should be inscribed for a good year", i.e. your name should be written down for a good year, or a good year should be inscribed under your name in God's book that he seals on *Yom Kippur*. This *liber scriptus* establishes everyone's fate for the coming year. To be accurate, there are three books: one for the righteous and one for the evil, which God seals already on *Rosh ha-Shanah*, and a third one for those whose case still needs to be considered and thus the decision is delayed until *Yom Kippur*. The greeting *Le-shanah tovah*, "Good year" is used in the ceremony not only on *Rosh ha-Shanah* but throughout the month of Elul. After *Rosh ha-Shanah*, however, a new greeting is used: *Gemar* (for women, *Gimri*) *hatimah tovah*, "Finish with a good decision!" or simply: *Gemar tov*, "Finish well!" One must never assume that the other's fate is not yet decided favorably. As for one's own fate, however, it should be considered undecided until *Yom Kippur*.

357. "Shofar."
Lino-cut by Imre Ámos

People customarily buy their synagogue seats or benches during the month before *Rosh ha-Shanah*. It used to be a seat for the entire year, but lately it is only meant for the High Holidays. The bench fee is considered part of the community tax. On the Sabbath and on holidays it is forbidden to carry money, therefore there is no collection in the synagogue. Pledges (*neder*) are made instead and the actual payment is on a weekday.

The major ritual event of *Rosh ha-Shanah* is the blowing of the *shofar*, *teki'at ha-shofar* (Numbers 29,1), that is why it is also called *yom teru'ah*, "the day of blowing". The *shofar* is blown as part of the synagogue ritual every weekday morning during the preceding month of Elul. The *shofar* is now a ritual object and it is covered or "hidden" until its turn comes. On the morning of *Rosh ha-Shanah* the sound of the *shofar* creates a special atmosphere. Blowing the *shofar* is not an easy task, one needs strong lungs and some practice to do it. It is a great honor to be asked to perform this role (*ba'al teki'ah*), and to listen to its sound is a *mitzvah*.

There are three modes of blowing the *shofar*: an extended, unbroken sound (*teki'ah*), three groaning sounds (*shevarim*) and nine short wailing (tremolo) sounds (*teru'a*). Different sequences of these three sounds are used in the *Rosh ha-Shanah* ceremony. During the first series (*teki'ot de-meyushav*), which starts with a *teki'ah–shevarim–teki'ah*, the congregation remains seated, during the second one, the *teki'ot de-me'umad*, which starts with *teki'ah–shevarim–teru'ah–teki'ah*, they stand up. There are other sequences, too. The last sound is always long and loud (Exodus 19,19), this is the "great tekiah (*teki'ah gedolah*)". During the ceremony the *shofar* is blown altogether one hundred times.

The instrument itself is very simple, it is made from the horn of a sheep, goat, antelope or gazelle. Only a kosher animal's horn is suitable. A cow horn may not be used because it reminds one of the golden calf. The best is a ram horn since it is a reminder of Abraham's sacrifice (Genesis 22,13). In the eighteenth and nineteenth centuries some artisans prepared quadrangular *shofars* with the application of steam- or hot-water presses. It is forbidden, however, to attach any kind of foreign material to the *shofar*, the word itself was understood as "void", therefore the *shofar* is not decorated either, except for carvings. It was a Jewish symbol in ancient times, like the *menorah* or the *lulav*.

According to the Biblical narrative Abraham sacrificed a ram instead of Isaac (*akedah*, "binding", Genesis 22,9); the smaller horn of this ram became the *shofar* of the Temple of Jerusalem. The "great *shofar*" (Isaiah 27,13) will sound at the arrival of the Messiah. In the Second Temple period in

Jerusalem the *shofar* was blown outdoors. It was sounded on every possible occasion, upon opening the synagogue door, before the arrival of the Sabbath, and so on, at least twenty times on weekdays and fifty times on a holiday. Since the age of the Talmud it has been used inside the synagogue as part of the ritual. The *shofar* marks the beginning of the new year and of the year of freedom or release (*yovel*). "You shall proclaim release throughout the land for all of its inhabitants" (Leviticus 25,10).

The best known prayer on *Rosh ha-Shanah*, the *U-netanne tokef* (*Unesane toykef*), is the description of daunted fear and of the Divine judgment. The simple text (an eleventh-century *piyyut*) evokes the day of judgment (*yom ha-din*), its melody in the Ashkenazi ritual is richly modulated.

> "Let us now relate the power of this day's holiness, for it is awesome and frightening. On it Your kingship will be exalted... It is true that You alone are the One who judges, proves, knows, and bears witness; who writes and seals... You will open the Book of Chronicles—it will read itself, and everyone's signature is in it. The great *shofar* will be sounded and a still, thin sound will be heard. Angels will hasten, a trembling and terror will seize them, and they will say: It is the Day of Judgment... All mankind will pass before You like members of the flock... On *Rosh ha-Shanah* will be inscribed and on *Yom Kippur* will be sealed... But repentance, prayer and charity remove the evil of the decree..."
>
> (From *The Complete Art Scroll Machzor: Rosh Hashanah*, Brooklyn, NY: Mesorah Publications, 1990, translated by R. Nosson Scherman)

Similar to this prayer are the "*Dies irae*", a hymn ascribed to Thomas of Celano (thirteenth century), and the *sequentia* following the *lectio* in the Roman Catholic *Missale* introduced by the Synod of Trident (1545–1563) and Pope Pius V (1566–1572). The notion of "day of wrath" originates from the Book of Zephania the prophet (Zephania 1,14–16), where also the *shofar* is mentioned (Zephania 1,16), that is, the *tuba* in the usage of "*Dies irae*", the *tuba mirum spargens sonum* ("the horn that makes a fearful sound...").

On New Year's day it is customary to eat "rich" and "sweet" foods (Nehemiah 8,10). The *hallah / barches* for *Rosh ha-Shanah* is round. It is dipped into honey instead of salt after the *kiddush*, so that the new year should be sweet. (Dipping the bread into honey lasts until the end of Sukkot, the final *hatimah*.) Another custom is to bake a ladder-shaped bread, to indicate that in the new year one's condition may change, it can go "up" or "down". It is customary to place "a head" (*rosh*) on the table, of a chicken, of a fish or a lamb, and everyone should eat at least a little of it. The desert is apples dipped in honey or apple pie, stewed apple. The custom of eating carrots on *Rosh ha-Shanah* can be understood only if we know that carrots in Yiddish are called *meren*, which also means to "increase", "multiply". Carrots can be eaten in any form, e.g. as *tsimes*. Walnuts and hazelnuts should be avoided, however. It is best not to sleep in the daytime because whoever is awake cannot be called to the final judgment.

Tashlikh is on the afternoon of the second day of *Rosh ha-Shanah*. The word means "throw away (your sins)" (Micah 7,18–19). Everyone should walk to the shores of a living water, one with fishes in it, because it—and only it—can purify you of your sins. (In the Diaspora only living waters are ritually clean, e.g. spring water, river, rain.) In Pest, too, Jews walk on this day to the Danube bank and empty one of their pockets, the pious ones even recite a blessing. This solemn, private act is what remained of the formerly merry, loud ceremony. In fact, nowadays in Pest, in the late afternoon of the second day, one can see people dressed elegantly, families or just fathers with their sons, scattered all along the Danube water-front... A poetic report on this, from Szeged in South Hungary, in prose:

> "On the bridge a sad, caftanned group is moving, – People praying here on the holiday eve, – Monotonous tune is humming over the water, – The East is celebrating, shabby and shivering in the cold."
>
> (Gyula Juhász, "A kis Tisza hídján" [On the Bridge across the Small Tisza], 1906)

Between *Rosh ha-Shanah* and *Yom Kippur* there are Ten Penitential Days, *aseret yemei teshuvah*. Repentance may still influence the final decision that will be made on *Yom Kippur*. Some people

358. *Tashlikh*. New Year's greeting card, ca. 1910

359. "Tashlikh." Lino-cut by Imre Ámos, 1940

360. "Wash away, River, our Sins". Engraving by Imre Ámos, 1930

consider the four days preceding *Rosh ha-Shanah* part of the Ten Penitential Days because, on the holidays in between, that is, on *Rosh ha-Shanah*, on Sabbath and on the day before *Yom Kippur*, fasting is forbidden. During the Ten Penitential Days fasting in not required, but one should withdraw from the world, possibly even stay away from work and contemplate (Isaiah 55,6). Penitence has three steps: the acknowledgment of sin (*hakkarat ha-het*), confession (*vidduy*) and the acceptance of its consequences, i.e. repenting and repairing. In this period the prayer *Avinu malkhenu*, "Our Father, our King" is recited every day during services. The Sabbath before *Yom Kippur* is called the Sabbath of return, *shabbat shuvah*. In traditional Ashkenazi communities the rabbi gives his moral sermon on the afternoon of that day, in Budapest, often on the eve.

3: A fast day, the fast of Gedaliah. After the conquest of Jerusalem Gedaliah was for a while the appointed governor, "king" of Judea. He was killed by members of the anti-Babylonian extremist party in ca. 582 B.C.E. (II Kings 25,22–25).

9, in the early morning or in the night before: Preparations for the greatest Jewish holiday, for *Yom Kippur* (*yom ha-kippurim / yomkiper / yonkiper*), start on the day before.

The *kapparot* (*kapporet*), "atonement" takes place early in the morning or during the preceding night. This is the only sacrificial ceremony in Judaism since the destruction of the Second Temple. It is of Babylonian origins. Rabbinical opinions had often objected to this practice for a long time but it could not be stopped. It is known in every Ashkenazi community, even if its practice is pretty much restricted to Orthodox communities by now. The men (*gever*) take a rooster (*gever*), the women take a hen (*tarnegol*, or better *tarnegolet*)—animals that had never been used for sacrifices in the Temple, and transfer their sins onto them. They grab the fowl by their feet and wave it three times around their heads while saying: "This is my exchange, this is my substitute, this is my atonement..." At the end the fowl is slaughtered. The ritual slaughterer (*oyfes shoykhet*) is usually very busy on this day. The fowl "sacrifice" is sometimes substituted by giving alms or by waving money the same way and then giving it as *tzedakah*.

A festive meal is taken in the afternoon, before sunset. Since *Yom Kippur* is a fast day, this meal is called *se'udah mafseket*, "last / concluding meal". It is a *mitzvah* to eat plenty. The Talmud says (Berakhot 8b) that to eat well before *Yom Kippur* is the same as to fast on *Yom Kippur*. A round *hallah / barches* is taken with the meal, decorated with "angel wings". The meal needs to be finished before sunset and the dishes washed and put away. It is customary to visit the graves of deceased relatives before *Yom Kippur*.

9, around sunset / 10, in the evening: *Erev Yom Kippur* or *Kol nidrei*. When the festive meal eaten in the afternoon is finished, people go to the synagogue for *Kol nidrei*. This prayer ("All vows...") needs to be said—or at least to be started—before sunset so that its words of repentance should refer to the day just about to end and the past year. *Kol nidrei* is recited three times after each other, at the beginning of the evening service, or rather it is sung, louder and louder. The synagogue is only slightly illuminated on that evening, only the *or neshamah*, "light of the soul" burns, which can be a large candle or an oil burner lasting 24 hours. The beautiful, moving melody of *Kol nidrei* is widely known, it is perhaps the best-known Jewish melody, variations on it were written by Max Bruch (cello and piano, 1880) and Arnold Schönberg (recitation, chorus and orchestra, 1938).

At the beginning of the ceremony two Torah scrolls are taken from the Ark. The first one is called *Sefer kol nidrei*. The *hazzan* and two older, prestigious members of the congregation face the congregation. Since only the *bet din* is entitled to release from a vow (*hattarat nedarim*), they are here to represent the *yeshivah shel ma'alah*, the heavenly chair of judgment. Even sinners and converts to other faiths (*meshummad / mesümed*) are allowed to join the communal prayer now. At some places the congregation breaks up into groups of four men, out of which three form the temporary *bet din* and the fourth man recites the prayer of apology. Then they switch roles.

The essence of the ceremony is asking and granting forgiveness. The exact meaning of the text has been a subject of debate for a long time. Medieval charges against the Jews were often based on this prayer. They misinterpreted its text, namely they thought that Jews can be released not only from their vows but also from business contracts and agreements. Therefore rabbinical authorities proclaimed that it can only refer to religious vows, oaths taken under pressure, unfulfilled pledges made to the Almighty or to oneself. The Biblical text (Deuteronomy 23,23) formulates only a general ethical principle. In the ethical interpretation *Kol nidrei* appeals for understanding: why one committed oneself to some great and noble deed but did not have the energy or the opportunity to make them come true. The nineteenth-century reform movements wanted to omit *Kol nidrei* from the liturgy altogether or to replace its text with another, but since both its text and its melody were the best known and most popular ones in the entire Jewish liturgy, this turned out to be impossible.

Another ritual song of the *Yom Kippur* ceremony is *Avinu malkhenu*, which, according to Talmudic tradition, follows the words of R. Akiva's spontaneous prayer.

The ceremony also includes general confessions (*vidduy*). Two prayers of confession, *Ashamnu*, "We committed transgression...", and *Al het*, "Because of the sins...", are recited ten or nine times respectively during the day. Both prayers are structured according to an alphabetical acrostic: 44 sins are listed, two under each letter in the Ashkenazi ritual. The longer one, *Al het*, is also called *vidduy gadol*, great confession. The punishment that people mete out to themselves is symbolical lashing (whipping). While reciting the prayer they beat their chest above the heart with closed fists, 39 times. The number is explained by ancient penal law. The Bible prescribes that persons punished lashing should receive "no more than 40" strokes (Deuteronomy 25,1–3). Later the Talmud fixed the number of lashings at 39 to make sure that the number prescribed by the Torah is not exceeded even by accident. Some especially devout persons asked to be scourged on the occasion. Everyone lay on their backs in the synagogue (Leviticus 26,1), which—following Isaiah 11,6—earlier used to be covered with hay on this day and—according to the 13 words in Psalm 78,38—the *shammes* or someone else, but definitely not one's own son, would beat everyone 3 times with 13 lashes. The text of the general confession incorporated into the Roman Catholic ceremony (*Confiteor*) is also based on this custom of self-flagellation: "I have sinned in thought, in word and in deed. (...) He beats himself on his chest, three times, saying: My sins, my sins, my very great sins... (*Mea culpa, mea culpa, mea maxima culpa*)." This passage was probably incorporated into the Catholic mass in the late Middle Ages. The Synod of Trident and the *Missale* (1570) of Pope Pius V canonized it in the liturgy for four centuries.

10, during the day: *Yom Kippur*. The rituals of *Yom Kippur* all have to do with expiation and purification (Leviticus 16,30). On this day, one should refrain from any activity that causes joy to the "soul". The Talmud (Yoma 73b) names five such pleasures: eating, bathing, using fragrant anointments, wearing leather shoes and pleasures of the flesh. That day offers a chance for people to apologize to their relatives, to friends whom they may have offended and accept the apology of others.

Yom Kippur is the only day that overrides even the sanctity of the Shabbat, it is *Shabbat ha-Shabbatot*, "Shabbat of (all) Shabbats", the greatest Shabbat. It is a fast day and prayers are recited all day long: *shaharit, musaf, minhah, neilah*. Maybe that is why *Yom Kippur* is also called *hosszú-nap*, "long day" in Hungarian. The *shofar* is sounded on that day, men are dressed in their *kittel* and a special buckle, women also tend to wear white. During the additional morning prayer (*musaf*) the hazzan invokes the original ritual (*avodah*) in the Temple (Leviticus 16). This day is all the more holy since it occurs but once a year. The congregations kneel down four times. (The word *barukh*, "blessed", which appears four times in the prayer, also means "to kneel down". This bending movement, by the way, involves lively swinging of upper body (*shokling* or *soklolni* in Hungarian), but one stands and kneels with legs closed. The *hazzan* is always helped, otherwise he would have to fall and jump up.) After that the *hazzan* together with all the kohanim present in the synagogue recite the priestly blessing. In the closing ceremony (*ne'ilah*) late in the afternoon the *Avinu malkhenu* sounds again. The congregation recites the *Shema* together. The blowing of the *shofar* marks the end of the day, the end of the fast. Members of the congregation greet each other after the service, like after the Seder, with the words: "Next year in Jerusalem."

It is customary to end *Yom Kippur* with smelling fragrant fruits, such as fresh apples or quince with cloves, used as some sort of *besamim*. (One may smell them all day long.)

15–22: *Sukkot*. The third pilgrimage holiday.

22: *Shemini Atzeret*.

23: *Simhat Torah*.

VIII: **Heshvan** (October / November), 29 or 30 days long

There is no holiday in this month.

IX: **Kislev** (November / December), 29 or 30 days long

25: The first day of *Hanukkah*. It is a semiholiday.

X: **Tevet** (December / January), always a "defective month", i.e. it consists of 29 days

10: A fast day in memory of the first day of the siege of Jerusalem during Nebukhadnezzar's war in 587 B.C.E. (II Kings 25,1; Jeremiah 52,4; Ezekiel 24,2).

XI: **Shevat** (January / February), always a "full" month, i.e. it consists of 30 days

15: *Tu bi-Shevat* (*Tu bishvat*). The New Year of trees. Semiholiday. On that day it is customary to eat as many different fruits as possible, but at least fifteen kinds (*peri hamishshah asar*). A kabbalistic tradition is to organize a *Tu bi-Shvat seder*, which by now has developed—parallel to the Passover Seder—its own ritual of four different cups of wine, four different sorts of fruit, texts to be read, etc.

XII: **Adar** (February / March), in a leap year it is "full" consisting 30 days, in a regular year, "defective", i.e. of 29 days

7: The memorial day of the birth and death of Moses. This is the holiday of the Hevrah Kaddisha.

13: *Ta'anit Esther*, Esther's fast. In memory of the three-day fast of the Jews (Esther 4,16).

14: First day of *Purim*. Semiholiday.

15: *Shushan Purim*, "Purim of Susa", the city of Queen Esther in the Bible. The Talmud (Megillah 1, 1) decrees that, according to Esther 9,18, cities that are surrounded by a wall, including Jerusalem, celebrate Purim one day later. This applied to medieval Buda, too.

In a leap year when Purim is in Adar II, the 15th of Adar I is only a "small Purim", *purim katan*. It is not a holiday proper but there are no eulogies, fasts, etc. held, either.

There is a saying, in Hungarian and in Yiddish: "It lasted from Esther's fast till Purim." (That is, one day only.) And a riddle on the same topic: "Which is the longer half of the year, from Esther's fast till Purim or from Purim till Esther's fast?"

XIII (only in a leap year): **Adar II (Adar sheni / bet)**, always a "defective" month, i.e. it consists of 29 days

*

And finally let us say a few words about some monthly holidays. Since the calendar follows the lunar cycle, one such celebration is the greeting of the new moon (*birkat / kiddush levanah*). It takes place on the first days of the month, on the first *motse-shabes* of the month when the new moon is clearly visible. After *havdalah* people take a candle and go out to an open space, in big cities this is usually the synagogue courtyard. If you look into the moon that night and, while standing on your toes or jumping up, say three times: "As I cannot reach you, my enemy should not be able to reach me either", and your life will not be in danger that month. From the *birkat levanah* grew out the expression *levone*-letters, that is, leaflets with the appropriate blessings printed in unusually big letters to assure that they could be read in the weak light of the new moon as well.

There is another holiday that one generally experiences only two or three times in a lifetime. This is the greeting of the Sun (*hammah*, "the hot one"), the *birkat / kiddush ha-hammah*, every twenty-eighth year. According to tradition and astronomy this is when the Sun arrives back to its original position "at the time of Creation". Talmudic literature reckons the date of Creation as the vernal equinox and according to their calculations the Sun-cycle, the "great circle (*mahzor gadol*)", starts every twenty-eighth year from the time of Creation. (28 years constitute the smallest cycle in which both weekdays and calendar dates repeat.) This "great circle" consists of altogether seven "heavenly days", i.e. seven times four earthly years. This holiday hails the onset of the new "great cycle" and confirms the promise that "the light of the Sun shall become sevenfold (...) and the LORD will bind up his people's wounds" (Isaiah 30,26). This ceremony is held always on the first day of Nisan, or actually on the Wednesday after it, on the fourth day of the week, when God, as one may know from the Bible (Genesis 1,14–19), created the Sun and put it on the sky. Since the beginning of the nineteenth century the Sun was greeted in the following years: in 1813 was the beginning of the two hundredth "great cycle", followed by 1841, 1869, 1897, 1925, 1953 (April 8), 1981 (March 18). The two-hundred-and-seventh cycle will begin on March 26, 2009, and so on.

362. "New Moon." Lino-cut by Imre Ámos

On April 6, 1897, the well-informed journal *Pesti Hírlap* reported in its "daily news" column about the greeting of the Sun that was going to take place at dawn on the following day:

"On this important day—which is nevertheless forgotten by the younger generation these days—observant Jews get up very early. They greet the sunrise on some high peak or in a courtyard, and gather in great numbers.

The Budapest Orthodox go up to Gellért Hill or János Hill,[10] and those for whom climbing these up is too much of an effort find themselves a site in the courtyard of Orczy House. They all have prayer-books in their hands and recite the designated chapters of the Psalms [Psalm 84,12; 72,5, etc.]. Polish Jews recite their prayer from a different book, and their prayers are much more numerous, too. Should we want to count how many Polish Jews there are in the capital, it would be the easiest to do it tomorrow morning, since they will all assemble in one place... Pious Jews regard this day as especially holy, and so those with an eye disease consider themselves especially lucky, if their doctors allow them to leave the dark room for the first time on that day, and they can catch their first glimpse of light from the rising sun. Thus tomorrow those who are interested can witness this Jewish ceremony. They only need to go as far as the courtyard of Orczy House. True, they will see neither the Sun from there, nor the sunrise; the celebrating crowds cannot see it either. But they will see the people who celebrate and sing, 'Blessed be the Almighty, king of the universe, who created the world', and who then have to wait another twenty-eight years for this ceremony again."

(16) Beyond Nagykörút, the Outer-Erzsébetváros

The construction of Nagykörút [Great Boulevard] changed the layout of the city just as radically as the construction of Andrássy út. The Municipality decided in 1871 to build a semicircular boulevard around Pest, along the old riverbed of the Danube, both ends of the semicircle meeting the new Danube bank. This new road only confirmed the eastern limits of Terézváros, which by then was marked by Nagymező utca. The part of the boulevard parallel to Nagymező utca was finished only at the end of the nineteenth century anyway. But the most significant change was the transfer of the railway station from Gyár utca (today Jókai utca) further up and out: the Western Railway Station was opened in 1877. It was no longer directly next to the Jewish quarter of Teréz- and Erzsébetváros. Quite a few buildings in Király utca, as well as some of the run-down buildings on the periphery of the Jewish quarter, had to be demolished to make room for the Nagykörút. The grand new buildings of the neighborhood gave the city an urbane, metropolitan appearance.

The Jewish quarter did not cease to be a focal point for the whole of Pest Jewry; this was from where Jews moved outwards, beyond Andrássy út, to Új-Lipótváros and even to the new quarter, which was now emerging beyond Nagykörút. The neighborhood of Révay utca attracted the rising Jewish bourgeoisie, employees and employers; Új-Lipótváros became the home of the urban middle-class, the intellectuals; the outer regions of Józsefváros were occupied by people who came to Pest from the provinces, while the poor moved to the outer regions of Erzsébetváros.

The name of István tér bears symbolic value. The name of Prince István (1817–1867), Palatine of Hungary in 1847–1848, was originally (in 1874) given to a square in Teréz- / Inner-Erzsébetváros. This square was renamed in 1907 after Gábor Klauzál (1804–1866), most certainly not against the wishes of the local Jews who—at least the elderly among them—still may well have remembered that Klauzál stood up for the Pest Jews in the anti-Jewish riots of 1848. The name István tér was given to another square beyond the Nagykörút, along István út, which was the continuation of Dohány utca towards the Városliget (City Park). Today this square is called Bethlen Gábor tér. By the late nineteenth century this area was inhabited largely by Jews; it seems that they brought the old name of István tér, which they were already used to, with them.

The Jewish quarter of Erzsébetváros kept spreading towards the East. It was the poor who moved outwards from the overcrowded center. The Orthodox synagogue or rather *shil* on Hunyadi tér belonged to the dairymen. The area from here to the *Központi Tejcsarnok* (Central Dairy Market) in Rottenbiller utca was the district of the poor, the "proletarians". Here stood the *Szegények Háza* or *Szegényápolda* (Poorhouse) at 7 Alsó Erdősor utca, with its back to Baromvásár tér (Cattle Market square) / Szegényház tér (Poorhouse square) (today Rózsák tere), the *Árvaház* (Orphanage) and the

---

[10] Gellért Hill is right in the middle of Budapest (235 m / ca. 770 feet), János Hill is a little way out (529 m / ca. 1735 feet).

363. Railway station in Gyár utca (today Jókai utca), the predecessor of the Western Railway Station, ca. 1870

364. Teréz körút with the Schossberger Palace in the foreground

Árva Leányház (Girls' Orphanage), too. Maps of the late nineteenth century indicate a Munkás utca (Workmen street). From the new Jewish institutions, just the *Siketnéma Intézet* (Institute for the Deaf and Dumb) was built on István tér itself. The streets here were boringly straight, lined by tenement houses with courtyards and external corridors, the toilet usually in the courtyard or at the end of the corridor. There were, of course, some better apartments on the second floor, some of them even with a bathroom. Employees, petty clerks and workers lived here. The social and financial status of the residents decreased towards Garay tér, where there was another market and another Orthodox synagogue in 48 Garay utca. Many Jews lived here, but the area was never an explicitly Jewish quarter. The market people went to the Garay utca synagogue, while workers, petty clerks and the like attended the synagogue on Bethlen Gábor tér; all of them were the typical petty bourgeoisie of the early twentieth century.

The synagogue on Bethlen Gábor tér was built by Baumhorn and his son-in-law, György Somogyi, at the site of the simple prayer-room of the Institute for the Deaf and Dumb. Stories, or rather story fragments, preserve the atmosphere around Bethlen Gábor tér. A woman recalled in 1994 that as a young girl in the late 1940s or early 1950s, she was occasionally asked on Friday nights to turn on the light in the building. Baumhorn already incorporated electric lights in his plan of the beautiful, large synagogue, he knew that the Neolog congregation would want illumination; but, according to tradition, Jews are not allowed to light lamps on the Sabbath, and so a *shabes goy*, a "servant for Saturday", a Christian had to be asked to do this favor. (Ironically, the pretty young girl in the story was Jewish.) This memory fragment is certainly not indicative of casual or secularized Jewish life. The memory of persecutions strengthened the Jewish identity of many survivors; for

365. Antal Fochs, the founder of the Institute for the Deaf and Dumb

some it was a religious identity, for others it was family background, customs, tradition. The people living in outer Erzsébetváros felt the impact of anti-Semitism on their own skin. They had to live with the destructive power of this impersonal, irrational, incited hatred, which operated even without Jews. The milieu was similar in Ferencváros, too, around the Páva utca synagogue.

Herminamező is not in the immediate vicinity of István út, but it belongs to the same slice of the city. Here are the Jewish institutions furthest from the city center: the *Aggok Háza* (Old Age Home), the *Vakok Intézete* (Institute for the Blind), the *Szeretetotthon* ("Almshouse", hospital and nursing home), the *Menhely* (Shelter). Herminamező is connected to Erzsébetváros by István út, which is the continuation of Dohány utca after the Aréna út (today Dózsa György út) intersection; this upper part of István út is now (from 1929 on) called Ajtósi Dürer sor. (Szent Domonkos utca, where the Jewish *Gimnázium* was built, is its side-street.) But neither geographically nor religion-wise does this area fit into Erzsébetváros. The buildings mark the Pest Israelite community's activity all over the city.

*

The Jewish quarter of Erzsébetváros spread towards the East quite naturally but there was one thresh-old to pass: the thin strip between Nagymező utca and Nagykörút.

Nagymező utca was the real borderline. This, by the way, was also the road taken daily by Jewish merchants arriving from Óbuda to reach Király utca from the Danube water-front. Originally Nagymező was the edge of the Jewish quarter, until the mid-nineteenth century the actual periphery of the city. By the end of the nineteenth century the press, entertainment and cultural district of the city grew up here. Mostly institutions of light entertainment: former taverns and restaurants became music-halls, former music-halls became elegant night clubs, cabarets, lounges, bars and variety theaters serving the entertainment needs of the wealthier bourgeoisie. The neighborhood of Nagymező utca had more such places than the whole city. But a more serious cultural forum, the Ernst Museum, was built up here too, on the western wing of Nagymező utca, at no. 8, at the edge of the Jewish quarter and the entertainment district.

Another category that underwent quick and radical transformation was the press. Small printing presses were replaced by new, larger printing houses and a whole press network emerged: daily papers, rotary press, morning and evening editions, etc. The vivid life of Nagymező (utca), also called the *boulevard* or the *Broadway* of Pest, the theater and newspaper district, did not lapse even during World War I or afterwards. New locations were added, but this remained the center.

Not only did the metropolitan entertainment industry of Pest grow out physically on the edge of the Jewish quarter, but many of its agents came from the Jewish quarter, too. Several members of the entertainment industry were of Jewish background: actors, artists, journalists. Most of them did not practice their professions as Jews, of course, but formed a new social stratum, that of the comedians, entertainers. One of the favorite places where they used to perform and socialize was the FÉSZEK Club founded in 1901. *Fészek* in Hungarian means "nest", but the Club's name is an acronym for *Festők, Építészek, Szobrászok és Egyéb Komédiások* [Painters, Architects, Sculptors and other Comedians]. Both meanings indicate what the place was like. The Club still exists at its original location at 36 Kertész utca, corner of Dob utca, in the building purchased in 1921 and architecturally adjusted to the purpose it serves.

Out of the Ghetto: a previously unknown entertainment business emerged on the edge of the Jewish quarter. The Budapest *boulevard* was created mostly by Jews. On Saturday mornings these "comedians" had hardly anything to do with Dohány utca, with the synagogue district or with Jewish tradition at all. They considered themselves Hungarian, cosmopolitan at best. They became Jewish only in 1938, forced by the (Anti-)Jewish Laws.

IX. Lipótváros, Új-Lipótváros

One of the main commercial centers had been, partly because of its proximity to the docks on the Danube, the Lipótváros, lying North of the Inner City, between the Pest Danube bank and Ország út (Károly körút–Bajcsy-Zsilinszky út). Land in the area was on the market since late in the eighteenth century. The district was named after King Leopold (Lipót) II (1790–1792) on the occasion of his coronation, but for quite some time it was just called *Új-váras* (*Újváros*), "new town". This northern extension of the historic kernel of Pest grew into a center of commerce and banking, a residential area of the upper class. Its further extension, Új-Lipótváros, first an industrial area, became a middle-class neighborhood. A kind of a *new-new* Jewish city, for that.

In the eighteenth century the link between Buda and Pest, between the banks of the Danube, was somewhat North of *Belváros* (Inner City), at the point where Deák Ferenc utca ends today. (This is the most narrow section of the river.) There was a "flying bridge" (*repülőhíd* in Hungarian) between the two banks since the late seventeenth century (1687). It consisted of two ferries, which were moved to and fro by the current of the river, along a rope spanning over the water. The "flying bridge" was in 1767 replaced by a pontoon, called *Hajóhíd* in Hungarian. The Pest bridgehead of the latter was first at the end of Kis Híd utca (today Türr István utca), and from 1787 on at the end of Nagy Híd utca (today Deák Ferenc utca). The pontoon was put together of planks over a row

369. The pontoon bridge between Buda and Pest. View of Pest from the Danube bank in Buda. Etching by János Blaschke, 1821

of boats, 46 or 47, later over 43 altogether. It was opened for vessels wishing to pass, and it was pulled to the shore (to a plot in Kis Híd utca) in the winter, to protect it from ice drifts. Its patron saint was St. John of Nepomuk. "The bridge was filled with people", wrote Ferenc Kazinczy upon crossing over to Buda during his visit to Pest in 1828. Indeed, the bridge was always busy—despite the toll. The *Hajóhíd* was standing until 1849, to be replaced by the *Lánchíd* (Chain Bridge). The harbor and docks where ships were unloaded and the market where the delivered wares were then sold was somewhat North of the Pest bridgehead. It was called *Rak-piac* (Loading Market) or *Kirakodó tér* (Unloading square), later Ferenc József tér (Francis Joseph square), today Roosevelt tér. After the *Lánchíd* was opened (1849), the extension of the *Rak-piac* and the original place of the Pest bridgehead was marked by two low stone pillars placed North and South of the new bridge (1857). Lipótváros, then the new commercial district of Pest, developed around *Rak-piac* and *Új Vásár tér* (New Market), today Erzsébet tér.

It was King Joseph II who ordered the construction of the enormous *Újépület* or *Cazárma* (*Neugebäude / Aedificium regium novum*) (New Building / Barracks) in 1786, under the guidance of János Hild (1766–1811), father of the architect József Hild. All of the northern suburb of Pest was constructed according to a consistent plan prepared in 1805. The area was divided into plots of similar size, a grid of streets, blocks of houses. The location of markets, fairs and docks was determined. Pest had already expanded considerably to the East by the development of Teréz-, József- and Ferencváros, and now Lipótváros was the first step in its growth towards the North.

A royal petition of the *Kereskedők Testülete* (Merchants' Corporation) of Pest in 1808 concluded that most Jews spent their days in cafés, offices and in the street in quest of what kind of merchandise was in demand and what was offered on the market. These services were rewarded with a fee by their customers, and they made business offers themselves. It was a quick grasp of the business opportunity that took the Jews from Király utca to the Rak-piac, to Lipótváros. The road leading from Rak-piac to Király utca was Lipót út / Fő utca / Híd utca / Nagy Híd utca, today Deák Ferenc utca.

Adolf Ágai describes in his memoirs how his family settled in Pest. The anecdote is part of his family history but it is also illustrative of general history. His great-grandfather left Istanbul together with his bride and, after an adventurous journey of four months, it was in Óbuda that they found a Jewish community, a *kahal* where they were finally able to stand under the *huppah*. Upon crossing the pontoon, Ágai writes, the bridal procession accidentally encountered Joseph II who lifted the bride's veil, looked into her eyes and gave her six gold coins of Körmöc as a wedding present.

"(...) And this relatively large sum of money became the foundation of my great-grandfather's affluence. He opened a store with Oriental goods. (...) Turkish pipes, chibouks, slippers, amber, tobacco leaves and similar merchandise were sold by a picturesque Sephardi Jew in a turban, uncle Benjamin, my great-grandfather's first-born son, who took the business over from his father and made it prosper, while my great-grandfather started dealing in Hungarian goods. He delivered wool to Silesia and hemp to the Balkans."

(*Az én dédatyámról* [About My Great-grandfather], 1907)

Soon the migration of the merchants themselves started: they moved closer to where the business was, closer to Lipótváros. They built up their warehouses here, rented apartments and offices. Lipótváros became their home as well as their work space. Figuratively speaking, the Jewish quarter moved to Lipótváros over Híd utca [Bridge Street], the "bridge" connecting Király utca with Lipótváros. The Jews of Óbuda crossed the river on the pontoon to go to the annual fair and later for their business, the stands on the market, every day.

The annual fair in Pest was a sort of an encounter between West and East. West was connected to the fair's location on the eastern bank of the Danube through the pontoon bridge. In 1790, for instance, some 12,000 wagons and carts delivered wares to Pest for the annual summer fair (Medardus, June 8), and ships arrived, too. Since much of the trading activity took place here, including signing contracts, delivery and payment, the commercial institutions were also founded in Lipótváros, from the beginning of the nineteenth century on.

On the southern side of the square stood the office building of the *Pesti Polgári Kereskedők Testülete* (Civil Merchants' Corporation of Pest), founded more than a century earlier, in 1699. (Its first name was *Pesti Szabad Polgári Kereskedők és Kalmárok Testülete*, Free Civil Tradesmen and Merchants' Corporation of Pest.) Its splendid new headquarters here was designed by József Hild (1826), the construction was finished by 1830. The Merchants' Corporation opened its Casino back in 1828.

Here is what the foundation document of the Hall of Commerce from 1828 says:

"This institution is founded with the intention (...) of providing space for Hungarian producers to meet with able merchants who would sell their products all over the wide world, so that they could discuss matters of the cultivation, use and sale of our natural resources, thereby developing Hungarian trade, increasing the wealth of the people and raising our country to the level of other commercially flourishing countries, turning our city into one of the most prominent trading centers of Europe."

The palace originally was called *Kereskedők Háza* (Merchants' House). On the ground floor of the new building, facing North, towards the Kirakodó tér, were the spacious rooms of the *Pesti Kereskedői Pitvar* (Pest Chamber of Commerce) or *Pesti Kereskedelmi Csarnok* (Pest Hall of Commerce) where producers, merchants and customers could meet and do business. This "Chamber" or "Hall" was the nucleus exchange market of Pest. It existed between the years 1831 and 1852. The successor of the Hall of Commerce, the first exchange market of Pest, called *Gabonacsarnok* (Grain Hall), was established in 1854. It occupied the rooms of its forerunner. The Merchants' House, Hild's Classicist building, the *chef d'oeuvre* of the architect, was renamed *Lloyd palota* (Lloyd Palace) after

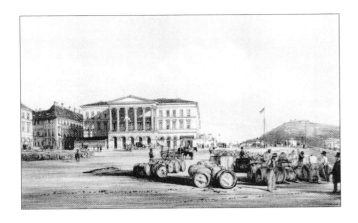
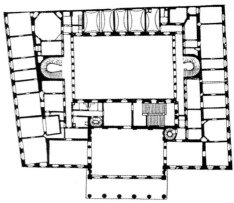

the *Pester Lloyd Gesellschaft / Pesti Lloyd Társulat* (Pest Lloyd Society), which was organized by the Pest merchant Jacob Kern in 1853 in order to supervise the commerce ethics and to foster professionalism in the trade. In a short period of time ca. 620 merchants joined the Lloyd Society. The Grain Hall was founded by the Lloyd Society. On the eastern, Dorottya utca side of the building there was a restaurant and café (*Börse* / Bourse Café, later *Lloyd Üvegszalon* / Lloyd Glass Saloon). After its foundation also the Commercial Bank rented office rooms in this building for a couple of years (on the second floor, with windows facing the Danube).

The rooms on the second floor were leased to the *Nemzeti Casino* (National Casino) between 1830 and 1860 and also Count István Széchenyi lived here for a few years (between 1832 and 1836). The Big Hall was used for balls, concerts and other prominent social events. (Cantor Denhof's concert performance, mentioned in Chapter III, above, also took place here.) The Upper House held its sessions in the Big Hall from 1861 to 1904, when the building of the Parliament was completed and it could occupy its permanent place there. The Hild building was severely damaged in World War II, so its owner, the Generali insurance company, razed it in 1948. Hotel Atrium Hyatt stands in its place today.

The *Pesti Áru- és Értéktőzsde* (Pest Exchange Market of Commodities and Stocks), the first institution to use the word *tőzsde*, "exchange market" in its name, was organized in 1864 with the aim "to foster selling and buying all kinds of trade commodities, uncoined gold and silver, money, bills, bonds, stocks, as well as signing contracts and agreements of security or shipping". The Pest Exchange Market and the Grain Hall merged in 1868. Five years later, in 1873, it moved to a new headquarters, to a building next block Southwest to the Lloyd Palace (the Hotel Forum stands on its place today). Its permanent halls—the Stock Exchange and the Grain Exchange—were built in 1903 on a part of the plot previously occupied by the *Neugebäude*. Vice-president, later president, of the Exchange Market was Zsigmond Kornfeld (1852–1909), another financial genius of the period. (In that building, the former *Tőzsdepalota*, 17 Szabadság tér, the Public TV headquarters are located today.)

Due to trade, Lipótváros was the largest, most modern and best developed quarter of Pest. An *Izraelita Kereskedők Testülete* (Israelite Trade Corporation) had been founded here back in 1824. The Civil Merchants' Corporation fostered the social integration of Jews, in accordance with the regulation of Act XXIX of 1840. In 1846 the wholesale merchants formed their own organization under the name *Pesti Nagykereskedők Testülete* (Corporation of Wholesale Merchants of Pest). The Corporation of Wholesale Merchants accepted anyone as a member who was ready to obey the statutes, regardless of religion, so there was no need for a separate Jewish trade corporation. By the late 1840s the number of members in the three trade corporations was as follows: Civil Merchants' Corporation: 245 members, Israelite Trade Corporation: 136 members, Wholesale Merchants' Corporation: 47 members. Naturally, there were Jewish members in the other two corporations as well.

"There is no doubt that the present high state of commerce in Hungary is the Jews' merit; furthermore, world history itself testifies that it was the Jews who did most for the flowering of European trade in general."

(Ignác Benedek, *Ne higyj a zsidó-falónak* [Don't Believe the Jew-baiter], Pest, 1848)

The separate Israelite Trade Corporation gradually became superfluous and was dissolved as early as in 1851. Its members joined either one of the two other corporations. Decades later, in 1899, the Civil Merchants' and the Wholesale Merchants' Corporations united under the name *Budapesti Kereskedelmi Testület* (Trade Corporation of Budapest).

The first major bank, the *Pesti Magyar Kereskedelmi Bank* (Hungarian Commercial Bank of Pest), was founded on the initiative of Móric Ullmann in 1841. The founding assembly meeting was held on April 30, 1842, in Lipótváros in the Hall of Commerce. In the beginning the Bank's headquarters was two or three rooms rented on the second floor of the Hild palace. In 1848 it moved from here to the house called "Két Török" [Two Turks]. Its first own building was built by József Hild on the northern edge of the *Színház tér* (today Vörösmarty tér) (1861). The Commercial Bank became the major financial institution of the country. After the *Ausgleich* or compromise of 1867, that Bank financed the coronation festivities, the center of which was on the *Kirakodó tér*, from that time on called Ferenc József tér (Francis Joseph square). It was them who first introduced saving accounts in Hungary (1880). Leó Lánczy (1852–1921), the director of the Commercial Bank from 1882 on, was perhaps the most legendary figure in the history of banking in Hungary. During his tenure, the Bank supported development of communication network (telephone, tram, railway, suburban railways, etc.) covering the whole country. Later the Commercial Bank built a new headquarters, designed by Zsigmond Quittner, on the corner of the Ferenc József tér (today Roosevelt tér) and Fürdő utca (today József Attila utca), in place of the *Duna Fürdő* or—like in Vienna—*Diana Fürdő* (Duna and Diana Bath, respectively) in the years between 1906 and 1918. This building is occupied by the Ministry of Interior today (3–4 Roosevelt tér), but on its corner facade the golden letters of the name of the original owner, the Commercial Bank, are still shining and there is also a slab with a commemorative inscription that refers to the previous Bath, to Count Széchenyi's stay there (1827 to 1832) and to the Bank. The Commercial Bank was nationalized on January 1, 1948, and liquidated in 1949.

From the mid-nineteenth century on Lipótváros was mostly inhabited by distinguished and wealthy Jews. Wahrmann, the Ullmanns, the Wodianers, and other well-to-do Jewish families all had a residence, apartment, office or business in Lipótváros. Strong family and business connections tied them to Vienna and to other industrial and commercial centers of the Austro-Hungarian Monarchy. They spoke German among themselves, and not Yiddish, and they were nurtured on German culture. Their territorial segregation in Lipótváros was due to their social and financial status, that is, to the riches, and not to their being Jewish.

In the last third of the nineteenth century a new generation of outstanding Jewish industrialists and bankers emerged. The emancipation law of 1867 opened their way also into high society. Mór Wahrmann was president of the *Budapesti Ipar- és Kereskedelmi Kamara* (Budapest Chamber of Industry and Commerce). Ferenc Chorin sr., grandson of R. Chorin of Arad, a lawyer by training,

372. Father and son: Ferenc Chorin sr. and jr.

was founder of the *Gyáriparosok Országos Szövetsége* (National Association of Industrialists, GYOSZ, 1902), with heavy interest in coal industry. He was an MP from 1867 on, and an appointed permanent member of the Upper House from 1903. He became a Christian. His son, Ferenc Chorin jr., went further in the footsteps of his father. Leó Lánczy (Magyarized from Lazarsfeld), the director of the Commercial Bank, backed him in matters of financing; he himself was interested in the steel and coal industries. After Wahrmann's death, Lánczy became the president of the Chamber of Industry and Commerce. He converted to Christianity. Zsigmond Kornfeld, son of a distiller in Bohemia, started his carrier as a bank clerk in Prague in 1878, being a business partner of the Viennese Rothschilds, who rescued the *Magyar Általános Hitelbank* (Hungarian General Credit Bank) from insolvency, he was invited to be president of the Credit Bank. It was he who cleared up the Hungarian

state debt in 1881 with the help of the Rothschilds. The Credit Bank became the de facto Hungarian National Bank. In 1891 Kornfeld joined the Budapest Stock Exchange as its vice-president. He learned Hungarian and it was on his initiative that the Exchange changed the language of its transactions from German to Hungarian. In 1899 Kornfeld became the president of the Stock Exchange, in 1902 he was appointed member of the Upper House, in 1909 he was created a baron. He remained Jewish, and in 1893 was elected vice-president of the Neolog community. However, his son, Baron Móric Kornfeld, converted to Christianity. Manfréd Weiss (1857–1922) founded first a canning factory in Csepel in 1877, and expanding it, established step by step the first Hungarian cartridge casing (1889) and cartridge factory (1892) and later a copper mill (1896), a foundry, a roll mill and a steel mill (1911); his Csepel arms factory, one of the largest in the Austro-Hungarian Monarchy at the outbreak of World War I, encompassing the entire process of arms manufacture, grew out from these first modest Csepel factories. He was appointed a baron in 1918. Yet he remained Jewish and generously supported Jewish social and medical institutions. The Deutsch (Hatvany) family, barons themselves, developed sugar beet growing and sugar industry. Most of the Jewish industrialists and bankers received titles and predicates of Hungarian nobility. With Jews and Judaism they stayed in contact only on the level of solidarity and welfare—yet on this level even in case they decided for the Christian religion.

The upper middle-class and upper-class bourgeoisie of Pest emerged from among the Jews of Lipótváros at the *fin-de-siècle*. Most of these Jews attended the Dohány Temple, to continue family tradition. Their forefathers were among the founders of the temple, their families have had a seat there for many decades. But they were also bound to the Dohány Temple because no other synagogue would have suited their yearning for religious liberalism and their social status. The Dohány Temple was the *primary* temple of the country, this is where the elite showed up.

(1) The Plan that Was Never Realized: The Lipótváros Synagogue

The Lipótváros synagogue or rather *temple*, as it was referred to from the very beginning, was never built. People started talking about it already around 1895, plans were made, there were debates over aesthetic issues, funds were raised; in 1898 a competition for the architectural design was announced, and the deadline was even extended, there even was a second competition. At the beginning, in 1889, Mór Wahrmann, the president of the community, and Ignác Goldziher, the secretary, submitted a letter of petition to the Municipality asking for plots in Lipótváros to build a Jewish school in the Lipótváros district. The *Neugebäude* was demolished, there were whole blocks at disposal. A year and a half later in 1893—Wahrmann died in the meantime—the new president, Zsigmond Kohner,

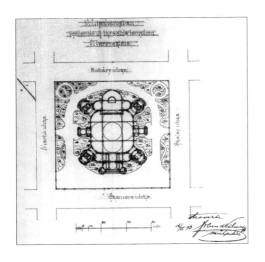

376. Lipótváros
Synagogue
Competition. Street
location. Plan by
Vilmos Freund

377. Lipótváros
Synagogue
Competition. Design
by Lipót Baumhorn

and Goldziher asked for extension of the plots in a new letter, since the community decided in favor of a new synagogue instead of a school. The Municipality donated six plots altogether for the new, representative synagogue, the third one in the capital, the first two being the "Dohány" and the "Rombach". The allocated plots were very close to the Parliament building, which was just under construction at that time, that is, they occupied the territory bordered by Szalay utca, Szemere utca, Markó utca and Koháry utca (today Nagy Ignác utca). (Eventually, the building of the Pest Central District Court was built here.)

The huge synagogue was meant to be a detached building, large enough to accommodate at least eighteen hundred men and the same number of women. An external staircase was to lead up to the women's gallery, there was to be an organ, a gallery and a rehearsal room for the choir, a prayer-room for weekdays, a room for the bride and groom, all kinds of service rooms, a drive-way, official residences. President Kohner headed the jury that was to decide the architectural competition. The jury consisted of the most distinguished architects of the time, with *no regard* to their religious persuasion. Among them were Ignác Alpár, Alajos Hauszmann, Frigyes Schulek and Imre Steindl, star architects of the period, Karl König, the architect of the Taborgasse synagogue in Vienna, the architect Wilhelm Stiassny, and representatives of the Jewish community and of the Municipality. The protocol of the jury's discussions states that representatives of the Jewish community did not vote since the artistic value of the competition works was to be judged. In March, 1899, after the jury's decision, as the envelopes that contained the names of the applicants were opened, it turned out that the joint competition work of two Christian architects won the first prize, that of Ernő Foerk (1868–1934) and Ferenc Schömer (code-name: "Alef").

378. Lipótváros
Synagogue
Competition. Ground
floor. Design by Béla
Lajta (Leitersdorfer)

379. Lipótváros
Synagogue
Competition. Design
by Béla Lajta
(Leitersdorfer)

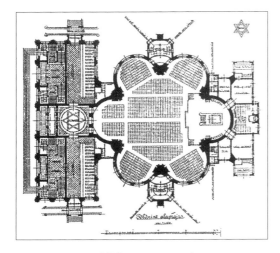

The second prize went to the work of Zoltán Bálint (1871–1939) & Lajos Jámbor (Frommer) (1869–1955) (code-name: "Moses") and the third prize to Béla Lajta (Leitersdorfer) (code-name: "Drawn hexagram 5659" [= 1899 C.E.]). The competition works of Izidor Scheer (later Gondos), László Vágó & József Vágó; of Géza Márkus; of Albert Schickedanz & Fülöp Herzog; of Lipót Baumhorn; of Vilmos Freund; and of Aladár Kármán & Gyula Ullmann were also honored and purchased. The jury and the critics were proud that Christian architects participated in the competition and even that they were the winners. In order to arrive at a final decision, a second competition was announced right in 1899, now for a narrower circle, and with a new jury, and the winning design was again that of Foerk (this time without Schömer). The works of Jámbor & Bálint and of Béla Lajta were also considered to be accepted.

All of the competition plans, even in the second round, far exceeded the available budget. Almost all the architects planned a huge temple covered by a dome. It seems that the triumph over the success of emancipation was felt not only by the community that ordered the plans, by the jury that made the decision but by the architects as well.

The deadline for the completion was set in the contract with the Municipality as March, 1903. On the request by the community it was prolonged until March, 1906. But nothing happened, except some deliberations and discussions within the community's leadership. A second extension for the implementation was given as March, 1908. In the meantime, new synagogues were built on Aréna út and in Páva utca, and finally the whole investment project was given up. The community was focusing on the corner of Dohány utca and the shortly opened lower section of Wesselényi utca, where the construction works of the community were started in the late 1920s.

380. Lipótváros Synagogue Competition. Proposed design by Zoltán Bálint & Lajos Jámbor

381. Lipótváros Synagogue Competition. The facade. Design by Albert Schickedanz & Fülöp Herzog

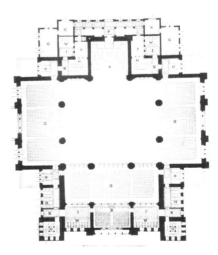

382. Lipótváros Synagogue Competition. Design by Izidor Scheer, László Vágó & József Vágó

383. Lipótváros Synagogue Competition. Second floor. Design by Ernő Foerk & Ferenc Schömer

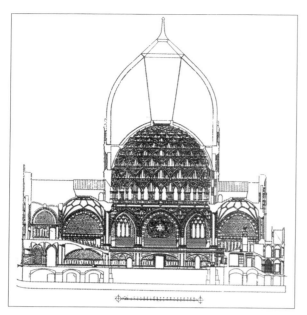

384. Lipótváros
Synagogue
Competition. Cross-
section of the dome
by Ernő Foerk &
Ferenc Schömer

The idea of the Lipótváros synagogue was completely forgotten after World War I, yet it would be inaccurate to say that the construction was hindered by the historical events. There were deeper reasons for it. The Lipótváros Temple was, unconsciously, intended to be the Jewish counterpart of the nearby Roman Catholic St. Stephen Basilica, both architecturally and from the point of view of urban planning. But it was superfluous. Another reason may have been of an aesthetic nature. The question of style and modern architectural functionalism was subject to an unending debate. The way the Moorish style had earlier been considered Jewish, was there a specific Jewish architectural form now? And how comfortable and well equipped did a modern synagogue have to be to match the needs of a modern, wealthy bourgeoisie?

Simon Meller (1875–1949), an art historian of the Szépművészeti Múzeum (Museum of Fine Arts), wrote a short study about the Lipótváros synagogue architectural competition, in which he expressed his dissatisfaction with the application of historical styles like the Gothic, Renaissance or Moorish, or even the Hungarian style. For him, all these were no more than imitations. In his view a modern building should by all means be constructed according to the modern concept of architectural functionalism.

"Our present-day Jewish temples are impractical, their ventilation is poor, the heating is insufficient. They are not comfortable and light enough, they are not modern enough. Let us imagine a huge temple interior where the walls and galleries are covered with plain wood, decorated with some modern ornaments that carry no meaning and thus do not violate any religious concepts. The ventilation, lighting and structure applies modern technology. (...) The sun glimmers through the double glass roofing and thus the beautiful color-harmony of the temple interior emanates a peaceful, serious and blissful mood."

(IMIT. *Yearbook*, 1900)

Meller's words echo the principles of Otto Wagner, the great Viennese architect who built his first synagogue in Rombach utca, in Budapest. Meller rejected style imitation and advocated universal architectural forms.

Only Béla Lajta's plan differed slightly:

"At the architectural competition of a new, great Jewish temple twenty-three or twenty-five years ago there was only one set of plans, which significantly differed from the others. This synagogue had a hexagonal ground-plan and one could see and hear from every angle. The congregation entered through magnificent stairs, its modern architecture was the embodiment of ancient Judaism, a perspective sketch with only a few lines, a white Oriental dome, which I will never forget. The serious questions posed in all the other plans (...) were resolved here by a single idea. This may not be the best of all plans, but it is a special and important one. It is a revelation to every architect. It is the creation of a young, unknown man whose talent revealed itself at once. (...) He gave expression to something that had lived in all of us, that we had not been able to formulate or even imagine, that we had desired and searched for."

(Béla Málnai, 1925)

The plans of the Lipótváros synagogue indicate that it would have been only a second Basilica, and that may be the reason why construction plans were finally dropped. But Meller's critical analysis, the functionalist program, continued to have an impact.

(2) The Library of the Hungarian Academy of Sciences

(9 Roosevelt tér, entrance from 1 Arany János utca)

The Library of the Hungarian Academy of Sciences is almost like a pilgrimage place for Hebraists, since its rich *Keleti Gyűjtemény* [Oriental Collection] includes the world-famous Kaufmann Collection. The wooden interior of the reading room is adorned with stylized Islamic ornaments, reflecting the Turkish traditions in Oriental studies and historiography in Hungary.

The collection was donated to the Academy by Róza Gomperz, the mother-in-law of Dávid Kaufmann, in memory of her daughter, Irma (1854–1905), and son-in-law, following her daughter's wish. The collection comprises some six hundred manuscripts and over a thousand old Hebrew books and prints, as well as close to a thousand scholarly works in the field of Oriental studies, and almost 700 manuscript fragments from the Cairo *Genizah*. Kaufmann acquired most of the old prints from a single collection in Mantova (Mantua) in 1895, from the library of Marco Montara, and the manuscripts, from the library of Gabriele Trieste, president of the Chamber of Commerce in Padua. It was his wife's dowry, which allowed him to give full vent to his passion for collecting manuscripts.

All the genres of medieval Jewish literature are represented in the Kaufmann Collection. There are even several Yemenite Hebrew manuscripts. Kaufmann himself started cataloguing his manuscripts and books but his untimely death prevented him from completing the job. Miksa (Max) Weisz finished the catalogue in 1906 and other scholars dealing with the manuscripts added notes to it later. Ever since Bacher's time several students of the Rabbinical Seminary chose texts from Kaufmann's collections for their dissertations, some were even published. Since 1959 the catalogue and even the texts have been made available to several large scholarly libraries all over the world on microfilm. Salamon Widder published the *piyyuts* from the *Genizah* in 1947 but other than that, only preparatory work has been done for the publication of the materials, and only a few more fragments got published. Scholars generally expected a complete catalogue of these to be done by Sándor Scheiber, but there was no trace of even a draft or notes in his literary remains, except, of course, his papers published over the years.

Some of the most famous manuscripts in the Kaufmann Collection are as follows.

385. *Ex libris* of Dávid Kaufmann

386. Róza Gomperz, mother-in-law of Dávid Kaufmann, the donor of the Kaufmann Collection to the Library of the Academy

387. Dávid Kaufmann

Megillah

Scroll of the Book of Esther. This is an eighteenth-century Northern Italian manuscript for synagogue use. The text of the scroll, with *tagim* but no vowel indications, is written within arches, decorated with garlands, flanked by twisted columns and topped by a balustrade. On the bottom, under each column of the text, vignettes illustrate the story. (See figs. V:4, V:5, V:6.) On one of these vignettes

Esther, according to a somewhat free interpretation of the text (Esther 8), falls at the feet of King Ahasuerus uncovering her breast. On another one we see Haman and his ten sons, who wanted to destroy the Jews, hanged. Their names (Esther 9,7–9) are written in a separate column with larger letters—this is the part where people are supposed to make noise as it is read by the *hazzan*. The leg of the last name's initial is extra long, indicating how tall the gallows were. Above every second column there are two winged putti, with inscribed shields in their

388. Winged putti in a manuscript of the Kaufmann Collection

hands. The inscriptions, Biblical quotations themselves, are only loosely related to the contents of the book. The text of the blessings recited before and after the reading of the *megillah* is written on a separate sheet, with vowel signs, and it is scrolled around the *megillah* like a protective cover. This scroll, almost four meters long, was published in facsimile edition in 1989. The beautiful scroll has a turned wooden rod and handle and a velvet case.

Mishnah

389. Mishnah.
A page from the Budapest manuscript with corrections (*haggahot*) on the margin

A complete manuscript of the *Mishnah* is a hefty volume of 286 parchment sheets. Apart from the fragments of the Cairo *Genizah* this is the oldest known copy of the Mishnah, completed around 200 C.E. This manuscript is from the first half of the thirteenth century, probably from Northern Italy. The text includes Palestinian vowel signs and there are corrections on the margin. It was published twice in facsimile, in 1929 in The Hague and in 1968 in Jerusalem, in reduced size. Ephraim E. Urbach (1912–1992), an authority on Talmudic tradition, a master of philology and history, an *amorah* of our times, a former student of the Breslau *Seminar*, and the former president of the Israel Academy of Sciences and Humanities, visited Budapest in December, 1988, on the occasion of the opening of the Center of Jewish Studies at the Hungarian Academy of Sciences. The elderly scholar was most interested in the Mishnah manuscript. He was clearly moved as it was placed in front of him in the library. He breathlessly opened it, looked up two words in the text, found them immediately. He examined the manuscript for a few minutes, looking at those details, which cannot be seen on a photocopy or facsimile, namely that the text and the corrections are by different hands. Finally, his face glowing with peaceful joy, he said that it was worthwhile for him to come to Budapest just for those two words. He had discovered Truth, the truth of the oldest manuscript.

Haggadah

The thin parchment codex of the *Pesah Haggadah* consists of 60 sheets. Apart from the text of the *Seder* ritual there are also 26 half- or whole-page miniatures depicting scenes of the exodus from Egypt and the *Seder* night. In addition, there are small miniatures, initials and drawings on every page and a few blank pages—the pictures intended to decorate these were left out for some reason. The headings are covered in gold leaf. There are vowel indications in the text and corrections on the margin, at one point even a note by the possibly Ashkenazi editor, which says "mistake of the scribe". The manuscript is a Sephardi, Catalonian work from the fourteenth century. The text was written by a Jewish scribe, the miniatures painted by a Christian illustrator. The codex had two facsimile editions, the first one was edited by Sándor (Alexander) Scheiber in Budapest in 1957, the second one by Gabrielle Sed-Rajna of Paris in 1990. In the meantime Bezalel Narkiss, the outstanding scholar of medieval Jewish illumination and art history (Jerusalem) established the original order of the codex sheets—since it was bound in the wrong order—and the library cleaned the manuscript. The second edition contains an art historical evaluation of the manuscript as well. This facsimile is a fully enjoyable medieval reading.

Mishneh Torah

The main work of Maimonides (R. Moshe ben Maimon / RAMBAM), the *Mishneh Torah*, the "quintessence of the Torah" (1180) is available in the Kaufmann Collection in two manuscript copies. One of them was written in 1310 in two volumes. The other consists of four folios, more than six-hundred dred parchment sheets, and it was completed by the scribe in 1296, after sixteen months of work. It is a masterfully written medieval Gothic book. In addition to the complete text of the *Mishneh Torah* the manuscript contains responsa to the book from 1413 on separate pages and corrections on the margin (*haggahot*). Sándor Scheiber and Gabrielle Sed-Rajna published a facsimile of its most beautiful pages, accompanied by a study, in 1980 in Hungarian and in 1984 in English.

The other, two-volume Maimonides manuscript includes Dávid Kaufmann's handwritten notes, as to how he got hold of the valuable manuscript. The fancier four-volume *Mishneh Torah* manuscript must have reached Budapest the same way. Here is an excerpt from the notes (according to the translation into Hungarian by Sándor Scheiber):

390. How did the valuable manuscripts reach Budapest? Dávid Kaufmann's handwritten note on the cover of the *Mishneh Torah* manuscript

"Who would have predicted that what David had seen in the palace of the Trieste brothers in Padua together with his good friend Dr. Osimo ז״ל [May his memory last] nineteen years ago, in the summer of 637 [= 1877 C.E.], he would see it again, and in his own apartment at that? It would be accurate to call these days Purim because my fate already gave me this treasure as a present: I got back this quintessence of magnificence and beauty, which I never expected to see again. I had already lost all hope that I would really own what I had bought from the Trieste brothers, because when the ten boxes containing this treasure reached the border at Udine, the customs officers did not let them pass but sent them back to Padua. There they were subject to inspection by the authorities and even Mr. L. was asked to give his opinion. Finally they ruled that 27 manuscripts, including some fairly valuable old books, had to remain in Italy, no one was allowed to take them out of the country. All efforts of the previous owners, especially of Dr. Trieste, to have the decision reversed proved in vain, though he went all the way to Rome with his request to "ransom the captives" [*pidyon shevuyyim*]. But in spite of these I did not give up the fight, I wanted to get what I had bought. I asked a friend of mine, an admirer of the rabbi of Ferrara, to travel to Padua and take the boxes. A few months later they sent two sacks filled with the most valuable books and other treasures to rabbi M., the brother-in-law of my relative, Dr. R., to Florence. He then tried to forward it under the name of my relative, K. But when the boxes reached Udine for the second time, they were again confiscated and I did not even know what had happened to them. My heart ailed from the pain caused by the endless and hopeless waiting. A few months later even the regulations were altered. Now it seemed completely impossible to get those 27 books out of Italy. Those applicants in whose case the authorities had already reached a decision and ruled out the option of an appeal could even be subject to punishment in case of further attempts. I gave up hope, but then, completely unexpectedly, help came. The Galleria [Laurentiana] in Florence overruled the previous decision of the authorities of Rome and they gave permission for the books to be taken out of the country. The highest official of the Laurentiana came to Florence personally to examine the books. And on Friday, Purim 656 [11th of Adar / February 28, 1896], I could finally take them home. A whole year after I learned that I could buy the books, which happened on February 28, 1895."[1]

[1] Purim in the previous year was celebrated on the 14th of Adar II (March 14, 1895). Kaufmann, while dating the events and his note according to the Jewish calendar, counted the time lapse according to the civil calendar.

Kaufmann commemorated this wonderful outcome not only in prose but in verse, too, on the cover of the complete Mishnah manuscript. He called it "Psalm of David", to give it a Biblical flavor. The "David" in the title is none other than himself as a psalmist. The poem consists of 15 lines, all of them ending in the same two syllables, -eret. The use of the suffix-rhymes, like in the text of *Akdamut*,[2] is masterful in its simplicity. Here is a prose translation of Kaufmann's "psalm":

"About joy, to the singer
Psalm of David

A script in my own handwriting, written with iron pen and lead, should commemorate that this treasury of magnificent objects has arrived to my house, to its greater glory, these jewels, valuable pearls and marbles were incarcerated and in fact, captured twice, causing me almost my death and ruination. I gradually lost all patience and hope, my soul was filled with worry and wrath. I thank you, Almighty, for this blessing and let the whole town rejoice and celebrate upon my glory, which is like the glory of the Queen, let Purim be a glorious festivity, a mass celebration.

Friday, Purim, 656 of the minor era.

Budapest, February 28, 1896
I, David, son of Yehudah, Kaufmann."

391. Dávid Kaufmann's "Psalm on joy"

The excited scholar and collector follows Jewish tradition in both these notes: in his use of terms and expressions, of Biblical quotations, in his reference to Purim and to "Lady" Esther, in the traditional dating. (The first word of the penultimate line of the verse is the date itself, as the points above it indicate.) The precious manuscripts were in good hands in his care.

Kaufmann inserted a similar note into the manuscript of a Mahzor as well. It was, no doubt, a great success that he could finally get the books through Italian customs.

Book of Secrets

Sefer ha-razim is a manuscript written on paper, a book of magic from late Antiquity, which was not a part of rabbinical literature. The text of the *Book of Secrets* or the *Book of Angel Raziel / Liber Razielis Angeli* was given to Noah at the time of the Flood just before he entered the ark, and it was used by him throughout his life, even after the Flood. The manuscript lists the names of the angels from the seven skies as well as prayers and magic spells to help or protect people. This is the best copy of the text showing the influence of Ancient Near Eastern spells.

The Buda Chronicle

The only extant copy of the *Megillat Ofen*, Izsák Schulhof's "Buda Chronicle" is also in the Kaufmann Collection, together with its German translation from 1800. It tells the life of Jews in Buda in the last period of the Turkish rule and the tragic events that happened to them during the siege and reconquest of the city by the Habsburg troops in 1686. The *Scroll* was copied by Eleasar Bendiner of Prague. Kaufmann acquired this manuscript in 1894 and he published a scholarly edition of the text already in the following year.

The correspondence of Ignác Goldziher, arranged chronologically, fills several shelves in the Library. There are Goldziher letters elsewhere in public collections, including the Széchényi Library, but all the letters from Goldziher's bequest are at the library of the Academy. In Goldziher's time

[2] *Akdamut / akdomus*, "introduction", "prologue". *Akdamut* is the title of the medieval introduction in verse in Aramaic to the weekly portion for the eve of Shavuot written by R. Meir ben Yitzhak, *hazzan* of Worms, in which every line ends with the syllable -ta.

the two major forms of international scholarly communication were the Orientalist conferences and private correspondence. Goldziher wrote about the conferences in great detail in his *Diary*, and his scholarly reports were published in the journal of the Academy. Apart from keeping in touch, private correspondence offered a good opportunity to discuss scientific questions at length. Goldziher wrote letters to and received letters from 1650 people, his bequest contains some 14,000 letters, most of them about his main research field, Arabic philology. Most of his correspondence was addressed to Theodor Nöldeke (1836–1930), an outstanding Semitic linguist and Orientalist of his time. Upon the considered advice of Aurél Stein the Library got hold of the photocopies of Goldziher's letters to Nöldeke from the bequest of the latter, and so the correspondence is almost complete; there are 217 letters written by Goldziher and 287 by Nöldeke.

This is what Nöldeke, a great admirer and friend of Goldziher, wrote after Goldziher's death, comparing some of the best Arabists:

"(...) I myself lacked the spirit of a genius, ever so lively in Goldziher and [Julius] Wellhausen, and so did my unforgettable friend de Goeje. We also had significant accomplishments, I can say without boasting, but the fire of genius was completely missing from our work."

In 1923, after Goldziher's death, his family sold his scholarly books to the library of the Hebrew University of Jerusalem, which was opened to the public just then. The Jerusalem library—now known as Jewish National and University Library—was founded as the Abrabanel Library in 1884; its collections were rather poor in the field of Islamic studies, etc. until that time. Goldziher's books went to Jerusalem. But the correspondence, according to the will of Goldziher's widow, was given to the Hungarian Academy of Sciences by their son, Károly Goldziher (1881–1955), mathematician, professor at the Technical University.

Another interesting special collection in the Library is the scholarly library of Sándor (Alexander) Scheiber.

"Sándor Scheiber collected and discussed scholarly publications, books and monographs from abroad with unfailing enthusiasm. The mystic and abstract character of most of these publications served Scheiber's goals perfectly: he could write and talk about them as he pleased, and thus he maintained a sense of keeping in touch with the outer world, of fighting isolation."

(Menahem Schmelzer, in: *A Scheiber-könyvtár katalógusa*, 1992)

After Scheiber's death his widow sold his books to the Library of the Hungarian Academy of Sciences. The collection comprises about five thousand titles and almost twice as many volumes, a third of which is in Hebrew, and the rest mainly in languages other than Hungarian, in the field of rabbinical literature, Jewish folklore and history. Scheiber also owned a large collection of books honoring great scholars published on their anniversaries (*Festschrift*); collecting these anniversary volumes was his well-known passion.

The Library of the Academy has been regularly acquiring books published in Israel, mainly scholarly books and literature, for a long time. It has had an exchange agreement with several Israeli libraries for many years. After Hungary stopped its diplomatic relations with Israel, this was the only place in Hungary, apart from the Rabbinical Seminary, where Hebrew *letters*, otherwise banned from public life, could enter.

*

In front of the building of the Hungarian Academy of Sciences stands the bronze statue of its founder, Count István Széchenyi (1791–1860), made by József Engel (1811–1901) in 1880.

Engel was an offspring of a rabbinical family from Sátoraljaújhely (*Ohel / Ihel* by its Hebrew and Yiddish names). He was to become a rabbi himself, attended the famous Yeshivah in Pozsony, but he was expelled because he was engaged more in wood-carving than in studying. The young man

392. Portrait and signature of József Engel

proved to be a talented pipe-carver. He went to Vienna, later to London and Rome. He was already an established Classicist sculptor, well known in England and Italy, when he won first prize in the competition for the statue of Széchenyi in 1866. Miklós Izsó and other prominent sculptors were among his competitors. He returned to Hungary only to prepare this statue. His studio at 1 Futó utca proved to be too small for the monumental statue, so he completed it in one of the rooms of the Riding Hall behind the National Museum. His first clay model collapsed due to some miscalculation. The final version, completed in 1870, was subject to mockery by his contemporaries. They said that on the model Széchenyi's gesture of founding the Academy was "sad"; they criticized every single detail. Nevertheless, in 1872, Engel won the next competition for the design of the plinth and the side figures of the statue, Minerva, Neptune, Vulcan and Ceres, the allegories of science, sailing, industry and agriculture, respectively. Hungarian public opinion did not accept the Classicist style and the mythological symbolism for a long time. After completing the statue of Széchenyi, "the greatest Hungarian", Engel never again won a competition, be it for public buildings like the Post Office or the Opera House or for national memorials like the Deák mausoleum, the statue of József Eötvös, the martyrs of Arad or of Ferenc Deák that he all applied for.

(3) Aurél Stein (1862–1943)

At 2 Tükör / Tüköry utca stood the house in which Aurél Stein was born. It was destroyed by a bomb in World War II. In the spacious apartments upstairs lived the Hirschler family: the parents, Márk Hirschler and his wife, their son, Ignác Hirschler, as well as their son-in-law, Náthán Stein and his wife, Anna Hirschler, whenever they were in Pest.

Next to Goldziher and Bacher, Aurél Stein is the third outstanding Hungarian scholar acknowledged all over the world of humanities. Only Sándor Kőrösi Csoma (1784–1842) could be compared to them as regards international reputation.

393. Aurél Stein

Márk, one of Stein's names, was the name of his grandfather on his mother's side. He must have been named after his grandfather, according to Jewish tradition, after his death. His other name, Aurél, was a name received in *baptism*. It was given to him in order to enable him to gain a footing in aristocratic Hungarian society, which was his father's ambition. Marcus Aurelius, the Roman emperor (161–180), was the symbol of tolerance. Aurél Stein, unlike Goldziher and Bacher, is to be regarded as Jewish only by birth, since his father, an educated businessman and bourgeois, had him baptized as soon as he was born. His Lutheran baptism was a sign of assimilation. Nevertheless, his education was governed by his uncle on his mother's side, Ignác Hirschler, and the much older brother, Ernő Stein was his immediate guardian, who greatly respected his younger brother's talent. In fact, Ernő was the one who handled the family's possessions instead of their father who had a tendency to give and purchase unnecessarily and was, therefore, untrustworthy from the point of view of business. As an adult, Ernő converted to the Protestant faith as well. He lived in Vienna and later in Galicia, not in Pest. The family only gathered on the occasion of holidays, otherwise they were in contact with each other through letters, almost exclusively in German. Ignác Hirschler, persevered in the Jewish tradition throughout, and never really mentioned religious matters in his letters to Ernő or Aurél Stein, perhaps not even when meeting them personally. He never lost sight of the ideals of classical German education, if it came to his nephew's education. He considered assimilation to be the only chance for Jewry to survive, entirely in the spirit of Neolog Judaism after the General Congress of 1868/69.

After primary school—having no family background in Budapest—Aurél Stein continued his studies in Germany (Dresden) and in Vienna, and only spent the summer holidays at home. Before taking his final examination, however, he came home and graduated in the Lutheran High School. He attended the school in the Deák tér building, and this was where he took his final examinations in 1879. Beforehand, during the summer holidays, he was already doing research in the nearby library of the Hungarian Academy of Sciences. As an advanced student of the High School, on the recommendation of Hirschler, member of the Academy, he spent all his spare time reading and studying in the library. The scenes of his further studies were already Vienna, Leipzig, Tübingen and London. He received financial support in the form of state scholarships granted by the minister, Ágoston Trefort. He came to Budapest once again to do his military service. He studied military cartography at the Ludovika Academy (1885/86), and made good use of his knowledge later in Asia. Otherwise he lived abroad continuously since 1886, although he was committed with all his heart to Hungary, to Hungarian culture and to the Academy, and came home on visits. During World War II, he helped all his relatives escape abroad.

His scientific interests drew him towards Asia; he became a student of the Sanskrit language, India, Kashmir, of the geography and history of Central Asia. A British subject, Sir Aurel Marc Stein spent most of his life on journeys of exploration. This tiny bookworm "crouching in the room (*Zimmerhocker*)", as Hirschler called him, spent several years on expeditions in Asia, on horseback, in tents, overcoming all the difficulties. Among other discoveries, he was the one who found the records of merchants, partly Jewish, who held regular commercial contacts between the Middle East and China in the centuries of the late Antiquity and in the Middle Ages. In his will he bequeathed his valuable library to the Hungarian Academy of Sciences. This collection brought foreign scientific publications of several decades into Hungary. Orientalists have been studying from Aurél Stein's books ever since.

His plaque (István Madarassy's work, 1976) is to be found on the new office building in the place of his former dwelling at 6–8 Arany János utca. His grave is in Kabul, Afghanistan.

(4) Kagál and the *Nyugat*

The corner house at 22 Nádor utca-9 Széchenyi utca housed Hotel Frohner, where members of the *Kagál* came together. The Kagál was an informal literary society at the end of the nineteenth century. Many though not all of its members were Jewish. Its establishment, at least its name, was due to anti-Semitism. After the Tiszaeszlár blood libel trial (1882–1883), Győző Istóczy (1842–1915), leader of the Anti-Semitic Party and member of Parliament, kept re-

394. Adolf Ágai, 1862

395. Portrait of Adolf Ágai, ca. 1875

ferring to a secret conspiracy or organization, which endeavored to realize the Jewish domination of the world. The word Kagál is actually the Magyarized form of *kagal*, the Russian pronunciation of the Hebrew *kahal / kehillah*, "community", "congregation". It was taken from the *Kagal's Book*, a pamphlet published and officially disseminated in 1869 by Yacov Brafmann, an agent of the Russian secret police. The word was then picked up and widely used in the terminology of political anti-Semitism in Western Europe. This is a good indication of where Istóczy and his Party took their anti-Semitic ideas from. But the Kagál of Pest was a table society of writers; they must have chosen this name out of ironic spite. What writer does not want to conquer the world, after all?

> "This mysterious name came in handy for us, though it was only later that we became aware of its meaning, or rather of what Istóczy meant by it. It was the Hebrew word *kohol*, which elicited his suspicions, turning his despair into unbound hatred... As far as we were concerned, its mysterious phonetic appeal was enough for us to appropriate it and thus we founded our 'firm' without any legal incorporation. This was all the more remarkable since we were not 'Jews' at all, that is, neither plaintiffs nor usurers."
>
> (Porzó / Adolf Ágai, *Utazás Pestről – Budapestre* [Journey from Pest to Budapest], 1912)

The Kagál was created by Adolf Ágai and the writers of *Borsszem Jankó*, the popular satirical magazine edited by Ágai. Among the members of the "society determined to pursue humor professionally" (András Hevesi) were Zoltán Ambrus (1861–1932), Andor Kozma (1861–1933) and others. "This was not a coffee-drinking company but a dinner-having one", wrote Ágai: company of Jews, non-Jews, writers and all kinds of artists who regularly had dinner together. "Simple Monday evenings occasionally turned into veritable symposia... There were times, during carnival, when the *Kagál* organized balls for ladies. There were theater performances, concerts by *kagalists* and by distinguished and world-famous artists, exhibitions and lots of other crazy manifestations, toasts given by beautiful lady-speakers over dinner, and finally, a dance."

Their meeting place was the Hotel Frohner, built according to Lőrinc Zofahl's plans in 1846. Frigyes Feszl added two floors to it and it was modeled again by János Frohner who opened a hotel in it in 1864. His guests were mainly of the upper-middle class. The murals of the ballroom on the second floor are by Károly Lotz. After World War II this magnificent Assembly Hall was barbarously divided into tiny rooms. Long ago, in the last years of his Pest sojourn, Baron Zsigmond Kemény (1814–1875) used to come here for lunch. Most of the delegates from the provinces attending the General Congress of 1868/69 stayed at Hotel Frohner. In 1883 György Holzwart acquired the hotel, but it was not until 1891 that he changed its name to Continental. The next owner, Gyula Weisz (1900–?), retained this name. The building was converted into a bank during World War I, in 1917, and this function of the building has not changed, though nowadays it is occupied by a different bank.

It was here in the Continental that in 1907–1908, Ernő Osvát and Miksa Fenyő began to organize the *Nyugat*, which was soon to become the most significant Hungarian literary journal of the twentieth century. The patrons of the journal were Ferenc Chorin sr. and jr., Baron Móric Kornfeld and Baron Lajos Hatvany. The latter, a writer and critic himself, was a great patron of Hungarian writers, of Endre Ady, among others. He was an offspring of the prosperous Deutsch / Hatvany-Deutsch / Hatvany family, owners of a sugar-mill in Hatvan.

(5) The Bourgeois Casino of Lipótváros (10 Nádor utca)

The Jewish bourgeois elite of Lipótváros had their separate social life with their own clubs, among which the *Lipótvárosi Polgári Casino* (Bourgeois Casino of Lipótváros) stood out. It was established in 1883 and called "a club" in a sophisticated English manner. Its Neo-Baroque palace at 10 Nádor utca–5 Zrínyi utca was designed by Vilmos Freund in 1895–1897 and was modeled and enlarged later according to László Vágó's plans. The Casino was only slightly behind the capital's most prominent clubs. Between 1927 and 1931 its president was Marcell Baracs (1865–1933), an MP, grandson of Lipót Lőw.

(He, too, used to live in Lipótváros, in 18 Mária Valéria utca.) Once, some time around 1928, Count István Bethlen (1874–1947), the Prime Minister and his cabinet spent an evening here listening to Gypsy music. The visit must have been intended as a symbolic gesture. The Casino supported art, organized concerts and exhibitions. It also announced competitions. It was for one of the competitions that Béla Bartók submitted his—by now famous—opera, "A kékszakállú herceg vára" (Duke Bluebeard's Castle) in 1911 (he did not win, to tell the truth). Presently the building is the club and Cultural Center of the Ministry of Interior.

The Casino also had a summer site at 46–48 Vilma királynő út / Városligeti fasor, built by József Vágó and László Vágó in 1912. (Today this is the headquarters of the Mineworkers' Trade Union.)

In 1941 the Casino had 1,800 members, out of whom 1,125 died during the war.

The Lipótváros Bourgeois Circle, which convened in the building on the corner of Arany János utca and Nagy Korona utca, was a somewhat more open society. Members of this society were mainly attorneys from the upper Lipótváros. Lectures were held here, too.

(6) The Pulitzer House

The Pulitzer family is of Moravian origin. One member of the family, a certain Izsák (Isaac) Politzer, a kosher butcher, lived in Buda during the first half of the eighteenth century. The next time the Jews were expelled from Buda, in 1746, he moved to Óbuda with his family. One of his descendants, Fülöp Pulitzer lived in Makó, southeastern Hungary, in the 1840s. He was a grain and produce merchant, worked diligently, had a high turnover of goods. He moved to Pest with his family in 1855. Initially he lived right next to the Új Vásár tér [New Market], at 6 Váci körút (Bajcsy-Zsilinszky út). The square was the parking lot of the Central Bus Terminal until 1997. A few years later, in 1858, he could already afford to move to a better area, to 2 Bálvány utca (today Október 6. utca). The tiny

396. Portrait of Joseph Pulitzer, 1887

Hild tér occupies this site today. By that time Fülöp Pulitzer was extremely well-off. His second child, József (1847–1911), was eleven years old. The following year the father died unexpectedly, and József, the eldest son, was too young to manage the great firm, which, consequently, soon went bankrupt.

József Pulitzer emigrated to the United States and joined the Union Army in Boston in 1864. As soon as the Civil War was over, he began to earn his living as a correspondent and journalist working for a German newspaper. After a while he bought his own paper in Saint Louis, Missouri. Later, in 1883, he bought another newspaper, the *World*, published in New York, and launched its afternoon edition, the *Evening World*. Under his management, both papers achieved financial success and made a name for themselves. For a short period he even tried his hand at politics, but eventually he contented himself with his role as newspaper proprietor, sympathizing with the Democrats. It was his newspapers and the rival Hearst papers, which created modern journalism in the United States. Persistent investigations, ingenious ferreting out of corruption, the pursuit of sensation, a good sense of business, a casual and entertaining style, timeliness—all these together gave the press its power status. Pulitzer, whose mother and father were both Jewish, whose name had been preserved in the *mohel*'s registry of the Makó Jewish community, who had presumably received the type of Jewish upbringing customary in ambitious bourgeois Jewish families at the time, never denied his Jewishness, but he did not establish contacts with any of the synagogues or Jewish organizations in the United States. He left his enormous fortune to Columbia University. Out of this money were founded the Columbia School of Journalism in 1912 and the Pulitzer Prize in 1917, awarded to particularly valuable literary and journalistic works. Since 1990, a private Foundation annually distributes Pulitzer Prizes in Hungary as well.

(7) Új-Lipótváros

The residents of Új-Lipótváros were different from the Jewish elite of Lipótváros. They were generally middle-class people, though the residents of the northern area of Lipótváros, bordering the southern edge of Új-Lipótváros, between Alkotmány utca and Szent István körút, in Honvéd utca, Szemere utca and beyond the boulevard, in Visegrádi utca, Csáky utca (today Hegedűs Gyula utca), Pannónia utca, and around Pozsonyi út were still relatively well-to-do. Previously, Lipótváros and Új-Lipótváros had belonged to the same district of the capital, it was only in 1930 that they were divided along the former Fegyvergyár utca / Lipót körút (today Szent István körút). The northern outskirts of Új-Lipótváros, the part North of Dráva utca was then attached to Angyalföld and, in 1937, it was named Magdolnaváros after the Regent's wife. The rest of Új-Lipótváros was called Szent István-város. (These names faded away during World War II and Új-Lipótváros regained its original name, though this is not used officially.) Today "old" Lipótváros and the Inner City together form the fifth district of the capital and "new" Lipótváros (Új-Lipótváros) together with Angyalföld are the thirteenth district.

Új-Lipótváros developed North of Lipótváros, in the area then called *Lipót-külváros* [Lipót-suburb], incorporating the southernmost section of the area North of Markó utca, between the Danube bank and the new *Nyugati pályaudvar* / Western Railway Station. There were storehouses and factories here, building material depots, later large industrial plants, for instance the new building of the Valero silk factory, a flooring or parquet factory and a sugar-mill. Furthermore, there were large mills. The first one was built in 1841, right beside the Valero plant. It was called the Pest Rolling Mill, later renamed József Rolling Mill, and was partially financed by Wodianer and Széchenyi. There were also the Budapest Rolling Mill, the Haggenmacher Rolling Mill, further away the Unió Rolling Mill, even further, near Wahrmann Mór utca / Victor Hugo utca, the Pannonia Rolling Mill, which was Mór Wahrmann's property, and started production in 1863, etc. And there were also storehouses, "Silos", built by Móric Ullmann, Sigel's grain- and market-hall, etc. The manufacturing industry of the northern part along the Pest Danube bank eventually developed around the first industrial plants of Lipót-suburb. Then the usage of the place-name was altered, and Nagykörút (Lipót körút) between the two parts of Lipótváros, starting at Margit híd (Margaret Bridge), was considered to be the borderline. The town planning of János Hild (1805) only regulated the construction in the area extending up to Markó utca. By the end of the nineteenth century, Lipótváros has already grown beyond Markó utca. Its character, however, has not changed significantly. Still, there is a certain difference between old Lipótváros and the blocks North of it. In place of the abandoned industrial plants, modern apartment buildings were erected in the years preceding World War I.

In Lipótváros and in Új-Lipótváros, the so-called Palatinus Houses with their new style brought about the first significant change in comparison with the Neo-Baroque architecture of the end of the century. By and large, these were all designed by Emil Vidor (1867–1952). Their name goes back to Palatine József's former landed property on Margit-sziget (Margaret Island). More precisely, this designation was applied to the buildings constructed by the Palatinus Building Stock Company and the Grünwald and Schiffer building agency. The sites were purchased in 1908 from Prince Joseph Habsburg (1872–1962) as part of the Government's project of taking over the Margit-sziget. The Palatinus Houses are to be found South of the Pest bridgehead of Margit híd, in 5 and 6–8 Falk Miksa utca (built in 1910/11), in 46 and 48 Nádor utca (1911), in 12 and 14 Honvéd utca (1912), in 4 Alkotmány utca (1912). On the place of a former Palatinus House, damaged in World War II, after the war a modern office building was built by the architects Gábor Preisich and others (1948), it housed first the Ministry of Interior, later the headquarters of the Hungarian Socialist Workers' Party (MSZMP), and now the Parliamentary Offices.

397. One of the Palatinus Houses on Rudolf tér (today Jászai Mari tér–Újpesti rakpart)

However, the majority of the Palatinus Houses, in the strict sense of the word, were built North of the bridgehead: in Rudolf tér (today Jászai Mari tér) / 12–18 Pozsonyi út (1912–1913), etc. These houses joined the two parts of Lipótváros together, as well as the two sides of Nagykörút. In fact, they signaled the beginning of modern architecture in this area.

More extensive construction projects North of the Palatinus Houses were undertaken only after World War I. By that time, official regulations provided for the construction of houses with a yard built around them. The intention was to create a uniform cityscape. The houses in the neighborhood of Lipótváros park (today Szent István park) were built around 1930. The park itself was established in 1935 and, similarly to the Lipótváros section of Nagykörút, it received its present name in 1937 on the occasion of the then forthcoming 900th anniversary of St. Stephen's death in 1038.

For about seventy-five years Új-Lipótváros has been referred to in Budapest as the *new-new* Jewish quarter. It is, indeed, newer than the *old-new* Jewish quarter, i.e. Erzsébetváros, nevertheless, it is *not* a *Jewish* quarter. It is, however, correct to say that indeed, Új-Lipótváros was designed and constructed, more or less, by Jewish engineers (or rather, engineers of Jewish origin), and the new houses have been occupied, more or less, by Jewish citizens (or rather, citizens of Jewish background).

The congregation of the synagogue in 3 Csáky utca / Hegedűs Gyula utca has been recruited from the Jewish citizens of Új-Lipótváros living in the northern parts of Lipótváros, and in the streets over the Körút. Apparently, the synagogue was built in order to meet a great demand. The Lipótváros Temple Association, which at the beginning of the twentieth century gathered to say their prayers in the Koháry / Nagy Ignác utca, moved from Lipótváros to Új-Lipótváros. Béla Vajda provided a room for prayer in a block of flats, later the community purchased the house, and fifteen years later (1927) the elder Lipót Baumhorn rebuilt it in its present form, adjusting his own, by that time somewhat old-fashioned, style to the technological possibilities of the time. Nevertheless, in Új-Lipótváros, members of the congregation were mostly conservative, rooted in the provinces. The provincial Jewry, the less educated Lipótváros Jews, were more attracted by the conservative character of the synagogue in Csáky utca than by the aristocratic liberalism of Dohány utca. There was no organ in Csáky utca; the table for Torah reading stood in the middle, the order of prayers was a bit archaic, too. Despite the proximity of the Orthodox house of prayer (in 3 Visegrádi utca), it was well-attended. The rabbi was Ármin Hoffer, a man of great erudition, in the first decades of the twentieth century. (József Schweitzer, his grandson, was for a time after World War II rabbi in his synagogue.) In general, the district temples in Pest (Nagy Fuvaros utca, Páva utca, Aréna út) were, by and large, similar, that is, far more traditional than the "Dohány". Those who did not attend synagogue very often were satisfied with Dohány utca, those who went daily, preferred to attended more conservative synagogues.

398. The Csáky utca synagogue

"On the High Holidays in autumn we went to the temple in Dohány utca on foot. We took a shortcut across Szabadság tér, and walked along either Bálvány utca (today Október 6. utca), Sas or Nagy Korona utca, where all the shops were closed. Hardly anyone turned up to buy anything, there was a Sunday-like atmosphere. In these streets, there were offices of textile factories and wholesalers, mainly Jewish. This was the case on Károly körút as well, where there were mainly stores selling ready-made clothing and broad-cloth... My father had a permanent seat as no. 4 in the 89th row. On arriving, I was surprised to see a little nameplate on the front part of the seat with my father's name engraved in it...The neighbors of our seat were always the same people. I thought they were all each other's friends or acquaintances as they were sitting next to one another. The only reason for this, however, was that they all had permanent seats, and naturally they always sat there. People sitting in the row in front of us, my father explained to me, were all in the textile business."

(Frigyes Brámer, 1978)

Taking also the synagogue in Rombach utca into account, it is not difficult to see that the community of Pest endeavored to preserve all nuances of the ritual.

The café was an extremely important institution for the Jewish citizens of Pest. Not only did they carry on conversations, they even conducted business here. Although there were stock markets, some deals, even big ones, were easier to make in informal ways. The café "Club" on the corner of Lipót körút and Csáky utca, already within the boundary of Új-Lipótváros, was a typical Jewish café. A little further towards Berlini tér (today Nyugati tér), where Lipót körút ran into Váci út, stood Vígszínház Café, another Jewish café. It was not kosher, but its owner as well as its guests were Jewish. There was also a cheaper, less elegant café nearby, owned by the Dairy Market. It was cheap because there were no fancy armchairs or plush sofas in it, only simple chairs. Afternoon snacks and even dinner was served here; the customers were mixed, but mostly poorer Jews.

People went food-shopping to the market, though the wealthier did not bother to do so. They could simply order everything from the nearby store in Falk Miksa utca. Elemér Szőke, the owner, would deliver anything, even milk and rolls early in the morning for breakfast. Beck's, Dávid Grünwald's and Pick's were similar stores right across the Vígszínház. There was pickled herring from the barrel, wine from the wine merchant, geese drawn and cleaned according to the customer's wish. Every one knew which stores kept kosher merchandise. One could buy milk, butter and sugar anywhere, it was only meat and Pesah foods to which they had to pay closer attention. The Orthodox standards were a little higher, they would trust only the items they purchased themselves.

In the interwar years the really wealthy Jews did not live in Lipótváros any more, but moved to the suburbs, to Pasarét, the Rózsadomb and also to the villas of Mátyásföld. Not even the modern houses of Új-Lipótváros were inhabited by the financial elite. It was the middle-class who lived here, and freelancers, creative intellectuals. Here lived the poet Miklós Radnóti, the journalist György Bálint, here was the apartment and studio of the ceramic artist Margit Kovács (1902–1977), the silver- and copper-work artist Margit Tevan (1901–1978), this is where the poet and translator István Vas (1910–1991) came to visit his friends. Doctors, engineers, teachers and journalists lived here as well. They must have been attracted by the modern, comfortable architecture of the houses, the urban surroundings, the beautiful Danube bank, the park. And a much stronger force must also have driven them here: their patients and customers lived here: the people who commissioned their works, the milieu, which enabled them to sustain themselves as artists.

In 1944 the authorities declared a few blocks in Új-Lipótváros the international ghetto, and here were most of those protected houses where those Jews lived who were not Hungarian citizens. The Jews living in Új-Lipótváros were generally wealthier than say the Jews living in the neighborhood of Garay utca. Papers that granted protection usually cost money, that is why more people here had foreign papers than in other neighborhoods.

The Jewish character of Új-Lipótváros was not a cause but a consequence. This district was by no means organized on the basis of who is Jewish and who is not. The construction of Új-Lipótváros was a typical example of how big cities kept expanding. Entrepreneurs bought the huge plots, architectural firms entered bids, young, talented architects who had studied abroad designed the individual buildings along the same style.

It was around the same time that Lágymányos (today the region around Móricz Zsigmond körtér in the eleventh district of Budapest) was built up. The percentage of Jews among the architects of Lágymányos and Új-Lipótváros was about the same. So the question arises, why is it, that Lágymányos was built in the more conservative Neo-Baroque style, while Új-Lipótváros was constructed according to the most contemporary European standards? Was it due to the fact that the population of Lágymányos was different, that it was inhabited mostly by Christian middle- and upper-middle class people? The late Gábor Preisich (1909–1998), during the past decades the grand old man of the society of architects of Budapest, who had been designing some of the houses himself, asserted that in Lágymányos the hands of the architects were bound by some Neo-Baroque buildings that had been built there earlier, and by the conservative taste of the Christian middle-class people living there, while the architects of Új-Lipótváros worked in a void and were free to plan according to their fantasy and the modern trends in order to meet the expectations of their Jewish customers.

(8) Alfréd Hajós Swimming Pool (Margit-sziget [Margaret Island])

The swimming pool was constructed in 1931, to the great glory of the architect, Alfréd Hajós. It was called *Nemzeti Sportuszoda* (National Sport / Olympic Swimming Pool), and was for decades, until 1975, the scene of Hungarian water sports. Swimming, diving and water-polo practices as well as competitions were held here, and it was favored by the general public, too. Though the pool is actually not in Új-Lipótváros, it is part of the same stylistic unit and today it belongs to the same district as well.

Alfréd Hajós (Guttmann) (1875–1955) was active as an architect mostly in the years preceding World War I. Some of his more famous buildings are the headquarters of the *Református Zsinati Iroda* (Calvinist Synodial Office, 21 Abonyi utca, built in 1909) and the *Vakok otthona* (Institute for the Blind, 7 Hermina út, built in 1912) in Budapest, and the Hotel "Arany Bika" [Golden Bull], built in 1910 in Debrecen. But he achieved some glory already earlier, as an athlete. He participated in the first modern Olympic Games in Athens in 1896 and won two gold medals, in one hundred and in 1000-meter free-style swimming. The Greek just called him the "Hungarian dolphin". He also played soccer with the *Budapest Torna Club* (Budapest Sports Club), he was an inside left, member of the national selection, and later captain of the National Soccer Team. At the 1924 Olympic Games in Paris one of his architectural plans designed together with Dezső Lauber won a silver medal. In the interwar period Hajós was actively involved in organizational work to further the Olympic movement and he endorsed the revival of the Olympic Committee after World War II. His apartment and office were on the third floor of 4 Báthory utca, facing Honvéd utca. "In his wonderfully beautiful apartment there were two large bright rooms facing the court-

399. The swimmer Alfréd Hajós (left) and marathon runner Gyula Kellner after they won Olympic medals. Photo, 1896

400. The National Olympic Swimming Pool. Competition design by Alfréd Hajós, ca. 1928

401. The National Olympic Swimming Pool, 1938

yard. In the summer all the doors between the rooms, halls and the cool winter-garden were kept open, forming a long corridor..."—wrote Győző Határ, a London-based Hungarian writer and one-time employee of the office, in his memoirs (*Életút* [A Life Story], 1988–1993).

In the staircase of his house and in the lobby of the Olympic Swimming Pool slabs commemorate the name of Alfréd Hajós.

*

Hajós was not the only Hungarian Jewish athlete who distinguished himself in swimming or some other sport. There is a whole book about Hungarian Jewish athletes, written in English by Andrew Handler in the United States. We agree with Handler who claims that it is probably in the area of sports that the role of Hungarian Jews is most difficult to determine. Many of the Jewish athletes competing under the Hungarian flag tried to conceal their background, there were only a few who proudly proclaimed their Jewishness. Most of the Hungarian Jewish athletes lived the life typical of an assimilated Jew. Handler lists some three hundred Hungarian Jewish athletes with more than one gold medal. Let us mention just a few. Jenő Fuchs (1882–1955) won Olympic gold medals in 1908 at London and in 1912 at Stockholm in fencing. Ferenc Mező (1885–1961) was a sports historian who won a gold medal at the 1928 Olympic Games for his book on the history of the ancient Olympic Games. (Before the Hungarian Olympic committee did not consider him worthy to be sent to the Games.) Béla Komjádi (1892–1933) was the coach of the Hungarian water-polo team that won several gold medals at European championships and other competitions in the late 1920s. In 1975 the new Olympic swimming pool was named after him. It stands on the Buda bank of the Danube (8 Árpád fejedelem útja), right where one of the Jewish cemeteries of Turkish Buda must have been. Attila Petschauer, a fencer, was member of the Olympic champion Hungarian team twice, in 1928 at Amsterdam and in 1932 at Los Angeles. Károly Kárpáti, a wrestler, defeated the German finalist at the 1936 Berlin Olympic Games in the Deutschlandhalle, in front of the Führer's very eyes. Endre Kabos won a gold medal both in team and in individual fencing at the 1936 Berlin Olympics. He died on November 4, 1944, when the Margit híd (Margaret Bridge) was blown up by the German Army. Ilona Elek (Schacherer), nicknamed "Csibi", also beat her German rival at the 1936 Berlin Olympics in fencing. She survived the war and remained the best in her branch for about another decade. In 1948 she won another Olympic gold medal at the London Olympic Games. Márton Bukovi was a soccer player with *Ferencvárosi Torna Club* (Ferencváros Sports Club, FTC), coach of the national selection team after World War II, sports-writer. Zsigmond Ádler was an outstanding boxing coach. Éva Székely, swimmer, the Hungarian "Madame Butterfly", became an Olympic champion in 1952 in Helsinki. She openly spoke and wrote about her Jewishness in her best-selling autobiography (*Sírni csak a győztesnek szabad* [Only the Winner May Cry], 1982), and revealed what had happened to her in 1944 (she survived the most difficult months in a house under Swiss protection).

The *Magyar Testgyakorlók Köre* (Hungarian Athletic Club, MTK) has been regarded a Jewish club in anti-Semitic circles, a view eventually shared by the general public. The truth of the matter was that the MTK, founded on November 9, 1888, in the villa of the Freudiger family in Városliget (between Hermina út and Stefánia út), always had many Jewish members, but it was never an explicitly Jewish athletic club.

Only zealous Zionists formed explicitly Jewish athletic clubs in Budapest. The founder of *Vívó és Atlétikai Club* (Jewish Fencing and Athletics Club, VAC) was Lajos Dömény (1880–1914) who also founded the Hungarian branch of *Keren Kayemeth* and the *Kadimah* Jewish boy scouts' group in 1913. (A Kadima group had been founded in Vienna three decades earlier, in 1882.) Its headquarters was at 26 Erzsébet körút. After World War I the union of scouts' groups rejected the application of *Kadimah* to join and so the oldest Hungarian Jewish scouts' group gradually fell apart and closed down by 1924. *Makkabi*, the alliance of Hungarian Jewish students, was formed in 1903. It was considered a sport club, too; its first president was the Talmudic scholar Sámuel Krausz. On the tenth anniversary of its foundation, in 1913, a group of one-thousand young Zionists, wearing top hats and white gloves, carrying the blue-white flag, marched to the *Keleti pályaudvar* / Eastern Railway Station to welcome David Wolfsohn, the president of the international Zionist organization. After World War I, as anti-Semitism grew stronger, members of the *Makkabi* organized a Jewish self-defense team to protect themselves from aggression.

Alfréd Brüll (1876–1944) was among the greatest patrons of Hungarian sport. He helped clubs and individual athletes to attend international competitions; he was also a personal friend to many. His home, the Brüll House, is at 115/B Üllői út; it was constructed by Géza Kiss in 1908–1909. The crypt of the Brüll family in the Kozma utca cemetery was made by the sculptor Alajos Stróbl. Alfréd Brüll himself was killed in Auschwitz.

It is somewhat ironic, yet symbolic of *fin-de-siècle* Hungarian national self-perception, that the concepts "ethnic Hungarian" and "ethnic Jewish" mixed. When creating the monument of the poet János Arany, to be placed in front of the National Museum, Alajos Stróbl (1856–1926), the most prominent sculptor of the period, modeled two of the side figures, the strong and heroic Miklós Toldi and Botond—symbolic figures of Hungarian national lore as created by Arany—after Dávid Müller, the celebrated athlete of the 1890s and Richárd Weisz, wrestler and Olympic champion, both Jewish and members of MTK.

X. Józsefváros, beyond the Boulevard

The region beyond József körút towards the East, what used to be the outer section of Józsefváros, but which today forms its center, has had a considerable Jewish population from the late nineteenth century on until the late 1950s. The Jews who lived here had a significant impact on the face of the city and local society. Népszínház utca and Nagy Fuvaros utca were inhabited by upper middle-class people, while poorer Jews lived in and around Teleki tér.

The building at 22 Népszínház utca, designed by Emil Vidor around 1906, was owned by the *Polgári Serfőzde* (Civil Brewery) and was called *Sörös palota* (Beer Palace). The poet and editor József Kiss (1843–1921) lived on its fourth floor towards the end of his life. Previously he had lived on the third floor of 17 Rökk Szilárd utca. It seems that in his old days he preferred a more peaceful area.

"If a colleague came by his house in the morning, he generally found the editor in bed. Actually it was not so much a bed as a wide cot, buried under and surrounded by carpets for prayer-stools, prayer-rugs, rugs to throw over camels or the merchandise on the caravan. Among and under these carpets hunkered the gnomic figure of the poet, enjoying them with his eyes and skin. The surrounding walls were decorated with the paintings of Rippl-Rónai, Mednyánszky, Nándor Katona, Adolf Fényes, Vaszary and Réti, some thirty-five or forty pieces. The poet would take extraordinary pride in showing them off to his visitors and discovering some fine detail every single day. (...) He furnished his study in Népszínház utca at the turn of the century almost like a gallery or a museum. It looked as if a rich art collector or a fashionable painter had lived there rather than a poet. He was certainly not the ascetic type. He believed he had the same right to live among comfortable armchairs, silk pillows, soft carpets, beautiful paintings and sculptures as a bank manager."   (Aladár Komlós, "Kiss József", in: Lajos Hatvany, Ed., *Beszélő házak*, 1957)

The rugs of József Kiss were a topic of conversation, even Dezső Kosztolányi wrote about them. "He throned on an immense bed in his study dimmed by Persian carpets, among silk pillows" (*Nyugat*, 1922).

"The life and work of József Kiss had the same significance in literature as the emancipation of Hungarian Jews had in politics. His Jewish poems and ballads opened Hungarian literature for us, they emancipated us literarily" (Lajos Szabolcsi, in: *Kiss József és kerekasztala*, Budapest, 1934, p. 192). József Kiss was a poet, a modern journalist and editor. His newspaper, *A Hét* [The Week] (editorial offices at 6 Erzsébet körút), launched in 1890, changed the tone of Hungarian literature completely. He expanded the poetry-reading public by turning a daily newspaper into an important literary organ. "He was a Jew, but an old one, already his great-grandfather lived in Hungary" (Gyula Krúdy). When he came to Pest as a young man, he immersed himself in the Jewish world of Király utca and its neighborhood. He could have become a *melammed*, they would have hired him from the Orczy House. His first poems and other writings reveal a strong secular Jewish identity. He never feared to speak out in debates over Hungarian or international Jewish issues. He expressed his views about the Tiszaeszlár blood libel trials in *Az ár ellen* [Against the Current] (1882) and about the pogroms in the Russian Pale in *Új Ahasvér* [New Ahasuerus] (1875) and *Odessza* (1905). "After the late 1880s he rarely talked about the Jewish community in his poems, he voiced his personal feelings instead. He seems to have felt that there was no further need to talk about Jewishness, that the debate over the Jewish question had abated. By then Hungarian Jews did not perceive themselves as a separate community, they did not feel like differentiating themselves and so they would not have accepted a poet who did so"—wrote Aladár Komlós in *Múlt és Jövő* in 1943.

As much as József Kiss became a secular literary personality, he still considered the translation of the prayers of the *Mahzor*, the holiday prayer-book, into Hungarian an important task. The Jewish community commissioned the translation from him in Mór Wahrmann's time and it was completed in 1888 (*Ünnepnapok* [Holidays]). His whole life long he bemoaned the fact that it was not accepted into the liturgy of the Dohány Temple. "The book has been out of print for over ten years now. I did not care to have it reprinted, and I will not do so in the future either. Why should I? For whom? Soon none of the old type of Jews will be left and the new Jews prefer songs about Mary", he wrote in 1914 on his 70th birthday, in a somewhat resigned tone. And yet the book was republished towards the end of his life, in 1921. The lasting value of the literary work of József Kiss is that it is rooted in the immediate experience of rural Jewish Hungary, the scene of his childhood. His works are a treasury of Jewish folklore that was heavily influenced by Hasidic lore, to which he was exposed growing up in Mezőcsát, a village in eastern Hungary. Sándor Scheiber collected the folklore from his works but he failed to include a novel by Kiss about Király utca, written under the pseudonym Rudolf Szentesi.

His grave is in the Kozma utca cemetery. The Jewish community erected his tombstone in 1930.

At 28/B Népszínház utca was the Wertheimer Nightclub (1886–1912). It was named after Lajos Wertheimer, the owner. It was a lower-class version of the nightclub. The program, put together by Lajos Bass, consisted of Polish–Jewish folksongs, Eastern-European Jewish tunes with Yiddish texts, showing Slavic musical influence—the secular Jewish music of the *shtetlakh*.

(1) Jewish Quarter of the Petit Bourgeois

The synagogue at 4 Nagy Fuvaros utca is in use today. It is furnished in Orthodox style but it is used by a Neolog community, services are held according to the Neolog ritual. Originally the building had

402. 4 Nagy Fuvaros utca. The ceiling of the prayer-room

belonged to the *Józsefvárosi Casino* (Casino of Józsefváros). The synagogue was built in the courtyard of the building in 1922, according to the design of Dezső Freund (1884–1960). The glass ceiling above the women's gallery indicates that the synagogue stands in a courtyard. There is a winter prayer-room in the building, and the large halls of the former casino are used for cultural events. There is even a kitchen that makes it possible to hold *Seder* evenings here for a number of people. Wooden plates with six-pointed stars are attached to the doors on the first and second floor, as decoration. The Jewish symbols became a central decorative element at the time of the construction of the synagogue.

Right across the street, on the second floor of the house at 3/B there is an Orthodox synagogue. Or rather, the vivid memory of an Orthodox synagogue in the mind of the people who live in that house. The building itself, as the inscription on the facade still tells us, used to belong to the "Kaufmann liquor, rum, vinegar and distillery". The synagogue was set up in two apartments combined. The larger one in the front became the men's section, the small one towards the back, accessible through the back stairs, the women's section. The synagogue was called the prayer-room of the *Écz Chájim Egylet* (Society, *etz hayyim*, "tree of life", the rod of the Torah scroll). In the spacious courtyard of the house a *Sukkah* was set up every fall, even in the years after World War II. This Orthodox synagogue was closed in the 1950s. Today, there are again two apartments in its place.

For the sake of a short digression here is an old joke about a Jewish Robinson.

"Having suffered a shipwreck, Rav Reuben Robinson, the only survivor of the catastrophe, finds himself on a desert island. He spends ten years here in solitude until finally a ship passing by the island notices his

smoke signals. As the captain steps ashore, he is proud to show him everything that he had built for himself in those ten years.

This is the synagogue where I pray every day, even if just by myself—he says—and that other one is for my adversary.

And the third one, my dear Rav Robinson, is this, a synagogue, too?—asks the captain.

Yes—replies Robinson scornfully—but I would never set foot in this one."

403. 3 Nagy Fuvaros utca. The building once housed an Orthodox synagogue

404. The entrance to the former Orthodox synagogue from the courtyard

This self-deprecating Jewish joke is, of course, not without foundation. In Budapest, for instance, in many places the synagogue and the temple, i.e. the Orthodox and the Neolog prayer-houses, are right next or very close to each other. After the 1868/69 General Congress the different Jewish religious factions expressed their distinctiveness in every way they could.

Everything necessary for traditional Jewish life was available in the neighborhood. There was a grocery at no. 4 and a bakery at no. 27—this is where women brought the *tshulent* on Friday afternoons so that it should be ready by the time the second *shabes* meal was to be served. (They say that only the Neolog Jews would bring their *tshulent* to the bakery, because you had to carry it home on *shabes*, which was forbidden... A *decent* Jewish household would have its own tshulent oven.)

A general store stood on the corner of Auróra utca and Bérkocsis utca. They say that on its wall it said: "PÁSZKA MACÓ." The two Hungarian names for *matzzah* were used next to each other so that the Orthodox and the hardly religious should both understand what was meant. The storekeeper wanted to attract a wide range of customers. His store was not strictly kosher, but eventually he separated dairy and meat products, to fulfill at least the basic requirements of *kashrut*. Yet the number of his customers gradually decreased and he went broke.

405. "PÁSZKA MACÓ." Formerly a grocery store on the corner of Auróra utca and Bérkocsis utca

406. Where the *shabes tshulent* was baked: formerly a bakery at 27 Nagy Fuvaros utca

407. Repair garage at the site of the former *kosheray* (28 Dankó utca)

A little further, at 28 Dankó utca, on the corner of Magdolna utca there was a *kosheray*, a ritual slaughterhouse. It was set up in a shed at the back of the courtyard-type building, with several small rooms. It looks the same today, though there is a new booth in place of the old one, and a service station has replaced the *kosheray*.

There are two kinds of ritual slaughter. In larger towns the slaughterer (*shohet / shoykhet*) specializes either in fowl (*oyfes shoykhet*) or in large animals, mainly cows (*gese shoykhet*). Since the purchase and slaughter of large animals like cows or sheep is a more complicated process, the slaughterhouse is generally not in the center of the town; but fowl needs to be slaughtered near to where the people live, where the rabbi is. Friday morning a good Jewish housewife (or husband) goes to the market and buys, among other things, chicken or a goose. Then she either takes them to the *shoykhet* herself or sends them over with the children. Should she find anything suspicious in the meat, an abnormal part or a clot of blood, she needs to consult the rabbi, who decides whether the meat may be eaten, or the whole piece has to be thrown away, or just the abnormal part.

A Yiddish proverb about the poverty of the *shtetl* says: *Mer shokhtim vi hiner*, "There are more slaughterers than hen".

Restaurants and cafés are also indispensable elements of urban life. There were some in this neighborhood, too, for instance the café of Henrik Pless at 10 Déri Miksa utca. It was a decent, spacious, elegant place with a middle-class public. Today a furniture store occupies the space. The reputation of the proprietors was questioned after the war. Rumor had it, though none knew for sure, that they had eaten horse-meat during the terrible winter of the siege of Budapest in the winter of 1944/45. This was considered cannibalism by the Jewish people in the neighborhood; for horse-meat is *treyf*, it is not "an animal with a split hoof" the consumption of which is forbidden by the Torah (Leviticus 11,2; Deuteronomy 11,6).

Pubs were numerous in the area, especially around the Teleki tér market. The *"Matróz csárda"* (Sailor's Inn) somewhat further on the left bank of the Danube, South of Ferenc József-híd / Szabadság-híd (Francis Joseph / Freedom Bridge), was considered a Jewish place. Whether it was kosher is rather doubtful.

(2) The Refuge of the Belzer Rebe in Pest (12 Köztársaság tér)

In Budapest there are not many memorials or monuments of Hasidim. There is one place, however, which should be marked, and that is the house at 12 Tisza Kálmán tér / Köztársaság tér, where R. Aaron Rokeach (Singer) (1880–1957), the Belzer *rebe* found refuge for about a year during World War II. Why did he hide here? Contemporaries must have known the answer. Based on an old directory we know that 3 Tisza Kálmán tér was the headquarters of the *A Budapesten Lakó Zsidó Galicziaiak Önsegélyező Egyesülete* (Aid Association of Galician Jews Living in Budapest). The neighborhood must have been an old "haven" for Hasidim and so the rebe fled to his people. Though probably coincidental, even the name of the square is of symbolic value. Kálmán Tisza (1830–1902), former Prime Minister and Minister of Interior, after whom the square was named, firmly rejected the anti-Semitic outbursts in Parliament during the Tiszaeszlár blood libel trials in 1882–1883. Doing so he indirectly supported the fight for the political rights of Eastern, Galician Jewry.

Belz (Ukraine, Galicia, near Lemberg / Lviv) had been an important center of Hasidism since the late eighteenth century. The first Belzer *tsadik* was R. Sholem (1779–1855), "the healer (*rokeah*)". He sought healing for the ailments of the soul in personal confession, going against the grain of Jewish tradition in general. For him men and (married) women were equal, he looked upon every Jewish couple as if they were Adam and Eve before the Fall.

408. Aaron Rokeach

"Tomorrow

It was before the Passover and while the Hasidim were drawing water for the baking of the unleavened bread, they called to one another: Next year in Jerusalem! Then R. Shalom said: Why not before next year? With this water which we are now drawing we may be baking unleavened bread in Jerusalem tomorrow on the day before the feast, and may eat it—if the Messiah comes to redeem us."

(Martin Buber, *Das verborgene Licht*, 1924 / *Tales of the Hasidim: The Later Masters*, translated by Olga Marx, New York: Schocken Books, 1947/1975)

R. Sholem's descendants all became famous for their ascetic life and for categorically rejecting any kind of formal innovation in the practice of Judaism. Not only did they oppose the Haskalah and reforms of Judaism but also the establishment of a central organization for Orthodox Jews, as well as the Zionist movement. The only known descendant of the family, or perhaps just of a *hosed* of the Belz rebe living in Máramaros, otherwise a man of fame who chose a civil life, was the Budapest and Viennese Isidor Kaufmann (1853–1921), painter of colorful Oriental or Orientalizing faces and scenes in Galicia.

Aaron Rokeach's father, Yissakhar Dov Rokeach (1854–1927), lived in Újfehértó during World War I and in Munkács for a few years after the war. József Patai visited the rebe in Belz still before World War I and recorded his memories of this visit upon the death of the rebe in 1927 in *Múlt és Jövő*. Patai's article makes it clear that the rebe functioned in the community like in a paying job; his followers, the Belzer Hasidim, some five or six thousand Jews, lived on the donations (*pidyon*), which the rebe received for blessing and advising those who visited him. Among his visitors were many *ingerishe yidn*, Hungarian Jews. The rebe of Munkács (*minkatsher rebe*) was actually his rival.

Already back in Belz, which belonged to Poland at that time, Aaron, Yissakhar's son, introduced extremely long services for his followers, unusual even by Orthodox standards. He had strong political influence through his followers: the Belzer Hasidim generally backed the Polish Government. He was considered the "chief-*rebe*" of Galicia by everyone in Poland, though there was no such official title or position. He was almost like a Jewish prince. His hundred-year-old synagogue is only to be completed when the Messiah comes, who will obviously pass through Belz on his way.

At the start of World War II Aaron and his family had to flee from Belz. In Przemysl his followers and his entire family, all seven of his children, were killed. Having passed through several ghettos in Poland, the last one being that in Bochnia (near Cracow), the rebe himself arrived via Verecke, the famous pass in the Carpathians, Ungvár, Kassa to Budapest in May 1943. It is said that he arrived in Budapest wearing a service uniform, that of a Hungarian general. Some say he was without his beard and with a broken heart. As a recent novel by István Gábor Benedek—a former student of the Rabbinical Seminary and now a journalist and writer—set forth in detail, the rebe was rescued to Budapest by people of General István Ujszászy (1894–1947?), the commander-in-chief of the Hungarian secret service. Three members of the Pest Orthodox community were behind the action, Márton Stern who ran a kosher restaurant in the Rumbach Sebestyén utca, Miksa Hollander (a merchant and *parnas* of the community) and József Salgó, an executive (*askan*) of the community. They sought the help of Margit Slachta, co-president of the Holy Cross Society and a Christian politician. Samu Stern, the president of the Neolog community, and Count István Bethlen, the former Prime Minister, were also cooperating.

The rebe lived as a recluse in Budapest. His first lodging was in Újpest, in the house of the municipal health officer, László Pesta, right opposite to the synagogue. The rebe was one of a large number of Polish Jews who found relative security in Hungary during World War II or who at least could flee to the West or to Palestine through Hungary. Did he wear his Hasidic clothing all the time?

Aaron Rokeach was finally able to escape to Palestine, probably via Temesvár, Romania, maybe as a member of one of the Zionist *excursions* (*tiyyul*). Or did he carry an official passport, a certificate? Some, including Niszel, the restaurant owner, say that he defrayed the costs of his escape and stayed in Pest with a large sum from his own money. The hiding of the Belzer rebe could not be such a big secret among his Hasidim or the authorities, after all. The Hasidim asked for his words and blessing, as an eyewitness, Tibor (Avraham) Helfer (1918–1998) told it. He must have received every kind of assistance from the Hungarian authorities that all the other refugees from Poland received, food stamps and the like. The Budapest center of the Polish Red Cross issued for him a Polish refugee identification card, Polish military uniform, and even gave him per diem of the refugees. For all this his name had to be on the official lists. Some even say that towards the end the Minister of Interior, Ferenc Keresztes-Fischer (1881–1948), sent a personal message to the rebe that he could not cover for him any longer.

It is said that the rebe said farewell to the Orthodox community, that on one Saturday evening, as the Shabbat was to go out, he gave a *shalesh-südes* for his folk in the Assembly Hall of the Orthodox community's headquarters.

There is another story about the departure of the rebe. They say that he left Budapest early in 1944; some specify the date as January 16, but what is known for sure is that it definitely happened before the German occupation on March 19, 1944. On the preceding day masses of Polish Hasidim are said to have gathered in the courtyard and in the street in front of his house, wearing traditional long, black coat, as if it were peace-time; thousands of them, waiting silently for a word from the rebe, just like on *shabes* in better times. R. Aaron appeared on the balcony for a short while and told his followers in Yiddish: *Blaybt shtilerheyt*, "Stay calm." On this day only mounted policemen could maintain order in the street.

R. Aaron's brother, the Bilgorai rebe, R. Mordechai also delivered a speech in front of the refugees in Pest in January, maybe on the very day the rebe left. Was it maybe in front of the same crowd of people? Was it him, only him, who gave the speech in question? He too, left, and he too encouraged the Hasidim to stay. As the word of the rebe is always the main guideline for the Hasidim, these words were taken literally. *Blaybt shtilerheyt*. Stay calm. You can stay, there is no need to worry, evil will not come here. And those who stayed were most probably seized during the frequent police raids in the following months, and since their citizenship was "unregulated", they were probably taken to a transit camp and deported with the next transport.

The gossip of the town in connection with the rebe's departure appeared in print back in those days, in the first and last issue of a publication intended to be a periodical called *Ha-Derekh* (Budapest: Nachum Uri Eisler, Shevat 13, 704 [January 28, 1944]) and also in a booklet: *Mashmi'a yeshu'ah* [Announcing Redemption] (Budapest: Meshullam Zalman Katzburg Printing House). Since the historical events came in quick succession then, there was no response to the critical voice. After the war the rebe was accused of having saved himself, leaving hundreds of thousands of his followers behind in the lurch.

Though this is only indirectly related to the story of the rebe, it should be mentioned that immediately after the German occupation of Hungary Keresztes-Fischer was arrested and sent to the Dachau concentration camp. General Ujházy died, after a long captivity in Russia, in a prison of the State Security in Budapest. Pesta, a non-Jewish medical doctor, bore high state and municipal offices after the war, his deed was never mentioned publicly. Helfer was, later, for decades, president of the Pest Orthodox Hevrah Kaddishah.

After the war Aaron Rokeach lived in Tel-Aviv and later in Jerusalem. He founded several *yeshivot* in Israel. The greatest Belzer yeshivah is in Jerusalem today, near Mahaneh Yehudah, but the present rebe, Aaron's younger cousin, has followers in Western Europe and in the United States, too. They even publish a newspaper. Some think that these *haredi*, rigorous Jews, are extremists.

Here is one of the memorable sayings of Aaron Rokeach:

"One can learn something good from everything. The Israeli *sherut*, the shared taxi, for instance, teaches you modesty. You can only get into it if you bow deeply."

Oral tradition preserved some other scenes as well, where the rebe had supposedly lived in Pest. An address where he used to stay was in the Jewish quarter, 32 Kertész utca. Inhabitants of the *Kupolás ház* (Domed House) at 56 Dohány utca, where the kosher slaughterhouse was, say that the Polish wonder-rebe was hiding in their house, this was where he survived the war. Others seem to know that his apartment was in Lujza utca. These data or just legends only confirm that the Belzer rebe was really someone, that his hiding in Pest was a noteworthy event in the eyes of many.

Until very recently Hasidism found no base in Budapest, there was no Jewish community or group, which would have considered the memory of the Belzer rebe their own. An *ohel* is generally erected over the tomb of Hasidic rabbis; the house in Józsefváros, which carries the memory of the Belzer rebe, was only a refuge.

(3) The Former Apartment of Sándor Scheiber (12 Kun utca, fourth floor, Apt. 27)

The former apartment of Sándor Scheiber is not a memorial open to the public. It is a simple one-bedroom apartment in a house on the corner of Teleki tér. The building used to be a fine one, even today it is one of the better houses of the neighborhood. There used to be a movie theater in it called *Népszínház-mozgó*. Jews were allowed to enter even in the summer of 1944, they could go to the first show every Wednesday and Friday. The site of the movie theater is an upholstery shop today. Lajos Scheiber (1867–1944) lived here, the rabbi of the Nagy Fuvaros utca community, and his family. His son, Sándor Scheiber remained in the apartment after the war, to keep tradition and also because it was conveniently near—in walking distance—to the Rabbinical Seminary. He lived there until his death.

There were thousands of books, all over the apartment. The bookcase, a fine piece of cabinetry, was almost collapsing under the weight of books, and there were books even on top of it, on his desk, piled up on the floor and on every possible piece of furniture. Scheiber had a very special personal relationship to his books and manuscripts. Gossips go around that he used to keep a book even underneath his prayer-book taking a glance at it between the prayers.

The pages came to life, he knew many by heart, the handwriting of the Cairo *Genizah* was alive in his head. This great collection of medieval manuscripts was found in 1896 immured in the ancient Ben Ezra Synagogue (882) in the Jewish quarter in Cairo's Old City (al-Fostat), in the synagogue where Maimonides used to pray. Scholars and collectors immediately put their hands on the find and the some one hundred and fifty manuscripts and fragments were scattered around the major museums of the world. Originally *genizah* was the treasury where the jewelry was kept at the Old Persian royal court; in the Middle Ages the term was used for one of the rooms of the synagogue where the *pasul*, defective holy texts and other Hebrew manuscripts were hidden. The Cairo materials had accumulated over several centuries, there were all kinds of Hebrew documents among them: Biblical and Talmudic texts, liturgical works, correspondence. But everything was in fragments, on loose pages, scrap paper. Scholarly research of the *genizah* had to start with the identification of the documents: what was written on the piece of paper or parchment and where could the rest of it be? Before the war Scheiber started doing *genizah* research at Cambridge, where the largest *genizah* collection is kept, though he knew that the *genizah* materials in the Kaufmann Collection had not been examined yet. He had the opportunity to visit all the major *genizah* collections of the world between New York and St. Petersburg, and wherever he went he found materials previously unknown to scholars. He recognized certain handwritings, he remembered individual pages, his mind joined together pieces of the *genizah* materials separated by oceans and continents. *Genizah* research was an essential part of his scholarly activity, this was what earned him international fame. Scholars from all over the world would send him their books, publications.

Scheiber's library was built up not only thanks to the international network of scholars, but also along his various interests. He was fascinated by contemporary *genizah* as well as by the old: Hungarian Jewish history, Hebrew inscriptions, manuscript fragments used for binding medieval codices, objects of Jewish folklore, the theme of Jewish wandering in literature and in folk customs. He collected anything that he came across in these areas—manuscripts, scrap papers, letters by József Kiss or Attila József. The uniqueness of manuscripts must have attracted him with magical force, he collected them just like books—whatever a modest apartment on the edge of the Inner City could contain!

(4) Sephardi Prayer-house (22 Teleki tér)

409. "Tshertkovo" shil (22 Teleki tér)

The synagogue on Teleki tér used to be called *Tshertkovo* or *Tshortkovo shil*. The name itself suggests that the "Sephardi" prayer-house was used not by Sephardi Jews but rather by Galician Hasidim. Tshertkov / Czertków or Czortków is a town in former Podolia, Ukraine, later Polish and Habsburg Galicia and today once again in the Ukraine. This is where the Rotschild (Rothschild) family comes from (though not everyone in Tshertkov was a Rotschild...). When David Moses Friedmann settled here in 1860, Tshertkov became an important Hasidic center. In the *shtetl* the synagogues and *shils* were traditionally built near the market. Pious, Hasidic merchants spent every free minute of theirs studying. Like in the *shtetl*, the spoken language on Teleki tér was Yiddish. The prayers and customs differed from the Ashkenazi *minhag* only insofar as Hasidism in general was influenced by Turkish Sephardim.

The entrance of the simple prayer-house is from the courtyard of a dwelling house.

(5) Teleki tér

Also the area around Teleki tér and Kun utca belongs to the Outer-Józsefváros. Most of this section was built up in the years after 1860. The *Józsefvárosi pályaudvar* (Józsefváros Railway Station), earlier called Hatvan–Losonc Railway Station, is in this neighborhood, on the segment of Orczy út (today Fiumei út). This used to be an important railway station for passenger traffic, but became a freight depot later.

The core of this section was most definitely the market. Originally it was called Baromvásár tér or Széna tér and fairs were held here. The Teleki tér market was for the poor, lower-middle-class population

410. The Jewish market, ca. 1920

411. "The railway station of the Pest-Losonc railroad in Pest" (Józsefváros Railway Station). Drawing by Gusztáv Zombory, 1865

412. The market on Teleki tér, 1946

what the New Market in the Inner City was for the wealthier. It was not just a flea-market but a permanent market with stalls. The flea-market was set up only in 1897 on the western edge of the square. In 1950 it was moved to Ecseri út and later to Nagykőrösi út, but then the market itself stayed on Teleki tér.

Early in the twentieth century the Jews of the neighborhood made a living at the market. Simple people, fairly new to the city, had a stall in Teleki tér. They had an organization as well, with headquarters in the *Zsibárus ház* (Peddler House). Most of them spoke Yiddish better than Hungarian, and so did their customers. This was the "haven" where Polish and Galician Jews coming to Pest in the early years of the twentieth century arrived; it was the "Lower East Side of Pest".

The term "from Teleki tér", whether used for merchandise or manners, was not exactly a compliment. But its basis was only the behavior at the market, because there was no lack of religious zeal here. The square was encircled by various little synagogues, prayer-houses, *shtiblakh*. Right on the corner, for instance, at 8 Lujza utca was the Polish synagogue (Szachre Pajlen, *sohrei Polin*, "Polish merchants"). Other prayer-rooms were at 1 and 5 Teleki tér, 3 and 7–9 Dobozi utca, 19 Erdélyi utca, 21 Lujza utca and more.

The Zsibárus Ház near Teleki tér is a U-shape block of houses embracing the corner house at 16 Lujza utca–40 Magdolna utca, 42–44 Magdolna utca, the corner house at 46 Magdolna utca, 21 Dobozi utca and 19 Dobozi utca. Peddlers, merchants lived here and here was their organization. This was the only place where the attack of the Arrow-cross men on October 15 and 16 was met by armed resistance.

(6) Anti-Semitic Party in the Pub

Mihály Kaiser's pub at no. 8 Teleki tér was one of the places where members of the *Antiszemita Párt* (Anti-Semitic Party) would meet in the years after the Tiszaeszlár trials. The Party's leaders were Győző Istóczy and Gyula Verhovay (1849–1906); they had considerable success at the elections in 1884, winning 17 seats. Their conspiracies were monitored by the police; reports by observers are preserved at the Budapest Municipal Archives.

Another place where they used to gather was the Lerch pub, and a third one, somewhat further away, Sverteczky's restaurant, then called "Fehér szegfű" (White Carnation) at 26 Práter utca.

Already at the next elections the success of the Anti-Semitic Party diminished; they won only six seats. Istóczy was regarded as some clown by the other MPs. Since they lost their political influence, their activities were confined to the sphere of the pub. Istóczy did not quite reach the middle of his life when he was forced to withdraw from politics altogether; he started editing his memoirs about his political career and spent the rest of his days translating Josephus Flavius (*The Jewish War*, 1900).

*

Whether it is a coincidence or not, the house right next to the former Kaiser pub, 10 Teleki tér, became an Arrow-cross headquarters in the fall of 1944. It was a transit camp; Jews who were seized in the streets of Budapest and in apartments were taken here, and to other houses in the square, including numbers 4–10. Raoul Wallenberg spoke up on behalf of a group of about fifty persons who were taken here from the international ghetto (15 Tátra utca) in December. He rescued a few people from here every day, but even he could not save everyone.

XI. Neighbors of the Pest Jewish Community

Though the Pest Jewish community was the largest one in the world anyway, it could have been even larger, had all the Jewish communities of the capital, Budapest, belonged to it. The significant Jewish community of Buda remained independent after the 1868/69 General Congress, and they retained this independence even after the unification of Pest, Buda and Óbuda—the creation of Budapest in 1873. The smaller Jewish communities of the once independent small towns around Budapest, for instance Újpest, also maintained their independence for a few more decades.

(1) Buda

The Buda Jewish community, which was founded for the second time late in the eighteenth century, thanks to the decrees of Joseph II, remained in existence until very recently.

During the last decade of its independent existence, immediately before World War II, three synagogues had belonged to it. The community's main temple at 5 Öntőház utca was designed by the architect Ignác Knabe in the "Moorish" style in 1865, possibly in the place of an—unknown—earlier prayer-house or prayer-room. It stood directly underneath the Castle facing the Danube and was clearly visible from the Pest side of the river; one can say that it had a distinguished location. Earlier there

416. The synagogue below the Castle under construction. The Öntőház utca synagogue, with scaffolding

was only a prayer-room in Buda and so the construction of a synagogue was a sign of the growth of the community. Though the costs of construction were collected only with some difficulty, the synagogue was soon completed. At the consecration ceremony on January 23, 1866, R. Meisel from the Dohány utca synagogue delivered a speech, in German. The rabbi of Óbuda categorically refused to attend the consecration of a "cult temple". R. Dessauer from Újpest, however, did appear. Not only the *hazzan* and the choir, but also some soloists sang. The festivity was concluded with the playing of the Hungarian national anthem. Participants of the se'udah (*Festessen*) paid for their own meal. The building was seriously damaged in World War II and later demolished by the authorities without hesitation. The houses on the odd-number side of the street still preserve the nineteenth century atmosphere of the neighborhood.

The Neo-Gothic building of the Újlaki synagogue (49 Zsigmond utca) was built in 1888 according to the plans of Sándor Fellner. Later an apartment house was built around it by the community. Currently this is the synagogue of the Buda branch of the Budapest community.

Immediately before World War I, in 1912, the Buda community announced a competition for the design of a large, distinguished synagogue. It was to accommodate 800 people downstairs and 600 on the balcony, with 60 places for morning prayer. Plans were sent in by Béla Lajta (he won the first prize), Imre Gombos (second prize), the Löffler brothers (third prize) as well as Dezső Jakab, but the war forestalled the very possibility of building a new synagogue.

The Constructivist building of the synagogue in Lágymányos / Kelenföld, then called *Szent Imre városi zsinagóga* (Synagogue of St. Emeric Quarter, 37 Lenke út / Bocskai út) was completed in 1936. It has been reconstructed since in a way that no trace of its original function remains. The only Jewish mark, a *menorah* on the iron fence, is hidden by a hedge. Today the building is owned by the *Tudományos Ismeretterjesztő Társulat* (Society for the Dissemination of Scientific Knowledge, TIT).

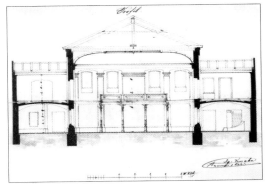

417. The facade of the Öntőház utca synagogue. Design by Ignác Knabe, 1865

418. The Öntőház utca synagogue. Cross-section

Buda Jews have always—occasionally or regularly—held services in private apartments as well, not just in the synagogue. For the High Holidays they sometimes rented the concert hall of the Budai Vigadó. The headquarters of the Buda community was at 12 Fő utca. They even published their own periodical, *Zsidó Élet* [Jewish Life]. The school of the Buda community was named after Károly Baracs (1868–1929), president of the community between 1921 and 1926. It was located at 1 Váli út, near the Körtér. Also Gábor Devecseri attended this school. The children's day care center was a few houses away, at 6 Váli út. The *Hevrah Kaddishah*'s offices were in the center of Buda, first at 4 Lánchíd utca, then at 16 Vérmező út. There was an old-age home in the green, suburban section of Buda, at 16/B Labanc út. The Buda community owned a building at 22 Keleti Károly utca—also the kosher cafeteria for the Jewish students of the Technical University was here.

A movement was started to unite the two communities around the mid-1930s, on the initiative of Pest but certainly supported by Buda Jews as well. The unity of Budapest stimulated contacts between the Buda and Pest Jewish communities; people from Buda went to Pest for the High Holidays, and many favored unification. Participants at a convention held at the Budai Vigadó on November 18, 1934 voted for unification. Bernát Heller, however, was of the opinion that a several-century-old community cannot liquidate itself. The unification finally took place after World War II, according to a decision of the convention of the Buda community on December 4, 1949, under state pressure. Real estate properties of the Buda community were handed over to the state. The community's office building went to one of the ruling parties, which very soon melted into the single

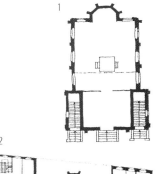

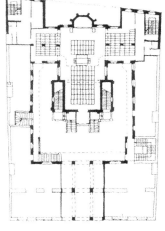

419. The ground-plan of the Újlaki synagogue (49 Zsigmond utca)
1: The original synagogue building
2: The synagogue with residential and community office buildings around it

420. The new synagogue of Buda. Competition design by Béla Lajta, 1912

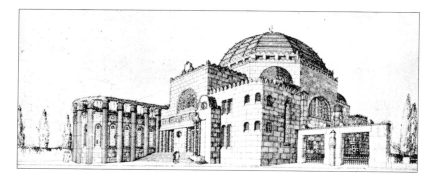

421. The new synagogue of Buda. Competition design by Sándor and Béla Löffler, 1912

422. Kelenföldi synagogue (37 Bocskai út). Ground-plan of the second floor

423. Kelenföldi synagogue

424. Kelenföldi synagogue. Hall in front of the second floor entrance to the synagogue

425. Interior of the Kelenföldi synagogue

ruling party. Thus, the Hungarian state became the owner of all the real estate holdings of the Buda Jewish community.

The Jewish cemetery next to the Farkasréti cemetery used to belong to the Buda Jewish community. This was the new Jewish cemetery, opened in 1895. The earlier Jewish cemetery in Víziváros was closed down in 1937. Arnold Kiss (1869–1940), Bertalan Edelstein (1876–1934), Artúr Geyer (1894–1976) and Imre Benoschofsky (1903–1970) are buried here, near the mortuary, in the row of the rabbis.

Artúr Geyer compiled the first bibliography (1958) of literature dealing with the persecution of Jews between 1938 and 1944. His book was confiscated before it could even leave the printer's and was sent immediately to the pulping mill, because he dared to list in his bibliography an article by József Darvas, a one-time populist writer who after 1956, at the height of the communist restoration, once again assumed important political roles. His article ("Őszinte szót a zsidókérdésben" [A Truthful Word about the Jewish Question], *Szabad Nép*, March 25, 1945) was considered to be an anti-Jewish attack by contemporaries. Darvas wrote about Jews returning from the concentration camps as follows: "(...) they learned to see the world divided into cadres and forced laborers. Now that things changed, they would like to be the cadres." He went so far as to write down such a word.

Imre Benoschofsky was the last rabbi of the independent Buda Jewish community. He came here from Pest, where he lived at 5 Teleki tér. His Buda apartment was at 7 Margit körút. After the unifi-

426. The Ark and the pulpit

427. *Parokhet* in front of the Ark

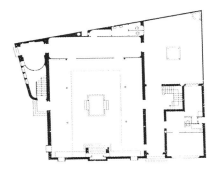
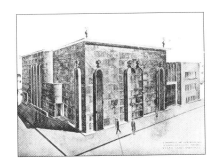

cation of the Buda and Pest communities he functioned as a deputy chief rabbi of the Dohány utca synagogue.

Sándor Ferenczi (1873–1933), psychoanalyst, the Hungarian apostle of Freud, is also buried here. Kornél Lánczos (1893–1974), nuclear physicist, one-time colleague of Albert Einstein, who wished to rest in Hungarian soil, was buried here, the *hesped* was given by Sándor Scheiber. On the gravestone of the architect László Vágó some of his works may be seen on the bas-relief, among them the Heroes' Temple. Even an arms manufacturer and member of the Upper House, Rudolf Frommer (1868–1936), designer and maker of the famous automatic pistol named after him, is buried here—*fegyverneki* Frommer according to his title of nobility ("armiger", to translate the place-name).

Also Bernát Heller rests in Farkasrét.

R. Pál Vidor (1909–1944) does not have a grave in Farkasrét, nor in any other cemetery. He was a talented member of the great generation who graduated from the Rabbinical Seminary in the 1930s. In his first scholarly work, published in 1932, he dealt with ancient Jewish philosophy; he analyzed the works of Philon of Alexandria. He became the rabbi of the Buda Jewish community, the Újlaki synagogue, in 1935. He died in a concentration camp.

The hospital of the *Hevrah Kaddishah* of Buda was at 16 Maros utca. This well-equipped institute was opened in 1931 with 43 beds. Its winding corridors, artful interior, sunny rooms, huge balcony facing South indicate the formerly cozy, safe atmosphere of the clinic. In the final months of World War II many people found refuge here, for shorter or longer periods. During the siege of Buda, on January 12, 1945, an Arrow-cross terror brigade broke into the hospital and massacred 92 people in the courtyard—patients, doctors, nurses and the whole staff. They applied their usual method of mass murder: they ordered the patients to dig a large pit and then shot the victims into it. It was the notorious "Pater Kun" (András Kun) who gave the men the command to shoot. "In the name of the Holy Christ, shoot!" The story

of the massacre was told by a nurse who miraculously survived the shooting; she climbed out of the pit from among the dead in the middle of the night. A few days later the neighboring building was hit by a bomb and it collapsed onto the mass grave.

A slab in the hall of the building commemorates this event in a Hungarian inscription and a Biblical quotation:

428. The Buda Orthodox synagogue. Ground-plan by Lajos Kozma, 1928

429. The Buda Orthodox synagogue. Design by Lajos Kozma, 1928

430. "The old-age home in Labanc út" (16/B Labanc út). Drawing by István Zádor, 1946

431. The hospital of the Buda Hevrah Kaddishah (16 Maros utca)

"The patients of this hospital,
its devoted, self-sacrificing doctors,
nurses and the whole staff
on January 12, 1945
became martyrs of our Jewish faith.
God of Mercy,
comfort our grieving heart,
heal the sick soul of mankind."

ובא לציון גואל
"He shall come as redeemer to Zion."
(Isaiah 59,20)

Today there is an ambulatory clinic in the building. Its beautiful, spacious garden is surrounded by bare walls, and further away by balconies of an apartment house. Flowers, grape, trees including some fruit-trees grace the courtyard, but the fruits are almost never picked. Rarely does anyone step in here, only those who know what happened here and come here to remember. The martyrs' grave is in the Óbuda cemetery.

Bernát Heller (1871-1943)

He lived in Buda, first at 77 Fő utca, later at the foot of the Rózsadomb, at 5 Bimbó út. He specialized in Jewish and Arabic folklore, probably under the influence of Goldziher, one of his masters.

432. Bernát Heller

In his main work, *Az arab Antar-regény* [The Arabic Antar Novel] (1918, German translation 1931), he discusses a medieval Arabic folklore book. Another one of his works, *A héber mese* [The Hebrew Tale] (ca. 1925), a well-written survey of the topic, just like the numerous scholarly background studies published mainly in foreign languages, is still a valuable introduction to this enchanting topic. In connection with Thomas Mann's *Joseph and His Brothers*, Heller published an article about "Thomas Mann, the Aggadist" in the *Évkönyv* of IMIT (1940), in which he discussed the great writer's deep spiritual commitment to the narrative methods of Talmudic literature and the *Aggadah*, stories supplementing or continuing some Biblical stories. This was not Heller's first study in the field; there were others before, like "The Relation of János Arany to Legend and Aggadah" (in: IMIT. *Évkönyv*, 1929). As a professor of the Rabbinical Seminary, he was famous for requiring his students to learn eight Biblical verses by heart every day, even on the Sabbath, on holidays and during vacation—since Torah study is allowed at any time. He held open house every Friday night, guests were offered cakes and tea, and they came exclusively to discuss scholarly topics. The description he gave of his other master, Mór Kármán, fits himself as well: "As the teacher of teachers, he did not limit his teaching to classes or conditions. His time, library, mind and soul were available to anyone at any time."

The dedication of Heller's gravestone, as is customary, was on his first *Jahrzeit*, it happened to take place on Sunday, March 19, 1944. Nobody, except maybe the Germans, could have foretold that it was going to be a fatal day. The master's students assembling around the grave came from all over, even from congregations in the countryside. On that evening Germans were already rounding up Jews from trains and railway stations. On his way home also the chief rabbi of Debrecen was asked to show his papers. As yet, the policeman was merciful to the scholar Pál Weisz (Meir Weiss). He said: "This time I'll let you go, dirty Jew, but hide in the toilet at every station." Sándor Scheiber could not return to his congregation in Dunaföldvár anymore.

*

There is a sort of a mystery around the Orthodox of Buda. It is hard to believe that "the pious (*yere'im*)" living in Buda went all the way to Pest, to the Kazinczy utca synagogue regularly. They must have had some prayer-rooms in Buda as well. There is, indeed, information about one in Mecset utca. In the interwar years there may have been plans even for the establishment of an independent Buda Orthodox community. The Freudigers are often mentioned as leaders of the "Buda community" in newspapers and memoirs.

Preparations were made for the construction of a syna-
gogue for the autonomous Orthodox community of Buda as well. The plans were designed by Lajos Kozma in 1928, having by that time already designed the synagogue in Kassa, and having learned his lesson from all the criticism. Kozma had also designed a few tombs, which adopted the shape of the tablets of the Law. Being a typographer, he had beautiful Hebrew calligraphy, much like Lajta. In his description of the design for the Buda synagogue Ernő Naményi stresses the courtyard particular, which has always been important for the Orthodoxy. "(Kozma) placed special emphasis on the artistic framing of the large synagogue courtyard." According to the critics, the defi-ciency of synagogue in Kassa was that it was not modern, that it was built in a historical, Neo-Classicist style. Like his fellow typographer and former customer, Imre Kner, the printer from Gyoma, also Kozma arrived from Art Nouveau at a new type of Neo-Classicism. Answering Vir-gil Bierbauer's criticism, Kozma argued that in Kassa he acted in accordance with his customers' request. His work was most probably determined by the architectural program of his customers in Buda as well. It was the Orthodox who insisted on a court-yard. Ultimately, the temple was not built.

433. Ábrahám óbudai Freudiger (see fig. 39, above) wearing Hungarian national gala dress. Photo, 1917

(2) Újpest

Újpest was for a long time an independent city, since 1950 it is the fourth district of Budapest. It was established exclusively by Jews. Around 1830 a large section of the estate of Count István Károlyi on the left bank of the Danube, North of Pest, was separated and rented out for planting vineyards. Thus a vine-growing community was created (István-hegy). Some Jews settled here, too, coming from other estates of Count Károlyi in Eastern Hungary. They were mainly artisans, first and fore-most of them, Izsák Lőwy (1793–1847), who is usually considered the founder of Újpest. Instead of Újmegyer, as the area was called in the beginning, he started referring to it as *Neupest* / Új-Pest (New Pest), and gave this name as the address of his factory and apartment in 1835. "My ideal is Pest, and only in Pest can an educated man easily find similar people. The prospering capital offers great opportunities for the enterprising spirit"—he wrote in a letter to his brothers. At first he intended to bring his sole leather factory, which he inherited from his father, to Pest but he was deterred by

434. Portrait of Izsák Lőwy

the difficulties of securing a residence permit and the interference of the guild of tanners. He could find a place for his enterprise more easily outside of Pest, anyway:

"This place is perfectly suitable for our purpose. It is right next to the Danube, beside the highway to Vác, less than half an hour from the capital. Though it is desolate, extremely desolate indeed, I am convinced that people will soon be attracted to come, if they can find employment here. They will surely grow attached to this place, if we treat them well. Dreariness will disappear, and we shall live among friends."

What Lőwy and his fellows had in mind was founding a "Jewish colony" in Újpest. For the realization of this plan, however, the leadership of the estate would have required at least a hundred and fifteen settlers, and there were not that many. It was Act XXIX of 1840, which made it possible for the three Lőwy brothers (Bernát, Izsák and Joachim) to purchase the territory that until then they had only been leasing for their factory. The Lőwys' enterprise developed quickly, and it became an important leather-processing factory. The inhabitants of Újpest, the majority of whom were Jews, established a real civil community on the basis of total equality (as far as religion and civil rights were concerned) of all inhabitants owning a dwelling. The citizens of the new town consciously ventured to carry out the political program of the French Enlightenment: "Liberty, Equality, Fraternity."

The first prayer-room in the new town was established in Izsák Lőwy's house. But very soon, in 1839, the Jewish community built a synagogue; in 1840 they opened their own school and, in 1844, they founded the first *Hevrah Kaddishah* on a plot granted by the owner of the estate, which was in the later Bocskay utca (today: Bocskai utca), on the corner of Part utca. Izsák Neuschloss was the first *hazzan*. Wedding ceremonies were performed in the synagogue and many came here even from Pest to stand under the *huppah*:

"Though this rough-and-ready synagogue was brand new, yet Izsák the tanner and his friends *daven*ed here with loud droning, according to the thousand-year-old tradition."

(Illés Kaczér, *Kossuth Lajos zsidaja* [The Jew of Lajos Kossuth], 1957)

Right after the foundation of the town Izsák Lőwy was elected the first magistrate of Újpest. Two decades after his death, in 1866, one of the main streets of Újpest (today Aradi utca—Kemény Gusztáv utca) was named after him. Recently, a little street by the old synagogue, the former Part utca was again named after him. The first rabbi came to Újpest as late as 1854. He was a certain Márkus Stern (?–1870), a distant relative of Goldziher.

Most of the other great factories of Újpest were founded by Jews, by locals, or others who had just moved here. Dániel Lőwy, son of Izsák Lőwy, established a manufacture for lumber products (Parquet and Veneer Factory). In the nineteenth century major firms were the wood processing plant of Izsák Neuschloss (1836), the leather factory of Gyula Wolfner and Co. (1841), the leather factory of the Mauthner Brothers and Co. (1887), Schreiber's vinegar factory, etc. There were cotton mills, cotton dyers, a ceramic and tile factory, parquet and shingle factory, all kinds of tanneries: sole leather, furniture leather, bag leather, and other articles of the garment trade, button and braid production, furthermore, a distillery, an ink manufacturing plant. All of these were founded by Jews moving to Megyer-Újpest.

Ignác Reich (1821–1887), president of the community, was one of the outstanding personalities of the spiritual life of Újpest Jewry. Previously he had been working in the Orthodox Central Office in Pest, and was a religion teacher as well. He was among the first to teach Hebrew through Hungarian.

He moved to Újpest in order to be able to avoid participation in the Jewish public affairs of the country. His great work, the three-volume *Beth-El—Ehrentempel verdienter ungarischer Israeliten* [Beth-El. Hall of Fame of Deserving Hungarian Israelites] (1856–1865) contains the biographies of prominent figures of Hungarian Jewry in modern times, up to the mid-nineteenth century. It is a particularly valuable work. The author describes almost everyone from his personal experience, and uses plenty of sources that have somehow disappeared since then. We have also used it as a source for our book. As far as literature is concerned, Reich's fame is not only connected to the five poems of *Honszerelmi dalok* [Patriotic songs] (Buda, 1848), but also to his Hebrew translation of the Hungarian national anthem by Ferenc Kölcsey.

Following the General Congress of 1868/69, the Újpest community decided in favor of an autonomous Orthodox status, but a Neolog community was also formed. The Orthodox synagogue was a bit further away, in Virág utca. Next to it there were a ritual bath (*mikveh*) and a slaughterhouse, both have been demolished since.

The new Neolog synagogue at 8 Beniczky utca / Berzeviczy Gergely utca was built by Ármin Hegedűs in 1896, according to the plans of Henrik Böhm (1867–1936). This building, too, has a courtyard. It is built in Romantic style, the outside walls are covered with yellow and brown bricks. There is a Hebrew and a Hungarian inscription on the facade.

ביתי בית תפלה יקרא לכל העמים

"For My House shall be called
A house of prayer for all peoples."
(Isaiah 56,7)

The interior design resembles a basilica; the women's galleries are on the two side walls. After the synagogue in Kecskemét was converted into an office building, its expensive organ was brought here, placed above the entrance hall. The organ altered the originally more conservative character of the temple, its location is also different from the way it was traditionally positioned in the Neolog synagogues of Hungary. The organ was usually placed above the ark, like in Dohány utca, deliberately to a different place than in Christian churches. Böhm and Hegedűs, the architects of the synagogue designed and constructed the city hall of Újpest (1899) as well, which is located near the synagogue.

The Újpest community established all the necessary institutions of Jewish life. They had their own bath, slaughterhouse, a new elementary school (1921), a cemetery. They even founded a women's club (1872), a girls' orphanage (18 József Attila utca / József utca—1895), a cultural center, a library, a soup-kitchen (1927) and an old-age home (19–21 Deák Ferenc utca) (1924). There was a separate committee, the (Solós Szeudósz Society [*shalosh se'udot*], "third meal") to organize the late Saturday afternoon gatherings. The community gave scholarships to students who studied abroad at the time of *numerus clausus* laws after World War I.

The building of the former Jewish school (in Venetianer Lajos utca) has been demolished. The cemetery, situated immediately to the North of the Angyalföld Railway Station at the southwestern edge of the public cemetery, at 8 Dugonics utca, was liquidated, and the graves were transferred to the parcel U of the Kozma utca cemetery. Its site has not been completely filled up so far.

Near to the Neolog synagogue, as several other examples from Pest show, there was an Orthodox *shtibl*. The house was, to say the full truth, a pub for cheap alcoholic beverages. The owner and manager of the pub, Reb Binyumen (Benjamin Berger), held a Yeshivah in a room on the second floor. Strange specialty of this Talmudic high school was that he and his students discussed the Aramaic and Hebrew texts in Hungarian, and not in Yiddish. Obviously, people who attended this school, were motivated enough to study seriously but had little background in the languages. The school was in use until the very last moment in 1944. Its address was: 119 Árpád utca; the *shtibl* was called "Kronstein".

In 1944 Újpest belonged to the countryside from the point of view of public administration. Its more than ten thousand Jews were forced into the Yellow-star Houses in the spring of 1944, and were later taken to the brickyard in Budakalász.

"(June 30, 1944): Yesterday the Jews of Rákospalota, Pestújhely and Erzsébetfalva were deported. Today it is Újpest's turn. I would rather not think about whose turn it will be tomorrow. Murder, murder, murder. (...) And the Hungarian Government loyalty performs the henchman's job. In Újpest, two gendarmes (*csendőr*) are posted in front of every yellow-star house, so that not a single one of Hitler's victims may escape. (...) Who is coming to our aid?"

(Miksa Fenyő, *Az elsodort ország* [The Country Swept Aside], 1946)

435. The Újpest synagogue. On the outer walls, the Deportation Memorial series. Design by Edith Kiss (Bán)

The deportation of the Jews of Újpest began on July 3, just a few days before the Regent ordered the suspension of deportations, and it ended a few days after the order. They were squeezed into freight cars (for cattle) in Békásmegyer and sent to Auschwitz. Only those escaped who had previously taken shelter in Pest.

On the inner side of the wall surrounding the synagogue courtyard there is a huge marble slab. Its inscription commemorates the martyrs of Újpest of 1944. Their list consists of more that 12,000 names. The monumental slab was designed by Mariann Kőrösi and installed in 1947.

On the same wall outside, around the corner of József Attila utca and Berzeviczy Gergely utca, a memorial of four large white stone reliefs is built into the wall. It depicts four scenes from the destiny of Újpest Jews: deportation (gendarmes with crane feathers on their cap herding the Jews into railway wagons); forced labor service (militia with Arrow-cross arm bands supervising the forced laborers); death row in Auschwitz (a soldier wearing swastika drives women and children with shaven heads into the gas-chambers); liberation of the ghetto (soldiers of the Red Army). This memorial is the work of Edith Kiss (Bán) and was unveiled in July, 1948.

Today the building of the synagogue complex comprises, beside the main hall, renovated in the 1990s, a little prayer-room for wintertime, a cultural center and the community office, as well as the well-equipped old-age home and asylum for mentally ill of the Budapest community.

Lajos Venetianer (1867–1922)

Venetianer was once a famous rabbi in Újpest. Like many of his contemporaries since the establishment of the Rabbinical Seminary, he too followed the classic track of the scholar-rabbi. He graduated

436. Portrait of Lajos Venetianer

from the Seminary, spent the customary year in Breslau, and earned a Ph.D. in humanities at the Budapest University. He started his rabbinic career in the countryside. In 1897 he was elected by the Újpest congregation to be the rabbi, and remained there until his death. He taught at the Rabbinical Seminary: religion, Biblical studies and Jewish history for the undergraduates and methodology of religious education and legal relations of the Jewish denomination in Hungary for the graduate students.

The former Liliom utca in Újpest bears Venetianer's name today.

His best known works are *A zsidóság szervezete az európai államokban* [The Organization of Jewry in the European States] (1901) and *A magyar zsidóság története* [The History of Hungarian Jewry] (1922). The latter work was reprinted a few years ago, but without the preface of the original edition, since its genuine confidence in the regency of Miklós Horthy was not justified by later events.

XII. Pest, 1944, Ghetto

(1) Laws against the Jews

The ghettoization of the Jews of Hungary began long before the fall of 1944. By the time the gates of the actual ghetto were closed, measures against Jews, *gezerot* as they were called in the Middle Ages, already had a history of about twenty years. Discrimination started with the *numerus clausus* law, Act xxv of 1920, promulgated on September 26, 1920. The term *numerus clausus* means "closed", or rather "limited number". The Act provided that from the 1920/21 academic year onwards only those would be admitted to universities and colleges "who were trustworthy from the point of view of morals and loyalty to the country, and even those only in limited numbers, so that the thorough education of each student could be ensured". The wording of the Act, sponsored by Count Pál Teleki (1879–1941), avoided the use of the term "Jew" and there is no trace of anti-Semitism in it; yet it closed the gates of Pest universities to young Jews. Instead of abilities it was "loyalty to the country", i.e. birth and background, that determined who may attend university. During the fall of the same year there were Jew-baitings at several universities; though spontaneous ones were not uncommon, this was the first time that they had been planned and organized in advance by associations in "defense of the race" such as *Turul* [mythical eagle of the ancient Hungarians] or *Ébredő Magyarok* (Awakening Magyars).

Those affected by discrimination went to study abroad (Vienna, Prague, Brno, etc.) in great numbers. Older people left to do research, never to return to Hungary. Among the professors who stayed abroad were Arnold Hauser (1892–1978), György Hevesi (1885–1966), Tódor / Theodor (von) Kármán (1881–1963), Károly Mannheim (1893–1947), János (von) Neumann (1903–1957), Leó Szilárd (1898–1964), Jenő Wigner (1902–1995), Ede Teller (1908–), and many others. (Tódor Kármán happened to be the son of Mór Kármán, who had rendered great services in modernizing the Hungarian teacher-training system and schools in the era of the Austro-Hungarian Dual Monarchy. The attribute *Praeceptor Hungariae* expressed his contemporaries' respect for him.) Many Hungarian scholars, who spent years of fruitful work abroad to avoid the *numerus clausus* law, were eventually awarded the Nobel prize.

Influenced by Zionism, Jewish engineers and students of the Technical University became increasingly enthusiastic for the idea of *aliyyah*. In June 1920, the first group of Hungarian engineers, members of the *Makkabi*, left for Palestine through Vienna. Several other illegal immigrants followed them, the second group of engineers in 1921. They were the first European engineer *halutzim*. The first modern cement works in Haifa were designed by an engineer invited from Budapest in 1925; and, by coincidence, he happened to carry out the job at the plant of another Pest engineer who emigrated at the same time. Hungarian engineers fleeing anti-Semitism in the 1920s played a key role in the architectural and technological modernization of Palestine, later Israel.

In 1920 the Palestine Office was established in Budapest (26 Erzsébet körút), the principal mission of which was to organize the *aliyyah*.

Explicit political anti-Semitism eased in the late twenties. After a while, the Government did not tolerate street atrocities anymore. During the last years of Count István Bethlen's decade as Prime Minister (1921–1931), the Government even relaxed the restrictions of the *numerus clausus* law (Act xiv of 1928).

Soon, however, partly under German influence, *restrictions* became once again official policy. Anti-Semitic utterances became common again, followed by pogroms and, a few years later, by further (Anti-)Jewish Laws.

In the years between 1934 and 1942 Fülöp Grünvald wrote lengthy annual reports on the condition of European Jewry for the IMIT Yearbook, continuing the tradition of Bertalan Edelstein's annual reviews. Year after year these accounts presented Europe, and especially Germany, in darker and darker color. Although they found the development of Jewish settlements in Palestine promising, they regarded the predicament of the Jews of Hungary as fast deteriorating.

The First (Anti-)Jewish Law (Act xv of 1938), passed on May 28, 1938, stated that "for the sake of social and economic balance" certain white-collar professions, such as that of journalists, actors, lawyers, doctors and engineers, could be practiced only by those who were members of the professional chamber. The number of Jews in each chamber could not exceed 20%. Contemporaries often referred to this Act as the "Act of balance". This Act, and the following ones, were called in Hungarian *zsidótörvény*, "Jewish Law"—this odd compound, with this strange spelling. They were essentially anti-Jewish legislation.

In an article in the April 14, 1938 issue of *Egyenlőség* János Vázsonyi (1900–died in Dachau, 1945), son of Vilmos Vázsonyi (1868–1926), the former Minister of Justice, wrote:

"Eighty to twenty. These are not election results, nor sports scores. It indicates no goal, only a kick, but a kick, that is not directed at a ball, a kick, which causes pain to many people. A few of the spectators in the stadium are cheering, the rest are clutching their heads in fright. Some find the result insufficient, they are howling in rage: keep on, keep on, keep on! Like pagans in the arena, when wild beasts were let on defenseless faithful. Eighty and twenty. Two numbers, which have gained new meaning in the past few days, two very telling numbers, which will soon be the cause of many complaints. Complaints of starving, of people who have lost their jobs. Bitterness and tears. Is this going to be the real solution? Will the Hungarians feel relieved? Will trouble decrease? Who dares to answer yes to all these questions? Eighty to twenty. This is the basis of the new law, the new law submitted by the Government at the last session of the Parliament. The new law that people started referring to as the *Jewish Law*."

On May 5, 1938, still during the parliamentary debate of the bill, Miklós vitéz[1] Makay, a Calvinist pastor and journalist, published a joint declaration against the "Act of balance" in *Pesti Napló*. It was signed by several non-Jewish writers and other leading intellectuals such as Béla Bartók (composer), István Bárczy (the Mayor of Budapest), József Berda (poet), Aurél Bernáth (painter), Imre Csécsy (politician), István Csók (painter), Géza Féja (writer), Noémi Ferenczy (Gobelin artist), Gyula Földessy (literary scholar), Aurél Kárpáti (literary critic), Károly Kernstok (painter), János Kmetty (painter), Zoltán Kodály (composer), Zsigmond Móricz (writer), Aladár Schöpflin (editor), Artúr Somlay (actor), Zoltán Szabó (writer), Jenő J. Tersánszky (writer), Béla Vikár (music scholar), Tibor Vilt (painter), Lajos Zilahy (writer) and others.

"All our contemporaries should consider their responsibility if, despite the protests of our conscience, a bill is enacted which some day all Hungarians will have to remember with shame."

There were altogether 59 signatures under the proclamation. Nevertheless, it was followed by no protests against the bill. On the contrary, in the Upper House debate the pontiffs of the Christian churches of Hungary backed the bill. Leading Hungarian populist writers did not sign the proclamation either, though they could have done so, not even Gyula Illyés (1902–1983). Péter Veres (1897–1970), a writer, a self-made man in literature and a leading politician in the populist movement, did not sign the text, but a copy of it, kept carefully through decades, was found in his literary remains. The populist movement that emerged in the late 1920s while striving for the rights and economical improvement of the Hungarian peasantry was rather mistrustful towards the urbanized strata of society, and first of all towards Jews.

[1] A hereditable title of honor, accompanied by landed property, granted by the Regent after World War I for military and political merits. It was to substitute for titles of nobility that the Regent was not entitled to grant. The *vitéz* were a kind of aristocracy around the Regent between the World Wars I and II.

The Act was promulgated with the usual closing formula: "I will observe this law (...) as the will of the nation, and will also make others do so. Undersigned: Miklós Horthy, Regent of Hungary; vitéz Béla Imrédy, Royal Prime Minister of Hungary."

On September 23, 1938, in the Gresham Palace (2 Mérleg utca), the Cabaret of Stage Writers run by László Békeffi (1891–1962), heir to the cabaret of Endre Nagy, presented its new show under the title: "Out with papers!" In February, 1939, it had its 200th performance. According to contemporary critics, this cabaret was a "dry comment on national politics". After a short while (April, 1940), the company had to move to 18 Révay utca (then Pesti Színház), and Békeffi himself was barred from practicing his profession (November 19, 1941). In 1943, he was taken to Sopronkőhida as a political prisoner, later to Dachau, yet he survived.

> "Instead of a critical review, more and more often one reads about who is Jewish, or whose wife is Jewish, etc. As if the art of the artist were not his religion and faith, with which he serves and honors humanity. These are troublesome times, indeed."
> (Imre Ámos, November 9, 1938)

Meanwhile, the Hungarian Royal Ministry of Agriculture issued a decree (on April 7, 1938), which stated that in public slaughterhouses "large animals may not be slaughtered, unless they have been appropriately stunned before being bled to death". Authorities had ordered preliminary intoxication already in 1928, but up to then ritual killing had been exempt from this obligation. Right before Passover the new decree made kosher slaughter (*shehitah*) impossible.

On March 11, Act II of 1939 was passed requiring everyone between ages 14 and 70 to perform national defense service (§ 87). Men unfit for military service between ages 21 and 24 were obliged to enlist for three months of forced labor service in a labor camp (§ 230). Those drafted started labor service already on July 15, 1939. Only later did the forced labor service (*munkaszolgálat* in Hungarian) acquire its special anti-Jewish connotation when on December 2, 1940, another decree was passed ordering Jewish draftees to be enrolled in special Jewish labor battalions. The legal basis for this discriminatory law was again created only later, by an executive order of April 17, 1941, and then by Act XIV of 1942, the new National Defense Law, adopted on July 31, 1942. The latter excluded Jews from all branches of the armed forces including the army, the gendarmes and the *levente* (military youth organization in Hungary, 1928-1944). Furthermore, it stated that "national defense service includes public labor service as well", and compelled Jews "to perform support functions in the army".

The first Jewish forced labor battalions were set up in the fall of 1941. A year later, in 1942, there were already ten forced labor battalions on the Eastern front in Ukraine with 250 people in each. Jewish labor battalions were labeled "100/n", while that of the politically unreliable elements were marked "400/n". The supervising staff was provided by the army. They are mostly remembered as extremely cruel. In Endre Bajcsy-Zsilinszky's opinion they were "a few hundred or thousand sadistic villains". (He was an MP opposing the Government politics, and later on was executed by the Arrow-cross men.) Forced labor battalions had the highest number of people in the fall of 1942. In those days, there were 152 labor battalions in operational areas; 130 of these were Jewish units, 16 were "political" (partially Jews, too), and 6 organized for road maintenance (Christians falling within the Anti-Jewish Laws). Another 152 forced labor battalions served in the rear, out of which 61 units were Jewish.

The Second (Anti-)Jewish Law (Act IV of 1939) was passed on May 5, 1939 in order to "prevent the expansion of Jews in public life and in the economy". It excluded Jews from public life (from the Parliament and other representative bodies), prohibited Jews from working for public corporations, from holding office in professional chambers, as newspaper editors, etc. It limited their participation in economic life and their rights to purchase or hold property. Furthermore, it reduced their numbers, in most white-collar professions even more strictly than prescribed by Act XV of 1938, to 6%.

Because of the First and the Second (Anti-)Jewish Laws, everybody had to document their origins. Hundreds of thousands of birth certificates were stamped as "Issued free of charge, in compliance with Act IV of 1939 (Order no. 7,720/1939, § 68)."

Here is what Count Pál Teleki, Royal Prime Minister of Hungary, declared at the debate of the (Anti-)Jewish Law in the Upper House on April 15, 1939.

"I support this bill based partly on my own conviction; I agree with its main points, by and large, but at the same time I must emphasize that had I submitted a bill drafted entirely by me, certain portions would have been much stricter. (...) This Act introduces the alien ideology [sic!] of race and blood into Hungarian legislation and mentality. (...) I have been convinced of the appropriateness of this attitude in its scientific and social aspects for more than twenty years now, as I have argued in words and writing."

There is a Yiddish proverb that sounds as if it were fashioned for Count Teleki: *A patsh farheylt zikh, a vort gedenkt zikh*, "The mark of a slap in the face will disappear, but words will be remembered."

After the bill had been presented in Parliament, all three Jewish community organizations (Neolog, Orthodox, Status quo) pointed out in a joint communiqué on January 12, 1939, that the bill violated the Hungarian constitution and was in contradiction with human rights, Divine law and with the most basic interests of the Hungarian nation. (The text of the communiqué was composed by Ernő Munkácsi.)

"If this Act is passed, hundreds of thousands of our people and our children will have to change their domicile. Our domicile, but not our homeland, for no human law can deprive us of our Hungarian homeland, just like none can deprive us of the worship of the Almighty. As none of the misfortunes which struck us over the millennia, no fire or flood, no scaffold or stake, neither galley nor handcuffs could sway us from our course, with the same persistence we will cling to our Hungarian homeland, the Hungarian language, which is our language and the history, which is part of our history. Just as our co-religionists exiled from Spain preserved their ancient Spanish language and the culture of their former homeland, we are going to await our acknowledgment and clearing, as well as the Hungarian resurrection."

On February 3, 1939, members of the Hungarist movement—followers of Ferenc Szálasi (1897–1946)—attacked people coming from the service in front of the Dohány utca synagogue. They threw a hand-grenade among the crowd injuring 22 people including some elderly, many of whom died from their wounds. It was partly because of the public outcry following the event that the movement was banned on February 24. Two weeks later, Prime Minister Count Pál Teleki permitted the members of the association to establish the Arrow-cross Party led by Ferenc Szálasi. In fact, since 1935 this movement has always had some kind of an organization under different names. Szálasi himself was in prison at that time (in the prison *Csillag*, Szeged).

The Third (Anti-)Jewish Law, Act xv of 1941, passed on August 8, 1941, introduced provisions to "defend the race". It prohibited marriage and sexual relations between Jews and non-Jews under penalty of imprisonment and other types of punishment. The concept "Jewish" was defined, unambiguously, in "racial" terms, as in the case of the German Nuremberg Laws (1935). As far as its wording is concerned, "this one appeared to be the most comprehensive (Anti-)Jewish Law in Europe" (Raul Hilberg).

Experts were quick to publish a 142-page long handbook on the decree entitled *The Act for Race Protection and Its Executive Provisions*, compiled and with explanatory notes by a certain dr. vitéz (...), secretary to the Minister of Justice (Budapest: Grill, 1941).

During the debate of the bill and even after it had been passed, leaders of the Christian churches expressed their concern that some members of their congregation, i.e. Jews who had converted to the Christian faith, were "re-Judaized" by the Act.

"I have never denied my Jewishness, I am *of the Jewish denomination* even today, though I do not feel *Jewish*. I have never been taught religion, it does not meet my needs, I do not practice it. Race, blood clot, roots, ancient sorrow trembling in the nerves and the like is but pure nonsense to me... My Jewishness is my *life-problem* only because circumstances, laws and the whole world made it my problem. It is a problem that has been forced upon me. Otherwise I am a Hungarian poet (...) and I do not care what the current Prime Minister may think... Should they disown me, should they accept me, my 'nation' will not cry out from the bookshelf saying 'get out of here, bloody Jew!' The land of my country will give me shelter. I still feel so today, in 1942, after three months of forced labor service and fourteen days of detention camp, (...) having been ousted from literature... And if they kill me? That would not change this fact either."

(Letter of Miklós Radnóti to Aladár Komlós, 1942)

In the summer of 1941 the *Magyar Élet Könyvkiadó* (Hungarian Life Publishing House), headed by Sándor Püski, published the second edition of the memoirs of the notorious examining judge at the Tiszaeszlár blood libel trials (*A tiszaeszlári bűnper. Bary József vizsgálóbíró emlékiratai* [The Tiszaeszlár Lawsuit. Memoirs of the Examining Judge József Bary]. The third edition of this rather biased book appeared in 1942, the fourth and fifth editions in 1944. The latter ones were published already after the deportation of the Jews from the provinces to Auschwitz, at the time of the massacres carried out by the Arrow-cross gangs. *Magyar Élet* had the work printed by firms once owned by Jews (Sylvester / Forrás Printing House). The reprinting after sixty years of these blatantly prejudiced memoirs were meant to be polemics against the statutory verdict and Károly Eötvös's documentary work: *A nagy per, mely ezer éve folyik, s még sincs vége* [The Great Trial that Has Been Going on for Thousand Years, and Has Not Yet Ended] (1904, new edition in 1968). Reviving the issue of blood libel from the nineteenth century amounted to anti-Semitic incitement at the time of the mass murder of Jews.

437. The Tiszaeszlár Lawsuit. Drawing by István Engel-Tevan, 1968

The—as it was often called—Fourth (Anti-)Jewish Law (Act XV of 1942), adopted on September 6, 1942, banned Jews from owning or purchasing land. Thus Hungarian citizens of Jewish faith or background were deprived of properties they had accumulated in the course of the past one hundred years on the basis of Act XXIX of 1840.

A yidish ashires iz vi a bintl shtroy, "Jewish wealth is like a bundle of straw"—says a Yiddish proverb.

After the Third and the Fourth (Anti-)Jewish Laws had came into force, chief executive officers, store managers, etc. were replaced by Aryan, i.e. non-Jewish, Christian people. The transfer of Jewish property to non-Jews was at that time called, "aryanization", just like in Germany.

"Dialogue between a young lady and an older woman on the streetcar:
    Have you taken it away from the Jew, my dear?
    Yes, we have, Aunt Magda.
    Did you ask for it, or did they give it?
    We asked for it and they gave it."

(Simon Kemény, *Napló* [Diary], March 21, 1942)

On November 27, 1942, during the parliamentary budget debate Endre Bajcsy-Zsilinszky (1886–1944) an MP who had earlier voted against the First and the Second (Anti-)Jewish Laws, reminded the representatives that he was "an old-time defender of the race from Szeged (1919/20)", that is, joined to the army led by Miklós Horthy in the first days of their insurrection, but pointed out the consequences of these Acts, namely that "certain robber instincts were bound to revive if people could seize the possessions of others just like that".

Since 1939 the *Magyar Izraeliták Pártfogó Irodája* (Office for Patronage of Hungarian Jews, in short, *Pártfogó Iroda* or MIPI), established in February 1938, operated in the building of the Institute for the Deaf and Dumb at 2 Bethlen Gábor tér. Initially it was the charity organization of the Pest Jewish community and the Hevrah Kaddishah but, from November on, all three Jewish community organizations of Hungary joined in and even the Zionist movement was represented.

The organization was established in order to help compensate for the financial losses caused by the (Anti-)Jewish Laws. They received some assistance from the *Joint* (American Joint Distribution Committee), and the rest of the money needed for its operation was raised by the *Országos Magyar Zsidó Segítő Akció* (National Hungarian Jewish Assistance Campaign, OMZSA). It was called the *Magyar Zsidók Szövetsége Szociális Osztálya* (Welfare Department of the Federation of Hungarian Jews), and in 1944, after the German occupation, to mark the difference in status: *Magyarországi* (of Jews in Hungary).

OMZSA was the most efficient solidarity organization in those days. Its work was coordinated by its vice-president, Géza Ribáry (1889-1942), a lawyer. Though Ribáry himself was not Orthodox, he managed to bring the Orthodox and the Neolog communities together thanks to his good relations with the Orthodox community. He was the one who composed the melody of "The OMZSA Song" on a poem by Ernő Szép.

The prose translation of the poem:

"Hear, hear Israel, fate strikes us and a sacrifice has to be made – The heart is bleeding, wounds are aching, a thousand mouths need food. – Little orphans disowned, in tattered coats, are waiting for our aid crying in despair: – Do not leave your brother, hear, hear Israel!"

(*OMZSA-Évkönyv*, 5703)

The publication in 1942 of the OMZSA *Haggadah* (reprinted in 1987), a valuable work printed in Dávid Löbl's Printing House, indicates that even in these difficult times the welfare organizations cared for the sustenance of Jewish spiritual life.

The Government issued Acts, decrees and regulations in quick succession, confining Jews, about 200,000–250,000 people in Budapest, to a ghetto-like existence even before the actual physical segregation. The ever more serious discrimination paralyzed the whole society in a short span of time. Before long, the whole capital became a ghetto.

(2) Theater of the Exiled

After the First (Anti-)Jewish Law Jewish intellectual life was forced to shrink. Any kind of activity was compelled to remain within the Jewish community. The Goldmark Hall and the cultural centers, the Jewish Museum, etc. were the only places where Jewish culture was permitted. Jewish authors could publish their works in the Jewish press only. By then it had also become impossible to leave, except to Palestine for another short while, but Palestine was an option only for those with strong Zionist feelings, like József Patai, who did leave. The life of the artists was not in danger yet, at least in the literal sense of the word. Until the spring of 1944 the political goal was merely the institutionalized isolation of Jews. But Jewish artists were expelled from general Hungarian culture by the laws, and Hungarian society at large excluded them, too. In the cultural and intellectual sphere the ghetto was set up before its actual walls were erected in Budapest.

It was an extraordinary event—and was seen as a courageous gesture—when Gyula Illyés published the works of Jewish writers in his journal *Magyar Csillag* (1941-1944), the continuation of the *Nyugat*. Among others, Zoltán Zelk (1906-1981)—son of a *hazzan* in Érmihályfalva, Transylvania— and Szilárd Darvas (1909-1961) published their poems here—poems sent home from the Eastern front where they were taken as forced laborers.

Due to the (Anti-)Jewish Laws, all artists of Jewish background lost their jobs. They had no opportunity to perform or exhibit, that is, to make a living. Soon after the First (Anti-)Jewish Law was passed in 1938, the Pest community, on the initiative of Géza Ribáry, applied for a permit to carry out the *Művészakció* (Initiative of the Artists). Keresztes-Fischer, Minister of Interior issued this permit on September 12, 1938, and soon the *Országos Magyar Izraelita Közművelődési Egyesület* (Hungarian Israelite Cultural Society, OMIKE), which had been active for three decades by then, extended its operations and started organizing performance opportunities for artists who had been deprived of such opportunities by the law. President of the OMIKE, Chief Rabbi Simon Hevesi has granted his full support to the Initiative of the Artists. Ribáry, the vice-president, became the moving spirit of the action.

Ribáry must have taken the idea of the Initiative of the Artists from the long tradition of matinees, poetry readings, cultural evenings and lecture series of the *Szabadegyetem* (Open University). It was not difficult to find a place for these programs; there were the Goldmark Hall, the Cultural Center of the Pest community, completed less than a decade earlier, and the Jewish Museum. The Goldmark Hall, like the cultural centers of individual synagogues, had been the scene of all kinds of performances ever since its construction, and by the beginning of 1938 it even staged complete plays. One of the performances was a Biblical drama by Leonid Andreev entitled "Curse", but the Purim celebration of the Rabbinical Seminary were also held here, e.g. on March 17, 1938, or a Hanukkah concert (December 19, 1938), etc. After the First (Anti-)Jewish Law this tradition only had to be institutionalized.

At first all kinds of programs were held as part of the Initiative of the Artists under the general title *Művész esték* (Cultural Evenings). Three places were used for the evening programs. In the Goldmark Hall (7 Wesselényi utca) drama performances and literary evenings were held. In the Cultural Center at 21/B Hollán Ernő utca—now called OMIKE *Kamaraszínház* (Chamber Theater)—musical evenings took place. In 2 Bethlen Gábor tér "varied programs" or shows were organized, like poetry readings, satirical evenings, solo performances, etc.

In the beginning, programs were held three times a week, on Saturdays, Sundays (often both in the afternoon and in the evening) and Tuesdays. In 1942 a fourth day was added, Thursday. For all that, there was hardly a larger room in any of the synagogues where performances would not have been held at least occasionally. There was the *Magyar Zsidók Egyesülete* (Association of Hungarian Jews) at 82 Király utca; the *Ügyvédi kör* (Attorney Club) at 2 Andrássy út; the *Kisiparosok köre* (Artisans' Club) at 19 Erzsébet körút; and the cultural halls of the district synagogues, e.g. at 4 Nagy Fuvaros utca, 39 Páva utca, etc.

Most of the operational expenses of the Initiative were covered, of course, by the Jewish community, but contributions came from "wealthier co-religionists" (*Egyenlőség*), too. Moreover, the organizers introduced subscription schemes, ensuring both audience and ticket sales for the whole season in advance. The performances were always sold out, all together around 20,000 people attended the programs each season.

Right the first Evening (November 11, 1939) was introduced by Ernő Szép, and he happened to be very active as a *konferanszié* (announcer or *compère*) all the following years. In the Goldmark Hall there were programs such as a memorial poetry reading of József Kiss (January 23, 1940), the Goldmark evenings (1940), literary recitals, press-shows on stage called *Eleven Újság* (Live Newspaper) (1940).

The performances of the opera section were initially in concert form, with piano accompaniment. Verdi's "Nabucco" was performed this way (January, 1939), and then Cézar Franck's "Rebecca" (February, 1940); Beethoven's "Fidelio" (with Erzsi Radnai as Leonora) (November 9, 1940); Halévy's "The Jewess" (with Dezső Ernster) (December, 1940); Gluck's "Orfeo" (with Oszkár Kálmán) (January 20, 1941); Mozart's "Die Entführung aus dem Serail" (with Oszkár Kálmán) (January 27, 1941).

To suit the technical requirements of a modern theater, the Goldmark Hall had to be altered to some extent. The reconstruction of the stage started soon after the first performances and was finished by October, 1941. Designers were the architect Zoltán Reiss and the graphic artist István Zádor. Spotlights, stage machinery and curtains were installed and the auditorium was slightly elevated in order to leave some space for the orchestra. Above the entrance door a huge golden letter was on the wall, a G standing for Goldmark. The new theater seated 372 people. In July, 1943 even a ventilator was installed so the performances continued in the summer, too.

After the reconstruction of the Goldmark Hall, the makeshift arrangement piano was replaced by an orchestra. From that time on, the program was equal to that of a regular opera house. Goldmark's "Sába királynője" became a hit in 1942, and again, in a new production, in 1943. Verdi's "Aida" was scheduled for March 2, 1944.

The first performances of the drama section were Hebbel's "Judith" (November 9, 1940) and Shloyme Anski's (1863-1920) "Dybuk" (both of them with Oszkár Beregi) (March 15, 1941). There were several pieces with Biblical or Jewish themes in the program, like Racine's "Esther" (Purim, 1942), and works by Hungarian Jewish authors as well, such as the plays of Lajos Szabolcsi ("Az áruló" [The Traitor], 1940, about Josephus Flavius, and "A király gyűrűje" [The King's Ring], 1941); or plays of Dezső Szomory and Ferenc Molnár. Still, on the whole the "Cultural Evenings" did not differ in any way from the standard repertoire of a good Budapest theater. Also "Hamlet" was staged (with Oszkár Beregi in the title role) (1943).

Concert performances were held on a regular basis. The genius of piano Annie Fischer (1914-1993) played Bach, Beethoven's Concerto for Piano in E-flat major "Emperor", etc.; Jenő Deutsch, a pupil of Bartók and Kodály, gave piano recitals (in late 1944 he disappeared in a forced labor camp). Pál Kadosa (1903-1983) (both as a composer and as a piano solist), Pál Lukács (1919-1981) (violin and viola), János Starker (1924-) (violoncello) scored great successes.

Special occasions were the Hungarian première of Bartók's "Divertimento" (December 8, 1941), or an evening in honor of Zoltán Kodály to celebrate his 60th birthday (December 7, 1942), where also the composer himself was present—"a true demonstration" according to an eyewitness. (Kodály's wife, Emma Sándor / Schlesinger, was Jewish.)

In addition to all these, a few times a year some great, festive events were set in the Dohány Temple or in the Heroes' Temple, like the performance of Händel's "Joshua" on November 16, 1939 (Erzsi Radnai, Dezső Ernster, Oszkár Beregi as narrator) and on May 2, 1940; Händel's "Judas Makkabäus" on June 23, 1941; or Händel's "Esther" on March 19, 1942.

Hebrew prayers or liturgical melodies were parts of any performance only in exceptional cases, like a "Kol Nidrei" sung by Dávid Ney (Friday, November 13, 1941) or "ritual melodies" performed by the cantor Béla Herskovits (October 24, 1942), both as parts of a theater performance. Sándor Fischer composed a song on the text and melody of the Seder night song "Had gadya"(1939). On the other hand, Purim and Hanukkah celebrations were regularly held in many different forms.

The artists who performed at the *Száműzöttek színháza* / "Theater of the Exiled" included Vilmos Komor (1895-1971) and Frigyes Sándor (1905-1979), conductors; the wonderful opera singers Dezső Ernster (1898-1981) (bass–baryton) and Dávid Ney (1905-1945) (tenor). Ernster left Hungary on the Kasztner train and later became a soloist of the Metropolitan Opera, New York; Ney died in Hörsching (Austria), in a concentration camp where he was taken from the ghetto of Kőszeg, Western Hungary. Oszkár Kálmán (1887-1971) was another excellent opera singer. Of the most prominent Hungarian actors Gyula Gózon (1885-1972), Erzsi Pártos (1907-), Imre Ráday (1905-1983) and József Tímár (Gerstner) (1902-1960) played here, as well as Oszkár Ascher (1897-1965) with prosa recitals, Béla Salamon (1885-1965) with humorous sketches, Alfonzó (József Markos / Markstein) (1912-1987) the satirist, Rodolfó (Rezső Gács) (1911-1987) the illusionist, and Zoli, the famous clown (Zoltán Hirsch) (1885-1944/45, Auschwitz)—the cream of Hungarian theater, film and entertainment.

The theater performed plays of Károly Pap, Dezső Szomory (Mór Weisz) (1869-1944), and Jenő Rejtő (Reich, pen-name on his parodistic dime novels: P. Howard) (1905-1943, died in forced labor). None of the actors had a contract, nor did they receive a salary. According to the regulations they were only entitled to receive *aid*.

The institutions of the Initiative of the Artists were run by eminent experts who had been dismissed from other theaters: Lajos Bálint (1886-1974), the former director of the National Theater, László Bánóczi (1884-1945), Zoltán Sándor and others. Oszkár Beregi formed a theater company from the actors arriving from different places; the artistic director of the opera program was Oszkár Kálmán, the conductors were Vilmos Komor and Sándor Fischer (1900–1995). (Maestro Fischer had lived in Budapest until his death. His two sons, Ádám and Iván Fischer, are prominent figures of international musical life.)

The Initiative of the Artists provided performance opportunities for about 700 artists who had lost their jobs, and with this also the hope to live, to make a living. The wonderful performances helped the Jews of Pest maintain a modicum of their rich and diverse secular culture.

"This is the only theater in which the (Anti-)Jewish Law still allowed Jewish directors, playwrights and actors to work"—wrote Károly Pap on the jacket of the 1940 edition at Tábor Publishing House of his new play, "Batsheba". Amazing spiritual power, incredible focus. Escape into Hungarian culture, into a Hungarian-Jewish life which hoped for protection by virtue of Hungarian citizenship. Escape into culture, into culture as the only possibility of life, of Jewish life. Belief, that Hungarian citizenship, civic and intellectual contribution to Hungarian culture would provide shelter or at least safe conduct in the ultimate emergency.

"The Goldmark Hall became a peculiar cultural ghetto. Jewish actors banished from the theaters performed dramas here, singers discharged from the Opera House staged whole operas, and the musicians organized such an orchestra that their concerts attracted personalities like Sergio Failoni, Aladár Tóth, and Zoltán Kodály, who came with his unforgettable wife, the grouchy, forthright and genial Mrs. Kodály, our *Emma néni* [Aunt Emma]. Their appearance at these concerts was, of course, not only a matter of artistic enjoyment but a political protest. These people—we may as well call them heroes—gave evidence that no prejudice could stop them."

(György Sándor Gál, *Atlantisz harangjai* [Bells of Atlantis], 1982)

As a part of the Initiative of the Artists, Zsigmond László (1893–1981), noted scholar of music history and poetics, organized a music academy, too. It was called the Goldmark Music Academy.

"God Almighty, what a school it was! Where Bence Szabolcsi would just drop by, silently, as a guest! But in spite of his modest, reserved conduct the invisible flame of his glorious spirit was there with him, burning like a sanctuary lamp. The minute he entered the largest room, which was now turned into a concert hall, the air started blistering around him—it was the presence of Spirit and Knowledge, of the kind of curiosity which makes man human. (...) He spoke gently, in a faint voice, which kept his students quiet, too. He spoke of the Goldmark-school, of Hungarian music. In his spontaneous talk there was no hint of the prevailing brutal laws, no trace of resentment or accusations—as if this coarse, hostile world did not exist out there. He did not refer to it with a single word, yet it was clear: these few years of yellow armbands, Jewish Laws and forced labor seem like a short intermezzo, a tiny fragment of time compared to the millennium through which Hungarian melodies have been flown from the Siberian desert to the Great Hungarian Plain, to the banks of the Danube and the Tisza, like a flag torn thousand times, though ultimately glorious...

"On the second occasion Szabolcsi came with a guest, Mária Basilides, and they gave an improvised concert. (...) Not only did they recall old tunes, but the landscape, too, where they were born, the people, who created these tunes, the plains and hills, which carried the tunes further, and a whole people who had been struck and imprisoned by fate ever so often and who could dream and sing even amidst the greatest poverty."

(György Sándor Gál, *Atlantisz harangjai* [Bells of Atlantis], 1982)

The last performance in the Goldmark Hall was on March 18, 1944, one day before the German occupation of Hungary. Then it was impossible to continue. The building itself, including the stage, was hit by a bomb during the siege of Budapest. It was rebuilt only in 1974. The Hall is in perfect condition and in regular use ever since, but the stage has not been rebuilt.

Károly Pap (1897-1945)

Pap was the son of a rabbi. His father, Miksa Pollák (1868–Auschwitz, 1944), chief rabbi of Sopron, edited the Hungarian prayer-book (*Avodat Yisra'el*, 1924), which has been used for decades by the Neolog community and is still in use. As a young man, Károly Pap was enthusiastic about revolu-

438. Károly Pap

tionary ideas. As a writer, he belonged to the circle of the *Nyugat* [West]. His novel entitled *Megszabadítottál a haláltól* [You Have Rescued Me from Death], published in 1932, presents Jesus as a Jewish revolutionary seeking a religion based on powerful emotions rather than ritual. His other novel, *Azarel* (1937), is about his own childhood. His grandfather's strictly Orthodox customs together with his father's temple-going religiosity beautifully illustrate Jewish life in countryside Hungary at the beginning of the century. His long essay called *Zsidó sebek és bűnök* [Jewish Wounds and Sins] (1935) was a self-tormenting reaction on the crisis of Jewish assimilation.

Following the publication of *Azarel*, the Hungarian Zionist Association held a so-called "literary trial" in the case of the novel. *Múlt és Jövő* reported on the trial in 1938. The prosecutor, Dénes Friedmann (1903-1944), rabbi of Újpest, a respected scholar, teacher at the Rabbinical Seminary, accused the novel of violating the fifth commandment ("Honor your father...", Exodus 20,12) by portraying the figure of the father, a rabbi, in a critical manner. The real problem, however, as Endre Sós—the expert at the trial—pointed out, was that it provided material for the enemies of the Jews. The defense quoted from R. Imre Benoschofsky's lecture on the novel:

> "The book depicts people, the Jews, in a masterly manner. (...) I can feel it: *numen adest.* (...) It is judged by a tribunal, but they do not ask whether this book is good, fair or true according to the criteria of authenticity, i.e. whether it is true from an artistic point of view. Instead they ask whether it is true word by word, whether it reflects life realistically. (...) Károly Pap's vision of Jewry is powerful, astounding and beautiful, consequently it is true."

The writer himself gave an impassioned defense of his novel during the trial.

> "(...) This book is cruel, indeed. Nevertheless, it was exactly with the aid of such cruelty that I was able to attain my objective. Namely, that my book should reach the depth of the Jewish soul at a level deeper than our economic and social anxieties, at the level of common eternal humanity. It is me who regrets most that this level is buried so deep in Jews, that the ruins of ghettos and assimilation buried it to such an extent that it became impossible to reach it with gentle hands. Who else could regret it more than me, the writer of the Jewish people? And how else could I be this writer, if I had not chiseled myself with the same cruel knife to wake up from my sleep under the ruins of lies, double lives and self-deception, as this novel chisels the Jewish reader."

439. Oszkár Beregi

Two plays of Károly Pap were performed in the Goldmark Hall, "Batsheba" (1940) and "Moses" (1944). The writer was deported to Bergen-Belsen where he disappeared.

Oszkár Beregi (1876-1966)

Beregi was a great Shakespearean actor, member of the Nemzeti Színház (National Theater) since 1899. He had a powerful voice and a dignified appearance. The *Ébredő Magyarok Egyesülete* (Association of Awakening Magyars) organized protests against him merely because he was Jewish. He left for abroad (Transylvania, Vienna, Berlin, the USA) and returned only in 1930 when, in a milder political climate, he felt safe. Although he could not return to the National Theater, he played with private companies (Magyar Színház / Hungarian Theater), Belvárosi Színház / Inner City Theater). In the Goldmark Hall he played King David in Károly Pap's "Batsheba", among others. He directed several performances and taught young actors. After World War II he returned to the scene of his former successes in the USA.

(3) Forced Labor Service

Soon after Hungary had entered the war on June 27, 1941, reserve labor service, in other words, forced labor service was introduced according to the provisions of Act II of 1939. This service concerned mostly Jews who were excluded from regular military service. Initially, the upper age limit was 25 years, which was raised to 37 in April 1943, to 48 in April 1944, and to 60 years on October 21, 1944. Supplied and equipped much worse than soldiers, captives of the forced labor battalions did hard physical work mainly on the Eastern front. They were deprived of their former military rank and were forced to wear a yellow armband. Many died under the terrible conditions or as a result of the brutality of the cadres (*keretlegény* in Hungarian).

> "(...) The *30-kilogram people* [ca. 66 pounds] form a separate community. These are the former Jewish forced laborers who had marched one thousand kilometers [ca. 625 miles] returning from Russia, who were driven into cattle wagons at one of the railway stations. The wagons were sealed and transported to Hungary. Upon arrival, these wagons remained idle on the rails for several days before they were opened at last. Skeletons staggered out of the enormous filth and stench, from among the corpses of their fellows who had died during the journey. The survivors are these *30-kilogram-people*, who had worked for 18 months in Russia under incredible, unbearable conditions... It was them who came home without any food or drink, in sealed cattle wagons, among the sick and dead. And it was them who were let out of this vicious prison four days after their arrival. They, the survivors, are the "30-kilogram-people". They will often be spoken of and written about all over the world, for there is hardly another case in the rich history of martyrdom comparable to theirs."
> (Simon Kemény, *Napló* [Diary], June 14, 1943)

Among those who died in forced labor service on the Eastern front were György Bálint, writer and journalist (1906–1943) and Attila Petschauer (1904–1943), Olympic champion in fencing. His torture happened to be ordered by one of his former Olympic teammates in Amsterdam.

The Hungarian Jewish manpower reserves attracted the attention of the German *Organisation Todt*, a labor army organized by Fritz Todt. On special request (February, 1943) he was authorized to use a unit of 3,000 persons who were sent to Serbia to work in the Bor copper mines. The agreement was signed on July 2, over the objections of the Minister of Defense, Vilmos nagybaczoni Nagy (1884–1976), after he resigned. The first Hungarian unit consisted mostly of Jews from the provinces but at the very end of May, in the first days of June 1944, several groups of Jewish captives wearing a yellow star and baptized Jews wearing a white armband were taken from Budapest as well, through transit camps in Vác and Jászberény. Their number was almost the same as that of the first Bor unit. They had to work "in the mountains" (Miklós Radnóti), under miserable circumstances until the German units were forced to retreat early in the fall of 1944.

Captives of the Bor forced labor battalions were then sent on their way, in several groups, towards German labor camps through Belgrade and Transdanubia in the middle of September, as the German army was retreating from the Balkans. In the first group there were younger people who were expected to work in Germany, the poet Miklós Radnóti among them. The second group was captured by Yugoslav partisans soon after they had left, thus they survived. Many of them found their way to Temesvár, and from there to other places in Romania; this was the group from which György G. Kardos (Klein) (1925–1997)—who was to become a writer—escaped to Palestine. Others, for instance Sándor Szalai, sociologist (1912–1983), the physician László Levendel (1919–1994), could return, in the tracks of the Soviet army through Makó and Szeged, to Budapest.

"(...) It was late night by the time we reached the village called Heidenau. Here six hundred other Jews joined us from other camps. Thus our number increased to three thousand and six hundred. It was the evening of *Rosh ha-Shanah*, and religious Jews had already started their prayer, as usual. We slept in the open air. It was very cold and nobody had more than a coarse blanket, we were all shivering. Morning came at last. Jews had been praying for a long time, even the *shofar* was blown, since we had one with us. Then we set off, and crossed Zagubica..."

(Zalman Teichman, "The Story of the Sad Journey from Bor to Cservenka-Temesvár" [A Memoir in Yiddish], 1945/1949)

In the Hungarian areas the first group was supervised by a Hungarian unit, yet some one thousand people from this group were shot by SS soldiers into the clay pit of the brickyard at Cservenka, Bácska County.[2] A few days later Raoul Wallenberg recorded the events of the Cservenka massacre and sent his report abroad. Those who arrived in Mohács on foot were driven into wagons and were transported further, under inhuman conditions, to Szentkirályszabadja, Veszprém County, to the labor camp set up at the airport. There they had to wait until the rest of the group arrived, then continued their journey in cattle cars or on foot, through the Bakony mountains and Győr towards Hegyeshalom, to the building site of the defense line along the border, or to German camps (Flossenburg, Sachsenhausen / Oranienburg, Bergen-Belsen).

One of the units was allowed a one-day rest on November 7 at the brickyard of the Benedictine Monastery in Pannonhalma. On November 9, however, they were West of Győr already, on the highway, near the village Abda. Radnóti was among them.

(4) The Era of Catastrophe,[3] I

From a letter of the Regent Miklós Horthy to the Prime Minister Count Pál Teleki dated October 14, 1940:

"(...) I have been an anti-Semite all my life. I find it unendurable that here in Hungary virtually all the factories, banks, properties, shops, theaters, newspapers and the entire economy should be in Jewish hands. Nevertheless, since I am convinced that the most important task of the Government is to improve the standard of living and become prosperous, it is impossible (...) to eliminate Jews, and replace them with incompetent, mostly worthless and big-mouth individuals. Otherwise we will go bankrupt... We cannot tolerate cruelty against Jews or their pointless humiliation in a sadistic manner since we shall need them later."

A dispatch of the German ambassador and plenipotentiary to Hungary sent to Berlin, dated June 1, 1944:

"The Hungarian Ministry of Interior has the intention of cleansing the area of Gödöllő of Jews earlier than the date determined in previous plans. This suggestion comes from someone in the Regent's circle. As the Regent's summer residence is in Gödöllő, they wish that the Regent should not have to see Jews there any-

[2] In his novel called *"Oly korban éltem én..."* [I Lived in Such an Era] (Budapest: Szépirodalmi Könyvkiadó, 1984), Imre Magyar (1910–1984), a physician and university professor, also recounted the events of Cservenka in detail (pp. 291–296).

[3] The years of World War II, the era of the systematic extermination of Jews, was named, as soon as it was over, *vészkorszak*, "Era of Catastrophe" by the Hungarian Jewish community. In Israel the term *Shoah*, or with the definite article, *ha-Shoah* ("total destruction", "disaster") was spread and accepted officially. The Hebrew word itself comes from the Bible (Isaiah 10,3). The usual English term, *Holocaust*, also derives from the Bible, from its Greek translation, where the word *holocauston / holocaustoma* is a technical term for a type of sacrifice, "that has been burnt entirely (*olah / olah ve-kalil*)" (see Genesis 8,20; Psalms 51,21, etc.). The figurative meaning is "that which has been destroyed in the fire". The English expression spread all over the world after the title of an American TV film in 1979.—In fact, it is impossible to find a *good*—fitting or suitable—word to denote the *evil* that happened.

more, that he should, at last, have the opportunity to experience the impact of the (Anti-)Jewish Laws personally."

Ottó Komoly's diary entry about his hearing by Miklós Horthy, jr. on September 15, 1944:

"Horthy jr. said: As a matter of fact, I have been an anti-Semite since I was born, by virtue of my education. This is how it was, how Jews were spoken of in our house. For instance, I found it completely impossible to marry a Jewish woman lest my children be of Jewish blood..."

*

The attitude of Hungarian authorities towards Jews living in Hungary, who were mainly Hungarian Jews, was adjusted to Nazi Germany's plan for the final solution (*Endlösung*) of the Jewish question, which was taking definite shape in the course of the war. Most of the significant Hungarian politicians, including the Regent, Miklós vitéz nagybányai Horthy himself, nurtured anti-Semitic attitudes or were at least indifferent towards the fate of the Jews. And all the leading officials would certainly have liked to get rid of Jews fleeing to Hungary from abroad.

Nevertheless the fate of Hungarian Jews, at least of those living in Budapest, differed from the fate of Jews in other satellite countries of Germany. It is a fact, though no symbolic meaning should be attributed to it, that in 1943 on the High Holidays, on *Rosh ha-Shanah* (September 30) and on Yom Kippur (October 9) policemen with white gloves directed traffic and maintained order in the region of the main synagogue in Dohány utca.

There was no other country in the large area under the sphere of influence of National-socialist Germany where Jews, Hungarian citizens and others, could remain out of reach of the efficient German organization established for the final solution of the Jewish question for as long as they did in Hungary. Here, even if only within the tight confines determined by the restrictive (Anti-)Jewish Laws, Jews lived in relative security, as one of the leaders of the Jewish Agency put it. Indeed, until the spring of 1944 the immediate danger to life was less in Hungary than anywhere else. On the other hand, there was no other country where, willingly cooperating with the Germans, the state played such an important and independent role in the deportation and murder of hundreds of thousands of its citizens, as the Hungarian Government did in the spring and summer of 1944. Of course, the fact that a state guarantees security to its citizens and protects their rights and lives in case of emergency, is no special merit, but a foremost duty. It was precisely by failing to perform this duty, by accepting the (Anti-)Jewish Laws, that Hungary violated her constitutional order and European traditions.

In 1944, when Hungary was already under German occupation, Hungarian political leaders still clung to the illusion of making independent political decisions. But whether the autonomy of the country was real or false, it does not diminish the responsibility of the Hungarian political leadership and the entire Hungarian nation for the destruction of 500,000 to 600,000 Hungarian Jews.

Nevertheless, it remains a fact that a part of Hungarian Jewry, at least of the Jews of Budapest, survived the war, even if in the midst of enormous sufferings.

SS Lieutenant-Colonel (*Obersturmbannführer*) Adolf Eichmann came to Budapest right after the Germans had occupied Hungary on March 19, 1944. He was the commander of the *Reichsicherheitshauptamt Sondereinsatzkommando* IV/B/4 or simply *Judenkommando*, a Gestapo unit established for special tasks and sent to Budapest from Mauthausen. Their headquarters were on Sváb-hegy (called Szabadság-hegy for several decades after World War II). They occupied several buildings for themselves and their Hungarian assistants in a remote part of the exclusive residential area just in the Buda woods, in the neighborhood of the former summer villa of Baron József Eötvös, the *Karthauzi-lak*—"Villa Seclusion", called after the title of a novel by Eötvös (1839–1841)—(14 Karthauzi utca) centered around the pension Majestic (2 Karthauzi utca, today 4/A Karthauzi utca) and Little Majestic (1 Evetke utca), a smaller building nearby, in a relatively concealed location. (On the side facade of the Little Majestic the big black letters of the building's original name may still be read out. The woodsheds, mentioned occasionally in the memoirs of forced laborers who were ordered here, are still there in the garden.) The Majestic, constructed shortly beforehand of bauxite concrete, then a fashionable material, became the general headquarters of Eichmann's commando in Hungary, shared with Péter Hain's delegation for a while. It was from here that Eichmann directed the last major operation of the supposedly final solution to the so-called Jewish question, the transportation of Hungarian Jewry into the concentration camps. He did it obsessively, and, given his previous performance, more skillfully than at his earlier posts.

The organizations led by Eichmann and Hain got hold of some other luxury hotels, pension condominiums in the immediate neighborhood as well, such as the Hotel Mirabel (6 Karthauzi utca), the *Rege üdülőszálló* (Rege Resort-hotel) (10 Rege utca), the pensions Lomnic (2 Evetke utca), *Új Majestic* (New Majestic), Bijou (24–26 Melinda út) and Melinda (30–32 Melinda út), the condominiums *Sváb-hegyi Társasház* (16 Melinda út), etc. The Hotel Bellevue (53 Béla király út) was also seized by the Gestapo. They could feel secure in the relaxed atmosphere of the Sváb-hegy. Nevertheless, they constructed a narrow route of escape for themselves, in order to avoid the heavy traffic on Istenhegyi út in case of an emergency. (At least this is what the people living in the neighborhood assumed. In any case, the little street between Melinda út and Mártonhegyi út has still no name. Only since very recently has it been linked organically to the city.) In November and December members of the *Judenkommando* drove groups of captives out of the houses on Melinda út, took them to the Széchenyi lookout and shot them. In the center of Pest Eichmann and his men used the building of Gólyavár for their purposes, which is located in the garden of the Faculty of Arts on Múzeum körút. Eichmann himself had an apartment on Rózsadomb, at 13 Apostol utca. The owner of the villa, Lipót Aschner (1872–1952), a banker and industrialist, president of the *Újpesti Torna Egylet* (Gymnastics Club of Újpest, UTE) was deported to Mauthausen. Forced laborers were ordered to work regularly in the villa. (Here he beat to death his gardener, a Jewish boy—this was the only murder with his own hand in that he was proven guilty in the trial in Jerusalem.) Dieter von Wisliceny, one of the officers of Eichmann's commando, was quartered with his soldiers on the 6th and 7th floors of the apartment building at 16 Szent István park.

One of the very first measures taken by the invading German authorities in Budapest, as in all the other places before, was to set up the *Zsidó Tanács* (Jewish Council / *Judenrat*). The headquarters

440. Portrait of Samu Stern

of the Jewish Council, made up of former leaders of the Jewish community, was in the community's office building at 12 Síp utca. Its president was Samu Stern, until then the president of the Pest Neolog community. He was replaced in October, when threats indicated that he was in immediate danger of life, by Lajos Stöckler. Within the confines determined by the Germans, they organized the everyday life of the Jews. The title of the newspaper in which they published announcements had to be changed from *A Magyar Zsidók Lapja* [Newspaper of Hungarian Jews] to *Magyarországi Zsidók Lapja* [Newspaper of Jews in Hungary] at German behest. Less than six weeks later the Jewish Council was transformed: the *Magyarországi Zsidók Szövetsége* (Association of the Jews of Hungary) and its *Ideiglenes Intéző Bizottság* (Temporary Executive Committee) were established (May 13). They fulfilled basically the same function as the Jewish Council. It was even referred to as the *II. Zsidó Tanács* (Second Jewish Council). The *III. Zsidó Tanács* (Third Jewish Council), whose real president was Stöckler, was formed on October 22.

The order of the prime minister compelling Jews to wear a six-pointed, bright canary-yellow star of 10 × 10 cm (4 × 4 inches) on the top left side of their clothing was issued on March 31 (Order no. 1,240 M.E. of 1944) and came into force on April 5. This medieval Jewish badge was thus revived, only now it meant death.

Prose translation of a poem by István Vas:

"April. There is a strange joke spreading: – I am supposed to wear a canary-yellow – Star above my heart. –
It was ordered by those Scythians – Who have invited the Goths here..."

(István Vas, "Április" [April], in *Márciustól márciusig* [From March till March], 1944/45)

Note:
Scythians: Hungarian nationalism boasted with Scythian origins of the nation, a historic myth popularized
by the medieval chronicles.

April 2: the American air force started bombing Budapest. Their first targets were the railway stations, the Manfréd Weiss weapons plant in Csepel, the region around Soroksári út, the Tököl airplane factory, etc. In the next two nights, it was the British who launched bomb attacks on similar targets. They even dropped firebombs, and a few bombs fell onto the Inner City as well. The timing of these bombings could hardly have been incidental. A few days before wearing the yellow star became obligatory, the Allies must have meant it as a warning. The official Hungarian propaganda was blaming the "Judeo-terrorists". Leaflets appeared in the streets demanding that a hundred Jews be executed for every dead Christian. (Let us not forget that this happened only three years after Hungary had entered the war voluntarily, under no pressure!)

April 5: the director of "Actio Catholica" reported to the Prince-Primate that "Our convents had to resist strong temptations as Jewish people wanted to hide away here. We told those appealing for our aid that they should not jeopardize Catholicism."

On the same day the Royal Prime Minister of Hungary specified in a decree the categories of people of Jewish origin who were granted an exemption from wearing a yellow star.
Exemption for baptized Jews was requested by the Holy Cross Society and their request was backed by the Archbishop of Esztergom (Cardinal Prince-Primate Jusztinián Serédi) and László Ravasz, Calvinist bishop (Dunamellék Church District) as well. According to the Prince-Primate wearing the yellow star, the sign of Jewish religion, meant for Christians "contradiction (to their faith) and heresy" (Circular to the Bench of Bishops, May 17). On another occasion, Serédi used in this connection the term "real apostasy", he had expressed this opinion already earlier in a letter to the Prime Minister dated May 10: "I must stress again and again with due emphasis that a distinction should be made between Christians of Jewish origin and people of the Jewish faith. (...) We owe at least that much to our Christian brothers." And even earlier, at the beginning of March, he wrote: "(...) Wearing a yellow star (...) would equal apostasy, and it is, therefore, intolerable; one should not expect anyone to wear the sign of a different religion." No wonder that even a report from the general headquarters of the SS (*Schutzstaffel*) in Hungary (a palace of the Barons Hatvany, 7 Werbőczy utca / Táncsics Mihály utca) stated that "(...) as a result of the nature of the church, the attention of the Prince-Primate is directed merely towards Jews who converted to the Christian faith." In consequence, a certain category of Christian Jews were exempted, namely those whose spouse was a non-Jew (*árja-párja*, "Aryan couples" as they were called in those days). Eventually the Prime Minister allowed Christian Jews to wear a little white cross under the yellow star (May 3).

441. Street in
Budapest, 1944

"As I came to the office this morning, – It was burning above my heart, – But another decree was published
– Which extinguished this yellow fire. – But I cannot get used to the idea, – neither that I do not wear it any
longer, – nor – that others still have to do so."

(István Vas, "Kivétel—Ugyanaz" [Exception—The Same], in: *Márciustól márciusig*
[From March till March], 1944/45)

April 7: The Ministry of Interior issued an order stating that "the Royal Government of Hungary would soon cleanse the country of Jews. This cleansing would be carried out by regions." It also forbade Jews to travel anywhere or at least they had to obtain a travel permit, which in the capital was issued by the police, in the countryside by the gendarmerie. The police had been arresting people at railway stations even earlier but, after the publication of the decree, they became even more diligent. Police and gendarmerie were now "practicing" all the procedures of deportation. For the time being they arrested only people without papers; a few months later, however, they were fully authorized to capture anybody. Jews were interned in the Kistarcsa detention camp, which soon became overcrowded. The Government forbade Jews to travel by car and restricted their travel by streetcar and bus as well. Before long, telephones installed in the house of Jews, bicycles and vehicles in possession of Jews were confiscated, and all the deposits and bank accounts of Jews were frozen. Furthermore, the decree imposed a curfew on Jews from 8 p.m. It also decided to "concentrate" Jews in ghettos which were set up in various places.

April 12: in order to provide accommodation for the victims of heavy bombings of a few days earlier, the Government demanded that the Jewish Council vacate and hand over 500 apartments within 24 hours. Eichmann arbitrarily increased the demand to 1,500 apartments. Afterwards authorities prohibited Jews, by decree, from using shelters in case of bomb attacks. Wallenberg wrote in an official dispatch to Stockholm on July 18, "Certain circles (...) are convinced that the presence of Jews offers some protection against bombings."

April 30: A government decree was issued "concerning the protection of Hungarian intellectual life against literary works written by Jewish authors". The decree enumerated the names of Jewish writers whose works were subject to confiscation and to removal from circulation. Later, on June 24, an additional list was published. All the libraries, including that of the Hungarian Academy of Sciences, prepared preliminary lists. "(...) Libraries of different associations, schools and other institutions,

shipped several hundred kilograms of Jewish books to Budapest. Books that had been discarded, were destined for pulping, and brought immediately to paper mills. Wagon-loads of filthy intellectual products were accumulated here. Over the past decades, these could corrupt and deprave Hungarian society without obstacle. It has all come to an end now, the Jewish book has ceased to be powerful. It has become mere material, an impotent mass of cellulose. Half a million Jewish books will be turned into nice white writing paper again. (...) The annihilation of the half a million Jewish books that have been collected will begin on Thursday at noon on the Budafok grounds of the *Első Magyar Kartonlemezgyár* (First Hungarian Cardboard Factory). This is going to be a solemn moment, indeed (...)"—wrote an extremist newspaper on June 14. Books written by the writers concerned were actually pulped on June 15. The writers included many of the most distinguished contemporary authors, such as Tibor Déry, Milán Füst, Frigyes Karinthy, Anna Lesznai, Ferenc Molnár, Miklós Radnóti, Zoltán Somlyó, Ernő Szép, Dezső Szomory and many others. The works of József Kiss were thrown into the pulping mill first. Some 450,000 volumes were destroyed altogether. The events were under

442-443. "Heavy stone wheels...", June 15, 1944

the auspices of Mihály vitéz Kolozsváry-Borcsa (1896–1946), under-secretary of state, government commissioner for press and intelligence affairs. A year before, Kolozsváry-Borcsa had published a voluminous reference book with the title *A zsidókérdés magyarországi irodalma* [Bibliography of Works on the Jewish Question in Hungary] (compiled in 1943, published in 1944). He could now make "good" use of his own catalogue for collecting books of Jewish subject.

May 15: The *Zsidókérdést Kutató Magyar Intézet* (Hungarian Institute for the Research of the Jewish Question) was opened ceremonially on the second floor of 4 Vörösmarty tér. Following the model of Germany, this institution was founded in accordance with a government order issued a month earlier, on April 15, "in order to study the Jewish question in Hungary regularly and scholarly, and to acquaint Hungarian public opinion with the Jewish question". "The Government decided to find the final solution to the Jewish question in the shortest time possible for these days", said the under-secretary of state, the person who signed the decree, in his opening speech. The Institute gathered a large number of volumes from the libraries of various Jewish institutions and from other collections, including the confiscated library of the synagogue of Pestszentlőrinc, which was the

legacy of Mihály Guttmann who passed away two years before. Torah scrolls and books were transported even from the devastated synagogues of the Carpatho-Ukraine. The Institute got hold of a part of the library of the Pest community as well. Materials were stored partly at the Vörösmarty tér premises of the Institute, partly on Rózsadomb, at 26 Bogár utca, and on Naphegy, at 31 Naphegy utca. Sándor Scheiber was able to save part of it from destruction.

444. Agents of the *Va'adah* in Pest. From left to right: Perec Révész, Hansi Brand, Rezső Kasztner, Ottó Komoly and Zvi Goldbart

"I was informed after the liberation that the villa on Rózsadomb had been destroyed in the bombings. As soon as I had the opportunity, I took a truck and went there with my students. We started digging among the ruins. I remembered the arrangement of the house and so I knew where to look for the Guttmann library. Indeed, we found many of the books, most of them in usable condition. Some were then transported to the United States by Guttmann's son, Henrik Guttmann, former teacher of the Seminary. The rest was used to fill in the gaps of the library of the Rabbinical Seminary. Unfortunately, the extensive index-card collection of *Clavis Talmudis*, Guttmann's life-work, of which only four volumes were published (1910–1930), was destroyed."

(In: *Magyar Könyvszemle*, 1970)

In the summer of 1944 Péter Hain (1895–1946), a detective-inspector responsible for the Regent's personal security since 1937, director of the state security department of the Budapest police headquarters since the German occupation, organized an exhibit somewhere on Sváb-hegy of the art treasures confiscated from Budapest Jews (e.g. the collections of Baron Hatvany, Baron Herzog, Káldi, Baron Kornfeld, Mauthner, estate of Baron Manfréd Weiss, etc.), which had been removed to the wine cellars at Budafok. Relatively precise descriptions of these works and some lists survived. Among them were paintings by El Greco, Gauguin, Goya, Rembrandt, Rubens, Tiepolo, Van Dyck, etc. The Germans put their hands on the residences of several wealthy Jews, e.g. the Mauthner Villa at 13 Lendvay utca, the Kornfeld Villa at 27 Lendvay utca, the Weiss and Chorin Villa at 114–116 Andrássy út, the Fenyő Villa at 44 Kútvölgyi út, the Herzog Villa at 93 Andrássy út. These villas were transformed into SS offices and all the valuable art works were to be taken to Germany. It was partly to prevent this process that on May 25 Dénes Csánky, painter, director general of the Museum of Fine Arts, was appointed government commissioner in charge of evaluating and preserving confiscated Jewish works of art (name of his Commission was in Hungarian: *Kormánybiztosság a zsidók*

445. Portrait of Ottó Komoly as a youth

zár alá vett műtárgyainak megőrzésére és számbavételére); this action actually served to keep some of these valuable art treasures, Persian rugs, jewelry, gems, etc., in the country. Csánky had previously asked several wealthy Jewish art collectors individually to offer paintings in their possession for the collection of the Museum. A few people deposited their collection in the Museum. Some of the paintings at Hain's disposal were taken over by the director general. Nevertheless, the Germans and Hain removed many of them; the "gold train" left the capital in December 1944, as the Red Army was closing in on Budapest. Passing Óbánya (next to Zirc) and Brennberg-bánya, the train reached Austria on March 30, 1945. A part of the Jewish art collections was in early 1945 captured by Soviet military authorities and remained in Soviet / Russian possession until today.

In the course of May and June, in accordance with German plans, the Hungarian gendarmerie deported the entire countryside Jewry, over 437,000 persons, who had been previously gathered, "concentrated" in camps. The first large "transport" of the well-organized action departed on May 15. The Hungarian State Railways (*Magyar Államvasutak*, MÁV) had been busy preparing the railway "rolling-stock" since the middle of April. The transit station was, in most cases, at a brickyard. The majority of trains, mostly freight cars, left for Auschwitz. There was no resistance.

"His Majesty the Regent told me that [the German authorities] demanded a large number of people for forced labor service from Hungary, and it was only with great effort that they could achieve that *Jews* should be given for this purpose instead of *Hungarian people*. And if they gave Jews to the Germans, the Government considered it appropriate to send their relatives as well, for it would have been unfair that the family of a man doing productive work and earning his living abroad should be provided for by the community at home. Thus a few hundred thousand Jews would get beyond the border. Nevertheless, not a single hair of their head would be hurt."

(László Ravasz, "Pro memoria" [notes on his audience with the Regent], April 28, 1944)

446. A postcard from *Waldsee* (Auschwitz), 1944

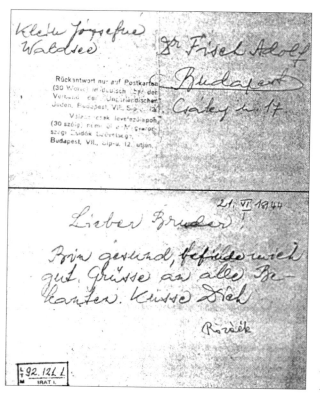

The deportations were organized and carried out by Hungarian state institutions; administration, police, gendarmerie. The non-Jewish population was watching the events mostly with indifference.

They had just started to round up the countryside Jewry when the first reliable news about Auschwitz reached Budapest. Between April 25 and 28, or a little later, during May, but definitely by early June, the Jewish community and some Zionist circles learned what was happening to those who had been deported from Slovakia. In Budapest, certain hints were dropped from which guesses could be made. For instance, the word *...witz* was to be found on a greeting card: Fülöp Freudiger, president of the Orthodox community of Buda, could decipher it under the word Waldsee with the aid of his textile magnifying glass, which he always kept on him. Then there was another postcard with two signatures: Joseph R'evim and Samuel Blimal-bisch—*re'evim* meaning "starving" and *beli malbish* "without clothes". Finally, here is the account of two inmates from Zsolna, Walter Rosenberg / Rudolf Vrba and Alfred Wetzler / Josef Lanik, who had escaped from Auschwitz.

"(...) From the end of the first transport it was clear to me that the aim of the organization of resistance was not rebellion but survival, the survival of the members of the resistance movement. I thought that if the truth became publicly known in Europe, first of all in Hungary, from where, I knew exactly, one million Jews were supposed to be transported to Auschwitz starting in May, it would start a resistance movement, which might have brought outside assistance for those in Auschwitz as well. We drew up the plans of our escape. I succeeded on April 7 [1944].

"Was that the most important reason why you escaped?

"Yes, indeed, I wanted to act immediately because of that. In other words, I knew I should not waste a single moment and that I had to escape as soon as possible in order to inform the world."

(Rudolf Vrba, in: Claude Lanzmann, *Shoah,* 1985)

Based on the account of the prisoners who had escaped the events were recorded in German in the office of the Jewish Council in Zsolna on April 26, 1944. It later became widely known as the Auschwitz Protocols and was soon sent through Bratislava to Budapest, to Kasztner and to others, such as the leaders of the Jewish Council. Freudiger received the Yiddish translation of the report from Michael Beer-Dow Weissmandel, rabbi of Bratislava. A month later, in June, the report of two more Auschwitz prisoners (Arnost Rosin and Czeslaw Mordowicz) was also recorded in Liptószent-miklós. It may have been sent to Pest as well.

Neither the Jewish Council nor the Orthodox community leaders or Zionist leaders announced the horrible news of Auschwitz; they concealed it entirely from the Hungarian Jewish public for a long time. In fact, they dreaded that others might suspect what they already knew. The helpless fear of community leaders and Zionists is well illustrated by the fact that even now, fifty odd years later, it is impossible to find out precisely who had received the Auschwitz Protocols and when. According to Bratislavians, Kasztner brought it with himself from Bratislava at the end of April. Kasztner himself only remembered to have taken it in his hands several weeks later in Pest. It is, however, a fact that when Kasztner went to Bratislava, he could already have read the German version of the report. It may have been he who provided a copy for the Pest community leaders, perhaps Freudiger's or Weissmandel's text, which may have been sent to him only after his visit to Bratislava. Nevertheless, for a long time Freudiger had not told anybody about it.

One of the copies of the Auschwitz Protocols was forwarded to Pest through the channels of the contacts of the Hungarian independence movement as well. A descendant of a Transylvanian rabbinic family, Calvinist Pastor József Éliás (1915–1995), the real leader of the "*Jó Pásztor*" *Bizottság* ("Good Shepherd" Committee) received it, perhaps at the beginning of May. In Budapest "Good Shepherd" was the only organization which, having become acquainted with the text of the report, took action. They had Mária Székely (later Mrs. Küllői-Rohrer) translate the Auschwitz Protocols into Hungarian; she did so in the attic of a friend's apartment (at 7 Érmelléki utca), which was a hiding place. The "Good Shepherd" tried to use the report to inform politically influential people, highest ranking leaders of Christian churches and the Regent's daughter-in-law, about the real purpose of the deportations. By the middle of May the leaders of the three Christian churches had already received the text of the Auschwitz Protocols. Ottó Komoly received it from the "Good Shepherd" as well.

Jewish leaders could not really expect to be heard by Hungarian politicians. Nevertheless, they prepared their translation of the report, too, and sent it to the Regent's younger son. It is hard to believe that Éliás and his group would not have known that the Regent and all the bishops spoke German. They must have intended to rouse the public opinion with the Hungarian translation. Jewish leaders had the Yiddish version (perhaps that of R. Weissmandel) translated into Hungarian; the Yiddish one could indeed not have been understood by anybody else but them. Laying the facts before those most directly concerned was delayed probably because both Christian clergymen and Jewish leaders hoped that it would soon have an impact on the highest level, i.e. they hoped for the Regent's rapid intervention. Thus, Horthy may have been informed about the Auschwitz Protocols from two independent sources, through his daughter-in-law, as well as through his younger son.

447. Miklós Krausz

Miklós (Moshe) Krausz, head of the Palestine Agency (Pro-Palestine Association of Hungarian Jews), the Pest representative of the Jewish Agency for Palestine since 1934, sent the Auschwitz Protocols abroad on June 18–19 through a Romanian diplomat passing through Pest. Representatives of the Vatican learned from Bratislava about the content of the report perhaps two weeks earlier. Nevertheless, it was only then that the news elicited the proper response. On June 20, in a monastery near Bratislava, a Vatican representative personally heard the account of prisoners who had escaped from Auschwitz. He promised to do his best to prevent further massacres at Auschwitz.

*

To contemplate serious resistance Hungarian Jewry would have needed external military assistance. The Allies took no definite measures in that respect, and their only undertaking proved unsuccessful. Supported by the British, the Jewish Agency for Palestine dropped a small group of parachutists (32 persons, two women among them) in Croatia in March. One of the women was Anna (Hana / Hannah) Szenes (1921–1944), daughter of Béla Szenes (1894–1927), a well-known writer and journalist. The poetic talent of Anikó, as she was called in the family, had developed quite early. Her poems written at the age of twelve were published in *Múlt és Jövő* in 1933. She was an ardent Zionist, made *aliyyah*, learned Hebrew, and wanted to take part in the liberation of Budapest Jews. The parachutists were caught as soon as they had crossed the border (June 7–13). Anikó, too, was imprisoned and taken to the Count Hadik Barracks (24–26 Horthy Miklós út, today Bartók Béla út). Several months later, already under the Arrow-cross regime, she was interrogated, sentenced to death and executed in the Margit körút prison on November 7. (For a long time, there was a vocational school in the building of the former garrison tribunal. It was pulled down around 1970 and replaced by the Ministry of Trade and Industry, which still occupies the building at 85 Margit körút.) They say that the corpse of Anna Szenes was asked for by the Pest Hevrah Kaddisah, yet nobody knows who buried her finally. Her grave was found in the Kozma utca cemetery thanks to the recollections of a non-Jewish cemetery gardener. Today there is but a cenotaph with a memorial (plot V/C, parcel 3/23). The mortal remains of Hannah were exhumed in March 1950 and the heroine of Israel, together with six fellow-parachutists, was laid to rest in the Heroes' Cemetery on Mount Herzl in Jerusalem.

Zionist organizations sent their request from Budapest to Switzerland, asking the Allies to drop bombs on the Kassa railway junction in order to block trains heading for Auschwitz. There was no response; the request had no effect, just as the Allies had not heeded previous request to drop bombs on Auschwitz.

It seemed that the only possible solution was negotiations. The prerequisite for these, however, was secrecy. Under the deteriorating military conditions, with a larger number of Jews, the Germans wanted to avoid another Warsaw ghetto revolt.

*

By then Hungarian Jewry had long been cut off from all international Jewish organizations. The official representative of the *Joint* had left the country already in December 1941. Only illegal organizations, such as various groups of the Zionist movement, were trying to help. Some of them continued to organize emigration. Betar (brit/berit Trumpeldor, "Trumpeldor Association"), one of these organizations, had been sending groups of emigrants through Romania regularly since 1938. They were preparing for a military struggle for independence and, therefore, needed manpower. Within six years, about 4,500 Hungarian *olim* reached Palestine with their aid. Once they set out on an old, worn-down ship, down the Danube. (The "Atid", meaning "Future", a steamboat registered in Hamburg, had taken emigrants to Palestine already in 1934. Wealthy passengers could even buy a passage on liners, regular lines. Nevertheless, the possibility of emigrating legally became more and more restricted. Consequently, Zionist organizations had to depend on their own daring.) *Betar* and various *halutz* underground movements such as *D'ror* (*dror / deror*, "freedom"), *Ha-Bonim* (*ha-bonim*, "builders"), *Ha-Noar Ha-Cioni* (*ha-no'ar ha-tziyyoni*, "youth of Zion"), *Makkabi Ha-Cair* (*makkabi ha-tza'ir*, "Makkabi youth"), etc., all played important roles. During 1942/43, since the Eastern front had been opened, ghetto rebellions had been suppressed and ghettos liquidated in Poland, and after deportations had begun in Slovakia, several Jews from foreign countries (Poland, Ukraine, Slovakia and Austria) were able to escape abroad, as refugees, through Hungary. Child-rescue organizations, which since 1942 had the permission of the British Government to organize regular emigration for children to Palestine with the assistance of the Jewish Agency, could still send a group of about fifty every month in the summer of 1944. These groups sometimes included older people as well. Nevertheless, by that time the British certificate of immigration was not sufficient anymore; to make *aliyyah* one needed all sorts of Hungarian permits as well. In the summer of 1943 Minister of Interior Keresztes-Fischer promised Rezső Kasztner through the mediation of Baron Miklós Wesselényi (1911–1980), at that time on the staff of the daily *Magyar Nemzet,* that they may appeal to him personally in exceptional cases. There were a few cases like that; for instance, in May 1944, there were six or seven hundred blank certificates available in the Budapest office of the *Va'adah.*

In May 1939 the British authorities controlling immigration to Palestine planned to issue altogether 75,000 permits for the entire period between 1939 and 1944. Of the 75,000 permits only 14,000 remained by the end of the summer of 1944. For a long time there was no other option than illegal immigration. An immigration permit was basically necessary only for being able to leave. It served as an identity card certifying that the person in question was registered by the authorities of the Palestinian British Mandate, and that she or he was thus under their protection. In principle, German and Hungarian authorities accepted these documents, consequently, they were even worth falsifying. In Budapest the number of certificates distributed by Zionist organizations quickly increased to 18,500 in the fall of 1944, but by that time it was no longer possible to leave with these papers. They could only be used as identification cards.

After March 19 there was no chance of evading the German authorities. Very rarely did smaller or larger groups actually succeed in leaving legally. There remained, however, some hidden paths, some secret trails (see Judges 5,6) until as late as August 1944.

The Relief and Rescue Committee, *Vaadat Ezra ve-Hacala / ha-Ezra Vehacala* [*va'adat ha-ezrah ve-hatzzalah*], abbreviated as *Vaada* [*va'adah*], had been established already in 1943 and was working continuously at 15 Semsey Andor utca, later at 12 Síp utca, under the leadership of Ottó Komoly (Nátán / Niszon Kahn) (1892–1945), architect and entrepreneur, captain in reserve, Rezső (Rudolf) Izrael Kasztner (1906–1957) and Jenő Joél Brand (1906–1964). In the name of the organization, the offshoot of Hungarian and Transylvanian Zionist movements, Brand and Kasztner started negotiations with the Gestapo in April. Their intention was to persuade the Germans to grant permission for Hungarian Jews to emigrate in return for equipment needed for the army, delivered from abroad. This was the *Blut für Ware* plan, which meant that they offered "wares for blood, for life", trucks for life. It was called "the great route" in the Zionist movement.

The "little route" was the secret path. Arranging for refugees to go abroad was called "excursions" (*tiyyul*, plural *tiyyulim*). They were organized by various Zionist groups. In Budapest they were loosely connected with Kasztner's and Brand's action. In return for a large amount of money, smugglers from the region of Békéscsaba led refugees with false "Aryan" papers at night through fields to northern Transylvania. Jehovah's Witnesses and members of the Nazarene communities living in great numbers in this part of the country helped unselfishly. In Nagyvárad (Oradea) and Kolozsvár (Cluj) also representatives of Zionist organizations helped them get over the Romanian border. At Torda, other agents were waiting for them. Only a few Hungarian Jews went on the "little road" and the majority of Slovakian Jews just wanted to get home—this was called re-*tiyyul*, i.e. "*excursion* back home". All in all, it was mostly Jews from Poland who took advantage of the assistance of Hungarian Zionists.

In early May, more than six hundred men and several women, mostly Jews arrested on streets and at railway stations in the provinces or picked out of detention camps, were taken from Pest to work in

Auschwitz-Birkenau. These people sent home postcards from a place called Waldsee. It sounded as if they had been in a small town somewhere in Austria. But the mysterious name of the place was fictitious and the cheerful texts of the postcards were all dictated by the Germans. Making workers send these postcards was meant to calm or to mislead public opinion back at home. This was obviously a test transport in preparation to the planned mass deportation of the Budapest Jews. By the time the Waldsee cards arrived in Pest, their senders may have already been burnt in the crematoriums.

At the beginning of the summer officials of the Jewish community began to distribute application forms for working in Germany. They hoped and promised that those having worked for a short while would be able to proceed as an organized group through Barcelona to Palestine. Indeed, on June 14 a large group of about 15,000 people from the provinces set out in six trains to go to work; instead of Germany they were supposed to be taken to Vienna. One of the trains, however, was directed towards Auschwitz by mistake, and another train that was destined to go to Auschwitz arrived at Strasshof (near Vienna) instead. Nevertheless, having worked under the supervision of the Gestapo in Vienna for a while, eventually everyone was taken to Bergen-Belsen or Auschwitz.

On June 28–29, 1944, 1,685 people from Hungary and Transylvania boarded a train at the Budapest-Rákosrendező Railway Station. Their journey was organized by Kasztner. They gathered in the assembly points of the International Red Cross, a few of them on Ménesi út, and the majority on the corner of Aréna út and Szabolcs utca, near the buildings of the Jewish Hospital and in the barracks built on the empty plot at 46 Columbus / Kolumbusz utca. Those coming from the countryside or Transylvania, mostly from Kolozsvár, had been waiting here all along. The Kasztner train departed from Pest on June 30, on Friday, and left the country at Hegyeshalom on July 7. According to the promise, i.e. the deal made with the Germans, they were to go to Switzerland. The train went to Bergen-Belsen instead. (This concentration camp was established by the Germans in order to gather Jews who were allowed to go abroad, and to start their exchange from here.) During their trip these people were subjected also to various types of psychological torture. The train stopped at a station and they could hear its name, *Auspitz*. (It was certainly said in German, the town's old Hungarian name being Pusztapécs.) They thought that after a week's journey the train was directed to *Auschwitz* by mistake. In Linz, they were informed that warm showers were available, consequently, they suspected gas chambers. The Germans were aware that they could have already known about the Auschwitz Protocols. But still, they escaped death. In Bergen-Belsen they were provided with a separate section in the camp, and they were supplied tolerably well. Only a few, exactly 318 people (for the mysterious number see Genesis 14,14), could go to Switzerland immediately, around the end of August; their train left from Bergen-Belsen on August 21. The majority were allowed to leave only on December 6–7, when the Germans were already hoping to make peace with the Allies in the near future. Fortunate passengers of the train went on to Haifa, Palestine, by way of Italy, immediately after their arrival to Switzerland. They spent the High Holidays already there, which must have been a wonderful experience for them. Members of the Kasztner group were let out of Hungary by the Germans only in exchange for a vast sum of ransom, 1,000 dollars per person. There were, however, some "free" passengers on the train, too. Part of the fortune collected in Kasztner's action was grabbed by Péter Hain. Kasztner hoped for an even greater deal, namely the exchange of the majority of Hungarian Jewry; even Eichmann did not reject this solution out of hand. Joél Brand traveled to Istanbul in order to organize the deal already in May, but the plan was never realized. Foreign charity institutions became mistrustful and they feared that if the Germans were given significant assistance, that might postpone the end of the war.

Joél (Joel or "Jajlis") Teitelbaum (1886–1979), the Satmar rebe, influential Hasidic leader in Hungary, was on board the Kasztner train, too. To the end of his life he remained strongly opposed to Zionism and the existence of the State of Israel, as are his followers, the Satmar Hasidim even today. In their opinion redemption should not be rushed and the Holocaust itself was a punishment for Israel's intention to realize what only the Messiah will realize. When one of the rebe's followers was asked what he thought of the fact that the rebe himself had been rescued by Zionists, he answered, "This may have been the only merit of the Zionist movement".

One of the well-known passengers on the Kasztner train was Lipót Szondi (1893–1986), the world famous psychologist. In Budapest his apartment was at 1 Anker köz. After the war he remained in Switzerland and continued his scientific activity there. His book on the murderer type of personality (*Kain. Gestalten des Bösen,* 1969; see also his *Moses. Antwort auf Kain,* 1973) can hardly be interpreted independently of his experiences of the year 1944.

More than half a century after Kasztner's beneficent activity, on October 14, 1998, a commemorative inscription was put on his former house (12 Váci utca).

The owners of the Csepel industrial complex and other major industrial plants, altogether forty-five members of the Baron Weiss, Chorin, Baron Kornfeld and Mauthner families, as well as about thirty members of the family of Fülöp (Pinhas) Freudiger, president of the Orthodox community of Buda and some other Orthodox people, managed to leave, too. The former were allowed to depart in June through Austria to Stuttgart by train, and from there by a Lufthansa flight to Portugal. In Lisbon the former—relieved just months before—Hungarian ambassador, Antal (Andor) Wodianer (1890–1964), helped them. The price of their release was to surrender a significant portion of their possessions, which Csepel being a weapons manufacturing plant was most desirable in the eyes of the Germans, to the Waffen-SS group of the Gestapo in the form of a 25-years lease contract. Formally, the "Jewish" members of the family gave up their share of the property to the "Aryan" members, and the family's entire industrial possessions were taken over, for "handling at their discretion", by the former *Révay udvar Bérház Rt.* [Révay courtyard Apartment Ltd.] located at 10 Révay utca. (This building has recently taken up the name *Házértékesítő és Kezelő Rt.* [House Seller and Maintenance Ltd.].) By that time the director of the corporation had long been a high-ranking SS officer. The Hungarian Cabinet was seriously concerned about the fact that the greatest Hungarian industrial complex was handed over to the Germans, but in vain. It was in the interest of the Germans that the family should be transferred abroad; evading Hungarian legislation and even the (Anti-)Jewish Laws they got hold of the greatest part of Hungarian arms manufacture.

Letter of Ferenc Chorin to the Regent of May 17, 1944:

"Perhaps you have been informed of the fact that I was under arrest for a few weeks in various places and conditions. (...) During that time, unfortunately, a string of decrees regulating the Jewish question, void of any legal basis, were published under the auspices of Your Serene Highness, most probably under pressure. These orders sequestered Jewish properties—though what really happened was confiscation, (...) and at the same time made all kinds of economic activities virtually impossible for Jews and those regarded as such, which I consider even graver at the moment. (...) I spent the last two weeks of my detention in so-called *Ehrenschutzhaft,* (...) and I met the economic group under the leadership of *Reichsführer* Himmler. (...) They offered to take the whole property of Manfréd Weiss into *treuhänderisch* handling. (...) The agreement served German interests since their ambition was to have the full potential of the largest Hungarian factory in the war's service. (...) I must emphasize, however, that our decision was not made due to our bitterness about the Government's measures, it is the result of careful consideration of the situation. We have not betrayed the interests of the country... It is true that part of our family regained their freedom, nevertheless they perhaps deserved it for their work in the past decades.

"I am saying farewell to Your Grace. (...) I have to give special thanks to you for the benevolence with which you have treated the efforts of the branch of industry that I have represented in Hungary for twenty years, of which you have always been so kind as to give evidence to me, and for which I have been, and will always be genuinely grateful."

The Freudigers set out towards Romania on August 9–10, by train, in exchange for a significant ransom. They received their passports in Romania, but more to the part it was their relation to Wisliceny, more specifically a box of candies with diamonds inside that made their journey possible. (Freudiger himself, nevertheless, had to have his beard cut off in order to be able to leave.)

(5) Yellow-star Houses

The plan of putting Budapest Jews into a ghetto arose already in April 1944, along with the "concentration" of provincial Jewry, but at that time Hungarian authorities believed that by settling Jews in one place, i.e. in a ghetto, they would leave the rest of the city at the mercy of the bombings of the Allies. They, therefore, deemed it more practical to mark out houses in several places of the capital, mostly in the neighborhood of important public buildings, railway stations and military targets. These houses, modeled on the *Judenhäuser* established in Germany in 1939, would accommodate Jews exclusively. The Jewish population would thus serve as hostages, as a form of protection against bombings. (As it turned out, bombs did not discriminate, but fell on Jewish houses too, even on the ghetto.) Eichmann and the Hungarian authorities eventually reached an agreement, after some wrangling. Within a week the entire Jewish population of the capital was made to move into only 1,840 apartments, instead of the 2,600 houses initially agreed upon. The approximately 19,000 Jewish apartments thus vacated were assigned to other people. The school building at 44 Wesselényi utca (240 beds), the headquarters of the Welfare Bureau (MIPI) located in the Institute for the Deaf and Dumb at 2 Bethlen Gábor tér (ca. 100–120 beds) and some of the buildings of the Boys' Orphanage (25–27 Vilma királynő út / Városligeti fasor, ca. 60 beds) were designated as emergency hospitals for Jews. The decree was signed by the Mayor of Budapest on June 16, to be implemented by June 21, i.e. within three days. The deadline was later postponed to June 24. The operation of moving people out of their homes was organized by the Jewish Council.

448. Posters and their readers, June 1944

"I do not think that there is another example in world history when close to 250,000 inhabitants of a single city would have moved into new apartments within eight days. (...) June 24 fell on a Saturday. Budapest was the scene of such a sight as not seen for centuries. The children of Israel carried their bags and baggage, pieces of furniture and articles for personal use, whatever they needed most, by carriage, handcarts, and wheelbarrows, and those who found nothing better, in bundles on their back, to the houses indicated. One day later, as a result of the curfew, services were no longer held in the temples at the right time. This had not happened since synagogues had been built. (...) Breaking the sanctity of the Sabbath, thousands of people were obliged to carry their luggage on this last day. They did so in order not to remain without shelter by the time evening fell, lest they should give pretext for SS-men and detectives making raids in the streets, to carry them off. It was a long summer evening. The setting sun still gave light to some of those moving into their new apartments, who in the precipitation of the last few minutes, escaped to their new home surreptitiously."

(Ernő Munkácsi, in: *Új Élet*, August 8, 1946)

449. Moving into the Yellow-star Houses, June 1944

A yellow star, 30 centimeters (12 inches) in diameter on a black background, had to be placed on the gate of every designated house. They were referred to as "Yellow-star Houses" after the

Jewish star, though sometimes they were called Jewish houses. "I resent that you declared our block of flats in Hajó utca [8–10 Fehér Hajó utca] a Jewish house, whereas there are several buildings in the capital which would be suitable for this purpose. You should not have put us to shame this way"—wrote the Lutheran Bishop Sándor Raffay in his annual report on November 22, 1944. Tenants could leave Yellow-star Houses only for two hours a day, later for a somewhat longer period, but exclusively in order to buy food and the like. People forced into these apartments were not allowed to leave Budapest at all. Everybody suspected that this "concentration", as in the case of Jews in the provinces, was but preparation for deportation.

Some of the Yellow-star Houses were 45 Úri utca; 4–6 Kígyó utca; 5 Galamb utca (this one was taken over by the German military commander on September 15); 18 Kossuth Lajos tér; 11/B Váci utca. And there were 1,835 others.

450. A Yellow-star House: 18 Kossuth Lajos tér (today Balassi Bálint utca)

(6) The Era of Catastrophe, II

By the end of May the German plans for the "concentration" of Budapest Jews was ready. Eichmann wanted to accomplish this job within one day, sometime in the second half of July. Details of the plan were mentioned in a dispatch dated May 26, 1944 by a counselor of the German Embassy, as well as in some recollections. The news that the SS had already worked out the plan of a "major operation" spread quickly. It was said that on a certain day the entire bus and streetcar traffic of Budapest would be stopped and all these vehicles be requisitioned to transport Jews. Help would be requested from the provinces as well, policemen, gendarmes, even mailmen and chimney sweeps, that is, anyone in a uniform, to help round up all the Jews of Budapest on one of the larger islands in the Danube. (As a matter of fact, Eichmann could have taken the idea of this insane plan from the Book of Esther, after Haman's plan to massacre the Jews.) But on June 30 the German ambassador, Edmund Veesenmayer, decided that they should wait with the execution of the plan. He sent a dispatch to Berlin on that day saying: "Small-scale special actions were carried out in the suburbs of Budapest as an introductory phase for the operation. Smaller Jewish transports of politicians, intellectuals, skilled laborers and Jews with large families are on the way." Otherwise they were to wait for another opportunity; the plan was again taken into consideration in August.

*

July 19: Immanuel Lőw, chief rabbi of Szeged, member of the Upper House, died in the emergency hospital set up in the building of the Jewish school at 44 Wesselényi utca. He lived in Szeged, he only stayed in his Pest apartment at 2 Vigadó tér on his occasional visits to the capital. The 91-year-old scholar was taken off the train on which the Jews of Szeged were deported to Auschwitz, he was first taken to a transit camp and then to a hospital. Sándor Scheiber visited him in his last days. Lőw was laid to rest in the Farkasrét cemetery on June 21; Sándor Scheiber and Imre Benoschofsky buried him. After the war, on April 23, 1947, he was exhumed and re-buried in Szeged, his home-town. He was the son and heir of Lipót (Leopold) Lőw; the main fields of his scholarly work were Talmudic literature, botany and zoology; his four-volume *Die Flora der Juden* (1924–1934) earned him international scholarly fame. He collected and published the works of his father; his own shorter papers—scattered in scholarly journals—were collected and edited by Sándor Scheiber (*Fauna und Mineralien der Juden*, 1969; *Studien zur jüdischen Folklore*, 1975).

The Rabbinate of Pest took care of R. Lőw in the days before his death and of his funeral later. What happened to him in his final days becomes clear from Sándor Scheiber's eulogies (*hesped*) over his grave.

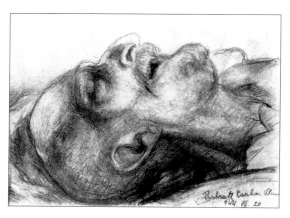

451. Immanuel Lőw on his death-bed. Drawing by Csaba Vilmos Perlott, June 20, 1944

At the grave of R. Lőw in 1944:

"The road to immortality and eternity leads through pain and suffering. The 90-year-old Immanuel Lőw, arriving to the door of immortality with faded eyes, did pay his entrance fee through that door. Upon arriving in Pest his first words were: *Ein tragisches Ende für Lőw.*"

At R. Lőw's exhumation in 1947:

"Immanuel Lőw, the greatest son of Szeged, to which he was faithful until his death, left his home town stigmatized, blind, barely able to walk, wearing his blue coat, carrying a single bag and a blanket on his arm. He returns now in white, with the eternal light in his eyes, accompanied by the respect of the scholarly world. (...) Abraham saw hell itself. His fate would not quite have matched that of the Patriarch, had Immanuel Lőw at the age of 90 not perceived the hell created by human evil on earth: the ghetto, hunger, the brickyard, the wagon, the transit camp on Aréna út. That is where I saw him again after so many years, as he was lifted into the ambulance of the emergency hospital. (...) I saw a man devastated at the end of his life whose pains were occasionally eased by the dormant mind. He saw his office in front of his eyes, and his library. He saw his temple and he murmured the prayer *U-netanne tokef.* He saw with his inner eyes the long rows of the victims of this horrible Jewish tragedy, among them the martyrs of his own congregation. And woe that *God's lion*, Immanuel Lőw, had to be among them..."

On R. Lőw's 25th *Jahrzeit* in 1969:

"(...) When I arrived to the transit camp in the Aréna út synagogue, the aged, blind, shattered scholar, just taken off the deportation train, was about to be transferred into an ambulance car. I handed him a bottle of warm soup. As the old man ate the soup with trembling hands, he said to me: Your soup is better than your (hand)writing. He was always angry with me for my tiny letters."

*

June 22: The Chief Mufti of Jerusalem sent a letter from Berlin to the Ministry of Foreign Affairs in Budapest requesting that the Hungarian Government prevent by all means the emigration of Hungarian Jews to Palestine, whether it was secret or official.

June 26: Responding to the separate requests of the Apostolic Nuncio Angelo Rotta, the representative or ambassador of the Vatican in Budapest, who was familiar with the Auschwitz Protocols, and of the American Congress, Pope Pius XII (1939–1958) appealed to the Regent of Hungary in an open telegram to spare the lives of Hungarian Jewry who had suffered that much.

June 26: In a message sent through the Swiss Embassy, Franklin D. Roosevelt, the President of the United States of America, reminded the Regent that Hungary would be held responsible for all the atrocities committed against Jews.

June 27/28: Several gendarme units arrived to Budapest unexpectedly. Some people anticipated a *coup d'état*. Two under-secretaries of state in the Ministry of Interior who favored even closer cooperation with the Germans were practically dismissed by the Regent. This event may have influenced his decision a few days later to deny permission for further deportations.

June 28: The Foreign Department of the US Congress issued an appeal to the countries allied with Germany and especially to Hungary to stop torturing the masses of innocent Jews.

June 30: Sweden's King Gustav V appealed to the Regent asking that Hungary treat the Jews according to its chivalrous tradition.

July 2: The aircraft of the Allies delivered the greatest air-raid against Budapest so far and this time the bombs fell not only on the industrial zones but also on the city itself. The bombardment must have been meant as a strong warning, but more towards the general goals of the war than to help the Jews of Budapest.

July 5, evening: in a state of panic, Prime Minister Döme vitéz Sztójay informed the ambassador of Germany that Hungarian secret agents in Bern were able to lay their hands on the dispatches of the British and the American Embassies, which revealed that there were detailed plans for the bombardment of Budapest and for the elimination of some political leaders in case the action against the Jews of the capital took place. (These reports were based on the messages of the *Va'adah*.)

July 7: The Prime Minister sent a letter to the Archbishop of Esztergom informing him that there would be no more deportations. On the following day the Prime Minister visited the Archbishop personally to confirm that the deportation of Budapest Jews had been suspended. Furthermore he told the Archbishop that should the deportations continue at a later date, Christians of Jewish background, that is Jews who had converted to the Christian faith, would be excluded, they could stay in Hungary. Also, Christian priests of Jewish background would be exempted from the obligation of wearing a yellow star.

July 8, Saturday: At night another train left the Békásmegyer local train station deporting the Jews from the suburbs around Budapest (Kispest, Pestszenterzsébet, Újpest), who were recently *concentrated* at the Budakalász brickyard, to Auschwitz. Similarly, Jews from Budapest and the suburbs who were gathered at the Pünkösdfürdő local train station or in the Monor brickyard, as well as those Jewish lawyers and journalists who were assembled in Csepel, were deported. With this the deportation of Hungarian Jews outside of Budapest was completed. According to official German records, over 437,000 people were sent in cattle cars, in altogether 147 trains towards Auschwitz. All the Jews from the suburbs (albeit separate administrative units) of Budapest, like Pestszentlőrinc, Rákospalota, etc. were also deported.

Early in July some young Zionists, with the understanding and probably even the support of some Jewish leaders from Síp utca, prepared flyers. In one of these flyers they appealed to the Christian society, in another one to the Hungarian nation and in the third one to the Jews of Budapest. The flyers revealed the truth about the deportation of the Jews of the provinces, hinted to the fact that this entailed their annihilation and appealed to the Hungarian nation to support the emigration of Jews. Budapest Jews were, on the other hand, instructed to resist deportation, even at the cost of their lives.

> "We are left to ourselves. (...) We should not be like a herd taken to the slaughterhouse. We should not allow ourselves to be carried to foreign places where we would be sent to the gas-chamber and the crematorium anyway. (...) Out to the street! Our slogan should be: We are not taking the death-train! (...) *Adonay, heye ozer lonu.* Let the Almighty come to our rescue."

The flyers were to be distributed through individually addressed envelopes. It seems, however, that only very few copies left the office of the Jewish community. Fülöp Grünwald (often spelled Grünvald on the title-page of his historical works) (1887–1964), a teacher at the Jewish Boys' *Gimnázium*, historian, on the staff of the Jewish Museum, participated in the production and distribution of the flyers. (The only known copies of the flyers are among the papers he left behind.) The only result was that by mid-August the producers of the flyers were arrested by the police and many in Síp utca were questioned. Those arrested were finally released on September 17, one day before Rosh ha-Shanah, the Jewish New Year.

July 11: The Mayor of Budapest ordered the registration of all the Jews who had converted to the Christian faith before August 1, 1941, and promised them certain privileges. On the following day the Government gave permission for the formation of an Association of Christian Jews (originally suggested to be called Christians of Jewish Descent) in Hungary (*Magyarországi Keresztény Zsidók / Zsidószármazású Keresztények Szövetsége*). Its president and principal activist was the writer Sándor Török (1904–1985). His apartment at 5 Bimbó út was one of the centers of Christian rescue work. Their motto was *Venite ad Me omnes*, "All should come to Me" (Matthew 11,28). Jews who converted were immediately removed from the jurisdiction of the Jewish authorities.

July 15: Eichmann managed to evade the order of the Regent and the Prime Minister to suspend deportations and entrained 1050 Jews from the Kistarcsa detention camp and 500 Jewish prisoners from the Rökk Szilárd utca prison (the Rabbinical Seminary). On July 19, on the second try, he even managed to dispatch the trains.

*

During the summer months there was a rush for conversion in Budapest. "In these difficult times thousands and thousands of Jews rush to get baptized", says the entry on July 26, 1944 in the records of the Jewish community. In his report to the Regent on June 21, 1944, the Secretary of State in the Ministry of Interior notes, "We have to confess that unfortunately it is Christian clergymen of all sorts who play the primary role in saving Jews. (...) These priests, pastors rescue Jews quoting the Christian principle of the love of one's neighbor." His complaint is obviously that they issue false baptismal certificates and baptize people solely to save them. In order to limit the number of conversions the authorities prescribed a waiting period and required a letter of release; the church required a longer period of learning before the conversion took place—the Roman Catholic church prescribed three months, the Calvinists, half a year.

From a report written by Bishop Sándor Raffay of the Lutheran Church on November 22, 1944,

"Thousands of Jews were flooding the parish offices often disturbing the peace and making it difficult to work. In order to somehow limit the number of admissions I ordered that only those Jews may convert in whose families there is already someone of the Evangelical faith, thus their conversion would be justified by the religious unity of the family; furthermore, those Jews whose life was in danger because of an illness or any other reason or those who were recommended by one of our church members on their own personal responsibility. With these limitations the number of conversions decreased radically. A longer period of learning and stricter requirements were an addition to these rules."

452. Lajos Stöckler

The Rabbinate strongly objected to the idea that the office organizing conversions should be located precisely at 12 Síp utca. Some Roman Catholic parishes issued false baptismal certificates. There were also several cases of falsification. After the war, in 1947, this was how Lajos Stöckler evaluated the activities of the Christian Jews, with a certain, if justifiable bias:

"Masses of people had hoped for better prospects and therefore responded to the call of the Association (of Christian Jews) to become its members. The actual outcome of the action was that people wearing a yellow star were divided into two camps. The new association engaged in broad organizational work, cooperating with the churches, of course. The support offered by the churches as part of this cooperation, however, was only intended for the converts, and even if there was joint action, the special interests were always made clear. The presumed advantages encouraged many to convert. Later it became clear that the Association did not accomplish anything apart from organizing. The short period of their activities stopped on October 15 and the excited masses were again left to the care of the Jewish Council."

The Scottish Mission, a Protestant (Calvinist) group whose missionary aim was to convert Jews, had been active in Budapest for over a century already, since 1841. Their headquarters at 49–51 Vörösmarty utca were open for everyone in these difficult times. Their leader, Jane Marianne Haining was arrested by the Gestapo and, despite the intercession of Bishop Ravasz, she was deported to Auschwitz. She issued baptismal certificates and later even hid people. The Jewish mission of the Norwegian Lutheran Church was in Zugló, at 14 Gyarmat utca, since 1902. It was mostly "Jews-for-Jesus" who came here, Jews who accepted Jesus as the Messiah but did not convert, did not give up their Jewishness. Naturally, the mission advocated conversion, too.

*

July 18: Through various channels the Hungarian Government conveyed the message to the embassies and consulates in Budapest that they would not prevent the International Red Cross from assisting Hungarian Jews in the ghettos and camps or from organizing the emigration of Jewish children.

July 30: *Tish'ah be-Av* services were held at the Dohány synagogue in peace; there was even a sermon.

August 2: The brickyard in Békásmegyer (Égető utca) was turned into a transit camp where Budapest Jews were assembled before they were deported.

August 19: Theodor Horst Grell, the secretary in charge of Jewish affairs at the German Embassy of Budapest, reported in a cable that, based on information from the Minister of Interior, the Government, with the permission of the Regent, would start the evacuation of Jews from Budapest on August 25.

> "The Regent only agreed to the removal of a certain number of Jews. The Government, however, decided that apart from the already separated group of Jews who had converted before January 1, 1941, those exempted, and the approximately 3,000 Jews who were chosen and exempted by the Regent personally, all Jews would be removed from Budapest. (...) The concentration would be carried out solely by the Hungarian gendarmerie, assembled specifically for that purpose."

Eichmann insisted that the deportation should take place five days earlier, on August 20, on St. Stephen's Day, the greatest holiday of official Christian Hungary.

August 21: The Budapest ambassadors of the neutral countries, headed by their Dean Angelo Rotta, held a consultation and wrote a protest letter to the Government.

> "The emissaries of the neutral countries accredited to Budapest are deeply disturbed by the recent information that the deportation of the entire Hungarian Jewry would soon begin. Though the real goal of the deportation is concealed by telling people that they are taken abroad for labor service, we became aware of what deportation actually means in most cases, and our information comes from absolutely reliable sources. In addition to voicing our sadness over the unfortunate fact that further deportations would destroy the reputation of Hungary once and for all, we, the emissaries of the neutral countries, led by the principles of human solidarity and Christian love, also consider it our duty to strongly protest against these morally erroneous, cruel and inhuman actions... We bid the Hungarian Royal Government to stop this procedure which should never have begun, for the honor of humankind."

August 24: After Romania deserted the war (on August 23), Eichman's Budapest Office was closed on the request of Géza vitéz csíkszentsimonyi Lakatos (1890-1967), the head of the new Hungarian Government. Eichmann himself left Budapest as well: he went to Velem in westernmost Hungary for a trip to the summer residence of the former under-secretary of state of the Ministry of Interior, who had been replaced in June. One of Eichmann's clerks, however, remained in Budapest scaring the Jewish Council to the extent that they asked the commander of the Hungarian gendarmerie to send Budapest Jews for forced labor service, in the hope that this would rescue them from deportation. The commander of the gendarmerie, however, had not yet completely given up the plan of deportation. He tried to find a place for a transit camp outside of Budapest and suggested Tura, Pest County for the purpose. But the Minister of Interior, at the request of Samu Stern and the Jewish Council, entrusted the International Red Cross with choosing the camp sight. The committee appointed by the Red Cross failed to find an appropriate spot even after an extended search. After Eichmann had left, Peter Hain also fled to Germany. An investigation proved that he had misappropriated the resources with which he was entrusted. In the months of the Arrow-cross rule Hain returned to Budapest, stayed at the "Majestic" and coordinated the anti-Jewish actions of the Arrow-cross.

September 7: The Government published an announcement that for the defense of Budapest all Jewish men older than 14 would be drafted for forced labor service.

Foreign embassies began distributing protective documents (passports, certificates) among the Jewish population of the capital. Earlier they had tried similar actions elsewhere to save Jews from

453. March of women, their hands up, in front of 58-60 Wesselényi utca. October–November, 1944

deportation. The Germans became aware of these actions. On July 14 one of Eichmann's clerks mentioned to the Jewish Council that all the Greek Jews had presented a Spanish passport. In any case, never before were there so many foreign documents issued.

Gábor Sztehlo wrote about the influx of people at the International Red Cross in September–October:

"The halls of the villa in Fillér utca looked almost like a Turkish bazaar. (...) The colorful scene was like a sketch of the old gentry Hungary. The dandified youth of Hungarian aristocracy was milling around in the building—it was fashionable to appear in the delegation. Then there was the financial aristocracy and a few members of wealthy Jewish families who were still in Hungary. At least half of the people crowding in the hall were employees of the delegation: young women were listed as secretaries, young men as messengers, errand boys, drivers. In particular there were a lot of drivers, since this was how people tried to save their cars from military requisition; they received a sticker which they displayed proudly on the windshield of their cars, and a certificate saying that they were couriers of the International Red Cross. Some even put the sticker on the side, back and top of their cars and then parked their cars for hours in the Inner City, in front of cafés, or they simply drove out to their estate in the countryside. But whenever a car was needed for our work, there was none around. When there was a rescue operation, I always had to take Born's huge Buick. The Delegate was sometimes enraged at the sight of these idlers, but could not even spare the time to chase them away; and the gallant young men could always swipe the secretaries off their feet.

"I may be judging the figures of this stage too harshly, but I knew their leaders too well: they were the dance partners of my sisters, I knew exactly what their opinions were, I read their thoughts like in an open book.

(...)

"When the Arrow-cross seized power, the mood of the crowd at the center of the delegation changed completely. The gay spirit of the dandified "golden youth" declined and they themselves disappeared—who knows where they went... Now it was only those really in need of help who were gathering in the fine halls in the evenings. Some were still making plans for the future, others were just sitting around, in despair."

(*Isten kezében* [In God's Hands], 1984)

454. Raid on Teleki tér, October 16, 1944

In the weeks between late August and mid-October some sort of relief was felt in Budapest. Several stores re-opened and the general mood improved. Some concession were made to Jews for the High Holidays. On Rosh ha-Shanah (September 18) the Jewish organizations were given permission to bring food for Jews who were imprisoned in detention camps and on Yom Kippur (September 28) many Jews were even released from certain camps. Also, the Minister of Interior suspended the curfew imposed on Jews for a few hours in the evening and in the morning on the holidays to enable people to attend services. It seemed that Jews in Budapest would not need to do anything to rescue themselves.

September 4: Registration started in the schools of the Jewish community. The Roman Catholic superintendent of schools announced

that from that time on no student obliged to wear the yellow star was allowed to enter their schools.

October 15: At noon the Regent announced that he had requested cease-fire from the Soviet army. The same evening, at around 9:30 p.m., Szálasi announced on the radio that the Arrow-cross Party had taken over. Lakatos as well as Horthy resigned. Ferenc Szálasi appointed himself the *nemzetvezető*, "Leader (like *Führer*) of the Nation" and formed a new government. Arrow-cross Party militants started their actions that very evening, as early as they could. A group of them showed up at 44 Wesse-

455. Yellow stars on winter-coats, October–November, 1944

lényi utca and shot into the building, towards the ceiling of the entrance hall, simply to terrify the people inside. Already at 9:15 p.m. an ambulance picked up a Jewish man on the corner of Csengery and Aradi utca, where he was shot.

On the following day the ambulance registered forty cases of Jews who were shot, almost a hundred on October 17 and at least twenty-five or thirty on each of the following days; the shootings took place along the Danube bank or on the bridges. The Arrow-cross started rounding up Jews at the Tattersall, the racetrack at 7 Kerepesi út. Buildings marked with the yellow star were blocked, Jews were not allowed to go out on the street for days. Whoever was still caught in the street or was driven out from the houses, and did not resist, like some did on Teleki tér, was taken to the Tattersall, never again to return. The new Minister of Interior made a threatening announcement: "I know nothing about Jews of the Roman Catholic, Evangelical or the Israelite faith, I only know people of the Jewish race. I do not acknowledge any kind of letter of exemption or foreign passport that a Jew of Hungarian citizenship had received from anywhere or anyone." Szálasi, by the way, took his oath of office in front of Cardinal Prince-Primate Jusztinián Serédi.

October 17: Jews captured by the Arrow-cross people in the streets, in houses and at the racetrack were taken to the Dohány utca and the Rumbach utca synagogues, which were now transformed into "concentration" camps. At times 6,000 people were squeezed into the synagogues. The Germans closed the Orthodox synagogue in Kazinczy utca. Services were held in the synagogues only after the ghetto was set up, first in Rumbach Sebestyén utca, starting December 15, and later also in Dohány utca.

(7) Death March

October 17: Eichmann returned to Budapest. Already on the following day he started organizing the deportations, stubbornly committed to pushing through his plan despite the conciliatory gestures of his immediate superior, Himmler. Sometime in October Heinrich Himmler gave orders to immediately halt the extermination of Jews, because he hoped that if the cruelties were stopped, the Allies would be willing to make peace or at least cease-fire. Eichmann, however, took no note of the political change and tried to proceed with the original plan, with vile passion. Eichmann agreed with the Hungarian Royal Minister of Defense that as a first step of the deportations they would move Budapest Jews to a *lager* near the capital, and set up a ghetto for the remaining Jews.

October 21: The Hungarian Royal Minister of Defense ordered every Jewish male between ages 16 and 60 and every Jewish female between ages 18 and 40 to participate in "forced labor for the defense of the country". They had to appear on October 23, 1944, at 8 o'clock in the morning, the men at the racetrack on Kerepesi út and the women at the sports hall on Erzsébet királyné útja.

"All Jews have to report, even those who are exempted, privileged, live in a mixed marriage or are of the Christian faith. (...) In order to be considered a foreign citizen you need to have a valid foreign passport.

"All Jews obliged to report should bring with them warm clothes, sturdy footwear, a blanket, a canteen, silverware, pots, washing implements, a backpack and food for three days.

"Caretakers and superintendents of all buildings are obliged to instruct Jews to report."

The words quoted above are from the bill. It was put into practice as follows:

"The building commander, Mr K., knocked on the door: Was I up? Sorry, but all gentlemen of Jewish origin must line up downstairs in the vestibule within thirty minutes. We should bring food for two days. I washed from the waist up, my younger brother shaved me (he too was coming); I gulped down a cup of herbal tea and a slice of bread (we were butterless), and swallowed about six plums. My sisters, having packed our rucksacks with whirlwind speed, now strapped mine on my shoulders, and placed the walking cane on a light blanket over my arm.

"There were already about thirty-five yellow stars in the lobby, men standing around in a vague formation facing the entrance, all loaded up, some with enormous, many-pocketed backpacks, plus four or five little parcels and boxes dangling from their hands. Most of the gentlemen were between 50 and 60 years old, a few under 50; some as old as 65, 70, 72 even. Upstairs, the building commander had made it clear, that there was no age limit, we all had to go."

(Ernő Szép, *Emberszag* (1945), translated by John Bátki, *The Smell of Humans. A Memoir of the Holocaust in Hungary* (Budapest, etc.: Central European University Press, 1994)

October 26: The Hungarian Royal Minister of Defense consented that certain persons, altogether seventy forced labor units, should carry out their work assignments in Germany (*Leihjude*). He also gave permission that those who were taken abroad to work should be accompanied by their families. Within a week the police rounded up 25,000 men and 10,000 women. At this time Auschwitz was already on the verge of elimination, because the Soviet troops were drawing ever nearer. Therefore Eichmann and the Hungarian Government chose another fate for the Hungarian captives. Most were sent off towards Hegyeshalom, on the western border of Hungary, on foot (*Fussmarsch*). They were supposed to build the defense line in front of Vienna, along the Hegyeshalom–Sopron–Kőszeg line: the Eastern Wall (*Ostwall*). Somewhat further South others were working on the Southeastern Wall (*Südostwall*). But before that trenches had to be dug around Budapest, East of the Danube, in Kispest, and later on the western side (Budafok, Albertfalva), and very soon also along the river Sió in Western Hungary. To distinguish these forced laborer units from those working for the army, these were called "defense-line Jews".

October 28: Armed Arrow-cross activists seized Ferenc Kálló, a Roman Catholic priest, from his apartment (Márvány utca), questioned and tortured him and, on the following day at dawn, they shot him into a ditch at the Budakeszi Sanatorium. Dean Kálló was the priest of the Garrison Hospital (Alkotás utca) and all military institutions in Buda belonged under his jurisdiction. Through his hospital contacts he could provide shelter for many, not just for Jews; he also provided life-saving documents for many. To commemorate the good deeds of the dean a street has been named after him in Buda, Kálló esperes utca, just under Sashegy.

October 29: A report of the International Red Cross from Budapest indicated that 50,000 Jews were taken for forced labor service to Germany, another 50,000 Jews were performing forced labor on the territory of Hungary, about one third of that number were working in Austria and Hungarian Jews were marching towards the Austrian border along all the roads, on foot.

At the same time a group of Jews left Bor and they were marching towards Germany. On their way they stopped in Szentkirályszabadja. This is where Miklós Radnóti wrote his last "postcard (*razglednica*)" into his notebook—his last poem, dated October 31, 1944.

"I fell beside him and his corpse turned over,
tight already as a snapping string.
Shot in the neck. 'And that's how you'll end too',
I whispered to myself, 'lie still, no moving.'
Now patience flowers in death. Then I could hear
'Der springt noch auf', above, and very near
Blood mixed with mud was drying on my ear."

(Miklós Radnóti, "Razglednicák, 4" [Postcards], translated by
Zsuzsanna Ozsváth and Frederick Turner)

456. With bundles of packages on Kerepesi út, by the walls of the cemetery, November, 1944

A few days later Radnóti and twenty-one of his fellow-captives were shot by a sergeant and four of the cadres, near Abda, into the dam across the river Rába. Radnóti's notebook was found in the pocket of his raincoat upon his exhumation on June 23, 1946. The *Bor Notebook* contains some of his greatest poems and fragments written during the last months of his life.

November 5: Overzealous officials sent the "defense line Jews", who were to work for the Germans, on their way towards Hegyeshalom a few days before they were supposed to leave. They were gathered in transit camps, in the brickyards of Óbuda.

Since the 1860s a whole chain of brickyards (*téglagyár* in Hungarian) had been built up along Bécsi út, close to the clay deposits. There was the Holzspach Brickyard at 15 Szépvölgyi út, approximately where the Measuring Instruments Factory is today; Kunwald Jakab Brickyard at 86 Bécsi út; the Nagybátony-Újlaki United Factory / Brickyard of the Újlaki Brick- and Lime-Burner at 134–136 Bécsi út—this was located at the southwestern edge of the area where the Óbuda housing project is today. A street name still refers to it: *Vályog utca* [Adobe Street]. The Bohn Brickyard was on the eastern hillside between Kiscell and Remetehegy, on the left side of Bécsi út, in today's *Tégla utca* (Brick Street). There was the Schossberger Brickyard and the Óbuda Lime-Burner and Brickyard on the right side of Bécsi út, South of Pomázi út; the Demjan Brickyard; the Brickyard on Aranyhegyi út, etc. *Fin-de-siècle* Budapest was built up with the bricks coming from these brickyards.

The largest and most significant of these brickyards was the Óbuda plant of the Nagybátony-Újlaki Brickyard at 134–136 Bécsi út. During World War II it was turned into a war factory. Only a few years earlier, in 1940, the deputy managing director of the factory was still a member of the Goldzieher / Goldziher family, Emil Lukács, a man of excellent organizing skills, who got baptized. He lived in a luxurious villa in Garas utca (no. 12, built by Andor Wellisch, 1914). He resigned in 1940, at the age of 70 and died of starvation in the fall of 1944.

The Nagybátony-Újlaki Brickyard was the largest transit camp in the fall of 1944. Thousands of people were brought here and thousands were sent off towards Germany on Bécsi út. Other transit camps were somewhat further, in the brickyards of Csillaghegy, Békásmegyer, Pilisborosjenő and Solymár, as well as in other towns that time outside of the administrative borders of Budapest, in Budafok, Albertfalva and Pünkösdfürdő, there on the athletic field. After World War II the brickyards of Óbuda were closed one by one, the last one, the Újlaki, in 1972. Since then new buildings have risen at these sites, and there is nothing to remind us of the tragic events of the fall of 1944.

All superintendents, caretakers and landlords in Budapest were obliged to keep track of Jews. They informed residents about the latest official regulations and sometimes informed the militia about the whereabouts of Jews. For days and days policemen were escorting groups of Jews to Óbuda. A gas explosion blew up the undermined Margit híd (Margaret Bridge), one of the main routes along which Jews were taken to Óbuda, on Saturday, November 4, around noon, but a pontoon was set up in its place in no time. Long lines of Jews rounded up from the streets or even chased out of protected houses were escorted or chased by the police to the brickyards of Óbuda, to the transit camps.

Prose translation of the poem:

"I left my refuge for one day: – I just wanted to see once more – The Hold utca, the Szabadság tér, – The cafés, the Chain Bridge. But – there was no time left for this. I saw – My mother. She could barely keep pace: – She was driven along with many others. – (...) A woman on the pavement – Told her son: See, the Jews – Are being driven there! The child was staring. – Among the guards there were only a few Swabians. Many – spoke with a zesty accent from Vas County, the Great Plain, or Nógrád County – And were cheering their prey in a victorious mood. – (...) – In the dark, in the pouring rain – My mother's tiny figure in black, – breathing hard, was walking – Towards Újlak."

(István Vas, "November", in: *Márciustól márciusig* [From March till March], 1944/45)

By November Jews were only permitted to be out on the streets between 10 and 12 in the morning. Even then they were sometimes picked up by the Arrow-cross. On November 16 the Arrow-cross raided the flea-market on Teleki tér. There were no Jewish vendors on the square anymore, but many Jews were still hiding in the houses of the neighborhood. Many were taken from their apartments or their hiding-place. They were only allowed to take a small bag with them. Once in the brickyards, very few could still be rescued by friends or acquaintances, with the help of the International Red Cross, the Swedish Embassy or officers of the Hungarian army. The widow and son of the poet Dezső Kosztolányi, who were taken to the brickyard on November 21, from their own apartment, were saved that way. Others received warm clothes or food from outside.

Mrs. Szenes writes:

"As the night fell, it started raining. We continued to march through the mud and the water (...) and finally we arrived to the brickyard in Óbuda. We were driven to the corridor around the burner which was so overcrowded that you could barely even stand. The walls of the burner kept us warm so at least the cold did not torture us all night long. It was impossible to sleep, and at dawn everyone was driven out into the courtyard. We were divided into groups of one hundred, four people in each row. The endless column of human beings started marching towards Austria. Civilian guards were ordered to accompany us, who made no secret out of their unhappiness at having to walk ten or twelve miles a day. They kept an eye on people so that none should escape, but they did not use force and from time to time they even allowed us to rest for five minutes."

Eichmann still insisted, and by now completely arbitrarily, that according to the original plan all Jews should be exterminated. The Hungarian authorities promised to hand over all Jews whom they could round up to the Germans, for forced labor service. And the *Fussmarsch*, as contemporaries called the deportation of these "lent" Jews, who had to march towards the border on foot, turned into a *Todesmarsch*, a death march. Those who reached Hegyeshalom were received by the Germans and even were given to eat—but to get there! Details of these death marches are known to us only from memoirs. One of the units left Pest on November 8 and arrived to Strasshof (near Vienna) seven days later, so they must have marched 18–20 miles a day. In her memoirs the mother of Hannah Szenes mentions that in the days after November 15 they had marched along Piliscsaba, Dorog, Szőny and Komárom, where she finally managed to escape. The groups leaving from Óbuda followed the "old" road to Vienna or one of the alternate routes (Dorog, Süttő, Szőny, Gönyű, Dunaszeg, Mosonmagyaróvár). In Süttő the captives slept on the cattle market, under the open sky, among

457. "Two people who could not go on." Water-color by Edith Kiss, 1945

horses, in Gönyű their night shelter was on a barge, in Mosonmagyaróvár they were pushed into a deserted factory building with no windows. At Gönyű two barges on the Danube were filled with people with dysentery; these were called the "death ships". At Hegyeshalom every morning a German (Gestapo) committee received the transports which arrived on the previous day. There were other reception points as well, for instance at Thurndorf. People who traveled from Vienna to Budapest at that time reported that two-thirds of the road between Vienna and Budapest were taken over by long lines of tired, agonizing people, that the ditches were filled with unburied dead bodies, people who died or were shot.

"(...) Along with Hungarian citizens of the Jewish faith members of our denominations, Christian Hungarians of Jewish origin are also sent on a long march, leading out of the country. Without regard for the old, the sick, fragile women or even tiny children, in the middle of the winter, they are forced to march all day long and spend the night along the cold road. We find human wrecks and sometimes even dead bodies along the roads, who had been left there tired, suffering."

(From a letter of Prince-Primate Cardinal Jusztinián Serédi to the "Leader of the Nation" Ferenc Szálasi of November 25, 1944)

The information gained from personal accounts was confirmed by the International Red Cross, which went on an inspection trip between November 23 and 27. "It was already dark at Gönyű and we saw with our own eyes how the gendarmes drove the Jews onto barges across a thin plank. Many of them fell into the ice-cold water"—says the report. Nándor Batizfalvy, a police commander who was even able to give some modest assistance to Wallenberg's rescue operations, informed the Swedish diplomat confidentially (on November 22) that 10,000 Jews had disappeared along the highways.

On November 19 the Hungarian Government tried to put an end to deportations, and a day later Szálasi himself prohibited the deportation of women on foot, but by then there was anarchy in Budapest and it was questionable whether anyone would obey his commands. The "infernal games", as Tibor Déry referred to the events in the title of his collection of short stories about the year of danger and hiding (Alvilági játékok, 1946), were already taking place. The deportations continued from Budapest even after November 21, only now again by train. Transports were sent from the Józsefváros Railway Station to Ravensbrück and Mauthausen for another few weeks. The last group of deportees, 1,200 inmates of the Toloncház (Detention Barracks), near to the Teleki tér, were sent off from Pest on December 22, on foot.

In the camps in Germany or Austria, in Mauthausen, where Jews arrived after marching for 20–25 days, they were housed in tents, not even barracks any more. Deportees who were sent off from Budapest were found around Nagycenk, Fertőrákos, Sopronbánfalva, Kőszeg and Reichenberg even in March 1945 in large numbers.

An excerpt from Antal Szerb's last letter to his wife, written on December 16, 1944:

"The place where we are now, Balf, is truly terrible, and we are in poor shape in every possible way. I lost all my faith, except that the war may be over soon. This is what keeps me going..."

The literary historian Gábor Halász (1901–March, 1945), writers György Sárközi (1901–January 8, 1945)—author of, among others, a novel about the Independence War of 1848/49—and Antal Szerb (1901–January 17 / March, 1945), author of a prize-winning popular history of Hungarian literature (1934): all of them died in a forced labor camp in Balf (near Sopron, Western Hungary). They were deported in the same transport. Friends tried to rescue them while still in one of the Óbuda brickyards, but they refused, saying that they trust the authorities of the Hungarian state. The folklore scholar János Honti (1910–March / April, 1945) died during the death march, near Kópháza. His last study sent back home was on "Orestes and Hamlet", signed from "bank of a ditch".

In Mauthausen, where the number of survivors was actually relatively high, more than 3,000 Hungarian Jews were murdered, mostly from Budapest. The camp was nicknamed Mordhausen.

On May 1, when the American troops were already very close, the Germans sent some of the surviving captives, among them 4,000 Hungarian Jews who had been transferred here from Auschwitz, on their way towards Günskirchen, on foot. By the time the Americans reached the camp five days later only a few hundred of the captives were alive. Géza Havas (1905–1945), journalist and poet from Budapest, who was deported to Mauthausen and then to Günskirchen from the Kőszeg concentration camp, died only a few hours before the liberation. In other German concentration camps the events of the final days were similar. Even in the last weeks, days and hours the deportees were harassed and tortured, transferred from one camp to another, without any logical reason, causing the death of many and immeasurable suffering to others.

(8) Righteous Gentiles

Hasidei ummot ha-olam.

This is the Hebrew term for the non-Jews who saved lives of Jews during the persecution. In Yiddish: *Hside umes ho-oylem*, "Righteous gentiles". True men (and women) among the people of the world. *Igaz emberek*, in Hungarian.

Friedrich Born (1903–1963)

Born arrived to Budapest on May 9, 1944, as the provisional delegate of the International Red Cross (of Bern), to become the head of the Budapest office. The Red Cross offered assistance to the inmates of prisons, concentration and internment camps. They protected refugees, hostages, people who had resettled or were of "dubious" citizenship. It was clear for everyone right from the beginning that the persecuted in Budapest were all Jews. The Red Cross was especially concerned with orphans and children temporarily separated from their parents.

Born's office was in Buda, in the Ernyey Villa at 51 Fillér utca, in the building of the Swiss commercial mission, the Bureau for Federal Foreign Trade Development by its official name.

458. Friedrich Born

"I have always appreciated the organizing ability and sense of order of the Swiss, but what I experienced over these few months is truly admirable. Though at first they started off clumsily enough and with too much circumspection, soon they continued to carry out their mission on a larger scale, systematically. It was precisely this initial attention to detail and caution which later made it possible for them to help with circumspection. They were disciplined, qualified and experienced, they knew people and coordinated their actions with others even in the biggest danger. They did not make a show out of their humanitarian sentiments but transformed them into organizational skills, and however hair-splitting they might have appeared in the eyes of many, they achieved enormous results with this method."

(Gábor Sztehlo, *Isten kezében* [In God's Hands], 1984)

Born deliberately avoided any cooperation with the Hungarian Red Cross. The managers of the office, even before his arrival to Pest, considered the Hungarian Red Cross "passive and intimidated. They don't care about the detainees, they are only waiting for the instructions of the authorities..." (April 15, 1944). Moreover, after the German occupation, the Hungarian Red Cross dismissed all its Jewish staff and volunteer workers.

From September, 1944 one of the offices of the International Red Cross, the so-called section "A", was at 4 Mérleg utca; it was directed by Ottó Komoly, who was taking care of Jews under the protection of the Red Cross. (The section "A" was actually the cover organization of the *Joint*.) Over 300 people were working in the office, all Jews, of course; the number of the staff shows how busy the organization was. They set up a special delivery group (35 people) to distribute Red Cross aid (food, medicine) among the destitute and to provide supplies for the hospitals. Their main task was to look after the children. They set up homes for the Budapest children, hosted children from the provinces in castles such as Csákvár and Ikervár, but they also took advantage of all other rescue opportunities in the course of their activities. When they ran short of the ready-made free passes and there were not enough seals either, they manufactured new seals in large amounts and copied new passes. It was also a task of section "A" to supply the ghetto's institutions with medicine and food, as far as possible. The neighboring building (6 Mérleg utca) was the center of the economic activities of the International Red Cross and the provisions for the institutions were organized from here.

The main office of the International Red Cross was at 52 Baross utca, another one was at 19 Munkácsy Mihály utca. There was a refugee camp at 46 Columbus utca (today: Kolumbusz utca). The documents were issued in Baross utca, including the fake ones. In Columbus utca, no. 60, on a parcel behind the big building of the Institute for the Deaf and Dumb, there were barracks for those waiting to emigrate, about 1,500 people or more. Abandoning his former residence at 3 Bérkocsis utca, Ottó Komoly moved here in the summer of 1944 for a few months. The camp was guarded by the SS until September 23, because they wanted to keep open the option of dealing with the Hungarian authorities based on the principle of "life for ware". The Red Cross took over the camp only when there were no chances for such exchanges any more. The Jewish orphanage was not a Red Cross institution but Born—on Komoly's mediation—granted permission for displaying the name and symbol of the organization on the building. This also contributed to the fact that, in the fall of 1944, the building on Vilma királynő út was considered a more or less safe place. The deportees' camp in the Óbuda brickyards was also under International Red Cross protection. At the request of Krizosztom Kelemen (1884-1950), chief abbot of Pannonhalma, the International Red Cross took the whole area of the Benedictine Monastery under its protection. Some of the Viennese death marches proceeded along the foot of Szent Márton Hill at Pannonhalma. The "masses of Jews driven in herds", as Kelemen phrased it, were given some food. A few adults and about a thousand children found shelter in the monastery during the fall. In Budapest, even months after the city's liberation, Born and his organization were practically the only ones to distribute food and medicine to the needy.

Born's impartiality towards the needy was interpreted as indifference by many. His independent decisions provoked discontent in Geneva. A colleague from the Geneva office, arriving to Pest at the beginning of December, blamed him for arbitrarily placing several thousand "private buildings" under Red Cross protection. The accusation was unjust because the number of the buildings in question could not have been more than a few dozen and they were all used for rescue purposes. According to an unbiased opinion Born was the most significant of all who rescued Jews in the fall of 1944.

In the spring of 1945 Friedrich Born was declared *persona non grata* by the new Hungarian Government and had to leave the country.

Carl Lutz (1895-1975)

Carl (Charles) Lutz, the Swiss consul in Budapest, played an important role in the rescue activities. He had good relations with the Germans, because in 1939/40, at the beginning of the war, he was in charge of the protection of German citizens who got stuck in Palestine and who were regarded as enemies by the British. Switzerland represented British interests in Hungary from the beginning of the war and so the issues of the Palestinian British Mandate belonged under the legation's authority as well. That was why Lutz could draw the offices organizing the emigration of Jews to Palestine under his jurisdiction. El Salvador was also represented by Switzerland, though only semiofficially. Quite often even the International Red Cross had to deal through the Swiss Embassy or the Swiss Consulate (17 Wekerle utca, today Hercegprímás utca).

The most important office of Consul Lutz's agency was at 12 Szabadság tér, in the building of the former American Embassy, at that time officially called the American Section of the Swiss

459. Charles Lutz, 1945

Embassy's Office for the Protection of Foreign Interests. Here he gave space to Miklós Krausz, who was handling the cases of those emigrating to Palestine. (Later Krausz moved his office to the nearby Glass House. After the war the building was returned to the Embassy.)

At the beginning of December 1944, when at the request of the Government most of the embassies left Budapest, Lutz remained. In consideration of his earlier personal merits, the Germans strictly instructed the Arrow-cross not to harm anyone in the ghetto while Lutz was in Pest. Some 25,000 people were given shelter in the all together 76 houses under the protection of the Swiss consulate.

To commemorate Lutz and his activities the Municipal Government of Budapest erected a statue (by Tamás Szabó) on a little square created next to the partition wall of the building at 12 Dob utca in 1991.

Angelo Rotta (1872–1965)

The Apostolic Nuncio, an elderly cardinal, was in office in Budapest since 1930, and the authority of the entire Roman Catholic Church and the Pope was behind him. Rotta did not agonize to protest in a note addressed to the Ministry of Foreign Affairs against the deportation of Jews from the provinces from the very first day, on May 15. He asked the Hungarian Government not to continue the war against the Jews that was in violation of the laws of nature and the commandments of God, and not to take steps which might force the Holy See and the conscience of the whole Christian world to protest.

460. Angelo Rotta in 1938, at the time of the Roman Catholic Eucharistic Congress held in Budapest

"I pray for the growth of this country every day, I pray that you should prosper, rejoice and be respected. But at the moment I am mostly concerned about the future. I fear that the injustice you are about to commit—let God shield us from it—shedding innocent blood might not bring God's blessing upon this country."

Rotta's conduct was exemplary at the time because while some leaders of the Roman Catholic Church in Hungary were reluctant to voice their objections clearly, or cared only about baptized Jews, he made no distinction between categories of persecuted. Though he specifically asked the Government to "exempt Christian Jews from the anti-Semitic regulations" (June 5, 1944), he took all the persecuted under his protection. He also appealed to the Vatican that they should try to pressure the Hungarian Government to take a clear stand. During the fall the office of the nuncio issued several thousand safe-conducts.

In 1992 the Hungarian Government and the Council of Roman Catholic Bishops erected a memorial slab in honor of Angelo Rotta on the wall of the building at 4–5 Dísz tér. Its inscription says: "He faithfully served his church during the hard years of the war and he took an active part in helping foreign refugees and those persecuted." There is not even a hint that the persecuted he had helped were Jews.

Margit Slachta (1884–1974)

At 69 Thököly út was the main convent of the *Szociális Testvérek Társasága* (Welfare Sisters Association). They maintained girls' homes which operated in the Catholic spirit here and at other locations. The Association was founded by Margit Slachta, the co-president of the Holy Cross Society. Under her leadership the Association gave shelter to thousands of persecuted Jews in its homes located in different parts of the town.

The *Szent Kereszt Egyesület* (Holy Cross Society) was the organization of converts, of Jews who converted to the Roman Catholic faith. It was founded in 1939 by Baron Móric Kornfeld (1882–1967), himself a convert. At this time its president was Baron Vilmos altorjai Apor (1892–1945), bishop of Győr, and its activities were organized by József Cavallier (1891–1970), a journalist. Their offices were at 10 Múzeum körút, conveniently close to the ghetto. From May 1944 on the eight-week-long preparatory courses for Jews who were to convert were held here, with some 40 people per group. It was here that an Arrow-cross patrol shot Cavallier on November 17. He was seriously wounded in the head but he survived. Apor, who in the summer of 1944 tried to arouse the conscience of the leaders of his church, became the victim of a Soviet bullet later.

461. Margit Slachta
462. Sára Salkaházi

On the left bank of the Danube, near Közraktár utca, at the Ferenc József Bridge (today Szabadság Bridge) and "Matróz csárda", a group of Jewish women were shot dead by some Arrow-cross militants on December 27, 1944. These women had been hidden in the girls' home nearby at 3 Bokréta utca, maintained by the religious order *Szociális Test-vérek* (Social Brethren) / *Katolikus Dolgozó Lányok Szövetsége* (Working Catholic Girls' Union), which belonged to Margit Slachta's organization. Together with the Jewish girls, the principal of the home, Sára Salkaházi (Schalkházi) (1899–1944) and a religion teacher, Vilma Bernovits were also killed.

A memorial slab was placed on the wall in 1989. Its inscription, unfortunately, fails to inform the reader about the sisters' role beyond vague generalities.

Gábor Sztehlo (1909-1974)

As a Lutheran pastor in Nagytarcsa and Budapest and hospital chaplain in Budapest from March to October 1944, Sztehlo was organizing the rescue of persecuted children in a rather peculiar way. In May 1944 Bishop Sándor Raffay appointed him to represent the Lutheran church at the "Good Shepherd" Committee. From this time on and especially after October 15, when József Éliás himself had to go into hiding, he supervised the activities of the child-rescue organization. This organization was part of the Budapest network of the International Red Cross.

463. Gábor Sztehlo with children in his arms

In the fall of 1944 Sztehlo set up temporary children's homes for relatively small groups of children in apartments at several locations, mainly in Buda. Upon his request some well-off families gave him their residences for that purpose and some mothers or other generous women personally not affected even offered to become the children's governesses. These homes were not always in villas, in many cases they were in apartments. In mid-October, when the Arrow-cross seized power, at Born's request Sztehlo and his family moved close to the office of the International Red Cross, into the villa of Ottó Légrády, the owner and general editor of the daily *Pester Lloyd* (to the upper, northwestern end of Lorántffy Zsuzsanna út). His office was moved to 44 Fillér utca. Around mid-September the children gathered by Sztehlo moved into the first apartment-home of the "Good Shepherd" in the house of Ottó Haggenmacher, a brewery owner and close relative of Sztehlo's wife, on Gellért-hegy at 16 Bérc utca. Gyula Muraközy, a Calvinist minister, opened the home officially by holding services there on October 5.

At the time of the ghetto the "Good Shepherd" Committee was functioning as the section "B" of the International Red Cross, though without using its badge so as not to draw attention to themselves.

From November on, some 1,700 children and about 400 adults were saved in Sztehlo's homes and by his engagement. "They were all baptized people of the Jewish race, but there were some who had not converted yet"—wrote Sztehlo in 1945. In the formulation of Emil Koren, however,

> "(...) Sztehlo's task was to help *converts*, Jews who were baptized. But as the need increased, he did not care any more whether the people he helped were baptized or not. He felt he had to help all the *persecuted* who had turned to him. (...)
>
> "(...) In many homes people from different social classes came together: aristocrats and proletarians, wholesale merchants and some petty bourgeoisie, illegal communists and rightists. For us all that mattered was whether their child needed help, whether he or she was persecuted or abandoned. If the answer was yes, we gave them shelter."

Pastor Koren's testimony is verified by recollections of the former children. According to these, the "Good Shepherd" never tried to gain over, let alone to convert or baptize them. In the "Good Shepherd" children's homes more than 400 assistants took care of the children; some of them were persecuted themselves. A good number of the rescued children are still alive, just past their prime.

Most of the 30 or 50 shelter-homes of the "Good Shepherd" Committee were located in the apparently less dangerous Buda. One of them was at 52 Városmajor utca, in a modern Bauhaus-style building designed by Gábor Preisich. In 1944/45 he lived in the house himself. 18 Jewish children and 8 mothers lived through the months of the Arrow-cross frenzy on the third floor of the building, in a large apartment and in the neighboring house (54 Városmajor utca). The director of the shelter was his wife, he himself became an employee, the heater of the home. Seventy people were hiding at 33 Lovas út, which earlier had sheltered some escaped French prisoners of war. Twenty-two girls found shelter at 37 Tamás utca, in the home of Tivadar Homonnay (1888–1964), the former Mayor of Budapest who resigned after the German occupation. In late December and early January Sztehlo moved some thirty children from the shell-struck houses to the cellar of his home, the Légrády villa on Lorántffy Zsuzsanna út, and was hiding them there while in the streets the Germans were shooting at the besieging Soviet troops.

Sztehlo's memorial plaque, the work of Tamás Vigh, was erected in 1984 in the Castle, on the outside wall of the German Lutheran Church at 28 Táncsics Mihály utca. (The church itself is the work of Mór Kallina from 1895.) The plaque was placed right next to the entrance of the vestry of Emil Koren, who actively assisted Sztehlo in his "Good Shepherd" mission. The commemorative inscription says:

> "Behold the olive-tree,
> Gábor Sztehlo's tree,
> planted on December 2, 1984, in Jerusalem,
> in the garden of the righteous gentiles."

Raoul Wallenberg (1912–1947?)

Raoul (Raul) Gustav Wallenberg, the Third Secretary of the Swedish Royal Embassy, arrived to Budapest on July 9, 1944. He was appointed "Humanitarian attaché" and was entrusted with a special task, namely to try by all possible means to save the lives of those who were persecuted by the National Socialists and whose lives were in jeopardy. He brought only 600 blank Swedish passports with him, for those 600 businessmen who had Swedish relatives. On top of that he was planning to help a wagonful of orphans escape to Sweden. Initially his trip appeared to be merely a risky adventure, but very soon it turned out to be a serious mission. Wallenberg quickly grew up to the challenge awaiting him in Budapest.

It seems that the idea of sending Wallenberg to Budapest was the brainchild of some representatives of the international Jewish organizations. Most probably they covered his costs as well. Wallenberg's appointment was formally based on an exchange of telegrams between King Gustav V and

Regent Miklós Horthy. It bears some symbolic meaning that before Wallenberg left for Hungary, R. Marcus Ehrenpreis recited the priestly blessing over the young diplomat who came from an aristocratic Calvinist family.

The Humanitarian Office of the Swedish Embassy was at 2–4 Üllői út, only two blocks from the edge of the ghetto. This is where the protective passes (*Schutzpass*) were issued, and here was the *Schützling Protokoll* too, the office in charge

464. Raoul Wallenberg's driving license issued in Budapest

of recording and trying to find missing persons. Initially this office was on Naphegy, at 2 Tigris utca, but they moved to Pest in October 1944. Both of these offices, like all other embassies and consulates later, were full of refugees. The Humanitarian Office used some other spaces as well, at 3 Mihály utca, at 3 Dezső utca, and 30 Ráth György utca in Buda; the Pest locations were at 15 Vámház körút and 1 Jókai utca. The Swedish Embassy itself was on the Gellért-hegy, at 10 Gyopár utca, but very soon they expanded, moving into the neighboring villa at 1/A Minerva utca (on the corner of Gyopár utca, today Kelenhegyi út, and Minerva utca). (Initially the protective passes were issued here.) The social care department worked at 16 Arany János utca and there was a food warehouse at 8 Szentkirályi utca. Wallenberg wanted to get as many people as possible out of the Yellow-star Houses and place them under the direct protection of the Embassy, so in November they started using more buildings, among others 16 Révay utca, where most of the Embassy staff lived, and 21–23 Személynök utca (today Balassi Bálint utca). All of these addresses were Wallenberg's offices. Others

who carried out the numerous tasks coordinated by Wallenberg were working in the Üllői út building and at 6 Harmincad utca. Here, the building of the Hazai Bank, even its safe room, was full of people protected by Wallenberg. Wallenberg himself often changed residences and had several addresses at the same time. The address given on his Hungarian driving license issued to him on November 8, 1944 was 6–11 Ostrom utca, but actually he stayed at the following apartments: 9/B Elek utca; 3 Dezső utca; 5 Madách Imre út, 6th floor (around Christmas); Har-

465. Raoul Wallenberg in his office, November 26, 1944. Photo by Tamás Veres

mincad utca; 17 Múzeum utca—6 Reviczky utca, a house with entrances from two streets (Károlyi Palace, today National Technical Library) (on New Year's Eve); then again Harmincad utca and finally probably at 16 Benczúr utca, one of the offices of the International Red Cross, section "T" (transport). In the end he did not stay at the same place two nights in a row.

Wallenberg was moving around the city with infinite personal courage in his small car (a Studebaker, license plate no. AY 152) driven by an equally courageous driver, Vilmos Langfelder, a Jewish man, engineer. A photographer, Tamás Veres, documented his actions comprehensively. Wearing a broad-brim Eden hat and a raincoat, later a blue winter-coat, Wallenberg always managed to show up exactly where he was needed; he came unarmed, but was always able to help. He quickly understood how things worked in Hungary, he learned how to deal with the Hungarian police, how to deal with benevolent or corrupt officials. He helped, acting quickly and firmly, by supplying food and medicine, passes and money, sometimes specifically by bribing. Towards the end of November he, like others, brought truckloads of food, medicine, warm clothing to the people on forced marches along the roads of Hungary towards the western border, easing their pain. Sometimes the supplies were delivered at night, distributed in pouring rain, at the light of small torches. At the end of

466. Statue in honor of Raoul Wallenberg by Pál Pátzay, 1949

November and beginning of December he had to go to the Józsefváros Railway Station every single day to try to retrieve from the deportation trains at least those who had Swedish documents or those to whom he could give such documents on the spot. On November 23, November 28 (this one is commemorated in György Somlyó's novel, *Rámpa*), December 10 and on some other trips as well he was even able to bring back a few people from Hegyeshalom, retrieve them from the death march. On Christmas eve Arrow-cross people gathered some people from the Swedish protected houses and put them in a train at the Józsefváros Railway Station—this was the last deportation train. Wallenberg managed to get these people off the train after it had already left. The gendarmes sometimes chased him away from the trains threatening him with their machine gun, on other occasions the Germans promised him a car accident. Yet his personal courage remained undaunted. He was last seen on January 17, 1945, around noon, in Budapest on the corner of Aréna út and Benczúr utca.

He was on his way to Debrecen, to the headquarters of the Red Army—only to disappear in a Soviet prison or concentration camp...

Wallenberg's figure has grown to become a symbol of the survival and rescue of the Jews of Budapest.

Honoring Wallenberg, a street on the territory of the international ghetto, the former Phönix utca, has been renamed after Wallenberg right in 1945 (Wallenberg utca, from 1946 on Raoul Wallenberg utca). A memorial plaque was placed there in 1989, a stylized portrait in bronze relief with a commemorative inscription, work of Gerő Bottos. A bronze statue of Wallenberg was made by Pál Pátzay in 1949, called "*Kígyóölő* / The Snake Killer". It was meant to stand also in the former international ghetto, in Szent István park, it was set up, but disappeared mysteriously in the night before its unveiling. After some time the statue showed up in Debrecen, in the courtyard of a pharmaceutical factory. Here, of course, the figure received a completely different meaning. A new statue of Wallenberg, work of Imre Varga, stands, for some unknown reason, in Buda, on Pasarét.

*

כל המאבד נפש אחת מישראל מעלה עליו הכתוב כאלו אבד עולם מלא
וכל המקיים נפש אחת מישראל מעלה עליו הכתוב כאלו קיים עולם מלא

"Whoever has caused a single soul to perish from Israel
Scripture imputes it to him
as though he had caused a whole world to perish.
And whoever saves alive a single soul from Israel
Scripture imputes it to him
as though he had saved alive a whole world."

(Mishnah, Sanhedrin 4,5—ed. by Hanoch Albeck,
English translation after Herbert Danby)

"Whoever has caused a single soul to perish from the mankind
Scripture imputes it to him
as though he had caused a whole world to perish.
And whoever saves alive a single soul from the mankind
Scripture imputes it to him
as though he had saved alive a whole world."

(Sanhedrin 4,5—ed. by Philip Blackman)

Carl Lutz, Sára Salkaházi, Margit Slachta, Gábor Sztehlo and Raoul Wallenberg were declared to be among the *hasidei ummot ha-olam* by the Yad Vashem, the institute for the preservation of the memory and the scholarly research of the Holocaust in Jerusalem. (For the name, *yad va-shem*, "hand and name" see Isaiah 5,4, referring to a memorial place.)

The same honorable title was given to the Italian cattle merchant from Trieste, Giorgio (Jorge) Perlasca (1910–1992) for his activities in Budapest. He came to Budapest on business back in 1943 and remained here after the Italian armistice. As an Italian, he was himself in danger in Budapest. He joined the Spanish Embassy staff, received Spanish citizenship on October 13, 1944, changed his Italian first name for the Spanish Jorge, and was engaged in supervising the Spanish protected houses. When the first secretary of the Spanish Embassy left Budapest on November 30, 1944, Perlasca started to act in the empty Embassy (11/B Eötvös utca) as if he were the Spanish attaché, as if he had real accreditation.

There were people in Budapest, too, who received this honor: the sculptor Béni Ferenczy (1890–1967) and his wife, Erzsébet Ferenczy; Sára Karig (1914–), later an outstanding translator and editor; the Lutheran pastor Emil Koren and his wife, Margit Koren (Podhradszky); the Calvinist pastor, Elek Máthé (1895–1968), instructor of Greek and Latin at the Calvinist High School, and his wife, Klára Máthé, who were both on the staff of the life-saving department of the International Red Cross during the war; László Michnay, President of the Adventist Church, who offered a shelter for 50 persecuted people in the home of the church on Dorozsmai út; the former Minister of Defense Vilmos nagybaczoni Nagy; the writer Géza Ottlik (1912–1990) (he received into his apartment the poet István Vas); the artist György Ruzicskay (1896–1993); the painter István Szőnyi (1894–1960), and his wife, Rózsa Szőnyi; and many others. For the time being, more than three hundred persons from Hungary are among the righteous gentiles of the world—including their family members, it comes to more than four hundred people all together.

(9) Protected Houses

November 15: In spite of all, the Government started to set up the ghetto. Since they had to respect the protective documents issued by foreign embassies, they ordered that people with such documents should move into separate houses designated for them. Based on agreements with the embassies of the neutral countries, these houses were under the protection of the country to which it belonged. This was why they were called "protected houses". Five houses were protected by the International Red Cross. The Arrow-cross Government hoped that in return for this gesture the neutral

countries would officially recognize Szálasi and his regime in Hungary, but this did not happen. The Jewish World Congress, however, issued a statement in November 1944 thanking the Vatican, Sweden and Switzerland for their extraordinary help in saving European Jews.

Most of the protected houses were in the "little ghetto", in the southern part of Új-Lipótváros, around Pozsonyi út and Szent István körút. Those holding an affidavit of a foreign country and waiting to leave Hungary had to move here, to the Palatinus Houses before November 20. This move caused some dissatisfaction, if not outrage, among the local Jewish

467. "Swedish" protected people on Szent István körút, December, 1944

population, because Jews not holding an affidavit had to move out of their own apartments and into houses marked with the six-pointed star in Erzsébetváros, in order to empty space for those holding one. Many were taken from the "little ghetto" straight to the brickyards, destined for forced labor service. Most people, however, tried to dupe the Arrow-cross militants, producing false affidavits or trying to hide. Those wishing to move into protected houses often could not find a place for themselves. There should have been more protected houses. Instead, more and more people were squeezed into the houses; soon there was not much difference between the conditions in the protected houses and the "large ghetto", which was opened two weeks later. In fact, as time passed, it seemed that the survival opportunities in the "large ghetto" were better.

Here are the addresses of some of the protected houses in the "little ghetto", according to a list of the gendarmerie from November 14, 1944.

6 Tátra utca: The primary office of the Swedish Embassy. This is where the cases of protected people were handled and the management of the protected houses organized: medical care, food and drugs, keeping contact with officials, mostly for the sake of locating people who had disappeared—taken captive by the Arrow-cross in the street or taken away from apartments. (According to their records only 52 out of 700 people reported missing were found, the others were most probably shot along the river bank by the Arrow-cross.) The office functioned until this area of the city was liberated on January 16.

14–16 Tátra utca: The hospital of the Swedish Embassy. It opened on December 2 with fifty beds, partially to relieve overcrowding at the Swedish emergency hospital at 13 Akácfa utca. There was an outpatient care, too. Anyone in need was admitted to this hospital. Many of those who collapsed during one of the death marches were brought here.

29 Wahrmann Mór utca (today Victor Hugo utca): Swedish hospital for contagious diseases.

7/A–B Hollán Ernő utca: Swedish protected houses

3 Kárpát utca: Swedish protected house

10/A, 14, 21, 23/A, 24 and 31 Katona József utca: Swedish protected houses

26, 28, 39 and 41 Katona József utca: Swiss protected houses

39 Légrády Károly utca (today Balzac utca): Swedish protected house; 43: Swedish protected house for Dutch citizens represented by Sweden; 48/B Swedish protected house for citizens of Argentina represented by Sweden

8, 15, 17/A–B and 36 Pannónia utca: Swedish protected houses

44 and 48 Pannónia utca: Spanish protected houses

7 Phönix utca (today Raoul Wallenberg utca): designated as a Swedish protected house, but occupied by Arrow-cross members

1, 3, 4, 5, 7, 10, 12, 14, 15–17 and 22 Pozsonyi út: Swedish protected houses

16 and 23 Pozsonyi út: protected houses of the International Red Cross

20, 24 and 30 Pozsonyi út: protected houses of the Vatican

28 Pozsonyi út: house "privileged" by the Regent (!), later a Swiss protected house

32, 33/A, 35, 36, 39, 40, 42, 49 and 54 Pozsonyi út: Swiss protected houses

35 Szent István park: Spanish protected house

40, 43 and 45 Sziget utca (today Radnóti Miklós utca): Swiss protected houses

41 Sziget utca: house privileged by the Regent (!)

4 Tátra utca: International Red Cross, later Swiss protected house

5/A Tátra utca: Swiss protected house

6, 12/A, 14 (second floor) and 15/A–B Tátra utca: Swedish protected houses

5 Újpesti rakpart: Portuguese protected house

7 Újpesti rakpart: Swiss protected house

32 Wahrmann Mór utca (today Victor Hugo utca): protected house of the Vatican

And so on.

The Regent issued privileges at special requests for some people who now fell under the (Anti-)Jewish Laws but who had outstanding scholarly, artistic, economic achievements to their credit or who filled prominent public roles. From March to June 1944 the Minister of Interior was in charge of these requests, afterwards the Prime Minister himself and, on August 22, the Prime Minister issued a general order regulating this issue. The office at 5 Tárnok utca issued such exemptions for altogether 3,000 people. After October 15 the Szálasi-government acknowledged only about one tenth of these, thus only one tenth of the exempted persons and their families were allowed to move into the houses privileged by the Regent. Altogether some 8,000 people enjoyed the protection of the Regent or the Minister of Interior, whether it was they themselves who fell under the current legal category of a "Jew" or their spouse. Among them were several prominent Hungarian scholars, such as András Alföldi, ancient historian, an expert on the archaeology of the Roman province of Pannonia; Ervin Baktay, expert on Indian art and civilization; Ödön Beke, linguist; the writer Marcell Benedek and his children; Géza Fehér, archaeologist, an expert on early Hungarian history; Dávid Raphael (Fokos-)Fuchs, linguist; Lipót Fejér, mathematician; Tibor Germán, professor of internal diseases; Károly Goldziher, a professor at the Technical University; Károly Marót, Greek classical philologist and professor of history of religions; Gyula Moravcsik, professor of Byzantinology and expert on Greek sources of Hungarian history; Frigyes Riesz, mathematician; Bence Szabolcsi, music historian; Károly Visky, expert on Hungarian folklore. Furthermore, there were some prominent writers and artists, among them Géza Csorba (sculptor), Adolf Fényes (painter) and Milán Füst (poet), as well as Gyula Gózon (actor), Miklós Ligeti, the sculptor of the statue (1903) of the first Hungarian chronicler, Anonymus located in Városliget (City Park), Mihály Székely (opera singer), Ede Telcs (sculptor), J. Jenő Tersánszky (writer), Leó Weiner (composer) and many others. Either themselves, or their wives were Jewish. None of them tried to flee. On November 15 the Arrow-cross regime ordered a review of the exemptions. Szálasi re-issued exemptions to only 70 people, his Minister of Interior, to another 501.

Instead of the writer Jenő Heltai (a relative of Herzl), his son and the actress Gizi Bajor submitted an application. When Heltai found out about it, he wrote the following letter to the under-secretary of state concerned:

"I do not have any special merits and I never requested any kind of privileges for myself. I have always accepted what fate had in store for me. I received many good things from this country in which I live, in whose language I write. Now I have to accept the bad, too. I would betray my entire past, if now, at the end of a long life, I appealed for a more favorable situation for myself than what is due to hundreds of thousands of my fellow-men. I will never do so, not even if those who love me and care about me suffer as a result. I am not handing in this request."

And from the will of J. Jenő Tersánszky, dated December 4, 1944:

"It is certainly possible that the henchmen of the present unlawful Hungarian Government (...) will kill me. They have an excuse to do so. My wife, with whom I spent twenty-four years sharing our work and mutually supporting each other, got baptized only after March 22, 1944, which was too late, according to the shameful and unlawful government decree. So far the exemption issued by the Horthy Government protected her at least to the extent that she could live with me in our apartment that we had obtained with hard work. This exemption was annulled on November 15 and now, according to the new regulation, my wife has to attach a yellow star upon her clothing and move out of our apartment into the ghetto within two days. (...) I decided with clear mind and strong will that I am going to resist the forces which are trying to take my wife away from me. If I manage to shoot at least one of these evil people, I will provide an example of what I think is now the just dessert of my fellow-Hungarians. (...) As a soldier who fought throughout the World War [I], I consider it my duty to make at least this exemplary gesture."

(Quoted by László Berza, in: *Évkönyv*, 1983/84)

The protected houses, the forced residence of exempted individuals, were not surrounded by any fence and were not watched by the police. They did not have a separate administration. And yet they were part of the ghetto, too. The people who lived here were persecuted, even if they were under international protection. As a matter of fact, protected houses enjoyed the same status as the Yellow-star Houses.

"In these once luxurious apartments, much like out there in the wagons, some 10–15 people piled up in each room; no *Lebensraum* was left to these bodies, whose vapors converged, in the mostly female essence of 'vital biological material'. This last phrase, as he found out at a later point, was used by the Grand Master of Deportation to denote the highly organized mass of human-shaped protein, the object of the Final Solution. The same person invented the first and primary slogan of the Final Solution: Cram them together, like herrings in a box. The comparison with the wagons, however, was a little hasty; it expressed the despair of the first moment rather than the actual situation. Here each body had some space of its own. It was tight, but there was even room to stretch our feet, usually lying on our coat and backpack. Heads to the wall and feet meeting in the middle of the room, but in a stretched position. It really wasn't as jam-packed as the wagons, not even as jam-packed as a herring box. And the door was open. (...) So here I am, at 39 Pozsonyi út."

(György Somlyó, *Rámpa* [The Ramp. A Novel], 1984)

The curfew imposed on Jews affected those in the international ghetto, too. They were, as the order said, "allowed to walk around the neighborhood between 8 and 9 a.m.". They could go as far as the Nagykörút, but there were armed Arrow-cross men everywhere in the streets.

There were some protected houses outside of the international ghetto, for instance at 21 Esterházy utca (today 3 Öt Pacsirta utca, Károlyi Palace) and the house across the street, no. 42 (today 2 Öt Pacsirta utca, Andrássy–Almásy Palace). Both were Swedish houses.

By the fall of 1944 all kinds of international identification documents were in circulation in Budapest, mostly in Hungarian and German, and most of them promised their owners a modicum of security. The best one was the regular foreign passport with hard cover. Moreover, some embassies issued temporary passports, valid for one trip only. And finally there were the Swiss protective passes (*Schutzbrief*), issued mostly at the Glass House as a result of the bright idea of Miklós Krausz, which certified that the person holding it was a Swiss citizen and thus under the protection of the Swiss Embassy. The Swedish protective passes (*skyddsbrev*) were similar. These three documents had a photo and a seal, naturally. An equally valid document was an emigration visa issued by Hungarian authorities or an immigration certificate to Palestine, which was issued by the Swiss Embassy from early June on. A more peculiar document was the collective passport. Each of them bore the names of 200 persons, later occasionally even a thousand, and those whose names were listed received a certificate (*Bescheinigung*) to prove it. Generally the collective passport covered entire families, too.

In a fury the German Embassy reported to Berlin on June 29 that the Swiss Embassy requested emigration documents for 7,000 families (for 40,000 persons) rather than 7,000 individuals, arguing that it was an oversight. By January, 1945 Wallenberg's office was even issuing "preliminary passports (*Vorpass*)" and "white passes" which attested that the passport of the person holding it was "in the making".

A Christian-Jewish quip from 1944:

"What does the inscription INRI mean on the cross?

"**I** am in transit to **N**azareth to **R**eorganize my **I**dentification papers. (*Indulok Názáretbe Rendezni az Iratokat.*)"

Foreign citizens had to report to the *Külföldieket Ellenőrző Országos Központi Hatóság* (Office for Aliens' Control, кеокн) regularly. This institution was actually set up in 1930 to control refugees and other foreign citizens staying in Hungary. The residence permits were issued by its officials, and always only for thirty days. Foreign citizens also received a certificate that, since they were not citizens of Hungary, they were not obliged to wear the yellow star as Hungarian laws required. This office was set up originally as a discriminating xenophobic measure, so following the enactment of the (Anti-)Jewish Laws it focused on Jews. The "homeless" and "refugees" who were to be controlled were for the most part Jews, anyway, from the Carpatho-Ukraine and Poland. The кеокн office was in the building of the *Vámház* (Customs Office) at 8 Fővám tér (today Budapest University of Economics). In the fall of 1944 it was a major undertaking for Jews to get there. Since they were not allowed to take the streetcar, they had to walk all the way from Pozsonyi út to Ferenc József híd (today Szabadság híd / Bridge), exposed to the violence of the Arrow-cross men.

The Swiss and Swedish Embassies were not the only places where passports and all kinds of identification papers were issued to persecuted Jews. The International Red Cross and the Vatican also supplied such documents, as well as the Spanish (11/B Eötvös utca) and the Portuguese Embassies (37 Váci utca) and consulates (initially on the Danube bank, later at 9 Zrínyi utca, finally in Hotel Ritz). El Salvador—represented by Georges Mandel-Mantello, first secretary of the Republic's consulate in Geneva, whose post was in Budapest since 1943—issued real citizenship certificates, not just passports, and Nicaragua also gave some protective passes.

These documents were usually not issued for free. After the War many people admitted that they simply could not afford to buy a *Schutzpass*.

There are no reliable data on how many foreign papers were issued altogether. The Swiss Embassy was probably the one to issue the largest number of documents—7,800 individual and 4 collective passports—but it was also the Swiss who acted on behalf of British and American citizens and on behalf of El Salvador, too. Finally Consul Lutz consented to the distribution of all 30,000 of the documents that were available. The Swedish Embassy issued 4,500 passports, other kinds of certificates and some 8,000 pieces of the *Schutzpass* which certified that the person holding it was listed on a collective passport. Beyond these photo identification documents they also issued some lists of people who were under protection, without a photo. These other kinds of documents were invented to protect the validity of real passports from false ones. Some 18,500 of the emigration certificates were issued. According to official data the Vatican issued 2,500 genuine passports (in reality it was 15,000), Portugal 700 (actually, 800) and Spain 100 passports. Turkey also issued a few protective documents.

Apart from the authentic documents all kinds of false documents were used. The papers of the International Red Cross were actually duplicates, anyway. At 65 Paulay Ede utca there was a printing house, where legal and illegal papers were printed alike. The Swedish *Schutzpass* was printed at the Antiqua Printing House with great care. Wallenberg always saw to it that the value of original Swedish papers should not be jeopardized by all kinds of forged ones, but he did not stop them from manufacturing more of the originals. Dávid Löbl's bibliophile printing house, the Officina, at that time under the direction of Imre Román, was able to produce all kinds of forms on short notice. But the most successful document makers were the Zionist co-workers of the International Red Cross.

The organization issued some 1,300 photo identification documents for its members, which were also protective documents. These co-workers were engaged full-time in producing documents. They printed in the Glass House, in attics and cellars and wherever they could. (Their haste sometimes resulted in carelessness: on one of the Swiss promissory notes they printed "Susse" instead of "Suisse"; the mistake brought some people into trouble.) Others prepared their own documents at home. There were forged document workshops all over the city.

Authentic Hungarian papers were in demand, too.

"Many forged papers were in use in those days, and if these were examined, it often had fatal consequences. Sára Karig learned all the tricks of document-making (...) She got hold of some original papers. They were mostly birth certificates, ecclesiastic and state ones, which proved our *Aryan* background. We used special chemicals to wash off the original data from the papers and filled in fresh data. Of course, we had to know what had been registered and in which way in the documents at their original place of issue. In my little room all the windows, mirrors and walls were covered with drying documents. Obtaining these chemicals was not an easy task in those days, either. The chemists knew exactly what these materials were good for."

(Mária Székely, apud: Sándor Szenes, *Befejezetlen múlt* [Unfinished Past], 1986)

Everyone tried to have several documents, to be on the safe side. Looking at the numbers it seems that most people were only able to get false papers. The number of false papers reached a couple of hundred thousand. (According to these data, everyone possessed at least a few of the documents, whether original or false.) The false Swiss papers alone numbered around 60,000. A passport, of course, was only useful in the protected houses and in the international ghetto. The real value of a false paper only revealed itself in the street, and as time passed it was increasingly a matter of luck which papers the Arrow-cross men accepted and which they did not.

On October 31 Carl Lutz and Raoul Wallenberg visited the Hungarian Ministry of Foreign Affairs, where they were informed that a decision was passed according to which, "to the greatest sorrow of the Hungarian Government, all Jewish persons would be treated equally after November 15". Indeed, these threatening words came true a few weeks later.

November 23: Officials ordered that Jewish children be removed even from the children's homes and moved into the ghetto. The International Red Cross insisted that children who are taken away from their care should be housed in buildings where the sanitary conditions were appropriate. By setting such entirely legitimate but in those times impossible requirements they were able to achieve that even those children who had already been moved into the ghetto could be taken back to the children's homes.

Gábor Sztehlo was allowed to enter the ghetto for negotiations with the Red Cross.

"A gloomy sight awaited me in the ghetto. I have seen so much poverty and anguish recently that I thought I was already used to it. But what I saw here was more than what I had ever seen before and very different, too. These people have reached this state during the past 3–4 months. The children, who had been running around happily only 4 months ago, were now standing back against the wall and watching anxiously the foreign black car. The women, dressed in clothes which had seen better days, turned towards the walls so that the guard should not see their inquisitive eyes. Apart from poverty, dirt and resignation, horror and fear ruled over this place, and this was the hardest to bear. The windows were generally of wood and paper, not glass. There was hardly a man visible in the desolate streets. (...) In the room where we arrived Hungarian policemen awaited us in blue uniforms. There were no Arrow-cross men or soldiers, it seemed that those were only guarding the ghetto at its wooden gates. The room was cold, dim and hostile as was the policeman who ordered the elders of the ghetto to be brought in. I will never forget that scene as those six or seven broken old men entered in their worn clothes, tired, sad..."

(*Isten kezében* [In God's Hands], 1984)

November 29: The Royal Hungarian Minister of Interior agreed to the request of the German authorities that Budapest supply further forced labor battalions to Germany. Among the people who were now destined to go on the *Todesmarsch* were some from the international ghetto as well as people with Swiss documents. Wallenberg managed to save the "Swedish" Jews. One of the transit camps from where the Ravensbrück transport left on December 1 was a lumberyard in Kőbánya, at 10 Kőbányai út.

(10) Red Danube

The Arrow-cross Party occupied several buildings around Budapest. 2 Szent István körút was taken over by the Arrow-cross, and so was 33/B Pozsonyi út, 7 Phönix utca, 12–14 Városház utca (the killers in Jókai utca came from here), 19 Teréz körút and 49 Erzsébet körút, where the section in charge of collecting the assets for the Party (*Vagyongyűjtő Osztály*) was located. There were Arrow-cross houses in Buda, too, for example at 48 Kapás utca, 37 Városmajor utca, 5 Németvölgyi út, etc. The main party building was 60 Andrássy út, the *Hűség Háza* (House of Fidelity), a notorious address already then. At the formation of the Hungarian National Socialist Party in 1937 Szálasi gave this address, the second floor, as the headquarters.

The Arrow-cross unleashed terror on the streets already on October 16. The people living at 14 Csengery utca were caught in the street and shot on the spot. Jews living at 31 Népszínház utca and 4 Teleki tér tried to resist, but they, too, were shot. Tisza Kálmán tér and Teleki tér were covered with corpses, bodies of those who tried to resist.

During the night of December 22, just before Budapest was completely surrounded, Eichmann left the capital by plane. The previous evening he paid his last visit to 12 Síp utca, without any apparent reason, in the company of armed soldiers. He may have meant it as a threat, to show that he was still there.

November 23: This was the first day that the case diary of the ambulance mentions that during the night someone was thrown into the Danube from the river bank, in front of 6 Margit rakpart (today Bem rakpart). From this day on executions were carried out regularly along the Danube bank at night, between Lánchíd (Chain Bridge) and Árpád híd (Árpád Bridge) as well as in Újpest, at Meder utca. The German authorities warned the Minister of Interior that these nightly shootings caused anxiety among the population and requested that they be suspended. The answer was that the Government had no influence over those events.

On December 27 a plenipotentiary of the "Leader of the Nation" returned—by a German courier airplane—to Pest to mobilize all Arrow-cross groups "in order to provide better protection for the city". But the Arrow-cross preferred to plunder. "All the Jews must be killed, and that's it", sounded the command from their "Leader". And the Arrow-cross units vied with each other to follow the order. These armed but unsupervised troops set out on raids from the Arrow-cross houses to the neighborhood of Pozsonyi út. Whomever they caught in the street was dragged to the Arrow-cross houses. After asking for people's documents the armed Arrow-cross militants often simply tore up the paper. Then they dragged people to the Danube bank and told them that they would not need those documents any longer, anyway.

The director of the Forensic Medical Institute declared after the war in a statement before the court:

"The Arrow-cross people killed their victims with bestial methods. Only very few were simply shot, most people were horribly tortured beforehand. Most people suffered for a long time before they died, as the terrible grimaces frozen on their faces seem to indicate. There were only few cases when the brain or the heart was shot; in most cases the cruel wounds indicate long sufferings. (...) On the corpses that were found naked, there were traces of beatings, bruises on the heads, faces. There were men and women of all age groups, even children and infants. These corpses were found and taken to the Institute a few days before Christmas. At that time (...) the police still made an effort to bring the corpses from the streets over here."

A survivor, Eva Bentley stated forty years later, in 1985 in London:

"Then the Danube was not blue but brown, red. Red from the blood of Jews."

After December 24, during the last weeks the regime of terror of the Arrow-cross reached its climax in Pest. They did not hesitate to attack the diplomatically protected houses in the international ghetto. At the end of December they dragged the residents of 30 Pozsonyi út to the street and shot them into the Danube. At dawn on January 8 and on the following days the 266 people who took refuge in the house at 1 Jókai utca (since then called "the death house") were taken to the Arrow-cross house in Városház utca. Some of them were then escorted to the ghetto, while others, some 180 persons, were intimidated, tortured, stripped of their clothing and of all their valuables and then shot in the courtyard of the house at 10 Petőfi Sándor utca or along the Danube bank. Many of those hiding in the neighboring buildings were murdered, too. The Swedish Embassy's food supply office was at 1 Jókai utca and, on the first floor, there used to be a restaurant. Many people tried to hide here in the final days of the war.

"(...) Her husband (...) was taken to the Danube bank in the winter of 1944. (...) He had stored his dearest treasure, his six exquisite pairs of shoes, all unique in their own way, wrapped in socks, to protect them from the tiniest grit of dust. He took them out of the socks occasionally and talked to them, while polishing them carefully. You can imagine that it was his shoes he was most concerned about, when he had to leave them on the icy Danube bank, because this pair has always been shiny... Years later my grandmother Liza noticed a similar pair of shoes on a man in the streetcar. Her heart started to pound faster, for she could have sworn that the shoes on the casually crossed legs of the man in the streetcar sitting right across had been his. She followed the man as he got off, and before the stranger could disappear in a building, she questioned him. He was smiling at her, as if he had been under some secret protection. In fact, before shutting the door in Liza's face, he was even so generous as to provide my grandmother with the information that he remembered someone from 1944, a weird fellow, who was already entirely naked, yet he was still holding on to his shoes, shouting that there must have been a misunderstanding, that he was a decorated Hungarian lieutenant in reserve." (Ágnes Hankiss, *Halottaskönyv* [Book of the Dead], 1993)

On a drawing of the artist Margit Anna, widow of Imre Ámos, lots of empty shoes are lined up on the Danube embankment: a graphic recollection.[4] In a recent novel the hero, a young girl, says passionately on the bank of Danube: "I do not want to know Yiddish!" (Zsuzsa Forgács, *Talált nő* [Woman Found], 1997).

On the Pest bank of the Danube, North of Margaret Bridge, there is a memorial for the victims of these murders. Further to the North, already in Angyalföld, close to Vizafogó, there is another memorial. Halfway between the two, on the western side of Bessenyei utca, in a small park right near the water the Hungarian Zionist Alliance and hundreds of their friends built a pyramid of stones in April 1994, in memory of the fighters and martyrs of the Zionist movement.

(11) The Glass House (29 Vadász utca)

Beyond the international ghetto there were some other buildings reserved for the protection of Jews, in the care of one of the foreign embassies or the International Red Cross. One such building was the *Üvegház* (Glass House), which had belonged to the Swiss Embassy. After July 24 it was officially called the *Svájci Követség Idegen Érdekek Képviselete Kivándorlási Osztály* (Swiss Embassy's Office for the Protection of Foreign Interests, Emigration Division).

---

[4] "Az elkésett Messiás, 1944. A Dunánál" [The Messiah Is Late, 1944. At the Danube], 1985 (Szentendre, "Imre Ámos" Museum, Margit Anna Collection).

Arthur Weiss, the manager of the company, offered the fine building—with the consent of the co-owners who had moved to Palestine already earlier—to the Swiss consulate for the purpose of housing the Palestine Office. This is how it became a refuge for so many. The Glass House as an institution was organized by the leaders of the *Va'adah*, Ottó Komoly and his deputies, back in June. The director of the office was Miklós (Moshe) Krausz, a Hungarian Orthodox and a committed Zionist, and

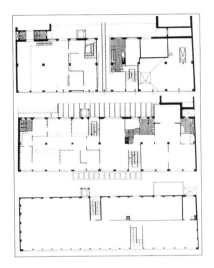

Mihály Salamon (1897–?), who was a leading figure in the rescue operations of the Mizrahi, the religious Zionist group. (The word *mizrahi* means "from the East", but the name of the movement comes from the abbreviation of *merkaz ruhani*, "spiritual center". This Zionist religious organization was formed in 1904 in Pozsony or Pressburg, today Bratislava, Slovakia.) Approximately fifty people were employed as staff. Theoretically only people already holding an immigration certificate were allowed to move in here, those who were about to leave for Palestine, or those waiting for a certificate; but then again who was not waiting for a certificate in those days? The certificate was often just an excuse to move into a safe place. But even this safe place had to be protected sometimes from the intervention of Polish and Slovak refugees and the undaunted *Ha-Shomer ha-Tza'ir* members. (By the end of September Weiss and Krausz were already about to call the police and have them thrown out of the building because they feared that their actions would threaten the relative security of other refugees, too.) Altogether some 3,000 people found asylum here in those infernal months. At times, around November, a police cordon guarded the building, not letting anyone to enter or to leave.

468. Facade of the Glass House, designed by Lajos Kozma, 1935

469. Glass House: ground-plan. From top to bottom: ground, second and third floors

470. Glass House: second floor hallway

471. Glass House: second floor, landing of the staircase

"The huge glass windows of the Glass House are glittering peacefully in the silence of the street. After the past weeks (...) this shiny little jewel and its deserted entrance among the massive stone walls somehow soothe the nerves. As you enter (...) you are confronted with unexpected dimensions. Left of the entrance a huge hall opens, in the back an enormous door, almost a gate, leads to the courtyard. This is a store, this is where customers must have been served. In the front corner of the room, left of the entrance, there is a small cabin, maybe the doorman's post or a tiny office. In the back to the right, close to the staircase, there is another cabin with a simple table. Behind the cabin a temporary handwritten poster: *Svájci követség idegen érdekeket képviselő osztálya* [Swiss Embassy's Office for the Protection of Foreign Interests]. (...) The whole room is made of glass. Doors, windows, walls—everything immaculately clean, made of transparent glass. Punctilious cleanliness all over the place. Narrow, winding, glowing glass steps lead from the spacious room to an improbably small passage. The walls of the staircase are covered with blocks of marble of different colors. The walls of the foyer, glittering like black diamond, are inscribed with raised golden letters announcing the owner, "Gyula Weiss Jr." and the year when his company came into existence. This foyer is so small that entering the two huge, impressive and surprisingly elegant halls on each side, it feels like "open sesame" in the tale. To the left is the conference room, an unexpectedly long and proportionately wide room, with glass windows to the street as well as to the courtyard. The white of the two sidewalls merges with the white of the ceiling and the built-in shelves and doors. There are only a few pieces of furniture which make the hall look even more elegant. In front of the glass wall facing the courtyard there is a desk, along the hall a long conference table with chairs, some stands at the side. The door is white from inside but it is glittering black on the outside. It opens only from the inside. It is a real conference hall. The enormous office to the right is made purely of glass to its least nook, even its bright chromium door. All around everything is made of glass. In the middle of the room, few meters from each other, are two square mirror-pillars reflecting passers-by in so many copies between the radiating metal frames that their function is hardly noticeable: they are coat-racks. In three corners of the hall there are three identical glass cabins, in the fourth one a tiny booth separated by stained-glass windows. The whole room with its two mirror-pillars and four glass cabins looks as if outstretched candelabra were shaking glass goblets. The room divided by the stained-glass window appears to have been a file-room, judging from its furniture. In front of it a small passage leads to a wash-basin alcove with multicolor tile walls. This is a display house. You can find here everything that the glass industry has to offer, in actual use. It is undeniably elegant, but with concern for the functional. Everything is glittering, clean, well tended. The floor is bright and smooth, the ceiling is like snow-white marble, the windows open silently, the mirrors and metal parts glitter like diamonds, as do the opaque white and dark black glass counters.

"The atmosphere is pleasant. It will be good to work here. To start the hopeless on a journey to the land of hope."

(Teri Gács, *A mélységből kiáltunk hozzád* [We Are Crying to You from the Abyss], 1946)

472. Lining up in front of the Glass House, summer of 1944

473. Lining up in front of the Glass House

In the second part of the account by the observer the lengthy description of the glitter and shimmer of the building is in sharp contrast to the fear and sufferings inside.

Only the description of the building itself was quoted above from the book of an eyewitness. The Glass House had a cellar as well, and part of this was the "Orthodox cellar" where some three hundred Orthodox Jews were living in the fall of 1944. Among them the Herzl Group formed a separate section, as did all the other movements. There was even a small stand down there where the daily prayers were recited at the usual hours of the day. Because of the many kids this was the liveliest part of the whole Glass House.

The Glass House actually plays a double role in the Jewish history of Budapest: as a protected house, which in spite of its special status brought sufferings, bloodshed and death; but also as a Jewish property, an example of the modern architecture of Lipótváros between the two wars.

The company was founded in 1896 as the mirror glass and window-pane wholesale store of Gyula Weiss Jr. The original nineteenth-century building burned down in 1930 and so the founder's son, Arthur Weiss, had a new house built in its place. Plans for the new building were made in 1935 by Lajos Kozma, an extraordinary figure of Hungarian Art Nouveau architecture, and the construction job was carried out by the "Dénes and Erős" company.

In the months of the Arrow-cross regime Arthur Weiss himself stayed at the Glass House and he directed some rescue operations from here, as some memoirs tell us. He managed to save the inhabitants of the Glass House from the last attack of the Arrow-cross. On December 31, 1944, some 40 to 50 armed Arrow-cross men blew up the entrance with a hand-grenade: they were in search of food. When they realized that they made a mistake, they forced some 600 people from the building onto the street; they even shot three people, Sándor Scheiber's mother among them. These people were already lined up to be taken to the Danube bank and shot there when Hungarian soldiers intervened, at the request of Weiss, and thus saved the lives of these people. On the next day someone disguised in a Hungarian soldier's uniform tricked him into leaving the building, took him to the Arrow-cross headquarters in Városház utca, tortured him and shot him into the Danube on the same day, January 1, 1945. Ottó Komoly was taken from his refuge at Hotel Ritz, where he moved only a few days earlier at the request of the hotel management, and was killed under similar circumstances.

In its current form the Glass House bears no resemblance to what it was like in the past. If we want to have at least a sense of what the Glass House looked like, let us rather take a glance at the foyer of the movie theater *Átrium* in Buda, at 55 Margit körút: this building was also designed by Kozma, in 1936, and it is also a sparkling mass of glass and mirrors.

(12) Terrible Responsibility

On November 26 the Calvinist Bishop László Ravasz asked the Roman Catholic Prince-Primate Cardinal Jusztinián Serédi and the Lutheran Bishop Sándor Raffay by way of a letter to sign a joint protest and send it to Szálasi:

"The sufferings of Hungarian Jews—some of our Christian fellows among them—cry out for help. I think that we can no longer delay the ultimate step, namely that the Christian churches of Hungary issue a joint protest against this terrible way of treating people. Our joint action, since it contradicts all our previous principles and practice, would emphasize all the more that fighting against the persecution of Jews is a universal human and general national obligation, and it would serve to underline the extraordinary urgency and importance of our protest."

Once again there was no joint action, and the leaders of the Christian churches wrote to Szálasi separately. Here is what Jusztinián Serédi wrote on November 25:

"In the solution of the so-called Jewish question, together with the honorable episcopacy, I have always kept in mind justice and the real interests of the Hungarian nation. For the sake of justice I have always rejected the idea of depriving people of their rights, may they be non-Jews, Hungarian citizens of Jewish origin or my own co-religionists of the Catholic faith, unless they had committed an individual crime which must be punished. When these Hungarian citizens are deprived of their legal rights without proving for each individual that he or she had committed some crime, it is not reasonable to argue that these Hungarian citizens of Jewish origin are being punished for the crimes that were committed by other citizens of Jewish origin against the Hungarian nation, because this would be a violation of the principle of individual responsibility, which has always been condemned by God's unwritten law as expressed in Roman Law [references in footnote], the Scripture containing written law [in a footnote: Ezekiel 18,3, etc.; Matthew 16,27] and Church Law which comprises both of these [references in footnote]. According to common sense each individual, including people of Jewish origin, can only be held responsible for a crime which they had committed and not for the crimes of others; consequently they cannot be punished for crimes which they had no part in, especially if by accepting the sanctity of baptism they had already left the community, that is, the Jewish community, which had committed the crimes. (...) The true interest of the Hungarian nation is, indeed, the enforcement of the justice and the elimination of injustice, because by passing such unjust decrees the Hungarian Government turns God and the entire Christian world against the Hungarian nation. And if our enemies took revenge later, just as unjustly as the Hungarian Government had treated its citizens of Jewish origin, not only on those who had issued these shameful decrees but even on those who had nothing to do with them and who had maybe even protested against them, then the Hungarian Government would not be in a position to protest, nor would be able to protect those Hungarian citizens who were suffering injustice; and it would have to bear the terrible responsibility not only in front of the nation and history but in front of God; the terrible responsibility for the turn of the nation's fate to its worse through these problematic decrees of the Government. (...) So far I have been able to get certain exemptions from the Jewish laws, especially for my Catholic followers. Now the present Government withdrew these exemptions even from Christians of Jewish origin and from other exempted people. In this last minute I protest against these unjust decrees, in the name of God's written and unwritten law, in the name of justice and the true interest of the Hungarian nation, in the name of fellow-bishops and myself."

Sándor Raffay, on November 25:

"As a bishop by God's grace and in the spirit of the Gospel of Jesus Christ I respectfully present a request that your honor stop or ease the often irrationally and extremely strict procedures related to the Jewish laws and decrees. My request is based on the LORD's commandment according to the Gospels, which says that we should love even our enemies. (...) For the sake of truth I have to emphasize that it is not just to punish each individual for the sin of a race. This is especially true of those who have already broken all ties with Judaism and are living now as members of the Christian Church. (...) The judgment of foreign Churches and societies strikes our sweet Hungarian homeland bitterly. It is not only in the name of truth, justice and Christian love that I am asking the Government of the state to ease the handling of Jews and especially of baptized Jews, but also because of my concern for the good name of the nation."

These protests were now much stronger and more general than ever before. The letters may have been follow-ups to previous personal meetings or other letters. This was certainly the case with Serédi who even refers to such a meeting—"as I elaborated on October 24 when we met in Esztergom". Their tone is emotional and serious, indicating compassion and responsibility. The three bishops—representatives of the three major Christian churches in Hungary—condemned collective punishment for the Jews, without asking the question if there was a collective sin at all and what exactly the "sin of the Jewish race", cited ever so often, may have been, that is, tacitly accepting the hostile presuppositions. As well grounded in theology as they were, none of them realized that in Ezekiel's words, quoted by Serédi, not only punishment, but also sin itself could only be individual. They tried to protect Jews from persecution within the ideological framework of anti-Semitism. Sincerely moved by the sufferings they were talking about, they still made a distinction between Jews and Christians of Jewish origin. One of their complaints was still that the previous exemption granted to Christians of Jewish background was now repealed. They still made a distinction between Jews who were Hungarian citizens and the Hungarian nation. It is questionable whether Szálasi could make anything out of Serédi's footnotes modeled on the encyclical letters of the Pope, of the rich Biblical references or of the quotes from the *Digesta* of Justinian (sixth century C.E.).

The letters were answered by the head of the civilian office of Szálasi on December 19, 1944, three weeks later. It said, "By order of the Leader of the Nation your request has been passed on to the Minister of Interior".

*

58 Pozsonyi út is a Calvinist church. It was consecrated in 1940, only a few years before the international ghetto was set up just a little to the South. The inscription on the facade says: SOLI DEO

GLORIA, "Glory be solely to God". Between 1940 and 1953 its minister was Albert Bereczky (1893–1966) who took part in some of the organizational work of the "Good Shepherd" Committee. (The "Good Shepherd" mission's sub-committee was set up on October 20, 1942, by the World Congress of the Hungarian Calvinist Church.) Other Calvinist co-workers were Gyula Muraközy sr. (1892–1961), then a minister of the Kálvin tér Calvinist Church and the president of the "Good Shepherd" Committee; László Márton Pákozdy (1910-1993), assistant minister, who was to become an outstanding Biblical scholar in Debrecen, later in Budapest at the Protestant (Calvinist) Theological Academy; József Éliás, the ecclesiastic secretary of the Committee, later the minister of the Nagyerdei Church in Debrecen, and many others. The *Szent Kereszt Egyesület* (Holy Cross Society) and the *Keresztény Zsidók Szövetsége* (Association of the Christian Jews of Hungary) cooperated with them, too. (Their headquarters were at 49–51 Vörösmarty utca, in the building of the Scottish Mission.) The tiny office and apartment of Éliás was at 5 Lázár utca, on the second floor. "His shelter was hidden in a dilapidated building; it was filled with all kinds of shabby furniture, but the people who came there were utterly enthusiastic", as Emil Koren described it somewhat later.

At the time of its foundation the "Good Shepherd" Committee's mission was to convert Jews to Christianity, but they also helped Christian children of Jewish origin, and by 1944 they did everything they could to help all Jewish children, all Jews, all the forced laborers and everyone who was persecuted. They closely cooperated with the International Red Cross, received significant financial support for their activities from them. It was this organization, more precisely Mária Székely, the secretary of Pastor Éliás, who prepared the Hungarian translation of the Auschwitz Protocols, and it was also them, more precisely Bereczky, Cavallier, Sándor Török and others, who took copies of the document to Horthy's daughter-in-law and the leaders of the three major Christian churches of Hungary, Sándor Raffay, László Ravasz and Jusztinián Serédi, back in the second week of May. It was certainly not their fault that these high church officials did not agree to protest jointly against this inhuman behavior, neither when the Hungarian deportations began nor later.

(13) In the Ghetto (December 5, 1944-January 18, 1945)

By the beginning of December 1944, most of the Yellow-star Houses had become empty. Their tenants, those who were still alive, had to move into the "big ghetto". Those who did not obey the ghetto decree could only go into hiding, exposing themselves to police-raids.

Borders of the ghetto comprised the core of Erzsébetváros, the old Jewish quarter. In general, the borderline went as follows: Dohány utca – Károly körút – Király utca – Nagyatádi Szabó utca (today Kertész utca), though it did not follow the street lines exactly, that is, it crossed courtyards or houses within each block along the plot-borders. The reason behind it was to ensure that houses opening to the border streets be not included in the ghetto. In addition, some specific buildings remained outside, like no. 8/A Klauzál utca, a laundry, or 7 Klauzál utca,

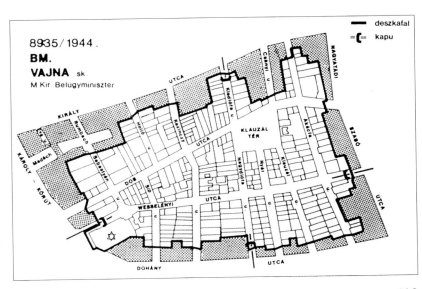

474. Official map of the Pest ghetto. The six-pointed star marks the Dohány utca synagogue

a brothel. All three main synagogues were within. The walls of the ghetto, high wooden fences all around, along the full length of streets, in the courtyards of buildings with a passage, were built quickly in the last days of November. (The work was done by the József Auguszt Construction Co.) There were gates at the intersections of Wesselényi utca and Károly körút, Wesselényi utca and Nagyatádi Szabó utca, Kis Diófa utca and Király utca, and at that of Nagy Diófa utca and Dohány utca. The gates were placed a few meters inside the street corner. The authorities gave no explanation as to why they had placed the gates opening towards the four cardinal points. The symbolism of the four points of the compass perhaps indicates that the intention was to create a model of an isolated world. In a recollection of Pál Szalai the "Leader of the Nation" was mentioned as referring to the four cardinal points with special emphasis.

The ghetto was closed on December 10. Its four gates were guarded from the outside by fully armed Arrow-cross men and SS soldiers. Non-Jews were not allowed to enter, not even in order to work there. In extraordinary and exceptional cases special entrance tickets into the area of the ghetto were issued by the police (at 3 Egyetem utca and, after the building here had been hit by a bomb, such tickets were distributed in the air-raid shelter of the City Hall).

On December 6, the Royal Ministry of the Interior of Hungary published a decree about changing the names of certain roads, streets and squares. "The family name of Jewish people" and "names with any type of Jewish connotation" had to disappear from the city map. At the beginning of the siege, there really was nothing more important to worry about than whose names the streets of Pest bore.

On December 10, the fourth floor of 12 Síp utca, i.e. the rooms of the president's office, built only fifteen years earlier, in 1928, were hit by a grenade. Many were wounded, others killed, and the archives were destroyed. The offices of the Jewish Council moved down to the second floor of the building.

The transfer of children from the city into the ghetto, even from houses under the protection of the International Red Cross, began on December 12. It was only with great difficulties, by alleging the danger of an epidemic, that it could be delayed until December 20. A few days later, however, the children could be taken back to many of the homes.

After the closing of the ghetto, section "A" of the International Red Cross could no longer continue its activities; even Red Cross employees were forced into the ghetto. There were altogether 162 apartment buildings in the area of the ghetto. In January 1945, the ghetto had 70,000 inhabitants on the average with fourteen people per apartment. Some people did not even have a place to sleep. The majority of the ghetto population were women, children and elderly men. Men who were able to work had been taken for forced labor service already earlier. The curfew after 4 p.m. ordered for Jews was in force in the area of the ghetto as well. There was no exit from the ghetto except for one small path. Upstairs in the Dohány synagogue there was a little door through which one could get into the building of the Jewish Museum, and the Museum itself opened to the street beyond the ghetto.

475. Miksa Domonkos, the commander of the ghetto, in his Hungarian captain's uniform

In the course of the altogether seven-week existence of the Pest ghetto administrative tasks were carried out by the Jewish Council, the headquarters of which were invariably at 12 Síp utca. The administration was managed by Miksa Domonkos (a captain of World War I, now in reserve). Wearing his uniform and stripes, with his self-confident manner, he could enforce his will even against policemen and the Arrow-cross. He was a brave man, born for organization. The area of the ghetto was divided into ten districts. Registration of inhabitants, organization of food distribution, running public services and taking care of children were the duty of district chiefs appointed by the Jewish Council. The ghetto security, almost 900 people altogether, recruited from the inhabitants of the ghetto, was responsible for maintaining internal order. These policemen's payment was an extra plate of soup every day. The International Red Cross maintained an office in the area of the ghetto, too.

Kitchens were run at the following locations: at 27 Dob utca, 41 Kazinczy utca (this was a supply store at the same time), 6 Rumbach Sebestyén utca (rooms of Márton Stern's restaurant), 14 Rumbach Sebestyén utca, 5, 12 and 22 Síp utca, on the corner of 18 Wesselényi utca and 22 Kazinczy utca (kosher restaurant of Mendel Weisz, also a supply store), 13 and 33 Wesselényi utca. There were bakeries at 15 Dob utca (owned by a certain Molnár), 22 Dob utca, 1 Holló utca, 25 Nagy Diófa utca and 9 Síp utca. There were a few private eateries, too, at least in the beginning, for example the *Szőlőskert korcsma* (Vineyard Inn) at 6 Wesselényi utca and a few other catering establishments owned by Christians, for instance a pub at 45 Akácfa utca, a candy store at 9 Dob utca, an eatery at 20 Dob utca, a coffee-house at 11 Wesselényi utca and a dairy shop at 26 Wesselényi utca.

Public and communal kitchens distributed about 60,000 portions of food daily. About one third of this quantity, 23,000 portions were prepared by the Orthodox Soup-kitchen, the center of which was at 13 Wesselényi utca. They had five large range boilers of 700 liters, each for mass cooking. Another quarter of the meals, about 15,000 portions, were cooked at Márton Stern's restaurant. In principle it was the Mayor's office that provided the ingredients, in practice, however, it was rather the International Red Cross.

Let us quote here from a note found among the papers of Miksa Domonkos about the catering possibilities and the actual portions distributed:

"**Provisions for the ghetto (December 1944)**

Monday:	bean soup with pasta	400 milliliters (14 ounces)
Tuesday:	dish of cabbage	300 milliliters (10.5 ounces)
Wednesday:	potato soup	400 milliliters (14 ounces)
Thursday:	dish of dried peas	300 milliliters (10.5 ounces)
Friday:	caraway-seed soup, pasta	400 milliliters (14 ounces)
Saturday:	tsholent	300 milliliters (10.5 ounces)
Sunday:	vegetable soup, pasta	400 milliliters (14 ounces)

"**Consumption of raw material for tsholent per 1000 persons:**

Fats:	5 [kilograms] (11 pounds)
Flour:	20 (44 pounds)
Beans:	110 (242 pounds)
Salt:	5 (11 pounds)
Onions:	5 (11 pounds)
Paprika (red pepper):	0.50 (1.1 pounds)
Black pepper:	0.20 (0.4 pound)
Garlic:	2 (4.4 pounds)

"**Calorie content:**

Children's portion:	931
General portion:	781
Portion for the sick:	1355

"*Note*: The minimum amount of calories needed by a non-working adult weighing 70 kilos is about 2200–2500."

Medical care for the inhabitants debilitated by the cold weather, lack of nutrition and long-term illness was a particularly serious problem. Hygienic conditions were terrible, garbage was not collected, water could be taken only from taps in the street, there was no gas, the inhabitants of the ghetto could light only small fires, from pieces of broken wooden furniture.

By May 1944 the Jewish hospital in Szabolcs utca was entirely taken over by the Germans. There was no real hospital in the area of the ghetto. Thus, temporary hospitals had to be set up in several places. Serious hospitals were established at two locations, at 44 Wesselényi utca (the school building was regarded as the central hospital) and, for a while, at 2 Bethlen Gábor tér. The Germans did not allow Jews to remove any medical equipment or instruments from the Szabolcs utca Jewish hospital. Furnishing the Wesselényi utca hospital was, therefore, a rather slow process. Nevertheless, bit by bit, partly transferring the equipment of the Jewish Hospital and Nursing Home, they succeeded in collecting almost everything that was needed, including an X-ray appliance and equipment for surgical operations. Even when there was no electricity in the building anymore, operations were still carried out by candle-light, and instruments were sterilized by the fires of wood and books collected from the Dohány utca synagogue and various other places. In the end, more than 500 people found shelter in the school building. The majority of the nurses and other staff were forced labor captives who had gone into hiding. Besides, about twenty smaller emergency clinics were in operation, for example, at 16, 18, 20, 27 and 30 Akácfa utca, 9, 12 Klauzál tér, 23 Klauzál utca (this is where the sick from the sanatorium for the tuberculosed were sent), 35 Klauzál utca, 11–13 Rumbach Sebestyén utca and 30, 33, 35, 37, 40 Wesselényi utca. The emergency clinic at 14 Rákóczi út, established spontaneously in November, was also connected with the Wesselényi utca hospital. The several hundred people living or taking shelter on the three floors of the building organized medical treatment themselves. Visiting hospitals outside the area of the ghetto, and even the one in the Wesselényi utca school, became increasingly difficult. Sick people could only be taken out of the ghetto through the wooden gates which were under guard. Part of the necessary medicine was collected from pharmacies in the neighborhood by purchasing agents in possession of the identity card of the International Red Cross. There were even homes for the aged in the ghetto, at 22 Akácfa utca and 32 Klauzál utca; day-cares and children's homes were at 32, 38 Akácfa utca, 11 Klauzál tér, and 10 Klauzál utca.

Children's education and religious life were maintained even under extraordinary circumstances. In the synagogues of Dohány utca and Rumbach Sebestyén utca, used as internment camps in the course of the previous months, religious services held on Friday afternoons and Saturday mornings throughout. The Chief Rabbi of the congregation was Zsigmond Groszmann (1880–1945). Ever since he was a young man he had been elucidating the history of the organizations of Pest Jewry and the administration of the Pest community in thorough studies based on original archival research. In these days he tried to remain a careful leader. On December 20, in an official letter, he asked for a "diary-like book" from the Jewish Council in order to record "rabbinical events". Apart from him, Ödön Kálmán (1886–1951), earlier rabbi of the independent community of Kőbánya, and Béla Berend (Presser) (1911–1987), previously the Chief Rabbi of Szigetvár, performed rabbinical duties in the ghetto, mostly burial ceremonies. Apart from the synagogues of Dohány utca and Rumbach Sebestyén utca, there were at least two other places of worship in public usage, namely, 31 Dob utca and 1 Holló utca. One of them being near the Orthodox synagogue, the other one near the "Rombach", initially they may have been instead of, or in addition to, those. They probably tried to preserve—as much as it was possible under the circumstances—the distinct ritual practices of the different religious tendencies.

476. Portrait of Zsigmond Groszmann

In the last few weeks, even the removal of the dead met with difficulties. Until the end of December it was still possible to use the cemeteries in Salgótarjáni utca and Kozma utca. In the latter one, a rabbi was staying permanently, he even slept there in order to perform burial ceremonies. The gardener of the cemetery, János Nyíri, directed funerals with great care, and tried to remember who had been buried and where. At the end of December, however, corpses could only be kept in Salgótarjáni utca. Because of the bombings not even hearses were allowed to leave the ghetto after the beginning of January and from then on dead bodies could only be placed within the walls of the ghetto. The earlier Orthodox *mikveh* at 40 Kazinczy utca was now a mortuary. (The mortuary of the international ghetto was at 32 Pozsonyi út.) After a time, the corpses of those who had passed away in the Wesselényi utca hospital could only be kept in the nearby Bucsinszky Café (30 Erzsébet körút, on the corner of Erzsébet körút and Wesselényi utca)—a famous gathering place for writers, journalists and Bohemians in the old days. There were two places marked for burials in the area of the ghetto. The first one was the middle of Klauzál tér, the other was the courtyard of Heroes' Temple, the small open area right next to the Dohány Temple. In this latter place more than 2,000 victims have been resting ever since. The name of the courtyard today is the Heroes' Cemetery after the temple next to it. At the very end, corpses had to remain unburied in the courtyard of 12 Síp utca and in the covered market on Klauzál tér.

On December 3 an armed group of Arrow-cross men attacked the barracks at 46 Columbus utca, which since the end of September had been under the auspices of the International Red Cross. The inhabitants of the camp were members of emigration groups organized by Zionists. Several people in the camp had firearms so they could resist, but the Arrow-cross men outnumbered them. Their leaders were executed on the spot.

On December 5 military operations of the Red Army to capture Budapest were launched from three directions. On December 10 the Government began its transfer towards the western borders. On December 11 German reinforcements arrived in Budapest. On December 16 another attack of the Red Army reached the capital directly. On December 24 the Soviets surrounded the city entirely. The siege of Budapest began.

On December 6 three armed men wearing Arrow-cross arm bands entered a children's home at 27–29 Orsó utca which was under the protection of the Spanish Embassy. There were about 120 children and several adults as nurses, maids or cooks staying in the home. The intruders stripped them naked, took away their belongings and tore up their safe-conducts. One of the representatives of the International Red Cross gave instructions loudly and shouted himself, so the Arrow-cross men mistook him for one of their own. In an unguarded moment he stepped outside through the gate and called policemen from the nearest station who then threw out the rowdy Arrow-cross men.

On December 7 the Budapest representatives of the neutral powers (the Vatican, Switzerland, Sweden, Spain, Portugal) established an office, *Département de coopération* at 3/B Tövis utca, which was to coordinate their rescue activities.

On December 12 Arrow-cross men carried away seventy children, thirty mothers and about ten "fathers" from the building at 29 Szent István körút, the Children's and Mothers' Home of the extremely active Swedish Red Cross under the leadership of chief representative Waldemar Langlet and his wife, Nina Langlet. Some of them were taken into the ghetto. On the same day, a few armed men carried out, though this time politely, an hour-long identity check of the nursing staff and patients of the "Alice Weiss" Hospital under the protection of the section "A" of the International Red Cross.

On December 15 the Government fled and the capital became the free prey of Arrow-cross bands. As a result, the activities of the Red Cross were banned. The various armed bands dwelling in Arrow-cross houses were no longer under control. They started the systematic murder of Jews all around the city. They broke into protected houses and even embassy buildings. On the following day all the banks were forced to open their safes. All the gold, jewels, gems and stocks kept there were confiscated for the National Bank.

477. Portrait of Waldemar Langlet

Inhabitants of the ghetto were appalled to learn on December 15 that a track branching off the rails of the streetcar turning from Nagymező utca into Király utca was laid down in Csányi utca, up to the wall of the ghetto. Everyone was sure that this was in preparation for deportation.

On December 15 at 6 o'clock in the evening an ambulance was called to the bookshop at 4 Kossuth Lajos utca. (In fact, there is still a bookstore at this address today.) On the previous day there had been an explosion in the store. The ambulance men found the corpses of eight men, Jewish forced labor captives, executed by a shot in the back of the head. They were called there after the explosion to clear the ruins. A note on their bodies said, "In revenge for blowing up an Arrow-cross bookstore".

After World War II, at the court hearing of rabbi Béla Berend's case at the National Council of the People's Tribunal, where he was relieved of the charge of being a war-criminal, some witnesses, among them R. József Katona (1909–1959), later Chief Rabbi of the Dohány utca synagogue, confirmed that "in those days Berend was regularly using the Hebrew greeting *nekamah*, meaning *revenge*, most probably to express his contempt and loathing towards Arrow-cross men."

During the night of December 20 the area of the ghetto was hit by several bombs. A few houses were seriously damaged, including 7 Kis Diófa utca (200 tenants), 9 Kis Diófa utca (106 tenants), 32 Dob utca (159 tenants), 43 Kazinczy utca (120 tenants), etc. Tenants of the destroyed buildings were put up in the Goldmark Hall.

On December 22 some Arrow-cross men forced Christian Jews staying in the building of the Scottish mission (49–51 Vörösmarty utca) into the ghetto. Furthermore, they carried out raids in the protected houses along Pannónia utca.

As a matter of fact, in these weeks almost all Christian institutions, including monasteries and schools, rescued and gave refuge to persecuted people, that is, runaway Jews. Men found shelter in the monastery of the Lazarist fathers (26 Nagyboldogasszony útja / Ménesi út), while there were mostly orphans and abandoned children in the convent of the *Irgalmas nővérek* (Sisters of Mercy), named after Saint Vincent (27 Nagyboldogasszony útja). In their Óbuda asylum (30 San Marco utca) there were minors, and in their school, the Ranolder Institute (23 Thaly Kálmán utca), there were little girls. In the convent of *Notre Dame de Sion* (1 Miasszonyunk útja / Meredek utca) a few women and children were accommodated, in the convent of the nuns of the *Isteni Szeretet Leányai* (Daughters of Divine Love) (12–14 Farkasvölgyi út) there were children, and in their cloister, the *Szent Margit Leánynevelő Intézet* (Szent Margit School for Young Ladies) (Knézich utca) there were adults and forced labor captives. In the "Szent Alajos" (St. Aloisius) monastery of the Salesian monks (79 Kiscelli út), where the director Mihály Kiss was just referred to as "the Chief Rabbi", there were men and boys, and in the women's hospital of the "Szent Erzsébet" (St. Elisabeth) order of nuns (41–43 Fő utca), women. Children were hiding in the *Collegium Josephinum* (34/A Vörösmarty utca); girls in the Pest house of the nuns of *Szűz Mária Társaság* (The Virgin Mary's Society), the *Collegium Marianum* (11 József utca); and men in the convent of the *Society of Jesus* (the Jesuits) (25 Mária utca). There were women and children in the nunnery of *Szent Szív Társaság* (Sacré Coeur Society) at 21 Ajtósi Dürer sor, in the *Sophianum Intézet* (Sophianum College) (1 Mikszáth Kálmán tér), which also belonged to the Sacré Coeur, as well as in the convent of the Society (87 Budakeszi út). Little girls were given refuge in the dormitory of the order of the *Isteni Megváltó Leányai* (Daughters of the Divine Savior) (*Szent Anna Kollégium* / St. Anna

478. Carl Ivan Danielssohn

Dormitory in 17 Horánszky utca), and girls could find shelter at the sisters of the *"Jó Pásztor" Egyházközség* ("Good Shepherd" Congregation)—albeit some of them only temporarily since Arrow-cross men carried off those in hiding, and others, luckily until the very end of the siege. The sisters of *Jézus Szíve Népleányok Társasága* (The Heart of Jesus Society of Folkgirls) issued protective documents in their convent in 14 Horánszky utca. The "white nuns", sisters of the convent on Miasszonyunk útja, were busy typing Vatican letters of protection for several weeks in the fall. Late in the fall, in the days of the death marches towards Hegyeshalom, after the Pest ghetto was blocked off, the monks Ferenc Köhler (Lazarist), Vince Tomek (Piarist), Lucius Havasi (Benedictine), Lénárd Deák Bárdos and Géza Izay (Jesuits) participated in rescue operations taking serious personal risks.

Apart from various other rescue operations of the Calvinist church, the *Magyar Keresztyén Leányegyesületek Nemzeti Szövetsége* (National Federation of Christian Girls' Associations of Hungary) (35 Bocskay út) in the immediate neighborhood of the synagogue of Lágymányos aided captives of the forced labor battalions transferred there, and gave shelter to several refugees in the women's home of the headquarters of the federation.

On December 23 representatives of neutral countries, those who had not yet left Budapest, met in the Castle district, in the palace of the apostolic nuncio. In their very last joint memorandum to the Royal Government of Hungary they protested against carrying children off into the ghetto. It was Nuncio Angelo Rotta of the Vatican, Ambassador Carl Ivan Danielsson of Sweden, Ambassador Harald Feller of Switzerland, Count Ferenc Pongrácz, the *chargé d'affaires* of the Portuguese Embassy and Giorgio (Jorge) Perlasca, the self-made *chargé d'affaires* of Spain, who signed the memorandum.

From the diary of Miksa Fenyő, hiding in Józsefváros, from December 23:

"There seems to be no end to the robbery and murder. No day goes by without a few dozen Jews dragged out of the ghetto on the slightest pretext, or on no pretext at all. At night they are shot to death along the banks of the Danube, to save the trouble of a burial. The same radical measures are applied against those non-Jews who have some quarrel with the Arrow-cross or, worse yet, with one or another of its members (by the way, the quarrel is rarely ideological; it is usually a matter of private property).

(...)

"If I had to name the foreign writer to whom I am the most indebted, to whom I owe hours that are worth years, who made my life so much richer, I would have to be Goethe. I wonder, if I ever return home from this miserable Odyssey of mine, I shall still find the good old Cotta edition of Goethe in my library. As a matter of fact, Goethe is worth of great appreciation, and I find it most regrettable that I cannot discuss the significance of this giant with Petőfi. For I believe that I could have convinced him about the paramount value of Goethe's works." (*Az elsodort ország* [A Country Swept Aside], 1946)

On December 24, on Christmas Eve according to the Christian calendar, on a Sunday, Arrow-cross men launched an unusually great number of raids on places of refuge for Jews outside of the ghetto, thus unwittingly reviving a medieval tradition. They treated Jewish children's homes with particular hostility.

The target of one of these Arrow-cross attacks was the Jewish Orphanage. During the German invasion, the Girls' and Boys' Orphanage had shriveled to a single building (25–27 Vilma királynő út / Városligeti fasor). There were about 130 boys and 60 girls under permanent care and lots of abandoned children in addition. At the end of the summer, the building at 5–7 Munkácsy Mihály utca was retrieved along with two more buildings nearby. The sign of the International Red Cross was displayed above the gates. The synagogue of the Vilma királynő út building was hit by a carpet-raid just the day before *Rosh ha-Shanah* (September 18). Part of the right wing collapsed, the temple room fell in, the ground-floor offices, the restaurant, dormitories, kitchen and storage-rooms were destroyed. So were the adults who stayed here, some forced laborers. In the morning of December 24 armed Arrow-cross men appeared in the building. They ordered chil-

479. The Radetzky Barracks (3 Bem József tér). In the fall of 1944 this was the headquarters of the Arrow-cross Party and of the Death's Skull Legion

dren into the courtyard and, under the pretext of checking their identity papers, they seized all their valuables, and threatened to shoot them dead. According to recollections, they shot some of the children, and sent the rest, together with adults, towards the Danube bank, or rather, as it turned out, through Ferdinánd híd (Ferdinánd Bridge leading over the tracks of the Western Railway Station) and the pontoon (replacing the blown-up section of the Margit híd), towards the Radeczky Barracks, headquarters of the *Halálfejes légió* (Death's Skull Legion), one of the major centers of the Arrow-cross Party in Buda. (Previously it was called Pálffy tér, at that time 3 Bem József tér; today this is the headquarters of the political party *Magyar Demokrata Fórum* [Hungarian Democratic Forum].) The director of the Orphanage tried to contact Wallenberg in the Vilma királynő út building, which was soon invaded by Arrow-cross men. He ran across town towards Wallenberg's office with a Christmas tree on his shoulder, which he bought in the street on the spur of the moment in order to divert suspicion. He could only talk to Wallenberg's secretary, Mrs. László Falk. It was perhaps exactly at that moment that Wallenberg was chasing by car the deportation trains which had just left the Józsefváros Railway Station. After a while a patrol of three men, one armed and two civilians, riding a motor-cycle with a side-car, stopped the march of the children from the orphanage at the Barracks. According to some recollections, they ordered Arrow-cross men to bring the children into the ghetto. They mistook *Síp utca*, the main street in the ghetto, for *Szív utca* and this was how the children were taken into the houses at 33 and 46 Szív utca instead of the ghetto. On the following day some of the orphanage children were herded towards the Danube bank by Arrow-cross men. There was an air-raid at the time so the Arrow-cross men started shooting at the airplanes. Those who could not drop out cautiously during this time were shot into the water from Új-Lipótváros or the docks at Újpest. Since the men had to economize on ammunition, they sometimes made three children stand behind each other. The bullet missed a few of them, hence they could escape. Two boys jumped into the water still before they got shot. Having swum in the icy waters of the Danube for a while, they touched land at the Parliament building and survived. Despite the reign of the Arrow-cross Party, nearly 1,200 Jewish children survived the Holocaust in the Orphanage.

In 1989 a slab was placed on the Munkácsy Mihály utca building: "In memoriam Mayor Lajos Gidófalvy (1901–1945) and the soldiers of the XIII/1 auxiliary *honvéd* battalion who rescued the tenants of the Jewish Boys' Orphanage. The orphanage had been under the protection of the International Red Cross, but was attacked by Arrow-cross men on December 24, 1944." There is another inscription informing the reader about Mayor Gidófalvy having been promoted posthumously to the rank of colonel by the Minister of Defense on May 10, 1991.

On December 24, 25 and 26 some posters of the Calvinist Church informed members of their congregations that on all three days of the holiday, at 9:30 in the morning, services would be held on the corner of Dob utca and Akácfa utca in the room of Polgár Café / Kazsimér's shop. Ironically, to these services they invited their Protestant and Baptist brothers as well.

On December 27–28, on Wallenberg's initiative and through the intervention of the Arrow-cross liaison to the police Pál Szalai (1915–1994), the Arrow-cross plenipotentiary of the "Leader of the Nation"—himself an old friend of Szalai's from their days as boy-scouts—ordered two officers and a hundred policemen to guard the ghetto. Policemen took over one of the Swedish houses of the international ghetto (6 Tátra utca), too. At times, Szalai and his policemen were able to repel the actions of the undisciplined gangs and even of the Hungarian military commander and of the German security service. In fact, these groups were not only after Jews in general, but were searching for certain individuals in particular. Their aim was to drive everybody into the ghetto and exterminate them all "with firearms on a certain day".

On December 28 armed Arrow-cross men and others dressed in SS uniforms attacked the hospital building at 2 Bethlen Gábor tér. Men were driven into the courtyard, women down to the basement. They seized the property of the sick and plundered the supply stores. On the following day everybody was taken to the women's gallery of the synagogue and was interned there for a whole day. On December 30 several young men were taken away from the building and shot in the nape in the basement of the Girls' School of Commerce in Wesselényi utca.

In the morning of December 30 eight armed men drove all the tenants, altogether 170 people, out of 21 Katona József utca, a Swedish protected house, to 60 Andrássy út. The people were kept in the courtyard for hours and then taken into the building where all their property and documents were taken away. At night, stripping everybody to their underwear, made them march barefoot via Andrássy út, Vilmos császár út, Alkotmány utca, Kossuth Lajos tér, Nádor utca and Zrínyi utca. There was not enough of them to kill everybody at once. At Zrínyi utca, they selected fifty men, among them Gedeon Richter (1872–1944), engineer and owner of a pharmaceutical plant (who, by the way, had an apartment nearby at 26 Ferenc József rakpart, today Belgrád rakpart), and shot them into the Danube at Zoltán utca. A few of them, however, as it turned out later, survived and fought their way to reach land at the Lánchíd. A group of armed troops frightened the Arrow-cross men who then accompanied the rest of their captives back to the "House of Fidelity". There they gave them half a kilogram (a pound) of bread and a small bowl of watery bean soup. On New Year's Eve most of them were taken to the ghetto.

At the beginning of January, 1945, news spread that the authorities of the Arrow-cross Party would soon transfer everybody to the "big ghetto". As a matter of fact, by that time even policemen cooperating with foreign representatives thought that a closed ghetto offered the greatest security. On January 3, however, Wallenberg was still protesting against the plan to the extraordinary Party commissioner and the German commanding general of Budapest (in Hotel Astoria). Referring to logistical difficulties he held the plan to be "insane and brutal from a humanitarian point of view". Nevertheless, on January 4 and in the course of the next few days Arrow-cross men liquidated the majority of the international ghetto. For two days they drove their captives in long rows along Lipótváros. The Swedish mission distributed the rest of their food and medicine supplies. Yet the plan of "concentration" was only partially carried out. On January 4 some Arrow-cross men rounded up all residents of the even side of Pozsonyi út (the one towards the Danube) and on the following day they rounded up everyone from the other side, too, but eventually left these people behind. Even if only in hiding, several people stayed in other, previously protected houses. Wallenberg offered some of his food supply even to the troops defending Budapest so that Arrow-cross men should respect the exterritoriality of embassy houses and buildings used by "a staff of Jewish origin" (the amount of food offered was never actually delivered).

The "Good Shepherd" could keep their children's homes under their own control until the very last moment. Although they often had to change their location in the besieged city, they did not have to bring children under their protection into the ghetto.

Here is an excerpt from a contemporary diary entry by a child (Tamás Kilényi) on January 3, 1945, about one of these moves (in this case from the home at 29 Bogár utca):

"(...) Three o'clock at night, we have to get up immediately, we are leaving. We all get a sugar cube. Two Hungarian soldiers come in. They are going to accompany us. We are leaving. We go outside. In the moonshine, we slip through the fence, and reach Bogár utca. Bombed out buildings everywhere. There are collapsed houses all along Bimbó út. Pieces of broken glass on the ground. We see fires burning in many places of the city. We reach Margit körút. No undamaged houses here, either. Through Széna tér, we reach Fillér utca [44 Fillér utca, the office of the "Good Pastor"]. Cannons and tanks everywhere. We grope our way among torn off wires, and this is how we reach Lorántffy út. (...) We lie flat on our stomach beside a wall. Bullets are whistling. (...) We go into reverend Sztehlo's house [Légrády Villa]. After knocking for a long time the door opens at last and we are let inside. We are led into a nice room where we soon go to bed. But we don't sleep yet, we eat sugar cubes. For breakfast there is caraway-seed soup with bread. After breakfast there was heavy firing so we went down to the cellar."

The rumor spread that Arrow-cross men intended to blow up the ghetto, and some picric acid had already been placed under certain buildings. There was no explosion, and no mines were found later, either, but it is not impossible that before the final destruction the Arrow-cross would have liked to carry out one more massacre, and the last muster was supposed to prepare this move.

On January 4 the headquarters of the ghetto security forces called upon competent guards to prevent the looting of the furniture of the Kazinczy utca synagogue.

On January 7 Lutz, Perlasca and Wallenberg paid a visit to the plenipotentiary representative of the Government and demanded that Arrow-cross men stop evacuating protected houses. Lajos Stöckler and Miksa Domonkos turned to Pál Szalai, the hero from the Arrow-cross ranks, for aid. The representative ordered two police officers and a unit of a hundred men to protect the ghetto.

On January 8 Lajos Stöckler, hiding in a Swedish office at 4 Üllői út, and the other residents of the house, altogether 166 people, were carried off by Arrow-cross men. At 41 Ferenc körút, which was called the "stripping room", their belongings were taken away and they themselves were to be taken to the Danube bank. Upon the strong protest of the police and Wallenberg they were finally let free.

From a report of R. Béla Berend on January 11:

"On Thursday evening around 22:45 a group of about 6 to 8 armed men, some in Arrow-cross uniforms, some in Hungarian and some in German military uniforms penetrated into the house at 27 Wesselényi utca.

They went straight to the air-raid shelter and verbally and physically abused the Jews they found there. Then they carried out a body search under the pretext of searching for firearms, and seized smaller personal belongings like fountain-pens, watches, matches, etc. First they fired warning shots into the air, then lined up and shot most of the people there: 26 women, 15 men and a little child. Most were shot in the head. Similar lootings and killings were committed at 29 Wesselényi utca, with one victim there. It seems that they were interrupted in their activity."

The various types of uniforms indicate that the ghetto, together with the rest of the city, became the prey of ordinary criminals and degenerate body-snatchers.

On January 12 rumor had it that armed Arrow-cross men and SS soldiers were gathering in the Hotel Royal (47–49 Erzsébet körút), to launch an attack on the ghetto in order to slaughter everyone. The attack was scheduled for January 15. Through the help of Pál Szalai, Wallenberg managed to arrange that the German commanding officer of the town, General Schmidthuber, prevented the massacre in the very last minute.

On January 14 the commander of the ghetto branch office of the state police and the liaison officer of the Arrow-cross Party requested the burial department of the Executive Committee of the Alliance of Hungarian Jews "to quicken the pace as far as burying the dead was concerned... Dead bodies are lying in the streets and in stores opening on the street for several days". Corpses had to be transferred to 44 Kazinczy utca, or buried in the ground at Klauzál tér, in the frost of the last days only stapled. On the order of the German authorities dead bodies had to be cleared away from the market hall of Klauzál tér. The instruction received by Miksa Domonkos was that "burials should be carried out with full force even earlier than the time determined for moving [i.e. the curfew], and if necessary, after dark, as well".

A strange episode from the last few days: On January 16–17, 1945, a Hungarian policeman in uniform presented himself to one of the (Jewish) ghetto guards at the gate (4 Wesselényi utca) saying that a battalion of policemen were quartered in the basement of the opposite building (the block of the former Viktória Insurance Company), probably, in the Broadway movie theater (later Film Museum, today the movie Broadway again), and they wanted to surrender to the Jewish gate guards.

On January 16 Russian military forces reached Új-Lipótváros and liberated the protected houses and the international ghetto. On January 18, around 9.00 a.m., the "big ghetto" was liberated as well. After a gun-battle with a smaller German unit the first Soviet soldiers made their way into the area of the ghetto from the Wesselényi utca gate through the air-raid shelter. The streets were empty. Soon afterwards, the gate to Dohány utca was opened. Still on that day and on the following one, thousands of people converged on the wooden fence surrounding the ghetto to knock it down.

About 70,000 people escaped death in the ghetto of Pest. After the war, the Jewish community published a thick printed volume with their names and full addresses. This is the very last conscription of Jews in Hungary: this time, a register of joy.

The liberation of the ghetto is commemorated by a simple stone slab put on the arcade wall of Wesselényi utca at the garden of Heroes' Temple. The slab was damaged by *evil hands* at the beginning of 1993, perhaps casting doubt on the legitimacy of the word *liberation* in connection with the Red Army. It was restored immediately on the basis of a photo.

On January 20 the building at 44 Wesselényi utca, the ghetto hospital, was hit by an artillery shell. Many died, including doctors, nurses and patients.

On February 17, 1945, the police station of the VIIth district reported that the burial of corpses from the area of the former ghetto had been finished on that day in the garden of "the Dohány utca Jewish temple". An excerpt from the report:

"At the location mentioned above altogether 2,281 corpses were buried in 24 common graves. Forty-five of these were shot in action (24 women and 21 men) and there were another 1,225 women and 1,011 men. The majority of the bodies had been dead for several weeks, many of them were entirely naked and could, therefore, be identified only partially. (...) Most of the dead were older people. (...) The lack of vehicles, the frozen state of the ground, the horror and reluctance of people made the burial work difficult."

A memorial *(Zakhor)* was erected in 1985 on the Dohány utca side of Heroes' Cemetery, by the arcades of the building of the Jewish Museum, roughly where the house in which Herzl was born used to be. The name *zakhor* (Deuteronomy 25,17–19) refers to the Ashkenazi ritual according to which on Yom Kippur and on the last day of certain other major holidays the dead and the martyrs of the congregation are remembered *(Yizkor)*. The small memorial of the Budapest ghetto was erected in 1990 in Wesselényi utca, in the little square between the Dohány Temple and the Heroes' Temple.

The Budapest National Committee, the highest authority in the days following the liberation of the capital, rescinded all the (Anti-)Jewish Laws by decree right after its establishment on January 21, 1945, as did the temporary Government on March 17, 1945, still in Debrecen, by passing an order of the prime minister (200/1945 M.E.). By the cease-fire agreement ratified by Act V of 1945 Hungary declared that she rescinded all (Anti-)Jewish Laws and the resulting restrictions. By Act XXV of 1946, passed on November 25, the Parliament repealed the (Anti-)Jewish Laws of the past era and established a foundation to support those having been persecuted because of their religion or Jewish background. The foundation did not carry out any meaningful activities and later even the Jewish properties that were once taken over by due process and were inventoried got lost somehow in the big sack of state finances.

480. The Red Cross Committee for investigating the atrocities committed by the Nazis and the Arrow-cross in the garden of the Dohány utca synagogue, February, 1945

The *Országos Református Szabad Tanács* (National Calvinist Free Council), was founded, among others, by Pastor Albert Bereczky, undersecretary of state after the war (1945–1946), later Calvinist bishop (of the Church District of Dunamellék, Budapest, 1948–1958)—a significant figure in his church who later played a controversial role in the political life of that era. Though many people participated in the Council's activity, it had no official status. Even before Act XXV of 1946 was passed by the Parliament, the convention of the Free Council in Nyíregyháza (August 14–17, 1946) had issued a statement which said as follows:

481. "Soup kitchen in Páva utca." Drawing by István Zádor, 1946

"We expiate together with our people, under the burden of our responsibility, for sins of omission and crimes committed against the Jews; we feel great empathy for the enormous sorrow carried by the entire surviving Jewry, for the sorrow that was caused by the loss of their beloved ones to inhumane extermination. Though belatedly, we apologize to the Hungarian Jewry in the presence of God."

The Free Council harshly criticized the official leadership of the Calvinist Church. Bishop László Ravasz responded by rejecting the apology. "The Protestant (Calvinist) Church of Hungary (...) did not ask the Jews to forgive simply because (...) it is not appropriate to apologize for someone else's crime..." (September 25, 1946). It was this remark, uttered by his own bishop and father-in-law, to which István Bibó alluded to in his study "Zsidókérdés Magyarországon 1944 után" [The Jewish Question in Hungary after 1944] (1948), where he wrote: "When an unofficial meeting of Hungarian clergymen explicitly begged for forgiveness of Jews in the name of the Hungarian nation and their own church, such a self-abasement was regarded as exaggerated and was rejected with a clear sound of irritation."

In 1960, however, Ravasz indulged in self-criticism because of his earlier views expressed during the debates in the Upper House and his behavior in the days of the persecution of Jews.

"I do admit one mistake of mine. One must not speak of Jewish faults when blind and beastly anti-Semitism puts a knife against the Jews' throat. At such a moment the knife must be wrested out of the murderer's hand. In this respect, I am guilty. *Mea culpa!*"

High-ranking leaders of other churches, who had not even been as firm as Ravasz was during his secret negotiations with the Government, did not apologize; they never uttered the words *Mea culpa*.

(14) Fateless

The story of those returning from the concentration camps and ghettos to Budapest during the spring and summer of 1945 is not connected to any specific street, square or area of the city.
The following passage from a novel by Imre Kertész has symbolic value:

"(...) A few steps further along the way I recognized our building. It still stood, in its entirety, in good shape. Inside the gate was the old smell. The shaky lift with its barred enclosure and the yellow, worn steps greeted me. Further up I was able to say hello to a familiar turn of the staircase in a particularly memorable moment. On reaching our floor, I rang the doorbell. It opened quickly but only slightly, stopped by a chain lock. That surprised me because I didn't recall such a contraption from the past. A strange face appeared in the door's chink: the sallow, bony face of a middle-aged woman peered out at me. She asked me who I was looking for, and I answered: I live here. No, she answered, we live here. She tried to shut the door but couldn't, because I had wedged my foot into it. I tried to explain to her: There must be some mistake, because I left from here, and most certainly we do live here. She, on the other hand, kept insisting that it was I who was mistaken, because without doubt they lived there, and with a kindly, polite, and sympathetic shaking of her head, she tried to close the door, while I tried to prevent this. For a second, though, I looked up at the number to be sure that I hadn't perhaps made a mistake, and my foot must have slipped then, because her attempt proved successful, and she slammed the door shut and turned the key twice."

(Imre Kertész, *Sorstalanság* [Fateless], written 1961, published in Hungary 1975,
English translation by Christopher C. Wilson & Katharina Wilson)

(15) Briha: A Chapter from the So Far Unwritten History of Hungarian Jews after World War II

"The miserable Hungarian Jewry, whose majority has already been destroyed, and who is now desperately fighting for its remaining life in the Gehenna of Pest, under Russian occupation can show its wounds only for a few weeks, even though the wounds are horrible indeed, and deserve all sympathy. The Russians are not especially moved by these wounds. The Russians are not enthusiastic about the Jews; true, they are not persecuting them either. And this is a huge difference. Nevertheless, after the first "disappointment" the Jews—as my rabbi said—will have to confine themselves to it: that they are not persecuted anymore for racial reasons and personally."

(Sándor Márai, *Ami a Naplóból kimaradt, 1945-1946* [That Was Left Out from the Diary], 1991)

Briha, berihah, "escape" is the Hebrew term used for the illegal emigration of the survivors (*she'er-it ha-peletah*) of the ghettos and concentrations camps to Palestine towards the end of World War II and in its aftermath, between 1944/45 and 1948. After the summer of 1945 one of the main crossroads of the mass exodus of the surviving Eastern and Central European Jews was Budapest.
The organization created by Aba Kovner (1918–1988), back when the Vilna ghetto still existed, also called *Brichah*, sent some emissaries (*shaliah*) to Budapest: Moshe Ben-David, Gaynor Jacobson and others. Masses of Jews arriving from Poland, Romania, the Soviet Union (even from Central

Asia) and Northern Europe, estimated by the number of people making illegal *aliyyot* to be about 250,000, arrived to Pozsony (Bratislava), Vienna or Budapest. Here they were organized in groups and sent, two trains a week, further to Salzburg, Tarvisio and from there, through various ports on the Mediterranean, to Palestine. (The operation bore the cover name *aliyyah bet*, "emigration no. 2", legal emigration being regarded as "no. 1".) Some of these people ended up in camps on the island of Cyprus, the ones whom the British authorities did not allow to land.

Among these *olim* there were some 15,000 Hungarian Jews. Leaders of the Pest Jewish community (first of all, Lajos Stöckler, the president) were always ready to help the organization in any way they could, and the Hungarian Government turned a blind eye to these actions because the *Joint* and other international organizations transferred the money to cover the expenses through the Hungarian National Bank. The border guards allowed the passengers on these special trains to cross the Hungarian border without a passport or any other document. In March, 1946 the Minister of Interior (László Rajk), the head of the *Katonapolitikai osztály* (Department of Military Politics or *katpol*), commander-in-chief of the border guard (György Pálffy), both prominent leaders of the Communist Party, and the Party's expert in economics (Zoltán Vas) decided to suspend these organized actions. Head of the operation in Budapest, Jonas Rosenfeld (Yonah Rosen) of the *Ezra*, was arrested by the State Security (April 9, 1946). The official explanation, publicized in newspapers, was that in the groups there were some Nazis trying to escape ("an exodus of Arrow-crossists"). (The only possible interpretation of this accusation could be that the former captives of concentration camps and ghettos were now helping the people who had tortured and held them captive escape from being held responsible.) After this the mass emigration of survivor groups was restricted and finally, on March 13, 1949, a committee was set up to dissolve Zionist organizations operating in Hungary. In May the police arrested ten Zionist leaders on the charge of helping illegal emigration. This measure not only ended any kind of open Zionist activity in Hungary, but also meant a serious danger to all the other Jewish organizations and to Jewish community life in general. It made further *aliyyot* from or through Hungary impossible. In the political trials of the fall of 1949 the communist politicians—who had tried to hinder the work of the Zionist organizations and cut the funds sent by international organizations to support the victims of persecutions—were now themselves accused of cooperating with Zionist leaders.

482. "Anikó Szenes Girls' Home." Drawing by István Zádor, 1946

The new regime, like the previous one some years earlier, limited the freedom of Jews first; and these restrictions, like before, led to a dictatorship over the whole Hungarian society.

XIII. Jewish Cemeteries

(1) Death

Jewish burial and mourning are prescribed by religious tradition in every detail, from the very moment of death. Though many may mourn the dead (*met*), only the immediate relatives are called mourners (*onen* or *avel*), that is, the parents, spouse, children, brother or sister (Leviticus 21,1–3).

The mourners have certain obligations related to dying (*gesisah*) and death. They may not leave a dying person (*goses* or *gajszesz* in Hungarian) alone, and it is a *mitzvah* to remain with the dying until his soul leaves his body (*yetzi'at neshamah*). The dead must be honored, too (*kevod ha-met*). It is customary to pour the water out of every dish when death occurs, at least from the glass or jar nearest to the dead (*niftar*, feminine *nifteret*). This is a symbolic act, to show that what has just happened is irrecoverable. In the Near East water was a great treasure. (In a Sumerian epic of Gilgamesh the death of god Dumuzi is signaled by water pouring out of a bag.) Pouring out the water symbolizes the greatness of the loss. A candle or light must be lit next to the dead to protect him (Proverbs 6,22). Where someone died all the mirrors must be covered or turned to the wall. The body is covered with black cloth (*mikhseh / mikhso / mekho*). Upon hearing the news of death one responds: *Barukh dayyan ha-emet*, "Blessed be the true judge".

The most important commandment is to bury the dead as soon as possible, on the same day if possible (Deuteronomy 21,23), but definitely before the Sabbath. Postponing the funeral constitutes lack of reverence towards the dead (*halanat ha-met*). Earlier, in small Jewish communities there was no obstacle to burial on the day the death occurred, but in modern Europe the authorities prohibited it, initially probably under Christian influence but later, in bourgeois societies, on rational grounds. Finally, by the eighteenth century, the custom of burying on the third day established itself in Jewish communities, too. (The three days reflect—through civil regulation in Europe—the lapse time between Jesus's death and resurrection as described in Matthew 28, etc.) In Hungary the authorities ruled against quick burial in 1827. Since this was a radical change compared to what Halakhah prescribed, there were debates on the issue for a long time. The Hatam Sofer was very much against the change. Mendelssohn's support was vital in the decision to accept the law. Later, it was David Einhorn who elaborated the arguments for the mortuary, already in the United States, in 1862.

A Jewish joke helps us understand why the authorities would not allow the dead to be buried immediately:

> "A Jewish coroner was asked how he could tell that someone had passed away. The old man answered calmly: Well, from how his folks cry..."
>
> (Máté Csillag, *Zsidó anekdoták kincseshaza* [Treasury of Jewish Anecdotes], 1925)

"Call the wailers to teach me some songs of bereavement"—reads the inscription on a fourteenth-century Jewish gravestone in Nagyszombat (quoted from Jeremiah 9,16). In large towns there are usually no wailers. People die in hospitals and, even if they die at home, the dead body is soon removed from the house. The custom of sitting vigil by the dead no longer prevails. Instead, *hashkavah* has been incorporated into the religious ritual; after the morning prayer the *hazzan* puts out the candles and sits in the last row of benches in the synagogue. The memory of wailing has been preserved in the language, however. The Biblical Hebrew wailing words, *hoy, hoy* or *oy, oy* (Jeremiah 22,18, etc.) and *ho, ho* (Amos 5,16) have been adopted by everyday usage. Nevertheless, the dead may not be left alone, there is always someone reading Psalms next to the dead until the funeral. Watching the dead (*shemirah*) is a religious commandment, the guard (*shomer*) is performing a *mitzvah*.

(2) The Hevrah Kaddishah

Burials used to be the task of the *Hevrah Kaddishah*, the Holy Society organized from members of the community for that purpose. Today this task has been taken over by clerks of the Jewish community. The pertinent ritual is still far stricter than the funerals of other religious communities.

The Hebrew word *hevrah* means "society", *hevrat kevarim* is a "society organized for burials". In the modern age the first Jewish burial societies (Latin *fraternitas*) were founded in German (Ashkenazi) communities in the sixteenth century. They were called *Hevra Kaddisha* in Aramaic, *Havurah* or *Hevrah kaddishah de-kevarim* in Hebrew or *Totenbruderschaft, Beerdigungsbruderschaft* or something similar in German. The ground rules of the *Hevrah* of Prague were written by R. Löw himself (1564), and this was to become the model. After a Moravian rabbi in the eighteenth century ruled in a decision that all Jewish communities should set up a Holy Society, these societies were established everywhere, and we can take it for granted that they existed even where the sources do not mention one specifically. According to the testimony of a goblet in the collection of the Jewish Museum in New York, Óbuda (or Buda?) had a *Hevrah Kaddishah* already in 1626; there was definitely one in Óbuda after 1770 and in Pest after 1788, even though it was but a few years earlier that Jews were allowed to live in Pest at all.

483. Table in the Ceremonial Hall of the Hevrah Kaddishah of Pest. Photo, ca. 1913

Originally the *Hevrah* was only in charge of performing the pious act (*gemilut hasadim*) of burial, but later it became a model for all kinds of civil self-aid and aid societies, and even for the institutional framework of self-aid in the society at large. The record book of the Jewish fraternities, called *Pinkas* (from the Greek *pinax*, "tablet"), set forth the basic principles, contained a list of members and records of their duties, accomplishments and obligations they might have failed to do. These old *Pinkas* books are the most important sources for the history of many Jewish communities. The volumes edited by the *Yad Vashem*, Jerusalem, on the history of the Jews in countries of Europe and on their losses and sufferings in the Holocaust are called *Pinkas*, too. (The volume on Hungary, *Pinkas ha-kehillot: Hungariyah*, was published in 1976.)

Members of the *Hevrah* contributed to its operation by their individual activities. They collected charity to cover the expenses. Each member was obliged to attend funerals. They organized ritual funerals and carried the coffin to the grave. They kept records of the deceased and of the funeral, noting the date of death (*Jahrzeit-Buch*); they organized memorial services (*hazkarah / hazkarat neshamot*), remembering the dead in the synagogue service (at Passover, Shavuot, Yom Kippur and Sukkot). (The word *Jahrzeit* is abbreviated in Hebrew as צ"י.) The Hevrah considered a noted *Jahrzeit*, Adar 7—the day of the death of Moses—as their own memorial day. For them this was a day of fasting and also a holiday. Members of the Hevrah visited the cemetery, checked their financial records and held a festive meal in the evening. Those whose date of death is not known are also traditionally remembered on this day.

484. "Bunch of grapes" goblet from the former collection of the Hevrah Kaddishah of Pest

The miniatures in the *Pinkas* of Nagykanizsa (1793), today at the Jewish Museum of Budapest, illustrate the activities of the *Hevrah Kaddishah*. The portrayal of eighteenth-century burial customs follows a model that was common in Central and Eastern Europe. At the exhibit of the Jewish Museum a couple of balls cut in half are on display, with a name on each of them: typical Jewish names, those of the members of the Burial Society, Yiddish or rarely German forms; the balls were used to cast lots for who would sit vigil by the dead and who would prepare the body for burial.

According to descriptions from the turn of the nineteenth and twentieth centuries, in those years the world's largest *Hevrah Kaddishah* was the Budapest one. Most of the community's social institutions, the hospitals, old-age homes and shelters were run by the *Hevrah*.

(3) Purification of the Dead

After the death sets in, the dead body needs to be covered and possibly placed on the floor. In large cities all the burial preparations take place in a funeral parlor, the body is to be brought here by the Hevrah Kaddishah as soon as possible.

In a ritual sense the dead is "not clean" (*tame / teme'ah, tüme* in Hungarian Yiddish). Therefore it has to be prepared for burial by the ceremony of purification (*tohorah / taharah / tahorah / tare*) or washing (*rehitzah / rekhitse*). In the cemetery there are usually three buildings for this purpose: two *tahorah* buildings or rooms, one for women and one for men, where the purification and dressing take place, and a mortuary. In the *tahorah* building there is a *tahorah* table; the body is laid on it with feet to the door. It is then washed in warm water which is heated on the spot. The body should never face downward. Great rabbis and scholars used to receive a "big washing (*rehitzah gedolah*)", that is their body was immersed in the *mikveh*. During the procedure Biblical verses are recited: Ezekiel 36,25, Zechariah 3,4, Song of Songs 5,11 or Song of Songs, Chapter 7 is read, etc. The verses that can be recited during washing are generally written on wooden or tin boards so that they can be read from there. At the end of the ritual it is said: "(It is) clean, clean, clean (*tahor, tahor, tahor*)."

The washing is followed by the dressing of the dead (*levishah*). A special comb is used to comb the hair, possibly a silver one, and similar is the tool for cleaning the nails, both ornamented with appropriate Hebrew inscriptions. There are a few such pieces held at the Jewish Museum. Women's hair is left free.

The dead are dressed in *takhrihim*, that is, in plain, white linen—called *kittel / kitl* or *sarganit / sarganes* (Latin *sargineum*), "shroud"—and in a white head-cover (Yiddish *heibli*). In addition to these, men are covered with their *tallit* and / or *tzitzit*, the latter is ritually mutilated, e.g. one of its fringes is cut off. People who died a violent death, for instance in an accident, or were victims of a shooting and the blood soaked into their clothes, they are buried without ritual washing and in the blood-stained clothes, because the blood is part of the body. Tradition frowns upon dressing the dead in fancy clothes (*halbashah*). It is customary to put pieces of a broken pot (*sherblakh*) and maybe a little earth or dust on the eyes and the mouth of the deceased. The arms are crossed on the chest, a weight is placed on the belly button and the legs are stretched out. Jewelry is not buried with the dead, but a wooden fork (*gepelah*) is placed into the hands to be crutches at the time of the redemption or to help them dig their ways out of the grave for the *gilgul*,[1] when the Messiah comes and all the dead "roll" to Jerusalem to be redeemed and enter the city through the Golden Gate following the Messiah (Ketubbot 111a). The head of the dead is placed upon a little pillow filled with earth from the Holy Land, as if he or she had been buried in the Holy Land (Deuteronomy 32,43); this has always been the ultimate wish of pious Jews in the Diaspora (*galut / goles*). The coffin (*aron*) is traditionally made of simple, rough wood, without any iron nails. It has to be closed immediately after the dead body is placed in it. The novelist Gyula Krúdy wrote upon the death of József Kiss that his "tiny corpse was resting among unplaned wooden planks, far from the city, in the Jewish cemetery", indicating that the poet was buried traditionally.

It is rare to find a description of the washing and the dressing of the dead. The following words are just the emotional notes of a friend and colleague:

"Lajos Vajda left us last night. (...) Being his close friends, Bandi [Endre Bálint] and I organized his funeral. We were there when he was dressed by two poor Jews in a tiny mortuary in Budakeszi. (...) He looked as if he were asleep and smiling, his body was not rigid at all, his hands were moving as the men washed him, as if he were alive. (...) We placed a little scrap of paper with some words of farewell into his burial clothes, above his heart."

(Imre Ámos, September 8, 1941)

---

[1] That is, "rolling of the soul (gilgul neshamot)": rolling of the dead to Jerusalem (when the Messiah blows the shofar); "transformation of the soul".

The funeral of the painter Lajos Vajda basically followed Jewish ritual. If he was washed by "two poor Jews", this must have happened according to the rules of the *Hevrah Kaddishah*, his "burial clothes" must have meant a *kittel*. The text on the "little scrap of paper", the friends' farewell, represented or replaced the words of the Psalms. In this instance three prominent Hungarian painters were brought together, after years of friendship, by the Jewish ritual.

(4) The Cemetery

The Jewish cemetery is called the "house of living (*beit hayyim*)", a euphemism (see Isaiah 26,19), the "house of graves (*beit ha-kevarot*)" (Nehemiah 2,3) or the "house of eternity" (*beit ha-olam*, Aramaic *beit almin*, Yiddish *bes oylem* or in Hungary *beszojlem*) (see Ecclesiastes 12,5), or simply *kevarot / kvores*, "graves". In the Middle Ages the Jewish cemetery was often referred to as *hortus Judaeorum*, the "Jews' garden" or *mons Judaicus*, "Jewish hill / mountain", referring probably to its site and position. Jews call the non-Jewish cemeteries *cvinter* (from the Greek *koimeterion*, Latin *coemeterium*, "resting place"). Jewish communities tended to open their cemeteries on a height or hill, and they usually did not mow the grass or prune the trees, but let the plants grow naturally around the graves. The state of the Salgótarjáni utca cemetery reveals several decades of lack of care, but it does appear rather natural.

The cemetery should traditionally be far removed from the town. A medieval example can be seen in Buda, where the cemetery was outside of the Jewish dwelling quarter on the Castle Hill, far below it (in Krisztinaváros and still further).

The mortuary (*ohel / ayhel*) is always at the entrance of the cemetery. (Its popular name is in Yiddish *tsiduk ha-din haysl / tzidduk ha-din-Haus*). *Kohanim* may not touch a corpse, thus they may not enter a cemetery either, may not be under the same roof with a corpse. Unless he himself is the mourner, a Kohen may not attend the funeral ceremony. Kohanim usually stand outside, in the door of the mortuary, behind an imaginary separation (*ezrat kohanim*). At some places a special path is built for them (*derekh kohanim*) between the graves out of brick, above the regular path, so that they may enter the cemetery. It is because of the *kohanim* that the highest limbs of trees are trimmed, for this would count as a "roof" and would thus make it forbidden for the kohanim to enter the cemetery at all.

485. Alms box of the Hevrah Kaddishah of Pest, modeled on a typical rabbinical grave

The graves of Kohanim and their families are generally in a segregated row next to the cemetery gate, so that they can visit the graves. A special place, usually in the front of the cemetery, is granted also for rabbis, as well as for community leaders, for leaders of the *Hevrah Kaddishah* and for Levites. Apart from that, graves are assigned in the order of death. At least six inches should be left between two graves, and if because of lack of space coffins are buried on top of each other, like in Prague, the same distance should be kept vertically. In case there is not enough space, a solid partition may be placed between coffins instead of keeping the distance. The iron fence we often see around graves is precisely this ritual partition. In Orthodox or strictly traditional communities there is generally a separate men's and women's side of the cemetery. Sometimes not even husband and wife can be buried next to each other, as it was the case of Dávid Kaufmann and Irma Gomperz in the Salgótarjáni utca cemetery, but there are exceptions. (The Shulhan Arukh, Yoreh de'ah 362/3 is permissive at this point.) It is not customary to bury in a common grave, unless it is a vault. It was exactly because of the traditional burial customs that family vaults came into fashion early in the twentieth century. Above some graves there is a roof held by columns, like a stone tent. This is not an arbitrary decorative element but the indication of an *ohel*, an indication that the deceased person was a pious Jew, a *hasid*. A real *ohel*, which is actually just a plain white house, is only built above the grave of a Hasidic *rebe*. Care must be taken not to bury enemies next to each other. Jews who had converted to another religion are usually buried in a corner of the cemetery. There is a separate place for still-born babies (*nefel*) or infants who died before they were one month old. There is no ritual mourning for them, either.

(5) Funeral

The funeral ceremony itself is "the acceptance of the verdict (*tzidduk ha-din*)". The prayers and the eulogy (*hesped*) are usually very short, though in case of a notable personality, if there are many speakers (*maspid*), the whole ceremony may last quite long. The ceremony generally ends with the text of Isaiah 25,8: "He will destroy death forever. My LORD God will wipe the tears away from all faces..."

You shall return to dust, says the Bible (Genesis 3,19), therefore one must bury into earth, possibly directly into earth. In former times the naked body of the deceased was just rolled into some linen. In many Jewish communities, even until World War II, no coffin was used for burial. At some places the lower plank of the coffin is removed from the grave, so that the body can come into direct contact with the earth. Another solution is to make holes in the coffin, to establish this contact at least symbolically.

Mourners rend their clothes, as did Jacob (Genesis 37,34) and David (II Samuel 13,31). Today the Ancient Near Eastern custom of rending is often replaced by symbolic cutting (*keri'ah*, in Yiddish *kerie shaydn*) or pinning a ribbon to the outer clothing. Since this is a ritual (Job 1,20), the mourners may not perform this cut, it has to be done for her or him, standing. At some places *keri'ah* is performed only at the funeral, but in Hungary this happens right when the death occurs. In case of the death of a parent the clothes are torn on the left side, near the heart, for other relatives on the right side. If clothes are changed during the week of mourning, the fresh clothes must be torn too, at least in case of a parent's death. In this case the torn clothes may not be mended later, while after someone else's death the torn clothes may be repaired a month later. Wearing black clothes or a black ribbon is a foreign mourning custom (*hukkat ha-goy*), the Jewish custom is tearing. It is forbidden to wear the prayer-shawl (*talit*) at the side of a dead person, whether at the cemetery, or even at the funeral, even though it is a ritual; this would ridicule the dead (*lo'eg la-rash*) who cannot perform this *mitzvah* any more.

The funeral is nothing but "accompanying the dead (*halvayat ha-met / levaye*)". Members of the *Hevrah* take the dead to the grave on their shoulders (*kattafim*); they are always men, even if the deceased is a woman, and even according to the Orthodox ritual. Accompanying the dead is a religious duty. Whoever catches sight of a funeral procession should join it at least for a little while; this is a truly pious deed (*hesed shel emet*), because it can never be returned (Rashi ad Genesis 47,29). For a funeral one has to approach the grave along the longest possible way. According to an ancient custom the funeral procession stops seven times before arriving at the grave and Psalm 91 is recited at every stop. Some people stop seven times even on the way back from the grave. Nowadays only three stops are left from the seven, and only at strictly traditional burials. In earlier times musicians, klezmers, used to accompany the funeral procession, especially in communities which had preserved Eastern traditions. This custom was dropped in Budapest a long time ago, just like the custom of apologizing (*mehilah*) to the dead in the name of Israel for all the evil that anyone had committed against her or him, which used to take place at the cemetery gate. Here is how a Hungarian newspaper reported on the funeral of Jacob Frank, the converted Podolian Messiah, in Offenbach, near Frankfurt am Main, just a few days after the event:

"Before the funeral procession started, everyone went up to the body one by one and, touching his feet with their hands (according to Jewish custom), they asked for his forgiveness. When this ceremony was over, the procession left for the cemetery. Ahead went the women dressed in white, holding burning candles, after them the children (...) and then the men. (...) The body was carried by 18 men. In front of him and after him went two men, their head uncovered. (...) At the grave (...) they all started crying and wailing loudly, but it stopped upon a single sign, and then the two old men recited a short prayer. (...) And when the coffin was let down into the grave, everyone threw a handful of earth upon it."

(In: *Hadi és más nevezetes történetek* [Military and Other Notable Stories], December 27, 1791)

The grave must be dug so that the head of the dead should be facing West and the feet East. As a sign of their sympathy, mourners touch the foot of the coffin at the grave, with both hands. They cry the Hebrew name of the deceased after him into the grave, so that he should remember it when he reaches the heavenly court. It is customary to throw a handful of earth into the grave. If a shovel is used, it should not be passed from hand to hand, everyone picks it up from the ground.

Once the grave is covered, the men traditionally line up in two rows and the mourners leave the site between those lines. It is only now that condolences are expressed.

"My great-grandfather (...) died at the age of 114, in a first floor apartment in the Schmiedunger House in Király utca. Not only Jews came to his funeral, but many Christians, flooding Király utca in its entire length as well as the neighboring streets. No one ever saw such a Jewish funeral in Pest before. And after the funeral, returning from the cemetery in his clothes torn from *keri'ah*, my 80-year-old grandfather threw ashes unto his head, fell on a chair and cried out in tears: He has stripped me of my glory! (Job 19,9)"

(Adolf Ágai, *Az én dédatyámról* [About My Great-grandfather], 1907)

(6) Mourning

Mourning (*evel*) is the obligation of immediate relatives. It takes place in four stages. The first stage, called *aninut*, is between the death and the funeral. The mourner, now called *onen*, eats alone during this period and he is exempt from all positive religious commandments, except that of sending the Purim-presents. If he has a job connected to ritual, if he is a *shakhter* for instance, he needs to organize his replacement.

The second stage of mourning, *avelut*, begins immediately after the funeral and lasts for seven days: this is called *shivah*. During these days the mourner, now called *avel / ovel*, sits on the floor (see II Samuel 13,31), or at least lower than normally, hence the term "to sit shivah". Even if he is not actually sitting for a whole week, he definitely does not attend to his regular occupation. A mourner may not wear leather shoes or jewelry, may not shave and must wear torn clothes. It is the mourners' obligation to say *Kaddish* three times a day. Since they need a *minyan* for this, in strictly Orthodox communities men are sent to the mourners' house three times a day at prayer so that ten men would be available. The rabbi of the community also visits mourners in his congregation. (Theodor Herzl mentions in his "Autobiography" that in 1878, when they were mourning his sister, Sámuel Kohn, chief rabbi of the Dohány synagogue, visited them.) The mirrors are still covered in the mourners' apartment, and a candle is kept burning for seven days. Mourners are only allowed to read those parts of the Bible which pertain to grieving, descriptions of bereavement, funerals, like Job or Lamentations.

The mourners' first meal after the funeral, the *se'udat havra'ah* should be prepared by friends or relatives. The mourners' bread (*lehem anashim*, Ezekiel 24,17), that is, all food, is to console the mourners (*nihum avelim*). There should be round foods in the meal, such as eggs, and now it is permitted to drink some wine, too (Jeremiah 16,7).

It is customary to visit the mourners during *shivah*. One should just sit down silently (Job 2,13) and say comforting words (Isaiah 41,1–2). On the Sabbath mourners may go to synagogue, but they should wait outside in the Hall until after the greeting of the Sabbath (*lekhah dodi*). One should not mourn on a holiday.

The third stage of mourning is the thirty days after the burial called *sheloshim* (Deuteronomy 21,13). In this period mourners return to their daily routine, but they do not go to parties, celebrations or other merry events, men do not have a shave. Major holidays suspend the *sheloshim*, these should be observed. The fourth stage of mourning, one year following the death, applies only to those who had lost a parent. The gravestone is erected at the end of this year, and the *Jahrzeit*, the death anniversary is observed every year. The *Jahrzeit* is traditionally a day of fast. A candle should burn in the house of the mourners all day long. In Hasidic communities, however, the *Jahrzeit* is considered a joyful day, since the deceased is coming closer to God year by year. Therefore the *Jahrzeit* is observed with merry celebrations (*hillulah*).

The memory of the deceased is preserved in the community, too. This is done in the framework of the ritual of *hazkarat neshamot* at *yizkhor*. Those whose parents are alive customarily leave the synagogue for this part of the service. When the name of the deceased is uttered, *Alav / alehah hashalom / olevasholem*, "May he / she rest in peace" is heard after it for some time. Saying *Kaddish* after the deceased is always the son's obligation. Therefore it is usually called the "orphan's (*yatom / yosom*) prayer". If one cannot say *Kaddish*, it is permitted to hire someone to do so. *Kaddish* can be said only in the presence of a *minyan*, i.e. ten men.

(7) Visiting the Grave

Visiting the grave is almost like a pilgrimage, except that it is not a visit to the grave of some unknown person. It is a special *mitzvah* to visit the cemetery on a fast day. Visiting parents' graves (*kever avot / keyveroves, keverovausz* in Hungarian) is a great *mitzvah* at all times, and it is mandatory on the *Jahrzeit*.

486. Visiting the grave

Men may enter the cemetery only with head covered. One must not bring flowers—that, too, is an alien custom. Instead, a little stone should be placed on the grave. If we have a request, possibly even from someone we do not know, we should just write it down on a piece of paper, sign it, carefully fold it, and stick the *kvitl* into the gravestone of a *rebe*, a *tzaddik*, who will take care of it. Prayer at a grave, like in the synagogue, is an act of praise or a request. At actual pilgrimage sites a memorial candle (*ner neshamah*) is lit next to the grave.

In the cemetery nothing must be for profit or serve private ends. It is forbidden to pick and eat the fruit of the trees, it is forbidden to eat or drink in general. The grass should not be cut, and if it is cut, it should by no means be used as fodder. The wild vegetation in older cemeteries, like in Amsterdam, Prague, Venice, Worms or elsewhere, appears to be due to lack of care, though it is just a way of keeping tradition.

Exhumation of the deceased is strongly prohibited by tradition, except if it is in the interest of the deceased. This is the case when a cemetery has to be abandoned. Late in the summer of 1944 the Kozma utca cemetery was hit by a bomb. Some graves were destroyed and bones were scattered. The Rabbinate ruled that they should be re-buried into one common grave, because this way the bones of a given person would definitely stay together until the *shofar* is blown.

Pogroms and the desecration of the Jewish cemetery used to occur together, at least in Russia. (Incidentally, the word *pogrom*, "destruction" comes from the Russian.) Thus sensitivity to the desecration of a Jewish cemetery has historical justification.

Upon leaving the cemetery one must wash hands ritually, pluck some grass and throw it backwards saying, "Let abundant grain be in the land" (Psalms 72,16); thus one's tracks vanish, so death will not find the person. Both of these customs are cleansing ceremonies.

(8) Gravestone, Inscription

It is an ancient custom to mark the site of burial (Genesis 35,20; II Samuel 18,18; Ezekiel 39,15). This mark can be a gravestone (*matzzevah*) or some other sign (*tziyyun*). The rabbis' gravestones are called *nefesh*, "soul". In Ashkenazi cemeteries we find mostly vertical gravestones (Greek *stele*). Jewish tombs are rarely surrounded by any structure, unless it is a famous rabbi's tomb. Family vaults are more popular in Neolog cemeteries, though it was a popular custom in ancient Jerusalem to bury family members in the same sepulcher. Gravestones are made, most probably since the Middle Ages, from "new", that is, previously unused materials; nor may gravestones be used for a different purpose later. Incorporating Jewish gravestones into the Buda Castle at the turn of the seventeenth and eighteenth centuries was actually an act of desecration, from a ritual point of view.

487. A family grave in the Csörsz utca Orthodox cemetery

The gravestone is customarily erected on the first *Jahrzeit*. In Jewish tradition it is forbidden to erect a gravestone without an inscription, for this would be a foreign god's symbol or sculpture, an *eidolon* or *idol*. The gravestone may be erected in various positions and thus the place of the inscription may vary, too. It is an old custom to put the marked stone towards the head of the corpse; Christian tradition also follows this custom. The inscription, traditionally only in Hebrew, must be on the "outern" (front) side of the gravestone. If a Yiddish, German or Hungarian inscription was added, this was generally shorter than the Hebrew one, mostly just the name of the deceased, and was written on the "back" side of the gravestone, the one facing the grave. In modern times, and especially in Neolog cemeteries, Christian customs have taken over. In Hebrew there is generally just a Biblical quotation, the Hebrew name of the deceased and the usual formula, and even these are written on the same side as the text in the Latin alphabet.

There is a Talmudic saying that reading gravestone inscriptions spoils the memory (Horayot 13b). This is not directed against inscriptions but rather a praise of living memory. It is a *mitzvah* not to let the name on the gravestone fade. There are some pious men, *hasidim*, all around the world, who go around in cemeteries and repaint the names on the graves, even those of unknown for them men.

Scholars often compose the inscription for their own grave themselves, as did Goldziher. Jewish tomb inscriptions are never completely stereotyped. They contain the name of the deceased and the exact date of his death according to the Jewish calendar; the *Jahrzeit* is calculated based on this date. But there are also some individual lines, a quotation, a Biblical phrase, to characterize the deceased, as well as some consoling words at the end. The words "*Shalom al Yisra'el* (Peace upon Israel)" (Psalms 125,5) are often added. Sometimes the Biblical quotation, name or date is hidden in an acrostic. Each inscription is an individual composition. The name of the mother of the deceased is usually written on the bottom line (it used to be uttered when saying *Kaddish*).

Abbreviations are common in the Hebrew text of gravestones. The following is a selection from the formulas used as abbreviations in burial inscriptions (listed according to their usual sequence on gravestones):

פ"נ	"Here lies buried (or hidden)" (*po nikbar / nitman*)
פ"ט	"Here lies (actually, hides)" (*po tamun*)
	(These three Hebrew expressions listed above correspond to the formula used on Greek or Roman gravestones: *entha de keitai / hic iacet*)
ה"ל	"Gone to eternity" (*halakh le-olamo / olamah*)
ר'	Rabbi / Rav / Reb / "Mr."
ח'	Scholar (*hakham*)
י"א	"Should (live) long (days)" (*yamim arukhim*) (used only if the father of the deceased is still alive)
ש"י	"His / Her Creator should guard Him" (*shomrehu yotzro / yotzrah*) (used only if the father of the deceased is still alive)
	or: "Blessed be his name" (*shemo yitbarekh*)
ז"ל	"Blessed be his / her memory" (*zikhro / zikhrah li-vrakhah*)
זצ"ל	"Blessed be the memory of the true man" (*zekher tzaddik li-vrakhah*) (Proverbs 10,7)
ע"ה	"May he / she rest in peace" (*alav / aleha ha-shalom*)
נ"ע	"He / She should find peace in Eden" (*nuho / nuhah eden*)
זלח"ה	"His / Her memory should live in eternity" (*zikhro / zikhrah le-hayyei ha-olam ha-ba*)
תנצב"ה	"His / Her soul should be bound into the bonds of life" (*tehi nafsho / nafshah tzerurah bi-tzeror ha-hayyim*) (I Samuel 25,29)
יצ"ו	"His / Her Rock and Redeemer should guard him / her" (*yishmerehu tzuro ve-go'alo / tzurah ve-go'alah*) (Psalms 19,15, etc.)
לפ"ק	"According to the minor era" (*li-frat katan*)
א"ס	*Amen, selah*
אאא	*Amen, amen, amen*
ססס	*Selah, selah, selah*

The dots above the letters of the inscription usually indicate an abbreviation or a date.

Here is one of the witty sayings of R. Shalom ben Tzvi ha-Levi, the Rayetzer *maggid* (d. 1830), published by a certain Nathan Dessauer. (Julius Dessauer was the rabbi of Újpest for a while around 1865; he published several collections of proverbs and sayings. Nathan was probably his pen-name, alluding to Lessing's "wise" Nathan.)

"How do we know that the world is getting worse year after year? From the gravestone inscriptions. These testify that only good people die. Consequently all the bad people are left alive."

(Nathan Dessauer, *Der jüdische Humorist*, Pest, 1865)

(9) Symbols on Gravestones

Jewish gravestones are more beautiful than palaces, says the Talmud (Sanhedrin 96b; see Matthew 23,29). "More beautiful" in this context means "precious", nevertheless they are often more beautiful, too. Seldom do we see so many bas-reliefs next to inscriptions as in Jewish cemeteries.

Jewish gravestones are traditionally not adorned with statues. Instead, symbols are carved on the stele. Adorning the gravestone is a modern custom; it is never emphasized at the expense of the inscription. The adornment of Sephardi gravestones is usually Biblical, for example, a motif from a story about a Biblical person who bears the same name as the deceased. Ashkenazi gravestones are more likely to indicate the status of the deceased. The face of the gravestone is often framed by an elaborate Baroque wreath. Two columns, Jakhin and Boaz on the two sides, and a tympanum or roof above them—such a composition is not just a frame for the gravestone but a tent, a stylized *ohel*, indicating that a true man, a *tzaddik* lies there. Other symbols are usually above the wreath. These can be references to the name of the deceased, plants or animals which in Hebrew or German represent his name, or the portrayal of his occupation, especially if this endowed him with a rank. It is always indicated if the person was a *Kohen* or a *Levite*. Finally these symbols may testify to personal virtues, to a pious and charitable life, or to the mode of his death if this was caused by an accident or a natural disaster. It is forbidden to portray human figures (see Exodus 20,4–5), not even in an allegorical form. Nevertheless, early in the nineteenth century statues of humans started to appear in the Jewish cemeteries of Pest. The Hatam Sofer himself denounced this new fashion (1832), though apparently to little avail.

Some of the symbols and their meaning,

ALMS-BOX:	he / she gave *tzedakah*
BEAR:	Ber, Beer, Dov
BOOK, BOOKS, BOOKSHELF:	scholar
BRICK-SHAPED BLANK SPACE:	reminder of the destruction of Jerusalem
BUNCH OF GRAPES:	fruitfulness, productive life
CANDLE:	pious woman
CARP:	Karpeles
CAT:	Katz
CROW:	died in a catastrophe
CROWN WITH TWO CHAINS:	goldsmith
CROWN:	good name (Pirkei Avot 4,17)
CROWN:	noble, high person (*ga'on*)
DEER:	Hirsch, Zevi, Ayyal
DOVE:	beautiful woman; Jonah
EAGLE:	Adler
FISH:	Fisch, Fish, Fischel, Fishl, Fischer
FLAME:	as LUCERNA
GRAPES:	Levi, Levite
HARP:	*hazzan*
HEART:	Herzl, Leyb; good-hearted, kind woman
HOUSE, COLUMN:	especially pure, chaste life
LAW (*shenei luhot*):	observant life
LION WITH SWORD:	doctor
LION:	Aryeh, Judah, Löw / Löb / Löbl, Leyb
LUCERNA:	sudden death
MENORAH:	"The life-breath of man is the lamp of the LORD" (Proverbs 20,27)
MORTAR AND PESTLE:	pharmacist
MOUSE:	Meisel
PALM:	true, honest person
PAROKHET:	rabbi
PITCHER (EWER) AND BOWL:	*ha-Levi*, a Levite's grave
POMEGRANATE (*rimmon*):	exceptional religious piety
SCISSORS:	Schneider
SCROLL AND PEN:	*sofer* / *soyfer*, Schreiber
SHIELD:	a life worthy of the distinguished ancestors
SHIP, SINKING SHIP:	death caused by tragedy
SHOFAR:	waiting for the Messiah
STAR OF DAVID (MAGEN DAVID)	
TENT:	rabbi, *rebe*
TORAH CROWN:	rabbi

TWO TABLETS OF THE TORAH SCROLL:	rabbi
TREE (sometimes with two human figures):	Adam and Havvah (Eve)
TWO CHAINS:	goldsmith
TWO COLUMNS:	pious life; Jakhin and Boaz, like before the Temple of Salomon (I Kings 7,21)
TWO HANDS WITH THE GESTURE OF THE PRIESTLY BLESSING:	*kohen*'s grave; blessing
TWO TORAH SCROLLS:	*talmid hakham*
WAILING WILLOW	
WOLF:	Wolf, Zeev

(10) The Old Orthodox Cemetery in Csörsz utca (55 Csörsz utca)

As in Germany at the time, during the nineteenth century the Jewish cemeteries of Pest were designated next to other large public cemeteries. As the city grew, new cemeteries were established further and further, always at the edge of the city, while the older cemeteries were taken over by development. Only a few former Jewish cemeteries survived, now testifying the former layout of the old city.

488. The Csörsz utca Orthodox cemetery. In the middle the *derekh kohanim*

The cemetery in Csörsz utca is now one of the oldest cemeteries in Budapest preserved in its original state. There have been no burials here since 1961. The tiny space is packed with graves, conveying an atmosphere of antiquity. The Orthodox community received this plot from the municipality in 1883 and the first funeral was held in 1890. Late in the nineteenth century this was the Jewish cemetery next to the Tabán and later the large Németvölgy public cemeteries. The former was gradually liquidated when the buildings in the lower section of Csörsz utca were built, the last ones being Hotel Novotel (1982) and the *Kongresszusi Központ* (Convention Center), only this small part of the cemetery remained untouched, squeezed between buildings. The street is at a higher level now, and the cemetery has been surrounded by walls; a few steps lead down to its entrance. It is possible that some of the graves were brought here from an earlier cemetery. The earliest grave, that of R. Shemuel Abeles, son of R. Josef Aryeh Abeles, dates from 1857.

Women's graves are mostly to the left of the narrow path leading through the cemetery (*derekh kohanim*), while the men are buried to the right of it. This traditional Orthodox arrangement is sometimes interrupted by graves where man and wife are buried next to each other, for instance, the grave of the óbudai Freudiger family, of husband and wife. This curious and rare double gravestone is behind the mortuary, in the corner of the cemetery. The husband's grave is decorated with hands raised for the priestly blessing, the wife's with a heart.

Another grave of the Csörsz utca cemetery held in high respect is that of Jacob Koppel Reich (1838–1929), the notable Orthodox chief rabbi. Over his grave there is a stone cover in the form of

a tent, the only kind of grave cover that is permitted by the Orthodox, and only in case of a distinguished individual. His gravestone is decorated with a crown. The inscription, strictly traditional, like on the other tombs of the cemetery, is on the "outer" side of the gravestone, towards the *derekh kohanim*.

R. Reich studied at the famous Pozsony / Pressburg *yeshivah* and married the daughter of one of the Hatam Sofer's students. When he accepted the invitation and moved to Budapest in 1889, he applied the ideas of his great master to the life of the Orczy House and later to the Kazinczy utca community: no concessions in religious life, but absolute loyalty to the state. He put great energy into organizing the life of the community. He founded a school called *Torat emet*, "Truth of the Torah", where secular subjects were also taught; the hospital of the community (*Szeretetkórház*) in 1920 in Buda, close to Városmajor, a city park, along with the *Aggok Háza* (Old-age Home) and *Szeretetotthon* ("Almshouse", nursing home) (*hekdesh*) of the Hevrah Kaddishah.

It was extraordinary even in those days that at the national assembly of the Orthodox community in 1905 Reich gave his address in Hebrew and not in Yiddish, the official language of the Orthodoxy (his Hungarian was rather poor, by the way). He was already over 80 when he was elected the Orthodox representative in the Upper House and symbolically occupied his seat as the oldest member of it.

Upon Reich's death in 1929 *Múlt és Jövő* published some of his sayings.

"R. Koppel Reich used to give a great eulogy on 7th of Adar every year, remembering all those who died during the preceding year. According to an ancient custom, the Hevrah Kaddishah would send him three gold coins as honorarium. Last year he was already too weak to give his *hesped*, but the Hevrah still sent him the three gold coins. Upon receiving it he smiled and told his secretary: Well, the proverb seems to be true, *silence is golden.*"

R. Koppel Reich's *Jahrzeit* is remembered by the Orthodox community up to the present day. Pilgrims often seek out his grave, and place a *kvitl* into the small stone tent over the grave. Some day even a real *ohel / ayhel* might be built over it.

Right next to the grave of R. Reich there is another noteworthy grave of the Csörsz utca cemetery, that of his son-in-law, R. Mordekhai Efrayim Fischel Zussmann (Sussmann) Sofer (1867–1942). He married the daughter of R. Reich in 1890. From 1914 on he was a *dayyan* and *maggid* beside his father-in-law. After R. Reich died, he became the rabbi of the congregation.

The father of R. Mordekhai Sussmann, Benjamin Zeev (Wolf) Sussmann Sofer (1825–1898), attended the *yeshivah* of the Hatam Sofer in Pozsony / Pressburg, and after the death of the latter, that of his son, the *Ketav Sofer*[2] (Abraham Samuel Benjamin Wolf, 1815–1871). At the time of the General Congress in 1868/69 he was appointed the *dayyan* of the Shas Hevrah congregation in Két Szerecsen utca (2 Paulay Ede utca), the antecedent of the Orthodox synagogue in Vasvári Pál utca.

Someone who actually could have been buried here but "rests with his fathers" (Genesis 15,15, etc.) in Pozsony, is R. Reich's predecessor, Hayyim ben Mordekhai Ephraim Fischel Sofer (1821–1886). He, too, used to be a pupil of the Hatam Sofer and Ketav Sofer. In 1879 he became the first rabbi of the Orthodox community of Pest and remained in this position until his death. He was one of the extreme Orthodox rabbis in Hungary, an ardent opponent of any kind of modernization, demanding that Neolog Jews be excommunicated and that their sons be refused circumcision.

Descendants of the great masters of the Pozsony *yeshivah*, Hatam Sofer and Ketav Sofer, first of all, the latter's son and successor in Pozsony, R. Simhah Bunem (the *Shevet Sofer*) (1842–1906); his other son, R. Simeon (the *Mikhtav Sofer*) (1850–Auschwitz, 1944), rabbi of Eger (Erlau); and his grandson, Akiva Sofer (the *Da'at Sofer*) (1878–1959), rabbi of Pozsony, were all in tight contact with the Hungarian Orthodox communities. Akiva Sofer attended a wedding of the Freudiger family (Katalin and Sámuel Vilmos von Freudiger) in Budapest in 1931.

*

The memorial plaque of the martyrs of the Orthodox hospital (64–66 Városmajor utca) commemorates a tragic day, January 14, 1945. Right next to it is the grave of Dániel Bíró, the head physician who was murdered along with the patients of the hospital.

A few days after the massacre in Maros utca, Sunday morning at 11 o'clock, a group of armed Arrow-cross men appeared in the Orthodox hospital in Városmajor utca.

An eye-witness, Emil Böszörményi Nagy accounted the events as follows:

"(...) They ordered that whoever could walk should get out of bed and get dressed. These persons were then sent down to the courtyard in small groups where they were ordered to turn around and then were shot in the back. Some were sent down to the coal storage room and were shot there. By four o'clock there were piles of dead in the courtyard. Then the Arrow-cross brothers continued their work in the sick wards. They went from ward to ward, killing everyone, old people, the seriously ill as well as little children. The director of the hospital was murdered on the spot, too. (...) On the following day an Arrow-cross man stood guard in front of the building and did not let anyone in. On Tuesday morning they poured gasoline over the bodies in the courtyard, which were covered with a red carpet, and set them on fire, together with the building. It burnt for two days. Some of the bodies burned completely, some were only partly charred. The

---

[2] His, and his descendants', honorary names, like that of the Hatam Sofer, refer to the titles of their Halakhic works, the plain meaning of the compounds being "writing of the scholar / Sofer".

corpses were later removed by the Soviet authorities, but a few limbs and human bones are still there in the ashes. There is, for instance, a woman's shoe with a charred foot in it. A few bones here and there. This is all that remained of the patients of the Dániel Bíró hospital today."

130 patients and 24 staff members of the hospital fell victim to the massacre. The building burned down completely; the ruins were cleared after the war and two apartment buildings were built on the spot since then. A small corner of the former plot is vacant even today: the little triangle at the intersection of Gaál József utca and Városmajor utca. A tiny, strange memorial stone is hiding in the grass among the shrubs and flowers, but the mysterious mirror writing on it refers to an event of private character.

A few days later, on January 19, 1945 the Arrow-cross men murdered the 90 elderly residents of the neighboring *Aggok háza / Szeretetotthon* on the corner of Városmajor utca and Alma utca. They had tried to liquidate this building twice before, they even lined up those who were able to walk in the street, but were interrupted and prevented from completing the massacre. On November 4, 1944 it was the police chief of Budapest who intervened and on November 11 the International Red Cross, Friedrich Born personally. But in January even the Red Cross was no longer in a position to be able to help.

"On January 19 a Christian employee of the *Szeretetkórház* went over to the school across the street which now gave home to the military hospital and asked the commander, a general, for protection. The general said (...) that he could not help. (...) Thus the employee told the elderly inhabitants of the institute, among whom there was barely anyone under seventy, to try to escape, to go wherever they could. Bombs were falling all day long, so the poor old people were afraid to leave. Nevertheless, four of them decided to go— in fact, they were the ones who survived. The other seventy remained and awaited their fate trembling. The Arrow-cross men arrived between 7 and 8 in the evening. They announced that the inhabitants had to be transported. They separated men and women and took the women to Városmajor. They lined them up near Szamos utca in three rows. Whoever could not walk was taken there in a wheelchair. Then the machine guns sounded. (...) Some did not die immediately, but were only wounded. They were begging their executioners to put an end to their lives. Upon this they threw three grenades among them. One exploded and lit the clothes. Finally the fire and the frost ended the job of the men."

These victims do not have a grave, only the cenotaph in the Csörsz utca cemetery preserves their memory. The Orthodox old-age nursing home functions even today (*Szeretetotthon*). Additional buildings have been erected next to the original one.

(11) The Cemetery in Salgótarjáni utca (6 Salgótarjáni utca)

The first and the second Jewish cemetery of Pest, the one on Váci út and in Lehel utca, no longer exist, buildings have been erected at these sites. The third Jewish cemetery of Pest, the one in Salgótarjáni utca, however, is still there. It is in the same condition as it was after the war. It is not used any more for new burials, but there are still people visiting its graves.

The Jewish cemetery in Salgótarjáni utca, located somewhat beyond the Outer-Józsefváros, is actually the eastern corner of the public cemetery on Köztemető / Fiumei út, but is separated from it by a stone wall. This partition, functioning as a ritual *mehitzah*, made it possible to reconcile Jewish tradition and state regulations. Similar fences divide all the other Jewish cemeteries of Budapest from the neighboring public cemeteries.

The cemetery in Salgótarjáni utca was opened in 1874. In the following decades this was the most distinguished burial place of the Pest Jewish community. Its entrance, designed by Béla Lajta, looks like a medieval castle. It has a high, pointed roof, a tower on the inner side and grates on the gate. Though someone still lives in the ruined building today, it looks more like some forgotten stage-prop for a Romantic play. The square mortuary, nothing but bare walls, is also the work of Lajta.

493. Entrance gate of the Salgótarjáni utca cemetery. Designed by Béla Lajta, 1908

494. The former mortuary of the Salgótarjáni utca cemetery. Designed by Béla Lajta, 1908

495. Stone candelabrum in front of the mortuary

"The atmosphere of the entrance and the domed mortuary of the old Jewish cemetery is unforgettable. Looking at the Hebrew inscriptions on the huge pylons, the enormous iron grates, the glittering-white Eastern dome above the golden-black interior of the mortuary we are overcome by a solemn, religious mood. This is art beyond architecture, (...) this is painting, which compels the visitor of the cemetery to feel pathos and anxious reverence."

(Béla Málnai, 1925)

The dome of the mortuary collapsed around 1970, but the iron gate and the huge menorah disappeared before that. The walls are still standing firmly, the structure of the building is recognizable. It is not divided into three, like the traditional Jewish mortuary. There is only one preparation room (*tahorah*), left of the entrance, with a large, undamaged, red marble *tahorah* table in it. The fireplace where the water was heated is still there, too. The women's *tahorah* must have been in the basement, for above the dressing room the ruins of the rabbi's room are to be found. The building was shortly declared a historic monument.

Two candelabra with a square stone base stand at the entrance of the building with the text of the burial liturgy inscribed on them. Above the gate there is another Hebrew inscription, in a kind of Art Nouveau fonts typical of Lajta; it says:

תשב אנוש עד דכא ותאמר שובו בני אדם
"You return man to dust; You decree: Return you mortals!"
(Psalms 90,3)

Above some of the letters of the text there are little circles; these are the letters which indicate the year of construction: 668, i.e. 1908. Above the exit towards the cemetery there is another inscription:

מה יקר חסדך אלהים ובני אדם בצל כנפיך יחסיון
"How precious is Your faithful care, O God!
Mankind shelters in the shadow of Your wings."
(Psalms 36,8)

On the right side of the building there is a red marble plaque also inscribed with the text of the funeral liturgy. Lajta even added the vowel signs to some of the words, making it look almost like a manuscript.

Burials have taken place here occasionally during World War II and even afterwards, until the late 1950s. This is where Sándor Scheiber buried his own parents, together, on February 14, 1945. His father, Lajos Scheiber, the rabbi of the Nagy Fuvaros utca synagogue from 1920 until his death, died in a hospital. His mother, Mrs. Scheiber, née Mária Adler, was murdered by Arrow-cross men in the "Glass House" one day after her husband's death.

This is where the assimilated Jewish middle-class, the Jewish bourgeoisie is buried. Not only they, of course, since the cemetery belonged to the whole Jewish community, but the visitor gets the sense of returning to the times of the Austro-Hungarian Dual Monarchy here. In the upper-middle class section just the gravestones are worth a fortune. The tombs of the (budai) Buday-Goldberger, the Weiss and the Hatvany-Deutsch families are the historical monuments of the Hungarian industrial elite of the period between the *Ausgleich* of 1867 and World War I. Of course, only those industrialists are buried here who did not give up the Jewish faith. Some of the vaults, like that of Baron Manfréd Weiss (1857–1922) and his wife, Alice Weiss née Wohl (1865–1904), contributors to several foundations, are of such monumental proportions that they appear somewhat comic. It is the grandeur and pomp of the millennial celebrations that the visitor senses here. Walking further to the rear, however, we find simple gravestones and the cozy atmosphere of an old Jewish cemetery.

In this cemetery of affluence special attention should be paid to the row of the Rabbinical Seminary and community leaders, for its modesty and simplicity, if nothing else. It is to the right of the mortuary and, notwithstanding the general custom, clearly somewhat behind the representative rows. Of the professors of the Seminary Mózes Bloch, Vilmos Bacher and Dávid Kaufmann are buried here, as well as Mayer Kayserling, Sámuel Löw Brill and other community leaders. Earlier the gravestones could be approached through the mortuary, thus the Hebrew inscriptions were on the "outside" of the stele, but by now this path is completely overgrown with bushes vegetation—that is why the graves of the inner rows appear to follow the model of the layout of Christian cemeteries.

496. Gate of the mortuary opening to the cemetery

497. Bronze gate of the mortuary

498. A *menorah* as candelabrum in the mortuary of the Salgótarjáni utca cemetery. Designed by Béla Lajta, 1908

Vilmos Bacher and his wife, née Ilona Goldzieher, the niece of Ignác Goldziher, are buried in the same grave. Their gravestone is the work of Béla Lajta. It is just about the only manifestation of the new period of modern Jewish gravestone art of Pest in this cemetery. Its style is a subdued version of Hungarian national Art Nouveau (*Sezession*). The Hebrew inscription echoes the words of Goldziher as he characterized his friend in his *Diary* at the time of their youth:

"His elevated poetic spirit was paired with a sober evaluation of life. He always clung to facts and concrete data, and never wanted to act against the realities of life."

The inscription on his grave is telling of the modesty of R. Benjamin Zeev. It testifies that he was a man who was able to maintain a balance between his talent and his aspirations. It says:

ה' לא גבה לבי ולא רמו עיני ולא הלכתי בגדלות ובנפלאות ממני

"O Lord, my heart is not proud nor my look haughty.
I do not aspire to great things or to what is beyond me."
(Psalms 131,1)

(12) The Cemetery in Kozma utca (6 Kozma utca)

The largest Jewish cemetery of Hungary is the Rákoskeresztúr Cemetery in Kozma utca. It is next to or rather part of the *Új Köztemető* (New Public Cemetery). The Jewish cemetery was opened in 1891, a few years after the public cemetery.

The large mortuary, divided into three, designed by Vilmos Freund, stands next to the entrance. The two side wings are the men's and the women's mortuary and service rooms, separate *tahorah* rooms; the middle part used to be the first class mortuary. The whole building was much fancier ("first class") once upon a time; the bronze chandelier and the carved wood furniture are the only remnants of its former pomp. The main entrance from the street leads to a hall which is no longer used as intended: it is the gallery or *cemetery of inscriptions* and signs. To the left are plaques commemorating victims of the Holocaust. Some of these were brought here from the provinces. To the right are stone slabs, building and commemorative inscriptions collected from the walls of synagogues, schools, orphanages and other buildings of the Jewish community that are now closed down, used for other purposes or demolished; there are memorial plaques of martyrs, of founders, builders and community presidents.

499. Mortuary of the Kozma utca Neolog cemetery: the main entrance from the street. Designed by Vilmos Freund, 1891

Right across the inner side of the *ohel* stands the memorial to the ten thousand martyrs of World War I. To the left is the L-shaped Martyrs' Memorial for the victims of the Holocaust, designed by Alfréd Hajós, erected in September, 1949. In front of the Wall of Remembrance there is a black marble vault, to the right of it a *menorah*. The two inscriptions on the wall, a Hebrew and a Hungarian one, have slightly different texts:

אחינו בני ישראל שמסרו נפשם על קדושת השב

"Our brothers, the sons of Israel,
who sacrificed their lives for the holiness of the Name."

"They were murdered by hatred—
their memory should be preserved by love."

Inscribed on the nine stone walls of the two-winged arcade memorial are tens of thousands of names, some of the about 600,000 Hungarian Jews who were murdered in the Holocaust and who are known by name. Many names were added later, in pencil. On both sides of the walls, above the names, there are Biblical quotations, from left to right:

כי עלה מות בחלונינו

"For death has climbed through our windows."
(Jeremiah 9,20)

וספדה הארץ משפחות משפחות לבד

"The land shall wail, each family by itself."
(Zechariah 12,12)

שמעתי ותרגז בטני לקול צללו שפתי

"I heard and my bowels quaked,
my lips quivered at the sound."
(Habakkuk 3,16)

הן אצעק חמס ולא אענה

"I cry, Violence!, but am not answered."

(Job 19,7)

העל זאת לא תרגז הארץ ואבל כל יושב בה

"Shall not the earth shake for this

and all that dwell on it mourn?"

(Amos 8,8)

מחוץ תשכל חרב ומחדרים אימה

"The sword shall deal death without,

as shall the terror within."

(Deuteronomy 32,25)

אז יבקע כשחר אורך

"Then shall your light burst through like the dawn."

(Isaiah 58,8a)

כי אבן מקיר תזעק

"For a stone shall cry out from the wall."

(Habakkuk 2,11)

ראה עניי וחלצני

"See my affliction and rescue me."

(Psalms 119,153)

ונתתי רוחי בכם וחייתם

"I will put My breath into you and you shall live again."

(Ezekiel 37,14)

בצר לי אקרא ה׳

"In my anguish I called on the Lord."

(II Samuel 22,7)

כבוד ה׳ יאספך

"The Presence of the Lord

shall be your rear guard."

(Isaiah 58,8b)

יחיו מתיך

"Let corpses arise!"

(Isaiah 26,19)

והילילו שירות היכל

"The songs in the palace will become cries of mourning."

(Amos 8,3)

ובמותם לא נפרדו

"Never parted in their death."

(II Samuel 1,23)

על אלה חשכו עינינו

"Because of these our eyes are dimmed."
(Lamentations 5,17)

כי לא תעזב נפשי לשאול

"For You will not abandon me to Sheol."
(Psalms 16,10)

איך נפלו הגבורים

"How have the mighty fallen!"
(II Samuel 1,19)

Behind the memorial there are two graves in which the remnants of Torah scrolls desecrated during World War II are buried. Near the memorial, in parcel A, are the mass graves of Jews murdered in the Holocaust. The dead are placed into mass graves according to the place of the massacres, where they were buried, and from where they were later exhumed. Among them are the martyrs of the ghetto of Pest from the mass grave on Klauzál tér and from the depositories of the last days.

The enormous territory of the cemetery was originally parceled to suit Jewish ritual requirements. In parcel A/4, behind the Wall of Remembrance, rest some scholarly rabbis, including Sámuel Kohn and Simon Hevesi (Dohány Temple), Illés Adler (Rombach utca synagogue) and Sándor Scheiber (Rabbinical Seminary). (R. Scheiber is buried in grave no. A/4 11–14/A.) Among the graves brought here from the Lehel utca cemetery are those of Israel and Judah Wahrmann. The grave of Ignác Goldziher (Isaac Judah ben Aaron Yom Tov by his Hebrew name) is in the row behind, in parcel 2; Goldziher was not a rabbi. Not far is the grave of the composer Márk Rózsavölgyi.

Also the Jewish martyrs of the Independence War of 1848/49 were reburied here. Their common memorial was designed by Béla Lajta. (See fig. 119 on p. 104, above.) The inscription on the stele says:

"This is the common grave of the soldiers of the Independence War of 1848/49. The Hevrah Kaddishah of Pest transferred their remains here from the Lehel utca cemetery (earlier called Váci út cemetery) which was opened in 1848, filled up by 1874 and liquidated by the authorities in 1910. Eternal, great centuries, stop and pay tribute to the ashes of Jewish heroes upon seeing these telling graves, crown them with laurel and tell them that their free homeland lives and flourishes till the earth exists."

500. Béla Lajta's plan for the arcades in the Kozma utca cemetery

Parcel 5/B is the parcel of artists and scholars. Many distinguished persons are buried here, such as Miksa Szabolcsi, the editor of *Egyenlőség*, and his wife—their vault is the work of Béla Lajta; the writers Sándor Bródy (1863–1924) and Ernő Szép, the opera singer Oszkár Kálmán, the actor Gyula Gózon, Andor Kellér (1903–1963) and Dezső Kellér (1905–1986), both writers and popular announcers (*konferanszié* or *compère*), the last two witnesses of the world of the cabaret, and numerous prominent figures of late nineteenth- and twentieth-century Hungarian art, the writer Tamás Kóbor, the painter Lipót Hermann, the historian Henrik Marczali (1856–1940), the Oriental scholar Ignác Kunos (1860–1945). These people are important figures of an imaginary Hungarian National Pantheon.

The death records of the Pest Jewish community since 1836 are available, only a few are missing. These records used to list the burials in the Rákoskeresztúr cemetery. Today the

greatest Hungarian Jewish biographical dictionary is concealed in these pages. The birth and death data of many, among them even some noted personalities, could be found only here, on the spot.

Both the Rákoskeresztúr and the Salgótarjáni út cemeteries were the places of display for the *nouveau riche*—more in harmony with other cemeteries of the period than with Jewish tradition. Whoever could afford it, commissioned gravestones from prominent artists. Béla Lajta alone designed over two dozen gravestones in the Rákoskeresztúr cemetery and several in the Salgótarjáni út cemetery. For a while he was the artistic consultant and supervisor of Jewish cemeteries.

The row of crypts next to the wall towards Kozma utca is an extraordinary sight. Near to the mortuary stand the crypts of the family Kornfeld (the financiers and industrialists), of the family Wellisch (the architect) and, in the opposite direction, of the family Goldberger (the textile manufacturers).

To the right of the mortuary stands the magnificent majolica sepulchral vault of the family Schmidl. It is actually an extraordinary piece of art history. Sándor Schmidl and his wife run a grocery and "colonial goods" store on 17 Károly körút. The crypt was built by their son, Miklós Schmidl, who took over the store after the death of the parents (1899 and 1904, respectively). The building was designed by Ödön Lechner and Béla Lajta in 1903, but was marked on the majolica base by the latter alone as "Béla Leitersdorfer architect" (1904). In any case, it is one of the earliest works of Lajta, designed following the tradition of Lehner, his master, but in its colors—the blue and golden background —modeled on the sepulcher of Galla Placidia in Ravenna. The majolica walls were the work of the Zsolnay porcelain and majolica factory in Pécs (South Hungary), the rich Art Nouveau flower decoration—glass and marble mosaic—was executed probably in the workshop of Miksa Róth. Recently a careful reconstruction by the Kőnig and Wagner Architects Co. (Tamás Kőnig, Péter Wagner, and others), in cooperation with the art historian Ferenc Dávid, restored the building to its original beauty (1998).

501. Sepulchral vault of the family Schmidl. Designed by Béla Lajta, 1904

(13) The New Orthodox Cemetery (12 Gránátos utca)

The cemetery of the Orthodox community currently in use, the Rákoskeresztúr Orthodox Cemetery, joins the Kozma utca cemetery on the North. Its wrought-iron gate opens next to the wall of the Neolog cemetery. There is a mortuary divided into three, with separate *tahorah* rooms for men and women. Rain-water is used here for the purification of the dead, prescribed for the *mikveh* as well.

The first row is the rabbinical row here too. Since Orthodox tradition does not allow the grave to be covered, there are only vertical gravestones here (*matzzevah / stele*), inscribed with names.

*

There are several other Jewish cemeteries on the territory of Greater Budapest, and not all of them are hidden behind new buildings. There is one in Budafok (6 Kinizsi utca–Temető utca, between the parcels 7 and 8 in the public cemetery); in Cinkota (Szabadföld út); in Csepel; in Kispest (6 Temető utca); in Mátyásföld / Nagyiccetelep (Pesti határút); in Nagytétény (40 Szentháromság utca); in Pestszentlőrinc (113 Sallai Imre utca); in Pestszenterzsébet (Temető sor); in Rákoscsaba (Göcsej utca); in Rákoshegy (Napkelet köz); in Rákosliget (Bártfai utca); in Rákospalota (Szentmihályi út); in Rákosszentmihály / Kisszentmihály (Rozsos utca) and elsewhere.

These cemeteries are probably the only remnants of the Jewish population in the formerly independent communities, which was wiped out by the deportations in 1944.

XIV. Jewish Life in Budapest Today

(1) Some Recent Events
Indicating the Changes in the Setting of the Jewish Community

The following section is by no means intended to be an all-comprehensive history of the Jews in Hungary in recent decades, let alone in the half-a-century after World War II. After the war Jewish history was basically a hidden history, and to write it, detailed in-depth research is necessary. Just from recollections, personal histories, newspaper articles it cannot be made comprehensive and coherent. Records of political influence and restriction—in cases, like in that of the Zionist trials, prosecutions—are buried in the archives of the State Security or the State Office for Church Affairs. On some significant moments only the treasures of foreign archives could shed light. After ca. 1984, the 40th anniversary of the Holocaust, trips to Israel, first of all, visits to relatives, were allowed much easier than before. In the last years of the communist regime the Jewish community was gradually allowed to bring about everything its lay or religious leaders dared to. People attended services, on the High Holidays synagogues were crowded, new Jewish organizations were established, the word *Jew / Jewish* started to be uttered in a positive sense. The aim here is simply to register visible, separate Jewish public life as it emerged from the seemingly homogeneous communist society and constituted itself after the change of regime in 1990. The following is just a kind of enumeration in chronological sequence—with some obvious preference for books. From the mid-1990s on, Jewish life has been so rich and flourishing that only a random selection of new developments can be recorded here.

1968

A year and a half after Hungary, following the Six-day War, broke off diplomatic relations with Israel, a novel by György G. Kardos, *Avraham Bogatir hét napja* [Seven Days in the Life of Avraham Bogatir] was published (Budapest: Magvető Publishing House) and it immediately became a best-seller. The novel is about Palestine from the perspective of the first *aliyyah*. It was received—despite the animosity of the period—as a vote for Israel.

1974

Hajtűkanyar [Hairpin Bend], a novel by Mária Ember about the deportation of Jews to forced labor camps (Strasshof, etc.) in the early summer of 1944 was published by Szépirodalmi Publishing House, Budapest. The novel contains documentary elements as well.

1975

A study by György Száraz, "Egy előítélet nyomában" [On the Tracks of a Prejudice] was published in the September issue of *Valóság*, an important in those years periodical of social sciences. A year later Magvető Publishing House published an extended version of it in book form, as part of a series called "Gyorsuló idő" [Accelerating Time]. Apart from the essay of István Bibó—written right after the war and unknown for the general public—Száraz's essay was the first serious discussion of the recent "Jewish wounds" (Károly Pap) and of the Hungarian tragedy, as the Holocaust was interpreted by the author.

1977

In the United States Andrew Handler published an anthology entitled *Ararát. A collection of Hungarian-Jewish Short Stories* (Cranbury, NJ: Associated University Press). Some of the pieces in this collection were English translations of texts which were hardly available even in Hungarian. For several decades the official view of the Budapest community and the general Jewish public opinion was that the intellectual achievements of Hungarian Jews should be evaluated and appreciated according to how well they served Hungarian national ends. Handler's anthology now indicated that Hungarian Jewish intellectuals do have a place in general Jewish culture as well.

1982

Sorsválasztók [Electors of Fate], a play by Gyula Illyés. The plot of the drama is that the protagonist, an actor, who has so far considered himself Hungarian ("Christian"), learns that he is Jewish. His mother was shot into the Danube by Arrow-cross men; the woman who raised him as her own child was actually the person who rescued him from a death march. Shaken as he is, he decides to emigrate to Israel immediately. The next twist in the play is when it comes to light that the whole story was simply made up by his mother in order to conceal the fact that her son was born before she got married. The actor may stay. In those days this play seemed courageous in the eyes of many, as it pried into certain social issues which had been suppressed for decades. Today, in hindsight, however, what the play seems to be emphasize is rather the separation of Jews-by-birth from the society at large. By doing so it anticipated—even if unintentionally—the extremist anti-Jewish political views of a decade later, according to which Jews should be excluded from Hungarian society.

1983

On December 25 a Jewish samizdat was published, the *Salom nyílt levele* [Open Letter of Shalom]. For nearly twenty years, since the Six-day War in 1967, there was no real Jewish press in Hungary, except for the dull *Új Élet*, the journal—or rather newsletter—of the *Magyar Izraeliták Országos Képviselete* (National Bureau of Hungarian Israelites, MIOK). The silence was broken by this publication. It had two issues, and then its successor, *Magyar Zsidó* [Hungarian Jew], a journal of the political opposition, had three issues in the years 1987 and 1988. It was the journalist György Gadó who stood behind these publications.

1984

Zsidóság az 1945 utáni Magyarországon [Jewry in Hungary after 1945], a collection of essays edited by Péter Kende, was published in the "Magyar Füzetek" series in Paris, containing papers by the sociologists Viktor Karády and András Kovács, the writer Iván Sanders, the historian Péter Várdy and others. This was the first time that Jewry as a social category and life experience became the subject of sociological analysis.

Zsidókérdés, asszimiláció, antiszemitizmus [Jewish Question, Assimilation, Anti-Semitism], a volume of studies on the Jewish question in Hungary in the twentieth century edited by Péter Hanák, was published by Gondolat Publishing House. The volume reprinted excerpts from the debate on the so-called Jewish question in 1917. The debate emerged from the answers on the inquiry of the periodical *Huszadik Század*. Hanák's volume also contained István Bibó's study from 1948, "Zsidókérdés Magyarországon 1944 után" [The Jewish Question in Hungary after 1944], the first in-depth analysis of the impact of the Holocaust on Hungary, of the Jews who escaped and of the society at large, of responsibilities and prospects. (An English translation of the seminal study was published in 1991.)

1985

A university periodical, *Medvetánc*, published (no. 2–3, 1985) a sociological study of Ferenc Erős, András Kovács and Katalin Lévai, "Hogyan jöttem rá, hogy zsidó vagyok? (Interjúk)" [How I Found out That I Was Jewish? (Interviews)].

A collection of articles edited by Róbert Simon, *Zsidókérdés Kelet- és Közép-Európában* [Jewish Question in Eastern and Central Europe], was published. This volume documents the debates on the so-called Jewish question from the sociological and political literature of the twentieth century.

Although it was published by the Department of Scientific Socialism of the Eötvös University, it was banned shortly after its publication, and all copies were withdrawn from circulation.

1986

Sándor Szenes published his book *Befejezetlen múlt. Keresztények és zsidók* [Unfinished Past. Christians and Jews], interviews with Christian clergymen who had resisted the Hungarian, German and Arrow-cross persecution of Jews. The second edition of the book (1994) included the complete text of the Auschwitz Protocols as it was translated in 1944 by Mária Székely (later Mrs. Küllői-Rohrer) on behalf of the "Good Shepherd" organization. It was the first printed publication of the Protocols in Hungarian.

1987

The Wallenberg family, Nicolas M. Salgo, then ambassador of the United States to Hungary, and the Municipality erected a statue in memory of Raoul Wallenberg in Pasarét, on the corner of Szilágyi Erzsébet fasor and Nagyajtai utca (a work by Imre Varga): A thin man in an overcoat, pushes apart robust walls of raw red marble with his right hand. There is a bas-relief on the reverse side of one of the walls, "Sárkányölő" (The Dragon Killer); next to it a Latin quotation reminds of Wallenberg's fate after the war: *Tempora si fverint nubila solus eris* (Ovidius, *Tristia* I, 9,6), it means: "If times become stormy, you will remain on your own." In 1990 somebody painted a six-pointed star with black paint on the surface of the marble. Though only faintly, its traces have remained visible since then.

1988

On January 1 the *MTA Judaisztikai Kutatócsoport* / Center of Jewish Studies at the Hungarian Academy of Sciences was formed.

On March 15 an Israeli information office was opened in Budapest, at the Swiss Embassy.

In the spring Gondolat Publishing House published the Hungarian translation of Randolph L. Braham's book, *A magyar Holocaust* [The Hungarian Holocaust]. The two thick volumes were not distributed initially, the book was available only at the office of the Jewish community. (The second, revised and enlarged edition was published in 1997.)

On November 20 the *Magyar Zsidó Kulturális Egyesület* (Hungarian Jewish Cultural Association, MAZSIKE) was formed. The numbering of membership cards started at 600 001, in a symbolic commemoration of the Hungarian Jewish victims of the Holocaust.

This was the year when the *Oneg Shabbat Klub*, later Association, was formed at the synagogue on Bethlen Gábor tér. The Club sponsors religious, cultural, and social programs mainly for young Jews. (Its address today is 15 István út, nearby.)

An anthology was published with the title *Múlt és Jövő* [Past and Future] at the end of this year, which became the first issue of the new series of the one-time famous Jewish cultural periodical, edited by József Patai in the interwar period.

In the course of this year the *Szohnut* (*sokhnut*, "agency"), the *Jewish Agency for Israel*, resumed its activities in Budapest. As the agency of the *Nemzetközi Cionista Szervezet* / *World Zionist Organization*, it arranges the emigration of Jews to Israel (*aliyyah*). It offers Hebrew language instruction, organizes study circles in Budapest, student vacations in Israel and helps those interested in studying at an Israeli university. All these activities are supposed to prepare for *aliyyah*.[1]

During the winter of 1988/89 a major debate evolved in Hungarian Jewish circles over the nationality status of Hungarian Jewry. The immediate cause of the debate was the elaboration of a law regulating the situation of national and ethnic minorities. The bill presented to Parliament listed the national minorities of Hungary and guaranteed certain collective rights to them. Hungarian Jewry was also offered a chance to accept this position, together with all the advantages of the regulation.

---

[1] *Aliyyah / aliya*, "going up"; *aliyyah le-regel*: "going up (to Jerusalem) on pilgrimage"; *aliyyah la-Torah / liye*: "going up to the Torah (to read from it)"; *aliyyah la-aretz*: "immigration to Israel", *alijázni* in Hungarian.

Some members of the Hungarian Jewish Cultural Association published an appeal urging people that those who consider themselves of Jewish nationality should declare it without ado on the questionnaire of the census due in January 1990. About five hundred persons responded to this request, and approximately 900 people joined the *Magyarországi Zsidók Nemzeti Szövetsége* (National League of Jews in Hungary) formed on December 11, 1990, on the first day of *Hanukkah*. All the other Jewish organizations maintained, at least tacitly, the stand taken at the 1868/69 General Congress, namely, that Jewish population in Hungary is not of a national character. Clearly they were influenced by the memory of the Holocaust, the (Anti-)Jewish Laws and the deportations. They were afraid that by accepting the status of nationality the integration of Jews into Hungarian society would be in jeopardy. On June 10, 1992, the Jewish community officially rejected this idea, they did not wish to change the present constitutional status of Jewry, but they did not exclude the possibility of changing their stand later. Finally, the law was passed (Act LXXVII of 1993) and it did not mention Jewry as a nationality, but it created the legal opportunity for groups of at least one thousand people to claim nationality status at any time.

1989

On June 15 the *Joint* reopened its Budapest office.

On June 16 former Prime Minister Imre Nagy and other martyrs of the 1956 revolution were reburied. At the memorial service, held on Heroes' square, the stairs and pillars of the Art Gallery wrapped in black canvas, the name of every victim of the reprisals following the revolution were read out loud. Although nobody had planned it that way, it was easy to realize that this ritual happened to be very similar to the tradition of reading out the list of Jewish martyrs in the synagogue (*mazkir neshamot* or *hazkarat neshamot*). That is, in this historic moment, in preparation for significant political changes, the Hungarian public accepted an element of the Jewish tradition as spontaneously revived in the context of the ceremony of national commemoration.

On July 10 the Budapest office of the *Zsidó Világkongresszus / Jewish World Congress* was opened.

In August a rabbi sent by the Lubavitch Hasidic community from Brooklyn, New York arrived in Budapest. In 1992 his congregation received the synagogue in Vasvári Pál utca. The building was restored during the summer of 1993 and reopened in the fall for the High Holidays. In 1998 a Yeshivah was opened there, with students from abroad as well as from Budapest.

In the academic year 1989/90 the instruction of Hebrew and Jewish studies started at the Faculty of Humanities of Loránd Eötvös University.

On September 18 the Foreign Minister of the State of Israel paid an official visit to Budapest. Diplomatic relations between Israel and Hungary, broken for twenty-two years, were now resumed. An Israeli Embassy was opened in Budapest and a Hungarian Embassy in Tel-Aviv.

On August 4, on the 77th anniversary of Raoul Wallenberg's birth, a memorial plaque was placed on the corner house of Wallenberg utca and Pozsonyi út (11 Wallenberg utca), the work of Gergő Bottos.

Magyarországi zsinagógák [The Synagogues of Hungary], a book by Anikó Gazda (1933–1990), an architect, was published by Műszaki Publishing House. Gazda describes Hungarian synagogues accurately, by means of a rich photo documentation and thorough historical research.

In November the first issue of *Szombat* [Sabbath], the review of the Hungarian Jewish Cultural Association, was published.

On December 19 the *Magyar–Izraeli Baráti Társaság* (Hungarian–Israeli Friendship Society) was founded on a meeting held in the building of the Hungarian Academy of Sciences.

1990

On January 14 the writer István Csurka, one of the most influential politicians of *Magyar Demokrata Fórum* (Hungarian Democratic Forum, MDF) at the time, read one of his "Sunday notes" over Radio Kossuth, with the title "Wake up, Magyars!" "Wake up, Magyars! You are being misled again! The revolution is over, we are back to Béla Kun's era, even if the new Lenin-boys happen to be reviling Lenin.

What may come next? Terror. Soldiers. Bloodshed and destruction"—he said. These words raised a public outcry. A week later the author protested against the charge of anti-Semitism. Yet his subsequent writings confirmed that the outcry was justified. Two years later, when, on August 20, 1992 Csurka published his notorious essay "A few thoughts concerning the two years that have passed since the change of regime and about the new program of MDF" in his journal *Magyar Fórum*, he was still the vice-president of MDF, the ruling party, and an MP. As a consequence of this essay, Csurka lost the support of the then Prime Minister, mainly out of career considerations, and it led to his dismissal from the governing party six months later. At the same time the article made it clear that his previous insinuations regarding the events of 1918/19 meant that Csurka identified Jews with Bolsheviks and, furthermore, that his intention was to frighten Hungarian society with the prospect of a Jewish rule of terror. Intellectual and political arguments of anti-Semitism gained certain legitimacy in Hungary in those days, and there were some startling examples of anti-Semitism in the streets as well. In his pamphlet and in one of his statements Csurka declared that he had no objections to Jews provided that they live in an Orthodox way, i.e. completely separate from Hungarian society, or that they emigrate to Israel. This remark echoes almost exactly the views of the representatives of political anti-Semitism in earlier times.—On June 24, 1878, Győző Istóczy argued that the Jewish people should be compensated for having been forced to leave their ravaged fatherland eighteen centuries earlier. Their original country, Palestine, should be reestablished and enlarged as an autonomous territory under the authority of the Sublime Porte or as an independent Jewish State. Thus the Jewish nation could come into existence, whose rapid expansion hinders European nations and threatens Christian civilization.—In 1921 Gyula Gömbös suggested that the Hungarian Government should contact the Zionist *Központi Iroda* / Central Office concerning the expulsion of the several hundred thousand Jews of Hungarian citizenship.—On October 16, 1944, Ferenc Szálasi was already talking about the final solution of the Jewish question in accordance with the basic principles of Zionism.—These are the earlier footsteps of anti-Jewish agitation in Hungary. What all three politicians found attractive in Zionism was that it made a sharp distinction between *Hungarians* and *Jews living in Hungary*, and that their intention was to resettle Jews in Palestine. It is clear, they thought, that Zionism may liberate Hungary from Jews. The events of 1944, that is, the Hungarian participation in the genocide perpetrated by the National-Socialists, resulted directly from the program of political anti-Semitism.

On March 19 a cantorial recital was held at the Budapest Opera House, and two days later at the Dohány utca synagogue. Continuing the tradition from before World War II, similar concerts had already been held regularly in Budapest since 1987, but this was the first time that synagogal music, the Pest *nusah*, was presented to a wider general public.

On April 1 the *Magyar Cionista Szövetség* (Hungarian Zionist Alliance) was founded. (This traditional name was later changed to *Magyarországi Cionista Szövetség* / Zionist Alliance in Hungary.)

In the summer the *Joint* founded a children's camp in Szarvas, a site of summer vacation and Jewish education, where young Hungarian instructors (*madrikh*) teach the youngsters basic Jewish knowledge. The camp became very popular among children in both Jewish proper and fully assimilated circles, just to name the extremes. Moreover, the camp became a component in the Jewish identity for the youth—campers and *madrikhim*—ever since. The camp is open also to groups of children from Eastern Europe. In the camp a *mashgiah* of Hungarian birth, from Bnei-Brak (Benei Berak), is employed, and according to all information the food is very tasty. In 1998 a synagogue was consecrated in the camp, replacing the former simple prayer-room.

On July 8 the memorial of the Budapest ghetto (a statue by Imre Varga) was unveiled in Wesselényi utca, on the little square between the Dohány utca synagogue and the Heroes' Temple. The square was surrounded by a fence in 1991. (In fact, this fence was planned already in the course of the 1930–1931 construction works, but it was not realized then.)

On September 1 teaching started at the *Masoret avot* American Endowment School located at 44 Wesselényi utca, and at the "Lauder Javne" Jewish Community School at 17–19 Lendvay utca. Later the "Lauder Javne", expanding, had to rent an extra school building in order to accommodate all its students. A temporary location was at 2–4 Tárogató út. In 1993 the Municipality granted them the rights

 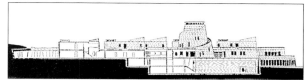

of a plot at 48 Budakeszi út, right next to the former Wodianer Villa, for 99 years, for the purpose of constructing a new school building here. The prize-winning architectural design, the work of Péter Sugár, Tamás Karácsony and Győző Szerényi displayed eclectic Middle-Eastern traits. For instance, traces of the Mount Scopus (*Har ha-Tzofim*) building of the Hebrew University and the tower block of the early medieval mosque of Samarra in Iraq (the *Malviyya*) can be recognized on drafts. On February 24, 1996 the new building of the "Lauder Javne" was inaugurated. The school was newly designed by Csaba Virág. Though original in every detail, the complex is a variant of the high-school or university campuses in Jerusalem and Israel. The central building is domed, the synagogue is located here.

502. Competition design of the planned "Lauder Javne" Jewish Community School by Péter Sugár, Tamás Karácsony and Győző Szerényi, 1993

In the academic year 1990/91 teaching started at Pedagogium, the teachers' training institute of the Rabbinical Seminary. The name reflects a series of lectures called *Szülők Pedagógiuma* (Parents' Pedagogium), initiated by the Pest community in 1933.

In one of the September issues of the periodical *Hitel* the next installment of Sándor Csoóri's essay called "Nappali Hold" [Daytime Moon] was published. A certain passage of the essay raised a long and rather heated debate in literary and political circles over the question of Jewish assimilation. Who assimilates whom? Do the Hungarians assimilate the Jews, like at the beginning of the twentieth century? Or is it today the Jews who assimilate Hungarians, as Csoóri suggests? This question implied that Jews in Hungary strive to assimilate the Hungarians. The debate grew acrimonious and cut a deep trench between the liberal-democratic and "populist-nationalist" (national democratic and, in some cases, chauvinistic and openly anti-Semitic) camps of Hungarian intellectuals. The basic question, however, was not raised by anyone in course of these passionate and often bitter debates. Namely, whether it is at all possible to live a full Jewish life in Hungary without any compulsion of assimilation. For instance, as a Hungarian citizen whose mother tongue is Yiddish or Hebrew, without any restrictions as a Hungarian? Is it possible to live in Hungary if someone is *different*, i.e. different from the ideal of one or another social group? Or rather, looking at the matter from the other perspective, do any of the social groups have the right to possess Hungary? Because he who arbitrarily declares those differing from him *different*, that is alien or inferior, inevitably means to own the whole country. This is how the persecution of Jews started in 1920 and in 1938. Nevertheless, the persecution of Jews was but one of the many possible forms of hatred directed at everything *foreign*, everything *different*.

On October 14 a memorial of Jewish martyrs killed during the Arrow-cross terror, the work of Anna Stein called "Égbe kiáltó" [Crying to the Heaven] (Genesis 4,10, etc.), was unveiled on the Danube bank, at the Pest foot of Margit híd.

Béla Tábor's book, *A zsidóság két útja* [The Two Ways of Jewry] was published by Pesti Szalon Publishing House for the second time. In the first edition of the book in 1939 Tábor was the first to formulate an alternative to assimilation, to suggest the possibility of living a full Jewish life in Hungary, to recognize the growth of a community that had just come to itself.

1991

In April the complete reconstruction of the Dohány utca synagogue started, with substantial financial support of the state.—After several years of continuing reconstruction, the synagogue was newly consecrated immediately before the High Holidays in 1996, on September 5.

On May 9 the Neolog Jewish community of Hungary adopted a new statute which changed the national and the Budapest organizations and elected a new leadership. Also, the term *izraelita / izr.*, "Israelite", used previously—from the early nineteenth century on—in the name of the community, was changed to *zsidó*, "Jewish". Thus the word *zsidó*, which in the past decades had attained a negative connotation, became once again a neutral item of Hungarian vocabulary.

Between June 11 and 17, Chaim Herzog, the President of the State of Israel, paid a state visit to Hungary. Next to the huge Hungarian national flag an equally huge Israeli flag was streaming on the facade of the Parliament building.

Zsinagógák és zsidó községek Magyarországon [Synagogues and Jewish Communities in Hungary], by Anikó Gazda, an architectural and statistical documentation of the history of Hungarian Jewry and of the role they played in the development of the cities, was published at the end of the year.

1992

Between September 20 and 23, Árpád Göncz, President of the Hungarian Republic, paid an official visit to Israel.

The Oriental Collection of the Library of the Hungarian Academy of Sciences published, in a separate volume, the catalogue of Sándor Scheiber's *Hebraica* and *Judaica* collection. Thus the precious collection that had been purchased from the family after the death of the former director of the Rabbinical Seminary was now opened for scholarly research.

1993

On March 11 the Constitutional Court of the Hungarian Republic ruled that Hungary did not fulfill Article 27, § 2 of the Paris Peace Treaty (enacted in Hungary as Act XVIII of 1947), which stated that in the case of those "who for racial, religious or any other reason had been the targets of harassment of a fascist nature either as individuals or as members of a community", and had passed away without a legal heir, their properties, rights and interests should be granted "to the organizations or communities representing these individuals". The Constitutional Court called upon Parliament to terminate the violation of the Constitution resulting from not fulfilling the law by December 31, 1993 at the latest. In fact, Act XXV of 1946, which repealed the (Anti-)Jewish Laws, ordered the Government to set up a committee, which was to elaborate recommendations on how to minimize or compensate for the disadvantages that had been suffered during the years of persecution. After this an *Országos Zsidó Kárpótlási Alap* (National Fund for the Compensation of Jews) was established, but never activated. Despite having passed several Acts compensating other social groups in course of their four years in office, members of Parliament elected in 1990 did not put an end to the dereliction. The Government took no real measures to fulfill the Paris Peace Treaty, nor did they take any steps to define the tasks and the scope of activities of a *Zsidó Helyreállítási Alap* (Jewish Restitution Fund), or to refund the frozen deposits, or to return the property that had been seized either illegally or by law from Jewish institutions or from Hungarian citizens being effected by the (Anti-)Jewish Laws. No effort was made to ease the consequences of personal damages either. Finally, on April 10, 1997 (Decree 1035/1997) the Government—explicitly referring to the Paris Peace Treaty and its enactment—founded the *Magyarországi Zsidó Örökség Közalapítvány* (Jewish Heritage in Hungary Public Foundation) in order to give support to persons "who for their Jewish descent had been the targets of harassment of a racial, religious or other fascist nature" and also to communities of these, if they are living and operating in Hungary. The aim is to reorganize the religious, cultural and educational networks of the concerned, strengthen their Jewish identity and, relating to individuals, to improve their social standing. The riches of the Foundation is 4 billion forints in compensation bills. Compensation of those who suffered in ghettos, concentration camps, by deportation or have lost their lives is still pending.

In the fall young intellectuals around the Rabbinical Seminary launched a series of lectures under the name *Yahalom Zsidó Szabadegyetem* (Yahalom Jewish Free University), reviving the tradition of the Pest Jewish community's *Szabadegyetem* (Jewish Free University) founded in 1932. The name *yahalom* (Ezekiel 28,13) means "precious stone", "jasper".

1994

On April 17 commemorations of the persecution of Jews and of the 50th anniversary of the Holocaust started in Hungary, with considerable national and international publicity.

On April 19 a pyramid was built of pebbles on the Danube bank, close to the northern border of the international ghetto of 1944 (Dráva utca) commemorating the Jewish martyrs who fell victim to the Arrow-cross terror.

On July 14, on the 90th anniversary of Theodor Herzl's death, the Municipality granted the name Herzl tér to the small square in front of the Dohány utca synagogue and the Jewish Museum (the place of Herzl's demolished house of birth).

On October 16 the *Magyar Zsidó Közösségi Ház* (Hungarian Jewish Cultural Center) was inaugurated at 16 Révay utca. The name was soon changed to *"Bálint" Zsidó Közösségi Ház* or simply "Bálint Ház" after the family Bálint (England) who donated a substantial part of the expenses. (In addition to the support from the *Joint* and the Central British Found). Some Jewish institutions were conveniently accommodated in the building, like "Yahalom"; the redaction of the journal *Szombat*; the "Forrás" (Spring) center of education and information; the Shalom Club of Holocaust survivors and their relatives; a Yiddish Club for native speakers and inquirers; public lectures are held, in the Main Hall on the ground floor and in the Hall of the second floor art exhibitions are organized, etc. The dormitory of the three Jewish high schools in Budapest is also operating here, on the third and fourth floors. The Bálint family wanted to remain in the background, and yet *Bálint Ház* became one of the most frequented words in the Jewish (socio-)dialect of Budapest.

In the fall the Yiddish Theater of Bucharest visited Budapest on the occasion of the Festival of Hungarian Theaters Abroad. They played in the Goldmark Hall in Yiddish, the play was translated simultaneously to Hungarian.

1995

In March the new permanent exhibition of the Jewish Museum was opened.

In the fall the Budapest Orthodox community opened a *beit midrash*, the *Budapest Kolel* (Circle) in its Dob utca building.

1996

On February 26 the 100th anniversary of Herzl's *Der Judenstaat* was commemorated by a conference organized by the Jewish Museum, the *Magyarországi Cionista Szövetség* / Zionist Alliance in Hungary and the "Yahalom".

On November 17–19, in the frame of the commemoration of the 1100th anniversary of the conquest of Hungary, a conference was organized by the Hungarian Holocaust Foundation with the general title "1100 Years of Coexistence".

In the fall the *Chabad Lubavitch Zsidó Nevelési és Oktatási Egyesület* (Chabad Lubavitch Jewish Heritage Center of Hungary) launched its kindergarten and day nursery (the only one in Hungary to date) Gan Menahem. Next year the Center set up its primary school called Beit Menahem. By establishing his *yeshivah* in the fall of 1998, the Lubavitch *rebe* set up a whole framework of Jewish education. Three new prayer-books have been published by them so far, Hebrew text and a full Hungarian translation, in a yearly sequence, with the titles as follows: *Sámuel imája. Zsidó imakönyv / Siddur. Tefillat Shemu'el* (1996); *Izrael fohásza. A zsidó újév imarendje / Zikhron Yisra'el Menahem. Mahzor le-Rosh ha-Shanah* (1997); *Sámson fohásza. Engesztelőnap imarendje / Gevurat Shimshon. Mahzor le-Yom Kippur* (1998).

1998

At the end of August the Jewish community organized a Summer Jewish Festival, the first one ever. In that frame, a Jewish Book Fair was held in front of the "Dohány". The first commercial catalog of Jewish books was edited and printed in Gyoma, at the Kner Publishing House.

In September the new school year started in the new school building of the Neolog community, the "Scheiber". The former "Anna Frank" moved out of the building in Rökk Szilárd utca, and that event gave the opportunity for starting the reconstruction of the 120-year-old building. Faculties and departments of the newly established Jewish University shall occupy the building, like the Rabbinical Seminary, Social Workers, Teachers of Religion (the former Pedagogium), Liturgy (school of cantorial art).

(2) What Is the Situation Today?

Jew or Israelite? A respected rabbi of Pest once said that a really committed Jew would never call himself or herself an Israelite. Nowadays the official usage has changed as well. Assimilation, the most important word in the Jewish history of the past one and half centuries in Hungary, has acquired a different meaning. Today complete social and cultural adaptation is a constitutional right; it is not an obstacle but rather a framework for the maintenance of Jewish life. Jewish religion may be practiced freely and there is a rich Jewish cultural life independent of it. It is even possible to participate in the Zionist movement. On the other hand, traditional anti-Semitism has emerged again, and manifested itself in rude forms, in verbal—and in some cases, physical—attacks.

For decades the occasional publication of the works of Jewish and Israeli authors in Hungarian translation has had a significant role in the preservation of Jewish cultural identity. The writings of Sholem Aleichem (1859–1916) achieved solid popularity. The mere news from the West about the musical and the film version of "Fiddler on the Roof" in 1960 and in 1968, respectively, created a sensation in Hungary, not to mention its performance by the *Fővárosi Operettszínház* (Municipal Operetta Theater) in 1972. (Ferenc Bessenyei, a very popular non-Jewish actor, playing the role of Tevye, was instructed by Sándor Scheiber himself during the rehearsals.) The fact that the musical was banned for a while after the Yom-Kippur War only enhanced its popularity. The response to the award of the Nobel Prize to Shemuel Josef Agnon (1888–1970) and Nelly Sachs (1891–1970) in 1966, the publication of their works in 1968, Else Lasker-Schüler's (1869–1945) volume of poems in 1972—all these were more than just cultural events. In a short period of time, a long sequence of books was published: volumes of Amos Oz and Itamar Jaoz-Kest, of Martin Buber, Franz Rosenzweig and Gershom Scholem, of Elie Wiesel, a short selection from the *Zohar*, novels of Abraham Malamud and Isaac Bashevis Singer became real best-sellers. For the time being, Hungarian literary culture—in which Jewish intellectuals have also found their place over the past century—is alive and well.

In recent years girls have started to wear the six-pointed star (*Magen David*) or the two letters of the Hebrew word *Hay*, "life", on their necklace. Some even wear a little gold or silver *mezuzah* on a necklace, even though it is not meant to be worn on the neck. These are little messages to the world, expressions of Jewish identity.

Traditionally, to live as a Jew means circumcision, observing halakhic regulations and paying the temple tax. All three points have, beside their strict meaning, figurative senses as well. Today in Budapest the observance of strictly ritual acts, like *berit millah* or *bar mitzvah*, falls far behind the number of people who show up in synagogues. Circumcisions or bar mitzvahs are regularly announced in the community's newspaper *Új Élet*, even if perhaps not all of them. Yearly a few dozen *brises* mean that a relatively high number of Jewish men is and remains uncircumcised. In the 1980s visitors from Israel or the US Jewish community did not trust *kashrut* in Hungary at all. In recent times Jewish identity in Hungary is constituted in concentric circles. Around the core Jewish society, the Jewish community or communities (Neolog, Orthodox, Lubavitch, Reform), there are circles of Jews with different identities. (a) A full Jewish life in terms of the Halakhah (circumcision, kashrut, community membership, tefillin, etc.). (b) Various forms of semi-Halakhic, more correctly, semi- or almost-secular Jewish life (often no circumcision, but some Talmud-Torah, services on High Holidays, the Hungarian column in the prayer-book, looking at the Hebrew letters with bad conscience). (c) Jewish nostalgia, emotional self-identification nurtured in the soil of an almost complete ignorance, but, on the other hand, combined with interest for, and striving after, knowledge (occasionally showing up in a synagogue, wearing *Magen David* or *Hay*, learning some Hebrew, traveling to Israel, etc.). (d) Judaism as a reminder of one's origins (a Hanukkah candlestick at home). (e) Cultural Judaism (preference for Jewish authors, films, etc., Jewish friends, interest for news of the Jewish society). (f) A fully secular Jewish identity, political Jewishness (no religion, but keen interest in the situation of the Jews, determined anti-anti-Semitism). (g) Rejecting or denying one's own Jewish background (people of Jewish descent who will not accept their Jewish origins, who reject any connection with Judaism, or Jews, or Israel—these are often held for Jews by the society at large).

While the traditional Neolog and Orthodox communities are maintaining their traditions, new in Budapest is the increasing influence and popularity of Lubavitch Hasidism. Their headquarters is the former Shas Hevrah synagogue in Vasváry Pál utca, but the impact of the very active rabbi, of his community and of his supporters from abroad is observable in almost every new development in Jewish society. The new series of prayer-books is a symbol of their increasing influence.

On the other edge, a young offspring of the American–British Reform movements is taking root in Budapest—though not as a continuity of previous Reform communities in Hungary. *Szim Salom* (*sim shalom*, "make piece") (Numeri 6,26) is a Hungarian variant of the British Progressive Movement. Their rabbi, the first lady as a rabbi in Hungary, received her ordination from the Leo Baeck College in London in 1998. For the time being, they come together for prayer in the former synagogue building in 48 Garay utca—beneath the umbrella of the Cultural Association. They received their Torah scroll from a private heritage, from a Hasid in a village in Eastern Hungary, through the help of their British connection. For the time being, the rabbis and community leaders more or less ignore them.

The community life of Budapest Jewry seems to start bustling, too. Educational institutions, clubs, youth organizations have been established such as the *Hasomér Hacair* (*ha-shomer ha-tza'ir*, "young guard"), *Hanoár Hacioni* (*ha-no'ar ha-tziyyoni*, "youth of Zion"), *Habonim Dror* (*ha-bonim*, "the builders" and *deror*, "freedom"), *Bné Akiva / B'nai Akiva* (*benei Akiva*, "sons of R. Akiva"), *Bné Brit / B'nai Brith* (*benei berit*, "sons of the covenant"), the *Hungarian Union of Jewish Students* (HUJS). The *Wallenberg Társaság*, though not explicitly Jewish, following the tradition of Raoul Wallenberg himself, supports minority rights.

The office of the *Joint* is in the building of the Jewish community in Síp utca. The busy office of the *Sokhnut*, the *Jewish Agency*, was for years at 27 Damjanich utca, and now it is in 17–19 Lendvay utca.

After several years of silence, in the 1990s Jewish press in Hungary is variegated. Besides the bi-weekly *Új Élet*, there are the monthly *Szombat* [Sabbath]; the monthly *Egység* of the Lubavitch community (circulation: ca. 13,000) and their weekly *Sábesz*; the monthly *Erec* of the Jewish Agency (circulation: ca. 14,000); the *Ígéret / Iggeret* (Promise / "letter"), newsletter of a synagogue (Nagy Fuvaros utca); a quarterly *Múlt és Jövő*, revived as a journal of Jewish culture; the *Remény*, journal of Jewish *belles-lettres*; and the respectful *Évkönyv*, recently edited by the Rabbinical Seminary (always published with some delay). Occasionally also other groups publish a "journal": a few pages, computer-printed or as a supplement to another journal, such was e.g. the *Córesz* ("trouble"), a satirical newsletter of the Union of Jewish Students or a newsletter of the Szarvas Camp.

In addition to the already existing "Anna Frank", the school of the Jewish community, other Jewish schools have opened their gates. These are the "Lauder Javne" and the American Endowment School (44 Wesselényi utca). The Jewish community's school moved to its new building in Laky Adolf utca, next block to the Jewish Hospital (38–40 Laky Adolf utca), in the fall of 1998, and in the new building it was renamed as *Scheiber Sándor Tanintézet* (Sándor Scheiber Educational Establishment). The new school is a replacement for the former *Zsidó Gimnázium*'s building in Abonyi utca. Its construction was financed in part by state and municipal subsidies. The building was designed by Péter Nyíri, in cooperation with Judit Görgényi interior designer. Stained-glass windows on the gallery towards the courtyard are works of the artist György Hegyi. Symbols of the twelve tribes again have the same role as they did sixty years earlier on the facade of the Goldmark Hall.

Thus, at the time of this writing (1998), there are three Jewish schools in Budapest, primary, secondary / high schools in one: the "Scheiber", the *Masoret avot* and the "Lauder Javne". These correspond more or less to the three main tendencies of Hungarian Jewry: the Neolog, the Orthodox and the secular ones. The "Scheiber" represents the old Neolog tradition in Jewish and secular education as it was established in Hungary in the nineteenth century, with all necessary improvements. The name of the Orthodox school refers to the tradition ("tradition of the fathers"), and that of the secular school, on the donor and on a town in Palestine (Yavneh / Jamnia), the seat of the first Sanhedrin after the destruction of the Temple where the reconstruction of Jewish religious life started. There is religious education in "Lauder Javne" as well, therefore the qualification as secular is true only to a limited extent. Religion here, by and large, means Jewish tradition, and it is in no direct correlation with religious observance. In addition to these schools with a high enrollment, some children certainly will attend the fourth Jewish school, that of the Lubavitch community.

The Jewish higher education is being completely reorganized in the late 1990s. The Jewish University, besides the newly established departments, is to embrace, after more than 120 years of existence, the Rabbinical Seminary and the recent Pedagogium, where the fifth regular class graduated in 1998.

Since the fall of 1989 there is a department (chair) for Hebrew studies at the Faculty of Humanities of the Loránd Eötvös University. Students can major in Hebrew and Jewish studies, and after ca. five years of study earn a degree (Master of Arts, MA). Theses have been written on the history of Hebrew grammars in Hungary; on the Halakhic status of Bibles printed by Christian typographers in the early modern period; on the Sabbatarian Simon Péchi's translation of the *Pirkei avot*; on the Hebrew treatises of R. Áron Chorin; on R. Moses Kunitzer's role in the reform of Hebrew, etc.

Oneg shabbat celebrations have been held recently on Saturday afternoons or evenings at several places. A widely popular *Oneg Shabbat* Club in Budapest is the one next to the Bethlen Gábor tér synagogue (15 István út). The custom of *oneg shabbats* is already of Israeli origin, the secular version of the Friday evening celebration. In Tel-Aviv, in the winter of 1929/30, Chaim Nachman Bialik (1873–1934) read out stories taken from the Talmudic tradition (*aggadah*), and explained them to a large audience on Saturday afternoons in the hall of the "Herzl" High School. (His adaptations of the *Aggadah* have become classical masterpieces of modern Hebrew prose since then.) Later a whole movement developed out of the initiatives of the poet. The Zionist *oneg shabbat*, in the spirit of Bialik, is a frame of the intellectual life connected with the Jewish tradition, and it may include the ritual of *havdalah* as well. Before World War II in Hungary it was the *Zsidó Gimnázium*, which first followed the initiative of Bialik and the *yishuv* in order to create a modern urban version of this custom. (The school organized a memorial evening on the occasion of Bialik's death.)

The Hungarian Jewish Cultural Association and the Hungarian Union of Jewish Students operate at 48 Garay utca, in the large first floor room of the former Orthodox synagogue. On Friday evenings various programs await the regular, or even occasional, visitor here. This is the place where the "Chagall" Gallery was established, a home to the works of Jewish artists, among others the group "Ayin" (*ayin*, "eye", "source"). On Saturday evenings in the *Oneg Shabbat* Club at 15 István út the public *havdalah* ceremony is followed by some social gatherings. And for Sunday afternoons there was the Hora Dance Club in the community center of Marcibányi tér, or in the Almássy tér Recreation Center. The *Hora*—ring dance of Jews who had settled in Palestine from the beginning of the twentieth century, still very popular in Israel—is basically the same as the Balkan *Kolo* or *Horo* dance. The Club recently found its place in the "Bálint Ház" (16 Révay utca).

The cantorial recitals, held annually in the spring or early summer in the Dohány utca synagogue or at the Vigadó, are regarded as significant musical events, as are the performances of the Budapester Klezmer Band. Klezmer music has become trendy anyway, guest performances of klezmer groups from abroad are very frequent. Muzsikás, a Hungarian folk music ensemble, plays Jewish music collected from Gypsies in Máramaros, with great success. They published a record, too.

Klezmer became popular in Budapest. There are at least three permanent bands here: Pannonia Klezmer Band, Budapester Klezmer Band and Di Nayer Kapelye Klezmer Band. The Hé-Band, an orchestra of the "Lauder Javne", plays Sephardi music. On an other level of entertainment, commercial Jewish pub music from Odessa is on the program of the ensemble "Vodku v glodku" (Vodka down the throat).

Books on Jewish topics, records, souvenirs, personal ritual accessories are available in the gift shop at 12 Síp utca and in the "Biblical World" Gallery (13 Wesselényi utca). The selection of the Gallery ranges from antiquities and original works of artistic value to usual merchandise, sometimes even to kitsch, as in similar outlets all over the world. The Gallery orders Jewish ritual objects—like Seder plate, hand-washer, Kiddush cup—with traditional Hungarian folk motifs from well-known Hungarian potters in a Transylvanian village. There are occasionally also art exhibitions and book launches in the rather small shop. In the summer there is a table with books and records at the entrance of the Jewish Museum as well. Recordings of Hungarian cantors recorded in the Dohány utca synagogue or in a studio are much in demand.

A consensus is beginning to take shape concerning the need for independent and characteristic Jewish cultural and scholarly institutions and collections in Budapest. In addition to the Jewish Museum, there is a need for a well-organized Hungarian Jewish Archive where historic documents would be properly preserved and made available for researches. A rich Jewish Library providing up-to-date information would also be indispensable; it does not exist yet, and with the temporary closing of the Rabbinical Seminary's library in 1998 the lack of a Jewish library became even worse.

The Hungarian Jewish Archives first received temporary accommodations in Síp utca. Their holdings embrace almost the entire history of Budapest Jewry from the end of the eighteenth century and their fonds from the provinces is extensive as well. The largest record groups are the papers of the Pest community in the aftermath of the 1868/69 General Congress. Its arrangement is still in progress, therefore it is not yet accessible for research purposes. Researchers may use the archive materials of the Jewish Museum, though, which is of considerable volume and great value, and the holdings of State Archives.

(3) Ashkenazi and Sephardi
—or How to Pronounce the Hebrew of the Bible?

In Budapest, Hungary, the answer to this question can only be given by tradition and practice. Central and East European Jews have always read Hebrew according to the Ashkenazi pronunciation, this is how they read the Torah and recited the prayers. In Hungary, where even the communities calling themselves Sephardi after the Turkish occupation were mostly of Ashkenazi—Hasidic origin, and certainly those who settled here later, the Sephardi pronunciation has no strong tradition in modern synagogue practice.

503. Portrait of Moshe Kunitzer

Hartwig (Naphtali Hirz) Wessely (1725–1805), who initiated the reform of Hebrew pronunciation, referred precisely to the fact (*Rehovot*, 1875) that the Sephardi people read out every phonetic symbol, even semitones of traditional texts, clearly, and claimed that their language sounded nicer than the Ashkenazi reading. "This (i.e. the Sephardi) pronunciation has been forgotten for a long-long time in our country." In Hungary, József Rájnis (1741–1812), a Jesuit teacher and poet, made a similar statement with an offensive, anti-Semitic overtone. In his opinion the accent ("barking", as he called it) of rabbis differed significantly from the original sounds of the ancient Jewish language (1781). Ashkenazim pronounce a few letters differently from the Sephardim, and there are numerous prevalent Ashkenazi accents as well: besides the received standard Ashkenazi of the Rabbinical Seminary, several of them are being used today in Budapest. In the "high-Ashkenazi", for instance, *o* is said instead of *a* and *au* instead of *o*, and in certain positions, like at the end of a word, the letter *tav* is pronounced as an *s* instead of *t*. They also stress syllables differently. Thus the first words of the Bible are read *Bereshit bara Elohim* in the Sephardi and *Böreishis boro Elauhim* in the Ashkenazi pronunciation. The difference is not a major one, but it is easy to recognize who reads according to which tradition even on the basis of a few words.

In Hungary there was an attempt to introduce Sephardi pronunciation already in the nineteenth century. Following German examples it was Moshe ben Menachem Kunitz (Kontz / Kunitzer) (1774–1837) of Óbuda, the rabbi of the Buda community from 1828 until his death, author of some valuable Talmudic works, a *Zohar* analysis (*Ben-Yohai*, 1815), and even a drama in Hebrew verse ("Beit Rabbi", 1805), who in 1818 published a rabbinic decision (*pesak*) which announced that the

Sephardi pronunciation should be used instead of the Ashkenazi in the synagogues. His main argument was that seven eighths of the world's Jewry prays using the Sephardi pronunciation. (This figure was somewhat exaggerated.) Kunitzer was in favor of reforms in general; he even supported the efforts of Áron Chorin. He studied in Prague and was held in high esteem. After his death it was suggested that the congregation of the *Altneuschul* in Prague mention three Moseses in the liturgy for the dead (*mazkir neshamot*), that is, Moses Maimonides, Moses Mendelssohn and Moses Kunitzer.

The activity of Kunitzer had no real result but, in spite of its failure, it indicates that representatives of the Haskalah were unanimously convinced that the Sephardi pronunciation, preserved by certain isolated Jewish groups through centuries, was closer to the original sound of the Hebrew language than the Ashkenazi one, the common language of European Jews, altered under German influence. In fact, representatives of the Jewish Enlightenment (*maskilim*) meant this linguistic archaization as a reform. Their intention was to purify Hebrew of linguistic formations they regarded as secondary. Interestingly enough, it happened to be R. Meisel who wrote Wessely's biography (1841). The Neolog movement paid attention to his initiatives.

The Torah and the prayers should always be read out clearly and distinctly, pronouncing every sound properly; this is a commandment, a *mitzvah*. A prayer which is not read out properly is invalid. The debate over pronunciation was never merely about linguistics; on the contrary, it concerned the very essence of traditional Jewish life.

At the beginning of the nineteenth century, it was the Sephardi pronunciation that seemed most suitable for distinguishing Hebrew from Yiddish. The Ashkenazi pronunciation adjusted, understandably, to the Yiddish sound system and intonation; it was nothing but Hebrew read with a Yiddish accent.

Nevertheless, Ashkenazi and Sephardi means more than simply two ways of pronouncing Hebrew. Behind these terms there are two great cultures of late medieval and modern Jewry. Both names come from the Bible, *Ashkenaz* from the Chart of Nations (Genesis 10,3), *Sefard / Sefarad* from the Book of the Prophet Obadiah (1,20). Ashkenaz comes from Jafet's family, he is the son of Gomer. In the names *Gomer* and *Ashkenaz* the Iranian mounted nations, the Cimmerians and the Scythians, can be recognized, who played such an important role in the history of the Near East and Asia Minor at the end of the seventh century B.C.E. *Sefarad* was the capital of the Lydian empire in the western region of Asia Minor. According to Assyrian and ancient Persian historical sources it was called Sparda, Sardeis according to Greek texts. The Sephardi *Halakhah* follows, more or less, the traditions of Babylonian Jewry, while the Ashkenazi customs revive the Palestinian traditions. The Jewry of the countries South of the Mediterranean region are considered Sephardi, including the Jews of Babylon, Yemen, South Arabia, North Africa and the Iberian Peninsula, and also the first Diaspora (*galut*) (sixth and fifth centuries B.C.E.) living continuously in this area, at the beginning in the eastern parts of the region. According to an old Sephardi tradition the Babylonian-Sephardi Jewry originates from Jerusalem, they are the descendants of the nobility of the city, offsprings of the captives transferred to Babylon by Nebukhadnezzar. This is the origin of the definitely aristocratic consciousness of Sephardi people, even in the nineteenth and twentieth centuries. *Ashkenazim* trace their ancestry to the Jewry of the Italian peninsula, from the time of the second Diaspora, in the first and second centuries C.E. The majority were Jews moving from the newly occupied province of Palestine to the core areas of the Roman empire. They migrated further reaching Western Europe via the Rhineland, first the French and German lands. During the Middle Ages they fled eastward because of the pogroms of the crusaders, and the expulsions as a result of epidemics, especially the Black Death of 1348. (The same epidemic was the cause of the expulsion of the Jews of Buda in the age of Louis Anjou.)

Lately, it has been said with some simplification that Sephardim are the Jews living in the countries of Islam, whereas Ashkenazim are those living in Christian countries. The decision of Rabbenu Gershom ben Judah around 1000, the interdiction of polygamy, and its consequences drew a sharp line of distinction between the Ashkenazi communities and the Sephardi people in Moslem countries who remained polygamous. After the Jews had been expelled from Spain in 1492, Ashkenazi and Sephardi communities started to live next to each other in Turkey, in the Balkans and in Buda as well. It became obvious then that even if only in matters of detail, there were many differences in their rituals and customs (*minhagim*), and it always took extra effort to harmonize them. A few difficult cases occurred in the sixteenth century in Buda as well. For instance, "Reuven" (i.e. *Peloni ben Almoni*[2] / NN or XY), a *kohen* from the holy congregation of Buda, whose wife gave birth to two sons, wanted to have another woman because his wife had become insane. She had to be kept locked up in a separate room, and although she regained her senses from time to time for a few weeks, she always relapsed into her illness again. It was impossible to live in the same house with her. The Ashkenazi rabbi of Salonika preferred, even in this case, to issue a letter of divorce (*get*). The *Shulhan Arukh*, the great Halakhic systematization of Josef Karo from 1565, became accepted in the Ashkenazi world only when Moshe Isserles (ca. 1525–1572), rabbi of Cracow, set the corresponding Ashkenazi decisions and customs (*Mappah*, 1569–1572) beside them in the form of remarks (*haggahot*). In other words, he laid his own table-cloth (*mappah*) on Karo's table (*shulhan*). Karo was *maran*, "our master" for the Sephardi people, whereas Ashkenazim only referred to him as *moram*, "their master".

It was precisely under the influence of Karo and Isserles, but also because of the contacts between Sephardim and Ashkenazim, that a certain leveling of the two traditions started following the sixteenth century. For instance, R. Noah of Buda ordered in 1619 that in the Safed yeshiva, founded by him and maintained from his donations, the number of Ashkenazi and Sephardi students should be equal. Nevertheless, uniformity has not come about, not even in Israel. There was, however, one field in which the Ashkenazi traditions prevailed in the whole Jewish world, and this was writing. Beside "Assyrian" or quadratic letters (*ketav merubba*) used for printing only, the Ashkenazi cursive script spread everywhere. It was adopted in the Sephardi world as well, and everyone uses it in Israel. But even these have Sephardi roots. According to Maimonides cursive script is needed so that the Hebrew alphabet, with which the Torah is written, would not be profaned or blasphemed.

In the first half of the nineteenth century, when various movements calling for the reformation of Jewish life were developing, the Sephardi culture seemed a real alternative for Ashkenazi Jewry. It appeared to be a means to overcome the Ashkenazi heritage which they regarded as backward. Preserving the spirit of traditions, they intended to modernize some aspects of Jewish ritual and lifestyle. The German–Jewish cult of Sephardi traditions had several elements. German romanticism attributed special value to historicism. The cult of antiquity manifested itself in several branches of culture. Folk culture was considered primordial rather than high culture. The idealization of Sephardi traditions meant also the rejection of Ashkenazi customs that were regarded as outdated. Their assessment now tended towards the other extreme, in contrast with the sixteenth century. At that time, Ashkenazi culture enjoyed higher status, since Ashkenazi Jews had not converted to any other religion, had not become *marranos*. Around 1500, when the first scholarly Hebrew grammar books were published in Europe, the authors naturally took the language of Jews living in France and Germany, that is Ashkenazi Hebrew, as the basis of their work, and Sephardi was regarded as a curiosity. In the epoch-making grammar book (*De rudimentis Hebraicis,* 1506) of Johannes Reuchlin (1455–1522), Ashkenazi Hebrew was the living language. It was only in the seventeenth century that European Hebraic scholars—the so-called "Christian Hebraists"—decided in favor of Sephardi reading. It was accepted by the great grammar (1817) of Wilhelm Gesenius (1786–1842) as well, which formed the basis of modern Hebrew linguistics. Its adherents in Pest were Bloch / Ballagi and Goldziher. Since the seventeenth century everyone considered Sephardi usage to be the scholarly standard and used it exclusively. Jewish scholarship (*Wissenschaft des Judentums*) was now committed to Sephardi, and it became the ideal for the initiatives of the reform movements. Those German Jews who wished to be emancipated and integrated into the non-Jewish environment definitely strove to be different from the "backward" Ashkenazi co-religionists. They wanted to leave out the verses that originated from the medieval "German" (i.e. Ashkenazi) environment (*piyyut*) from

---

[2] For the name see Ruth 4,1.

504. Torah ornaments (*rimmonim*) from the former Pest Sephardi community

the ritual and prayer-books, since these remained alien to the Sephardi world. Nevertheless, the debate was not just about pronunciation and the *Mahzor*, but also about Jewish way of life. The invitation of Mayer Kayserling, a Sephardi scholar, to Dohány utca was in harmony with the German scale of values.

The idealization of the "Moorish" style was also brought to Budapest by the preference for Sephardi culture. Those who commissioned the designs for the new synagogues as well as those who visited the temples regarded it not as Hispanic Arabian architecture, not even as Oriental tradition (which, incidentally, they also found attractive, even though the Iberian peninsula was by no means the East). What the style implied was the Sephardi world. Behind this phenomenon there stood the efforts of the reform movement. Yet the Sephardi pronunciation was not accepted by the moderately reform-minded Jewish public of Pest, neither when Kunitzer suggested its use, nor along the practice of the "Central Reform Association" (Einhorn and Einhorn).

There were, however, a few real Sephardi communities in Hungary, even after the Turkish occupation. There were some persons with Arab-sounding names, such as *Almuslin,* found already in the earliest census of Jews in Pest in 1791. The word itself means "Moslem". Similar names are *Elkan* (*kohen*), the name of famous furriers at the Orczy House and *Albachary* (*bahur*), merchants on Erzsébet tér. In both cases, the Hebrew word used as a name is combined with an article. There were several "Swiss men" (in German *Schweitzer*) among the Jews of Óbuda. They were referred to as the *marranos,* but even if their ancestors happened to have lived in a Christian disguise, they certainly lived a Jewish life. Whether they were *marranos* or not, there were many Sephardim among the Jews coming from the Balkans, from Switzerland or France. Nevertheless, their assimilation into Ashkenazi Jewry was a rather fast process in Hungary. It started in the provinces (Nagykároly: 1818, Temesvár: 1833). As their number decreased, gradually their separate *minyan* folded up everywhere and those who remained joined the Ashkenazi *minyen.* The nineteenth-century Spanish Sephardi community did not survive in Budapest either. Following World War I the Ashkenazi traditions became generally accepted here as well. According to one of the journalists of *Egyenlőség* (1934), however, in the neighborhood of Király utca, "the careful observer may often notice pure Spanish Jewish features, occasionally even hear a few Spanish words".

The last traces of real Sephardi Jews in Budapest were found in 1944. The Spanish ambassador's deputy (Angel Sanz-Briz), leaving Hungary, reported to his Government on December 14, 1944:

"The undersigned managed to establish the fact that there was a limited number of Sephardi people living in Budapest. They had migrated here from the former Ottoman empire and had preserved their Spanish language. They number 45. We issued a regular [Spanish] passport for them, in which we recorded the 45 persons mentioned above. (...) I expounded to the [Hungarian] Foreign Ministry that the protection of the Sephardim had always been the traditional policy of the Spanish authorities and that this had always been respected by the countries in which the Jewish question was raised."

As a matter of fact, the name Sephardi referred to the Hasidim of Central and Eastern Europe. Eastern European Hasidism evolved along the teachings of Yitzhak Luria (1534–1572), "the divine (*ha-elohi*) rabbi". Certain elements of the Sephardi liturgy of Safed were adopted and naturalized together with his teachings. They could not change the Ashkenazi pronunciation, though, and they retained several Ashkenazi customs as well. After all, Hasidism added but nuances to the Ashkenazi ritual.

Scholars of the early nineteenth-century Hebrew language reform accepted the Sephardi pronunciation as the standard, as did the inhabitants of the Palestinian Jewish colonies (*yishuv*) by the end of the nineteenth century, and this practice was adopted and confirmed by Zionism as well. The Sephardi pronunciation has spread in Israel, too. Modern Hebrew is based on it and it became generally accepted in the synagogue ritual as well. Over the past few decades the linguistic *nusah* has slowly adjusted to it, in the teaching of the language as well as in Bible reading, at some places even in the synagogue. In the 1950s the leadership of the Hungarian Jewish community strictly forbade the Sephardi pronunciation which sounded similar to modern Hebrew. It was even forbidden at the Rabbinical Seminary, lest they be accused of Zionism and thus invite political or police intervention. Those who study Hebrew these days may learn both pronunciations, yet the attraction and impact of the Israeli intonation is powerful. In synagogues, the Ashkenazi pronunciation still is in use, but younger people, including students of the Rabbinical Seminary, switch to the Sephardi–Israeli reading they got accustomed during their stay in Israel. While the Ashkenazi pronunciation creates a kind of isolation from Jews abroad, on the other hand, it is a traditional value and should be preserved. There is no better solution than to know both.

(4) The Yiddish in Pest

In Pest, just like everywhere else in the Ashkenazi world, the "Jewish tongue" was Yiddish for a long time. Jews spoke in the Jewish tongue, i.e. in Yiddish (*yid* means "Jew"), as opposed to Hebrew (*leshon kodesh / loshn-koydesh*), the holy tongue, which was used for sacred purposes. Yiddish is written with Hebrew characters. It is called *mame-loshn*, mother tongue, if for no other reason, because most women did not know any other language. It emerged on the lips of Jews living in Germany in the Middle Ages, in the tenth and eleventh centuries, and has been developing continuously ever since. In Eastern Europe it came under strong Slavic influence and various Yiddish dialects emerged. "The whole *jargon* consists of dialects, even the written language, even if a common written form has been agreed upon"—wrote Franz Kafka in 1912.

There is no doubt that in the Middle Ages Jews who lived in Buda spoke Judeo-German, i.e. Yiddish. Those who left Buda for Turkey spoke Yiddish, too. During the Turkish occupation another Jewish language, Judeo-Spanish came to be used in certain circles in Buda. The chronicle of the 1683 siege of Buda called *Eyn sheyn nay lid fun Ofen*, "A Nice Song from Buda", was written in Yiddish, too—the tongue in which the general European Jewish public could be addressed at the time. Among the important early remnants of Yiddish literature there is a piece from Buda, too, the *Naye maysebukh*, "New Stories" printed by Jonathan ben Jacob in 1697.

The decline of Yiddish in Pest paralleled the rise of bourgeois Jewry and of their Magyarization. For a while, around 1840, there were still two ways for assimilation and a choice between Hungarian or German for the linguistic acculturation of Yiddish-speaking Jews. In the 1840s Jews arriving to Pest from Germany or Moravia were more likely to lean towards the everyday use of German rather than Hungarian; for them there was a second linguistic shift a few decades later when they learned Hungarian. There were, of course, some who chose Hebrew, if only as a written language for the time being. They were the advocates of Hebrew language reform and the creators of modern literature in classical Hebrew, etc. In the first half of the nineteenth-century Pest and Western Hungary, reaching as far as Pozsony / Pressburg or Vienna, had a rich Hebrew literature; poetic works and treatises were written in large numbers. Jews from Eastern Hungary, the *interlendish* Jews, were clinging to their Yiddish more faithfully; for most of them abandoning the Yiddish language would have been tantamount to abandoning community life. In Pest all three languages, Yiddish, German and Hungarian, were used alongside each other for a short while in the synagogue as well as for social contacts. The language of the 1868/69 General Congress was mostly German. Later Neolog Jewry committed itself firmly to Hungarian, while Orthodoxy was equally firm about maintaining Yiddish as the language to be used in the synagogue and in the home. If there was any attempt to break away from this it was generally towards Hebrew, as in the case of R. Koppel Reich. The language of assimilation was initially German but, after the last third of the nineteenth century, it became Hungarian. German was maintained only as a second language, mainly to be used at home. After the split of Orthodox and Neolog Jewry the prestige of Yiddish declined quickly. But the continued presence of Yiddish in everyday usage at home and in public is demonstrated by the existence of a Pest Jewish socio-dialect in which the Yiddish element is equal to the Hebrew. In the bourgeois Pest, the Magyarized Jewish society had less and less respect for Yiddish, they considered it the *jargon* of the *galiciánerek* / in German *Galizianers*, of the *kaftánosok* / *kaftanniks*. By then *maggidim* no longer came to Pest, sermons were held in Hungarian or in German in the synagogues and a Yiddish *droshe*—like those of Benjámin Fischer in the "Rombach" twice a year—was rarely heard. Yiddish was only referred to as a *jargon* for decades. Everyone understood it, but if a child picked up a Yiddish word at school and uttered it at home, the smile usually froze upon the parents' lips.

In Pest Yiddish the culture of the kaftanniks was only accepted as a form of low-class entertainment:

> "As long as (the Jewish joke) makes fun of our Israelite compatriots in the Hungarian tongue, be it on stage, in writing or in drawing, their complaints are great. But when it comes to jesting about the *ingverishe* [from Ungvár] Polish-Yiddish accent or dances and gestures, they seem to be enchanted. The urban Jewish type is but the broker and the banker. (...) But what the Galician *klezmorim* and jesters had brought to us from across the border is something completely different! That is of real artistic value in content and form. (...) And may their farces be occasionally coarse for the refined ear, they are always witty, humorous and entertaining . (...) It is just that you need to be educated to understand it! The difficulties of the dialect are enhanced by the tricks of the Gemarah. Without knowing the rituals, customs and other intimate secrets the audience can get pretty bored."
>
> (Porzó / Adolf Ágai, in: *A Hét*, 1890)

505. A page from the manuscript of József Holder, from his Yiddish translation of "The Tragedy of Man" by Imre Madách

In Pest there was no real secular Yiddish culture, literature, theater, as in Warsaw in the first decades of the twentieth century or in the Russian Pale (*tehum ha-moshav / tkhum ha-moyshev*). There is little information about how the evenings were spent in the pubs, restaurants and cafés of Teleki tér and its neighborhood, but maybe Yiddish was heard there more often than elsewhere in town.

The only significant Yiddish poet in Pest was József Holder (1893–1944), from the Carpatho-Ukraine. His poems and some of his translations of Hungarian poems into Yiddish are still well known, but his main work, the Yiddish translation of a Hungarian national classic from the year 1859/60, the *Az ember tragédiája* [The Tragedy of Man] by Imre Madách, *Di tragedie funem mentshn* was never published in full. Holder starved to death in the Budapest ghetto in early January, 1945.

But as much as the *jargon* was looked down upon by many, in the interwar years still everyone knew at least a little of it. Imre Ámos notes in his diary, for instance, that when he and his wife, Margit Anna, visited Marc Chagall in Paris in 1937, it was with the help of some words borrowed from the *jargon* that they were able to communicate.

A truly remarkable remnant of the Western Yiddish spoken in Pest is a poem, or rather a translation of a Hungarian poem into Yiddish. Let us quote the first two verses from it, according to a recently printed critical edition by Ádám Nádasdy (1998), reproducing the spelling used by the extant manuscripts, which were all written in Latin characters.

"Melach Edward, der englische
Kümmt geritten auf zej' Ferd:
La'mach kücken, zogt er esaj,[3]
Wos is dos Ländele wert?

"Gibt's daj e Flüss im Überflüss?
Ün Hei ün Wâzen gnüg?
Dos Spritzen daj vün Brüderblüt
Hat dos eppes genützt?"

The title of the poem is "Die chasónem vün Wales, vün Jankele Gold". It is none other than the Yiddish translation of a nineteenth-century Hungarian classic, of a poem by János Arany, "A walesi bárdok" [The Bards of Wales], written in 1857.

The typewritten manuscript has been going around in Budapest for the past decades, yet its origin remains mysterious. A copy of it was found among the papers of Soma Braun (1890–1944), the prominent folklorist and sociologist, who died as a forced laborer. This funny translation, or rather parody, of the Arany poem may have been composed sometime in the first decades of the twentieth century, possibly after World War I, and even though the surviving cabaret programs do not indicate it, it may have been a great stuff for entertainment in the literary circles of Budapest, in a social environment where the earlier *heimish* Yiddish became already *outlandish*; Yiddish was already nothing more than a well-known exotic remnant.

In the 1960s Miklós Hutterer, a linguist, researcher of the German dialects spoken in Hungary who, though of German origin, grew up in the Orczy House and learned Yiddish in the street, was still able to collect some original Jewish folklore in the Jewish tongue around Wesselényi and Dob utca.

The Yiddish language is a relic, though a living relic in some places. In Orthodox or Hasidic circles it is still used every day, even in Pest. Yiddish may revive one day among others, too, in a wider circle.

(5) Jewish Hospitality

Kosher dining has never been a problem in Pest. There were several kosher restaurants, the most famous one probably Stern's restaurant at 6 Rombach utca / Rumbach Sebestyén utca. It was *glatt*-kosher, strictly Orthodox. It was open on Sabbath, but customers did not pay—nobody was carrying money anyway. Of course, customers had to pay the bill in advance or after Sabbath. The former rooms of Stern's restaurant have been altered during reconstruction so radically that it is impossible to recognize them anymore.

Today those who keep kosher can buy their groceries in the neighborhood around Klauzál tér and Kazinczy utca. There are stores selling kosher food as well as a few kosher restaurants.

Kosher meat can be purchased at butcher shops under supervision of the rabbinate.[4] These are, for the time being: the butchery, sausage factory and food store of Dezső Kővári at 41 Kazinczy utca; the Orthodox poultry store and bakery (28 Kazinczy utca); the Orthodox butchers at 35 Dob utca and 16 Visegrádi utca; the Neolog butchers at 11 Klauzál tér and 6 Eötvös utca.

---

[3] An addition in a manuscript: (...) cu zejn samesz.
[4] The certificate (*hekhsher*) testifies that responsibility rests with a rabbi qualified and authorized to control the whole process of preparing the food.

The Kőváry butchery's history can be documented in detail. It is now eighty-odd years old. Its owners were as follows:

Adolf Heuffel: 1914–1926
Izidór Rebenwurzel and Mihály Berkovits: 1926–1935
Salamon and Izidór Rebenwurzel: 1935–1957
Mihály Berkovits: 1957–1971
Mrs. Berkovits: 1971–1973
Dezső Kővári: 1973–

The Orthodox store at 28 Kazinczy utca also carries bread and *hallah* (*barches*), as well as spices, soft drinks, etc. The Rothschild kosher food store (32 Rákóczi út) and its other stores carry a wide range of kosher products from abroad, first of all, from Israel, including wines. These stores (4 Szent István körút, 19 Teréz körút, 9 Károly körút) mark out the former Jewish quarters of the city. Some non-alcoholic beverages in Hungary, like a certain grape juice (*traubi* in Hungarian) or coke, do not need a *hekhsher*. (Yet on the *traubi* there is one.) Attentive buyers can detect the mark of the American Orthodox Union on some imported foods. *Matzzah* (*matses*) is baked—since ever—at the *Fővárosi Sütőipari Vállalat* (City Bakery), once called *Pászka Kft.*, at 26 Tüzér utca, and in a small bakery in Kis Diófa utca. Recently *matzzah* imported from Israel became an article of prestige before Passover, but regular stores carry *matzes* through the year.

Wine can be purchased at the "Verpeléti" Orthodox kosher wine cellar (16 Klauzál tér). György G. Kardos mentioned in his short stories repeatedly the tall blond lad who used to sell the wine here in the 1950s, when non-Jews would come more often than Jews.

As for restaurants, there is an Orthodox kosher restaurant "Hanna" at 35 Dob utca (in the courtyard, on the second floor of the Orthodox community building). One can immerse here in the atmosphere of a traditional Friday evening or Saturday noon and have a taste of the Central-European Jewish kitchen. They serve traditional *tsholent* and *gefilte fish*. "Hanna" used to be the name of kitchen of the Jewish community for children. It was located that time at 32 Kertész utca. A fine restaurant of the mid-1990s, the "Shalom" at 2 Klauzál tér, also operated under rabbinical supervision, but it was closed because of financial insufficiency. A new Orthodox kosher restaurant opened in Hotel King's (27–29 Nagy Diófa utca).

There is a Jewish pastry shop in Budapest, Fröhlich's at 22 Dob utca. Traditional delicacies are offered there, like *kindli* and *flódni*.

Still, the largest Jewish restaurant in Budapest is the community's central kitchen, the *Szeretetkonyha* (39 Páva utca), a restaurant, a *mensa* and a *tamhuy* combined. It serves the whole Jewish community of the capital, delivering food to dining-halls of the institutions. Since the "Scheiber" Neolog school was opened, the kitchen of the latter, with an Orthodox *hekhsher*, took over its functions, perhaps temporarily only.

Earlier, in the 1980s, the only place with Jewish-type—meaning non-kosher—food was Kádár's at 10 Klauzál tér. In the 1990s some new restaurants and fast-food stores of this type were opened. In these one may have a taste of the typical foods of the Mediterranean and the Near East, of their Israeli version, such as *falafel*, *hummus*, *shwarma*, *pita*, and try food imported from Israel, e.g. olives or dates, wines or beer. Such a place is the Carmel Cellar, a restaurant at 31 Kazinczy utca, a next-door neighbor of the Orthodox synagogue. It is a very popular place indeed, capitalizing on curiosity for the Jewish kitchen; the food there is at best "kosher-type". The *Falafel Faloda* (Eatery or Salad Bar) (53 Paulay Ede utca) serves only vegetarian food, without a *hekhsher*, "almost kosher", but reliable in this category. There was at one time a general store "Made in Tel-Aviv" at 9 Klauzál tér; or the falafel place called "Cabar" (from *cabar / sabre*, "cactus", "born in Israel") at 25 Irányi utca, or the "Golden Gastronomia" at 8 Bécsi utca. The situation changes quickly; these days restaurants open and close down frequently. Once the demand arises, there will surely be more Jewish restaurants and stores.

A Yiddish proverb says: *Hun iz gut tsu esn banand, ikh un di hun*, "When eating a chicken it is best if it's just the two of us, me and the chicken."

Because of their great importance in the recent cultural history of Budapest, two cafés should be mentioned. One of them is Café "Terminus" at 54 Teréz körút, where Mihály Székely (1901-1963), the great bass opera singer used to spend time. Earlier it was the steady "hangout" of Jenő Heltai and Ferenc Molnár, the latter wrote his play "Hattyú" [The Swan] here.

The other café, the famous "New York" / "Hungária", a café and restaurant, is located at 9-11 Erzsébet körút, in the New York Palace. It was built according to the architectural design of Alajos Hauszmann (1847-1926) and was opened in 1894. The ceiling is decorated with the frescos of Károly Lotz and Gusztáv Magyar-Mannheimer (1859-1937). In the interwar years it was rented and later bought by Vilmos Tarjáni (1881-1947), a journalist who came to be internationally known because of his reports on criminal cases. The New York Café was regularly visited by the literary establishment of Budapest in those years. The editorial meetings of *Nyugat* were held on the gallery.

The "Kis Pipa" (Little Pipe) (38 Akácfa utca) is just a restaurant and pub in the Jewish quarter. Its sole celebrity was Rezső Seress (1889-1968) at the piano. A survivor of the Pest ghetto became a popular salon musician; he was playing piano in bars for decades, first in "Miniatűr" in a luxurious neighborhood of Buda (Buday László utca), then in the "Kis Pipa". His popular song "Szomorú vasárnap" [Sad Sunday] became a world hit. Unnoticed by the society at large, he died (committed suicide) in 1968.

(6) Tshulent and Gefilte Fish

At the beginning of the era of contemporary fashion cookbooks, Zorica Krausz (Mrs. Péter Herbst) published her book *Magyarországi zsidó ételek* [*Jewish Dishes in Hungary*] (Budapest: Minerva, 1984). Later the book had a second, fancier edition, but the first one was a real social event. It was not customary to talk about Jewish things publicly before, in fact, it was not possible. And a Jewish cookbook is never just about food. It necessarily deals with Jewish customs, Jewish life. The author described traditional Jewish culinary customs with almost ethnographic accurateness. Her book was actually more about Hungarian *minhag* in the disguise of a cookbook. (As a matter of fact, a disproportionately long introduction described the Jewish home and the holidays, explained essential details of the kashrut, etc.) In those days this was the only publication on the topic in Hungary, so it created a minor sensation. The Jewish readers were dissatisfied with only one detail of the book, namely that the recipes were written in the past tense. But the uproar was actually a good sign: traditional life could not be written about in the past tense.

All kinds of dishes are described in the book. Some are items known throughout the Ashkenazi world and beyond, others are typically eaten only by Hungarian Jews. There are also dishes prepared differently in Hungary than elsewhere in Jewish Eastern Europe. Instead of recipes, here is a list of some typical dishes.

barhesz (*barkhes*): braided white bread (like *hallah*), preferably sprinkled with poppy seeds
belek: stuffed goose breast
cibel, ejer-cibel / *ejer mit cibel* (*eyertsibl*): boiled eggs crushed or smashed and mixed with onions, goose fat, sometimes even with liver, and spices; in Hungarian called *lengyeltojás*, "Polish (that is, Polish-Jewish) eggs" or *zsidótojás*, "Jewish eggs"
cimesz / *cimmesz* (*tsimes* / *tsimmes*): pearl barley cooked with carrots and potato, seasoned with salt, black pepper, nutmeg and sugar
delkl / *delkli*: cottage cheese pie, sometimes with plum jam or preserve
ejerkihli (*eyerkikhl*) / *ejerkuhni*: sweet egg dough
ejnmáh (*eynmakh*): garlic sauce
false fis (*falshe fish*): a kind of gefilte fish, made from poultry or veal, in aspic
fárvli (*farvl, farfl*): egg barley, steamed

506. Gingerbread (*leykekh*) with the letters of the Hebrew *alefbet*

feferbájgli (*feferbaygl*): dough spiced with black pepper

flódni (*fladn*): cake filled with layers of poppy seed, apples, plum-preserve and nuts

galuszka (*galushka*): doughnut

gánef / ganef: sausage-shaped *kugli* (that is, false sausage)

gehakte herring: salt herrings with apples, onions and eggs

gehakte léber: baked chicken liver ground and mixed with onions, eggs and melted chicken fat

glingl: veal lungs ground and cooked

griven / gribenesz: cracklings from poultry fat

grojpláh/ (*groyplakh*): fried and cooked pearl barley with onion rings

halzli: goose neck (skin) stuffed with ground meat and baked crispy

hremzli / kremzlah / kremslakh: pancakes from potato or *matzo* meal, stuffed with fruit, sweetened

inarsz (*inars*): goose fat with garlic and paprika, chilled

ingberlakh: dry cookies made of *matzo* meal, spiced with ginger

kárst (*karsht*): bread baked from corn meal

kindli: cookie roll filled with nuts or poppy seed, honey and raisins

kiske (*kishke*): veal intestines filled with potatoes, steamed and dried

kolacs (*kolatsh*): yeasted sweet buns with cinnamon (*kalács, kolacky*)

krancli (*krantsl*): pastry rings with beaten egg whites and sugar

krepláh / krepleh (*kreplakh*): dumplings stuffed with minced meat

krézli (*krezli*): veal sausage baked

kropp: poultry (goose or turkey) neck (skin) stuffed with ground meat and baked crispy (like *halzli*)

krót mit bondleh (*krot mit bondlekh*): cabbage with beans cooked separately and then mixed

krotzip: cabbage soup

kugel / kugli: grated potatoes mixed with eggs, salt, paprika and baked

lékoch / lejkeh / lebkuchen (*lekakh / leykekh*): honey cookies with almonds, nuts or dried fruit, honey-cake, honey-and-spice cake

lingenvurst (*lingenvursht*): goose pouch filled with giblets, rice, eggs and steamed.—Or: goose lungs filled in veal intestines, steamed and dried

lokshnkugli (*lokshn kugel*): pasta, made with eggs

loksn (*lokshn*): broad egg noodles (*lokshn*) baked and sweetened.—*brate lokshn*: *lokshn* cut into broad stripes

macsanka (*matshanka*): poultry (goose) aspic

mandelbrot, komishbrot: almond cookies

mandlen: soup noodles

mezonot (*mezoynes*): little cookies

milc (*milts*): milt

pce (*ptskha*): jelly from calf's foot with garlic, on *barches*

safre fis (*shafre fish*): fish aspic

smalcbájgli (*shmaltsbaygel*): schmaltz pie rings

tejgel / tejglakh (*teyglakh*): pellets of dough with honey, ginger, nutmeg, covered with beaten egg whites and baked

vajszkinlah (*vayskinlakh*): vanilla and lemon cookies

zaftbarsten (*zaftbarshten*): beef fried in goose fat with vegetables

zatterka: corn and wheat meal dough with milk

Nevertheless, one or two Jewish dishes must be described in detail, as well. A real Jewish food is *gefilte fish*, "stuffed fish" (*gefüllte Fisch*). It is not only a basic Jewish food but is also considered a decisive factor in historical linguistics, since the borderline between the territories where Eastern and Western Yiddish were spoken is a culinary borderline, too. West of this line *gefilte fish*, and some kinds of meat, too, were prepared with sugar, East of it with black pepper. Geographically this line is somewhere along the Polish-Lithuanian border.

There is more than one way to prepare *gefilte fish*. Its name comes from the basics of preparing the dish, namely that the fish is removed from its skin, is mixed with onions, garlic, spices, eggs and some *hallah* or *hallah* crumbs and is then stuffed back into the skin. The basic spices are salt and black pepper, but some people use grated lemon peel, nutmeg, parsley, thyme, marjoram, *paprika* or red pepper, etc. The stuffing can be different, too; for instance, it can be mixed with cooked carrots or root parsley, mushrooms, nuts, etc. *Gefilte fish* can be fried in butter or baked in sour cream, it can be poached. The best way is to make it from *csuka* (pike or hake), if available. But it will be very tasty if made from another fish as well, only that the fish should be big enough and one should be skillful enough with its skin.

507. "About Preserves." Title page of the cookbook of the *rebetsen* Mrs. Lajos Venetianer

Gefilte fish is usually eaten on Friday night, as part of the "first meal on the Sabbath". It must be prepared in time so that it is ready by the time the sun sets. If it is eaten after *shabes*, like in Hasidic communities at the *rebe*'s table, it becomes a pretty late dinner, since they only start making it after *havdalah*. True, this is the main idea of the meal.

Another basic food without which there is no Jewish life is *tsholent* (*cholent, sholent, tshulent, sólet* in Hungarian, perhaps from the French *chaulette*). In Hebrew it is simply called *hamin*, i.e. "warm (food)". This is the "second meal on the Sabbath", heavy, festive. You need to have some good beans to make a good *tshulent*, possibly small white ones. The beans need to be soaked for at least a day and a half. You need to put it on (*zetsen*) Friday afternoon and keep in a warm oven till Saturday noon. It is best to bake the *tshulent* in a pot, possibly a special *tshulent* pot. We should put some beef, smoked goose breast together with its skin, onions, and crushed garlic into the pot, too, and add just enough water to cover it. Some people make it with barley, millet or potatoes. "Wheat *tshulent*" is eaten once a year, around January–February. It is the week of *shabbat shirah*, the "Sabbath of the Song", i.e. of the Song of the Red Sea (*shirat ha-yam*) when it comes to reading the story of Moses and Miriam in the Torah, the weekly Torah portion of Exodus 10–17. At this time some of the wheat is to be used from the *shmire matses*. On top of the *tshulent* some also put an egg, in its shell, or some *kugl*. Whether we bake our *tshulent* at home or at the bakery, the fire should be low, since the meat and the beans need to soften slowly, their flavors need to grow and mingle. And let's not forget, what we are making is not a bean soup or some other ordinary bean dish. It is real *tshulent*, in which every single bean is soft and dry, and if our *tshulent* turns out well, we should be able to feel the taste of the whole dish in every tiny little bean.

XV. The Invisible Jewish Budapest

This is the most difficult chapter of this book.

In fact, it is an impossible undertaking. To describe that which is *not visible*, and to write about that which is *not Jewish*; yet which we still see, because we live in it, and which still is Jewish, although those who built, shaped and formed it, did not do so as Jews, even though they were Jewish in origin and most of them in religion as well, and—at least those who lived long enough to suffer it—they certainly were Jewish in their fate. They suffered the consequences of the (Anti-)Jewish Laws passed after 1938.

"The Jews made Budapest for us"—wrote Endre Ady in his famous article entitled "Korrobori" in 1917. As the pronoun "us" indicates, this Budapest was not "Jewish", but "Hungarian". It looked Hungarian, and was accepted as such by contemporary popular opinion. Posterity does not know anymore how to put the question, yet it has been put in many ways: What is Jewish in modern Budapest? But because those who established the modern city, its buildings and its spiritual life, its atmosphere and its character, were labeled Jews, and as such were expelled from their Hungarian identity—not only expelled, but destroyed—, their works are qualified as Jewish as well, retrospectively, at least when distinguishing one historical element of the cultural unity.

In the last third of the nineteenth century the Jewish presence had a clear influence on the townscapes of most smaller Hungarian towns: the buildings of the Jewish community, both in their use of space and their contemporary style, brought modern urbanization into the heart of the old towns. This was not entirely the case with Budapest. Here the structure of the city had already been formed by the time of the emancipation law; at most, some parts of the districts lying beyond the Nagykörút and the outermost districts could evolve independently from the old city. In these districts, for example in Kőbánya, the synagogue's role in forming the cityscape is evident. In the inner areas of the city, however, the structure of the city was altered by modernization only in some respects, for example the street network. Andrássy út and the Nagykörút are good examples. But neither in these changes to the cityscape, nor in the replacement of old buildings by newer, larger, and more modern ones did Jewish influence prevail.

At the beginning of the twentieth century Hungarian architects were the children of emancipation—assimilated, Hungarian, even if they were Jewish by descent or by ties to the Jewish community. What matters, of course, is not whether they were Hungarian patriots or proud Hungarian citizens, but that they attended the same schools and learned the same technical and artistic styles as their non-Jewish colleagues, or perhaps, in some cases, even more recent ones. The late nineteenth-century Neo-Baroque face of Budapest's inner districts was not Jewish in style, but was the reflection of contemporary Hungarian society, including the Jewish financial and industrial elite. Hungarian noble–feudal values and aesthetics along with the modern technology are what shaped the Neo-Baroque districts around the Inner City. In part, this was the work of Jewish-born or Hungarian Jewish citizens, but what they contributed was their talents rather than their Jewish heritage. The turn-of-the-century art, Art Nouveau, *Sezession* or *Jugendstil*, combined contemporary forms with various traditional Hungarian stylistic elements in architecture.

Looking back it seems unbelievable, yet true: Béla Lajta, and others as well, whose Jewish affiliation was obvious, made extensive use of the romantic, largely fictitious Hungarian national ornaments of József Huszka (1854–1934), of the illustrations for the folk-art album by Dezső Malonyai (1866–1916). Lajta was Jewish, like his colleagues, but perhaps the most harmoniously Hungarian at the same time. Every one of them was Jewish to his own degree, the Jewish community of Pest and the smaller towns accepted them as Jews, chief rabbi Hevesi was proud of them, and some of their orders came from Jewish circles, too. But what they produced was certainly not Jewish art. In the phrase "Hungarian Jewish" (or "Hungarian-Jewish"), the word "Jewish" acquired a meaning only later, when the Jews who had accepted Hungary as their home were abandoned by their homeland, in fact, were cast out; and when, still later, their wish to assimilate to Hungarian society was thrown at them as an accusation.

The *part* that Jews played in shaping the face of the city is easy to recognize: it is visible in the Jewish community buildings and institutions. The *contribution*, however, of the Jewish bourgeoisie to the life of the city is for the most part invisible, and this is precisely because it was their contribution as Hungarian citizens.

(1) Houses, All Over the City

Simon Hevesi wrote in the text of a lecture delivered at the *Izraelita Magyar Irodalmi Társulat* (Israelite Hungarian Literary Society) in 1909:

> "Jewish abilities today could vie with the Greek and Roman masters of architecture. (...) Look around in the capital of your homeland, look at the sequence of developmental milestones: the proud palace of the Hungarian Royal Ministry of Finance is the work of Sándor toronyi Fellner; the Hall of Commerce is Kármán's and Ullmann's creation; Alfréd Wellisch's noble concepts are embodied in the Main State Secondary / High School in Tavaszmező utca. On the banks of the Danube the Gresham Palace proves to the competence of Zsigmond Quittner, the Palace of the Adriatic Navigation Society claims Vilmos Freund as its creator; and if you still haven't seen it, go look at the new Jewish Institute for the Blind, truly a masterpiece, a lasting memorial in praise of Béla Leitersdorfer; you know the works of Lipót Baumhorn, the grandmaster of Jewish temple construction, and we haven't even mentioned the creations of Révész and Kollár, of Géza Márkus, of László and József Vágó, and many other eminent Hungarian architects, the cornerstones of architectural development in the Hungarian capital." (In: IMIT. *Évkönyv*, 1909)

When Hevesi read his paper it was meant to promote self-reflection, to enhance the knowledge and appreciation of Jewish contributions in contemporary Jewish society. Today, in retrospect, his proud enumeration sheds light on the invisible Jewish Budapest.

Let us name here just the most important works of the Jewish architects mentioned by Hevesi:

Lipót Baumhorn (1860-1932)

He really was the grandmaster of synagogue construction, as Hevesi said. Synagogues built by Baumhorn can be found across all of pre-World War I Hungary, the most famous among them being the one in Szeged (1902–1904), the synagogue of R. Immanuel Lőw. Baumhorn's works in Budapest:

508. Lipót Baumhorn

Angyalföld synagogue: on the corner of Aréna út / Dózsa György út and Tüzér utca, built in 1908

Bethlen Gábor tér synagogue: 2 Bethlen Gábor tér, in the building of the Institute for the Deaf and Dumb (reconstruction, in cooperation with his son-in-law, the architect György Somogyi); built in 1931

Csáky utca synagogue: 3 Csáky utca / Hegedűs Gyula utca (Baumhorn reconstructed here, in 1927, a synagogue designed and built by Béla Vajda into the courtyard of an apartment house in 1911)

Ferencváros synagogue: 29 Páva utca, on the corner of Páva utca and Tűzoltó utca; built in 1923–1924 (here Baumhorn himself designed every detail, down to the smallest details of the murals)

Sándor toronyi Fellner (1857-1944)

"The proud palace of the Hungarian Royal Ministry of Finance"—thus Hevesi. The building he referred to is 6 Szentháromság tér, built between 1901 and 1904 (currently the conference center of the *Kulturális Innovációs és Továbbképző Vállalat* / Cultural Innovation and Management Training Co.). Fellner's other works in Budapest:

Duna-palota (Duna Palace) or Hotel Ritz: Mária Valéria utca (today 12-14 Apáczai Csere János utca), built in 1911-1912 (burnt down in the last days of the siege of Pest, in January, 1945)

Igazságügyminisztérium (Ministry of Justice): 16 Markó utca, built in 1918 (today *Legfelsőbb Bíróság* / Supreme Court)

Apartment building: 1 Duna utca, built in 1904

Villa: 21 Benczúr utca, built in 1906

Vilmos Freund (1846-1920)

"On the banks of the Danube (...) the palace of the Adriatic Navigation Society"—thus Hevesi. With this acknowledgment Hevesi made a minor mistake: the building referred to actually is the headquarters of the *Magyar kir. Folyam- és Tengerhajózási Rt.* (Hungarian Royal River and Maritime Navigation Co.), Alsó Duna-sor / 11 Apáczai Csere János utca. However, it is a work of Géza Aladár Kármán and Gyula Ullmann, and not of Freund. Nor was the "palace of the Adriatic Navigation Society" (*Adria Hajóstársaság*) (16 Szabadság tér) built by Freund, it is a work of Artúr Meinig (ca. 1898). On the other hand, Freund built the palace of the "Adriatic" in Fiume (Rijeka, Croatia).

Vilmos Freund was one of the Monarchy's best-known architects. He obtained his diploma in architecture from the Technical University of Zurich, with Gottfried Semper (1803-1879), the master of Neo-Classicist architecture. In Pest he became a landlord, owning various pieces of real estate (including a bathhouse), a businessman, among the highest tax-payers of the town and a member of the capital's Magistrate for decades. As an architect he was employed by people of his own status, other high tax-payers. His style, like the taste of his customers, was varied, Neo-Renaissance and Neo-Baroque.

The mistake made by Hevesi notwithstanding, many works of Freund can be identified in Budapest:

Izr. Polgári Fiúiskola (Israelite Boys' Higher Elementary School): 44 Wesselényi utca, built in 1896

Izr. Siketnémák Országos Intézete (Israelite Institute for the Deaf and Dumb): 2 Bethlen Gábor tér, built in 1876. The synagogue, in the current configuration, was installed only later in the building's right wing, according to the design of Lipót Baumhorn and György Somogyi in 1931 (today "Gusztáv Bárczi" Training College for Teachers of Handicapped Children)

Lipótvárosi Polgári Kaszinó (Bourgeois Casino of Lipótváros): 10 Nádor utca-5 Zrínyi utca, built in 1895-1897

Zsidó Kórház (Jewish Hospital): 33-35 Szabolcs utca, built in 1888-1889, as well as the "Zsigmond and Adél Bródy" Children's Hospital, built in 1897 (today a part of the "Imre Haynal" University of Health Sciences complex)

Funeral parlor of the Isr. / Jewish cemetery, 6 Kozma utca, built in 1891

Géza Aladár Kármán (1871-1939)

"Kereskedelmi Csarnok"—thus Hevesi. The building he referred to is: *Magyar Kereskedelmi Csarnok* (National Hall of Commerce) at 11 Szabadság tér, built in 1899-1901 (today a part of the building complex belonging to the Embassy of the United States).

Kármán usually worked together with Gyula Ullmann. Some of their works in Budapest:

Magyar kir. Folyam- és Tengerhajózási Rt. (Hungarian Royal River and Maritime Navigation Co.) headquarters: Alsó Duna-sor / 11 Apáczai Csere János utca. Today the MAHART (*Magyar Hajózási Rt.* / Hungarian Shipping Co.) headquarters

Ullmann House: 10 Szabadság tér, built in 1899–1901 (today, like next to it the *Kereskedelmi Csarnok*, 11 Szabadság tér, is a part of the complex of the United States' Embassy)

Kánitz Áruház (Kánitz Department Store): 12 Szabadság tér, built in 1899–1901. These two houses, and the former *Kereskedelmi Csarnok* between them (11 Szabadság tér), occupying a wing of the former *Neugebäude*, were built in the same time, right after the latter was demolished

Fischer üzletház (Store and Office Building): 10 Bécsi utca, built in 1909–1912

Hermes Magyar Általános Váltóüzlet (Hungarian General Bill Co.): 5 Petőfi Sándor utca, built ca. 1905

Király-bazár (Király Bazaar): 3–5 Károlyi Mihály utca, built in 1899–1902 (today a retail and apartment complex)

Pesti Izr. Nőegylet Leány Árvaháza (Girls' Orphanage of the Israelite Women's Association of Pest: 29 Uzsoki utca (formerly 5 Jókai út), built in 1901. (The building was purchased by the *Országos Munkásbiztosító Pénztár* / National Workers' Insurance Company in 1927 and after renovation and expansion this became its Central Hospital. Today it is the Uzsoki utca Hospital)

Wertheimer és Frankl Áruház (Department Store): 6 Hold utca, built in 1900–1901

Groedel Villa: 28 Lendvay utca, built in 1900–1901. After World War II it was the headquarters of the *Állami Egyházügyi Hivatal* (State Office for Church Affairs), and now, that of a political party

Kármán Villa: Villa of Géza Aladár Kármán, 19 Bajza utca, built in 1908–1909

Weiss Buildings: 4, 10 and 12 Lipót körút / Szent István körút, built in 1903–1904

József Kollár (1870-1943)

Kollár usually worked together with Sámuel Révész; most of their works were apartment houses and villas. Their works in Budapest:

Központi Zálogház (Central Pawn Shop): 30–32 Lónyai utca, built in 1901–1903

Modern és Breitner Áruház (Department Store) and apartment house: 23 Deák Ferenc utca, built in 1910–1912 (today a retail and apartment complex)

Ugriai-Nasici Fabank (Timber Bank): 21 Nádor utca, built in 1910

Apartment houses: 37 Akácfa utca (owner: Antal Rakovszky), built in 1909; 7 Báthory utca, built ca. 1905; 8 and 20 Hegedűs Gyula utca, built ca. 1909; 20 Lovag utca, built ca. 1906–1907; 10 Zichy Jenő utca (owner: dr. Weisz), built ca. 1903

Lähne House: 11/B Váci utca, built in 1912 (today a retail and apartment complex)

Basch Villa: 44 Városligeti fasor, built ca. 1912

Révész Villa: 40 Városligeti fasor, built ca. 1911

Béla Lajta / Leitersdorfer (1873-1920)

"The new Jewish Institute for the Blind, truly a masterpiece"—thus Hevesi. The building he referred to is that at 60 Mexikói út (1908).

Béla Lajta was a member of a wealthy family: his father, Lipót Leitersdorfer, was one of the highest tax-payers of Budapest (a *virilis*, "well-to-do"). Lajta chose architectural design as a career instead of following the family tradition, the construction business. He studied at the Budapest Technical University and later traveled and worked abroad for many years. Returning home he took long study tours in Transylvania and Northern Hungary, inspired

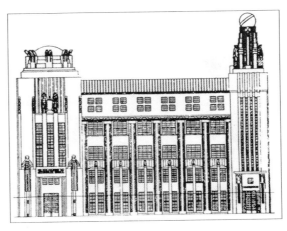

510. Municipal Advanced School of Commerce (11 Vas utca). Design of the facade by Béla Lajta, 1909

511. Stage design by Béla Lajta for Goldmark's opera "The Queen of Sheba" at the Hungarian Opera House, 1914/15

in part by his chosen mentor, Ödön Lechner (1845–1914) and Malonyai, and by his own interest in folk art, that had been awakened abroad. He worked for a time alongside Lechner, and his vision was inspired by his master, too: the establishment of a national architecture. "He came home with the pledge that he would help to make our architecture Hungarian; that if one comes here, one should find Hungarian-speaking houses, and from these one should learn to speak Hungarian" (János Hock, 1904). Lajta developed his personal variant of Art Nouveau, the organic unity of Middle-Eastern elements, Hungarian folk-art motifs and luxurious modernism. He designed not only buildings, but many tombs, stores, interiors of homes, furniture, decorations, the craft works of the Institute for the Blind (e.g. the impressive door-knobs) and even letters of inscriptions. He designed scenery for Goldmark's opera "The Queen of Sheba" at the Hungarian Opera House (1914). Lajta strove for the *Gesamtkunst* ideal of Art Nouveau. He boldly adapted forms and motifs which were associated with specific materials and functions to other materials and other functions. "He encouraged artists to apply the forms of Hungarian folk art found on woodcarvings, dishes, cloaks, flasks, and tulip-covered cabinets not only in decoration but in construction as well, and argued that out of this would grow the Hungarian architectural style" (János Hock). Lajta applied motifs of embroidery as decoration in architecture, to mention just one case of his applications. Today the extensive use of Hungarian popular motifs in his art seems exaggerated to some extent. Lajta's stone relief gate decorations (School of Trade, Institute for the Blind, *Szeretetház* / Nursing Home) are as if his trademarks, as are his beam-roof structures which remind us of the Transylvanian high, shingled roofs, built for deep snow. He frequently used Jewish symbols as design motifs when applicable, together with, and equal to, Hungarian folk-art motifs. "He was passionate about the Hungarian ideal, he was in possession of the wisdom of those who had traveled extensively, and his motto was return to the solemn tranquillity of Judaism"—as the art historian Pál Nádai characterized him (ca. 1925). His final major work, the Jewish Secondary / High School, was completed after his death, but those who finished it remained faithful to the essence of his design. Around 1910 Lajta also worked with Lajos Kozma who continued and renewed his artistic ambitions. Some of Lajta's works in Budapest:

512. Store building of the firm Leitersdorfer and Son (5 Szervita tér). Designed by Béla Lajta, 1912

Bárd Zeneműbolt (Bárd Music Store) (interior design): 4 Kossuth Lajos utca, built in ca. 1900 (still a bookstore)

Hecht Jónás és Fia Nagykereskedés (Jonas Hecht and Son Wholesale Building), portal: 14 Szent István tér, built in 1907 (today headquarters of the *Magyar Külkereskedelmi Bank* / Hungarian Foreign Trade Bank)

Henrik and Rezső Leitersdorfer Business House: 5 Szervita tér (today Martinelli tér), built in 1911/1912 (today Rózsavölgyi and Co. Music Store)

Községi Felső Kereskedelmi Iskola (Municipal Advanced School of Commerce): 11 Vas utca, built in 1909–1912 (today "István Széchenyi" School of Commerce). This building is a masterpiece of reinforced-concrete constructivism. Miksa Róth (1865–1944) prepared the stained-glass windows, as well as the mosaic decorations, the latter ones together with the painter Bertalan Pór, in 1912

Parisiana: 35 Paulay Ede utca, built in 1909 (see Ch. VII, 6, above)

Salgótarjáni utca Jewish Cemetery: entrance and mortuary,

built in 1908-1910, as well as numerous tombs, among them Vilmos Bacher's (1913)

Zsidó Gimnázium: on the corner of Abonyi utca and Szent Domonkos utca / Cházár András utca, built in 1914–1931 (see Ch. VIII, 8, above)

Kozma utca Isr./Jewish cemetery: monument of honor for the heroes of the Independence War of 1848/49 (built in 1912); monument of relocation of the old Jewish cemetery (1912); graves, the most famous among them being the sepulchral vault of the family Schmidl, designed together with Ödön Lechner, but built perhaps on his own (1904); the gravestone of Henrik Lajta, his relative (its design is identical with that of the Bacher gravestone in the Salgótarjáni utca cemetery) (1921)

Apartment house of the *Erzsébetvárosi Takarékpénztár* (Erzsébetváros Savings Bank): 18 Rákóczi út, built in 1911–1913 (today a retail and apartment complex)

Harsányi House: 19 Népszínház utca, built in 1911/1912

Villa Leitersdorfer: 7 Völgy utca, built in 1903

Villa of Dezső Malonyai: 5 Izsó utca, built in 1905–1907

And so on.

Géza Márkus (1872-1912)

At the beginning of his career, Márkus worked in the studio of Vilmos Freund. His best-known and most valuable work is probably the *Cifraház / Cifrapalota* (Fancy House) in Kecskemét (1903), a casino and apartment house, right beside the Neolog synagogue; on the wall of the casino's former big hall (today a museum and gallery of contemporary art) there is a huge, magnificent peacock. Some of Márkus's works in Budapest:

Király Színház (Király Theater): 71 Király utca, built in 1905 (see Ch. V, 1, p. 165, above)

Pedestal of the Vörösmarty statue: Vörösmarty tér, built in 1908

Népopera [People's Opera] (today "Erkel" Theater): 30 Köztársaság tér, built in 1910–1911

Zsigmond vágfalvi Quittner (1857-1918)

The "Gresham Palace", referred to by Hevesi, is at 5–6 Roosevelt tér. Built according to Quittner's plans in 1907 for the London-based insurance company "The Gresham"; also the Vágó brothers contributed to the execution plans.

This huge house was one of the first examples of a *plaza*-type space within a larger building in Budapest: a covered, generally glass-roofed, one- or two-story high interior space, which brings public space, the street, inside the building—a walk-through courtyard. In Hungarian it is called *passzázs* or *bazár*. In the case of the Gresham Palace four buildings are connected in a T-shape by an arched glass roof; small stores open to the inside courtyard-street. Above the intersection of the two interior alleys there is a bell-shaped, glass-tiled dome. At the three street entrances (Zrínyi utca, Ferenc

József tér / Roosevelt tér, Mérleg utca) peacock-patterned iron grates served as fences and gates. The walls of the gallery were covered with patterned majolica tile from the Zsolnay factory in Pécs. The tile and the stained-glass windows lent a Middle-Eastern atmosphere to the whole passageway, although the individual motifs are actually Hungarian. The statues decorating the walls are works of Géza Maróti (Rintel) (1875–1941) and Ede Telcs (1872–1948), the stained-glass windows are by Miksa Róth.

Quittner, like many of his contemporaries, was not simply a designer and architect, but more of a building contractor. He owned important real estate property in Zugló. His buildings are characterized by unusual skill and care, but always are accommodated to the official style. Some of his works in Budapest:

Fasor Szanatórium (Sanatorium): 9–11 Városligeti fasor, built in 1890
Mentők (Ambulance) headquarters: 22 Markó utca, built in 1890
Pesti Magyar Kereskedelmi Bank (Hungarian Commercial Bank of Pest) headquarters: 3–4 Ferenc
    József tér / Roosevelt tér, built in 1906–1907 (today Ministry of Interior)
Phoenix Biztosító Társaság (Phoenix Insurance Co.) headquarters: Bécsi utca.
Apartment house of the *Magyar Hírlapírók Nyugdíjintézete* (Hungarian Journalists' Pension Fund):
    16 Alkotmány utca, built in 1889
Palace of Count megyeri Krausz: 12 Andrássy út, built in 1884
Kozma utca Isr. / Jewish cemetery: Mór Wahrmann's mausoleum, built in 1892

In the basement of the Gresham Palace (entrance from 2 Mérleg utca) opened his famous Podium Cabaret Endre Nagy (1877–1938) in the fall of 1921. It was a room of the restaurant belonging to József Fészl jr. where there was space for more than three hundred guests. These shows of the entertainer and writer-to-be—just one of his several ventures into cabaret and satire—were on for a year and a half, until January 1923.

Blanka Pécsi (later Péchy) (1894–1988) also performed in the Cabaret. (Later she was a leading actress in the Goldmark Hall, and even later, in the 1960s, the *grande dame* of poetry recital, she initiated contests in correct and beautiful pronunciation of Hungarian.)

This Cabaret is where a famous long-living theatrical dialogue series—dialogues between Sokrátesz (sic!, meaning in this distorted form in Hungarian "heaping on much") and Plato ("platform"), later between Hacsek and Sajó—was started, satirical dialogues on political issues built on nonsensical talk, a purely verbal Stan and Pan.

Sámuel Révész (Rosenfeld) (1877–1928)

From ca. 1900 on, Révész worked as an architect with József Kollár (1869–1943). After World War I he established a tapestry studio on his own.

Gyula erényi Ullmann (1872–1926)

Ullmann worked with Géza Aladár Kármán. It was him who directed the renovation of the Óbuda synagogue in 1900.

József Vágó (1877–1947) and László Vágó (1875–1933)

The Vágó brothers had been working together until 1911—that is why Simon Hevesi mentioned them together. Later their ways parted. After World War I László Vágó continued to work without his brother and remained an architect of distinction in his own right.

József Vágó became the head of the architectural directorate during the *Tanácsköztársaság* (Hungarian Soviet [Councils'] Republic) in 1919; afterwards he was forced to emigrate because of his political role. Among his most important successes abroad was the shared first prize in the architectural competition for the Palace of the League of Nations in Geneva (1926); he and several others took part in the preparation of the final plans and in the construction, too. After his return home, around 1930, he remained completely in the background; he was not accepted into the *Mérnöki Kamara* (Chamber of Engineering) and could not even officially call himself an architect. In the telephone directory he listed himself as "private entrepreneur, the designer of the Palace of the League of Nations in Geneva". He worked mainly on large-scale urban planning designs (Vigadó tér, the Pest and Buda bridgeheads of the Chain Bridge, Károly körút–Erzsébet sugárút). Most of his plans remained on paper, though some were actually published: *Az újjáépülő Tabán* [Rebuilding Tabán] (1934); *Budapest művészi újjáépítése Vágó József elgondolása szerint* [The Artistic Reconstruction of Budapest according to the Concepts of József Vágó] (1936).

Just one dwelling house of József Vágó was actually built: the home and studio of Lóránt Basch, the lawyer of *Nyugat* and a curator of the Baumgarten Foundation, the house at 48/B Városmajor utca (1934). This house, like his brother's last buildings, was characterized by Constructivism and a fine Italian style; large wall surfaces, simple geometric forms and rounded arches. The house is a variation, to some extent, of the Heroes' Temple. Recent alterations have unfortunately ruined its harmonic image.

Some Vágó works in Budapest (JV below means József Vágó; an LV, László Vágó):

Árkád Bazár (Bazaar) / *Illés Játékáruház* (Toystore) (JV–LV): on the corner of Dohány utca and Síp utca (22 Dohány utca–3 Síp utca), built in 1908–1909 (today Metro Club)

Gutenberg Otthon: *A Magyarországi Könyvnyomdászok és Betű-öntők Segélyegyletének bérháza* (apartment house of the Hungarian Printers and Type-casters' Aid Society) (JV–LV): Főherceg Sándor tér / 4 Gutenberg tér, built in 1906

Késmárky és Illés Áruház (Department Store) (LV): Kossuth Lajos utca, built in 1897

Lipótvárosi Casino Nyári Helyisége (Bourgeois Casino of Lipótváros' Summer Premises) (JV): 46–48 Vilma királynő út / Városligeti fasor, built in 1912

516. The facade of the former National Salon (Erzsébet tér). Designed by József and László Vágó, 1906

Nemzeti Szalon (National Salon) (JV–LV): Erzsébet tér, built in 1906 (demolished in 1960)

Apartment houses (JV-LV): 16–18 Síp utca (owner: Izsák Braunstädter), built in 1902–1903; 2 Boáros tér, built in 1905; 14 Bartók Béla út, built in 1903; 17 Visegrádi utca, built in 1903, etc.

Grünwald Villa (JV): 1 Ostrom utca, built in 1914–1916

Schiffer Villa (JV): 19/B Munkácsy Mihály utca, built in 1911

Alfréd Wellisch (1854–1941)

"Tavaszmező utca Main State Secondary / High School"—thus Hevesi. The building he referred to is: *Tavaszmező utcai Állami Főgimnázium* at 17 Tavaszmező utca, in Outer-Józsefváros, built in 1894 (today "Kálmán Kandó" College of Electrical Engineering).

Wellisch called himself an architect and architectural contractor. As a contractor he acquired some truly important blocks and building sites in Terézváros and Új-Lipótváros, and even further out in Angyalföld. Among them were the house at 49 Nagymező utca, which he planned and built in 1892. For a while he may even have lived here, but sold it in 1910. His further plots and / or houses: 16 Sziget utca / Radnóti Miklós utca; 53 and 60 Visegrádi utca; the entire odd-numbered side of the lower Gömb utca, etc. Real estate was for him not simply a means to increase his personal wealth; it also was a chance for the architect to free himself from the stipulations of customers so that he could build according to his own artistic taste and following the concept for the development of the city. It is true that he himself hardly took advantage of these opportunities. He also built for his father, Nathan Wellisch, the Wellisch family crypt himself (Kozma utca Isr. / Jewish cemetery), in 1904. Some of his works in Budapest:

Izr. Fiú Árvaház (Isr. Boys' Orphanage), Fasor / Városligeti fasor building: 25–27 Városligeti fasor, built in 1900. (Later largely remodeled.) The Boys' Orphanage itself was established by the Jewish community two years after the Girls' Orphanage, in 1869

Salgótarjáni Kőszénbányák Rt. (Salgótarján Coal Mining Co.) headquarters: 25 Arany János utca, built in 1905–1907

Apartment houses: 34 Király utca (owner: Countess [Géza] Teleki), built in 1914; 25–27 Paulay Ede utca, built in 1889–1891

Wellisch House: 4 Kossuth Lajos tér, built in 1911. (Later a ministry building, today the Housing Authority)

Wellisch Villa (Sándor and Gyula Wellisch): 21 Zugligeti út. (Ignác Goldziher vacationed here for many years)

*

Many names are missing from Simon Hevesi's list which might well have been included, even from among the architects of the early twentieth century: for example, Ferenc Fischer (1871–1921), Ármin Hegedűs, Dezső Jakab (1864–1932), Marcell Komor (1868–1944), Béla Löffler (he lived in the Middle East and for a time in Palestine after World War I, and in Hungary he disappeared from public view) and his older brother Sándor Löffler; Géza (Rintel) Maróti (1875–1941); Ernő Román (1883–1959) and Miklós Román (1879–1945); Emil Vidor and many others; and, of course, all Jewish architects from subsequent decades are missing.

The few names mentioned by chief rabbi Hevesi should be enough, however, to indicate the dimensions of the *contribution* of Jewish architects to the look of Budapest.

(2) Hebrew or Yiddish Loanwords in Hungarian

Mókembé—says the Hungarian slang of Budapest, that is, "place B.", variant: *Mohambé*, using a Yiddish word, *mokem*, "place" (Hebrew *makom*). Hebrew and Yiddish vocabulary had a direct impact on Hungarian for about two centuries.

Every distinct social group, may it be as small a unit as a family, will surely develop its own inside language, at least a few words, which probably nobody else understands and nobody else needs to use anyway. These familiar jargons, used in narrow circles or spreading into the surrounding society, enrich the language of the society at large by variant terms and phrases which are connected to the history of that group, their way of life and customs.

The words in the following list are loanwords, words that were—or still are—used in everyday Hungarian, first of all in the metropolitan center, in Budapest. An exception is the classical elements of the list, which became parts of the spoken language via Latin, the Christian church or the sophisticated usage of intellectuals. The rest—actually, most of the words—is used in the language of the street, in the slang. In any case, about one third of the vocabulary of slang in Central Europe is of Hebrew or Yiddish origin. (Yiddish was called in Pest, following the usage in Germany, simply "jargon".) On the other hand, many Hebrew, Hebrew-Yiddish and German-Yiddish words entered Hungarian not directly through the Jewish "jargon"—though some loanwords certainly came with the Jews—but rather through the trans-national vernacular of the thieves in Eastern Europe and the Austro-Hungarian Dual Monarchy, the so-called *hebre* language. These words might not be polite or distinguished terms, but they are always functional; they are a convenient means of communication used by the stratified—but never completely segregated—lower or marginal circles of the society in a metropolis. In its vocabulary Budapest still preserves the memory of the languages spoken by Jews in Pest in the eighteenth and nineteenth centuries, Yiddish and German.

The following vocabulary is a list of words and phrases rooted either in the Hebrew of the Bible, or in the Jewish "jargon" of Budapest, or in the trans-national slang. These terms are of Hebrew, Yiddish, German or Slavic (first of all, Polish) origin. Terms that mock Jews by imitating Yiddish are not included; these certainly do not belong to the vocabulary of Jewish origin. Detailed explanation follows a term only in cases where it is necessary or if this is a logical supplement to other parts of the present book. Terms explained elsewhere in the book are not commented on here again. Nor are regular Hungarian words in the Jewish "jargon" included, which might have acquired a specific meaning, such as *bejön–kimegy* ("comes in"–"goes out", i.e. the day, Sabbath or holidays), *betér* ("enter", i.e. to enter the Jewish community, to convert to Judaism), or *pontozott* ("dotted", i.e. Hebrew text with dots, the vowel signs).

Most words also have other ways of pronunciation than the ones listed here. In case of the words of Yiddish origin the aim here was to preserve their phonology, even if this meant spelling them with obvious mistakes, if one can speak of a mistake relating to words that never were—or rather, were only in exceptional cases—used in writing. The spelling of the lemmata reflects the Hungarian orthography, etymologies try to follow the *Encyclopaedia Judaica* and the YIVO standards, respectively.

abrakadabra: "spell", "nonsensical talk" (Aramaic)

ádámcsutka, "Adam's apple"

aher: "after", "afterwards"; *ahrem:* "in the back" (Hebrew *ahor,* "behind", Yiddish *akhren*); *ahremből:* "from the back", "slyly"

ahér: "other", "different", "stranger" (Hebrew *aher*)

ahszor: "cruel" (Hebrew *akhzar,* Yiddish *akher*)

ajser: "rich" (Hebrew *ashir*)

ajvé: "oh!" (Yiddish *oy, vey,* German *Weh,* "pain")

alefbét, alefbész: "ABC", "basic knowledge"

ámen: "Amen", "it is over" (Hebrew *amen*)

amhórec: "boorish person (not versed in religion)" (Hebrew *am ha-aretz,* "people of the land / countryside", Yiddish *amorets*)

auszgetippelt: "exactly this" (German *ausgetippelt*)

avle: "injustice" (Hebrew *avlah,* "evil")

azesz: "impertinence" (Hebrew *azzut*); *azeszpónem:* "impertinent, insolent person" (Hebrew *azzut panim*)

bájesz: "house" (Hebrew *bayit*); *bájzli:* "shank", "cheap tavern"

baldóver: "important person" (Hebrew *ba'al davar,* "someone in charge of the affair")

balek: "credulous man" (Turkish / Yiddish *balik,* "a fish") (slang)

balhé: "scandal" (Hebrew *ballahah,* "fright", "terrible thing")

barchesz / barhesz: "braided white bread (hallah)" (Hebrew *berakhot,* "blessings")

barkochba, barkochbázik: a guessing game ("twenty-one questions") named after Bar Kokhbah (Kosebah) (second century C.E.). It has been, and still is, an extremely popular game in Budapest ever since the early twentieth century

bárzli: "railway" (Hebrew *barzel,* "metal", "iron")

bé: "two" (the numerical value of the second letter of the Hebrew alphabet, *bet,* is two) (slang)

bechóved: "honorable", "distinguished" (Hebrew *be-kavod,* "in respect")

behemót: "huge" (Hebrew *behemah,* plural *behemot*)

bencsol, bencsolás: "reciting a blessing" (Yiddish *bentshen,* from Latin *benedictio*)

betámt: "attractive", "admirable", "charming"; *támja van:* "he / she has *tam*", "charm" (Hebrew *ta'am,* German–Yiddish)

bócher: "rabbinical student", "young man occupied with study of the Talmud" (Hebrew *bahur,* "bachelor", "unmarried man")

bóvli / bóvel: "worthless / cheap merchandise" (from the Hebrew city-name *Babel / Bavel,* Yiddish *Bovel*)

böhöm: "immensely (big)" (Hebrew *behemah*)

brahi: "joke", "kidding", "teasing" (Yiddish); *brahiból:* "as a joke"; *brahira:* "spontaneously", "inconsiderately"

brajgesz / brojgesz: "angry", "furious" (Hebrew *be-rogez,* "in anger")

branef / bronef: "brandy" (Yiddish).—A Jewish proverb says: "The holiday brandy (*jantevbranef*) tastes good on a weekday, too."

cadik, "saintly man" (Hebrew *tzaddik,* "pious", "true")

cefet: "sick" (Hebrew *zefet*) (see *züfec*); *cefetül érzi magát,* "feels miserable"

cholile: "God forbid" (Hebrew *halil / halilah,* "profane", "vulgar") (*hasz ve-holile*)

córesz: "trouble", "difficulty", "annoyance" (Hebrew *tzarah,* plural *tzarot*) *dá:* "four" (the numerical value of the fourth letter of the Hebrew alphabet, *dalet,* is four) (slang)

dafke: "in spite", "nevertheless" (Hebrew–Aramaic–Yiddish *davka / dafke,* "clinging to", "exactly that")

dálesz / dallesz: "poverty", "nothing" (Hebrew *dallut,* "poverty")

davenen, davenol: "to pray", "he / she prays" (from the Latin *deus, divus, divinus, divinatio*)

délinyitás: "opening (of a store) at noon", a pun in Hungarian, a robbery by breaking in the door (from Hebrew *delet,* "door", "gate") (slang)

déverol: "talks" (Hebrew *davar,* "word")

dibbe: "slander" (Hebrew *dibbah*)

diberöl: "talks", "accuses" (Hebrew *dibber,* "he talked")

dibuk: "wandering soul", "ghost" (Hebrew *dibbuk,* Yiddish *dibuk*)

diró: "apartment" (Hebrew–Yiddish *dirah / dire*) (slang)

éca, écesz: "advice", "idea" (Hebrew *etzah,* plural *etzot*); *éceszgéber:* "the person who gives advice or ideas" (German)

éden: "splendor" (from the name of the Garden of Eden, Genesis 2,8 ff.)

ejdim: "witness" (Hebrew *ed,* plural *edim*) (slang)

elpaterol: "gets rid of someone or something" (Hebrew *patar,* "dismiss", Yiddish *poter,* "free of")

elpénecol: "to miss", "to fail (one's luck)" (Yiddish *penets,* "section", "slice")

emesz: "true!", "right!" (Hebrew *emet,* "truth", Yiddish *emes*) (slang)

észer: "greedy", "rapacious" (Hebrew / Yiddish)

frájer: "naive", "innocent", "foolish" (as opposed to *hóhem*) (German *freier* / Yiddish *freyer*)

fuser: "bungler" (German–Yiddish)

gaj: "destruction", "hell" (Hebrew *gay, gayeh,* "the inside of something", "valley"); *gajra megy:* "to become devastated"

gajd, gajdol: "noise", "to sing loudly / confused" (Hebrew *gad*)

gajdesz: "destruction"; *gajdeszba küld:* "destroys", "kills"

gajsesz / gajszesz: "seriously sick / dying person" (Hebrew *goses,* Yiddish *goyses*); *gajszenol:* "he is dying"

gajve: "conceit", "arrogance", "haughtiness" (Hebrew *ge / ge'eh,* feminine *ge'ah,* "proud", Yiddish *gajvedik,* "arrogant", "haughty")

galiciáner: "Oriental", "Jew from Galicia", "simpleton" (derogatory)

ganef: "thief", "burglar", "swindler", "deceiver" (Hebrew *gannav*)

gezeresz: "wailing", "weeping", "raid", "pogrom" (Hebrew *gezerah,* plural *gezerot,* "edict", "decree", "an order affecting only certain Jewish communities", "prohibition", "anti-Semitic actions", Yiddish *gsere,* "debate")

gi: "three" (the numerical value of the third letter of the Hebrew alphabet, *gimel,* is three) (slang)

glatt-kóser: "food according to the strictest ritual prescriptions". It is called *glatt,* "smooth", because this qualification is only given to beef if upon slaughtering the cow its lungs are found to be "smooth", i.e. there was no blood clots in it. (The Hebrew word for *glatt-kosher* is *halakh*)

goj / gaj: "non-Jewish man" (Hebrew *goy,* "people", "foreign people")

gojlem / gólem: "corpulent", "portly", "sluggish" (Hebrew *golem,* "clay", "material"); *lejminer gojlem:* "clay *golem*", "a complete blockhead"

gólesz: "exile", "Diaspora" (Hebrew *galut*)

gyehenna: "purgatory", "limbo", "Hell" (Hebrew *Ge-Hinnom,* the valley South of Old Jerusalem).—According to the Bible and the Jewish tradition, this was the location of the sacrificial altar, where children were taken "through fire", a purification rite (Jeremiah 7,31; 19,1–5, on the prohibition of the rite see Leviticus 18,21; 20,3–5). In Jewish tradition even the fire of Ge-Hinnom is not burning on Sabbath

hadova: "empty speech" (Hebrew *ha-davar,* "the word")

hajlakol: "leaves", "flees" (Hebrew *halakh,* "went") (slang)

hajlem: "hospital" (Hebrew *holim,* "sick people") (slang)

hákhám: "wise man", "rabbi" (Hebrew *hakham*)

hakni, "barnstorming" (Hebrew *ha-kol,* "everything")

halef: "knife" (Hebrew *halaf*, knife used for ritual slaughter)

halleluja: "Halleluyah", "joy" (Hebrew *hallelu-Yh*, "the LORD be praised")

handlé: "peddler" (German *Händler* / Yiddish *hendler*)

happol: "grab", "extort" (Yiddish *hapn*, "to grab")

hapsi: "man", "free" (in the sense of *frejer*) (Hebrew *hofshi*)

haszene / haszne: "wedding celebration" (Hebrew *hatunnah*).—A Yiddish proverb says: *Liber a mise hasene vi a sheyne levaye*, "Better a nasty wedding than a nice funeral"

haver / havér / háver: "friend" (Hebrew *haver*, "fellow", "associate", "a man versed in Halakhah", "colleague"); *havrusze:* "gang of thieves" (Hebrew–Aramaic *havruta*)

házer balhé: "catching in the act" (Hebrew *hizzer*, "enclose") (slang)

hé / hesz / kész, "policeman", "investigator" (slang) (Yiddish *he*)

hebre nyelv (language): "slang" (Hebrew)

heder / héder: "pad", "room", "chamber" (the traditional Jewish elementary school) (Hebrew *heder*, "room"); *héderol:* "sleeps", "crashes out" (slang)

herót: "fear", "trouble" (Hebrew *haratah*, Yiddish *harote*, "regret"); *herótom van:* "I had enough", "I am bored of it"

hések: "theater" (Hebrew *heshek*, "pleasure")

hevra: "gang" (slang) (Hebrew *hevrah*)

hipis: "body searching", "rummaging in a room" (Hebrew *hippus*, "searching", that is, looking up the weekly portion in the Torah scroll) (slang)

hirig: "beating" (Hebrew *hereg*, "killing", "murder", Yiddish *hargenen*, "to kill"); *hirigel:* "beats"; *hargenol:* "beats", "batters"

hochmec / hohmec: "know-it all" (Hebrew *hokhmah*, "wisdom"); *hochmecol / hohmecol:* "knows everything better"

hóhem: "smart", "bright", "cunning person", "clever" (as opposed to *frájer*) (Hebrew *hakham*)

hosszúnap, "long day" (Yom Kippur)

hozsánna, hozsánnázik: "praise", "praising" (Hebrew *hosha-na,* "o help!" / *hoshannah*)

hucpa, hücpe: "impertinence" (Hebrew–Yiddish)

icig, "Jew" (from the name *Yitzhak* / Isaac, Yiddish *Itzig*)

ise: "wife (Hebrew *ishshah*, "woman", Yiddish *ishe,* "wife")

ivré: "Hebrew reading"

jajem: "tip" (Hebrew *yayin*, Yiddish *yayim,* "wine"); *borravaló,* "(money) for wine" in Hungarian

jampec: "weirdo", "person dressing in weird clothes" (Yiddish *yampots,* "crazy", "fool") (Slavic)

jarmelke, "(Jewish) headgear"

jatt: "handshake", "bait", "bribe" (Hebrew *yad*, "hand"); *jattol:* "shakes hands", "gives money"

jebuzeus: a derogatory term used in swearing (*Azt a jebuzeusát!*) (the name of Jerusalem in the Bible before David conquered it, Jebus, Judges 19,10, etc., hence the name of its original population) (Latin)

Jehova: the mistaken reading of the four Hebrew letters of God's name (Yhwh) in European languages, of medieval origin

jichesz: "(fine) lineage", "excellence". —A Jewish saying: The best *yikhes* is knowledge (of the Talmud), only followed by Kohanite or Levite descent

jubileum: "(round) anniversary" (Hebrew *yobel / yovel*, the year following the period of seven times seven years, the *shemittah,* "debt forgiveness", i.e. the "fiftieth year")

kabala: "mascot", "superstition" (Hebrew *kabbalah,* "taking over", "tradition")

kajak: "strength" (Hebrew *koah*, Yiddish *koyekh, koykhes*); *kajakos:* "strong, energetic"

kajle: "sick" (Hebrew *holeh*, Yiddish *khoyle*)

káli: "girl", "sweetheart (of a thief)" (Hebrew *kallah,* "bride") (slang)

kasa: "good", "excellent", "great" (Hebrew *kasher*)

kaserol: "he is explaining himself", "making up excuses"

kerub (plural *kerubim*): "Cherub"

kibic: "observer", "outsider", someone who meddles in things without participating in them (e.g., in playing cards) (Yiddish *kibetser*, German *Kiebitz*)

klezmer: "(Jewish) musician"

knasz: "punishment" (for breaking a contract) (Latin *census*)

kóbi: "Jew" (derived from the name Jacob)

kóli: "lie" (Hebrew *kol*, "voice") (slang)

kóser: "good", "of good quality" (Hebrew *kasher / kosher,* "ritually appropriate")

kóved: "honor", "respect" (Hebrew *kavod*).—
There is a Jewish joke about koved. A visitor
inquires about the president of the Jewish
community from its
members. Everyone
tells him that the
president is a
scoundrel, a dishon-
est man. Finally he
meets the president
himself and asks
him what the com-
munity members
are like. He is told
that they are all
scoundrels, dishon-
est people. "If so,
asks the guest, why
did you accept to be
the *rashekol* of these
scoundrels?"—
"Believe me, just for
the *koved* I get from
them."

517. Elevator fence in
35 Dob utca, the
Orthodox community
building. Photo, 1997

lájle: "night" (Hebrew *laylah*)

lébecol: "to live an easy / lighthearted life",
"take it easy" (German *leben* / Yiddish *lebn*,
"to live")

lében: "dear" (attached to names, in addressing someone), e.g. *rebelében:* "Dear rabbi!"

leff: "superiority", "self-confidence" (Hebrew
lev, "heart") (slang)

lejm: "stealing", "begging"; *lejmol:* "gets something by constant begging", "bugging" (Yiddish)

macesz / máci: "unleavened bread" (*matzzah,
matzzot, matzes*)

macher: "fixer", "a skillful organizer" (German).
—A *gantser (groyser) makher,* "an influential
person" (Yiddish)

mahlajka: "scandal", "controversy" (Hebrew
mahloket, Yiddish *makhloykes*)

májem, in májemben hagy: "to leave someone
in lurch" (Hebrew *mayim,* "water")

majré: "fear" (Hebrew *mora,* Yiddish *moyre*);
majrés: "anxious person"; *majrézik,* "is afraid of"

mammon: "(monetary) wealth" (Hebrew)

mamzér / mamzer: "bastard", "illegitimate
child" (Hebrew)

manna: "manna" (Hebrew)

markecol: "steals from a drunken or sleeping
person"

masefa: "fortune-teller" (Hebrew *mekhashshe-
fah,* Yiddish *makhsheyfe,* "witch")

maustot: "dead", "goner" (Hebrew *mot* and
German *tot*)

mázli: "good luck" (Hebrew *mazzal,* Yiddish
mazl)

mecije: "found object", "good deal", "bargain"
(Hebrew *metziah*)

medine: "region", "landscape" (Hebrew *medinah,* "country") (slang)

melák: "huge / massive man" (Hebrew
melekh, "king")

meló: "work", "job" (Hebrew *melakhah,*
Yiddish *melokhe,* German *Maloche*)

menetekel: "warning" (Aramaic) (Daniel 5,25)

meruba: "Hebrew (and Arab) letters", "quadratic (script)" (Hebrew *merubba*)

messiás: "redeemer", "Saviour" (Hebrew
mashiah, "anointed")

mesüge: "crazy person" (Hebrew *meshugga* /
Yiddish *meshuge*)

mész: "banishment (from Budapest)" (Hebrew
met, Yiddish *mes,* "dead", "corpse")

meszira: "denouncing", "informing (against
someone)", "accusing a Jew (to the non-
Jewish authorities)"

mismás: "facelift", "glossing over"

mispóche: "(large) family", "relatives" (Hebrew
mishpahah)

mísz / móusz: "ugly", "awkward", today rather
"nasty", "unkindly" (Yiddish *mies, a mieser,*
feminine *a miese*)—A Yiddish proverb says:
*Az di moyd iz mies, zogt zi az der shpigl iz
shuldig,* "If a woman looks ugly, she says it's
the mirror's fault"

míszmachol: "detest / depress someone"

mókem: "city" (Hebrew *makom,* Yiddish
mokem, "place") (slang)

mókemplácc, "the square in the city", that is,
Teleki tér (Yiddish *mokem* and German
Platz)

móles: "drunk" (Hebrew *male,* "filled up");
bemólézott: "he is tipsy"

moloch: "all-consuming idol"; "(votive) sacrifice", "God requiring human sacrifice" (in
Jerusalem in Ge-Hinnom) (Hebrew *molekh*)

mószerol, bemószerol: "denounces", "informs
(against someone)", "gives someone away"
(Hebrew *moser,* "denouncer", "someone
who denounces / accuses a Jew to the non-
Jewish authorities")

nazir: "Christian", "monk"

nebich, nebach, neboch: "poor thing", "unfortunately", "sorry"

noha / noah: "wine (made from wild grapes)" (from the name of Noah, see Genesis 9,20)

nü?: "so?", "what's up?" (in Jewish jokes)

óberhóhem: "a person who always knows everything better" (German *ober-* with the Hebrew *hakham*, Hungarian *hóhem*).—A Jewish saying explains the word as follows: "He is even smarter than God, for God knows everything, but he knows everything better"

onánia: "masturbation", "onanism"; in its original sense: "coitus interruptus" (from the name of Onan, Genesis 38,9)

osz-posz: "exactly the same"; "empty, meaningless talk" (from Hebrew *ot be-ot,* "letter to letter")

pacák: "man" (Yiddish *patsef*)

pajesz / pájesz "sidelocks of Jewish men (usually worn long and curled)" (Hebrew *pe'ah* (plural *pe'ot,* Yiddish *pejesz,* "edge", "end", "corner".—According to a Biblical precept (Leviticus 19,27) it is forbidden to cut the sidelocks. By the Orthodox this prohibition is strictly observed even today, in Hungary in a more or less symbolic form

pé: "mouth" (Hebrew *peh*)

plédlizik: "escapes", "survives" (Hebrew–Yiddish *peletah / pleyte*)

pléte: "bankruptcy", "breakdown"; *pléte megy:* "goes bankrupt" (German–Yiddish *Pleite / pleyte*)

pólisi: "Jew from the Polish frontier region" (derogatory)

pónem: "person" (Hebrew *panim,* "face")

póter: "free", "released" (Hebrew–Yiddish *poter*) (slang)

rabbi

rahedli: "a lot of", "a bundle of" (German)

rebach / reibach / revach: "profit", "unusually large gains" (Hebrew *ravah,* "grow", Hebrew–Yiddish *revah / revekh*)

rüfke: "easy woman", "(Jewish) whore" (from the Hebrew name *Rivkah,* "Rebecca", Genesis 22,23, etc. / Yiddish *rifke*).—Stories go around that in 1944 an Arrow-cross demonstration was held below the Castle Hill, at the Regent's residence, shouting: "Rebecca, out of the Castle", a hint on the Wodianer family, his wife's (indirect) "Jewish" (former Jewish) relatives

sábeszdekli: "Shabbat headgear"

sábesz-goj: "servant (of the Jews)", "a non-Jew hired to perform tasks that Jews are not allowed to do on the Sabbath"

samesz: "faithful / loyal servant" (Hebrew *shammash,* Yiddish *shames*)

sátán: "Satan", "devil" (Hebrew *satan,* "attacker", "accuser")

sém / sén / sejn: "name", "fame", "personal description (at the police)" (Hebrew *shem,* "name") (slang)

séró: "hair" (Hebrew *se'ar*)

siker: "drunk" (Hebrew *shikkor,* Yiddish *shiker*)

siksze / sikce: "Christian girl" (Hebrew *shikkutz*)

sisera, sisere-had: "populous army", "idle people" (from the name of Sisra, see Judges 4,2, etc.)

slemil / slimázel: "unlucky fellow" (German and Yiddish *schlimm,* "bad" and Hebrew *mazzal,* "luck"; from Yiddish, the German–Hebrew–Russian *Schlimm-mazlnik / Schlimmezalnik*)

smonca: "empty talk", "chatter", "gossip" (Yiddish *shmontse*)

smucig: "stingy" (German *schmutzig* / Yiddish *shmutsik*)

smukk: "jewel", "(false) pearl" (from German *Schmuck* / Yiddish *shmuk*)

smúz: "chat", "gossip" (Hebrew *shemu'ah,* "hearsay", "news", Yiddish *shmues,* "conversation", "chat", *shmuesn,* "to talk"); *smúzol:* "talks (in a low voice in synagogue during prayer)", "(he / she) chats"

snóder: "donation (in the synagogue)" (Hebrew *she-nadar,* "he who makes an offer for the synagogue")

sóher: "stingy", "has no money"

sojvet: "judge" (Hebrew *shofet*) (slang)

sólet: tshulent

srác: "boy", "little boy" (Hebrew *sheretz,* "swarming one")

stika, stikában: "secret", "secretly" (Hebrew *shetikah,* "in silence")

stikli: "trick" (Yiddish *shtikl,* "piece", "case")

sügér: "crazy" (after the Hebrew *meshugga* / Yiddish *meshüge*)

száh: "a lot" (Hebrew–Yiddish *sakh*) (slang)

szajré: "stolen things" (Hebrew *sahar,* "purchase", Yiddish *skhoyre,* "goods")

szasszerol: "search", "guess" (Yiddish)

szeráf: "Seraph" (Hebrew)

szombat: "Saturday" (Hebrew *shabbat*)

tachlesz / tachlisz: "result", "essence", "serious reason", "serious business" (Hebrew *takhlit*)

tám (1): "simpleton" (Hebrew *tam*)

tám (2): "charm", "grace" (Hebrew *ta'am*)

tapenol: "to touch", "tap", "pat", "stroke" (Yiddish *tapn*)

tarhál: "begs for money" (from Hebrew *tirhah*, Yiddish *tirhe*)

tof: "good" (Hebrew *tov*)

tofel: "unclean", "used", "old" (Hebrew *tafel*, "plain")

tóhesz: "bottom" (Hebrew *tahat*, "below", Yiddish *tokhes*, "bottom")

tóhuvabóhu: "chaos" (*tohu va-bohu*, Genesis 1,2)

topis: "dressed carelessly / in rags"

tré: "trashy", "outworn" (from *tréfe*, *tréfli*)

tréfe: "not kosher" (Hebrew *terefah*)

tréfi: "catching in the act" (slang) (Hebrew *terefah*, here: "pray of a beast")

tréfli: "worthless", "useless"

trenderli: "peg-top", "tee-totum", a toy (the game is usually played on Hanukkah) (*dreidel / sevivon*)

tróger: "seasonal worker (who delivers / carries things)", "dishonest person", "bum" (German *Träger*, Yiddish *troger*)

tüme: "(Christian) temple" (Yiddish *tume*) (Hebrew *tuma'ah*, "impurity")

vastartalék: "iron reserve", a calque in some European languages (e.g. German *eisernes Vieh*) from a rabbinic (Mishnah) term, in Hebrew: *tzon barzel,* "iron animal (literally, sheep) / thing"; the part of the woman's dowry, which remains her personal property and which is returned to her, should her husband die or divorce her

volf: "six" (the numerical value of the sixth letter of the Hebrew alphabet, *vav,* is six) (slang)

zebaoth, "God" (Hebrew *tzeva'ot,* YHWH *tzeba'ot,* "LORD of the troops"

zóf: "silverware" (Hebrew *zahav,* "gold") (slang)

züfec / züfesz: "bad luck", "fear", "beating" (Hebrew *zefet*); *züfecel:* "beats up someone" (slang)

zsinagóga: "synagogue" (Greek *synagoge,* "assembly", "house of assembling")

(3) The Jewish Joke

Jokes should not be analyzed and lectured about but told and laughed at. We certainly do not want to talk about them in generalities, but one who does not appreciate the Jewish joke of Pest (*hokhmah, vits, leytsones*), cannot appreciate Jewish Budapest either. Jewish jokes have been an integral part of the city for the past one hundred years, as is the funny, witty language or the cabaret which developed in the same urban milieu. And the reverse of this statement is also true: the Jewish joke would not be the same without Budapest. True, Pest is not the only home of the Jewish joke; its kind can be located more exactly within the polygon formed by Vienna–Pozsony (Pressburg)–Budapest–Warsaw–Cracow–Lemberg (Lviv). Jokes, including Jewish jokes, are like the air—borders do not block their way, they penetrate everywhere, they are the same everywhere. But it does make a difference, whether one breathes the air in Budapest or somewhere else, and the same international joke has a different flavor if told in Budapest. The material and background of Jewish jokes come from Eastern European life itself, from the customs, conditions and traditions. Without knowing these one may not understand the jokes, either. An essential element of the Jewish joke is language—Yiddish, German, and even Hungarian as used by Jews, sometimes artificially but deliberately Judaized, loaded with references to Jewish life, sometimes miming Yiddish syntax as well. When told aloud, the comic effect is raised even by intonation. The Jewish joke has also recreated the humor, irony and self-directed irony over endless, perpetual Halakhic debates preserved in classical Jewish textual tradition; it also replicates the witty arguments of *pilpul,* the arguments hidden in questions, the dialectics, logical reasoning that aims to establish a balance between opposing ideas, the *hilluk.* "Discovering the comic effect of automated wisdom, of playing the wise guy [*óberhóchem*] was the unique achievement of the Jewish joke"—wrote Aladár Komlós in 1934.

One of the basic types of Jewish jokes is, indeed, the *pilpul*-type. In these jokes the unexpected comic effect derives from a certain situation; one element becomes important for its own sake, over-shadows the importance of other elements and thus turns into its own opposite, destroying itself.

In a novel of Illés Kaczér (Katz) (1887–1980), already quoted, which takes place around 1830, the market place can clearly be identified as the Jewish Market. Someone stole a kerchief from one of the stands. The merchant was just discussing with the owner of the next stand which kerchiefs were better, the ones sold by Goldberg or by Elkán, both wholesale dealers from Szerecsen utca. If the quality of the kerchiefs was not good enough, the village women would bring them back at the next fair. When the merchant discovers that a kerchief was stolen, he just laughs. His neighbor is aston-ished, "Someone steals from you and you are just laughing?—Of course I am laughing—at least nobody will complain about this one." This is the basic pattern, and there are innumerable variations on it.

"Two passengers are standing on the deck of a ship which has just stranded. One of them is wailing.

"*Oy-vey*, it's going to sink!

"What are you wailing for? This ship isn't yours, is it?"

(László Kabos, 1985 / István Y. Kertész, 1993)

"A Jew wearing caftan visits the famous Neolog rabbi, the German R. Kayserling, and complains to him that his daughter is going to get married on that day, that even the *huppah* is ready, but the groom wants to with-draw from the marriage because a little bit is still missing from the dowry. He asks the rabbi to help, if he can. Kayserling gives him the missing sum instantly. The *kaftannik* gratefully thanks the rabbi and on his way out he recites a prayer: *Riboynoy shel oylom*, LORD of the Universe, please do not accept this as a *mitsve* from this *apikoyres*, this heretic."

(Máté Csillag, Zsidó anekdoták kincsesháza [Treasury of Jewish Anecdotes], 1925)

"A matchmaker visits the rich, confirmed bachelor and wants to talk him into a marriage.

"You see, what is your life like? You eat in restaurants all the time and sit in cafés all day long, and in the evening when you come home you have no one to talk to. What kind of life is this? Look at me! I am a poor man. I run around all day long to earn a living. In the evening when I go home tired, my children come to greet me, all eight of them, and they ask, 'Daddy, what did you bring for us?' My wife asks me questions, too. The baby starts to cry, the bigger children start shouting, my wife just talks and talks, the baby just cries and cries... Eh, if only I never knew what marriage was!" (Máté Csillag, 1925)

"The beggar says: Mister, I come to you every Friday. You always used to give me ten crowns for *shabes*, and now you are only giving five?

"You see, I got married last week and I married a poor girl. I need to save some money now.

"The beggar: He is getting married at my expense! What an impertinence!" (Máté Csillag, 1925)

Another category of urban Jewish jokes originating probably from Pest is the type where the source of comic effect is the difference between Jewish lifestyles—between Orthodox and Neolog, between observant and non-observant.

"The judge says: You shameless! Is it not bad enough that you go around stealing, but you steal on Saturday, when you people have a holiday!

"The prisoner: But please, sir... I am not Orthodox."

(Adolf Ágai, Abrincs. 150 jordány vicc [150 Jordanian Jokes], Budapest: Athenaeum, 1879)

The title of Ágai's book calls for explanation. *Jordány*, or *jordán* (Jordanian), or just *dán* (Danish), distorted from the Hungarian name of the river Jordan, are mildly derogatory terms for Jews.

"The Jewish tenant wished to speak with the landlord. When he entered the landlord's apartment, he took off his hat, but another little hat remained on his head. As he was about to leave, the landlord noted: I just noticed that you are wearing a little hat. In Budapest it is only bishops and other church dignitaries who wear such head covers. You are not a bishop, I take it.

"Excuse me, Sir, but according to the precepts of our religion we may never uncover our heads.

"It is hard to believe what you are saying, for I have met many Jews in my life, but none of them was wearing such a hat.

"It may very well be so, but those Jews were probably Neolog, not Orthodox.

"Isn't it the same? Who are those Neolog?

"Fie! They are even worse than the Christians."

(Avrom Reitzer, *Masel tov*, ca. 1900)

"You are eating *treyf* on Yom Kippur! Aren't you ashamed?

"What can I do? Is there any kosher restaurant open?"

(*Oj, wie kóser, oj, wie fájn*, 1903)

"A young man visits Rabbi Koppel Reich and asks him to issue the papers necessary for conversion to the Christian faith for him.

"Look, my friend, I don't like to deal with such things. Why don't you go to a Neolog rabbi—he can issue these papers for you just as soon.

"You are sending me to that *goy*? Then I'd rather not convert at all!"

(Máté Csillag, 1925)

Jokes are shaped in the process of telling. They attain a final form, but this form is changed again and again every time the joke is retold, always adjusted to the context. That is why we hear Pest jokes with specific settings, historical characters, even jokes which already have been written down. A Yiddish proverb says: *In troyerike tsaytn blit leytsones*, "In sad times jokes flourish." (The Yiddish word *leytsones* is of Hebrew origin, *latzon* in Hebrew means "riddle".) If there is an opportunity, the joke pattern is reanimated and sounds as fresh as if it had just been invented. Yet it has a history.

"Three gentlemen are sitting in a café. As they are sitting next to each other, they strike up a conversation which is soon directed towards politics. To figure out who the others are they inquire about each other's religion. I, says one of them, am in favor of *numerus clausus*. I denounce it, says the other one. My father denounces it too, says the third man, but I am in favor of it."

(Imre Nagy, *A bölcs rabbi tréfái* [Jests of the Wise Rabbi], 1923)

"One of our co-religionists hurries home along the Körút [Nagykörút], when four young men step in front of him and say:

"Your identification papers, Jew!

"If you already know that I am a Jew, gentlemen, what do you need to see my papers for?"

(Imre Nagy, 1923)

Let us close this section with a Jewish joke from Pest and an excerpt from a novel which tries to interpret history within the framework of a Jewish joke.
The joke:

"The public school teacher asks little Samu why makes Budapest the most modern city in Hungary.

"Because this is where the most Neolog are."

(Máté Csillag, 1925)

And the section from the novel:

"(...) Doctor H. sighed deeply and sat down on the bunk.

"As a reward, I am going to tell you a joke, all right? Two Jews are traveling on a train...

"You have to change the words—said Silberstein.—Five thousand Jews are traveling on the train. Or, if it's more convenient this way, eighty Jews are traveling in a wagon.

"But this way the punch line won't fit.—Doctor H. looked at him sadly.

"I am afraid that you are never going to be able to tell these jokes again. The punch line will just not fit anymore."

(Mária Ember, *Hajtűkanyar* [Hairpin Bend], 1974)

István Örkény also used this joke in his fake film-script called *Forgatókönyv* [Script] (1979). He had a Jewish woman, fleeing in 1944 during the Arrow-cross terror with a Swedish passport, tell the joke.

(4) Corpus Juris Hungarici

After the late nineteenth century the intellectual and artistic *contribution* of Jews to Hungarian literature, scholarship, the arts or even music had become more or less invisible, identical with it. The *Zsidó lexikon* [Jewish Lexicon] compiled by Péter Ujvári in 1929 was still quite informative on this topic. After the Holocaust several competent public figures tried to sum up the losses. Sándor Scheiber, László Kardos and others, the authors of a volume of studies (*She'erit Yisra'el*, 1946) edited by Imre Benoschofsky assessed the situation and opportunities from the Jewish point of view. László Bóka, the editor of the volume called *Magyar mártír írók antológiája* [Anthology of Hungarian Martyr Writers] (1947) accepted the premise applied earlier by Gyula Illyés in his literary journal *Magyar Csillag*: the indissoluble unity of Hungarian literary life. So far nobody has investigated the role of the institutions of intellectual life, institutions which are more closely tied to location, in our case Budapest, than individual creative work itself. Actually, it is only the IMIT's *Évkönyv* (until 1948) and later the *Évkönyv* of MIOK, edited by Sándor Scheiber, that indicate the Jewish *contributions*, and more recently the "yearbooks" of the Rabbinical Seminary of Hungary, published rather irregularly. Real Jewish institutions used by a wider public—periodicals, concerts, exhibitions or literary evenings—have only begun to emerge recently.

Writers with a Jewish background were listed and their original names identified all-comprehensively in 1944 in the list of Jewish authors compiled by the authorities—in order to ban their books.[1] After that, after the tragic events that followed, it was almost impossible to speak of a writer as Jewish. A recent conference, organized by the circle of young Jewish intellectuals around "Yahalom" (1996), shed light on the problems of drawing the borders (that is, borders between Hungarian and Hungarian-Jewish or Jewish-Hungarian literature). A similar attempt was made in arts with the monumental "Diaspora (and) Art" exhibition in the Jewish Museum (1997) and with a conference parallel to it. In the field of music, Sándor Scheiber, and after him a Transylvanian–Israeli composer (Ervin Junger), compiled an extensive data-base on Béla Bartók's Jewish connections and a musicologist (Judith Frigyesi) analyzed Bartók's music, in part from the background of Jewish intellectual life in early twentieth-century Budapest. Instead of giving an enumeration, list of names, catalog of titles, etc., it should only be mentioned here, emblematically, that Bartók in exile, in the United States, writing his "Concerto" (1943), a masterly work of a homesick artist, referred to Budapest by using a popular melody, "Szép vagy, gyönyörű vagy, Magyarország" ("You are nice, you are beautiful, oh Hungary"), from the operetta "A hamburgi menyasszony" [The Bride from Hamburg] (1926) by Zsigmond Vincze (1874–1935), a Jewish composer.

As is done all along this book, only the historical perspective of this topic will be analyzed. Like above, in the chapter about buildings, a documentary text will be quoted here, just to signal the Jewish *contribution* in a field which is otherwise rarely mentioned, without trying to be all-comprehensive.

*

[1] Randolph L. Braham (re-)edited the list of Hungarian and foreign Jewish authors whose works were banned in his *The Politics of Genocide* (1994), II, pp. 1385 ff.

The "most Hungarian area of scholarship", as the lawyer Ernő Munkácsi (1896–1950)—son of the linguist Bernát Munkácsi, a leader (secretary-general) of the Pest Jewish community—put it, is law.

> "Those seventy years, during which Hungarian Jews were allowed to work in the field of Hungarian jurisprudence, were very short. Nevertheless we are proud of what we have accomplished in that time, bringing growth and progress to Hungarian legislature. The spirit of emancipation inspired Hungarian Jewry and thus many of our men chose to pursue this most Hungarian field. (...) Károly Csemegi, the former major of the Independence War of 1848/49, later Privy Councilor, president of the Supreme Court, the person who after a hundred years of preparation created the first Hungarian Code of Criminal Law, the code through which the state practices its constitutional rights most often and most effectively, was also one of us. (...) And it was Dezső Márkus, judge of the Country Court, also one of our men, who edited the complete Hungarian Law Digest, issued on the occasion of the celebrations of the millennial existence of the Hungarian state, and he wrote thousands and thousands of Latin footnotes and glosses on these several-century-old Hungarian laws, the most peculiar flowers of Hungarian spirit and intellect. He who wishes to find out anything about old Hungarian law cannot do so without Dezső Márkus."
>
> ("Búcsú a magyar zsidó bíráktól" [Farewell to the Hungarian Jewish Judges],
> in: *Küzdelmes évek*, Budapest: Libanon, 1943)

Károly Csemegi (1826-1899)

518. Károly Csemegi

His original family name was Nascher. He studied at the Piarist schools in Szeged and Pest, then at the Faculty of Law in Pest. He fought in the Independence War of 1848/49 as a major, he organized his own infantry and cavalry unit. He was captured and imprisoned at Temesvár and spent six more months in the Nádor Barracks in Buda (2 Nádor tér, today Kapisztrán tér). Earlier he was a county deputy clerk. He started his second career as a lawyer at Arad, and he achieved national fame in this field. (He got baptized.) After the Austro-Hungarian compromise or *Ausgleich* of 1867 he was employed in the Ministry of Justice, became an under secretary here, and was eventually appointed president of the Supreme Court in 1879. He formulated the laws concerning the judicial system, the power of the judge (Act IV of 1869) and about the attorney organization (Act XXXIII of 1871); these were to form the basis of modern law in Hungary. It was during his years at the Supreme Court that several modern methods of prosecution were introduced, e.g. hearing both parties, defense, oral proceedings, etc. Nevertheless, his main work is the Code of Criminal Law (Act V of 1878; Act XL of 1879), which has determined Hungarian criminal law until today. It was published in France, too, in 1885.

Dezső Márkus (1862-1912)

Márkus started his career as a lawyer. He was employed by the Ministry of Justice (1894) and became a judge of the Supreme Court (1911). He edited Law reports, wrote commentaries to laws. His magnum opus is the series *Magyar törvénytár–Corpus Juris Hungarici* [Hungarian Code of Laws] launched in 1896, which remained for decades, until the end of World War II, the official edition of Hungarian laws. He also edited and annotated, in Latin, the classic of Hungarian law, Werbőczy's *Hármaskönyv* (*Tripartitum opus juris consuetudinarii*, 1517). Márkus never abandoned the Jewish faith.

(5) Still Visible, But Not What It Used to Be

> "The population of the town (...) is not entitled to sell the synagogue (*beit ha-keneset*), only on condition that if they request it, it needs to be given back to them. (...) They may sell it unconditionally, too, but may not by any means sell it for the following four purposes: bath, workshop, ceremonial place and washroom. (...) The sacredness (*kedushah*) of the synagogue does not cease, even if it is destroyed. If grass grows on it, nobody should cut it, because of the grief of the soul (*agmat nefesh*)"

—as written in the Mishnah (Megillah 3,1–3).

There have always been debates about what to do with abandoned synagogue buildings, what should come in their place. Around the end of the second century C.E. the Mishnah did take into consideration that synagogues may have to be sold, if they are not used, that they may be destroyed. But it prescribes for the population of the town that the building used earlier for rituals should not be used for profane purposes (public bath), for practical ends (workshop), for the ritual of other religions or for lowly purposes. The "grief of the soul" will guard over the memory of the holy purpose of the place.

*

The following is not meant as a complete list by any means. It is just a few examples, one from Buda and some from Pest.

Buda

37 Bocskai út: The Science Studio of TIT, the Society for Dissemination of Scientific Knowledge. This used to be the Szent Imre-városi synagogue, i.e. the synagogue of Lágymányos / Kelenföld. The former "new" synagogue of the Buda community was built in 1936 according the plans of Ede Novák (1888–1951) and István Hamburger. After World War II the Jewish community sold it and, around 1965, it was reconstructed to meet the needs of the new owner. It became an ordinary office building. The one-time synagogue and community office building became unrecognizable. Only those familiar with the history of the building know that the lecture hall on the second floor was once a synagogue. As much as one can tell from photographs, its interior must have been decorated with geometrical forms, it may have been similar to the Heroes' Temple, only simpler. The only detail of the former synagogue which has survived is the wrought-iron fence on the Bocskai út side.

Kőbánya

7–9 Cserkesz (Cserkész) utca: The former synagogue of the Kőbánya Jewish community, together with the community office building and dwelling house right next to it, was designed by Richárd Schöntheil (1874–?) in 1909–1911. The synagogue is a major attraction of the otherwise architecturally undistinguished district. After World War II it was used as a warehouse and as a theater; it was used, repaired and damaged by Hungarian Television. Currently a Christian religious community is trying to take care of it. It is enough to look at the building—at its two corner towers, at the spire decorated with the typical flower pattern of Hungarian Art Nouveau over the dome, at the ashlar, brick and concrete walls— to realize immediately that it must have been a synagogue, even without knowing Baumhorn's style.

519. The synagogue in Kőbánya, Cserkesz utca. Designed by Richárd Schöntheil, 1911

520. Interior of the former synagogue in Kőbánya, after the reconstruction in 1991. Today a Christian ecumenical temple of the Humanitarian Foundation in the custody of the Evangelical Pentecostal Church

Pest

5–7 Munkácsy Mihály utca (earlier Epreskert utca): the building is currently occupied by a company called Centrál Hotel Co. Earlier it was a guest-house of the Hungarian Socialist Workers' Party, and before that, dormitory of the highest party school of the Hungarian Communist Party (later Hungarian Workers' Party). Today, after several restorations, the original building is not recognizable at all. Once it had belonged to the Girls' Orphanage of the Pest Jewish community, established in 1867. It also used to function as an apartment house for a while. After World War I there were plans to rebuild it into a secondary school for girls; this plan was not carried out. In 1937 the building was reconstructed according to the plans made by Alfréd Hajós. In 1944 it was used by the Orphanage. In the early 1990s the Jewish community exchanged its virtual rights on it for the building in 16 Révay utca, where the "Bálint Ház" was accommodated.

25–27 Városligeti fasor (earlier Vilma királynő út): currently the building is the experimental telecommunications plant of the Mechanical Laboratory. Originally it was the Boys' Orphanage of the Pest Jewish community. The Orphanage was established in 1869 and operated at several locations. At first its address was 6 Holló utca, then 5–7 Epreskert utca / Munkácsy Mihály utca, and finally it was moved here. After World War II it was combined with the Girls' Orphanage at 35 Délibáb utca–88 Dózsa György út. The building in Városligeti fasor was built according to the plans of Alfréd Wellisch in 1900. The Jewish community wanted to reconstruct it after World War I but this only happened after World War II, and then according to the plans of Alfréd Hajós.

2 Bethlen Gábor tér: "Gusztáv Bárczi" Training College for Teachers of Handicapped Children. The red brick building was originally the Israelite Institute for the Deaf and Dumb, built in 1877 according to the plans of Vilmos Freund. Later the Institute for the Blind moved here, too, mainly for financial reasons. Before World War II the Israelite Women's Association belonging to the synagogue of the district maintained a soup-kitchen and a children's playhouse in the huge building. During World War II several Jewish institutions moved here, since they were expelled from their original sites. In 1944 there was even a temporary hospital here.

521. The Israelite Institute for the Deaf and Dumb on Bethlen tér. Designed by Vilmos Freund, 1877

522. The interior of the Bethlen tér synagogue. Designed by Lipót Baumhorn, 1931

The synagogue, located in the wing towards István út, was built according to the design of Lipót Baumhorn and his son-in-law, György Somogyi, in 1931. This survived in an exceptionally good condition and in its original form and function—the rostrum (bimah) in the middle, the women's gallery with a separate entrance. Above its gate a Hebrew inscription, often seen on synagogues, says: "This is the gateway to the Lord—the righteous shall enter through it" (Psalms 118,20); indicating that the prayer-house is that gateway to the Lord. Behind the synagogue there is a Cultural Center with a separate entrance through the courtyard (17 István út) where currently the *Oneg Shabbat* Club holds its meetings.

55 Dózsa György út: Fencing club (Honvéd / Budapest Soldiers' Sports Association). This

used to be the synagogue at 26 Tüzér utca / Aréna út, East of the Jewish cemetery. The synagogue was built according to the design of Lipót Baumhorn, and was consecrated in 1908, just before the High Holidays, on September 25. The building was slightly damaged during World War II and has deteriorated ever since. Around 1980 it was remodeled and transformed into a fencing club. The blue walls together with the red bricks give the building an exotic image. Whoever has seen any synagogue will immediately recognize that this

523. The Angyalföld / Aréna út synagogue (55 Dózsa György út). Today a fencing room

building used to be one, too. In the Cultural Center behind the synagogue there is a prayer-room even today. Of the original Jewish community institutions the *matzzah* bakery still, despite all the changes, works in the neighborhood, at 26 Tüzér utca.

Not far from here, in Lehel utca, there used to be another Jewish cemetery. It was used by the Jewish community in the nineteenth century, after its second cemetery was closed down in 1808, until about 1874 when the cemetery in Salgótarjáni utca was opened. This is where Márk Rózsavölgyi was buried originally, along with the Jewish heroes of the 1848/49 War of Independence, as well as several noted rabbis. The municipality decided to eliminate this cemetery in 1907; they wanted to build an elementary school in its place. It was still there when the synagogue on Aréna út was opened, but it was eliminated soon afterwards. The graves were removed to the

524. "Gravestones in the old Jewish cemetery of Pest." Drawing by Gergely Pörge, 1908

525. In the old Jewish cemetery of Pest, ca. 1908

526. In the old Jewish cemetery of Pest. On the right, the synagogue on Aréna / Dózsa György út is visible

527. In the old Jewish cemetery of Pest

528. Stele in the Kozma utca cemetery commemorating the former Jewish cemetery of Pest. Design by Béla Lajta

Kozma utca Isr. / Jewish cemetery. The memory of the cemetery is preserved only on some photographs. In place of the former cemetery, on the territory surrounded by Aréna út / Dózsa György út–Lehel utca–Taksony utca–Tüzér utca, there is a school and some dwelling houses.

33–35 Szabolcs utca: "Imre Haynal" University of Health Sciences. This used to be the *Zsidó Kórház* (Jewish Hospital) or *A Pesti Izr. Hitközség Alapítványi Közkórháza* (Foundational Public Hospital of the Pest Israelite Community). Its buildings, dedicated in 1889, seven all together, were nationalized by the state in 1950. A few years later, in 1956, the up-to-date, well-equipped complex was handed over to the *Orvostovábbképző Intézet* (Medical School) and its clinic, and it remained the number one medical institution of Hungary ever since. Recently it was named "Imre Haynal" University of Health Sciences, after Imre vitéz váradi Haynal (1892–1979, professor of heart diseases. In Kolozsvár (Cluj), where he was director of the clinic for internal diseases, helped Jews to escape.)

Originally the Jewish Hospital lay on the territory bordered by Aréna út / Dózsa György út, Vágány utca, Bókay János tér and Szabolcs utca. Beyond Bókay tér there was the independent Francis Joseph Commercial Hospital. It was joined to the Jewish Hospital already in the times of the Medical School, at the cost of eliminating Bókay tér. But the nice park and the building still do not form an integral part of the hospital complex.

The "Imre Haynal" University of Health Sciences has taken over two other formerly separate Jewish medical institutions as well, both of which stood on the former Bókay tér. One of them was the *Bródy Zsigmond és Adél Gyermekkórház* ("Zsigmond and Adél Bródy" Children's Hospital) at

529. Bust of Alice csepeli Weiss in the Hospital and Old-age Home of the Pest Hevrah Kaddishah (57 Amerikai út)

1 Bókay tér, the other one the *Weiss Alice Gyermekágyas Otthon közkórház* ("Alice Weiss" Maternity Home Public Hospital) on the other side of the square, at 4 Bókay tér.

The Children's Hospital was founded by the journalist Zsigmond Bródy (1840–1906) in memory of his wife. (They used to live at 18 Alkotmány utca, marble steps were leading up to their second floor apartment.) It was built according to the design of Vilmos Freund in 1897. It remained in the care of the Jewish community and in 1920 it was joined to the Jewish Hospital. In 1933 the original foyer of the building was remodeled and a synagogue was established there, designed by György Somogyi. Today the building is used by the Pediatric Clinic II of the "Imre Haynal" University.

The Maternity Home was founded in 1910 by the industrialist Manfréd Weiss, to preserve his wife's name. Organizationally it was under the auspices of the Jewish Women's Association of Pest. At its foundation it was a private institute, from 1926 a public hospital and from 1945, part of the Jewish Hospital. The original entrance from Bókay tér was framed by two pairs of columns. Some details of the building, e.g. the golden mosaic niche on the staircase landing and the stained-glass window, are telling of its original luxury and the generosity of the founder. (Originally the niche held a bust of Alice csepeli Weiss.) Today it is the Gynecological Clinic and Maternity Ward of the "Imre Haynal" University.

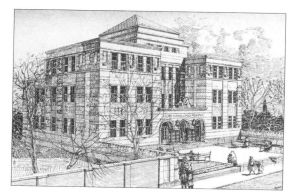

530. The Aladár and Józsa Kaszab Polyclinic (Vágány utca)

The *Tüdőgondozó Intézet* (Tuberculosis Institute), founded by József Bródy and his wife, née Fanny Weiszburg, had belonged to the Jewish Hospital from the start. The *Poliklinika* or "Aladár Kaszab and his wife, née Józsa Weiszkopf" Polyclinic in Vágány utca was also part of the Jewish Hospital.

Kaszab, an industrialist (screw factory) and later the president of the Jewish community, founded the Polyclinic in 1925 to enable the doctors of the hospital to care for outpatients and accept medical interns. Its building was designed by Ernő and Miklós Román.

József Patai wrote about the Polyclinic as follows:

"The palace of good hearts where thousands and thousands find a cure for their aches and pains, and nobody inquires about their background, about their God."

The Jewish Hospital has always treated Jewish as well as non-Jewish patients—this was even specified in its foundation rules. At least two-fifth but sometimes up to fifty percent of its numerous patients were non-Jews, and in this sense the Polyclinic was a public health institution.

531. The Girls' Home of the Jewish Women's Association of Pest (149 Hungária körút)

149 Hungária körút: Budapest Traffic Police Department headquarters. The police took over this building in 1951, after it had been damaged by machine gunfire and burnt out during World War II. The building was remodeled in 1969, but its new form, a simple block house, is just as insignificant as it was originally—as far as we can tell from old photographs. Higher-rank police officers working in the building benevolently told in 1993 that there used to be a "nunnery" here before, and they refer to the corridor surrounding the square courtyard as the "cloisters".

There is a separate building in the courtyard, opening from Hungária körút: the cultural center of the traffic police. The first floor of this building used to be the synagogue of the *Leányotthon* (Girls' Home) of the Jewish Women's Association of Pest; its ground plan and walls are still in their original state. During the reconstruction of the police headquarters it was simply surrounded by a new, square building, and additional floors were built on top of it. The former synagogue is a tiny, octagonal independent building with a hall at its entrance and with a trapezoid gallery.

532. The former synagogue in the old building of the Girls' Home (149 Hungária körút). Today, after reconstruction, the cultural center of the Traffic Police Department

This plot was originally the site of the two buildings of the István út Sanatorium or *Cottage* Sanatorium. The two buildings used to stand next to each other, partly on today's István út. They were designed by János Szabó. The Girls' Home was set up by the Jewish Women's Association in 1923; they provided room and board for poor, single Jewish young women at a very low cost. The Association bought the building in the same year, and a few years later, in 1926, the Girls' Orphanage (*Mädchen Waisenhaus* or *Hirsch báró Leánymenhely* / "Baron Hirsch" Girls' Home) moved here from 5 Jókai utca. The necessary reconstruction of the building, according to the plans of Izidor Stärk, was carried out by the company of Fehér & Dános. The synagogue must

533. Old-age Home. Entrance, with the original Hebrew inscription (see also next page)

534. The Old-age Home of the Hevrah Kaddishah (167 Hungária körút)

535. Old-age Home. The former synagogue

have been built at that time, too. The Orphanage occupied the second and the third floors, the Girls' Home was on the fourth floor, with 120 and 40 places, respectively.

167 Hungária körút: Currently the Chronic Department of the Uzsoki utca Hospital. Originally it was the *Sínylők Menháza* (Shelter of the Suffering), then an *Aggok Háza* (Old-age Home). It was established by the foundation of Ármin Kann in 1869. The building was designed by Vilmos Freund and built between 1891 and 1893. The annexes were ready only a few years later, in 1902. In 1925 the Pest Hevrah Kaddishah modernized the building according to the plans of József Mann and Emil Vidor; they added a third floor, installed central heating, etc.

The former synagogue is in the rear of the building, separated, on the second floor. The rectangular building is perpendicular to the main building; it has twelve huge windows and Neo-Classicist half columns on the walls. The iron lights are clearly made from the former six-arm wall lamps of the synagogue. There is a separate entrance to the gallery, its beautiful wrought-iron fence is original, too. This room currently serves as the library of the hospital. Right next to the synagogue a door opened onto the large balcony. Above the entrance of the building there used to be a Biblical quotation. Its Hebrew and Hungarian text is discernible on photographs:

אל תשליכני לעת זקנה ככלות כחי אל תעזבני

"Do not cast me off in old age;
when my strength fails, do not forsake me."
(Psalms 71,9)

The Hospital District of Béla Lajta

The above name is no more than our own improvization, but we think it does have some justification. On the southwestern edge of Herminamező [Hermina meadow], a section of the fourteenth district named after the daughter of Palatine József, a whole block of important hospital buildings of the

536. Institute for the Blind. Plan of Béla Lajta, 1905

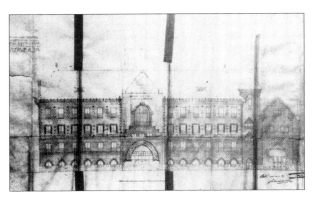

Jewish community were designed by Béla Lajta. Though the hospital district around Mexikói út–Amerikai út and the office buildings of the Jewish community on Hungária körút were divided by railway tracks (built in 1847), Herminamező was still one organic unit, and so were the Jewish institutions of this area.

60 Mexikói út: *Mozgásjavító Általános Iskola és Diákotthon* (Movement Correction Elementary School and Student Home).

Originally the *Vakok Tanintézete* (School for the Blind), founded by Ignác (Izsák) lovag[2] Wechselmann and his wife, Zsófia Neuschloss, in 1901. Wechselmann (1828–1903) was a successful contractor; he was the only Jewish member of the architect's guild of Pest in 1863. He was the contractor for several major construction projects, including Förster's plans of the Dohány Temple and several works of Miklós Ybl (the University Library, other university buildings, the *Vámház* / Customs House, the *Várkert* / Castle Garden, etc.). Since he had no children, he left a considerable part of his wealth for the purpose of building a school for blind children; half of the school was to be used for the education of Jewish children, the other half for Christians. The institute, named after its founder and donor, was designed by Béla Lajta (Leitersdorfer)—this was his first major work completed on his own. The construction started in 1905 and was finished in 1908. The stained-glass windows are work of Miksa Róth, the copper and iron pieces are by Jenő Galambos, the stone carvings, by György Weisinger. During its reconstruction in 1993 several sections were added to the building and its interior was altered to a great extent, but at least the main gate was restored in its original form.

537. Institute for the Blind (60 Mexikói út). Main entrance

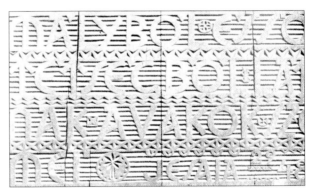

The main entrance, covered by a semicircular roof, is a wooden gate. Its whole surface is decorated with Hungarian folk-art motifs and inscriptions written in stylized type resembling the Braille-script—also Lajta's design. The inscriptions are all Biblical quotations about blindness: "I will lead the blind..." (Isaiah 42,16); "The LORD restores sight to the blind" (Psalms 146,8); "Who gives man speech? Who makes him dumb or deaf, seeing or blind?" (Exodus 4,11); "You shall not insult the deaf, or place a stumbling block before the blind" (Leviticus 19,14); "In that day, the deaf shall hear..." (Isaiah 29,18). On the two sides of the gate there are two huge iron pillars with eternal lights.

At the beginning the Institute could house seventy-five people. In 1926 the foundation was forced to sell the building and so the Institute for the Blind traded places with the Institute for the Deaf and Dumb. (Deaf and dumb, in Hebrew *heresh*, are to be protected and helped according to Jewish tradition. Certain Halakhic restrictions are applicable, but it is forbidden to "curse", that is, to humiliate them, see Leviticus 19,14.) They were now using the building on Bethlen Gábor tér together with other Jewish institutions; OMIKE was here for a while and so did the Joint. During World War II the building as well as the large empty space behind it was used as a detention camp, barracks were set up, in part precisely for handicapped Jews.

After the war it was used by the Foreign Language College and then by an elementary school. The Movement Correction Elementary School and Student Home occupies it since 1952. Though this institute is not the actual successor of the Institute for the Blind but of the Home for Disabled Children (1903), they do keep up the memory of the Jewish foundation. The original name of the institute can still be made out from the traces of the letters on the facade. The two original marble

538. Institute for the Blind. A *menorah* on the iron fence, designed by Béla Lajta

539. Institute for the Blind. Detail of the inscription on the main entrance gate. Letters designed by Béla Lajta, 1905

---

[2] "Knight", a title of nobility.

540. Institute for the Blind. *Menorah* and inscription on the main entrance gate

541. Institute for the Blind. Side door, entrance to the gym

542. Institute for the Blind. Iron *menorah* column in front of the gym

slabs with the original inscriptions from the foundation are still there on the walls at the entrance. All but one of the original inscriptions in the wrought-iron fence outside the building, also written in stylized Braille-script, are missing.

"He who visits the Wechselmann Institute for the Blind or the Old-age Home will immediately sense (Lajta's) excellent talent for composition. The expanded, spacious rooms, wide corridors, lots of light, happy colors and Hungarian decorations are telling of his spirit. But his elaborate care left its traces on his buildings, too. As he adjusted the stairs and the banisters to the insecure steps of the small blind children, as he created warm, bright rooms for the old and sick, and there are flowers everywhere, on the windows, on iron grates, in the garden and even on the walls."
(Pál Nádai, ca. 1940)

The synagogue of the Institute was once in an annex to the right of the main building, to which a tower was attached. Today it is occupied by the school's gym. In spite of the complete reconstruction, the original function of the room is still obvious. There is an entrance to it from the Institute and another from the street. The latter retained its original form, albeit in poor condition, but the original decoration, the Jewish symbols, the gate with a tent-shaped top and its early twentieth-century Orientalizing modern style iron decoration are still there. Even the glass window of the gate is

543. Hospital and Old-age Home of the Pest Hevrah Kaddishah (57 Amerikai út). Designed by Béla Lajta

544. Moses. Statue by Ede Telcs (1911) on the facade of the Hospital and Old-age Home

the original, its pattern shows a *menorah*. This gate is not in use currently, it is protected by big trees which were planted there exactly for this purpose.

57 Amerikai út: National Neurosurgical Research Institute. The E-shaped hospital building was designed by Béla Lajta in 1911. At its foundation it was the *Szeretetház* (Old-age Home) of the Hevrah Kaddishah (*Gyógyíthatatlan Betegek Intézete* / Institute for the Incurably Sick) with 75 beds; during World War I it housed the military hospital of the Red Cross; since 1919 a well-equipped sanatorium occupied a part of it, with 60 beds (*Szeretetkórház*).

Every little detail of the building has Lajta's imprint on it. The entrance to the left, the nicer gate leads to the synagogue. Its original form and its interior are known only from photos. (Directors of the Institute today think that there was a mortuary in it.) The stone reliefs of the gate are decorated with Jewish motifs (six-pointed star, *menorah*) and references to Biblical stories (serpent and tree, Noah's Ark), all in Lajta's favorite Hungarian folk-art style. Above the main entrance there is a statue of Moses by Ede Telcs. The other side-gate is decorated with a relief, too. Both side-gates are protected by a semicircular copper roof. The staircases appear to be towers. Above them the intricate wood beam structure is a refined version of Transylvanian Hungarian folk architecture. The two pairs of columns of the main entrance

are decorated with a row of *menorah*s. The inscriptions on the marble slabs on the foyer wall were turned towards the wall during the last reconstruction in 1985. The section of the plate-rods of the grated fence show the "*zikkurrat* motif". The wrought-iron grates as well as the gates were made in the smith workshop of József Hahmann. The whole building is protected as a historic monument.

546. Entrance hall of the Hospital and Old-age Home in its original condition, with the building inscriptions. (Today the marble slabs are turned inwards)

547. Hospital and Old-age Home. Side entrance (on the southeastern front of the building)

548. The former synagogue of the Hospital and Old-age Home. Designed by Béla Lajta

Next to it, on the back side of the plot at 55 Amerikai út (entrance from 42 Laky Adolf utca) was the Pulmonary Unit of the Uzsoki utca Hospital; since 1993 it is part of the Jewish Hospital. Originally it was the *Felnőtt Vakok Intézete* (Adult Institute for the Blind) of the Pest Hevrah Kaddishah, opened in 1923, with 75 beds. On the facade of the building the initials "P.Ch.K." refer to the owner.

The present Jewish Hospital is right next to it, at 53 Amerikai út. Originally this was the *Menedékház* (Shelter) of the Pest Hevrah Kaddishah, founded by Gyula Hoffer and his wife, Szerén Krámer, in 1914. "Home for the old, the blind and for impoverished merchants", in other words a shelter for whoever needed it. It was built in 1918. Its original name is discernible on the wall of the "back" wing, along with the year of its foundation, 1914. We can tell from old photographs that the Shelter could once be approached through the courtyard of the Old-age Home. Between 1919 and 1925 there were emergency apartments here and then it was again used by the Hevrah Kaddishah for its original purpose. It was hit by a bomb during World War II. The original building was rebuilt to some extent, but mostly it was extended by another section towards Mexikói út and, in 1989–1990, a new wing was added, also parallel to Mexikói út.

549. Home for the Blind of the Pest Hevrah Kaddishah (55 Amerikai út)

550. Home for the Blind. Facade (towards Amerikai út and the Old-age Home)

551. Home for the Blind. Inner (back) courtyard towards Laky Adolf utca

János Szevera was a former owner of the two plots, the same person who rented the Orczy Café. Around 1860 he built a restaurant on this plot, which later became very popular as the garden-restaurant *Az Amerikaiakhoz* (At the sign of the Americans), owned by Ferenc Druska. After his death, around 1910, Móric Weisz rented it from the widow. Later the Hevrah Kaddishah bought the plot from Mrs. Druska.

Not far from here, at 27 Erzsébet királyné útja, there is a one-story Neo-Classicist house, built around 1890, the property of Miksa Grauer, the owner of a distillery and a Jewish community leader. This was one of the first Hevrah Kaddishah buildings in the neighborhood, probably a shelter, too. Later the employees of the Amerikai út hospital district stayed here.

The three hospital and care buildings of the Hevrah Kaddishah, the Old-age Home, the Shelter and the Adult Institute for the Blind, all three charity institutions—modern versions of the *hekdesh*—were located around a single courtyard, almost like community buildings joining around the synagogue courtyard. The building complex was surrounded by pleasant gardens, a garden path and benches. The garden probably reached as far as Korong utca. The patients of these institutions were generally here for an extended period, sometimes permanently. They lived in a pleasant environment. The Hevrah Kaddishah really took care of those in need.

The reconstruction of the synagogue of the present Jewish hospital was made possible by the funds left behind by Lipót Herman in 1984. The noted painter had always exhibited paintings with Jewish topics, which he remembered from his childhood. Nevertheless, it was a great surprise when, after his death, a series of color drawings were found among his papers, depicting Yiddish proverbs. Mária Ember published them in 1988 in a volume entitled *Jár-kel, mint zsidóban a fájdalom* [Walks about, as Pain Does in a Jew].

552. The Shelter of the Pest Hevrah Kaddishah. Street facade (53 Amerikai út)

553. The Shelter. Courtyard facade

Rákospalota

77 Régi Fóti út: Warehouse and Workshop of the National Széchényi Library. Originally it was a synagogue built in 1927. The external appearance of the building was not changed during its reconstruction in 1985, but all Jewish religious symbols were removed. One of its stained-glass windows survived. The synagogue had a courtyard, too.

Nagytétény

56/B–58 Nagytétényi út: Warehouse of the National Technical Information Center and Library. Nagytétény became incorporated into Budapest only in 1950, before that it was an independent town. Its old, once remarkable Orthodox Jewish community comprised some fifty families. Its baroque synagogue, built at the beginning of the nineteenth century, is used as library stacks today. Reconstruction became absolutely necessary, but it left the ark, the women's gallery, as well as the Holocaust memorial in the courtyard, the four trees, untouched. The original Hebrew and Hungarian inscription above the former synagogue entrance is still there:

ממזרח שמש עד מבואו מהלל שם ה׳

"From East to West the name of the Lord is praised."
(Psalms 113,3)

*

More synagogues disappeared from the map of Budapest after World War II than during the war, during the persecution of Jews. Some buildings were abandoned; nobody from their former congregations survived, no one returned. Other buildings were simply confiscated by the state, regardless of earlier events, or of the numbers and needs of the surviving Jewish community of Budapest, as if the Jewish community had to make up for what had happened in 1944. Other synagogues were sold by the Jewish community, or by the official leaders of the Jewish community. Those were hard days, they may have acted under duress, not out of conviction, maybe to cover the cost of maintaining the remaining property. During the past half a decade most of the institutions of the Jewish community, the hospitals, several synagogues, and so on, have become public property.

By now only the "grief of the soul" remains, the memories, and everyone—"the whole population of the town"—has to bear the responsibility.

XVI. Comments on the Illustrations

When selecting the illustrations to this book, it was not the main concern of the authors and of the editor to make new photos by any means, nor that each and every illustration be of high quality. They thought it more important to reproduce available old photographs, even if these were not the best or the most beautiful. Old photos are documentary evidence themselves, many of them being the single surviving relic of long-perished buildings or of buildings transformed beyond recognition, while others reflect an earlier condition than what may be seen today. These old photos are, in a certain sense, archaeological finds, similarly to most of the portraits published here for the first time or re-published. Old photo-documents are also part of the history charted in this book: they are part of it in their own right. And also part of this history are the photographers who are rarely, if ever, remembered as far as the Jewish history of Pest is concerned.

Several photos have been adopted from the pages of the old series of the *Múlt és Jövő*. At the time, József Patai programmatically collected documentation on the entire historical heritage of the Jews in Hungary, similarly to the historical relics of Jews in other countries. His personal "museum of Jewish Hungary in photos" is an inexhaustible treasury.

Despite the efforts of the authors and of the editor, it has often proved impossible to provide data on the photographs other than the source from which they have been taken. In several cases the name of photographer remained unknown.

The following remarks on the illustrations offer some explanations to the photographs; in some cases these notes are rather lengthy, while in others they have been kept brief; in any case, they are not merely a technical supplement to the book, but an organic part of it. Names of the photographers, etc., as well as source of the photos are indicated.

Measures are in centimeters (cm); 1 cm = 0.4 inch.

Abbreviations

BI&SchS	Ilona Benoschofsky & Alexander (Sándor) Scheiber, Eds., *The Jewish Museum of Budapest* (1989)
BTM	Budapesti Történeti Múzeum / Budapest Historical Museum
BTM: KM	Budapesti Történeti Múzeum, Kiscelli Múzeum
CsZs&DZ	Photo collection of Zsigmond Csoma & Zita Deáky, Budapest
EZ	Zoltán Egyed
FA	Aliona Frankl
FBA	Annie Fischer-Bánó
FA&LLL	Aliona Frankl & László Lugo Lugosi
FSzEKt.: BpGy.	Fővárosi Szabó Ervin Könyvtár, Budapest Gyűjtemény / Metropolitan Ervin Szabó Library. Budapest Collection
Gazda	Anikó Gazda, *Zsinagógák és zsidó községek Magyarországon* [Synagogues and Jewish Communities in Hungary] (Hungaria Judaica, 1) (Budapest: MTA Judaisztikai Kutató csoport, 1991)
GCs	Csaba Gedai
Gerszi	Teréz Gerszi, *A magyar kőrajzolás története a XIX. században* [History of Lithography in Nineteenth-century Hungary] (Budapest: Akadémiai Kiadó, 1960)
Grüsse	Ferenc Kollin & János Sediánszky, *Budapesti üdvözlet* [Greetings from Budapest] (Budapest: Helikon Kiadó, 1983) / *Grüsse aus dem alten Budapest* (Budapest: Corvina, 1988)
HL	Lipót Herman, *Jár-kel, mint zsidóban a fájdalom*. Drawings of Lipót Herman (Budapest: Origo-Press, 1988)
JL&FÁ	László Jaksity & Árpád Farkas
LE	Endre Lábass

MA	András Márkus
MéJ	*Múlt és Jövő*
MKVM	Magyar Kereskedelmi és Vendéglátóipari Múzeum / Hungarian Museum of Commerce and Catering
MNM	Magyar Nemzeti Múzeum / Hungarian National Museum
MNM Ét.	MNM Éremtára / Numismatic Collection
MNM: KRO	MNM: Középkori Régészeti Osztály / Department of Medieval Archaeology
MNM: LTM	MNM: Legújabbkori Történeti Múzeum / Museum of Modern History
MNM: MTKcs.	MNM: Magyar Történelmi Képcsarnok / Hungarian Historical Gallery
MNM: TFt.	MNM: Történeti Fényképtár / Historical Photo Archives
MOL	Magyar Országos Levéltár / Hungarian National Archives
MTA Kt.	A Magyar Tudományos Akadémia Könyvtára / Library of the Hungarian Academy of Sciences
MZsM	Magyar Zsidó Múzeum / Hungarian Jewish Museum
NZL&MI	László Z. Nagy & István Móricz
SzM–XX	Szépművészeti Múzeum, XX. századi Alapítvány / Museum of Fine Arts, Twentieth-century Art Foundation

A Hakdome

1. **Street vendors on Teleki tér**, 1912. The man on the right is wearing a *kapote*. (By the way, the Yiddish word *kapote* is the same as Hungarian *kabát*, both of them come from a Slavic language.) Photo: János Müllner, 1912. MNM: LTM. Photo Archives. (Inv. no. 59,891 ad 762/1948.)—Reproduction by JL&FÁ.

I. Castle Hill

2. **Mint**. Woodcut by Hans Burgkmair d. Ä. (1473–1531) for *Der Weisskunig*, the fictionalized (auto-)biography of Emperor Maximilian I (1493–1519), edited by Max Treitzsaurwein, the royal scribe, 1515. From: László Zolnay, *Kincses Magyarország. Középkori művelődésünk történetéből* [Treasures of Hungary. Facets of Our Cultural History in the Middle Ages] (Budapest: Magvető, 1977).

3. **Denarius of King Stephen (István) V** (1270–1272). Obverse. Enlargement. In the mint-mark or *tzurat ha-matbe'a*, the "picture (mint mark)" / "writing", the Hebrew letter *alef* can be seen. László Réthy, *Corpus nummorum Hungariae*, I (Budapest: M. Tud. Akadémia, 1899), no. 297. MNM Ét. (Inv. no. N.II.409.)—Photo: GCs.

4. **Denarius of King Stephen (István) V**. Obverse and reverse. Original size. Diameter: 1.3 cm. László Réthy, *Corpus nummorum Hungariae*, I, no. 297. MNM Ét. (Inv. no. N.II.409.)—Photo: GCs.

5. **Denarius of King Béla IV** (1235–1270). Obverse. Enlargement. In the mint-mark the Hebrew letter *pe* can be seen. László Réthy, *Corpus nummorum Hungariae*, I, no. 244. MNM Ét. (Inv. no. 4/B918-4.)—Photo: GCs.

6. **Denarius of Béla IV**. Obverse. Enlargement. In the mint-mark the Hebrew letter *mem* can be seen.

László Réthy, *Corpus nummorum Hungariae*, I, no. 241. MNM Ét. (Inv. no. Sz.I.54.9.)—Photo: GCs.

7. **The two Jewish streets and synagogues in the Castle Hill** of Buda. Map. From: László Zolnay, *Buda középkori zsidósága és zsinagógáik* [Jews in the Medieval Buda and Their Synagogues] (Budapest: Budapesti Történeti Múzeum, 1987).

8. **The earliest Jewish gravestone of Buda**, erected at the head of "Rav Pesah, son of Rav Peter", 5038 (= 1278 c.e.). Height: 68 cm, width: 72 cm. BTM. (Inv. no. 639.) Part of the exhibition showing the history of Budapest. From: Alexander Scheiber, *Jewish Inscriptions in Hungary* (1983), no. 21.—Photo: FA&LLL, 1994.

9. **Jewish gravestones** from the excavations in Buda on display in the former Lapidarium in the Round Bastion of the Fishermen's Bastion, which once housed the former collection of stone relics of the Municipal Museum (today the Budapesti Történeti Múzeum / Budapest Historical Museum). Second from the right: gravestone of Lady Freudel (see fig. **I:8**, and Ch. I, 14, below). From: MéJ (1933).—Repr.: NZL&MI.

10. **The new Jewish street** (today Táncsics Mihály utca) and the two synagogues on Castle Hill.
   1: The "small" synagogue (26 Táncsics Mihály utca)
   2: The "great" synagogue (23 Táncsics Mihály utca)
   3: The archway between the two buildings (see fig. **30**, below)

11. **A former memorial slab** commemorating the old Jewish street on the Castle Hill. Unveiled by the *Magyar Tudományos Akadémia Régészeti Bizottsága* (Archaeological Committee of the Hungarian Academy of Sciences), 1866/1868. From: MéJ (1937).—Repr.: NZL&MI.

The slab was originally placed on the wall of one of the houses on Szent György tér or in Szent György utca. According to Sámuel Kohn, it was "2 Szent György utca" (*A zsidók története Magyarországon*, 1884). The memorial slab was removed long ago and, in fact, also its place has disappeared in the meantime. The house on whose walls the slab was originally placed (in 1868, rather than in 1866 as suggested by the inscription itself) was purchased by Prince (Archduke) Josef Habsburg (1872–1962), together with the neighboring house (1892); later he demolished the houses (1902) and built his own palace. According to Endre Liber's catalogue of the memorial slabs in Budapest the slab was still visible "on the wall of the palace owned by Royal Duke Josef"; see *Budapest szobrai és emléktáblái* [Monuments and Commemorative Slabs of Budapest] (1934), p. 464. The palace was severely damaged in World War II and was demolished after the war. In a recent survey of historic monuments in Budapest the inscription of the slab is described as "unknown"; see Miklós Horler, *et al., Budapest műemlékei* [Historic Monuments of Budapest], I (1955), p. 588. It would thus seem that this photograph is the only surviving record of the former memorial slab.

The Hungarian inscription on the slab no. V runs in translation as follows:

"V.

"This street was called *zsidó utca* [Jewish street] until the reign of Sigismund (1424), *sz. Zsigmond utca* after the foundation of the church and provostship of St. Sigismund, and *vár utca* after the expulsion of the Turks in 1686. In this street, among others, the following owned houses: canonry of the St. Sigismund from 1424, Palatine Imre Perényi until 1518, and Tamás Pécsi until 1536.

"Archaeological Committee of the Hungarian Academy of Sciences, 1866."

"*sz. Zsigmond*": St. Zsigmond or Sigismund, after whom Zsigmond utca was named, was the patron saint of King and Emperor Sigismund (Zsigmond). His chapel ("the church of St. Zsigmond's provostship") stood on the northern side of Szent György tér.

On the initiative of Lajos György Arányi (1812–1877), a physician and university professor, around 1864 the Archaeological Committee of the Hungarian Academy of Sciences decided to mark the historic

monuments on Castle Hill with memorial slabs. The inscription on about four or five of the twenty slabs also mentions that the given area was settled by Jews in the Middle Ages. The texts on these slabs were edited by scholars of the period, such as Gusztáv Wenzel (1812–1891), a historian of law and university professor, Jakab Rupp (1800–1879), the erudite archivist, Ferenc Toldy (1805–1875), literary historian and university professor, and their work was greatly assisted by Flóris Rómer (1815–1889), a Benedictine monk, archaeologist and university professor, all of whom—with the exception of Rupp—were members of the Hungarian Academy of Sciences. These slabs—foreshadowing the spirit of the emancipation law (Act XVII of 1867)—clearly outlined the old and the new Jewish quarter in the Castle Hill district. Eight of the twenty slabs have since been lost (some without a trace), but the ones that have survived have been fully restored by the Municipal Inspectorate of Historic Monuments (1978). Arányi himself was a passionate antiquarian, and he collected a small museum in his home. For the history of the Jews in Buda he may become interested, beside that, perhaps also for personal reasons: he had family ties to the famous violinist József Joachim (1831–1907). For the history of the memorial slabs of the Academy see Anna B. Kaiser, "A budai Vár történelmi emléktábláiról" [About the Historical Commemorative Slabs of the Castle Hill of Buda], *Műemlékvédelem*, 22 (1978), pp. 302–306.

Other inscriptions referring to a Jewish presence on the Castle Hill:

Dísz tér (Inscription no. XIII). Its text runs:

"That part of the present-day Dísz tér, lying between the former Szent János kapu [St. John Gate], today Vizi kapu [Water Gate], the former Zsidó kapu [Jewish Gate] or Völgy kapu [Valley Gate], today Fehérvári kapu [Fehérvár Gate], where there was no guard post before and during the Turkish period, was called Szombathely (*vicus Sabbathi*). (The Bécsi kapu was called Szombat gate...) Archaeological Committee of the Hungarian Academy of Sciences 1866."

4 Hess András tér (today "Fortuna" restaurant and bar) (Inscription no. XX):

"This square was in olden times called Szent Miklós tér [St. Nicholas Square]. Bécsi utca, starting from here, used to be called Szent Miklós utca and later, (new) Zsidó utca [Jewish street] (...) Archaeological Committee of the Hungarian Academy of Sciences 1866."

7 Bécsi kapu tér (former residence of Baron Lajos Hatvany) (Inscription no. IX):

"Bécsi kapu [Vienna gate] was named by the Turks after 1541. It was formerly called Szombat gate. Under the reign of Charles (Károly) I the greater royal residence (*magna curia regis*) stood here, after it was transferred from Óbuda to Castle Hill. (...) Bécsi kapu utca was called Zsidó utca [Jewish street] under the Turks. The synagogue stood near the Vienna gate. Archaeological Committee of the Hungarian Academy of Sciences 1866."

12. **Pointed hat** (*Judenhut*) as a Jewish badge in a medieval prayer-book. A *hazzan* blowing the *shofar* during the New Year service. (See fig. **357**, below.) Oriental Collection of the MTA Kt. Kaufmann Collection. *Deutsches Machsor* (*Minhag Ashkenaz*) (Cat. no. A. 388), vol. II, p. 12, verso.—MTA Kt. Microfilm Archives and Photo Laboratory. Photo: Mrs. Tibor Kolthay.

13. **Portrait, probably of Jacob** (Jákob) **Mendel**, "Prefect of the Jews (*obrister der judischhait*)", on the seal of a document, a contract, 1496, published in: *Magyar-Zsidó Oklevéltár* (Monumenta Hungariae Judaica), I, no. 94. Enlargement (1 : 2.5). MOL. (Inv. no. 1496.24,575/D.1.24,757; now lost or misplaced.) Photo: Bernát Kumorovitz. From: András Kubinyi, *et al.*, *Budapest története a későbbi középkorban és a török hódoltság idején* [History of Budapest in the Late Middle Ages and in the Period of the Turkish Occupation] (1973).—Repr.: NZL&MI.

14. **Portrait of "Mandl Jvd"** (Mendel) on his green wax seal on a document, a receipt, 1496, published in: *Magyar-Zsidó Oklevéltár*, I, no. 166. Kassa (Košice, Slovakia), State Archives. (Old cat. no. B.572.) From: Ernő Munkácsi, *Libanon* (1941); Daniel M. Friedenberg, *Medieval Jewish Seals from Europe* (1987).—Repr.: NZL&MI.

15. "**Wedding procession of King Matthias** (Mátyás) and Beatrix to Buda in 1476." Lithograph by Béla Vizkelety, 1864. Béla Vizkelety's (1825–1864) work is "one of the finest historical graphic works of the period" (Teréz Gerszi). It shows the Jews awaiting the royal couple with a banner, a Torah scroll and the Two Tablets of the Law. (Instead of the customary two scrolls, there is only a single Torah scroll. The numbers of the Ten Commandments begin on the left tablet, in accordance with Christian practice.) The Jews all wear a striped prayer-shawl (*tallit*). The group is headed by the Prefect Jacob Mendel (wearing a prayer-shawl and riding a horse, with a straight-blade sword in his hand). The theme was no doubt drawn from Bonfini, and the artist's choice suggests that by the mid-nineteenth century the Jews in Hungary were searching for common strands with Hungarian historical tradition. The setting may correspond to the present-day Tabán. Lithograph; printed by [Alajos] Rohn & [Vilmos] Grund, 1864. 38.5 × 56 cm. MNM: MTKcs. (Inv. no. MTKCs. 1628.) Gerszi, pp. 92, 212, *sub* Vizkelety, no. 9 and fig. 94. Black-and-white photo in the MZsM.—Repr.: NZL&MI.

16. **Ground-plan of the "great" synagogue** on the Castle Hill, Buda. Reconstruction based on the excavations in 1964/65. Drawn by Aurél Budai. From: Aurél Budai, "Az elásott zsinagóga" [The Buried Synagogue], *Szombat*, 4 (1992), no. 8, pp. 4–5; "Középkori zsinagógák Budán" [Medieval Synagogues in Buda], MéJ, New Series, 4 (1993), no. 2, pp. 28–33.

Babits Mihály sétány (formerly called *An der langen Wand* / Várbástya / Bástyasétány / Horthy Miklós bástyasétány), in part lying over the rear gardens and buildings of medieval houses, attained its present form in 1936. Some of the buildings in the back courtyards were no doubt built against the fortification walls from the Middle Ages, the "great" synagogue being one of them.

17. **Cross-section of the "great" synagogue**. Design for the reconstruction of the building. Drawn by Aurél Budai. From: László Zolnay, *Buda középkori zsidósága és zsinagógáik* [Jews in the Medieval Buda and Their Synagogues] (Budapest: Budapesti Történeti Múzeum, 1987).

18. **Interior of the "great" synagogue**. Reconstruction of the building; timber ceiling version. The platform between the first and second pillars shows the original position of the rostrum or *bimah / almemor*. (If the figure on the right is a woman, as suggested by the drawing, it reflects a rather anachronistic view.) Drawn by Aurél Budai. From: MéJ (1993)

19. **Interior of the "great" synagogue**. Reconstruction, vaulted ceiling version. Drawn by Egon Pfannl. From: László Zolnay, *Buda középkori zsidósága és zsinagógáik* [Jews in the Medieval Buda and Their

Synagogues] (Budapest: Budapesti Történeti Múzeum, 1987).

20. **Remains of the southern, longitudinal wall** of the "great" synagogue, as revealed by the excavations in 1964/65. (The facade of the building on the former Zsidó utca.) The date, indicated by the letters *shin* and *alef* on the central pillar, is 301 (= 1541 C.E.). An excavation photo was published by Melinda T. Papp, *Acta Technica* (1970), p. 224, no. 16. From: László Zolnay, *Buda középkori zsidósága és zsinagógáik* [Jews in the Medieval Buda and Their Synagogues] (Budapest: Budapesti Történeti Múzeum, 1987).

21. **The Hebrew date inscription** on a central pillar in the "great" synagogue: *shin* and *alef*. (The mark between the two letters indicates abbreviation.) From: László Zolnay, *Buda középkori zsidósága és zsinagógáik* [Jews in the Medieval Buda and Their Synagogues] (Budapest: Budapesti Történeti Múzeum, 1987).

22. **Theological dispute between Christian and Jewish scholars**. Both parties draw their arguments from the Bible. The Jews are wearing *Judenhut*. Woodcut by Thomas Anshelm (ca. 1465–1524), a Swiss-German artist, late fifteenth century.—Jost Ammann, *Handwerker und Stände* (Frankfurt a. M., 1568).

At the height of his career, Anshelm lived in Pforzheim, in the same town as Johannes Reuchlin. Reuchlin spared no effort to win over Jews to Christian messianistic beliefs. Anshelm's woodcut illustrates the *dialogue*.

23. **Fragment of a page from a Hebrew codex**, possibly from Buda. The text on it is I Chronicles 1. Single page of a three-column Hebrew Bible codex, with a micrography of Hebrew letters depicting Adam (only his hand is visible) and Eve holding an apple (*rimmon*, "pomegranate"). Parchment (about two-thirds of the folio page that was recycled as cover filling of another book), thirteenth century. Formerly in the Festetich Archives (Keszthely), today MZsM. (Inv. no. Ipm.–64.633.) Published by Sándor Büchler, in: *Libanon* 7 (1943), fig. 15, *ante* p. 65; Sándor Scheiber, *Héber kódexmaradványok...* [Fragments of Hebrew Codices...] (1969). From: BI&SchS.—Repr.: NZL&MI.

24. **Imre Szerencsés's note in a Hebrew manuscript** (a commentary on Genesis), p. 1, recto. The text (top, right), written with Rashi letters: "This book belongs to me, and this is my name: Shelomo Shneur." From: Sándor Scheiber, *Folklór és tárgytörténet* [Essays on Jewish Folklore and Comparative Literature], II (1977).

According to Scheiber, Szerencsés recorded his name also on the title page of the manuscript, and beside it, the numeral 14, most likely denoting the serial number of the book in his library. "Who has learnt Torah, and whose fortune became the Torah"—reads another note of his on the last page.

The other remark (top, center) was added by a subsequent owner of the book: "3. Shelomo from Dubno" (Dubno, Volhynia; today Ukraine); the person in question was a follower of Moses Mendelssohn, who strongly criticized the Hasidic way of life (late eighteenth century). Jew's College, London. (Inv. no. 20.)

25. **The Fortunate One** (*fortunatus*). Man sitting under a canopy, on a wide, throne-like armchair, holding a thick money-pouch, with pages standing in front of him. The name *"Andolosia"* perhaps refers to Spain (Andalusia). Woodcut, sixteenth century. László Zolnay identified the man as Imre Szerencsés of Buda. From: László Zolnay, *Kincses Magyarország. Középkori művelődésünk történetéből* [Treasures of Hungary. Facets of Our Cultural History in the Middle Ages] (Budapest: Magvető, 1977).

26. **Jews and Turks defending Buda** against King Ferdinand's army, 1541. The siege was led by Wilhelm Roggendorf, a general of King Ferdinand (1526–1564). On the left, one of the men holds a banner depicting the *Judenhut*; on the right, a banner with a cross is held by the enemy. *"Warhafftige Anzeygung wie es im Leger vor Ofen ergangen ist.* M. D. XLI." Ilona Hubay, *Magyar és magyar vonatkozású röplapok, újságlapok, röpiratok az Országos Széchényi Könyvtárban* [Leaflets and Flyers pertaining to Hungary in the Collection of the National Széchényi Library], 1480–1718 (Budapest, 1948), no. 179. From: László Zolnay, *Buda középkori zsidósága és zsinagógáik* [Jews in the Medieval Buda and Their Synagogues] (Budapest: Budapesti Történeti Múzeum, 1987).

27. **Hebrew manuscript from Buda**: Yehudah ben Meir ha-Kohen, *Selihot mi-kol ha-shanah*. Place and date in the first colophon of the manuscript: *Oven* 403 (= 1643 C.E.). (The date is indicated by some of the letters dotted from above in the text of the colophon.) Paper manuscript with Turkish illumination. Mainz, Stadtbibliothek. From: Sándor Scheiber, *Héber kódexmaradványok...* [Fragments of Hebrew Codices...] (1969).—Repr.: NZL&MI.

28. **Hebrew manuscript from Buda**: Yehudah ben Meir ha-Kohen, *Selihot mi-kol ha-shanah*. Place and date in the second colophon of the manuscript:

Oven ha-birah (Fortress Buda), "in the five-thousand-four-hundred-and-third year" (= 1643 C.E.). Paper manuscript with Turkish illumination. Mainz, Stadtbibliothek. From: Sándor Scheiber, *Héber kódexmaradványok...* [Fragments of Hebrew Codices...] (1969).—Repr.: NZL&MI.

29. **Efraim ha-Kohen**, *Sha'ar Efraim*—first section of responsum 94, with the question: May a *kohen* enter the "great" synagogue if it is connected to the house on the opposite [side of the street] by an archway spanning over the Jewish street?—From the printed edition (Lemberg, 1887; reprint: Jerusalem, 1973).

30. **Covered passage-way in the Jewish street in Buda**. (Based on Efraim ha-Kohen's responsum 94.) (Schematic reconstruction.)—Drawn by Tamás Dezső.

The reconstruction is based on the assumption that a "roof" and perhaps a balustrade or side-wall was erected over the passage-way in order to provide passage from the building on one side of the street to the other side. R. Efraim's text suggests a reconstruction along these lines. It is, however, also possible that the arch had originally functioned as a buttress between opposing buildings, a practice that was quite common in medieval towns. The arch was covered with thatch in order to protect it from the rain. It is nonetheless a fact that R. Efraim specifically speaks of a passage between the two buildings; remains of the door, which opened onto the small bridge, have been identified during the excavations of the building.

31. **Hebrew inscriptions on the wall** of the "small" synagogue, mid-seventeenth century. Medieval Jewish Prayer-house.—Photo: FA, 1993.

32. **Inscription on Lady Sarah's gravestone**, 416 (= 1656 C.E.). Height: 59 cm, width: 51.5 cm. BTM: Medieval Jewish Prayer-house. (Inv. no. 114.) From: Alexander Scheiber, *Jewish Inscriptions in Hungary* (1983), no. 78.—Repr.: FBA.

33. **Map of Buda Castle** from the time of the siege, 1684. ("*Prospect der Festung Ofen, wie solche zu sehen von Alt Ofen wehrender Belagerung Anno 1684.*") The view is from Óbuda, i.e. from the North. According to the legend, no. 4 (the towered building on the right) is the *Iuden Kirch*, "Jewish Temple" (in fact, the Maria Magdolna Church). Engraving by an unknown artist, perhaps based on a drawing by a contemporary eye-witness, Louis Nicolas d' (/ von) Hallart. MZsM. (Inv. no. T.–64.1781.) MNM: MTKcs. From: Árpád Károlyi, *Buda és Pest visszavívása 1686-ban...* [The Recapture of Buda

and Pest in 1686] (1886), p. 201; and in that book's new edition, for the 250th anniversary revised by Imre Wellmann (Budapest: Budapest Székesfőváros kiadása, 1936), p. 137; MéJ (1934).—Repr.: NZL&MI.

The glaring error made by the cartographer suggests that the "temple" of the Buda Jews was known even beyond their community.

34. **The victorious troops plunder, pillage and shed blood** in Buda recaptured from the Turks, 1686. "The conquest of Buda (*Die Eroberung von Ofen*)." At the bottom of the picture, the title is set in a cartouche: "*Budam expugnatam janissariorum sanguine exundantem direptioni tradit Victor Carolus V. 2. Sept. 1686*", "Buda, captured and watered with the Janissaries' blood, is yielded to plunder by the victorious Charles V, September 2, 1686." Tapestry. 450 × 695 cm. Vienna, Kunsthistorisches Museum. (Inv. no. IX/13.) From: Rotraud Bauer, *Historische Schlachten auf Tapisserien aus dem Besitz des Kunsthistorischen Museums Wien. Ausstellung in Schloss Halbturn, 1976* (Eisenstadt: Amt der Burgenländischen Landesregierung, Kulturabteilung, 1976).

For the Habsburg dynasty the recapture of Buda in 1686 marked the end of the Turkish expansion in Europe. The series of medallions glorifying the Austrian Emperor Leopold I (1657–1705) (see fig. **35**, below) served to enhance imperial splendor and was part of the huge international reception of this momentous event. The military commanders, too, basked in the glory of the campaign.

Some of the relics commemorating the main events and individual episodes of the military campaign are relevant to the history of the Buda Jews; based on the collection in the Jewish Museum, these were published in Patai's *Múlt és Jövő* in the interwar period, but they were otherwise neglected in the recent publications that appeared on the 300th anniversary of the event (1986). The photographs published in MéJ were not accompanied by more detailed descriptions and thus the tapestries relating to history of the Jews will be described here at some length.

The general of the wars against the Turks, the real hero of the campaign was Prince Charles (V) of Lorraine (1643–1690); in order to commemorate the remarkable victory, his son, Prince Leopold Joseph Charles (1679–1729) had two series of tapestries (gobelin) woven, based on designs by French artists in the royal workshop in Nancy, under the supervision of Charles Mité (Mitté) (?–1736), the court weaver. These tapestries depicted episodes of the momentous events, the great battles, in the relatively new genre of the representational art of the royal courts, modeled on the art of the court in Versailles. Leopold Joseph's fondness for grand and precious carpets of artistic value can be attributed to his wife who was related to Louis XIV, the Sun King. The design of these carpets was modeled on sketches made by Charles / Karl Herbel (ca. 1659-1702), a painter from Lorraine. Herbel was, for a long period of time, part of the Prince's entourage, and the Prince perhaps took him along on his campaigns, enabling him to work on the spot. (Some of the sketches have survived; they are now housed in the Hofburg Museum of Innsbruck, Charles's former seat.) The tapestries were brought to Vienna on the occasion of the wedding of Maria Theresa and Francis Stephen, Prince of Lorraine, later Emperor Francis I (1745-1765), held in 1736; these remained in imperial possession and they were still used as decorations for court and ecclesiastic functions as late as the Austro-Hungarian Dual Monarchy. In the age of the Dual Monarchy the imperial court displayed two pieces from both series in the Castle of Buda, in the wing of the royal palace built in 1896-1903 by Alajos Hauszmann, above the staircase and in the buffet hall. These four tapestries were still in Buda in the interwar period, until the end of World War II. (A few pieces of the series were shown in temporary exhibitions, some staged in Budapest, after World War II.)

All four carpets kept in Budapest disappeared without a trace after World War II. The latter is the only one which has turned up, appearing on the antiquities market in Switzerland. It eventually ended up in Nancy (Musée Historique Lorraine). It was no doubt taken to the West and sold for profit by persons who in the summer and fall of 1944 had access to the treasures of the Royal Palace. The story, should its details ever come to surface, will no doubt be even more mysterious than that of the Hungarian royal crown.

Two of these tapestries have an indirect relevance to Jewish history in that they depict the plundering of the captured town: on both carpets, the Jewish quarter of Buda can be made out in the background and the depiction of the merciless destruction confirms the gruesome details in Izsák Schulhof's account in Hebrew.

The first, smaller series (1703-1710) incorporated 5 relatively small tapestries: three of them are now in Vienna (Kunsthistorisches Museum), two were brought to Buda in 1903. One of these was no. 2 in

the series. Interestingly enough, in Hungary nobody seems to have been offended by its title, nor by its symbolic message: "The destruction and plundering of Buda (*Pillage et saccagement de Bude/Die Plünderung von Ofen*)."

This tapestry, most likely based on Herbel's cartoon, was woven in Mité's workshop. The same composition was reproduced in an oil painting by an unknown painter, perhaps also by Herbel or—as previously thought—by F. J. Textor; entitled *"Buda vi capta et ferro et igne vastata*, Buda, Occupied by force, Devastated by Iron and Fire", it is now in the Hofburg Museum in Innsbruck. (Inv. no. J-7-7811.)

Before it reached Buda, the tapestry was exhibited on the 200th anniversary of the siege (1886), as well at the millennial exhibition (1896). Its picture was first published by Károlyi & Wellmann, *Buda és Pest visszavívása* (1936), p. 379. It reached a wider audience, however, through the engraving based on the oil painting by Gusztáv Morelli (1848-1909), now in the collection of the Hofburg in Innsbruck, published also in *Az osztrák-magyar Monarchia írásban és képben: Magyarország* [The Austro-Hungarian Monarchy in Text and in Pictures: Hungary], III (Budapest: M. kir. Államnyomda, 1893).

The second, larger series, which originally comprised 19 large tapestries, was designed by renowned French artists of the period. The tapestries were in part woven in the royal workshop (1709-1718) and in part in the La Malgrange factory in Nancy. The carpet shown here, depicting "The Recapture of Buda (*Die Eroberung von Ofen*)", is no. 13 in this series. In Hungary it was first published in *Vasárnapi Újság*, 33 (1886), no. 34 (August 22), p. 545. It was based on a chalk drawing (petit carton) (29.6 × 45.3 cm) by Jean-Baptiste Martin / Martin-des-Batailles (ca. 1659-1735), entitled *"Le sac de la ville de Bude"*, now in the Albertina in Vienna (Inv. no. 10,096). Both the design and the tapestry were made in Nancy (1713). In accordance with earlier views, Árpád Károlyi attributed the design ("sketch")— erroneously, as it turns out—to the renowned painter of battle scenes, Adam Franz van der Meulen (1632-1690).

The two tapestries showing the plundering and ransacking of Buda (no. 2 in the smaller series and no. 13 in the larger series), somewhat unusually, portray the bloodbath and cruelties of the siege and in this respect they confirm Izsák Schulhof's account of the same events. Both tapestries—in this case no. 13 of the larger series—

show the streets of the Castle Hill, viewed from Szent György tér. Charles, Prince of Lorraine, is shown riding his horse a little to the right from the center of the picture.

In the background lies the Jewish quarter of Buda with the Zsidó utca (Jewish street), burning houses and corpses on the street. In fact, the decisive battle of the siege was fought in the Zsidó utca, at its northern end: Abdurrahman, the Pasha of Buda, tried to hold up the besieging troops, himself falling in battle. The most bloody events of the battle have been recorded by Johann Dietz of Brandenburg, an army doctor in the besieging army: "...Not even the babies in their mother's wombs were spared. All were sent to their deaths. I was quite horrified by what was done here. Men were far more cruel to each other than wild beasts (*Bestien*)." Wellmann himself (Károlyi & Wellmann, p. 374) felt the need to quote Izsák Schulhof to confirm these words.

There is a rich special literature on the engravings and tapestries depicting the recapture of Buda; most reliable among these is György Rózsa, *Schlachtbilder aus der Zeit der Befreiungsfeldzüge* (Budapest: Akadémiai Kiadó, 1987).

35. **Turk and Jew** (wearing a *Judenhut*) in the Buda mint. A sarcastic medal minted on the occasion of the recapture of Buda, 1686. On the obverse: a furnace, beside which stand a turbaned Turk putting a crucible into the furnace and a Jew (wearing a *Judenhut*) working the bellows. Made by Martin Brunner of Nuremberg (1659–1725). Silver, bronze, copper and tin coins, 4.2 cm in diameter. From: MéJ (1937).—Repr.: NZL&MI.

There are three German inscriptions on the coin.

On the obverse: "*Wer distillirt nun Geld zum Fried. Weil Türck und Iud des Krieges müd.*" In translation: "Who for peace now distills money. Both Jew and Turk of war are weary."

On the reverse, a four-line poem:

"Ofen gehört für Leopold.
Mahumeth ist das Glück abhold.
Verlieret Ofen samt dem Gold,
dafür man Frieden kauffen solt.
An. 1686."

In translation: "Buda will now be Leopold's, – Mahomet's chances are lost, – lost is Buda, gone is the gold, – with which peace could have been bought. An(no) 1686."

Along the edge: "*Durch diesen Streit das Turcken Reich steht auf der Neig.*" In translation: "In this strife the Turkish empire will lose its stride."

For this coin, and several other issues minted on the occasion of the 1686 siege, see Ödön Gohl, *Budapest emlékérmei*, I: *Buda 1686-iki visszavételének emlékérmei* [Commemorative Medallions from Budapest, I: Commemorative Medallions of the Recapture of Buda in 1686] (Offprint from *Budapest Régiségei*, vols 6–7) (Budapest, 1899), no. 73; Lajos Huszár, *A régi magyar emlékérmek katalógusa a legrégibb időktől 1850-ig* [Catalogue of Old Hungarian Commemorative Medallions from the Earliest Times to 1850], I: *Történeti érmek*, 3. *Újkor* (1657–1705) [Medallions on Historical Events, 3. (Early) Modern Times (1657–1705)] (Az éremgyűjtők szakkiadványsorozata, 5. csoport, no. 12) (Budapest: Magyar Éremgyűjtők Egyesülete, 1975), no. 520.

36. **A Jewish flyer urging the redemption of the Jews** captured in Buda, 1686. A *news*-letter by Sender (Alexander / Sándor) Taussig / Tauszk of Prague. Print. Formerly: Breslau, Stadtbibliothek. From: MéJ (1937).—Repr.: NZL&MI.

The woodcut decorating the print depicts Moses on Mt. Sinai, surrounded by Jews in the desert—that is, as the message suggests, delivered from the Egyptian slavery.

The text (top right of picture):

"Moses was designated as a redeemer (*go'el*), and he is the first among the redeemers. But I too am perhaps one of them. For I have redeemed [from the Holy community of Oven] those who have remained and escaped (*she'erit ha-peletah*) (I Chronicles 4,43) from death unto life. May my God record this as my good deed."

I:1. **Castle Hill**: **Interior of the Medieval Jewish Prayer-house** (the former "small" synagogue). For the Hebrew inscriptions on the wall see fig. **31**, above.—Photo: FA, 1993.

I:2. **Jewish male attire from Transylvania**, seventeenth century. The dress has a definite Turkish character. Transylvanian Jews, invited there from the Turkish-occupied territories by Prince Gábor Bethlen (1613–1629), were for the greater part of Sephardi origin—from Spain in olden times, living in Turkey after the expulsion. According to Bethlen's Charter of Privilege (1623) they were forbidden to wear Christian clothing, hence they followed their own tradition that adopted some Turkish elements. (Fur caps, baggy trousers, slippers, kaftans, while women wore necklaces strung with gold coins, a type common in the Balkans.) The costume of the Sephardi Jews of Buda no doubt resembled this costume. Drawing from an English costume-book. *The True & Exact Dresses & Fashions of All the Nations in Transylvania*. London, British Library, Manuscript Collections, Add. MSS 5257, no. 49: "*A Jew Merchant*". Drawing by an unknown English (?) artist, ca. 1700. From: Géza Galavics, József Jankovics & Ágnes Várkonyi, *Régi erdélyi viseletek. Viseletkódex a XVII. századból* [Old Transylvanian Costumes. A Costumes Album from the Seventeenth Century] (Budapest: Európa Könyvkiadó, 1990). CsZs&DZ. (Inv. no. CsZs. 9/1.)

On another "Hungarian Jew" in a Turkish-type costume see a watercolor picture, probably from a similar Costume album, in the Jerusalem Institute for Islamic Art, dated from 1587, in: Esther Juhasz, Ed., *Sephardi Jews in the Ottoman Empire. Aspects of Material Culture* (Jerusalem: The Israel Museum, 1990), Plate 22a.

I:3. **Jewish female attire from Transylvania**, seventeenth century. *The True & Exact Dresses & Fashions of All the Nations in Transylvania*. London, British Library etc., no. 50: "*A Jew's Wife*". From: Géza Galavics, József Jankovics & Ágnes Várkonyi, *Régi erdélyi viseletek* [Old Transylvanian Costumes] (1990). CsZs&DZ. (Inv. no. CsZs. 9/2.)

I:4. **Sword, engraved with Hebrew inscription**, and its scabbard, seventeenth century. From the former collection of Count Manó Andrássy in the Andrássy-Almássy Palace at 42 Esterházy utca–13 Múzeum utca (today 2 Esterházy utca). MZsM. Length: 84 cm, width of blade: 3 cm. (Inv. no. Ipm.–64.1110.) Alexander Scheiber, *Jewish Inscriptions in Hungary* (1983), no. 148.—Photo: FA&LLL, 1994.

I:5. **Hebrew inscription on the sword blade**. (For the text see pp. 12 f., above.) MZsM.—Photo: FA&LLL, 1994.

I:6-7. **A wedding ring with Hebrew inscription** (one word to the right of the "tent" or "roof", the other to the left): *Mazzal tov*, "Good luck." (See p. 38, above.) Diameter: ca. 3 cm, thickness: ca. 1.7 cm. MNM: KRO. (Inv. no. 9/1861.) From: Alexander Scheiber, *Jewish Inscriptions in Hungary* (1983), no. 147.—Photo: FA&LLL, 1994.

I:8. **Inscription on Lady Freudel's gravestone**, 432 (= 1672 c.e.). (See pp. 36 ff., above.) Height: 163 cm, width 67 cm. BTM: Medieval Jewish Prayer-house.

(Inv. no. 120.) From: Alexander Scheiber, *Jewish Inscriptions in Hungary* (1983), no. 87.—Photo: FA&LLL, 1994.

II. Óbuda

37. **Portrait of R. Pinhas Leib Freudiger**, *dayyan* of Óbuda. From: MéJ (1933).—Repr.: NZL&MI.

The Freudiger family moved to Óbuda from Moravia, sometime around the last third of the eighteenth century. Pinhas Leib received his family name, according to family tradition, because of his talent as a preacher in Óbuda: he was named *Prediger*, "preacher", receiving or adopting the name *Freudiger* in consequence of Joseph II's Germanization decree.

According to the decrees in effect during the eighteenth century in Moravia—in the Czech-Moravian province—and confirmed by Maria Theresa (1748), only one son in each Jewish family that had a residence permit was allowed to marry. If other sons in the family chose to marry, their residence permit was revoked. Many of those affected by this decree moved to Hungary, where this restriction did not apply, often just with the intent of circumventing this decree. The Moravian background—German language and culture, industrial profession, trade ventures and contacts in German-speaking countries—characterized a significant portion of Hungarian Jewry.

38. **Portrait of Mózes óbudai Freudiger**. From: MéJ (1911).—Repr.: NZL&MI.

The Freudiger family became an owner of the Lindenbaum textile plant when Mózes Freudiger married into the Lindenbaum family.

39. **Portrait of Ábrahám óbudai Freudiger**, president of the Budapest Orthodox community. From: MéJ (1924).—Repr.: NZL&MI.

For Ábrahám Freudiger wearing Hungarian national gala dress see fig. **433**, below.

40. **The Óbuda synagogue**, ca. 1899. Candelabra, a brick and iron fence in front of the building. The buildings of the Jewish community and various residential buildings are next to the synagogue. From: *The Jewish Encyclopedia*, 1 (New York & London: Funk & Wagnalls, 1906).—Repr.: NZL&MI.

41. **The Óbuda synagogue**, ca. 1920. The new ornamentation of the tympanum was designed by Gyula Ullmann in 1900, when the synagogue was renovated. There were residential buildings on both sides of the synagogue. Photo. 9 × 12 cm. BTM: KM. Photo Archives. (Inv. no. 730.)—Repr.: MA.

A similar photo of the Óbuda synagogue, but with a huge menorah in front of the building, from 1930 (BTM), was published recently by Éva Gál, in: Csongor Kiss & Ferenc Mocsy, Eds., *Óbuda évszázadai* [Centuries of Óbuda] (Budapest: Kortárs Kiadó, 1995), p. 382; *Budapesti Negyed,* no. 8 (1995).

42. **The Óbuda synagogue**, ca. 1960. From: Miklós Horler, *et al., Budapest műemlékei* [Historic Monuments of Budapest], II (1962).—Repr.: NZL&MI.

The rapid deterioration of the building's exterior following World War II, despite some renovation work in 1947, may be observed, if this photo is compared to the one published by József Katona in 1949, in *A 90 éves Dohány-utcai templom* [The 90-year-old Dohány utca Temple] (1949), Pl. VI, no. 10.

43. **The Óbuda synagogue**, 1981. Photo: Carol H. Krinsky. From: Carol H. Krinsky, *Europas Synagogen. Architektur, Geschichte und Bedeutung* (Stuttgart: Deutsche Verlags-Anstalt, 1988).—Repr.: NZL&MI.

44. **Interior of the Óbuda synagogue**. The original part of the building, view from the East (the Ark). There is a partition screen (*mehitzah*) in front of the women's gallery. The rostrum or *bimah* stands at the center of the synagogue. From: Miklós Horler, *et al., Budapest műemlékei* [Historic Monuments of Budapest], II (1962).—Repr.: NZL&MI.

45. **Rostrum or bimah / almemor** in the Óbuda synagogue. From: Miklós Horler, *et al., Budapest műemlékei* [Historic Monuments of Budapest], II (1962).—Repr.: NZL&MI.

46. **The former building of the Óbuda synagogue** now occupied by the studio of the Hungarian Television, 1993. The huge aluminum container in front of the building has been an eyesore for years.—Photo: FA&LLL, 1992.

47. **Ground-plan of the Óbuda synagogue**, showing the additions in 1822. From: Gazda.

48. **Ark-shaped wall candelabrum** from the former Jewish Museum of Óbuda (formerly 9 Zichy utca). Earlier in the Simon Weisz collection. From: MéJ (1915).—Repr.: NZL&MI.

49. **The sermon of R. Moshe Minc** (Moses Münz) at the consecration of the Óbuda synagogue. The title page of the published version reads: "Holiday sermon on the occasion of the consecration of the magnificent prayer-house of the Holy community of *Oven*, belonging to the Yeshurun community—may God protect it—, held by the leader of the *beit din* and the leader of our community (...) Moshe Minc", etc. (Wien: Anton Strauss k. k. [königlich-kaiserlicher] privil. [privilegisierter] Buchdrucker, 1822).—

Yeshurun mentioned here is Israel (Deuteronomy 32,15). For R. Münz's portrait see fig. **74**, below. Library of the Rabbinical Seminary, Budapest.—Repr.: FBA.

In the center of the title page, left, the stamp of R. Sám(uel) (Löw) Brill of Pest can be seen.

50. **Torah shield** from the former Jewish Museum of Óbuda. The place of the plaque showing the weekly portion (*shilt*) is empty. MZsM. (Inv. no. Ipm.-64.83.) From: Miklós Horler, *et al., Budapest műemlékei* [Historic Monuments of Budapest], II (1962).—Repr.: NZL&MI.

Generally, a plaque inscribed with the word *Shabbat* was used for the normal weekly portion, and separate *shiltim*, each with two names, were made for the holidays.

51. **Torah crown** from the Óbuda synagogue, 1806. Each of the two *rimmonim*, "pomegranates", have twelve bells, arranged in three rows. There is a Hebrew inscription engraved on the base of the crown: "A pious donation to the Holy congregation of Óbuda in the year 566 according to the minor era (= 1806 C.E.)." Partially gilt silver, embossed, chased. With a Pest hallmark from the years 1774–1781; mark of János Mihály Schwager. Height: 43.5 cm. (Inv. no. Ipm.-64.45.) Photo: László Szelényi. From: BI&SchS.—Repr.: NZL&MI.

The crown (*keter*) on the Torah scroll, on the curtain of the Ark, etc. reflects the status of the Torah, as legally binding: the strength of the Torah is at least equal to the power of the King. The pomegranates (*rimmonim*) topping the staves (*etz hayyim*) of the Torah scrolls represent the Garden of Eden in the East (Genesis 2,8 ff.). There are two *rimmonim* because the scroll is rolled onto two staves.

52. **Torah pointer** (*yad*) from the Óbuda synagogue, 1837. The inscription engraved on the stem reads: "Holy Society of (Ó)buda (*Oven*)." Length: 29 cm. MZsM. (Inv. no. Ipm.-64.81.) Silver, chased. With an Óbuda hallmark (1836): mark of Fülöp Adler. Photo: László Szelényi. From: BI&SchS.—Repr.: NZL&MI.

The chain at the upper end of the *taitel* (*teitelboym*) or *yad* is used for hanging the pointer onto the left stave of the scroll (containing the next portion of the text) after the dressing of the Torah.

53. **Torah finials**: *rimmonim*, "pomegranates", from the Óbuda synagogue, ca. 1800. With a Pest hallmark (ca. 1800): mark of Ferenc Pasperger. Both *rimmonim* have bells. An engraved Hebrew inscrip-

tion around the base runs: "Piously donated to the Holy Society (Hevrah Kaddishah) of Óbuda by Mordekhai Blau, son of Akiva—of blessed memory—and by his wife Fradl (Freudel), daughter of Mendel, in the year 600 according to the minor era (= 1840 C.E.)." (A later engraving, probably by the occasion of the donation.) Height: 43 cm. MZsM. (Inv. no. Ipm.-64.67/1-2.) Photo: László Szelényi. From: BI&SchS.—Repr.: NZL&MI.

54. **Torah shield** from the Óbuda synagogue, 1840. In the center, the Two Tablets of the Law (*shenei luhot*) with the first words of the Ten Commandments. The inscription in the plate (*shilt*): *Pesah*. (The two sides of similar *shilts* are usually inscribed with the words *Sukkot* and *Pesah*.) The edge of the upper, bell-shaped part is inscribed with a Hebrew text: "To the Holy Society of Óbuda in the year 600 according to the minor era (= 1840 C.E.)." With a Viennese hallmark: mark of Friedrich Laubenbacher d. J. 50 × 32.5 cm. MZsM. (Inv. no. Ipm.-64.53.) Photo: László Szelényi. From: BI&SchS.—Repr.: NZL&MI.

55. **Portrait of Leó budai Buday-Goldberger**, 1941. MNM: LTM. Photo Archives. (Inv. no. 34,871.)—Repr.: JL&FÁ.

56. **The visit of His Majesty Francis Joseph I** at the Goldberger factory in Óbuda, 1857. From Winter's Jewish calendar [*Illustriertes israelitisches Jahrbuch*, 1859]. From: MéJ (1916); László Kállai, *A 150 éves Goldberger-gyár* [The 150-year-old Goldberger Industrial Plant] (1935).

A number of valuable lithographs with Jewish themes were published by the printing house of Sámuel Winter (1824–1903), a lithographer active in Pest. These include a portrait of R. Löw (Arszlán) Schwab (1857) (see fig. **121**, below), that of Gyula Rózsavölgyi (1859, 1861), the charter of the Hevrah Kaddishah with a view of the Jewish hospital in Pest, etc. See Gerszi, p. 217.

57. **The kosher restaurant** (*Gasthaus*) of M. Guttman in Óbuda (28 Zsigmond utca), early twentieth century. Beside it, workshop of a cabinet-maker and the shop of Stowasser, the "imperial and royal provisioner and musical-instrument maker"; on the left, the shop of a scrap-iron merchant on the corner. The signboard of the restaurant has the word *kosher* painted in Hebrew letters. There is a gas lamp in front of the restaurant. Photo. 6 × 9 cm. MNM: LTM. Photo Archives. (Inv. no. 22,861.)—Repr.: MA.

The Stowasser store sold products of that renowned musical instrument factory in Buda; the

company, founded by János Stowasser in 1770, was located at the corner of Lánchíd utca and Sikló utca, and had just a few employees, working with painstaking craftsmen's techniques. It had a standing contract with the Opera House and the army. It remained active until World War II.

58. **Jewish courtyard** (*Judenhof*) in Óbuda. Street view, early twentieth century. From: MéJ (1933).—Repr.: NZL&MI.

59. **Portrait and signature of József Manes Oesterreicher.** From: Ignaz Reich, *Beth-El*, I (1868).

60. **Facade of the building used as the Jewish school**, Óbuda, 1774. *Faciale des so genanten Gemein Müllnerischen Juden Hauses in Alt-Ofen*, "The facade of the Jewish house called community mill in Óbuda." From: Éva Gál, in: *Évkönyv*, 1975/76.

61. **Design of the future Jewish school** for the rebuilding of the Hollitscher House in Óbuda, 1789. From: Éva Gál, in: *Évkönyv* 1975/76.

Erklärung / Explanation:

A: *Grundriss der zu errichten angetragenen Schulgebäude*, "Ground-plan for the school building to be built."

B: *Der Juden Gemeinde zu benützen verbleibender Zinstheil*, "Premises remaining in the use of the Jewish community."

C: *Provil nach der Lienie am m(eridian)*, "Section along the m(eridian) line."

62. **Beaker of the Hevrah Kaddishah** of Óbuda, eighteenth century. Partially gilt silver, engraved and embossed. The Hebrew inscriptions run as follows: "This chalice belongs to the Holy Society of Óbuda, crafted in 509 (= 1749 C.E.)."—"Donated by the noble Gumpel, the noble Wolf and the noble Gershom, three officials (*katzin*) of the Holy Society."—"A gift for eternal time to the Hevrah Kaddishah from me, Moses Hollitscher, in the year 638 according to the minor era (= 1878 C.E.)." The mark on the rim: IM (?). Height: 16.2 cm, diameter 9.5 cm, 7.7 cm. MZsM. (Inv. no. Ipm.-64.130.) Photo: László Szelényi. From: BI&SchS.—Repr.: NZL&MI.

63. **Goblet from the Óbuda synagogue**, early eighteenth century. With an engraved Hebrew inscription: "Property of the Hevrah Kaddishah of Óbuda, 1874." Embossed silver. With a Buda hallmark (1851): mark of József Gretschl jr. Height: 28.5 cm, diameter: 9.5 cm, 11.5 cm. MZsM. (Inv. no. Ipm.-64.68.) Photo: László Szelényi. From: BI&SchS.—Repr.: NZL&MI.

64. **Tankard from the Óbuda synagogue**, eighteenth century. Engraved Hebrew inscription under the

rim: "Behold the old tankard. Purchased by the officials of the Hevrah Kaddishah of Óbuda in the year 552 (= 1792 C.E.)." Embossed silver. With an Augsburg hallmark: mark of MS (?). Height: 21.5 cm, diameter: 9.5 cm, 10.5 cm. MZsM. (Inv. no. Ipm.-64.136.) Photo: László Szelényi. From: BI&SchS.—Repr.: NZL&MI.

65. **Gravestones in the old Jewish cemetery** in Óbuda, Laktanya utca, ca. 1920. Photo: Mór Erdélyi. From: Miklós Horler, *et al.*, *Budapest műemlékei* [Historic Monuments of Budapest], II (1962).—Repr.: NZL&MI.

66. **Mortuary in the Laktanya utca cemetery**. From: MéJ (1934).—Repr.: NZL&MI.

67. **Gravestones in the Laktanya utca cemetery**, ca. 1920. Photo: Mór Erdélyi. 6 × 9 cm. MNM: LTM. Photo Archives. (Inv. no. 22,135.)—Repr.: MA.

68. **Triple gravestone** (husband, wife, child) in the Laktanya utca cemetery, 1796. From: MéJ (1933).—Repr.: NZL&MI.

69. **"The former Jewish cemetery in Óbuda"**, that is, the Pálvölgyi Jewish cemetery. Drawing of Imre Ámos, 1936. Ink, brush. 39.6 × 32.5 cm. SzM-XX. (Inv. no. V.P.31.)

70. **"The cemetery at the feet of Mount Matthias (Mátyás-hegy)"** (that is, the Pálvölgyi Jewish cemetery). (For the location of the cemetery see fig. **II:4**, below.) Photo: Richárd Margittay. From: MéJ (1938).—Repr.: NZL&MI.

71. **"The cemetery under Mount Matthias"** (that is, the Pálvölgyi Jewish cemetery). Photo: Richárd Margittay. From: MéJ (1938).—Repr.: NZL&MI.

72. **Portrait of R. Gyula Wellesz**. From: Sándor Scheiber, *Folklór és tárgytörténet* [Essays on Jewish Folklore and Comparative Literature], I (1977).—Repr.: NZL&MI.

73. **Portrait of R. Moshe Abeles**, *dayyan* of Óbuda. From: MéJ (1933).—Repr.: FBA.

74. **Portrait of Moshe Minc** (Moses Münz), chief rabbi of Buda (*"Ober Rabbiner zu Ofen"*). The original Hebrew inscription of the portrait reads: "Rabbi, great *ga'on*, renowned person (*mefursam*)." Portrait by Sámuel Lehnhardt (ca. 1790–after 1840). Engraving by János Donát (1744–1830). MZsM. From: MéJ (1916).—Repr.: NZL&MI.

75. **R. Aaron Chorin's advice to his generation**: Title pages of two of his books.

Left: *Davar be-itto. Ein Wort zu seiner Zeit* (Wien: Anton Strauss k. k. privil. Buchdrucker, 1820). The text of the title page says: "Advice to his generation. What is correct (literally: 'good')? It is made up of two components. The (one) component is Torah (i.e. the teaching), the (other) component is piety (*avodah*). For my brethren, the Children of Israel. For those who know Hebrew: in their tongue, for those who do not understand Hebrew words, in Ashkenazi (i.e. Yiddish)." The author's name on the title page (spelt according to the Yiddish): *Aharon Horiner*. Library of the Rabbinical Seminary, Budapest.—Repr.: FBA.

Right: Title page of Chorin's book published in Prague: *Sefer Emek ha-shaveh* (1803). The title, as noted also by the censor allowing its publication, refers to a Biblical toponym (Genesis 14,17): After vanquishing the kings of the East who had attacked the cities around the Dead Sea (Genesis 14), Abram (Abraham) is greeted with bread and wine by Melchizedek (*Malki-tzedek*), king of Salem. Library of the Rabbinical Seminary, Budapest.—Repr.: FBA.

76. **Portrait of Aaron Chorin**, chief rabbi of Arad. From: MéJ (1917).—Repr.: NZL&MI.

II:1. **Óbuda: Town map**. *Buda és Pest térképe* [Map of Buda and Pest], 1831. (Detail.) The building farthest to the North of the town on the right bank of the Danube is perhaps the Óbuda synagogue. E. K. Fruhwirth & Leó Torsch, after Sámuel Blaschnek. 61.5 × 90.5 cm (the entire map). Gerszi, p. 139, sub Fruhwirth, no. 2. MNM: MTKcs. (Inv. no. MTKCs. T.3419.)—Photo: NZL&MI, 1994.

II:2. **The Temple of the Israelites in Óbuda**: "*Az izraeliták temploma Óbudán / Der Israelitische Tempel in Altofen.*" Count Karl [Károly / Carlo Pino] Vasquez, *Buda és Pest szabad királyi várossainak tájleírása* [Topography of Free Royal Cities of Buda and Pest]. Prepared in 1837. Printed in 1838. Sheet II: Franz Weiss's color picture in the frame around the map (in the left lower corner). Four sheets (out of six) of the oversize (83.5 × 64 cm) map were reproduced in a recent book by Szilvia Andrea Holló, *Budapest régi térképeken, 1686-1896* [Budapest on Old Maps, 1686-1896] (Budapest: Officina Nova, 1994); this sheet in no. 10, pp. 36-37. MNM: MTKcs. (Inv. no. MTKCs. T.1383.)—Photo: NZL&MI, 1994.

Recently Éva Gál has published valuable new information on the early history of the Jewish community and its synagogue in Óbuda, based on her archival researches. The Jews were apparently settled in the community by Count Péter Zichy (ca. 1710); in one of his handwritten notes he lists that among his merits in bringing prosperity to Óbuda was "the transportation of Jews thereupon". The first Jewish judge in Óbuda was Marcus Mandel from (Pilis-) Vörösvár. According to the census of 1727, the twenty-four Jewish families had their own teacher (this was no doubt a *melammed* who, as shown by the difficulties in connection with staffing the schools set up following the decree of Joseph II in the late eighteenth century, had no secular training). The community also had a ritual slaughterer. By this time, the prayer-house for which license was given by Zsuzsanna Bercsényi, Péter Zichy's widow, had also been built. However, the inheritance strife that broke out between the widow and the son born to Zichy from his earlier marriage also affected the Jewish community. The son, Count Ferenc Zichy, at the time the canon of the Nagyvárad Roman Catholic bishopric, wanted to seize Óbuda for himself. His men attacked the Jewish school at Óbuda and he forced the residents of the town to participate in the attack. The Royal Court of Appeal later ordered an investigation; the statements of the witnesses contain valuable information: "They set upon that school with axes and iron hooks. (...) Whatever they found there, they seized as booty. (...) Whoever found something, could take it freely." "A Jew by the name Hirsl (Hirschl) in the school was stabbed by the soldiers with their guns." Lakits, priest of the Óbuda Roman Catholic parish, who was also present at the destruction of the school (i.e. of the *shul*, the prayer-house), had to leave after this incident. Zsuzsanna Bercsényi continued to extend seignorial protection over the Jewish community which she later confirmed in a contract (1732). After her death her son, Count Miklós Zichy, and after his death his widow, Erzsébet Bercsényi, maintained the legal relation with the Óbuda Jewish community and there were no serious disputes even after the community came under the control of the Crown. The Óbuda synagogue is itself proof of its legal status.

II:3. **Ark curtain** (*parokhet*) from the Óbuda synagogue, 1772. Green silk velvet, decorated with relief embroidery, with green silk and metal thread. Donated by the Boskovitz family. The letters above the lions holding the crown are the Hebrew letters K"T, an abbreviation for *keter Torah*, "Crown of the Torah". 242 × 164 cm. MZsM. (Inv. no. Ipm.–64.1475.) —Photo: FA, 1994.

II:4. **Óbuda: Location of the old "Israelite cemetery"** (Pálvölgyi Jewish cemetery) in the Pálvölgy-Mátyás-hegy–Zöldmál triangle. (For photos of the

cemetery see figs. **70–71**, above.) *Budapest székes-főváros és környékének térképe* [Map of the Capital Budapest and Its Vicinity] (Eggenberger-féle könyvkereskedés: Hoffmann & Vastagh, 1909). (Detail.)— Repr.: NZL&MI.

III. Király utca: The Old-Old Jewish Quarter of Pest

77. **"The *Újpiacz*** [New Market / Erzsébet tér] in Pest." Drawing by Rudolf Alt (1812–1905), 1845. On the right, the houses of the former Fürdő utca (today József Attila utca). From: *Buda-Pest. Előadva 32 eredeti rajzolatban Alt Rudolf által* [Buda-Pest. Presented in 32 Original Drawings by Rudolf Alt]. Drawn by [Franz Xaver] Sandmann, published by János Rauch (Pest: Konrád Adolf Hartleben, 1845). 15.8 × 21.1 cm. MNM: MTKcs. (Inv. no. MTKCs. T.2844-Alt színtelen.)—Photo: NZL&MI, 1994.

78. **Market on the Pest quay** on the Danube bank in the 1840's. In the background the Gellért-hegy. Lithograph after a drawing by Henrik Weber in Gábor Prónay, *Skizzen aus dem Volksleben in Ungarn*, 1855. FSzEKt.: BpGy. From: Éva Faragó, *A reformkori Buda-Pest* [Buda-Pest in the Reform Period] (Budapest: Enciklopédia, 1996), p. 66.

79. **View of the Orczy House** from Károly körút. Photo: György Klösz. MNM: LTM. Photo Archives. (Inv. no. 2150.)—Repr.: MA.

80. **The southern courtyard of the Orczy House** with the gate from Károly körút. Photo. From the collection of the Hungarian Jewish Archives.

81. **The southern courtyard of the Orczy House**, a gravestone store at the outer wall of the synagogue (see figs. **84** and **98**, below). Photo. From the collection of the Hungarian Jewish Archives.

82. **The northern courtyard of the Orczy House**, the corner left to the "Choir Temple". Photo. From the collection of the Hungarian Jewish Archives.

83. **The northern courtyard of the Orczy House**, the Károly körút–Király utca corner. Photo. From the collection of the Hungarian Jewish Archives.

84. **The southern courtyard of the Orczy House**, 1928. The side of the middle wing (left) without the corridor along the southern wall of the synagogue. The corridor with the iron railing on the second floor led to the entrance of the synagogue, which was on the second floor of the middle wing and originally had one level only. The windows on the third floor opened from the gallery, added in 1829. For the gravestone store (left) see figs. **81**, above, and **98**, below. Photo. 9 × 12 cm. MNM: LTM. Photo Archives. (Inv. no. 1020.)—Repr.: MA.

85. **The synagogue in the Orczy House** (in the middle wing). The two-story interior space, viewed from the northwestern corner of the gallery. The *bimah / almemor*, enclosed within a wooden railing and raised above the pews by a few steps, can be seen in the front, while the Ark can be seen in the background. The *bimah* is set at a distance of six to seven rows of pews from the Ark. The pews are provided with *Ständer*-type reading desks. The interior of the synagogue was lit by a row of electric lamps hanging from the ceiling; these were obviously later additions. Photo, 1928. 18 × 24 cm; 24 × 36 cm. MNM: LTM. Photo Archives. (Inv. no. 167; 17,793.) —Repr.: MA.

Another photo of this synagogue, made before the Orthodox congregation moved to another place, has also survived; see József Katona, *A 90 éves Dohány-utcai templom* [The 90-year-old Dohány utca Temple] (1949), Pl. VIII, 14.

86. **The northern courtyard of the Orczy House**, during its demolition, ca. 1936, view from the Király utca entrance. The two windows on the left, on the second and third floors, are those on the northern wall of the synagogue. Photo: Richárd Margittay. From: MéJ (1938).—Repr.: NZL&MI.

87. **Tribute to Salomon Sulzer**. A Hebrew poem by Josef Lőwy, printed in Gross-Kanizsa / Nagykanizsa, by Ph. Fischel, 1866. Published by György Landeszman, "Lőwy József héber üdvözlő költeménye" [Josef Lőwy's Verse Greeting in Hebrew], *Évkönyv*, 1979/80 (Budapest: MIOK, 1980), pp. 245–247.

88. **Portrait of Karl Ed. Denhof**. From: Ignaz Reich, *Beth-El*, II (1868).

89. **A synagogal cantor** (*hazzan*). From Moshe Leib Wolf Trebitsch's handwritten prayer-book. MZsM. (Inv. no. 64.629.) From: *Évkönyv* 1983/84; Sándor Scheiber, *Folklór és tárgytörténet* [Essays on Jewish Folklore and Comparative Literature], III (1984).—Repr.: NZL&MI.

90. **Portrait of David Strelisker** / Strelisky / Brod. Contemporary painting. MZsM. (Inv. no. Képz.-64.2132.) From: MéJ (1916).—Repr.: NZL&MI.

91. **The northern courtyard of the Orczy House**. In the middle the western facade of the former "Choir Temple", which could be entered from the corridor on the second floor. The third floor was the level of the (women's) gallery. The semicircular window lit the barrel vault of the synagogue. Photo, ca. 1930. 9 × 12 cm. MNM: LTM. Photo Archives. (Inv. no. 1021.)—Repr.: MA.

92. **Interior of the "Choir Temple"**, viewed from the gallery. After the Temple was abandoned in 1859, the barrel vault was replaced with a horizontal fake-ceiling. From: MéJ (1933).—Repr.: NZL&MI.

93. **Interior of the "Choir Temple"**, 1928. Viewed from the same angle as fig. **92**, left. By this time the building was used as a textile warehouse. The photo was taken from the northeastern corner of the "Temple" and shows the southern side, the western entrance from the courtyard and the junction of the southern and western galleries. Photo. 18 × 24 cm. MNM: LTM. Photo Archives. (Inv. no. 168.)—Repr. MA.

94. **Demolition of the Orczy House**. Photo: Richárd Margittay. From: MéJ (1938).—Repr.: NZL&MI.

The demolition of the "Jewish courtyard (*Judenhof*)" was begun from the southern side of the residential wing on Károly körút. The photo allows a view into the southern courtyard, onto the front, that is, onto western part of the cross-wing, which, like the wing on Károly körút, contained apartments.

95. **The Orczy House**. Passage between the two courtyards, at the western end of the first floor section of the middle wing, viewed from the northern courtyard. The doorway on the right is the entrance to the northern courtyard from Károly körút, opening onto a stairway leading to the corridor from which the "Choir Temple" and the synagogue could be approached. From: MéJ (1933).—Repr.: NZL&MI.

96. **The Orczy House**. Ground-plan based on the map shown in fig. **III:2**, below. (Reconstructed by Ferenc Dávid.) Roofs and buildings.—Drawn by Tamás Dezső.

    1: Northern courtyard

    2: Southern courtyard

    3: Synagogue (see fig. 85, above)

    4: "Choir Temple" (see figs. **91–93**, above, and **III:6**, below)

    5: The Jewish school / "Israelitische National-schule" (?)

97. **The Orczy House**. View and angle of the surviving photos. (Reconstructed by Ferenc Dávid.)—Drawn by Tamás Dezső.

Figs. **79**, above, and **98–99**, below, were shot from Károly körút

    1: Fig. **84**

    2: Fig. **86**

    3: Fig. **91**

    4: Fig. **95**

98. **The Orczy House from the Károly körút**. In the front, the Orczy Café, further the gate to the south-

ern courtyard and to its left a shop (Arnold Weisz). (There are signboards above the gate: one for a hairdresser's, and others for smaller shops in the courtyard, including a gravestone store for which see figs. **81** and **84**, above.) The building of the Anker Insurance Co. (see fig. **200**, below) can be seen in the background (on the site of the former Gyertyánffy House). Photo, ca. 1915. 24 × 36 cm. MNM: LTM. Photo Archives. (Inv. no. 17,827.) From: *Európai Utas* (1992), no. 1.—Repr.: MA.

99. **The Orczy House** from the Károly körút, with the Orczy Café, 1935. (The text of the signboard is illegible.) There is a gas lamp in front of the Café. From: Béla Bevilaqua Borsody & Béla Mazsáry, *Pest-budai kávéházak* [Cafés of Pest and Buda] (1935).—Repr.: NZL&MI.

100. **The Orczy Café**, 1935. The mirror on the left originates from the former Privorszky Café that stood on the southern side of Vigadó tér and was opened in 1869 by Ferenc Privorszky, one of the most renowned café proprietors of contemporary Pest; Privorszky hoped that his Café would be his most brilliant enterprise. However, he went bankrupt, for the revenues from this Café, located near the Vigadó and other elegant nightclubs, did not cover the expenses on luxury items. A part of the furnishings was purchased by the new lessee of the Orczy Café. Photo. From: *Európai Utas* (1992), no. 1.—Repr.: NZL&MI.

The career of the Café's earlier lessees indicates that in the mid-nineteenth century the "Orczy" ranked right behind the elegant cafés in the Belváros (Inner City) and that progress from here would have meant a hotel and café in the Inner City, the southern areas of the Lipótváros, the Danube bank promenade or on the Régi Színház tér (today Vörösmarty tér).

An extension of the Orczy Café proper was a "garden" restaurant or café in the southern courtyard of the Orczy Ház; this "garden" can be clearly recognized on a surviving photo (fig. **80**, above), in the corner of the courtyard.

101. **The last lessees of the Orczy Café**, the Strasser family. From: *Európai Utas* (1992), no. 1.—Repr.: NZL&MI.

102. "**The building of the Piarists on Városház tér**", a colored lithograph by Adolf Tikáts (1872-1956). The three-story building of the *Collegium Pestiense* can be seen on the left (the eastern wing of the building on the Váci utca of today and its southern side facing the Erzsébet híd), with the shops of the

so-called "Vas-udvar" [Iron Court] (today 4 Pesti Barnabás utca) in the middle and with the tower of the Greek Orthodox Church (today 2/B Petőfi tér) in the background. MNM: MTKcs. (Inv. no. MTKCs. T.8956.)—Repr.: NZL&MI.

103. **Torah translation of Móric Bloch** (Mór Ballagi). Two pages of the text and the Hebrew title page of the book. Printed in Buda, with the font of the Hungarian Royal University [= Egyetemi Nyomda], 1841. The two pages: chapter 5 of Deuteronomy / *Devarim* (the beginning of the section containing the Ten Commandments). The Hebrew title page has the author's Hebrew name: *Mordekhay Blokh*, Buda appears as *Ofen* and the Egyetemi Nyomda, as *Kenigl. ungarische uniferzit. bikhdrickeraj*. Loránd Eötvös University, Faculty of Humanities, Library of the Department of Assyriology and Hebrew Studies.

104. **Mór Ballagi, a Member of Parliament**. MNM: LTM. Photo Archives. (Inv. no. 28,306—65.438.)—Repr.: JL&FÁ.

105. **Mór Wodianer**. A drawing by Josef Kriehuber (1800-1876), a well-known Viennese artist, 1847. Printed by József Tyroler. MNM: MTKcs. (Inv. no. MTKCs. 53.182.)—Photo: NZL&MI, 1994.

106. **Albert Wodianer**. MNM: LTM. Photo Archives. (Inv. no. 66,148.)—Repr.: JL&FÁ.

107. **Béla Wodianer**. Photo. From: MéJ (1998).

108. **Portrait of Márk Rózsavölgyi**. Lithograph by Miklós Barabás (1810-1898), the most popular graphic artist of the period. Printed in *Nemzeti képcsarnok a Pesti Divatlaphoz* [National Portrait Gallery for the *Pesti Divatlap*], (1844), no. 6. MNM: MTKcs. Gerszi, p. 126, *sub* Barabás, no. 285. From: MéJ (1911).—Repr.: NZL&MI.

109. "**The National Theater in Pest**." Drawing by Rudolf Alt, 1845. The facade of the building on Kerepesi út (today Rákóczi út); the Inner City with Hatvani utca (today Kossuth Lajos utca) in the background. From: *Buda-Pest. Előadva 32 eredeti rajzolatban Alt Rudolf által* [Buda-Pest. Presented in 32 Original Drawings by Rudolf Alt] (1845). 17.4 × 27 cm. MNM: MTKcs. (Inv. no. MTKCs. T.3442-Alt színtelen / black-and-white.)—Photo: NZL&MI, 1994.

110. **The grave of Márk Rózsavölgyi** in the former Jewish cemetery on Váci út (or Lehel utca). Drawing by Gergely Pörge (1858-1930), 1908. 34.8 × 26 cm. MNM: MTKcs. (Inv. no. MTKCs. T.9026.)—Photo: NZL&MI, 1994.

111. **The Valero Courtyard in Király utca**. Designed by József Hild, 1824. From: Jenő Rados, *Hild József* (1958).

112. **The statutes of the Society to Disseminate the Hungarian Language** among the Israelites of the Country (or: Homeland), 1847.

113. **Portrait of Ignác Einhorn (Ede Horn).** Painting by József Borsos (1821–1883). MZsM. From: MéJ (1935).—Repr.: NZL&MI.

114. **Memorial tablet of Ede Horn** on the house where he was born (Vágújhely / Nové Mesto nad Váhom, Slovakia), by Kornél Sámuel (1883–1914), 1912. From: MéJ (1913).—Repr.: NZL&MI.

115. **Portrait and signature of R. David Einhorn.** Daguerrotypie, Pest, 1852. Einhorn's clothing resembles the pastor's robe of the German Protestants. From: Kaufmann Kohler, Ed., *David Einhorn Memorial Volume. Selected Sermons and Addresses* (New York: Bloch, 1911).

The photo was probably made by Lipót Strelisky in his studio that opened in 1843.

The *David Einhorn Memorial Volume* (1911) also contains the original German texts of three of his sermons from Pest. These are the following (according to their serial number in the volume): (II) Inaugural address: January, 1852 (text: Genesis 25,23); (xxxv) *Shavu'ot*, 5612 (= 1852 C.E.) (text: Psalms, 8–10); (xxxvII) Destruction of Jerusalem (*Tish'ah be-Av*), 5612 (= 1852 C.E.) (text: Gen. 50, 50–53).

116. **Recruitment of a Jew** into the National Guard, 1848. From: György Spira, *A pestiek Petőfi és Haynau között* [People in Pest between Petőfi and Haynau] (Budapest: Enciklopédia Kiadó, 1998), p. 789.

117. **An advertisement for József Tyroler** steel and copper engraver's Pest Royal Patented Steel and Copper Printing Shop. The frame (anti-clockwise from the upper right corner) shows the process of printing from the conception of a poem to its printing. Colored copper engraving. 16.5 × 23.5 cm. MNM: MTKcs. (Inv. no. MTKcs. 4411. Vegyes tárgyú reklámlapok [Advertisement leaflets].)—Photo: NZL&MI, 1994.

118. **Portrait of Ferenc Deák.** Etching by József Tyroler, 1848. 26.4 × 18.3 cm. MNM: MTKcs. (Inv. no. MTKcs. 1105.)—Repr.: NZL&MI.

119. **Memorial of the Jewish soldiers** who fell in the War of Independence of 1848/49. Kozma utca Jewish (Neolog) cemetery. Designed by Béla Lajta. From: Béla Lajta, in: *Magyar Iparművészet* (1914). For the translation of the text see p. 444, below.— Repr.: NZL&MI.

III:1. **Óbuda, Újlak, Buda and Pest.** A map by Karl Vasquez, *Buda és Pest szabad királyi várossainak tájleírása* [Topography of Free Royal Cities of Buda and Pest] (1838), sheet I: Detail of the map with the pontoon bridge. (On the latter, see fig. **369**, below.) Szilvia Andrea Holló, *Budapest régi térképeken, 1686-1896* [Budapest on Old Maps, 1686-1896] (Budapest: Officina Nova, 1994), no. 10, pp. 34–35. MNM: MTKcs. (Inv. no. MTKcs. T.1382.)—Photo: NZL&MI, 1994.

III:2. **Neighborhood of the Károly Barracks and the Orczy House.** József Homolka, *Budapest fő- és székváros legújabb térképe* [The Newest Map of the Capital Budapest] (1882, new edition: Eggenberger-féle könyvkereskedés, 1896). (Detail.)—Photo: NZL&MI, 1994.

The ground-plan of the Orczy House survived on this map only. The map also shows the synagogues in Rombach utca and Dohány utca, as well as the Boys' Orphanage in Holló utca. The building of the Rabbinical Seminary can be seen a little further, at the corner of Rökk Szilárd utca and Bérkocsis utca. Although not visible on this detail, the map also shows an Institute for the Blind in Király utca, which is identical with the Jewish Institute for the Blind (see fig. **210**, below).

52 Kazinczy utca: "Zion", shown under this address, was no doubt some sort of association, perhaps the *Zion Jótékonysági Egylet* (Zion Charitable Association), which later moved to a new location; this map dates from too early a period for that the "Zion" in Kazinczy utca be affiliated with an Austrian association by the same name (*Zion: Verbund der österreichischen Vereine für Colonisation Palästinas und Syriens*, founded in 1892).

III:3. **Theresienstadt / Terézváros.** Apartment blocks and gardens between Kerepesi út and Király utca in what later became the Erzsébetváros. Karl Vasquez, *Buda és Pest szabad királyi várossainak tájleírása* [Topography of Free Royal Cities of Buda and Pest] (1838), sheet I. (Detail.) The section shown here is rotated to the right by 90° and thus the orientation is changed: in fact, the Terézváros district lay East-Northeast of the "K. K. Invaliden Haus" / Károly Barracks (and not left, as here). Szilvia Andrea Holló, *Budapest régi térképeken, 1686-1896* [Budapest on Old Maps, 1686-1896] (Budapest: Officina Nova, 1994), no. 10, pp. 34–35.

The streets around Király utca were the following (according to the names on the map): *Land Strasse* (Ország út / Károly körút), *Tabaks Gasse* (Dohány utca; the by-pass or shortcut nature of the street can be especially well made out on the map), *Pfeiffer*

Gasse (Sipos / Síp utca), *Kreutz Gasse* (Nagy Kereszt / Kazinczy utca), *Nussbaum Gasse* (Diófa / Nagy Diófa utca), *Sommer Gasse* (Nyár utca), *Kleine Feld Gasse* (Csányi utca and Klauzál utca), *Akazien Gasse* (Akácfa utca), *Gärtner Gasse* (Kertész utca), *Valero Gasse* (Kürt utca), *Rumbach Gasse* (Rumbach Sebestyén utca), *Schwarz Adler Gasse* (Holló utca), *Kerepescher Gasse* (Rákóczi út), *Felber Gasse* (outer section of Dohány utca), *Drey Trommel Gasse* (Három Dob utca / Dob utca), *Königs Gasse* (Király utca). This corresponds more or less to the *old-new* Jewish quarter. MNM: MTKcs. (Inv. no. MTKCs. T.1382.)—Photo: NZL&MI, 1994.

III:4. Tannery. By an unknown artist, early nineteenth century. Colored lithograph. 7.5 × 8.9 cm. MNM: MTKcs. (Inv. no. MTKCs. 297/1950. Gr. V/1/2-90.)—Photo: NZL&MI, 1994.

III:5. Sexton (*shammash / shames*) **holding the gavel** used for summoning the congregation to prayer (*Schulklopfer*). Jewish costume from Western Hungary, 1808. MZsM. (Inv. no. Ipm.-64.629.) Sándor Scheiber, *Folklór és tárgytörténet* [Essays on Jewish Folklore and Comparative Literature], III (1984); CsZs&ZD. (Inv. no. CsZs. 13/2.)

III:6. The Temple of the Israelites in Pest / "*Die Tempel der Israeliten in Pesth*", by Antal József Strohmayer, 1833. The interior of the "Choir Temple" in the Orczy House, from the western (back) wall. The Ark is on the eastern side and above it there is a Hebrew inscription similar to the one on the *shivviti* tablets (Psalms 16,8). Beside differences in the ground-plan, several elements of the interior—such as the Ark and the inscription above it—recall the *Stadttempel* and *Chorschul* (Seitenstettengasse) in Vienna. Colored lithograph. 19.3 × 25 cm. MNM: MTKcs. (Inv. no. MTKCs. T.5301.-Budapest)—Photo: NZL&MI, 1994.

III:7. Sámuel Wodianer's house: "*Sámuel Wodianer háza / Das Samuel Wodianer'sche Haus.*" Karl Vasquez, *Buda és Pest szabad királyi várossainak tájleírása* [Topography of Free Royal Cities of Buda and Pest] (1838), sheet III: Franz Weiss's colored frame picture (on the right). Szilvia Andrea Holló, *Budapest régi térképeken, 1686-1896* [Budapest on Old Maps, 1686-1896] (Budapest: Officina Nova, 1994), no. 10, pp. 38-39. MNM: MTKcs. (Inv. no. MTKCs. T.1384.)—Photo: NZL&MI, 1994.

III:8. Rudolf Wodianer's house on the Danube: "*Wodianer Rudolf háza a duna mellett / Das Rudolph Wodianer'sche Haus an der Donau.*" Karl Vasquez, *Buda és Pest szabad királyi várossainak*

tájleírása [Topography of Free Royal Cities of Buda and Pest] (1838), sheet IV: Franz Weiss's colored frame picture (on the right). Szilvia Andrea Holló, *Budapest régi térképeken, 1686-1896* [Budapest on Old Maps, 1686-1896] (Budapest: Officina Nova, 1994), no. 10, pp. 40-41. MNM: MTKcs. (Inv. no. MTKCs. T.1385.)—Photo: NZL&MI, 1994.

III:9. J. A. Valero's silk factory in Király útsza: "*Valero J. A. selyemgyára a királyútszában / J. A. Valero's Seidenfabrik in der Königsgasse.*" Karl Vasquez, *Buda és Pest szabad királyi várossainak tájleírása* [Topography of Free Royal Cities of Buda and Pest] (1838), sheet III: Franz Weiss's colored frame picture (on the left). Szilvia Andrea Holló, *Budapest régi térképeken, 1686-1896* [Budapest on Old Maps, 1686-1896] (Budapest: Officina Nova, 1994), no. 10, pp. 38-39. MNM: MTKcs. (Inv. no. MTKCs. T.1384.)—Photo: NZL&MI, 1994.

III:10. Coat-of-arms of the Wodianer family, 1844. The seemingly expressionless late Baroque decoration in fact contains several motifs reflecting the Wodianers' trade in tobacco and other commodities, such as the ship (for the shipping of tobacco from the South) and hop-vine, as well as explicitly Jewish motifs such as the cock (*tarnegol*), the Levitic pitcher (ewer) and bowl (?) and the six-pointed star. The otherwise customary heraldic lion also harmonizes with these motifs. MOL. From the *Liber regius*. (DL 97.652.)—Photo: FA, 1994.

IV. The Jewish Triangle in Pest

120. **The "Jewish Triangle" in Pest.** Budapest, (Inner-) Erzsébetváros. From: Gazda.
   The "triangle":
      1: Synagogue in Dohány utca, 1859
      3: Synagogue in Rumbach Sebestyén utca, 1872
      4: Orthodox synagogue in Kazinczy utca, 1913
   Other places of interest of the Jewish community:
      2: Heroes' Temple, 1931
      5: Hungarian Jewish Museum, 1931
      6: Graveyard, 1944/45
      7: Goldmark Hall, 1931
      8: Ghetto Memorial, 1985
      9: Holocaust Memorial, 1989

121. **Portrait of R. Löw (Arszlán) Schwab.** Lithograph, printed by Sámuel Winter. From: *Budapesti Negyed*, no. 8 (1995).

122. **Dohány utca synagogue.** Design by Frigyes Feszl, 1851. Colored lithograph. Druck u(nd) Verlag v(on) [Mór] Engel u(nd) [Ignác] Mandello, Pesth. Lith(ographie) v(on) [Franz] X(aver) Sandmann.

46 × 61.8 cm. MOL. (Cat. no. T.14–Tervek a Kereske-delmi Minisztérium anyagából, file 2, fol. 148.) From: Dénes Komárik, *Feszl Frigyes* (1993).

123. **Dohány utca synagogue**. Colored engraving by Ludwig Rohbock, 1859. From: *Budapest és környéke eredeti képekben* [Budapest and Its Vicinity in Original Pictures]. Drawings by Lajos (Ludwig) Rohbock. Text by János Hunfalvy (Pest, 1859–Printed in Darmstadt by Gusztáv György Lange). 12.8 × 15.7 cm. MNM: MTKcs. (Inv. no. MTKCs. T.6994.)–Repr.: NZL&MI.

Another drawing of the synagogue by Rohbock: MNM: MTKcs. (Inv. no. MTKCs. T.3063.)

124. **The original ground-plan of the Dohány utca synagogue**. Ground floor. (For the current layout see fig. **333**, below.) From: Gazda.

125. **Dohány utca synagogue**. Engraving by G. M. Kurz, 1860, probably after an earlier drawing (C. Schumann?). (See also fig. **127**, below.) *Illustriertes Jahrbuch für Ernst & Scherz* (1860). MZsM. (Inv. no. Képz.-65.1610.) BTM. From: MéJ (1916); Andrew Handler, *Dori* (1983); Ines Müller, *A Rumbach Sebestyén utcai zsinagóga* (1993).–Repr.: NZL&MI.

126. **Dohány utca synagogue** and the neighboring houses, ca. 1890. On the signboards here entirely different names figure than the ones on another photo (see fig. **146**, below). Photo: György Klösz. From: *Budapest anno...* (1979).–Repr.: NZL&MI.

127. **Ludwig Phillippson's choral work** for the consecration of the Dohány utca synagogue, 1859. (For the engraving on the title page of the printed version see fig. **125**, above.) MZsM. From: MéJ (1916).–Repr.: NZL&MI.

The composer, Ludwig Phil(l)ippson (1811–1889), was a well-known rabbi in Magdeburg and one of the leading advocates of the reform of the ritual in Germany, he was the founder and editor of *Allgemeine Zeitung des Judentums* (1837). He was also known for his Bible translations. His early commitment for the Dohány utca synagogue was motivated by the reform efforts.

128. **The original design for the facade** of the Dohány utca synagogue, drawn and signed by József Hild, 1857. (See also fig. **IV:4**, below.) Photo. 12 × 9 cm. BTM: KM. Photo Archives. (Inv. no. 805.)–Repr.: MA.

129. **Mór Friedmann, chief cantor** (*hazzan*) of the Dohány utca synagogue. (In the title of the picture: M. J. Friedmann.) Lithograph by Miklós Barabás, 1860. (Printed by Reiffenstein & Rösch in Vienna.) 46 × 38.3 cm. MZsM. (Inv. no. Képz.-65.2593.)

MNM: MTKcs. (Inv. no. MTKCs. T.1281.) Gerszi, p. 122, *sub* Barabás, no. 103. From: MéJ (1913).–Repr.: NZL&MI.

There is also a lithograph of Friedmann by Vilmos Grund (see Gerszi, p. 146, *sub* Grund, no. 50), as well as by György Suhajdy (1875) (see Gerszi, p. 203, *sub* Suhajdy, no. 29). The cantor seems to be a well-known or even popular figure in the society at large.

130. **Consecration ceremony** of the Dohány utca synagogue, 1859. Engraving by Alajos Fuchsthaller (ca. 1815–1863): "*Innere Ansicht des Pester isr. Tempels während des Gottesdienstes am 6. Sept., 1859.*" The man in the middle of the group on the platform (the chief cantor?) is holding a Torah scroll. MNM: MTKcs. (Inv. no. MTKCs. T.5315.) From: MéJ (1931).–Repr.: NZL&MI.

The original form of the Ark in the Dohány utca synagogue is shown in this engraving. The new organ pipes, added in the early twentieth century, considerably changed the appearance of the synagogue's interior. (Originally the Ark, its form recalling a tent, had wholly hidden from view the organ pipes.)

This engraving can no doubt be seen as a *visual reportage* of the consecration ceremony of the synagogue.

131. "**Memorial services for László Teleki** in the Israelite temple of Pest on June 6, 1861 / "*Die Teleki-Gedächtnisfeier im Pester israel. Tempel am 6. Juni 1861.*" Lithograph by Ede Langer. 25.1 × 30.3 cm. *Allgemeine illustrierte Judenzeitung*, Beilage zu Nr. 28 (1861). Gerszi, p. 157, *sub* Langer, no. 14. MNM: MTKcs. (Inv. no. MTKCs. T. 4420.) From: MéJ (1916).–Repr.: NZL&MI.

Count László Teleki (1811–1861) died (committed suicide) on May 8. The memorial services, a month later, were a gesture symbolizing Jewish participation in the political life of Hungary.

132. **Interior of the Dohány utca synagogue**. The new organ pipes are flanking the tenth of the Ark. Photo, ca. 1900. From: *Budapesti Negyed*, no. 4 (1994), p. 36.

133. **A *parokhet* for weddings** in the Dohány utca synagogue, with the *huppah* in the center. MZsM. (Inv. no. Ipm.-64.1519.) From: MéJ (1933).–Repr.: NZL&MI.

134. "**A seat for prayer**", reservation for a year in the "Temple" of Pest, i.e. in the "Choir Temple" in the Orczy House, 1845/46. Bottom: signature of the community treasurer, Elias Abeles. Framed with etchings of Biblical scenes: Moses striking water

from the rock (Exodus 17; Numeri 20,7–11); Moses, Miriam and the copper serpent (Numeri 21); quails (Exodus 16,13; Numeri 11,31 ff.); gathering of manna (Exodus 16,11–35). Paper, steel engraving. 14 × 9 cm. MZsM. (Inv. no. V.-64.821.) From: MéJ (1931); BI&SchS.—Repr.: NZL&MI.

135. **Farkas Alajos Meisel**, the first rabbi of the Dohány utca synagogue. Lithograph by Miklós Barabás, 1859. Published and printed in Pest: Gebrüder Pollák, 1859. (In the title: Dr. Meisel W. A. [Wolf Alois].) Gerszi, p. 125, *sub* Barabás, no. 235. MNM: MTKcs. From: MéJ (1933); József Katona, *A 90 éves Dohány-utcai templom* [The 90-year-old Dohány utca Temple] (1949), Pl. II, 2.—Repr.: NZL&MI.

There is another lithograph of Meisel by József Marastoni (1867, see Gerszi, p. 173, *sub* Marastoni, no. 303).

136. **Sámuel Kohn as the central figure** on a tableau of the *A magyar ifjú Izrael* [Young Hungarian Israel], 1868. He wears the hat of the rabbis' priestly robes. From: Ignaz Reich, *Beth-El*, I (1868). From: MéJ (1915).

137. **Portrait of Sámuel Kohn**, ca. 1875. From: József Katona, *A 90 éves Dohány-utcai templom* [The 90-year-old Dohány utca Temple] (1949).—Repr.: NZL&MI.

138. **Sámuel Kohn in the 1900s**, wearing a *yarmulke*. Photo: Rákos (18 Erzsébet tér). Hungarian Jewish Archives.

139. "**Chief Rabbi Sámuel Kohn**, of the Dohány Temple, in cloak, on the occasion of the Millennial procession (1896)". MNM: LTM. Photo Archives. (Inv. no. 77,842.)—Repr.: JL&FÁ.

140. **Lifting of the Torah scroll** (*hagbahah*). Imre Ámos, "A tóraadás ünnepe" [Festival of Giving the Torah], 1940. The celebration of giving the Torah (*zeman mattan Torateinu*) is *Shavu'ot*. Yet the Torah scroll here is inscribed with the word *Bereshit*, the portion to be read on *Simhat Torah*. Lino-cut. 34 × 27 cm. From: [*Ünnepek.*] *Ámos Imre 14 eredeti metszete* [Holidays. Fourteen Original Lino-cuts by Imre Ámos] (1940) (after no. 5 in the series).

141. **Portrait of Ignác Hirschler**, 1868/69. From the tableau of the General Jewish Congress (see fig. **143**, below).

142. **The law of emancipation** (Act XVII of 1867).

143. **Tableau of the participants of the General Jewish Congress**, 1868/69. MZsM. (Inv. no. T.64.1810.) From: MéJ (1915)—Repr.: NZL&MI.

144. **The scene of the General Jewish Congress**: the County Hall in Pest. Rudolf Alt, "Vármegyeház Pesten" [County Hall in Pest], ca. 1853. From: *Festői megtekintések Budára és Pestre. Malerische Ansichten von Ofen und Pest*. Nach (der) Natur gezeich(net) v(on) R. Alt. Lithog(raphie) v(on) [Franz] X(aver) Sandmann. Verlags Eigenthum v(on) L. T. Neumann in Wien. Vervielfältigung ausschl(iesslich) vorbehalten. Ged(ruckt) b(ei) J. Rauh [ca. 1853] (no. 14 in the series). 19.5 × 26.4 cm. MNM: MTKcs. (Inv. no. MTKCs. T.4036-Alt színes.)—Photo: NZL&MI, 1994.

145. **The scene of the Orthodox convention** after they left the General Jewish Congress: Hotel Tigris. Rudolf Alt, "Vendéglő a Tigrishez" [At the sign of the tiger], ca. 1853. The hotel stood at the intersection of Szél utca and Fürdő utca on József tér (today 5 Nádor utca). From: Rudolf Alt, *Festői megtekintések Budára és Pestre. Malerische Ansichten von Ofen und Pest* (ca. 1853). (No. 10 in the series.) 19 × 26.4 cm. MNM: MTKcs. (Inv. no. MTKCs. T.4032-Alt színes.)—Photo: NZL&MI, 1994.

146. **The house where Theodor Herzl was born**, next to the Dohány utca synagogue. The signboards (from left to right): "Abeles" (on the neighboring house), "Ign. Lederer & Sohn"; "David Lőwinger", etc. On the opposite side: "Julius Neugebauer". MNM: LTM. Photo Archives. (Negative. 52/60/11. Inv. no. 17,821.) 24 × 36 cm.—Repr.: MA.

It is unknown which floor and which apartment was inhabited by the Herzl family—perhaps the third one.

The Abeles / Abelesz family, one of the oldest Jewish families of Pest, were related to the Herzls: Jacob Herzl's mother-in-law (Johanna Diamant) was an Abeles girl. In the earlier nineteenth century the Jewish community of Pest—and in particular, the synagogue in the Orczy House—always had an official from the Abeles family. Jacob Herzl's father-in-law, Hermann (Herschel / Haschel) Gabriel Hirsch [Zwi / Tzvi] Diamant (1805–1871) was likewise an affluent merchant in Pest. One of his brothers-in-laws, Wilhelm (Vilmos) Diamant fought in the Independence War of 1848/49 and, as far as the family knows, was promoted to the rank of lieutenant.

147. **Theodor Herzl. A childhood photo**, 1865. Photo: Izsó Kohn, "photo-writer in Pest". From: MéJ (1925).—Repr.: NZL&MI.

148. **Theodor Herzl's parents with their two children**, ca. 1870. Photo. From the former Emil Víg collection (Újvidék / Novi Sad, Yugoslavia). From: MéJ (1926).—Repr.: NZL&MI.

Jacob Herzl is about 35 years old on the photo; as a grown-up, his son bore an uncanny resemblance to him. The girl, Pauline Herzl (1859–1878), was much beloved by her brother, and he involved her in his literary activities. The book on the table, in front of Theodor Herzl's mother, is not merely a piece of the décor: Jeanette (Nanette) Herzl, née Diamant (1837–1911), the youngest daughter of Hermann Hirsch Diamant, an affluent clothier who lived in Váci utca in the Inner City, was an educated middle-class woman, well versed in German culture, with a strong interest in literature. She introduced her son to classical German literature.

149. Theodor Herzl's sketches on one of his school essays, 1874. The Central Zionist Archives, Jerusalem: Herzl Archives. From: MéJ (1941).

150. The Herzl family's new home on the Danube bank: the *Thonethof* (Mária Valéria utca, the house on the corner of 10 Apáczai Csere János utca–3 Vigadó tér), 3rd floor. Postcard. From: Grüsse.– Repr.: NZL&MI.

The exact address of the Herzl family in Lipótváros is known from Theodor Herzl's *bar mitzvah* invitation.

151. Herzl as a student of the Lutheran High School, 1876. From: Andrew Handler, *Dori* (1983).

152. Herzl's advocate at the Sublime Porte: Ármin Vámbéry, oriental scholar and traveler, university professor. From: Sándor Scheiber, *Folklór és tárgytörténet* [Essays on Jewish Folklore and Comparative Literature], III (1984).–Repr.: NZL&MI.

The name "Schlesinger", which Herzl used for Vámbéry in his letters and in his diary, also crops up in the text of the *Altneuland* (1902) (Ch. I/2).

153. Theodor Herzl's letter to Adolf Ágai, 1889. From: MéJ (1936).

154. Facade of the Rumbach Sebestyén utca synagogue, 1981. Photo: Carol H. Krinsky. From: Carol H. Krinsky, *Europas Synagogen* (1988). Repr.: NZL&MI.

155. Facade and towers (Yakhin and Boaz) on the street front of the Rumbach Sebestyén utca synagogue. Detail. (After the restoration.) Photo: FA&LLL, 1992.

156. Frieze on the facade of the Dohány utca (!) synagogue before the recent restoration. Photo: FA&LLL, 1992.

157. The Two Tablets of the Law (*shenei luhot*) on the facade of the Rombach utca synagogue after restoration. Photo: FA&LLL, 1992.

158. The "Moorish" ornamentation of the Rombach utca synagogue tower. Detail. Photo: FA&LLL, 1992.

159. Interior of the Rombach utca synagogue, ca. 1895. The *dukhen* and the *ner tamid* can be seen in the foreground, with the rostrum or *bimah / almemor* and the entrance in the background, and the women's gallery above and in a semicircle around the entrance. Photo: György Klösz. MNM: LTM. Photo Archives. (Inv. no. 23,077.) From: Ines Müller, *A Rumbach Sebestyén utcai zsinagóga* [The Synagogue in Rumbach Sebestyén utca] (1993). Repr.: MA.

160. Ground-plan of the Rumbach Sebestyén utca synagogue. From: Gazda.

161. Interior of the Rumbach Sebestyén utca synagogue. Photo, ca. 1949. Photo Archives of the *Országos Műemlékvédelmi Hivatal* (National Office for the Preservation of Historic Monuments). (Inv. no. 27,417.)

The same photo is published in Ines Müller, *A Rumbach Sebestyén utcai zsinagóga* (1993), p. 39, no. 29.

162. The former Ark in the Rumbach Sebestyén utca synagogue, 1974. Photo: Edit Szilágyi. Hild–Ybl Foundation Archives.

163. The former *bimah* and the *shulhan* in the Rumbach Sebestyén utca synagogue, 1988. The *bimah* is to the right, the *shulhan* is displaced from its original position. (For its original position see fig. **159**, above.) (The upper part of an Ark, from another synagogue—perhaps from the Orczy House—can be seen in the background.) Photo: Ines Müller, *A Rumbach Sebestyén utcai zsinagóga* (1993).–Repr.: NZL&MI.

164. The northeastern corner of the women's gallery in the Rumbach Sebestyén utca synagogue, 1971. (It is the corner near the *dukhan*; see also fig. **159**, above.) Photo: Edit Szilágyi. From: Ines Müller, *A Rumbach Sebestyén utcai zsinagóga* (1993).–Repr.: NZL&MI.

165. Portrait of R. Mózes Feldmann. From: MéJ (1943).–Repr.: NZL&MI.

166. Portrait of R. Illés Adler. From: MéJ (1943).– Repr.: NZL&MI.

167. Portrait of R. Benjámin Fischer. From: MéJ (1926).–Repr.: NZL&MI.

168. The Rumbach Sebestyén utca synagogue, with the octagon, from the courtyard, prior to its renovation, 1988. (For the interior of the octagon or "dome" see figs. **159** and **161**, above.) Photo: Ines Müller. From: Ines Müller, *A Rumbach Sebestyén utcai zsinagóga* (1993).–Repr.: NZL&MI.

169. The Rumbach Sebestyén utca synagogue, with the octagon, from the courtyard, 1991, after its renovation. Photo: Ines Müller. From: Ines Müller, *A Rumbach Sebestyén utcai zsinagóga* (1993).—Repr.: NZL&MI.

170. **Interior of the Rumbach Sebestyén utca synagogue**: the Ark (by the eastern wall) and the *bimah* (in the center), already in a state of disrepair, ca. 1985. Photo: Ágnes Hávorné Takách. From: Anikó Gazda, *Magyarországi zsinagógák* (1989); Ines Müller, *A Rumbach Sebestyén utcai zsinagóga* (1993).—Repr.: NZL&MI.

171. **Plaque on the eastern wall** in the prayer-room of the Nagy Fuvaros utca synagogue. The inscriptions on it run as follows: "I have set the LORD always before me" (Psalms 16,8); "Know before whom you are standing; it is the King of kings, the Holy one, be He blessed" (Berakhot 28b); "A prayer without intention is like the body without soul" (Isaiah Horowitz, *Shenei luhot ha-berit*: Tamid), etc. — Photo: LE, 1991.

172. **Pitcher (ewer) and bowl of the Levites**. An inscription is engraved under the rim of the jug: "Donated as a memorial by the learned Shelomo Rosenthal and his wife, Khayele. May their souls be bound in the bond of life. In the year 605 according to the minor era (= 1845 C.E.). Hevrah Kaddishah, Pest." The quote is from I Samuel 25,29. These ritual vessels no doubt passed into the ownership of the Hevrah Kaddishah directly after Salamon Rosenthal's death. They had apparently been acquired from Vienna by his father, Naftali Rosenthal. Was the family *ha-Levi*? With Vienna hallmarks (1757): mark of FL (Frantz Lintzberger) (pitcher) and of PD (?) (bowl). MZsM. Height: 18.5 cm (pitcher), 3.5 cm (bowl). (Inv. no. Ipm.–64.15; –64.16.) Photo: László Szelényi. From: BI&SchS.—Repr.: NZL&MI.

173. **All one needs for the morning prayers**: *tallit*, prayer-book (*Siddur*) and *tefillin* (in a velvet bag) on a table in the winter prayer-room of the Kazinczy utca synagogue.—Photo: FA, 1992.

174. **Laying of the *tefillin*** (the *tefillin shel yad*). Imre Ámos, "Tefillin". Lino-cut. 34 × 27 cm. From: [*Ünnepek.*] *Ámos Imre 14 eredeti metszete* [Holidays. Fourteen Original Lino-cuts by Imre Ámos] (1940).

From a ritual point of view, the drawing is slightly incorrect: the *tefillin shel yad* must first be wound around the arm and only then is the *tefillin shel rosh* placed on the forehead; the *bayit*, "house", the box-like part of the phylacteries, has to be tightened first, and then the *retzu'ah* wound.

175. **Arrangement of the *tefillin* boxes**. Explanatory diagrams from the manuscript of Maimonides'

Mishneh Torah. MTA Kt. Oriental Library, Kaufmann Collection. (Cat. no. A. 77.) Vol. I, p. 60, verso. MTA Kt. Microfilm Collection and Photo Laboratory, Photo: Mrs. Tibor Kolthay.

176. **The Orthodox school building** in the courtyard of the Kazinczy utca synagogue. The inscription on the facade: "School of the aut. (= *autonom* / autonomous) Orthodox community of Budapest." Designed by Sándor Löffler & Béla Löffler. From: MéJ (1913).—Repr.: NZL&MI.

177. **Facade of the Orthodox school**, with clock. From: MéJ (1924).—Repr.: NZL&MI.

178. **Maharam (Morenu ha-rav Moshe) Trebitsch**, a graduate from the *Hatam Sofer*'s yeshivah. Photo, from a tableau. From: *Judea* (1925). CsZs&DZ. (Inv. no. CsZs. XVIII/12.)

R. Trebitsch is mentioned in Pinhas Zelig Schwartz's comprehensive gazetteer of Hungary, the (*Sefer*) *Shem ha-gedolim* (Paks, 1913; reprint: Brooklyn, NY: Jerusalem Publishing, 1959), p. 157, no. M/36; according to the entry, R. Trebitsch was well-versed in the Torah and was extremely pious (*yir'at ha-Shem*), an outstanding person in the town of *Ofen* (Óbuda).

179. **The office building** of the Orthodox community of Pest in Dob utca. Designed by Sándor Löffler and Béla Löffler. From: MéJ (1913).—Repr.: NZL&MI.

180. **Interior of the Kazinczy utca synagogue**.— Photo: FA, 1992.

181. **Entrance and detail of the facade** of the Kazinczy utca synagogue, 1913. The (pseudo-) rosette window is decorated with a *menorah*. The Hebrew inscription under the frieze (incomplete on the photo): "How awesome is this place! this is none other but the house of God, and this is the gate of heaven" (Genesis 28,17). Designed by Sándor Löffler & Béla Löffler. From: MéJ (1913).—Repr.: NZL&MI.

Several photos of the consecration ceremony of the Kazinczy utca synagogue, as well as of the other buildings of the Pest Orthodox community, appeared in MéJ; these include pictures of the synagogue (see figs. **182, 184–186, 188–189,** below), the office building (see fig. **179,** above) and the school (see fig. **176,** above). The journal devoted several articles to the "Kazinczy" also in later issues.

182. **Entrance Hall with an ornamental fountain** in the Kazinczy utca synagogue. (Restoration works were started in 1997.) The inner side of the main entrance can be seen to the right. Designed by Sándor Löffler & Béla Löffler. From: MéJ (1913).— Repr.: NZL&MI.

183. Interior with the Ark in the Kazinczy utca synagogue. Drawing by Sándor Skutetzky & József Porgesz for the architectural competition, 1910. Collection of János Gerle. From: János Gerle, *et al.*, *A századforduló magyar építészete* [Hungarian Architecture at the Turn of the Century] (1990).

184. Interior of the Kazinczy utca synagogue with the *bimah / almemor* and the entrance to the left. Designed by Sándor Löffler & Béla Löffler. From: MéJ (1913).—Repr.: NZL&MI.

185. The Ark and the eastern wall in the Kazinczy utca synagogue. There is a tower-like wooden pillar on both sides of the Ark: Yakin and Boaz (I Kings 7,21, etc.). Designed by Sándor Löffler & Béla Löffler. From: MéJ (1913).—Repr.: NZL&MI.

186. Door of the Ark in the Kazinczy utca synagogue. (The photo published in MéJ was entitled "Altar-door".) There is an inscription in the center of the curtain (*parokhet*) above the door: "Holy to G(od) (*Kodesh le-*H′ [= *le-ha-Shem*]". Designed by Sándor Löffler & Béla Löffler. From: MéJ (1913).—Repr.: NZL&MI.

The door of the Ark is usually covered with a *parokhet*. A photo of the original *parokhet*, embroidered with the Two Tablets of the Law (*shenei luhot*) set between two "tulip" candlesticks, was published in MéJ (1913) (described there as "altar-curtain").

187. Winter prayer-room in the Kazinczy utca synagogue, with the *Siddur* used by the reader (*sheliah tzibbur*) on the table (*omed*) in the foreground. The directives of the local congregation were inscribed above the *shivviti* and *mizrah* tablets.

> "With the help of God (*ha-Shem*). According to the ruling of the just *bet din* and the magistrates and officials of the local community. Anyone *going down* to the Ark (*tevah*) may only pray in the Ashkenazi *nusah*, in accordance with the directives (*takkanah*) of the founders, of blessed memory, of the local Holy community."

The expression "to go down (to the Ark)" traditionally means that the person praying in front of the Ark, i.e. the *omed*, fulfills the words of Psalm 130: "Out of the depths have I cried unto thee, o Lord" (Psalms 130,1).—Photo: FA&LLL.

188. Interior of the Kazinczy utca synagogue: barrel vaulted ceiling, viewed from the second-floor gallery, with the entrance in the background. Designed by Sándor Löffler & Béla Löffler. From: MéJ (1913).—Repr.: NZL&MI.

189. Interior of the Kazinczy utca synagogue: view from the steps of the Ark (MéJ called them "steps of the altar"), viewed from the West. Designed by Sándor Löffler & Béla Löffler. From: MéJ (1913).—Repr.: NZL&MI.

190. Ritual bathing (*mitzvat niddah*). Miniature, parchment book, eighteenth century. The pages of the book measure 8 × 10.5 cm; the miniature, ca. 4 × 4 cm. MZsM. (Inv. no. Ipm.–64.626.) *Seder birkat ha-mazon...*, "Order of blessings at the table, prepared and written by the scribe Meshullam who is called Zimel, in Polna [today in Bohemia], 511 (= 1751 C.E.)", p. 18, verso. From: *Seder birkat ha-mazon / Grace after Meals / Asztali áldás* (Facsimile edition, Budapest: Helikon, 1991).

Halakhah prescribes three positive ritual commandments (*mitzvot*) for women: (a) *hadlakah*, lighting candles on Friday evening, (b) *hallah*, setting aside a portion of the dough, (c) *niddah*, ritual purity. (Of the three religious commandments, the last is also the third in frequency.)

191. The back outern wall of the Kazinczy utca synagogue, with the frame of the wedding canopy (*huppah / hüpe*). (Viewed from the office building on the opposite side.)—Photo: FA&LLL, 1993.

192. Frame of the wedding canopy (*huppah*) in the courtyard of the Kazinczy utca synagogue. (Used also as the tent at *Sukkot*.)—Photo: EZ, 1994.

193. The courtyard of the Kazinczy utca synagogue: view from beside the *huppah* frame. The inscription on this side reads: "The voice of the bride..."—Photo: EZ, 1994.

194. A printed wedding invitation, in which the groom announces the wedding. The invitation is decorated with a scene of the wedding ceremony: the blessing recited over the wine. Musicians stand on the right: a violinist, a cellist, a cymbal or zither player, as well as a jester (*marshalik*), wearing a pointed hat. Above the canopy, a putto blows the words of the good wishes with his trumpet: "*Mazel tov.*" The text of the invitation can be seen at the bottom: "The groom, (...) [name], will marry the bride, (...) [name], in wedding ceremony (literally: under the *huppah* and with *kiddushin*) according to the religion (*dat*) of Moses and Israel, on the day of (...) [date]. Partake in my happiness and come to the wedding (*mishteh*, 'feast'), which I shall hold." The personal data had to be filled out by hand. The musicians (*klezmorim*) on the left form an ideal Klezmer band. Print, late eighteenth century. (With the name of the artist and the engraver.) MZsM. From: MéJ (1933).—Repr.: NZL&MI.

IV:1. Position of the hands when reciting the Priestly Blessing (*birkat kohanim*). Stained-glass window in the synagogue of the Rabbinical Seminary.—Photo: FA. 1994.

IV:2. The Dohány utca synagogue, ca. 1860. The doors of the shops on the ground floor of the houses next to the synagogue can be seen quite well; the overall appearance is considerably more pleasing than on later photos (see figs **126** and **146**, above). Colored lithograph. 34 × 43 cm. MNM: MTKcs. (Inv. no. MTKCs. T.5289.)—Photo: NZL&MI, 1994.

IV:3. Colored bricks and ornamental pattern on the exterior of the Dohány utca synagogue during the renovation, 1994.—Photo: EZ, 1994.

IV:4. Design of the synagogue on the curtain of the Ark in the Dohány utca synagogue. The Ark and the curtain were both designed by Frigyes Feszl. The curtain shows the facade of the synagogue according to the original design (see fig. **128**, above).—Photo: EZ, 1994.

The photo documents that during the recent renovation the Ark was protected by a huge plastic sheet.

IV:5. Ark in the Dohány utca synagogue. Designed by Frigyes Feszl.—Photo: EZ, 1994.

IV:6. Eternal light (*ner tamid*) **in the Dohány utca synagogue.** Designed by Frigyes Feszl.—Photo: EZ, 1994.

IV:7. Torah scrolls in the Ark of the Dohány utca synagogue.—Photo: FA&LLL, 1992.

IV:8. Stained-glass window in the Rumbach Sebestyén utca synagogue.—Photo: FA, 1994.

IV:9. Pillar in the Rumbach Sebestyén utca synagogue. (Detail.) (Cast-iron pillar supporting the women's gallery.) (After the recent renovation.)—Photo: FA, 1994.

V. Erzsébetváros

195. The outer edge of the Jewish quarter around Király utca: "Nagymező utca with the Terézváros Church." Painting by Albert Schickedanz, ca. 1880. Oil. MNM: LTM. (Inv. no. 14,848.)

196. Gömöry House, 12 Király utca. Once the "Arany Oroszlán" [Golden Lion] apothecary, it was later called (after its new owner) "Török Gyógyszertár" and even Török House. Photo, ca. 1935. 10 × 15 cm. MNM: LTM. Photo Archives. (Inv. no. 319.)—Repr.: MA.

The apartment of Azriel Brill was on the second floor of this house, and his son, R. Sámuel Löw Brill, a *dayyan* of the Dohány utca synagogue, also lived here. (See pp. 113 f., above.)

197. 25–27 Király utca. Small shops, among others: *Trenk testvérek kóser füstölthús és szalámi gyára. Gyári raktár* (Kosher smoked meat and salami factory of the Trenk Brothers. Factory outlet). On the signboard the word *kosher* is written in Hebrew letters. The owner of the *Király Áruház* (Király Department Store) was a certain Goldberger. The person in the right corner of the photo is most likely a porter. Photo. 6 × 9 cm. MNM: LTM. Photo Archives. (Inv. no. 21,823.)—Repr.: MA.

198. 3 Király utca. Shops. From right to left (according to the signboards): porcelain, cheese (Dávid Drucker), bandage- and truss-maker (Márk Fried), *Táncz tanintézet* (Dancing school) (Engel), *Szállítási bizomány* (Delivery) (Wald brothers), etc. The word *kosher* and other inscriptions in Hebrew can be seen on the signboard beside the entrance to the cheese shop. Photo, ca. 1900. Photo: Antal Weinwurm. 24 × 36 cm. MNM: LTM. Photo Archives. (Inv. no. 17,797.)—Repr.: MA.

199. Porter. The inscription on the band around the cap reads "*Gepäck Träger*", with the identification number. Drawing by Hermann Struck. From: *Vasárnapi Újság*. CsZs&DZ. (Inv. no. CsZs. 94/1/2.)

200. The Anker House. Drawing by Gergely Pörge, "Az Anker-udvar Pesten" [The Anker Court in Pest], 1908. (See fig. **98**, above.) 29.7 × 37.3 cm. MNM: MTKcs. (Inv. no. MTKCs. T.9009.)—Photo: NZL&MI, 1994.

201. A Jew in Pest, Váci utca, the Inner City. Cartoon by Mihály Szemlér (1833–1904), ca. 1860. From: *Budapesti Negyed*, no. 8 (1995).

202. Pekáry House, 47 Király utca, 1859. Colored engraving by Ludwig Rohbock, *Budapest és környéke eredeti képekben* [Budapest and Its Vicinity in Original Pictures] (1859). MNM: MTKcs. (Inv. no. MTKCs. T.3038.)—Photo: NZL&MI, 1994.

203. Pekáry House, 47 Király utca, ca. 1896. Photo: György Klösz. From: *Budapest anno...* (1979).—Repr.: NZL&MI.

204. License issued to a Jewish peddler (*Hausir Jude*) by the Pest Municipal Magistrate, 1821. The license was valid only for the days of the weekly market and only for Kecskeméti utca (Ketschkemether Gasse, in the Inner City). The peddler was, according to the license, not allowed to occupy an area larger than "one fathom (*Klafter*)" long and "three feet" wide (ca. 2 × 1 m or 6.5 × 3 feet); he could not sell his wares from a stand, only from a blanket spread on the ground; he could not have more wares than what he would carry on his back tied into a pack and he could not sell his wares elsewhere than in the appointed area, e.g. on the streets of the city or in houses. See fig. **206**, below. MZsM. From: MéJ (1916).—Repr.: NZL&MI.

205. **The Király utca** near the Terézváros Church. Photo, ca. 1900. From: *Budapesti Negyed*, no. 4 (1994).

206. **Jewish peddler** carrying a pack that complies with the license of the Pest Municipal Magistrate (see fig. **204**, above). *Képes Világ* (1868), II, p. 805. From: Zita Deáky, Zsigmond Csoma & Éva Vörös, Eds., *"...és hol a vidék zsidósága?... Történeti és néprajzi tanulmányok* ["...And Where is the Jewry of the Province?..."] Historical and Ethnographic Studies]. (Centrál-Európa alapítványi könyvek, 2; Budapest, 1994), p. 94. CsZs&DZ. (Inv. no. CsZs 93/3/9.)

207. **Mór Grossmann**'s shop "Gilt Ball" for linen and lingery, 28 Király utca, ca. 1910. Advertising on the partition wall recovered in 1997. Courtesy by Anna Perczel.—Photo: LE.

208. "**Handlé**" [Peddler]. Drawing of a Jewish peddler by János Jankó (1833–1896). *Vasárnapi Újság* (1867), p. 624. From: Miklós Létay, *Az utca népe Pest-Budán 1848-1914* [People of the Street in Pest and Buda, 1848–1914] (Budapest, 1993).

209. **Traffic and the throng in Király utca**. Drawing by Karl Klič (1841–1926), ca. 1868. *Borsszem Jankó*. From: Károly Vörös, *Budapest története a márciusi forradalomtól az őszirózsás forradalomig* [History of Budapest from the Revolution in March (1848) until the Revolution of the Michaelmas Daisy (1918)] (Budapest: Akadémiai Kiadó, 1978).

210. **Building of the (Israelite) Institute for the Blind**, 64 Király utca, ca. 1900. A Hungarian and Hebrew text is inscribed on the building at the Gyár utca corner of the building: "Imaház. *Bet ha-midrash*" (Prayer-house), and beside the entrance from Király utca: "*Kosher*". The latter one was either a restaurant or a butcher. The Music Academy was later built on the site of this building. Photo. 6 × 9 cm. MNM: LTM. Photo Archives. (Inv. no. 21,281.)—Repr.: MA.

211. **Imre Kálmán**. Photo, 1912. From: *Budapesti Negyed*, no. 8 (1995).

212. **Boy wearing a Purim mask**, carrying *shlakhmones*, a food gift (*mishlo'ah manot*) in one hand and a rattle in the other. Imre Ámos, "Purim". Linocut. 34 × 27 cm. From: [*Ünnepek.*] *Ámos Imre 14 eredeti metszete* [Holidays. Fourteen Original Linocuts by Imre Ámos] (1940).

213. "**On Purim you may do as you like**, but after the holiday we will know who behaved improperly (*Purim darf man alles tun, nach Jantef stellt sach eraus, wer e Asesponem war*)." Color chalk-drawing by Lipót Herman to illustrate a Jewish saying. 12.3 × 16 cm. From: HL.

214. **4 Holló utca**. The home of Ignác Goldziher and Sámuel Kohn. Floor mosaic in the shape of a six-pointed star on the ground floor in the stairway. Photo: FA&LLL, 1993.

215. **Vitus Srágó Feis Phoebus Goldzieher** (?–1844), Ignác Goldziher's grandfather. (The name *Srágó / Schraga*, Aramaic *sheraga*, "lamp", corresponds to Hebrew *Uri*, "light", "bright", and was often rendered as *Phoebus*; the latter's Yiddish variant is *Feyvush / Feysh, Feyvl*; all these are Jewish variants of the same name and not different names.) From: MéJ (1938).—Repr.: FBA.

216. **R. Nathan Mayer (Meir) Goldziher**, Vitus Goldzieher's third son, Ignác Goldziher's uncle. Oil painting by Julius Hamburger (1830–?), a Viennese painter, 1869. From the bequest of Mrs. Vilmos Bacher. From: MéJ (1938).—Repr.: NZL&MI.

Vitus Goldzieher's library of rabbinical works was, for the greater part, inherited by Nathan Goldzieher; some of the books, however, went to Ignác Goldziher. In his Diary the latter mentions that these books formed the core (*Grundstock*) of his collection of Hebrew books.

217. **R. Meir Hirsch Henrik Goldziher** (1816–1884), Vitus Goldzieher's second son, Ignác Goldziher's oldest uncle. Photo: Nándor Pál. Colored photo; formerly in the possession of Mrs. Sándor Büchler. From: MéJ (1938).—Repr.: NZL&MI.

218. **Izsák Goldzieher** (1820–1892), Vitus Goldzieher's youngest son, Ignác Goldziher's uncle and father of the ophthalmologist Vilmos Goldzieher (1849–1916), head of the Ophthalmology Department in the "Szent Rókus" Hospital.

Izsák Goldzieher's younger daughter, Ilona (1860–1931) became Vilmos Bacher's wife. Margit Herzog, his older daughter's daughter, married Lajos Blau. Vilmos Goldzieher's daughter, Klára Románné Goldzieher (1881–1962), was acknowledged as a handwriting expert, graphologist and a research scholar on left-handedness. From: MéJ (1938).—Repr.: NZL&MI.

219. **Mrs. Adolf Goldziher** née Katharina Gütl Berger (1814–1884), Ignác Goldziher's mother. One of Ignáz Goldziher's Hebrew names was after her father, Izsák (Yitzhak) Berger. Photo: Nándor Pál. From: MéJ (1938).—Repr.: NZL&MI.

220. Adolf Goldziher (1811–1874), the oldest son of Vitus Goldzieher, Ignác Goldziher's father. Oil painting, formerly in the possession of Mrs. Sándor Büchler. From: MéJ (1938).—Repr.: NZL&MI.

221. Mrs. Nátán Glück, née Mária Goldziher (1852–1884), Ignác Goldziher's younger sister. Photo, formerly in the possession of Mrs. Sándor Büchler. From: MéJ (1938).—Repr.: NZL&MI.

Mária Goldziher's second daughter, Aranka, who was—for a time—brought up in Ignác Goldziher's house, married Sándor Büchler.

222. A certificate by Moses Schreiber, chief rabbi of Pozsony (the *Hatam Sofer*) (1828). The document entitled the addressee to bear the title *haver*, i.e. acknowledged that he had acquired the necessary erudition in Jewish traditional literature.

"(...) The above mentioned *bahur* studied here in our *yeshivah* for some time, and all of it has been finished finely; his taste has not gone bad, nor has his smell become unpleasant, for he found delight in the Torah of the LORD, that is what he matters day and night, he does not turn to the streets and children of our days, nor—God forbid—to the liars. Since he fears God all day and does not move from the tenth of the Torah, and the knees of the wise, or dear friendships, his thoughts are the thoughts of the Torah, he guards it in order to add to it, and not to tear away from it, from the holy laws of Life. Let us rely upon his honor, let us call him, in the honor of the wise, by a new name: the colleague (*haver*). Rav Aharon (son of our above mentioned master, Rav Fleish), let him strengthen in the Torah and worship.

"This is how I spoke in the Holy community of Pressburg, on Wednesday, the 26th of Adar, in the year 188 according to the minor era [= 1828 C.E.].

The modest (*ha-katan*) Moshe Sofer, from F(rank)f(urt am) M(ain)."

The title *haver* was an official recognition of exceptional merit in Torah learning, equivalent to a *yeshivah* graduation diploma. The date shows that the *bocher* left the Pozsony *yeshivah* at the age prescribed by tradition. That Adolf Goldziher studied throughout his life is repeatedly mentioned in his son's, Ignác Goldziher's, *Diary*. From: MéJ (1939).

223. Ignác Goldziher's childhood pledge to his father, 1862. From: MéJ (1939).

"The undersigned hereby pledges that as of today he will forever forsake his bad deeds and leave the paths of evil. He will strive to keep the commandment to honor his father and mother as it is written in the Torah of Moses: Honor thy father and thy mother: that thy days may be long (*Shemot* [Exodus] 20,12). And I shall not be like the servant who serves his master for a reward, but like the servant who serves not for reward, but out of the fear of God. May my father, my distinguished teacher, forgive me all my sins and disaffections which I have committed against him or was false to him unto this day.

"Stuhlwb. [Stuhlweissenburg / Székesfehérvár], on the 4th day [Wednesday] of *Aharei mot* [weekly portion, Leviticus 16–18] in Nisan, 622 (= 1862 C.E.), the year of repentance, of the abandonment (of sins) and of eternal forgiveness.

Jichák Leib Goldziher".

Ignác Goldziher was preparing for his *bar mitzvah* ceremony that year, which may explain the last words of the date formula of his pledge.

224. Adolf Goldziher's letter to his son (October 5, 1868), in the time when Ignác set off for his first university study trip abroad (Berlin). According to his *Diary*, he found the letter hidden in his suitcase. The father's request was that he should piously keep the anniversary of his grandparents' death: "With this virtuous deed your glory will rise and you will see Zion and Jerusalem rebuilt." From: MéJ (1939).

225. "**My son, Yitzhak** (Itzig) Leib, was born to me in a good hour (*le-sha[ʾah] tovah*) on the holy Sabbath, in the week of the *Hukkat-Balak* weekly portion (Numbers 19,1–22,1 and 22,1–25,9) on the 12th of Tammuz, 610 according to the minor era [= 1850 C.E.]. May it be God's will that as you have been privileged to introduce your son into the covenant, so may you also be privileged to bring him to the Torah with its commands, to the wedding canopy, and to a life of good deeds."—"My son, Ignatz, was born on June 22, 850." Note by Ignác Goldziher's father in Hebrew and German, respectively. From: Sándor Scheiber, *Folklór és tárgytörténet* [Essays on Jewish Folklore and Comparative Literature], III (1984).

Ignác Goldziher's Hebrew names were Yitzhak Yehudah ben Aharon Yom Tov. Both the last name (*Jom Tov*) and the name *Leib* mentioned here occur among the names of the great-grandparents: Jom

Tov Lipman Goldzieher was Vitus Goldzieher's father, while Kalonymus (Kálmán) Júda Lőb Goldzieher was his father-in-law.

Births were traditionally recorded by the father in the prayer-book of his wife, which he had given to her as a gift on the day of their wedding. According to the traditional formula, the child was always born "under a good sign / on a good day", and similarly part of this formula was that the boy "should be raised to the Torah, to the *huppah* and to good deeds", i.e. that he should live to see the *bar mitzvah*, the wedding and the various stages of manhood.

226. **Ignác Goldzieher delivers his *bar mitzvah* sermon** in the Székesfehérvár synagogue, 1863. (The photo was apparently made at a photographer's studio with stage props.) From: MéJ (1934).—Repr.: NZL&MI.

227. **Ignác Goldzieher at age 16**, 1866. Photo dedicated to his sister. From: MéJ (1938).—Repr.: NZL&MI.

228. **Ignác Goldzieher upon receiving his doctor's degree** (Dr. phil.) in Leipzig, 1870. From: MéJ (1937).—Repr.: NZL&MI.

229. *Ex libris*, **"from the books", of Ignác Goldzieher.** From: *Évkönyv*, 1979/80.

230. **Ignác Goldzieher's last photo**, 1920. From: MéJ (1937).—Repr.: NZL&MI.

231. **Portrait of Sándor Büchler** at the time he wrote his major work, *A zsidók története Budapesten...* [History of the Jews in Budapest...] (1901). Photo: Bienenfeld & Tsa. (25 Király utca). Hungarian Jewish Archives.

A photo of Sándor Büchler also appeared in MéJ (1914).

232. **Wholesale and retail stationery** of Vilmos Kohn jr., 1901. On the signboard: "Paper, stationery, drawing instruments and school supplies, printing works, wholesale, retail", etc. (Kerepesi út / 61 Rákóczi út). MNM: LTM. Photo Archives. (Inv. no. 52,334.)—Repr.: JL&FÁ.

233. **The publishing house of the Singer and Wolfner Co.** (10 Andrássy út), ca. 1912. The company was founded in 1885 by Sándor Singer, József Wolfner [jr.] and József Wolfner sr. From: *Budapesti Negyed*, 1 (1993), p. 156.—Repr.: NZL&MI.

234. **Interior of the Singer and Wolfner publishing house**, 1912. Designed by Géza (Rintel) Maróti. (Since perished.) From: *Új Idők* (December 8, 1912), title page.—Courtesy by Ferenc Dávid.

235. *Mezuzah*. **Margit Tevan's work.** The word *Shaddai* is set within the circle on the right; on the left, the lion of Judah (Genesis 49,9). Gilt copper. Photo: Juci Laub. From: MéJ (1936).—Repr.: NZL&MI.

236. *Havdalah*. The man holds a spice-box (*besamim*) (see fig. **V:2**, below), the boy, a braided *havdalah* candle. Imre Ámos, "Habdala". Lino-cut. 34 × 27 cm. From: [*Ünnepek.*] *Ámos Imre 14 eredeti metszete* [Holidays. Fourteen Original Lino-cuts by Imre Ámos] (1940).

237. **Children with *matzzot*.** Greeting card for Passover (*pesah*), 1908. Text: "Let all who hunger enter and eat." (Quote from the Haggadah, the text of the service or *seder* at the dining table.) 14 × 9 cm. From András Szántó's postcards collection.

238. **Passover on a page of the Kaufmann Haggadah.** On the right: Preparations for the holiday. On the left: Family at the Seder table. The ceremony is led by the head of the family. Miniature from a hand-written Pesah Haggadah, Spain (Catalonia), fourteenth century. MTA Kt. Oriental Library, Kaufmann Collection. (Cat. no. A. 422.) Fol. 2, recto.— MTA Kt. Microfilm Collection and Photo Laboratory. Photo: Mrs. Tibor Kolthay.

239. **Seder plate** (*ke'arah*) and rack to hold *matzzah*. The uppermost tray, the Seder plate, has five small bowls for the prescribed foods. Turned wood. Hungarian, mid-nineteenth century. MZsM. (Inv. no. Ipm.-66.52.)—Photo: FA&LLL.

240. **Elijah's chair** (*Kisse shel Eliyahu*) from the Óbuda synagogue. The backs are decorated with six-pointed stars. Carpenter's work from Pest, 1827. MZsM. (Inv. no. Ipm.-64.2201.) From: MéJ (1933).—Repr.: NZL&MI.

241. **A housewife asks the rabbi** to check the ritual purity of her chicken. Drawing by Lipót Herman to illustrate the Jewish saying: *Wen Scheile, schon trefe*, "If there is a question, it is surely not kosher." Colored chalk-drawing. 8.8 × 11.8 cm. From: HL.

242. **The kosher-border on István tér** (today Klauzál tér). Goose is sold on the right side, pork on the left. (The view is from Dob utca.) From: Porzó / Adolf Ágai, *Utazás Pestről - Budapestre* [Journey from Pest to Budapest] (1912).

243. **Signboard of the Orthodox kosher butchery**, 41 Kazinczy utca. Courtesy by Anna Perczel. Photo: LE.

244. **Mug with two handles for ritual hand-washing** (*netilat yadaim*). Tinned brass, embossed. Hungarian, eighteenth century. Height: 13.5 cm. MZsM. (Inv. no. Ipm.-64.352.) Photo: László Szelényi. From: BI&SchS.—Repr.: NZL&MI.

245. **The Budapest Talmud Association's** house in Vasvári Pál utca. Courtesy by Anna Perczel. Photo: LE.

246. **Interior of the Vasvári Pál utca synagogue.** The Ark, with the partition (*mehitzah*) in the foreground, after the renovation (1993).—Photo: FA&LLL, 1994.

247. *Etrog* **container**, with an engraved Hebrew inscription: "Acquired by the officials of the local charity (institutions) in the Holy community of Óbuda. In the year 625 (= 1865 c.e.), on the holiday of Sukkot." (The inscription was probably engraved on the lid later.) Embossed silver. With a Buda hallmark (1883): mark of József Károly Gretschl sr. Height: 7 cm, width: 9 cm, length: 14.5 cm. MZsM. (Inv. no. Ipm.-64.345.) Photo: László Szelényi. From: BI&SchS.—Repr.: NZL&MI.

248. **Holiday of the Tabernacles**. Palm frond, myrtle twigs, willow branches and *etrog* (here in the container). Imre Ámos, "Sátoros ünnep" [Holiday of the Tabernacles]. Lino-cut. 34 × 27 cm. From: [*Ünnepek.*] *Ámos Imre 14 eredeti metszete* [Holidays. Fourteen Original Lino-cuts by Imre Ámos] (1940). 29 × 22.5 cm. SzM–XX.

Of this picture, a variant in ink is also known. The man holds the *lulav* in his right hand and the *etrog* in the left. In terms of the ritual, the print of the lino-cut (here), which is symmetrical with the ink drawing, is the correct one.

Another element of the *Sukkot* ritual is illustrated in one of Imre Ámos's main works, an oil painting: "Sátoros ünnep (Zsidó férfi ünnepi csokorral)" [Feast of the Tabernacles. A Jewish Man with the Festive Branch] (1933), showing the man in the ceremonial procession. Ámos gave this painting to József Patai (1935), from whom it reached the collection of the MZsM. (Inv. no. Képz.-64.2332.)

V:1. **Betrothal plate**. The Hebrew inscription (*Mazel tov*, "Good luck") is repeated several times, and also appears on the stave of the *huppah*. Porcelain. MZsM. (Inv. no. Ipm.-64.786.)—Photo: FA&LLL, 1993.

V:2. **Spicebox** (*besamim*) for the ritual of bidding farewell to the Sabbath (*Havdalah*). The box has two tiers and is modeled on a tower. The first tier has a movable door and balcony, the second one has double windows. (For its use see fig. **236**, above.) Silver filigree. Óbuda (?), late eighteenth century. Height: 32 cm. MZsM. (Inv. no. Ipm.-64.71.)—Photo: FA&LLL, 1993.

V:3. **Setting aside a portion of the dough** (*mitzvat hallah*), the second of the religious obligations of women (Numbers 15,20). This rite is in remembrance of the offering in the Temple. Miniature, in a parchment book, eighteenth century. Size of pages: 8 × 10.5 cm, size of miniature: 4 × 3.5 cm. MZsM. (Inv. no. 64.626.) *Seder birkat ha-mazon*. Polna, 511 (= 1751 c.e.), p. 17, verso. From: *Seder birkat ha-mazon / Grace after Meals / Asztali áldás* (Facsimile edition, Budapest: Helikon, 1991).

V:4. **Purim in the synagogue**: when Haman's name is mentioned, everyone stamps their feet and boos. On the women's gallery, musical instruments are used for making noise. Miniature in a *Megillah* [Scroll (of the Book of Esther)] from Italy, mid-eighteenth century. 5 × 15 cm. MTA Kt. Oriental Library, Kaufmann Collection. (Cat. no. A. 14.) Fly-leaf, col. I, bottom of the column.

V:5. **Purim. Sending a gift of food** (*mishloah manot*). The two persons are evidently carrying the two trays laden with food to each other, and both seem to be in a hurry. Miniature in a *Megillah* [Scroll (of the Book of Esther)] from Italy, mid-eighteenth century. 5 × 15 cm. MTA Kt. Oriental Library, Kaufmann Collection. (Cat. no. A. 14.) Megillah, col. XV, bottom of the column.

V:6. *Droshe*, **with a moral lesson**. Miniature in a *Megillah* from Italy, mid-eighteenth century. 5 × 15 cm. MTA Kt. Oriental Library, Kaufmann Collection. (Cat. no. A. 14.) Megillah, col. XVI, bottom of column.

V:7. *Seder* **plate**. The eight medallions on the rim contain words reminding of the successive events of the *Seder* celebration. Hand-painted Herend porcelain, mid-nineteenth century. The leader of the ceremony washes his hands before the *Seder*. On the left, an elderly man sits in an armchair, here serving as the *hesebet*. Seder plate. Diameter: 36 cm. MZsM. (Inv. no. Ipm.-64.425.)—Photo: FA&LLL, 1994.

V:8. **Celebration of the *Seder* and the meal**. A *Judenstern*-type lamp hangs from the ceiling. *Seder* plate. Hand-painted Herend porcelain, mid-nineteenth century. Diameter: 23 cm. MZsM. (Inv. no. Ipm.-64.426.)—Photo: FA&LLL, 1994.

One technical feature of the lamps known as *Judenstern*, "Jewish star" was that—despite their relatively high oil consumption—their receptacle could hold enough oil without the need to refill on the Sabbath and other holidays. The name comes from their form, modeled on a six-, eight- or twelve-pointed star. The *Judenstern* was a variant of a fairly widespread type of lamps in the late medieval–early modern period, which survived in Jewish households even after it had disappeared elsewhere.

VI. Józsefváros

249. **Building of the Rabbinical Seminary**, 1877. Engraving. *Magyarország és a nagyvilág* (1877), no. 41.

250. **József Freund of Óbecse**, the founder of the boarding school of the Teachers' College and the Rabbinical Seminary, wearing Hungarian national gala dress. From: MéJ (1918).—Repr.: NZL&MI.

251. **József Freund of Óbecse and his wife** in the Holy Land, dressed as Beduins. From: MéJ (1928).—Repr.: NZL&MI.

252. **Lajos Blau as a student** of the Rabbinical Seminary, ca. 1885. There is a prayer-shawl (*tallit*) on his shoulders. From: MéJ (1941).—Repr.: NZL&MI.

253. **Lajos Blau as a field rabbi** in his military uniform. From: MéJ (1941).—Repr.: NZL&MI.

254. **The "Eastern Wall"** in the Rabbinical Seminary's synagogue.—Photo: FA, 1993.

The two large marble slabs flanking the Ark contain the names of the "benefactors of the Seminary"; these include Vilmos Bacher, Moses Bloch, József Freund (of Óbecse), Ignác Goldziher, Izsák Goldzieher, Zsigmond Gomperz (Róza Gomperz's husband), Ignác Hirschler, Mór Wahrmann, Sándor Wahrmann.

255. **Portrait of R. Gyula Fischer.** Drawing by Raphael (György) Patai, 1929. From: Raphael Patai, *Apprentice in Budapest* (1988).

256. **Portrait of R. Ármin Hoffer.** Drawing by Raphael (György) Patai, 1929. From: Raphael Patai, *Apprentice in Budapest* (1988).

257. **Ceremonial Hall of the Rabbinical Seminary,** with portraits of the rectors and professors of the Seminary. Upper row (from left to right): Moses Bloch, Vilmos Bacher, Ignác Goldziher, Dávid Kaufmann, Lajos Blau, Bernát Heller, Mihály Gutmann, Simon Hevesi, Lajos Venetianer, Ármin Hoffer, Mózes Richtmann. Lower row (from left to right): Miksa Weisz, Sámuel Löw Brill, Bertalan Edelstein, Miksa Klein, Zsigmond Groszmann, Gyula Fischer, Arnold Kiss, Dénes Friedmann, Sándor Scheiber, László Salgó. The portraits are arranged in a more or less chronological order.—Photo: FA&LLL, 1993.

After the Hall was repainted in 1993, the portraits were put back in a slightly different order.

258. **Former office of the director** of the Hungarian Jewish Archives in the Rabbinical Seminary. There is a *parokhet* on the wall and one hanging in front of the bookcase. The archive materials in the room and the small museum collection were gathered, following Sándor Scheiber's intentions, by R. György Landeszman, the former director of the Archives.—Photo: FA&LLL, 1992.

259. **Portrait of Moses Bloch.** From: MéJ (1929); Moshe Carmilly-Weinberger, Ed., *The Rabbinical Seminary of Budapest* (1986).

260. **Two Hebrew translations** from Hungarian by Simon Bacher: "Hymnus" [Anthem] by Ferenc Kölcsey (the first stanza) and "Fóti dal" [Song of Fót. A Convivial Song] by Mihály Vörösmarty (the first two stanzas).

261. **Vilmos Bacher as a field rabbi** during the occupation of Bosnia, 1878. From: MéJ (1914).—Repr.: NZL&MI.

262. **Vilmos Bacher in his study.** Photo, ca. 1910. The original is in the collection of the family.—Repr.: NZL&MI.

263. **Portrait of R. Ernő Róth,** 1942. From the tableau showing the teachers and students of the years 1937–1942, 1942. Office of the Rabbinical Seminary, Budapest.—Repr.: NZL&MI.

264. **Jewish gravestone from Aquincum** (?). Detail (see fig. **265**, below). A *menorah* and Jewish names written in Greek letters can be seen between the human figures on the Roman relief. MNM: (Inv. no. 62.70.1.)—Photo: FA&LLL, 1994.

265. **Jewish gravestone from Aquincum** (?). Height: 181 cm, width: 76 cm. MNM: (Inv. no. 62.70.1.) Until recently, it was exhibited in the aula of the National Museum, to the right of the main stairway. (Now in the newly established Lapidarium.) From: Alexander Scheiber, *Jewish Inscriptions in Hungary* (1983), no. 2.—Photo: FA&LLL, 1994.

266. **Three engraved *menorahs*** and Judeo-Greek inscriptions on the Jewish gravestone from Aquincum (?). From: Alexander Scheiber, *Jewish Inscriptions in Hungary* (1983), no. 2.

VI:1. **The former desk of the professor** in the main class-room of the Rabbinical Seminary. (Following the renovation in 1993.)—Photo: FA&LLL, 1993.

VII. Terézváros

267. **Portrait of Mór Wahrmann.** From the tableau of the General Jewish Congress, 1868/69 (see fig. **143**, above).

268. **Portrait of Mór Wahrmann.** From: Ignaz Reich, *Beth-El*, III, 1 (1882).

269. **Mór Wahrmann.** Cartoon from *Borsszem Jankó*. From: Géza Buzinkay, *Mokány Berczi és Spitzig Itzig... A magyar társadalom figurái az élclapokban 1860 és 1918 között* [Figures of the Hungarian Society in Satiric Newspapers between 1860 and 1918] (Budapest: Magvető Könyvkiadó, 1988).

270. **Miksa Falk,** editor-in-chief of the *Pester Lloyd* and Hungarian language teacher of Queen Elisabeth, wife of King and Emperor Francis Joseph. Photo, ca. 1880. From: *Budapesti Negyed*, no. 8 (1995).

271. **The Pannonia Steam Mill,** 1864. Originally in Pannónia utca. Drawing by an unknown artist. *Ország Tükre* (1864), no. 5. Gerszi, p. 219, no. 122. Reprinted in: Károly Vörös, *Budapest története a*

márciusi forradalomtól az őszirózsás forradalomig [History of Budapest from the Revolution in March (1848) until the Revolution of the Michaelmas Daisy (1918)] (1978).

272. **Mór Wahrmann dozing off** at a private concert given by the [Jenő] Hubay–[Dávid] Popper quartet, ca. 1888. Caricature by János Jankó in *Borsszem Jankó*. From: MéJ (1937).

273. **Mausoleum of Mór Wahrmann**. Planned by Zsigmond Quittner, 1892. From: Zsigmond Quittner, *Építő Ipar* (1900).—Repr.: NZL&MI.

274. **The *Párisi Nagy Áruház*** (Department Store) on Andrássy út. Postcard. From: Grüsse.—Photo: NZL&MI, 1994.

275. **"Grand promenade on the roof** of the *Párisi Nagy Áruház*." Postcard. From: Lajos Csordás, "Budapest ezer lapban elbeszélve" [Budapest's History Told on Thousand Cards], in: *Népszabadság* (November 7, 1998), p. 40.

276. **The Parisiana Nightclub**. Design by Béla Lajta, 1908. The original inscription on it says: "Modified blueprint of the nightclub that is to be built on the plot at Budapest, Szerecsen utca, cadastral number 3876, owned by Mrs. Adolf Friedmann, née Amália Schwarz." Signature: "Béla Lajta, architect. Budapest, 10 Pálma utca." Fővárosi Önkormányzat, Magas-építési tervtár (Municipal Government, Architectural Engineering Archives). (Cadastral no. 29,320.) From: Ferenc Dávid, *et al.*, *A Parisiana újjáépítése* [The Reconstruction of the Parisiana] (1991).

277. **The facade of the Parisiana**, ca. 1910. From: János Gerle, *et al.*, *A századforduló magyar építészete* [Hungarian Architecture at the Turn of the Century] (1990); Ferenc Dávid, *et al.*, *A Parisiana újjáépítése* [The Reconstruction of the Parisiana] (1991).

278. **The facade of the Theater** in Paulay Ede utca after the 1991 restoration.—Photo: FA&LLL, 1994.

279. **Foyer of the *Blaha Lujza Színház*** ("Lujza Blaha" Theater). Design by László Vágó, 1921. From: Ferenc Dávid, *et al.*, *A Parisiana újjáépítése* [The Reconstruction of the Parisiana] (1991).

280. **Portrait of Miksa Szabolcsi**. From: MéJ (1911).—Repr.: NZL&MI.

281. **Portrait of József Patai**. Photo, ca. 1915. From: Raphael Patai, *Apprentice in Budapest* (Salt Lake City: University of Utah Press, 1988), p. 331.

282. **Regular guests of Café Japán**, ca. 1912, among them the artists Pál Szinyei Merse (second from the left) and József Rippl-Rónai (with a cane). Ödön Lechner, Károly Ferenczy and Károly Kernstok were also among the regulars.

283. **Ground-plan of the Dessewffy utca synagogue**. From: Gazda.

284. **The new marble *almemor*** of the Bikur Cholim synagogue in Dessewffy utca, ca. 1935. From: MéJ (1936).—Repr.: NZL&MI.

285. **An advertisement of the restaurant Niszel**. The Hebrew spelling of the word Orthodox in the term "*orth. kosher*" reflects the usage in Hungarian.

VII:1. Terézváros. A map by Karl Vasquez, *Buda és Pest szabad királyi várossainak tájleírása* [Topography of Free Royal Cities of Buda and Pest] (1838), sheet IV. (Detail.) The map clearly shows that the building up of the neighborhood North of Király utca (*Königs Gasse*) was at that time—decades before the demolition work preceding the construction of Sugár út (Andrássy út)—fairly homogenous. The streets in question are as follows: *Zwey Mohren Gasse* (Két Szerecsen utca / Paulay Ede utca); *Elbogen Gasse* (Könyök utca), which extended to Gyár utca and marked the line of the first section of the later Sugár út / Andrássy út; *Rettig Gasse* (Retek utca / Révay utca); *Lazarus Gasse* (Lázár utca), etc. The word *Synagogen*, "synagogues" appears above the area between Király utca–Rombach utca–Három Dob utca (*Drey Trommel Gasse*)–Ország út (*Land Strasse*). Szilvia Andrea Holló, *Budapest régi térképeken, 1686-1896* [Budapest on Old Maps, 1686-1896] (Budapest: Officina Nova, 1994), no. 10, pp. 40-41. MNM: MTKcs. (Inv. no. MTKCs. T.1385.)—Repr.: NZL&MI.

VII:2. Interior of the "Paris" department store (*Párisi Nagy Áruház*), ca. 1910. Colored postcard. 9 × 13.9 cm. MNM: MTKcs. (Inv. no. MTKCs. 61.16.)—Photo: NZL&MI, 1994.

VII:3. 23 Andrássy út. Staircase of the Wahrmann Palace.—Photo: FA&LLL, 1993.

VII:4. Wahrmann Palace. Etched-glass window in the staircase.—Photo: FA&LLL, 1993.

VII:5. Wahrmann Palace. Wrought-iron handrail in the staircase. (Detail.)—Photo: FA&LLL, 1993.

VII:6. Courtyard of the Dessewffy utca synagogue. To the right, the entrance to the synagogue; to the left, the stairs leading to the women's gallery. The photo was taken during the recent renovation work.—Photo: FA&LLL, 1993.

VIII. The Pest Jewish Community

286. **12 Síp utca.** Office building of the Budapest Jewish community. On the facade there is a fairly recent inscription: *Budapesti Zsidó Hitközség,*

"Jewish community of Budapest" (not shown on the photo).—Photo: FBA, 1994.

287. **Entrance to the office building** of the Jewish community, view from the courtyard. There is a memorial slab on the right: "*Yizkor* [Remember]. The martyrs of this house (1941–1944). They were true to the Jewish community, unto their death. Let us be true to their memory, unto our death." The magnetic door in the entrance is part of the security check equipment installed in 1993.—Photo: FBA, 1994.

288. **The presidential table in the Assembly Hall**, recently with the Hungarian and Israeli flags on the right side. The *menorah* in the center, similarly to the one in front of the Knesset in Israel, is modeled on Titus' triumphal arch in Rome. On the left, the portrait of Ármin Neuwelt (signed by H. Weiss, 1929).—Photo: FBA, 1994.

289. **Mór Szitányi Ullmann**, a former Board member of the Pest Jewish community. (The portrait was painted after his baptism.) From: Vera Bácskai, *A vállalkozók előfutárai* [Forerunners of Entrepreneurs] (Budapest: Magvető Könyvkiadó, 1989).

290. **Portrait of Sáje Wolf Schossberger**. From the tableau of the General Jewish Congress, 1868/69 (see fig. **143**, above).

291. **Portrait of Ignác Hirschler**. CsZs&DZ. (Inv. no. CsZs. 94/2/13.)

292. **Portrait of József Kőrösi** (Kőrösy). From: Károly Vörös, *Budapest története a márciusi forradalomtól az őszirózsás forradalomig* [History of Budapest from the Revolution in March (1848) until the Revolution of the Michaelmas Daisy (1918)] (1978).

293. **At the door of a Dob utca Orthodox prayer-room**. Photo, ca. 1910. From: *Budapesti Negyed*, no. 8 (1995).

294. **Leaving Judaism**. "Mr. Meshumed and Mrs. Meshumed", that is, a convert and his spouse. Cartoon in *Üstökös*, late nineteenth century. From: MéJ (1916).—Repr.: NZL&MI.

295. **Outside corridor in 17 Síp utca**. Courtesy by Anna Perczel. —Photo: LE, 1997.

296. **The Hunyadi tér synagogue**. Prayer-room of the Hazkarah Prayer-association. To the right, the railing (*mehitzah*) separating the women's space. The Hebrew name of the Prayer-association is recorded on a memorial slab from the fall of 663/1902: *Hevrat mazkir neshamot*, "Society for the remembrance of the (deceased) souls." Vilmos Vázsonyi, an MP, was an "honorary member and attorney" of the Association.—Photo: FA&LLL, 1992.

297. **Manfréd Weiss**, the generous benefactor of several foundations, with his family. His wife, Alice Weiss née Wohl, and their children, from right to left, Elza, Marianne, Jenő, Alfonz. Photo, ca. 1893. MNM: LTM. From: *Budapesti Negyed*, 1 (1993), p. 49.—Repr.: NZL&MI.

The photo was taken at the time when Manfréd Weiss' Csepel arms factory was one of the largest in the Austro-Hungarian Monarchy at the outbreak of World War I. His foundations for the support of several Jewish welfare institutions were all established in memory of his wife (see figs. **529** and **547**, below).

Marianne Weiss later married Baron Móric Kornfeld. Elza Weiss married Alfréd Mauthner.

298. **Buildings of the Jewish hospital** on the corner of Aréna út and Szabolcs utca, 1896/97. Designed by Vilmos Freund, 1888–1889.—Courtesy by András Losonci, director and head surgeon.

299. **A pavilion of the Jewish hospital**, 1896/97.— Courtesy by András Losonci, director and head surgeon.

300. **Sick-ward in the Jewish hospital**, 1896/97.— Courtesy by András Losonci, director and head surgeon.

301. **Entrance to the former prayer-room of the Jewish hospital**. The inscription above the entrance: "*Imaház / Beit ha-keneset*." From: MéJ (1935).—Repr.: NZL&MI.

302. **Interior of the prayer-room** of the Jewish hospital. From: MéJ (1935).—Repr.: NZL&MI.

303. **Title page of a Hungarian–Hebrew–German primer** for the Jewish public schools: Sámuel Kohányi, *Első hangoztató és olvasókönyv* [First Reader]. *A magyar-német-héber olvasókönyvnek I. része* [First Part of the Hungarian-German–Hebrew Reader] (Pest: Pesti Izráelita Magyar Egylet, 1861).— Országos Széchényi Könyvtár (National Széchényi Library). (Inv. no. 302,620.)

304. **Temporary building of the Jewish Girls' High School** (5-7 Munkácsy Mihály utca), ca. 1920. From: MéJ (1923).—Repr.: NZL&MI.

305. **Design for the plannned reconstruction** of the Jewish Girls' High School, 1923 (for the existing building see fig. **304**, above).

The plans of reconstruction of the existing temporary building were apparently thwarted by the decision of the Jewish community to build the High School for Girls next to the High School for Boys, on the plot at Szent Domonkos utca and Abonyi utca. From: MéJ (1923).—Repr.: NZL&MI.

306. **The synagogue in the Mɪᴋéꜰᴇ school** and dormitory for apprentices (48 Damjanich utca). From: MéJ (1927).—Repr.: NZL&MI.

307. **Memorial leaf in honor of Moses Montefiore** on the occasion of his visit to Pest in 1863 (lithographic printing house of Mór Deutsch). The inscription is a traditional Hebrew micrography: the letters are arranged into the shape of the Two Tablets of the Law, outlining the text of the Decalogue. The accompanying text in the frame:

> "The face of Moshe Montefiore: the image of the faithful messenger, the emissary of the Creator. Your name is the same as your teacher's: *Mosheh rabbeinu*; your way (is) the same as your ancestor's: *Avraham avinu*. You reside at the king's court, on the Island of Britain [here: *ziyyim ve-kittim*, see Daniel 11,30]. Your authority is as R. Eleazar ben Arakh's, the royal prince, to convert those who have deviated. (…) It is a joy for us, the Pest community, that you shall sojourn within our boundaries. He comes among us to see his brethren…", etc.

Montefiore, like Abraham in the Bible (Genesis 12,1–6), was on this occasion traveling to the Holy Land. Eleazar ben Arakh (second century c.ᴇ.) was a sage of the Talmudic period who held that the greatest virtue was kindness (Pirkei Avot, 2,9). MZsM; Hungarian National Gallery. From: MéJ (1934).

A portrait of Montefiore was also printed by the lithographic printing house of Lipót Wellisch in the last third of the nineteenth century.

308. **Moses Montefiore's letter** to the Pest Hevrah Kaddishah, expressing his thanks that its emissaries visited him on his 99th birthday.

> "(…) Gratitude and a blessing that you have visited me, that you have honored me with your kind visit and have extended your blessing on the occasion of my ninety-ninth birthday, on the eighth day of Heshvan… [Marheshvan / November 8, 1883]."

The letter was obviously written by a scribe, but it was signed by the patriarch himself in Latin letters, writing his first name Moshe in Hebrew. From: MéJ (1931).

309. **Bernát Munkácsi** on a field trip in the Ural (Russia), where he pursued his linguistic studies among Finno-Ugrian peoples, the supposed relatives of Hungarians. Photo, 1885. From: Hungarian Jewish Archives.

310. **Main entrance of the *Zsidó Gimnázium* /** Jewish Secondary / High School on the original plan of Béla Lajta, 1913/14. From: MéJ (1918).—Repr.: NZL&MI.

311. **Facade of the Jewish High School** in Szent Domonkos utca. Plan by Béla Lajta, 1913/14. From: Ferenc Vámos, *Lajta Béla* (1970).—Repr.: NZL&MI.

312. **The entrance from Szent Domonkos utca** on the design by Ármin Hegedűs & Henrik Böhm, 1928. From: *Tér és Forma* (1931).—Repr.: NZL&MI.

313. **Hall of the Jewish High School**, second floor. In the back the doors of the synagogue. Designed by Ármin Hegedűs & Henrik Böhm. From: *Tér és Forma* (1931); MéJ (1932).—Repr.: NZL&MI.

314. **Main entrance of the Jewish High School** (in Szent Domonkos utca). Designed by Ármin Hegedűs and Henrik Böhm, based on Béla Lajta's original design. Decorated with two *menorahs* in brick relief, and with floral designs. Photo: Ernő Bánó. From: Dénes Györgyi, Ed., *Új magyar építőművészet* [New Hungarian Architecture], I (Budapest: Budai István, 1935).—Repr.: NZL&MI.

315. **Interior of the synagogue** of the Jewish High School. The photo must have been taken shortly after its completion as the furnishing—e.g. the Ark—is not complete yet. From: MéJ.

316. **The synagogue of the Jewish High School**. Interior, view from the entrance. The railing of the *bimah* can be seen in the center. Photo: Ernő Bánó. From: MéJ.

317. **The synagogue of the Jewish High School**. Photo, ca. 1935. Interior, seen from the gallery. Pews, the *bimah / almemor* and the Ark. The crossbeams are inscribed with Biblical quotations. These are as follows (from the doors to the Ark). Row 1: "Hearken unto the cry and to the prayer, which Thy servant prayeth before Thee" (I Kings 8,28 / II Chronicles 6,19). Row 2: "Enter into His gates with thanksgivings, and into His courts with praise: Be thankful unto Him, and bless his name" (Psalms 100,4). Row 3: "Let us come before His presence with thanksgiving, and make joyful noise unto Him with psalms (*bi-zemirot*)" (Psalms 95,2). Row 4: "Lᴏʀᴅ, I have loved the habitation of Thy house, and the place (*makom*), where Thy glory (*kavod*) dwelleth" (Psalms 26,8). Row 5 probably was inscribed—as far as one can see it on this photo—

with the first sentence of the *Shema Yisra'el*. Photo, ca. 1935. MNM: LTM. Photo Archives. (Inv. no. 07–15,003.)—Repr.: MA.

318. **Charity** (*tzedakah / tsdoke*). Stained-glass window in the synagogue of the Jewish High School. The Hebrew text: "Righteousness delivers from death" (Proverbs 10,2). The name of the donor, Aladár Kaszab and his wife, née Józsa Weiszkopf, is recorded in Hebrew and Hungarian in the two bottom lines of the text. In the year of the donation (1928) Kaszab was elected the president of the community; these windows were probably a—smaller—part of his *shnoder*. From: MéJ (1932).—Repr.: NZL&MI.

319. **The inner courtyard** of the Jewish High School. The staircase is at the center, the windows of the synagogue can be seen between the staircase and the chimney of the boiler-house. Photo: Ernő Bánó. From: MéJ (1935).—Repr.: NZL&MI.

320. **The staircase**, view from the courtyard. From: *Tér és Forma* (1931).—Repr.: NZL&MI.

321. **The entrance to the gym** from the courtyard in the Girls' High School. Above the gate, the figure of a lion in brick relief by Manó Rákos: "The lion of Judah" (Genesis 49,9). From: *Tér és Forma* (1931).—Repr.: NZL&MI.

322. **Sticker in the books presented as awards** at the end of the school year in the Jewish High School, 1931. The sticker shows the main entrance in Szent Domonkos utca, designed by Béla Lajta (see fig. **310**, above). By the fall of 1931, the entire complex of the school had been completed. The gift *ex libris* was signed by the director, Salamon Goldberger and by the teacher of the Hungarian language, Simon Gedő. From: *Évkönyv* [Yearbook], 1979/80.

Simon Gedő (1882–1957) is known for his essays on German literature and his (mostly unpublished) translations, including Martin Buber's *Hasidic tales*.

323. **The entrance to the Girls' High School**. On the columns: Rachel, Miriam and Esther in brick relief, each identified with their names in Hebrew. From: MéJ (1932).—Repr.: NZL&MI.

324. **Middle-Eastern type bazaar** at the corner of Dohány utca and Wesselényi utca, on the plot where the Jewish Museum was built later. The bazaar was established after Wesselényi utca was extended westwards to Károly körút (Dohány utca) in 1897. On the right, beside the Dohány utca synagogue, the partition wall of the old office building of the

Jewish community rises. On the left, the building of the old school (see fig. **335**, below), on the site of the eventual Goldmark Hall. From: MéJ (1930).—Repr.: NZL&MI.

325. **The Károly körút wing** of the Dohány utca synagogue: left, the old office building of the Jewish community (original appearance), 1930, prior to the demolition of the frontal part of this annex. (The building was partly demolished, including two windows on the left, frontal side, and the arcades beneath; see the ground-plan, fig. **333**, below.) The iron railing in front of the main entrance extended across the square (today a side-walk). From: MéJ (1930).—Repr.: NZL&MI.

326. **Competition design by Béla Tauszig** (Taussig) & Miklós Róth for the planned building on the corner of Dohány utca and Wesselényi utca. From: *Tér és Forma* (1929); MéJ (1929).—Repr.: NZL&MI.

327. **Design by Marcell Komor & János Komor** for building over the plot on the corner of Dohány utca and Wesselényi utca. From: *Tér és Forma* (1929); MéJ (1930).—Repr.: NZL&MI.

328 **Design by Dezső Jakab & Aladár Sós** for building over the plot on the corner of Dohány utca and Wesselényi utca. (Code-word: "Hit és Haza" [Faith and Homeland].) From: *Tér és Forma* (1929); MéJ (1930).—Repr.: NZL&MI.

329. **New buildings in Wesselényi utca**. Designed by Marcell Komor & János Komor. (In the background, the tower of the Dohány utca synagogue.) From: *Tér és Forma* (1929); MéJ (1930).—Repr.: NZL&MI.

330. **Design by Ernő Román**. (Code-word: "Hősök emléke" [In Memory of Heroes].) From: *Tér és Forma* (1929); MéJ (1929). Repr.: NZL&MI.

331. **The first design by László Vágó** for the planned building on the corner of Dohány utca and Wesselényi utca. From: *Tér és Forma* (1929).—Repr.: NZL&MI.

332. **Design by Ferenc Faragó & György Polacsek** for building over the plot on the corner of Dohány utca and Wesselényi utca. From: *Tér és Forma* (1929). Repr.: NZL&MI.

333. **The new ground-plan of the Dohány utca synagogue** after the reconstruction. Below the rule: the demolished part of the building. (See also fig. **124**, above.) After Gazda.—Drawing by Tamás Dezső.

334. **Arcades in the Károly körút wing** of the Dohány utca synagogue, which was later demolished. On the right, arcades towards the courtyard in front of the synagogue; in the back, right, door to the staircase of the synagogue's northern tower; in the back,

behind the glass door, the still empty plot (today the Heroes' Garden). From: MéJ (1930).—Repr.: NZL&MI.

335. Backyard of the Dohány utca synagogue, where the Heroes' Temple was to be built. View from the corner of Wesselényi utca and Rumbach Sebestyén utca. The hut stands roughly on the site of the present-day Ghetto Memorial. On the right, the old school building (see fig. **324**, above). From: MéJ (1930).—Repr.: NZL&MI.

336. Competition design by László Vágó for the reconstruction of the corner of Dohány utca and Wesselényi utca, 1929. (Code-word: "5689", that is, the year 1929 according to the Jewish calendar.) From: MéJ (1930).—Repr.: NZL&MI.

337. Reconstruction of the corner of Dohány utca and Wesselényi utca. From: MéJ (1930).

> 1: Dohány utca synagogue
> 2: Heroes' Memorial Temple (today Heroes' Temple)
> 3: Cultural Center (today the Jewish Museum)
> 4: Heroes' Garden (today Memorial Garden)
> 5: Goldmark Hall, etc.

338. The Cultural Center next to the Dohány utca synagogue (today the Jewish Museum). Design by László Vágó & Ferenc Faragó. There are here 12 (7 + 5) arcades on the planned building. From: Egyenlőség (1930); MéJ (1930).—Repr.: NZL&MI.

339. The Cultural Center on the corner of Dohány utca and Wesselényi utca (today the Jewish Museum). From: Tér és Forma (1931).—Repr.: NZL&MI.

340. Heroes' Temple. Competition design by Ferenc Faragó & György Polacsek. (Code-word: "Pietas".) From: Tér és Forma (1929).

341. Heroes' Temple. Competition design by Ferenc Faragó. From: MéJ (1930); Tér és Forma (1931).—Repr.: NZL&MI.

342. Heroes' Temple. Competition design by Ferenc Faragó (another version) (according to the article published in Tér és Forma it was designed by Faragó & Deli [Sándor Deli]). From: MéJ (1930); Tér és Forma (1930).—Repr.: NZL&MI.

343. Heroes' Temple: the arcades in Wesselényi utca. Design by László Vágó & Ferenc Faragó. Photo: János Röckel. From: Tér és Forma (1931); Dénes Györgyi, Ed., Új magyar építőművészet [New Hungarian Architecture], I (1935).—Repr.: NZL&MI.

344. The facade of the Heroes' Temple. Design by László Vágó & Ferenc Faragó. Photo: János Röckel. From: Tér és Forma (1931); Dénes Györgyi, Ed., Új magyar építőművészet [New Hungarian Architecture], I (1935). Repr.: NZL&MI.

345. View of the entrance to the Heroes' Temple from the arcades in the garden. Design by László Vágó & Ferenc Faragó. Photo: János Röckel. From: Tér és Forma (1931); Dénes Györgyi, Ed., Új magyar építőművészet [New Hungarian Architecture], I (1935).—Repr.: NZL&MI.

346. View of the entrance to the Heroes' Temple from the arcades in Wesselényi utca. Design by László Vágó & Ferenc Faragó. Photo: János Röckel. From: Dénes Györgyi, Ed., Új magyar építőművészet [New Hungarian Architecture], I (1935).—Repr.: NZL&MI.

347. Heroes' Temple: portico with colonnade on the Wesselényi utca side of the garden. Design by László Vágó & Ferenc Faragó. Photo: János Röckel. From: Dénes Györgyi, Ed., Új magyar építőművészet [New Hungarian Architecture], I (1935).—Repr.: NZL&MI.

348. Memorial inscription above the entrance in the Heroes' Temple. After a photo: EZ, 1994.

349. Jewish Museum. Stained-glass windows in the central exhibition hall, main floor. From: MéJ (1933).—Repr.: NZL&MI.

350. Portrait of Bernát Mandl. From: MéJ (1939).—Repr.: NZL&MI.

351. Pass issued to Fülöp Grünwald (address: 131 Hungária körút) by the Jewish Council in 1944. From: Kollaboráció vagy kooperáció [Collaboration or Cooperation] (1990).

352. Goldmark Hall, designed by Béla Tauszig, ca. 1929. From: Egyenlőség (1930).—Repr.: NZL&MI.

353. The Twelve Tribes of Israel. Design for the ornamentation of the Wesselényi utca facade of the Goldmark Hall. The sequence here reflects the final one: Reuben in the upper right corner, followed by Simeon, and Levi in the lower right corner, followed by Judah, etc. From: Egyenlőség (1930).—Repr.: NZL&MI.

354. Facade of the Goldmark Hall on the Wesselényi utca side. The Twelve Tribes of Israel.—Photo: FA&LLL.

355. Asher, Naphtali, Joseph, Benjamin. The Goldmark Hall, the Wesselényi utca facade. (Detail.) The lower row of the relief.—Photo: FA&LLL.

356. The first luah of Pest, 5608 / 608 (= 1848 c.e.), from the 3rd of Elul (September / St. Michael's month) to the 3rd of Tishri (October / All Saints' month). The calendar follows the sequence of the secular year (in this case, from September, 1848 on). Included are the weekly portions, the Jewish, Roman Catholic and Protestant holidays. In 1848, the New Year, Rosh ha-Shanah of the year 609 (1st of Tishri) fell on September 28, a Thursday. From: *Első magyar zsidó naptár és évkönyv 1848-ik szökő-évre* [First Hungarian Jewish Calendar and Yearbook for the Leap Year 1848].

357. *Shofar* **in the New Year's ritual.** (See fig. **12**, above.) "Shofar" by Imre Ámos. The word *teki'ah*— perhaps referring to the "great *teki'ah*"—is written on the book lying on the table, a real *shtot*. Lino-cut. 34 × 27 cm. [*Ünnepek.*] *Ámos Imre 14 eredeti metszete* [Holidays. Fourteen Original Lino-cuts by Imre Ámos] (1940).

358. *Tashlikh.* **New Year's greeting card**, ca. 1910. The caption is in Hebrew: a quote from the Book of Micah (7,19), and the words of the traditional New Year's greeting. From: András Szántó's postcards collection.

359. *Tashlikh.* Imre Ámos, "Taslich". Lino-cut. 34 × 27 cm. From: [*Ünnepek.*] *Ámos Imre 14 eredeti metszete* [Holidays. Fourteen Original Lino-cuts by Imre Ámos] (1940).

360. *Tashlikh.* Imre Ámos, "Vidd el, folyó, a mi bűneinket" [Wash away, River, our Sins]. Copper engraving, 1930. 49.8 × 26.3 cm. Imre Ámos's bequest. Photo: István Petráss. From: Katalin Perényi, *Ámos Imre* (Budapest: Corvina, 1982).—Repr.: NZL&MI.

361. "**Kapparah.**" Early morning before the Day of Atonement. Lino-cut by Imre Ámos. 34 × 27 cm. [*Ünnepek.*] *Ámos Imre 14 eredeti metszete* [Holidays. Fourteen Original Lino-cuts by Imre Ámos] (1940).

362. **Greeting of the New Moon.** "Újhold" [New Moon] by Imre Ámos. Lino-cut. 34 × 27 cm. [*Ünnepek.*] *Ámos Imre 14 eredeti metszete* [Holidays. Fourteen Original Lino-cuts by Imre Ámos] (1940).

363. *Vasúti indóház* (**railway station**) in Gyár utca (today Jókai utca), the predecessor of the *Nyugati pályaudvar* (Western Railway Station), ca. 1870. Built by the *Magyar Középponti Vasúttársaság* (Central Hungarian Railroads Co.) (1844). *Budapesti Híradó*, 1845. From: Imre Miklós, *A magyar vasutasság oknyomozó történelme* [The Cause and Effect History of Hungarian Railroads] (A történet-írás könyvei, 1) (Vác: Kapisztrán Nyomda, 1937).

364. **Teréz körút with the Schossberger Palace** in the foreground (1–5 Teréz körút, on the corner of Király utca and Teréz körút), ca. 1890. The carriage of the streetcar can be seen in front of the house. Drawing by Henrik Schmahl (1846–1913). From: Károly Vörös, *Budapest története a márciusi forradalomtól az őszirózsás forradalomig* [History of Budapest from the Revolution in March (1848) until the Revolution of the Michaelmas Daisy (1918)] (1978).

365. **Antal Fochs**, the founder of the Institute for the Deaf and Dumb. From: MéJ (1918).—Repr.: NZL&MI.

366. **Israelite Institute for the Deaf and Dumb** on István tér / Bethlen Gábor tér. The building is enclosed by a fence and lamp-posts stand in front of it. István út is paved with cobblestones. (For the former appearance of the square see fig. **521**, below.) From: MéJ (1918).—Repr.: NZL&MI.

367. **The former synagogue** of the Institute for the Deaf and Dumb. Interior. The *parokhet* is decorated with a Torah crown. (For its appearance following the rebuilding, see fig. **522**, below.) From: MéJ (1918).—Repr.: NZL&MI.

368. **Ferenc Molnár and Jenő Heltai**, writers of fame and popularity. Photo, ca. 1910. From: Géza Buzinkay, *Budapest képes története* [History of Budapest in Pictures](Budapest: Corvina, 1998).

VIII:1. "**Who is the mightier of the two?** The *rashekol* or the king?" Lipót Herman's colored chalk drawing to illustrate a Jewish saying. 12.5 × 13 cm. From: HL.

VIII:2. **Mór** [Mózes / Móric] **Ullmann's new house** on the Danube bank: "*Ullmann új háza a dunaparti kirakó révnél.*" (The site of the building is today occupied by the office building at 7–8 Roosevelt tér, between Vigyázó Ferenc utca and Zrínyi utca.) Karl Vasquez, *Buda és Pest szabad királyi várossainak tájleírása* [Topography of Free Royal Cities of Buda and Pest] (1838), sheet I. Franz Weiss's colored frame picture (in the upper row). Szilvia Andrea Holló, *Budapest régi térképeken, 1686–1896* [Budapest on Old Maps, 1686–1896] (Budapest: Officina Nova, 1994), no. 10, pp. 34–35. MNM: MTKcs. (Inv. no. MTKCs. T.1382.)—Photo: NZL&MI, 1994.

VIII:3. **Hunyadi tér synagogue**: reading desk (*shulhan*) and the Ark.—Photo: FA&LLL, 1992.

VIII:4. **Zionist badges.** Six-pointed star, inscribed in Hebrew letters: *Tziyyon*, "Zion". The inscription on the round badge: "Your people, Israel, is the only one on the earth" and "One Torah, one Law (*mishpat*)." The dots above the letters indicate the date: 672 (= 1912 C.E.). MNM Ét. Collection of Badges. (Inv. no. 56/931–6, Star of David; 65/939–3, round badge.)—Photo: FA&LLL, 1994.

VIII:5. **Label of the "Zion" schnapps.** The Hebrew inscription: "Be thankful unto Him and bless His name. For its taste (*ta'amo*) is good." The first sentence is a quotation from the Book of Psalms (100,4). (In the Bible, the pronoun obviously refers to God, on the label, in a more profane vein, to the cordial.) The last word on the label is in fact *ta'amor*, with *tet* and *alef*, but this does not make sense; the letter *resh* at the end of the word is probably superfluous. A word like *ta'amo*, with *tet*, *ayin* and *mem* would mean "taste", that is, "...its taste is good". *Non liquet*. There can be no doubt that this facetious inscription tried to create the impression that it was a Biblical or Talmudic quotation; there is a German word under the Hebrew legend: "*Siehe* IV. 5" (?). The words following the quotation from the Book of Psalms recalls the description of the fruits in the Garden of Eden (Genesis 2,9) whose use for business purposes was traditional. The melancholic man, sipping his drink and grieving over Zion, is sitting in a posture characteristic of Hungarians in a pub. Label on the cordial bottle of the Salamon Bloch Co. 16 × 7 cm. MKVM. The label was on display at the exhibition "*...és hol a vidék zsidósága?...* ["...And Where is the Jewry of the Province?..." in the Magyar Mezőgazdasági Múzeum (Hungarian Agricultural Museum) in 1994. CsZs&DZ.—Photo: FA&LLL, 1994.

VIII:6. From the collections of the Jewish Museum: Curtain (*parokhet*) of the Ark, 1826. 236 × 164 cm. MZsM. (Inv. no. Ipm.-64.1463.)—Photo: FA&LLL, 1994.

VIII:7. Ark in the Heroes' Temple.—Photo: FA&LLL, 1994.

VIII:8. From the collections of the Jewish Museum: Marriage contract (*ketubbah*). Verona, 5441 (= 1680/81 C.E.). The frame is decorated with the signs of the Zodiac. Height: 72 cm, width: 52.5 cm. MZsM. (Inv. no. Ipm.-64.1250.)—Photo: FA, 1994.

VIII:9. Lantern in the Heroes' Temple.—Photo: EZ, 1994.

VIII:10. Memorial inscription above the entrance to the Heroes' Temple.—Photo: EZ, 1994.

IX. Lipótváros, Új-Lipótváros

369. The pontoon bridge between Buda and Pest. View of Pest from the Danube bank in Buda. Jews of Óbuda, commuting between their home and the market in Pest, crossed the river on this bridge. Etching by János Blaschke, 1821, in: Franz (Ferenc) Schams, *Vollständige Beschreibung der königlichen Freystadt Pesth in Ungern* (Pest: Hartleben, 1821). From: Éva Faragó, *A reformkori Buda-Pest* (Budapest: Enciklopédia, 1996).

On the bridge, a tax was due upon crossing. Only the nobles and civil servants were granted exemption. A report in the *Pesti Hírlap* from 1842 (September 22)

mentions the case of a Jewish physician who was compelled to pay the tax, his standing notwithstanding; as an intellectual, he—a *honorácior* in Hungarian—was nearly a nobleman.

370. *Kirakodó tér* or *Rak-piac*. In the background the building of the Civil Merchants' Corporation of Pest (later Lloyd Palace). Rudolf Alt, "A Kereskedelmi Kar épülete Pesten / Casino in Pesth" [The Building of the Commercial Corps in Pest], ca. 1853. *Festői megtekintések Budára és Pestre. Malerische Ansichten von Ofen und Pest* (ca. 1853) (no. 5 in the series). Etching. 18.5 × 26.2 cm. MNM: MTKcs. (Inv. no. MTKCs. T.4027-Alt színes.)—Repr.: NZL&MI.

371. Lloyd Palace. Ground-plan of the second floor. From: Jenő Rados, *Hild József* (1958).

372. Father and son: Ferenc Chorin sr. and jr. Photo: Koller, 1900. MNM: TFt. From: *Budapesti Negyed*, no. 8 (1995).

373. Baron Zsigmond Kornfeld. Photo Strelisky, 1905. MNM: TFt. From: *Budapesti Negyed*, no. 8 (1995).

374. Baron Manfréd Weiss. Photo Strelisky, ca. 1910. MNM: TFt. From: *Budapesti Negyed*, no. 8 (1995).

375. Baron Ferenc Hatvany and Baron Lajos Hatvany. Photo, ca. 1900. Petőfi Irodalmi Múzeum. Photo Archives. From: *Budapesti Negyed*, no. 8 (1995).

376. Lipótváros Synagogue Competition. Street location. Plan by Vilmos Freund. Budapest Municipal Archives. From: *Budapesti Negyed*, no. 18/19 (1997–1998).

The competition announcement specified: "1800–1800 seats for men and women. Sanctuary (with the usual layout) and *almemor*, Ark and 18 seats, organ gallery behind the Sanctuary for a choir with 80 members and a separate stairway. Side areas: lobby, two halls for wedding guests, two rooms for the employees of the synagogue, a rehearsal room, spacious entrance-hall with cloakrooms and conveniences, and a superintendent's and two servant's quarters above. Stairs and stairways, central heating, ventilation and electric lights. Costs: 2 million, free choice of style."

In his review of the design submitted for the competition, Ludwig (Lajos) Hevesi came to the same conclusion as Simon Heller, in a study that appeared in *Évkönyv* (1900): "We should not build synagogues in any of the historical styles, but should rather erect modern buildings. Historical styles are becoming extinct. (...)" Etc. (In: *Pester Lloyd*, April 7, 1899.)

377. Lipótváros Synagogue Competition. Design by Lipót Baumhorn. (Code-word: "Hit és Remény"

[Faith and Hope].) Hungarian Jewish Archives. (Inv. no. 81.145.) From: *Budapesti Negyed*, no. 18/19 (1997–1998).

378. Lipótváros Synagogue Competition. Ground floor. Design by Béla Lajta (Leitersdorfer). (Code-word: "Rajzolt ötszög" [Designed Pentagon].) (3rd prize.) *Építő Ipar* (1899). From: *Budapesti Negyed*, no. 18/19 (1997–1998).

379. Lipótváros Synagogue Competition. Design by Béla Lajta (Leitersdorfer). (Code-word: "Rajzolt ötszög" [Designed Pentagon].) (3rd prize.) From: *Egyenlőség* (1899), Supplement to the March 19 issue; *Építő Ipar* (1899); Ferenc Vámos, *Lajta Béla* (1970); János Gerle, *et al., A századforduló építészete* [Hungarian Architecture at the Turn of the Century] (1990).—Repr.: NZL&MI.

380. Lipótváros Synagogue Competition. Proposed design by Zoltán Bálint & Lajos Jámbor. (Code-word: "Mózes".) (2nd prize.) From: *A Magyar Mérnök- és Építész-Egylet Közlönye* (1899).—Repr.: NZL&MI.

381. Lipótváros Synagogue Competition. The facade. Design by Albert Schickedanz & Fülöp Herzog. (Code-word: "Hétágú gyertyatartó" [Seven-arm Candelabrum].) (The jury recommended the purchase of this design.) From: Anikó Gazda, *Magyarországi zsinagógák* (1989); Ines Müller, *A Rumbach Sebestyén utcai zsinagóga* (1993).

382. Lipótváros Synagogue Competition. Design by Izidor Scheer, László Vágó & József Vágó. (Code-word: "Nyolc lépcsőház" [Eight Staircases].) Magyar Építészeti Múzeum (Hungarian Museum of Architecture). *Der Architekt* (1899). Photo: Gábor Barka. From: *Budapesti Negyed*, no. 18/19 (1997–1998).

383. Lipótváros Synagogue Competition. Second floor. Design by Ernő Foerk & Ferenc Schömer. (Code-word: "Alef".) (1st prize.) From: *A Magyar Mérnök- és Építész-Egylet Közlönye* (1899).—Repr.: NZL&MI.

384. Lipótváros Synagogue Competition. Cross-section of the dome by Ernő Foerk & Ferenc Schömer. (Code-word: "Alef".) (1st prize.) BTM: KM. Nyomtatványtár, Collection Foerk. Photo: Judit Szalatnyai. From: *Budapesti Negyed*, no. 18/19 (1997–1998).

385. *Ex libris* **of Dávid Kaufmann** in the Library of the Hungarian Academy of Sciences. The catalogue number indicates a manuscript.

386. Róza Gomperz, mother-in-law of Dávid Kaufmann, the donor of the Kaufmann Collection to the Library of the Hungarian Academy of Sciences. The caption to the photo in MéJ: "(...) founder of the Jewish women's teachers' training college". From: MéJ (1917).—Repr.: NZL&MI.

387. Dávid Kaufmann. From: *Zsidó Plutarchos*, II (Népszerű zsidó könyvtár, 19) (ca. 1925).—Repr.: NZL&MI.

388. Winged putti in a manuscript of the Kaufmann Collection. The inscription in the shield-shaped field under the crown: *Shalom lakhem. Al tir'u,* "Peace be to you, do not fear." (Joseph's words of greeting to his brothers when they returned after finding the money in their sacks; see Genesis 43,23. A suitable ending to the events recorded in the Book of Esther.) Miniature in a *Megillah* (Book of Esther) from Italy, mid-eighteenth century. 11 × 18 cm. MTA Kt. Oriental Library, Kaufmann Collection. (Cat. no. A. 14.) Megillah, col. XVI (the last column), above the text.

389. *Mishnah.* **A page from the Budapest manuscript** with corrections (*haggahot*) on the margin. MTA Kt. Oriental Library, Kaufmann Collection. (Cat. no. A. 50.)—MTA Kt. Microfilms and Photo Laboratory. Photo: Mrs. Tibor Kolthay.

390. How did the valuable manuscripts reach Budapest? Dávid Kaufmann's handwritten note on the inner cover of the *Mishneh Torah* manuscript. MTA Kt. Oriental Library, Kaufmann Collection. (Cat. no. A. 78.) Vol. I, cover.—MTA Kt. Microfilms and Photo Laboratory. Photo: Mrs. Tibor Kolthay.

391. Dávid Kaufmann's "Psalm on joy". Handwritten note on the cover of the Mishnah manuscript. MTA Kt. Oriental Library, Kaufmann Collection. (Cat. no. A. 50.) Vol. I, cover.—MTA Kt. Microfilms and Photo Laboratory. Photo: Mrs. Tibor Kolthay.

392. Portrait and signature of József Engel. From: *Beth-El*, II (1868); MéJ (1917).

393. Aurél Stein. Photo, ca. 1920. MNM: LTM. Photo Archives. (Inv. no. 25,772.)—Repr.: JL&FÁ.

394. Adolf Ágai, 1862. (The photo was taken in a photographer's studio.) From: MéJ (1916).—Repr.: NZL&MI.
Ágai was originally called Adolf Rosenzweig; both Ágai and Porzó were pen-names.

395. Portrait of Adolf Ágai, ca. 1875. Photo: Ferenc Kozmata. MNM: LTM. From: MéJ (1912).—Repr.: NZL&MI.

396. Portrait of Joseph Pulitzer, 1887. From: *The Curio* (1887); *The New Encyclopaedia Britannica*, 9 (1974/1985).

397. One of the Palatinus Houses on Rudolf tér (today 5–6 Jászai Mari tér—1–3 Újpesti rakpart), view from the Danube bank. Postcard, ca. 1920. From: Grüsse.—Repr.: NZL&MI.

398. **Interior of the Csáky utca synagogue** (today Hegedűs Gyula utca). The rebuilding was planned by Lipót Baumhorn & György Somogyi. The rostrum or *bimah* stands at the center. From: MéJ (1936).—Repr.: NZL&MI.

399. **The swimmer Alfréd Hajós** (left) and **marathon runner Gyula Kellner** (1871-1940) after they won Olympic medals. Sportmúzeum / Sports Museum. Photo: Gyula Jelfy, 1896. From: *Budapesti Negyed*, 8 (1995).

400. **The National Olympic Swimming Pool.** Competition design by Alfréd Hajós, ca. 1928. (Code-name: "Olympia".) From: *Tér és Forma* (1929).—Repr.: NZL&MI.

401. **The National Olympic Swimming Pool.** Designed by Alfréd Hajós. From: Dénes Györgyi, Ed., *Új magyar építőművészet* [New Hungarian Architecture], II (Budapest: Budai István, 1938).—Repr.: NZL&MI.

X. Józsefváros, beyond the Boulevard

402. **4 Nagy Fuvaros utca.** The ceiling of the prayer-room with a lamp.—Photo: LE, 1991.

403. **3 Nagy Fuvaros utca.** The building once housed an Orthodox synagogue.—Photo: LE, 1991.

404. **The entrance to the former Orthodox synagogue** from the courtyard (3/B Nagy Fuvaros utca). Photo: LE, 1991.

405. "**PÁSZKA MACÓ.**" Formerly a grocery store on the corner of Auróra utca and Bérkocsis utca.—Photo: LE, 1991.

406. **Where the *shabes tshulent* was baked:** formerly a bakery at 27 Nagy Fuvaros utca.—Photo: LE, 1991.

407. **Repair garage at the site of the former *kosheray*** (28 Dankó utca). The plot of the former kosher butchery.—Photo: LE, 1991.

408. **Aaron Rokeah.** From: István Gábor Benedek, "A csodarabbi ismeretlen megmentője" [The Unknown Rescuer of the Rebe], in: *Népszabadság* (June 21, 1997), p. 26.

409. "**Tshertkovo**" *shil* (22 Teleki tér). The main wall of the prayer-room is inscribed with the words "Guardian of Israel! Preserve the remnants of Israel that Israel should not perish!" Photo: Mrs. Ágnes Hávorné Takách. From: Anikó Gazda, *Magyarországi zsinagógák* (1989).—Repr.: NZL&MI.

410. **The Jewish market** (Tisza Kálmán tér, today Köztársaság tér), ca. 1920. The eastern half of the market, view from the North-Northeast. (On the original, full photo also the building of the Detention Barracks can be seen behind the booths in the far

background on the right.) MNM: LTM. Photo Archives. (Inv. no. A/45.)—Courtesy by Anna Perczel.

411. "**The railway station of the Pest–Losonc railroad in Pest**" (*Józsefvárosi pályaudvar* / Józsefváros Railway Station). Engraving by an unknown artist after a drawing by Gusztáv Zombory (1835-1872), 1865. MNM: MTKcs. (Inv. no. MTKCs. T.61.32.)—Repr.: NZL&MI.

412. **The market on Teleki tér,** 1946. In the background: the road of Népszínház utca and the houses 1-5 Teleki tér (numbered from right to left) (no. 1 at the corner of Teleki tér and Erdélyi utca). The signboards have since been replaced; "Gyarmat-áruk" (Colonial goods) by "Élelmiszer" (Groceries), "Patika" (Pharmacy) by "Gyógynövény" (Herbs); etc. Photo. FSzEKt.: BpGy. (Inv. no. 1116/29.)—Courtesy by Anna Perczel.

413. **Stores, workshops and a peddlers' cart** (15-19 Teleki tér). The signboards: "Strausz bőr áruház / kereskedés, cipészkellékek" [Strausz leather-wares / store, shoemaker's items], "Fa és szén" (Wood and coal), "1 kg edény 1 [forint (?)]" [1 kg dishes 1 (forint ?)], "Krausz S. Zsigmond férfiruha szabóság" (Zsigmond S. Krausz men's tailoring), etc. A dray packed with various household belongings waits on the street. MNM: LTM. Photo Archives. (Inv. no. 19.020.)—Repr.: MA.

414. **Crowd in front of the Teleki tér booths,** 1946. The cemetery extend and the road of Fiumei / Kerepesi út on the left, the booths on the right. Photo, 1946. FSzEKt.: BpGy.—Courtesy by Anna Perczel.

415. **Wine, beer and brandy shop.** Pub run by Károly Velekey (12 Teleki tér). Founded in 1896. Photo: Mór Erdélyi. MNM: LTM. Photo Archives.—Courtesy by Anna Perczel.

X:1. Ark in the prayer-room of the Nagy Fuvaros utca synagogue. The inscription on it: "From East to West the name of the LORD (in the center, with capital letters: JHWH) is praised" (Psalm 113,3).—Photo: LE, 1991.

X:2. Interior of the Nagy Fuvaros utca synagogue: the rostrum (*bimah / almemor*), view from the eastern wall (from the Ark). For the front side of the plaque with the order of prayers see fig. **X:3**, next.

X:3. Plaque with the order of prayers in the Nagy Fuvaros utca synagogue in front of the reading desk.—Photo: LE, 1991.

The prayers are the ones to be recited at the conclusion of each reading from the Torah, before and after every *aliyyah*: "Blessed be the LORD (YY) who is blessed for all eternity. Blessed art Thou, Lord our God, Ruler of the Universe. Thou hast chosen us from all the peoples and given us Thy Torah. Blessed art Thou, giver of the Torah." Etc.

X:4. *Parokhet* **in the Nagy Fuvaros utca synagogue.** (Detail.) Crown of the Torah (*keter Torah*).—Photo: LE, 1991.

X:5. 14 Fecske utca. Six-pointed star stained-glass window in the staircase.—Photo: LE, 1991.

X:6. 7–9 Dobozi utca. There was an Orthodox prayer-room in the courtyard wing of the building.—Photo: LE, 1991.

XI. Neighbors of the Pest Jewish Community

416. The synagogue below the Castle under construction. The Öntőház utca synagogue, with scaffolding. From: Imre Miklós, *A magyar vasutasság oknyomozó történelme* [The Cause and Effect History of Hungarian Railroads] (Vác: Kapisztrán Nyomda, 1937).

A few photographs of the ruins of this synagogue can be found in the Jewish Museum, dating from the period immediately following World War II, prior to its demolition (1945/46). Photo: Blahos. 9 × 14 cm. (Inv. no. Foto-70.53–55.)

417. The facade of the Öntőház utca synagogue. Design by Ignác Knabe: "*Plan über den neuzubauenden israelitischen Cultus-Tempel in Ofen* (Budapest, Öntőház utca 5–7), 1865." Facade. Budapest Municipal Archives. (Inv. no. BMT 403/XV.302–403.)—Repr.: Mrs. Gábor Pechan.

418. The Öntőház utca synagogue. Cross-section. Design by Ignác Knabe, 1865. Budapest Municipal Archives. (Inv. no. BMT 403/XV.302–403.)—Repr.: Mrs. Gábor Pechan.

419. The ground-plan of the Újlaki synagogue (49 Zsigmond utca). From: Gazda.

    1: The original synagogue building

    2: The synagogue with residential and community office buildings around it

420. The new synagogue of Buda. Competition design by Béla Lajta, 1912 (1st prize). From: MéJ (1912); Ferenc Vámos, *Lajta Béla* (1970).—Repr.: NZL&MI.

421. The new synagogue of Buda. Competition design by Sándor Löffler & Béla Löffler, 1912 (3rd prize). From: *Építő Ipar* (1912); MéJ (1912); János Gerle, *et al.*, *A századforduló magyar építészete* [Hungarian Architecture at the Turn of the Century] (1990).—Repr.: NZL&MI.

422. Kelenföldi synagogue (37 Bocskai út). Ground-plan of the second floor, with the hall of the synagogue and the offices of the community. From: Gazda.

423. Kelenföldi synagogue. The building immediately upon completion, without the fence. The main entrance with its flight of steps, from Zsombolyai utca. Designed by Ede Novák & István Hamburger, 1936. From: MéJ (1936).—Repr.: NZL&MI.

424. Kelenföldi synagogue. Hall in front of the second floor entrance of the synagogue. Designed by Ede Novák & István Hamburger, 1936. From: MéJ (1936).—Repr.: NZL&MI.

425. Interior of the Kelenföldi synagogue. The Hebrew inscriptions behind the Ark and the *dukhan* on the main wall contain quotations from the *Kedushshah* / Book of Isaiah (6,3): "Holy, holy, holy is the Lord of the armies / hosts (Jhwh *tzeva'ot*): the whole earth is full of His glory." The rostrum or *bimah* stands in the center, a practice—theoretically—acceptable for the conservative tradition. From: MéJ (1936); József Katona, *A 90 éves Dohány-utcai templom* [The 90-year-old Dohány utca Temple] (1949).—Repr.: NZL&MI.

426. The Kelenföldi synagogue: the Ark and the pulpit. Designed by Ede Novák & István Hamburger. From: MéJ (1936).—Repr.: NZL&MI.

Another, even more close-up photo of the Ark and the pulpit was later published in: MéJ (1939).

427. The Kelenföldi synagogue: *parokhet* in front of the Ark. According to the embroidered text on the *parokhet* and the *mappah*, the "Temple" had been founded by Samu Schwarcz, the president of the district. Above the Ark are the Two Tablets of the Law (*shenei luhot*). The late Orientalizing Art Nouveau decoration (date palms) ensured the uniform style of the building and its furnishings. From: MéJ (1939).—Repr.: NZL&MI.

428. The Buda Orthodox synagogue. Ground-plan by Lajos Kozma. (See fig. **429**, right.) From: Ernő Naményi, *Templom és iskola* (1929).

429. The Buda Orthodox synagogue. Design by Lajos Kozma, 1928. (For the ground-plan see fig. **428**, left.) On the left, under a small balcony, the entrance to the stairway leading to the women's gallery. The legible part of the Hebrew inscription on the main facade: "(...) this is [none] other but the House of God (*beit Elohim*), and this..." (Genesis 28,17). From: Ernő Naményi, *Templom és iskola* (1929).—Repr.: NZL&MI.

430. "Labanc úti Szeretetotthon [The Old-age home on Labanc út]" (16/B Labanc út). Drawing by István Zádor, 1946. From: *Zádor István 32 litográfiája (Az*

Országos Zsidó Segítő Bizottság munkájáról 1945 után) [32 Lithographs by István Zádor (About the Activity of the National Jewish Aid Committee)] (Budapest: no publisher [American Joint Distribution Committee], 1946), no. 31. 24.6 × 31.5 cm. MNM: MTKcs. (Inv. no. MTKCs. 78.77.)—Repr.: NZL&MI.

431. The hospital of the Buda Hevrah Kaddishah (16 Maros utca).—Courtesy by András Losonci, director and head surgeon.

432. Bernát Heller. From: Sándor Scheiber, *Folklór és tárgytörténet* [Essays on Jewish Folklore and Comparative Literature], I (1977).—Repr.: NZL&MI.

433. Ábrahám óbudai Freudiger (see fig. **39**, above) wearing Hungarian national gala dress. Photo, 1917. From: Martin Pollack, *Des Lebens Lauf. Jüdische Familien-Bilder aus Zwischen-Europa* (Wien–München: Christian Brandstätter, 1987).

The photo was taken from a family album. The album also contains valuable information on the Freudigers' family relations. The wife of Ábrahám Freudiger was a great-granddaughter of the *Hatam Sofer* and the sister of Akiva Sofer (1878–1959), the rabbi and *rosh yeshivah* in Pozsony (Pressburg / Bratislava); there is in the album also a photo of the wedding of Ábrahám Freudiger's son, Sámuel Vilmos Freudiger (1931). At the luxurious wedding held in a hotel restaurant the men and women guests sat at separate tables; Akiva Sofer was sitting left to the head of the family.

434. Portrait of Izsák Lőwy. From: Ignaz Reich, *Beth-El*, I (1868).

435. The Újpest synagogue. On the outer walls, the Deportation Memorial series. Designed by the artist Edith Kiss (née Bán) (1905–1966). For a long time the identity of the artist remained unknown, and other names were in circulation. Her oeuvre was recently rediscovered by Helmut Bauer (Berlin).—Photo: FA&LLL, 1992.

436. Portrait of Lajos Venetianer. From: MéJ (1915).

XI:1. Share issued by the Buda Jewish community for building a synagogue (1907) in units of 100 korona, with a total value of 100,000 korona. The serial number of this share is 93. The picture of a synagogue can be seen on the left (although the building resembles the Frankfurt synagogue consecrated in 1860, it nonetheless seems to be imaginary). There is an inscription above the building: "And let them make me a sanctuary; that I may dwell among them" (Exodus 25,8). 22.5 × 32 cm. Courtesy by Lajos Pallós. MNM Ét. Collection of

Securities. (Inv. no. 82.571.1.)—Photo: FA&LLL, 1994.

XI:2. Újpest in the early twentieth century. *Budapest székes-főváros és környékének térképe* [Map of the Capital Budapest and Its Vicinity] (Eggenberger-féle könyvkereskedés: Hoffmann & Vastagh, 1909). (Detail.)—Repr.: NZL&MI.

XII. Pest, 1944, Ghetto

437. The Tiszaeszlár Lawsuit (blood libel trial). Drawing by István Engel Tevan, 1968 (illustration on the jacket of the new edition of the book on the trial written by the lawyer of the defendant). From: Károly Eötvös, *A nagy per* [The Great Trial], II (Budapest: Szépirodalmi Könyvkiadó, 1968).

438. Károly Pap. Photo. Petőfi Irodalmi Múzeum. Photo Archives.

439. Oszkár Beregi. Photo: Angelo Photos. MNM: LTM. Photo Archives. (Inv. no. 67,741 ad 1930/1955.)—Repr.: JL&FÁ.

The younger brother of Oszkár Beregi, Ármin Beregi (1879–1953), was a Zionist leader in Hungary, head of the Palestine Office between 1925 and 1935, when he left for Palestine. The Beregi family was related to the family of Theodor Herzl. The family background explains Oszkár Beregi's commitment to Zionism.

440. Portrait of Samu Stern. From: *Kollaboráció vagy kooperáció* [Collaboration or Cooperation] (1990).

441. Street in Budapest, 1944. From: Israel Gutman, Ed., *Encyclopedia of the Holocaust* (New York: MacMillan, etc., 1990).

442–443. "Heavy stone wheels...", June 15, 1944. Mihály Kolozsváry-Borcsa ceremoniously launched the pulping of books by Jewish writers in the First Hungarian Cardboard Factory of Pest. Excerpts from his speech on that occasion: "When the events of March nineteenth occurred, I considered my first duty the elimination of the poisonous Hebrew letters from Hungarian literature. I undertook the role of the book-burner, often condemned and deemed barbarous by the liberals, because this literature has to be torn out from Hungarian intellectual life." The headline of the report: "*Harmincöt mázsás kőkerekek...*", in translation: "Seven thousand pounds of stone wheels have begun to grind half-a-million Jew-books [*sic*!, *zsidókönyv* in Hungarian]..." MNM: LTM. Photo Archives. (Inv. no. 16,142.)—Repr.: JL&FÁ.

444. Agents of the *Va'adah* in Pest. From left to right: Perec Révész, Hansi Brand, Rezső Kasztner, Ottó

Komoly and Zvi Goldbart. From: *Kollaboráció vagy kooperáció* [Collaboration or Cooperation] (1990).

445. Portrait of Ottó Komoly as a youth. From: Sándor Szenes, *Befejezetlen múlt* [Unfinished Past] (1986).

446. A postcard from *Waldsee* (Auschwitz), 1944. From: Mária Ember, Ed., *Siratóének* [Funeral Song] (Budapest, 1994). Translation of the German text: "June 21, 1944. Dear Brother! I am healthy, I feel well. Greetings to all acquaintances. I kiss you. [Signature (by a different hand):] Rózáék."

447. Miklós Krausz. Photo. From: Szabolcs Szita, Ed., *Magyarország 1944. Üldöztetés—embermentés* [Hungary 1944. Persecution and Rescue] (Budapest, 1994).

448. Posters and their readers, June 1944. The poster announced the decree of the Mayor concerning inventorization of the movable property of the Jews (June 6). MNM: LTM. Photo Archives. (Inv. no. 9014/A–2413.)—Repr.: JL&FÁ.

449. Moving into the Yellow-star Houses, June, 1944. The ministerial decree 1610/1944 came into effect. MNM: LTM. Photo Archives. (Inv. no. 54,475; 77,224.)—Repr.: JL&FÁ.

450. A Yellow-star House: 18 Kossuth Lajos tér (today Balassi Bálint utca). MNM: LTM. Photo Archives. (Inv. no. 77,216.)—Repr.: JL&FÁ.

451. Immanuel Lőw on his death-bed. Drawing by Csaba Vilmos Perlott, June 20, 1944. The drawing was ordered from the artist by Sándor Scheiber. Pencil, paper. 24.5 × 32.1 cm. MZsM. (Inv. no. Képz.–64.2087.) Photo: László Szelényi. From: BI&SchS.—Repr.: NZL&MI.

452. Lajos Stöckler. Photo. From: Szabolcs Szita, Ed., *Magyarország 1944. Üldöztetés—embermentés* [Hungary 1944. Persecution and Rescue] (Budapest, 1994).

453. March of women, their hands up, in front of 58-60 Wesselényi utca. They are wearing winter-coats, even though the weather is sunny. Photo, late October–November, 1944. The prisoners are escorted *out* of the city, towards Rottenbiller utca, probably to the Óbuda brickyard. The arched doorway is 58 Wesselényi utca; the building in the right corner of the photo has since been replaced by the back wall of the (temporary) National Theater. From: Szabolcs Szita, *Haláleröd* [Death Fortress] (1989).

454. Raid on Teleki tér, October 16, 1944. Two men on the right—assaulting an old man—are wearing Hungarian military caps (uniforms?). From: Szabolcs Szita, *Haláleröd* [Death Fortress] (1989).

455. Yellow stars on winter-coats, October- November, 1944. From: Szabolcs Szita, *Haláleröd* [Death Fortress] (1989).

456. With bundles of packages on Kerepesi út, by the walls of the cemetery, in November, 1944. The densely-packed march is escorted towards the Keleti pálya-udvar (Eastern Railway Station), their destination probably being Margit híd and the Bécsi út. From: Randolph L. Braham, *A magyar Holocaust* [The Politics of Genocide. The Holocaust in Hungary], II (1988).

457. "Two people who could not go on." Water-color by Edith Kiss, 1945. From: Mária Ember, Ed., *Siratóének* [Funeral Song] (Budapest, 1994).

458. Friedrich Born. Photo. From: *Friedrich Born. "A Righteous among the Nations"* (Jerusalem: Yad Vashem, 1988).

459. Charles Lutz, 1945. By the ruins of the British Embassy, 1 Werbőczy utca (today 1 Táncsics Mihály utca) now housing the (National Office for the Preservation of Historic Monuments). From: Szabolcs Szita, *Haláleröd* [Death Fortress] (1989).

460. Angelo Rotta in 1938, at the time of the Roman Catholic Eucharistic Congress held in Budapest. MNM: LTM. Photo Archives. (Inv. no. 41,318.)—Repr.: JL&FÁ.

461. Margit Slachta. Photo. From: Sándor Szenes, *Befejezetlen múlt* (Budapest, 1986).

462. Sára Salkaházi. Photo. From: Sándor Szenes, *Befejezetlen múlt* (Budapest, 1986).

463. Gábor Sztehlo with children in his arms, 1945. MNM: LTM. Photo Archives. (Inv. no. 58,951.)—Repr.: JL&FÁ.

464. Raoul Wallenberg's driving license issued in Budapest. From: *Heti Világgazdaság* (1994).

465. Raoul Wallenberg in his office. His wall calendar shows the date November 26, 1944. Photo: Tamás Veres. MNM: LTM. Photo Archives. (Inv. no. 77,100; 92,352.)—Repr.: JL&FÁ.

Veres, that time an amateur photographer, accompanied Wallenberg on his actions. Most of the photos about Wallenberg's accomplishments in Budapest were shot by him. Later, in the United States, he became a professional photographer.

466. Statue in honor of Raoul Wallenberg by Pál Pátzay, 1949. Photo. MNM: TFt. From: Sári Garai, Ed., *"... hogy a budapesti Wallenberg-kiállítás emléke fennmaradjon"* [Be the Memory of the Wallenberg Exhibition in Budapest Alive] (Budapest, 1994).

467. "Swedish" protected people on Szent István körút, December, 1944. The march is moving towards the ghetto. MNM: LTM. Photo Archives. (Inv. no. 16,162.)—Repr.: JL&FÁ.

468. Facade of the Glass House, designed by Lajos Kozma, 1935. Photo: Zoltán Seidner. From: Dénes

Györgyi, Ed., *Új magyar építőművészet* [New Hungarian Architecture], I (1935).—Repr.: NZL&MI.

469. **Glass House**: ground-plan. From top to bottom: ground, second and third floors. From: László Beke & Zsuzsa Varga, *Kozma Lajos* [Lajos Kozma] (Budapest: Akadémiai Kiadó, 1968).

470. **Glass House**: second floor hallway. The initials W. Gy. (Gyula Weisz) can be seen on the floor and on wall tiles behind the glass door. Photo: Zoltán Seidner. From: Dénes Györgyi, Ed., *Új magyar építőművészet* [New Hungarian Architecture], I (1935).—Repr.: NZL&MI.

471. **Glass House**: second floor landing of the staircase, with a view through the windows onto the courtyard. Photo: Zoltán Seidner. From: Dénes Györgyi, Ed., *Új magyar építőművészet* [New Hungarian Architecture], I (1935).—Repr.: NZL&MI.

472. **Lining up in front of the Glass House**, summer of 1944. MNM: LTM. Photo Archives. (Inv. no. 45,698.) From: Jenő Lévai, *Zsidósors Magyarországon* [Jewish Fate in Hungary] (1948); Randolph L. Braham, *A magyar Holocaust* [The Politics of Genocide. The Holocaust in Hungary], II (1988).

473. **Lining up in front of the Glass House**, summer, 1944. The sign of the International Red Cross can be seen on the door, A man wearing a Hungarian military uniform stands beside the car. Photo: Charles Lutz (!). From: Szabolcs Szita, *Haláleröd* [Death Fortress] (1989).

474. **Official map of the Pest ghetto**. (Its caption refers to the office of the "Hungarian Royal Minister of Interior".) The six-pointed star marks the location of the Dohány utca synagogue. From: Randolph L. Braham, *A magyar Holocaust* [The Politics of Genocide. The Holocaust in Hungary], II (1988).

deszkafal: wooden fences, board wall

kapu: gate

475. **Miksa Domonkos**, the commander of the ghetto, in his Hungarian captain's uniform. Photo. From: Szabolcs Szita, Ed., *Magyarország 1944. Üldöztetés —embermentés* [Hungary 1944. Persecution and Rescue] (Budapest, 1994).

476. **Portrait of R. Zsigmond Groszmann** (wearing his priestly robe). From: József Katona, *A 90 éves Dohány-utcai templom* [The 90-year-old Dohány utca Temple] (1949).—Repr.: NZL&MI.

477. **Portrait of Waldemar Langlet**. From: Szabolcs Szita, *Haláleröd* [Death Fortress] (1989).

478. **Carl Ivan Danielsson**. Photo. From: Péter Bajtay, Ed., *Emberirtás, embermentés* [Killing Men, Rescuing Men] (Budapest, 1994).

479. **The Radetzky Barracks** (3 Bem József tér). In the fall of 1944 this was the headquarters of the Arrow-cross Party, and of the Death's Skull Legion. Postcard. From: Grüsse.—Repr.: NZL&MI.

480. **The Red Cross Committee** for investigating the atrocities committed by the Nazis and the Arrow-cross in the garden of the Dohány utca synagogue, February, 1945. The man in the center, wearing an armband of the Red Cross (!), is perhaps R. László Salgó. MNM: LTM. Photo-Archives. (Inv. no. 16,034.)—Repr.: JL&FÁ.

481. "**Soup kitchen in Páva utca**." Drawing by István Zádor, 1946. From: *Zádor István 32 litográfiája (Az Országos Zsidó Segítő Bizottság munkájáról 1945 után)* [32 Lithographs by István Zádor (About the Activity of the National Jewish Aid Committee)] (Budapest: no publisher [*American Joint Distribution Committee*], 1946), no. 27. 24.6 × 31.5 cm. MNM: MTKcs. (Inv. no. 78.73.)—Repr.: NZL&MI.

482. "**Anikó Szenes Girls' Home**." Drawing by István Zádor, 1946. On the wall hangs a portrait of Anikó Szenes wearing her uniform. The meeting was perhaps part of a Zionist training course (*hakhsharah*). From: *Zádor István 32 litográfiája (Az Országos Zsidó Segítő Bizottság munkájáról 1945 után)* [32 Lithographs by István Zádor (About the Activity of the National Jewish Aid Committee)] (Budapest: no publisher [*American Joint Distribution Committee*], 1946), no. 8. 24.6 × 31.5 cm. (Detail.) MNM: MTKcs. (Inv. no. 78.54.)—Repr.: NZL&MI.

XII:1. "**It's hard to be a Jew**" / "*Schwer is zü sein e jid*, 1944." Drawing by Lipót Herman to illustrate a Jewish saying. 11.8 × 15.5 cm. From: HL.

XII:2. "**Do not leave your brother behind**!" An OMZSA poster, ca. 1940. Managing editor: Géza Ribáry. From: *OMZSA-Évkönyv, 5703* (= 1942/43 C.E.).—Repr.: NZL&MI.

XII:3. **The Nagybátony-Újlaki Brickyard**. Water-color by Adolf Tikáts, ca. 1910. MNM: MTKcs. (Inv. no. MTKCs. 59.453.)—Repr.: NZL&MI.

While this may not be the building in question, the detention camps from where the deportees were led out to the Bécsi út resembled the one shown here.

The most complete list of the Újpest brickyards is given by Walter Endrei, "Óbuda ipari létesítményei" [Industrial Establishments in Óbuda], in: *Tanulmányok Budapest múltjából*, 21 (1979), pp. 325–359; Miklós Lévai, in: Csongor Kiss & Ferenc Mocsy,

Eds., *Óbuda évszázadai* [Centuries of Óbuda] (Budapest: Kortárs Kiadó, 1995), pp. 533 f.

XIII. Jewish Cemeteries

483. Table in the Ceremonial Hall of the Hevrah Kaddishah of Pest, ca. 1913. There is an alms box on the table, modeled on a rabbi's grave (identical to the one shown on fig. **485**, below), Torah ornaments (including several *rimmonim*), candlesticks and goblets (one is identical to the piece shown in fig. **484**, below). From: MéJ (1913).

484. "Bunch of grapes" goblet from the former collection of the Hevrah Kaddishah of Pest. Embossed and partially gilt silver, early seventeenth century. Inscribed with the following text: "Pious donation to the Hevrah Kaddishah of Pest, Leib Pollák, 596 according to the minor calendar (= 1836 C.E.)." With a Nuremberg hallmark: mark of Georg Müller. Height: 35 cm, diameter: 7.7 cm, 9 cm. MZsM. (Inv. no. Ipm.–64.132.) Photo: László Szelényi. From: BI&SchS.–Repr.: NZL&MI.

485. Alms box of the Hevrah Kaddishah of Pest, modeled on a typical rabbinical grave (see e.g. fig. **490**, below). Engraved with scenes of death on the front of the "gravestone": the sick-bed, vigil beside the corpse laid on the ground, the washing of the dead, and scenes of the funeral: four men carrying the body wrapped in linen and placed on a bier. Silver, engraved and chased. The box bears engraved Hebrew inscriptions: "Made at the expenses of the Hevrah Kaddishah charitable treasury (*kuppat ha-tzedakah*) of the respected Holy Society of the city, commissioned by the representative (*aluf*) Moshe Leib (...) and Josef (...), officials, and Aizik and Avrom Pollák (Pollack) (?), deputy-officials (*unter-gabbaj*). The Holy Society of Pest. (...)"– "Righteousness delivers from death" (Proverbs 10,2). Our Anointed (*mashiah*) will come soon. He will destroy death forever" (Isaiah 25,8). The numerical value of the marked letters in the first quote (Proverbs 10,2) is 563 (= 1803 C.E.). With a Pest hallmark (1803): mark of Tamás Trautzl. Height: 15.5 cm. MZsM. (Inv. no. Ipm.–64.485.) Photo: László Szelényi. From: BI&SchS.–Repr.: NZL&MI.

486. Visiting the grave. A photo published in Patai's *Múlt és Jövő*.

487. A family grave in the Csörsz utca Orthodox cemetery. The gravestone in the center shows a pair of hands in the position for the priestly blessing.–Photo: FA&LLL, 1993.

488. The Csörsz utca Orthodox cemetery. In the middle the *derekh kohanim*.–Photo: FA, 1992.

489. Portrait of Jacob Koppel Reich. Photo: Sándor Kertész. From: MéJ (1929).–Repr.: NZL&MI.

490. Grave of Jacob Koppel Reich in the Csörsz utca Orthodox cemetery. Left to it the grave of Mordekhai Efraim Fischel Sussmann Sofer. –Photo: FA, 1994. The inscription of R. Reich's gravestone runs as follows:

"Here lies (literally: is concealed, *poh tamun*) our master, our teacher, our rabbi, the holy rabbi, the *ga'on*, the famed person (*mefursam*) of the entire Jewish Diaspora (*tefutzot Yisra'el*), prince of the Torah, father of scholars, greatest of preachers (*darshan*), our master and teacher, son of R. Jehezkiel, a blessing on his true and saintly memory, grandson of the sainted R. Kopl Harif [Jacob Altenkunstadt]. The span of his life was ninety-two years. For seventy years he preached Torah and thirty-nine (years) he spent at the head of the local Orthodox congregation (*adat yere'im orthodoksim*) in the city of Budapest (*ir ha-birah Budapesht*). He was famed throughout the world. (...) His excellence was honored by the king, for his merits he was honored with the title of royal councilor." Etc.

491. The former hospital and outpatient care of the Orthodox community at 64–66 Városmajor utca (corner of Városmajor utca and Gaál József utca), also called "Dániel Bíró" Hospital after its head surgeon. From: MéJ (1926).–Repr.: NZL&MI.

492. The Old-age Home (*Szeretetház*) of the Orthodox community at 2 Alma utca (corner of Városmajor utca and Alma utca). Design by Miksa Grünwald. From: MéJ (1937).–Repr.: NZL&MI.

493. Entrance gate of the Salgótarjáni utca cemetery. Designed by Béla Lajta, 1908.–Photo: FA, 1994.

494. The former mortuary of the Salgótarjáni utca cemetery, designed by Béla Lajta, 1908. From: Ferenc Vámos, *Lajta Béla* (1970).–Repr.: NZL&MI.

Today there is a fence along the graves covered with concrete beside the wall of the building. The row of graves of the Rabbinical Seminary's professors community officials lies on the right side of this fence, and the gravestones in that row face the mortuary (the ritual building).

495. Stone candelabrum in front of the mortuary in the Salgótarjáni utca cemetery. (See also fig. **XIII:16**, above.) Designed by Béla Lajta, 1908. From: MéJ (1911).—Repr.: NZL&MI.

496. **Gate of the mortuary** opening to the cemetery in the Salgótarjáni utca cemetery.—Photo: FA&LLL, 1993.

497. **Bronze gate of the mortuary** in the Salgótarjáni utca cemetery, designed by Béla Lajta, 1908. From: Ferenc Vámos, *Béla Lajta* (1970).—Repr.: NZL&MI.

498. **A** *menorah* **as candelabrum** in the mortuary of the Salgótarjáni utca cemetery. Designed by Béla Lajta, 1908. From: Ferenc Vámos, *Béla Lajta* (1970).—Repr.: NZL&MI.

499. **Mortuary of the Kozma utca Neolog cemetery**: the main entrance from the street. Designed by Vilmos Freund, 1891.—Photo: FA&LLL, 1992.

500. **Béla Lajta's plan for the arcades** in the Kozma utca cemetery. From: Ferenc Vámos, *Béla Lajta* (1970).—Repr.: NZL&MI.

501. **Sepulchral vault of the family Schmidl**. Designed by Béla Lajta, 1904. From: György Szegő, "Megújult a Schmidl-sírbolt" [The Schmidl Vault Was Renewed], in: *Népszabadság* (November 10, 1998), p. 32.

XIII:1. **The Golden Book** (*pinkas*) of the Nagykanizsa *Gemilut Hasadim* Hevrah Kaddishah from the year 5552 (= 1792/93 C.E.). Recorded and illustrated in Nagykanizsa by Jitzhak Eizik of Kabold (Kobersdorf, Austria). Manuscript on paper book, 299 pages, black leather binding with silver mounts. It contains the statutes (*takkanot*) of the Hevrah and excerpts from medieval Hebrew works, such as the *Sefer hasidim*, "Book of the Pious", *Massekhet Ge-Hinnom*, "Treatise of Gehenna", the *Shulhan Arukh*, and Moshe Zacuto's *Tofteh-arukh*, "Fiery furnace", a description of punishments in the hell (for the title see Isaiah 30,33), as well as a membership list and the names of the benefactors of the Jewish hospital in Nagykanizsa.

Illustration to the description of hell (*Ge-Hinnom / Tofet*). Color miniature. Width (with frame): ca. 34 cm. MZsM. (Inv. no. Ipm.-64.1067.)—Photo: FA&LLL, 1994.

XIII:2. **Dying**. On the left side of the sickbed stands a physician, on the right an official of the Hevrah Kaddishah. The skeleton represents Death: a drop of poison falls from his sword onto the lips of the dying man. The legend: "Death approaches relentlessly." The Golden Book of the Hevrah Kaddishah in Nagykanizsa, 1792/93. MZsM.—Photo: FA&LLL, 1994.

XIII:3. **Vigil by the deceased**. The corpse is placed on the ground and is covered. The windows of the

room are thrown open. The vigilant reads the funerary prayers. Above the corpse are the words (from the prayer-book held by the vigilant): "Rest in peace, sleep in peace, until the Consoler comes, who blows [the *shofar* (?)]." The Golden Book of the Hevrah Kaddishah in Nagykanizsa, 1792/93. MZsM.—Photo: FA&LLL, 1994.

XIII:4. **Washing the dead body**. One of the men holds a wooden fork (*gepelah*), which will be placed in the hand of the deceased. The other man combs the beard. Three men are praying, one of them holds an alms box. All are members of the Hevrah Kaddishah. A plaque inscribed with prayers can be seen on the wall and in the hand of one person. The Golden Book of the Hevrah Kaddishah in Nagykanizsa, 1792/93. MZsM.—Photo: FA&LLL, 1994.

XIII:5. **On the way to the cemetery**. The deceased is laid on a wagon drawn by two horses. The men in the funeral procession in other illustrations depicting the funeral, wear secular clothes, top hats, triangular hats; only a few have hats with upturned brims. The Golden Book of the Hevrah Kaddishah in Nagykanizsa, 1792/93. MZsM.—Photo: FA&LLL, 1994.

XIII:6. **Burial**. In front of the mortuary. The corpse was wrapped into his *kitl* and will be buried without a coffin. The Golden Book of the Hevrah Kaddishah in Nagykanizsa, 1792/93. MZsM.—Photo: FA&LLL, 1994.

XIII:7. **In the cemetery**. The members of the Hevrah pile up the grave mound. The Golden Book of the Hevrah Kaddishah in Nagykanizsa, 1792/93. MZsM.—Photo: FA&LLL, 1994.

XIII:8. **Condolences**. The mourner passes between the double line of the men who are present. The Golden Book of the Hevrah Kaddishah in Nagykanizsa, 1792/93. MZsM.—Photo: FA&LLL, 1994.

XIII:9. **Sitting** *shivah*. A mourner sits on the ground during the seven days of mourning (*shivah / süve*). He wears a black skullcap, a *yarmulke* (*pileolus*). He holds the Bible in his hand which, according to the accompanying legend, is opened at the Book of Job. The low table is laid out with his first meal (*se'udat havra'ah*: bread, a boiled egg and wine. The mirror in the room is covered. The Golden Book of the Hevrah Kaddishah in Nagykanizsa, 1792/93. MZsM.—Photo: FA&LLL, 1994.

XIII:10. **Black balls for drawing lots** (*goral*) in a silver collection plate. The balls are inscribed with names of the Burial (Holy) Society's members: "*reb* Shemuel Tzintz", "*reb* Avrohom Jung", "*reb* Glik", "*reb* Jacob Frid", "*reb* Hofman", "*reb* Tzvi Engel Segal", etc. The lots were drawn in order to determine who would perform the tasks connected with the burial of the deceased. Eighteenth century. MZsM. (Inv. no. Ipm.-64.519; 64 pieces.)—Photo: FA&LLL, 1994.

The plate in which the balls were placed was a collection plate. The inscription around the rim records the name of the donor: the *katzin* Jacob Gruber, the president (*gabbai*) of the local *tzedakah*, Pest, in the year 620 (= 1860 C.E.). Silver. With a Pest hallmark: mark of Pál Cseh. Height: 8 cm, diameter: 20 cm. MZsM. (Inv. no. Ipm.-64.848.)

XIII:11. *Derekh kohanim* in the Csörsz utca cemetery.—Photo: FA&LLL, 1993.

XIII:12. Salgótarjáni utca cemetery. The entrance house, view from inside the cemetery. Designed by Béla Lajta, 1908.—Photo: FA, 1994.

XIII:13. The entrance house from closer.—Photo: FA, 1994.

XIII:14. The entrance of the mortuary, from the entrance house. Designed by Béla Lajta, 1908.—Photo: FA&LLL, 1994.

In the background the gravestone of Vilmos Vázsonyi (1868-1926)—a former minister of Justice, member of the Hevrah Kaddishah—can be seen through the missing gate; the grave stood in the small open area in front of the exit. Designed by Géza Maróti (Rintel), 1926. Vázsonyi, a truly democratic politician, was the person in the Jewish community of Pest who achieved the most; in the high politics he always sided with the community.

XIII:15. Stone table for washing the dead body (*taharah*) and fireplace for heating water in the mortuary of the Salgótarjáni utca cemetery. Designed by Béla Lajta, 1908.—Photo: FA&LLL, 1994.

XIII:16. Candelabrum in front of the mortuary in the Salgótarjáni utca cemetery, 1994. (For its original appearance see fig. **495**, above.)—Photo: FA&LLL, 1994.

XIII:17. Funeral prayers on the wall of the mortuary (right side) in the Salgótarjáni utca cemetery. Red marble stele.—Photo: FA&LLL, 1994.

XIII:18. Old graves in the Salgótarjáni utca cemetery.—Photo: FA&LLL, 1993.

XIII:19. Gravestone of Vilmos Bacher and his wife in the Salgótarjáni utca cemetery. Front side (!) with inscriptions in Hebrew.—Photo: FA&LLL, 1994.

XIII:20. Gravestone of Vilmos Bacher and his wife in the Salgótarjáni utca cemetery. Reverse side (!) with inscriptions in Hungarian. Designed by Béla Lajta, 1912.—Photo: FA&LLL, 1994.

XIII:21. Gravestone of Henrik Lajta in the Kozma utca cemetery, 1921.—Photo: FA&LLL, 1994.

Henrik Lajta was Béla Lajta's older brother and the family wished to erect a gravestone designed by the younger brother. The gravestone was made after one of Lajta's very last designs, Vilmos Bacher's gravestone. Only the inscription was changed.

XIII:22. The Salgótarjáni utca cemetery.

XIV. Jewish Life in Budapest Today

502. Competition design of the planned "Lauder Javne" Jewish Community School by Péter Sugár, Tamás Karácsony & Győző Szerényi, 1993. From: *Szombat* (1993), no. 2.

503. Portrait of R. Moshe Kunitzer. From: Ignaz Reich, *Beth-El*, II (1868).

504. Torah ornaments (*rimmonim*) from the former Pest Sephardi community. The inscriptions on the upper and lower rims are as follows: "Tzvi Hersh, son of David, 'May his Creator protect him', 362 according to the minor era (= 1602 C.E.)."—"The Sephardi congregation in Pest." Embossed copper with engraved ornamentation. The two spheres of the *rimmonim* are soldered separately. Height: 34 cm. MZsM. (Inv. no. Ipm.-64.386.) Alexander Scheiber, *Jewish Inscriptions in Hungary* (1983), no. 153. Photo: László Szelényi. From: BI&SchS.—Repr.: NZL&MI.

Tzvi Hersh ben David, who donated the Torah ornaments to the Sephardi congregation in Pest, had a German name (Hirsch). Was he a "Sephardi" *Hasid*?

505. A page from the manuscript of József Holder, from his Yiddish translation of "Az ember tragédiája" [The Tragedy of Man] by Imre Madách. Xerocopy. Loránd Eötvös University, Faculty of Humanities, Library of the Department of Assyriology and Hebrew Studies.

506. Gingerbread (*leykekh*) with the letters of the Hebrew *alefbet*. There are initials in the lower left corner: FR (?). Cast of an eighteenth-century gingerbread mold. From the collection of Béla Lajta. Photo. From: MéJ (1915).—Repr.: NZL&MI.

A short explanation signed by P. J. (József Patai) accompanied this photo in MéJ. According to it, in the late eighteenth century non-Jewish bakers tried to win the favors of Jewish customers by using Hebrew letters (Jewish bakers could not be members of the Gingerbread Bakers' Guild). Béla Lajta had an impressive collection of gingerbread molds, as well as other items of folk art and handicrafts.

The designer of the gingerbread mold followed the Ashkenazi pronunciation in marking the consonants, as shown by the letters *bet, kaf* and *tav*. In the case of these letters, the explosive pronunciation (*b, k, p* and *t*), marked by a dot, the *dagesh*, and the spirant pronunciation (*v, kh, f* and *s*) were both indicated, whereas in the case of two other letters (*gimel* and *dalet*) which traditionally also have two different pronunciations, the explosive / spirant pronunciation was not marked since these do not play a role in Ashkenazi pronunciation.

507. **"About Preserves."** Title page of the cookbook of the *rebetsen* Mrs. Lajos Venetianer: *A befőttekről. Gyümölcs, főzelék és saláta épen való eltartása. Édes és sós sütemények* [About Preserves. Preservation of Fruits, Vegetables and Salads in a Perfect Condition. Sweet and Salty Cookies] (Újpest & Budapest: Ritter Nyomda, no date). MKVM.—Repr.: NZL&MI.

XV. The Invisible Jewish Budapest

508. **Lipót Baumhorn.** Photo. From: Ruth Ellen Gruber, *Upon the Doorposts of Thy House. Jewish Life in East-Central Europe, Yesterday and Today* (New York, etc.: John Wiley & Sons, 1994).

509. **The former** *Pénzügyminisztérium* / **Ministry of Finance** (6 Szentháromság tér) Designed by Sándor toronyi Fellner, 1904. Postcard. From: Grüsse.—Repr.: NZL&MI.

510. **Municipal Advanced School of Commerce:** (11 Vas utca). Design of the facade by Béla Lajta, 1909. From: János Gerle, et al., *A századforduló magyar építészete* [Hungarian Architecture at the Turn of the Century] (1990).

511. **Stage design** by Béla Lajta for Goldmark's opera "The Queen of Sheba" at the Hungarian Opera House, 1914/15. In the two winged figures (*seraf* or *kerub*) Lajta merged the motifs taken from European artistic tradition with the representational modes of the recent archeological finds from the Near East. On the two sides of the stage *menorah*-like candelabra. From: Ferenc Vámos, *Lajta Béla* (1970).—Repr.: NZL&MI.

512. **Store building of the firm Leitersdorfer and Son** (5 Szervita tér). Designed by Béla Lajta, 1912. (On the second floor of the building there was a pension.) From: Ferenc Vámos, *Lajta Béla* (1970).—Repr.: NZL&MI.

513. **Entrance of Rózsavölgyi and Co. Music Store** in the store building of the firm Leitersdorfer and Son (5 Szervita tér). Designed by Béla Lajta, 1912. Above the door, stylized arms of Austria and Hun-

gary, with an inscription underneath: "Imperial and Royal (...) court merchants." The inscription of the signboard says "Rózsavölgyi and Co. Musical scores, books, theater tickets, pianos." From: Ferenc Vámos, *Lajta Béla* (1970).—Repr.: NZL&MI.

514. **Decoration (pomegranate / tulip)** on the facade of the Jewish High School, designed by Béla Lajta. The inscription says: "A study by Béla Lajta. With fraternal respect, HA (= Ármin Hegedűs)." From: MéJ (1932).—Repr.: NZL&MI.

515. **The Király Theater.** In front of the building the star actress of the period, Sári Fedák (1879–1955). Photo, 1912. From: Tamás Gajdó, Péter Korniss & György Szegő, *Színházkutatás* [Research into a Theater] (Budapest: Thália Színház, 1988).

516. **The facade of the former National Salon** (Erzsébet tér). Designed by József and László Vágó, 1906. Postcard, ca. 1910. From: Grüsse.—Repr.: NZL&MI.

517. **Elevator fence** in 35 Dob utca, the Orthodox community building. Photo: LE, 1997.

518. **Károly Csemegi.** Drawing. From: Márton Vida, Ed., *Ítéljetek! Néhány kiragadott lap a magyar-zsidó életközösség könyvéből* [Be Judges! Pages from the Book of the Hungarian–Jewish Life Community] (Budapest, 1939), p. 27.

519. **The synagogue in Kőbánya**, Cserkesz utca. Designed by Richárd Schöntheil, 1911. Photo. From: Tamás Gajdó, Péter Korniss & György Szegő, *Színházkutatás* [Research into a Theater] (1988).

520. **Interior of the former synagogue in Kőbánya**; after the reconstruction in 1991. Today a Christian ecumenical temple of the Humanitarian Foundation in the custody of the Evangelical Pentecostal Church. Above the (former) "Ark" there is a Hebrew and a Hungarian inscription, the second period of the *Shema Yisra'el*: "Love the LORD (YHWH), your God" (Deuteronomy 6,5).—Photo: FA, 1993.

In the synagogue originally there was the following inscription: "Be of the disciples of Aaron, loving peace and pursuing peace, loving humankind and drawing them to the Torah" (Pirkei Avot, 1,12).

521. **The Israelite Institute for the Deaf and Dumb** on Bethlen tér. Designed by Vilmos Freund, 1877; reconstruction plan of the synagogue by Lipót Baumhorn and György Somogyi, 1931. After World War II the building was reconstructed by Alfréd Hajós. (See also fig. **366**, above.) Photo, ca. 1900, 6 × 9 cm. MNM: LTM. Photo Archives. (Inv. no. 22.696.)—Repr.: MA.

522. **The interior of the Bethlen tér synagogue**, designed by Lipót Baumhorn, 1931. (For its original condition see also fig. **367**, above.) From: MéJ (1936); József Katona, *A 90 éves Dohány-utcai templom* [The 90-year-old Dohány utca Temple] (1949).—Repr.: NZL&MI.

523. **The Angyalföld / Aréna út synagogue** (55 Dózsa György út). Today a fencing room. Designed by Lipót Baumhorn, 1908.—Photo: FA, 1992.

524. "**Gravestones in the old Jewish cemetery of Pest**" (the Lehel utca—Aréna út Jewish cemetery). Drawing by Gergely Pörge, 1908. 25.9 × 34 cm. MNM: MTKcs. (Inv. no. MTKCs. T.9025.)—Repr.: NZL&MI, 1994.

The drawing seems to have been made after the photo on fig. **525**, right.

525. **In the old Jewish cemetery of Pest** (Lehel utca). The new graves here are more or less situated in accordance with tradition; the gravestone is in front of the grave, the Hebrew inscription, on its outer side. Photo, [ca. 1908]. From: MéJ (1911).

526. **In the old Jewish cemetery of Pest**. In the background (on the right) the facade of the synagogue on Aréna / Dózsa György út is already visible. Photo, [ca. 1908]. 21 × 27 cm. MNM: LTM. Photo Archives. (Inv. no. 183.)—Repr.: MA.

From the position of the graves and the synagogue one can tell that most graves in the old cemetery were positioned, in full harmony with the tradition, along the East–West line, that is, the head of the dead towards West, the stele at the head, the Hebrew inscription on the outer side of the stele, also facing West.

527. **In the old Jewish cemetery of Pest**. In the foreground, old graves marked only with a stele and its inscription. Photo, [ca. 1908]. 21 × 27 cm. MNM: LTM. Photo Archives. (Inv. no. 185.) From: MéJ (1911)—Repr.: MA.

528. **Stele in the Kozma utca cemetery** commemorating the former Jewish cemetery of Pest (in Váci út, later Lehel út). Design by Béla Lajta, 1912. On top of the stele a willow (like a stylized upside-down *menorah*); on the side, tulip patterns. Photo: "[Antal ?] Weinwurm jr. & Co. (6 Ó utca)." From: Béla Lajta, in: *Magyar Iparművészet* (1914).—Repr.: NZL&MI.

The inscription runs as follows:

"1912. This is the common resting place of the mortal remains of those who were originally buried in the Jewish cemetery on the old Váci út, later Lehel út, which was opened in 1808, closed in 1874 and, due to an official decree, liquidated in 1910. They were exhumed by the

Hevrah Kaddishah and re-buried here with due respect. Blessed be their ashes."

529. **Bust of Alice csepeli Weiss**, née Wohl, in the Hospital of the Pest Hevrah Kaddishah. This statue was probably set up in the hall of the Hospital (57 Amerikai út) (see fig. **546**, below); for the entrance of the women's division of the Hospital and Old-age Home, above which one may read the name of Alice Weiss, see fig. **547**, below. There was probably a similar statue in the niche on the staircase landing in the Maternity Home, too. (For a photo of Alice Weiss with her family see fig. **297**, above.) From: MéJ (1928).—Repr.: NZL&MI.

530. **The** "**Aladár and Józsa Kaszab**" **Polyclinic** (2 Vágány utca). Drawing signed by "Román". Today the building is the Outpatient Clinic of the "Imre Haynal" University of Health Sciences; designed by Ernő & Miklós Román, 1925. From: MéJ (1925).—Repr.: NZL&MI.

531. **The Girls' Home and Shelter** of the Jewish Women's Association of Pest / *A Pesti Izr. Nőegylet Leányotthon- és Leánymenhelye* (149 Hungária körút), designed by Izidor Stärk, 1926. Photo: Mór Erdélyi. From: MéJ (1926).

532. **The former synagogue** in the old building of the Girls' Home and Shelter (149 Hungária körút). Today after reconstruction, the cultural center of the Traffic Police Department. From: MéJ (1926).—Repr.: NZL&MI.482.

533. **Old-age Home** (nursing home) / *Aggok háza*. Entrance, with the original Hebrew inscription. (For its text see p. 492, below.) From: MéJ (1935).—Repr.: NZL&MI.

534. **The Old-age Home** of the Hevrah Kaddishah (167—or 167-169, according to the number on the photo—Hungária körút). Designed by Vilmos Freund, 1891-1893. Photo: Ernő Bánó. From: MéJ (1928)—Repr.: NZL&MI.

535. **Old-age Home**. The former synagogue. From: MéJ (1935)—Repr.: NZL&MI.

536. **Institute for the Blind** / *Vakok tanintézete* (60 Mexikói út). Plan of Béla Lajta, 1905. From: Ferenc Vámos, *Lajta Béla* (1970).—Repr.: NZL&MI.

537. **Institute for the Blind** (60 Mexikói út). Main entrance. Designed by Béla Lajta, 1905-1908. From: Ferenc Vámos, *Lajta Béla* (1970).—Repr.: NZL&MI.

538. **Institute for the Blind**. A *menorah* decoration on the iron fence. Designed by Béla Lajta. From: Ferenc Vámos, *Lajta Béla* (1970).—Repr.: NZL&MI.

539. Institute for the Blind. Inscription on the main entrance gate (Isaiah 29,18, mistakenly quoted as 29,48 in the inscription). (Detail.) Carved wooden plaque. From: Ferenc Vámos, *Béla Lajta* (1970).—Repr.: NZL&MI.

540. Institute for the Blind. *Menorah* and inscription on the main entrance gate. Carved wooden plaque. From: MéJ (1911).—Repr.: NZL&MI.

541. Institute for the Blind. Side door, entrance to the gym. From: Ferenc Vámos, *Lajta Béla* (1970).—Repr.: NZL&MI.

The separate entrance and the *menorah* decoration of the gate indicate that this room must have had a different function originally. It must have been used as a ceremonial hall. Contrary to the opinion expressed in this book and based on contemporary reports of *Egyenlőség*, Ferenc Dávid is of the opinion that this room could not have been used as a synagogue. His conclusion is corroborated by the decision of the Institute's founder to have an equal number of Jewish and non-Jewish students here. Nevertheless, it is hard to imagine that at the time of the foundation of the Institute they would not have provided the facilities for communal religious services for the Jewish children who were living at the Institute. Maybe services were held in the gym, hence the expressive synagogue-like decoration, without the room actually being a synagogue. The children living at the Institute, being blind, could not have formed a *minyan* just by themselves anyway. Holding services in the gym of a school, first of all, High Holiday services, was—and is—not unusual in Budapest.

542. Institute for the Blind. Iron *menorah* column in front of the gym. (For its position see fig. **541**, left.) From: MéJ (1911)—Repr.: NZL&MI.

543. Hospital and Old-age Home (nursing home) of the Pest Hevrah Kaddishah / *A Pesti Chevra Kadisa Szeretetháza* (57 Amerikai út). Designed by Béla Lajta. From: Ferenc Vámos, *Lajta Béla* (1970).—Repr.: NZL&MI.

544. Moses. Statue by Ede Telcs (1911) on the facade of the Hospital and Old-age Home. From: MéJ (1911)—Repr.: NZL&MI.

545. Hospital and Old-age Home / *Szeretetház*. Wall decoration next to the northwestern gate. From: Ferenc Vámos, *Lajta Béla* (1970).—Repr.: NZL&MI.

This adorned gate must have been the entrance to the former synagogue of the Hospital and Old-age Home.

546. Entrance hall of the *Szeretetház* / Hospital and Old-age Home in its original condition, with the building inscriptions. Today the marble slabs are turned inwards. On the right side, there is an inscription, written in Lajta's typical capital letters, as follows: "The construction of the Hospital and Old-age Home of the Pest Hevrah Kaddishah was started in the spring of 1908 and completed in the spring of 1911. At the time of the construction the leaders of the Holy community were (...), etc." The bust of Alice csepeli Weiss (fig. **529**, above) may have stood next to the staircase. Photo: Ernő Bánó. From: MéJ (1928)—Repr.: NZL&MI.

547. Hospital and Old-age Home / *Szeretetház*. Side entrance (on the southeastern front of the building). Entrance to the women's division bearing the name of Alice csepeli Weiss. The inscription above the door was gouged out during a recent remodeling. From: Ferenc Vámos, *Lajta Béla* (1970).—Repr.: NZL&MI.

548. The former synagogue of the Hospital and Old-age Home or *Szeretetház*. Designed by Béla Lajta. From: Ferenc Vámos, *Lajta Béla* (1970).—Repr.: NZL&MI.

The *Múlt és Jövő* (1928) published several other photos of the synagogue.

549. Home for the Blind / *Vakok Otthona* of the Pest Hevrah Kaddishah (55 Amerikai út), 1914. (See also fig. **550**, right, view from closer.) From: Ferenc Vámos, *Lajta Béla* (1970).—Repr.: NZL&MI.

550. Home for the Blind / *Vakok Otthona*. Facade (towards the Amerikai út and the Old-age Home). (See also fig. **549**, left.) From: MéJ (1935).—Repr.: NZL&MI.

The facade of the building has been somewhat altered by a later remodeling. The stairs have been demolished, the gate is replaced by a window and the inscriptions are gone, too, except for the date over the entrance (1914) and the little six-pointed star. The courtyard is filled with the newly built annexes of the Jewish Hospital.

551. Home for the Blind / *Vakok Otthona*. Inner (back) courtyard (42 Laky Adolf utca). From: MéJ (1935)—Repr.: NZL&MI.

After several reconstructions, today the former back front (currently: street front) of the building has little to do with its original appearance. In place of the covered portico of the upper floor there is a roof; the entrance stairs have been demolished; the gate is replaced by a window; the former courtyard is paved over with concrete. The inner courtyard has been transformed into a back entrance. Ever since this building has become part of the current

Jewish Hospital (1994), this is where the delivery men load and unload their cargo daily.

552. The Shelter / *Menedékház* of the Pest Hevrah Kaddishah (53 Amerikai út). Street facade (towards the Amerikai út). From: MéJ (1935).—Repr.: NZL&MI.

The building of the *Menedékház* (Shelter) was originally probably T- or L-shaped, the courtyard wing was built perpendicular to the Amerikai út wing. The entrance opened from the courtyard wing. The reconstruction after World War II radically changed the facade towards Amerikai út. The inscriptions have been taken off, too. Only the order of the windows reminds of the original character of the building.

553. The Shelter / *Menedékház*. Courtyard facade (towards the Old-age Home). From: MéJ (1935).—Repr.: NZL&MI.

The reconstructions and the new buildings have changed the courtyard facade of the Shelter com-pletely. The original main entrance of the courtyard wing towards the Old-age Home is blocked. The entrance to the current Jewish Hospital is from the other side of the building on this picture. A new wing has been added to the corner step-out on the right of this picture occupying most of the original courtyard. There are annexes on the opposite side, the courtyard and the entire space have disappeared completely. The original inscriptions on the facade can only be seen from the side, from the windows on the right wing.

A completely new development in this neighborhood is the new school building built 1998. The *Scheiber Sándor Tanintézet* (Sándor Scheiber Educational Establishment) at 38–40 Laky Adolf utca, close to the current Jewish Hospital complex, helped the place regain its caring and benevolent Jewish face.

XVII. Bibliography

A határ és a határolt. Töprengések a magyar-zsidó irodalom létformáiról [Of the Borders and the Enclosed. Thoughts about the Life Forms of Hungarian-Jewish Literature], ed. by Petra Török (Budapest: Az Országos Rabbiképző Intézet Yahalom Zsidó Művelődéstörténeti Kutatócsoportja, 1997)

Adalékok a belső Terézváros történetéhez [Contributions to the History of Inner Terézváros] (Budapest: Budapesti Városszépítő Egyesület, 1982)

Adalékok a Belső-Erzsébetváros történetéhez [Contributions to the History of Inner Erzsébet-város] (Budapest: Budapesti Városszépítő Egyesület, 1983)

Adalékok a Belső-Józsefváros történetéhez [Contributions to the History of Inner Józsefváros] (Budapest: Budapesti Városszépítő Egyesület, 1985)

Adalékok a Lipótváros történetéhez [Contributions to the History of Lipótváros], I-II (Budapest: Budapesti Városszépítő Egyesület, 1988)

Adalékok a Népköztársaság útja történetéhez [Contributions to the History of Népköztársaság útja / Andrássy út] (Második kiadás, Budapest: Budapesti Városszépítő Egyesület, 1988)

Ágai, Adolf, "Az én dédatyámról" [About My Great-grandfather], in: IMIT. *Évkönyv*, 1907 (Budapest: Franklin, 1907), pp. 26–42

Almási, János, "Budapest történeti topográfiája a német megszállás időszakában" [Historical Topography of Budapest in the Period of the German Occupation], in: Gyula Vargyai & János Almási, Eds., *Magyarország, 1944: Német meg-szállás* (Budapest: Nemzeti Tankönyvkiadó & Pro Homine–1944 Emlékbizottság, 1994), pp. 123–146

Asaf, Uri, "Christian Support for Jews during the Holocaust in Hungary", in: Randolph L. Braham, Ed., *Studies on the Holocaust in Hungary* (East European Monographs, 301) (New York: Columbia University Press, 1990), pp. 65–112

Avenary, Hanoch, Ed., *et al.*, *Kantor Salomon Sulzer und seine Zeit* (Sigmaringen: J. Thorbecke, 1985)

Babits, Mihály, "Baumgarten Ferenc és alapítványa" (1927) [Ferenc Baumgarten and His Foundation], in: *Esszék, tanulmányok*, II (Budapest: Szép-irodalmi Könyvkiadó, 1978), pp. 164–165

Bácskai, Vera, "A pesti zsidóság a 19. század első felében" [Jews in Pest in the First Half of the Nineteenth Century], in: András Kovács, Ed., *Zsidók Budapesten = Budapesti Negyed*, 3, no. 2 (Summer, 1995), pp. 5–21

Bácskai, Vera, "Jewish Wholesale Merchants in Pest in the First Half of the Nineteenth Century", in: Michael K. Silber, Ed., *Jews in the Hungarian Economy, 1760-1945* (Jerusalem: The Magnes Press, 1992), pp. 40–49

Bácskai, Vera, *A vállalkozók előfutárai. Nagykereskedők a reformkori Pesten* [Forerunners of Entrepreneurs. Merchants in Pest in the Reform Period] (Budapest: Magvető Könyvkiadó, 1989)

Bajtay, Péter, *Emberirtás – embermentés. Svéd követ-jelentések 1944-ből. Az Auschwitzi Jegyzőkönyv* [Genocide—Rescue Activities. Reports of the Swedish Ambassador from 1944. The Auschwitz Protocol] (Budapest: Katalizátor Iroda, 1994)

Balassa, József, "Magyar zsidó dialektus" [Hungarian Jewish Dialect], in: IMIT. *Évkönyv*, 1898 (Budapest: Lampel & Wodianer, 1898), pp. 114–117 (There is no "Hungarian-Jewish dialect that would be an obstacle to the full language assimilation")

Bán, Éva, "Lisszabon–Budapest–Berlin, 1944-1945. Portugál mentőakció Budapesten. Dokumentumok" [Lisboa–Budapest–Berlin, 1944-1945. Portuguese Rescue Activity. Documents], *Valóság*, 35, no. 7 (1992), pp. 91–106

Bányai, Viktória [Viktória Pusztai], "Hebrew Literature in Hungary in the Epoch of Haskalah", in: *Studia Judaica*, 6 (1997), pp. 169–176

Barna, Jónás & Fülöp Csukási, *A magyar-zsidó felekezet elemi és polgári iskoláinak monográfiája* [Monograph of the Primary and Higher Elementary Schools of the Hungarian-Jewish Denomination], I-II (Budapest: Corvina Nyomda, 1896)

Baron, Salo W., "Aspects of the Jewish Communal Crisis in 1848", in: *Jewish Social Studies*, 14 (1952), pp. 99–144

Baron, Salo W., "The Impact of the Revolution of 1848 on Jewish Emancipation", in: *Jewish Social Studies*, 11 (1949), pp. 195–248

Barta, Mór, "Bibliai kifejezések és közmondások a magyarban" [Biblical Idioms and Proverbs in Hungarian], in: IMIT. *Évkönyv*, 1913 (Budapest: Franklin, 1913), pp. 87–106

Beer, Iván, "Magyarországi zsidó exlibrisek" [Jewish Ex-libris in Hungary], in: *Évkönyv*, 1979/80 (Budapest: MIOK, 1980), pp. 3–59

Bence, György, *A magyarországi zsidók története az előidőktől a zsidó vallás recepciójáig* [History of Jews in Hungary from the Beginnings until the Reception of the Jewish Religion] (Manuscript, 1988)

Benedek, István Gábor, *Ez lett a vesztünk, mind a kettőnk veszte...* [This Was Our Fate, the Fate for Both of Us...] (Budapest: Magyar Könyvklub, 1998) (A novel about the rescue of the Belz rebe)

Benedek, István Gábor, "Öt lövés a történelemre" [Five Shots at the History], *Népszabadság* (August 24, 1996), p. 23 (About the Attempt in Front of the Dohány utca synagogue, April 3, 1931)

Benoschofsky, Ilona & Alexander [Sándor] Scheiber, Eds., *The Jewish Museum of Budapest* (Budapest: Corvina, 1987)

Benoschofsky, Ilona & Elek Karsai, Eds., *Vádirat a nácizmus ellen. Dokumentumok a magyarországi zsidóüldözés történetéhez, I: 1944. március 19 - 1944. május 15* [Indictment against Nazism. Documents on the History of Persecution of the Jews in Hungary, I: March 19–May 15, 1944] (Budapest: MIOK, 1958)

Benoschofsky, Ilona & Elek Karsai, Eds., *Vádirat a nácizmus ellen. Dokumentumok a magyarországi zsidóüldözés történetéhez, II: 1944. május 15 - 1944. június 30* [Indictment against Nazism. Documents on the History of Persecution of the Jews in Hungary, II: May 15–June 30, 1944] (Budapest: MIOK, 1960)

Benoschofsky, Ilona, "Fejezetek a Magyar Zsidó Múzeum történetéből" [Chapters from the History of the Hungarian Jewish Museum], in: *Évkönyv*, 1981/82 (Budapest: MIOK, 1982), pp. 48–76

Benoschofsky, Ilona, "Miért maradt el a budapesti zsidók deportálása?" [Why Was the Deportation of the Jews of Budapest Cancelled?], in: *Új Élet Naptár*, 1960-1961 / 5720-5721 (Budapest: MIOK, 1960), pp. 62–64

Benoschofsky, Ilona, *The History of Jewry in Hungary* (Budapest: Central Board of Hungarian Jews, 1988)

Benoschofsky, Imre, "Emlékek a Szemináriumból" [Memories from the Rabbinical Seminary], in: *Évkönyv*, 1970 (Budapest: MIOK, 1970), pp. 74–105

Benoschofsky, Imre, Ed., *Se'erit Jisra'el - Maradék zsidóság. A magyarországi zsidóság 1945/46-ban* [Remnants of Israel. The Jews in Hungary in 1945-1946] (Budapest: A Budai Izraelita Aggok és Árvák Menházegyesülete, 1946)

Ben-Tov, Arieh, *Holocaust. A Nemzetközi Vöröskereszt és a magyar zsidóság a második világháború alatt* [Holocaust. The International Red Cross and the Hungarian Jewry during World War II] (Budapest: Dunakönyv Kiadó, 1992)

Berger, Joel, Ed., *Udim. Zeitschrift der Rabbinerkonferenz in der Bundesrepublik Deutschland*, 16 (5752/53–1992). *Gewidmet dem Andenken von Prof. Dr. Abraham Naftali Zwi Ernst Roth...*

Berkovits, György, "A gyarmat. Újpest történeti szociográfiája, 1835-1868" [The Colony. Historical Sociography of Újpest], *Valóság*, 24, no. 8 (1981), pp. 32–50

Bernstein, Béla, "Reformmozgalmak a magyar zsidóság körében 1848-ban" [Reform Movements among the Hungarian Jewry in 1848], in: IMIT. *Évkönyv*, 1898 (Budapest: Lampel & Wodianer, 1898), pp. 251–265

Bernstein, Béla, *A negyvennyolcas magyar szabadságharc és a zsidók* [The Independence War of 1848 and the Jews]. With a foreword by Mór Jókai (1898; second, revised edition, Budapest: Tábor, 1939)

Berza, László, Ed., *Budapest történetének bibliográfiája*, II: *1686-1950. Városleírás, városépítés – Budapest egészségügye, Budapest fürdőváros* [Bibliography of the History of Budapest, II: 1686-1950. Description of the City. City Building—Public Health. Spa Budapest] (Budapest: Fővárosi Szabó Ervin Könyvtár, 1963); IV: *1686-1950. Társadalom* (1965), pp. 322–325: "Jewish Emancipation"

Bevilaqua Borsody, Béla & Béla Mazsáry, *Pest-budai kávéházak. Kávé és kávésmesterség, 1535-1935. Művelődéstörténeti tanulmány*, I–II [Cafés in Pest-Buda. Coffee and Coffee-making, 1535-1935] (Budapest: Athenaeum, 1935)

Bibó, István, "The Jewish Question in Hungary after 1944", in his *Democracy, Revolution, Self-Determination*. Selected writings, ed. by Károly Nagy, translated by András Boros-Kazai (Atlantic Studies on Society in Change, 69) (Boulder, Colo.: Social Science Monographs, 1991)

Bierbauer, Virgil, "A kassai templom - Kozma Lajos műve" [The Church of Kassa—A Work of Lajos Kozma], in: *Tér és Forma*, 2 (1929), pp. 414–415 — Reply of Kozma: "Az építészeti kritikáról" [On Architecture's Criticism], l. c., pp. 456-457

[Bierbauer, Virgil], "A pesti izraelita hitközség Dohány uccai építkezése" [The Construction of the Dohány utca Synagogue of the Pest Israelite Community], in: *Tér és Forma*, 4 (1931), pp. 335-342

Blau, Lajos [Ludwig], *Brill Sámuel Lőw, a pesti rabbiság elnöke. 1814-1897* [Sámuel Lőw Brill, the Head of the Rabbinate of Pest] (Budapest, Athenaeum, 1902)

Bodor, Ferenc, "Az Orczy Kávéház" [The Orczy Café], in: *Európai Utas*, 3 (1992), no. 1, pp. 7-10

Bodor, Zsigmond, "Horn Ede emlékezete" [Memory of Ede Horn], in: IMIT. *Évkönyv*, 1914 (Budapest: Franklin, 1914), pp. 114-117

Bojár, Iván András, "Lauder iskola: különös, keleti légkör – Tegnapi győztesekből mai áldozatok" [The Lauder School: Strange, Oriental Atmosphere—From Yesterday's Winners Victims of Today], *Népszabadság* (March 29, 1996), p. 32 (On planning and construction anomalies at the "Lauder Javne")

Bona, Gábor, "Az 1848-49-es honvédsereg zsidó születésű tisztjei" [Jewish Officers of the 1848-49 Army (A Study and Documents)], *Múlt és Jövő*, New Series, 10 (1998), no. 1, pp. 59-87

Bonfini, Antonio, *Rerum Ungaricarum decades / A magyar történelem tizedei* (Budapest: Balassi Kiadó, 1995), Hungarian translation by Péter Kulcsár.—Excerpts: *Mátyás király* [King Matthias], translated by László Geréb (Budapest: Magyar Helikon, 1959); "II. Ulászló" [King Ladislaus II], translated by Péter Kulcsár, in: Péter Kulcsár, Ed., *Humanista történetírók* (Budapest: Szépirodalmi Könyvkiadó, 1977), pp. 122-286

Borsa, Béla, "Reneszánszkori ünnepségek Budán" [Renaissance Festivals in Buda], in: *Tanulmányok Budapest múltjából*, 10 (1943), pp. 13-53

Borsa, Béla, *Ismeretlen, egykorú német leírás Mátyás és Beatrix házasságáról* [An Unknown Contemporary German Description of the Wedding of King Matthias and Beatrix] (Specimina Dissertationum Facultatis Philosophicae (...) Universitatis (...) Quinqueecclesiensis, 188 / A Német Intézet értekezései, 19) (Pécs, 1940)

Borsos, Béla, "Zichy utca 9. Óbudai Izr. Hitközség gyűjteménye" [The Collection of the Israelite Community of Óbuda], in: Horler Miklós, *et al.*, *Budapest műemlékei*, II (Magyarország műemléki topográfiája, 6) (Budapest: Akadémiai Kiadó, 1962), pp. 492-498

Braham, Randolph L., *A magyar Holocaust* (Budapest: Gondolat & Wilmington: Blackburn International, 1988) (With a foreword by T. Iván Berend, quoting in full a review article by György Ránki on the original English edition: "A magyar Holocaust" [The Hungarian Holocaust], in: *Élet és Irodalom*, June 18, 1982.) — Second, revised and enlarged edition: *The Politics of Genocide. The Holocaust in Hungary*, I-II (Social Science Monographs) (New York: Columbia University Press, 1994); in Hungarian: *A népirtás politikája. A Holocaust Magyarországon*, I-II (Budapest: Belvárosi Könyvkiadó, 1997)

Braham, Randolph L., Ed., *Hungarian-Jewish Studies* (New York: World Federation of Hungarian Jews, 1973)

Brámer, Frigyes, "A budapesti gettó utolsó két hete" [The Last Two Weeks of the Budapest Ghetto], in: *Évkönyv*, 1975/76 (Budapest: MIOK, 1976), pp. 9-17

Brámer, Frigyes, "Koncentrációs tábor a Rabbiképző épületében" [Concentration Camp in the Building of the Rabbinical Seminary], in: *Évkönyv*, 1971/72 (Budapest: MIOK, 1972), pp. 219-228

Brámer, Frigyes, "Zsidó élet Pesten a század elején" [Jewish Life in Pest at the Beginnings of the (Twentieth) Century], in: *Évkönyv*, 1977/78 (Budapest: MIOK, 1978), pp. 91-95

Braun, Róbert, Klára Czike & Erika Lencsés, "Madách sétány: Ellentmondások, dilemmák" [Madách Promenade. Contradictions, Dilemmas], in: *Kritika* (1993), no. VIII, pp. 22-24

Budáné Juhász, Katalin, *A mi városunk - Erzsébetváros* [Our Town—Erzsébetváros] (Budapest: Karakó Kiadó, 1994)

Budapest lexikon [Lexicon of Budapest] (Budapest: Akadémiai Kiadó, 1973); second, corrected and enlarged edition, ed. by László Berza, I-II (Budapest: Akadémiai Kiadó, 1993)

Buza, Péter, *Herminamező. Fejezetek egy városrész történetéből* [Herminamező. Chapters on the History of a City Quarter] (Budapest: Herminamező Polgári Köre, 1992)

Buzinkay, Géza, *Mokány Berczi és Spitzig Itzig, Göre Gábor mög a többiek... A magyar társadalom figurái az élclapokban 1860 és 1918 között* [Figures of the Hungarian Society in Satiric Newspapers between 1860 and 1918] (*Magyar Hírmondó*) (Budapest: Magvető Könyvkiadó, 1988)

Büchler, Sándor, "A Goldzieherék családfájáról" [On the Genealogy of the Goldzieher Family], in: *Múlt és Jövő*, 27 (1937), pp. 336-339; 28 (1938), pp. 18-20, 51-52, 82-83, 113-114, 152-153, 184-185

Büchler, Sándor, "A magyar nyelv terjeszkedése a zsidók között" [Spread of the Hungarian Language among the Jews], in: IMIT. *Évkönyv*, 1905 (Budapest: Franklin, 1905), pp. 259–264

Büchler, Sándor, "Egy középkori héber könyvillusztráció" [A Medieval Hebrew Book-illustration], in: *Libanon*, 7 (1943), p. 65

Büchler, Sándor, *A zsidók története Budapesten a legrégibb időktől 1867-ig* [History of the Jews in Budapest from the Earliest Times until 1867] (Az IMIT kiadványai, 14) (Budapest, 1901)

Carmilly-Weinberger, Moshe, Ed., *The Rabbinical Seminary of Budapest, 1877-1977. A Centennial Volume* (New York, Sepher-Hermon Press, 1986)

Chorin, Ferenc [jr.], *A Magyar Gyáriparosok Országos Szövetsége közgyűlései alkalmából tartott serlegbeszédek, 1927-1938* [Addresses Delivered to the General Assemblies of the National Association of Industrialists] (Gyoma: Kner, 1938)

Cohen, Asher, *The Halutz Resistance in Hungary, 1942-1944* (New York: Columbia University Press, 1986)

Cohen, Yitzchok Yosef, *Hakhamei Hungariyah ve-ha-sifrut ha-toranit bah / Sages of Hungary and her Torah Literature* (Jerusalem: Machon Yerushalayim, 5755 (!) [1997])

Csánki, Dezső, *Rajzok Mátyás király korából* [Drawings from the Age of King Matthias] (Magyar Könyvtár, 34, no. 333) (Budapest: Lampel & Wodianer, 1903), pp. 36–63: "Mátyás király menyegzője" [Wedding of King Matthias]

Cseh, Gergő Bendegúz, "Az Országos Zsidó Helyreállítási Alap létrehozásának körülményei és működése (1947-1989) [The National Jewish Restitution Fund. Its Founding and Activity], *Levéltári Közlemények*, 65 (1994), pp. 119–127

Csemegi, József, "Az óbudai zsidótemplom" [The Jewish Temple in Óbuda], in: *Budapest*, 3 (1947), pp. 108–111; also separately: *Az óbudai zsidótemplom* (A "*Budapest*" könyvtára, 11) (Budapest, 1947)

Csergő, Hugó, "Három magyar zsidó nemzedék" [Three Hungarian Jewish Generations], in: OMZSA-*Évkönyv*, 5703 (1942/43) (Budapest: Országos Magyar Zsidó Segítő Akció / Löbl Dávid és Fia Könyvnyomda, 1942)

Csillag, András, "Joseph Pulitzer's Roots in Europe: A Genealogical History", in: *American Jewish Archives*, 39 (1987), (48) 49–68

Csillag, István, "A régi pesti zsidókórház" [The Old Jewish Hospital in Pest], in: *Évkönyv*, 1977/78 (Budapest: MIOK, 1978), pp. 96–99

Csillag, István, "Hirschler Ignác ifjúkori arcképéhez" [On the Portrait of Ignác Hirschler in His Youth], in: *Évkönyv*, 1979/80 (Budapest: MIOK, 1980), pp. 92–100

Csillag, Máté, *Zsidó anekdoták kincsesháza* [Treasury of Jewish Anecdotes], introduction by Ármin Frisch (1925); new edition, with a foreword by István Domán (Budapest: Sós Antikvárium & Orpheus, 1991)

Dávid, Ferenc, "Tisztelgés Lajta Béla emlékének. A Parisiana újjáépítése" [Homage to the Memory of Béla Lajta. The Reconstuction of Parisiana], in: *A Parisiana újjáépítése. Az Országos Műemléki Felügyelőség Magyar Építészeti Múzeumának kiállítása* (Budapest, 1991)

Dávid, Ferenc, "Zsinagóga a mellékutcában" [A Synagogue in the Side Street], in: *Beszélő*, New Series, 4, no. 38 (1993. szeptember 25), p. 28

Deáky, Zita, "Egy körrendelet margójára. (A bor szerepe a körülmetélés ritusában)" [On the Margin of a Decree. The Role of Wine in the Circumcision Rite], in: *Néprajzi Látóhatár*, 2 (1993), pp. 203–208

Dernschwam, Hans, *Erdély. Besztercebánya. Törökországi útinapló* [Transylvania. Besztercebánya. Travel Diary of Turkey / *Tagebuch einer Reise nach Konstantinopel*]. Hungarian translation edited by Lajos Tardy (Bibliotheca Historica) (Budapest: Európa Könyvkiadó, 1984)

Domjan, Thomas, "Der Kongress der ungarischen Israeliten 1868-1869", in: *Ungarn Jahrbuch*, 1 (1969), pp. 139–162

Eck, Nathan, "The March of Death from Serbia to Hungary (September, 1944) and the Slaughter of Cservenka", in: *Yad Vashem Studies*, 2 (1958), pp. 255–294

Einhorn, Ignaz [Ede Horn], *Die Revolution und die Juden in Ungarn. Nebst einem Rückblick auf die Geschichte der Letztern* (Leipzig, 1851)

Einhorn, Ignaz [Ede Horn], *Grundprinzipien einer geläuterten Reform im Judenthum* (Pest, 1848)

Eisner, Jenő, *Az izraelita hitfelekezet[et] és hitközségeket érintő törvények és rendeletek gyűjteménye* [Collection of Laws and Decrees concerning the Israelite Denomination and Communities] (Karcag: Kertész József Könyvnyomdája, 1925) (A catalog of the Orthodox communities, including their statutes and the decrees relating to their structure)

Ember, Mária, Sári Garai & Tamás Kovács, "*...Hogy a budapesti Wallenberg-kiállítás emléke fennmaradjon*" [Be the Memory of the Wallenberg

Exhibition in Budapest Alive] (Wallenberg-füze-
tek, 1) (Budapest: no publisher, 1994) [Catalog
of the exhibition commemorating Raoul Wallenberg, 1994]

Ember, Mária, Ed., *Siratóének. Antológia*
[Funeral Song. An Anthology] (Budapest: Private
edition, 1994)

Eötvös, József, "A zsidók emancipációja"
[The Emancipation of Jews] (1840), recently in:
Eötvös, *Reform és hazafiság* (Budapest: 1978), I,
207–256, and separately, e.g. *A zsidók emancipációja*, [edited by] Gábor Szigethy (Gondolkodó
magyarok) (Budapest: Magvető Könyvkiadó, 1981)

Evlia Cselebi török világutazó magyarországi utazásai,
1660-1664 [The World-traveler Evliya Chelebi's
Travels in Hungary], translated (in 1904) by Imre
Karácson, (re-)edited by Pál Fodor (Budapest:
Gondolat, 1985)

Fabó, Bertalan, "Tyroler József. A Kossuth-bankók réz-
metszője. (Vázlat)" [József Tyroler. The Engraver of
the Kossuth Bank Notes. (A Sketch)], in: IMIT.
Évkönyv, 1910 (Budapest: Franklin, 1910), pp. 162–170

Fazakas, István, *Jasszok, zsarók, cafkavágók.
Életképek a vagányvilágból, ó- és új argószótár*
[Dictionary of Old and New Argot] (Budapest:
Fekete Sas Kiadó, 1991)

Fekete, Lajos, "Ofener Kaufleute zur Zeit der
Türkenherrschaft", in: *Die Welt des Islams*.
Sonderband (1941), pp. 98–108

Fekete, Lajos, *Budapest a törökkorban* [Budapest in
the Turkish Period] (Budapest története, 3)
(Budapest: Kir. M. Egyetemi Nyomda, 1944)

Feldmájer, Péter, "Bitter Restitution", *Szombat*, 10
(August, 1998 / Iyyar, 5758), pp. 2–4

Felkai, László, *A budapesti zsidó fiú- és a leány
gimnázium története* [History of the Jewish Boys'
and Girls' High School] (Budapest: Anna Frank
Gimnázium, 1992)

Ferkai, András, *Buda építészete a két világháború
között. Művészeti emlékek* [Architecture of Buda
between the World Wars I and II] (Budapest: MTA
Művészettörténeti Kutató Intézet, 1995)

Feuer, Istvánné [Rózsa Tóth], "Magyarországi közép-
kori zsinagógák az általános európai fejlődés
tükrében" [Medieval Synagogues in Hungary with
Respect to Their Place in the European
Development], in: *Évkönyv*, 1971/72 (Budapest:
MIOK, 1972), pp. 43–61

Fisch, Henrik, *Keresztény egyházfők felsőházi beszé-
dei a zsidókérdésben* [Speeches of the Heads of
Christian Churches in the Upper House on the

Jewish Question] (in the discussions of the First
Anti-Jewish Law in 1938 and of the Second one in
1939) (Budapest: published by the author, printed
at Neuwald I. Utódai Könyvnyomda, no date [1947])

Freudiger, Fülöp (Philip), *et al.*, "Report on Hungary:
March 19–August 9, 1944", in: Braham, Randolph
L., Ed., *Hungarian-Jewish Studies* (New York:
World Federation of Hungarian Jews, 1973)

Freudiger, Fülöp, "Five Months", in: Randolph
L. Braham, Ed., *The Tragedy of Hungarian Jewry.
Essays, Documents, Depositions* (New York:
Institute for the Holocaust Studies of the City
University of New York, 1986), pp. 75–146

Friedenberg, Daniel M., *Medieval Jewish Seals from
Europe* (Detroit: Wayne State University Press,
1987), pp. 311–332: "Hungary"

Friedrich, Klára, "Tyroler József, a magyar szabadságharc rézmetsző-művésze" [József Tyroler, the
Engraver of the Hungarian War of Independence],
in: IMIT. *Évkönyv*, 1939 (Budapest: Franklin, 1939),
pp. 253–261

Frigyesi, Judit, *Béla Bartók and Turn-of-the-Century
Budapest* (Berkeley, etc.: University of California
Press, 1998)

Friss, Ármin, *Magyar-zsidó oklevéltár* (Monumenta
Hungariae Judaica), I: 1092–1539 (Budapest:
Wodianer F. és Fiai, 1903)

Fürst, Aladár, "Buda visszafoglalásának zsidó irodalmi
emlékei" [Jewish Literary Monuments on the
Reconquest of Buda], in: IMIT. *Évkönyv*, 1936
(Budapest: Franklin, 1936), pp. 168–184

Füst, Milán, "Kosztolányi és a zsidóság" [Kosztolányi
and the Jewry], in: *Múlt és Jövő*, 27 (1937), p. 83

Füzesi, Róbert, *Színház az árnyékban* [Theatre
in the Shadow] (Budapest: KoLibri, 1990)

Gábor, Eszter, "A két világháború közötti magyar
építészet tendencia-váltása" [Changing Paradigms
in the Hungarian Architecture between the World
Wars I and II], in: *Ars Hungarica*, 12 (1984),
pp. 93–100

Gábor, Eszter, "A lipótvárosi zsinagóga pályázata"
[Design Competition of the Lipótváros Syna-
gogue], *Budapesti Negyed*, 5, no. 4/6, and 6, no. 1
(Winter, 1997–Spring, 1998), pp. 5–47

Gadó, János, "Torah-reading Sociologist Wanted.
Jewish Schools / Education in Hungary before
and after 1989", *Szombat*, 10 (August, 1998 /
Iyyar, 5758), pp. 15–19

[Gadó, János], "Unofficial Statistics on the Hungarian Jews", *Szombat*, 10 (August, 1998 / Iyyar,
5758), p. 5

Gál, Éva, "Adalékok az óbudai zsidók XVIII. századi történetéhez" [Contributions to the History of the Jews in Óbuda in the Eighteenth Century], in: *Évkönyv*, 1975/76 (Budapest: MIOK, 1976), pp. 101–121

Gál, Éva, "Az óbudai uradalom zsidósága a 18. században" [The Jewry of the Óbuda Manor in the Eighteenth Century], in: *Századok*, 126 (1992), pp. 3–34

Gál, Éva, "Az óbudai zsinagóga" [The Óbuda Synagogue], in: Csongor Kiss & Ferenc Mocsy, Eds., *Óbuda évszázadai* (Budapest: Kortárs Kiadó, 1995), pp. 382–384

Gál, Éva, "Zsidók Zsámbékon a XVIII. században" [Jews in Zsámbék in the Eighteenth Century], in: *Évkönyv*, 1983/84 (Budapest: MIOK, 1984), pp. 142–156

Gál, Éva, *Az óbudai uradalom a Zichyek földesurasága alatt, 1659-1766* [The Óbuda Manor under the Zichy Landlords] (Budapest: Akadémiai Kiadó, 1988)

Gál, Éva, *Óbuda, 1541-1848* (Tanulmányok Óbuda történetéből, 3) (Budapest: Budapest Főváros III. kerületének Önkormányzata, 1990)

Garai, George, *The Policy toward the Jews, Zionism and Israel of the Hungarian Communist Party, 1945-1953* (Thesis, London School of Economics and Political Science, 1979) (Manuscript)

Gazda, Anikó, "A zsidók elhelyezkedése a településben. – A magyarországi zsinagógák ismertetése: Budapest. Peremvárosok" [The Location of the Jews in the Settlement. Survey of the Synagogues in Hungary: Budapest and Suburbs], in: László Gerő, Ed., *Magyarországi zsinagógák* (Budapest: Műszaki Könyvkiadó, 1989), pp. 48–53, 215–255

Gazda, Anikó, *Zsinagógák és zsidó községek Magyarországon. (Térképek, rajzok, adatok)* [Synagogues and Jewish Communities in Hungary. (Maps, Drawings, Data)] (Hungaria Judaica, 1) (Budapest: MTA Judaisztikai Kutatócsoport, 1991)

Gergely, R., Ed., *Microcard Catalogue of the Rare Hebrew Codices, Manuscripts and Ancient Prints in the Kaufmann Collection* (Budapest: Akadémiai Kiadó, 1959)

Gerle, János & György Somogyi, "Baumhorn Lipót zsinagógái" [The Synagogues of Lipót Baumhorn], in: *Évkönyv*, 1979/80 (Budapest: MIOK, 1980), pp. 355–365

Gerle, János, *A pénz palotái* [Palaces of the Money] (Budapest: Városháza, 1994)

Gerle, János, András Ferkai, Mihály Vargha & Zsuzsanna Lőrinczi, *Építészeti kalauz. Architectural Guide. Architecture in Budapest from the Turn-of-the-Century to the Present* (Budapest: 6 BT, 1997)

Gerle, János, Attila Kovács & Imre Makovecz, *A századforduló magyar építészete* [The Hungarian Architecture at the Turn of the Century] (Budapest: Szépirodalmi Könyvkiadó & Bonex, 1990)

Gerő, Ödön, "A pesti izr. hitközség fiúreálgimnáziuma és leánygimnáziuma" [The Boys' Real-Gymnasium and Girls' High School of the Israelite Community of Pest], in: *Tér és Forma*, 4 (1931), pp. 343–350

Geyer, Artúr, "Az első magyarországi deportálás" [The First Deportation from Hungary], in: *Új Élet Naptár*, 1960-1961 / 5720-5721, pp. 75–82

Giladi, David, *Pesti mérnökök – Izrael országépítői* [Engineers of Pest—Builders of Israel] (Budapest: Ex libris & Múlt és Jövő, 1992)

Goldhammer, Leo, "Jewish Emigration from Austria-Hungary in 1848-1849", in: *YIVO Annual of Jewish Social Science*, 9 (1954), pp. 332–362

Gonda, László, *A zsidóság Magyarországon, 1526-1945* [Jews in Hungary, 1526-1945] (Budapest: Századvég Kiadó, 1992)

Grossmann, Alexander, *Nur das Gewissen. Carl Lutz und seine Budapester Aktion. Geschichte und Porträt* (Wald-Zürich: Verlag im Waldgut, 1986)

Groszmann, Zsigmond, "A magyar zsidók zsinati törekvései" [Synodial Aspirations of the Hungarian Jewry], in: Simon Hevesi, *et al.*, Eds., *Jubileumi emlékkönyv Blau Lajos (...) 65. születésnapja (...) alkalmából* (Budapest: Franklin, 1926), pp. 190–198

Groszmann, Zsigmond, "A Pesti Izr. Hitközség története" [History of the Pest Israelite Community], in: A Pesti Izr. Hitközség fennállása 125. évfordulójának megünneplése (Budapest: Pesti Izr. Hitközség, 1925), pp. 55–86

Groszmann, Zsigmond, "A pesti kultusztemplom" [The Choir Temple of Pest], in: *Magyar-Zsidó Szemle*, 40 (1923), pp. 86–94

Groszmann, Zsigmond, "A pesti zsidó gyülekezet alkotmányának története" [History of the Constitution of the Pest Jewish Community], in: Mihály Guttmann, *et al.*, Eds., *Emlékkönyv Hevesi Simon (...) papi működésének negyvenedik évfordulójára* (Budapest, 1934), pp. 126–172 (and offprint)

Groszmann, Zsigmond, "A pesti zsidó község megszilárdulásának korából" [From the Period of the

Consolidation of the Pest Jewish Community], in: *Magyar-Zsidó Szemle*, 50 (1933), pp. 261–267

Groszmann, Zsigmond, "A pesti zsidóság második nemzedéke" [The Second Generation of Jews in Pest], in: Hevesi Simon, *et al.*, Eds., *Zikkaron Jehuda. Tanulmányok Blau Lajos (...) emlékére* (Budapest: Neuwald Nyomda, 1938), pp. 127–139

Groszmann, Zsigmond, "A pesti zsidóság vezetői" [Leaders of the Jews in Pest], in: *Magyar-Zsidó Szemle*, 56 (1939), pp. 51–57

Groszmann, Zsigmond, "Az izraelita Magyar Egylet törekvései" [Efforts of the Israelite Magyar(izing) Society], in: *Libanon*, 3 (1938), pp. 39–43

Groszmann, Zsigmond, "Hirschler Ignác" [Ignác Hirschler], in: IMIT. *Évkönyv*, 1941 (Budapest: Franklin, 1941), pp. 143–158

Groszmann, Zsigmond, "Magyar szó a zsinagógában" [Hungarian Word in the Synagogue], in: *Egyenlőség*, 54, no. 24 (1934. május 5), p. 13

Groszmann, Zsigmond, "Meisel pesti főrabbi kora" [The Age of Meisel, Chief Rabbi of Pest], in: IMIT. *Évkönyv*, 1933 (Budapest: Franklin, 1933), pp. 100–113

Groszmann, Zsigmond, "Milyen volt száz éve a pesti zsidóság?" [The Jews in Pest a Hundred Years Ago], in: *Egyenlőség*, 54, no. 14 (1934. január 27), pp. 10–11

Groszmann, Zsigmond, *A magyar zsidók a XIX. század közepén (1849–1870). Történelmi tanulmány* [Hungarian Jews in the Mid-nineteenth Century. (A Historical Study] (Budapest: Egyenlőség, 1917)

Groszmann, Zsigmond, *A magyar zsidók V. Ferdinánd alatt (1835–1848)* [Hungarian Jews during the Reign of Ferdinand V] (Budapest: Egyenlőség, 1916)

Groszmann, Zsigmond, *A pesti zsinagóga* [The Synagogue of Pest] (Offprint from: *Egyenlőség*, December 12 and 19, 1915) (Budapest: Magyar Könyvnyomda és Könyvkiadóvállalat, 1915)

Groszmann, Zsigmond, *A recepciós mozgalom politikai története* [Political History of the Reception Movement] (Offprint from: *Egyenlőség*, October 31, 1915) (Budapest: Magyar Könyvnyomda és Könyvkiadóvállalat, 1915)

Gruber, Ruth Ellen, *Upon the Doorposts of Thy House. Jewish Life in East-Central Europe, Yesterday and Today* (New York, etc.: John Wiley & Sons, 1994), pp. 139 ff.: "Synagogues Seeking Heaven: Looking for Lipót Baumhorn"

Grünvald, Fülöp, "A buda-várhegyi zsidó község háromszoros pusztulása" [Three Destructions of the Jewish Community of Buda–Castle Hill], in: *Múlt és Jövő*, 27 (1937), pp. 116–118

Grünvald, Fülöp, "A Buda-várhegyi zsinagóga és zsidó temető helye török időkben" [The Synagogue of Buda–Castle Hill and the Jewish Cemetery in the Turkish Period], in: Sándor Scheiber, Ed., *Volume in Honour of Prof. Bernhard Heller* (Budapest, 1941), pp. 164–169

Grünvald, Fülöp, "A héber feliratú díszkard. (A Praefectus Judaeorum kardja?)" [Sword of Honour with Hebrew Inscription. (Sword of the Prefect of the Jews?)], in: *Új Élet*, 9 (1953), no. 12

Grünvald, Fülöp, "A magyar zsidó múlt historikusai" [Historians of the Hungarian Jewish Past], in: IMIT. *Évkönyv*, 1934 (Budapest: Franklin, 1934), pp. 208–225

Grünvald, Fülöp, "A zsidó ifjúság a magyar szabadság harcban" [The Jewish Youth in the Hungarian War of Independence], in: IMIT. *Évkönyv*, 1948 (Budapest: no publisher, 1948), pp. 193–206

Grünvald, Fülöp, "Egy pesti zsidó ifjú levele 1848 április havában" [Letter of a Pest Jewish Youngster in April, 1848], in: *Libanon*, 7 (1942), pp. 120–121

Grünvald, Fülöp, "Jura Judaeorum. A hétszáz éves oklevél a magyarországi zsidóság jogairól" [The 700-years-old Charter (of Béla IV) on the Rights of the Jews in Hungary], in: *Új Élet*, 7, nos. 47 & 48 (1951)

Grünvald, Fülöp, "Mandl Bernát, 1852–1940" [Bernát Mandl], in: IMIT. *Évkönyv*, 1942 (Budapest: Franklin, 1942), pp. 183–191

Grünvald, Fülöp, "Néhány vonás az 1838-as pestbudai árvíz rajzához" [Contributions to the History of the Flood in Pest-Buda in 1838], in: *Libanon*, 3 (1938), pp. 43–47

Grünvald, Fülöp, "Oesterreicher Manes József", in: *Évkönyv*, 1973/74 (Budapest: MIOK, 1974), pp. 55–58

Grünvald, Fülöp, "Pesti levél Hochmuth Ábrahámnak 1848. március 17-éről" [A Letter from Pest to Abraham Hochmuth on March 17, 1848], in: *Libanon*, 8 (1943), pp. 72–74

Grünvald, Fülöp, *A zsidók története Budán. Vázlat* [History of the Jews in Buda. A Sketch] (Budapest: Phoebus Nyomda, 1938)

Grünwald, Fülöp, "A magyar történelem zsidó művelői" [Jewish Historians of the Hungarian History], in: *Ararát. Magyar zsidó évkönyv az 1940. évre* (Budapest: Országos Izr. Leányárvaház, 1940, 5700/1), pp. 135–140

Grünwald, Fülöp, "A zsidó települések múltja magyar földön" [History of Jewish Settlements in Hungary], in: *Ararát. Magyar zsidó évkönyv az 1942. évre*

(Budapest: Országos Izr. Leányárvaház, 1942–5702/3), pp. 64–71

Grünwald, Leopold, *Toldot hakhmei Yisra'el. Biographie des R. Efraim Kohn aus Wilna (...) und das Leben der Juden in Ofen unter der Herrschaft der Türken...* (Cluj: Wainstein, 1924)

Grünwald, Miksa, *Zsidó biedermeier* [Jewish Biedermeier] (Minerva Könyvtár, 113) (Budapest, 1937)

Grünwald, Philipp, "Die Porträt-Siegel der Judenpräfekten Ungarns", in: Israel Klausner, Raphael Mahler & Dov Sdan, Eds., *N. M. Gelber Jubilee Volume* (Tel-Aviv, 1963), pp. 285–292

Guttmann, Mihály, "Bloch Mózes" [Moses Bloch], in: IMIT. *Évkönyv,* 1911 (Budapest: Franklin, 1911), pp. 101–110; new edition, with additions, in: *Zsidó Plutarchos,* II (Népszerű zsidó könyvtár, 19) (Budapest, no date [ca. 1925]), pp. 43–54

H. Gaal, Adorján, "A Budapest-lipótvárosi zsidó templom" [The Jewish Temple of Budapest-Lipótváros], in: *A Magyar Mérnök- és Építész-Egylet Közlönye,* 33 (1899), pp. 125–130

H. Boros Vilma, *Stein Aurél ifjúsága. Hirschler Ignác és Stein Ernő levelezése Stein Aurélról, 1866–1891* [The Youth of Aurél Stein. Correspondence of Ignác Hirschler and Ernő Stein about Aurél Stein, 1866–1891] (A Magyar Tudományos Akadémia Könyvtárának kiadványai, 61) (Budapest, 1970)

Hajnóci, R. József, [Ed.], *A magyar zsidók közjoga. Betű- és számsoros útmutató a magyarhoni izraeliták felekezeti ügyeinek törvényes szervezetében* [The Constitutional Law of the Hungarian Jews. Alphabetic and Numerical Index to Legal Organization of Denominational Affairs of Israelites in the Hungarian Homeland] (Lőcse: published by the editor, 1909)

Handler, Andrew, *An Early Blueprint for Zionism. Győző Istóczy's Political Anti-Semitism* (East European Monographs, 261) (New York: Columbia University Press, 1989)

Handler, Andrew, *Dori. The Life and Times of Theodor Herzl in Budapest (1860–1878)* (Judaic Studies Series) (Alabama: The University of Alabama Press, 1983)

Handler, Andrew, *From the Ghetto to the Games: Jewish Athletes in Hungary* (East European Monographs, 192) (New York: Columbia University Press, 1985)

Haraszti, György, "A Rumbach utcai zsinagóga és hívei" [The Rumbach utca Synagogue and Its Congregation], in: Ines Müller, *A Rumbach Sebestyén utcai zsinagóga* (1993), pp. 103–119

Haraszti, György, "Jakab budai zsidó vallomása az ostromlott Buda belviszonyairól" – "Zsidó ének a budai zsidóság ostrom alatti és utáni sorsáról" [Confession of Jacob, Jew in Buda, about the Inner Situation in Buda during the Siege—Jewish Song on the Fate of the Jews in Buda during and after the Siege], in: Ferenc Szakály, Ed., Buda visszafoglalásának emlékezete, 1686 (Budapest: Európa Könyvkiadó, 1986), pp. 501–509, 511–525

Haraszti, György, "Szép új dal Budáról" [A Nice New Song about Buda], in: *Keletkutatás,* Spring, 1987 (Budapest: Kőrösi Csoma Társaság, 1987), pp. 66–82

Haraszti, György, *Magyar zsidó levéltári repertórium,* I: *Hazai levéltárak zsidó vonatkozású anyagának áttekintése a kiadott levéltári segédletek alapján* [Directory of Archival Holdings Relating to the History of Jews in Hungary: Hungarian Archives] (Hungaria Judaica, 2) (Budapest: MTA Judaisztikai Kutatócsoport, 1993)

Háy, Gyula, "Kozma Lajos, ahogy ma látjuk" [Lajos Kozma As We See Him Today], in: *Tér és Forma,* 2 (1929), pp. 278–287

Házi, Jenő, "A budai zsidók sorsa 1686-ban" [The Fate of the Jews of Buda in 1686], in: Sándor Scheiber, Ed., *Magyar-Zsidó Oklevéltár* (Monumenta Hungariae Judaica), XVII (Budapest: MIOK, 1977), pp. 9–18

Hegedüs, Géza, "Egy Goldziher-unoka családi emlékei" [Family Recollections of a Goldzihers' Grandson], in: *Évkönyv,* 1981/82 (Budapest: MIOK, 1982), pp. 194–210

Hegedüs, Géza, *Előjátékok egy önéletrajzhoz* [Preludes to an Autobiography] (Budapest: Szépirodalmi Könyvkiadó, 1982)

Herbst Péterné Zorica Krausz, *Magyarországi zsidó ételek* [Jewish Dishes in Hungary] (Budapest: Minerva, 1984)

Herzl, Theodor, *Briefe und Tagebücher,* 1: *Briefe 1866–1895,* bearbeitet von Johannes Wachten (Berlin, etc.: Propyläen, 1983)

Herzl, Theodor, *Briefe und Tagebücher,* 2–3: *Zionistisches Tagebuch,* I–II, bearbeitet von Johannes Wachten & Chaya Harel (Berlin, etc.: Propyläen, 1983–1985)

Hetényi Varga, Károly, "A magyar katolikus egyház az üldözöttekért (1944–1945)" [The Hungarian Catholic Church for the Persecuted (1944–1945)], in: Szabolcs Szita, Ed., *Magyarország 1944* (1994), pp. 115–149

Hevesi, Lajos, *Karczképek az ország városából* [Sketches from the Capital of the Country] (Budapest: Cserő Gyula Ödön Könyvkereskedése, no date [1876])

Hilberg, Raul, *Perpetrators, Victims, Bystanders. The Jewish Catastrophe 1933-1945* (New York: HarperCollins, 1992) / *Täter, Opfer, Zuschauer: Die Vernichtung der europäischen Juden 1933-1945* (Frankfurt a. M.: Fischer, 1992)

Hilberg, Raul, *The Destruction of the European Jews* (1961) / *Die Vernichtung der europäischen Juden 1933-1945* (Frankfurt a. M.: Fischer Taschenbuch Verlag, 1990)

Holló, Szilvia Andrea, *Budapest régi térképeken, 1686-1896* [Budapest on Old Maps, 1686-1896] (Budapest: Officina Nova, no date [1994])

Horák, Magda, Ed., *"Ősi hittel, becsülettel a hazáért!" OMIKE - Országos Magyar Izraelita Közművelődési Egyesület, 1909-1944* ["In Traditional Faith and Honesty for the Homeland!" OMIKE—Hungarian Israelite Cultural Society] (Budapest: Háttér Kiadó, 1998)

Horler, Miklós, *et al.*, *Budapest műemlékei*, I-II [Historic Monuments of Budapest] (Magyarország műemléki topográfiája, 4 & 6) (Budapest: Akadémiai Kiadó, 1955, 1962)

Hutterer, Claus Jürgen, "Jiddisch in Ungarn", in: A. Starck, Ed., *Westjiddisch. Mündlichkeit* (Sprachlandschaft, 11) (Aarau, etc., 1994), pp. 43-60

Hutterer, Miklós (Claus Jürgen Hutterer), "The Phonology of Budapest Yiddish", in: *The Field of Yiddish* (The Hague: Mouton, 1965), pp. 116-145

Iványi, Béla, "Középkori regeszták a magyar zsidóság múltjára vonatkozólag" [Medieval Abstracts (of Charters) on the Past of the Hungarian Jewry], in: IMIT. *Évkönyv*, 1948 (Budapest: no publisher, 1948), pp. 74-88

Iványi, Béla, *Buda és Pest sorsdöntő évei, 1526-1541* [The Fatal Years of Buda and Pest, 1526-1541] (Budapest, 1941) (offprint from *Tanulmányok Budapest múltjából*, 9)

Jár-kel, mint zsidóban a fájdalom [Illustrating Sayings on Jews]. Drawings of Lipót Herman, with an introduction by Mária Ember (Budapest: Origo-Press, 1988) [According to R. Y. István Kertész, Lipót Herman illustrated Jewish sayings and proverbs from the collection edited by Imre Nagy, *Zsidó közmondások* [Jewish Proverbs] (Budapest: Az Ojság, 1930).]

Járy, Péter, "A kétszázéves Freund-család" [About the Two-hundred-year-old Freund Family.], in: *Évkönyv*, 1975/76 (Budapest: MIOK, 1976), pp. 167-175

Jenei, Károly, *et al.*, *A Pamutnyomóipari Vállalat Goldberger Textilnyomógyárának története 1784-től* [History of the Goldberger Textile Factory from 1784 on] (Budapest: Magyar Történelmi Társulat Üzemtörténeti Szakosztály, 1970)

Jólesz, Károly, *Miért? Zsidó törvények és szokások magyarázata* [Why? Explanation of Jewish Laws and Customs] (No place, no publisher, no date [Budapest, 1991])

Jólesz, Károly, *Zsidó hitéleti kislexikon* [Lexicon of Jewish Religious Life] (Budapest: MIOK, 1985)

Junger, Ervin, *Bartók és a zsidó diaszpora. Adatok Bartók Béla művészi és társadalmi kapcsolataihoz* [Bartók and the Jewish Diaspora. Data on Béla Bartók's Artistic and Social Contacts] (Budapest: MTA Judaisztikai Kutatócsoport, 1997)

Kalauz Felső-Magyarország vasútain Budapesten és a Dunán utazva [Guide Book for Traveling on the Railways of Upper Hungary, Budapest and the Danube] (Budapest: Pesti Könyvnyomda, 1873)

Káldy-Nagy, Gyula, "Száműzetés vagy áttelepítés? A budai zsidók történetéhez 1526-ban" [Exile or Resettlement? Contribution to the History of Jews of Buda in 1526], in: *Évkönyv*, 1979/80 (Budapest: MIOK, 1980), pp. 192-196

Kállai, László, *A 150 éves Goldberger-gyár* [The 150-year-old Goldberger Factory] (Budapest: Textil-Ipar Újság kiadása, 1935)

Kapronczay, Károly, "Lengyel zsidó menekültek Magyarországon a második világháború idején" [Jewish Refugees from Poland in Hungary during World War II], in: *Évkönyv*, 1985-1991 (Budapest: Országos Rabbiképző Intézet, 1991), pp. 199-206

Kárpótlás és kárrendezés Magyarországon, 1989-1998 [Indemnification and Compensation in Hungary, 1989-1998], compiled by Sándor Berényi, *et al.* (Budapest: Napvilág Kiadó, 1998)

Karsai, Elek, Ed., *"Fegyvertelen álltak az aknamezőkön..." Dokumentumok a munkaszolgálat történetéhez Magyarországon*, I-II [Documents to the History of the Forced Labor Service in Hungary] (Budapest: MIOK, 1962)

Karsai, Elek, Ed., *Vádirat a nácizmus ellen. Dokumentumok a magyarországi zsidóüldözés történetéhez*, III: 1944. május 26-1944. október 15 [Indictment against Nazism. Documents to the History of the Persecution of the Jews in Hungary, III] (Budapest: MIOK, 1967)

Karsai, Elek & Miklós Szinai, "A Weiss Manfréd-vagyon német kézbe kerülésének története" [History of the Forfeiture of Manfréd Weiss's

Wealth by Germans], in: *Századok*, 95 (1961), pp. 680-719

Katona, József, "A Dohány utcai templom" [The Dohány utca Temple], in: *Új Élet Naptár*, 1960-1961 / 5720-5721, pp. 41–46

Katona, József, *A 90 éves Dohány-utcai templom* [The 90-year-old Dohány utca Temple]—Fülöp Grünvald & Ernő Naményi, *Budapesti zsinagógák* [Synagogues in Budapest] (Budapest: Országos Magyar Zsidó Múzeum, 1949)

Katz, Jacob, "A végzetes szakadás. Orthodox és neológ szétválás a magyar zsidóságban: A szakadás eredete, befolyása és következményei" [The Disastrous Schism. Separation of Orthodox and Neolog in the Hungarian Jewry. Roots, Impact and Consequences of the Schism], in: *Múlt és Jövő*, New Series, 2 (1991), no. 1, pp. 49–55

Katzburg, Nathaniel, *Hungary and the Jews. Policy and Legislation, 1920-1943* (Ramat-Gan: Bar-Ilan University Press, 1981)

Kaufmann, Dávid, "Budavár visszafoglalásának egy szemtanúja és leírója" [An Eyewitness of the Reconquest of Buda and His Account], in: IMIT. *Évkönyv*, 1895 (Budapest: Lampel & Wodianer, 1895), pp. 63–92

Kaufmann, Dávid, *A zsidók utolsó kiűzése Bécsből és Alsó-Ausztriából, előzményei (1625-1670) és áldozatai* [The Last Expulsion of the Jews from Vienna and Lower Austria, Its Antecedents (1625–1670) and Its Victims] (Budapest, 1889)

Kaufmann, David, *Die Erstürmung Ofens und ihre Vorgeschichte nach dem Berichte Isak Schulhofs. Megillath Ofen* (Trier: Sigmund Mayer, 1895)

Kayserling, Mayer, "Luzzatto és a magyarországi zsidó tudósok" [Luzzato and the Jewish Scholars in Hungary], in: IMIT. *Évkönyv*, 1901 (Budapest: Franklin, 1901), pp. 315–333 (On Salamon Rosenthal)

Kellér, Andor, *Mayer Wolf fia. Wahrmann Mór életregénye* [Wolf Mayer's Son. Biography of Mór Wahrmann. A Novel] (Budapest: published by the author, no date [ca. 1941])

Kepecs, József, Ed., *A zsidó népesség száma településenként (1840-1941)* [Statistics of the Jewish Population by Settlements (1840–1941)] (Budapest: Központi Statisztikai Hivatal, 1993)

Kertai Friedrich, Klára, "Tyroler József" [Joseph Tyroler], in: *Évkönyv*, 1979/80 (Budapest: MIOK, 1980), pp. 220–229

Kertész, Imre, *Fateless* [*Sorstalanság*, 1961 / 1975], English translation by Christopher C. Wilson & Katharina Wilson (Evanston, Ill.: Northwestern University Press, 1992)

Kertész, Ödön, "A százhat esztendős MIKÉFE első negyedszázada" [The First Decades of the 106-year-old MIKÉFE], in: *Évkönyv*, 1948 (Budapest: no publisher, 1948), pp. 273–293

Kertész, Y. István, *Gitli néni tésztája - avagy elmélkedés zsidó viccekről* [Dough of Aunt Gitli—Reflections on Jewish Jokes] (Budapest: Gazdasági Média Kiadói Kft., 1993)

Kiss, Arnold, "Jargon irodalom és költészet" [Literature and Poetry in Jargon / Yiddish], in: IMIT. *Évkönyv*, 1908 (Budapest: Franklin, 1908), pp. 41–80

Klein, Isaac, *A Guide to Jewish Religious Practice* (New York & Jerusalem: The Jewish Theological Seminary of America, 1992)

Kohlbach, Bertalan, "Folklore a zsinagógában" [Folklore in the Synagogue], in: IMIT. *Évkönyv*, 1930 (Budapest: Franklin, 1930), pp. 175–193

Kohlbach, Bertalan, "Sütemények a zsidó szertartásban" [Cakes in the Jewish Rite], in: IMIT. *Évkönyv*, 1914 (Budapest: Franklin, 1914), pp. 144–162

Kohn, Sámuel, "Az óbudai zsidó hitközség a múlt század közepe felé" [The Jewish Community of Óbuda towards the Middle of the Last Century], in: *Magyar-Zsidó Szemle*, 8 (1891), pp. 254–259

Kohn, Sámuel, *A zsidók története Magyarországon a legrégibb időktől a mohácsi vészig* [The History of Jews in Hungary from the Beginning until the Battle at Mohács] (Budapest: Athenaeum, 1884)

Kohn, Sámuel, *Héber kútforrások és adatok Magyarország történetéhez* [Hebrew Sources and Data to the History of Hungary] (Budapest: Athenaeum / Zilahy Sámuel, 1881; reprint: Budapest: Akadémiai Kiadó, 1990)

Kollaboráció vagy kooperáció? A budapesti Zsidó Tanács [Collaboration or Cooperation? The Jewish Council of Budapest], ed. by Mária Schmidt (Budapest: Minerva, 1990) [Memoirs by Fülöp Freudiger, Ottó Komoly, Samu Stern, Lajos Stöckler and some related documents]

Komárik, Dénes, "A pesti Dohány utcai zsinagóga építése" [The Building of the Dohány utca Synagogue of Pest], in: *Művészettörténeti Értesítő*, 40 (1991), pp. 1–16

Komárik, Dénes, "A Dohány utcai zsinagóga építése" [The Building of the Dohány utca Synagogue], in: András Kovács, Ed., *Zsidók Budapesten = Budapesti Negyed*, 3, no. 2 (Summer, 1995), pp. 31–40

Komárik, Dénes, *Feszl Frigyes (1821-1884)* [Frigyes Feszl (1821-1884)] (Budapest: Akadémiai Kiadó, 1993)

Komlós, Aladár, "Az asszimiláció kora. A magyar irodalom és a zsidók" [The Age of the Assimilation. Hungarian Literature and the Jews], in: IMIT. *Évkönyv*, 1940 (Budapest: Franklin, 1940), pp. 170-201

Komlós, Aladár, "Három zsidó megy a vonaton. A zsidó vicc" [Three Jews Are Traveling on the Train. The Jewish Joke], in: IMIT. *Évkönyv*, 1934 (Budapest: Franklin, 1934), pp. 227-243

Komlós, Aladár, "Kiss József emlékezete, vagy: A zsidó költő és a dicsőség" [The Memory of József Kiss, or the Jewish Poet and the Glory], in: IMIT. *Évkönyv*, 1932 (Budapest: Franklin, 1932), pp. 49-73

Komlós, Aladár, "Magyar-zsidó írók 1848-ban" [Hungarian-Jewish Writers in 1848], in: IMIT. *Évkönyv*, 1848 (Budapest: no publisher, 1948), pp. 187-192

Komlós, Aladár, "Zsidó költők a magyar irodalomban" [Jewish Poets in the Hungarian Literature], in: *Ararát. Magyar zsidó évkönyv az 1942. évre* (Budapest: Országos Izr. Leányárvaház, 1942–5702/3), pp. 163-169

Komlós, Aladár, "Zsidóság, magyarság, Európa" [Jews, Hungarians, Europe], in: *Ararát. Magyar zsidó évkönyv az 1943. évre* (Budapest: Országos Izr. Leányárvaház, 1943 / 5703-4), pp. 24-27

Komoly, Ottó, "The Diary of Ottó Komoly: August 21-September 16, 1944)", in: Braham, Randolph L., Ed., *Hungarian-Jewish Studies* (New York: World Federation of Hungarian Jews, 1973), pp. 147-250

Komoróczy, Géza, "Pious Anti-Semitism in the Centuries of Darkness and Light", *Budapest Review of Books*, 7, no. 3 (Fall, 1997), pp. 124-129 (On Hungarian translations of Paolo Sebastiano Medici's book on Jewish customs)

Komoróczy, Géza, "Das Judentum in Budapest im Dualismus", in: Tibor Fényi, Ed., *Budapest 1896. Ein Millennium im K.u.K.-Rahmen* (Wien: Ungarisches Kulturinstitut in Wien, 1996), pp. 26-38

Komoróczy, Géza, "Mit veszített a magyar zsidóság 1944-ben - mit veszített a magyar társadalom?" [What is the 1944 Loss of Hungarian Jewry—What Is the Loss of the Hungarian Society?], in: Mária Ember & Éva Mayer, Eds., *Mi minden veszett el itt...* (Budapest: Friedrich Ebert Stiftung, 1996), pp. 34-40

Koren, Emil, "Emlékezés Sztehlo Gáborra" [Recollection of Gábor Sztehlo], in: *Holocaust Füzetek*, no. 2 (no date [1993]), pp. 38-45

Kőrösi, József, *Budapest nemzetiségi állapota és magyarosodása az 1881-diki népszámlálás eredményei szerint* [National Composition and Magyarization of Budapest according to the Census of the Year 1881] (Budapest: M. T. Akadémia Könyvkiadó-hivatala, 1882)

Kőrösi, József, *Die Hauptstadt Budapest im Jahre 1881. Resultate der Volksbeschreibung und Volkszählung vom 1. Januar 1881*, I-III (Berlin: Puttkammer und Mühlbrecht, 1881-1883)

Kőrösi, József & Gustav Thirring, *Die Hauptstadt Budapest im Jahre 1891. Resultate der Volksbeschreibung und Volkszählung*, I-III (Berlin: Puttkammer und Mühlbrecht, 1894-1898)

Kőrösy, Ferenc, "A Kőrösy család és a vele kapcsolt családok" [The Kőrösy Family and Related Families], in: *Évkönyv*, 1983/84 (Budapest: MIOK, 1984), pp. 200-218

Kőszegi, Ábel, *Töredék. Radnóti Miklós utolsó hónapjainak krónikája* [Fragment. Chronicle of the Last Months of Miklós Radnóti] (Mikrokozmosz füzetek) (Budapest: Szépirodalmi Könyvkiadó, 1972)

Kovács András, Ed., *Zsidók Budapesten* [Jews in Budapest] = *Budapesti Negyed*, 3, no. 2 (Summer, 1995)

Krauss, Samuel, "The Jewish Rite of Covering the Head", in: *Hebrew Union College Annual* 19 (1946), pp. 121-168

Krausz, Sámuel, "Magyar zsidók a Balkánon" [Hungarian Jews on the Balkans], in: IMIT. *Évkönyv*, 1932 (Budapest: Franklin, 1932), pp. 137-156

Krausz, Sámuel, "Zsidó kéziratok a régi budai könyvtárban" [Jewish Manuscripts in the Old Library of Buda], in: IMIT. *Évkönyv*, 1900 (Budapest: Lampel & Wodianer, 1900), pp. 193-204

Krinsky, Carol H., *Europas Synagogen. Architektur, Geschichte und Bedeutung* (Stuttgart: Deutsche Verlags-Anstalt, 1988) / *Synagogues of Europe* (New York: The Architectural History Foundation, 1985)

Kubinyi, András, "A zsidóság története a középkori Magyarországon" [History of the Jews in Hungary in the Middle Ages], in: László Gerő, Ed., *Magyarországi zsinagógák* (Budapest: Műszaki Könyvkiadó, 1989), pp. 19-27

Kubinyi, András, "Fejezetek a magyarországi zsidóság középkori történetéből" [Chapters from the

Medieval History of the Jews in Hungary], in: *Az Országos Rabbiképző Intézet Évkönyve, 1992–1995* (Budapest, 1995), pp. 115–142

Kubinyi, András, "Spanyol zsidók a középkori Budán" [Spanish Jews in Medieval Buda], in: Sándor Scheiber, Ed., *Magyar-Zsidó Oklevéltár* (Monumenta Hungariae Judaica), XII (Budapest: MIOK, 1969), pp. 19–26

Lackó, Miklós, "A zsidó értelmiség a Holocaust előtt" [Jewish Intellectuals before the Holocaust], in: *Magyar Tudomány*, New Series, 39 (1994), pp. 651–658

Lackó, Miklós, "Zsidók a budapesti irodalomban" [Jews in the Literature of Budapest], in: András Kovács, Ed., *Zsidók Budapesten = Budapesti Negyed*, 3, no. 2 (Summer, 1995), pp. 107–126

Lajta, Béla, "A temető művészete" [The Art of the Cemetery], in: *Magyar Iparművészet*, 17 (1914), pp. 112–122

Lakatos, Lajos, "Magyar zsidó cigányok" [Hungarian Jewish Gypsies], in: IMIT. *Évkönyv*, 1910 (Budapest: Franklin, 1910), pp. 197–206

Langlet, Nina, *A svéd mentőakció, 1944* [The Swedish Rescue Action] (Budapest: Kossuth Könyvkiadó, 1988)

Lazarus, Adolf, "Sulzer Salamon. Születésének századik évfordulójára" [Salomon Sulzer. On the 100th Anniversary of His Birth], in: IMIT. *Évkönyv*, 1905 (Budapes: Franklin, 1905), pp. 121–125

"Lector Judaeus" [= Fülöp Grünwald (?)], "A magyar zsidóság száz év előtt. Statisztikai kistükör" [The Hungarian Jewry Hundred Years Ago. A Statistical Survey], in: Jenő Nádor, Ed., *Magyar zsidók könyve 1943–5703* (Budapest: OMIKE, 1943), pp. 5–35 — Reprint: *Újból és mindörökké* (Gyoma: Kner Múzeum és Könyv Alapítvány, no date [1994])

Lévai, Jenő, *A pesti gettó csodálatos megmenekülésének hiteles története* [The Authentic History of the Wonderful Escape of the Pest Ghetto] (Budapest: Officina, no date)

Lévai, Jenő, *Fehér könyv. Külföldi akciók magyar zsidók megmentésére* [White Book. Actions from Abroad for the Rescue of Hungarian Jews] (Budapest: Officina, 1946)

Lévai, Eugene [Jenő], *Black Book on the Martyrdom of Hungarian Jewry* (Zurich: The Central European Times Publishing Co. & Vienna: The Panorama Publishing Co., 1948)

Lévai, Jenő, *Fekete könyv. A magyar zsidóság szenvedéseiről* [Black Book on the Martyrdom of Hungarian Jewry] (Budapest: Officina, 1946)

Lévai, Jenő, *Írók, színészek, zenészek, énekesek regényes életútja a Goldmark-teremig. Az OMIKE Színháza és művészei* [Romantic Career of Writers, Actors, Musicians, Singers until the Goldmark Hall. The OMIKE Theatre and Its Artists] (Budapest, 1943)

Lévai, Jenő, *Raoul Wallenberg* (Budapest: Magyar Téka, 1948³; reprint: Budapest: Állami Könyvterjesztő Vállalat & Maecenas, 1988)

Lévai, Jenő, *Szürke könyv. Magyar zsidók megmentéséről* [Gray Book. On the Rescue of Hungarian Jews] (Budapest: Officina, 1946)

Lévai, Jenő, *Zsidósors Magyarországon* [Jewish Fate in Hungary] (Budapest: Magyar Téka, 1948)

Levendel, László, "A túlélő" [The Survivor], in his *A túlélő* (Budapest: Főnix Alapítvány, 1993), pp. 46–59

Lőw, Leopold, "Schicksale und Bestrebungen der Juden in Ungarn" (5606/7 / 1846/47), in: Leopold Lőw, *Gesammelte Schriften*, hrsg. von Immanuel Lőw (Szegedin, 1898) (reprint, Hildesheim & New York: Olms, 1979), pp. 371–435

Magyarországi zsidó hitközségek, 1944 április. A Magyar Zsidók Központi Tanácsának összeírása a német hatóságok rendelkezése nyomán [Jewish Communities in Hungary, April, 1944. Data from a Census Organized by the Central Council of Hungarian Jews on the Order of German Authorities]. Editor-in-chief Joseph Schweitzer, edited by Kinga Frojimovics (Hungaria Judaica, 6), I–II (Budapest: MTA Judaisztikai Kutatócsoport, 1994)

Mahler, Eduard, *Handbuch der jüdischen Chronologie* (Grundriss der Gesamtwissenschaft des Judentums) (Leipzig: Gustav Fock, 1916)

Majoros, Valéria, "Lajta Béla síremlék- és temetőművészete" [Sepulchral Art of Béla Lajta], in: *Ars Hungarica*, 11 (1983), pp. 165–184, figs. 80–91

Majsai, Tamás, "A kőrösmezei zsidódeportálás 1941-ben" [Deportation of the Jews in Kőrösmező], in: *A Ráday Gyűjtemény Évkönyve*, 4–5 (1984–1985), pp. 59–86; "Iratok..." [Documents]: l. c., pp. 195–245

Majsai, Tamás, "A protestáns egyházak az üldözés ellen" [The Protestant Churches against the Persecution], in: Szabolcs Szita, Ed., *Magyarország 1944* (1994), pp. 150–184

Málnai, Béla, "Lajta Béla emlékének" [To the Memory of Béla Lajta] (1925) (A copy of the type-written manuscript in the Hungarian Jewish Archive; published *apud:* Ferenc Vámos, *Lajta Béla*, 1970, pp. 362–366)

Mandel, S., "A nehéz kézműveket és a földmívelést a magyarországi izraeliták közt terjesztő egylet történetének vázlata" [A Historical Sketch about the Society for Disseminating Difficult Crafts and Agriculture among Hungarian Israelites], in: Pál Tencer, Ed., *Album*, I (Pest, 1869), pp. 14–25

Mandl, Bernát, "A magyarhoni zsidók tanügye II. József alatt" [Education of the Jews in Hungary under Joseph II], in: IMIT. *Évkönyv*, 1901 (Budapest: Franklin, 1901), pp. 166–220

Mandl, Bernát, "Adalék néhány Magyarországban szereplő középkori zsidó történetéhez" [Contribution to the History of Some Medieval Jews in Hungary], *Magyar-Zsidó Szemle*, 35 (1918), pp. 58–65

Mandl, Bernát, "Régi zsidó pecsétekről" [On Old Jewish Seals], in: IMIT. *Évkönyv*, 1904 (Budapest: Franklin, 1904), pp. 282–293

Mandl, Bernát, "Zsidó pecsétek és érmek" [Jewish Seals and Coins], in: *Múlt és Jövő*, 5 (1915), pp. 304–306

Mandl, Bernát, *A magyarországi zsidó iskola a 19. században* [The Jewish School in Hungary in the Nineteenth Century] (Budapest, 1909)

Mandl, Bernát, *Das jüdische Schulwesen in Ungarn unter Kaiser Josef II* (Frankfurt a. M., 1903)

Mandl, Bernát, *Magyar-Zsidó Oklevéltár* (Monumenta Hungariae Judaica), II: 1540–1710 (Budapest: IMIT, 1937)

Marcus, Jacob Rader, *The Jew in the Medieval World. A Source Book: 315–1791* (Cincinnati: Hebrew Union College Press, 1938; reprint: 1990), pp. 261–269 (Sir Paul Rycaut)

Márton, Lajos, "Zsidó lovasküldöttség Hunyadi Mátyás esküvőjén" [Mounted Delegation of Jews at the Wedding of Matthias Hunyadi], in: *Erdélyi Zsidó Évkönyv*, 6 (1940/41), pp. 66–69

McCagg, William O., Jr., *A History of Habsburg Jews, 1670–1918* (Bloomington & Indianapolis: Indiana University Press, 1989)

McCagg, William O., Jr., *Jewish Nobles and Geniuses in Modern Hungary* (East European Monographs, 3) (Boulder: East European Quarterly / New York: Columbia University Press, 1972)

Mérei, Gyula, "Wahrmann Mór" [Mór Wahrmann], in: IMIT. *Évkönyv*, 1943 (Budapest: Franklin, 1943), pp. 313–343

Miskolczy, Ambrus, "Az 1849-i magyar zsidóemancipációs törvény és ismeretlen iratai" [The Jewish Emancipation Act of 1849 and Unknown Documents Relating to It], *Múlt és Jövő*, New Series, 10 (1998), no. 1, pp. 8–41

Moess, Alfréd, *Pest megye és Pest-Buda zsidóságának demográfiája 1749-1846* [Demography of Jews in Pest County and Pest-Buda between 1749 and 1846] (A magyarországi zsidó hitközségek monográfiái, 2) (Budapest: MIOK, 1968)

Mohács emlékezete. A mohácsi csatára vonatkozó legfontosabb magyar, nyugati és török források [Memory of Mohács. The Most Important Hungarian, Western and Turkish Sources concerning the Battle at Mohács (1526)] (Budapest: Európa Könyvkiadó, 1973³)

Móricz, Zsigmond, "Café Orczy Kávéház. Egy százötven éves kávéház" [Café Orczy. A Hundred-and-fifty-year-old Café] (1935), in his *Riportok*, II: 1930–1935 (Budapest: Szépirodalmi Könyvkiadó, 1990), pp. 496–498

Müller, Ines, *Die Otto Wagner-Synagoge in Budapest* (Wien: Löcker Verlag, 1992); in Hungarian translation: *A Rumbach Sebestyén utcai zsinagóga. Otto Wagner fiatalkori főműve Budapesten* (Hungaria Judaica, 4) (Wien: Löcker Verlag & Budapest: MTA Judaisztikai Kutatócsoport, 1993)

Munkácsi, Ernő, "Emlékezéseim a Rombach-utcai templom fénykorára" [My Recollections on the Golden Age of the Rombach utca Temple], in: *Múlt és Jövő*, 33 (1943), pp. 9–10

Munkácsi, Ernő, "Mendel prefektus hiteles portréja" [Authentic Portrait of Prefect Mendel], in: *Libanon*, 6 (1941), pp. 82–83

Munkácsi, Ernő, *Hogyan történt. Adatok és okmányok a magyar zsidóság tragédiájához* [How it Happened. Data and Documents to the Tragedy of the Hungarian Jewry] (Budapest: Renaissance, 1947) (Published excerpts in Hungarian translation from the Auschwitz Protocol)

Nádai, Pál, "Van-e zsinagóga-stílus" [Does Exist Any Synagogue-style?], in: *Zsidó évkönyv az 5689. bibliai évre* (Budapest, 1928/29), pp. 162–166

Nádasdy, Ádám, "A walesi bárdok tréfás jiddis fordítása" [Amusing Yiddish Translation of "The Bards of Wales", A Ballad by János Arany], *2000*, 10, no. 10 (October, 1998), pp. 46–60

Nagy, Loránt, "Adatok a késő Árpád-kori pénzek kormeghatározásához" [Data to the Chronology of Coins from the Late Árpád Age], in: *Numizmatikai Közlöny*, 72/73 (1973/74), pp. 43–47

Nagy, Sz. Péter, *A Kasztner-akció, 1944* [The Kasztner Action, 1944] (Budapest: Rejtjel Kiadó, 1995)

Naményi, Ernő, *Templom és iskola. Kozma Lajos építészeti munkáiból összeállította és kísérő szöveggel ellátta – – [Temple and School. From the Architectural Works of Lajos Kozma compiled by – –] (Budapest: Múlt és Jövő, 1929)

Naményi, Ernő, "Vallásos reformmozgalmak Magyar országon" [Religious Reform Movements in Hungary], in: *Ararát. Magyar zsidó évkönyv az 1941. évre* (Budapest: Országos Izr. Leányárvaház, 1941, 5701-2), pp. 137–141

Narkiss, Bezalel & Gabrielle Sed-Rajna, *Illuminated Manuscripts of the Kaufmann Collection* (Index of Jewish Art. Iconographical Index of Hebrew Illuminated Manuscripts, 4) (Budapest: The Library of the Hungarian Academy of Sciences, Jerusalem: The Israel Academy of Sciences and Humanities & Paris: Institut de Recherche et d'Histoire des Textes, 1988)

Neumann, Ede, "Kayserling M." [M. Kayserling], in: IMIT. *Évkönyv,* 1906 (Budapest: Franklin, 1906), pp. 71–129

Orbán, Ferenc, *Magyarország zsidó emlékei, nevezetességei* [Jewish Sites and Sights in Hungary] (Budapest: Panoráma, 1991)

Orbán, Ferenc, *Zsidó élet Magyarországon / Jewish Life in Hungary,* 1996 / 5756 (Budapest: Makkabi, 1996)

Pach, Zsigmond Pál, *et al.,* ["A magyar zsidóság statisztikája"] [Statistics of the Hungarian Jewry] in: *A Zsidó Világkongresszus Magyarországi Képviselete Statisztikai osztályának Közleményei,* nos. 1-14 (1947–1949)

Parczel, József, *Az óbudai izraelita templom restaurálásának története* [History of the Restoration of the Israelite Temple in Óbuda] (Budapest: Bichler I. könyvnyomdája, 1901)

Pásztor, Mihály, *A százötven éves Lipótváros* [The Hundred-and-fifty-year-old Lipótváros] (Statisztikai Közlemények) (Budapest: Budapest Székesfőváros Házinyomdája, 1940)

Patai, József, "Herzl gyermekkori magyar írásai" [Hungarian Writings of Herzl from His Childhood], in: *Múlt és Jövő,* 31 (1941), pp. 54–56

Patai, József, *Harc a zsidó kultúráért* [Struggle for the Jewish Culture] (Budapest: Múlt és Jövő, 1937)

Patai, Raphael, *Ignaz Goldziher and His Oriental Diary. A Translation and Psychological Portrait* (Detroit: Wayne State University Press, 1987)

Patai, Raphael, *The Jews of Hungary. History, Culture, Psychology* (Detroit: Wayne State University Press, 1996)

Perczel, Anna, *et al., Budapest, VIII. kerület, Közép-Józsefváros északi városnegyed, részletes rendezési terv,* I: Műleírás [Budapest, the Eighth District,

Middle Józsefváros Northern Quarter, Detailed Arrangement Plan] (Manuscript; Budapest: VÁTI Rt., 1994)

Perczel, Anna, *Pest régi zsidónegyede: Belső-Erzsébetváros – Belső-Terézváros építészeti értékei, lakóházai* [The Old Jewish Quarter of Pest: Architectural Values and Dwelling Houses in the Inner Erzsébetváros and Inner Terézváros] (Manuscript, 1998)

Peterdi, Andor, "Orczy-kávéház" [The Orczy Café], in: *Múlt és Jövő,* 24 (1934), pp. 333–334

Pietsch, Walter, "A zsidók bevándorlása Galíciából és a magyarországi zsidóság" [Jewish Immigration from Galicia and the Hungarian Jewry], in: *Valóság,* 31, no. 11 (1988), pp. 46–59

Pollack, Martin, *Des Lebens Lauf. Jüdische Familien-Bilder aus Zwischen-Europa* (Wien–München: Verlag Christian Brandstätter, 1987)

Pollak, K., *Josephinische Actenstücke über Altofen* (Wien: Moritz Maisner, 1902) (Offprint from Die Neuzeit, 1902, nos. 5-9) (Statutes of the Óbuda Jewish community, 1787)

Pólya, Jakab, *A budapesti bankok története az 1867-1894. években* [History of the Banks in Budapest in the Years between 1867 and 1894] (Budapest: Márkus Samu, 1895)

Pólya, Jakab, *A Pesti Polg. Kereskedelmi Testület és a Budapesti Nagykereskedők és Nagyiparosok Társulata története* [The Civil Merchants' Corporation of Pest and the Corporation of Wholesale Merchants of Budapest. Their History] (Budapest: Franklin, 1896)

Porzó (Adolf Ágai), *Utazás Pestről - Budapestre, 1843-1907. Rajzok és emlékek a magyar főváros utolsó 65 esztendejéből* [Journey from Pest to Budapest, 1843-1907] (1908) (Budapest: Pallas, 19123) (reprint, Budapest: Fekete Sas Kiadó, 1998)

Preisich, Gábor, "Budapest építészete a két világháború között" [The Architecture of Budapest between the Two World Wars], in: *Épités- és Közlekedéstudományi Közlöny,* 11, no. 3/4 (1967), pp. 461–524

Preisich, Gábor, *Budapest városépítésének története* [History of the Architecture of Budapest] (Budapest: Műszaki Könyvkiadó, I: *Buda visszavételétől a kiegyezésig* (1960); II: *A kiegyezéstől a Tanácsköztársaságig* (1964); III: *1919-1969* (1969); IV: *1945-1990* (1998)

Purin, Bernhard, Ed., *et al., Salomon Sulzer. Kantor, Komponist, Reformer. Katalog zur Ausstellung* (Wien: Jüdisches Museum der Stadt Wien, 1991)

Quittner, Zsigmond, "Három síremlék" [Three Sepulchral Monuments], in: *Építő Ipar* 24, no. 3 (1202) (1900. január 18), pp. 15(-18)

R–Z, "A Dohány uccai 'Hősök temploma' tervpályázat" [Design Competition of the Heroes' Temple in Dohány utca], in: *Tér és Forma*, 4 (1931), pp. 35–44

Rádóczy, Gyula, "A héber betűjeles Árpád-házi pénzek-hez" [Hebrew Letters on the Coins of the Árpád Dynasty], in: *Numizmatikai Közlöny*, 70/71 (1971/72), pp. 33–37

Radnóti, Miklós, *Foamy Sky. The Major Poems of - -*. Selected and Translated by Zsuzsanna Ozsváth & Frederick Turner (Princeton, NJ: Princeton University Press, 1992)

Rados, Jenő, *Hild József. Pest nagy építőjének élet-műve* [József Hild. Œuvre of the Great Architect of Pest] (Budapest: Akadémiai Kiadó, 1958)

Reich, Ignaz, *Beth-El. Ehrentempel verdienter unga-rischer Israeliten*, I (1856; Pest: Aloiz Bucsánszky, 1868^2), II (Pest: A. Bucsánszky, 1868^2), III, Heft 1 (Budapest: Eduard Neumayer, 1882)

Reményi Gyenes, István, *Ismerjük őket? Zsidó szár-mazású nevezetes magyarok arcképcsarnoka* [Do We Know Them? Famous Hungarians of Jewish Origin] (Budapest: Ex Libris Kiadó, 1997^2)

Reményi Gyenes, István, "Zsidók az 1848–49-es szabadságharcban. Magyarhon igaz fiai" [Jews in the Independence War of 1848–49. True Sons of the Hungarian Homeland], *Magyar Nemzet* (April 2, 1998), p. 12 (On the original name of Frigyes Korányi)

Remete, László, "Az Országos Rabbiképző Intézet könyvtárának rekonstrukciójáról" [On the Reconstruction of the Library of the Rabbinical Seminary], in: *Évkönyv*, 1985–1991 (Budapest: Országos Rabbiképző Intézet, 1991), pp. 389–401

Remete, László, "Deportált könyvek" [Deported Books], *Szombat*, 6, no. 8 (Cheshvan, 5755 / October, 1994), p. 35

Révay, József & Aladár Schöpflin, *Egy magyar könyv-kiadó regénye* [Story of a Hungarian Publishing House] (Budapest: Franklin, no date [ca. 1930]) (History of the Franklin Publishing House, into which the Wodianer's merged)

Richtmann, Mózes, "Magyarországi hírek az álmessi-ásokról" [Hungarian Reports on False Messiahs], in: *Magyar-Zsidó Szemle*, 24 (1907), pp. 147–156

Roboz, Ottó, "A Zsidó Fiúárvaház Vöröskeresztes Otthona" [The Red Cross Home of the Jewish Boys' Orphanage], in: *Évkönyv*, 1983–1984 (Buda-pest: MIOK, 1984), pp. 275–292

Rónai, László, *A magyar katolikus egyház története 1939-ben* [History of the Hungarian Catholic Church in 1939], I (Budapest: Új Ember, 1995)

Ronén, Ávihu, *Harc az életért. Cionista (Somér) ellenállás Budapesten, 1944* [Struggle for Life. Zionist (Shomer) Resistance in Budapest, 1944] (Budapest: Belvárosi Könyvkiadó, 1998)

Rürup, Reinhold, "The European Revolutions of 1848 and the Jewish Emancipation", in: Werner Mosse, *et al.*, Eds., *Revolution and Evolution: 1848 in German-Jewish History* (Tübingen: J. C. B. Mohr, 1981), pp. 1–54

Ságvári, Ágnes, Ed., *Holocaust Budapest 1944* (Budapest: The Jewish Agency for Israel, 1994) (City map)

Ságvári Ágnes, Ed., *Archival Documents on Data concerning Jewish Holocaust in Hungary* (No place, no publisher, no date [1996])

Ságvári, Ágnes, Ed., *The Holocaust in Hungary. Methodology and Content of the Series of Pub-lications "The Holocaust in Hungary" in Hun-garian* (Budapest: Magyar Auschwitz Alapítvány, 1994)

Salgó, László, "Emlékek a Zsidó Gimnázium első évtizedéből" [Recollections of the First Decade of the Jewish High School], in: *Évkönyv*, 1970 (Budapest: MIOK, 1970), pp. 107–115

Salgó, László, "Goldberger Salamon. Születésének 100. évfordulója alkalmából" [Salamon Goldberger. On the Occasion of the 100th Anniversary of His Birth], in: *Évkönyv*, 1979/80 (Budapest: MIOK, 1980), pp. 286–291

Sanders, Ivan, "Ősi legendák, modern történelem – zsidó témák Kaczér Illés műveiben" [Old Legends, Modern History—Jewish Themes in Works of Illés Kaczér], *Szombat*, 6, no. 1 (January, 1994 / Shevat, 5754), pp. 36–42

Sanders, Ivan, "Oriental Flower in Pest", *Budapest Review of Books*, 5, no. 2 (Summer, 1995), pp. 19–24 (A review article on the first, Hun-garian edition of the present book)

Sándor, Anna, "Oesterreicher Manes József arcképé-hez" [To the Portrait of Manes József Oester-reicher], in: *Évkönyv*, 1979–1980 (Budapest: Országos Rabbiképző Intézet, 1980), pp. 292–300

Sándor, Vilmos, "A budapesti nagymalomipar kialakulása (1839–1880)" [Development of the Milling Industry in Budapest], in: *Tanulmányok Budapest múltjából*, 13 (1959), pp. 315–423

Scheiber, Sándor, "A héber betűjeles Árpád-házi pénzekhez" [Hebrew Letters on the Coins of the

Árpád Dynasty], in: *Numizmatikai Közlöny*, 72/73 (1973/74), p. 91

Scheiber, Sándor, "A magyar zsidóság szellemi élete a századfordulótól. Kitekintéssel Bartók Bélára" [Intellectual Life of Hungarian Jewry from the Turn of the Century. With an Outlook on Béla Bartók], in his *Folklór és tárgytörténet*, III (1984), pp. 151–218

Scheiber, Sándor, "Goldziher Ignác", in: Simon Róbert, Ed., Goldziher Ignác, *Az iszlám kultúrája* (Budapest: Gondolat, 1981), II, pp. 1065–1082; new edition, with additions, in his *Folklór és tárgytörténet*, III (1984), pp. 537–565

Scheiber, Sándor, "La cultura ebraica ungherese e Béla Bartók", in: *L'anima e la forme* (Milano: Electa, 1981), pp. 222–231

Scheiber, Sándor, "Tanítómesterek a hagyomány láncolatával" [Masters of Teaching along the Chain of the Tradition], edited by Géza Komoróczy, in: *Múlt és Jövő*, New Series, 1, no. 1 (1990), pp. 33–38 (His commemorative sermons over Vilmos Bacher, Ignác Goldziher and Immanuel Lőw)

Scheiber, Sándor, "Zsidó könyvek sorsa Magyarországon a német megszállás idején" [Fate of Jewish Books in Hungary during the German Occupation], in: *Magyar Könyvszemle*, 86 (1970), pp. 233–235

Scheiber, Sándor, "Zsidó küldöttség Mátyás és Beatrix esküvőjén" [Jewish Delegation at the Wedding of Matthias and Beatrix], in: *Múlt és Jövő*, 33 (1943), pp. 107–108

Scheiber, Sándor, "Zsidó néprajzi adatok Kiss József műveiben" [Jewish Folklore Data in the Works of József Kiss], in: IMIT. *Évkönyv*, 1948 (Budapest: no publisher, 1948), pp. 101–123

Scheiber, Sándor, "Zsidók említése Ottendorff Henrik útleírásában 1663-ban" [References to Jews in the Travel Diary of Henrik Ottendorf in 1663], in: *Libanon*, 8 (1943), pp. 64–65

Scheiber, Sándor, *Folklór és tárgytörténet* [Essays on Jewish Folklore and Comparative Literature], I–II (Second, enlarged edition, Budapest: MIOK, 1977); III (1984)

Scheiber, Sándor, *Héber kódexmaradványok magyarországi kötéstáblákban. A középkori magyar zsidóság könyvkultúrája* [Hebräische Kodexüberreste in ungarländischen Einbandstafeln. Die Buchkultur der ungarischen Juden im Mittelalter] (Budapest: MIOK, 1969) (pp. 13 ff.: Seal of Jacob Mendel; pp. 110–144: Buda)

Scheiber, Sándor, *Magyar zsidó hírlapok és folyóiratok bibliográfiája* (1847–1992) [Bibliography of Hungarian Jewish Newspapers and Journals (1847–1992)]. Edited from the manuscript of the author by Livia Scheiberné Bernáth and Györgyi Barabás, complemented by Györgyi Barabás (Hungaria Judaica, 3) (Budapest: MTA Judaisztikai Kutatócsoport, 1993)

Scheiber, Sándor, *Magyarországi zsidó feliratok a III. századtól 1686-ig* [Jewish Inscriptions in Hungary. From the 3rd Century to 1686] (Budapest: MIOK, 1960).—See a review on it by Mózes Richtmann, *Antik Tanulmányok*, 9 (1962), pp. 136–139 — Corrected and enlarged edition: *Jewish Inscriptions in Hungary. From the 3rd Century to 1686* (Budapest: Akadémiai Kiadó / Leiden: E. J. Brill, 1983)

Schellyei, Anna, *Budapest zsidó arca* [Jewish Aspect of Budapest] (Budapest: B'nai B'rith, no date [ca. 1996])

Schiller, József, *A strasshofi mentőakció története és előzményei (1944–1945)* [The Strasshof Rescue Action, Its History and Antecedents (1944–1945)] (Budapest: Gordius Könyvek, 1996)

Schmelzer, Hermann Imre, "Ötven év távlatából" [Fifty Years On], in: *Múlt és Jövő*, New Series, 5 (1994), no. 2, pp. 63–65

Schmelzer, Hermann Imre, "Wellesz Gyula (1872–1915)", in: *Évkönyv*, 1983/84 (Budapest: MIOK, 1984), pp. 348–355

Schmidt, Mária, "Mentés vagy árulás? Magyar zsidó önmentési akciók a második világháború alatt" [Rescue or Treason? Hungarian Jewish Self-rescue Actions during World War II], in: *Medvetánc* (1985), no. 2/3, pp. 111–125; new edition in her *Diktatúrák ördögszekerén* (Budapest: Magvető, 1998), pp. 188–209

Scholem, Gershom, *Sabbatai Sevi. The Mystical Messiah 1626–1676* (Bollingen Series, 93) (Princeton, NJ: Princeton University Press, 1973) (p. 565, etc.: on his followers in Buda)

Schőner, Alfréd, *A Dohány utcai zsinagóga* [The Dohány utca Synagogue] (Budapest: MIOK, 1989)

Schulhof, Izsák, *Budai krónika (1686)* [Chronicle of Buda]. Translated from Hebrew by László Jólesz. With a postscript by Ferenc Szakály (Bibliotheca Historica) (Second, corrected edition, Budapest: Magyar Helikon, 1981) — See a review on the first edition by György Haraszti, *Századok*, 115 (1981), pp. 236–240

Schwarcz, Miksa, *Kohen Efrájim ó-budai rabbi élete és responsumai* [R. Efraim Kohen. His Life and His Responsa] (Budapest: Márkus Samu, 1887)

Schweitzer, Gábor, "Miért nem kellett Herzl a magyar zsidóknak? A politikai cionizmus kezdetei és a magyarországi zsidó közvélemény" [Why Hungarian Jews Did Not Accept Herzl. Beginnings of Political Zionism and the Opinion of Hungarian Jews], in: *Budapesti Negyed*, 2, no. 2 (1994), pp. 42–55

Schweitzer, József, "A pesti Rabbiképző megalapítása a responzum-irodalomban" [Foundation of the Rabbinical Seminary of Pest in the Responsa Literature], in: *Évkönyv*, 1977/78 (Budapest: MIOK, 1978), pp. 329–342

Schweitzer, József, *A zsidóság a magyar művelődés századaiban* [Jewry in the Centuries of Hungarian Culture] (Művelődéstörténet – vallástörténet továbbképző füzetek, 4) (Budapest: Budapesti Műszaki Egyetem, 1994)

Siklódi, Csilla, *et al.*, *Jews in Hungarian Sports. Exhibition of Museum of Physical Education and Sports, Budapest* (Tel-Aviv: Maccabi World Games, 1993)

Silber, Michael K., "A zsidók társadalmi befogadása Magyarországon a reformkorban: A kaszinók" [Social Reception of Jews in Hungary in the Period of Reforms], in: *Századok*, 126 (1992), pp. 112–141 / "The Entrance of Jews into Hungarian Society in *Vormärz*: the Case of the 'Casinos'", in: Jonathan Frankel & Steven J. Zipperstein, Eds., *Assimilation and Community. The Jews in Nineteenth-century Europe* (Cambridge, etc.: Cambridge University Press, 1992), pp. 284–323

Silber, Michael K., "A pesti radikális reformegylet 1848–1852 között" [The Social Composition of the Pest Radical Reform Society, 1848–1852], *Múlt és Jövő*, New Series, 10 (1998), no. 1, pp. 125–142

Simon, László, *Zsidókérdés a magyar reformkorban, 1790–1848, különös tekintettel a nemzetiségre* [The Jewish Question in the Period of Reforms, 1790–1848, with Special Regard on the Nationality] (A debreceni m. kir. Tisza István Tudományegyetem Magyar Történelmi Szemináriumának közleményei, 6) (Debrecen: Bertók Lajos, 1936)

Simon, Róbert, "Goldziher Ignác. Adalékok a nemzeti és a polgári fejlődés alternatíváinak és egy tudomány születésének közép-kelet-európai összefüggéseihez" [Ignác Goldziher. On the Alternatives of National and Civil Progress and on the Birth of a Science in Its Central-Eastern European Setting], in: *Magyar Filozófiai Szemle* 26, no. 3 (1982), pp. 336–379

Simon, Róbert, *Ignác Goldziher. His Life and Scholarship as Reflected in His Works and Correspondence* (Budapest: Library of the Hungarian Academy of Sciences & Leiden: E. J. Brill, 1986) (Correspondence between Goldziher and Theodor Nöldeke)

Sisa, József, "A Rumbach utcai zsinagóga, Otto Wagner ifjúkori alkotása" [The Rumbach utca Synagogue. An Early Work of Otto Wagner], in: *Ars Hungarica*, 10 (1982), pp. 43–49

Spiegel, Jehuda, "A magyarországi zsidóság kapcsolata Erec Jiszráéllel a nemzedékek során" [Ties between Hungarian Jewry and Eretz Israel through Generations], *apud:* Giladi, David, *Pesti mérnökök – Izrael országépítői* (1992), pp. 17–23

Spiegler, Gyula Sámuel, *Adalékok Budapest székesfőváros történetéhez. Teréz- és Erzsébetváros* [Data to the History of Budapest, the Capital of Hungary] (Budapest: Kellner, 1907)

Spiegler, Gyula Sámuel, *Budapest-Erzsébetváros története* [History of Budapest-Erzsébetváros] (Budapest: Dobrowsky és Frankl, 1902)

Spira, György, *A pestiek Petőfi és Haynau között* [People in Pest between Petőfi and Haynau] (Budapest: Enciklopédia Kiadó, 1998)

Spitzer, Schlomo, "Der Einfluss des Chatam Sofer und seiner Pressburger Schule auf die jüdischen Gemeinden Mitteleuropas im 19. Jahrhundert", in: *Studia Judaica Austriaca*, 8 (1980), pp. 111–121

Statute und Beschlüsse des am 10. Dezember 1868 eröffneten Landes-Congresses der Israeliten in Ungarn und Siebenbürgen (Pester Buchdruckerei Actien-Gesellschaft, 1869)

Stern, Samu (Samuel), "A Race with Time: A Statement", in: Braham, Randolph L., Ed., *Hungarian-Jewish Studies* (New York: World Federation of Hungarian Jews, 1973), pp. 1–47

Strbik, Andrea, *Héber nyelvtanok Magyarországon. A Magyarországon kiadott, magyar szerzők által írt vagy magyar nyelvű héber nyelvtanok bibliográfiája (1635–1995)* [Hebrew Grammars in Hungary. Bibliography of the Hebrew Grammars Published in Hungary or Written by Hungarian Authors (1635–1995)] (Hungaria Judaica, 10) (Budapest: MTA Judaisztikai Kutatócsoport & Osiris Kiadó, 1999)

Szabó, Ferenc, Ed., *Terézváros Budapest szívében* [Terézváros in the Heart of Budapest] (Budapest: Terézvárosi Művelődési Közalapítvány, no date [1998])

Szabolcsi, Bence, "A magyarországi zsinagógai ének kultúrföldrajzi helyzete" [The Hungarian Synagogal Chant in Its Cultural-Geographical Setting], in: *Ararát Évkönyv. Zsidó magyar almanach az 1939. (5699-5700.) évre* (Budapest: Pesti Izraelita Leányárvaház, 1939), pp. 121-125

Szabolcsi, Bence, "A zsidóság története Magyarországon" [History of the Jewry in Hungary], *apud:* Simon Dubnov, *A zsidóság története az ókortól napjainkig.* Translated from the original Yiddish by Bence Szabolcsi (Budapest: Tábor, 1935, 1941[5]), pp. 335-359 (reprint, Budapest: Gondolat & Bethlen Gábor Könyvkiadó, 1991[6]), pp. 227-254; and in: *Szombat*, 2 (1990), nos. 1-6

Szabolcsi, Bence, "Hogyan kellene megújítani istentiszteletünk zenei részét?" [About Reforming the Musical Aspect of Our Synagogal Service], in: *Ararát. Magyar zsidó évkönyv az 1941. évre* (Budapest: Országos Izr. Leányárvaház, 1941, 5701-2), pp. 115-118

Szabolcsi, Lajos, *Két emberöltő. Az Egyenlőség évtizedei (1881-1931). Emlékezések, dokumentumok* (ca. 1942) [Two Generations. Decades of the Periodical *Egyenlőség* (1881-1931). Memoirs, Documents] (Hungaria Judaica, 5) (Budapest: MTA Judaisztikai Kutatócsoport, 1993)

Szakály, Ferenc, "Oppenheimer Sámuel működése, különös tekintettel magyarországi kihatásaira" [Activity of Samuel Oppenheimer with Special Regard on Its Impact in Hungary], in: Sándor Scheiber, Ed., *Magyar-Zsidó Oklevéltár* (Monumenta Hungariae Judaica), XIV (Budapest: MIOK, 1971), pp. 31-78

Szamota, István, *Régi utazások Magyarországon és a Balkán-félszigeten* [Old Travels in Hungary and in the Balkans] (Budapest: Franklin, 1891), pp. 100-108, no. IX (Peter Eschenloer); pp. 131-146, no. XIII (Pierre Choque)

Szegő, György, Levente Thury & Róbert B. Turán, Eds., *Diaszpóra (és) művészet. Diaspora (and) Art* (Budapest: Magyar Zsidó Múzeum, 1997)

Szekeres, József, *A pesti gettók 1945 januári megmentése. "A magyar Schindler"- Szalay Pál visszaemlékezései és más dokumentumok alapján* [The Rescue of the Ghettos of Pest. The "Hungarian Schindler"—Memoirs of Pál Szalay and other Documents] (Budapest: Budapest Főváros Levéltára, 1997)

Szemere, Samu, "A zsidóság az 1848-49-es szabadságharcban" [The Jewry in the Independence War of 1848-49], in: IMIT *Évkönyv*, 1848 (Budapest: no publisher, 1948), pp. 183-186

Szenes, Chana, *Élete, küldetése és halála* [Her Life, Mission and Death], edited by Elisheva Danzig (Tel-Aviv: Hákibuc Hámeuchád, 1954

Szenes, Katherine, "On the Threshold of Liberation. Reminiscences", *Yad Vashem Studies,* 8 (1970), pp. 107-126

Szerb, Antal, "Baumgarten Ferenc" [Ferenc Baumgarten] (1937), in: *A varázsló eltöri pálcáját* (Expanded edition, Budapest: Magvető Könyvkiadó, 1961), pp. 181-190

Szirtes, Zoltán, *Temetetlen halottaink, 1941. Körösmező, Kamenyec-Podolszk* [Our Unburied Deads, 1941. Körösmező, Kamenetz-Podolsk] (Budapest: no publisher, 1996)

Szita, Szabolcs, *Haláleröd. A munkaszolgálat és a hadimunka történetéhez* [Fortress of Death. On the History of Forced Labor Service] (Budapest: Kossuth Könyvkiadó & Állami Könyvterjesztő Vállalat, 1989)

Szita, Szabolcs, *Utak a pokolból. Magyar deportáltak az annektált Ausztriában, 1944-1945* [Ways from the Hell. Hungarian Deportees in Austria, 1944-1945] (Budapest: Metalon Manager Iroda, 1991)

Szita, Szabolcs, Ed., *Magyarország 1944. Üldöztetés – embermentés* [Hungary 1944. Persecution and Rescue] (Budapest: Nemzeti Tankönyvkiadó, 1994)

Sztehlo, Gábor, *Isten kezében* [In the Hands of God] (Budapest: A Magyarországi Evangélikus Egyház Sajtóosztálya, 1984; second edition, 1986)

Szűts, László, *Bori garnizon* [Garrison in Bor] (Budapest: Renaissance, no date [1945])

T. Papp, Melinda, "Baudenkmäler im mittelalterlichen Judenviertel der Budaer (Ofner) Burg", in: *Acta Technica*, 67 (1970), pp. 205-225

Takács, Pál, "A hetvenötéves budai zsidótemplom" [The 75-year-old Jewish Temple in Buda], in: *Múlt és Jövő*, 31 (1941), pp. 171-172

Tardy, Lajos, "Egy reformkori svéd utazó és a magyar zsidóság" [A Swedish Traveler in the Reform Period and the Hungarian Jewry], in: *Évkönyv*, 1983/84 (Budapest: MIOK, 1984), pp. 366-368

Tardy, Lajos, "Néhány adat Mendel Jakab prefektus működéséhez és a budai zsidóság konstantinápolyi életéhez" [Some Data on the Activity of the Prefect Jakab Mendel and on the Life of the Jewry from Buda in Constantinople], in: *Évkönyv*, 1979/80 (Budapest: MIOK, 1980), pp. 397-412

Tátrai, Zsuzsanna, "Purimi szokások" [Customs of Purim], in: Ildikó Kríza, Ed., *A hagyomány kötelékében. Tanulmányok a magyarországi zsidó folklór köréből* (Budapest: Akadémiai Kiadó, 1990), pp. 149–155

Telegdi, Bernát, "Werbőczy István a zsidó temetőben" [István Werbőczy in the Jewish Cemetery], in: *Egyenlőség*, 54, no. 48 (1934. december 15), p. 14

Török, András, *Nagy Budapest könyv* [The Big Budapest Book] (Budapest: Corvina, 1998)

Török hadak Magyarországon. Kortárs török történet-írók naplójegyzetei [The Turkish Army in Hungary. Diary Notes of Contemporary Turkish Historians]. Translations by József Thury, edited and commented by Gábor Kiss (Budapest: Panoráma, 1984)

Trunk, Isaiah, *Judenrat. The Jewish Councils in Eastern Europe under Nazi Occupation* (Lincoln: University of Nebraska Press, 1972)

Turán, Robert B., *Jewish Guide to Hungary* (Budapest: Polgár Kiadó, 1997)

Ujvári, Péter, Ed., *Zsidó lexikon* [Jewish Lexicon] (Budapest, 1929; reprint: no place, no date [Budapest, ca. 1987])

[*Ünnepek.*] *Ámos Imre 14 eredeti metszete* [Holidays. 14 Original Lino-cuts by Imre Ámos]. Foreword by Géza Ribáry. Explanations by Ernő Naményi (Budapest: Ámos Imre / Hungária Rt., 1940)

Vadász, Ede, "Adalékok a Wahrmann-, Szófer-(Schreiber-), gorlicei Weiss- és Fischmann-családok származási adataiból; a családok kiválóbbjainak életrajzaihoz is" [Genealogical Data of the Wahrmann, Sofer (Schreiber), gorlicei Weiss and Fischmann Families, also Contributions to the Biographies of the Prominent Members of the Families], in: *Magyar-Zsidó Szemle*, 24 (1907), pp. 327–356

Vámos, Ferenc, *Lajta Béla* [Béla Lajta] (Budapest: Akadémiai Kiadó, 1970)

Váradi, László, "Külföldi diplomáciai mentési kísérletek a budapesti zsidóságért" [Diplomatic Attempts from Abroad to Rescue the Jews of Budapest], in: *Medvetánc* (1985), no. 2/3, pp. 99–110

Varga, László, "A magyarországi zsidóság megsemmi-sítése, 1944-1945" [Destruction of the Hungarian Jewry, 1944-1945], in: *Évkönyv*, 1983/84 (Budapest: MIOK, 1984), pp. 389–420

Varga, László, "Manfréd Weiss: The Profile of a Munitions King", in: Michael K. Silber, Ed., *Jews in the Hungarian Economy, 1760-1945* (Jerusalem: The Magnes Press, 1992), pp. 196–209

Varga, László, "Ungarn", in: Wolfgang Benz, Ed., *Dimension des Völkermords. Die Zahl der jüdischen Opfer des Nationalsozialismus* (München: R. Oldenbourg Verlag, 1991), pp. 331–351

Venetianer, Lajos, *A magyar zsidóság története a honfoglalástól a világháború kitöréséig, különös tekintettel gazdasági és művelődési fejlődésére* [History of the Hungarian Jewry from the Conquest of the Homeland until World War I, with Special Regard on Their Economic and Cultural Development] (Budapest, 1922; reprint: Budapest: Könyvértékesítő Vállalat, 1986)

Vértes, Róbert, *Magyarországi zsidótörvények és rendeletek, 1938-1945* [Anti-Jewish Laws and Decrees in Hungary, 1938-1945] (Budapest: Polgár Kiadó Kft., 1997)

Vidor, Pál, "Üzenet a kitérőknek" [Message to the Apostates], in: *Ararát. Magyar zsidó évkönyv az 1942. évre* (Budapest: Országos Izr. Leányárvaház, 1942–5702/3), pp. 17–22

Viharos (Ödön Gerő), *Az én fővárosom* [My Capital] (Budapest: Révai, 1891)

Vörös, Károly, "A budapesti zsidóság két forradalom között" [The Jews of Budapest between Two Revolutions], in: *Kortárs*, 30 (1986), no. 12, pp. 100–117; new edition in his *Hétköznapok a polgári Magyarországon* (Társadalom- és művelő-déstörténeti tanulmányok, 22) (Budapest: MTA Történettudományi Intézete, 1997), pp. 187–205

Vörös, Károly, "A Király utca története" [History of the Király utca], in: *Budapest*, 19 (1981), Part 1: "...Dől Rákosról be a homok" [The Sand is Storming from Rákos], no. 4, pp. 32–35; Part 2: "Tüzes a bor, tüzes a lány..." [Fiery Is the Wine, Fiery Is the Girl], no. 5, pp. 38–41; Part 3: "...És éltek együtt, és éltek egymásból" [They Lived together, and They Lived from Each Other], no. 6, pp. 39–41

Vörös, Károly, "Mór Wahrmann: A Jewish Banker in Hungarian Politics in the Era of the Dual Monarchy", in: Michael K. Silber, Ed., *Jews in the Hungarian Economy 1760-1945* (Jerusalem: Magnes Press, 1992), pp. 187–195 / "Wahrmann Mór – Egy zsidó politikus a dualizmus korában" [Mór Wahrmann—A Jewish Politician in the Age of the Dual Monarchy], in: András Kovács, Ed., *Zsidók Budapesten = Budapesti Negyed*, 3, no. 2 (Summer, 1995), pp. 22–30

Vörös, Károly, *Budapest legnagyobb adófizetői, 1873-1917* [The Largest Tax-payers of Budapest] (Budapest: Akadémiai Kiadó, 1979)

Vörös, Károly, *Egy világváros születése* [Birth of a Metropolis] (Budapest: Kossuth, 1973)

Vörös, Károly, Ed. (and the chapters on the period between 1849 and 1918 written by), *Budapest története a márciusi forradalomtól az őszirózsás forradalomig* [History of Budapest from the Revolution in March (1848) until the Revolution of the Michaelmas Daisy (1918)] (Budapest története, 4) (Budapest: Akadémiai Kiadó, 1978)

Vrba, Rudolf, "The Preparations for the Holocaust in Hungary: An Eyewitness Account", in: Randolph L. Braham, *et al.*, Eds, *The Holocaust in Hungary. Fifty Years Later* (New York: Columbia University Press, 1997), pp. 227–283

Waktor, Andrea, "A XIX. századi családmodell működése és változásai a Ballagi család levelezésének tükrében" [Family Models in the Nineteenth Century, Their Operation and Changes in the Mirror of the Correspondence of the Ballagi Family], *Sic itur ad astra. Az Eötvös Loránd Tudományegyetem Bölcsészettudományi Kara történészhallgatóinak és a Magyar Történészhallgatók Egyesületének kiadványa*, (1995), no. 1 / 2, pp. 43–92

Weisz, Miksa [Max], "Kayserling M. emlékezete" [Memory of M. Kayserling], in: IMIT. *Évkönyv*, 1929 (Budapest: Franklin, 1929), pp. 169–194

Weisz, Max, *Katalog der hebräischen Handschriften und Bücher in der Bibliothek des Professors Dr. David Kaufmann* (Frankfurt a. M.: J. Kaufmann, 1906)

Widder, Salamon, "A héber nyelvújítás" [The Hebrew Language Reform], in: IMIT. *Évkönyv*, 1933 (Budapest: Franklin, 1933), pp. 173–185

Widder, Salamon, "Színes ablakok. A zsidó fiúgimnázium templomának ablakai" [Stained-glass Windows. Windows of the Temple in the Jewish Boys' High School], in: *Múlt és Jövő*, 15 (1925), p. 301

Winkler, Ernő, *Adalékok a zsidó eskü (juramentum more judaico) középkori történetéhez, 2: A zsidó eskü Magyarországon* [The Jewish Oath in the Middle Ages in Hungary] (Budapest: Neuwald Nyomda, 1927)

Yahil, Leni, *The Holocaust. The Fate of European Jewry, 1932–1945* (New York / Oxford: Oxford University Press, 1990)

Yahil, R., "Raoul Wallenberg: His Mission and His Activities in Hungary", in: *Yad Vashem Studies*, 15 (1983), pp. 7–54

Zakar, Péter, "Tábori rabbik 1848–49-ben" [Field Rabbis in 1848–49], *Múlt és Jövő*, New Series, 10 (1998), no. 1, pp. 88–102

Zeke, Gyula, "A budapesti zsidóság lakóhelyi szegregációja a tőkés modernizáció korszakában (1867–1941)" [Dwelling Place Segregation of the Budapest Jewry in the Period of Capitalist Modernization], in: *Hét évtized a hazai zsidóság életében* (Budapest: MTA Filozófiai Intézet, 1990), I, pp. 162–199

Zeke, Gyula, *A magyarországi zsidóság a századfordulón (1895–1919)* [Hungarian Jews at the Turn of the Century] (Manuscript, 1989)

Zeke, Gyula, "A nagyvárosi kultúra új formái és a zsidóság" [New Types of Culture in Metropoles and the Jews], in: András Kovács, Ed., *Zsidók Budapesten = Budapesti Negyed*, 3, no. 2 (Summer, 1995), pp. 90–106

Zolnay, László, *Buda középkori zsidósága és zsinagógáik* [Jews in the Medieval Buda and their Synagogues] (Budapest: BTM, 1987)

Zolnay, Vilmos & Mihály Gedényi, *A régi Budapest a fattyúnyelvben* [The Old Budapest in the Slang] (Budapest: Fekete Sas Kiadó, 1996)

Zsoldos, Jenő, "Irodalmunk zsidószemlélete: Hetényi János" [Attitude to the Jews in Our Literature: János Hetényi], in: *Libanon*, 3 (1938), pp. 131–138

Zsoldos, Jenő, "Mendelssohn a magyar szellemi életben" [Mendelssohn in Hungarian Intellectual Life], in: IMIT. *Évkönyv*, 1933 (Budapest: Franklin, 1933), pp. 173–185

Zsoldos, Jenő, "Vajda Péter zsidószemlélete" [Péter Vajda's Attitude to the Jews], in: *Libanon*, 1 (1936), pp. 41–50

Zsoldos, Jenő, *1848–1849 a magyar zsidóság életében* [1848–1849 in the Life of Hungarian Jewry] (Budapest: A Pesti Izr. Hitközség Leánygimnáziumának és Ipari Leányközépiskolájának 48-as Ifjúsági Bizottsága, 1948)

Index

The indexes below were generated by the word processor, and their mechanical character was not changed essentially by edition. Spelling inconsistencies in the text of the book, due to its documentary character, or a few mistakes are tacitly or *expressis verbis* corrected here.

Below, page numbers are referred to with regular numerals (111); black-and-white photos, illustrations and figures in the text and/or comments on them (pp. 498–545, above), with italics (*222*); and color illustrations (pp. 229–252, above) and comments on them, by the numbers of the chapters and serial numbers of the photos, with bold (**III:3**).

1. Index of Personal Names

This index refers just to the *names* mentioned in the book, and not necessarily to the *person* him/herself, though some cross-references may help with the identification.

In case of some so-called Magyarized family names also the original—in general, German—name is indicated, especially if the person in question himself was the one who changed the family name. (After marriage, women bore their husband's full name until very recently, as customary in Hungary.) Magyarization meant a certain degree of social integration and assimilation, it gave a Hungarian civil identity to the person, and this alone bears historical information. Extensive lists of names, even those from later periods, e.g. deportation lists from 1944, show that Magyarization of names was very much restricted, it was wide-spread in the upper-middle class and among intellectuals. References to the original names can serve as a potential data-base to study linguistic patterns of integration and/or codes of maintaining a degree of Jewish identity. Hebrew or synagogue names, where they are known, are registered here as well.

In some cases birth or death dates are indicated in this index. Missing data shed light on the fact that there is no up-to-date Jewish biographical dictionary for Hungary. A couple of dates could be recovered only from burial matriculas, gravestones, obituaries in newspapers, etc. The persecution of Jews destroyed lines of continuity, and by methods of historiography only dim traces can be recovered.

2. Index of Cities and Towns

The main entry below, in general, is the historical name used in the text itself. Contemporary names, if different, and variant forms are indicated as cross-references. Former separate towns around Buda, Óbuda and Pest, now incorporated in the capital, are registered along with street names in Index 3.

3. Index of Budapest Street Addresses

The following index registers names of districts or neighborhoods and streets of the capital, also street addresses, names of houses and of institutions, as far as they can be tied to an exact street address. Historical and recent street names are identified only up to a reasonable degree. (A recent compilation, György Mészáros, Ed., *Budapest teljes utcanévlexikona* [Complete Lexicon of Street Names of Budapest], Budapest: Dinasztia Kiadó & Gemini Budapest Kiadó, 1998, proved to be very useful in this respect.) In certain cases (cemeteries, hospitals / nursing and old-age homes / shelters, soup-kitchens, orphanages, schools, synagogues), thematic group indexes are presented, without otherwise aiming at a detailed subject index.

Also Available from CEU Press

The Smell of Humans
A Memoir of the Holocaust in Hungary
Ernő Szép

"An author whose voice is well worth discovering."   John Klier, Slavonica

Szép's tone is a meld of stupefaction and irony. Without overtly condemning or succumbing to despair, he describes a series of events of progressively grosser infamy.

Published 1994
204 pages
1-85866-014-9   cloth $40.95 / Ł25.95
1-85866-011-4   paperback $20.95 / Ł12.95

Memoir of Hungary
Sándor Márai

This scathing, at times humorous, and always insightful memoir by the exiled Hungarian novelist Sándor Márai provides one of the most poignant and human portraits of life in Hungary between the German occupation in 1944 and the consolidation of Communist power in 1948.

Published 1996
428 pages
1-85866-064-5   paperback $24.95 / Ł15.50

Jewish Claims Against East Germany
Moral Obligations and Pragmatic Policy
Angelika Timm

Published February 1998
280pages
963-9116-04-1   cloth $49.95/ Ł31.00

The above books are available at all good bookshops or:
UK & Western Europe - Plymbridge Distributors Ltd. Tel.: 44-1752-202-301
US & Canada - CUP Services Tel.: 1-607-277-2211
Other Regions - CEU Press Tel.: 36-1-327-3138